central america
on a shoestring

Carolyn McCarthy, Greg Benchwick, Joshua Samuel Brown, Alex Egerton,
Matthew D Firestone, Kevin Raub, Tom Spurling, Lucas Vidgen

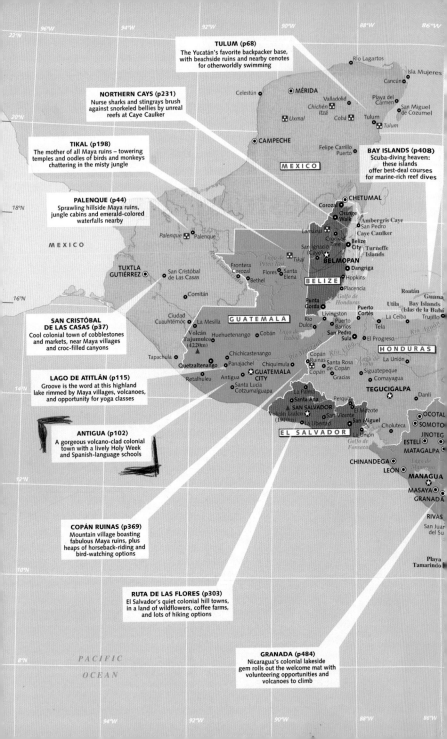

TULUM (p68)
The Yucatán's favorite backpacker base, with beachside ruins and nearby cenotes for otherworldly swimming

NORTHERN CAYS (p231)
Nurse sharks and stingrays brush against snorkeled bellies by unreal reefs at Caye Caulker

TIKAL (p198)
The mother of all Maya ruins – towering temples and oodles of birds and monkeys chattering in the misty jungle

PALENQUE (p44)
Sprawling hillside Maya ruins, jungle cabins and emerald-colored waterfalls nearby

BAY ISLANDS (p408)
Scuba-diving heaven: these islands offer best-deal courses for marine-rich reef dives

SAN CRISTÓBAL DE LAS CASAS (p37)
Cool colonial town of cobblestones and markets, near Maya villages and croc-filled canyons

LAGO DE ATITLÁN (p115)
Groove is the word at this highland lake rimmed by Maya villages, volcanoes, and opportunity for yoga classes

ANTIGUA (p102)
A gorgeous volcano-clad colonial town with a lively Holy Week and Spanish-language schools

COPÁN RUINAS (p369)
Mountain village boasting fabulous Maya ruins, plus heaps of horseback-riding and bird-watching options

RUTA DE LAS FLORES (p303)
El Salvador's quiet colonial hill towns, in a land of wildflowers, coffee farms, and lots of hiking options

GRANADA (p484)
Nicaragua's colonial lakeside gem rolls out the welcome mat with volunteering opportunities and volcanoes to climb

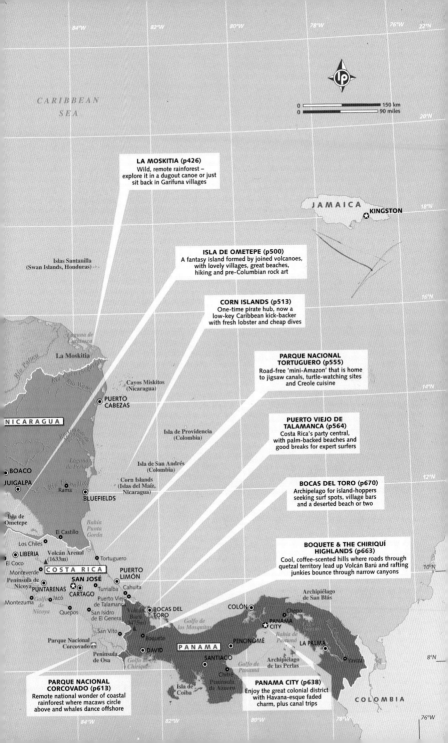

LA MOSKITIA (p426)
Wild, remote rainforest –
explore it in a dugout canoe or just
sit back in Garífuna villages

ISLA DE OMETEPE (p500)
A fantasy island formed by joined volcanoes,
with lovely villages, great beaches,
hiking and pre-Columbian rock art

CORN ISLANDS (p513)
One-time pirate hub, now a
low-key Caribbean kick-backer
with fresh lobster and cheap dives

**PARQUE NACIONAL
TORTUGUERO (p555)**
Road-free 'mini-Amazon' that is home
to jigsaw canals, turtle-watching sites
and Creole cuisine

**PUERTO VIEJO DE
TALAMANCA (p564)**
Costa Rica's party central,
with palm-backed beaches and
good breaks for expert surfers

BOCAS DEL TORO (p670)
Archipelago for island-hoppers
seeking surf spots, village bars
and a deserted beach or two

**BOQUETE & THE CHIRIQUÍ
HIGHLANDS (p663)**
Cool, coffee-scented hills where roads through
quetzal territory lead up Volcán Barú and rafting
junkies bounce through narrow canyons

**PARQUE NACIONAL
CORCOVADO (p613)**
Remote national wonder of coastal
rainforest where macaws circle
above and whales dance offshore

PANAMA CITY (p638)
Enjoy the great colonial district
with Havana-esque faded
charm, plus canal trips

Responsible Travel

Central America overflows with those incredible 'What? Where? You did what?' places that can, well, change your life. But visitors can bring changes for the destinations too – some of which are not good. In the last 50 years, the region has seen the erosion of traditional customs, deforestation, and rising illicit drug use and prostitution. Sometimes tourism is a culprit. Ecotourism has caught on, particularly in Costa Rica, saving many hectares of forest from the saw. Still, ecotourism is an often abused buzzword. Here are a few ways to help.

TIPS

- **Go overland** Take buses, not planes – if coming from the USA, consider taking a bus across Mexico.
- **Give right** Handouts to kids encourage begging; give directly to schools or clinics instead.
- **Buy local** Try to eat and stay at family-owned places and use community-owned services.
- **Cold showers** Avoid hot showers if water is heated by a wood fire.
- **Never litter** Carry out all your trash when camping or hiking, and pick up trash when you can.
- **Respect local traditions** Dress appropriately when visiting local churches or traditional communities.
- **Be curious** Ask locals about ways to avoid mistakes some travelers make – let us know what you learn.

INTERNET RESOURCES

www.eco-indextourism.org Many links on sustainable travel.
www.ecotourism.org Links to ecofriendly businesses.
www.planeta.com Includes a free 93-page e-book.
www.tourismconcern.org.uk UK-based organization dedicated to promoting ethical tourism.
www.transitionsabroad.com Focuses on responsible travel.

VOLUNTEER

Volunteering is the new travel – some tips follow; see p723 for more.

- Preserve turtle-nesting sites – from poachers and reckless tourists – at Refugio de Vida Silvestre La Flor (p499) in Nicaragua or Costa Rica's Parque Nacional Tortuguero (p555).
- Ask around at volunteer hubs including Quetzaltenango (p139) in Guatemala and Boquete (p663) in Panama.
- Teach English: options include Comarca de Kuna Yala (p690) in Panama and San Salvador (p277) in El Salvador.

Central America Highlights

The green cuff links between North and South America, these seven compact countries, plus the southern strip of Mexico, would be easy to skip on a map, yet they represent a true back-packers' paradise, a complex web of cultures, ancient ruins, tropical wildlife and adventure. The perfect place to dream a little dream. For starters, summit a volcano, traipse through jungle to Maya pyramids, or surf the waves along gold-sand beaches. Learn to dive for dirt cheap or take bargain Spanish classes in a cool colonial town. Or just remember to slow down in a Maya, Kuna or Mískito village, where old-world traditions stroll into present day.

UROS RAVBAR

① ISLA HOLBOX (MEXICO)

It's the feeling, the quietness of having the sea all around. Here, you can go in the sea and bathe at any time of day. And it's a very safe place. It's small. It's not crowded. And even in the 'season' you can find your spot (see boxed text, p60).

Sandra, Traveler, Germany

TIKAL (GUATEMALA)

Approaching Tikal's Gran Plaza (p202) early in the morning before the tour buses arrive, you get the sensation you've stumbled upon some long-buried secret. The radiant centerpiece of an ancient Maya capital occupied for some 16 centuries, it's a testament to the cultural and artistic heights scaled by this amazing jungle civilization.

Lucas Vidgen, Lonely Planet Author, Australia

3

RICHARD I'AN

ROBERT HARDING PICTURE LIBRARY LTD / ALAMY

2

GARÍFUNA CULTURE (BELIZE)

Soak up Garífuna culture in Dangriga (p250), where local drum-makers work under beachside *palapas* (thatched-roof shelters), restaurants serve *hudut* (plantains mashed into a paste), and *punta* music jams happen right outside your guesthouse.

Joshua Samuel Brown, Lonely Planet Author, USA

IMAGE SOURCE / AL

4

PARAGLIDING OVER LAGO DE ATITLÁN (GUATEMALA)

It was like holding a live map, where everything in the planning stage of your trip comes to life in front of you. The memories of the places I'd already seen came to me vividly, and the places I visited after the flight came to me in pictures I'd preserved in my memory while aloft (see p115).

José Fernández, Traveler, Mexico

COPÁN (HONDURAS)

As central features of a once sprawling city, the massive temples and sculpted palaces of Copán (p374) were conceived as mountains and cut from mountains…the integration of human and natural landscapes is explicit, alluring and mind-bending.

Dr Allan Maca, Traveler, USA

SEAN CAFFREY

SURFING (EL SALVADOR)

Wow, I really don't know where to start with Playa El Tunco (p294), it's that good. It's undoubtedly the best break for all levels of gung-ho surfers in El Salvador, plus it has peaceful huts alongside the beach that are affordable for all types of traveler.

Trent, Traveler, Australia

PAUL KENNEDY

MARGIE POLITZER

VOLCÁN MADERAS, ISLA DE OMETEPE (NICARAGUA)

Hiking up into the clouds surrounded by jungle on Volcán Maderas (see p500) is such a great experience that reaching the summit brings mixed emotions – you don't want the adventure to end.

Ben Shimon, Traveler, USA

PARQUE NACIONAL CORCOVADO (COSTA RICA)

Costa Rica's ultimate outdoor experience is anything but a walk in the park. At Corcovado (p613), with the proper gear, ample supplies and a healthy appetite for adventure, you can leave behind the tourist crowds and lose yourself in the wilds.

Matthew D Firestone, Lonely Planet Author, USA

RALPH HOPP

DAVE AND SIGRUN TOLLERTON / ALAMY

9

8

PAVONES (COSTA RICA)

Pavones (p614) is one of my favorite surf spots in the world, even though it doesn't attract as much attention as other, more famous beaches. I like that it's difficult to get to and a bit of an unknown, though the waves here never seem to disappoint.

Daniel, Traveler, Germany

10 PANAMA CITY (PANAMA)

DIEGO LEZA

Panama City (p638) is high-octane Latin America with *ceviche* (marinated seafood), casinos and stacked skylines. Sure, the traffic resembles a boa constrictor digesting one megalithic meal, but people are real here and beauty lives in the skewed rhythms, incongruous visions and fiery concrete sunsets.

Carolyn McCarthy, Lonely Planet Author, USA

Contents

The Authors

CAROLYN MCCARTHY   Coordinating Author, Panama

Author of 10 travel guides, Carolyn McCarthy has been writing about the Americas since 1998. Panama, memorable for its warm tropical downpours, fried snappers, rainforest and sharks, has become one of her favorites. Her other Lonely Planet titles include *Chile*, *Trekking in the Patagonian Andes*, *Panama* and *South America on a Shoestring*. A former Fulbright fellow, Carolyn's writing has appeared in *National Geographic*, the *Boston Globe* and other publications. She lives in southern Chile. Follow her Americas blog at www.carolynswildblueyonder.blogspot.com.

GREG BENCHWICK   Mexico's Yucatán & Chiapas

Greg first visited the Yucatán Peninsula on a family trip back in the early '80s. He's been coming back regularly ever since. When he's not writing about sustainable travel or Latin America, Greg loves to explore the wild areas of his native Colorado with his wife and their three-legged Turkish street dog. To see videos from Greg's adventures, check out his website, www.soundtraveler.com.

JOSHUA SAMUEL BROWN   Belize

American-born and USC Annenberg/Getty Arts Journalism fellow Joshua Samuel Brown has lived in Taiwan, Hong Kong and China since 1994, and has traveled extensively around America, Canada and Belize. His features have appeared in an eclectic variety of publications around the globe, including the *South China Morning Post*, *Business Traveler Asia*, *Clamor Magazine* and *Cat Fancy*. To date, Joshua has coauthored four travel guides for Lonely Planet. His debut book, *Vignettes of Taiwan*, is available at bookstores in Asia, through Amazon or at www.josambro.com. Google 'Snarky Tofu' to follow Joshua's strange journey around the world.

LONELY PLANET AUTHORS

Why is our travel information the best in the world? It's simple: our authors are passionate, dedicated travelers. They don't take freebies in exchange for positive coverage so you can be sure the advice you're given is impartial. They travel widely to all the popular spots, and off the beaten track. They don't research using just the internet or phone. They discover new places not included in any other guidebook. They personally visit thousands of hotels, restaurants, palaces, trails, galleries, temples and more. They speak with dozens of locals every day to make sure you get the kind of insider knowledge only a local could tell you. They take pride in getting all the details right, and in telling how it is. Think you can do it? Find out how at **lonelyplanet.com**.

ALEX EGERTON   Nicaragua

A journalist by trade, Alex has been hanging around in Central America for almost a decade, teaching at universities, contributing to magazines and searching for the perfect fried cheese. He currently divides his time between suburban Managua and Bluefields, where he lives in a recording studio and writes about all things Caribbean. Alex is also actively involved in a project promoting sustainable tourism in remote indigenous communities in Nicaragua. While on the road for this guide, Alex twice bought medicine from persuasive pharmaceutical salesmen on intercity buses, but has yet to try either pill.

MATTHEW D FIRESTONE   Costa Rica

Matthew is a trained anthropologist and epidemiologist, though he postponed his academic career to spend his youth living out of a backpack. To date he has authored more than 20 guidebooks for Lonely Planet, and covered far-flung destinations from the Darién Gap to the Dead Sea. When he's not in graduate school, out in the field or on assignment, he likes to spend his time exploring the American West with his parents, or catching up with the in-laws in the foothills of Mt Fuji.

KEVIN RAUB   Honduras

Kevin Raub grew up in Atlanta and started his career as a music journalist in New York, working for *Men's Journal* and *Rolling Stone* magazines. The rock 'n' roll lifestyle took its toll, so he needed an extended vacation and took up travel writing. He accepted the Honduras gig a few weeks before all hell broke loose, but went anyway. Though he was stopped nine times at police checkpoints, he soldiered on, canvasing the country in his rented Mitsubishi pick-up truck, which he managed to only get stuck once, deep in a dead-end mountain road between Marcala and La Esperanza. This is his eighth Lonely Planet title.

TOM SPURLING   El Salvador

When Tom Spurling last visited Central America, he left his passport at a Nicaraguan hostel and got red-taped at the border. For this guide he explored every craggy, volcanic corner of El Salvador, making hit-and-write missions to guerrilla strongholds and Rasta bars armed with acidophilus and very full briefs. On behalf of Lonely Planet, Tom has now linguistically butchered Spanish, Turkish, Hindi and outback Queensland's rising inflection. His best travel experience was working on a project supported by the Planet Wheeler Foundation in rural South Africa. He lives in Melbourne with his wife and son who indulge his inability to pack light or travel safe.

LUCAS VIDGEN   Guatemala

Lucas has been traveling and working in Latin America for 15 years. He currently lives in Quetzaltenango, Guatemala, where he sits on the board of directors of NGO Entre Mundos and publishes the city's leading culture and nightlife magazine, *XelaWho*. Having contributed to various books for Lonely Planet, Lucas now mostly divides his time between Central and South America. He is a regular contributor to Lonely Planet titles *Nicaragua*, *Argentina*, *South America on a Shoestring* and *Central America on a Shoestring*. His Spanish is OK, but he misses potato cakes and his mum.

CONTRIBUTING AUTHOR

Dr David Goldberg wrote the Health chapter. He completed his training in internal medicine and infectious diseases at Columbia-Presbyterian Medical Center in New York City, where he has also served as voluntary faculty. At present he is an infectious-diseases specialist in Scarsdale, New York, and the editor in chief of the website MDtravelhealth.com.

Itineraries

Central America's slim figure – with a curve here and there – gives just a little room for creative looping itineraries. The easiest way, time willing, is going from top to bottom (or bottom to top). That said, a few multicountry trips with one gateway can be taken without much backtracking. To see it all (essentially a combination of everything that follows), give yourself at least three months. If you only have two or three weeks, though, you're best sticking with a country or two. Or just drop in and see where the wind directs you.

See p726 for information on 'open-jaw' air tickets to Central America, and p732 for the duration of some major bus trips.

NORTHERN LOOP
Guatemala, Mexico, Belize, Honduras & El Salvador

This route loops through much of the region's northern highlights, starting from **Guatemala City** (p89). Head straight to colonial **Antigua** (p102) for a few days, doing a volcano climb and perhaps a crash course in Spanish. Then get a chicken bus to other highland sites; at stunning **Lago de Atitlán** (p115) skip the gringoburg of Panajachel for a few days of hiking and swimming from an atmospheric base such as hippie-friendly **San Marcos La Laguna** (p128), before continuing on to **Chichicastenango** (p131) to see the famous Maya market. Pad your budget and venture north to Mexico on a 'Chiapas loop' to witness modern Maya life at the mountain town of **San Cristóbal de Las Casas** (p37) and the Maya ruins amid the jungle at **Palenque** (p44). Visit the riverside ruins

Mountains, jungle, beaches, ruins: this diverse route is classic Central America, summoning culture, adventure and serious relaxation. Feel free to linger in one place and save a slice or three for the next trip.

of **Yaxchilán** (p48) en route to the mother of Maya sites, **Tikal** (p198), back in Guatemala. Bus east to Belize, stopping for a Frisbee golf round at a jungle base outside hilly **San Ignacio** (p245), before splashing into the Caribbean's wonderful reefs at laid-back **Caye Caulker** (p231).

Cay-hop south, stopping at offbeat **Hopkins** (p253) or more mainstream **Placencia** (p255), before boating to Guatemala's **Lívingston** (p184) to take a serious jungle boat trip along the **Río Dulce** (p188).

Cross into Honduras and head for the cobblestone town of **Copán Ruinas** (p369), offering river-tubing trips, horseback rides over mountains, and the namesake ruins. Bus to **Gracias** (p381), and thank the colonial town for its proximity to a quetzal-rich national park.

Southward in El Salvador, stop in kitschy mountain town **La Palma** (p323) for hikes over high-up log bridges. Bypass San Salvador for the Pacific 'surf villages' of **La Costa del Bálsamo** (p293), where you can get cheap surf lessons. Catch a Guatemala City bus from San Salvador.

SIDE TRIPS

If you're big on ruins, detour from Palenque to colonial **Mérida** (p53), stopping at **Uxmal** (see boxed text, p56), then visit **Chichén Itzá** (p56) and **Tulum** (p68). Bus to Belize, then go west to Tikal.

If you've 'done Mexico,' though, skip it. From Chichicastenango head to **Nebaj** (p136) for day hikes and a few days in **Quetzaltenango** (p139) to explore volcanoes and traditional villages. Head north past Huehuetenango into the stunning wilds of the Ixcán region and make your way east, stopping in for a dip at the sublime **Laguna Lachuá** (see boxed text, p170) en route to the crossroads for either **Cobán** (p165) or Tikal.

Need more water? Before Copán, detour to the party-activities hub of **La Ceiba** (p395) and boat to the **Bay Islands** (p408) for some diving.

SOUTHERN LOOP
Costa Rica, Panama & Nicaragua

Nicaragua and Panama frame the more tourist-trodden Costa Rica. Starting in **San José** (p534), take the bus-and-boat trip to the English-speaking Caribbean coast and turtle country at **Tortuguero** (p555), then boat and bus back south to the party-surf town of **Puerto Viejo de Talamanca** (p564). Cross into Panama and boat out to the Caribbean archipelago of **Bocas del Toro** (p670) for island-hopping and surfing. Then head to Central America's cosmopolitan capital, **Panama City** (p638), with its Havana-like charm and a look at the **Panama Canal** (p653). Bus west, via David, to the cool coffee highlands around **Boquete** (p663) and look out over the Pacific *and* Caribbean from atop **Volcán Barú** (p667).

Bus back to Costa Rica, taking the ferry from Puntarenas for checking out the boho hangout of **Montezuma** (p592) on Península de Nicoya, near swimming holes, wilderness beaches and surfing in **Mal País** (p595). Get back to Puntarenas to reach Nicaragua's double-volcano **Isla de Ometepe** (p500), after hammock swings and rum at fun but gringofied **San Juan del Sur** (p496), then visit colonial **Granada** (p484), with volcanoes and eerie night hiking. Bus, via Managua, to Rama for a boat to Bluefields and a boat out to **Little Corn Island** (p515) for serious snorkeling and kick-back time. Retrace your steps to Managua for a direct bus back to San José.

SIDE TRIPS

For an alternative return to Costa Rica from Nicaragua, cross the border at Los Chiles, after a boat ride along the **Río San Juan** (p507). In Costa Rica, bus via Ciudad Quesada to **La Virgen** (p577), a rafting highlight.

HOW LONG?

Minimum: 5 to 8 weeks

WHEN TO GO?

Any time; just before or after peak season (December to April) misses most crowds and tropical storms

BUDGET?

US$25 to US$40 per day, US$10 more at beach towns and in Mexico and Belize

HOW LONG?

5 to 7 weeks

WHEN TO GO?

Any time; just before or after peak season (December to April) misses most crowds and tropical storms

BUDGET?

US$20 to US$40 per day, more at beach towns

Get the 'wow' of Central American wildlife in the more expensive (and popular) Costa Rica, before the 'whoa now' jolt of the authentic, less touristy countries next door. Both are touted as the 'new Costa Rica,' with volcanoes and rich coastlines, but you'll probably love them for other reasons.

In Panama, take a chill beach-and-surf detour to **Playa Venao** (p684) on the Península de Azuero. If you have a splurge fund, consider an unreal adventure near the **Darién Gap** (p694), or fly to the fascinating Kuna-inhabited islands known as **Comarca de Kuna Yala** (p690).

ACTION ALL THE WAY!

Seize the great outdoors on this slender isthmus with volcanoes, mountains, rivers and waves. If you've never surfed or gone diving, no excuses! Central America is the place to learn.

Starting in Guatemala's highlands, get into the regional swing with a guided bike ride around **Antigua** (p109). Chicken-bus it to wee **Nebaj** (p136) and arrange a three-day hike through the Cuchumatanes mountains to **Todos Santos** (p153). From colonial Quetzaltenango, set aside two days to climb Central America's highest point, **Volcán Tajumulco** (p142).

Bus via Guatemala City to Honduras' **Copán Ruinas** (p369), a touristy hub with horseback rides and famous ruins. Campers should head to **Parque Nacional Montaña de Celaque** (p384), near Gracias, and take butterfly-lined paths to campsites in the cloud forest. Bus to **La Ceiba** (p395), Honduras' activities and party center, with canopy tours and rafting trips on the Río Cangrejal. Boat out to the **Bay Islands** (p408), for snorkeling or reef dives and certification courses.

Southwest in El Salvador, stop in artsy **Suchitoto** (p319) and go by horseback to former FMLN hideouts at Volcán Guazapa. Pass on the capital for **La Libertad** (p291), the nation's surf capital. Bus to Nicaragua, stopping in colonial **León** (p476) for a climb up and slide down a nearby volcano. Give a couple of days at least for **Isla de Ometepe** (p500), a volcano island in a sea-sized lake with hikes up to – and past – the clouds.

HOW LONG?

5 to 7 weeks

WHEN TO GO?

Generally dry season (December to April); mountain hikes will get sloppy (and dangerous) in peak rainy season (September and October), while rains can dampen Bay Islands' trips November to February

BUDGET?

Guides for hikes or dives add to costs; count on US$40 to US$50 per day

Central America is a paradise for the active – surfing, diving, hiking and boating easily rank in the region's top highlights. This trip – from Guatemala City to Panama City – assumes an 'open-jaw' ticket.

Costa Rica is flooded with options. DIY canoe rides through the **Tortuguero** (p555), accessed via Río San Juan, remains a Central America highlight. In the south, **Parque Nacional Chirripó** (p609) has a well-marked two-day trail to the country's highest mountain, with a bunkhouse way up.

In Panama, detour from David to **Boquete** (p663), near Volcán Barú and rivers to raft. Brush up on your surf skills at one of the region's best waves, at **Santa Catalina** (p681). Before you end your trip, get some Rollerblades to traverse the causeway along the mouth of the Panama Canal near **Panama City** (p643). Or just see a flick.

'I ONLY HAVE TWO WEEKS!'

Laments such as this crop up all the time: 'I want to see Central America but only have a couple weeks; where should I go?' The best advice is sticking with some highlights in a country or two. Perhaps sample 'tomorrow's Central America' in El Salvador and Nicaragua; many first-timers often do Guatemala. An 'open-jaw' ticket – flying into one place and out of another – helps you get the most out of your time.

Apart from choosing a sample from the earlier itineraries, here are a couple of stabs at what you can accomplish in just 14 days.

Box Ticker: Panama to Guatemala

All of Central America in 14 days? You nuts? OK. Here's a way to see most countries, traveling overland and mostly by day.

Start with two nights in **Panama City** (p638) – see the canal and colonial Casco Viejo. Bus 15 hours to **San José** (p534), arriving at 3am on the Tica Bus. Taxi to one of the hostels with a pool; do a day trip to **Parque Nacional Braulio**

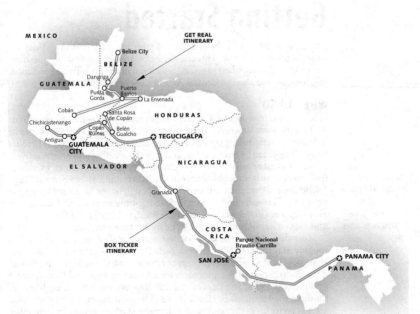

Carrillo (p550) to climb a volcano. Get the morning bus for a 10-plus-hours trip to Nicaragua's colonial wonder **Granada** (p484) for a couple of nights wandering past the plaza's mango trees and to take a canopy tour down a volcano. Wake up *early* for a long day: get the Tegucigalpa bus (roughly 10 hours) and a Copán Ruinas bus (seven more), and allow yourself two full days' rest in **Copán Ruinas** (p369) – but not forgetting the nearby Maya ruins. Get a shuttle bus (six hours) to **Antigua** (p102) for the last couple of days in the volcano-studded highlands, hopefully squeezing in a day trip to the **Chichicastenango market** (p132). End the trip in Guatemala City.

With just two weeks up your sleeve, you can make a mad dash and try to see as much as you can, or just take it very, very easy soaking up a culture that doesn't ever hurry.

Get Real: Belize to Honduras

Wherever you go, travel's ultimate highlight is the local people you meet. This trip – from Belize City to Tegucigalpa – sticks with traditional villages where long-rooted traditions live large. Hang out with the Garífuna in **Dangriga** (p250), best during the Garífuna Settlement Day festival (November 19), then sing songs with a Maya family at a homestay outside **Punta Gorda** (p260).

Ferry to Puerto Barrios, Guatemala, and bus to **Cobán** (p165) to stay in the cloud forest for a couple of days with a Q'eqchi' family.

Bus east into Honduras, where you can hang out on the beach and try local coconut bread at low-key Garífuna villages such as **La Ensenada** (p394), then bus from **Santa Rosa de Copán** (p379) to see the Lenca market at cliff-hugging **Belén Gualcho** (see boxed text, p384). It's a seven-hour bus ride to Tegucigalpa.

Getting Started

Preparing a trip is half the fun, even if your itinerary gets tossed out the window once you arrive. This chapter helps answer the first big questions for a trip, including when to go and what kind of cash you'll need. For more information, see also the Central America Directory (p710).

WHEN TO GO

When are you free? Any time of year will be pretty good (as long as a hurricane isn't on the same itinerary). Beaches are best for a dip around February; the hills remain refreshingly cool around August. However, the seasons here are less distinguished by temperature, and more by weather and tourist activity.

Peak tourist season coincides with the dry season – known as *verano* (summer), which is roughly between Christmas and Easter's Semana Santa celebrations (attractions in themselves). Though hotels fill up and raise their prices, you'll usually find a room even in big-time tourist destinations such as Antigua in Guatemala, or Cancún in Mexico. Either side of this period – mid-November or mid-April – can be the best time to visit.

Most days during the rainy or wet season, called *invierno* (winter) – roughly May through November or early December – are blessed with variable pockets of sunshine and cheaper airfares. Often a suddenly blackened sky will drop rain in the afternoon for an hour or two, and then clear up again. But flooding and days of rain can happen, particularly problematic for those mountain hikes. Hurricanes and tropical storms are an even more serious concern, as they can last for days (most often coming in September and October up and down the Caribbean coast) and affect the whole region.

For climate charts of select cities in Central America, see p714; see also Climate in the Directory of each country chapter.

COSTS & MONEY

Central America is not an expensive place to travel. Guatemala, Honduras and Nicaragua are the cheapest countries to visit, with El Salvador and Panama comprising the second tier. Travel costs in Belize, Costa Rica and Mexico are a jump up from other Central American countries (particularly those Mexican

---

10 TIPS TO STAY ON A BUDGET

- Always ask the price before agreeing to any services.
- Eat set lunches in local markets, buy boiled corn from street vendors – cut back on those tempting Western breakfasts (at US$4 a pop and up).
- Walk around – from bus stations, to museums across town – to save on using taxis.
- Team up with fellow travelers – solo travelers often pay the same as a couple does, and a group of three or four sharing a hotel room can work out cheaper than staying in a hostel.
- Cut back on the *carves* (beer), partyers. A buck or two per bottle adds up.
- Avoid repeatedly buying small bottles of water; buy water in bulk, drink boiled water or bring a purifier.
- Go 2nd-class; cheaper buses – those stuffed ex–US school buses painted in bright colors – can be up to 50% cheaper.
- Slow down. Slower travel means less transport, more time to figure out the cheap deals.
- See fewer countries – fewer countries means fewer entry visas and less distance to travel.
- Skip Mexico, Costa Rica, Belize and Caribbean party towns – all are pricier.

WHAT TO TAKE

Almost everything can be found in towns of significant size in Central America. However, some items can be hard to find or expensive to the point of offense.

- An alarm clock for early buses (and many do leave early).
- Books for leisure time or waiting for transport. However, book exchanges in big cities and traveler hangouts have new and used books in English.
- Camping gear if you plan to camp; bring it all (except fuel for the stove) as equipment is over-priced and not always available.
- Condoms and birth-control pills are available in larger towns, but it's convenient to bring your own.
- A flashlight is definitely needed for powerless beach huts and checking out ruins.
- Photocopies: copy your passport, airline ticket, any visas and traveler's check numbers; pack these separately from the originals.
- A snapshot or two of the family back home will be appreciated by your new Central American friends.
- Rain gear: a thin waterproof jacket and a rainproof sack for your pack is a godsend; you may be dry in the bus, but your pack on top can get soaked.
- Repellent: best found in larger towns and cities.
- A Latin American Spanish phrasebook (see p741).
- A universal sink plug and clothesline for washing laundry and hanging up wet clothes.
- A water filter/purifier for camping or just potable water.

---

buses!), but even in these countries you can still usually find dorm beds for as low as US$10 to US$15, and a bed in a guesthouse for US$25 to US$40.

How Much Do You Need?

In general, it's possible to get by on a daily budget of US$15 (in Guatemala) to US$40 (in Mexico or Belize). This range is a bare minimum per day, involving staying in a hostel with free breakfast and internet access, having a simple lunch and dinner, seeing an attraction and riding a few hours to the next town. Bring more than you think you'll need and allow yourself the means for a splurge now and then for nice meals, drinks and hotels with air-con, as well as for a snorkel trip, a tour or a guide. Staying in a reasonable hotel room with air-con will cost you an extra US$15/20 for Nicaragua/Mexico. Sample costs are provided on the first page of each country chapter.

How to Carry Money

It's wise to store some spare US dollars in case of an emergency – at least a couple days' budget. ATMs are widely available in the region; though, if your personal identification number (PIN) is more than four digits, ask your bank if it will be accepted before heading off. For general information on money for the region, see p719, as well as the Money section in each country's Directory.

Foreigner Prices

Museums and national parks throughout Central America often charge higher admission fees for foreign tourists. It's sometimes about twice what the locals pay, but still pretty cheap. Keep in mind what the locals earn before complaining. Some places may offer student discounts, otherwise don't haggle; they're set prices.

HOW MUCH?

Bottle of beer US$0.70-3

Bus ride (3hr) US$3.50-10

Dorm bed US$6-15

Hotel double US$8-35

Internet access per hr US$1-2

Set lunch US$3-5

PRETRIP INSPIRATION

Film

A bit of celluloid can whet the appetite for Central America. The region has been a playground for big-budget films, but let's face it, *Apocalypto* and *Jurassic Park* offer little insight into Latin American culture.

Watch out for more non-Hollywood films being made here. *Looking for Palladin* (2008), written and directed by Andrzej Krakowski and shot in Antigua, gives a good sense of the street. The award-winning *La casa de enfrente* (2003), directed by Tonatiúh Martínez, delves into such gritty subjects as corruption and prostitution; it's part of the new wave of Guatemalan filmmaking.

Director Paz Fabrega won international awards for 2010's *Agua fría de mar* (Cold Sea Water), the Costa Rican story of a young couple and a seven-year-old girl from opposite sides of the social spectrum. *Sin nombre* (Nameless) was a 2009 Sundance prize winner about gangs and illegal immigration that opens in Honduras.

The first Panamanian-made commercial film was 2009's *Chance,* a worthy tropical comedy about class shenanigans, told by two maids. Also from Panama, *Burwa dii Ebo* (The Wind and the Water), an official 2008 Sundance selection, follows an indigenous Kuna teenager who moves to Panama City. Though yet to be commercially distributed, it has also won awards in Toronto and Chile.

The 2008 Salvadoran war film *Sobreviviendo Guazapa* (Surviving Guazapa), directed by Roberto Davila, is a kind of Central American *Rambo*. *Walker* (1987) is Nicaraguan director Alex Cox's unconventional take on the adventures of Central America's most infamous megalomaniac, shot on location in Nicaragua.

Classics include Woody Allen's spoof *Bananas,* and *The Mosquito Coast* (starring Harrison Ford), set in Honduras and shot in Belize.

Literature

Travelers along the Maya route have the perfect introduction to these fascinating ancient civilizations with Michael D Coe's *Breaking the Maya Code.*

More than just a travelogue, Salman Rushdie's *The Jaguar Smile: A Nicaraguan Journey* is a witty and opinionated account of his visit during the revolution.

Costa Rica: A Traveler's Literary Companion offers 26 short stories that capture the soul of the county. *The Last Flight of the Scarlet Macaw* is Bruce Barcott's account of one activist making a difference in Belize.

The Soccer War by Ryszard Kapuscinski is an entertaining and harsh account of the 100-hour war between Honduras and El Salvador. Paul Theroux's excellent *The Mosquito Coast* prompted the film about the American family in the heart of darkness. For a sense of the elephantine undertaking of the Panama Canal, read the 700-page *The Path Between the Seas* by David McCollough (also handy as a yoga block).

For more book suggestions, see p713, as well the Books sections in each country's Directory.

Internet Resources

- Visit **Mundo Maya online** (www.mayadiscovery.com) for articles, Maya legends and information on the region.
- Surf **Ecotravels** (www.planeta.com), with arresting articles, reference material and links.
- Find **community-based tourism** (www.redturs.org) initiatives.
- Fabulous **El Salvador blog** (www.luterano.blogspot.com) has great insights.
- Check out **Amnesty International** (www.amnesty.org) reports on Central America.
- Compare famous Central American rums via expert reviews at **Ministry of Rum** (www.ministryofrum.com).

See also p718 for a list of useful online sources.

DOS & DON'TS

■ Do tip 10% at restaurants unless a service charge has been included.

■ Do use the formal *usted* to address locals until they use *tú* first.

■ Do read up on recent history – many locals may be suffering from recent civil wars that your country may or may not have contributed to – it's worth knowing beforehand.

■ Don't go into shops shirtless or in a bikini – though the beach may be nearby, some communities are offended by informal attire.

■ Don't expect everything to rush at New York pace.

■ Don't take photographs of religious ceremonies or people without asking.

CONDUCT

There are a few things to keep in mind about 'being good' in Central America. Remember that life here probably goes at a slower pace than yours back home. See also Responsible Travel (p4).

Introductions

A simple *buenos días* or *buenas tardes* ('good morning' or 'good afternoon' to English speakers) should preface your conversation, including simple requests. When you enter a room, even a public place such as a restaurant or waiting room, it's polite to make a general greeting to everyone. It's also nice to say hello to your bus mate (and your bus mate's chicken).

Indigenous People

The term *indio* or *india* used to refer to indigenous people is generally considered offensive; the word *indígena* for indigenous men and women is widely used.

Dress

It's worth paying attention to your appearance here. Latin Americans on the whole are very conscious of appearance, grooming and dress; it's difficult for them to understand why a foreign traveler (assumed to be rich) would dress scruffily, when even impoverished Central Americans do their best to look neat. Your relations can be smoother if you're looking spick-and-span. This also applies to dealings with the officials (ie immigration personnel and police).

Casual dress is becoming more acceptable, though. You may see local women wearing miniskirts – an unthinkable occurrence in the not-so-distant past – but not everyone appreciates this attire, and some locals may find it offensive. As a foreigner, it's a good idea to steer toward the conservative, so as not to offend. A general rule is to notice what the people around you wear and dress accordingly.

Shorts are usually worn by both sexes only at the beach and in coastal towns. You'll notice that many local women swim with T-shirts over their swimming suits, and you may want to do the same or be prepared to receive a lot of male attention *and* a sunburn. See p724 for more suggestions for women travelers.

Show particular reserve in how you're dressed when entering churches. Shorts, short skirts and tank tops are a definite no-no.

Another consideration about your appearance is safety. Even cheap imitation jewelry (much less a video camera dangling around your neck) spells wealth to many would-be thieves, particularly in the capital cities. See p715 for more on basic travel safety.

24

Snapshots

CURRENT EVENTS

When the cogs of the world economy creaked to a halt in 2008, Central America felt it like a cut of lifeblood to its veins. Throughout the region, foreign manufacturing companies closed shop or cut staff, tourist numbers dipped, and the constant influx of cash from family members working abroad nearly dried up. It was like a switch was pulled on the great machine of international commerce.

The question now is how to recover. But before Central America prospers, it will have to settle for something even more essential – namely stability. A 2009 UN report cited Central America as the region with the highest non-political crime worldwide. According to the report, both strong-arm and soft-touch approaches have failed and must evolve toward a 'smart' strategy of citizen security that includes preventive and coercive actions.

This might be easier said than done. The issue of security is perhaps nowhere more paramount than in Guatemala, where police corruption is a major problem and crime is steadily on the rise. In Mexico, the mobilization of the military to counteract drug trafficking has triggered violent backlash, though it's mostly in the north. Yet the perception of violence, added to the initially hyped outbreak of the H1N1 'swine flu' virus, has dealt a severe blow to Yucatán's resort areas.

El Salvador took a left turn in 2009, when the Frente Farabundo Martí para la Liberación Nacional (FMLN) party rose to power for the first time since its inception as a guerrilla resistance movement. The change is considered a major victory for democratic process and reconciliation in El Salvador, but whether the administration – led by former TV journalist Mauricio Funes – can live up to its promises of political transparency and widespread social change, remains to be seen. Gang violence has topped the headlines.

In any other region, the above would be enough dramatic fodder. But the biggest story of 2009 was the twilight coup staged on June 28, 2009 in Honduras. It turned out that the armed forces had been following orders from the supreme court to detain and remove President Manuel Zelaya from office. Accused of treason and abuse of office, Zelaya had also forged a cozy alliance with Venezuela's Hugo Chávez that made many fear a permanent power kick. While tensions simmered, Honduras held transparent democratic elections in November 2009, electing Nationalist party candidate Porfirio 'Pepe' Lobo, a center-right conservative considered the polar opposite of Zelaya.

Panama had already bucked the Latin American leftist trend by electing conservative supermarket-magnate Ricardo Martinelli president in May 2009. But the biggest news in Panama has been the US$5 billion project to expand the canal. This massive makeover (slated for 2014) should bring on more canal traffic and allow larger vessels for a much-needed boost to the economy.

Belize has been publicly debating the potential benefits of oil exploration versus the risks of environmental damage. With Central American economies struggling, natural resources are more at risk than ever for large-scale mining, hydroelectric dams and deforestation.

The silver lining in these hard times is the opportunity to stand back and take stock. Runaway development in the region, made possible through big foreign investments, has stalled. Even with the ratification of the Central American Free Trade Agreement (Cafta), criticisms abound; only time will tell if free trade is the right direction for the region. In the meantime the public is keeping a close eye on its Central American leadership.

Thomas E Skidmore's *Modern Latin America* has a 48-page summary of Central America's contemporary history. Costa Rican Héctor Pérez-Brignoli's *A Brief History of Central America* is a readable 222-page overview of the region.

Go to www.amnesty.org for Amnesty International reports on Central America.

HISTORY
Most believe the first Central Americans were people from Asia who migrated around 20,000 years ago across the frozen Bering Strait from Russia to Alaska and down through the Americas. Others argue that seafaring Asians crossed to present-day California only about 11,000 years ago. Either way, things have gotten decidedly more tense in the last few thousand years. Natural disasters, such as hurricanes, volcanic eruptions and mudslides, wrecked settlements, while rival city-states battled each other. Then the Europeans showed up.

Europeans, Meet 'Americans'
By the time the first Europeans with shiny helmets arrived in Central America – Christopher Columbus (Cristóbal Colón to his Spanish crew) made it here in 1502 – the region's greatest civilizations had already dissipated into the jungle (see p32).

Most of the 'Indians' who did meet the Spanish lived in small tribes, as corn farmers or hunter-gatherers. Other than a few scattered highland towns, and larger ones at present-day Managua and Granada in Nicaragua, nothing here rivaled the power centers of the Aztecs or Incas of the time.

Conquest & Colonization
The Spanish conquistadors – mostly poor, illiterate criminals sniffing out get-rich schemes – moved in independent factions, sometimes warring against each other. The first Spanish settlement in Central America was established in Panama in 1509, but further conquests were put on snooze. Instead, Panama served as a base for Francisco Pizarro's takeover of the Inca Empire in Peru. Meanwhile, in February 1519, Hernán Cortés landed at the isle of Cozumel and led his savage attacks on Mexico to the north.

Also in 1519 Pedro Arias de Ávila settled Panama City and began a bloody trip north while displaying incredible cruelty to the indigenous population. In 1524 he established León and Granada in today's Nicaragua, while Cortés' brutal lieutenant Pedro de Alvarado waged his own takeover of the Guatemala and El Salvador areas. With control over the region up for grabs, the two forces inevitably clashed in present-day Honduras.

Amid this, indigenous tribes fought each other, the Spanish (though some fought *with* the Spanish against rival clans) and smallpox (in present-day Mexico about 90% of the indigenous population died in the first 75 years of Spanish occupation). Many who weren't killed became slaves.

Eventually 'Guatemala' (Central America, including Chiapas but not Panama) was established as part of the viceroyalty of Mexico (then called Nueva España). The indigenous population was subjected to violent rule, tempered slightly after pleas to King Carlos V of Spain by Dominican friar Bartolomé de Las Casas in 1542. A colonial capital was established at Antigua in 1543. After a 1773 earthquake destroyed it, a new capital was created at Guatemala City.

According to the Maya calendar, time is cyclical and divided into 5200-year *kalpas* (eras) that end in destruction. The present era is set to end, by global annihilation, on December 23, 2012.

Independence
Colonial trade restrictions and governments run exclusively by European-born Spaniards eroded the patience of many *criollos* (people born in Latin America of Spanish parentage). The first Central American revolt, following Mexico's the previous year, flared in San Salvador in 1811 (led by priest José Matías Delgado and Manuel José Arce), but was quickly suppressed. By 1821 Mexico's viceroy, Agustín de Iturbide, defected to the rebels, and Guatemala's leaders reluctantly signed the first acts of independence. Spain finally let go for good on September 15, 1821. Guatemala was annexed by Iturbide's forces; conservatives welcomed the union. But Delgado and Arce staged a brief revolt in El Salvador (they even wanted to join the USA!).

Learn how one company's tropical meddling 'set the template for capitalism' in *Bananas: How the United Fruit Company Shaped the World*, by Peter Chapman.

Iturbide's reign was soon overthrown, and Central American states declared independence from Mexico in 1823 (Chiapas stayed with Mexico). The federation of five states – Guatemala, Honduras, El Salvador, Nicaragua and Costa Rica – had a brief, shaky existence (though they did manage to abolish slavery decades before the USA did). Arce became the first president, but succumbed to dictatorial tendencies and was overthrown. In 1837 a largely indigenous mob marched on Guatemala City and the federation dissolved in 1838, with the republics setting out on their own. See the History sections in individual country chapters for details on how they panned out.

An Era of Intervention

On September 21, 1981, the colony of British Honduras officially became the independent nation of Belize.

Starting in 1823 with the Monroe Doctrine (a policy of 'America for the Americas'), the USA has butted in on many of Central America's affairs. William Walker notoriously tried to take over the region in the mid-19th century and spurred on the era of 'banana republics,' the unfortunate tag for some of the region's more bendable governments. As bananas started bringing in big money, the US-funded United Fruit Company took control in 1899. In 1954, when the Guatemalan government planned to break up large estates into small private plots, the CIA orchestrated an invasion from Honduras. Soon after, the Guatemalan civil war broke out, leading to 200,000 deaths.

Throughout the 1970s and '80s, the sovereignty of the small nations of Central America was limited by their northern neighbor, the US. Big sticks, gun boats and dollar diplomacy were instruments of a Yankee policy to curtail socialist politics, especially the military oligarchies of Guatemala, El Salvador and Nicaragua.

In 1979, the rebellious Sandinistas toppled the American-backed Somoza dictatorship in Nicaragua. Alarmed by the Sandinistas' Soviet and Cuban ties, fervently anticommunist President Ronald Reagan, elected in 1981, decided it was time to intervene. The Cold War arrived in the hot tropics.

The Contra war escalated throughout the 1980s. Reagan began funding the counter-revolutionary Contras, operating out of Honduras and eventually out of Costa Rica as well. Soviet and Cuban military and economic aid poured in for the Sandinistas. After the US Congress rejected further military aid for the Contras in 1985, the Reagan administration secretly continued funding them through a scheme in which the CIA illegally sold weapons to Iran and diverted the proceeds to the Contras. When the details leaked out, the infamous 'Iran-Contra Affair' blew up.

After many failed peace initiatives, the Costa Rican president, Oscar Arias Sánchez, finally came up with an accord that was signed in August 1987 by the leaders of Costa Rica, El Salvador, Nicaragua, Guatemala and Honduras. Arias was given the Nobel Peace Prize the same year.

Modern Currents

'If we cannot export goods, we will keep exporting people.'

OSCAR ARIAS SÁNCHEZ, EX-PRESIDENT OF COSTA RICA AND WINNER OF THE 1987 NOBEL PEACE PRIZE

Central America is undergoing rampant urbanization. According to a UN estimate, the years since 1970 have seen all countries in the region except Guatemala move from a largely rural-based society to a predominately urban one. This is nowhere more evident than in El Salvador, which has the highest population density in the region.

With more land used for timber and cattle, villagers and farmers are feeling the squeeze. In addition, real estate is on the rise, thanks to both remittances and international retirement communities. Increasingly, those without means – and some estimates suggest 34% of Central America lives below the poverty line – are simply heading for the city (if not to the USA via Mexico).

Joining the new arrivals to Central American capitals have been convicted criminals, sent back home from the USA (as mandated by new legislation)

following any gang-related convictions. Unsurprisingly, the growing reports of gang activity and murder in Central America occur mostly in urban areas. The most infamous gang is the Mara Salvatrucha (or MS-13), a highly organized, multinational gang founded in Los Angeles, with more than 100,000 members.

Politics, meanwhile, swings both left and right. In Nicaragua former president and Sandinista leader Daniel Ortega was voted back in office in 2007 (using pink as a campaign color!), while El Salvador has elected many ex-FMLN guerrillas to its congress and even the presidency. On the other hand, the civil war–era, right-wing leader of Guatemala, José Efraín Ríos Montt, sought a term in congress in 2007, while a survivor of one of Montt's ordered raids, Maya writer Rigoberta Menchú, ran for president.

In politics, a key issue has been the Central American Free Trade Agreement (Cafta), an arrangement to open the local economies of Costa Rica, El Salvador, Guatemala, Honduras, Nicaragua and the Dominican Republic to US trade and investment, which went into effect on January 1, 2009. Proponents of Cafta tout its economic benefits, including increased access to US markets and the prospects of job creation. Critics argue that the accord does not protect Costa Rica's small farmers and domestic industries, which would inevitably struggle to compete with the anticipated flood of cheap US products.

THE CULTURE
People
Along the northern Pacific slopes are heavy populations of indigenous groups (more than half of Guatemala is Maya) and *ladinos* or *mestizos* (people of mixed indigenous and Spanish ancestry). It changes gradually to the south, as European features become more noticeable. In Costa Rica *criollos* account for more than 95% of the population. On the Caribbean, descendents of Africans dominate populations, while communities of Mennonites (in Belize) and Asians (throughout) add to the mix.

Official website www.pancanal.com offers webcams of the Panama Canal in action, cool cargo data and the lowdown on the US$5 billion expansion.

INDIGENOUS PEOPLES
Today all Central American countries have groups, larger or smaller, of *indígenas* (indigenous people). The largest surviving groups are the Maya communities of Guatemala, Belize, and Mexico's Chiapas and Yucatán Peninsula. Communities in the Guatemalan highlands (Chichicastenango and Lago de Atitlán, among others), and San Cristóbal de Las Casas, in Chiapas, are known for traditional costumes, such as goat-fur vests and striped blouses.

In Honduras and Nicaragua are many other indigenous groups, including the Tolupanes (Jicaque), Pech (Paya), Tawahka (Sumo), Lenca, Chortí and Miskito peoples. Nicaragua is also home to the Rama. El Salvador has small numbers of Izalco and Pancho, descended from the Pipil. Costa Rica has few native inhabitants, but they include the Boruca, Cabécar, Guatuso and Terraba. In Panama there are significant groups of Ngöbe-Buglé, Kuna and Chocóes, which are broken into two groups, the Emberá and the Wounaan, who still live deep in the Darién Gap. Panama's Kuna are a particular success story, since they run their area as an autonomous zone of 400 islands on the Caribbean coast and control all revenue and tourism investment.

Food Culture in Central America is much more than a simple cookbook. Written by anthropologist Michael R McDonald, it examines almost every conceivable aspect of food in Central America.

Throughout the past 500 years, many indigenous groups have given up traditional dress and language for the cell phone–toting urban, *ladino* society. Others live as independently as governments will allow and transform what's introduced to fit into their own customs.

PEOPLE OF AFRICAN DESCENT
Black people inhabit much of the Caribbean coast and many are descended from Africans brought to the West Indies (primarily Jamaica) as slaves. Black

Creoles (of mixed British and African descent) account for most of Belize's population. The Spanish brought many slaves to the region, especially to Panama, but most came from the Caribbean during the 19th century as laborers (not slaves) to work on banana plantations.

Along the northern coast, the Garífuna have descended from West African slaves and Carib indigenous people. They were transplanted to Honduras in 1797 from the Caribbean island of St Vincent, eventually establishing communities in Belize, Guatemala, Honduras and Nicaragua.

Say indígena (indigenous) in Central America and not indio (Indian), a term which is outright offensive to some (particularly in Costa Rica).

Arts
LITERATURE
Poetry's huge. Nicaraguan poet Rubén Darío (1867–1916) lived a debaucherous life (eg waking up hungover and married), but spoke for much of Latin America with his own *modernismo,* political-style. His provocative 'To Roosevelt' criticized the US president (Theodore, not Franklin) following the US invasion of Panama in 1903. He wrote: 'Our America, trembling with hurricanes, trembling with Love: zero men with Saxon eyes and barbarous souls, our America lives…Be careful.' *Stories and Poems/Cuentos y poesías* is a bilingual collection of his works.

El Salvador's Roque Dalton García (1935–1975) was also a radical poet and was eventually executed by fellow communists, who may have wrongly taken him for a CIA spy. *Miguel Marmol* is a collection of his works in English.

Guatemalan Miguel Ángel Asturias (1899–1974) won the Nobel Prize for Literature in 1967 for his representation of Latin American dictators in *El señor presidente.*

A K'iche' Maya writer from Guatemala, Rigoberta Menchú (b 1959), won the 1992 Nobel Peace Prize for her incredible recount of the Guatemalan civil war in *I, Rigoberta Menchú: An Indian Woman in Guatemala.* It later ignited controversy when some elements of the book were claimed to be false (which she acknowledged). Menchú has received death threats for years, which kept her in exile, but she returned to make a bid for the presidency in late 2007.

And We Sold the Rain: Contemporary Fiction from Central America (1988; edited by Rosario Santos) is a great collection of 20th-century writings from regional authors, with indigenous people a major theme.

MUSIC
Music is everywhere. Throughout much of the region everyone seems to love the xylophone-like marimba, proudly believed to be a Guatemalan invention. A Maya instrument, the *chirimía* (like an oboe) can still be heard in churches in the Guatemalan highlands. Salsa is huge everywhere, with big bands frequently playing outdoor shows for late-night plaza-packing crowds. Panamanian Rubén Blades is one of the world's best known *salseros* and songwriters, though perhaps better known for his acting in films such as *Once Upon a Time in Mexico.*

In recent years, reggae, reggaetón and other Afro-Caribbean sounds have increasingly spilled out from the Caribbean coastline to more stereos throughout the region. The Garífuna's drum-heavy traditional music, called *punta,* is made with conch shells, maracas and serious hip-shaking; it's based on West African traditions.

To learn how women have increasingly added to the Central American literary scene, see Writing Women in Central America: Gender & Fictionalization of History by Laura Barbas-Rhoden.

Religion
Roman Catholicism, introduced by the Spaniards, has since been Central America's principal religion, while Protestant sects have been predominant in British-influenced Caribbean areas. Things have been tipping more toward Protestantism in the past couple of decades, however, as waves of translated Bible-toting missionaries representing various evangelical religions (as well as Jehovah's Witnesses, Mennonites, Mormons and Seventh-Day Adventists) arrive with humanitarian projects. The Church of Scientology even opened a location in Managua. Some missionaries go to simply build schools, clinics or

LOCAL LORE

Understanding the traditions and lore of any region is key to understanding the heart and spirit of its people. Here are our favorites from each Central American country:

- **Belize – Mosquito** A Belizean legend tells of 'Mosquito' and 'Wax' being friends until Wax borrowed US$5 and didn't pay it back. Wax avoided Mosquito for months, until one day Mosquito found him and Wax jumped into the nearest hole to hide – an ear. Ever since, Mosquito buzzes around ears trying to collect the debt.

- **Costa Rica – La Negrita** Costa Rica's mysterious 'Black Virgin' (now the country's patron saint) is a statuette of an indigenous Virgin Mary, first found in 1635. According to tradition, whenever it's taken it reappears at the spot where it was originally – at La Basílica de Nuestra Señora de Los Ángeles (p551), built in her honor in 1824.

- **El Salvador – La Siguanaba** This mythical hottie seduces men, then turns grotesque and whorish, causing her victims to drop dead or go batty. La Siguanaba travels with her mischievous little boy Cipitío, who approaches women washing at rivers and hurls rocks at them.

- **Guatemala – La Llorona** This is the legend of a beautiful peasant woman who, jilted by her lover, drowned his children in the local river. Grief-stricken, she then drowned herself. Late at night, near water, you can sometimes hear her wailing, bemoaning the loss of the children.

- **Honduras – Little Virgin** She's just longer than your finger – but what a fuss she's caused! Found centuries ago in a cornfield, the 6cm-tall wooden statue of the Virgin of Suyapa is thought to have healing powers. When thieves seized her, there was a nationwide hunt until she was found in the men's room of a Tegucigalpa restaurant (see p348).

- **Mexico – Chamula** Folks in the Maya village San Juan Chamula (p43) believe that foreigners – whom they call 'Germans' – reach their village by 'following the lightning,' which 'leads to gold.' Newborns are carefully kept out of strangers' sight. If you should see one, the mother will ask you to kiss her baby *inmediatamente* to ensure no bad spirits are exchanged.

- **Nicaragua – La Carretanagua** This ghostly oxcart makes a hideous racket going down *pueblo* streets at the darkest hours of the darkest nights, driven by a skull-faced phantom (meaning someone in the village will die during the night). It is perhaps connected to folk memories of Spanish plunderers arriving with teams of oxen.

- **Panama – Teribe** According to the Teribe tribe, *indios conejos* (literally 'rabbit Indians') are nocturnal warriors who live deep in the jungle. They are pale-white with stripes on their backs and dwarfish in size, like giant rabbits. Although they are nearly invincible under cover of night, they can easily be killed if ambushed while sleeping during the day.

help rebuild after a natural disaster; many programs, however, openly work to convert. Some missionaries sermonize in plazas, criticize the 'unbelief' of 'ancestral worship' and keep tabs on millions of 'unreached people.'

Ethnic groups, however, continue to practice and preserve their traditional religions, sometimes fused with Catholicism. Maya beliefs and folk remedies, for example, have long been 'tolerated' by Catholic priests. Here, animist beliefs and chicken sacrifices freely merge with the (occasional moonshine-drinking) saints. The Garífuna of the region's Caribbean coastal areas continue to practice their traditional African-based religion, emphasizing the worship of ancestral spirits, in addition to Christianity.

Good times to hear Garífuna's *punta* music and dance are at Honduras' festivals and Belize's Garífuna Settlement Day (November 19).

ENVIRONMENT
The Land

Considering its diversity, Central America is remarkably small, measuring just 523,780 sq km (about the size of France or Texas; approximately 2% of Latin America) with never more than 280km separating the Caribbean Sea and the Pacific Ocean.

For an extensive, search-
able database of photo-
graphs of pre-Columbian
ceramics, have a look at
www.mayavase.com.

Created from four shifting tectonic plates over millions of years, Central America is the new kid on the block. As the world's major continental plates were slowly drifting into current positions from the Pangea landmass, this region surfaced from the sea and somersaulted snugly as a skinny, altruistic, 2400km land bridge between the two bigger Americas. Central America's two major plates (Cocos and Caribbean) still go at it, colliding at 10cm per year (geological light speed). Some day, far off, Central America may even split into two.

All that tectonic action helped create 300-plus volcanoes and one of the world's most active volcano zones. Guatemala's Volcán Fuego is one of the fieriest. Many volcanoes burp lava or ash on a regular basis, and bigger eruptions occur. Even 'extinct' ones sometimes erupt, as Costa Rica's Volcán Irazú did in 1963. El Salvador's Volcán Izalco emerged from ground level to its 1910m apex in the past 250 years.

Earthquakes rock the region as well. Over the years, San Salvador has been rebuilt nine times, and Antigua (Guatemala) has still not fully recovered from its 1773 quake.

Several cordilleras (mountain ranges) stretch for hundreds of kilometers down the Central American strip, broken by valleys and basins with fertile volcanic soil. Narrow, slightly sloping plains run along the coasts. When hurricanes or tidal waves hit, mudslides are common.

Wildlife

Central America's diverse and abundant animal and plant species owe much to the region's 'bridge' position between North and South America. Hundreds of continental runaways and migrators, such as jaguars and oak trees, have spilled into Central America – and stuck around.

ANIMALS

Volcano freaks can access
photos and updated
details at www.rci.
rutgers.edu/~carr.

Central America has 7% of the world's species on just 0.5% of the world's landmass. Costa Rica, Panama and Belize, in particular, are known for their abundant wildlife.

Many mammals can be discovered in the jungle: monkeys (spider, howler, squirrel), cats (jaguar, puma, ocelot), sloth, anteaters, bats and agoutis (simply fantastic creatures). Even more impressive is the number of birds that live or migrate here. More than 900 species have been recorded in Panama alone. The many birds of the region include toucans, macaws, parrots, harpy eagles and hummingbirds. Lucky visitors can spot a quetzal (ket-*sahl*), the national bird (and inspiration for the currency) of Guatemala and an important Maya symbol. These 35cm-long birds have bright green, red and white feathers; the March-to-June breeding season is the easiest time to spot one. Bird-watchers should consult Louie Irby Davis' *A Field Guide to the Birds of Mexico and Central America.*

If you see a turtle-nesting
site, do not startle the
fragile newborn by flash-
ing your camera in its
face – even if operators
say it's OK, it is *not*.

The areas in and around rivers, lakes and coastlines are home to many fish species. Amphibians and reptiles include sea, river and land turtles, crocodiles, frogs (watch out for the poisonous arrow frog) and iguanas.

Only a few of the many snake species are poisonous, notably the shy and tiny coral snake and large *barba amarilla* (or fer-de-lance). Some spiders such as the tarantula can be as big as a human face.

Deforestation and hunting have left a mark on many species, such as the quetzal, with some species facing extinction.

PLANTS

There are five major types of vegetation zones in Central America, all influenced by differing altitudes, climates and soils.

SAVING THE ENDANGERED SEA TURTLES *Matthew D Firestone*

Of the seven kinds of sea turtles, four frequent Central America's beaches: olive ridley, leatherback, green and hawksbill. All four species, classified as endangered or critically endangered, face an imminent threat of extinction.

Habitat destruction is a huge problem. With the exception of the leatherbacks, these species return to their natal beach to nest. Development or artificial lighting (including flashlights) kills the mood – and the reproductive cycle. Leatherbacks have their own problems. The Leatherback Trust estimates that 63% of all Pacific leatherbacks get hooked by commercial fishing loglines, resulting in a 15% to 18% death rate.

Hunting and harvesting eggs are also responsible for declining populations. Since the enforcement of bans requires lots of nighttime beach patrols during turtle-nesting season, this is an area where travelers can pitch in. See individual country chapters for more information.

On the Caribbean coast, up to 850m, tropical rainforest has canopies of tall trees and lush ground cover. The Pacific coastal strip (and northern Belize) is home to tropical dry forest, with trees and shrubs parched brown during the dry season.

Higher up, from 850m to 1650m, the cooler climate is home to a mixed upland forest of evergreens, pines and deciduous oaks. One of the loveliest terrains, just higher up again, is the cloud forest. The extreme humidity helps keep tall trees from drying out, which also protects a herb- and moss-covered floor from direct sunlight.

A few areas above 3000m have alpine vegetation, with short grasses (such as the Chilean *páramo* in Costa Rica) and flowering herbs.

National Parks & Reserves

Central America has some 250 national parks, nature reserves and other protected areas. The most remote parks – such as Reserva de Biosfera Maya that comprises much of northern Guatemala – include vast areas with no infrastructure. Meanwhile, some of the most popular parks (such as Costa Rica's Parque Nacional Manuel Antonio) are touristed to the point of threatening the environment.

Environmental Issues

Central America's position between two oceans (and their hurricanes and tropical storms) makes its environment particularly vulnerable. Humans have an impact too. Deforestation of tropical rainforest – the 'lungs of the planet' – continues at a reckless pace. In 1950 about 60% of Central America was covered by tropical forest; only half remains today. Some 95% of El Salvador's original forest is gone, while Guatemala reportedly clears 3% to 5% of its Reserva de Biosfera Maya (in El Petén) annually. Hamburgers are as much to blame as timber, as the expansion of livestock farms increases. In addition, deforestation has led to soil erosion, which results in severe flooding and mudslides, as evidenced by Hurricane Stan in 2005.

Nonetheless, scientists believe millions of additional species remain undiscovered, including plant species potentially important for pharmaceutical purposes. Central America still has some incredible wilderness areas where the forests remain largely unexplored, for example the Darién region of Panama. The forests are also still home to indigenous peoples, such as the Miskito in Honduras and Nicaragua, and the Emberá and Wounaan of Panama.

Occasionally new problems are not human fault, such as in early 2007, when a waterborne fungal disease wiped out several amphibian groups in Panama, including the rockhopper frog. The chytrid virus is posing a

A few worthy books include *The Good Alternative Travel Guide*, Mark Mann's *The Community Tourism Guide* and Adrian Forsyth's entertaining *Tropical Nature: Life and Death in the Rain Forests of Central and South America*.

serious threat to amphibians worldwide, with scientists racing to protect species and study the cause.

Meanwhile, ecotourism remains a buzzword. Organizations of national parks and reserves are devoted to helping conserve and protect natural environments, but in many cases where resources have developed past the point of sustainability, 'ecotourism' has become a true misnomer.

THE MAYA

It's not a contest, but of the New World's three biggest pre-Columbian civilizations (Aztec, Inca and Maya), Maya is usually considered the greatest. During its peak (around AD 750), possibly 10 million people thrived in stone cities of up to 200,000 inhabitants. The Maya's turf sprawled over much of present-day southern Mexico, Guatemala, Belize, El Salvador and Honduras (making up the Ruta Maya). The Maya elite used hieroglyphs to record battles, reigns, beliefs and precise planetary movements. Atop towering blood-red pyramids were vaulted temples adorned with bas-relief tributes to the gods. Many Maya from neighboring cities who saw these impressive pyramids were soon tortured and executed: the captured were not treated kindly.

Much remains unknown about the Maya, however. New theories are rolled out regularly, particularly as to why, at the peak of power, the Maya world suddenly collapsed.

History

During the Maya Preclassic period (2000 BC to AD 250), the first prototypes for the great art to come were drafted at cities such as the giant El Mirador (Guatemala). Two masterful calendars were developed: a 260-day year, and a 365-day *haab* ('vague' year), with five dreaded unlucky days at the end of 18 20-day months. The earliest known use of the calendar dates from 36 BC.

Maya cities as we know them best took shape during the Classic period (AD 250–900), when Palenque, Tikal, Cobán and Copán flourished. Pyramids skyrocketed, topped with ornate stone roof combs, not the thatched huts atop most central Mexican sites.

Then, in the late-Classic period (AD 800–900), came the collapse. Cities were abandoned, population numbers diminished; those who remained lived in small hut communities scattered about the region. Common theories for what happened include overpopulation, war between city-states, revolution and drought.

Most Postclassic (AD 900–1524) activity occurred in the Yucatán (notably Chichén Itzá), based on a union of overtaken Maya and their new lords from the north, the Toltecs.

At the time of the Spanish conquest, Tulum was still occupied, but the heyday of Maya civilization was clearly past, with the giant cities lost in jungle. Still, the weakened Maya put up some of the toughest resistance to the Spanish in the Americas.

Put in a little time to help the environment by volunteering. Near Tikal, there are opportunities with local wildlife projects (see boxed text, p192). In Panama, you can help sea-turtle populations by monitoring nesting sites (see boxed text, p683). See p723 for more on volunteering.

The Academia de Lenguas Mayas website (www.almg.org.gt) is packed with information about Maya languages, legends, music and ceremonial sites.

READING UP ON MAYA HISTORY

The best introduction to Maya history is Mayanist Michael D Coe's enduring *The Maya,* while his surprisingly engaging *Breaking the Maya Code* reviews the wacky, bitchy world of Mayanists. Much of what we do know about the Maya comes from a Spaniard who destroyed hundreds of priceless Maya books and idols in the 16th century. Friar Diego de Landa, a Franciscan, was ordered by his superiors to write a detailed book on Maya customs and took a stab at a Maya alphabet. Much is described in his *Yucatán Before and After the Conquest.*

Beliefs & Rituals

According to the *Popol Vuh* (aka the 'Maya Bible'), which was written postconquest by the K'iche' Maya, it took the great god K'ucumatz three tries to get humans right. The first two failures involved making people from mud, then wood, before humans were successfully made from ground corn and water.

Corn, or maize, has always played a huge role for the Maya. Some even tattooed their faces to resemble kernels. A surprising crucifix-like shape on monuments actually symbolizes corn husks. Even now, some Catholic churches in the region have altars to maize.

Another part of worship was sacrifice, which wasn't limited to slaves and captured foes; children, dogs and squirrels were also offerings for the many Maya gods. Some ceremonies involved painful rituals such as women slicing their tongues and threading them with thorn-studded rope, or men jabbing needles into their penises.

Other painful procedures where merely cosmetic, such as tying flat boards to infants in order to flatten foreheads. Some Maya skulls have been found with hundreds of small holes in them.

The so-called 'last unconquered tribe' of the Maya are the 700 or so Lacandón who live in primitive communities in Chiapas' jungles in south Mexico. After much resistance, many of these Maya, known for their long hair with bangs and white robes, are changing their religious beliefs, largely the result of missionaries.

Modern Currents

Some visitors are surprised to learn that the Maya are very much alive in northern Central America and southern Mexico, rebounding from the disease and destruction the European colonists introduced 500 years ago. The native languages, such as Yucatec and K'iche', are still widely spoken, and populations are growing. Estimates suggest there are six million Maya today. Guatemala is said to be 40% Maya, and Mexico's biggest indigenous population is that of the Yucatec in the Yucatán Peninsula.

These population figures, however, don't mean the struggle for equality ended with independence from Spain in 1821. In 1847 the War of the Castes erupted in the Yucatán, with Maya rebels nearly driving out Europeans for good. More recently, the Guatemalan civil war in the 1980s saw some 400 Maya villages wiped out by government troops and paramilitaries. In Chiapas in 1994, a guerrilla force of chiefly Tzotzil and Tzeltal Maya kicked off the Zapatista 'revolution' – seeking more say in how public land is used in the wake of Nafta (North American Free Trade Agreement).

Over the generations, many alien products and ideologies have been absorbed into daily life, without completely replacing traditional ways and beliefs. For generations, the Chamula community outside San Cristóbal de Las Casas in Mexico used *chicha* (a corn-based drink) to help them burp out evil spirits in holy places; after the Spanish introduced Catholicism, and the Americans Coca-Cola, the Chamula simply began using bottles of the fizzy soda in cathedrals where, on occasion, a chicken is sacrificed.

Everything you need to know about the ancient ball game played by the Maya is available at www.ballgame.org.

'I blame two things for the recent decay of the local Maya traditions: cell phones and missionaries.'

SAN CRISTÓBAL DE LAS CASAS (MEXICO) RESIDENT

Mexico's Yucatán & Chiapas

Caught between the relentless beat of progress and the echoing shouts of tradition, the Yucatán Peninsula, plus its highlands neighbor of Chiapas, stand at the crossroads. On one side you have the brawny megaresorts with their oft-preposterous pomp and circumstance, on the other are the proud, steadfast traditions of the Maya, the mystery of the ceremonial centers created by their ancestors, and the Old World allure of colonial masterpieces like Mérida, Campeche and San Cristóbal de Las Casas. And in between, on every peroxide-blonde beach and every patch of jungle still echoing with the roars of howler monkeys, beats the heart of Ixchel, the earth goddess, marveling at her remarkable creation.

Despite overzealous development, the natural beauty of this region abides with verdant jungle hideaways, freshwater limestone sinkholes (known locally as cenotes), and the giant Mesoamerican Reef. Found just offshore from Quintana Roo, this is the world's second-largest barrier reef, making the Caribbean coast a snorkeling and beach destination par excellence.

FAST FACTS

- **Area** Yucatán state 39,340 sq km; Quintana Roo 50,351 sq km; Campeche 56,798 sq km; Chiapas 74,211 sq km; 220,700 sq km in total

- **Budget** US$40 to US$50 per day
- **Capital** Mexico City
- **Costs** Budget room US$15 to US$40, three-hour bus ride US$10, set lunch US$4
- **Country Code** ☎ 52
- **Languages** Spanish and two dozen Maya languages
- **Money** US$1 = M$13 (Mexican pesos)
- **Population** eight million (Yucatán, Quintana Roo, Campeche and Chiapas states)
- **Seasons** high (July and August, December to March), low (rest of the year)
- **Time** GMT minus six hours; GMT minus five hours during daylight-saving time

TRAVEL HINTS

It's easy to take day trips to big-time archaeological sites like Uxmal and Chichén Itzá, but by staying in local communities near these sites, you are more likely to have a positive impact on the local economy – plus, you'll gain a unique perspective.

OVERLAND ROUTES

From Mexico you can loop into Guatemala – from San Cristóbal de Las Casas to Quetzaltenango, or to Tikal via Palenque – and into Corozal, Belize, from Chetumal, south of Tulum.

HIGHLIGHTS

- **Chichén Itzá** (p56) Explore the age-old ruins and find out why they named this 'the seventh modern wonder of the world.'
- **Tulum** (p68) Stroll along long stretches of white-sand beach and the nearby Maya ruin; though it's no longer a quiet backpacker hub, there are still cheap sleeps and plenty of space.
- **San Cristóbal de Las Casas** (p37) Pull on a sweater and sip fresh espresso in the cool, mountainous 'Zapatista capital,' one of the Americas' finest colonial-era towns.
- **Mérida** (p53) Put your best salsa foot forward during the more-than-lively, street-spilling weekend fair in this Spanish-colonial wonder near Maya ruins and seldom explored estuaries.
- **Off the beaten track** (p71) Adventure out to the untouched and out-of-the-way fishing village Punta Allen, which lies within a protected reserve and offers snorkel trips to dolphin hangouts.

CURRENT EVENTS

In the 2006 national election, PAN's (Partido de Acción Nacional) Felipe Calderón narrowly defeated the left-leaning López Obrador of the Partido de la Revolución Democrática (PRD). Obrador's supporters alleged fraud, kicking off massive national protests, which have since quieted. And then came Calderón's mobilization of the military to counteract Mexico's drug-trafficking problem, which triggered more backlash (especially in Mexico's northern states). The perception of violence – coupled with the 2009 outbreak of the H1N1 'swine flu' virus – drastically affected visitation to the Yucatán's resort areas. And while the real risk of the virus is far more mild than the media hype would have had us believe, the resorts continue to struggle. Combine that with the worldwide economic crisis that rocketed into full force that year, and you have the makings of a real disaster.

HISTORY

The Maya set up many city-states across the broad south of Mexico, though the population and activity had declined before the Spanish arrived. (For more on Maya history, see p32.) A couple of Spaniards – Diego de Mazariegos in present-day Chiapas, and Francisco de Montejo in the Yucatán – had the area under Spanish control by the mid-16th century. Mexico won independence from Spain in 1821, and pulled in Chiapas from the United Provinces of Central America in 1824.

Long oppressed by Spaniards and *criollos* (Latin Americans of Spanish lineage), the Maya rose in the War of the Castes in 1847, leading to destroyed churches and many massacres. The brimming sense of inequal-ity didn't settle with peace in 1901. As Nafta (North American Free Trade Agreement) kicked into effect in 1994, the mainly Maya Zapatistas stormed San Cristóbal de Las Casas. Their struggle has quieted down in recent years, now that they run seven autonomous zones (called *caracoles*, literally 'snails') outside San Cristóbal. But it's not over.

THE CULTURE

Travelers often comment on the open, gentle and gregarious nature of the people of the Yucatán, especially the Yucatecan Maya. Here, more than elsewhere in Mexico, it seems you find a willingness to converse, a genuine interest in outsiders, while the obsequious attitude often encountered elsewhere in the country is absent. This openness is all the more remarkable when you consider that the people of the Yucatán Peninsula have fended off domination by outsiders for so long – a situation that persists today.

TRANSPORTATION

GETTING THERE & AWAY
Air

Most visitors to the Yucatán arrive by air. Air routes are structured so that virtually all international flights into the region pass through a handful of 'hub' cities: Dallas/Fort Worth, Houston, Los Angeles, Mexico City, Miami or New York. The majority of flights into the peninsula arrive at busy **Aeropuerto Internacional de Cancún** (CUN; ☎ 998-886-0047; www.cancun-airport. com). The region's other gateways are **Cozumel** (CZM; ☎ 987-872-2081; www.asur.com.mx), **Chetumal** (CTM; ☎ 983-832-0898), **Mérida** (MID; ☎ 999-946-1530; www.asur.com.mx) and Campeche (CPE).

AIRLINES FLYING TO/FROM THE YUCATÁN

Air Berlin (airline code AB; ☎ in Germany 01805-73-7800; www.airberlin.com; hub Dusseldorf)

American Airlines (airline code AA; ☎ 800-904-6000; www.aa.com; hub Dallas); Cancún (☎ 998-866-0086)

Continental Airlines (airline code CO; ☎ 800-900-5000; www.continental.com; hub Houston); Cancún (☎ 998-866-0006)

Delta Airlines (airline code DL; ☎ 800-123-4710; www.delta.com; hub Atlanta); Cancún (☎ 998-866-0660)

Frontier Airlines (airline code F9; ☎ in USA 800-432-1359; www.frontierairlines.com; hub Denver)

Northwest (airline code NW; ☎ 800-907-4700); Cancún (☎ 998-866-0044)

TACA Airlines (airline code TA; ☎ 800-400-8222; www.taca.com; hub San Salvador); Cancún (☎ 998-866-0008)

Boat & Bus

Mexico borders Guatemala and Belize to the south, and there is an array of border crossings between them.

From Quintana Roo, travelers can connect to buses to Belize (or on to Flores, Guatemala) via Chetumal (see boxed text, p71), just north of Corozal, Belize. At the time of writing, each person leaving Belize for Mexico needed to pay a US$18.75 exit fee. All fees must be paid in cash (in Belizean or US currency), and officials usually won't have change for US currency.

From Chiapas, there are three major border crossings to Guatemala. Southeast of Palenque, at Frontera Corozal, it's possible to boat over to Bethel and get a bus; tour packages ease the uncertainties of this journey (see boxed text, p47). South of San Cristóbal de Las Casas, the best way into Guatemala is at Ciudad Cuauhtémoc, near La Mesilla, Guatemala (see boxed text, p43). Another option is crossing into Guatemala from the Mexican border town of Tapachula, further southwest.

GETTING AROUND
Air

Flights from other parts of Mexico arrive at the airports of Campeche, Mérida, Cancún,

---

DEPARTURE TAX

A departure tax equivalent to about US$48 is levied on international flights from Mexico. It's usually included in the price of your ticket, but if it isn't, you must pay in cash during airport check-in. Ask your travel agent in advance.

THE ZAPATISTAS

To learn more about the Zapatistas, check out www.ezln.org.mx (in Spanish). Further background is available in *The Zapatista Reader,* an anthology of writers from Octavio Paz and Gabriel García Márquez to the Zapatista leader Marcos himself, as well as at **SiPaz** (www.sipaz.org) and **CMI** (www.chiapas.indymedia.org) websites.

Cozumel, Playa del Carmen, Ciudad del Carmen, Chetumal and Tulum. Another useful gateway for the region is Tuxtla Gutiérrez, which services San Cristóbal de Las Casas in Chiapas. There are two taxes on domestic flights: IVA, the value-added tax (15%), and TUA, an airport tax of about US$12. In Mexico, the taxes are normally included in quoted fares and paid when you buy the ticket. If you buy the ticket outside Mexico, though, you will have to pay the TUA when you check-in in Mexico.

The national carriers for domestic and international flights include the following:

Aeroméxico (airline code AM; ☎ 800-021-4010; www.aeromexico.com; hub Mexico City); Campeche (☎ 981-823-4044); Cancún (☎ 998-287-1860); Mérida (☎ 999-920-1293)

Mexicana de Aviación (airline code MX; ☎ 800-801-2010; www.mexicana.com; hub Mexico City); Cancún (☎ 998-881-9090)

Boat

Ferries connect Cancún with Isla Mujeres and Playa del Carmen with Isla Cozumel. Ferries also go to Isla Holbox from north of Cancún. Most visitors to Yaxchilán go by boat.

Bus

Mexico's bus system is luxurious, with frequent services (unlike much of Central America's); many buses have air-con, toilets, reserved seating and movies. And you pay for it – prices are substantially higher than in the rest of Central America.

Buses in the Yucatán rarely fill, but try to reserve ahead for night buses between the Yucatán and Chiapas. You can book some 1st-class buses through **Ticket Bus** (☎ 800-702-8000; www.ticketbus.com.mx).

UNO (☎ 800-702-8000; www.uno.com.mx), **ADO GL** (☎ 800-702-8000; www.adogl.com.mx) and **OCC** (☎ 800-822-2369; www.occbus.com.mx) provide luxury services. **ADO** (☎ 800-802-8000; www.ado.com.mx) sets the 1st-class standard. The biggest 2nd-class companies are Mayab, Oriente and **Noreste** (☎ 800-280-1010; www.noreste.com.mx).

First-class buses typically cost around M$40 per hour of travel (70km to 80km). Deluxe buses may cost just 10% or 20% more than 1st class, or about 60% more for super-deluxe services such as UNO. Second-class buses cost 10% or 20% less than 1st class.

Note that there have been occasional highway robberies on overnight buses over the years. You can store bags in the secure luggage hold.

Car & Motorcycle

To rent a car or scooter you'll need to show a valid driver's license (your country's license is OK) and a major credit card.

Local Transportation

Many locals prefer piling into vans or *colectivos* (shared taxis or minibuses), which travel on shorter routes. They cost about the same as a 2nd-class bus, but *colectivos* go more frequently.

CHIAPAS

Chilly pine-forest highlands, sultry rainforest jungles and attractive colonial cities exist side by side within Mexico's southernmost state, a region awash with the legacy of Spanish rule and the remnants of ancient Maya civilization. The state has the second-largest indigenous population in the country, and the modern Maya of Chiapas form a direct link to the past, with a traditional culture that persists to this day. Many indigenous communities rely on subsistence farming and have no running water or electricity, and it was frustration over lack of political power and their historical mistreatment that fueled the Zapatista rebellion, putting a spotlight on the region's inequities.

SAN CRISTÓBAL DE LAS CASAS

☎ 967 / pop 250,000 / elev 1940m

Set in a gorgeous highland valley surrounded by pine forest, the colonial city of San Cristóbal (cris-*toh*-bal) has been a popular travelers' destination for decades. It's a pleasure to explore its cobbled streets and markets, soaking up the unique ambience and the wonderfully clear highland light. Medium-sized San Cristóbal also boasts a comfortable blend of city and countryside, with restored century-old houses giving way to grazing animals and fields of corn.

Surrounded by dozens of traditional Tzotzil and Tzeltal villages, San Cristóbal is at the heart of one of the most deeply rooted indigenous areas in Mexico. A great base for local and regional exploration, it's a place where ancient customs coexist with modern luxuries.

Orientation

San Cristóbal is very walkable, with straight streets rambling up and down several gentle hills. The Pan-American Hwy (Hwy 190, Blvr Juan Sabines, 'El Bulevar') runs through the southern part of town, and nearly all transportation terminals are on it or nearby. From the OCC bus terminal, it's six blocks north up Insurgentes to the central square, Plaza 31 de Marzo. Heading east from the plaza, Calle Real de Guadalupe, which remains pedestrian-only for a few blocks, has a concentration of places to stay and eat. A longer pedestrian mall, the Andador Turístico (or Andador Eclesiástico), runs up Avs Hidalgo and 20 de Noviembre from the Arco de El Carmen in the south to the Templo de Santo Domingo in the north, crossing Plaza 31 de Marzo en route. The Cerro de San Cristóbal and Cerro de Guadalupe lord over the town from the west and east, respectively.

Information

Banamex (Insurgentes 9; ☺ 9am-4pm Mon-Sat) Has an ATM; exchanges dollars and euros.
El Locutorio (☎ 631-4828; Av 20 de Noviembre 20A; ☺ 9am-9pm) Inexpensive international calls.
Hospital Amigo del Niño y de la Madre (☎ 678-0770; Insurgentes) General hospital with emergency facilities.
Lavandería Las Estrellas (Real de Guadalupe 75; per kg M$10; ☺ 8:30am-7pm Mon-Sat)
Main post office (Allende 3; ☺ 7:30am-7pm Mon-Fri, 8:30am-3:30pm Sat)
Municipal tourist office (☎ 678-0665; Palacio Municipal, Plaza 31 de Marzo; ☺ 8am-9pm)

Dangers & Annoyances

Because of incidences of assault on female passengers, women riding alone in taxis at night should take extra precautions.

Sights

PLAZA 31 DE MARZO

The leafy main plaza is a fine place to take in San Cristóbal's unhurried highland atmosphere. On the north side of the plaza, the **cathedral** was begun in 1528 but wasn't completed till 1815 because of several natural disasters. Sure enough, new earthquakes struck in 1816 and 1847, causing considerable damage, but it was restored again between 1920 and 1922. The gold-leaf interior has five gilded altarpieces featuring 18th-century paintings by Miguel Cabrera.

The **Hotel Santa Clara**, on the plaza's southeast corner, was built by Diego de Mazariegos, the Spanish conqueror of Chiapas. His coat of arms is engraved above the main portal. The house is a rare secular example of plateresque style in Mexico.

CERRO DE SAN CRISTÓBAL & CERRO DE GUADALUPE

Want to take in the best views in town? Well, you'll have to work for them, because at this altitude the stairs up these hills can be punishing. Churches crown both lookouts, and the Iglesia de Guadalupe becomes a hot spot for religious devotees around the Día de la Virgen de Guadalupe (December 12). These areas are not considered safe at night.

TEMPLO & EX-CONVENTO DE SANTO DOMINGO

Located just north of the center, the 16th-century **Templo de Santo Domingo** (admission free; 6:30am-2pm & 4-8pm) is San Cristóbal's most beautiful church, especially when its facade catches the late-afternoon sun. The baroque frontage, with its outstanding filigree stucco work, was added in the 17th century and includes the double-headed Hapsburg eagle, symbol of the Spanish monarchy in those

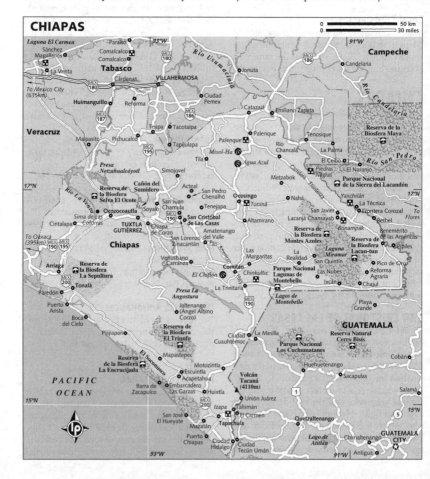

CHIAPAS

DANGERS & ANNOYANCES IN CHIAPAS

Drug trafficking and illicit northbound immigration are concerns along the border regions with Guatemala, and military checkpoints are frequent on the Carretera Fronteriza along the Guatemalan border from Palenque to the Lagos de Montebello. These checkpoints generally increase security for travelers, though it's best to be off the Carretera Fronteriza before dark. For similar reasons all border crossings with Guatemala are places you should aim to get through early in the day.

Indigenous villages are often extremely close-knit, and their people can be suspicious of outsiders and particularly sensitive about having their photos taken. In some villages cameras are, at best, tolerated – and sometimes not even that. You may put yourself in physical danger by taking photos without permission. If in any doubt, ask first.

Occasional flare-ups occur between Zapatista communities and the army or anti-Zapatista paramilitaries. If you plan to travel off the main roads in the Chiapas highlands, the Ocosingo area or far-eastern Chiapas, take local advice about where to avoid going. Unknown outsiders might also be at risk in these areas because of local political or religious conflicts.

---

days. The interior is lavishly gilded, especially the ornate pulpit.

Around Santo Domingo and the neighboring **Templo de la Caridad** (built in 1712), Chamulan women and bohemian types from around Mexico conduct a colorful daily crafts market. The ex-monastery attached to Santo Domingo contains two interesting exhibits: one is the weavers' showroom of Señora Jolobil; the other is the **Centro Cultural de los Altos** (☎ 678-1609; Calz Lázaro Cárdenas s/n; admission M$41; ☯ 10am-5pm Tue-Sun), which boasts a Spanish-language museum on the history of the San Cristóbal region.

NA BOLOM

A **museum and research center** (☎ 678-1418; www.nabolom.org; Guerrero 33; view house only regular/student/senior M$35/20/20, 1½hr tour in English or Spanish M$45; ☯ 9am-8pm, tour 4:30pm Tue-Sun), Na Bolom is dedicated to the study and support of Chiapas' indigenous cultures and natural environment, and has community and environmental programs in indigenous areas. Its library of more than 9000 books and documents is a major resource on the Maya.

MERCADO MUNICIPAL

For a closer look at local life – and an assault on the senses – visit San Cristóbal's busy municipal **market** (☯ 7am-5pm), eight blocks north of the main plaza between Utrilla and Belisario Domínguez.

MUSEO DE LA MEDICINA MAYA

This award-winning **museum** (☎ 678-5438; www.medicinamaya.org; Av Salomón González Blanco 10; admission M$20; ☯ 10am-6pm Mon-Fri, to 5pm Sat & Sun) introduces the system of traditional medicine used

by many indigenous people in the Chiapas highlands.

ARCO & CENTRO CULTURAL EL CARMEN

The **Arco de El Carmen**, at the southern end of the Andador Turístico on Av Hidalgo, dates from the late 17th century and was once the city's gateway. The ex-convent just east is a wonderful colonial building, with a large peaceful garden. It's now the **Centro Cultural El Carmen** (Hermanos Domínguez s/n; admission free; ☯ 9am-6pm Tue-Sun), hosting art and photography exhibitions and the occasional musical event.

CAFÉ MUSEO CAFÉ

This **cafe and coffee museum** (☎ 678-7876; MA Flores 10; admission M$25; ☯ 8am-10pm; ☏) is a venture of Coopcafé, a grouping of more than 17,000 small-scale (mainly indigenous) Chiapas coffee growers.

MUSEO DEL ÁMBAR DE CHIAPAS

The **Museo del Ámbar de Chiapas** (Chiapas Amber Museum; ☎ 678-9716; www.museodelambar.com.mx; Plazuela de la Merced; admission M$20; ☯ 10am-2pm & 4-7:30pm Tue-Sun) explains all things amber (with information sheets in English and other languages) and displays and sells some exquisitely carved items and insect-embedded pieces.

Courses

El Puente Spanish Language School (☎ 678-3723; www.elpuenteweb.com; Real de Guadalupe 55; individual/group per week M$2450/2200) offers language courses. **La Casa en el Árbol** (☎ 674-5272; www.lacasaenel arbol.org; Real de Mexicanos 10; classes individual/group per hr M$143/91, 7-day homestay M$1885) Socially committed school that teaches Tzeltal and Tzotzil as well as Spanish. It offers lots of out-of-school activities and is also a base for volunteer programs.

Tours

Recommended tour agencies offering a variety of trips include the following:

Explora (☎ 674-6660; www.ecochiapas.com; 1 de Marzo 30; ◷ 9:30am-2pm & 4-8pm Mon-Fri, 9:30am-2pm Sat)
Otisa (☎ 678-1933; www.otisatravel.com; Real de Guadalupe 3C)

Festivals & Events

Semana Santa The crucifixion is acted out on Good Friday in the Barrio de Mexicanos in the northwest of town.

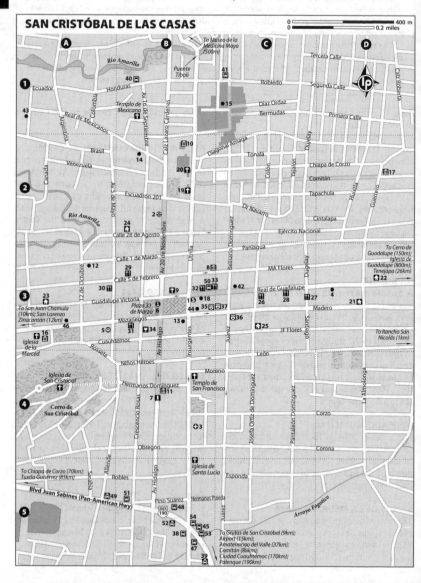

SAN CRISTÓBAL DE LAS CASAS

Feria de la Primavera y de la Paz (Spring and Peace Fair) Easter Sunday is the start of the weeklong town fair, with parades, musical events, bullfights and so on.

Festival Internacional de las Culturas (www.conecultachiapas.gob.mx) In mid- to late October, this free weeklong cultural program keeps hopping with music, dance and theater.

Sleeping

Rancho San Nicolás (☎ 678-0057; jultov@hotmail.com; Prolongación León, Ranulfo Tovilla 47; campsites per person with/without car M$70/50, r without bathroom per person M$70, cabañas per person M$70, d villas M$300; P ☎) Past cornfields and grazing horses, this spot on the edge of town is a tranquil dose of the *campo* (countryside) in the city.

Hostal Rincón de los Camellos (☎ 116-0097; www.loscamellos.over-blog.com; Real de Guadalupe 110; dm M$80, s/d/tr/q M$220/280/330/400, without bathroom M$160/220/270/340; ☎) A clean, tranquil little spot run by a welcoming French-Mexican trio. The brightly painted rooms are set around two patios, with a grassy little garden out back. A small kitchen has free drinking water and coffee.

Posada Ganesha (☎ 678-0212; www.ganeshaposada.com; 28 de Agosto 23; dm M$100, s/d/tr without bathroom M$150/250/300, all incl breakfast; ☎) An incense-infused *posada* (guesthouse) trimmed in Indian fabrics, this is a friendly and vibrant place to rest your head, with daily yoga classes, a simple guest kitchen and a pleasant new lounge area. The free-standing *cabaña* (cabin) room is especially nice.

Posada México (☎ 678-0014; www.hostellingmexico.com; Josefa Ortiz de Domínguez 12; dm M$100, r with/without bathroom M$360/280, tr with/without bathroom M$480/420, all incl breakfast; ✗ 🖳 ☎) A large courtyard compound with stunning mountain views, this HI-affiliated hostel has pretty gardens, good bright rooms and dorms (one for women only), a kitchen, a pool table, a DVD library, lots of comfy terraces, patios and lounges and a small new bar. A 10% discount available for HI card-holders.

Hostel Las Palomas (☎ 674-7034; www.laspalomas hostel.com; Guadalupe Victoria 47; dm M$120, r with/without bathroom M$500/250, all incl breakfast; ✗ 🖳 ☎) Bask in the sunny courtyard of this colonial building, where the private en-suite rooms have a fireplace and skylights. Dorms (some with queen-sized beds for budget-minded couples) come equipped with lockers and in-room bathroom, while private rooms with shared bathroom are simpler.

B&B Le Gite del Sol (☎ 631-6012; www.legitedelsol.com; Madero 82; s/d/tr/q M$250/300/390/460, without bathroom M$160/200/300/400, all incl breakfast; P ✗ 🖳 ☎) A bountiful breakfast complements simple rooms with radiant sunflower-yellow floors.

Eating

Self-caterers can stock up at the centrally located **Super Más** (Real de Guadalupe 22; ☽ 8am-9:30pm) market, plus a handy cluster of **fruit and vegetable shops** on Dugelay between Madero and MA Flores.

Arez (☎ 678-6308; Real de Guadalupe 29; wraps M$25-45, mains M$60-90; ☺ noon-11pm; ☒ Ⓥ) Lamb shawarma and other delicious dishes grace the menu of this new Lebanese falafel spot. Try the 'barbecue Arez,' with grilled beef, chicken, onions and peppers.

TierrAdentro (☎ 674-6766; Real de Guadalupe 24; set menu M$35-73; ☺ 8am-11pm; ☒ ☏) A popular gathering center for coffee-swigging, laptop-toting locals, this large indoor courtyard restaurant and cafe is a comfortable place to while away the hours. It's run by Zapatista supporters, who hold frequent cultural events and conferences on local issues here. A simple yet delicious *menú compa* (M$35) rotates daily, with hearty offerings like rice and beans with handmade tortillas.

La Casa del Pan Papalotl (☎ 678-7215; Centro Cultural El Puente, Real de Guadalupe 55; mains M$40-68; ☺ 8:30am-10pm Mon-Sat; ☒ Ⓥ) This excellent courtyard vegetarian restaurant does a particularly filling buffet lunch from 1pm to 5pm (M$80). Fresh bread and locally grown organic ingredients are staples here.

Mayambé (☎ 674-6278; 5 de Mayo 10; set menu M$40, mains M$45-95; ☺ 9:30am-11pm; Ⓥ) This superb courtyard restaurant boasts a wonderful range of Asian, Middle Eastern and Mediterranean dishes on the menu, including plenty of vegetarian options.

Namandí Café & Crepas (☎ 678-8054; Mazariegos 16C; crepes M$55-75; ☺ 8am-11pm; ☒ ☏) Nattily attired waiters serve baguette sandwiches, pastas and good coffee at this large, modern cafe and restaurant.

L'Eden (☎ 678-0085; Hotel El Paraíso, 5 de Febrero 19; mains M$58-120; ☺ 7am-11pm) This quality restaurant's tempting European and Mexican menu includes *fondue suiza*, *sopa azteca* and succulent meat dishes.

Drinking & Entertainment

La Covacha (Crescencio Rosas 2B; ☺ 7pm-midnight) Sidle up to the tree-trunk tables at this Cuban mojito bar for a drink. A few other worthwhile bars are located on the same block.

Multiforo Las Velas (Madero 14; ☺ 8pm-3am Thu-Sat) Live music and dancing start around 11pm, and circus and theater performances occasionally take a turn.

Latino's (☎ 678-9927; Madero 23; admission Thu-Sat M$25-30; ☺ 8pm-3am Mon-Sat) Where the city's *salseros* gather to groove.

Laska (Madero 12) Dim and funky, with crazy designs climbing up the walls, this artsy and intimate new club features soulful *trova* (Latin American protest folk).

Getting There & Away

A fast toll *autopista* (expressway; M$38 for cars) zips here from Chiapa de Corzo. An increased military and police presence has reduced the number of highway holdups on Hwy 199 between Ocosingo and Palenque, but it's still probably best to travel along this stretch of road during daylight hours.

AIR

San Cristóbal's airport, about 15km from town on the Palenque road, has no regular passenger flights; the main airport serving town is at Tuxtla Gutiérrez. Three daily direct OCC minibuses (M$125) run in both directions between the Tuxtla airport and San Cristóbal's main bus terminal; book in advance.

Mexicana (☎ 678-9990; Madero 8A) sells flights from Tuxtla Gutiérrez.

BUS, COLECTIVO & VAN

There are around a dozen terminals, mostly on or just off the Pan-American Hwy. The most important one is the 1st-class **OCC terminal** (☎ 678-0291; cnr Pan-American Hwy & Insurgentes), also used by ADO and UNO 1st-class and deluxe buses, and 2nd-class Transportes Dr Rodolfo Figueroa (TRF). Tickets for all these lines are sold at **Ticket Bus** (☎ 678-8503; www.ticketbus.com.mx; Real de Guadalupe 24; ☺ 8am-10pm) in the center of town.

First-class **AEXA** (☎ 678-6178) and 2nd-class Ómnibus de Chiapas share a terminal on the south side of the highway; and various vans and *colectivo* taxi services have depots on the highway in the same area.

For Guatemala, most agencies offer daily van service to Quetzaltenango (M$300, eight hours), Panajachel (M$300, 10 hours), Antigua (M$400, 12 hours) and Flores (from Palenque, M$500).

Destination	Cost (M$)	Duration (hr)
Campeche	372	11
Cancún	720-856	16-18
Ciudad Cuauhtémoc (Guatemalan border)	80	3½
Guatemala City	330	11
Mérida	532	13
Mexico City (TAPO)	350-1060	13-14
Palenque	80-166	5
Villahermosa	232	7-8

GETTING TO THE GUATEMALA HIGHLANDS

The best way to reach Guatemala is via the convenient **Ciudad Cuauhtémoc–La Mesilla** border. A blip of a border town, Ciudad Cuauhtémoc is the last and first place in Mexico on the Pan-American Hwy. Comitán is 83km north, and the Guatemalan border post is 4km south at La Mesilla. Taxis (M$10 *colectivo*, M$30 private) ferry people between the two sides. There are banks and money changers on both sides of the border, which closes to car traffic from 9pm to 6am.

A few OCC buses to Ciudad Cuauhtémoc from San Cristóbal de Las Casas (M$80, 3½ hours) run from noon to 10pm, or you can get to Comitán and pick up onward transportation there. Frequent vans, *combis* and buses from Comitán (M$30 to M$38, 1½ hours) run about every 20 to 30 minutes, 5am to 5pm.

From La Mesilla, mototaxis (M$3/Q2) can drop you off at the bus depot. Buses leave at least 20 times daily from 6am to 6pm for Huehuetenango (Q20, two hours) and Quetzaltenango (Q15, 3½ hours), where you can find onward connections to Guatemala City.

For the reverse trip, see p154.

CAR

San Cristóbal's only car-rental company, **Optima** (☎ 674-5409; optimacar1@hotmail.com; Mazariegos 39) rents cars for M$450 per day and M$2700 per week.

Getting Around

Combis (minibuses; M$4.50) go up Crescencio Rosas from the Pan-American Hwy to the town center. Taxis within town cost M$20 (M$25 at night).

Friendly **Los Pingüinos** (☎ 678-0202; www.bike mexico.com/pinguinos; Ecuador 4B; 10am-2:30pm & 3:30-7pm Mon-Sat) rents good-quality mountain bikes with lock and maps and can advise on good and safe routes.

Croozy Scooters (☎ 631-4329; Belisario Domínguez 7; scooter hire 5/9/24hr M$190/290/350, bicycle hire per 24hr M$100; 9am-6pm Tue-Sun) rents bicycles and well-maintained Italika CS 125cc scooters.

AROUND SAN CRISTÓBAL

The inhabitants of the beautiful Chiapas highlands are descended from the ancient Maya and maintain some unique beliefs, customs and costumes.

During the day, walking or riding by horse or bicycle along the main roads to San Juan Chamula and San Lorenzo Zinacantán should not be risky; however, it's not wise to wander into unfrequented areas or down isolated tracks.

Transportation to most villages goes from points around the Mercado Municipal in San Cristóbal. *Combis* to San Juan Chamula (M$9) leave from Calle Honduras frequently from 4am to about 6pm; for Zinacantán, *combis* (M$12) and *colectivo* taxis (M$14) go at least hourly, from 5am to 6pm, from a yard off Robledo.

San Juan Chamula

pop 3000 / elev 2200m

Chamulan people are a fiercely independent Tzotzil group, more than 80,000 strong. Their main village, San Juan Chamula, 10km northwest of San Cristóbal de Las Casas, is the center for some unique religious practices.

Outsiders can visit San Juan Chamula, but a big sign at the entrance to the village strictly forbids photography inside the village church or at rituals. Do *not* ignore these restrictions; the community takes them very seriously. Nearby, around the shell of an older church, is the village **graveyard**, with black crosses for people who died old, white for the young, and blue for others.

Sunday is the weekly **market**, when people from the hills stream into the village to shop, trade and visit the main church.

Next to the main plaza, **Templo de San Juan** (Chamula's main church) is ghostly white, with a vividly painted arch of green and blue. You must obtain tickets (M$20) at the **tourist office** (7am-6pm), beside the plaza, before entering the church.

San Lorenzo Zinacantán

pop 3700 / elev 2558m

The orderly village of San Lorenzo Zinacantán, about 11km northwest of San Cristóbal, is the main village of the Zinacantán municipality (population 45,000). Zinacantán people, like Chamulans, are Tzotzil.

A small **market** is held on Sundays until noon, and during fiesta times. The huge central **Iglesia de San Lorenzo** (admission M$15) was rebuilt following a fire in 1975. Photography is banned in the church and churchyard. The

MEXICO'S YUCATÁN & CHIAPAS

small thatch-roofed **Museo Jsotz' Levetik** (admission by donation), three blocks below the central basketball court, covers local culture and has some fine textiles and musical instruments.

PALENQUE

☎ 916 / pop 85,000

Deservedly one of the top destinations of Chiapas, the soaring jungle-swathed temples of Palenque are a national treasure and one of the best examples of Maya architecture in Mexico. Modern Palenque town, a few kilometers to the east, is a sweaty, humdrum place without much appeal except as a jumping-off point for the ruins, though a recent makeover has spiffed up a few blocks of the main road near the park. Many people prefer to base themselves at one of the forest hideouts along the road between the town and the ruins, including the funky travelers' hangout of El Panchán.

History

The name Palenque (Palisade) is Spanish and has no relation to the city's ancient name, which may have been Lakamha (Big Water). Palenque was first occupied around 100 BC, and flourished around AD 630–740. The city rose to prominence under the ruler Pakal, who reigned from 615 to 683. Archaeologists have determined that Pakal is represented by hieroglyphics of sun and shield, and he is also referred to as Sun Shield (Escudo Solar). He lived to the then-incredible age of 80.

Pakal's son Kan B'alam II (684–702), who is represented in hieroglyphics by the jaguar and the serpent (and is also called Jaguar Serpent II), continued Palenque's expansion and artistic development. During Kan B'alam II's reign, Palenque extended its zone of control to the Río Usumacinta, but was challenged by the rival Maya city of Toniná, 65km south. Kan B'alam's brother and successor, K'an Joy Chitam II (Precious Peccary), was captured by forces from Toniná in 711, and probably executed there. Palenque enjoyed a resurgence between 722 and 736, however, under Ahkal Mo' Nahb' III (Turtle Macaw Lake), who added many substantial buildings.

After AD 900, Palenque was largely abandoned.

Orientation

Hwy 199 meets Palenque's main street, Av Juárez, at the Glorieta de la Cabeza Maya, an intersection with a large statue of a Maya chieftain's head, at the west end of the town. From here Av Juárez heads 1km east to the central square, El Parque. The main bus stations are on Av Juárez just east of the Maya statue.

A few hundred meters south from the Maya statue, the paved road to the Palenque ruins, which are 7.5km away, diverges west off Hwy 199. This road passes the site museum after about 6.5km, then winds on about 1km further uphill to the main entrance to the ruins.

Accommodations are scattered around the central part of town and along the road to the ruins. The commercial heart of town, where you'll hardly ever see another tourist, is north of the center along Velasco Suárez.

Information

There are more than a dozen cybercafes; in-town rates run from M$8 to M$10 per hour.
Banamex (Av Juárez 62; ☺ 9am-4pm Mon-Sat)
Clínica Palenque (☎ 345-0273; Velasco Suárez 33; ☺ 9:30am-1:30pm & 5-8pm)
Lavandería La gotAzul (Independencia; per kg M$10) Do your laundry here.
Post office (Independencia; ☺ 8am-8:30pm Mon-Fri, to noon Sat)
Tourist information kiosk (El Parque; ☺ 9am-2pm & 6-9pm Mon-Fri)
Tourist information office (☎ 345-0356; cnr Av Juárez & Abasolo; ☺ 9am-9pm Mon-Sat, 9am-1pm Sun)

Sights
PALENQUE RUINS

Ancient **Palenque** (admission M$51; ☺ 8am-5pm, last entry 4:30pm) stands at the precise point where the first hills rise out of the Gulf coast plain, and the dense jungle covering these hills forms an evocative backdrop to Palenque's exquisite Maya architecture. Hundreds of ruined buildings are spread over 15 sq km, but only a fairly compact central area has been excavated. The forest around these temples is still home to howler monkeys, toucans and ocelots. The ruins and surrounding forests form a national park, the Parque Nacional Palenque, for which you must pay a separate M$22 admission fee at Km 4.5 on the road to the ruins.

Palenque's **Museo de Sitio** (Site Museum; ☎ 345-2684; Carretera Palenque-Ruinas Km 7; admission free with ruins ticket; ☺ 9am-4:30pm Tue-Sun) is worth a wander, as it displays finds from the site and interprets, in English and Spanish, Palenque's history. Official site **guides** (2hr tour for up to 7 people in Spanish/English/French/Italian M$600/1105/1105/1105) are available by the entrance.

Transportes Chambalú (☎ 345-2849; Hidalgo) and **Transportes Palenque** (cnr Allende & Av 20 de Noviembre) run *combis* to the ruins about every 15 minutes from 6am to 6:45pm daily (M$10 each way). They will pick you up or drop you off anywhere along the town-to-ruins road. (Be aware that the mushrooms sold by locals along the road to the ruins from May to November are of the hallucinogenic variety.)

As you enter the site, a line of temples rise in front of the jungle on your right, culminating about 100m ahead at the **Templo de las Inscripciones** (Temple of the Inscriptions), the tallest and most stately of Palenque's buildings. From the top, interior stairs lead down into the tomb of Pakal (closed indefinitely to avoid further damage from the humidity

exuded by visitors). Pakal's jewel-bedecked skeleton and jade mosaic death mask were moved from the tomb to Mexico City, and the tomb was recreated in the Museo Nacional de Antropología (from where the priceless death mask was stolen in 1985), but the carved stone sarcophagus lid remains at the Museo de Sitio.

Diagonally opposite the Templo de las Inscripciones is **El Palacio** (The Palace), a large structure divided into four main courtyards, with a maze of corridors and rooms. Soon after the death of his father, Kan B'alam II started designing the temples of the **Grupo de las Cruces** (Group of the Crosses). All three main pyramid-shaped structures surround a plaza southeast of the Templo de las Inscripciones. The **Templo del Sol** (Temple of the Sun), on the

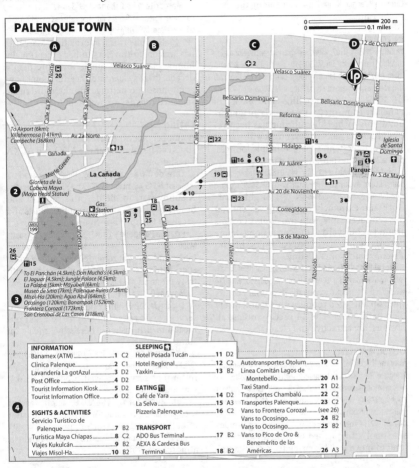

PALENQUE TOWN

INFORMATION	
Banamex (ATM)	1 C2
Clínica Palenque	2 C1
Lavandería La gotAzul	3 D2
Post Office	4 D2
Tourist Information Kiosk	5 C2
Tourist Information Office	6 D2

SIGHTS & ACTIVITIES	
Servicio Turístico de Palenque	7 B2
Turística Maya Chiapas	8 C2
Viajes Kukulcán	9 B2
Viajes Misol-Ha	10 B2

SLEEPING 🛏	
Hotel Posada Tucán	11 D2
Hotel Regional	12 C2
Yaxkin	13 B2

EATING 🍴	
Café de Yara	14 D2
La Selva	15 A3
Pizzería Palenque	16 C2

TRANSPORT	
ADO Bus Terminal	17 B2
AEXA & Cardesa Bus Terminal	18 B2
Autotransportes Otolum	19 C2
Linea Comitán Lagos de Montebello	20 A1
Taxi Stand	21 D2
Transportes Chambalú	22 C2
Transportes Palenque	23 C2
Vans to Frontera Corozal	(see 26)
Vans to Ocosingo	24 B2
Vans to Ocosingo	25 B2
Vans to Pico de Oro & Benemérito de las Américas	26 A3

west side of the plaza, has the best-preserved roofcomb at Palenque. Steep steps climb to the **Templo de la Cruz** (Temple of the Cross), the largest and most elegantly proportioned in this group.

South of the Grupo de las Cruces is the **Acrópolis Sur**, where archaeologists have recovered some terrific finds in recent excavations. It appears to have been constructed as an extension of the Grupo de las Cruces, with both groups set around what was probably a single long, open space.

Sleeping

The first choice to make is whether to stay in or out of Palenque town. Most out-of-town places, including **El Panchán** (www.elpanchan.com; Carretera Palenque-Ruinas Km 4.5), are along the road to the ruins.

IN TOWN

Yaxkin (☎ 345-0102; www.hostalyaxkin.com; Prolongación Hidalgo; hammocks/dm M$60/150, r with air-con & bathroom M$250, r with fan & without bathroom M$180, s/d/tr/q cabañas with air-con & bathroom M$300/440/540/740; ☒ ☒ ☐ ☜) Channeling laid-back El Panchán from pretty La Cañada neighborhood, this former discotheque has been revamped into a modern new hostel with a guest kitchen, table-tennis table, multiple lounges, and a swank restaurant and bar.

Hotel Regional (☎/fax 345-0183; hotelregional@hotmail.com; Av Juárez 119; r with air-con M$450, s/d/tr/q with fan M$200/250/300/350; ☒ ☜) Bright paintwork and extremely bright murals enliven this central cheapie, with two floors of rooms around a courtyard with a turtle pond. Some upstairs rooms have nice balconies, but no air-con. Bathrooms are tiny.

Hotel Posada Tucán (☎ 345-1859; ismahpt@hotmail. com; Av 5 de Mayo 3; r/tr with air-con M$300/350, with fan M$250/300; ☒) Textured walls in primary colors spice up fair-sized rooms with TV and nicely tiled bathrooms. The 14 breezy rooms, all upstairs, are attractive and clean.

OUTSIDE TOWN

Mayabell (☎ 341-6977; www.mayabell.com.mx; Carretera Palenque-Ruinas Km 6; hammock shelters or campsites per person M$50, hammocks to rent M$20, small vehicles without hookups M$30, vehicle sites with hookups M$170, cabañas without bathroom M$300, r with air-con/fan M$850/650; ☐ ☒ ☒) Once you see the sprawling jungleside pool – frequented by monkeys – you'll long to move in. This spacious grassy camp-

ground is just 400m from the site museum and has lots of clean and comfortable sleeping options, plus an enjoyable restaurant.

Jungle Palace (www.elpanchan.com; El Panchán, Carretera Palenque-Ruinas Km 4.5; d/tr cabañas with bathroom M$200/250, s/d/tr cabañas without bathroom M$100/120/180) A basic option in El Panchán, the Jungle Palace offers rudimentary though well-screened cabins with fans, some of which back onto a stream.

El Jaguar (☎ 341-8209; www.elpanchan.com; Carretera Palenque-Ruinas Km 4.5; s/d cabañas with bathroom M$160/200, without bathroom M$100/120; ☐) Just across the road from El Panchán, and under the same ownership as Chato's Cabañas, El Jaguar has more open grounds and the same creek running through it.

Margarita & Ed Cabañas (☎ 348-4205; El Panchán, Carretera Palenque-Ruinas Km 4.5; cabañas M$240, r/tr/q with air-con M$370/450/600, r/tr with fan M$270/320; ☐ ☒ ☒) Full of local information, Margarita has welcomed travelers to her exceptionally homey place in the jungle for more than a decade. Bright, clean and cheerful rooms have good mosquito netting, and the more rustic screened *cabañas* are well kept too.

Eating

A number of inexpensive stands and sit-down spots can be found near the ADO and AEXA bus stations.

Café de Yara (☎ 345-0269; Hidalgo 66; snacks & breakfast M$45-66, mains M$60-90; ☻ 7am-11pm; ☜) A sunny start to the day, this modern and beautiful corner cafe has great breakfasts and excellent Chiapas-grown organic coffee.

Pizzería Palenque (☎ 345-0332; Av Juárez 168; pasta M$50-55, pizzas from M$68; ☻ 1-11pm) Light wood tables and a recent remodel have added some sparkle to this very popular pizza place with tasty pies and pastas.

Mayabell (☎ 341-6977; Carretera Palenque-Ruinas Km 6; mains M$55-90) This open-sided restaurant serves a good range of *antojitos* (snacks) and meat and fish dishes. There's live music on some evenings.

La Selva (☎ 345-0363; Hwy 199; mains M$58-165; ☻ 11:30am-11:30pm) Palenque's most upscale restaurant serves up well-prepared steaks, seafood, salads and *antojitos*.

Don Mucho's (☎ 341-8209; El Panchán, Carretera Palenque-Ruinas Km 4.5; mains M$60-120) The hot spot of El Panchán, Don Mucho's provides great-value meals in a jungle setting, with a candlelit atmosphere at night.

GETTING TO FLORES, GUATEMALA

The trip between Palenque and Flores (near Tikal) is easiest on a full-transportation package (two buses and boat) from a Palenque travel agency. The packaged tour usually includes an air-conditioned van to Frontera Corozal, a river launch up the Río Usumacinta to Bethel in Guatemala, and a public bus on to Flores. This takes 10 or 11 hours altogether, for around M$350. Two-day packages to Flores, visiting Bonampak and Yaxchilán en route, cost around M$1100.

Tour agencies in Palenque servicing the route:

Servicios Turísticos de Palenque (☎ 345-1340; www.stpalenque.com; cnr Avs Juárez & 5 de Mayo)

Transportes Chambalú (☎ 345-2849; Hidalgo)

Turística Maya Chiapas (☎ 345-0798; www.tmayachiapas.com.mx; Av Juárez 123)

Viajes Kukulcán (☎ 345-1506; www.kukulcantravel.com; Av Juárez 8)

Viajes Misol-Ha (☎ 345-1614; Av Juárez 148)

Otherwise, you can do it on your own. If you can't get a bus or *combi* direct to Frontera Corozal, get one to Crucero Corozal, 16km southeast of San Javier on the Carretera Fronteriza, where *colectivo* taxis (M$25 per person) and occasional vans (M$25) run to Frontera Corozal. The *ejido* (communal landholding) hits up visitors entering or leaving Frontera Corozal for a M$15 per person toll; keep your ticket for exiting unless you're continuing on to Guatemala.

Autotransporte Chamoán vans run hourly from Frontera Corozal *embarcadero* (wharf) to Palenque (M$70, 2½ to three hours), with the last departure at 5pm.

Lanchas (small motorboats) leave for Bethel (40 minutes upstream) on the Guatemalan bank of the Río Usumacinta, and for La Técnica, directly opposite Frontera Corozal. **Lancha organizations** (boat to Bethel for 2/3/4/7/10 people M$350/450/550/600/750) have desks in a thatched building near the *embarcadero*, and all charge the same prices. *Lanchas* to La Técnica go on a *colectivo* basis of M$15 per person. Information in Frontera Corozal is unreliable on onward buses within Guatemala, but about three to five daily buses from La Técnica to Flores (Q40, five to six hours) leave until 5pm, stopping for immigration in Bethel. You can also go directly from Bethel to Flores (Q35, 4½ hours).

For information on crossing from Guatemala, see boxed text, p197.

Drinking & Entertainment

La Palapa (☎ 105-0047; Carretera Palenque-Ruinas Km 5; ☽ to 3am) As freaky fun as it gets in these parts, this alfresco 'jungle lounge' has DJs spinning reggae, salsa and electronica.

Getting There & Away

Though an increased military and police presence has made this route pretty safe, highway holdups still occasionally occur on Hwy 199 between Palenque and San Cristóbal de Las Casas. It's not advisable to travel on this road at night.

Palenque's airport, 3km north of town along Hwy 199, didn't have commercial traffic for years, but in 2010 **Aerotucán** (www.aerotucan.com.mx) began a twice-weekly passenger service (as well as pricier charters) to Tuxtla Gutiérrez.

ADO (☎ 345-1344; Av Juárez) has the main bus terminal, with deluxe and 1st-class services, an ATM and left-luggage facilities; it's also used by OCC (1st-class) and TRT (2nd-class) buses. **AEXA** (☎ 345-2630; Av Juárez 159), with 1st-class buses, and Cardesa (2nd-class) are 1½ blocks east, with an onsite internet cafe. Vans

to Ocosingo wait on Calles 4a and 5a Poniente Sur, near the bus terminals, and leave when full. **Transportes Palenque** (cnr Allende & Av 20 de Noviembre) runs vans to Tenosique, which has onward connections to Guatemala.

Daily departures include the following:

Destination	Cost (M$)	Duration (hr)
Campeche	242	4½-5½
Cancún	250-668	11-13
Mérida	364	8
San Cristóbal de Las Casas	80-166	5
Tulum	478-566	11
Villahermosa	50-102	2½

Getting Around

Taxis wait at the northeast corner of El Parque and at the ADO bus terminal; they charge M$50 (M$70 at night) to El Panchán or Mayabell, and M$60 to the ruins. *Combis* (M$10) from the center ply the ruins road until about 6:45pm.

BONAMPAK, YAXCHILÁN & THE CARRETERA FRONTERIZA

The ancient Maya cities of Bonampak and Yaxchilán, southeast of Palenque, are easily accessible thanks to the Carretera Fronteriza, a good paved road running parallel to the Mexico–Guatemala border, all the way from Palenque to Lagos de Montebello, around the fringe of the Lacandón Jungle. Bonampak, famous for its frescoes, is 148km by road from Palenque; the bigger and more important Yaxchilán, with a peerless jungle setting beside the broad and swift Río Usumacinta, is 173km by road, then about 22km by boat.

The Carretera Fronteriza is the main thoroughfare connecting a number of excellent ecotourism projects including some in the Lacandón village of Lacanjá Chansayab (see boxed text, opposite page). For information on other ecotourism projects in the area, check out www.laselvadechiapas.com.

Dangers & Annoyances

Drug trafficking and illegal immigration are facts of life in this border region, and the Carretera Fronteriza more or less encircles the main area of Zapatista rebel activity and support, so expect numerous military checkpoints along the road and from this area to Palenque and Comitán. For your own security, it's best to be off the Carretera Fronteriza before dusk.

Tours

The **Mesoamerican Ecotourism Alliance** (www.travelwithmea.org) organizes all-inclusive trips to the region, including the Lacandón villages of Nahá and Metzabok.

GETTING THERE & AWAY

From Palenque, vans run to Frontera Corozal (M$70, 2½ to three hours, hourly), and to Benemérito de las Américas (M$80, 3½ hours, every 40 minutes from 4am to 5pm), leaving from a small terminal behind the Maya statue.

Línea Comitán Lagos de Montebello (Map p45; ☎ 916-345-1260; Velasco Suárez s/n), a few blocks west of Palenque market, also runs hourly vans to Benemérito (M$60, 11 times daily from 3:30am to 2:45pm), with the first five continuing round the Carretera Fronteriza to Lagos de Montebello (M$200, seven hours to Tziscao) and Comitán (M$225, eight hours).

All these services stop at San Javier (M$50, two hours), the turnoff for Lacanjá Chansayab and Bonampak, 140km from Palenque, and at Crucero Corozal (M$60, 2½ hours), the intersection for Frontera Corozal.

There are no gas stations on the Carretera Fronteriza, but plenty of entrepreneurial locals sell reasonably priced gas from large plastic containers. Look for homemade '*Se vende gasolina*' signs.

Bonampak

The site of **Bonampak** (admission M$41; 8am-4:45pm) spreads over 2.4 sq km, but all the main ruins stand around the rectangular Gran Plaza. Never a major city, Bonampak spent most of the Classic period in Yaxchilán's sphere of influence. The most impressive surviving monuments were built under Chan Muwan II, a nephew of the Yaxchilán's Itzamnaaj B'alam II, who acceded to Bonampak's throne in AD 776. The 6m-high **Stele 1** in the Gran Plaza depicts Chan Muwan II holding a ceremonial staff at the height of his reign. He also features in **Stele 2** and **Stele 3** on the Acrópolis, which rises from the south end of the plaza.

However, it's the vivid frescoes inside the modest-looking **Templo de las Pinturas** (Edificio 1) that have given Bonampak its fame – and its name, which means 'Painted Walls' in Yucatec Maya.

The Bonampak site abuts the Reserva de la Biosfera Montes Azules, and is rich in wildlife.

GETTING THERE & AWAY

Bonampak is 12km from San Javier on the Carretera Fronteriza. The first 3km, to the Lacanjá Chansayab turnoff, is paved, and the rest is good gravel/dirt road through the forest. Taxis will take you from San Javier or the Lacanjá turnoff to the ruins and back for M$80 per person, including waiting time. Private vehicles cannot pass the Monumento Natural Bonampak entrance, 1km past the Lacanjá turnoff, but you can rent bicycles there for M$60 for three hours, or take a *combi* to the ruins for M$70 round trip. Free lockers are available at the park entrance.

Yaxchilán

Jungle-shrouded **Yaxchilán** (admission M$49; 8am-4:30pm, last entry 3:30pm) has a terrific setting above a horseshoe loop in the Río Usumacinta. The control this location gave it over river commerce, and a series of successful alliances and conquests, made Yaxchilán one of the most important Maya cities from the Classic period in the Usumacinta region. Archaeologically,

Yaxchilán is famed for its ornamented facades and roofcombs, and its impressive stone lintels carved with conquest and ceremonial scenes. A flashlight is helpful for exploring some parts of the site.

Howler monkeys (saraguates) inhabit the tall trees, and are an evocative highlight. You'll almost certainly hear their visceral roars, and you stand a good chance of seeing some. Spider monkeys, and occasionally red macaws, can also be spotted here at times.

Yaxchilán peaked in power and splendor between AD 681 and 800 under the rulers Itzamnaaj B'alam II (Shield Jaguar II, 681–742), Pájaro Jaguar IV (Bird Jaguar IV, 752–68) and Itzamnaaj B'alam III (Shield Jaguar III, 769–800). The city was abandoned around AD 810. Inscriptions here tell more about its 'Jaguar' dynasty than is known of almost any other Maya ruling clan. The shield-and-jaguar symbol appears on many Yaxchilán buildings and steles; Pájaro Jaguar IV's hieroglyph is a small jungle cat with feathers on its back and a bird superimposed on its head.

At the site, drinks are sold at a shack near the river landing. Most of the main monuments have information boards in three languages, including English.

As you walk toward the ruins, a signed path to the right leads up to the **Pequeña Acrópolis**, a group of ruins on a small hilltop – you can visit this later. Staying on the main path, you soon reach the mazy passages of **El Laberinto** (Edificio 19), built between AD 742 and 752, during the interregnum between Itzamnaaj B'alam II and Pájaro Jaguar IV. Dozens of bats

---

DIY: EXPLORE MORE OF CHIAPAS

Try out some of these DIY adventures:

- **Agua Azul & Misol-Ha** These spectacular water attractions – the thundering cascades of Agua Azul and the 35m jungle waterfall of Misol-Ha (www.misol-ha.com) – are both short detours off the Ocosingo–Palenque road.

- **Amatenango del Valle** The women of this Tzeltal village by the Pan-American Hwy, 37km southeast of San Cristóbal, are renowned potters.

- **Chiapa de Corzo** Set 12km east of Tuxtla Gutiérrez on the way to San Cristóbal, Chiapa de Corzo is a small and attractive colonial town with an easygoing, provincial air. Set on the north bank of the broad Río Grijalva, it's the main starting point for trips into the **Cañón del Sumidero**.

- **Grutas de San Cristóbal** The entrance to this long cavern is among pine woods 9km southeast of San Cristóbal, a five-minute walk south of the Pan-American Hwy.

- **Lacanjá Chansayab** The largest Lacandón Maya village is 12km from Bonampak. Its family compounds are scattered around a wide area, many of them with creeks or the Río Lacanjá itself flowing past their grassy grounds. Check out www.ecochiapas.com/lacanja (in Spanish) for information on visiting the region.

- **Lagos de Montebello** The temperate pine and oak forest along the Guatemalan border east of Chinkultic is dotted with more than 50 small lakes of varied hues. The nearby **Chinkultic ruins** add to the mystery.

- **Laguna Miramar** Ringed by rainforest 140km southeast of Ocosingo in the Reserva de la Biosfera Montes Azules, this is one of Mexico's most remote and exquisite lakes.

- **Ocosingo** A respite from both the steamy lowland jungle and the chilly highlands, the bustling regional market town of Ocosingo sits in a gorgeous and broad temperate valley midway between San Cristóbal and Palenque. The impressive Maya ruins of **Toniná** are just a few kilometers away.

- **Reserva de la Biosfera El Triunfo** The luxuriant cloud forests high in the remote Sierra Madre de Chiapas are a bird-lover's paradise.

- **Reserva de la Biosfera La Encrucijada** This large biosphere reserve protects a 1448-sq-km strip of coastal lagoons, sand bars and wetlands.

- **Sima de Las Cotorras** (☎ 968-689-0289; simacotorras@hotmail.com) A dramatic sinkhole punching 160m wide and 140m deep into the earth, about 1½ hours' drive from Tuxtla Gutiérrez.

find shelter under the structure's roof today. From this complicated two-level building you emerge at the northwest end of the extensive **Gran Plaza**.

Though it's difficult to imagine anyone here ever wanting to be any hotter than they already were, **Edificio 17** was apparently a sweathouse. About halfway along the plaza, **Stele 1**, flanked by weathered sculptures of a crocodile and a jaguar, shows Pájaro Jaguar IV in a ceremony that took place in AD 761. **Edificio 20**, from the time of Itzamnaaj B'alam III, was the last significant structure built at Yaxchilán; its lintels are now in Mexico City. **Stele 11**, at the northeast corner of the Gran Plaza, was originally found in front of Edificio 40. The bigger of the two figures visible on it is Pájaro Jaguar IV.

An imposing stairway climbs from Stele 1 to **Edificio 33**, the best-preserved temple at Yaxchilán, with almost half of its roofcomb intact. The final step in front of the building is carved with ball-game scenes, and splendid relief carvings embellish the undersides of the lintels. Inside is a statue of Pájaro Jaguar IV, minus the head, which it lost to treasure-seeking 19th-century timber cutters.

From the clearing behind Edificio 33, a path leads into the trees. About 20m along this path, fork left uphill; go left at another fork after about 80m, and in 10 minutes or so, mostly going uphill, you'll reach three buildings on a hilltop: **Edificio 39**, **Edificio 40** and **Edificio 41**.

GETTING THERE & AWAY

River launches take 40 minutes running downstream from Frontera Corozal, and one hour to return. *Lancha* (small motorboat) outfits, with desks in a thatched building near the Frontera Corozal *embarcadero* (wharf), all charge the same prices for trips (return journey with 2½ hours at the ruins for two/three/four/seven/10 people M$680/780/800/950/1300), though boats from **Escudo Jaguar** (☎ 502-5353-5637; www.escudojaguarhotel.com) may be cheaper. *Lanchas* normally leave frequently until 1:30pm or so, and it's sometimes possible to hook up with other travelers or a tour group to share costs.

THE YUCATÁN

Those who say there's no street cred or authenticity in the Yucatán haven't spent much time away from the Playa del Carmen and Cancún pedestrian malls with 'one tequila, two tequila, three tequila…floor' T-shirt shops. Stretching like a giant, flat limestone thumb between the turquoise Caribbean and murky Gulf of Mexico, the broad Yucatán overflows with local culture.

Yucatán state has Mexico's highest concentration of indigenous people (about 60%). Inland, visit steamy Mérida, a lively colonial-era city built with stones from Maya pyramids. Or you can cruise down to Campeche, where a well-preserved colonial center awaits. Throughout the peninsula, Maya ruins such as Tulum, Edzná, Uxmal and Chichén Itzá get most visitors, while early morning arrivals at Cobá or Dzibilchaltún often have the pyramids to themselves. Beach-wise, you'll find the best sand and snorkeling spots along the Caribbean coast in Quintana Roo.

CAMPECHE
☎ 981 / pop 211,700

Campeche is a colonial fairyland, its walled city center a tight enclave of perfectly restored pastel buildings, narrow cobblestoned streets, fortified ramparts and well-preserved mansions. Added to Unesco's list of World Heritage Sites in 1999, the state capital has been so painstakingly restored you wonder if it's a real city.

Orientation & Information

Though the bastions still stand, the walls have been mostly razed and replaced by Av Circuito Baluartes, which rings the city center as the walls once did. The streets in the central grid follow a numbered sequence: inland-oriented streets have odd numbers and perpendicular ones have even numbers.

All of the hostels provide online services, and 'cybers' abound in the center.

Central post office (cnr Av 16 de Septiembre & Calle 53; ☯ 8:30am-3:30pm Mon-Fri)

Cruz Roja (Red Cross; ☎ 815-2411; cnr Av Las Palmas & Ah Kim Pech) Some 3km northeast of downtown.

Kler Lavandería (Calle 16 No 305; per kg M$10; ☯ 8am-6pm Mon-Fri, 8am-4pm Sat) Laundry.

Secretaría de Turismo (State Tourist Office; ☎ 127-3300; www.campeche.travel; Plaza Moch Couoh; ☯ 8am-9pm) Tourist info.

Sights & Activities
PLAZA PRINCIPAL

Shaded by spreading carob trees, and ringed by tiled benches and broad footpaths radiating from a belle-epoque kiosk, Campeche's

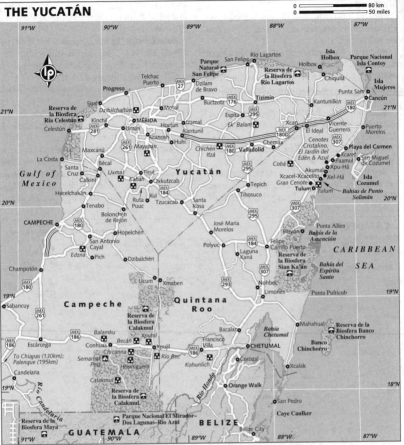

THE YUCATÁN

appealingly modest **Plaza Principal** started life in 1531 as a military camp. Dominating the plaza's east side is the two-towered **Catedral de Nuestra Señora de la Purísima Concepción** (admission free; ⏰ 7am-noon & 4-6pm). Across the plaza, **Centro Cultural Casa Número 6** (Calle 57 No 6; admission M$5; audio guide M$10; ⏰ 9am-9pm) is a prerevolutionary-era mansion that is worth the visit to get an idea of how the city's high society lived back then.

BALUARTES

After a particularly blistering pirate assault in 1663, the remaining inhabitants of Campeche set about erecting protective walls around their city. Following the wall around the city is a great way to visit a number of museums and sites in one day. Among the favorite stops are two main entrances which connected the walled compound with the outside world – the **Puerta del Mar** (Sea Gate; cnr Calles 8 & 59), which opens onto a wharf, and the **Puerta de Tierra** (Land Gate; Calle 18; admission free; ⏰ 9am-9pm), which is now the venue for a sound-and-light show.

Designed to protect the Puerta del Mar, the **Baluarte de Nuestra Señora de la Soledad** contains the fascinating **Museo de la Arquitectura Maya** (Calle 8; admission M$31; ⏰ 9am-7:30pm Tue-Sun), the one must-see museum in Campeche.

Behind Iglesia de San Juan de Dios, the **Baluarte de San Pedro** (cnr Avs Circuito Baluartes Este & Circuito Baluartes Norte; admission free; ⏰ 9am-9pm) houses the **Galería y Museo de Arte Popular** (Museum & Gallery of Folk Art; admission free; ⏰ 9am-9pm Mon-Sat, 9am-2pm Sun), which displays indigenous handicrafts.

Sleeping

Campeche's three hostels all offer bicycle rentals, complimentary breakfasts and tours of archaeological sites.

Hostal La Parroquia (☎ 816-2530; www.hostalparroquia.com; Calle 55; dm M$90, d/q without bathroom M$210/320; 🖳 📶) Half a block from the Plaza Principal, Campeche's newest hostel resides in a magnificent late-1500s mansion.

Monkey Hostel (☎ 811-6605; www.hostalcampeche.com; cnr Calles 10 & 57; dm M$100, r without bathroom M$240; 🖳 📶) You can't beat the view of the plaza and cathedral from Campeche's longest-established and most popular hostel.

Hostal del Pirata (☎ 811-1757; piratehostel@hotmail.com; Calle 59 No 47; dm M$100, r with/without bathroom M$270/240; 🖳) A block from the Puerta de Tierra, this hostel is ensconced in Campeche's historical center, and the building itself is a 17th-century relic.

Hotel Colonial (☎ 816-2222; Calle 14 No 122; s M$175, d M$210-238; 🔀) Time stands still within this stubbornly low-tech establishment, the budget travelers' haven for six decades.

Eating

Mercado Principal (Av Circuito Baluartes Este; ⏱ 7am-5pm) Across the street from the Baluarte de San Pedro, and offers terrific snacks.

Parador Gastrónomico de Cockteleros (Av Costera; shrimp cocktails M$40-100, fish M$50-90; ⏱ 9am-6:30pm) This complex on the north end of the *malecón* (waterfront promenade), 4.5km from the Plaza Principal, is the place to sample local seafood.

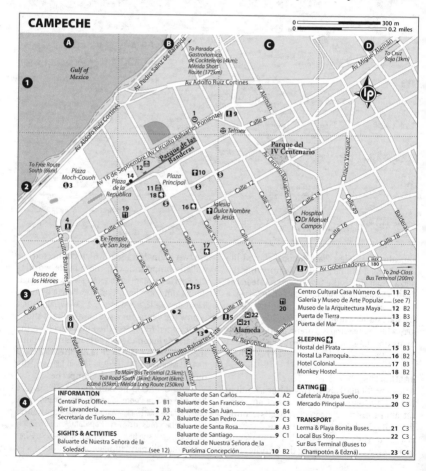

CAMPECHE

0 — 300 m
0 — 0.2 miles

Centro Cultural Casa Número 6	**11** B2
Galería y Museo de Arte Popular	(see 7)
Museo de la Arquitectura Maya	**12** B2
Puerta de Tierra	**13** B3
Puerta del Mar	**14** B2

SLEEPING
Hostal del Pirata	**15** B3
Hostal La Parroquia	**16** B2
Hotel Colonial	**17** B3
Monkey Hostel	**18** B2

EATING
Cafetería Atrapa Sueño	**19** A2
Mercado Principal	**20** C3

TRANSPORT
Lerma & Playa Bonita Buses	**21** C3
Local Bus Stop	**22** C3
Sur Bus Terminal (Buses to	
Champotón & Edzná)	**23** C4

INFORMATION
Central Post Office	**1** B1
Kler Lavandería	**2** B3
Secretaría de Turismo	**3** A2

SIGHTS & ACTIVITIES
Baluarte de Nuestra Señora de la Soledad	(see 12)
Baluarte de San Carlos	**4** A2
Baluarte de San Francisco	**5** C3
Baluarte de San Juan	**6** B4
Baluarte de San Pedro	**7** C3
Baluarte de Santa Rosa	**8** A3
Baluarte de Santiago	**9** C1
Catedral de Nuestra Señora de la Purísima Concepción	**10** B2

DIY: EXPLORE MORE OF CAMPECHE

Leave the guidebook behind and head out into the less explored corners of Campeche. Here are some ideas to get you started:

- **Calakmul** (☎ 555-150-2073; admission M$41, road maintenance fee per car M$40, local tax per person M$40; ⏰ 8am-4:30pm) It's tough to get to this remote Maya site, which is surrounded by Mexico's largest biosphere reserve, but it's well worth the extra expense.

- **Chenes Sites** Northeastern Campeche state is dotted with more than 30 sites in the distinct Chenes style, recognizable by the monster motifs around the doorway.

- **Edzná** (admission M$41; ⏰ 8am-4:30pm) The closest major ruins to Campeche – and some of the most impressive in the entire peninsula – are easy to reach on a day trip from town.

Cafetería Atrapa Sueño (☎ 816-5000; Calle 10 No 260; mains M$50-100; ⏰ 9am-8pm; **V**) This little hippie bistro – complete with a Zen garden out back – features a good selection of vegetarian fare.

Entertainment

There's invariably someone performing on the Plaza Principal every Saturday and Sunday evening from around 6:30pm. For Campeche's hottest bars and clubs, head 1km south from the city center along the *malecón* past the Torres del Cristal.

Getting There & Away

AIR

The airport is 6km southeast of the center. **Aeroméxico** (☎ 800-021-4010) flies to Mexico City at least twice daily.

BUS

Campeche's **main bus terminal** (☎ 816-2802; Av Patricio Trueba 237), usually called the ADO or 1st-class terminal, is about 2.5km south of Plaza Principal via Av Central.

The **2nd-class bus terminal** (☎ 816-2802; Av Gobernadores 289), often referred to as the 'old ADO' station, is 1.5km east of the Mercado Principal.

Destination	Cost (M$)	Duration (hr)
Cancún	372-466	7
Mérida via Bécal	136-162	2½
Mérida via Uxmal	94-105	4½
Mexico City	966-1144	17
Palenque	242	6
San Cristóbal de Las Casas	354-494	9

Getting Around

Local buses originate at the market or across Av Circuito Baluartes from it and go at least partway around the Circuito before heading to their final destinations. The fare is M$4.50. Taxis charge a set rate of M$25 (M$35 after dark) for rides within the city; by the hour they're around M$100.

MÉRIDA

☎ 999 / pop 781,100

Since the Conquest, Mérida has been the cultural capital of the entire peninsula. At times provincial, at others *muy cosmopolitano*, it is a town steeped in colonial history, with narrow streets, broad central plazas, and the region's best museums. It's also a perfect hub city to kick off your adventure into the rest of Yucatán state. There are cheap eats, good hostels and hotels, thriving markets, and goings-on just about every night somewhere in the downtown area.

Orientation & Information

Mérida's sequentially numbered grid makes finding your way easy. Even-numbered streets run north–south; odd-numbered streets run east–west. The Plaza Grande – between Calles 60 and 62, and Calles 63 and 61 – is a 10-minute walk north from the few bus stations. Banks and ATMs are easy to find in the center.

City tourist office (☎ 942-0000; Calle 62, Plaza Grande; ⏰ 8am-8pm Mon-Sat, to 2pm Sun) Offers free walking tours of the city at 9:30am.

Hospital O'Horán (☎ 924-4800/1111; Av de los Itzáes)

Lavandería La Fe (☎ 924-4531; Calle 64 btwn Calles 55 & 57; ⏰ 8am-6pm Mon-Fri, to 2pm Sat) Laundry.

Nómadas Travel (☎ 948-1187; www.nomadastravel.com.mx; Prolongación Paseo de Montejo No 370, Colonia Benito Juárez Norte) Books flights and offers services for student travelers.

Post office (☎ 928-5404; Calle 53 No 469; ⏰ 9am-4pm Mon-Fri, for stamps only 9am-1pm Sat)

MEXICO'S YUCATÁN & CHIAPAS

Sights

Try to be in Mérida for the all-day fair every Saturday and Sunday. For sights near Mérida, see boxed text, p56.

Plaza Grande (or *zócalo*) is rimmed by Mérida's main historic buildings, most built from disassembled Maya pyramids. The most obvious ones are the 42m towers of the **Catedral de San Ildefonso** (Mesoamerica's oldest cathedral, dating from 1598) – much of its interior was destroyed during the Mexican Revolution (1910–29). Next door is the worthwhile **Museo de Arte Contemporáneo Ateneo de Yucatán** (Macay; ☎ 928-3236; Calle 60 btwn Calles 61 & 63; admission free; ⏱ 10am-5:15pm Wed-Mon, to 7:15pm Fri & Sat), with rooms highlighting local artist Fernando Castro Pacheco.

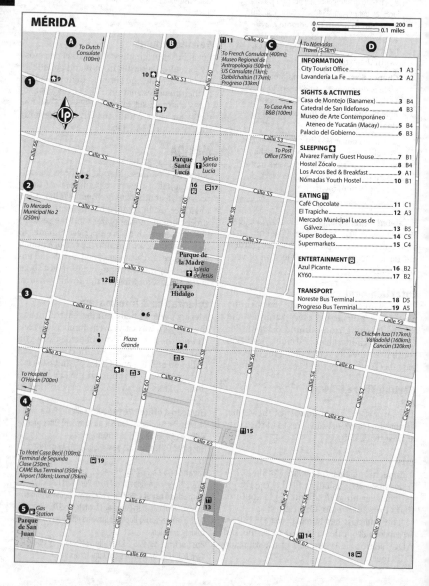

MÉRIDA

0 ——— 200 m
0 ——— 0.1 miles

INFORMATION
City Tourist Office 1 A3
Lavandería La Fe 2 A2

SIGHTS & ACTIVITIES
Casa de Montejo (Banamex) 3 B4
Catedral de San Ildefonso 4 B3
Museo de Arte Contemporáneo
  Ateneo de Yucatán (Macay) 5 B4
Palacio del Gobierno 6 B3

SLEEPING 🏠
Alvarez Family Guest House 7 B1
Hostel Zócalo 8 B4
Los Arcos Bed & Breakfast 9 A1
Nómadas Youth Hostel 10 B1

EATING 🍴
Café Chocolate 11 C1
El Trapiche 12 A3
Mercado Municipal Lucas de
  Gálvez 13 B5
Super Bodega 14 C5
Supermarkets 15 C4

ENTERTAINMENT 🎭
Azul Picante 16 B2
KY60 .... 17 B2

TRANSPORT
Noreste Bus Terminal 18 D5
Progreso Bus Terminal 19 A5

At the south end of the square, you can walk into the courtyard of the home of the founding conquistadors at the **Casa de Montejo** (Calle 63), dating from 1549 and now a Banamex bank. Also go past the armed guards at the 1892 **Palacio del Gobierno** (Calle 61), facing the plaza's northeast corner, to see Pacheco's impressive wall-sized murals upstairs.

Nine blocks north of the plaza, the great **Museo Regional de Antropología** (☎ 923-0557; cnr Paseo de Montejo & Calle 43; admission M$41; ☻ 8am-5pm Tue-Sun), in the ornate Palacio Canton, explains why the Maya deformed their children's skulls, and displays jewelry, carvings and artifacts (with explanations in English).

Several blocks south of the plaza, the sprawling **Mercado Municipal** (btwn Calles 56 & 56a, south of Calle 65) is a fascinating area to wander about.

Sleeping

Hostel Zócalo (☎ 930-9562; hostal_zocalo@yahoo.com. mx; Calle 63 No 508; dm M$100, r with/without bathroom M$350/280; ☐ ☎) Great location and a beautiful old colonial building make this hostel unique. It has firm beds, and a big buffet breakfast is included. The service can be a bit gruff and you may have problems getting hot water.

Nómadas Youth Hostel (☎ 924-5223; www.nomadas travel.com; Calle 62 No 433 at Calle 51; dm M$109, s with/without bathroom M$268/199, d M$328; P ☐ ☎ ☎) This is Mérida's backpackers' central, and the best hostel in the city. There are mixed and women's dorms, as well as private rooms. It even has free salsa classes and an amazing pool out back.

Hotel Casa Becil (☎ 924-6764; hotelcasabecil@yahoo. com.mx; Calle 67 No 550C btwn Calles 66 & 68; s/d with fan M$250/280, d with air-con M$300-350; ☻) Almost a hostel but not quite, the Casa Becil's friendly owner calls it a 'BBC,' which stands for bed, breakfast and coffee. It offers very inexpensive, clean rooms, and a fully equipped kitchen downstairs.

Alvarez Family Guest House (☎ 924-3060; www. casaalvarezguesthouse.com; Calle 62 No 448 btwn Calles 51 & 53; s/d with fan M$350/400, d with air-con M$500-600; P ☻ ☎ ☎) Impeccably clean and in a family home, this 'hostel plus' offers a friendly, one-of-the-family ambience, nice showers, spotless bathrooms and in-room fridges.

Casa Ana B&B (☎ 934-0005; www.casaana.com; Calle 52 No 469 btwn Calles 53 & 51; r incl continental breakfast M$520; ☻ ☎ ☎) Though out of the way, Casa Ana is an intimate escape and the best budget B&B in town.

Eating

A few blocks east of the Plaza Grande are side-by-side **supermarkets** (Calle 56) as well as a branch of **Super Bodega** (cnr Calles 67 & 54a), a market–department store chain.

our pick **Mercado Municipal Lucas de Gálvez** (cnr Calles 56a & 67) This is where Mérida's least expensive eateries are located. Choose between all your favorite Yucatecan dishes, maybe even some *cochinita pibil* (pork marinated in chillies, wrapped in banana leaves and pit-cooked or baked).

Mercado Municipal No 2 (Calle 70) 'Número Dos' is a less crowded, but still cheap and good market on the north side of Parque de Santiago.

El Trapiche (☎ 928-1231; Calle 62 No 491 btwn Calles 59 & 61; mains M$26-50; ☻ 8am-midnight) A great, centrally located place, El Trapiche has cheap Mexican eats in a casual environment.

Café Chocolate (Calle 60 No 442; set lunch M$59, mains M$45-80; ☻ 7am-midnight Mon-Sat; V) The food is excellent at this colonial cafe.

Drinking & Entertainment

Mérida offers many folkloric and musical events in parks and historic buildings, put on by local performers of considerable skill. The website www.yucatantoday.com offers monthly news and often highlights seasonal events.

Take a cab to the Prolongación de Montejo, where you'll have your choice of bumping discos and uberchic lounges. In the center, visit **KY60** (Calle 60 btwn Calles 55 & 57; admission free; ☻ 9pm-3am), with good pool tables and reasonably priced beer, or **Azul Picante** (Calle 60 btwn Calles 57 & 55; ☻ until late), a salsa bar.

Getting There & Away

Mérida's tiny but modern airport is 10km southwest of the Plaza Grande off Hwy 180 (Av de los Itzáes). Check out www.ticketbus. com.mx for good ticket info. Following are some of the terminals, the bus lines operating from them and areas served.

MEXICO'S YUCATÁN
& CHIAPAS

CAME bus terminal (☎ reservations 924-8391; Calle 70 btwn Calles 69 & 71) Mérida's main bus terminal has mostly 1st-class buses.

Noreste bus terminal (Calle 67 btwn Calles 50 & 52) Second-class Noreste, Sur and Oriente bus lines use this terminal.

Progreso bus terminal (Calle 62 No 524 btwn Calles 65 & 67) A separate terminal serving Progreso.

Terminal de Segunda Clase (Calle 69) ADO, Mayab, Oriente, Sur and ATS run mostly 2nd-class buses to various points in the state and around the peninsula.

Destination	Cost (M$)	Duration (hr)
Campeche (short route)	105-162	2½-3½
Cancún	179-418	4-6
Celestún	47	2
Chichén Itzá	90-94	1¾-2½
Izamal	20-25	1½
Mexico City (Norte)	1088	19
Palenque	242-366	8-9
Playa del Carmen	414	4½-8
Progreso	14	1
Ruta Puuc (round trip)	132	8
Tulum	194	4
Uxmal	41	1-1½
Valladolid	78-128	2½-3½

CHICHÉN ITZÁ

If carvings of skulls and heart-eating eagles, or skeleton-filled cenotes and nine-level pyramids don't satisfy you, come for the acoustics of a Pink Floyd show, as regular clapping echoes attest. Chichén Itzá is one of Mexico's most famed archaeological sites, even if you are not allowed to climb any of the temples. Most of the lodgings, restaurants and services are ranged along 1km of highway in the village of Pisté, to the western side of the ruins. It's 1.5km from the ruins' main entrance to the first hotel, Pirámide Inn, which is one of your best bets to stay the night.

The **site** (Mouth of the Well of the Itzáes; admission M$111, parking M$20, sound-&-light show M$40, guide M$500-600; ☼ 8am-6pm summer, 8am-5:30pm winter), 41km west of Valladolid, was a modest late-Classic town before war-torn Toltecs from Tula, in central Mexico, conquered it in AD 987. An unlikely harmony followed, with experienced Maya architects masterfully adhering to the imagery of the Toltec feathered-serpent cult of Quetzalcóatl (Kukulcán in Maya). The city was abandoned around 1224.

To explore the site, start from the Great Plaza, about 100m beyond the gate. In the

ASK A LOCAL

We asked Mérida local Monica Trujillo where to go for the best quick trips out of town. For more tips, check out www.red ecoturismo.com or www.yucatantoday.com.

- **Celestún** They have an amazing bird-watching tour here in the estuary (eight hours, M$250 per person).
- **Cuzamá** There are three incredible cenotes that you get to by horse-drawn carriages (eight hours, M$200 for a group of four people).
- **Dzibilchaltún & Progreso** You can stop at the ruins and the cenote in the morning, continuing on to the beach at Progreso just in time for afternoon cocktails (four hours, M$80 per person).
- **Uxmal & Ruta Puuc** You can see all of these sites – including Uxmal – in a day (eight hours, M$350 per person). Or continue your journey with a visit to **Mayapán** and the **Loltún caves**.

Monica Trujillo, Mérida

middle, the imposing **El Castillo** (The Castle) pyramid is designed to represent the Maya calendar in stone and is famous for the moving serpent illusion on its staircase, visible during the spring and autumn equinoxes. Inside the pyramid is a pre-Toltec pyramid with a red jaguar throne, reached by a sweat-box chamber – now closed.

Just northeast (back to the left as you enter the plaza) is Gran Juego de Pelota, the biggest **ball court** in Mesoamerica. The acoustics are terrific: try chatting with a friend on opposite sides.

Across the plaza from El Castillo is a 300m path north to **Cenote Sagrado** (Sacred Cenote), where some 50 skeletons have been found.

Back in the plaza, on the eastern end, stands the impressive **Templo de los Guerreros** (Temple of the Warriors), with a *chacmool* (Maya sacrificial stone) looking over the warrior-carved columns. Behind is the shady **Grupo de las Mil Columnas** (Group of the Thousand Columns). Beyond, a path leads through the forest past the **Mercado** (Market), with a sunken courtyard rimmed by columns and a lone palm out of step.

The path leads past a replica of a traditional home, then another goes a few hundred meters south to the unusual **Caracol** (Snail), once used as an observatory (and a rare building you can climb). Just beyond is the **Edificio de las Monjas** (Nunnery).

Getting There & Away

Oriente's 2nd-class buses pass through Pisté bound for Mérida (M$70, 2½ hours) hourly between 8:15am and 4:15pm. Hourly Oriente buses to Valladolid (M$20, 50 minutes) and Cancún (M$90, 4½ hours) pass between 7am and 5:30pm. There's also 2nd-class service to Tulum (M$78, three hours) and Playa del Carmen (M$112, four hours). First-class buses serve Mérida (M$90 to M$94, 1¾ hours, 2:25pm and 5pm), Cancún (M$108, 2½ hours, 4:30pm) and Tulum (M$101, 2½ hours, 8am and 4:30pm). *Colectivos* to Valladolid (M$20, 40 minutes) pass through town regularly.

VALLADOLID

☎ 985 / pop 45,900

Also known as the Sultaness of the East, Yucatán's third-largest city is known for its quiet streets and sun-splashed, pastel walls. It certainly is sultry, and it's worth staying here for a few days or even a week, as the provincial town makes a great hub for visits to Río Lagartos, Chichén Itzá, Ek' Balam, and a number of nearby cenotes.

Sights

The **Templo de San Bernardino & Convento de Sisal** (☺ 8am-noon & 5-9pm) are about 700m southwest of the plaza. They were constructed between 1552 and 1560 to serve the dual functions of fortress and church.

Museo de San Roque (Calle 41; admission free; ☺ 9am-9pm), between Calles 38 and 40, has models and exhibits on the history of the city and the region.

There are also numerous cenotes in the area. **Cenote Zací** (Calle 36; admission M$25; ☺ 8am-6pm) is the worst of the bunch. A bit more enticing but less accessible is **Cenote Dzitnup** (Xkekén; admission M$25; ☺ 8am-5pm), 7km west of the plaza. Across the road, about 100m closer to town, is **Cenote Samulá** (admission M$25; ☺ 8am-6pm), a lovely cavern pool with *álamo* roots stretching down the walls. To get here, rent a bike from **Antonio 'Negro' Aguilar** (☎ 856-2125; Calle 44 btwn Calles 39 & 41; ☺ 7am-7pm) for about M$10 per hour. Shared vans departing from in front of Hotel María Guadalupe (on Calle 44) go to Dzitnup for M$10.

Sleeping & Eating

Hostal Los Frailes (☎ 856-5852; www.hostaldelfraile. com; Calzada de los Frailes No 212C; dm with air-con/fan M$130/90, r M$220; ✱ 💻 🛜) In an old converted *casona* (mansion), this hostel has less of a groovie traveler vibe, but is nonetheless a good option.

Hostel La Candelaria (☎ 019-858-562-267; www. hostelvalladolid.com; Calle 35 No 201F; dm M$100, r without bathroom M$250, all incl breakfast; 💻 🛜) A friendly place right on a quiet little square, this hostel can get a little cramped and hot, but there are two kitchens, a cozy garden area complete with hammocks, a girls-only dorm, and plenty of hangout space, making this the best hostel in town.

Bazar Municipal (cnr Calles 39 & 40) This place at the plaza's northeastern corner is a collection of market-style shops, popular for their big, cheap breakfasts.

Getting There & Away

The main **bus station** (cnr Calles 39 & 46) is two blocks west of the plaza. Frequent buses go to Cancún (M$78 to M$128, two hours), Mérida (M$88 to M$128, two hours) and Chichén Itzá (M$20 to M$44, 45 minutes).

Colectivos for Pisté and Chichén Itzá (M$20, 40 minutes) leave across the road from the ADO bus terminal, and for Tizimín (M$30, 40 minutes) from the eastern side of the main plaza. *Colectivos* for Ek' Balam

---

DIY: EXPLORE MORE OF YUCATÁN STATE

There are a lot of gaps on the maps of this vast state. Here are some DIY ideas to get you started.

- **Río Lagartos** Head to this little fishing village on the gulf coast to kick off adventures into a nearby nature reserve (excursions cost about M$100 per person). On your way down, stop at the well-preserved **Ek' Balam site** (admission M$31, guide M$250; ☺ 8am-5pm).

- **Izamal** The yellow city has heaps of unexplored ruins nearby.

- **Ticul to Tihosuco** Part of the route is called Ruta de los Conventos (Route of the Convents), as each of these tiny villages has a cathedral or church, many in beautiful disrepair.

(M$40) leave from the corner of Calles 44 and 37.

CANCÚN

☎ 998 / pop 526,700

Unlike many cities in the world, Cancún just isn't afraid. It's unabashed and unapologetic, and in that lies its high-gloss charm. So send in the Maya dancers, swashbuckling pirates and beer-chugging US Spring Breakers. Cancún can take it. But can you?

Enduring Cancún means following the locals: stay and eat in the *centro* (downtown area), take the local bus out with packed lunch to hop onto the resorts' beaches, and return later that day for drinks in town.

Orientation

Cancún's Zona Hotelera, home to the resorts and beaches, is set along Blvd Kukulcán, which curves around a curved sandy spit (actually an island). Ciudad Cancún, just west, is home to *el centro* (downtown), around Av Tulum between the bus station and Av Cobá. The airport is 8km south of downtown. All sites in this section are in downtown unless otherwise specified.

Information

The Cancún Visitors Bureau has an informative website, www.cancun.travel. Internet cafes in downtown Cancún are plentiful, speedy and cheap, costing M$10 per hour or less. There are several banks with ATMs on Av Tulum, between Avs Cobá and Uxmal.

Centro Médico Caribe Cancún (☎ 883-9257; Av Yaxchilán 74A; ⏱ 24hr)

City tourism office (☎ 887-3379; www.cancun.gob. mx; Av Cobá; ⏱ 8am-6pm Mon-Fri, 9am-2pm Sat)

Lavandería Tulum (Av Tulum; per kg M$16) Laundry.

Main post office (☎ 884-1418; cnr Avs Xel-Há & Sunyaxchén; ⏱ 8am-6pm Mon-Fri, 9am-1pm Sat)

Nómadas Travel (☎ 892-2320; www.nomadastravel. com; Av Cobá 5; ⏱ 10am-2pm & 3:30-7pm Mon-Fri, 10am-2pm Sat) This downtown agency has good deals for students.

Pay-in-advance lockers (per 24hr M$90) At the airport, just outside customs at the international arrivals area.

Tourist police (☎ 885-2277)

Sights & Activities

MAYA RUINS

In the **Zona Arqueológica El Rey** (admission M$39; ⏱ 8am-5pm), on the west side of Blvd Kukulcán between Km 17 and Km 18, there's a small temple and several ceremonial platforms. **Yamil Lu'um** (admission free) sits atop a beachside knoll in the parklike grounds between the Park Royal and the Westin. To reach the site, visitors must pass through either of the hotels flanking it or approach it from the beach (the easiest way) – there is no direct access from the boulevard.

BEACHES

Under Mexican law, travelers have the right to walk and swim on every beach throughout the country, except those within military compounds. In practice, it is difficult to approach many stretches of beach without walking through the lobby of a hotel, particularly in the Zona Hotelera – just pretend you own the place.

Starting from Ciudad Cancún in the northwest, all of Isla Cancún's beaches are on the left-hand side of the road (the lagoon is on your right). The first beaches are **Playa Las Perlas**, **Playa Juventud**, **Playa Linda**, **Playa Langosta**, **Playa Tortugas** and **Playa Caracol**; after rounding Punta Cancún, the beaches to the south are **Playa Gaviota Azul**, **Playa Chac-Mool**, **Playa Marlin**, the long stretch of **Playa Ballenas** and finally, at Km 17, **Playa Delfines**.

GETTING INTO TOWN

From the Airport

White Riviera city buses to Ciudad Cancún (M$40) leave the airport about every 20 minutes between 5:30am and 11:30pm, stopping at both the domestic and international terminals.

Grayline Express *colectivos* (M$195) depart for the Zona Hotelera and downtown from in front of the international terminal every 15 minutes, while cheaper ADO shuttles leave from the domestic terminal for downtown (M$40) or Playa del Carmen (M$100).

From the Bus Station

Cancún's **bus terminal** (cnr Avs Uxmal & Tulum) is within walkable distance from all the downtown accommodations listed for Cancún.

CANCÚN CENTRO

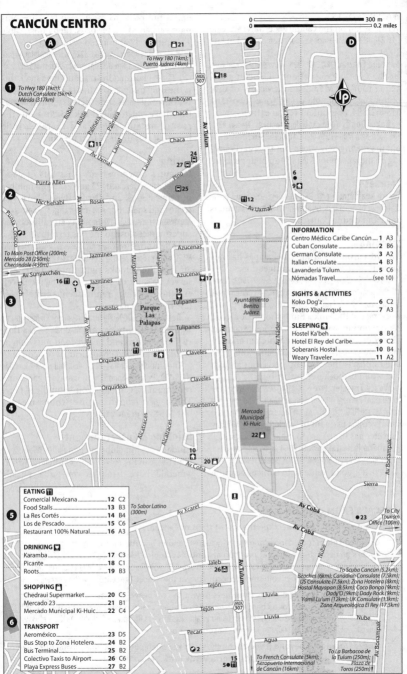

0 _____ 300 m
0 _____ 0.2 miles

To Hwy 180 (1km);
Puerto Juárez (4km)

To Hwy 180 (1km);
Dutch Consulate (5km);
Mérida (317km)

To Main Post Office (200m);
Mercado 28 (250m);
Checandole (450m)

Parque
Las
Palapas

Ayuntamiento
Benito
Juárez

Mercado
Municipal
Ki-Huic

To Sabor Latino
(300m)

To City
Tourism
Office (100m)

To Scuba Cancún (5.2km);
Beaches (6km); Canadian Consulate (7.5km);
US Consulate (7.5km); Zona Hotelera (8km);
Hostal Mayapan (8.5km); Coco Bongo (9km);
Dady'O (9km); Dady Rock (9km);
Yamil Lu'um (12km); UK Consulate (13km);
Zona Arqueológica El Rey (17.5km)

To French Consulate (5km);
Aeropuerto Internacional
de Cancún (16km)

To La Barbacoa de
la Tulum (250m);
Plaza de
Toros (250m)

INFORMATION
Centro Médico Caribe Cancún **1** A3
Cuban Consulate **2** B6
German Consulate **3** A2
Italian Consulate **4** B3
Lavandería Tulum **5** C6
Nómadas Travel.......................(see 10)

SIGHTS & ACTIVITIES
Koko Dog'z **6** C2
Teatro Xbalamqué........................... **7** A3

SLEEPING
Hostel Ka'beh **8** B4
Hotel El Rey del Caribe.................. **9** C2
Soberanis Hostal **10** B4
Weary Traveler **11** A2

EATING
Comercial Mexicana **12** C2
Food Stalls **13** B3
La Res Cortés **14** B4
Los de Pescado **15** C6
Restaurant 100% Natural.............**16** A3

DRINKING
Karamba **17** C3
Picante **18** C1
Roots...**19** B3

SHOPPING
Chedraui Supermarket.................**20** C5
Mercado 23 ....**21** B1
Mercado Municipal Ki-Huic.........**22** C4

TRANSPORT
Aeroméxico **23** D5
Bus Stop to Zona Hotelera..........**24** B2
Bus Terminal **25** B2
Colectivo Taxis to Airport **26** C6
Playa Express Buses.....................**27** B2

WATER SPORTS

Work began on the **Cancún Underwater Museum** (☎ 848-8312; www.asociadosnauticoscancun.com) in late 2009.

Scuba Cancún (☎ 849-5226; www.scubacancun.com.mx; Blvd Kukulcán Km 5.2) offers a Cancún snorkeling tour for M$377 and a variety of dive options at reasonable prices (one-/two-tank M$702/884, equipment rental extra).

Koko Dog'z (www.kokodogz.com; Av Náder 42-1; ☺ noon-8pm Mon-Fri, to 6pm Sat) sells surfboards – but the surfing here sucks – or try wakeboarding on the lagoon for M$1950 an hour per boat.

Courses

Teatro Xbalamqué (☎ 887-3828, ext 509; http://teatro xbalamque.blogspot.com; cnr Jazmines & Av Yaxchilán) offers yoga and drama courses.

Sleeping

The area around Parque Las Palapas has numerous hostels and other budget digs.

Hostel Ka'beh (☎ cell phone 998-892-7902; hostel kabeh@gmail.com; Alcatraces 45; campsites per person M$50, dm M$120; ☒) This brand new hostel is still working out the kinks. But it should be a good central option, with air-con, a book exchange, nice common areas, a shared kitchen and immaculately clean *azulejo*-tiled bathrooms. The one oddity is the blow-up beds, but at least you won't be bothered by bedbugs.

Weary Traveler (☎ 887-0191; www.wearytraveler hostel.com; Palmera 30; dm with air-con/fan incl breakfast buffet M$110/100; ☒ ☒ ☐) The cramped shared rooms could use a bit of work, but the Weary Traveler has the basics to make a good hostel.

Soberanis Hostal (☎ 884-4564; www.soberanis.com.mx; Av Cobá 5; dm/d incl continental breakfast M$120/595; ☐ ☞) It's good value with a nice location,

and a fun place to meet friends. All rooms have very comfortable beds, tiled floors, cable TV and nicely appointed bathroom.

Hostal Mayapan (☎ 883-3227; www.hostalmayapan.com; Blvd Kukulcán Km 8.5; dm incl breakfast M$200-240; ☒ ☐ ☞) Located in an abandoned mall, this is the only budget spot in the Zona Hotelera. It's new and lacks some details – for instance, they have yet to build a kitchen – but the rooms are superclean and there's a little hangout spot in an atrium upstairs.

Eating

Cancún's downtown area has lots of good budget eats. Mercados 23 and 28 have a number of tiny eateries, and Parque Las Palapas has some food stalls. For self-catering, try **Comercial Mexicana** (cnr Avs Tulum & Uxmal), a centrally located supermarket close to the bus terminal.

La Res Cortés (cnr Calles Alcatraces & Orquideas; mains M$20-80; ☺ 6pm-2am) This amazing little open-air restaurant looks right onto a park, and serves up some of the city's best tacos, as well as other offerings reminiscent of the street fare in Guadalajara.

Restaurant 100% Natural (Cien por Ciento Natural; ☎ 884-0102; Av Sunyaxchén; mains M$40-180; ☺ 7am-11pm; Ⓥ) Vegetarians and health-food nuts delight at this health-food chain near Av Yaxchilán.

Checándole (☎ 884-7147; Av Xpujil 6 SM 27; mains M$50-130; ☺ noon-8pm) If you can only eat at one restaurant in Cancún, you should eat here. The *menú del día* (fixed three-course meal) is just M$45 – great value.

Drinking & Entertainment

Ciudad Cancún clubs are generally mellower than those in the rowdy Zona Hotelera, which generally have drink-'til-you-puke specials

---

ESCAPE FROM CANCÚN

Here are some top tips to escape the tourist traps of Cancún.

▪ **Down to Tulum** (p68) Stop along the way at lost cenotes and **Akumal's Laguna Yal-Kú**. There's an expensive volunteer program at **Centro Ecológico Akumal** (☎ 984-875-9095; www.ceakumal.org). Further south, **Flora, Fauna y Cultura** (☎ 984-871-5273; www.florafaunaycultura.org) offers extended low-cost volunteer opportunities at the Xcacel-Xcacelito beach reserve.

▪ **Isla Holbox** It's best if you have three days to visit this off-beat Gulf coast island. Come May through to September for a chance to swim with a whale shark. **Hostel Ida y Vuelta** (☎ 984-875-2358; www.camping-mexico.com/home_uk.htm; campsites M$80, hammocks M$90, dm M$100, r M$550, bungalows with kitchen M$600; ☞) is your best budget bet.

▪ **Nuevo Durango & beyond** If you ask nicely, locals will often put you up in a *palapa* (thatched palm leaf–roofed shelter). Check out **Puerta Verde** (www.puertaverde.com.mx) for more info.

> ### SPLURGE
>
> **Hotel El Rey del Caribe** (☎ 884-2028; www.
> elreydelcaribe.com; cnr Avs Uxmal & Náder; s/d
> M$975/1105; ⊠ ⊞ ⊠ ⊠) El Rey is a true
> 'eco-tel' that composts, employs solar col-
> lectors and cisterns, uses gray water for the
> gardens and even has a few composting
> toilets. This is a beautiful spot with jungle-
> style courtyard, azure swimming pool and
> a small Jacuzzi.

from around M$200 to M$300. Downtown,
stroll along Av Yaxchilán down to Parque Las
Palapas and you are sure to run into something (or somebody) you like.

CIUDAD CANCÚN

Karamba (☎ 884-0032; cnr Azucenas & Av Tulum;
⊗ 10pm-6am Thu-Sun) Come here for a varied crowd of
gays, lesbians and cross-dressers.

Picante (Av Tulum 20; ⊗ 9pm-6am) A longtime
neighborhood gay bar.

Plaza de Toros (cnr Avs Bonampak & Sayil) Has several bars.

Roots (☎ 884-2437; Tulipanes 26; Fri & Sat M$50;
⊗ 6pm-1am Mon-Sat) Pretty much the hippest bar in
Ciudad Cancún.

Sabor Latino (☎ 892-1916; cnr Avs Xcaret & Tankah;
women/men M$40/60, Wed free; ⊗ 10:30pm-6am,
closed Sun-Tue low season) On the 2nd floor of Chinatown
Plaza, this is another happening club.

ZONA HOTELERA

Coco Bongo (☎ 883-5061; Forum Mall; ⊗ 10:30pm-
5am) This is often the venue for MTV's Spring Break coverage.

Dady'O (☎ 800-234-9797; Blvd Kukulcán Km 9; ⊗ 10pm-
4:30am) One of Cancún's more elaborate dance clubs.

Dady Rock (☎ 883-3333; Blvd Kukulcán Km 9;
⊗ 5:30pm-3:30am) A steamy rock-and-roll club.

> ### ASK A LOCAL
>
> We got together with Cancún local Vanessa
> Trava and 10 of her closest friends to see
> where Cancún's professionals choose to dine.
>
> ■ **La Barbacoa de la Tulum** If you love
> tacos, head to this cheap cantina at the
> Plaza de Toros.
>
> ■ **Los de Pescado** (Av Tulum 32; meals M$20-
> 99; ⊗ 10am-5:30pm) Order *ceviche* or tacos
> with a beer or two at one of downtown's
> best budget spots.
>
> *Vanessa Trava, Cancún*

Getting There & Away

AIR

About 8km south of the city center, **Aeropuerto
Internacional de Cancún** (Cancún International Airport;
☎ 886-0047) is the busiest in southeast Mexico.
See p35 for details.

BOAT

There are several points of embarkation for
Isla Mujeres from Cancún by boat. From
Punta Sam it costs M$18 (M$220 for a car),
from Puerto Juárez M$35, and leaving from
the Zona Hotelera the cost is about M$135.

BUS

The **bus terminal** (cnr Avs Uxmal & Tulum) offers 1st-
and 2nd-class service. Across from the bus
terminal, a few doors from Av Tulum, is the
ticket office and miniterminal of **Playa Express**
(Pino). It runs shuttle buses down the Caribbean
coast to Tulum approximately every 30 minutes until early evening.

Destination	Cost (M$)	Duration (hr)
Chetumal (to Belize)	244-294	5½-6½
Chichén Itzá	108	3-4
Mérida	256-318	4-6
Mexico City	1264-1466	24
Palenque	562-688	12-13
Playa del Carmen	24-38	1-1¼
Tulum	82-108	2¼-3
Valladolid	128	2-3

Getting Around

Riviera buses (Aeropuerto Centro) head south
on Av Tulum to the airport. *Colectivos* head
to the airport from a stand in front of the
Hotel Cancún Handall on Av Tulum, about
a block south of Av Cobá. They charge M$25
per person and leave when full. The official
rate for private taxis is M$150.

To reach the Zona Hotelera from downtown, catch any bus with 'R1,' 'Hoteles' or
'Zona Hotelera' signs displayed on the wind-
shield as it travels along Av Tulum toward Av
Cobá, then eastward on Av Cobá. The one-
way fare is M$7.50. To reach Puerto Juárez
and the Isla Mujeres ferries, catch a Ruta 13
('Pto Juárez' or 'Punta Sam'; M$7.50) bus
heading north on Av Tulum.

Cancún's taxis don't have meters – fares are
set, but always agree on a price before getting
in. From downtown to Punta Cancún is M$80
to M$100, to Puerto Juárez M$30 to M$40.

Rental-car agencies with facilities at the airport and La Isla Shopping Village in the Zona Hotelera include **Alamo** (☎ 886-0179), **Avis** (☎ 883-4583, 01-800-288-8888), and **Hertz** (☎ 01-800-709-5000, cell phone 998-111-3997).

ISLA MUJERES
☎ 998 / pop 14,000

If you are going to visit just one of Quintana Roo's islands, Isla Mujeres (Island of Women) is probably the place for you. It's not as crowded as Cozumel, yet offers more to do and see than chiller-than-thou Holbox. Sure, there are quite a few ticky-tacky tourist shops, but folks still get around by golf cart and the crushed-coral beaches are better than those of Cozumel or Holbox.

The name Isla Mujeres goes at least as far back as Spanish buccaneers, who (legend has it) kept their lovers in safe seclusion here. Today some archaeologists believe that the island was a stopover for the Maya en route to worship their goddess of fertility, Ixchel, on Isla Cozumel.

Orientation & Information

The island is 8km long, 150m to 800m wide and 11km off the coast. You'll find most of the restaurants and hotels in the town of Isla Mujeres, with the pedestrian mall on Hidalgo serving as the focal point. The ferry arrives in the town proper on the island's northern tip.

HSBC Bank (Av Rueda Medina)

Internet cafe (cnr Matamoros & Guerrero; per hr M$10; 🕑 9am-10pm Mon-Sat)

Lavandería Automática Tim Pho (☎ 877-0529; cnr Juárez & Abasolo; 🕑 7am-9pm Mon-Sat, 8am-2pm Sun) Laundry.

Medical Center (Guerrero btwn Madero & Morelos)

Police (☎ 877-0082)

Post office (☎ 877-0085; cnr Guerrero & López Mateos; 🕑 9am-4pm Mon-Fri)

Tourist information office (☎ 877-0767; Av Rueda Medina; 🕑 8am-8pm Mon-Fri, 9am-2pm Sat & Sun)

Sights

If you want a break from the water, bus or bike to the **Isla Mujeres Tortugranja** (Isla Mujeres Turtle Farm; ☎ 888-0705; Carretera Sac Bajo Km 5; admission M$30; 🕑 9am-5pm) south of town. The turtle farm has pools and protected shores for turtles and their eggs.

The dramatic **Punta Sur** (admission M$50), at the southern tip of the island (8km from town), has a romantic lighthouse but has been tacki-

fied with cartoonish figures put alongside a severely worn Maya ruin.

Activities

SWIMMING

The best swimming on the island is conveniently found in town at **Playa Norte** (North Beach; northwest to be precise). The lagoon separating the Avalon Reef Club from the rest of the island has a great shallow swimming spot known as **Yunque Reef**.

About 7km south of town, skip the touristy nature park of Playa Garrafón and opt for its northerly neighbor **Hotel Garrafón de Castilla** (☎ 877-0107; Carretera Punta Sur Km 6; admission M$30; 🕑 9am-5pm).

DIVING & SNORKELING

Within a short boat ride of the island there's a handful of lovely dives, such as Barracuda, La Bandera, El Jigueo, Ultrafreeze and Manchones. You can expect to see sea turtles, rays and barracuda, along with a wide array of hard and soft corals. To protect and preserve the reefs, a M$20 fee is charged for all diving and swimming.

Snorkeling with whale sharks (M$1170 to M$1250) just off Isla Holbox is the latest craze. Folks at the following dive shops can arrange your trip.

Mundaca Divers (☎ 999-2071; mundacadivers@gmail.com; Madero 10) offers dives for M$585 (one tank) to M$780 (two tanks) and snorkeling tours from M$325. They also have an office at the Avalon Reef Club. **Sea Hawk Divers** (☎ 877-1233; seahawkdivers@hotmail.com; Carlos Lazo) has similar prices.

The fisherfolk of Isla Mujeres have formed a cooperative to offer snorkeling tours of various sites from M$260, including the reef off Playa Garrafón, and day trips to Isla Contoy for M$715. You can book through the **Fisherman's Cooperative Booth** (☎ 877-1363; Av Rueda Medina) in a *palapa* steps away from the dock.

Sleeping

Between mid-December and March, many places are booked by midday. If planning to linger longer, watch for 'Rooms for Rent' signs.

ourpick **Poc-Na Hostel** (☎ 877-0090; www.pocna.com; cnr Matamoros & Carlos Lazo; dm with air-con/fan M$155/100, r with air-con & bathroom M$350, r without bathroom M$270; ✕ 💻 🖤) Moments away from one of the island's nicest beaches and decorated with shells and hibiscus flowers, Mexico's oldest youth hostel also ranks among the country's best.

Hotel Roca Teliz (☎ 877-0804; www.islamujeresonline.com.mx; cnr Hidalgo & Abasolo; s with air-con/fan M\$390/250, d with air-con/fan M\$390/280; ✷ ❑ ✺) Good budget digs, especially for solo travelers, the 'Rock' has a cool central courtyard, dark but clean rooms, and is located right on the Hidalgo pedestrian mall. Prices drop like a rock in low season.

Hotel Caribe Maya (☎ 877-0684; Madero 9; d with air-con/fan M\$350/280; ✷) The old blue tiles need replacing, but this place offers rooms that, though a bit musty, are solid value even in high season.

Eating

Inside the remodeled **Mercado Municipal** (Town Market; Guerrero) are a couple of stalls selling hot food at low prices.

Mañana (☎ 877-0555; cnr Matamoros & Guerrero; dishes M\$20-70; ✷ 8am-4pm; **V**) A good-vibe place with colorful hand-painted tables, superfriendly service and some excellent veggie options.

Viva Cuba Libre (Hidalgo; mains M\$60-90; ✷ 5pm-midnight Tue-Sun) It competes for decibel levels with neighboring restaurants, but really, we all like Cuban *son* more than bad disco remixes, don't we?

La Lomita (Juárez; mains M\$60-230; ✷ 9am-10:30pm Mon-Sat) The 'Little Hill' serves good, cheap Mexican food in a small, colorful setting between Allende and Uribe.

Mininos (Av Rueda Medina; mains M\$70-140; ✷ 11am-9pm) A tiny, colorfully painted shack with a sand floor, right by the water.

Entertainment

Isla Mujeres' highest concentration of nightlife is along Hidalgo.

La Luna (Guerrero; ✷ 7am-3am or later) Some say it's the best in town.

Playa Sol (Playa Norte; ✷ 9am-10pm or later) A happening spot day and night.

Poc-Na Hostel (cnr Matamoros & Carlos Lazo; ✷ sunset-sunrise) A beachfront joint with bonfires and more hippies than all the magic buses in the world.

Getting There & Away

There are several points of embarkation to reach Isla Mujeres from Cancún by boat. From Punta Sam and arriving just south of town, it costs M\$18 (M\$220 for a car). Ferries

from Puerto Juárez (M\$35) and the Zona Hotelera (M\$135) arrive in town.

In Cancún, to reach Puerto Juárez and the Isla Mujeres ferries, catch a Ruta 13 ('Pto Juárez' or 'Punta Sam'; M\$7.50) bus heading north on Av Tulum.

Getting Around

A number of shops rent bikes for about M\$30/120 per hour/day. **David** (☎ cell phone 998-223-1365; Av Rueda Medina near Abasolo) has a decent selection.

Mopeds cost M\$130 per hour, while golf carts are M\$200 per hour; rent them at **Pepe's Moto Rent** (☎ 877-0019; Hidalgo btwn Matamoros & Abasolo).

Local buses depart about every 25 minutes from the ferry dock and head along Av Rueda Medina, stopping along the way. Taxi rates are set by the municipal government and posted at the taxi stand just south of the passenger ferry dock.

PLAYA DEL CARMEN
☎ 984 / pop 100,400

Playa del Carmen is the hippest city in all of the Yucatán Peninsula. Sure, the waters aren't as clear as those of Cancún or Cozumel – and daily cruise-ship visits are starting to spike the numbers on the ticky-tacky scale – but nevertheless, this remains a fun spot to indulge and escape.

Orientation & Information

Playa is mostly laid out on an easy, one-way grid. Quinta Av (pronounced '*keen*-ta'), or 5 Av, is the most happening street in town.

Banamex (cnr Calle 12 & 10 Av)

Centro de Salud (☎ 873-0493; cnr 15 Av & Av Juárez)

Gigalav Laundry & Internet (Calle 2 No 402; ✷ 8am-10pm Mon-Sat) Conveniently has both an internet cafe (M\$10 per hour) and a laundry (M\$15 per kilo).

Post office (cnr 20 Av & Calle 2; ✷ 9am-4pm Mon-Fri)

Tourist police kiosk (☎ 873-2656; Plaza Mayor; ✷ 24hr)

Activities

Prices for diving and snorkeling are similar at most outfits: resort dives M\$1300, one-tank M\$637, two-tank M\$1027, cenote M\$1287, snorkeling M\$377, whale-shark tour to Isla Holbox M\$3120 and open-water certification M\$4485.

Alltournative (☎ 803-9999; www.alltournative.com; 5 Av btwn Calles 12 & 14; ✷ 9am-7pm Mon-Sat) Offers tour packages.

Dive Mike (☎ 803-1228; www.divemike.com; Calle 8) Between 5 Av and the beach.

Scuba Playa (☎ 803-3123; www.scubaplaya.com; Calle 10) A PADI five-star resort.

Courses

International House (☎ 803-3388; www.ihrivieramaya. com; Calle 14) has Spanish classes (M$2860) and offers residence-hall stays (M$390 per night) and homestays (M$455 per night). **Playa Lingua del Caribe** (☎ 873-3876; www.playalingua.com; Calle 20) offers Spanish and Maya classes.

Sleeping

Travelgarden (☎ 873-0068; Av Juárez; dm/s/d M$120/250/350; 🛜) A half-block from the beach, this decent budget bet lacks a little in the cleanliness department, but has two *palapa*-style 'dorm rooms' with two or three beds in each and some small rooms with private bathroom.

Hostel Río Playa (☎ 803-0145; www.hostelrioplaya. com; Calle 8; dm incl breakfast M$140-160, r without bathroom M$450-500; 🔀 🖵 🛜) The best budget buy in town, the Río offers easy access to the beach and a women's-only dorm. It also has a shared kitchen, a cool rooftop bar and hangout area – with a remarkably shallow pool – and air-con in all rooms.

Hostel Playa (☎ 803-3277; www.hostelplaya.com; Calle 8; dm/d/tr M$145/420/550) While it's a bit away from the center, this is one of Playa's standby hostels. The best thing about this place is the ambience: it has a huge, central common area,

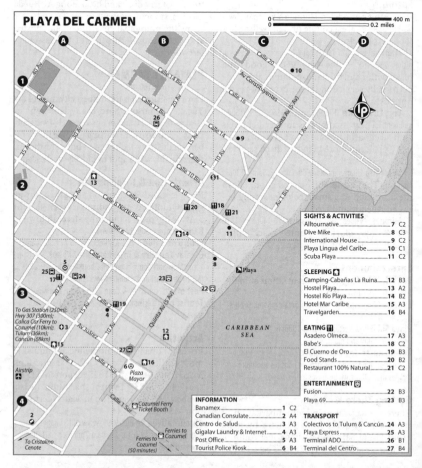

PLAYA DEL CARMEN

0 — 400 m
0 — 0.2 miles

CARIBBEAN SEA

To Gas Station (250m); Hwy 307 (300m); Calica Car Ferry to Cozumel (10km); Tulúm (36km); Cancún (68km)

Airstrip

To Cristalino Cenote

Ferries to Cozumel

Ferries to Cozumel (50 minutes)

Plaza Mayor

Cozumel Ferry Ticket Booth

SIGHTS & ACTIVITIES		
Alltournative	**7**	C2
Dive Mike	**8**	C3
International House	**9**	C2
Playa Lingua del Caribe	**10**	C1
Scuba Playa	**11**	C2

SLEEPING 🏠		
Camping-Cabañas La Ruina	**12**	B3
Hostel Playa	**13**	A2
Hostel Río Playa	**14**	B2
Hotel Mar Caribe	**15**	A3
Travelgarden	**16**	B4

EATING 🍴		
Asadero Olmeca	**17**	A3
Babe's	**18**	C2
El Cuerno de Oro	**19**	B3
Food Stands	**20**	B2
Restaurant 100% Natural	**21**	C2

ENTERTAINMENT 🎭		
Fusion	**22**	B3
Playa 69	**23**	B3

INFORMATION		
Banamex	**1**	C2
Canadian Consulate	**2**	A4
Centro de Salud	**3**	A3
Gigalav Laundry & Internet	**4**	A3
Post Office	**5**	A3
Tourist Police Kiosk	**6**	B4

TRANSPORT		
Colectivos to Tulum & Cancún	**24**	A3
Playa Express	**25**	A3
Terminal ADO	**26**	B1
Terminal del Centro	**27**	B4

DETOUR: CRISTALINO CENOTE

On the west side of the highway south of Playa del Carmen is a series of wonderful cenotes. Among these is **Cristalino Cenote** (adult/child M$40/20; 🕑 6am-5:30pm), just south of the Barceló Maya Resort. It's easily accessible, only about 70m from the entrance gate, which is just off the highway. Two more sinkholes, Cenote Azul and El Jardín del Edén, are just south of Cristalino along the highway, but Cristalino is the best of the three.

---

great kitchen, and both beer and spirits are allowed until 12:30am, when people either head to bed or go out to the clubs.

Camping-Cabañas La Ruina (☎ 873-0405; Calle 2; campsites or hammock spaces per person M$150; d with/without bathroom M$400/300; 🔀) Pitch your tent or hang your hammock in a large lot near the beach. This is the least appealing of the budget offerings.

Hotel Mar Caribe (☎ 873-0207; maldonadomarta19@gmail.com; cnr 15 Av & Calle 1; r with air-con/fan M$600/400; 🔀) A simple, secure and very clean nine-room place with mostly fan-cooled rooms (three rooms have air-con).

Eating

Head out of the tourist zone to find cheap, quality eats such as great grilled chicken from **Asadero Olmeca** (mains M$30; 🕑 7am-6pm), next to the Tulum-bound *colectivos*. There are lots of cheap food stands on 10 Av between Calles 8 and 10, near the center.

El Cuerno de Oro (cnr Calle 2 & 10 Av; set meals M$38, mains M$75-99; 🕑 7am-10pm) Hearty, home-style set meals are served in this casual eatery near the bus terminal.

Babe's (Calle 10; mains M$50-100; 🕑 noon-11:30pm Mon-Sat, 5-11:30pm Sun; V) Babe's serves some excellent Thai food, including a yummy *tom kha gai* (chicken and coconut-milk soup) brimming with veggies. There's another Babe's along the Nueva Quinta between Calles 28 and 30.

Restaurant 100% Natural (☎ 873-2242; cnr Quinta Av & Calle 10; breakfast M$58-68, mains M$100-184; 🕑 7am-11pm; V) The trademarks of this quickly establishing chain – fresh juices, salads, various vegetable and chicken dishes and other healthy foods – are delicious and filling.

Entertainment

The party generally starts on Quinta Av, then heads down toward the beach on Calle 10.

Playa 69 (Callejón off Quinta Av btwn Calles 4 & 6; www.rivieramayagay.com; 🕑 until late Tue-Sun) A gay dance club.

Fusion (Calle 6; 🕑 until late) Groove out by the beach under that Playa moon at Fusion.

Getting There & Away

BOAT

Ferries to Isla Cozumel (M$140 one way, 30 minutes) leave at 6am, 8am, 9am, 10am, 11am, 1pm, 3pm, 5pm, 6pm, 7pm, 9pm and 11pm. Buy tickets at the booth on Calle 1 Sur.

BUS

Playa has two bus terminals. The newer one, **Terminal ADO** (20 Av), just east of Calle 12, is where most 1st-class buses arrive and depart. The old bus station, **Terminal del Centro** (cnr Av Juárez & Quinta Av), gets all the 2nd-class (called *intermedio* by lines such as Mayab) services. **Playa Express** (Calle 2 Norte) offers quick service to downtown Cancún for M$34.

COLECTIVOS

Colectivos are a great option for cheap travel southward to Tulum (M$35, 45 minutes). They depart from Calle 2 near 20 Av when full (about every 10 or 15 minutes) from 5am to 10pm. From the same spot, you can grab a *colectivo* to Cancún (M$30).

Destination	Cost (M$)	Duration (hr)
Aeropuerto Internacional de Cancún	90	1
Chetumal (to Belize)	154-258	5-5½
Chichén Itzá	218	3-4
Cobá	72	1-1¾
Mérida	286	5
Palenque	642	12-13
San Cristóbal de Las Casas	816	16-18
Tulum	48-65	1
Valladolid	94-120	2½-3½

ISLA COZUMEL

☎ 987 / pop 73,200

An immensely popular diving spot since 1961 (when Jacques Cousteau, led by local guides, showed its spectacular reefs to the world), Cozumel lies 71km south of Cancún. Measuring 53km by 14km, it is Mexico's largest island. Called Ah-Cuzamil-Peten (Island of Swallows) by its earliest inhabitants, Cozumel has become a world-famous diving and cruise-ship destination.

Maya settlement here dates from AD 300. During the Postclassic period, Cozumel flourished as a trade center and, more importantly, a ceremonial site. Every Maya woman living on the Yucatán Peninsula and beyond was expected to make at least one pilgrimage here to pay tribute to Ixchel, the goddess of earth, fertility and the moon, at a temple erected in her honor.

Orientation & Information

San Miguel de Cozumel is the island's only town. There are ATMs, banks and internet joints on the plaza.

Clínica Médica Hiperbárica (Hyperbaric Chamber; ☎ 872-1430; Calle 5 Sur) Between Av Rafael Melgar and Av 5 Sur.

Del Mar Lavandería (Av 20 Sur btwn Av Benito Juárez & Calle 1 Sur; per load M$65)

Post office (cnr Calle 7 Sur & Av Rafael Melgar; ⏰ 9am-4:30pm Mon-Sat)

Tourist office (2nd fl, Plaza Mayor; ⏰ 8am-3pm Mon-Fri)

Sights

Exhibits at the fine **Museo de la Isla de Cozumel** (☎ 872-1434; Av Rafael Melgar; admission M$36; ⏰ 8am-5pm) present a clear and detailed picture of the island.

In order to see most of the island you will have to rent a vehicle or take a taxi; cyclists will need to brave the regular strong winds.

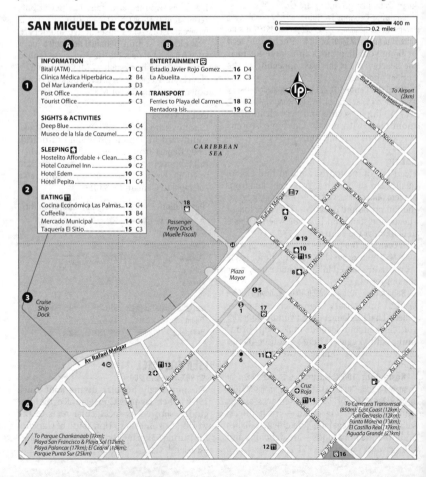

SAN MIGUEL DE COZUMEL

0 — 400 m
0 — 0.2 miles

INFORMATION
Bital (ATM) **1** C3
Clínica Médica Hiperbárica **2** B4
Del Mar Lavandería **3** D3
Post Office **4** A4
Tourist Office **5** C3

SIGHTS & ACTIVITIES
Deep Blue **6** C4
Museo de la Isla de Cozumel....**7** C2

SLEEPING
Hostelito Affordable + Clean....**8** C3
Hotel Cozumel Inn **9** C3
Hotel Edem **10** C3
Hotel Pepita **11** C4

EATING
Cocina Económica Las Palmas...**12** C4
Coffeelia **13** B4
Mercado Municipal **14** C4
Taquería El Sitio.......................**15** C3

ENTERTAINMENT
Estadio Javier Rojo Gomez **16** D4
La Abuelita **17** C3

TRANSPORT
Ferries to Playa del Carmen......**18** B2
Rentadora Isis...........................**19** C2

CARIBBEAN SEA

Passenger Ferry Dock (Muelle Fiscal)

Plaza Mayor

Cruise Ship Dock

Blvd Aeropuerto Internacional

To Airport (2km)

To Parque Chankanaab (7km); Playa San Francisco & Playa Sol (12km); Playa Palancar (17km); El Cedral (18km); Parque Punta Sur (25km)

To Carretera Transversal (850m); East Coast (12km); San Gervasio (12km); Punta Morena (13km); El Castillo Real (17km); Aguada Grande (21km)

The following route will take you south from San Miguel, then counterclockwise around the island.

The **Parque Chankanaab** (admission M$208; 7am-6pm) is a popular snorkeling spot. A taxi from town costs M$130 one way.

The Maya ruin of **El Cedral** is the oldest on the island. It's the size of a small house and has no ornamentation, but it costs nothing to visit and it is easy to reach. It's 3.5km down a signed paved road that heads off to the left (east) a kilometer or two south of Nachi-Cocom's access road, hiding amid a forest of pole structures painted yellow and white and erected as souvenir stalls.

About 17km south of town, **Playa Palancar** is another great beach, where you can rent snorkel gear and kayaks.

The southern tip of the island has been turned into a rather overpriced 'ecotouristic' **Parque Punta Sur** (872-0914; admission M$130; 9am-5pm).

The eastern shoreline is the wildest part of the island and presents some beautiful seascapes and many small blowholes. Swimming is dangerous on most of the east coast because of riptides and undertows. With a bit of care you can sometimes swim at Punta Chiqueros, Playa Chen Río and Punta Morena. As you travel along the coast, consider stopping for lunch or a drink at the Rasta Bar (Km 29.5), El Galeón (Km 43.1) or Coconuts (Km 43.5). El Galeón rents surfboards and boogie boards for M$200 and M$70 per hour, respectively.

Beyond where the east-coast highway meets the Carretera Transversal, intrepid travelers can walk toward **Punta Molas**, the island's northeastern point, accessible only by foot. About 17km up the road are the Maya ruins known as **El Castillo Real**, and a few kilometers further is **Aguada Grande**.

The Maya complex of **San Gervasio** (admission M$90; 7am-4pm) are Cozumel's only preserved ruins. San Gervasio is thought to have been the site of the sanctuary of Ixchel, goddess of fertility, and thus an important pilgrimage site at which Maya women worshipped.

Activities

The top dives in the area include **Santa Rosa Wall**, **Punta Sur Reef**, **Colombia Shallows** and **Palancar Gardens**. Prices vary, but in general expect to pay about M$950 for a two-tank dive, M$910 for an introductory 'resort' course and M$5460 for PADI open-water certification. Good snor-

keling can be found at Casitas and Dzul-Há. Snorkelers are required to pay M$20 for park admission. The best snorkeling sites are reached by boat; a half-day boat tour will cost from M$400 to M$650. Contact **Deep Blue** (872-5653; www.deepbluecozumel.com; cnr Av 10 Sur & Calle Dr Adolfo Rosado Salas) for diving and snorkeling trips.

Sleeping

our pick **Hostelito Affordable + Clean** (869-8157; Av 10 Norte btwn Av Benito Juárez & Calle 2 Norte; www.hostelito.com; dm M$156, d/q M$455/650;) The name says it all: Hostelito is affordable *and* clean. Upstairs you'll find a great terrace, kitchen and common area, as well as a four- to six-person dorm and two doubles.

Hotel Edem (872-1166; Calle 2 Norte No 124; s/d with fan M$200/250, d with air-con M$350;) Great location and saintly rates make the Edem a prime deal. It has a turtle-filled fountain and a friendly Siamese cat, and the no-nonsense *señora* keeps the doors locked after 9pm.

Hotel Cozumel Inn (872-0314; mariocozumelinn@hotmail.com; Calle 4 Norte; s/d with fan M$290/350, d with air-con M$400;) A green building with 26 well-maintained rooms with good beds, and a small swimming pool.

Hotel Pepita (872-0098; Av 15 Sur; r M$385;) The owner, Maria Teresa, takes pride in her work, and it shows. This is the best economical hotel in the city. It's friendly, with well-maintained rooms grouped around a garden.

Eating

The cheapest option are the little market *loncherías* (lunch stalls) next to the Mercado Municipal on Calle Dr Adolfo Rosado Salas between Avs 20 and 25 Sur.

Taquería El Sitio (Calle 2 Norte; tacos & tortas M$15-30; 7am-1pm) Head over here for scrumptious tacos and *tortas* (sandwiches).

our pick **Coffeelia** (872-7402; Calle 5 Sur; breakfast M$55-76, mains M$45-75; 7:30am-11pm Mon-Sat, 8am-1pm Sun;) A great way to start or finish the day: head over to Coffeelia for warm smiles and delicious food – and great coffees, including espressos. Thursday is story night in the pleasant garden area.

Cocina Económica Las Palmas (cnr Calle 3 Sur & Av 25 Sur; set meals M$55; 9:30am-7pm Mon-Sat) This place packs up with locals come lunchtime. And while it gets hotter than Hades, you'll love the *chicharrones* (fried pork rinds) and Maya favorites like *poc chuc* (slow-roasted pork) on offer.

Entertainment

Cozumel's nightlife is quiet and subdued. Try the plaza or around the cruise-ship dock first.

Estadio Javier Rojo Gomez (cnr Calle Dr Adolfo Rosado Salas & Av 30 Sur) Hosts rock concerts and *lucha libre* (professional wrestling) matches.

La Abuelita (cnr Calle 1 Sur & Av 10 Sur) Grab a drink with the locals at the 'little grandma.'

Getting There & Away

AIR

Some airlines fly direct from the USA; European flights are usually routed via the USA or Mexico City. See p35 for more info on carriers.

BOAT

Passenger ferries run to Isla Cozumel from Playa del Carmen. Unless you're driving your own car, take the Playa passenger ferries offered by **México Waterjets** (www.mexicowaterjets.com) or **Ultramar** (www.granpuerto.com.mx). Both services cost M$140 one way, and there's normally a passenger ferry every hour to and from Cozumel, depending on the season. The ferries run from 6am to midnight.

Getting Around

BICYCLE

A full day's bicycle rental typically costs M$90 to M$160 (depending on season). Ask at your hotel.

CAR & SCOOTER

Car-rental rates start at around M$500 all-inclusive. For scooters and motorcycles, you'll pay anywhere from M$220 to M$500 per day. Try **Rentadora Isis** (☎ 872-3367; Av 5 Norte), between Calles 2 and 4 Norte, and make sure you check the fine print.

TAXI

Fares in and around town are M$34 per ride, to the Zona Hotelera M$80, and a day trip around the island costs M$700 to M$1000; luggage may cost extra.

TULUM

☎ 984 / pop 14,800

Tulum's spectacular coastline – with its confectioner-sugar sands, jade-green water, balmy breezes and laid-back international vibe – make it one of the top beaches in Mexico. Where else can you get all that *and* a dramatically situated Maya ruin? There is

one big drawback. The town center, where the really cheap eats and sleeps are found, sits right on the highway, making it feel more like a truck stop than tropical paradise. This said, both Cobá to the west and the massive Reserva de la Biosfera Sian Ka'an to the south make good day trips.

Orientation & Information

Spread-out Tulum has three parts: the rapidly developing town, where buses and *colectivos* pull in, the ruins (a couple of kilometers north), and the Zona Hotelera (3km east). The bus terminal is toward the southern end of town. Watch your valuables on the beach, and bring a lock if you plan to stay in the no-frills beachfront *cabañas*.

Tulum Pueblo has Telmex pay phones, internet cafes, numerous currency-exchange booths (one with an ATM), two **HSBC banks** (☽ 8am-5pm Mon-Sat) and a **post office** (Av Tulum; ☽ 9am-3:30pm Mon-Fri).

Sights & Activities

TULUM RUINS

Seeing Mexico's most-visited Maya site atop surf-splashed Caribbean cliffs, it's not hard to imagine a Postclassic Maya or two asking for a transfer here. These days the location of the relatively small roped-off **ruins** (admission M$51; ☽ 8am-4:30pm) may be more impressive than the site itself. Many visitors charge through them as a dip on the beach awaits behind. A M$20 train takes you to the ticket booth from the entrance, or just hoof the 300m. Taxis from town charge M$40. There's a less-used foot entrance from the north side of the Zona Hotelera.

Tulum is believed to have been an important port town during its Postclassic heyday (AD 1200–1521). Named by the Spanish, Tulum means 'wall' in Maya. The site's original name was Zama, or 'Dawn' – watch the sunrise to realize why. Tulum was one of Mexico's last ancient cities to be abandoned, about 75 years after the Spanish conquest.

To explore the ruins, pass the ticket booth and enter the compact rectangular site near its northwestern corner. Heading east you pass the **Casa del Cenote** (House of the Cenote), named for the small pool at its southern base. Above, you can look over the site – set just south on a waterfront bluff is the **Templo del Dios del Viento** (Temple of the Wind God). Past it is the biggest site, **El Castillo** (The Castle), whose Toltec-style *kukulcanes* (plumed serpents) are evidence of the late Postclassic period. Just south are the steps down to the beach, and above are many cliffside vantage points for your camera.

West, roughly in the middle of the site, the interesting two-story **Templo de Las Pinturas** (Temple of the Paintings) features relief masks (and murals on its unapproachable inner wall).

DIVING & SNORKELING

Cenote Dive Center (☎ 876-3285; www.cenotedive.com; Av Tulum) is a recommended outfit specializing in guided cave dives, and cenote and cave snorkeling trips.

Snorkeling or swimming right from the beach is possible and fun, but be extra careful of boat traffic.

Courses

About 8km south of the T-junction in the Zona Hotelera, **Ocho Tulum** (☎ 140-7870; www.mexico kantours.com) offers daily yoga classes (M$200). Also inquire here about kiteboarding packages. Four-hour courses cost M$3250, while M$7150 gets you 10 hours of instruction.

Sleeping

TULUM PUEBLO

Most hostels in town have free bikes for their guests.

Weary Traveler (☎ 871-2390; www.wearytraveler hostel.com; Av Tulum; dm M$120, r M$325; 🞩 🖳 🛜) Turn right out of the bus station and walk one block south to this fun hostel. A great place to meet friends, the Weary Traveler is known for its full breakfast.

Hotel El Crucero (☎ 871-2610; www.el-crucero.com; Crucero Ruinas; dm with bathroom M$130, d with air-con/ fan M$585/390; 🞩 🖳) You'll feel welcome and well taken care of at this friendly hotel. Dorm rooms have bathrooms and lockers, while air-con rooms are done up in themes, such as the Mexican Mural, Jungle Room and the Lizard Lounge.

Rancho Tranquilo (☎ 871-2784; Av Tulum s/n; dm M$150, r with/without bathroom M$350/250, r with air-con M$600; 🞩 🖳 🛜) A nice option for those looking for hostel-type lodging, Rancho Tranquilo offers a mix of *cabañas*, dorms and rooms in a low-key, lushly landscaped garden.

Villa Matisse (☎ 871-2636; shuvinito@yahoo.com; Av Satelite No 19; d M$650; 🛜) Funky patchwork quilts add a splash of color to the glaringly white, clean rooms at the Matisse.

ZONA HOTELERA

Hostel Maria Sabina (☎ 873-0113; ecohosteltulum@ gmail.com; dm M$150, cabaña without bathroom M$500) About 10km south of the T-junction, this is the best budget buy in the Zona Hotelera, with two dorms and six private *cabañas*. It's a little Jonestown feeling, but you get a shared kitchen, a large cenote onsite, plus free use of the kayaks, snorkel gear and bikes.

Cabañas Playa Condesa (r with/without bathroom M$550/300) Just 1km north of the T-junction, this group of thatched *cabañas* is a great budget deal. Along with the basic rooms – which are actually rather clean – you also get mosquito nets (believe us, you'll need them).

Zazil-kin (☎ 124-0082; www.hotelstulum.com; cabañas with/without bathroom M$750/400; 🞩 🛜) This popular place is a 10-minute walk from the ruins. It has a dive center, a basketball court, a restaurant-bar-disco and a nice stretch of beach.

Eating

The places listed here are in Tulum Pueblo. In the Zona Hotelera, head to one of the hotels for good eats. Two small supermarkets provide an alternative to eating out: Stop 'n' Go, 100m east of Hwy 307 on the road to Cobá, and Super Mar Caribe, about four blocks north of the bus terminal.

El Mariachi (Av Tulum btwn Orión & Centauro; mains M$65-109, tacos M$9; ⏰ 7am-3am) Popular with locals and tourists alike, this open-air spot delivers yummy slow-cooked pork *enchiladas* (stuffed pastries), fresh grilled fish and about every cut of meat you could imagine.

ourpick Salsalito Taco Shop (Orión btwn Avs Andromeda & Tulum; mains M$79-125, tacos M$20) Far enough removed from the main strip that you won't be sucking in exhaust fumes, this *palapa*-style eatery has great fish and shrimp tacos, prepared with loads of cabbage and freshly chopped carrots on top.

La Nave (☎ 871-2592; Av Tulum; mains M$80-160; ⏰ Mon-Sat) Perched over Av Tulum, this open-air Italian joint is perpetually packed.

Drinking & Entertainment

Caribe Swing (Av Tulum) is a locals' watering hole. Come to **Divino Paraíso** (Av Tulum) on Tuesday nights for free salsa lessons.

Getting There & Away

When leaving Tulum, you can wait at Crucero Ruinas for intercity buses and the *colectivos* to Playa del Carmen.

If you're headed for Valladolid, make sure your bus is traveling the short route through Chemax, not via Cancún. *Colectivos* leave from Av Tulum for Playa del Carmen (M$35, 45 minutes) and Punta Allen (2pm).

Destination	Cost (M$)	Duration (hr)
Cancún	82	2
Chetumal (to Belize)	120-164	3½-4
Chichén Itzá	78-118	3½
Cobá	36	45min
Mérida	194	4
Playa del Carmen	48	1
Valladolid	70	2

Getting Around

Except for the shuttles operated from the youth hostels, there are no *colectivos* out to the beach. Taxi fares are fixed and pretty cheap; a ride from either of the two taxi stands in Tulum Pueblo (one south of the bus terminal, which has fares posted; the other four blocks north on the opposite side of the street) to the ruins costs M$40. Fares to most *cabañas* mentioned here are M$50 to M$70.

AROUND TULUM
Gran Cenote

A little more than 3km from Tulum on the road to Cobá is **Gran Cenote** (snorkeling M$100), a worthwhile stop on your way between Tulum and the Cobá ruins. A taxi from downtown Tulum costs around M$60 one way, or it's an easy bike ride.

Cobá

A Classic-era Maya city set deep in tropical jungle, the fascinating Cobá **ruins** (admission M$51; 8am-5pm), 48km northwest of Tulum, are more linked with distant Tikal than Tulum or Chichén Itzá. Cobá was home to 55,000 Maya at its peak (AD 800–1100). Many amazing regional *sacbeob* (stone-paved avenues) led here. The longest one runs 100km to Yaxuna, near Chichén Itzá. The name – from the Maya word *koba* (believed to mean 'ruffled waters') – likely refers to the reedy, croc-filled lakes in the area.

Be at the gates when they open and you may not see another person for two hours. You can rent bikes for M$30 per day after 8am. If you walk through the jungle trails, expect to stay a minimum of three hours at the site.

Only a few of the estimated 6500 structures have been excavated. The four principal groups are spaced apart. Approximately 100m along the main path is **Grupo Cobá**, with an enormous pyramid and corbelled-vault passages. After 500m, the road forks: the left leads to the Nohoch Mul pyramid, the right to Grupo Macanxoc. Either way passes the **Conjunto Pinturas** (Collection of Paintings), 100m further, which has a couple of stelae.

If you're conscious of time, skip **Grupo Macanxoc**, 500m away (which has a few eroded stelae depicting women from Tikal) and head northeast past the **Grupo Nohoch Mul** and continue to the right (east) to the semicircular Xaibé structure, the juncture of four *sacbeob*. To the north, past a couple of structures, you'll see the 42m-high **Nohoch Mul** (Big Mound), a pyramid you can climb to look over the jungle canopy. It's a 1.5km, half-hour walk back to the entrance gate.

SLEEPING

Hotel y Restaurante El Bocadito (☎ 985-106-9822; r with air-con/fan M$350/150; ☒) Just north of the Laguna Cobá, at the entrance to town, this place has very basic rooms, all with private bathrooms.

Hotelito Sac-bé (☎ 984-206-7140; r with air-con/fan M$450/350; ☒) Clean and friendly, the Sac-bé is on the opposite side of the street from El Bocadito and about 100m closer to the main road heading out of town.

GETTING THERE & AWAY

Most buses serving Cobá stop at El Bocadito – a 10-minute walk (past the lake) from the ruins. Buses continue on to Valladolid and Chichén Itzá.

Reserva de la Biosfera Sian Ka'an

More than 5000 sq km of tropical jungle, marsh, mangroves and islands on Quintana Roo's coast have been set aside by the Mexican government as a large biosphere reserve. In 1987 the UN classified it as a World Heritage Site – an irreplaceable natural treasure.

There's an **entrance gate** (admission M$23) to the reserve about 10km south of Tulum. At the gate, there's a short nature trail taking you to a rather nondescript cenote (Ben Ha).

Entering the reserve by land on the road to Punta Allen, you pass **Boca Paila Camps** (☎ 984-871-2499; www.cesiak.org; r M$1300-1500), where you can check out the turtle rescue (M$325) or rent a kayak (M$425). About 1km further south is the **Centro de Visitantes Reserva de la Biosfera**

> **DETOUR**
>
> Punta Laguna, 20km northeast of Cobá on the road to Nuevo Xcan, is a fair-sized lake with a small Maya community nearby. A **tourist cooperative** (☎ 986-107-9187; www.puntalaguna.org) charges M$50 for entry to the lake area and about M$250 per hour for guided visit. There's no public transportation here.
>
> The villages of **Mahahual** and **Xcalak** make for tempting (though pricey) beachside excursions south from Tulum. And, on your way to Belize, it's definitely worth your time to stop for a day or two along the shores of the beautiful **Laguna Bacalar**.

Sian Ka'an, where you'll find some natural-history exhibits along with a watchtower.

At the end of the road, **Punta Allen** (40km south from Tulum) is known primarily for its catch-and-release bonefishing; tarpon and snook are very popular sportfish as well. An hour's tour of the lagoon, including turtles, bird-watching and a quick snorkel, costs M$400 to M$600. Ask at your hotel about tours. There are no ATMs or internet cafes in town.

At the entrance to town, the beachfront **Hotel Costa del Sol** (☎ 984-113-2639; Punta Allen; campsites M$200, r M$1130) has quaint fan-cooled bungalows and a laid-back feel. The restaurant is pretty decent, and there's karaoke on weekend nights.

GETTING THERE & AWAY
Community Tours Sian Ka'an (☎ 984-871-2202; www.siankaantours.org; Av Tulum, Tulum) runs tours from Tulum that include pickup in the Zona

Hotelera. Trips cost between M$910 and M$1300. You can also enter the reserve by taking a **colectivo** (☎ 984-115-5580; M$200) out of Tulum: one leaves daily from downtown Tulum at 2pm and arrives about three hours later.

MEXICO DIRECTORY

ACCOMMODATIONS
If you're dorming it, a bunk is M$100 to M$130; if you go 'private,' Quintana Roo rates (around M$300 or $500 for a double) are higher than in the rest of the Yucatán Peninsula and Chiapas (about M$200 or M$300). You'll need a towel and soap for many cheap stays; most hostels provide sheets, though many lack mosquito nets (but not mosquitoes). Some places on the beach and in Palenque charge around M$50 to M$100 for a space for a tent or hammock. Accommodations prices are subject to two taxes: *impuesto de valor agregado* (IVA, or value-added tax; 15%) and *impuesto sobre hospedaje* (ISH, or lodging tax; 2% in most states). Many budget establishments only charge these taxes if you require a receipt.

Prices in this chapter are for high season, generally December to March, plus Semana Santa and, sometimes, summer (July and August).

ACTIVITIES
Diving the Yucatán is a big highlight, with great dives off the entire Quintana Roo coast, especially Isla Cozumel (p67). Also fun is snorkeling or diving in cenotes between Playa del Carmen (p63) and Tulum (p69). You can

> **GETTING TO BELIZE**
>
> Visitors heading south to Belize must change buses in **Chetumal**, the capital of Quintana Roo state. It's a hmm-and-go type of place, except for the remarkable **Museo de la Cultura Maya** (☎ 983-832-6838; Av Héroes; admission M$50; ☷ 9am-7pm Sun-Thu, 9am-8pm Fri & Sat), simply the best museum on Maya culture. The comfortable **Hotel Ucum** (☎ 983-832-0711/6186; Av Mahatma Gandhi 167; d with air-con/fan M$380/200; P ☒ ☒) is nearby.
>
> Chetumal's **main bus terminal** (near Avs Insurgentes & Belice) has frequent connections to Palenque and up the coast. From here regular direct buses leave for Corozal (M$35), Orange Walk (M$50) and Belize City (M$105), and five buses go on to Flores, Guatemala (M$300). From the Nuevo Mercado Lázaro Cárdenas there are 2nd-class buses to Belize.
>
> **Gibson Tours & Transfers** (www.gibsonstoursandtransfers.com) charges US$25 to the border and US$50 to Corozal. Though pricier than a bus, its taxi can wait for you and it can assist with border formalities.
>
> Be prepared to show evidence of the payment of your 'nonimmigrant fee' (see boxed text, p75) to leave Mexico. See boxed text, p242, for information on crossing into Mexico from Belize.

rappel into one at Ek' Balam (see boxed text, p57). There are kayak trips at the Reserva de la Biosfera Sian Ka'an (p70). In the highlands you can arrange good bike trips from San Cristóbal de Las Casas (p37).

BOOKS
If you're venturing north to Oaxaca, Mexico City or further inland on the Yucatán Peninsula, pick up Lonely Planet's *Mexico* or *Cancún, Cozumel & the Yucatán* guides.

BUSINESS HOURS
Most stores geared to locals (not tourists) are open from 9am to 7pm, with an hour or two off for lunch, Monday to Saturday. Tourist-related businesses usually don't take a break for siesta (this includes tourist offices).

CLIMATE
It's always hot in the Yucatán and around Palenque. The wet season, from May to October, makes the air sticky and hot. The hurricane season lasts from June to November, with most of the activity from mid-August to mid-September. In the Chiapas highlands, temperatures cool considerably, hovering between 10°C (50°F) and 20°C (68°F) all year.

For climate charts, see p714.

CUSTOMS
The normal routine when you enter Mexico by air is to complete a customs declaration form (which lists duty-free allowances), then place it in a machine. If the machine shows a green light, you pass without inspection. If a red light shows, your baggage will be searched.

DANGERS & ANNOYANCES
Despite often alarming media reports and official warnings for Mexico in general, the Yucatán Peninsula and Chiapas remain a safe place to travel, and with just a few precautions you can minimize the risk of encountering problems. Be wary of your belongings on night buses, on the beach and in crowded markets.

Enjoy yourself in the ocean, but beware of undertows and riptides on any beach. Women traveling alone, even pairs of women, should be cautious about going to remote beach and jungle spots. Cocaine and marijuana are prevalent in Mexico, and possession of small amounts for personal consumption has been legalized – this said,

there's still a lot of violence that goes along with drug trafficking, and the easiest way to avoid problems related with this is by avoiding the drugs. If you get busted using or transporting illegal drugs, your consulate will not help you.

DISCOUNT CARDS
The ISIC student card, the IYTC card for travelers under 26, and the ITIC card for teachers can help you obtain reduced-price air tickets to or from Mexico at student- and youth-oriented travel agencies. Staying at hostels affiliated with the Hostelling International (HI) saves about M$10 per night.

EMBASSIES & CONSULATES
Many embassies or their consular sections are in Mexico City; Cancún is home to several consulates, and there are some diplomatic outposts in Mérida as well.

Belize (☎ 983-832-1934; Av San Salvador 566, Fraccionamiento Flamboyanes, Chetumal)

Canada Cancún (off Map p59; ☎ 998-883-3360; 3rd fl, Local 330, Plaza Caracol II, Blvr Kukulcán Km 8.5, Zona Hotelera); Playa del Carmen (Map p64; ☎ 984-803-2411; playadelcarmen@canada.org.mx; Av 10 Sur btwn Calles 3 & 5 Sur)

Cuba Cancún (Map p59; ☎ 998-884-3423; Pecari 17); Mérida (☎ 999-944-4215; Calle 1-D No 32, Colonia Campestre)

France Cancún (off Map p59; ☎ 998-147-7448; consulat-cancun@aol.com; Blvr Colossio 760, SM 311); Mérida (off Map p54; ☎ 999-930-1500; Calle 60 No 385)

Germany (Map p59; ☎ 998-884-1898; Punta Conoco 36, SM24, Cancún)

Guatemala Ciudad Hidalgo (☎ 962-698-0184; 9a Calle Oriente 9, Colonia San José); Comitán (☎ 963-110-6816; 1a Calle Sur Poniente 35); Tapachula (☎ 962-626-1252; 5a Norte 5)

Italy Cancún (Map p59; ☎ 998-884-1261; Alcatraces 39, SM22)

Netherlands Cancún (off Map p59; ☎ 998-884-6284; nlconsulcancun@prodigy.net.mx; Calle Reno 45, SM20, M20); Mérida (off Map p54; ☎ 999-924-3122; Calle 64 No 418)

UK (off Map p59; ☎ 998-881-0100; The Royal Sands, Blvr Kukulcán Km 13.5, Zona Hotelera, Cancún)

USA Cancún (off Map p59; ☎ 998-883-0272; 2nd fl, No 320-323, Plaza Caracol Dos, Blvr Kukulcán, Zona Hotelera); Mérida (off Map p54; ☎ 999-942-5700; Calle 60 No 338-K, btwn Calles 29 & 31; Colonia Alcalá Martín)

FESTIVALS & EVENTS
Día de los Reyes Magos (Three Kings' Day, or Epiphany) January 6.

Día de la Candelaría (Candlemas) Held on February 2; commemorates the presentation of Jesus in the temple 40 days after his birth.

Carnaval A big bash preceding the 40-day penance of Lent, Carnaval takes place during the week or so before Ash Wednesday (which falls 46 days before Easter Sunday; late February or early March).

Semana Santa Held throughout Holy Week (starting on Palm Sunday, or Domingo de Ramos), with solemn street processions.

Día de la Independencia (Independence Day) On September 16, the anniversary of the start of Mexico's War of Independence in 1810.

Festival Cervantino Barroco San Cristóbal de Las Casas puts on a great art fair in late October or early November.

Día de Todos los Santos (All Saints' Day) and **Día de los Muertos** (Day of the Dead) On November 1 and 2, Mexico's most characteristic fiesta.

Día de la Virgen de Guadalupe (Day of the Virgin of Guadalupe) A week or more of celebrations throughout Mexico leads up to December 12, the day in honor of the Virgin who appeared to an indigenous Mexican, Juan Diego, in 1531.

Posadas From December 16 to 24, nine nights of candlelit parades re-enact the journey of Mary and Joseph to Bethlehem.

Día de Navidad (Christmas) December 25.

FOOD

Look out for *comidas corridas* or *comidas económicas* – these basic set meals, served for lunch (and into the afternoon), are widespread and cheap (M$30 to M$50). They usually come as soup, a meat dish with rice, a drink and dessert. Restaurants tend to keep long hours – often 7am to 10pm or midnight daily.

GAY & LESBIAN TRAVELERS

Cancún and Playa del Carmen are the biggest destinations. Here are a few websites with gay-friendly listings and other useful tips:

www.aquiestamos.com Cancún listings.

www.gay.com In-depth 'guides' to Cancún, Playa del Carmen and Mérida.

www.gaymexico.net Cancún link includes info on a gay parade.

HOLIDAYS

The chief holiday periods are Christmas to New Year, Semana Santa (the week leading up to Easter and up to a week afterward) and mid-July to mid-August. Other holidays:

Día de la Constitución (Constitution Day; February 5)

Día del Trabajo (Labor Day; May 1)

Cinco de Mayo (May 5)

Día de la Independencia (Independence Day; September 16)

Día de la Raza (Columbus Day; October 12)

INTERNET ACCESS

Internet cafes are easy to find in all places listed in this chapter other than Punta Allen and the far-flung ruins. It costs about M$10 to M$15 per hour to get behind a machine.

LEGAL MATTERS

Mexican law presumes an accused person is guilty until proven innocent. If you're arrested, you have the right to notify your embassy or consulate.

Road travelers should expect occasional police or military checkpoints. They are normally looking for drugs, weapons or illegal migrants.

MAPS

Quality regional maps include the highly detailed **ITMB** (www.itmb.com) 1:500,000 *Yucatán Peninsula Travel Map* and the sketchier **Guía Roji** (www.guiaroji.com.mx) 1:1,000,000 scale *Maya World* (M$60), showing all of the peninsula and parts of Tabasco and Chiapas. A good internet resource is **Maps of Mexico** (www.maps-of-mexico.com), with detailed maps of all the states.

MONEY

The Mexican peso (M$) is divided into 100 centavos.

The best way to get pesos in Mexico is from widely available ATMs *(cajeros automáticos)*, which use the Cirrus and Plus systems. You can cash money or traveler's checks at banks or at many *casas de cambio* (exchange offices). It's generally possible to change Canadian dollars, euros and British pounds.

Not many cheap accommodations or restaurants accept credit cards, but most travel agencies selling air tickets do.

Mexico's *impuesto de valor agregado* (IVA; value-added tax) is levied at 15%. By law the tax must be included in prices quoted to you and should not be added afterward.

Costs are higher in the Yucatán than in Chiapas. At most restaurants, a 10% tip is expected; some resort towns expect US levels of 15%.

Exchange Rates

The table, following, shows currency exchange rates at the time this book went to press.

Country	Unit	M$
Australia	A$1	10.84
Canada	C$1	12.38
Euro zone	€1	15.87
Japan	¥100	14.18
New Zealand	NZ$1	8.75
UK	£1	18.76
USA	US$1	12.93

POST

Post offices are typically open Monday to Friday, and Saturday morning. Post offices will hold letters for you as *lista de correos* (mail list) for up to 10 days, or poste restante (longer).

RESPONSIBLE TRAVEL

Tourists wreak havoc on coral reefs off the Yucatán shore. Some highly promoted beach parks, such as Xcaret (not included in this chapter), receive criticism for their dolphin shows and damage to the ecosystems.

Maya communities remain richly traditional. Be careful when visiting such communities; *never* take photos unless you have permission as it's deeply offensive, nor should you photograph objects such as saints in churches, which are regarded as sacred by the Maya.

Try to buy products – hammocks, handicrafts, coffee – directly from the sources, or from shops that represent them.

STUDYING

Spanish-language schools are more expensive in Mexico than in the rest of Central America. San Cristóbal de Las Casas (p39) has the most developed language-school scene, but there are also schools in Playa del Carmen (p64).

TELEPHONE

Local phone calls are cheap, but domestic long-distance and international calls can be expensive unless you call from *casetas telefónicas* (or *locutorios*; call offices where an on-the-spot operator connects the call for you), which offer international calls from M$3 or M$5 per minute. Voice Over Internet Protocol (VOIP) calling like Skype is available from many internet cafes and is a great money-saver.

Area codes have three digits and local numbers have seven. To call Mexico from abroad, dial your international access code, then ☎ 52 (Mexico's country code), followed by the area code and the seven-digit number. To call abroad from Mexico, dial ☎ 00, followed by country code, area code and number. To call long-distance in Mexico, dial ☎ 01, followed by the three-digit area code and the local number.

Collect calls are very costly. For a Mexican domestic operator, dial ☎ 020; for an international operator, dial ☎ 090. For Mexican directory information, dial ☎ 040.

Cell Phones

The most widespread cell-phone system in Mexico is **Telcel** (www.telcel.com). Amigo cards, for recharging Telcel phones, are widely available from newsstands and minimarts.

Phone Cards

To use a Telmex card phone, you need a phone card known as a *tarjeta Ladatel*. These are sold at kiosks and shops everywhere – look for the blue-and-yellow signs that read '*De venta aquí Ladatel*.'

Calls from Telmex card phones cost M$1 per minute for local calls; M$4 per minute long-distance within Mexico; M$5 per minute to the USA or Canada; M$10 per minute to Central America; M$20 per minute to Europe, Alaska or South America; and M$25 per minute to Hawaii, Australia, New Zealand or Asia.

TOILETS

These vary, but are generally never horrendous, and you pay for what you get (usually M$2). Bus stations often keep quite clean toilets.

TOURIST INFORMATION

'Tourist information' in many places means handing out brochures (and maybe plugging tours). Municipal- and state-run tourist offices are set up in most towns; some have English-speaking staff, of varying usefulness.

State-run websites include the following:

Campeche (☎ 981-811-9229, 800-900-2267; www.campeche.travel)

Chiapas (☎ 961-617-0550, 800-280-3500; www.turismochiapas.gob.mx)

Quintana Roo (☎ 983-835-0860; http://sedetur.qroo.gob.mx)

Tabasco (☎ 993-316-3633, 800-216-0842; www.visitetabasco.com)

Yucatán (☎ 999-930-3760; www.mayayucatan.com)

VISAS & DOCUMENTS

Citizens of many countries (including the USA, Canada, EU countries, Australia, New

PAID YOUR 'NONIMMIGRANT FEE' YET?

Though the tourist card itself is issued free of charge, you will need to pay a tourist fee of about M$200, called the *derecho para no inmigrante* (DNI; nonimmigrant fee), before you leave the country. If you enter Mexico by air, however, the fee is included in your airfare. If you enter by land, you must pay the fee at a bank in Mexico at any time before re-entering the frontier zone on your way out of Mexico (or before you check in at an airport to fly out of Mexico).

Zealand and Japan) do not presently require visas to enter Mexico as tourists. The list does change, however; check with a Mexican embassy or consulate, or at www.lonelyplanet.com for up-to-date information.

When entering Mexico, all tourists must obtain a tourist card (*forma migratoria para turista*; FMT) from Mexican immigration. Officers will write in the length of your stay; although the maximum is 180 days for most nationalities, let the officer know how long you want to stay, as they sometimes put in fewer days than the maximum. If that happens, the stay can be extended to the maximum at an immigration office for free, or beyond the maximum for about M$200. If you lose the card, you'll (supposedly) have to pay a fine of about M$420.

Travelers under 18 are sometimes required to show notarized consent forms from their parents. Officials are less likely to ask for this than airline staff when boarding. If you're under 18, check with a Mexican consulate before you go.

VOLUNTEERING

Volunteering is an amazing way to give back and learn from your trip. There are volunteer programs in sea-turtle preservation in Akumal and Xcacel-Xcacelito (see boxed text, p60). And you can always look for opportunities at your local hostel or language school. Most programs require a minimum commitment of at least a month, and some charge high fees.

Guatemala

Guatemala is a magical place. If you're into the Maya, the mountains, the markets or any of a million other things, you're bound to be captivated. People come and they stay. Or they leave and return. There's almost too much going on here, and even the shortest trip down the road takes you to completely different places, with new challenges and surprises. Don't be surprised if you hear yourself saying, 'we'll have to come back and do that, *next time.*'

Want to surf in the morning and learn Spanish in the afternoon? No problem. Descend a volcano, grab a shower and hit the sushi bar for dinner? You can do that. Check out a Maya temple and be swinging in a beachside hammock by sunset? Easy.

Guatemala's got its problems, but they mainly keep to themselves (although if you go looking for trouble, who knows what you'll find). More than 10 years after the official end to the civil war, this isn't the scary place that your mother fears it is. Travel here – once fraught with danger and discomfort – is now characterized by ease; you can do pretty much whatever you want, and your experience will only be limited by your imagination and time.

FAST FACTS

- **Area** 108,890 sq km (smaller than the US state of Louisiana; a bit bigger than England)
- **Budget** US$20 to US$40 per day
- **Capital** Guatemala City
- **Costs** Budget hotel in Guatemala City US$15, bottle of beer US$2, three-hour bus ride US$3, set lunch US$3.50
- **Country Code** ☎ 502
- **Languages** Spanish, Maya
- **Money** US$1 = Q8.2 (quetzals); US dollars readily accepted
- **Population** 15 million
- **Seasons** Dry (October to May), wet (June to September)
- **Time** GMT minus six hours

TRAVEL HINTS

Pack light, and you can put your backpack inside the bus. Everything is negotiable (almost).

OVERLAND ROUTES

From Mexico enter Guatemala at Ciudad Hidalgo–Tecún Umán or Ciudad Cuauhtémoc–La Mesilla. From El Salvador enter via Anguiatú; from Honduras via Agua Caliente; and from Belize via Benque Viejo del Carmen.

HIGHLIGHTS

■ **Tikal** (p198) Ignore the tour groups – this is the country's number-one tourist attraction for good reason.

■ **Antigua** (p102) Eat, drink and sleep well while studying Spanish and climbing volcanoes near Guatemala's most cosmopolitan and picturesque city.

■ **Lívingston** (p184) See another side of Guatemala in this Garífuna enclave on the Caribbean.

■ **Semuc Champey** (p171) Find out why people call this the most beautiful spot in the whole country.

■ **Best journey** (p188) Take a spectacular boat ride down a jungle-walled canyon of Lívingston–Río Dulce.

■ **Off the beaten track** (p129) Explore the lovely, traditional lakeside village of San Juan La Laguna.

GUATEMALA

CURRENT EVENTS

In late 2007, Álvaro Colom of the center-leftist Unidad Nacional de la Esperanza was elected President of Guatemala. Colom followed on from Oscar Berger's example of steady, minimalist governance and the country's infrastructure improved significantly, but allegations of back-room deals and political favoritism dogged Colom throughout his term.

The major political scandal of Colom's term was what came to be known as the Rosenberg Case. In May of 2009, Guatemala City lawyer Rodrigo Rosenberg was shot. Two days later a video surfaced, showing Rosenberg himself stating that if he was murdered it would be because he had evidence incriminating President Colom and his government in a corruption scandal.

The video screened worldwide and opposition parties were quick to act, staging massive demonstrations calling for Colom's resignation. Then it got really weird. First it was found that Rosenberg's friends and cousins had masterminded the assassination, and then investigators claimed that Rosenberg himself, depressed and distraught, had ordered the hit. While many seeking to make political mileage out of the event dispute the investigation's findings, the incident has all but faded into the background.

The major concern for all Guatemalans is security. An estimated 5% of murders in the country are prosecuted and daily newspapers regularly feature body counts of 10 and upwards for Guatemala City alone. The *Prensa Libre* reports the number of kidnappings per year has quintupled in the last decade, while annual murder rates have skyrocketed from 2904 to 6498. The police, understaffed and under-resourced, struggle in the face of rising crime, unaided by the fact that over the same period they've had 14 directors, one of whom has been accused of stealing US$300,000 seized in a cocaine raid.

Violence against women has long been a concern in Guatemala and while Congress passed down tough new penalties for femicide (the assassination of women) in 2008, critics label them useless in a country where so many murders go unsolved.

Contrary to the growing trend of lawlessness, human-rights campaigners have secured victories in bringing civil-war criminals to justice – ex-colonel Marco Antonio Sánchez Samayoa was sentenced to 53 years in prison for his part in the murder of eight farmers in 1981.

At the time of writing it looks like former President Portillo will be brought to justice, too – having evaded prosecution for years, he was finally charged by the USA for laundering money using US banks, and looks set to be extradited and put on trial there.

HISTORY

Earliest estimates put humans in what is now Guatemala as far back as 11,000 BC. The prevailing theory is that they got here by walking across an ice bridge from Siberia. Once their traditional food sources (mammoths, wild nuts and berries) began to dry up, these early inhabitants became farmers, domesticating corn, beans, tomatoes, chilies, turkeys and dogs for the dinner table. The improvement in the stability of the food supply led to population growth, an improvement in agricultural techniques, the development of early art forms

GUATEMALA

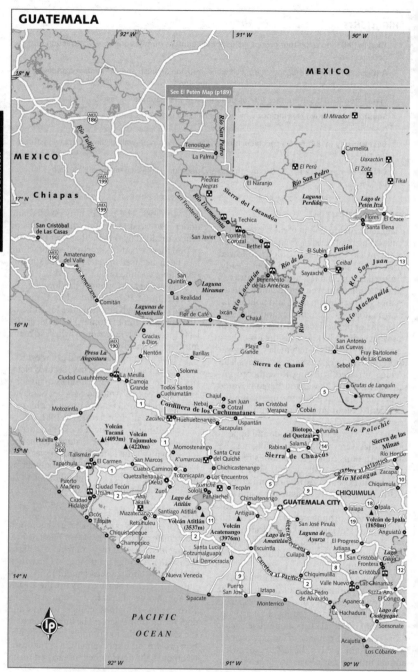

and a language that is traceable to what many Maya speak today.

Maya astronomers count the present era as starting at 3114 BC. Archaeologists generally put the birth of the Maya civilization (the Preclassic period) at around 2000 BC.

Rise & Fall of the Maya

Further developments in agriculture and increases in population gave these early civilizations time and resources to develop artistic and architectural techniques.

Between 800 BC and AD 100 population centers such as El Mirador in El Petén and Kaminaljuyú grew with trade and conquest and hundreds (if not thousands – many are yet to be uncovered) of temples and ceremonial centers were built. Guatemala's most famous Maya site, Tikal, came into its own around the start of the Classic period – AD 250.

The history of these – and many other – city states was troubled at best, characterized by broken military alliances, food shortages and droughts. The best not-too-academic reading on this time is in Simon Martin's and Nicholas Grube's *Chronicle of the Maya Kings and Queens*.

By the time the Spanish arrived, Maya civilization was already in trouble. Some centers, such as El Mirador had already been abandoned and others such as Tikal and Quiriguá had shrunk to the size of minor towns. Theories suggest that many abandoned El Petén in favor of the highlands, setting up capitals in K'umarcaaj, Iximché, Zaculeu and Mixco Viejo.

Relocation didn't bring peace, though – soon Toltec tribes, having abandoned the Yucatán, moved in and began to take control. Infighting among tribes, overpopulation and the resulting strain on the food supply combined to make conditions very favorable to the Spanish when they arrived in 1523.

Conquest & Colonization

The Spanish didn't just walk on in, as many think. Spirited resistance was met, most notably from the K'iche' (in a famous battle led by Tecún Umán, near present-day Quetzaltenango). In yet another sad episode in Guatemalan history, the neighboring Kaqchiquel not only refused to join forces with the K'iche', they actually joined the Spanish and fought against them.

It didn't take long for the Spanish to shaft the Kaqchiquel, though, and pretty soon most of the Maya were under Spanish control, the exceptions being the Rabinal (who have largely maintained their culture) and the Itzáes, who, hidden out on the island of Flores in El Petén were unconquered until 1697.

The 19th Century

During the short existence of the United Provinces of Central America, liberal president Francisco Morazán (1830–39) instituted reforms aimed at correcting three persistent problems: the overwhelming power of the Church; the division of society into a Hispanic upper class and an indigenous lower class; and the region's impotence in world markets.

But unpopular economic policies, heavy taxes and an 1837 cholera epidemic led to an indigenous uprising that brought conservative Rafael Carrera to power. Carrera ruled until 1865 and undid much of Morazán's achievements. His government allowed Britain to take control of Belize in exchange for construction of a road between Guatemala City and Belize City. The road was never built, and Guatemala's claims for compensation were never resolved.

The liberals regained power in the 1870s under president Justo Rufino Barrios, a coffee-plantation owner who embarked on a program of modernization – constructing roads, railways, schools and a modern banking system. Barrios also did everything possible to encourage coffee production, including promoting forced relocation and labor. Succeeding governments generally pursued the same policies of control by a wealthy minority and repression of opposition.

The Early 20th Century

From 1898 to 1920, Manuel Estrada Cabrera ruled as a dictator. He fancied himself an enlightened despot, styling himself the 'Teacher and Protector of Guatemalan Youth,' seeking to turn Guatemala into a 'tropical Athens' by bringing culture to a backward land. At the same time, however, he looted the treasury, ignored education and spent millions on the military.

When Estrada Cabrera was overthrown, Guatemala entered a period of instability that ended in 1931 with the election of General Jorge Ubico, who modernized the country's health and social welfare infrastructure but was forced into exile in 1944.

Philosopher Juan José Arévalo came to power in 1945, establishing the nation's social security system, a bureau of indigenous affairs, a modern public health system and liberal labor laws. His six years as president saw 25 coup attempts by conservative military forces.

Arévalo was succeeded in 1951 by Colonel Jacobo Arbenz Guzmán, who looked to break up estates and foster high productivity on small farms. But the US supported the interests of large companies such as United Fruit, and in 1954 (in one of the first documented covert CIA operations) the US government orchestrated an invasion from Honduras led by two exiled Guatemalan military officers. Arbenz was forced to step down and land reform never took place. Violence, oppression and disenfranchisement ensued, fueling the formation of left-wing guerrilla groups and fomenting discord.

Civil War

During the 1960s and '70s, economic inequality and the developing union movement forced oppression to new heights. Amnesty International estimates that 50,000 to 60,000 Guatemalans were killed during the political violence of the 1970s. Furthermore, the 1976 earthquake killed about 22,000 people and left about a million homeless.

In 1982 General José Efraín Ríos Montt initiated a 'scorched earth' policy, which is believed to have resulted in the extermination of the populations of over 400 villages at the hands of the military. President Ríos Montt, an evangelical Christian, was acting in the name of anti-insurgency, stabilization and anticommunism. An estimated 15,000 people, mostly Maya men, were tortured and massacred; 100,000 refugees fled to Mexico. In response, four guerrilla organizations united to form the URNG (Guatemalan National Revolutionary Unity).

In August 1983 Ríos Montt was deposed in a coup led by General Oscar Humberto Mejía Victores, but human-rights abuses continued. It was estimated that more than 100 political assassinations and 40 abductions occurred every month during this time. The US suspended military aid, and 1985 saw the election of civilian Christian Democrat Marco Vinicio Cerezo Arévalo – but not before the military secured immunity from prosecution and control of the countryside.

The 1990s

In 1990 Cerezo Arévalo was succeeded by Jorge Serrano Elías, who reopened dialogue with the URNG. But the talks collapsed,

Serrano's popularity declined, and he came to depend more on the army for support. On May 25, 1993, Serrano carried out an *autogolpe* (self-coup), suspending the constitution and ruling by decree. Although supported by the military, the coup was unsuccessful and Serrano was forced into exile. Congress elected Ramiro de León Carpio, an outspoken critic of the army, to complete Serrano's term.

In March 1995 the US again suspended aid, due to the government's failure to investigate the murder or disappearance of US citizens in Guatemala. These cases included the 1990 murder of Michael Devine and URNG leader Efraín Bámaca Velásquez (the latter's wife, US attorney Jennifer Harbury, had been conducting a protest since his disappearance in 1992). Eventually it was revealed that he had been murdered.

The Signing of Peace Accords

In 1996 Álvaro Enrique Arzú Irigoyen of the middle-right PAN (Partido de Avanzada Nacional) was elected. In December he and the URNG signed peace accords ending the 36-year civil war – a war in which an estimated 200,000 Guatemalans were killed, a million were left homeless and untold thousands 'disappeared.'

The accords called for accountability for the armed forces' human-rights violations and resettlement of one million refugees. They also addressed the identity and rights of indigenous peoples, health care, education and other basic social services, women's rights, the abolition of compulsory military service and the incorporation of the ex-guerrillas into civilian life.

It's been a rocky road since the war's end. Bishop Juan Gerardi, coordinator of the Guatemalan Archbishop's Human Rights Office (Odhag), was beaten to death outside his home in 1998. In May 1999 a minuscule 18% of the population voted in a referendum that asked whether constitutional reforms integral to the peace process should be implemented. The majority of those voters were opposed to the reforms and the process stalled.

The greatest challenge to peace stems from inequities in the power structure. It's estimated that 70% of the country's arable land is owned by less than 3% of the population. According to a UN report, the top 20% of the population has an income 30 times greater than the bottom 20%. Or, as most Guatemalans will tell you, there are seven families who 'own' Guatemala.

Guatemala in the 21st Century

Any hopes for a truly just and democratic society have looked increasingly frayed in the years since 1996. While international organizations, from the European Parliament to the Inter-American Commission on Human Rights (IACHR), regularly criticize the state of human rights in the country, Guatemalan human-rights campaigners are threatened or simply disappear on a frighteningly regular basis. The major problems – poverty, illiteracy, lack of education and health care (all much more common in rural areas, where the Maya population is concentrated) – remain a long way from being solved.

The 1999 presidential elections were won by Alfonso Portillo of the conservative Frente Republicano Guatemalteco (FRG). Portillo was seen as a front man for FRG leader, Efraín Ríos Montt. The national anticorruption prosecutor, Karen Fischer, fled the country in 2003 in the face of threats received when she investigated Panamanian bank accounts allegedly opened for President Portillo. At the end of his presidency Portillo too fled the country, in the face of allegations that he had diverted US$500 million from the treasury to personal and family bank accounts.

El Periódico newspaper printed an article in 2003 arguing that a 'parallel power structure' involving Ríos Montt had effectively run Guatemala ever since he had been ousted as president 20 years previously. Within days, the paper's publisher and his family were attacked by an armed gang of 12. Days later, Ríos Montt himself was granted permission by Guatemala's constitutional court to stand in the 2003 elections, despite the fact that the constitution banned presidents who had taken power by coup in the past, as Ríos Montt had in 1982.

In the end Guatemala's voters dealt Ríos Montt a resounding defeat, electing Oscar Berger of the moderately conservative Gran Alianza Nacional as president. Berger managed to stay relatively untouched by political scandal, critics saying this was because he didn't really do *anything*, let alone anything bad.

Hurricane Stan hit the country in October 2005, causing massive devastation and loss of life. The country's infrastructure, never wonderful, was torn apart as roads and villages were buried under landslides, and bridges, electricity, power and phone lines went down.

Cafta (the Central America Free Trade Agreement, or *Tratado de Libre Comercio* – TLC in Spanish) was ratified by Guatemala in 2006. Supporters claim it frees the country up for greater participation in foreign markets, while detractors state that the agreement is a bad deal for the already disenfranchised rural poor.

THE CULTURE
The National Psyche
You'll be amazed when you first reach Guatemala just how helpful, polite and unhurried Guatemalans are. Everyone has time to stop and chat and explain what you want to know. Most Guatemalans like to get to know other people without haste; feeling for common ground and things to agree on.

What goes on behind this outward politeness is harder to encapsulate. Few Guatemalans exhibit the stress, worry and hurry of the 'developed' nations, but this obviously isn't because they don't have to worry about money or employment. They're a long-suffering people who don't expect wealth or good government but make the best of what comes their way – friendship, their family, a good meal, a bit of good company.

Outwardly, it appears that family ties are strong, but beneath the surface you may find that the real reason that three generations live together in one house has more to do with economics than affection.

Guatemalans are a religious bunch – agnostics and atheists are very thin on the ground. People will often ask what religion you are quite early in a conversation. Unless you really want to get into it, saying 'Christian' generally satisfies. Orthodox Catholicism is gradually giving way to evangelical Protestantism among the *ladinos* (persons of mixed indigenous and European race), with the animist-Catholic syncretism of the traditional Maya always present. See also opposite page.

Some say that Guatemala has no middle class, just a ruling class and an exploited class. It's true that Guatemala has a small, rich, *ladino* ruling elite whose main goal seems to be to maintain wealth and power at almost any cost. It also has an indigenous Maya population, comprising more than half the total population, which tends to be poor, poorly educated and poorly provided for, and has always been kept in a secondary role by the ruling elite.

But as well as these two groups, there's a large group of poor and middle-class *ladinos*, with aspirations influenced by education, TV, international popular music and North America (of which many Guatemalans have direct experience as migrant workers) – and maybe by liberal ideas of equality and social tolerance. This segment of society has its bohemian/student/artist circles whose overlap with educated, forward-looking Maya may hold the greatest hope for progress toward an equitable society.

Lifestyle
The majority of Guatemalans live in one-room brick or concrete houses, or traditional *bajareque* (see Architecture, p84), with roofs of tin, tiles or thatch. They have earth floors, a stove/fireplace and minimal possessions – often just a couple of bare beds and a few pots. Thus live most of Guatemala's Maya majority, in the countryside, in villages and in towns.

The few wealthier Maya and most *ladino* families have larger houses in towns and the bigger villages, but their homes may still not be much more than one or two bedrooms and a kitchen that also serves as a living area. Middle-class families in the wealthier suburbs of Guatemala City live in good-sized one- or two-story houses with gardens. The elite few possess rural as well as urban properties – for example a comfortable farmhouse on the Pacific Slope, or a seaside villa on the coast.

Despite modernizing influences, traditional family ties remain strong. Extended-family groups gather for weekend meals and vacations. Old-fashioned gender roles are strong too: many women have jobs to increase the family income but few have positions of power. Homosexuality barely raises its head above the parapet: only in Guatemala City is there anything approaching an open gay scene, and that is pretty much for men only.

Traveling in Guatemala you will encounter a much wider cross-section of Guatemalans than many Guatemalans ever do, as they live their lives within relatively narrow worlds. The Guatemalans you'll meet on the road will also tend to be among the most worldly and open-minded, as a result of their contact with tourists and travelers. If you spend time studying Spanish or volunteering, you stand an even higher chance of meeting Guatemalans interested in learning – in other cultures, in music and the arts, in improving the position of women, the indigenous and the poor.

The CIA's World Factbook states that 7.5 million Guatemalans – about half the population – live in poverty. The official national minimum wage is only Q56 (about US$7) per day – and not everyone is entitled even to this. An established school teacher can earn around Q1800 (about US$225) per month. Poverty is most prevalent in rural, indigenous areas, especially the highlands. Wealth, industry and commerce are concentrated overwhelmingly in sprawling, polluted Guatemala City.

People

The great majority of Guatemala's 15 million people live in the highland strip from Guatemala City to Quetzaltenango, the country's two biggest cities. Many towns and large villages are dotted around this region. Some 49% of the population lives in towns and cities, and 40% are aged under 15.

Some 41% of Guatemalans are indigenous, but this line is blurred as many people have indigenous blood, but some choose not to describe themselves as such. Nearly all of this indigenous population is Maya, although there is a very small population of non-Maya indigenous people called the Chinka' (Xinca) in the southeastern corner of the country. The four biggest Maya groups, the K'iche' (Quiché), Mam, Q'eqchi' (Kekchí) and Kaqchiquel are most densely concentrated in the Highlands. The rest of Guatemala's population is nearly all *ladinos* – descended from both the Maya and European (mostly Spanish) settlers. There are also a few thousand Garífuna (descended from Caribbean islanders and shipwrecked African slaves) around the Caribbean town of Lívingston.

Maya languages are still the way most Maya communicate, with approximately 20 separate (and often mutually unintelligible) Maya languages spoken in different regions of the country. It's language that primarily defines which Maya people someone belongs to. Though many Maya speak some Spanish, it's always a second language – and there are many who don't speak any Spanish.

RELIGION

Roman Catholicism is the predominant religion in Guatemala, but it is not the only religion. Since the 1980s evangelical Protestant sects, around 58% of them Pentecostal, have surged in popularity, and it is estimated that 30% to 40% of Guatemalans are now Evangelicals. These numbers continue to grow as evangelical churches compete hard for further souls.

Catholicism's fall can also be attributed in part to the civil war. Catholic priests were (and still are) outspoken defenders of human rights, and attracted persecution from dictators at the time, especially from Ríos Montt. As a result, many Catholic churches in rural areas simply closed down during this time and evangelical ones moved in to fill the vacuum.

The number of new evangelical churches in some towns and villages, especially indigenous Maya villages, is astonishing. You will undoubtedly hear loud Guatemalan versions of gospel music pouring out of some of them as you walk around, and in some places loudspeakers broadcast the music and its accompanying preaching across entire towns.

Catholicism in the Maya areas has never been exactly orthodox. The missionaries who brought Catholicism to the Maya in the 16th century permitted aspects of the existing animistic, shamanistic Maya religion to continue alongside Christian rites and beliefs. Syncretism was aided by the identification of certain Maya deities with certain Christian saints and survives to this day. A bizarre example is the deity known, among other things, as Maximón (see boxed text, p126).

The Maya still worship at a number of places sacred since ancient times, bringing offerings and sacrificing chickens to gods who predate the arrival of the Spanish. Each place has its own different set of gods – or at least different names for similar gods.

Visitors might also be able to observe traditional Maya ceremonies in places such as the Pascual Abaj shrine at Chichicastenango, the altars on Laguna Chicabal outside Quetzaltenango, or El Baúl near Santa Lucía Cotzumalguapa, but a lot of traditional rites are off-limits to foreigners.

ARTS

Literature

Guatemalan writer Miguel Ángel Asturias won the Nobel Prize in literature in 1967. Best known for his thinly veiled vilification of Latin American dictators in *El señor presidente*, Asturias also wrote poetry (collected in *Sien de alondra*, published in English as *Temple of the Lark*). Other celebrated Guatemalan writers include poet Luis Cardoza y Aragón and short-story master Augusto Monterroso. Gaspar Pedro Gonzáles' *A Mayan Life* is claimed to be the first novel written by a Maya author.

Music

Music is a very important part of Guatemalan society, and a source of pride is that the marimba (xylophone) may have been invented here (although some claim it was brought from Africa by slaves). The Maya also play traditional instruments including the *chirimía* (of Arabic origin and related to the oboe) and reed flute.

Guatemalan tastes in pop music are greatly influenced by the products of other Latin American countries. Reggaetón is huge – current favorites being Pitbull, Wisin & Yandel and Calle 13. The only record label seriously promoting new Guatemalan artists (mostly in the urban/hip-hop vein) is Guatemala City–based UnOrthodox Productions (www.uo productions.com).

Guatemalan rock went through its golden age in the '80s and early '90s. Bands from this era such as Razones de Cambio, Bohemia Suburbana and Viernes Verde still have their diehard fans. The most famous Guatemalan-born musician is Ricardo Arjona, who has lived in Mexico since the '90s.

Architecture

Modern Guatemalan architecture, apart from flashy bank and office buildings along Guatemala City's Av La Reforma, is chiefly characterized by expanses of drab concrete. Some humbler rural dwellings use the traditional wall construction known as *bajareque* (stones, wooden poles and mud). Village houses are increasingly roofed with sheets of tin instead of tiles or thatch – less aesthetic but also less expensive.

The ancient Maya ruins and Spanish colonial structures in Antigua are impressive works of architecture. Interestingly, Maya embellishments can be found on many colonial buildings (such as the lotus flowers adorning Antigua's La Merced).

Weaving

Guatemalans make many traditional *artesanías* (handicrafts), both for everyday use and to sell. Crafts include basketry, ceramics and wood carving, but the most prominent are weaving, embroidery and other textile arts practiced by Maya women.

The *huipil* (a long, sleeveless tunic) is one of several types of garment that have been worn since pre-Hispanic times. Other colorful types include: the *tocoyal,* a woven head-covering often decorated with bright tassels; the *corte,* a piece of material 7m or 10m long that is used as a wraparound skirt; and the *faja,* a long, woven waist sash that can be folded to hold what other people might put in pockets.

Colorful traditional dress is still predominant generally in the heavily Maya-populated highlands, but you'll see it in all parts of the country. The variety of techniques, materials, styles and designs is bewildering to the newcomer, but you'll see some of the most colorful, intricate, eye-catching and widely worn designs in Sololá and Santiago Atitlán, near the Lago de Atitlán, Nebaj in the Ixil Triangle, Zunil near Quetzaltenango, and Todos Santos and San Mateo Ixtatán in the Cuchumatanes mountains.

SPORTS

The sport that most ignites Guatemalans' passion and enthusiasm is football (soccer). Though Guatemalan teams always flop in international competition, the 10-club Liga Mayor (Major League) is keenly followed by reasonably large crowds. The two big clubs are Municipal and Communications, both from Guatemala City. The *Clásico Gringo* is when teams from Quetzaltenango and Antigua (the two big tourist towns) play. The national press always has details on upcoming games. Admission to games runs from Q20 for the cheapest areas and Q100 and up for the best seats.

ENVIRONMENT
The Land

Consisting primarily of mountainous forest highlands and jungle plains, Guatemala covers an area of 109,000 sq km. The western highlands hold 30 volcanoes, reaching heights of more than 4200m southwest of Huehuetenango. In the Cuchumatanes range northwest of here, land not cleared for Maya *milpas* (cornfields) is covered in pine forests, although these are dwindling rapidly.

The Pacific Slope holds rich coffee, cacao, fruit and sugar plantations. Down along the shore the volcanic slope meets the sea, yielding vast, sweltering beaches of black volcanic sand.

Guatemala City lies at an altitude of around 1500m. To the north, the Alta Verapaz highlands gradually give way to El Petén, whose climate and topography is similar to the Yucatán: hot and humid or hot and dry. Southeast of El Petén is the banana-rich valley of the Río Motagua, dry in some areas, moist in others.

Guatemala is at the confluence of three tectonic plates, resulting in earthquakes and volcanic eruptions. Major quakes struck in 1773, 1917 and 1976. Its dynamic geology includes a tremendous system of surface-level and subterranean caves. This karst terrain riddles the Verapaces region and has made Guatemala a popular spelunking destination. Surface-level caves have been used for Maya ceremonies since ancient times.

Wildlife
ANIMALS
The country's abundance of animals includes 250 species of mammal, 600 bird species, 200 species of reptile and amphibian, and numerous butterflies and other insects.

The national bird, the resplendent quetzal, is often used to symbolize Central America. Though small, the quetzal is exceptionally beautiful. The males sport a bright red breast, brilliant blue-green across the rest of the body and a spot of bright white on the underside of the long tail.

Other colorful birds include toucans, macaws and parrots. Boasting the ocellated turkey (or 'Petén turkey') – a large, impressive, multicolored bird reminiscent of a peacock, Tikal is a bird-watching hot spot, with some 300 tropical and migratory species sighted to date. Several woodpecker species, nine types of hummingbirds and four trogon species are just the beginning of the list. Also in the area are large white herons, hawks, warblers, kingfishers, harpy eagles (rare) and many others.

Although Guatemala's forests host several mammal and reptile species, many remain difficult to observe. Still, visitors to Tikal can enjoy the antics of the omnipresent *pizotes* (coatis, a tropical mammal related to raccoons) and might spy howler and spider monkeys.

Other mammals deeper in the forest include jaguars, ocelots, pumas, peccaries, agoutis, opossums, tapirs, kinkajous (nocturnal arboreal mammals), *tepezcuintles* (pacas, white-spotted brownish rodents), white-tailed and red brocket deer, armadillos and very large rattlesnakes. Reptiles and amphibians in the rest of Guatemala include at least three species of sea turtle (leatherback, *tortuga negra* and olive ridley) and two species of crocodile (one found in El Petén, the other in the Río Dulce). Manatees also frequent the waters around Río Dulce.

PLANTS
Guatemala has over 8000 plant species in 19 different ecosystems, ranging from coastal mangrove forests to mountainous interior pine forests to high cloud forests. In addition, El Petén supports a variety of trees, including mahogany, cedar, ramón and sapodilla.

The national flower, the *monja blanca* (white nun orchid), is said to have been picked so much that it's now rare in the wild. Nevertheless, the country has around 600 species of orchid, a third of which are endemic.

Guatemala also has the perfect climate for *xate* (*sha*-tay), a low-growing palm that thrives in El Petén and is prized in the developed world as a flower-arrangement filler.

National Parks & Reserves
Guatemala has 92 protected areas, including biosphere reserves, national parks, protected biotopes, wildlife refuges and private nature reserves. Even though some areas are contained within other, larger ones, they amount to 28% of the national territory.

Many of the protected areas are remote and hard to access by the independent traveler; the table (p87) shows those that are easiest to reach and/or most interesting to visitors (but excludes the volcanoes, nearly all of which are protected, and areas of mainly archaeological interest).

Environmental Issues
Environmental consciousness is not largely developed in Guatemala, as vast amounts of garbage strewn across the country will quickly tell you. Despite the impressive list of parks and protected areas, genuine protection for those areas is harder to achieve, partly because of official collusion to ignore the regulations and partly because of pressure from poor Guatemalans in need of land. Deforestation is a problem in many areas, especially El Petén, where jungle is being felled at an alarming rate not just for timber but also to make way for

cattle ranches, oil pipelines, clandestine airstrips, new settlements and new maize fields cleared by the slash-and-burn method.

On the more populous Pacific side of the country, the land is mostly agricultural or given over to industry. The remaining forests on the Pacific coastal and highland areas are not long for this world, as local communities cut down the remaining trees for heating and cooking fuels.

Nevertheless, a number of Guatemalan organizations are doing valiant work to protect their country's environment and biodiversity. On the following page are some good resources for finding out more about Guatemala's natural parks and protected areas.

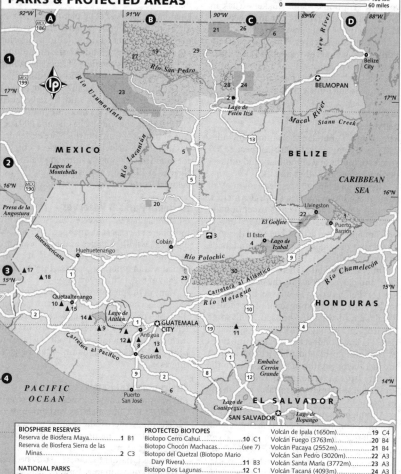

PARKS & PROTECTED AREAS

BIOSPHERE RESERVES
Reserva de Biosfera Maya.................**1** B1
Reserva de Biosfera Sierra de las
    Minas..**2** C3

NATIONAL PARKS
Parque Nacional Grutas de Lanquín...**3** C3
Parque Nacional Laguna del Tigre......**4** B1
Parque Nacional Laguna Lachuá........**5** B2
Parque Nacional Mirador-Río Azul......**6** C1
Parque Nacional Río Dulce..................**7** D2
Parque Nacional Sierra del
    Lacandón...**8** B1
Parque Nacional Tikal........................**9** C1

PROTECTED BIOTOPES
Biotopo Cerro Cahuí........................**10** C1
Biotopo Chocón Machacas.............(see 7)
Biotopo del Quetzal (Biotopo Mario
    Dary Rivera).....................................**11** B3
Biotopo Dos Lagunas.......................**12** C1
Biotopo Laguna del Tigre.................**13** B1
Biotopo San Miguel La Palotada......**14** C1

VOLCANOES
Volcán Acatenango (3976m)...........**15** B4
Volcán Agua (3766m)......................**16** B4
Volcán Atitlán (3537m)...................**17** B4
Volcán Chicabal (2900m)................**18** A3

Volcán de Ipala (1650m)..................**19** C4
Volcán Fuego (3763m)....................**20** B4
Volcán Pacaya (2552m)...................**21** B4
Volcán San Pedro (3020m)..............**22** A3
Volcán Santa María (3772m)...........**23** A3
Volcán Tacaná (4093m)...................**24** A3
Volcán Tajumulco (4220m)..............**25** A3

OTHER AREAS
Área de Protección Especial Punta de
    Manabique.......................................**26** D2
Refugio de Bocas del Polochic.........**27** C3
Refugio de Vida Silvestre Petexbatún.**28** B2
Reserva Natural Monterrico-Hawaii..**29** B4

GUATEMALA'S MAJOR PARKS & RESERVES

Protected Area	Features	Activities	Best Time to Visit	Page
Parque Nacional Tikal	diverse jungle wildlife among Guatemala's most magnificent Maya ruins	wildlife-spotting; seeing Maya city	year-round, Nov-May drier	p198
Parque Nacional Laguna del Tigre	remote, large park within Reserva Maya; freshwater wetlands; El Petén flora and fauna	wildlife-spotting including scarlet macaws, monkeys, crocodiles; visiting El Perú archaeological site; volunteer opportunities at Estación Biológica Las Guacamayas	year-round, Nov-May drier	p207
Parque Nacional Mirador-Río Azul	national park with Reserva Maya; El Petén flora and fauna	jungle treks to El Mirador archaeological site	year-round, Nov-May drier	p207
Parque Nacional Río Dulce	beautiful jungle-lined lower Río Dulce between Lago de Izabal and Caribbean; manatee refuge	boat trips	year-round	p188
Parque Nacional Grutas de Lanquín	large cave system 61km east of Cobán	visiting caves, swimming, seeing bats; don't miss the nearby Semuc Champey lagoons and waterfalls	year-round	p170
Biotopo del Quetzal	easy-access cloud-forest reserve; howler monkeys, birds	nature trails, bird-watching, possible quetzal sightings	year-round	p165
Biotopo Cerro Cahuí	forest reserve beside Lago de Petén Itzá; Petén wildlife including monkeys	walking trails	year-round	p197
Refugio de Vida Silvestre Bocas del Polochic	delta of Río Polochic at western end of Lago de Izabal; Guatemala's second-largest freshwater wetlands	bird-watching (more than 300 species); howler-monkey observation	year-round	p180
Reserva Natural Monterrico-Hawaii	Pacific beaches and wetlands; birdlife, turtles	boat tours, bird- and turtle-watching (turtle nesting)	Jun-Nov	p162

GUATEMALA

Arcas (off Map p92; Asociación de Rescate y Conservación de Vida Silvestre; ☎ 7830-1374; www.arcasguatemala. com; Km 30, Calle Hillary, Lote 6, Casa Villa Conchita, San Lucas Sacatepéquez, Guatemala) NGO working with volunteers in sea-turtle conservation and rehabilitation of El Petén wildlife.

Asociación Ak' Tenamit (www.aktenamit.org) Guatemala City (off Map p92; ☎ 2254-1560; 11a Av A 9-39, Zona 2); Río Dulce (☎ 5908-3392) This Maya-run non-governmental organization works to reduce poverty and promote conservation and ecotourism in the rainforests of eastern Guatemala.

Cecon (Map p92; Centro de Estudios Conservacionistas de la Universidad de San Carlos; ☎ 2331-0904; www. usac.edu.gt/cecon, in Spanish; Av La Reforma 0-63, Zona 10, Guatemala City) Manages six public *biotopos* and one *reserva natural*.

Conap (Map p92; Consejo Nacional de Áreas Protegidas; ☎ 2238-0000; http://conap.online.fr; Edificio IPM, 5a Av 6-06, Zona 1, Guatemala City) The government arm in charge of protected areas.

Fundación Defensores de la Naturaleza (off Map p92; ☎ 2310-2900; www.defensores.org.gt; 2a Av 14-08, Zona 14, Guatemala City) NGO that owns and administers several protected areas.

Planeta (www.planeta.com/guatemala.html) Focuses on sustainable tourism in Guatemala.

ProPetén (☎ 7867-5296; www.propeten.org; Calle Central, Flores, El Petén) NGO that works in conservation and natural resources management in Parque Nacional Laguna del Tigre.

Proyecto Ecoquetzal (☎ 7952-1047; www.ecoquetzal. org; 2a Calle 14-36, Zona 1, Cobán, Alta Verapaz) Works in forest conservation and ecotourism.

TRANSPORTATION

GETTING THERE & AWAY

Air

Guatemala's two major international airports are in Guatemala City (Aeropuerto Internacional La Aurora; p99) and near Flores and Santa Elena (Aeropuerto Internacional Mundo Maya; p196).

Destinations include Atlanta, Belize City, Cancún, Havana, Houston, Los Angeles, Madrid, Managua, Mexico City, Miami, Newark, Panama City, San José (Costa Rica) and San Salvador.

Airlines serving Guatemala have offices in Guatemala City. Many also have offices in Aeropuerto Internacional La Aurora. The internet-based **Spirit Airlines** (NK; www.spiritair.com) also flies between the US and Guatemala.

Land

Guatemala is linked to Chiapas (Mexico) by two official highway routes; to Belize by one road route (see p199); and to Honduras and El Salvador by numerous overland routes (see p184 and p176).

The most popular and easily accessible entry points to Guatemala from Mexico are at Tecún Umán–Ciudad Hidalgo, and at La Mesilla–Ciudad Cuauhtémoc. More adventurous routes take you by country bus and riverboat from Yaxchilán in Chiapas via the Río Usumacinta or the Río de la Pasión to El Petén. For information on these and other routes, see p197, p154 and p155.

Direct international bus routes from Guatemala City include: Belize City, Managua (Nicaragua), San Salvador (El Salvador), Tapachula (Mexico), Tegucigalpa and other Honduran destinations. See p99 for more details.

DEPARTURE TAX

A US$30 departure tax (plus US$3/Q25 airport security tax) is charged on all international flights leaving Guatemala. The departure tax is usually (but not always) included in the price of your ticket; the security tax must always be paid separately in quetzals or dollars. All passengers on domestic flights are charged a Q10 departure tax, payable at the airport.

Sea & River

On the Caribbean coast, boats leave Punta Gorda (Belize) for Puerto Barrios and Lívingston. Generally, sea passage is easiest to and from Puerto Barrios, as this is an active transit point. No car ferries are available. See p183 for details.

Three river crossings connect Chiapas, Mexico, to El Petén, Guatemala. These are good alternatives for travelers visiting Palenque and Tikal in one trip. All involve a combination of bus and boat travel. See boxed text, p197, for details.

GETTING AROUND

Air

There are various domestic airports around the country, but the only *scheduled* domestic flights operating at the time of research are between Guatemala City and Flores, run by the following companies:

Grupo TACA (☎ 2470-8222; www.taca.com; Hotel Intercontinental, 14 Calle 2-51, Zona 10)

TAG (☎ 2380-9401; www.tag.com.gt; Aeropuerto Internacional La Aurora)

Bicycle

Cycling is coming into its own in Guatemala. You can join biking tours or take to the hills independently. Bicycles can be rented in Antigua, Flores, Panajachel and Quetzaltenango. Remember that size matters on Guatemalan roads and as a cyclist nobody will be yielding to you.

Boat

Speedy *lanchas* (small motorboats) are becoming the norm for transportation on Lago de Atitlán and between Puerto Barrios, Lívingston and Río Dulce, replacing bigger, cheaper ferries.

A few of Guatemala's natural reserves and archaeological sites are accessible only – or preferably – by water.

Bus

Buses go just about everywhere in Guatemala, and where they don't, you'll find minivans and trucks picking up the slack. Fares are generally cheap (around Q10 per hour or less), although comfort levels vary. If you can't bear another jaunt on a 'chicken bus,' ask if there is a Pullman service available. These larger, coach-style buses are way more comfortable, run between major destina-

WARNING

While bus travel at night in Guatemala is rarely a good idea for anybody, it is strongly advised that solo female travelers not catch buses – Pullman or 'chicken' – at night time, the exceptions being the overnight buses traveling between Guatemala City and Flores. There have been no incident reports regarding those services.

Basically, what you want to avoid is being the last person on the bus when it arrives, if it's going to arrive at night.

tions and only cost slightly more than the 2nd-class buses.

If you're traveling light, keep your luggage with you inside the bus. Otherwise, heave it onto the roof or stuff it into the luggage compartment and keep your eye on it.

Long-distance buses rarely have working toilets, but usually stop for 20-minute meal and relief breaks at appropriate times. If not, drivers will stop to let you fertilize the roadside.

Car & Motorcycle

Although few people do, it's possible to hire a car in Guatemala City (at the airport), Antigua, Cobán, Flores and Quetzaltenango. You can hire motorcycles in Antigua and San Pedro La Laguna. For general information about driving around the region, see p732.

Hitchhiking

Hitchhiking in the Western sense of the word is not practiced in Guatemala because it is not safe. However, where the bus service is sporadic or nonexistent, pick-up trucks and other vehicles serve as public transportation. Stand by the side of the road, hold your arm out and someone will stop. You are expected to pay the driver as if it were a bus, and the fare will be similar. This is a safe and reliable system used by locals and travelers; get used to severe overcrowding.

Local Transportation

Local buses (available only in Guatemala City and Quetzaltenango) are crowded and cheap. Few Guatemalan taxis are metered, and fares can be exorbitant. If you don't like the price quoted, walk away. Then go back and bargain. Then walk away again. Repeat process until a reasonable price is established.

Also whizzing around streets are tuk-tuks, three-wheeled motor taxis that visitors to Asia will be familiar with. Rides in these are generally cheap (under Q10 per person) and can be hair-raising, particularly if your driver has not yet entered puberty.

GUATEMALA CITY

pop 1.1 million / elev 1500m

Depending on who you talk to, Guatemala's capital (known universally as 'Guate') is either big, dirty, dangerous and utterly forgettable or big, dirty, dangerous and fascinating. Either way, there's no doubt that there's an energy here unlike that found in the rest of Guatemala, and the extremes that categorize the whole country are in plain view.

It's a place where dilapidated buses belch fumes next to BMWs and Hummers, where skyscrapers drop shadows on shantytowns, and where immigrants from the countryside and the rest of Central America eke out a meager existence, barely noticed by the country's elite.

This is the cultural capital of Guatemala – the writers, the thinkers, the artists mostly live and work here. All the best museum pieces go to the capital, and while nearly every city-dweller dreams of getting away to Antigua or Monterrico for the weekend, this is where they spend most of their time, a fact reflected in the growing sophistication of the restaurant and bar scenes.

ORIENTATION

Guatemala City, like almost all Guatemalan towns, is laid out according to a logical grid system. Avenidas run north–south; calles run east–west. Streets are usually numbered from north and west (lowest) to south and east (highest); building numbers run in the same directions, with odd numbers on the left side and even on the right heading south or east. However, Guatemala City is divided into 15 *zonas*, each with its own version of the grid. Thus 14a Calle in Zona 10 is a completely different street several miles from 14a Calle in Zona 1, though major thoroughfares such as 6a Av and 7a Av cross several zones.

Addresses are given in this form: '9a Av 15-12, Zona 1,' which means '9th Av above 15th St, No 12, in Zona 1.' The building will be on 9th Av between 15th and 16th Sts, on the right side as you walk south. Beware of anomalies, such as diagonal *rutas* and *vías* and wandering *diagonales*.

Short streets may be suffixed 'A,' as in 14a Calle A, running between 14a Calle and 15a Calle.

Maps

Intelimapas' *Mapa Turístico Guatemala*, Inguat's *Mapa Vial Turístico* and International Travel Maps' *Guatemala* all contain useful maps of Guatemala City.

Instituto Geográfico Nacional (☎ 2248-8100; www.ign.gob.gt; Av Las Américas 5-76, Zona 13; ⊙ 9am-5pm Mon-Fri) Sells 1:50,000 and 1:250,000 topographical maps of all parts of Guatemala (Q60 each).

Sophos (☎ 2419-7070; Plaza Fontabella, 4a Av 12-59, Zona 10) One of the most reliable sources of maps.

INFORMATION

Bookstores

Sophos (☎ 2419-7070; Plaza Fontabella, 4a Av 12-59, Zona 10) Relaxed place to have a coffee and read while in the Zona Viva. A good selection of books in English on Guatemala and the Maya, including guidebooks and maps.

Vista Hermosa Book Shop (☎ 2369-1003; 2a Calle 18-50, Zona 15) Ditto.

Emergency

Asistur (☎ 1500; 24hr) Tourist assistance and tourist police liaison.

Internet Access

Inexpensive internet cafes are pretty much everywhere.

Café Internet Navigator (14a Calle, Zona 1; per hr Q6; ⊙ 8am-8pm) East of 6a Av.

Web Station (2a Av 14-63, Zona 10; per hr Q5; ⊙ 10am-midnight Mon-Sat, noon-midnight Sun) One of the cheapest in the Zona Viva.

Laundry

Lavandería El Siglo (12a Calle 3-42, Zona 1; ⊙ 8am-6pm Mon-Sat) Charges Q40 to wash, dry and fold per load.

Medical Services

Guatemala City has many private hospitals and clinics. Public hospitals and clinics provide free consultations but can be very busy. To reduce waiting time, try to be there before 7am.

Farmacia del Ejecutivo (☎ 2238-1447; 7a Av 15-01, Zona 1; ⊙ 24hr) This pharmacy accepts Visa and Master-Card.

Hospital Centro Médico (☎ 2332-3555, 334-2157; 6a Av 3-47, Zona 10) Recommended private hospital with some English-speaking doctors.

Hospital General San Juan de Dios (☎ 2253-0443/7; 1a Av at 10a Calle, Zona 1) One of the city's best public hospitals.

Money

Take normal precautions when using ATMs.

ABM (☎ 2361-5602; Plazuela España, Zona 9) Changes euros into quetzals.

American Express (☎ 2331-7422; Centro Comercial Montufar, 12a Calle 0-93, Zona 9; ⊙ 8am-5pm Mon-Fri, to noon Sat) In an office of Clark Tours.

Banco de la República (Aeropuerto Internacional La Aurora; ⊙ 6am-8pm Mon-Fri, 6am-6pm Sat & Sun) Currency exchange services and a MasterCard ATM. On the airport departures level.

Edificio Testa (cnr 5a Av & 11a Calle, Zona 1) Visa, MasterCard and Amex ATMs.

MasterCard ATM (Hotel Stofella, 2a Av 12-28, Zona 10)

Visa ATMs Zona 1 (cnr 5a Av & 6a Calle) Opposite Parque Centenario; Zona 10 (2a Av) South of 13a Calle.

Post

Main post office (7a Av 11-67, Zona 1; ⊙ 8:30am-5pm Mon-Fri, to 1pm Sat) In the huge yellow Palacio de Correos. There's also a small post office at the airport.

Tourist Information

Inguat Main tourist office (☎ 2331-1333, 2331-1347; informacion@inguat.gob.gt; 7a Av 1-17, Zona 4; ⊙ 8am-4pm Mon-Fri) Located in the lobby of the Inguat (Instituto Guatemalteco de Turismo) headquarters in the Centro Cívico. The office has limited handout material, but staff

---

GETTING INTO TOWN FROM THE AIRPORT

Aeropuerto Internacional La Aurora is in Zona 13, in the southern part of the city, 10 to 15 minutes from Zona 1 by taxi, 30 minutes by bus. See p101 for a warning on city buses and details on getting to and from the airport by bus.

Taxis wait outside the airport's arrivals exit. 'Official' fares are Q60 to Zona 9 or 10, Q85 to Zona 1, Q250 to Antigua, but in reality you may have to pay a bit more. Be sure to establish the destination and price before getting in. Prices for taxis *to* the airport, hailed on the street, are likely to be lower – around Q50 from Zona 1. For Antigua, shuttle minibuses are more economical than taxis if there's only one or two of you.

are extremely helpful; Aeropuerto Internacional La Aurora
(☎ 2331-4256; arrivals hall; ⏰ 6am-9pm)

DANGERS & ANNOYANCES

Street crime, including armed robbery, has increased in recent years. Use normal urban common sense: don't walk down the street with your wallet bulging out of your back pocket, and avoid walking downtown alone late at night. Work out your route before you start so you're not standing on corners looking lost or peering at a map; pop into a cafe if you need to find your bearings. It's safe to walk downtown in the early evening, as long as you stick to streets with plenty of lighting and people. Stay alert and leave your valuables in your hotel. Don't flaunt anything of value, and be aware that women and children swell the ranks of thieves here. The incidence of robbery increases around the 15th and the end of each month, when workers get paid.

The area around 18a Calle in Zona 1 has many bus stations and even more lowlifes and hustlers. Nearly half of Zona 1's robberies happen here, the worst black spots being the intersections with 4a, 6a and 9a Avs. This part of town (also a red-light district) is notoriously dangerous at night; if you are arriving by bus at night or must go someplace on 18a Calle at night, take a taxi.

The more affluent sections of the city – Zonas 9 and 10, for example – are safer, but don't let your guard down. Thieves have figured out that rich people hang out in fancy areas, and so sometimes work the area in groups of two or three. The Zona Viva, in Zona 10, has police patrols at night. But even here, going in pairs is better than going alone. Never (never!) try to resist if confronted by a robber.

The red city buses are temptingly cheap, particularly if you have to cross town, but there are so many stories of robberies, pickpockets and even shoot-outs that it is not advised to catch them. An exception are the new green Transmetro buses which have a policeman on board at all times – for more information on this service, see p102.

For a warning on solo female travelers traveling on intercity buses, see p89.

SIGHTS

The major sights are in Zona 1 (the historical center) and Zonas 10 and 13, where the museums are grouped. If you're in town on a Sunday, consider taking the Transmetro's

SubiBaja (ticket free; ⏰ 9am-2pm) self-guided tour. Modern, air-con Transmetro buses run a circuit passing every 20 minutes, with 10 stops including the Parque Central, Centro Cívico, La Aurora Zoo (and museums), the Zona Viva, Pasos y Pedales, Cuatro Grados Norte and Mapa en Relieve. Volunteer guides give an onboard commentary and each bus is staffed by a member of the Transit Police. It's an excellent way to see many of these sights without worrying about public transportation or taxis.

Zona 1
PARQUE CENTRAL

Most of the notable sights in Zona 1 are near the Parque Central (officially the Plaza de la Constitución), which is bounded by 6a and 8a Calles and 6a and 7a Avs.

Every town in the New World had a plaza used for military exercises, reviews and ceremonies. On the plaza's northern side would be the *palacio de gobierno* (colonial government headquarters). On another side, preferably east, was a church (or cathedral). The other sides of the square could house additional civic buildings or imposing mansions. Parque Central is a good example of this classic town plan.

Visit on Sunday, when locals stroll, play in the fountains, gossip, neck and groove to salsa music. Otherwise, try for lunchtime or late afternoon. You'll be besieged by shoeshine boys, Polaroid photographers and sellers of kitsch.

PALACIO NACIONAL DE LA CULTURA

On Parque Central's north side is the magnificent **Palacio Nacional de la Cultura** (☎ 2253-0748; cnr 6a Av & 6a Calle; admission Q30; ⏰ 9am-11:45am & 2-4:45pm Mon-Sat), built at enormous cost by dictator/president Jorge Ubico (1931–44). It's the third palace to stand here. It often hosts revolving exhibitions featuring contemporary Guatemalan artists.

You can go wandering independently, or else free tours take you through a labyrinth of gleaming brass, polished wood, carved stone and frescoed arches (painted by Alberto Gálvez Suárez). Notable features include the 2-ton gold, bronze and Bohemian-crystal chandelier in the reception salon, and two Moorish-style courtyards.

CENTRO CULTURAL METROPOLITANO

This surprisingly avant-garde **cultural center** (1st fl, Palacio de Correos, 7a Av 11-67, Zona 1; ⏰ 9am-5pm Mon-Fri) hosts art exhibitions, book launches, handicraft workshops and film nights.

GUATEMALA

GUATEMALA CITY

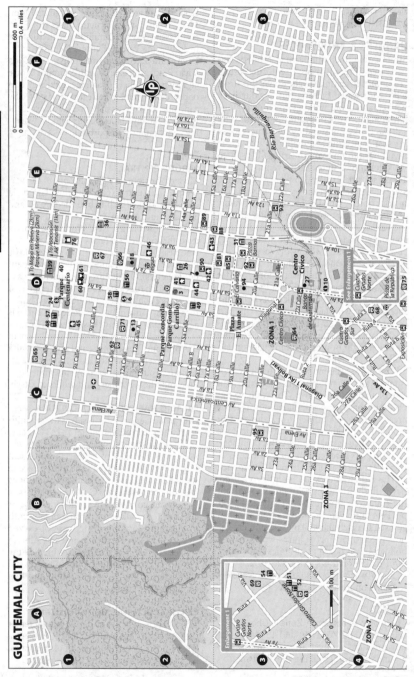

GUATEMALA

Enlargement 2

0   100 m

86

73   53   23

91   25

5a Calle

70

To Vista Hermosa Book Shop (1.5km);
King Quality & Comfort Lines (1.6km)

59

ZONA 5

Río Negro

38
33

Universidad
Francisco
Marroquín

ZONA 10

Diagonal 6

78

4

16

19

47

74

8a Calle

Hotel
Stofella   14

See Enlargement 2

21

To Belican Embassy (300m);
German Embassy (500m);
French Embassy (800m);
Productos Mundiales (1km);
Honduran Embassy (1.3km)

2a Calle (Boulevard Vista Hermosa)

Calle Mariscal Cruz

Diagonal 6 (Av de la Barranquilla)

Torre del
Reformador

ZONA 4

Terminal

29   32

8

Av la Reforma

22   15

50

55

7

87

20

IGSS Zona 9

28

Plazuela
España

Plaza
España

Montúfar

Tívoli

Liberación

1

Av de la Castellana

Parque
Centroamérica

ZONA 9

2

30

Diagonal 12 (Boulevard Liberación)

Parque
Aurora

177

ZONA 13

35

34   37

To Belican Embassy (300m);
To Aeropuerto
To Estación Del Norte;
To Xelajuraz (150m);
Instituto Geográfico Nacional (400m)

To Aeropuerto
Internacional La Aurora (500m);
Jungle Flying Tours (1.5km);
Salvadoran Embassy (2km);
Cuban Embassy (2.5km); X-Park (4km)

To Hostal Los Lagos (150m);
Patricia's Guesthouse (1km);
Aeropuerto Internacional
La Aurora (1km)

ZONA 8

ZONA 8

40 Calle

Av 13a

Diagonal 1 (Av Bolívar)

To Transportes Rebuli (1km);
Transportes Álamo (2km);
Los Halcones (3km);
Arcas (20km)

82   84

To Tica-Bus (2km);
Centro Sur (6km)

Aguilar Batres

Calle Real de Petapa

To USAC (250m)

5   6   7   8

CASA MIMA

This wonderfully presented **museum and cultural center** (8a Av & 14a Calle; 9am-12:30pm & 2-6pm Mon-Fri, 9am-5pm Sat) is set in a house dating from the late 19th century. The owners of the house were collectors with eclectic tastes ranging from French neo-Rococo, Chinese and art deco, to indigenous artifacts. The place is set up like a functioning house, filled with curios and furniture spanning the centuries.

MERCADO CENTRAL

Until it was destroyed by the earthquake of 1976, the **central market** (9a Av btwn 6a & 8a Calles; 7am-6pm Mon-Sat, 6am-noon Sun), east of the cathedral, was where locals bought food and other

necessities. Reconstructed in the late 1970s, the new *mercado* specializes in touristy items such as cloth, carved wood, worked leather and metal, basketry and other handicrafts. Except for the odd tour group, not that many tourists make it here – if you're a hard bargainer, you might get a good deal. Vegetables and other daily needs are on sale on the lower floor – check it out for a sensory overload. The city's true 'central' food market is in Zona 4.

MUSEO DE FERROCARRIL

The **railway museum** (www.museodelferrocarril guatemala.com; 9a Av 18-03; admission free; 9am-12:30pm & 2-4pm) is one of the city's more intriguing museums. Documented here are the glory days of the troubled Guatemalan rail system, along with some quirky artifacts, like hand-drawn diagrams of derailments and a kitchen set up with items used in dining cars. You can go climbing around the passenger carriages, but not the locomotives.

MUSEO NACIONAL DE HISTORIA
The **national history museum** (☎ 2253-6149; 9a Calle 9-70; admission Q50; ☺ 9am-5:30pm Mon-Fri) is a jumble of historical relics with an emphasis on photography and portraits. Check the hairstyles of the 19th-century politicos.

Zona 2
Zona 2, north of Zona 1, is a mostly middle-class residential district, though its northern end holds the large Parque Minerva, which is surrounded by golf courses, sports grounds and the buildings of the Universidad Mariano Gálvez.

PARQUE MINERVA
Minerva, the Roman goddess of wisdom, technical skill and invention, was a favorite of President Manuel Estrada Cabrera. Her park is a placid place, good for walking among the eucalyptus trees and sipping a cool drink. However, watch out for pickpockets and purse-snatchers.

The prime sight here is the **Mapa en Relieve** (Relief Map; Av Simeón Cañas Final; www.mapaenrelieve.org; admission Q25; ☺ 9am-5pm), a huge relief map of Guatemala. Constructed in 1904 under the direction of Francisco Vela, the map shows the country at a scale of 1:10,000, but the height of the mountainous terrain has been exaggerated to 1:2000 for dramatic effect. You may note that Belize features on the map – a hangover from the fact that most Guatemalans consider this to be Guatemalan territory. The Mapa en Relieve and Parque Minerva are 2km north of Parque Central along 6a Av, but that street is one way heading south.

Centro Cívico Area
The civic center complex, constructed during the 1950s and '60s, lies around the junction of Zonas 1, 4 and 5. Here you'll find the Palace of Justice, the headquarters of the Guatemalan Institute of Social Security (IGSS), the Banco del Quetzal, the city hall and the Inguat headquarters. The Banco del Quetzal building bears high-relief murals by Dagoberto Vásquez depicting the history of his homeland. City Hall holds a huge mosaic by Carlos Mérida.

On a hilltop across the street from the Centro Cívico is the **Centro Cultural Miguel Ángel Asturias** (www.teatronacional.com.gt; 24a Calle 3-81, Zona 1), which holds the national theater, a chamber theater and an open-air theater, as well as a small museum of old armaments.

Other than the Centro Cívico, this area is known mostly for the pedestrianized **Cuatro Grados Norte** (Vía 5 btwn Rutas 1 & 3, Zona 4) area – a few traffic-free blocks filled with restaurants, bars and cultural centers.

Zona 10
East of Av La Reforma, the posh Zona 10 holds two of the city's most important museums, both in large new buildings at the Universidad Francisco Marroquín.

Museo Ixchel del Traje Indígena (☎ 2331-3739; www.museoixchel.org; 6a Calle Final; admission Q20; ☺ 8am-6pm Mon-Fri, 9am-1pm Sat) is named for Ixchel, wife of Maya sky god Itzamná and goddess of the moon, women, reproduction and textiles, among other things. Photographs and exhibits of indigenous costumes, textiles and other crafts show the incredible richness of traditional highland art. If you enjoy seeing Guatemalan textiles, you must make a visit to this museum.

Behind it is the **Museo Popol Vuh** (☎ 2361-2301; www.popolvuh.ufm.edu; 6a Calle Final; adult/child Q20/6; ☺ 9am-5pm Mon-Fri, 9am-1pm Sat), where well-chosen polychrome pottery, figurines, incense burners, burial urns, carved-wood masks and traditional textiles fill several exhibit rooms. Other rooms hold colonial paintings and wood and silver objects. A faithful copy of the Dresden Codex, one of the precious 'painted books' of the Maya, is among the most interesting pieces. This is an important collection, especially given its precolonial emphasis.

The Universidad de San Carlos de Guatemala has a large, lush **Jardín Botánico** (Botanical Garden; Calle Mariscal Cruz 1-56; admission Q10; ☺ 8am-3:30pm Mon-Fri, 8am-noon Sat) on the northern edge of Zona 10. The admission includes the university's **Museo de Historia Natural** (Natural History Museum) at the site.

If you're here on a Sunday, check out **Pasos y Pedales** (☺ 10am-3pm Sun), a wonderful municipal initiative that sees the Av de las Americas (Zona 10) and its continuation, Av la Reforma in Zona 13, blocked off to traffic for 3km and taken over by jugglers, clowns, in-line skaters, dogwalkers, food vendors, t'ai chi classes, skate parks and playgrounds for kids. It's great place to go for a walk (or you

GUATEMALA

can hire bikes or in-line skates on the street) and a very relaxed, sociable side of the city that is rarely otherwise seen.

Zona 13

The major attraction in the city's southern reaches is Parque Aurora, with its zoo, children's playground, fairgrounds and several museums. One of the museums, the Moorish-looking **Museo Nacional de Arqueología y Etnología** (☎ 2475-4399; www.munae.gob.gt; Sala 5, Finca La Aurora; admission Q60; ☼ 9am-4pm Tue-Fri, 9am-noon & 1:30-4pm Sat & Sun), has a collection of Maya artifacts from all over Guatemala, including stone carvings, jade, ceramics, statues, stelae and a tomb. Models depict the ruins at Tikal and Zaculeu. Exhibits in the ethnology section highlight the various indigenous peoples and languages in Guatemala, with emphasis on traditional costumes, dances and implements of daily life.

Facing it is the **Museo Nacional de Arte Moderno** (☎ 2472-0467; Sala 6, Finca La Aurora; admission Q50; ☼ 9am-4pm Tue-Fri, 9am-noon & 1:30-4pm Sat & Sun), which holds a collection of 20th-century Guatemalan art, especially paintings and sculpture.

Nearby is the **Museo Nacional de Historia Natural Jorge Ibarra** (☎ 2472-0468; 6a Calle 7-30; admission Q50; ☼ 9am-4pm Tue-Fri, 9am-noon & 2-4pm Sat & Sun), whose claim to fame is its large collection of dissected animals. Several hundred meters east of these museums is the city's official handicrafts market, the **Mercado de Artesanías** (Crafts Market; ☎ 2472-0208; cnr 5a Calle & 11a Av; ☼ 9:30am-6pm), just off the access road to the airport. It's a sleepy place where shopkeepers display the same items available in hotel gift shops.

La Aurora Zoo (☎ 2472-0894; www.aurorazoo.org.gt; 5a Calle; adult/child Q20/10; ☼ 9am-5pm Tue-Sun) is not badly kept as zoos go, and the lovely, parklike grounds alone are worth the admission fee.

About 10-minutes' drive south of the airport is **X-Park** (☎ 2380-2080; www.xpark.net; Av Hincapié Km 11.5; admission Q15; ☼ 11am-7pm Tue-Fri, 10am-9pm Sat, 10am-7pm Sun), a very well-constructed 'adventure sports' park. A taxi here from Zona 10 should cost around Q30.

SLEEPING
Zona 1

Shoestringers tend to head straight for Zona 1. Prices in Guate are higher than in the rest of the country, but there are a few bargains. Many of the city's cheaper lodgings are 10 to 15 minutes' walk south from Parque Central.

Hotel Fenix (☎ 2251-6625; 15a Calle 6-56; s/d Q70/100) Zona 1's classic budget hotel has found a new home, just around the corner from where it used to be. The building's actually more atmospheric than the last, and rooms here are still a very good deal.

Hotel Ajau (☎ 2232-0488; hotelajau@hotmail.com; 8a Av 15-62; s/d Q150/190, without bathroom Q70/110; P ☐) If you're coming from or going to Cobán, the Ajau's the obvious choice, being right next door to the Monja Blanca bus station. It's still a pretty good deal, anyway, with lovely polished floor tiles and cool, clean rooms.

Hotel Quality Service (☎ 2251-8005; www.quality guate.com; 8a Calle 3-18; s/d incl breakfast Q170/230; P ☐ ☜) There's a pleasing, old-timey feel about this place, which is balanced perfectly by the modern-but-not-overly-so rooms. The pick of the bunch near the park.

Hotel Spring (☎ 2230-2858; www.hotelspring.com; 8a Av 12-65; s/d from Q180/260, without bathroom s/d Q110/140; P ☐) With a beautiful courtyard setting, the Spring has a lot more style than other Zona 1 joints. It's central and has quiet sunny patios. The 43 rooms vary greatly, but most are tall, spacious and clean. Have a look around if you can. All rooms have cable TV. It's worth booking ahead.

These are OK, too:

Hotel Capri (☎ 2232-8191; 9a Av 15-63; s/d Q120/170, without bathroom Q80/120; P) A modern four-story number in a decent location. Get a room away from the noisy street out front.

Chalet Suizo (☎ 2251-3786; www.hotelchaletsuizo.com; 7a Av 14-34; s/d Q150/200, without bathroom Q100/150; P ☜) Spacious, simple rooms in a modern building. Good deal for the price.

Zonas 10 & 13

Xamanek Inn (☎ 2360-8345; www.mayaworld.net; 13a Calle 3-57, Zona 10; dm/d incl breakfast Q120/280; ☐ ☜) A welcome option in the often-overpriced Zona Viva area is this comfy little hostel. Dorms are spacious and airy, separated into male and female. Rates include free internet. There's a book exchange, kitchen use and a cheery little backyard.

Guesthouses are springing up all over the place in a middle-class residential area in Zona 13. They're very convenient for the airport, and staff will pick you up or drop you off there. There are no restaurants out here, but these places offer breakfast and have the complete lowdown on home-delivery fast food in the area.

Patricia's Guest House (☎ 2261-4451; www. patriciashotel.com; 19 Calle 10-65, Zona 13; s/d Q130/260, without bathroom Q115/230, incl breakfast; P 🖳 🛜) Relaxed and comfortable, with a sweet little backyard where guests can hang out. Also offers private transportation around the city and to bus stations.

Hostal Los Lagos (☎ 2261-2809; www.loslagoshostal. com; 8a Av 15-85, Zona 13; dm Q160, s/d Q250/500, incl breakfast; P 🖳) The most hostel-like of the near-the-airport options. Dorms are airy and spacious and there are a couple of reasonable-value private rooms.

EATING

Cheap eats are easily found, as fast food and snack shops abound. To really save money, head for Parque Concordia, in Zona 1 bounded by 5a and 6a Avs and 14a and 15a Calles, whose west side is lined with stalls serving sandwiches and snacks at rock-bottom prices from early morning to late evening. Fine dining is concentrated in Zona 10.

Zona 1

Dozens of restaurants and fast-food shops are strung along and just off 6a Av between 8a and 15a Calles.

Restaurante Rey Sol (11a Calle 5-51; mains Q20-30; ☯ 8am-5pm Mon-Sat; V) Good, fresh ingredients and some innovative cooking keep this strictly vegetarian restaurant busy at lunchtimes.

Café de Imeri (6a Calle 3-34; mains Q27-40; ☯ 8am-7pm Tue-Sat) Completely out of step with the majority of Zona 1 eateries, this place offers interesting breakfasts, soups and pastas. The list of sandwiches is impressive and there's a beautiful little courtyard area out back.

Café-Restaurante Hamburgo (15a Calle 5-34; set meals Q30-50; ☯ 7am-9:30pm) This bustling spot facing the south side of Parque Concordia serves good Guatemalan food, with chefs at work along one side and orange-aproned waitresses scurrying about. At weekends a marimba band adds atmosphere.

Restaurante Long Wah (6a Calle 3-70; mains Q40-60; ☯ 11am-10pm) With friendly service and decorative red-painted arches, the Long Wah is a good choice from Zona 1's other concentration of Chinese eateries, in the blocks west of Parque Centenario.

Bar-Restaurante Europa (Local 201, Edificio Testa, cnr 5a Av & 11a Calle; mains Q40-60; ☯ 8am-8:30pm Mon-Sat) This comfortable, relaxed bar-restaurant has good-value food – try chicken cordon bleu for dinner, or eggs, hash browns, bacon and toast for breakfast.

Picadily (cnr 6 Av & 11a Calle; mains Q40-80; ☯ lunch & dinner) Right in the thick of the 6a Av action, this bustling restaurant does OK pizzas and pastas and good steak dishes. The place is clean and street views out of the big front windows are mesmerizing.

Zona 4

La Esquina Cubana (cnr Vía 5 & Ruta 1, Cuatro Grados Norte; mains Q30-60; ☯ lunch & dinner Tue-Sun) For authentic Cuban dishes, washed down with some very tasty mojitos, try this laid-back little spot out the back of the parking area.

Del Paseo (Vía 5 1-81, Cuatro Grados Norte; mains Q50-100; ☯ lunch & dinner Tue-Sun) This spacious, artsy, bistro serves good Mediterranean-style food and wine goes for Q30 a glass.

Kabala (Vía 5, Cuatro Grados Norte; mains Q60-120; ☯ lunch & dinner Tue-Sun) The best Japanese restaurant for miles around is at this 'fusion' place (we're not quite sure what they're fusing with). It doubles as a cocktail bar later on.

Zona 10

A string of (mostly) nameless *comedores* (basic eateries) opposite the Los Proceres mall serve the cheapest eats in Zona 10. There's nothing fancy going on here – just good, filling eats at rock-bottom prices.

Panes del Sol (1 Av 10-50; mains Q20-40; ☯ lunch & dinner) Home-style Guatemalan food served in more or less formal surrounds can be hard to come by in Zona 10, but this place does it well at good prices. Tables are set in the eatery at the side of a *kiosko* (small store).

Cafetería Patsy (Av La Reforma 8-01; set lunches Q25; ☯ 7:30am-8pm) A bright, cheerful place popular with local office workers, offering subs, sandwiches and good-value set lunches.

Kakao (2a Av 13-44; mains Q60-150; ☯ lunch & dinner Tue-Sun) Set under a *palapa* (thatched palm-leaf shelter), and with a soft marimba soundtrack, this is Zona 10's best *típica* (regional) food restaurant. The atmosphere and food are both outstanding.

DRINKING & ENTERTAINMENT
Zona 1

Staggering from bar to bar along the darkened streets of Zona 1 is not recommended, but fortunately there's a clutch of good drinking places all within half a block of each other just south of Parque Central.

Las Cien Puertas (Pasaje Aycinena 8-44, 9a Calle 6-45) This superhip (but not studiously so) little watering hole is a gathering place for all manner of local creative types and other colorful characters. It's in a shabby colonial arcade that is sometimes closed off for live bands.

El Gran Hotel (www.elgranhotel.com.gt; 9a Calle 7-64) The down-market renovated lobby of this classic ex-hotel is one of downtown's better-looking bars. There's poetry, live music and film nights throughout the week – check the website for details.

El Portal (Portal del Comercio, 6a Av; ⏲ 10am-10pm Mon-Sat) This atmospheric old drinking den serves fine draft beer (around Q15 a mug) and free tapas. Ché Guevara was once a patron. To find it, enter the Portal del Comercio arcade from 6a Av a few steps south of Parque Central.

Zona 10

The best place to go bar-hopping is around the corner of 2a Av and 15a Calle – there's plenty of places to choose from – check and see who's got the crowd tonight.

Bajo Fondo (15a Calle 2-55) One of the more atmospheric little bars in the area, this place has good music and the occasional spontaneous jam session.

Zona 12

For a seriously down-to-earth night out, you should go out partying with the students from USAC, Guatemala's public university. The strip of bars along 31a Calle at the corner of

---

GAY & LESBIAN VENUES

Don't get too excited about this heading: there are a couple of places worthy of mention for men, and nothing much for women.

Genetic (Ruta 3 No 3-08, Zona 4; ⏲ 9pm-1am Fri & Sat) This used to be called Pandora's Box, and has been hosting Guatemala's gay community since the '70s, though it gets a mixed crowd and is one of the best local venues for trance/dance music. It has two dance floors, a rooftop patio and a relaxed atmosphere. Friday is 'all you can drink.'

Black & White Lounge (www.blackand whitebar.com; 11a Calle 2-54, Zona 1; ⏲ 7pm-1am Wed-Sat) A well-established gay disco-bar in a former private house near the downtown area, often with strippers.

Club SO36 (www.clubso36.com; 5a Calle 1-24, Zona 1; ⏲ 4-10pm) A combination bar, strip club and gay cinema.

11a Av, just near the main entrance to the university all offer cheap beer, loud music and bar junk food. Like student bars all over the world, they're busy any time of day, but nights and weekends are best. A taxi out here from the center should cost about Q50 if it's not too late.

Live Music

La Bodeguita del Centro (12a Calle 3-55, Zona 1; Sun-Thu free, Fri & Sat Q25-60) There's a hopping, creative local scene in Guatemala City, and this large, bohemian hangout is one of the best places to connect with it. There's live music of some kind almost every night from Tuesday to Saturday, usually starting at 9pm.

Rattle & Hum (4a Av & 16 Calle, Zona 10) One of the last places in Zona 10 to still be hosting live music, this Australian-owned place has a warm and friendly atmosphere.

TrovaJazz (www.trovajazz.com; Vía 6 No 3-55, Zona 4) Jazz, blues and folk fans should look into what's happening here.

Box Lounge (15a Calle 2-53) With live DJs Tuesdays to Saturdays, this is one of the best spots in town to connect with Guatemala's growing electronic music scene.

Discotecas

La Estación Norte (Ruta 4, 6-32, Zona 4) As far as mega-discos go, this one around the corner from Cuatro Grados Norte is kind of interesting. It's done out in a train theme, with carriages for bars, and platforms for dance floors. Dress well, but not over the top.

El Círculo (7a Av 10-33, Zona 1; ⏲ 7pm-1am Wed-Sat) One of the most reliable dance floors in the downtown area. The crowd is mostly young, and the music is mostly latina, along the lines of salsa, merengue and reggaetón. Occasional live music.

Zona 10 has a bunch of clubs attracting 20-something local crowds along 13a Calle and adjacent streets, such as 1a Av. The area's exclusivity means that door staff are well versed in the old 'members only' routine. If you want to try your luck, the universal rules apply: dress up, go before 11pm and make sure your group has more women than men in it. Check flyers around town for special nights.

Here are a couple to get you started:

Kahlua (cnr 15a Calle & 1a Av, Zona 10) For electronica and bright young things.

Mr Jerry (13a Calle 1-26, Zona 10) For salsa and merengue.

Arts

Two very good cultural centers in Cuatro Grados Norte host regular theatrical performances and other artistic events. It's always worth dropping in or checking their websites to see what's on.

The English-language *Revue Magazine* (www.revuemag.com) has events details, although it focuses more on Antigua. Your hotel should have a copy, or know where to get one. Free events mags in Spanish come and go. At the time of writing, *El Azar* (www. elazarcultural.blogspot.com) had the best info. Pick up a copy at any cultural center listed here. Movie and other listings can be found in the *Prensa Libre* newspaper.

IGA Cultural Center (Instituto Guatemalteco Americano; ☎ 2422-5555; www.iga.edu; Ruta 1, 4-05, Zona 4) This hosts art exhibitions and live theater.

Centro Cultural de España (☎ 2385-9066; www. centroculturalespana.com.gt; Vía 5, No 1-23, Zona 4) The Spanish cultural center hosts an excellent range of events, including live music, film nights and art exhibitions, mostly with free admission.

Centro Cultural Miguel Ángel Asturias (☎ 2332-4041; www.teatronacional.com.gt; 24a Calle 3-81, Zona 1) Cultural events are also held here.

SHOPPING

Mercado de Artesanías (Crafts Market; ☎ 2472-0208; cnr 5a Calle & 11a Av, Zona 13; ⏰ 9:30am-6pm), a sleepy official *mercado* near the museums and zoo, sells similar goods to those in the Mercado Central (p94), in less crowded conditions.

For fashion boutiques, electronic goods and other developed-world paraphernalia, head for the large shopping malls such as **Oakland Mall** (www.oaklandmall.com.gt; Diagonal 6, 13-01, Zona 10).

For a more everyday Guatemalan experience, take a walk along 6a Av between 8a and 16a Calles in Zona 1. This street is always choked with street stalls noisily hawking everything from pirated DVDs and CDs to shoes, underwear and overalls. Once the **Plaza El Amate** (cnr 18a Calle & 4a Av, Zona 1) is opened, the plan is to move all these unofficial vendors here.

GETTING THERE & AWAY
Air

Guatemala City's **Aeropuerto Internacional La Aurora** (code GUA; ☎ 2321-5050) is the country's major airport. All international flights to Guatemala City land and take off here. At the time of writing, the country's only *scheduled*

domestic flights are between Guatemala City and Flores. **Grupo TACA** (☎ 2470-8222; www.taca.com; Hotel Intercontinental, 14a Calle 2-51, Zona 10) makes two round-trip flights daily (one in the morning, one in the afternoon), plus an extra flight four mornings a week which continues from Flores to Cancún (Mexico) and flies back from there via Flores in the afternoon. **TAG** (☎ 2380-9401; www.tag.com.gt; Aeropuerto Internacional La Aurora) offers one flight daily, leaving Guatemala at 6:30am and returning from Flores at 4:30pm.

Tickets to Flores cost around Q1330/2245 one way/round trip with Grupo TACA and Q1150/1980 with TAG, but some travel agents, especially in Antigua, offer large discounts on these prices.

Bus

Buses from here run all over Guatemala and into Mexico, Belize, Honduras, El Salvador and beyond. Most bus companies have their own terminals, some of which are in Zona 1. The city council has been on a campaign to get long-haul bus companies out of the downtown area, so it may be wise to double check with Inguat (p90) or your hotel about the office location.

INTERNATIONAL BUS SERVICES

The following companies offer daily 1st-class bus services to international destinations. Many longer-distance trips require a compulsory overnight stop in one of the other Central American capitals, which can add to the overall price. Check the websites for departure times and details.

Hedman Alas (☎ 2362-5072/6; www.hedmanalas. com; 2a Av 8-73, Zona 10) Covers various destinations in Honduras, including Copán (Q291, five hours), San Pedro Sula (Q374, eight hours), La Ceiba (Q433, 12 hours) and Tegucigalpa (Q433, 12 hours).

King Quality & Comfort Lines (☎ 2369-7070; www.king-qualityca.com; 18a Av 1-96, Zona 15) Goes to San Salvador (El Salvador; Q210, five hours), Managua (Nicaragua; Q460 to Q740, 14 hours), San José (Costa Rica; Q625 to Q1200, 30 hours), Tegucigalpa (Honduras; Q516 to Q824, 36 hours) and San Pedro Sula (Honduras; Q616 to Q933, 30 hours).

Línea Dorada (☎ 2415-8900; www.lineadorada.com. gt; cnr 10a Av & 16 Calle, Zona 1) Has services to Belize City (Belize; Q350, 15 hours), Chetumal (Mexico; Q415, 23 hours) and Tapachula (Mexico; Q150, seven hours).

Pullmantur (☎ 2367-4746; www.pullmantur.com; Holiday Inn, 1a Av 13-22, Zona 10) Goes to San Salvador (El Salvador; Q290, 4½ hours) and Tegucigalpa (Honduras; Q516, 10½ hours).

GUATEMALA

Rutas Orientales (☎ 2253-7282; www.rutasorientales. com; 21 Calle 11-60, Zona 1) Has departures to San Pedro Sula (Honduras; Q200, nine hours).

Tica Bus (☎ 2473-0633; www.ticabus.com; Calz Aguilar Batres 22-55, Zona 12) Covers San Salvador (El Salvador; Q125, five hours), Tapachula (Mexico; Q125, five hours), Tegucigalpa (Honduras; Q250, 35 hours), Managua (Nicaragua; Q430, 28 to 35 hours), San José (Costa Rica; Q566, 53 to 60 hours) and Panama City (Panama; Q790, 76 hours).

Transportes Galgos Inter (☎ 2232-3661; www. transgalgosinter.com.gt; 7a Av 19-44, Zona 1) Runs to Tapachula (Mexico; Q205, five to seven hours) and can book connections to as far north as the US.

NATIONAL PULLMAN BUS SERVICES
The following bus companies have Pullman services to Guatemalan destinations. For a warning on solo female travelers traveling on intercity buses, see p89.

ADN (☎ 2251-0050; www.adnautobusesdelnorte.com; 8a Av 16-41, Zona 1) For Flores.

Fortaleza del Sur (☎ 2230-3390; Calz Raúl Aguilar Batres 4-15, Zona 12) Covers the Pacific Coast.

Fuente del Norte (☎ 2238-3894; www.autobuses fuentedelnorte.com; 17a Calle 8-46, Zona 1) Covers the whole country.

Hedman Alas (☎ 2362-5072/6; www.hedmanalas.com; 2a Av 8-73, Zona 10) Goes to Antigua.

Línea Dorada (☎ 2415-8900; www.lineadorada.com. gt; cnr 10a Av & 16 Calle, Zona 1) Luxury buses to the Petén region, Quetzaltenango, Huehuetenango, Río Dulce etc.

Litegua (☎ 2220-8840; www.litegua.com; 15a Calle 10-40, Zona 1) Covers the east and Antigua.

Los Halcones (☎ 2432-5364; Calz Roosevelt 37-47, Zona 11) For Huehuetenango.

Monja Blanca (☎ 2238-1409; www.tmb.com.gt; 8a Av 15-16, Zona 1) For Cobán and points in between.

Rapidos del Sur (☎ 2232-7025; 20 Calle 8-55, Zona1) For the Pacific coast and El Petén.

NATIONAL PULLMAN SERVICES FROM GUATEMALA CITY

Destination	Cost (Q)	Duration (hr)	Departures	Frequency	Company
Antigua	40	1	2pm & 6pm	2 daily	Litegua
	50	1	7pm	1 daily	Hedman Alas
Biotopo del Quetzal	43	3½	4am-5pm	half-hourly	Monja Blanca
Chiquimula	35	3	4:30am-6pm	hourly	Rutas Orientales
Cobán	50	4½	4am-5pm	half-hourly	Monja Blanca
El Carmen	65	7	12:15am-6:30pm	half-hourly	Fortaleza del Sur
Esquipulas	50	4½	4:30am-5:30pm	half-hourly	Rutas Orientales
Flores/Santa Elena	110	10	nonstop	hourly	Fuente del Norte
	150-190	8	10am-9pm	3 daily	Línea Dorada
	120	10	6am & 9pm	2 daily	Rapidos del Sur
	150	8	9pm & 10pm	2 daily	ADN
Huehuetenango	65	5	noon & 4pm	2 daily	Los Halcones
	90	5	6:30am & 10:30pm	2 daily	Línea Dorada
La Mesilla	130	7	6:30am & 10:30pm	2 daily	Línea Dorada
Melchor de Mencos	125-170	11	9pm & 10pm	2 daily	Fuentes del Norte
Panajachel	40	3	5:15am	1 daily	Transportes Rebuli
Poptún	115	8	11:30am, 10:30pm & 11pm	3 daily	Línea Dorada
Puerto Barrios	60-90	5	3:45am-7pm	half-hourly	Litegua
Quetzaltenango	65	4	8:30am-2:30pm	4 daily	Transportes Galgos
	60	4	6:15am-5:30pm	4 daily	Alamo
	70	4	4am & 2:30pm	2 daily	Línea Dorada
	55	4	6:30am-5pm	hourly	Transportes Marquensita
Retalhuleu	70	3	9:30am-7:30pm	5 daily	Fuentes del Norte
Río Dulce	60	4	6am-4:30pm	half-hourly	Litegua
Sayaxché	135	11	5:30pm & 7pm	2 daily	Fuentes del Norte
Tecún Umán	55	6	6am-6pm	hourly	Fortaleza del Sur

2ND-CLASS BUS SERVICES FROM GUATEMALA CITY

Destination	Cost (Q)	Duration (hr)	Departures	Frequency	Departs
Antigua	5	1	7am-8pm	every 5min	Calz Roosevelt btwn 4a Av & 5a Av, Zona 7
Chichicastenango	12	3	5am-6pm	hourly	*parada*, Zona 8
Ciudad Pedro de Alvarado	25	2½	5am-4pm	half-hourly	Centra Sur
Escuintla	15	1	6am-4:30pm	half-hourly	Centra Sur
Huehuetenango	50	5	7am-5pm	half-hourly	*parada*, Zona 8
La Democracia	20	2	6am-4:30pm	half-hourly	Centra Sur
La Mesilla	75	8	noon	1 daily	*parada*, Zona 8
Monterrico	40	4	10:20am-2:20pm	hourly	Centra Sur
Panajachel	30	3	7am-5pm	half-hourly	*parada*, Zona 8
Salamá	30	3	5am-5pm	hourly	17a Calle 11-32, Zona 1
San Pedro La Laguna	35	4	2pm, 3pm & 4pm	3 daily	*parada*, Zona 8
Santa Cruz del Quiché	35	3½	5am-5pm	hourly	*parada*, Zona 8
Santiago Atitlán	25	4	4am-5pm	half-hourly	*parada*, Zona 8
Tecpán	7	2	5:30am-7pm	every 15min	*parada*, Zona 8

Rutas Orientales (☎ 2253-7282; www.rutasorientales. com; 21 Calle 11-60, Zona 1) Covers the east.
Transportes Álamo (☎ 2471-8646; 12 Av 'A' 0-65, Zona 7) For Quetzaltenango.
Transportes Galgos Inter (☎ 2253-4868; www.trans galgosinter.com.gt; 7a Av 19-44, Zona 1) For Quetzaltenango.
Transportes Marquensita (☎ 2451-0763; 1a Av 21-31, Zona 1) For Quetzaltenango.
Transportes Rebuli (☎ 2230-2748; www.toursrebusa. com; 23a Av 1-39, Zona 7) For Panajachel.

Pullman Bus Departures
See the table, left, for specifics on national Pullman services from Guatemala City.

2ND-CLASS BUS SERVICES
The table above lists all 2nd-class bus ('chicken bus') services. Most Pacific Coast services leave from Centra Sur, a large terminal on the southern outskirts of the city which is connected to the center by Transmetro buses (see boxed text, p102). Buses for the Western Highlands leave from a series of roadside *paradas* (bus stops) on 41a Calle between 6a and 7a Avs in Zona 8.

Shuttle Minibus
Door-to-door minibuses run from the airport to any address in Antigua (usually Q80 per person, one hour). Look for signs in the airport exit hall or people holding up 'Antigua

Shuttle' signs. The first shuttle leaves for Antigua about 7am and the last around 8pm or 9pm. Shuttle services from Guatemala City to popular destinations such as Panajachel and Chichicastenango (via Antigua – both around Q180) are offered by travel agencies in Antigua – see p103 for contact details.

GETTING AROUND
Bus
Due to alarming increases in (often violent) crime on Guatemala City's red city buses, it is pretty much universally accepted that tourists should only use them in case of dire emergency. The major exception to this is the TransMetro system of green, articulated buses (see boxed text, p102). This may all change as a new system of prepaid, security-camera monitored buses called Transurban comes into effect sometime in 2010, but critics of the system say that the new buses will be more of the same. Catch them or not, if you spend any time out and about in Guatemala City, especially Zona 1, its buses will become a major feature of your existence as they roar along in large numbers belching great clouds of black smoke. Jets flying low over the downtown area intermittently intensify the cacophony.

Buses will stop anywhere they see a passenger, but street corners and traffic lights are your best bet for hailing them – just hold out your hand. Buses cost Q1.10 per ride in the

GUATEMALA

GUATEMALA

TRANSMETRO

In early 2007, in answer to growing concerns about traffic congestion and insecurity on urban buses, Guatemala City inaugurated the TransMetro system. TransMetro buses differ from regular old, red urban buses because they are prepaid (the driver carries no money, thus reducing risk of robberies), travel in their own lanes (not getting caught in traffic jams), only stop at designated stops and are new, comfortable and bright green.

The first route to be opened connects the Centro Cívico in Zona 4 to Centra Sur, a new bus terminal where the majority of buses for the Pacific Coast now depart. At the time of writing, the Central Corridor route, connecting Zona 1 with Zonas 9 and 10, was about to be inaugurated.

Crime has got so bad on Guate's regular red buses that travelers are advised not to use them, but TransMetro buses are safe, fast and comfortable. All rides cost Q1, payable at the bus stop before boarding. If you'd like to try one out for free, consider catching a SubiBaja bus (see p91) on any Sunday.

daytime: you pay the driver or his helper as you get on. Don't catch them at night.

For the thrillseekers out there, these are the most useful routes:

Zona 1 to Zona 10 (Bus 82 or 101) Travels via 10 Av, Zona 1, then 6a Av and Ruta 6 in Zona 4 and Av La Reforma.
Zona 10 to Zona 1 (Bus 82 or 101) Travels via Av La Reforma then 7a Av in Zona 4 and 9a Av, Zona 1.
Airport to Zona 1 (Bus 82) Travels via Zonas 9 and 4.
Zona 1 to Airport (Bus 82) Travels via 10a Av, Zona 1 then down 6a Av in Zonas 4 and 9.

Taxi

Plenty of taxis cruise most parts of the city. Fares are negotiable; always establish your destination and fare before getting in. Zona 1 to Zona 10, or vice versa, costs around Q40 to Q60. If you want to phone for a taxi, **Taxi Amarillo Express** (☎ 2232-1515) has metered cabs that often work out cheaper than others, though true *capitaleños* (capital-city residents) will tell you that taxi meters are all rigged and you get a better deal by bargaining.

ANTIGUA

pop 58,150
Guatemala's tourism showpiece, Antigua remains far more than a tourist attraction. A place of rare beauty, major historical significance and vibrant culture, it's the country's one must-visit destination.

A former capital – the seat of government was relocated to Guatemala City following several major earthquakes during the colonial period – Antigua boasts an astonishing catalog of colonial relics in a magnificent setting. Its streetscapes of pastel facades under terracotta roofs unfold amid three volcanoes: Agua (3766m), Fuego (3763m) and Acatenango (3976m). Designated a Unesco World Heritage Site and with an ideal climate, it's a splendid place for walking (though it can get chilly after sunset). While many old ecclesiastical and civic structures are beautifully renovated, others retain tumbledown charm, with fragments strewn about parklike grounds and sprays of bougainvillea sprouting from the crumbling ruins.

Thanks to the dozens of Spanish language schools that operate here, Antigua has become a global hot spot as well, boasting fine dining, plenty of colonial-chic accommodations and an aggressively cosmopolitan nightlife. But the foreign presence by no means dominates the atmosphere. Antigua remains a vibrant Guatemalan town, its churches, plazas and markets throbbing with activity.

Perhaps the real miracle of Antigua is its resilience. Despite the destructive forces that have conspired against it – earthquakes, volcanic eruptions and floods, followed by virtual abandonment and centuries of neglect – the town has reemerged with a vengeance, buoyed by the pride of its inhabitants.

HISTORY

Antigua was founded on March 10, 1543, and served as the colonial capital for 233 years. The capital was transferred to Guatemala City in 1776, after Antigua was razed in the earthquake of July 29, 1773.

The town was slowly rebuilt, retaining much of its traditional character. In 1944 the Legislative Assembly declared Antigua a national monument, and in 1979 Unesco declared it a World Heritage Site.

Most of Antigua's buildings were constructed during the 17th and 18th centuries, when the city was a rich Spanish outpost and the Catholic church was ascending to power. Many handsome, sturdy colonial buildings remain, and several impressive ruins have been preserved and are open to the public.

ORIENTATION
Volcán Agua is southeast of the city and visible from most points; Volcán Acatenango is to the west; and Volcán Fuego (Fire) – easily recognizable by its plume of smoke and red glow – is to the southwest. These three volcanoes (which appear on the city's coat of arms) provide easy reference points.

In Antigua compass points are added to the avenidas and calles. Calles run east–west, so 4a Calle west of Parque Central is 4a Calle Poniente; avenidas run north–south, so 3a Av north of Parque Central is 3a Av Norte.

Most buses arrive at the Terminal de Buses, a large open lot just west of the *mercado*, four blocks west of Parque Central along 4a Calle Poniente.

INFORMATION
Bookstores
Dyslexia Books (1a Av Sur 11) Mostly used books, mainly in English.
Rainbow Reading Room (7a Av Sur 8) Thousands of used books in English and Spanish for sale, rent or trade.

Emergency
Asistur (☎ 5978-3586; asisturantiguaguatemala@gmail. com; 6a Calle Poniente Final; ☷ 24hr) The helpful tourism assistance agency acts as a police liaison for tourists.

Internet Access
Aside from an abundance of affordable cybercafes, wi-fi is available in restaurants, cafes and elsewhere – even the Parque Central is a wireless hot spot.
Conher (☎ 5521-2823; 4a Calle Poniente 5; per hr Q10) All-purpose communications center, offering printing, scanning and CD burning.
Funky Monkey (Monoloco, 5a Av Sur 6, Pasaje El Corregidor; per hr Q8; ☷ 8am-12:30am) The latest of Antigua's cybercafes.

Laundry
Laundromats are easy to find; most charge Q6 per pound to wash, dry and fold.
Quick Laundry (6a Calle Poniente 14; ☷ 9am-6pm Mon-Sat, 9am-2pm Sat)

Media
The Antigua-based *Revue Magazine* (www. revuemag.com) runs about 90% ads, but has reasonable cultural events information. It's available everywhere. *La Cuadra* (www.la cuadraonline.com), also Antigua-based, mixes politics with irreverent commentary.

Medical Services
Farmacia Ivori Select (☎ 7832-1559; 4a Calle Poniente 33; ☷ 24hr) Pharmacy.
Hospital Privado Hermano Pedro (☎ 7832-1197; Av de La Recolección 4; ☷ 24hr) Near the bus station, a private hospital that offers 24-hour emergency service and accepts foreign insurance.

Money
Banco Industrial (5a Av Sur 4; ☷ 9am-7pm Mon-Fri, 9am-1pm Sat) Has a reliable ATM and changes US dollars (cash and traveler's checks). Another useful BI ATM is inside Café Barista (p113), across the square.
Citibank (cnr 4a Calle Oriente & 4a Av Norte; ☷ 9am-4:30pm Mon-Fri, 9:30am-1pm Sat) Gives Visa (not MasterCard) cash advances. A second branch, one block east, changes US dollars and euros.
Visa & MasterCard ATM (5a Av Norte) Facing Parque Central.

Post
Post office (cnr 4a Calle Poniente & Calz de Santa Lucía Norte) West of Parque Central, near the market.

Telephone
Most internet cafes offer cut-rate international calls, though Skype calls may be even cheaper.
Conher (☎ 5521-2823; 4a Calle Poniente 5) Charges Q0.75 per minute to USA or Europe.

Tourist Information
Antigua Guatemala: the City and its Heritage, by long-time Antigua resident Elizabeth Bell, is well worth picking up at a bookstore. It describes all of the city's important buildings and museums, and neatly encapsulates Antigua's history and fiestas.
Inguat (☎ 7832-3782; 2a Calle Oriente 11; info-antigua@inguat.gob.gt; ☷ 8am-5pm Mon-Fri, 9am-5pm Sat & Sun) Inside a colonial mansion near the Capuchinas convent, the tourist office has free city maps, bus information and helpful, bilingual staff.

Travel Agencies
Everywhere you turn in Antigua, you'll see travel agencies offering tours to interesting sites around Antigua and elsewhere in

GUATEMALA

ANTIGUA

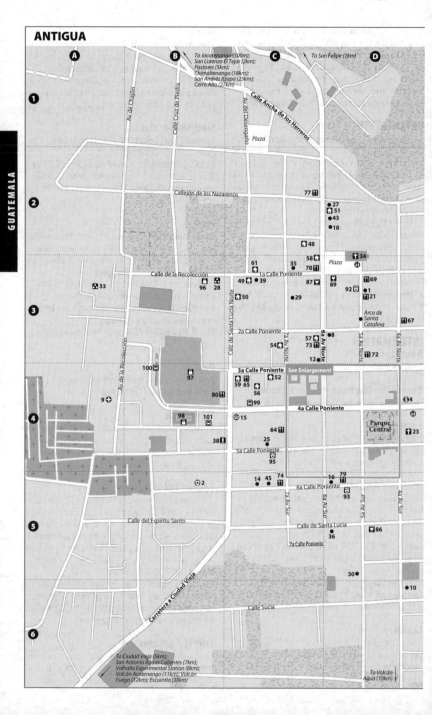

To Jocotenango (500m);
San Lorenzo El Tejar (2km);
Pastores (5km);
Chimaltenango (18km);
San Andrés Itzapa (25km);
Cerro Alto (27km)

To San Felipe (1km)

To Ciudad Vieja (5km);
San Antonio Aguas Calientes (7km);
Valhalla Experimental Station (8km);
Volcán Acatenango (11km); Volcán
Fuego (12km); Escuintla (38km)

To Volcán
Agua (10km)

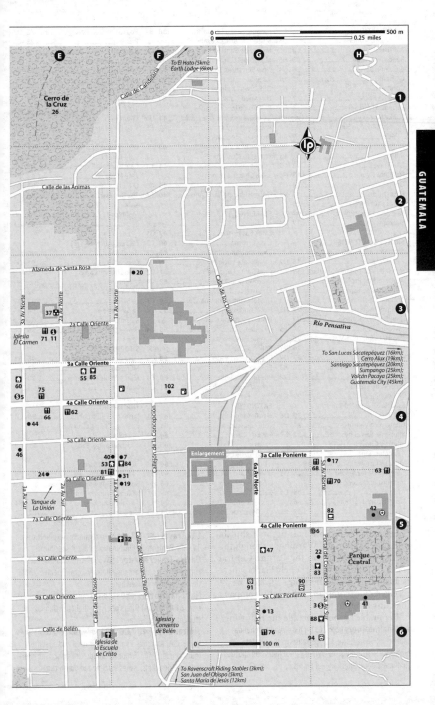

GUATEMALA

Guatemala, international flights, shuttle minibuses and more. Warning: although the agency gRuta Maya on the Parque Central claims to be 'operated by Lonely Planet,' there is absolutely no connection – in fact, we've received more complaints about this company than any other in town.

Reputable agencies include the following:

Adrenalina Tours (☎ 7832-1108; www.adrenalina tours.com; 5a Av Norte 31) Specialists in the western highlands; can arrange everything from tours and shuttles to domestic and international flights.

LAX Travel (☎ 7832-1621; laxantigua@intelnett.com; 3a Calle Poniente 12) International flight specialist.

Onvisa Travel Agency (☎ 5909-0160; Calz de Santa Lucía Norte 7; onvisatravel@hotmail.com) Operates shuttles to Copán and elsewhere.

National Travel (☎ 7832-8383; antigua@nationalgua. com; 6a Av Sur 1A) Offers one-way flights, including student and teacher fares.

Sinfronteras (☎ 7720-4400; www.sinfront.com; 5a Av Norte 15A) Arranges a variety of cultural and adventure tours, primarily for European groups. Sells discount international air tickets; issues student and youth cards.

DANGERS & ANNOYANCES

Antigua generally feels safe to walk around but muggings do occur, so don't let your guard down completely. This holds doubly true after the bars close at 1am, when muggers are on the lookout for inebriated visitors. After 10pm, consider taking a taxi back to your lodgings, especially if you're female. Pickpockets work the busy market, doing overtime on paydays at the middle and end of the month. December (bonus time) brings a renewed wave of robberies.

Some of the more remote hiking trails have been the scene of muggings, though stepped-up police patrols have reduced the likelihood of such incidents in recent years. If you're planning on hiking independently to any of the volcanoes, check with Asistur (p103) about the current situation.

SIGHTS
Parque Central

The gathering place for locals and visitors alike, on most days the plaza is lined with villagers selling handicrafts to tourists; on Sunday it's mobbed and the streets on the east and west sides are closed to traffic. Things are cheapest late Sunday afternoon, when the peddling is winding down.

The plaza's famous fountain was built in 1738. At night, mariachi or marimba bands play in the park.

PALACIO DE LOS CAPITANES GENERALES

Begun in 1558, the Captain-Generals' Palace was the governmental center of all Central America from Chiapas to Costa Rica until 1773. The stately double-arcaded facade, which marches proudly along the southern side of the Parque, was added in the early 1760s.

CATEDRAL DE SANTIAGO

On the park's east side, Catedral de Santiago was founded in 1542, damaged by earthquakes many times, badly ruined in 1773 and only partially rebuilt between 1780 and 1820. In the 16th and early 17th centuries, Antigua's churches had lavish baroque interiors, but most – including this one – lost this richness during post-earthquake rebuilding. Inside, a crypt contains the bones of Bernal Díaz del Castillo, historian of the Spanish conquest, who died in 1581. If the front entrance is closed, you can enter at the rear or from the south side.

PALACIO DEL AYUNTAMIENTO

The City Hall, on the north side of the park, dates mostly from 1743. In addition to town offices, it houses the **Museo de Santiago** (☎ 7832-2868; admission Q30; ☉ 9am-4pm Mon-Fri, 9am-noon & 2-4pm Sat & Sun) in the former town jail, exhibiting furnishings, artifacts and weapons from colonial times. Next door is the **Museo del Libro Antiguo** (Old Book Museum; ☎ 7832-5511; admission Q30; ☉ 9am-4pm Tue-Fri, 9am-noon & 2-4pm Sat & Sun), with exhibits of colonial printing and binding, including a replica of Guatemala's first printing press, which began work here in the 1660s.

UNIVERSIDAD DE SAN CARLOS

Now in Guatemala City, San Carlos University was founded in Antigua in 1676. What used to be its main building (built in 1763), half a block east of the park, houses the **Museo de Arte Colonial** (Museum of Colonial Art; ☎ 7832-0429; 5a Calle Oriente 5; admission Q50; ☉ 9am-4pm Tue-Fri, 9am-noon & 2-4pm Sat & Sun), with some expressive sculptures of saints, and paintings by leading Mexican artists of the era, such as Miguel Cabrera and Juan de Correa.

Churches & Monasteries

Once glorious in their gilded baroque finery, Antigua's churches have suffered indignities from both nature and humankind. Rebuilding after earthquakes gave the churches thicker walls, lower towers and belfries, and bland interiors, and moving the capital to Guatemala City deprived Antigua of the population needed to maintain the churches in their traditional glory. Still, they are impressive. In addition to those noted here, you'll find many others scattered around town in various states of decay.

IGLESIA Y CONVENTO DE NUESTRA SEÑORA DE LA MERCED

At the north end of 5a Av is **La Merced**, Antigua's most striking colonial church. La Merced's construction began in 1548. Improvements continued until 1717, when the church was ruined by earthquakes. Reconstruction was completed in 1767, but in 1773 an earthquake struck again and the convent was destroyed. Repairs to the church were made from 1850 to 1855; its baroque facade dates from this period. Inside the **monastery ruins** (admission Q5; ☉ 8:15am-5:45pm) is a fountain 27m in diameter – possibly the largest in Central America.

GUATEMALA

IGLESIA DE SAN FRANCISCO

The town's next most notable church is **San Francisco** (cnr 8a Calle Oriente & Calle de los Pasos). It dates from the mid-16th century, but little of the original building remains. Rebuilding and restoration over the centuries have produced a handsome structure. All that remains of the original church is the resting place of Hermano Pedro de San José Betancourt, a Franciscan monk who founded a hospital for the poor and earned the gratitude of generations. He died here in 1667; his intercession is still sought by the ill, who pray here fervently.

LAS CAPUCHINAS

The Iglesia y Convento de Nuestra Señora del Pilar de Zaragoza, usually called **Las Capuchinas** (cnr 2a Av Norte & 2a Calle Oriente; adult/student Q30/15; ☺ 9am-5pm), was founded in 1736 by nuns from Madrid. Destroyed repeatedly by earthquakes, it is now a museum, with exhibits on religious life in colonial times. The building has an unusual structure of 18 concentric cells around a circular patio.

CHURCH RUINS

A massive ruin at the west end of 1a Calle Poniente, the **Iglesia y Convento de la Recolección** (Av de la Recolección; admission Q30; ☺ 9am-5pm), is among Antigua's most impressive monuments. Built between 1701 and 1708, it was destroyed in the 1773 earthquake.

Near La Recolección is the **Colegio de San Jerónimo** (cnr Calz de Santa Lucía & 1a Calle Poniente; adult/student Q30; ☺ 9am-5pm), also called the Real Aduana, which was built in 1757 by friars of the Merced order. Because it did not have royal authorization, it was taken over by Spain's Carlos III in 1761. In 1765 it was designated for use as the Royal Customhouse, but was destroyed in the 1773 earthquake.

Monumento a Landívar

At the west end of 5a Calle Poniente is the Landívar Monument, a structure of five colonial-style arches set in a little park. The poetry of Rafael Landívar, an 18th-century Jesuit priest, is esteemed as the colonial period's best, even though he wrote much of it in Italy after the Jesuits' expulsion from Guatemala. Landívar's Antigua house was nearby on 5a Calle Poniente.

Mercado

At the west end of 4a Calle Poniente, across Calz de Santa Lucía Norte, sprawls the **market** (☺ Mon, Thu & Sat) – chaotic, colorful and always bustling. The frenzied mornings are the best time to come.

Cerro de la Cruz

On the town's northeast side is the **Hill of the Cross**, offering fine views over Antigua and south toward Volcán Agua. Don't come here without a tourist police escort (see Asistur, p103), as it's notorious for muggers. The tourist police was formed because of robberies here; reportedly no crime against tourists has taken place on the hill since.

ACTIVITIES

Two professional, established and friendly outfits offering a big range of activities are **Old Town Outfitters** (☎ 5399-0440; www.adventureguatemala.com; 5a Av Sur 12C) and **Guatemala Ventures** (☎ /fax 7832-3383; www.guatemalaventures.com; 1a Av Sur 15). Drop by either place to chat about possibilities.

Climbing the Volcanoes

All three volcanoes overlooking Antigua are tempting challenges but how close you can get to **Volcán Fuego** depends on recent levels of activity. In many ways the twin-peaked **Volcán Acatenango**, overlooking Fuego, is the most exhilarating summit. For an active-volcano experience many people take tours to **Volcán Pacaya** (2552m), 25km southeast of Antigua (a 1½-hour drive).

Get reliable advice about safety before you climb, for example from Inguat (see p103), regarding the possible dangers from volcanic activity as well as from armed robbers preying on tourists along some trails. In general the weather and the views on all the volcanoes are better in the morning. Take sensible precautions: wear adequate footwear (volcanic rock can be very rough on shoes), warm clothing and, in the rainy season (May to October), some sort of rain gear. Carry a flashlight in case the weather changes; it can get as dark as night when it rains on the mountain – though it's better not to go at all if rain is expected. Don't neglect food and water.

It's advisable to go with a reputable agency (see above). **Agua** trips with Guatemala Ventures (Q810) drive to the end of the dirt road, well beyond the village of Santa María de Jesús. The summit is about two hours' walk from this point (against five hours from the village).

One-day Pacaya trips, with 1½ to two hours' walking uphill and one to 1½ hours down, cost around Q350, including lunch and an English-speaking guide. With luck you'll be able to look down into the active crater. Various travel agencies (see p103) run bargain-basement, seven-hour Pacaya trips daily for Q80 (leaving Antigua at 6am and 2pm); food and drinks are not included, nor is the Q40 admission to the Pacaya protected area.

Cycling

Old Town Outfitters (☎ 5399-0440; www.adventure guatemala.com; 5a Av Sur 12C) offers a range of mountain-bike tours at all levels of difficulty, including the two-day Pedal & Paddle Tour (Q1750 to Q2500), which includes kayaking and hiking at Lago de Atitlán.

Guatemala Ventures (☎ /fax 7832-3383; www.guate malaventures.com; 1a Av Sur 15) also offers some bike tours, from intermediate to expert levels. It does half- or full-day rides through the Antigua Valley (Q1075), two-day bike-and-kayak trips to Lago de Atitlán (Q1550 per person) and weeklong jaunts encompassing volcanic slopes, highland forest and Pacific mangroves, as well as Lago de Atitlán (Q8600). Another, lazier option, is its trip up Cerro Alto in a minibus with a coast back down on a mountain bike (Q250).

If you'd rather pedal off on your own, **Ox Expeditions** (☎ 7832-0074; www.guatemalavolcano.com; 1 Av Sur 4B) rents out quality mountain bikes at Q30 per hour.

Horseback Riding

Ravenscroft Riding Stables (☎ 7830-6669; 2a Av Sur 3, San Juan del Obispo), 3km south of Antigua on the road to Santa María de Jesús, offers English-style riding, with scenic rides of three, four or five hours in the valleys and hills around Antigua. Rides cost Q205 per hour per person for experienced riders, Q250 for beginners. You need to be fairly fit. Reservations and information are available through the **Hotel San Jorge** (☎ 7832-3132; 4a Av Sur 13). Reach the stables on a bus bound for Santa María de Jesús (p114).

Volunteering

Any of the Spanish schools listed can help you find volunteer work, even if you're not studying there. **EntreMundos** (www.entremundos.org) and **Idealist** (www.idealist.org) both have free, searchable databases listing Antigua opportunities. **Proyecto Mosaico Guatemala** (☎ 7832-0955; www. promosaico.org; 3a Av Norte 3; ☼ 10am-4pm Mon & Tue, Thu & Fri, to 2pm Wed) is an Antigua-based NGO that

places volunteers with projects. It charges a Q450 registration fee.

COURSES
Cooking

The **Antigua Cooking School** (☎ 5944-8568; www. antiguacookingschool.com; 5a Av Norte 25B; 4hr class Q520) offers classes in traditional Guatemalan cuisine, preparing classics such as corn tamales, *subanik* (stew made with vegetables, chilli, chicken, turkey and pork), *pepián* (chicken and vegetables in a piquant sesame and pumpkin-seed sauce) and *chuchitos* (small tamales). Classes are available Monday through Saturday.

El Frijol Feliz (☎ 7882-4244; www.frijolfeliz.com; 7a Calle Poniente 11; 3hr class Q330) offers hands-on instruction on preparing Guatemalan meals; students may choose their own menu.

Dancing

You can learn to dance at several places around town. Both **Salsa Chapina Dance Company** (☎ 5270-6453; 6a Calle Poniente 26) and **New Sensation Salsa Studio** (☎ 5033-0921; 1a Calle Poniente 27) offer one-on-one instruction in salsa, merengue, *bachata* (a partnered dance originating in the Dominican Republic) and cha-cha.

Language

Antigua is world-famous for its many Spanish-language schools. Prices, teacher quality and student satisfaction vary greatly, so shop around. Ask for references and talk to ex-students. Inguat (p103) has a list of reputable schools, including the following:

Academia de Español Probigua (☎ 7832-2998; www.probigua.org; 6a Av Norte 41B) Well-regarded, nonprofit school that donates the school's profits to establish and maintain libraries in rural villages.

Academia de Español Sevilla (☎ /fax 7832-5101; www.sevillantigua.com; 1a Av Sur 17C) This school has a good free activity program, and offers a shared student house as a sleeping option.

Academia de Profesores Privados de Español (☎ /fax 7882-4284; www.appeschool.com; 1a Calle Oriente 15) Also offers courses for tourism, educational and healthcare personnel, and an opportunity to study in the outlying village of San Juan del Obispo.

Centro Lingüístico Maya (☎ 7832-0656; www. clmaya.com; 5a Calle Poniente 20) Large, professionally managed, slightly pricier institute with 30 years' experience training diplomatic personnel and journalists.

Cima Del Mundo (☎ 7832-3327; www.cdmschool.com; 6a Av Norte 45) Donates profits to and offers volunteer

GUATEMALA

opportunities with Niños de Guatemala school for low-income kids in nearby Ciudad Vieja.

Escuela de Español Cooperación (☎ 5812-2482; www.spanishschoolcooperacion.com; 7a Av Norte 15 B) A highly recommended school run as a cooperative, ensuring teachers get paid fairly.

Escuela de Español San José el Viejo (☎ 7832-3028; www.sanjoseelviejo.com; 5a Av Sur 34) Professional school accredited by Guatemalan Ministry of Education, set in superb gardens with tennis court, pool and own tasteful accommodations.

Instituto Antigueña de Español (☎ 7832-7241; www.spanishacademyantiguena.com; 1a Calle Poniente 10) A highly recommended school, only hiring experienced teachers. It can arrange volunteer work in the area, too.

Ixchel Spanish School (☎ /fax 7832-0364; www.ixchelschool.com; 7a Calle Poniente 15) Comfortable, welcoming school with enjoyable group activities and lush garden.

Proyecto Lingüístico Francisco Marroquín (☎ /fax 7832-1422; www.spanishschoolplfm.com; 6a Av Norte 43) Antigua's oldest Spanish school, run by a nonprofit foundation working to preserve Maya languages and culture. Also offers instruction in Maya languages.

Classes start Mondays at most schools, though you can usually be placed with a teacher any day of the week. The busiest seasons are January, and April to August – some schools request advance reservations for these times. Instruction is usually one-on-one and costs between Q750 to Q1515 per week for four hours of classes daily, five days per week. You can enroll for up to 10 hours a day of instruction. Most schools offer room and board with local families, where you'll often have your own room, usually with shared bathrooms, for around Q700 per week (including three meals daily except Sunday). Homestays are supposed to promote the 'total immersion' concept of language learning, but often there are several foreigners staying with one family and separate mealtimes for students and the family. Make a point of inquiring about such details if you really want to be totally immersed.

Antigua is not for everyone who wants to study Spanish; there are so many foreigners about, it takes some real discipline to converse in Spanish rather than your native tongue. Many enjoy this social scene, but if you think it will bother you, consider studying in Quetzaltenango (Xela), El Petén or elsewhere, where there are fewer foreign students and more opportunities to dive into Spanish.

TOURS

Inguat-authorized guides around the Parque Central offer city walking tours, with visits to convents, ruins and museums, for Q100 to Q160. Similar guided walks are offered daily by travel agencies (see p103). Also on offer are trips to the surrounding villages and coffee plantations for around Q200.

Elizabeth Bell, a local scholar of Antigua history, or her knowledgeable associates, lead three-hour cultural walking tours of the town (in English and/or Spanish) on Tuesday, Wednesday, Friday and Saturday at 9:30am, and on Monday and Thursday at 2pm. The cost is Q160. Reservations can be made through **Antigua Tours** (☎ /fax 7832-5821; www.antiguatours.net; 5a Av Norte 6), inside Café El Portal (Portal del Comercio 6) off the Parque Central; groups congregate at the park's fountain at the appointed hour. Bell and company also do tours to the nearby villages, visiting weaving workshops and Maya shrines.

Nearly all the agencies listed on p103 offer tours to more distant places, including Tikal, the Cobán area, Monterrico, Chichicastenango and Lago de Atitlán. Two-day trips to Tikal, flying from Guatemala City to Flores and back, start at around Q3600 per person. A hectic one-day Tikal tour costs Q2415 round trip. Two-day land tours to Copán (some including Quiriguá and Río Dulce) are between Q1300 and Q3420 per person, depending on the number of participants, standard of accommodations and guide availability.

On long-distance tours be sure of what you are paying for – some of the cheaper 'tours' simply amount to shuttling you to Guatemala City then popping you on a public bus.

CATours (☎ 7832-9638; www.catours.co.uk; 6a Calle Oriente 14) offers two-day motorbike tours to Lago de Atitlán or Monterrico from Q1385.

FESTIVALS & EVENTS

Antigua really comes alive in **Semana Santa** (Holy Week), when hundreds of people dress in purple robes to accompany the most revered sculptural images from the city's churches in daily street processions remembering Christ's crucifixion and the events surrounding it. Dense clouds of incense envelop the parades and the streets are covered in breathtakingly elaborate *alfombras* (carpets) of colored sawdust and flower petals.

The fervor and the crowds peak on Good Friday, when an early morning procession departs from La Merced church, and a late afternoon one leaves from Iglesia de la Escuela de Cristo. There may also be an enactment of the crucifixion in Parque Central. Have ironclad Antigua room reservations well in advance of Semana Santa, or plan to stay in Guatemala City or another town and commute to the festivities.

Processions, *velaciones* (vigils) and other events actually go on every weekend through Lent, the 40-day period prior to Holy Week. Antigua's tourist office has schedules of everything, and the booklet *Lent and Holy Week in Antigua*, written by Elizabeth Bell, gives explanations.

It seems that Guatemala City's entire population of pickpockets decamps to Antigua for Semana Santa; they target foreign tourists especially.

SLEEPING

When checking a budget establishment, look at several rooms, as some are much better than others.

Asistur (☎ 5978-3586; asisturantiguaguatemala@gmail.com; 6a Calle Poniente Final; **P** ⊛) You can park an RV or pitch a tent on the grounds of Asistur, the tourist police. There's no charge, but it's appreciated if campers contribute items such as tools or bug spray. There are toilets, showers and electric hookups.

Dionisio Guest House (☎ 5644-9486; ciuisis@yahoo.com; 3a Calle Poniente Callejón; dm with/without bathroom Q45/40, d/tr Q120/150, with bathroom Q150/200; ▣ ⊛) The most relaxed of four guesthouses along a little cul-de-sac, featuring spanking clean and nicely decorated rooms along a sunny terrace, a well-supplied kitchen and a cozy lounge area.

Jungle Party Hostal (☎ 7832-0463; www.junglepartyhostal.com; 6a Av Norte 20; dm Q50; ⊛) With bar service, hammock hangouts and the famous all-you-can-eat Saturday barbecue, the Jungle Party has a great atmosphere, and the smiling staff know exactly what's needed by travelers.

Black Cat Hostel (☎ 7832-1229; www.blackcathostels.net; 6 Av Norte 1A; dm Q60, d/tr Q150/225, all incl breakfast) Though the dorms are cramped and you can't use the kitchen, this place is always hopping. Plenty of tours are on offer, plus free movies and good local advice.

our pick Yellow House (☎ 7832-6646; yellowhouseantigua@hotmail.com; 1a Calle Poniente 24; s/d without bathroom Q75/130; ▣) Simple but thoughtfully designed and ecologically conscious, this makes a superior budget choice. Rooms

vary, but comfy beds, recessed lighting, and mosquito-screened windows are the norm.

Casa Jacaranda (☎ /fax 7832-7589; hyrcasajacaranda@gmail.com; 1a Calle Poniente 37; dm Q82, s/d without bathroom Q165/287; ▣ ⊛) Rooms at this original, mellow new hostel are simple but pleasing. Four-bed dorms leave plenty of elbow room, and the shared bathrooms are thoughtfully designed. A grassy patio under a jacaranda tree makes for a tranquil retreat.

Hotel la Casa de Don Ismael (☎ /fax 7832-1932; www.casadonismael.com; 3a Calle Poniente 6, Lotificación Cofiño 2a Callejón; s/d without bathroom Q120/175; ⊛) This homey, humble guesthouse is hidden down a small side street and overseen by its kind, cordial namesake. Seven rustic rooms share three hot-water bathrooms, and there's a pleasant roof terrace.

Posada Don Diego (☎ 7832-1401; posadadondiego@gmail.com; 6a Av Norte 52; s/d Q160/285, without bathroom Q110/185; ▣ ⊛) Located behind a cafe/doughnut purveyor just across from La Merced, Don Diego's place has a handful of comfortable, simply furnished rooms facing a patch of lawn with stone fountain. The pricier rooms have TV.

Casa Cristina (☎ 7832-0623; www.casa-cristina.com; Callejón Camposeco 3A; s/d downstairs Q185/224, upstairs Q224/275; ⊛) There are just a dozen rooms at this comfy little two-story hotel on a pretty backstreet near La Merced. All are quaintly appointed with indigenous bedspreads, brushed-on pastels and wood-stained furniture, and the roof terrace (only open till 8pm) makes a nice retreat. *Muy tranquilo.*

Casa Santa Lucía No 3 (☎ 7832-1386; 6a Av Norte; r Q186) Step back in time, down arched hallways with heavy exposed beams, to reach the well-maintained paint-dappled rooms equipped with blasting hot showers. Though the staff could be a tad more communicative, it's a great location, just north of La Merced.

Antigua hotels can fill up fast. Here are some more options:

Hostal Umma Gumma (☎ 7832-4413; umma gumma@itelgua.com; 7 Av Norte 15; dm/s/d without bathroom Q40/60/120, s/d with bathroom Q85/170; ▣) Lovably run-down, sociable hostel with good kitchen and great rooftop terrace.

Kafka (6a Av Norte 40; dm incl breakfast Q50; ⊛) Basic but clean dorms downstairs from a popular bar. The ones at the rear are quietest.

El Hostal (☎ 7832-0442; elhostal.antigua@gmail.com; 1a Av Sur 8; dm Q75-90; s/d/tr Q120/220/300; ⊛) Half a dozen neatly kept rooms and dorms with sturdy single beds or well-spaced bunks, set around a cheery little patio/cafe.

GUATEMALA

Hotel Burkhard (☎ 7832-4316; hotelburkhard@ hotmail.com; 3a Calle Oriente 19A; r Q100) Tiny hotel with a dozen compact, fancifully decorated rooms on two levels.

Posada Juma Ocag (☎ 7832-3109; Calz de Santa Lucía Norte 13; s/d/tr Q120/140/200) Comfortable and creatively decorated. Good rooftop patio and well-tended little garden. Reservations in person only.

Casa Santa Lucía No 2 (☎ 7832-7418; Calz de Santa Lucía Norte 21; s/d Q120/180; **P**) Sparklingly clean rooms with plenty of colonial charm.

EATING

The cheapest eating in town is the good, clean, tasty food served from street stalls a block west of Parque Central in the early evening. Small restaurants north of the bus station on Alameda de Santa Lucía do good-value set lunches for around Q25. Note that most formal restaurants in Antigua whack on a 10% tip before presenting the bill. It should be itemized, but if in doubt, ask.

Guatemalan

In the early evening, Doña María takes up her post in front of La Merced, at the top of 5a Avenida, and serves fine tamales and *chuchitos*, laced with hot sauce and pickled cabbage, along with bowls of *atol blanco* (corn-based hot beverage). Talk about comfort food!

Casa de Las Mixtas (3a Callejón; mains Q20-30; ☒ breakfast, lunch & dinner) For down-home Guatemalan fare with a bit of style, try this family-run operation on a quiet backstreet across from the market. Aside from their namesake snack – *mixtas* are Guatemalan-style hot dogs, wrapped in tortillas – they also do *paches* – like tamales, but made of mashed potatoes instead of corn dough – and offer a range of set breakfasts.

ourpick Tienda La Canche (6a Av Norte 42) A hole in the wall if there ever was one, the restaurant, behind a 'mom and pop' store, consists of two tables with floral tablecloths. There are a couple of traditional options daily, such as *pepián de pollo* (a hearty chicken stew containing chunks of potato), accompanied by a tray of thick tortillas and half an avocado.

Restaurante Doña Luisa Xicotencatl (☎ 7832-2578; 4a Calle Oriente 12; sandwiches & breakfast dishes Q30-40) Probably Antigua's best-known restaurant, this is a place to enjoy the colonial patio ambience over breakfast or a light meal. The attached bakery sells all kinds of bread and rolls: banana bread comes hot from the oven around 2pm daily.

Café La Escudilla (4a Av Norte 4; pastas Q44, mains Q68-80; ☒ 8am-midnight Wed-Mon; 🛜 **V**) This is an inexpensive patio restaurant with tinkling fountain, lush foliage and some tables under the open sky. The food on offer is simple but well prepared and there are plenty of vegetarian options, as well as economical breakfasts.

La Cuevita de Los Urquizú (☎ 4593-5619; 2a Calle Oriente 9D; lunch combos Q60; ☒ lunch & dinner) Sumptuous *típico* food is the draw here, all kept warming in earthenware pots out front, making it almost impossible to go past. Choose from *pepián*, *kaq'ik* (spicy turkey stew), *jocón* (green stew of chicken or pork with green vegetables and herbs) or other such Guatemalan favorites, and you'll get two accompaniments (Q60).

There's plenty more *típico* food around:

Doña María Gordillo Dulces Típicos (4a Calle Oriente 11) Ground zero for traditional Guatemalan sweets, just as popular with the locals.

La Cenicienta (5a Av Norte 7; slice of pie Q20) An old-fashioned pastry shop selling irresistible cheesecake, pineapple upside-down cake, almond torte and macadamia nut pie. Good coffee, too.

Posada de Don Rodrigo (5a Av Norte 17; mains Q120-180; ☒ breakfast, lunch & dinner) Good seafood crepes, steaks and sausages with a subtle Guatemalan accent, served up in a gorgeous courtyard.

International Cuisine

El Papaturro (☎ 7832-0445; 2 Calle Oriente 4; pupusas Q25, mains Q60-95; ☒ lunch & dinner) For *pupusas* (cornmeal mass stuffed with cheese or refried beans), *rellenitos* (stuffed green plantains) and other Salvadoran staples, this homey spot run by natives of Guatemala's southern neighbor serves authentic dishes and good steak plates in a relaxed courtyard.

Travel Menu (6a Calle Poniente 14; mains Q25-32; ☒ noon-7:30pm Tue-Sun; **V**) Not nearly as unimaginative as the name would imply, this

---

SPLURGE IN PARQUE CENTRAL

As carpenter, antique restorer and occasional xylophone player, Luis Méndez Rodríguez is the auteur of the **Posada San Sebastián** (☎ 7832-2621; snsebast@hotmail. com; 3a Av Norte 4; s/d/tr Q374/498/580; 🛜). Each of the uniquely appointed nine rooms displays his knack for finding and refurbishing art and furniture. Big bathrooms with tub are a bonus, as are the use of a kitchen, roof terrace and a pretty little courtyard garden.

little bar-restaurant serves food that you may have been craving (chow mein, curry, etc) in an intimate candlelit environment. Its motto: 'small place, big portions.'

Y Tu Piña También (1a Av Sur 10B; sandwiches & salads Q30-35;   7am-8pm Mon-Fri, 8am-7pm Sat & Sun;   ) A tempting array of healthy sandwiches (served on wholewheat, pita or bagel), salads and crepes. Good breakfasts, too: omelets, waffles and abundant fruit salads, plus excellent coffee.

Rainbow Café (7832-1919; 7a Av Sur 8; breakfast Q40, mains Q40-60;   8am-midnight Mon-Sat, 7am-11pm Sun;   ) Fill up from an eclectic range of all-day breakfasts, curries, stir-fries, Cajun chicken, guacamole and more, and enjoy the relaxed patio atmosphere.

Casa de Corea (5550-0771; 7a Av Norte 2; main Q40-50;   10am-9pm Mon & Wed-Fri, noon-9pm Sat & Sun) This Korean-owned eatery, with guest-generated graffiti covering the walls, has all the Seoul food you need. Wash down your kim chi or *sundubu jjigae* (chili-spiked stew of tofu and shellfish) with a Korean beer or some rice wine.

El Sabor del Tiempo (7832-0516; 5a Av Norte & 3a Calle; mains Q55-80;   lunch & dinner) One of the town's more atmospheric eateries, done out in rich woods and antique fittings. The menu features good Italian-themed dishes like rabbit in white wine (Q60) and there's draft beer on tap.

Bistrot Cinq (7832-5510; 4a Calle Oriente 7; mains Q100-130;   6pm-11pm Mon-Thu, noon-11pm Fri-Sun) This is the date-night favorite, a faithful replica of its Parisian counterparts, offering zesty salads and classic mains like trout amandine and filet mignon. Check the blackboard for exciting nightly specials. Be sure to make it down for Sunday brunch (served noon to 3pm).

World-food options abound in Antigua:

Wiener (Calz Santa Lucía Norte 8; mains Q35-60;   lunch & dinner) Serving what's possibly the biggest wiener schnitzel you've ever seen, alongside some good-value set lunches.

Sabe Rico (7832-0648; 6a Av Sur 7; sandwiches & salads Q40;   8am-7pm Mon & Wed, 11am-3pm Tue, 8am-8pm Thu-Sat, 9am-4pm Sun) For tasty salads and sandwiches, freshly baked breads, brownies and fine wines.

Pushkar (7979-7848; 6a Av Norte 18; curries Q45-79;   lunch & dinner) Excellent curries, tandoori and thalis served in a stylish lounge or atmospheric patio.

Gaia (5 Av Norte 35A; mains Q58-90;   lunch & dinner) Covers the Middle East, with good couscous and falafel on offer, as well as *sheeshas* (water pipes, Q95).

Sunshine Grill (5964-7620; 6a Av Norte 68; pizzas Q60-140;   Wed-Mon) Amazing pizzas, good French fries, graffiti-covered walls and a karaoke jukebox.

DRINKING
Cafes

Café Barista (4a Calle 12;   7am-10pm;   ) Though some may be dismayed to see this sleek, modern franchise on the Parque Central's northwest corner, true coffee aficionados should head here for Antigua's finest lattes and cappuccinos, made with Guatemalan coffee varieties.

Café Condesa Express (Portal del Comercio 4;   6am-6:30pm) For a quick caffeine fix, hit this outlet on the west side of the Parque Central, or its more formal parent operation, accessed through the bookstore.

Bars

Antigua's bar scene is jumping, except for the nationwide law that says that all bars must close at 1am. Many people roll in from Guatemala City for a spot of Antigua-style revelry on Friday and Saturday.

Kafka (6a Av Norte 40) This expat haven, named enigmatically after the Czech surreal novelist, has an intimate rooftop bar where bonfires blaze nightly. 'Happy Hour' goes till closing time.

Monoloco (5a Av Sur 6, Pasaje El Corregidor) The atmosphere can get pretty rowdy here after hours, with plenty of newcomers filing in. The two-level place (open-air upstairs, with benches and long tables) has scores of TVs tuned to the big game.

El Muro (3a Calle Oriente 19D;   Mon-Sat) 'The Wall' is a friendly neighborhood pub with a range of beers, an eclectic menu of snacks and plenty of sofas to lounge around on. Music, which tends toward '70s and '80s rock (think Pink Floyd), is kept low enough for conversation.

Café No Sé (1 Av Sur 11C) This downbeat little bar is a point of reference for Antigua's budding young Burroughs and Kerouacs. It's also the core of a lively music scene, with players wailing from a corner of the room most evenings.

Reds (1a Calle Poniente 3) Across the way from La Merced, Reds is a low-key clubhouse that draws a refreshingly mixed crowd, often more Guatemalan than gringo. Come here to shoot pool (tourneys on Thursday nights), drink cut-rate mojitos and/or watch sports TV.

JP's Rumbar (7882-4244; 7a Calle Poniente;   Thu-Tue) Hailing from New Orleans, JP serves great gumbo alongside the rum, plus a heaping helping of second-line jazz and blues. The cream of Antigua's music scene perform here nightly.

ENTERTAINMENT
Discotecas
La Casbah (☎ 7832-2640; 5a Av Norte 30; admission Q30; ☻ 8:30pm-1am Tue-Sat) This two-level disco near the Santa Catalina arch has a warm atmosphere, is reportedly gay-friendly and quite a party most nights.

La Sin Ventura (5a Av Sur 8; ☻ Tue-Sat) The liveliest dance floor in town is packed with Guatemalan youth toward the weekend. There's live salsa and merengue on Thursday nights.

Arts & Concerts
Proyecto Cultural El Sitio (☎ 7832-3037; www.elsitio cultural.org; 5a Calle Poniente 15) This arts center has lots going on, from concerts and plays (some in English) to photo exhibits, music workshops and film screenings. Stop by to check the schedule.

La Sala (6a Calle Poniente 9; ☻ Tue-Sun) Crowds pour into this boisterous hall, with murals of frenetic dancers, for live rock, blues or reggae – or maybe it's the cheap liquor. Bands hit the stage nightly around 9pm.

Cinema & TV
Cine Lounge La Sin Ventura (☎ 7832-0581; 5a Av Sur 8; snacks Q20-30; ☻ noon-8:30pm Tue-Sat) Antigua's only proper cinema projects videos of recent Hollywood (not dubbed) and Spanish-language releases on a big screen all day long, with nightclub-style seating. The movies are free; just pay for food and drinks. To see what's playing, check the board outside.

Proyecto Cultural El Sitio (☎ 7832-3037; www.elsitio cultural.org; 5a Calle Poniente 15) Shows arthouse and documentary films on Wednesday and Thursday.

Bagel Barn (5a Calle Poniente 2) Projects videos of Hollywood and Spanish-language films every evening from around 5pm.

For North American and European sports on TV, check the programs posted at **Café 2000** (6a Av Norte 2), **Reds** (1a Calle Poniente 3) and **Monoloco** (5a Av Sur 6, Pasaje El Corregidor).

SHOPPING
Nim Po't (www.nimpot.com; 5a Av Norte 29) This shop boasts a huge collection of Maya dress, as well as hundreds of masks and other wood carvings. This sprawling space is packed with *huipiles* (long embroidered tunics), *cortes* (wraparound skirts), *fajas* (waist sashes) and more, all arranged according to region, so it makes for a fascinating visit whether you're in the market or not.

Casa del Tejido Antiguo (1a Calle Poniente 51; admission Q5; ☻ 9am-5:30pm Mon-Sat) Claiming to be the only place in Antigua managed by indigenous people, this is another intriguing place for textiles; it's like a museum, market and workshop rolled into one, with exhibits on regional outfits and daily demonstrations of backstrap weaving techniques.

Mercado de Artesanías (Handicrafts Market; 4a Calle Poniente; ☻ 8am-8pm) At the west end of town by the main market, this market sells masses of Guatemalan handicrafts – mostly not top quality but with plenty of colorful variety in masks, blankets, jewelry, purses and so on. Don't be afraid to bargain.

GETTING THERE & AROUND
Bus
Buses to Guatemala City, Ciudad Vieja and San Miguel Dueñas arrive and depart from a street just south of the market. Buses to Chimaltenango, Escuintla, San Antonio Aguas Calientes and Santa María de Jesús go from the street outside the west side of the market. If you're heading out to local villages, it's best to go early in the morning and return by mid-afternoon, as bus services drop off dramatically as evening approaches.

To reach highland towns such as Chichicastenango, Quetzaltenango, Huehuetenango or Panajachel (except for the one direct daily bus to Panajachel), take one of the frequent buses to Chimaltenango, on the Interamericana Hwy, and catch an onward bus from there. Making connections in Chimaltenango is easy, as many friendly folks will jump to your aid as you alight from one bus looking for another.

Chimaltenango (Q5; 45min; 19km; every 15min 6am-6pm)

Escuintla (Q8; 1hr; 39km; every half hour 5am-4pm)

Guatemala City (Q8; 1hr; 45km; every few minutes 5am-6:30pm); Litegua (☎ 7832-9850; www.litegua.com /litegua; 4a Calle Oriente 48) Offers Pullman service (Q40) from its office at the east end of town at 10am and 4pm.

Panajachel (Q36; 2½hr; 146km; 1 Pullman bus daily at 7am by Transportes Rebulli) Departs from Panadería Colombia on 4a Calle Poniente, half a block east of the market.

Shuttle Minibus

Numerous travel agencies (see p103) offer frequent and convenient shuttle services to places such as Guatemala City, Aeropuerto Internacional La Aurora, Panajachel and Chichicastenango. They also go less frequently (usually on weekends) to places further afield, including Río Dulce, Copán Ruinas (Honduras) and Monterrico. These services cost a lot more than ordinary buses (for example, around Q80 to Guatemala City, as opposed to Q8 on a chicken bus), but they are comfortable and convenient, with door-to-door service at both ends.

Taxi & Tuk-Tuk

Taxis and tuk-tuks wait where the Guatemala City buses stop and on the east side of Parque Central. An in-town taxi ride costs around Q25; tuk-tuks are Q10. Note that tuk-tuks are not allowed in the center of town; you'll have to hike a few blocks out to find one.

THE HIGHLANDS – LAGO DE ATITLÁN

Guatemala's most dramatic region – the highlands – stretch from Antigua to the Mexican border northwest of Huehuetenango. Here the verdant hills sport emerald-green grass, cornfields and towering stands of pine, and every town and village has a story.

The traditional values and customs of Guatemala's indigenous peoples are strongest in the highlands. Maya dialects are the first language, Spanish a distant second. The age-old culture based on maize (from which the Maya believe that humans were created) is still alive; a sturdy cottage set in the midst of a thriving *milpa* (cornfield) is a common sight. And on every road you'll see men, women and children carrying burdens of *leña* (firewood), to be used for heating and cooking.

The poster child for Guatemala's natural beauty, the volcano-ringed Lago de Atitlán, has been attracting tourists for decades. Surrounded by small villages, the lake deals with its popularity well, although a major bacteria outbreak in late 2009 alerted inhabitants to the perils of rapid growth (see p117). The only place that feels really played out is Panajachel – the other villages maintain a

---

EXPLORE MORE AROUND ANTIGUA

There's enough in Antigua to keep you going for weeks, but the surrounding countryside has its attractions, too.

- **Earth Lodge** (☎ 5664-0713; www.earthlodgeguatemala.com; dm Q35, cabin s/d/tr Q90/140/165) Set on a 16-hectare avocado farm in the hills above Jocotenango, the Earth Lodge is fast becoming a backpacker must-do. See the website for transportation details.

- **San Lorenzo El Tejar** Worth the 25-minute ride northwest to soak in its popular hot springs.

- **Pastores** This is ground zero for leatherwork and the the place to come for handmade cowboy boots and stock whips.

- **Cerro Alux** (www.cerroalux.com) Near the village of San Lucas Sacatepéquez is this hilltop ecopark with interpretive trails and good bird-watching opportunities.

---

quiet air, while offering a reasonable degree of comfort.

DANGERS & ANNOYANCES

Although most visitors never experience any trouble, there have been incidents of robbery and worse in the highlands. The most frequent sites for robberies are unfortunately some of the most beautiful – the paths that run around Lago de Atitlán. The security situation is forever changing here – some months it's OK to walk between certain villages, then that route suddenly becomes dangerous.

If you do plan to go walking, use common sense – don't take any more money than you need, or anything that you really don't want to lose. Walk in groups of at least six, and (one piece of local advice) consider taking a machete along (for deterrent purposes only, naturally). If you do run into trouble, don't resist – chances are your life is worth more than your camera.

GETTING THERE & AROUND
The Highlands

The curvy Interamericana Hwy, also known as Centroamérica 1 (CA-1), passes through the highlands on its way between Guatemala

City and the Mexican border at La Mesilla. Driving the 266km between Guatemala City and Huehuetenango can take five hours, but the scenery is beautiful. The lower Carretera al Pacífico (Hwy CA-2), via Escuintla and Retalhuleu, is straighter and faster; it's the better route if you're trying to reach Mexico as quickly as possible.

The Interamericana is thick with bus traffic. As most places you'll want to reach are off the Interamericana, you may find yourself waiting at junctions such as Los Encuentros and Cuatro Caminos to connect with a bus or pick-up. Travel is easiest on market days and in the morning. By mid or late afternoon, buses may be scarce, and short-distance local traffic stops by dinnertime. On remote routes,

you'll probably be relying more on pick-ups than buses for transportation.

Lago de Atitlán

Following the Interamericana 32km west from Chimaltenango, you'll reach the turnoff for the back road to Lago de Atitlán via Patzicía and Patzún. The area around these two towns has been notable for bandit activity in the past (as has the other back road, which runs from Cocales on the CA-2 to San Lucas Tolimán), so stay on the Interamericana to Tecpán, the starting point for a visit to the ruined Kaqchiquel capital of Iximché (*eesh-im-chay*; see p123).

Another 40km west along the Interamericana from Tecpán is the Los Encuentros

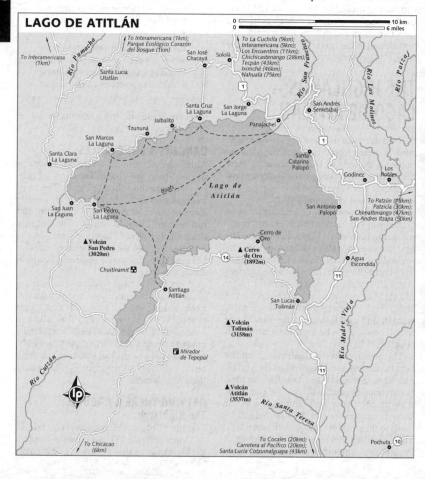

LAGO DE ATITLÁN

0 — 10 km
0 — 6 miles

To Interamericana (1km);
Parque Ecológico Corazón
del Bosque (1km)

To La Cuchilla (9km);
Interamericana (9km);
Los Encuentros (11km);
Chichicastenango (28km);
Tecpán (43km);
Iximché (46km);
Nahualá (75km)

San José Chacayá
Solalá

To Interamericana
(1km)

Río Pamacha

Santa Lucía
Utatlán

Santa Cruz
La Laguna

San Jorge
La Laguna

San Andrés
Semetabaj

Río San Francisco

Río Los Molinos

Río Patzaj

Jaibalito

Tzununá

Panajachel

San Marcos
La Laguna

Santa Clara
La Laguna

Boats

*Lago de
Atitlán*

Santa
Catarina
Palopó

Godínez

Los
Robles

San Juan
La Laguna

San Pedro
La Laguna

San Antonio
Palopó

To Patzún (18km);
Patzicía (30km);
Chimaltenango (47km);
San Andrés Itzapa (50km)

▲ Volcán
San Pedro
(3020m)

Chuitinamit

Cerro de
Oro

▲ Cerro
de Oro
(1892m)

Agua
Escondida

Santiago
Atitlán

San Lucas
Tolimán

Río Madre Vieja

▲ Volcán
Tolimán
(3158m)

Mirador
de Tepepul

Río Cutzán

▲ Volcán
Atitlán
(3537m)

Río Santa Teresa

To Chicacao
(6km)

To Cocales (20km);
Carretera al Pacífico (20km);
Santa Lucía Cotzumalguapa (43km)

Pochuta

junction. It's a new town serving people waiting to catch buses. The road to the right heads north to Chichicastenango and Santa Cruz del Quiché. From the Interamericana a road to the left descends 12km to Sololá and another 8km to Panajachel, on the shores of Lago de Atitlán.

If you are not on a direct bus, you can get off at Los Encuentros and catch another bus or minibus, or flag a pick-up, from here down to Panajachel or up to Chichicastenango; it's a half-hour ride to either place.

The road from Sololá descends through pine forests, losing more than 500m in elevation on its 8km course to Panajachel. Sit on the right for breathtaking views of the lake and volcanoes.

PANAJACHEL
pop 19,900 / elev 1595m

The busiest and most built-up lakeside settlement, Panajachel ('Pana' to pretty much the entire country) has developed haphazardly and, some say, in a less than beautiful way. Several different cultures mingle on Panajachel's dusty streets.

Ladinos and gringos control the tourist industry. The Kaqchiquel and Tz'utujil Maya from surrounding villages come to sell their handicrafts to tourists. Tour groups descend on the town by bus for a few hours or overnight.

Its excellent transportation connections and thumping nightlife make it a favorite for weekending Guatemalans. During the week, things quiet down, but the main street, Calle Santander, remains the same – internet cafe after handicrafts store after restaurant after travel agent, but you need only go down to the lakeshore to understand why Pana attracts so many visitors.

Information

BOOKSTORES
Bus Stop Books (Centro Comercial El Dorado, Calle Principal; ◷ 8am-1:30pm Wed-Mon, 8am-6pm Tue) A good selection of mainly used books to swap and buy and a small selection of guidebooks.

Gallery Bookstore (Comercial El Pueblito, Av Los Árboles) Sells and exchanges used books, and sells a few new ones, including some Lonely Planet guides.

Libros del Lago (Calle Santander) Has an excellent stock of books, including Latin American literature in English and other languages on Guatemala, the Maya and Mesoamerica, plus maps and guidebooks.

EMERGENCY
Asistur (☎ 5874-9450; Edificio Las Manos, Av El Tzalá, Barrio Jucanyá)

Disetur (Tourist police; ☎ 5531-3982; Playa Pública) The station is in a small building near the Santiago boat dock.

INTERNET ACCESS
Standard rates are Q5 to Q10 an hour; typical hours are 9am to 10pm daily, perhaps shorter on Sunday.

EVIL BLOOM

In late 2009 during an unusually warm spell, a massive bloom of cyanobacteria covered the turquoise waters of Lago de Atitlán with malodorous sheets of brownish sludge. Cyanobacteria occurs naturally in oceans and lakes, but the ecological imbalance of Lago de Atitlán following decades of unchecked development created the conditions for their proliferation.

The primary cause was increased nutrients, provided by agrochemicals from surrounding communities, which flow into the lake as runoff with the rains. Bacteria gobble these phosphorous-rich chemicals up like Pac-Men and as temperatures rose, the organisms bloomed and died, leaving thick mats of smelly crud.

The news hit tourism operators hard, but more gravely threatened the surrounding communities, for whom the lake has traditionally been a source of water, food and income. Within a month, the blight had receded and the lake returned to its usual pristine state, raising hopes that this was just a cyclical phenomenon. Whether the cyanobacteria caused permanent damage is uncertain. No dead fish were found, and initial tests by UC Davis found the bloom did not pose health risks, though they advised continuous monitoring of lake-fish quality.

People were back swimming and diving within a few months, which by all accounts is safe to do. Still, the blight was viewed as a symptom of an ailing ecosystem. The federal government pledged funding for proper sewage treatment facilities, and some of the more progressive tourism providers banded together to implement their own anti-phosphate campaign. For more information on their efforts, see www.savelakeatitlan.blogspot.com and www.lakeatitlanhealth.com.

Get Guated Out (Comercial El Pueblito, Av Los Árboles)
Standard internet operation.
Multiservicios J&M (Calle Rancho Grande)

LAUNDRY

Lavandería Il Bucato (Centro Comercial El Dorado, Calle
Principal; ☺ 9am-6:30pm Mon-Sat) Costs Q30 for up to
5 pounds.

MEDICAL SERVICES

The nearest hospital is at Sololá.
Centro de Salud (☎ 7762-1158; Calle Principal;
☺ 8am-6pm Mon-Fri, 8am-1pm Sat) Medical clinic.

MONEY

Banco Agromercantil (cnr Calles Principal & Santander;
☺ 9am-6pm Mon-Sat, 9am-1pm Sun) For traveler's checks.

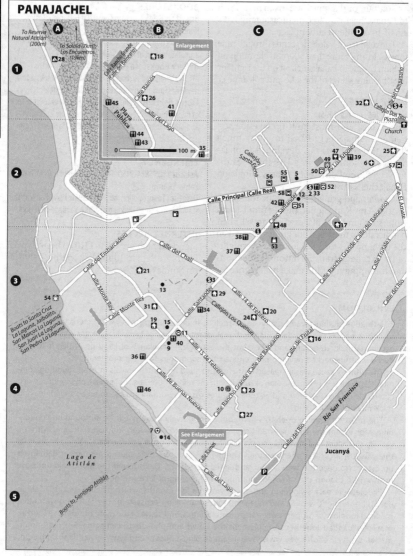

Banco Industrial (Comercial Los Pinos, Calle Santander; 9am-4pm Mon-Fri, 9am-1pm Sat) Visa-card advances.

Banrural (Calle del Campanario; 9am-5pm Mon-Fri, 9am-1pm Sat) Changes traveler's checks.

POST

Post office (cnr Calle Santander & Calle 15 de Febrero) About 200m from the lake.

Realworld Export (☎ 5634-5699; Centro Comercial San Rafael, Calle Santander) Courier service that arranges bulk shipments from multiple handicrafts buyers to reduce charges, an economical solution for shipment of larger items.

TELEPHONE

Some cybercafes and travel agencies located on Calle Santander offer moderately cheap phone

GUATEMALA

To San Lucas Tolimán (24km)

Market

Town Hall

Calle de la Navidad

Av El Tzalá

Calle El Amate

To Santa Catarina Palopó (4km); San Antonio Palopó (9km); Ixímché (40km)

INFORMATION		
Asistur	1	F2
Banco Agromercantil	2	D2
Banco Industrial	3	C3
Banrural	4	D1
Bus Stop Books	(see 5)	
Centro Comercial El Dorado	5	C2
Centro de Salud	6	D2
Disetur	7	B4
Gallery Bookstore	(see 39)	
Get Guated Out	(see 39)	
Inguat	8	C3
Lavandería Il Bucato	(see 5)	
Libros del Lago	9	B4
Multiservicios J&M	10	C4
Post Office	11	B3
Realworld Export	(see 8)	

SIGHTS & ACTIVITIES		
Jabel Tinamit	12	C2
Jardín de América	13	B3
Kayak Rentals	14	B4
Realworld Paragliding	(see 8)	
Roger's Tours	15	B3

SLEEPING		
Apartamentos Sulita	16	D4
Casa Linda	17	D2
Casa Loma	18	B1
Hospedaje El Viajero	19	B3
Hospedaje García	20	C3
Hospedaje Santo Domingo	21	B3
Hotel El Sol	22	F4
Hotel Jere	23	C4
Hotel Larry's Place	24	C3
Hotel Maya-Kanek	25	D2
Hotel Posada Viñas del Lago	26	B1
Hotel Tzutujil	27	C4
Hotel Visión Azul	28	A1
Mario's Rooms	29	C3
Posada Los Encuentros	30	E3
Posada Monte Rosa	31	B3
Villa Lupita	32	D1

EATING		
Atlantis	33	D2
Cafe Bombay	34	B3
Cook Shacks	35	B2
Deli Jasmín	36	B4
Deli Llama de Fuego	37	C3
El Patio	38	C3
Guajimbo's	(see 37)	
La Rostícería	39	D2
Las Pitayas	40	B4
Los Pumpos	41	B1
Pana Pan	42	C2
Restaurante Catamarán	43	B2
Restaurante Chichoy	44	B2
Restaurante Taly	45	B1
Sunset Café	46	B4

DRINKING		
Pana Lounge	47	D2
Pana Rock Café	48	C2
Solomon's Porch	(see 5)	

ENTERTAINMENT		
Chapiteau	49	D2
El Aleph	50	D2
La Terraza	51	C2
Rumba	52	D2

SHOPPING		
Comerciales de Artesanías Típicas Tinamit Maya	53	C3

TRANSPORT		
Embarcadero Tzanjuyú	54	A3
Main Bus Stop	55	C2
Microbuses y Taxis San Francisco Booth	56	C2
Pick-ups to Santa Catarina Palopó & San Antonio Palopó	57	D2
Rébuli	58	C2

calls – around Q2/3.50 a minute to call a land-line/cell phone in North America or Central America, and Q3/4.50 a minute to Europe.

TOURIST INFORMATION

Inguat (☎ 7762-1106; info-panajachel@inguat.gob.gt; Centro Comercial San Rafael Local 11, Calle Santander; ☒ 9am-1pm & 2-5pm) This tourist office is on the main street. There are a few brochures available and staff can answer straightforward questions.

Sights & Activities

The **Reserva Natural Atitlán** (☎ 7762-2565; www.atitlan reserva.com; adult/child Q45/25; ☒ 8am-5pm) is down the spur leading to Hotel Atitlán and makes a good day trip. The well-designed nature reserve has trails, an interpretive center, zip lines, camping, a butterfly farm, small shade coffee plantation, lots of monkeys and an avi-ary. For longer stays, there are some excellent rooms with private decks, and camping.

Lago de Atitlán offers phenomenal **hiking** and **cycling**. You can walk from Panajachel to Santa Catarina Palopó in about an hour, continuing to San Antonio Palopó in about another hour; it takes only half as long by bicycle, on hilly roads. Or take a bike by boat to Santiago Atitlán, San Pedro La Laguna or another village to start a tour of the lake. Several places along Calle Santander rent bicycles. **Roger's Tours** (☎ 7762-6060; www.rogerstours.com; Calle Santander) rents quality mountain bikes for Q40/250 per hour/day and leads a variety of cycling tours (Q415 to Q500 including helmet, guide and lunch).

Paragliding is Atitlán's latest growth indus-try – in Pana you can hook with the highly recommended **Realworld Paragliding** (☎ 5634-5699; realworldparagliding@gmail.com; Centro Comercial San Rafael, Calle Santander), who charges Q665 per flight, which takes 20 minutes to an hour, depending on wind conditions and passenger preferences.

Kayaks are available for rent (Q30 per hour) from the pier at the foot of Calle del Rancho Grande.

Visitors short on time should consider a **boat tour** around the lake. Boats leave the Playa Pública quay daily at 8:30am and 9:30am for tours to San Pedro La Laguna (where you stop for about 1½ hours), Santiago Atitlán (1½ hours) and San Antonio Palopó (one hour). Both return at 3:30pm. Cost is Q100 for either tour. Travel agencies along Calle Santander offer more expensive tours (around Q540 per person), which may include weaving demon-strations, visits to the shrine of Maximón in Santiago Atitlán (see p126), and so on.

Courses

Panajachel has a niche in the language-school scene. Two well-run schools are **Jardín de América** (☎/fax 7762-2637; www.jardindeamerica.com; Calle del Chalí) and **Jabel Tinamit** (☎ 7762-6056; www.jabeltinamit.com; Callejón Las Armonías). Both have ample gardens and good atmosphere. Four hours of one-on-one study five days per week, including a homestay with a local family, will cost around Q1400 per week. The latter institute also offers courses in Kaqchiquel and Maya weaving.

Festivals & Events

The festival of **San Francisco de Asís**, held on October 4, is celebrated with massive drink-ing and fireworks.

Sleeping

Budget travelers here will rejoice at the profu-sion of family-run *hospedajes* (guesthouses). They're simple – perhaps two rough beds, a small table and a light bulb in a bare boarding room – but cheap. Most provide clean toilets and some have hot showers. More expensive hotels offer generous discounts for longer stays.

Hotel Visión Azul (☎ 5759-7321; eugestra@yahoo.com; Finca San Buenaventura; campsite per person Q35; ☎ ☒) This semi-secluded location just out-side town is the best camping option around. Set amid well-tended, lakefront gardens. Campers have access to sheltered grilling areas, hot showers and kayaks. Rooms with private terraces are available.

Hotel El Sol (☎ 7762-6090; www.panamuraoka.com; Carretera a Santa Catarina Palopó; dm Q50, s/d/tr Q150/200/250; ☒ ☎) Along the road to Santa Catarina, this modern, Japanese-owned hos-tel offers an eight-bed dorm and five private rooms. Good sushi and a Japanese tub fed by natural hot springs add to the appeal.

Hospedaje El Viajero (☎ 7762-0128; s/d Q60/100) El Viajero is at the end of a short lane off lower Calle Santander, making a peaceful yet central location. There's nothing fancy here, but the rooms are spacious and bright and there's plenty of balcony seating. You can use a cooker, microwave and fridge, and there's laundry service and free drinking water.

Villa Lupita (☎ 5054-2447; Callejón Don Tino; s/d Q60/120, without bathroom Q40/70) Family-run Lupita is great value for staying in the town center. Facing a plaza below the church, it's removed from the tourist drag. Accommodations are basic but clean and a flower-filled patio softens the environment.

Hospedaje García (☎ 7762-2187; Calle 14 de Febrero; s/d Q80/150, without bathroom Q50/80) The best of the rooms here are actually the cheaper ones – they're about twice the size of the others and have balconies looking out onto the patio.

Hotel Maya-Kanek (☎ 7762-1104; Calle Principal; s/d Q75/130; P) Bare-bones basic (but comfortable) rooms line a cobbled courtyard with flitting hummingbirds and fanciful skeleton-shaped benches.

Hotel Jere (☎ 7762-2781; www.hoteljere.com; Calle Rancho Grande; s/d Q80/100; P 💻) The Jere's big, tasteful rooms are another class act in this part of town. Everything is enlivened by textiles, photos, maps and informative posters, and you can book shuttle buses and lake tours on the spot.

Mario's Rooms (☎ 7762-2370; www.mariosrooms.com. gt; Calle Santander; s/d Q90/160, without bathroom Q60/110; 💻) A long-time favorite with return visitors, Mario's smallish rooms are arranged on two floors facing a plant-filled courtyard, and have blasting-hot showers.

Hotel Larry's Place (☎ 7762-0767; Calle 14 de Febrero; s/d Q100/150; P) Set back from the road behind a wall of vegetation, Larry's Place offers good-sized, cool rooms in a sylvan setting. Furnishings are tasteful and the balconies welcome, though they lack views.

Hotel Tzutujil (☎ 7762-0102; www.panajachel.com/tzu tujil.htm; Calle Rancho Grande; s/d Q100/200, without bathroom Q60/120) Down a narrow alley through cornfields, the Tzutujil is a solitary structure with balconies, arched windows and a spiral staircase to a roof terrace. On the downside, the boxy rooms are of a low-budget standard, with lumpy beds and dodgy electric showers behind a partition.

Posada Los Encuentros (☎ 7762-1603; www.los encuentros.com; Callejón Chotzar 0-41; s/d Q249/332, with kitchen Q415/498) Just across the river is this 'ecocultural B&B,' featuring seven cozy rooms in a relaxed home, plus a volcanically heated pool, medicinal plant garden, sunning terrace and fitness center.

Pana offers up plenty more cheap sleeps:

Hospedaje Santo Domingo (off Calle Monte Rey; s/d Q20/30, with bathroom Q50/70) The cheapest rooms are basic wood-plank affairs, but there are better shared-bathroom doubles in a newer, two-story block. Lovely grassy patio. No phone.

Casa Linda (☎ 7762-0386; Callejón El Capulin; s/d Q100/130, without bathroom Q49/98) Spotless little rooms

around a tranquil garden at this establishment. Get one upstairs for a breezy balcony.

Hotel Posada Viñas del Lago (☎ 7762-0389; www. hotelvinasdelago.com; Playa Pública; s/d Q100/150; P) This garishly painted hotel, just steps from the lakefront, offers basic rooms with great views (the best are units 21 to 23).

Casa Loma (☎ 7762-1447; Calle Rancho Grande; s/d Q100/150, without bathroom Q50/100) Basic wood-plank rooms and a sweet grassy lawn area.

Posada Monte Rosa (☎ 7762-0055; Calle Monte Rey; s/d Q100/150) Well-decorated, good-sized rooms. No phone reservations.

Apartamentos Sulita (☎ 4055-7939; Calle del Frutal 3-42; cabins per week Q1040) Cute little one- or two-person cabins with kitchen, lounge, bathroom and one bedroom.

Eating

The cheapest places to eat are by the beach at the mouth of the Río San Francisco. The cook shacks on the shore have rock-bottom prices, as do the food stalls around the parking lot. Across the street, you can fill up for Q30 at any of several little restaurants, all of which offer priceless lake views. Taco and fried-chicken stalls also proliferate along Calle Santander every afternoon and evening. You might try the appropriately named Humo en Tus Ojos, last spotted near the intersection of Calle Principal and Calle Santander; this is where the cops eat.

For food shopping, there's the Despensa Familiar, at the north end of Calle El Amate.

Pana Pan (Calle Santander 1-61; pastries Q7; ☺ breakfast & lunch) Cinnamon rolls, banana and chocolate muffins, and whole-wheat bread make a call here obligatory. Take away or sit down with a coffee.

La Rostería (Av Los Árboles; mains Q25-40; ☺ 8am-10pm Mon-Sat) Run by a cheerful Canadian dude, 'the rotisserie' specializes in spit-roasted chicken, served at a street-side terrace. A quarter chicken, fries and coleslaw will set you back Q25.

Deli Jasmín (Calle Santander; items Q25-45; ☺ 7am-6pm Wed-Mon) This tranquil garden restaurant serves a range of healthy foods and drinks to the strains of soft classical music. Breakfast is served all day, and you can buy whole-wheat or pita bread, hummus or mango chutney to take away.

Atlantis (Calle Principal; mains Q40-60; ☺ breakfast, lunch & dinner) This cafe-bar serves excellent submarines (Q35) alongside more-substantial meals. The back garden is the place to be on a balmy night.

Guajimbo's (Calle Santander; mains Q40-70; ☺ breakfast, lunch & dinner) This Uruguayan grill is one of Pana's best eateries, serving generous meat and chicken dishes with vegetables, salad, garlic bread and rice or boiled potatoes. You won't leave hungry. There are vegetarian dishes too, good-value breakfasts, and bottomless cups of coffee.

Café Bombay (Calle Santander; mains Q45; 🕙 11am-9pm Wed-Mon; **V**) This cozy joint plays up the international angle, with creative vegetarian dishes from 14 countries: everything from spinach lasagna to miso to curries, and there's even a veggie version of that Guatemalan classic *pepián* (served with veggies, rice and *chuchito*).

Sunset Café (cnr Calle Santander & Calle del Lago; mains Q50-65; 🕙 lunch & dinner) This open-air eatery at the lake end of Calle Santander has great vistas and serves meat, fish and vegetarian dishes. With a bar and live music nightly, it's the place to enjoy those phantasmagoric volcano sundowns.

If you're looking for cheap with a view, check out the touristy restaurants crowding the east end of Calle del Lago, such as Restaurante Taly, Restaurante Catamarán or Restaurante Chichoy, all with decks overlooking the lake. Los Pumpos, up at street level, reportedly has the best quality and variety. All the beach restaurants serve seafood and *caldo de mariscos* (shellfish stew), though lake fish has not been served since an outbreak of bacteria in late 2009 (see boxed text, p117).

More good, cheap eats along Calle Santander? No problem:

Las Pitayas (Calle Santander) Freshly squeezed fruit juices and *licuados* (fruit shakes), including the refreshing *panatonic* (lemon juice, ginger and mint). For food, it's got panini and wraps.

Deli Llama de Fuego (Calle Santander; items Q25-45; 🕙 7am-10pm Thu-Tue) The same excellent menu as Deli Jasmín, served under a *llama de fuego* (African tulip) tree.

El Patio (Plaza Los Patios, Calle Santander; mains Q35; 🕙 breakfast, lunch & dinner) Popular with locals for lunch. Try to make it on a Monday for the *caldo de res* (a broth with large chunks of meat and veggies), served with all the trimmings.

Drinking

Pana Rock Café (☎ 7762-2194; Calle Santander) This is a good place to start, continue or finish your night's imbibing, with a seemingly endless happy hour. The classic rock may not be to your liking, but two mixed drinks for Q25 is hard to argue with.

Pana Lounge (Av Los Árboles) The action at this low-lit bar revolves around the pool table (Q40 per hour) and the beer (Q40 per *cubetazo*, ie bucket of five bottles).

Solomon's Porch (Calle Principal; 🕙 lunch & dinner) The balcony overlooking Calle Santander is a great place for a few drinks, accompanied by big-screen TV, wireless internet and live music.

Entertainment

If salsa's your thing, drop by restaurant **La Terraza** (Edificio Rincón Sai, Calle Santander), a haven for salsaphiles, especially on Friday and Saturday nights when guest instructors conduct workshops. Classes are Q100 per hour (half that for long-termers).

Chapiteau (Av Los Árboles; admission from Q20) If you've got your dancing legs on, check out this strobe-lit disco-bar in the middle of Pana's Zona Viva (nightlife zone).

El Aleph (Av Los Árboles) DJs keep the multitudes moving with a spirited mix of reggaetón, merengue, electronica and salsa. Beer is cheapest by the bucket (aka *cubetazo*).

Rumba (Calle Principal) Opposite the start of Av Los Árboles, Rumba is a large disco-bar playing thumping Latin pop, popular with the Guatemalan teens and 20-somethings who descend on Pana during weekends and vacations.

Shopping

Stores and stalls along Pana's Calle Santander have some of the best prices for souvenirs in the country. Freelance vendors and artisans also set up tables or blankets, especially on weekends. Booths also adorn the beach end of Calle Rancho Grande.

Comerciales de Artesanías Típicas Tinamit Maya (🕙 7am-7pm) One of Guatemala's most extensive handicrafts markets, this market sells traditional clothing, jade, leather items, wood carvings and more. You can get good deals if you're patient and bargain.

Getting There & Away
BOAT

Passenger boats for Santiago Atitlán (35 minutes) depart from the Playa Pública (public beach) at the foot of Calle Rancho Grande. All other departures leave from the Embarcadero Tzanjuyú, at the foot of Calle del Embarcadero. Frequent canopied *lanchas* go counterclockwise around the lake, stopping in Santa Cruz La Laguna (15 minutes), Jaibalito, Tzununá, San Marcos La Laguna (30 minutes), San Juan La Laguna and San Pedro La Laguna (45 minutes). The last boat departs around 7:30pm. To the villages along the lake's eastern shore, there are no public boat services; take a bus or pick-up instead (see below).

One-way passage anywhere on Lago de Atitlán costs Q20, though local inhabitants are charged much less. Some travelers get indignant about this two-tiered system, but it's been institutionalized and complaints generally fall on deaf ears. Ignore all middlemen and negotiate the fare directly with the captain.

BUS

The town's main bus stop is where Calle Santander and Calle Real meet, across from the Banco Agromercantil. Rébuli buses depart from the Rébuli office on Calle Real. For most destinations further afield, it's best to catch one of the many buses to Los Encuentros and find a connection there. To get to Santa Catarina Palopó, get a pick-up (Q3, 20 minutes) at the corner of Calles Principal and El Amate.

The table, p124, lists direct departures from the main bus stop. These are all chicken buses, although there is some Pullman leaving at 11am daily for Antigua (Q35, 2½ hours), continuing on to Guatemala City (Q35, 3½ hours).

SHUTTLE MINIBUS

Tourist shuttle buses take half the time of buses, for several times the price. You can book at any of the travel agencies on Calle Santander. The **Microbuses y Taxis San Francisco booth** (☎ 7762-0556; www.mitasfa.com; Calle Principal) also sells shuttle-bus seats. Despite advertised lists of departures, real shuttle schedules

GUATEMALA

SIDE TRIPS FROM PANA

Sololá

Nine steep kilometers uphill from Panajachel, Sololá's Friday **market** – a local, rather than a tourist, affair – is one of the highlands' best. The plaza next to the cathedral comes ablaze with the colorful costumes from a dozen surrounding villages, and neatly arranged displays of meat, vegetables, fruit, housewares and clothing occupy every available space.

Every Sunday morning the **cofradías** (Maya religious brotherhoods) parade ceremoniously to the cathedral for their devotions. On other days, Sololá sleeps.

Santa Catarina Palopó

Four winding kilometers east of Panajachel lies Santa Catarina Palopó. Here, narrow streets paved in stone blocks run past adobe houses with roofs of thatch or corrugated tin, and the gleaming white church commands your attention. It's interesting to imagine that this is what all the lakeside villages would once have been like. If you really like it here, there are simple, inexpensive places to stay and eat. Most people drop in for the day, particularly looking to buy one of the luminescent indigo *huipiles* (long embroidered tunics) you see around Lago de Atitlán.

San Antonio Palopó

Continuing past Santa Catarina for 5km gets you to San Antonio Palopó, a larger but similar village where men and women in traditional clothing tend their terraced fields and clean mountains of scallions by the lakeshore. The **Hotel Terrazas del Lago** (☎ 7762-0157; www.hotelterrazasdellago.com; s/d Q180/240; 🛜) is an attractive hotel with some great views.

Iximché

Off the Interamericana near the small town of Tecpán lie the ruins of **Iximché** (admission Q50; 🕙 8am-4:30pm), capital of the Kaqchiquel Maya. Set on a flat promontory surrounded by cliffs, Iximché (*eesh*-im-chay; founded in the late 15th century) was easily defended against attack by the hostile K'iche' (Quiché) Maya. They had no such luck against the Spanish.

Entering the archaeological site, visit the museum (closed Monday) on the right, then continue to the four ceremonial plazas, which are surrounded by temple structures up to 10m high, and ball courts. Some structures have been uncovered: the original plaster coating is still in place on a few.

Any bus traveling on the Interamericana can drop you at the turnoff for Tecpán, from which it's about a 1km walk (or, if you're lucky, a short ride on an urban bus) to the center of town (Tecpán). 'Ruinas' microbuses to the site (Q2.50, 10 minutes) leave hourly from the plaza.

GUATEMALA

BUSES FROM PANAJACHEL

Destination	Cost (Q)	Duration	Departures	Frequency
Chichicastenango	20	1½hr	7am-3pm	5 daily
Cocales	15	2½hr	6:30am-5pm	4 daily
Guatemala City	25	3½hr	5am-1pm	6 daily
Los Encuentros	5	35min	6am-7pm	frequent
Quetzaltenango	30	2½hr	7am-2pm	3 daily
San Lucas Tolimán	10	1hr	5:30pm	1 daily
Sololá	3	15min	6am-7pm	frequent

depend on how many customers there are, so try to establish a firm departure time before parting with money. Typical fares: Antigua (Q125), Chichicastenango (Q58), Guatemala City (Q183), San Cristóbal de Las Casas (Mexico; Q332) and Quetzaltenango (Q166).

SANTIAGO ATITLÁN

South across the lake from Panajachel, on the shore of a lagoon squeezed between the volcanoes of Tolimán and San Pedro, lies Santiago Atitlán, known to everybody as Santiago. It's the most workaday of the lake villages, home to Maximón (mah-shee-*mohn;* see boxed text, p126), who is paraded around during Semana Santa – a good excuse to head this way during Easter. The rest of the year, Maximón resides with a caretaker, receiving offerings. He changes house every year, but he's easy enough to find by asking around. If that's too much work, local children will take you to see him for a small tip.

Although the most visited village outside Panajachel, Santiago clings to the traditional lifestyle and clothing of the Tz'utujil Maya. The best days to visit are Friday and Sunday, the main market days, but any day will do.

Walking to and from San Pedro La Laguna is not recommended, unless the security situation improves, since this remote route has a robbery risk.

Orientation & Information

The street straight ahead from the dock leads up to the town center. Every tourist walks up and down this street, so it's lined with craft shops and art galleries.

There's a Cajero 5B ATM at Banrural, a block west of the plaza.

You'll find a lot of fascinating information about Santiago at www.santiagoatitlan.com (in English).

Sights

At the top of the slope is the main square, flanked by the town office and a huge centuries-old **church**. Within are wooden statues of the saints, each of whom gets new handmade clothes every year.

On the carved pulpit, note the figures of corn (from which humans were formed, according to Maya religion), as well as a literate quetzal bird and Yum-Kax, the Maya god of corn. A similar carving is on the back of the priest's chair.

A memorial plaque at the back commemorates Father Stanley Francis Rother, a missionary priest from Oklahoma; beloved by the local people, he was murdered in the church by ultraright-wing death squads in 1981.

During the civil war, Santiago became the first village in the country to succeed in expelling the army, following a notorious massacre of 13 villagers on December 2, 1990. The site of this massacre, where troops were encamped, is now the **Parque de Paz** (Peace Park), about 500m beyond Posada de Santiago.

There are many rewarding **day hikes** around Santiago. Unfortunately, owing to the security situation, it's highly advisable to go with a guide – ask in your hotel for a reputable one. You can climb any of the three **volcanoes**, the **Mirador de Tepepul** (a lookout), about 4km south of Santiago, or the **Cerro de Oro**, some 8km northeast. Guides for all the above hikes charge around Q200 per person.

The **Cojolya Association of Maya Women Weavers** (☎ 7721-7268; www.cojolya.org) has a small museum of backstrap loom weaving. Demonstrations are offered and there's a small shop.

Aventura en Atitlán (☎ 5811-5516; wildwestgua@yahoo.com) offers well-recommended **horseback rides** to the Mirador de Tepepul and elsewhere, for Q450 to Q620. Most rides include a gourmet meal. It does guided hikes, too.

Sleeping & Eating

Hotel Tzanjuya (☎ 5590-7980; s/d Q55/100) Up the hill on the main street, this modern tiled hotel is reasonable value. You get a choice of lake or volcano views. It is prohibited, as signs point out, to spit on the walls here.

Hotel Lago de Atitlán (☎ 7721-7174; r Q75-85) Go four blocks uphill from the dock then turn left to this hotel, whose reception is in the hardware store next door. It's a modern five-story building (rather an anomaly in this little town). Rooms are bland but mostly bright, many having large windows with decent views. Go up on the rooftop for great sunsets.

Posada de Santiago (☎ 7721-7366; www.posadadesantiago.com; cottages d/tr Q540/623, ste from Q705, s/d Q249/374; P □ ☎) Striking a balance between rustic charm and luxury, the long-standing *posada* (guesthouse or country-style inn) makes a nice retreat. Seven cottages and three suites are set around gardens stretching up from the lake. Some less expensive rooms are in a two-story building. The restaurant serves delicious, natural fare. The *posada* is 1.5km from the dock. Catch a tuk-tuk (Q5) or hire a *lancha* over to the hotel dock (Q70).

Restaurante El Gran Sol (mains Q35-40) Two blocks up from the dock on the left, this family-run establishment is a good bet for breakfast, lunch or snacks, with a spiffy kitchen and lovely thatched-roof terrace. The Mexican-born proprietor loves to cook – ask her to make one of her specials.

There are plenty of cheap *comedores* above the market next to the plaza.

Getting There & Away

Boats leave regularly from Santiago's main dock for Panajachel (Q20, 35 minutes) and San Pedro La Laguna (Q25, 45 minutes).

Buses to Guatemala City (Q40, 3½ hours) leave from the main square regularly from 3am to 3pm.

SAN PEDRO LA LAGUNA
pop 10,000

It all comes down to what you're looking for – price wars between competing businesses keep San Pedro among the cheapest of the lakeside villages, and the beautiful setting attracts long-term visitors whose interests include (in no particular order): drinking, fire twirling, African drumming, Spanish classes, volcano hiking and hammock swinging.

While this scene unfolds at the lakefront, up the hill San Pedro follows more traditional rhythms. Clad in indigenous outfits, the predominantly indigenous *pedranos* (as the locals are called) congregate around the market zone. You'll see coffee being picked on the volcano's slopes and spread out to dry on wide platforms at the beginning of the dry season.

Orientation & Information

San Pedro has two docks. The one on the south side of town serves boats going to and from Santiago Atitlán. Another dock, around on the east side of town, serves boats going to and from Pana. At either, walk uphill to reach the center of town. Alternatively, from the Santiago dock, you can take your first right and follow the path for about 15 minutes to the other side of town. Along this path is where a lot of the tourist-oriented businesses start up. To take this route coming from the Panajachel dock, take your first left and then a right down the lane that runs beside a store called Las Estrellitas.

There's a 5B ATM just up from the Panajachel dock on the left. You can exchange US dollars and traveler's checks at **Banrural** (☽ 8:30am-5pm Mon-Fri, 9am-1pm Sat) in the town center. It also has a MasterCard ATM. There's internet access at D'Noz, Casa Verde Internet and the Internet Café, just up the street from the Panajachel dock. The typical access rate is around Q8 per hour. Call North America/Europe for Q2/4 at Casa Verde Tours, or use Skype at any of the above internet cafes.

Zuyuva (☽ noon-4pm Thu-Mon) is a secondhand bookstore with a decent selection of fiction and Guatemala titles. An alley opposite the Museo Tz'unun Ya' leads there.

Sights & Activities

Looming above the village, **Volcán San Pedro** (3020m) almost asks to be climbed by anyone with a bit of energy and adventurous spirit. The volcano has recently been placed within an ecological park to minimize environmental damage caused by hikers and also improve the security situation, which wasn't great before. **Excursion Big Foot** (☎ 7721-8203; 7a Av, Zona 2), 50m to the left at the first crossroads up from the Panajachel dock, has a track record of responsibility and departs at 3am when there are at least six people (Q100 each).

Another popular hike goes up the hill to the west of the village that is referred to as **Indian Nose** – its skyline resembles the profile

GUATEMALA

THAT'S ONE SMOKIN' GOD

The Spanish called him San Simón, the *ladinos* (persons of mixed indigenous and European race) named him Maximón and the Maya know him as Rilaj Maam (ree-lah-*mahm*). By any name, he's a deity revered throughout the Guatemalan highlands. Assumed to be a combination of Maya gods, Pedro de Alvarado (the Spanish conquistador of Guatemala) and the biblical Judas, San Simón is an effigy to which Guatemalans of every stripe go to make offerings and ask for blessings. The effigy is usually housed by a member of a *cofradía* (Maya religious brotherhood), moving from one place to another from year to year, a custom anthropologists believe was established to maintain the local balance of power. The name, shape and ceremonies associated with this deity vary from town to town, but a visit will be memorable no matter where you encounter him. For a small fee, photography is usually permitted, and offerings of cigarettes, liquor or candles are always appreciated.

In Santiago Atitlán, Maximón is a wooden figure draped in colorful silk scarves and smoking a fat cigar. Locals guard and worship him, singing and managing the offerings made to him (including your Q10 entry fee). His favorite gifts are Payaso cigarettes and Venado rum, but he often has to settle for the cheaper firewater Quetzalteca Especial. Fruits and gaudy, flashing electric lights decorate his chamber; effigies of Jesus Christ and Christian saints lie or stand either side of Maximón and his guardians. Fires may be burning in the courtyard outside as offerings are made to him.

In Nahualá, between Los Encuentros and Quetzaltenango, the Maximón effigy is à la Picasso: a simple wooden box with a cigarette protruding from it. Still, the same offerings are made and the same sort of blessings asked for. In Zunil, near Quetzaltenango, the deity is called San Simón but is similar to Santiago's Maximón in custom and form.

San Jorge La Laguna on Lago de Atitlán is a very spiritual place for the highland Maya; here they worship Rilaj Maam. It is possible that the first effigy was made near here, carved from the *palo de pito* tree that spoke to the ancient shamans and told them to preserve their culture, language and traditions by carving Rilaj Maam (*palo de pito* flowers can be smoked to induce hallucinations). The effigy in San Jorge looks like a joker, with an absurdly long tongue.

In San Andrés Itzapa near Antigua, Rilaj Maam has a permanent home, and is brought out on October 28 and paraded about in an unparalleled pagan festival. This is an all-night, hedonistic party where dancers grab the staff of Rilaj Maam to harness his power and receive magical visions. San Andrés is less than 10km south of Chimaltenango, so you can easily make the party from Antigua.

---

of an ancient Maya dignitary. **Asoantur** (☎ 4379-4545), an association made up of 25 Tz'utujil guides from the local community, will lead a minimum of two people up there for around Q150 per person. It also offers cultural tours of San Pedro and nearby coffee plantations, horseback-riding tours, and kayak, bicycle and motorbike rentals. It operates from a hut on the lane up from the Pana dock.

Once you've watched the sunset, one of the best places to be is soaking in the solar-heated tubs at **Los Termales** (8:30am-11:55pm; Q35 per person), down a small path next to the Buddha Bar. Book ahead so it has a pool already hot when you arrive.

If you're wary of the lake water quality, have a swim at **La Piscina** (adult/child Q20/10; 11am-dusk Tue-Sun;), 50m up from the Santiago dock, a global gathering place that revolves around a pool. Weekends are busiest with barbecues and Bocce ball.

Several **walks** between San Pedro and neighboring villages make terrific day trips, although armed muggings on the lonely roads between villages are not uncommon. See the warning on p115. You can walk west to San Juan La Laguna (30 minutes), San Pablo La Laguna (1½ hours), San Marcos La Laguna (three hours), Jaibalito (five hours) and finally, Santa Cruz (all day). From the last three you can easily hail a *lancha* back to San Pedro until around 3pm.

Kayaks are available for hire (Q15 per hour), turning right from the Pana dock.

Hatha yoga sessions (Q30) are held Monday to Saturday at 9am in a circular garden along the path below the Buddha Bar.

Courses
LANGUAGE

The standard price for four hours of one-on-one Spanish-language classes, five days a week, is Q550 to Q600. Accommodations with a local family, with three meals daily (except Sunday) typically costs Q500. Schools can also organize other sleeping options.

Cooperativa Spanish School (☎ 5398-6448; www. cooperativeschoolsanpedro.com) Run as a cooperative (therefore guaranteeing fair wages for teachers); a percentage of profits goes to needy families around the lake. After-school activities include videos, conferences, salsa classes, volunteer work, kayaking and hiking. This school comes highly recommended. The office is halfway along the path between the two docks.

Escuela Mayab (☎ 5098-1295; franciscopuac@yahoo. com) Down a laneway coming off the street between the two docks, this well-organized school holds classes under shelters in artistically designed gardens. Activities include videos, kayaking and horse treks, though tuition is cheaper without these things. Escuela Mayab is associated with a medical clinic in Chirijox and can organize volunteer work for doctors, nurses and assistants.

OTHER COURSES

Pick up a brush at **Chi Ya'a** (☎ 5636-0176; www. chiyaa.weebly.com; per hr Q30), where local artist Gaspar shows how to create oil paintings in the Maya bird's-eye view and from-behind styles. The studio is at the waterfront just below Los Thermales.

Grupo Ecológico Teixchel (☎ 5932-0000; teixchel@ gmail.com 🕒 8:30-noon & 2-6pm) is a Tz'utujil women's collective that sells fair-trade woven goods and offers weaving classes for Q25 per hour (not including materials).

Sleeping

NEAR THE PANA DOCK

Hospedaje Xocomil (☎ 5598-4546; s/d Q40/80, without bathroom Q25/50) Up the lane to the right about 50m past Hotel Gran Sueño, this family-run place is in the basic backpacker category, but the staff are kind and there's a kitchen for guests' use.

our pick Hotel Gran Sueño (☎ 7721-8110; 8a Calle 4-40 Zona 2; s/d Q75/125) Beyond a plant-draped entryway and up a spiral staircase are bright rooms with colorful abstract designs and more style than elsewhere. Rooms 9 and 11 are fantastic lake-view perches. The hotel is up the street to the left of Hotel Mansión del Lago.

Hotel Mansión del Lago (☎ 7721-8124; www. hotelmansiondellago.com; 3a Vía & 4a Av, Zona 2; s/d/tr Q75/150/225) Straight up from the Pana dock is this concrete monster. Large rooms are done up in a cloud motif, with wide balconies looking right at the Indian's Nose.

Hotel Nahual Maya (☎ 7721-8158; 6 Av 8 C-12; r Q100; P) The forest of rooftop rebar somewhat mars the Mediterranean villa motif, but the rooms are sparkling clean and homey and have little balconies with hammocks out front.

BETWEEN THE DOCKS

Zoola (☎ 5847-4857; http://zoolapeople.com; dm Q30, s/d Q60/100, without bathroom Q40/70) 'Laid-back' is the operable phrase at this Israeli-run establishment, a place to crash after a Middle Eastern feast at the adjoining restaurant. Reached down a long, jungly boardwalk opposite the Museo Tz'unun Ya,' it features eight brightly colored rooms around a peaceful garden. There's a two-night minimum stay.

Hotelito El Amanecer Sak'cari (☎ 7721-8096; www. hotelsakcari.com; 7a Av 2-12, Zona 2; s/d Q160/260; P 🛜) On the left just after Cooperativa Spanish School, the efficient Sak'cari has clean, tangerine-colored rooms with lots of shelves and wood paneling. Rooms at the rear are best, with big balconies overlooking a vast landscaped lawn.

Hotel Mikaso (☎ 5973-3129; www.mikasohotel.com; 4a Callejon A-88; d/tr/ste Q374/457/580) The only real upmarket hotel in San Pedro, this prominent tower stands proudly by the lakefront. Big, colonially furnished rooms cooled by ceiling fans ring a garden bursting with birds-of-paradise. The rooftop bar/Spanish restaurant boasts fantastic lake views (see p128).

NEAR THE SANTIAGO DOCK

Hotel Peneleu (☎ 5925-0583; 5a Av 2-20, Zona 2; s/d Q35/50, without bathroom Q15/30) It doesn't look like much from the outside, but once you get past the dirt yard, you'll find a clean, modern hotel with some of the best budget rooms in town. Try to get No 1 or 2, which are up top, with big windows overlooking the lake. To find it, go 80m up Calle Principal from Hotel Villasol, then along the street to the left.

Hotel Villa Cuba (☎ 7959-5044; www.hotelvillacuba. com; Camino a la Finca, Zona 4; s/d Q60/120) A large, modern hotel on grounds that sweep down to the lake. The seven rooms are well furnished, swimming is good here, and it's only a tuk-tuk away from the bar and restaurant scene. To find it, take the first road to the left up from the dock and continue for 2km.

Eating

Prices are low in San Pedro La Laguna, but if you're hurting, there are a bunch of *comedores* up the hill in the main part of town.

NEAR THE PANA DOCK

There are plenty of places to get your grub around the Pana dock.

Shanti Shanti (8a Calle 3-93; mains Q20-25; ☺ breakfast, lunch & dinner) With terraced seating cascading down to the lakeside, this makes a pleasant perch for hippie staples like falafel, curried veggies and hearty soups.

Alegre Pub (8a Calle 4-10; mains Q30-60; ☺ breakfast, lunch & dinner) Near the Pana dock, the Alegre is always, well, *alegre* (happy), with a real British pub feel – drinks specials, a Sunday roast and trivia nights. There are free movies twice a week in the way laid-back rooftop garden and loads of free, reliable tourist info. The big breakfast fry-up will make Brits weep with homesickness.

D'Noz (☎ 5578-0201; 4a Av 8-18; mains Q36-45; ☺ breakfast, lunch & dinner) Another popular hangout, D'Noz, right up from the Pana dock, is San Pedro's closest thing to a cultural center, with free movies, a big bar and a lending library. The menu spans the globe from Asian fusion to French quiche to Tecpán sausage.

BETWEEN THE DOCKS

ourpick Café La Puerta (☎ 4050-0500; mains Q25-35; ☺ breakfast & lunch) It's not just the lakefront setting (just below Hotel Mikaso) that makes this such an appealing spot for breakfast and bird-watching, but also the abundant, natural fare. For lunch, they feature Mexican burritos, tacos and quesadillas.

Buddha (☎ 4178-7979; 2a Av 2-24; mains Q35-40; ☺ lunch & dinner, closed Tue) The Eastern-inspired Buddha can be enjoyed on various levels – downstairs there's a pool table and boisterous bar, upstairs a restaurant doing convincing versions of Thai, Indian and other Asian dishes, and up top a thatched-roof lounge for hookah smoking.

Ventana Blue (mains Q35-46; ☺ dinner Wed-Sun) There are just four tables at this cozy bistro at a bend in the path between the docks. Created by Santa Cruz La Laguna native Santos Canel, the brief but exciting menu features an array of Asian and Guatemalan dishes, from Thai coconut curries to *jocón* (chicken and vegetables in a cilantro sauce).

Mikaso (4a Callejon A 1-88; mains Q60-Q85; ☺ breakfast, lunch & dinner) This rooftop restaurant specializes in Iberian fare, with a nice range of Spanish *bocadillos* (appetizers) on freshly baked baguettes. If you want the paella, the chef needs 24 hours' notice.

Drinking & Entertainment

El Barrio (7a Av 2-07, Zona 2; ☺ 5pm-1am) This cozy little bar on the path between the two docks has one of the most happening happy hours in town, with food till midnight and drinks till 1am. There's a good cocktail and snacks list and a couple of chilled-out outside areas.

Alegre Lounge (8a Calle 4-10) Has a range of ridiculously cheap drinks specials, plus sports, movies and Wii competitions on the big screen.

Freedom Bar (8a Calle 3-95, Zona 2; ☺ to 1am) The hardest-partying bar in town, the Freedom has good lounging areas, a pool table, a (relatively) huge dance floor and often hosts guest DJs on weekends. It's on the first street to your right coming up from the Pana dock.

While many *pedranos* spend their evenings shouting the lord's praises at evangelical congregations, visitors go to the movies. At the Panajachel dock, D'Noz and the Alegre Lounge show films most nights, as does Buddha between the docks, and Mikaso hosts its own little *cinema paradiso* Wednesday (English) and Sunday (Spanish) nights at 8pm.

Getting There & Away

From the rest of the lake, it's easiest to reach San Pedro by passenger boats. If you're headed toward Quetzaltenango there are buses (Q35, three hours) from San Pedro's Catholic church, up in the town center, at 5am, 5:30am and 8am. There are also buses to Guatemala City, but it's quicker to catch a boat to Panajachel, then a bus from there.

Travel agents around the Pana dock offer daily shuttles to Antigua (Q83), Guatemala City (Q166), Monterrico (Q166) and San Cristóbal de las Casas (Mexico; Q249), among other places.

SAN MARCOS LA LAGUNA
pop 3000

Without any doubt this is the prettiest of the lakeside villages. The flat shoreline here has paths snaking though banana and coffee plantations, and avocado trees. The town has become something of a magnet for hippies-with-a-purpose, who believe the place has a particular spiritual energy, and is an excellent place to learn or practice meditation, holistic therapies, massage, Reiki and other spiritually oriented activities.

Whatever you're into, it's definitely a great place to kick back and distance the everyday world for a spell. Lago de Atitlán is beautiful and clean here, with several little docks you can swim from.

There's a community information board in front of the San Marcos Holistic Center with postings on events and housing options. You'll find plenty of useful information and web links at www.atitlanresource.com. Get online at **Prolink** (9am-7pm Mon-Sat, 10am-5pm Sun; per hr Q12), across from the Paco Real hotel.

Activities & Courses

Guy (☎ 5854-5365), at Restaurante Tul y Sol along the lakefront trail, offers paragliding rides (Q665) in the mornings from Santa Clara La Laguna down to San Juan. It's an exhilarating ride offering some great photo opportunities.

The town's greatest claim to fame is **Las Pirámides Meditation Center** (☎ 5205-7151; www.laspiramidesdelka.com), on the path heading inland from Posada Schumann. Every structure on the property is built in a pyramid shape and oriented to the four cardinal points. Among the many physical (eg yoga, massage) and metaphysical (eg tarot readings, channeling) offerings is a one-month lunar meditation course that begins every full moon and cov-ers the four elements of human development (physical, mental, emotional and spiritual). Most sessions are held in English. The last week of the course requires fasting and si-lence by participants. Nonguests can come for meditation or hatha yoga sessions (Q30) Monday to Saturday.

Accommodations in pyramid-shaped houses are available for Q150 per day and are only offered to people interested in joining the course. This includes the meditation course, use of the sauna and access to a fascinating multilingual library. A restaurant serves veg-etarian fare. The best chance to get a space is just prior to the full moon. Las Pirámides has a private dock; all the *lancheros* know it and can drop you here.

The best swimming is off the rocks, west of the village. From Aaculaax (see p130) follow the trail down to the rocky outcrop and make your way to the best dive perch. (Locals advise you to have someone watch your things while you're swimming).

Sleeping

Hotel El Unicornio (http://hotelunicorniosm.8m.com; s/d incl breakfast Q50/100) A favorite with the budget-con-scious, El Unicornio has eight rooms in small, thatched-roof A-frame bungalows among verdant gardens, sharing hot-water showers, nice hangout areas, a sauna and an equipped kitchen. To get here turn left past Hotel La Paz,

---

EXPLORE MORE OF LAGO DE ATITLÁN

Crowds of tourists getting to you? The lake still has a few untouched corners that are well worth checking out:

- **Jaibalito** Accessible only by boat or on foot, this little village between San Marcos and Santa Cruz hosts one of the country's most magical hotels, **La Casa del Mundo** (☎ 5218-5332; www.lacasadelmundo.com; r with/without bathroom Q550/288), with gorgeous gardens, swimming holes and a hot tub overhanging the lake. There's great food on offer and the nearby **Club Ven Acá** (pasta Q40, mains Q80), a bit to the east, which also offers a fusion menu (Q20), purple-basil mojitos, hot tub and infinity pool.

- **San Juan La Laguna** A 10-minute tuk-tuk ride (and another world away) from San Pedro, this little village is definitely still keeping it real, but with enough comforts for your average traveler, like a couple of good budget hotels, some good places to eat, a weaving cooperative or two and even a couple of Spanish schools.

- **Parque Ecológico Corazón del Bosque** This community-run **ecopark** (☎ 7723-4140; www.corazondelbosque.com; Km 145 Carretera Interamericana; adult/child Q5/3; 8am-6pm), 45 minutes from Panajachel, offers great bird-watching and hiking on 45 hectares of land covering the highest point in the surrounding countryside. Good meals and simple cabins are on offer. Microbuses, every half hour from Sololá to Novillero (Q6), can drop you at the entrance; or take any bus plying the Interamericana between Los Encuentros (Q5, 15 minutes) and Quetzaltenango.

or walk along the lakeside path and turn right after Las Pirámides Meditation Center.

Hotel La Paz (☎ 5702-9168; lapazcolection@hotmail.com; r per person Q50-60) Along a side path off the track behind Posada Schumann, the mellow La Paz has rambling grounds holding two doubles and five dormitory-style rooms. All are in bungalows of traditional *bajareque* with thatched roofs, and some have loft beds. The organic gardens and vegetarian restaurant, traditional Maya sauna and morning yoga sessions (Q30) are additional attractions.

Aaculaax (☎ 5287-0521; www.aaculaax.com; r Q100-395, ste from Q700) An artful, atmospheric hotel that looks like it grew out of the rock by itself, this place is constructed using recycled materials, such as old bottles. Each room is unique, and most have good lake views. There's a bar-chill-out area on the top floor with board games and comfy seating.

Posada del Bosque Encantado (☎ 5208-5334; www.hotelposadaencantado.com; s/d Q120/160) Set in jungle-like grounds that could well be an enchanted forest, the rooms here strike a good balance between rustic and stylish. Each room has a loft with a double bed and another bed downstairs. Walls are mud brick, beds are big and firm, and there are hammocks strewn around the place.

Eating & Drinking

A couple of *comedores* around the plaza sell tasty, good-value Guatemalan standards.

Comedor Susy (Parque Central; set lunch Q30; ☺ breakfast, lunch & dinner) AKA Comedor Mi Marquensita, this 'mom and pop' store on the central plaza is where many expats go for a cheap, home-cooked meal, which might explain why tofu dishes pop up among the chicken and pork chops.

Moonfish (mains Q25-40; ☺ 7am-6pm Wed-Mon; Ⓥ) After a morning dive off the rocks, stroll up the path to Moonfish with a lakeside terrace. Hippie-friendly fare includes tempeh sandwiches, tofu scrambles, and fresh salads with ingredients from the adjacent garden.

Restaurante Fe (mains Q80; ☺ breakfast, lunch & dinner) This recently inaugurated restaurant, a short walk toward the lake from the Paco Real, features a sophisticated Asian-influenced menu, with exotic items like banana-smoked chicken on creamed cabbage and Caesar salad garnished with eel. The thatched-roof bar makes a nice perch, especially to marimba accompaniment on Sundays.

Blind Lemon's (www.blindlemons.com; mains Q35; ☺ lunch & dinner; ☎) Named after one of owner Carlos' blues heroes, this hangout in a colonial-style mansion brings the Mississippi Delta to Atitlán, with weekly blues jams by Carlos and special guests. The menu features chicken platters, Cajun-blackened fish, pizza, burgers and other gringo comfort food. It's at the top of the western path.

Getting There & Away

The last dependable boat back to Jaibalito, Santa Cruz and Panajachel usually goes about 5pm.

A paved road runs east from San Marcos to Tzununá and west to San Pablo La Laguna and Santa Clara La Laguna, until it meets the road running from the Interamericana to San Pedro. You can travel between San Marcos and San Pedro by pick-up, with a transfer at San Pablo.

SANTA CRUZ LA LAGUNA
pop 5680

For all practical purposes this place consists of four hotels spread along the lakeside near the dock: it's the earthiest of the lake options, and also the home of the lake's scuba-diving outfit, ATI Divers. The main part of the village is uphill from the dock.

ATI Divers (☎ 5706-4117; www.laiguanaperdida.com/ati_divers.php) offers a four-day PADI open-water diving certification course (Q1835), as well as a PADI high-altitude course and fun dives (Q250/415 for one/two dives) for certified divers, including one in a volcano caldera. The outfit is based at La Iguana Perdida hotel.

Good walks from Santa Cruz include the beautiful lakeside walking track between Santa Cruz and San Marcos (about four hours one way). You can stop for a beer and a meal at La Casa del Mundo en route (see p129). Or you can walk up the hill to Sololá, a 3½-hour walk one way.

Sleeping & Eating

La Iguana Perdida (☎ 5706-4117; www.laiguanaperdida.com; dm Q25-35, r Q240-300, s/d without bathroom Q70/90; ▣) The first place you'll see coming off the dock offers a range of rooms, from primitive (electricity-free dorm in an A-frame cabin) to luxurious (new adobe structure with stylish furnishings, lake-view windows and balconies). Meals are served family-style, with everyone eating together; a three-course dinner is Q50. You always have a vegetarian choice, and everything here is on the honor system: your tab is totaled up when you leave.

Hotel Isla Verde (☎ 5760-2648; www.islaverde atitlan.com; s/d Q332/374, without bathroom Q249/291; 🛜) A 10-minute walk west of the dock along the lakefront trail brings you to this lovely group of cabins dotted around the hillside. Decoration is simple, but pleasing, and the restaurant (featuring jaw-dropping views) serves excellent meals.

Getting There & Away
Boats can stop here coming from either San Pedro or Panajachel. Make sure you tell the captain as you get on, though – it's not a regular stop. If you're going to Hotel Isla Verde, get dropped off at its dock to avoid the walk.

THE HIGHLANDS – QUICHÉ

A largely forgotten little pocket of the country. Most visitors to this region are on a quick in-and-out for the famous market at Chichicastenango. Further to the north is Santa Cruz del Quiché, the departmental capital; on its outskirts lie the ruins of K'umarcaaj (or Gumarcaah), also called Utatlán, the last capital city of the K'iche' (Quiché) Maya. More adventurous souls come for the excellent hiking around Nebaj.

CHICHICASTENANGO
pop 66,000 / elev 2172m

Surrounded by valleys, with nearby mountains looming overhead, Chichicastenango seems isolated in time and space from the rest of Guatemala. When its narrow cobbled streets and red-tiled roofs are enveloped in mists, it's magical.

Chichi is a beautiful, interesting place with shamanistic and ceremonial undertones despite gaggles of camera-toting tour groups. *Masheños* (citizens of Chichicastenango) are famous for their adherence to pre-Christian religious beliefs and ceremonies. You can readily see versions of these old rites in and around the Iglesia de Santo Tomás and at the Pascual Abaj shrine on the outskirts of town.

Chichi has always been an important trading town, and its Sunday and Thursday markets remain fabulous. If you have a choice of days, come on Sunday, when the *cofradías* often hold processions.

History
Once called Chaviar, this was an important Kaqchiquel trading town long before the Spanish conquest. Just prior to the arrival of the conquistadors, the Kaqchiquel and the K'iche' (based at K'umarcaaj near present-day Santa Cruz del Quiché) went to war. The Kaqchiquel abandoned Chaviar and moved to Iximché, which was easier to defend. The conquistadors came and conquered K'umarcaaj, and many of its residents fled to Chaviar, which they renamed Chugüilá (Above the Nettles) and Tziguan Tinamit (Surrounded by Canyons).

These names are still used by the K'iche' Maya, although everyone else calls the place Chichicastenango, a foreign name given by the conquistadors' Mexican allies.

Information
Most banks change US dollars and traveler's checks. Chichi's many banks all stay open on Sunday.

Banco Industrial (🕙 10am-2pm Mon, 10am-5pm Wed & Fri, 9am-5pm Thu & Sun, 10am-3pm Sat) Has a Visa/ MasterCard ATM.

Banrural (5 Av & 5 Calle; 🕙 9am-5pm Sun-Fri, 8am-noon Sat)

Inguat (☎ 7756-2022; 7a Calle 5-43; 🕙 8am-noon daily, plus 2-6pm Mon-Sat) Chichi's Inguat office, on the block east of the plaza, provides information and maps (Q5), plus internet access (Q5 per hour).

MG Internet (5a Av 5-70; per hr Q5) Provides internet facilities upstairs.

Post office (4a Av 6-58) Northwest of the main plaza.

Dangers & Annoyances
Like any small town, Chichi is fairly hassle-free to walk around. Be aware, though, that pickpockets love the jammed streets of market days. Ignore touts offering assistance in finding a hotel: showing up at a hotel with one means you'll be quoted a higher price, as the hotel has to give them a kickback.

Sights & Activities
Make sure you check out the fascinating **mural** that runs alongside the wall of the town hall on the east side of the plaza – it's dedicated to the victims of the civil war and tells the story of the war using symbology from the *Popol Vuh* (a book compiled by members of the Maya nobility soon after the Spanish Conquest).

Inguat-authorized guides in beige vests charge Q50 for a **village tour**, Q100 for a walk to Pascual Abaj.

MARKET
Maya traders from outlying villages come to Chichi on Wednesday and Saturday evenings in preparation for the indigenous market, one of Guatemala's largest. You'll see them carrying bundles of long poles up to the square, then laying down their loads and spreading out blankets to cook dinner and sleep in the arcades surrounding it.

Just after dawn on Sunday and Thursday, the poles are erected into stalls, which are hung with cloth, furnished with tables and piled with goods.

In general, the tourist-oriented stalls sell carved-wood masks, lengths of embroidered cloth and garments; these stalls are around the market's outer edges in the most visible areas. Behind them, the center of the square is devoted to locals' needs.

Most stalls are taken down by late afternoon. Prices are best just before the market breaks up, as traders would rather sell an item cheap than carry it back with them.

Arriving in town the day before the market in order to pin down a room is highly recommended. In this way, too, you'll be able to get up early for the action. Otherwise, you can come by bus, or by market-day shuttle buses which come from Antigua, Panajachel and Guatemala City, returning in early afternoon.

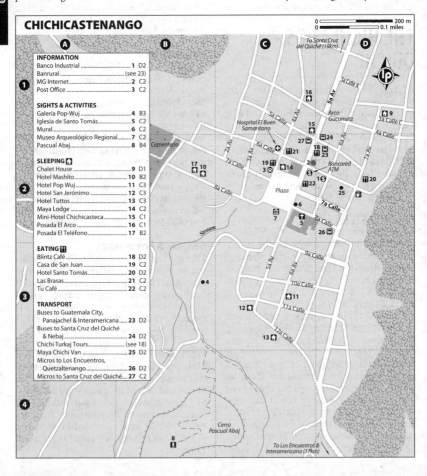

CHICHICASTENANGO

0 ———— 200 m
0 ———— 0.1 miles

INFORMATION
Banco Industrial 1 D2
Banrural .... (see 23)
MG Internet 2 C2
Post Office 3 C2

SIGHTS & ACTIVITIES
Galería Pop-Wuj 4 B3
Iglesia de Santo Tomás 5 C2
Mural 6 C2
Museo Arqueológico Regional 7 C2
Pascual Abaj 8 B4

SLEEPING
Chalet House 9 D1
Hotel Mashito 10 B2
Hotel Pop Wuj 11 C3
Hotel San Jerónimo 12 C3
Hotel Tuttos 13 C3
Maya Lodge 14 C2
Mini-Hotel Chichicasteca 15 C1
Posada El Arco 16 C1
Posada El Teléfono 17 B2

EATING
Blintz Café 18 D2
Casa de San Juan 19 C2
Hotel Santo Tomás 20 D2
Las Brasas 21 C2
Tu Café 22 C2

TRANSPORT
Buses to Guatemala City,
 Panajachel & Interamericana 23 D2
Buses to Santa Cruz del Quiché
 & Nebaj 24 D2
Chichi Turkaj Tours .... (see 18)
Maya Chichi Van 25 D2
Micros to Los Encuentros,
 Quetzaltenango 26 D2
Micros to Santa Cruz del Quiché ... 27 C2

To Santa Cruz
del Quiché (19km)

Hospital El Buen
Samaritano

Cementerio

Arco
Gucumatz

Bancared
ATM

Plaza

Stream

Cerro
Pascual Abaj

To Los Encuentros &
Interamericana (17km)

GUATEMALA

The market starts winding down around 3pm or 4pm.

IGLESIA DE SANTO TOMÁS

Although officially Catholic, this simple **church** (cnr 5a Av & 8a Calle), dating from about 1540, is more often the scene of rituals that are only slightly Catholic and more distinctly Maya. The front steps of the church serve much the same purpose as did the great flights of stairs leading up to Maya pyramids. For much of the day (especially on Sunday), the steps smolder with copal incense, while indigenous prayer leaders called *chuchkajaues* (mother-fathers) swing censers containing *estoraque* (balsam) incense and chant magic words in honor of their ancestors and the ancient Maya calendar.

It's customary for the front steps and door of the church to be used only by important church officials and by the *chuchkajaues,* so you should go around to the right and enter by the side door.

Inside, the floor of the church may be spread with pine boughs and dotted with offerings of corn, flowers and bottles of liquor. The candles and offerings on the floor are in remembrance of the ancestors, many of whom are buried beneath the church floor just as Maya kings were buried beneath pyramids. Photography is not permitted in this church.

MUSEO ARQUEOLÓGICO REGIONAL

In the arcade facing the square's south side is the **Museo Arqueológico Regional** (5a Av 4-47; admission Q5; ☺ 8am-12:30pm & 2-4:30pm Tue-Sat, 8am-2pm Sun), which exhibits ancient clay pots and figurines, flint and obsidian (glass formed by the cooling of molten lava) arrowheads and spearheads, copper ax heads, *metates* (grindstones for maize) and a jade collection.

PASCUAL ABAJ

On the town's outskirts is the Pascual Abaj (Sacrifice Stone), a local shrine to Huyup Tak'ah, the Maya earth god. Said to be hundreds – perhaps thousands – of years old, the stone-faced idol has suffered numerous indignities at the hands of outsiders, but locals still revere it. *Chuchkajaues* come here regularly to offer incense, food, cigarettes, flowers, liquor and Coca-Cola to the earth god. They may even sacrifice a chicken – all to express their thanks and hope for the earth's continuing fertility. The site also offers nice views of the town and valley.

Tourists have been robbed walking to Pascual Abaj – it's best to go in a group or with an Inguat guide. To get there, walk down the hill on 5a Av from the Santo Tomás church, turn right onto 9a Calle and continue downhill along this unpaved road, which bends to the left. At the bottom of the hill, when the road turns sharply right, bear left and follow a path through the cornfields, keeping the stream on your left. Signs mark the way. Walk to the buildings just ahead, which include a farmhouse and a **mask-making workshop**.

Walk through the farm buildings to the hill behind, then follow the switchbacking path to the top and along the ridge. Soon you'll reach a clearing and see the idol in its rocky shrine. The squat stone crosses near it have many levels of significance for the Maya, only one of which pertains to Christ. The area of the shrine is littered with past offerings, and the bark of nearby pines has been stripped away in places to be used as fuel in the incense fires. On the way back to town, you might stop into the **Galería Pop-Wuj** (☎ 7756-1324), a studio/gallery/art institute on the right-hand side.

Festivals & Events

Quema del Diablo (Burning of the Devil; December 7) Residents burn their garbage in the streets to release the evil spirits within. Highlights include a marimba band and a daring fireworks display that has observers running for cover.

Feast of the Immaculate Conception (December 8) Don't miss the early-morning dance of the giant cartoon characters in the plaza.

Feast of Santo Tomás (December 13–21) When pairs of brave (or crazy) men fly about at high speeds suspended from a pole.

Sleeping

As Chichi has few accommodations, arrive early on Wednesday or Saturday if you want to secure a room before market day.

Posada El Teléfono (☎ 7756-1197; 8a Calle A 1-64; s/d Q30/60) Not exactly luxury, but the rooms here are comfortable enough and good value for the price. The view of the town's technicolor cemetery from the rooftop is a draw in itself.

Mini-Hotel Chichicasteca (☎ 7756-2111; 5a Calle 4-42; s/d without bathroom Q40/80) This hotel's adequately clean rooms with bare brick walls are a decent budget choice. It's conveniently located for both the bus stop and plaza.

Hotel Tuttos (☎ 7756-1540; hoteltuttos@yahoo.com; 12a Calle 6-29; dm 50, s/d Q100/200) Up the hill, away from the chaos of the market area, the Tuttos has good-sized, fairly clean rooms. The terrace and rooms out back have great views over the valley and the attached pizzeria comes recommended.

Chalet House (☎ 7756-1360; www.chalethotel guatemala.com; 3a Calle C No 7-44; s/d incl breakfast Q150/200; 🛜) A cozy option with good beds, homey touches and private hot-water bathrooms. Rooms get better the further upstairs you go – ask to see a few.

Posada El Arco (☎ 7756-1255; 4a Calle 4-36; s/d Q150/200) Near the Arco Gucumatz, this is one of Chichi's more original accommodations. Rooms are decorated with Maya weavings, colonial bedsteads and sparkly bathrooms, and the lovely garden has fine mountain views. Reservations recommended.

Maya Lodge (☎ 7756-1167; 6a Calle A 4-08; s/d Q209/259; Ⓟ) Right on the plaza, this has a colonial atmosphere though it's a bit frayed at the edges. Adorned with woven rugs and Maya-style bedspreads, the 10 rooms are set alongside a patio dotted with rosebushes.

Some more options:

Hotel Mashito (☎ 7756-1343; 8a Calle 1-72; s/d Q50/100, without bathroom Q40/80) Plain but comfortable rooms in a big family house.

Hotel San Jerónimo (☎ 7756-1838; Final de 5a Av; Q50/100) Plain but spotless, with firm beds, fine window frames, and lovely balconies in some rooms.

Hotel Pop Wuj (☎ 7756-2014; hotelpopwuj@yahoo. com; 6a Av 10-18; s/d Q100/200, without bathroom Q75/150) Stylish rooms with tile floors and huge, comfy beds. Room rates may be negotiable.

Eating

On Sunday and Thursday, eating at the cook shops in the center of the market is the cheapest way to go. Don't be deterred by the fried-food stalls crowding the fringe – dive into the center for wholesome fare. On other days, look for the little *comedores* near the post office on the road into town.

Tu Café (5a Av; mains Q30-50; 🕒 breakfast, lunch & dinner) The *plato vegetariano* here is soup, rice, beans, cheese, salad and tortillas, for a reasonable Q30. Add *lomito* (a pork fillet) and it becomes a *plato típico*.

Las Brasas (6a Calle 4-52; mains Q45-60; 🕒 breakfast, lunch & dinner) *Parrillas* (grilled meats) are the thing at this semiformal upstairs hall. A gut-stuffing platter of char-grilled sausage, chicken or steak comes with halved potatoes, tortillas, rice, country cheese and black beans.

Casa de San Juan (☎ 7756-2086; 4a Av 5-58; mains Q60; 🕒 breakfast, lunch & dinner) The San Juan is one of the few eateries in town with style – art on the walls and the tables themselves, jugs of lilies, wrought-iron chairs – and its wide-ranging menu is great, too. Balcony tables overlook the market.

Blintz Café (☎ 7755-1672; 5a Calle 5-26; 🕒 7:30am-9:30pm) Yes, you can find decent espresso in Chichi – plus smoothies and a variety of crepes – at this chic locale inside a shopping center above the Hotel Chugüilá.

Hotel Santo Tomás (7a Av 5-32; 3-course dinners Q110; 🕒 breakfast, lunch & dinner) One of Chichi's best-looking hotels features a sumptuous dining room staffed by waiters in colonial farmers' outfits. A marimba band plays at market-day lunchtimes and the evenings before.

Getting There & Away

Buses tend to arrive and depart from the corner of 5a Calle and 5a Av – just listen out for the guys yelling the name of your destination. On market days, however, buses may stop at the corner of 7a Av and 9a Calle, to avoid the congested central streets.

Antigua (3½hr; 108km) Take any bus heading for Guatemala City and change at Chimaltenango.

Guatemala City (Q30; 2½hr; 145km) Every 20 minutes from 3am to 5pm.

Los Encuentros (Q7; 30min; 17km) Take any bus heading south for Guatemala City, Panajachel, Quetzaltenango and so on. Otherwise, frequent microbuses to Los Encuentros (Q5) leave from in front of the Telgua building on 7a Av.

Nebaj (103km) Take a bus to Santa Cruz del Quiché and change there.

Panajachel (Q10; 1½hr; 37km) Buses at 9am, 11:30am, 12:30pm and 1pm; or take any southbound bus and change at Los Encuentros.

Quetzaltenango (Q20; 3hr; 94km) Nine buses between 4:30am and 1pm; or take any southbound bus and change at Los Encuentros. Frequent micros (Q20) pass the Telgua building until 7:30am, then hourly till noon.

Santa Cruz del Quiché (Q7; 30min; 19km) Buses depart every 20 minutes, 5am to 7pm. Micros to Quiché leave from 5a Calle on the west side of 5a Av between 6am and 11pm.

Chichi Turkaj Tours (☎ 7742-1359; 5a Av 5-24), inside the Hotel Chugüilá, and **Maya Chichi Van** (☎ 7756-2187; 6a Calle 6-45) offer shuttles to Guatemala City (Q190), Antigua (Q125), Panajachel (Q140) and Quetzaltenango (Q125) on Monday and Friday at 9am and Sunday and Thursday at 5pm, with a minimum of five passengers.

SANTA CRUZ DEL QUICHÉ

pop 30,050 / elev 1979m

The capital of the Quiché department, Santa Cruz – which is usually called 'El Quiché' or simply 'Quiché' – is 19km north of Chichicastenango. This small, dusty town is quieter and more typical of the Guatemalan countryside than Chichicastenango. Saturday is the main market day, making things slightly more interesting and way more crowded.

Quiché's **tourist office** (☎ 7755-1106; turismoen quiche@gmail.com; ☺ 8am-4:30pm Mon-Fri), inside the town hall, provides good information and a baroquely detailed map. **Banrural** (☺ 8am-5:30pm Mon-Fri, 8am-2pm Sat, 8am-noon Sun), at the plaza's north end, changes euros and has a Cajero 5B ATM. Get online at **Bear Net** (0 Av 7-52; ☺ 8am-8:30pm), 1½ blocks south of the plaza.

The best time to be here is mid-August during the **Fiestas Elenas** (www.fiestaselenas.com), a week of festivities and a proud display of indigenous traditions. It all leads up to the *convite feminino*, when El Quiché's women don masks and dance up a storm to marimba accompaniment.

K'umarcaaj

The **ruins** (admission Q30; ☺ 8am-4:30pm) of the ancient K'iche' Maya capital are 3km west of El Quiché. The kingdom of Quiché was established in late Postclassic times from a mixture of indigenous people and Mexican invaders. Around 1400, King Gucumatz founded his capital here at K'umarcaaj and conquered many neighboring cities. Eventually, the kingdom of Quiché extended its borders to Huehuetenango, Sacapulas, Rabinal and Cobán, even coming to influence the peoples of the Soconusco region in Mexico.

Once Pedro de Alvarado had defeated the K'iche', they invited him to visit their capital, where they secretly planned to kill him. Smelling a rat, Alvarado rallied his allies (including the anti-K'iche' Kaqchiquel), and together they captured the K'iche' leaders, burnt them alive and destroyed K'umarcaaj.

The history is more interesting than the ruined site, of which little remains but a few grass-covered mounds. Still, the site – shaded by tall trees and surrounded by defensive ravines – is a beautiful place for a picnic and is also still used by locals as a religious ritual site.

Gray 'Ruinas' microbuses depart for K'umarcaaj from in front of the cathedral in Santa Cruz every 20 minutes (Q1). The last one back is at 6:50pm.

Sleeping & Eating

The main hotel district is along 1a Av (Zona 5) north of the bus terminal, with at least five hotels within two blocks, and two more on either side along 9a Calle. As always, the area around the market is the prime hunting ground for budget grub.

Posada Santa Cecilia (☎ 5332-8811; 1a Av & 6a Calle; s/d Q75/170) Conveniently placed above an espresso vendor just south of the main plaza, this modern establishment offers a handful of bright, spiffy units with comfy beds and pretty quilts.

Hotel Rey K'iche' (☎ 7755-0827; 8a Calle 0-39, Zona 5; s/d Q100/180; 🖥) Between the bus station and plaza, the Rey K'iche' offers well-maintained, brick-walled rooms around a quiet interior. There's a decent cafe upstairs.

Café San Miguel (2 Av 4-42; sandwiches Q12; ☺ 8am-8pm) Opposite the cathedral, this little bakery-cafe is a popular gathering place, with good coffee and freshly baked goods on offer.

Restaurante El Chalet (2a Av 2-29, Zona 5; mains Q49-60; ☺ breakfast, lunch & dinner) The specialty here is grilled meats, served with homemade salsa. Dining is in pleasant gardens beneath an arbor. It's a few blocks east of the big clock tower.

Getting There & Away

Many buses from Guatemala City to Chichicastenango continue to El Quiché. The last bus from El Quiché heading south to Chichicastenango and Los Encuentros leaves mid-afternoon.

El Quiché is the jumping-off point for the somewhat remote reaches of northern Quiché, which extend all the way to the Mexican border. Departures from the bus station include the following:

Chichicastenango (Q6; 30min; 19km) Frequent microbuses depart from the southwest corner of the main plaza.
Guatemala City (Q30; 3hr; 163km) Buses every 15 minutes, 3am to 5pm.
Huehuetenango (Q25; 2hr; 173km) Microbuses every half hour from 6am to 5:30pm.
Los Encuentros (Q15; 1hr; 36km) Take any bus heading for Guatemala City.
Nebaj (Q25; 2hr; 75km) Five buses via Sacapulas, 8:30am to 5pm. Microbuses run from 5:30am to 8pm.
Sacapulas (Q10; 1hr; 45km) Take any bus or micro bound for Nebaj or Uspantán.

Uspantán (Q25; 2¼hr; 75km) Microbuses every 20 minutes from 6:30am to 8pm.

NEBAJ

pop 35,900 / elev 2000m

Set deep in a bowl in the dramatic, largely untouched Cuchumatanes mountains, Nebaj's foreigner population consists of equal parts hard-core hikers and volunteers who work with the desperately poor communities in the surrounding countryside.

The locals, removed from modern influences, proudly preserve their ancient way of life. They make excellent handicrafts (mostly textiles) and the Nebaj women wear beautiful *huipiles*.

Nebaj's remote location has been a blessing and a curse. The Spaniards found it difficult to conquer and in more recent times, guerrilla forces made the area a base of operations, drawing strong measures from the army to dislodge them – particularly during the short, brutal reign of Ríos Montt. The few surviving inhabitants of these villages either fled across the border into Mexico or were herded into 'strategic hamlets' (settlements constructed to enable the army to keep inhabitants from having contact with the guerrillas). Refugees are still making their way back home here.

Information

The **tourist office** (☎ 7755-8182; ⊗ 8am-5pm Mon-Sat, 8am-noon Sun), inside the Mercado de Artesanías, can answer any question as long as it's posed in Spanish.

Banrural, on the Parque Central, changes traveler's checks; the Cajero 5B ATM is in the town-hall building, opposite the Parque. The **post office** (5a Av 4-37) is one block north of the Parque. **La Red** (El Descanso Bldg, 3a Calle, Zona 1), offers internet access. Otherwise, try **System-IC** (Calz 15 de Septiembre; ⊗ 8am-8pm). Log on to www.nebaj.com for good information on hiking, volunteering, studying, etc in the area.

Festivals & Events

Nebaj's annual **festival**, coinciding with the Assumption of the Virgin Mary, runs for 10 days in mid-August.

Activities

Guias Ixil (☎ 5847-4747; www.nebaj.com; El Descanso Bldg, 3a Calle, Zona 1) offers half-day walks to **Las Cataratas** (Q75 for one person, plus Q25 for each extra person), a series of waterfalls

north of town, or around town with visits to the **sacred sites** of the *costumbristas* (people who still practice non-Christian Maya rites). Guias Ixil also leads three-day treks over the Cuchumatanes to Todos Santos Cuchumatán (see p153) and many others – see the website for details.

Las Cataratas is easy enough to reach on your own: walk 1.25km past the Hotel Ileb'al Tenam along the Chajul road to a bridge over a small river. Immediately before the bridge, turn left (north) onto a gravel road and follow the river. Walking downriver for 6km, you'll pass several small waterfalls before reaching a larger waterfall about 25m high.

The group **Laval Iq'** (☎ 7755-8337; www.region ixil.com; 6a Av & 8a Calle) is comprised of former civil war combatants from 19 Ixil communities. Not only do these guides know the trails better than anyone, they also have lots of tales to tell about the region's turbulent history. They offer various hikes to far-flung corners of the region. Treks of two/three/four days cost Q700/1130/1580 per person, including transportation, meals and lodging at community-run lodges.

If you prefer to hike on your own, take a copy of the *Guía de Senderismo Región Ixil* (Q50), on sale at the Mercado de Artesanías. It has detailed descriptions and maps (in Spanish) for 20 treks in the Ixil region.

Courses

Nebaj Language School (☎ 5311-9100; www.nebaj.com/nebajlanguageschool.html; El Descanso Bldg, 3a Calle, Zona 1) charges Q600 for 20 hours a week of one-to-one Spanish lessons, including some hiking

---

EXPLORE MORE OF QUICHÉ

Nebaj is the jumping-off point for many picturesque hikes around Quiché. Here are just a few options:

▪ **Cocop**, one of the worst hit of all villages in the civil war, is an easy four-hour hike from Nebaj.

▪ Stay in community-run lodges on a three-day loop through **Xeo**, **Cotzal** and **Ak'Txumbal**.

▪ Catch a bus or pick-up to **Salquil Grande**, then take a gorgeous two-hour stroll past waterfalls to the village of **Parramos Grande**.

---

and cultural activities. Homestays, with two meals a day, cost Q500 a week.

Sleeping & Eating

Media Luna Medio Sol (☎ 5749-7450; www.nebaj.com/hostel.htm; 3a Calle 6-15; dm Q35, r per person Q45; ☎) This hostel offers three six-bed dorm rooms and one private room, sharing toilets and showers. There's table tennis, a sauna and kitchen facilities to keep you busy.

Hotel Ileb'al Tenam (☎ 7755-8039; Calz 15 de Septiembre; s/d Q55/95, without bathroom Q30/55; **P**) At the northeast edge of town (500m from the Parque). The hotel features two sections: a long wooden house with simple rooms along a plank veranda; and at the rear, an 'annex' with more modern rooms around a tranquil patio.

Popi's Restaurant (5a Calle 6-74; mains Q22-40; ☺ breakfast, lunch & dinner) This low-key bakery/hostel bakes bread and pies and whips up gringo comfort foods, including three-egg omelets, granola and burritos.

Comedor Dámaris (4a Calle; meals Q30; ☺ lunch & dinner) The set lunch here might be a tasty *caldo de res*, half an avocado, tortillas and a soft drink.

El Descanso (El Descanso Bldg, 3a Calle, Zona 1; mains Q30-50; ☺ breakfast, lunch & dinner) Sharing a property with the Nebaj Language School, this cozy restaurant features a bar, lounge areas and good music in Nebaj's most alternative ambience. It serves a range of snacks, salads and soups.

Shopping

You can buy a huge range of local textiles inside the **Mercado de Artesanías** (cnr 7a Calle & 2a Av, Zona 1).

Getting There & Away

Microbuses bound for Santa Cruz del Quiché, via Sacapulas, go every half hour from 4am until 5pm (Q25, two hours), departing from behind the church at the corner of 5a Av and 7a Calle. To head west to Huehuetenango or east to Cobán, change at Sacapulas. Micros to Cobán depart at 5am and noon from the Quetzal gas station at 15 de Septiembre, but see the warning (see boxed text, p138).

SACAPULAS TO COBÁN

Heading east out of Sacapulas, the road meanders up sadly deforested slopes before reaching the village of **Uspantán**. Rigoberta Menchú, the 1992 Nobel Peace Prize laureate, grew up in the Quiché area, a five-hour walk from Uspantán. Be aware that Menchú and her oft-controversial politics are not universally loved around here.

If you're headed to Cobán by bus (Q30, four hours), you may end up spending the night in Uspantán, as the last minibus leaves town at 4pm. It can get very cold here. **Hotel La Villa Maya** (☎ 5423-4493; 6a Calle 2-17; s/d Q25/50, with bathroom Q55/100; **P**) is a humble, motel-style guesthouse, with clean rooms behind a row of bright-yellow pillars decorated with Maya motifs. **Hotel Posada Doña Leonor** (☎ 7951-8041; 6a Calle 4-25; s/d/tr Q75/130/165; **P** ☎) offers a lot more comfort. Banrural on the plaza changes US dollars.

Along with the Huehue–Sacapulas leg of the same highway, the Uspantán–Cobán road (see East Toward Cobán, p155) is one of the most gorgeous rides in Guatemala. Sit on the left for views, but first read the warning (see boxed text, p138).

WESTERN HIGHLANDS

Dramatic scenery, traditional villages, excellent hiking and the travelers' oasis of Quetzaltenango are what really shine in this region. Roads and buses are some of the worst in the country, making travel tough but rewarding.

For introductory information on the highlands, see p115.

CUATRO CAMINOS

Heading westward from Los Encuentros, the Interamericana Hwy twists and turns ever higher into the mountains, bringing increasingly dramatic scenery and cooler temperatures. After 59km you come to the important highway junction known as Cuatro Caminos (Four Roads), where you can continue north (straight on) to Huehuetenango (77km), turn east to Totonicapán (12km) or turn southwest to Quetzaltenango (13km). A new ring road – constructed but not opened at the time of writing will allow vehicles traveling to Quetzaltenango to bypass this junction.

Buses pass through Cuatro Caminos about every half hour from 6am to 6pm on their way between Quetzaltenango and Totonicapán.

TOTONICAPÁN

pop 94,700 / elev 2500m

San Miguel Totonicapán is a pretty Guatemalan highland town known for its

---

ROAD OUT

Renowned for its incredible views, highway 7W was until recently the most direct route from Huehuetenango to Cobán. But in late 2008, disaster struck when a mountain collapsed atop the road, leaving its east end in shambles.

There's been no official attempt at rebuilding, but locals have carved out a hastily constructed detour that's generally considered unsafe. Buses from Uspantán to Cobán regularly plow through the debris anyway, despite the dangers. By all accounts, it's a hair-raising journey and things worsen when it rains and drivers refuse to risk the gap, making passengers hike through the mud for 2km to continue the journey.

A saner alternative is backtracking via Guatemala City, a loss of about four hours but an infinite gain in peace of mind, or taking the alternative route (see p155).

---

artisans. Shoemakers, weavers, tinsmiths, potters and woodworkers all make and sell their goods here. Market days are Tuesday and Saturday; it's a locals' **market**, not a tourist affair, and it winds down by late morning.

Flanking Totonicapán's 'parque' (as the plaza is called) are the requisite **colonial church** and a wonderful **municipal theater**, built in 1924 in the neoclassical style and restored in recent years.

Sights & Activities

Casa de la Cultura Totonicapense (☎ 5630-0554; kiche78@hotmail.com; 8a Av 2-17; admission free), a short walk from the lower plaza, holds displays on indigenous culture and crafts. It also administers a wonderful 'Meet the Artisans' program that allows tourists to meet artisans and local families, observing how they live, work and play. A one-day program, requiring two weeks' advance booking, includes visits to various craft workshops (including potters, carvers of wooden masks and musical instruments, and weavers), a bit of sightseeing, a marimba concert and a traditional lunch in a private home. Rates are Q475/540/630 per person in groups of four/three/two participants, or 655/770/900 including a stay with a local family and two meals.

An alternative program, costing Q250/288/328 per person for four/three/

two participants, takes you on foot to nearby villages to visit community development projects, natural medicine projects, schools, craft workshops and Maya sacred sites. Tours in English are available on request.

Encompassing some 13 hectares of old-growth forest northeast of Totonicapán, the **Sendero Ecológico El Aprisco** (☎ 7766-2175; admission Q20; ⏰ 8am-4pm) makes for some delightful hiking. Well-marked trails traverse the community-run reserve. Pick-up trucks head this way from the east end of 7a Calle. Alternatively, the Casa de la Cultura Totonicapense can organize trips to the reserve at Q165 per person.

Festivals & Events

Apparition of the Archangel Michael (May 8) Features fireworks and traditional dances.

Feria Titular de San Miguel Arcángel (Name-Day Festival of Archangel St Michael; September 24–30) Peaks on September 29.

Festival Tradicional de Danza (late October – dates vary) Totonicapán keeps traditional masked dances very much alive with this festival.

Sleeping & Eating

The Casa de la Cultura Totonicapense can arrange stays with local families at Q345/410/490 per person in groups of four/three/two, including dinner and breakfast.

Hospedaje Paco Centro (☎ 7766-2810; 3a Calle 8-18, Zona 2; s/d Q35/70) Practically hidden inside a shopping center a couple blocks from the lower plaza, this sternly managed place has big, tidy rooms of three to four beds each.

Hotel Totonicapán (☎ 7766-4458; www.hoteltotonicapan.com; 8a Av 8-15, Zona 4; s/d Q150/275) The fanciest digs in town are reasonable for the price, with big, modern rooms featuring carpeted floors, a few bits of furniture and some good views.

Restaurante Bonanza (7a Calle 7-17, Zona 4; meals Q40-60; ⏰ 7am-9pm; 🛜) Totonicapán's most conventional restaurant is a meat-and-tortillas sort of establishment, where bow-tied staff deliver heaping helpings of steak, chicken and seafood.

Getting There & Away

'Toto' buses from Quetzaltenango depart every 20 minutes or so (Q5, one hour) throughout the day from the Rotonda on Calz Independencia (passing through Cuatro Caminos). The last direct bus to Quetzaltenango leaves Toto at 6:30pm.

QUETZALTENANGO (XELA)

pop 159,700 / elev 2335m

Quetzaltenango – which the locals kindly shorten to Xela (*shell*-ah), itself an abbreviation of the original K'iche' Maya name, Xelajú – may well be the perfect Guatemalan town – not too big, not too small, enough foreigners to support a good range of hotels and restaurants, but not so many that it loses its national flavor. The Guatemalan 'layering' effect is at work in the downtown area here – once the Spanish moved out, the Germans moved in and their architecture gives the zone a somber, some would say Gothic, feel.

Xela attracts a more serious type of traveler – people who really want to learn Spanish, and then stay around and get involved in myriad volunteer projects on offer.

It also functions as a base for a range of spectacular hikes through the surrounding countryside – the constantly active Santiaguito and highest-point-in-Central-America Tajumulco volcanoes, and the picturesque, fascinating three-day trek to Lago de Atitlán to name a few.

History

Quetzaltenango came under the sway of the K'iche' Maya of K'umarcaaj in the 14th century. Before that it had been a Mam Maya town.

With the formation of the Federation of Central America in the mid-19th century, Quetzaltenango initially decided on federation with Chiapas and Mexico, instead of with Central America. Later, the city switched alliances and joined the Central American Federation, becoming an integral part of Guatemala in 1840. The late-19th-century coffee boom augmented Quetzaltenango's wealth. Plantation owners came to buy supplies, and coffee brokers opened warehouses. The city prospered until 1902, when a dual calamity – an earthquake and a volcanic eruption – brought mass destruction.

Still, Xela's position at the intersection of the roads to the Pacific Slope, Mexico and Guatemala City guaranteed it some degree of affluence. Today it's again busy with commerce.

Orientation

The heart of Xela is the Parque Centro América, shaded by old trees, graced with neoclassical monuments and surrounded by the city's important buildings.

The main bus station is Terminal Minerva, on 7a Calle, Zona 3, on the western outskirts and next to one of the city's main markets. First-class bus lines have their own terminals.

Minibuses run between Terminal Minerva and Parque Centro América – listen for helpers yelling 'parque' or 'terminal' respectively.

Information

BOOKSTORES

North & South (Map p142; 8 Calle & 15 Av 13-77, Zona 1) Broad selection of titles on Latin America, politics, poetry and history. Also plenty of new and used guidebooks and Spanish student resources.

Vrisa Books (Map p142; 15a Av 3-64) Excellent range of secondhand books in English and European languages, including Lonely Planet guides; plus a rental library (Q20 per book per week). It also rents out bikes for touring (see p143).

EMERGENCY

Asistur (Tourist Assistance; ☎ 4149-1104)
Policía Municipal (☎ 7761-5805)

INTERNET ACCESS

It only costs Q5 to Q6 per hour to get online here. See the publication *XelaWho* for a wi-fi hot-spot finder.

Café Digital (Map p140; Diagonal 9 19-77A, Zona 1)
Xela Pages (Map p140; 4 Calle 19-48, Zona 1)

INTERNET RESOURCES

Xela Pages (www.xelapages.com) Packed with information about Xela and nearby attractions. Also a useful discussion forum.

LAUNDRY

It costs around Q5 to wash and dry 1kg loads here.

Rapi-Servicio Laundromat (Map p142; 7a Calle 13-25A, Zona 1; ⏰ 8am-6:30pm Mon-Sat)

MEDIA

The following English-language publications are available free in bars, restaurants and cafes around town.

EntreMundos (www.entremundos.org) Published every two months by the Quetzaltenango-based organization of the same name, this newspaper has plenty of information on political developments and volunteer projects in the region.

XelaWho (www.xelawho.com) Billing itself as 'Quetzaltenango's leading Culture & Nightlife Magazine,' this little monthly lists cultural events in the city, with some fairly irreverent takes on life in Guatemala in general.

GUATEMALA

GUATEMALA

QUETZALTENANGO

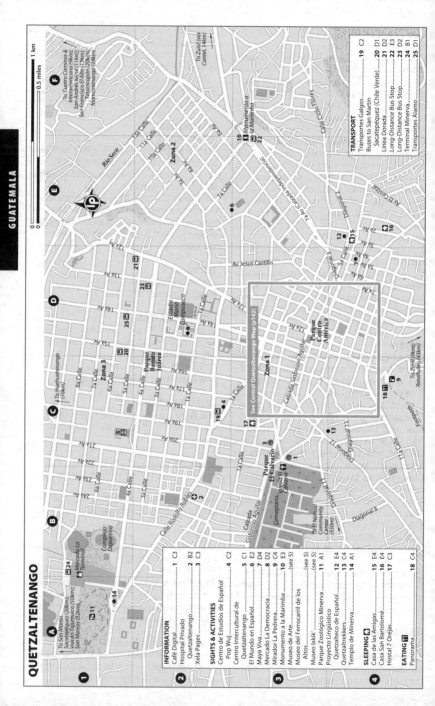

MEDICAL SERVICES
Both of the following hospitals maintain a 24-hour emergency service.

Hospital Privado Quetzaltenango (Map p140; ☎ 7761-4381; Calle Rodolfo Robles 23-51) Usually has an English-speaking doctor on staff.

Hospital San Rafael (Map p142; ☎ 7761-4414; 9a Calle 10-41, Zona 1)

MONEY
Parque Centro América is the place to go for banks. **Banco Industrial** (Map p142; ⊙ 9am-6:30pm Mon-Fri, 9am-1pm Sat) has branches on the north and east sides of the plaza. Both change traveler's checks and give advances on Visa; the latter, in the *municipalidad* (town hall) building, has an ATM on the Plus network. There's a Cajero 5B ATM in the Edificio Rivera just north of the *municipalidad*.

POST
Main post office (Map p142; 4a Calle 15-07, Zona 1) Central location, east of the Telgua office.

TELEPHONE
Café Digital and Xela Pages offer cheap international calls. For local calls, there are four card phones outside **Telgua** (Map p142; cnr 15a Av A & 4a Calle).

TOURIST INFORMATION
Inguat (Map p142; ☎ 7761-4931; ⊙ 9am-5pm Mon-Fri, 9am-1pm Sat), at the southern end of Parque Centro América, is hit or miss, with staff attitudes ranging from helpful to clueless.

There's a plethora of tourist maps circulating; look for them at internet cafes, language schools and hotels. Although they're essentially advertising flyers, the better ones, such as Xelamap (www.xelamaponline.com) include plenty of useful information, including an events calendar, hiking options and current bus fares.

Sights
PARQUE CENTRO AMÉRICA
This plaza and its surrounding buildings are pretty much all there is to see in Xela proper. At its southeast end, the Casa de la Cultura holds the **Museo de Historia Natural** (Map p142; ☎ 7761-6427; 7a Calle; admission Q6; ⊙ 8am-noon & 2-6pm Mon-Fri, 9am-5pm Sat & Sun) which has exhibits on the Maya, the liberal revolution in Central American politics and the Estado de Los Altos, of which Quetzaltenango was the capital. Marimbas, weaving, taxidermy and other local lore also claim places here.

The once-crumbling **cathedral** (Map p142) has been rebuilt (well, its facade, anyway) in the last few decades. Up the block, the **municipalidad** (Map p142) follows the grandiose neoclassical style so favored as a symbol of culture and refinement in this wild mountain country. On the plaza's northwest side, the palatial **Pasaje Enríquez** was built to be lined with elegant shops, but as Quetzaltenango has few elegant shoppers, it instead houses an assortment of travel agencies, language institutes, cafes and one major bar.

OTHER SIGHTS
On 1a Calle is the impressive neoclassical **Teatro Municipal** (Map p142), which stages regular performing arts productions, from international dance recitals to the crowning of La Señorita Quetzaltenango.

Check out the **Mercado La Democracia** (Map p140; 1a Calle, Zona 3), 10 blocks north of Parque Centro América, for the hustle of a real Guatemalan city market.

About 3km northwest of Parque Centro América, near the Terminal Minerva bus station and another big market, is **Parque Zoológico Minerva** (Map p140; ☎ 7763-5637; Av Las Américas 0-50, Zona 3; admission free; ⊙ 9am-5pm Tue-Sun), a zoo-park with a few monkeys, coyotes, raccoons, deer and Barbary sheep. Outside the zoo on an island in the middle of 4a Calle stands the neoclassical **Templo de Minerva** (Map p140), built by dictator Estrada Cabrera to honor the Roman goddess of education and to inspire Guatemalans to new heights of learning.

Quetzaltenango's railroad station, 1km east of the Templo de Minerva along 4a Calle, lay dormant for years until the city converted it into the **Centro Intercultural de Quetzaltenango** (Map p140; cnr 4a Calle & 19 Av, Zona 3), with schools of art and dance and three fine museums. The **Museo Ixkik'** (Map p140; admission Q25; ⊙ 9am-1pm & 3-6pm) is devoted to Maya weaving and traditional outfits. The **Museo de Arte** (Map p140; ⊙ 8am-noon & 2-6pm) holds 200 paintings by Guatemala's leading modernists, including Efraín Recinos, Juan Antonio Franco and the landscape artist José Luis Álvarez. And the **Museo del Ferrocarril de los Altos** (Map p140; admission Q6; ⊙ 8am-noon & 2-6pm) covers the ambitious rail project that connected Quetzaltenango to the Pacific coast but operated for just three years in the period between 1930 and 1933.

The **Mirador La Pedrera** (Map p140), a 3km (or Q30) taxi ride from the center, offers a fine view of the city.

Activities
HIKING
Volcán Tajumulco (4220m) is the highest point in Central America and a challenging two-day hike from Quetzaltenango. Volcán Santiaguito (2488m) and Volcán Santa María (3772m) can also be ascended.

All of the following tour companies charge around Q370 for a two-day trip to Tajumulco, Q150 for full-moon ascents of Santa María, Q650 for the three-day treks between Quetzaltenango and Lago de Atitlán, and Q1350 for the five-day Nebaj–Todos Santos Cuchumatán jaunt across the Cuchumatanes mountains.

Hike & Help (Map p142; ☎ 7765-0883; www.fdiguate.org; 15 Av 7-41, Zona 1) Uses profits from hikes to fund educational projects in poor rural communities.

Kaqchikel Tours (Map p142; ☎ 5010-4465; www.kaqchikeltours.com; 7a Calle 15-36, Zona 1) Also does a challenging two-day hike right up close to the active Volcán Santiaguito (Q600).

Monte Verde Tours (Map p142; ☎ 7761-6105; www.monte-verdetours.com; 13a Av 8-34, Zona 1) Does a variety of volcano hikes and offbeat tours around Xela.

Quetzaltrekkers (Map p140; ☎ 7765-5895; www.quetzaltrekkers.com; Diagonal 12 8-37, Zona 1) Volunteer-run organization that supports a local school for kids from low-income families. It offers a range of other trips – see its website for details.

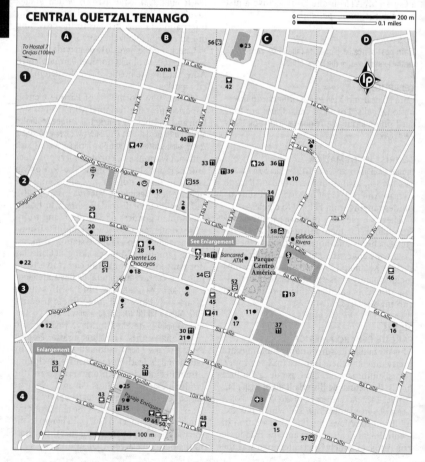

CENTRAL QUETZALTENANGO

CYCLING

Cycling is a great way to explore the surrounding countryside or commute to Spanish class. Fuentes Georginas (p148), San Andrés Xecul (p148) and the steam vents at Los Vahos (p148) are all attainable day trips. **Vrisa Books** (Map p142; 15a Av 3-64) rents mountain and town bikes for Q40/100/200 per day/week/month; it also offers cycling tours to some of the above destinations.

Courses

DANCE & WEAVING

The highly recommended dance school **Salsa Rosa** (Map p142; Diagonal 11 7-79) gets top marks for its fun atmosphere and professionalism. Group and private salsa and merengue classes are offered. If you're just looking to make a night of it, the dance club **La Parranda** (see p146) offers free salsa classes Wednesdays from 9pm.

Trama Textiles (Map p142; ☎ 7765-8564; trama.textiles@yahoo.com; 3a Calle 10-56, Zona 1) offers backstrap weaving classes and operates a fair-trade fabrics shop. For a simple demonstration of techniques it charges Q35. Ten hours of instruction costs Q325 and students produce a scarf; 20 hours of classes costs Q650 and produces an embroidered table runner.

LANGUAGE

In recent years, Xela has become well known for its Spanish-language schools. Unlike Antigua, Xela is not overrun with foreigners, but it does have a small student social scene. **Xela Pages** (www.xelapages.com/schools.htm) has information on many of the schools here.

Most of the city's Spanish schools participate in social-action programs with the local K'iche' people and provide students with an opportunity to get involved. The standard price is Q920/1050 per week for four/five hours of instruction per day, Monday to Friday. Add around Q330 for room and board with a local family. Some places charge up to 20% more for tuition from June to August, and many require nonrefundable registration fees, particularly when booking in advance from overseas. College students may be able to take classes for academic credit.

The following are among the many reputable schools:

Casa Xelajú (Map p142; ☎ 7761-5954; www.casaxelaju.com; Callejón 15, Diagonal13-02, Zona 1) One of the biggest, also offering classes in K'iche', and college credit.
Celas Maya (Map p142; ☎ 7761-4342; www.celasmaya.edu.gt; 6a Calle 14-55, Zona 1) Also offering classes in K'iche' set around a garden courtyard.
Centro de Estudios de Español Pop Wuj (Map p140; ☎ /fax 7761-8286; www.pop-wuj.org; 1a Calle 17-72, Zona

GUATEMALA

1) Pop Wuj's profits go to development projects in nearby villages, in which students can participate. The school also offers medical and social-work language programs.

El Mundo en Español (Map p142; ☎ 7761-3256; www.elmundoenespanol.org; 8 Av Calle B A-61, Zona 1) The extended family environment here is intended to promote natural language learning; most students reside on the premises. Located in a residential neighborhood east of the center.

El Nahual Community Center (off Map p140; ☎ 7765-2098; www.languageselnahual.com; 28 Av 9-54, Zona 1) Runs some excellent, grass-roots community projects in which students can participate, such as teaching underprivileged kids and maintaining an organic community garden.

El Quetzal Spanish School (Map p140; ☎ 7765-1085; www.elquetzalspanishschool.com; 10a Calle 10-29, Zona 1) One of the few indigenous-run businesses in town, offering plenty of activities and a reading room.

Escuela de Español Miguel de Cervantes (Map p142; ☎ 7765-5554; www.learn2speakspanish.com; 12a Av 8-31) Friendly owner, attractive learning environment in a historic building, onsite accommodations available (see below right).

Inepas (Instituto de Español y Participación en Ayuda Social; Map p142; ☎ 7765-1308; www.inepas.org; 15a Av 4-59) Students can participate in a variety of worthy projects, including a Unesco-recognized rural school. Offers a selection of inexpensive accommodations besides homestays.

Madre Tierra (Map p142; ☎ 7761-6105; www.madre-tierra.org; 13 Av 8-34, Zona 1) Classes held in the courtyard of a classic colonial house. Activities include conferences with guest speakers from the community.

Proyecto Lingüístico Quetzalteco de Español (Map p140; ☎ /fax 7763-1061; www.plqe.org; 5a Calle 2-40, Zona 1) This collectively managed and politically minded institute also runs the Escuela de la Montaña, a limited-enrollment language-learning program on an organic coffee *finca* near Xela, where participation in local culture and volunteering are strongly encouraged.

Utatlán Spanish School (Map p142; ☎ 7763-0446; www.xelapages.com/utatlan; Pasaje Enríquez, 12a Av 4-32, Zona 1) Young and energetic, with plenty of parties and activities.

Volunteering

EntreMundos (Map p142; ☎ 7761-2179; www.entremundos.org; El Espacio, 6a Calle 7-31, Zona 1; ☻ 1-5pm Mon-Thu) is an excellent resource for volunteers seeking projects (and vice versa). The free searchable database on its website has details of hundreds of positions. If you'd like to drop in for more personalized service, it asks for a Q25 contribution. The organization also regularly seeks volunteers for capacity building workshops for NGOs and to produce its bimonthly newspaper.

Tours

A professional and amiable outfit, **Adrenalina Tours** (Map p142; ☎ 7761-4509; www.adrenalinatours.com; Pasaje Enríquez, Zona 1) provides a range of trips in the Xela area and little-visited parts of the department of Huehuetenango. **Altiplano's Tour Operator** (Map p142; ☎ 7766-9614; www.altiplanos.com.gt; 12a Av 3-35, Zona 1) offers some interesting half-day tours to indigenous villages and markets, colonial churches and coffee plantations around Xela. Both tour operators offer tours to Takalik Abaj (p157).

Tranvía de los Altos (Map p142; ☎ 7765-5342; www.tranviadelosaltos.com) is a pseudo-streetcar that does various circuits of the city, complete with knowledgeable commentary (in Spanish) and cheesy sound effects. Two-hour tours (Q70 per person) start at 11am and 3pm. English-language tours (Q125) are available with two days' notice.

Maya Viva (Map p140; ☎ 7761-6408; www.amaguate.org; 5a Av & 6a Calle 6-17, Zona 1) is a community tourism program that seeks to empower Maya women in the countryside. Visitors learn about customs, traditions and daily activities in rural communities near Quetzaltenango.

Festivals & Events

Xela Music Festival (late March or early April) Organized by the Alianza Francaise, this one- or two-day festival sees city streets blocked off, as local musicians play on five or six stages around the downtown area.

Feria de la Virgen del Rosario (Feria Centroamericana de Independencia; September 15–22) Xela's big annual party. Residents kick up their heels at a fairground on the city's perimeter and there's plenty of entertainment at selected venues around town.

Juegos Florales Centroamericanos (mid-September) The prizes in this international Spanish-language literary competition hosted by the city are awarded in mid-September, too.

Sleeping

All of the places listed here are in Zona 1.

Miguel de Cervantes Guesthouse (Map p142; ☎ 7765-5554; www.learn2speakspanish.com; 12 Av 8-31, Zona 1; r per person incl breakfast Q48; ☐ ☎) The nine guest rooms at the MdC Spanish school are spiffy wood-and-concrete affairs, set around one of the cutest courtyards in Xela. When there's water pressure, the showers in the shared bathrooms rock. Even if you're not taking classes, you can join in the student activities.

Guest House El Puente (Map p142; ☎ 7761-4342; 15a Av 6-75, Zona 1; s/d Q50/100, without bathroom Q40/80) The four rooms here surround a large garden; three share well-used bathroom facilities. Connected to the Celas Maya Spanish school, it's often occupied by language learners who congregate in the kitchen.

our pick **Los Chocoyos** (Map p140; ☎ 7761-6497; www.centroculturalloschocoyos.com; 7a Calle 15-20, Zona 1; r per person Q60; ☜) One component of a multi-use cultural center, this guesthouse offers serious discounts for longer stays. The eight split-level rooms have a bedroom upstairs, a lounge with TV downstairs. The guest kitchen is one of the best in town.

Black Cat Hostel (Map p142; ☎ 7756-8951; www.black cathostels.net; 13a Av 3-33, Zona 1; dm incl breakfast Q60, r Q160; ☜) A great place to stay if you're looking to meet up with other travelers, featuring a sunny courtyard, a bar-restaurant and lounge/TV area. Though sparsely furnished, the rooms are done in soothing colors with nice wood floors.

Hostal 7 Orejas (Map p140; ☎ 7768-3218; www.7orejas. com; 2a Calle 16-92, Zona 1; dm incl breakfast Q95) A cordially managed, scrupulously maintained hostel on a quiet street northwest of the center. The spacious, fresh-smelling rooms each have three queen-sized beds and carved-wood chests for storage. Music, movies and cocktails keep guests occupied upstairs at the El Orejón lounge.

Casa Doña Mercedes (Map p142; ☎ 7765-4687; cnr 6a Calle & 14a Av 13-42, Zona 1; s/d Q170/280, without bathroom Q86/175) In the heart of downtown, this tranquil little guesthouse is quite luxurious for the price, with plenty of colonial style. The shared bathroom accommodations are actually the better way to go here.

Casa San Bartolomé (Map p140; ☎ 7761-9511; www. casasanbartolome.com; 2a Av 7-17, Zona 1; s/d/tr Q205/287/328; ☜) In the family for generations, this atmospheric old residence has been converted into a cozy B&B. There are six rooms, three apartments (with kitchens) and a cottage. All have beautiful furniture and modern art. An elaborate breakfast is served on the lovely rear terrace. Long-termers get substantial discounts.

Xela has plenty of other fine options:

Casa de las Amigas (Map p140; ☎ 7763-0014; 5a Calle 2-59, Zona 1; r Q25-35) Simple rooms with homey atmosphere and kitchen facilities.

Hostal Don Diego (Map p142; ☎ 5308-5106; www. hostaldondiegoxela.com; 6a Calle 15-12, Zona 1; dm Q45, s/d from Q55/100; ☜) Sparely furnished rooms with good firm beds around a sunny courtyard. Reduced rates for weekly or monthly stays.

Eating

Quetzaltenango has a good selection of places to eat in all price ranges. Cheapest are the food stalls on the lower level of the central market, where snacks and main-course plates are sold for Q10 or less. One very popular breakfast locale is Doña Cristy (Map p142), serving *atol de elote* (a hot maize beverage), empanadas and *chuchitos*.

LATIN AMERICAN CUISINE

Café Canela (Map p142; 7a Calle 15-24; meals Q15; ☽ breakfast, lunch & dinner Sun-Fri) This unassuming lunch joint has yummy home-cooked fare by gregarious Nicaraguan owner/chef Marta. There are three daily specials to choose from, with one veggie option.

Café Sagrado Corazón (Map p142; 14a Av 3-08, Zona 1; meals Q25; ☽ 6:30am-7pm) This hole-in-the-wall eatery is a good place to try Guatemalan home cooking, with regional specialties like *pepián* and *jocón*. Meals are truly filling, coming with soup, *tamalitos* (miniature tamales), rice, potatoes, avocado and salad.

Casa Ut'z Hua (Map p142; 12a Av 3-05; meals Q25-30; ☽ breakfast, lunch & dinner) Delicious, authentic Guatemalan and Quetzalteco dishes are the draw at this kitschily decorated country hut.

Maya Café (Map p142; 13 Av 5-48; mains Q25-30; ☽ 7am-6pm) Plenty of *típica* Xela fare on offer at this locally popular dining hall. Try the *quichom*, a spicy chicken concoction. Lunch comes with soup and a juice.

INTERNATIONAL CUISINE

Al-Natur (Map p142; 13a Av 8-34 A; ☽ 9am-7:30pm Mon-Sat, 1-7pm Sun; ☜) For politically correct snacks, head here: all sandwiches, milkshakes, cappuccinos and pastries are organically grown, fair-trade approved and/or produced by cooperatives.

Casa Antigua (Map p142; 12a Av 3-26; sandwiches Q28; ☽ noon-9pm Mon-Sat, 4-9pm Sun; ☜) Sandwiches are big, chunky affairs and there are plenty of steaks flame-grilled out front at this casual eatery near the Parque. Seating is at sturdy wooden tables along a pleasant patio.

Panorama (Map p140; ☎ 5319-3536; 13a Av A; meals Q40-80; ☽ dinner Wed-Fri, lunch & dinner Sat & Sun) This Swiss-owned restaurant (a 10-minute slog up the hill at the south end of town) does good set meals and Swiss raclette cheese. The view is amazing and the setting is romantic.

Royal Paris (Map p142; ☎ 7761-1942; 14 Av A 3-06; salads Q45; ☽ lunch & dinner; ☜) Overseen by the French consul herself, this bistro ought to be authentic, and the escargots, baked camembert and filet mignon approach Parisian standards. There's live folk and jazz Wednesday, Friday and Saturday nights (when reservations are a good idea).

Casa Babylon (Map p142; 5a Calle 12-54; mains Q50-85; breakfast, lunch & dinner Mon-Sat; V) With the widest menu in town, the Babylon is a travelers' favorite. Dishes run from big, tasty sandwiches to Guatemalan classics to more exotic fare such as fondue and Middle Eastern fare.

our pick Sabor de la India (Map p142; 15 Av 3-64; mains Q60-70; noon-10pm Tue-Sun; V) What is surely the most authentic Indian fare in the country is made here by a friendly fellow from Kerala. Servings are huge; the *thalis* – assortments of curried veggies – are recommended.

Plenty more in this category, too:

Café El Árabe (Map p142; 4a Calle 12-22, Zona 1; mains Q55; noon-midnight; V) Authentic Middle Eastern food, freshly made pitas and plenty of vegetarian choices.

Restaurante Cardinali (Map p142; 14a Av 3-25; pastas Q60; mains Q125; lunch & dinner) Homemade pasta, good pizzas and an extensive wine list.

Drinking & Entertainment

The live music scene is particularly strong in Xela. For details on what's on, pick up a copy of *Xela Who* or check www.xelawho.com. All of the following are in Zona 1.

CAFES

Coffee plays an important part in Xela's economy, and there's no shortage of places where you can grab a cup.

Café La Luna (Map p142; 8a Av 4-11; 9:30am-9pm Mon-Fri, 4-9pm Sat;) La Luna is a comfortable, relaxed place to hang out and eat a cake, salad or sandwich. The hot chocolate is the specialty – the coffee is so-so. Choose any of several rooms: decor is in similar vein to Café Baviera but the music is classical instead of jazz.

Café Baviera (Map p142; 7761-5018; 5a Calle 13-14 7am-8:30pm;) This European-style cafe has good coffee, roasted on the premises, and is a decent place for breakfast or a snack (crepes, croissants, soups and salads, Q30 to Q40). The wooden walls are hung with countless photos and clippings on Xela and international themes.

Café El Cuartito (Map p142; 13a Av 7-09; 11am-11pm Wed-Mon; V) Xela's hippest cafe does a good range of snacks and juices, and coffee just about any way you want it. Weekends it often has DJs spinning laid-back tracks, and there's always art on the walls by local contemporary artists.

That's not nearly all, folks:

El Infinito Lounge (Map p142; 7a Calle 15-18; 11am-11pm Mon-Sat;) Cool art, tofu snacks, hip music, bubble tea, board games and great coffee – more like this please.

Time Coffee Shop (Map p142; 7768-3467; Pasaje Enríquez, 12 Av 4-52; 8am-8pm Tue-Sun;) A stylish and central little spot, with views out onto the park.

Café El Balcón del Enríquez (Map p142; Pasaje Enríquez, 12 Av 4-40; breakfast, lunch & dinner) The food and coffee at this outdoor, upstairs cafe are only so-so, but the views are spectacular.

BARS

Salón Tecún (Map p142; Pasaje Enríquez; 8am-1am) Busy all day and night with a healthy (but not *that* healthy) crowd of Guatemalans and foreigners; the Tecún claims to be the country's longest-running bar (since 1935). Good bar snacks and gringo comfort food, including probably the best burgers in town.

Pool & Beer (Map p142; 12a Av 10-21; 6pm-1am Tue-Sun) The pool tables are worn, the cues crooked, but this slackers' clubhouse remains a friendly and refreshingly non-trendy spot. If the tables are occupied, you can be the DJ, choosing from the PC's 30,000 odd tracks.

Ojalá (Map p142; 15 Av A 3-33; 5pm-1am Tue-Sat;) A fun clubhouse for a predominately global clientele, Ojalá has a series of comfy salons centering on a colonial patio where various events take place (trivia contests, live music). Local microbrews (Q40) are among the quaffs available at the lovely bar.

Arguile (Map p142; 13a Av 7-31; noon-1am Mon-Sat;) Nominally a Middle Eastern snack bar, after hours Arguile becomes a trendy lounge, where a mixed Guatemalan/foreigner crowd smoke hookahs (Q50) or dance to the DJs.

DANCE CLUBS

La Parranda (Map p142; 14a Av 4-47; cover charge Fri & Sat Q20; Wed-Sat) This glitzy, strobe-lit disco offers free salsa classes on Wednesday nights (basic and intermediate); other evenings have guest DJs and drinks giveaways.

La Rumba (Map p142; 13a Av; Wed-Sat) The big dance floor at this highly popular hall fills up fast, with plenty of Guate-gringo/a couples teaching each other how to salsa, merengue and *cumbia* (Colombian dance).

ARTS

The recently inaugurated **Casa No'j** (Map p142; 7768-3139; www.casanoj.blogspot.com; 7a Calle 12-12;

8am-5pm Mon-Sat), off the Parque's southwest corner, is Xela's premier cultural center. Besides staging photo and art exhibits, it also hosts film, theater and poetry festivals throughout the year. Check its blog for upcoming events.

Another happening space, the **Centro Cultural Los Chocoyos** (Map p142; www.centroculturalloschocoyos. com; 7a Calle 15-20) regularly stages performance events, including plays and concerts.

Other recommendations:

Teatro Municipal (Map p142; 1a Calle) Cultural performances are presented at this beautiful venue.

Teatro Roma (Map p142; 14a Av A) Facing Teatro Municipal; sometimes screens interesting movies.

Cinema

Though there's no proper movie house in the center of town, a number of venues run weekly film series, including Ojalá, Time Coffee Shop and Royal Paris, as well as El Orejón, the lounge inside the Hostal 7 Orejas. In addition, the **Blue Angel Video Café** (Map p142; 7a Calle 15-79; Q10) shows Hollywood films nightly at 8pm, besides serving a nice range of vegetarian meals, herbal teas and hot chocolate. See *XelaWho* for schedules.

Getting There & Away

BUS

For 2nd-class buses, head out to the **Terminal Minerva** (Map p140; 7a Calle, Zona 3), a dusty, noisy, crowded yard in the west of town. Buses leave frequently for many highland destinations. Leaving or entering town, some buses make a stop east of the center at the *rotonda*, a traffic circle on Calz Independencia, marked by the Monumento a la Marimba. Getting off here when you're coming into Xela saves the 10 or 15 minutes it will take your bus to cross town to Terminal Minerva.

First-class companies heading for Guatemala City have their own terminals (listed below). Cheaper 2nd-class buses depart Terminal Minerva for Guatemala City (Q35) every 10 minutes, 5am to 5pm, but make many stops and take longer.

First-class services for Guatemala City:

Linea Dorada (Map140; 7767-5198; www.linea dorada.info; 12 Av & 5 Calle, Zona 3) Two deluxe buses (Q70), 4am and 2:30pm; door-to-door shuttle service for passengers getting the early departure (Q25 from Zona 1).

Transportes Álamo (Map140; 7763-5044; 14 Av 5-15, Zona 3) Seven Pullman buses, from 4:30am to 4:45pm.

Transportes Galgos (Map140; 7761-2248; Calle Rodolfo Robles 17-43, Zona 1) Pullmans at 4am, 8:30am and 12:30pm.

All the buses in the table below depart from Terminal Minerva. Buses for Almolonga and Zunil have an additional downtown stop at the corner of 8a Av and 10a Calle, southeast of Parque Centro América. Those for San Martín Sacatepéquez (Chile Verde) also stop at 6a Calle, two blocks north of Parque Benito Juárez.

BUSES FROM QUETZALTENANGO

Destination	Cost (Q)	Duration	Departures	Frequency
Almolonga	2.50	40min	5:30am-5pm	every 15min
Chichicastenango	40	3hr	9am-3:30pm	hourly
Ciudad Tecún Umán (Mexican border)	25	3hr	5am-6pm	hourly
Cuatro Caminos	3	15min	5:30am-5pm	every 15min
Huehuetenango	20	2hr	5:30am-7pm	every 15min
La Mesilla (Mexican border)	15	3½hr	5am-4pm	hourly
Momostenango	7	1½hr	5:45am-7pm	every 15min
Panajachel	25	3hr	10am-4:30pm	hourly
Retalhuleu	13	1½hr	4:30am-7:30pm	every 10min
San Andrés Xecul	3.50	40min	6am-3pm	every 15min
San Francisco El Alto	9	1½hr	5:45am-7pm	frequent
San Martín Sacatepéquez (Chile Verde)	5	1hr	6am-3pm	every 15min
Totonicapán	5	1hr	5:45am-7pm	every 20min
San Pedro La Laguna	35	4hr	10am-4pm	every 2hr
Zunil	4.50	1hr	6:30am-5:30pm	every 10min

GUATEMALA

To get to Antigua, catch any Guatemala City–bound bus passing Chimaltenango and change there. To get to the Mexican border at El Carmen/Talismán, take a bus to San Marcos (Q10, two hours, every 30 minutes), then another to Malacatán (Q15, two hours) and finally a collective taxi (Q5) or microbus to El Carmen (Q4).

SHUTTLE MINIBUS

Adrenalina Tours (Map p142; ☎ 7761-4509; www.adren alinatours.com; Pasaje Enríquez, Zona 1) and **Monte Verde Tours** (Map p142; ☎ 7761-6105; www.monte-verdetours. com; 13a Av 8-34, Zona 1) run shuttle minibuses to many destinations including Guatemala City (Q290), Antigua (Q210), Chichicastenango (Q140), Panajachel (Q115), and San Cristóbal de las Casas (Mexico; Q290).

Getting Around

Inguat (Map p142; ☎ 7761-4931; ☽ 9am-5pm Mon-Fri, 9am-1pm Sat) has information on city bus routes. City buses charge Q1.25, doubling the fare after 7pm and on holidays. Frequent mini-buses run between Terminal Minerva and the downtown area. The Rotonda bus stop on Calz Independencia is also served by 'Parque' microbuses running to the center.

Taxis wait at the stand on the north end of Parque Centro América. Bargain hard. Cab fare between Terminal Minerva and down-town is around Q30.

AROUND QUETZALTENANGO (XELA)

The beautiful volcanic countryside around Quetzaltenango makes for exciting day trips and getting out there is as simple as hopping on one of the buses serving the traditional villages that pepper this region.

Market days in surrounding towns include Sunday in Momostenango, Monday in Zunil, Tuesday and Saturday in Totonicapán and Friday in San Francisco El Alto.

Fuentes Georginas

This is the prettiest natural **spa** (☎ 5904-5559; www.lasfuentesgeorginas.com; adult/child Q25/15; ☽ 8am-5:30pm) in Guatemala. Here, pools of varying temperatures are fed by hot sulfur springs and framed by a high wall of tropical vegetation. Fans of Fuentes Georginas were dismayed when a massive landslide destroyed several structures (including the primary bathing pool) in 1998 and crushed the statue of the Greek goddess that previously gazed upon the pools. After restoration, spa regulars realized the landslide had opened a new vent.

As a result, the water here is hotter than ever. Although the setting is intensely tropi-

---

EXPLORE MORE AROUND QUETZALTENANGO (XELA)

Looking for more unpolished village life? Three places close to Xela are well worth the minimal effort required:

- **Los Vahos** These rough-and-ready **sauna/steam baths** (admission Q10; ☽ 8am-6pm), about 3.5km from downtown Xela, make for a good short hike. Take an Almolonga-bound bus and get off at the road to Los Vahos, which is marked with a small sign. From here it's a 2.3km uphill walk. Altiplano's Tour Operator (see p144) organizes hikes up here. The views are remarkable.

- **San Andrés Xecul** Surrounded by fertile hills about 10km northwest of Xela, this small town boasts perhaps the most bizarre **church** anywhere – technicolor saints, angels, flowers and climbing vines share space with whimsical tigers and monkeys on its shocking-yellow facade. Regular buses (Q3.50, 40 minutes) run between Xela and San Andrés.

- **Zunil** This pretty agricultural market town is set in a lush valley and dominated by a towering volcano. The white colonial church gleams above the red-tiled and rusted-tin roofs of the low houses. The town has a particularly photogenic **church**, and is also home to the **Cooperativa Santa Ana** (☽ 7am-7pm) handicrafts cooperative in which over 600 local women participate. Other draws include the weekly market held on Mondays and the image of **San Simón**, an effigy of a local Maya hero venerated as a (non-Catholic) saint. The effigy is moved each year to a different house; ask anyone where to find San Simón. You'll be charged a few quetzals to visit him and take pictures (see p126). Buses running between Zunil and Xela (Q4.50, one hour) stop on the main road, beside the bridge.

cal, the mountain air keeps the temperature deliciously cool all day.

The site has a **restaurant** (meals Q60-75; ☺ 8am-7pm), and three sheltered picnic tables with cooking grills (bring your own fuel). Down the valley are seven rustic **cottages** (per person Q95), each with a shower, a barbecue area and a fireplace to ward off the mountain chill at night. Included in the price of the cottages is access to the pools all day and night. Trails here lead to two nearby volcanoes: **Volcán Zunil** (three hours each way) and **Volcán Santo Tomás** (five hours each way). Guides (essential) are available for either trip. Ask at the restaurant.

GETTING THERE & AWAY

Fuentes Georginas offers daily shuttles to the site (Q75 round trip, including entrance fee), leaving at 9am and 2pm from its **office** (Map p142; ☎ 7763-0596; 5a Calle 14-14) in Quetzaltenango. They return at 1pm and 6pm.

Alternatively, take any bus to Zunil, where pick-up trucks wait to give rides up to the springs, a half hour away (Q100, including a 1½-hour wait while you soak).

San Francisco El Alto
pop 41,000 / elev 2582m

High on a hilltop overlooking Quetzaltenango stands San Francisco El Alto, Guatemala's garment district. Every inch is jammed with vendors selling sweaters, socks, blankets, jeans and more. Bolts of cloth spill from overstuffed storefronts, and that is on the quiet days! On Friday the town explodes as the real **market** action kicks in. The large plaza, surrounded by the church and *municipalidad* and centered on a cupola-like *mirador* (lookout), is covered in goods. Stalls crowd into neighboring streets, and the press of traffic is so great that a special system of one-way roads is established. Vehicles entering the town on market day must pay a small fee.

This is regarded as the country's biggest, most authentic market, but it's not nearly as heavy with handicrafts as are the markets in Chichicastenango and Antigua. Beware of pickpockets and stay alert.

Around mid-morning when the clouds roll away, panoramic views can be had throughout town, especially from the church roof. The caretaker will let you up.

Banco Reformador (2a Calle 2-64) changes traveler's checks and has a Visa ATM.

San Francisco's big party is the **Fiesta de San Francisco de Asís**, celebrated around October 4 with traditional dances such as La Danza de Conquista and La Danza de los Monos.

Hotel Vista Hermosa (☎ 7738-4010; 2a Calle & 3a Av; s/d Q60/120, without bathroom Q30/60) does indeed have beautiful views from its big, comfortable rooms.

For food, **El Manantial** (2a Calle 2-42; mains Q30), a couple of blocks below the plaza, is pleasant and clean, serving steaks and a few *comida típica* dishes.

Buses to San Francisco leave Quetzaltenango (passing through Cuatro Caminos) frequently throughout the day (Q9, 1½ hours). Because of San Francisco's one-way streets, you'll want to get off on 4a Av at the top of the hill (unless you like walking uphill) and walk toward the church. To go back, buses run downhill along 1a Av.

Momostenango
pop 59,000 / elev 2259m

Beyond San Francisco El Alto, and 35km from Quetzaltenango, Momostenango is Guatemala's famous center for *chamarras* (thick, heavy woolen blankets). The villagers also make ponchos and other woolen garments. As you enter the plaza, you'll see signs inviting you to watch blankets being made and purchase the finished products. The best time to do this is market day, Sunday; haggle like mad. A basic good blanket costs around Q100, perhaps twice as much for an extra-heavy 'matrimonial.'

On market days, the streets will be thronged and so buses will often leave you on 3a Calle. It's about a five-minute walk to the plaza from here – follow the crowd or head toward the church spires.

Momostenango is also noted for its adherence to the ancient Maya calendar and traditional rites. Ceremonies coordinated with the important dates of the calendar take place in the hills about 2km west of the plaza. It's not easy for travelers to witness these rites, though try Takiliben May Wajshakib Batz (see p150).

INFORMATION
Banco Reformador (1a Calle 1-3, Zona 1; ☺ 9am-5pm Mon-Fri, 9am-1pm Sun) Changes traveler's checks and has a Cajero 5B ATM.

Centro Cultural (☺ 8am-6pm Mon-Fri, 8am-1pm & 2-5pm Sat) Is good for tourist information. In the *municipalidad* building.

SIGHTS & ACTIVITIES

Momostenango's **Los Riscos** (The Crags) are peculiar geological formations on the edge of town. The eroded pumice spires rise into the air like something from *Star Trek*. To get there, go one block south of the plaza and head downhill on 3a Av, Zona 2. Turn right at the bottom of the hill, go left at a fork (signed 'A Los Riscos'), then after 100m turn right along 2a Calle and walk 300m to Los Riscos.

Takiliben May Wajshakib Batz (☎ 7736-5537; wajshkibbatz13@yahoo.es; 3a Av 'A' 6-85, Zona 3), just past the Texaco at the entrance to town, teaches classes in Maya ceremonies. Its director, Rigoberto Itzep Chanchavac, a Maya priest, does horoscopes (Q40) and private consultations and hosts ceremonial workshops. His **chuj** (traditional Maya sauna; per person Q100; ⏲ 4-6pm Tue & Thu) requires advance bookings.

FESTIVALS & EVENTS

Picturesque **diablo (devil) dances** are held in the plaza a few times a year, notably on Christmas Eve and New Year's Eve. The homemade devil costumes can get quite campy and elaborate: all have masks and cardboard wings, and some go the whole hog with fake-fur suits and heavily sequined outfits. Dance groups gather in the plaza with a five- to 13-piece band, drinking alcoholic refreshments during the breaks. For entertainment, they are at their best around 3pm, but the festivities go late into the night.

The annual fair, **Octava de Santiago**, is celebrated from July 28 to August 2.

SLEEPING & EATING

Accommodations are very basic.

Hospedaje y Comedor Paclom (☎ 7736-5174; 2a Av & 1a Calle, Zona 2; r per person Q25) This serviceable *hospedaje*, a block uphill from the first plaza, has rooms facing a courtyard crammed with plants and birds.

Hotel Otoño (☎ 7736-5078; gruvial.m@gmail.com; 3a Av 'A' 1-48, Zona 2; r per person Q100; P) Momostenango's one 'luxury' lodging has 14 modern rooms with glossy tiled floors and huge bathrooms with balconies or picture windows taking in the surrounding hills.

Restaurante La Cascada (1a Calle 1-35, Zona 2; meals Q30; ⏲ breakfast, lunch & dinner) A bright and clean upstairs eatery serving good-value set meals. The food is simple and filling, and there are some good views of the church spires and surrounding hills.

GETTING THERE & AWAY

You can get buses to Momostenango from Quetzaltenango's Terminal Minerva (Q7, 1½ hours), from Cuatro Caminos (Q6, one hour), or from San Francisco El Alto (Q5, 45 minutes). Buses run about every 15 minutes, with the last one back to Quetzaltenango normally leaving Momostenango at 4:30pm.

Laguna Chicabal

This magical lake is nestled in a crater of the Volcán Chicabal (2900m). The 'Center of Maya-Mam Cosmovision,' it's an intensely sacred place and a hotbed for Maya ceremonies. Maya priests come from all over to make offerings here, especially around May 3. Visitors are definitely not welcome at this time; do not visit Laguna Chicabal during the first week of May.

The lake is about a two-hour hike from **San Martín Sacatepéquez** (also known as Chile Verde), a friendly, interesting village about 25km from Xela and notable for the traditional dress worn by the village men. To get to the lake, head down from the highway toward town and look for the sign on your right (you can't miss it). Hike 45 minutes uphill through fields and past houses until you crest the hill. Continue hiking downhill for 15 minutes to the ranger station, where you pay a Q15 entrance fee. From here, it's another 30 minutes uphill to a *mirador* and then a whopping 615 steep steps down to the edge of the lake. Start early for the best visibility; clouds and mists envelop the volcano and crater by early afternoon.

The thick vegetation ringing the lake hides picnic tables and sublime campsites. Treat the lake with the utmost respect.

Frequent buses run between Quetzaltenango and San Martín Sacatepéquez (Q5, one hour) until 4pm.

HUEHUETENANGO

pop 144,900 / elev 1909m

Mostly a stopping-off point for more interesting places, Huehue (*way*-way) offers few charms of its own, but some people do love it for its true Guatemalan character. Either way, there are enough eating and sleeping options here to keep you happy, and the sight of the Cuchumatanes mountain range (highest in Central America) in the background makes for some striking scenery.

The lively *indígena* (traditional) market is filled daily with traders who come down

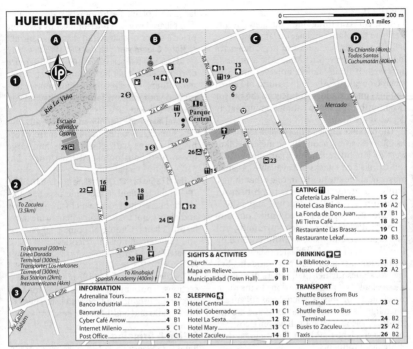

HUEHUETENANGO

EATING 🍴
Cafetería Las Palmeras...............**15** C2
Hotel Casa Blanca......................**16** A2
La Fonda de Don Juan..............**17** B1
Mi Tierra Café...........................**18** B2
Restaurante Las Brasas.............**19** C1
Restaurante Lekaf.....................**20** B3

DRINKING 🍷🍸
La Biblioteca...........................**21** B3
Museo del Café........................**22** A2

SIGHTS & ACTIVITIES
Church...**7** C2
Mapa en Relieve..........................**8** B1
Municipalidad (Town Hall).............**9** B1

SLEEPING 🛏
Hotel Central.............................**10** B1
Hotel Gobernador.......................**11** C1
Hotel La Sexta............................**12** B2
Hotel Mary................................**13** C1
Hotel Zaculeu.............................**14** B1

INFORMATION
Adrenalina Tours............................**1** B2
Banco Industrial..............................**2** B1
Banrural...**3** B2
Cyber Café Arrow............................**4** B1
Internet Milenio..............................**5** C1
Post Office.....................................**6** C1

TRANSPORT
Shuttle Buses from Bus
  Terminal................................**23** C2
Shuttle Buses to Bus
  Terminal................................**24** B2
Buses to Zaculeu.......................**25** A2
Taxis.......................................**26** B2

GUATEMALA

from surrounding villages. Surprisingly, the market area is about the only place you'll see traditional costumes in this town, as most of its citizens are *ladinos* wearing modern clothes. Coffee growing, mining, sheep raising, light manufacturing and agriculture are the region's main activities.

For travelers, Huehue is usually a leg on the journey to or from Mexico – the logical place to spend your first night in Guatemala. The town is also the perfect staging area for forays deeper into the Cuchumatanes or through the highlands on back roads.

Orientation & Information

The town center is 4km northeast of the Interamericana, and the bus station is off the road linking the two, about 2km from each. Almost every service of interest to tourists is in Zona 1 within a few blocks of the Parque Central.

Huehue has no official tourist office, but folks in the *municipalidad* can generally answer any queries.

Adrenalina Tours (☎ 7768-1538; www.adrenalina tours.com; 4a Calle 6-54) Leads a bunch of interesting tours

and hikes throughout the region, and offers shuttle service to key destinations (see p155).

Asistur (☎ 5460-7042) Can come to your assistance in a jam.

Banrural (3a Calle 6-16; 🕑 8:30am-4pm Mon-Fri, 9am-4pm Sat) Has a whopping two Cajero 5B ATMs and they change euros. There are other ATMs at Banco Industrial, a block further north, and at the Banrural on Av Kaibal Balam, 100m east of the bus terminal.

Cyber Café Arrow (1a Calle 5-08; per hr Q5; 🕑 8am-10pm)

Internet Milenio (4a Av 1-54; per hr Q5; 🕑 8am-6pm Mon-Sat, 9am-1pm Sun)

Post office (2a Calle 3-54; 🕑 8:30am-5:30pm Mon-Fri, 9am-1pm Sat) Is half a block east of Parque Central.

Sights & Activities
PARQUE CENTRAL

Huehuetenango's main plaza is shaded by old trees and surrounded by the town's imposing buildings: the *municipalidad* (with its band shell on the upper floor) and the huge colonial church. The plaza has its own little **Mapa en Relieve** of Huehuetenango Department.

ZACULEU

With ravines on three sides, Zaculeu ('White Earth' in the Mam language), a late Postclassic religious center, occupies a strategic defensive location that served its Mam Maya inhabitants well. It finally failed, however, in 1525, when Gonzalo de Alvarado (cousin of Pedro) and his conquistadors laid siege to the site for two months. It was starvation that ultimately defeated the Mam.

The parklike **Zaculeu archaeological zone** (admission Q50; ☺ 8am-6pm), about 200 sq meters, is 4km west of Huehuetenango's main plaza. Cold soft drinks and snacks are available. A small museum at the site holds, among other things, skulls and items found in a tomb beneath Estructura 1, the tallest structure at the site.

Restoration by the United Fruit Company in the 1940s has left Zaculeu's pyramids, ball courts and ceremonial platforms covered by a thick coat of graying plaster. Many of the restoration methods were not authentic, but the work goes further than others in making the site look as it might have done to the Mam priests and worshipers when it was still an active religious center. All that's missing are the colorful frescoes that must have once covered the exterior. The buildings show a great deal of Mexican influence.

Buses to Zaculeu (Q2.50, 20 minutes) leave about every 30 minutes (between 7:30am and 6pm) from in front of the school at the corner of 2a Calle and 7a Av. Make sure they're going to 'Las Ruinas' – Zaculeu is the name of a community, too. A taxi from the town center costs Q30 one way. One hour is plenty of time to look round the site and museum.

Courses

Xinabajul Spanish Academy (☎ 7764-6631; academia xinabajul@hotmail.com; 4a Av 14-14, Zona 5) offers one-to-one Spanish courses and homestays with local families. It's two blocks east of the bus station and two blocks south of the Interamericana.

Festivals & Events

Fiestas Julias (July 13–20) This special event honors La Virgen del Carmen, Huehue's patron saint.
Fiestas de Concepción (December 5–6) Honoring the Virgen de Concepción.

Sleeping

Hotel Central (☎ 7764-1202; 5a Av 1-33; r per person Q30; P) This rough-and-ready little number might be to your liking. Rooms are simple,

large and plain. Bathrooms are downstairs. The pillared wooden interior balcony gives the place a sliver of charm and it sure is central.

Hotel Gobernador (☎ /fax 7764-1197; 4a Av 1-45; s/d Q35/60, with bathroom Q52/80; P) A little maze of rooms (don't get lost!), some much better than others – check your bed for sponge factor and your window for openability and you should be happy.

Hotel Mary (☎ 7764-1618; 2a Calle 3-52; s/d Q80/130; P) This large, older hotel has sparely furnished rooms with comfy beds and large green-tiled bathrooms. At least one – No 310 – features a balcony.

Hotel La Sexta (☎ 7764-1488; 6a Av 4-29; s/d Q85/140; P) Cubicles flank either side of a barnlike interior here, cheered up a bit by tropical birds and plants, not to mention aquamarine faux-leather chairs. Choose a room as far back as you can – street noise is relentless.

Hotel Zaculeu (☎ 7764-1086; www.hotelzaculeu.com; 5a Av 1-14; s/d Q115/225; P ☐) This 125-year old hotel has oodles of character and 36 big rooms in two sections. Those in the 'new section' are a bit pricier but brighter and more stylish. There's a lovely patio and laid-back bar here, too.

Eating & Drinking

Hotel Casa Blanca (7a Av 3-41; salads Q20, steaks Q50; ☺ breakfast, lunch & dinner) For lovely surroundings, you can't beat the two restaurants at this classy hotel, one indoors, the other in the garden. On Sunday mornings there's a popular breakfast buffet for Q30.

our pick Cafetería Las Palmeras (4a Calle 5-10; mains Q25; ☺ breakfast, lunch & dinner) On the southern part of the Parque Central, this is a popular spot. The open-air upper-floor dining room has views over the park. The *caldo de pollo criollo* (Q25) brims with chicken, *güisquil* (squash) and corn.

Mi Tierra Café (4a Calle 6-46; mains Q25-40; ☺ breakfast, lunch & dinner) An informal cafe-restaurant serving good homemade soups and burgers. It also takes a good crack at some international dishes, muffins and a range of other goodies. Good, cheap and filling set lunches are available.

Restaurante Lekaf (☎ 7764-3202; 6a Calle 6-40; pizzas Q35-100; ☺ 10am-11pm) This modern, airy dining hall has a varied menu, including sandwiches, pizza and seafood. There's live music (marimba, folk) Thursday to Sunday evenings.

Restaurante Las Brasas (4a Av 1-36; steaks Q40-55; ☺ breakfast, lunch & dinner) With a good combination of steaks, seafood stew and chop suey on offer, this retro diner should satisfy most appetites. Its specialty is Cuchumatán lamb.

La Fonda de Don Juan (2a Calle 5-35; pizzas Q47-97; ☻ 24hr) The place for Huehue's night owls and early risers, La Fonda serves varied Guatemalan and international fare, including good-value pizzas.

Museo del Café (7a Av 3-24; ☻ Mon-Sat) This recently inaugurated 'museum' serves some of Huehue's best coffee, and displays antique coffee-processing paraphernalia. You can roast your own beans for purchase if that's what you're into. Ask about coffee plantation tours.

La Biblioteca (6a Calle 6-28; ☻ 6pm-1am Tue-Sat, 11am-4pm Sun) Popular with middle-class Guatemalans, this music and sports bar has various cozy nooks on two levels.

Getting There & Away

The bus terminal is in Zona 4, 2km southwest of the plaza along 6a Calle. It's a trash-ridden, chaotic place, where a number of companies ply the same routes, though information is not posted in any coherent fashion. Microbuses leave from the south end of the station.

Two lines with a Pullman service to Guatemala City depart from their own private terminals.

Línea Dorada (☎ 7768-1566; www.lineadorada.info; Av Kaibil Balam 8-70) Departs 2:30pm, 11pm and midnight (Q90). Also has Pullman services to the Mexican border via La Mesilla, leaving at 4:30am.

Transportes Los Halcones (☎ 7765-7986; 10a Av 9-12, Zona 1) Departs 2am, 4:30am, 7am and 2pm (Q65).

There are 2nd-class bus and minibus services leaving from the bus terminal (see below). To get to Antigua, take a Guatemala City–bound bus and change at Chimaltenango. For Panajachel take a Guatemala City bus and change at Los Encuentros. For Nebaj, go to Sacapulas or Aguacatán and change there.

If you can't make one of the early morning departures for Todos Santos Cuchumatán, there are sporadic microbuses going to Tres Caminos (the Todos Santos junction), from which onward transportation is available. These depart from the El Calvario gas station at the corner of 1a Av and 1a Calle. After 11am, buses run roughly every half hour till 2pm, then hourly until 5pm.

Also, **Andrenalina Tours** (☎ 7768-1538; www. adrenalinatours.com; 4a Calle 6-54) offers daily shuttle services headed to Nebaj (Q165), Quetzaltenango (Q165), Panajachel (Q250) and elsewhere.

AROUND HUEHUETENANGO
Todos Santos Cuchumatán
pop 3500 / elev 2450m

Way up in the highlands, Todos Santos is as raw as Guatemalan village life gets – dramatic mountain scenery, mud streets, beans and tortillas and everything shut by 9pm. There are a couple of language schools operating here and this is the end point for the spectacular hike from Nebaj (see p142). Hiking is also good in the local hills. Saturday is market day, with a smaller market on Wednesday. The notorious post-market inebriation ritual has faded into history since dry laws took over (the November 1 celebrations – see p154 –

2ND-CLASS BUSES FROM HUEHUETENANGO

Destination	Cost (Q)	Duration	Departures	Frequency
Almolonga	2.50	40min	5:30am-5pm	every 15min
Aguacatán	8	30min	6am-7pm	every 20min
Barrillas	50	7hr	2am-10pm	every 10min
Cuatro Caminos	15	1½hr	6am-7pm	every 20min
Gracias a Dios (Mexican border)	30	5hr	10am-4pm	4 daily
Guatemala City	50	5hr	6am-5pm	every 30min
La Mesilla (Mexican border)	20	2hr	6am-6pm	every 15min
Quetzaltenango	20	1½hr	6am-4pm	hourly
Sacapulas	20	1½hr	11:30am & 12:45pm	2 daily
Santa Cruz del Quiché	25	2½hr	5am-5:30pm	every 15min
Soloma	25	2½hr	2am-10pm	hourly
Todos Santos Cuchumatán	25	2½hr	4am-6am	4 daily

GUATEMALA

GETTING TO CIUDAD CUAUHTÉMOC, MEXICO

Four kilometers separate the Mexican and Guatemalan immigration posts at La Mesilla and Ciudad Cuauhtémoc, and you'll have to drive, walk, hitch or take a tuk-tuk (Q4) between them. The strip in La Mesilla leading to the border post has a variety of services, including a police station, post office and a Banrural.

Moneychangers at the border give a good rate if you exchange your dollars for their pesos or quetzals, a terrible one if you want dollars for your pesos or quetzals.

If you get marooned in La Mesilla, try the very basic **Hotel Mily's** (☎ 7773-8665; s/d Q120/160; 🅿). Bargaining may be in order. Onward connections are available from the border post east to Huehuetenango and northwest to Comitán (Mexico).

See p43 for information on crossing the border from Mexico.

---

now being the only permissible time to get smashed).

The post office and Banrural are on the central plaza. The bank changes US dollars and traveler's checks.

Viajes Express (☎ 5781-0145; rigoguiadeturismo@ yahoo.com; 🕑 8am-6pm Mon-Sat, noon-6pm Sun) offers internet access (Q6 per hour) and shuttle services (see opposite). It's next door to Hotel Mam.

If you're coming to Todos Santos in winter, bring warm clothes.

COURSES

Todos Santos' one language school, the **Hispanomaya** (☎ 5163-9293; http://academiahispanomaya. org), is a nonprofit that funds scholarships for village kids to go to high school in Huehue. The standard weekly price for 25 hours' one-on-one Spanish tuition is Q985, which includes lodging and meals in a village home. Also included are two guided walks, a seminar on local life, and movies. The school also offers classes in Mam and Maya weaving (Q15 per hour).

The Hispanomaya is opposite the Museo Balam, down a side street one block east of the plaza.

FESTIVALS & EVENTS

Todos Santos is famous for the annual horse races held on **El Día de Todos los Santos** (November

1), the culmination of a week of festivities and an all-night male dancing and *aguardiente* (sugarcane liquor) drinking spree on the eve of the races. Traditional foods are served throughout the day and there are mask dances.

SLEEPING & EATING

You can arrange **homestays** (r per person Q30, with 3 meals Q45) through the language school whether or not you're studying. You'll get your own bedroom, and share the bathroom and meals with the family.

Hotelito Todos Santos (☎ 5327-9313; r Q125, s/d without bathroom Q45/90) Along a side street that goes off to the left a few meters up the hill beside the plaza. This budget option has small and bare, but well-scrubbed, rooms with tiled floors and firm beds.

Hotel Casa Familiar (☎ 5580-9579; romanstoop@ yahoo.com; s/d Q150/200) Undergoing major renovations at the time of writing, this central lodging has the town's coziest rooms, with hardwood floors, window frames, traditional textile bedspreads, good hot showers and plenty of blankets. New features include a common room with fireplace and a roof deck with a *chuj* (traditional Maya sauna).

Comedor Martita (meals Q20; 🕑 breakfast, lunch & dinner) This simple family-run *comedor*, opposite Hotel Mam, serves great food prepared with fresh ingredients in a dining room with views over the town and valley.

Comedor Katy (meals Q22; 🕑 breakfast, lunch & dinner) Women in traditional garb attend to pots of *pepián* and chicken soup bubbling over glowing embers at this similarly rustic cook shack just below the central plaza. Tables on the terrace overlook the market.

ENTERTAINMENT

Hispanomaya shows movies on Guatemalan, Maya and Latin American themes in the evening. The English-language documentaries *Todos Santos* and *Todos Santos: The Survivors,* made in the 1980s by Olivia Carrescia, are particularly fascinating to see here on the spot. They focus on the traditional life of Todos Santos and of the devastation and terror of the civil war, when, by some accounts, 2000 people were killed in the area. There's a small charge (usually about Q10) for nonstudents.

GETTING THERE & AWAY

Buses and microbuses depart from the main street between the plaza and the church.

GETTING TO MEXICO

Getting to Ciudad Hidalgo (Mexico) via Ciudad Tecún Umán (Guatemala)
This is the better and busier of the two Pacific Slope border crossings; a bridge links Ciudad Tecún Umán with **Ciudad Hidalgo**. The border is open 24 hours, and banks change US dollars and traveler's checks. Several basic hotels and restaurants are available, but there's no real point in lingering here.

Minibuses and buses between here and Guatemala depart until about 6pm along the Carretera al Pacífico to **Coatepeque, Retalhuleu, Mazatenango, Escuintla** and **Guatemala City**. Direct buses to **Quetzaltenango** (Q25, three hours) leave until about 2pm. If you don't find a bus to your destination, take one to Coatepeque or, better, Retalhuleu, and change buses there.

On the Mexican side, buses run from Ciudad Hidalgo to the city of **Tapachula** (M$15, 50 minutes) every 10 minutes, 4:30am to 10pm.

Getting to Talismán (Mexico) via El Carmen (Guatemala)
A bridge across the Río Suchiate connects El Carmen with **Talismán**. The border is open 24 hours. It's generally easier and more convenient to cross at Ciudad Tecún Umán; there are few services at El Carmen, and those are very basic. Most buses between here and the rest of Guatemala go via **Ciudad Tecún Umán**, 39km south, then along the Carretera al Pacífico through **Coatepeque, Retalhuleu** and **Escuintla**. On the way to Ciudad Tecún Umán most stop at **Malacatán** on the road to San Marcos and Quetzaltenango, so you could try looking for a bus to **Quetzaltenango** there, but it's more dependable to change at **Coatepeque** (Q20, two hours from El Carmen) or Retalhuleu.

On the Mexican side, minibuses run every 10 minutes between Talismán and **Tapachula**, from 5am to 9pm (M$10).

About 10 buses leave for Huehuetenango (Q25, 2½ hours) between 5am and 7am, then run roughly hourly until 4pm. **Adrenalina Tours** (p151) offers shuttle service from Huehuetenango on Saturdays (Q165). In Todos Santos, **Viajes Express** (☎ 5781-0145; rigoguia deturismo@yahoo.com; ⏱ 8am-6pm Mon-Sat, noon-6pm Sun) has shuttles to Huehuetenango (Q100), Panajachel (Q250) and La Mesilla (Q150) – prices given assume six passengers.

East Toward Cobán

The road from Huehuetenango to Cobán is rarely traveled and is often rugged, particularly since a major landslide buried a section of it, making a hair-raising detour necessary (see boxed text, p138). Starting early and with several transfers, you can make the 150km trip in one day. It's well worth it for the views of highland life along the way.

If the detour sounds too sketchy for you, another option is to catch a Barrillas-bound bus from Huehue (Q50, seven hours), probably stay the night in one of the basic but doable hotels there, then head on to Playa Grande (Q50, four hours) in a pick-up truck. There are reasonable hotels in Playa Grande, too. If you've got some time on your hands, consider stopping off at the **Parque Nacional** **Laguna Lachuá** (see p170), to the east of Playa Grande. From Playa Grande there are regular buses to Cobán (Q50, four hours), which pass by the entrance to the park.

THE PACIFIC SLOPE

Divided from the highlands by a chain of volcanoes, the flatlands that run down to the Pacific are known universally as La Costa. It's a sultry region – hot and wet or hot and dry, depending on the time of year, with rich volcanic soil good for growing coffee at higher elevations, and palm-oil seeds and sugarcane lower down.

Archaeologically, the big draws here are Takalik Abaj and the sculptures left by pre-Olmec civilizations around Santa Lucía Cotzumalguapa.

The culture is overwhelmingly *ladino*, and even the biggest towns are humble affairs, with low-rise wooden or concrete houses and the occasional palm-thatched roof.

Guatemalan beach tourism is seriously underdeveloped. Monterrico is the only real contender in this field, helped along by a nature reserve protecting mangroves and their inhabitants. Almost every town on the beach has places to stay, although more often than not they're very basic affairs. Sipacate gets the best waves and is slowly developing as a surf resort, although serious surfers find much more joy in Mexico or El Salvador.

RETALHULEU
pop 42,350 / elev 240m

Arriving at the bus station in Retalhuleu or Reu (ray-oo) as it's known to most Guatemalans, you're pretty much guaranteed to be underwhelmed. The neighborhood's a tawdry affair, packed out with dilapidated wooden cantinas and street vendors.

The town center, just five blocks away, is like another world – a majestic, palm-filled plaza, surrounded by some fine old buildings. Even the city police get in on the act, hanging plants outside their headquarters.

On the outskirts are the homes of wealthy plantation owners, impressive weekend getaways and the gated communities that are springing up all over the country.

The main reason most people visit the town is for access to the Takalik Abaj site (see opposite), but if you're up for some serious downtime, a couple of world-class fun parks are at IRTRA (www.irtra.org.gt), just down the road.

Orientation & Information

The town center is 4km southwest of the Carretera al Pacífico, along Calz las Palmas, a grand boulevard lined with towering palms. The bus terminal (10a Calle btwn 7a & 8a Avs) is northeast of the plaza. To find the plaza, look for the twin church towers and walk toward them.

There is no official tourist office, but people in the municipalidad (6a Av) facing the east side of the church, do their best to help.

Banco Agromercantil (5a Av) Facing the plaza, changes US dollars and traveler's checks and has a MasterCard ATM.

Banco Industrial (cnr 6a Calle & 5a Av) Changes US dollars and traveler's checks, gives cash advances on Visa cards and has a Visa ATM.

Internet (cnr 5a Calle & 6a Av; per hr Q5) Provides internet access.

Sights & Activities

The Museo de Arqueología y Etnología (6a Av 5-68; admission Q15; ⏰ 8am-12:30pm & 2-5pm Tue-Sat, 9am-12:30pm Sun) is a small museum with archaeological relics. Upstairs are historical photos and a mural showing the locations of 33 archaeological sites around Retalhuleu.

You can swim (admission Q15) at Siboney Hotel (out on the Carretera al Pacífico) even if you're not staying there.

Tours

The local tour operator, ReuXtreme (☎ 5202-8180; www.reuxtreme.com; 4a Calle 4-23, Zona 1), in the Hostal Casa San Martín, offers kayaking trips, bird-watching and nature walks, tours of local archaeological sites and shuttles to Antigua, Quetzaltenango and Panajachel, among others.

Sleeping

Posada de San Nicolás (☎ 7771-4386; posadasannicolas reu@hotmail.com; 10a Calle 8-50, Zona 1; per person with fan/air-con Q80/100; 🅿) The best budget deal in town, these are simple, clean rooms. A couple of blocks from the bus stop.

AGROTOURISM AROUND RETALHULEU

With so many beautiful *fincas* (farms) in gorgeous rural settings, it was only a matter of time before agrotourism started to take hold in Guatemala. This is seriously low-impact tourism – often you can stay in the original farmhouse and tours basically consist of walking around the property. These are all working farms – if you're planning on staying, get in touch a few days in advance to let them know you're coming. See the websites for transportation details.

Aldea Loma Linda (☎ 5724-6035; www.aldealomalinda.com; r per person without bathroom volunteers/visitors Q25/50) A beautiful village nestled in the southern foothills of the Santa María volcano. Accommodations are basic but comfortable and volunteer work is available.

Finca Santa Elena (☎ 7772-5294; www.fincasantaelena.com; Km 187 Carretera a Quetzaltenango; s/d without bathroom Q125/250; 🖥) One of the most easily accessible *fincas* in the region offering wonderfully informative tours. Accommodations is in the lovely wooden farmhouse.

Comunidad Nueva Alianza (☎ 5348-5290; www.comunidadnuevaalianza.org; dm/s/d without bathroom Q65/85/170; 🖥) Set on a hillside overlooking the coast, this farm has gorgeous views and a great hike to a nearby waterfall. Short tours are information-packed and there are various short- and long-term volunteer positions available.

our pick Hostal Casa San Martín (☎ 7771-6136; www.hostalcasasantamaria.com; 4a Calle 4-23, Zona 1; s/d from Q120/240; ✗ ⊛ ⊠) One of the more atmospheric options in town, this small hotel offers eight cool and spacious rooms with minimal but tasteful decorations. The small swimming pool in the courtyard is a good place for a dip.

Hotel Posada Don José (☎ 7771-0180; www.hotel posadadedonjose.com; 5a Calle 3-67, Zona 1; s/d Q260/330; ℗ ✗ ⊠) A beautiful colonial-style hotel built around a huge swimming pool. Swan dives from the top balcony are tempting, but probably unwise. Rooms are spacious and comfortable; the hotel is slowly remodeling here, so it's worth having a look at a few before deciding.

Eating & Drinking

Reu seems to be slightly obsessed by pizza – 5a Av north of the plaza is almost wall-to-wall pizzerias.

Cafetería La Luna (5a Calle 4-97; lunch incl drink Q20, dinner Q30; ⊙ breakfast, lunch & dinner) Opposite the west corner of the plaza, this is a town favorite for simple but filling meals in a low-key environment.

Lo de Chaz (5a Calle 4-65; mains Q25-40; ⊙ breakfast, lunch & dinner) A simple place off the plaza, serving breakfasts, icy beer, soups, snacks and seafood.

Aquí me Quedo (5a Calle 4-20; ⊙ Wed-Sat 10pm-1am) Your best bet for a few drinks in a lively atmosphere without bursting your eardrums is this friendly little upstairs bar with a great balcony that catches the odd breeze.

Getting There & Away

Most buses traveling along the Carretera al Pacífico detour into Reu. Departures include the following:

Champerico (Q9; 1hr; 38km) Buses every few minutes, 6am to 7pm.

Ciudad Tecún Umán (Q13; 1½hr; 78km) Services every 20 minutes, 5am to 10pm.

Guatemala City (regular/Pullman Q45/70; 3hr; 196km) Services every 15 minutes, 2am to 8:30pm.

Quetzaltenango (Q11; 1hr; 46km) Buses every 30 minutes, 4am to 6pm.

Santa Lucía Cotzumalguapa (Q22; 2hr; 97km) Some Escuintla- or Guatemala City–bound buses might drop you at Santa Lucía; otherwise get a bus to Mazatenango ('Mazate') and change there.

Shared taxis (Q5) are the best way to get to El Asintal (for Takalik Abaj). Look for station wagons with 'Asintal' painted on the windscreen around the bus stop and plaza.

PARQUE ARQUEOLÓGICO TAKALIK ABAJ

The active archaeological dig at Takalik Abaj (tah-kah-*leek* ah-*bah*, K'iche' for 'standing stone') is 30km west of Retalhuleu. Large Olmecoid stone heads discovered here date the site as one of the earliest in the Maya realm. The **site** (admission Q50; ⊙ 7am-5pm) has yet to be restored and prettified, so don't expect a Chichén Itzá or Tikal. But if you want to see archaeology as it's done, pay a visit. This site is believed to be one of the few places where the Olmec and Maya lived together.

To reach Takalik Abaj by public transportation, catch a shared taxi from Retalhuleu to El Asintal (Q5, 30 minutes), which is 12km northwest of Retalhuleu (Reu) and 5km north of the Carretera al Pacífico. Less frequent buses leave from a bus station on 5a Av A, 800m southwest of Reu plaza, about every half hour, 6am to 6pm. Pick-ups at El Asintal provide transportation on to Takalik Abaj (Q5) 4km further by paved road. You'll be shown around by a volunteer guide, whom you will probably want to tip. You can also visit Takalik Abaj on tours from Quetzaltenango (p144).

CHAMPERICO

The most accessible beach from Xela, Champerico isn't a bad place for a quick dip, although the rubbish-strewn sand and heavy undertow are definite turnoffs. It's a good place to avoid on weekends when the place packs out, but midweek is much mellower. A string of beachfront *comedores* serve good-value seafood dishes.

SPLURGE NEAR TAKALIK ABAJ

Set on the grounds of a working farm 2km past the entrance to the Takalik Abaj, the **Takalik Maya Lodge** (☎ 2333-7056; www.takalik.com; package/B&B per person Q620/370) is by far the most comfortable place to stay in the area. Sleeping options include the old farmhouse, or newly constructed 'Maya style' houses set in the forest. Package rates include meals and tours of the coffee, macadamia and rubber plantations, as well as guided horseback-riding tours of the waterfalls on the property and the archaeological site. Any pick-up from El Asintal passing Takalik Abaj will drop you at the entrance.

GUATEMALA

EXPLORE MORE OF THE PACIFIC COAST

The coast is, logically, all about the beach. The two most popular beach spots for travelers happen to be the ones closest to Quetzaltenango and Antigua – Champerico and Monterrico respectively, and they suffer for their popularity, both with foreign and Guatemalan tourists.

There are, however, plenty of little beach towns that are worth considering, where quite often you'll have the place to yourself:

- **Tilapita** Literally a one-hotel village, this is a great place to get away from it all and take a couple of mangrove tours while you're at it.

- **Tulate** The coastline's gentle slope into the ocean makes this one of Guatemala's best swimming beaches.

- **Chiquistepeque** A mellow little beach town that's way off the beaten track. A community literacy program that operates here is always looking for volunteers.

Beware of strong waves and an undertow if you go in the ocean, and stay in the main, central part of the beach. If you stray too far in either direction you put yourself at risk from impoverished, potentially desperate shack dwellers who live toward the ends of the beach; tourists have been victims of violent armed robberies here. Most beachgoers come on day trips, but there are several cheap hotels and restaurants. **Hotel Maza** (☎ 7773-7180; r with fan/air-con Q125/250; ✖), on the beachfront, is the best bet. The last buses back to Quetzaltenango leave at about 6pm, a bit later for Retalhuleu.

SANTA LUCÍA COTZUMALGUAPA
pop 95,300 / elev 356m

A very ordinary coastal town, Santa Lucía stretches haphazardly over a couple of hills. The pace is sleepy and there's no real reason to be here, except to check out the remarkable archaeological sites outside of town, where huge, severe stone heads sit nestled among sugar plantations.

The local people are descended from the Pipil, an indigenous culture known to have historical, linguistic and cultural links with the Nahuatl-speaking peoples of central Mexico. During the early Classic period, the Pipil grew cacao, the currency of the time. They were obsessed with the Maya-Aztec *juego de pelota* (ball game) – it's thought that the players had to try to keep a hard rubber ball airborne using any part of their body other than their hands, head or feet – and with the rites and mysteries of death. Pipil art, unlike the flowery, almost romantic Maya style, is cold and severe, but it's finely done. Just how these 'Mexicans' ended up in the midst of Maya territory remains unexplained.

Orientation & Information

Santa Lucía Cotzumalguapa is northwest of the Carretera al Pacífico. In its main square, several blocks from the highway, are copies of some of the region's famous carved stones. The town has a few basic hotels and restaurants.

The main archaeological sites to visit are Bilbao, a *finca* right on the outskirts of town; Finca El Baúl, a large plantation further from town, at which there are two sites (an interesting hilltop site and the *finca* headquarters); and Finca Las Ilusiones, which has collected most of its findings into a museum near the *finca* headquarters.

Taxi drivers in Santa Lucía's main square will take you around all three sites for about Q200 without too much haggling. In this hot and muggy climate, riding at least part of the way is a very good idea. If you do it all on foot and by bus, pack a lunch; the hilltop site at El Baúl is perfect for a picnic.

Banco Industrial (cnr 4a Av & 4a Calle), a block north of the park, changes US dollars and traveler's checks and has a Visa ATM.

Sights & Activities
BILBAO STONES

This ceremonial center flourished about AD 600. Plows have unearthed (and damaged) hundreds of carved stones during the last few centuries; thieves have carted off many others. In 1880 many of the best stones were removed to museums abroad.

Known locally as simply *Las Piedras* (The Stones), this site actually consists of several sites deep within a sugarcane *finca*. To get there you leave town northward on the road passing Iglesia El Calvario. From the intersection past the church, go 2.7km to a fork in the road just beyond a bridge; the fork is marked by a sign saying 'Los Tarros.' Take the right-hand fork, passing a settlement called Colonia Maya on your right. After you have gone 1.5km from the Los Tarros sign, a dirt track crosses the road: turn right here, between two concrete posts. Ahead now is a low mound topped by three large trees: this is the **hilltop site**. After about 250m fork right between two more identical concrete posts,

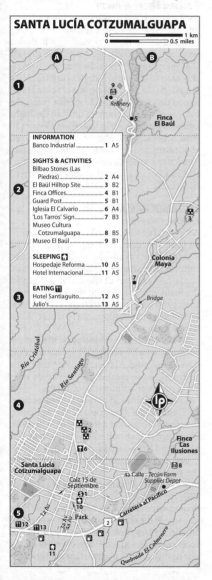

SANTA LUCÍA COTZUMALGUAPA

0	1 km
0	0.5 miles

INFORMATION
Banco Industrial 1   A5

SIGHTS & ACTIVITIES
Bilbao Stones (Las
   Piedras) 2   A4
El Baúl Hilltop Site 3   B2
Finca Offices......................... 4   B1
Guard Post............................ 5   B1
Iglesia El Calvario 6   A4
'Los Tarros' Sign.................... 7   B3
Museo Cultura
   Cotzumalguapa.................. 8   B5
Museo El Baúl 9   B1

SLEEPING
Hospedaje Reforma 10   A5
Hotel Internacional 11   A5

EATING
Hotel Santiaguito...............12   A5
Julio's.................................13   A5

and follow this track around in front of the mound to its end after some 150m, and take the path up on to the mound, which is actually a great ruined temple platform that has not been restored.

Although some stones are badly worn, others bear Mexican-style circular date glyphs and more mysterious patterns that resemble those used by people along the Gulf Coast of Mexico near Villahermosa.

To continue to El Baúl, backtrack to where you turned right just beyond Iglesia El Calvario. Buses to El Baúl pass this point every few hours; you can also hitch. If driving, you'll have to return to the town center along 4a Av and come back out on 3a Av, as these roads are one way.

FINCA EL BAÚL

Just as interesting is the **hilltop site** at El Baúl, an active place of worship for locals. Some distance from the site along another road, next to the *finca* headquarters, is the *finca*'s private **museum** (admission free; ☺ 8am-4pm Mon-Fri, 8am-noon Sat), containing stones that were uncovered on the property.

El Baúl is 4.2km northwest of El Calvario church. From the church (or the intersection just beyond it), go 2.7km to a fork in the road just beyond a bridge; look for the 'Los Tarros' sign – buses will go up to here. Take the right fork (an unpaved road). From the Los Tarros sign it's 1.5km to the point where a dirt track crosses the road; on your right is a tree-covered 'hill' in the midst of flat fields. It's actually a great, unrestored temple platform. Make your way across the field and around the hill's south side, following the track to the top. If you have a car, you can drive to within 50m of the top. If you visit this hilltop site on a weekend, you may find worshipers here; people have been coming to pay homage to the idols for over 1400 years.

Of the two stones here, the great grotesque **half-buried head** is the more striking. The elaborate headdress, 'blind' eyes with big bags underneath, beaklike nose and smug grin seem at odds with the blackened face and its position, half-buried in the ancient soil. The head is stained with candle wax, liquor, and the smoke and ashes of incense fires – all part of worship. The other stone is a relief carving of a figure surrounded by circular motifs that may be date glyphs. A copy of this stone is in Santa Lucía's main square.

GUATEMALA

From the hilltop site, backtrack 1.5km to the fork with the Los Tarros sign. Take the other fork this time, and follow the paved road 3km to the headquarters of Finca El Baúl. (If you're on foot, you can walk from the hilltop site back to the unpaved road and straight across it, continuing on the dirt track. This will eventually bring you to the asphalt road that leads to the *finca* headquarters. When you reach the road, turn right.) Buses trundle along this road every few hours, shuttling workers between the refinery and the town center.

Approaching the *finca* headquarters (6km from Santa Lucía's main square), cross a narrow bridge. Continue uphill and you will see the entrance on the left, marked by a machinegun pillbox. Beyond, you pass workers' houses and a sugar refinery on the right, and finally come to the headquarters. Ask permission to visit the museum and a guard will unlock the gate. **Museo El Baúl** (admission free; ☺ 8am-4pm Mon-Fri, 8am-noon Sat) comprises a very fine open-air collection of Pipil stone sculpture collected from around Finca El Baúl's sugarcane fields.

Within the gates are numerous sculpted figures and reliefs found on the plantation, some of which are very fine.

MUSEO CULTURA COTZUMALGUAPA

This indoor **museum** (admission Q25; ☺ 8am-4pm Mon-Fri, 8am-noon Sat) is very close to Bilbao – set in the *finca* that controls the Bilbao sugarcane fields – but, paradoxically, access is more difficult. Your reward is the chance to view hundreds of objects that have been collected from the fields over the centuries.

About 1.5km east of the town center on Carretera al Pacífico, shortly before the Tecún farm-supplies depot, take a side track 400m to the left (north) to find the museum.

Sleeping & Eating

Hospedaje Reforma (4a Av 4-71; s/d Q40/70) This hotel has exactly three things going for it: it's cheap, central and the patio is decorated with stuffed boars' heads. And if you like sleeping in dark and airless little concrete cells, make that four.

Hotel Internacional (☎ 7882-5504; Callejón los Mormones; s/d Q90/140; [P] [☺]) Down a short lane (signposted) off Carretera al Pacífico is the best budget hotel in town. It has clean, good-sized rooms with a fan, cold showers and a TV. Air-conditioning costs Q70 extra.

Julio's (Carretera al Pacífico Km 90.5; mains Q30-50; ☺ breakfast, lunch & dinner) An excellent little local

diner out on the highway, serving satisfying breakfasts and good-value set meals.

Hotel Santiaguito (☎ 7882-5435; Carretera al Pacífico Km 90.4; mains Q30-80) The restaurant at this hotel, on the highway on the west edge of town, is a good option, and there's a swimming pool that nonguests can use for Q20 per day.

Getting There & Away

As the Hwy CA-2 now bypasses Santa Lucía, lots of buses don't come into town. Coming to Santa Lucía from the east, you'll almost certainly need to change buses at Escuintla (Q9, 30 minutes). From the west you'll probably have to change at Mazatenango (Q13, 1¼ hours). At Cocales, 23km west of Santa Lucía, a road down from Lago de Atitlán meets the CA-2, providing a route to or from the highlands. Eight buses daily run from Cocales to Panajachel (Q22, 2½ hours, 70km), between about 6am and 2pm. At the time of writing there were reports of robberies along this stretch of road; ask around about the current situation.

LA DEMOCRACIA
pop 6580 / elev 165m

A sleepy little village on the way to the beach, La Democracia makes it on the map for further investigation into the mysterious, ancient culture that carved the heads found around Santa Lucía. More of these can be seen in the main square here, and the local museum has a surprisingly good collection of artifacts, considering its location. There is a 5B ATM on the main plaza.

At the **Monte Alto archaeological site**, on the outskirts of La Democracia, huge basalt heads have been found. Although cruder, the heads resemble those carved by the Olmec near Veracruz several thousand years ago.

Today these heads are arranged around La Democracia's main plaza. As you come into town from the highway, follow signs to the *museo,* which will lead you left, then left again, and left yet again.

Facing the plaza, along with the church and the modest Palacio Municipal, is the small, modern **Museo Regional de Arqueología** (☎ 7880-3650; admission Q30; ☺ 8am-4pm Tue-Sat), which houses some fascinating archaeological finds. The star of the show is an exquisite jade mask. Smaller figures, 'yokes' used in the ball game, relief carvings and other objects make up the rest of this small but important collection.

Sleeping & Eating

Guest House Paxil de Cayala (☎ 7880-3129; s/d without bathroom Q50/100) Half a block from the plaza, La Democracia's only place to stay is OK for the night, with big, mosquito-proofed rooms.

Burger Chops (mains Q25-45; ☺ breakfast, lunch & dinner) Also just off the square, this is as close as the town gets to a restaurant.

The flour tortillas stuffed with meat from the little roadside stands around the plaza are delicious, and a bargain at Q15.

Getting There & Away

The Chatía Gomerana company runs buses every half hour, 6am to 4:30pm, from the Centra Sur terminal in Guatemala City to La Democracia (Q20, two hours) via Escuintla. From Santa Lucía Cotzumalguapa, catch a bus 8km east to Siquinalá and change there.

SIPACATE

An hour and a half down the road from Santa Lucía is Guatemala's surf capital. Waves here average 6ft (2m), the best time being between December and April. The town is separated from the beach by the Canal de Chiquimulilla. Oddly unexploited, the beach here has only a couple of hotels, the budget choice being **El Paradon** (☎ 4593-2490; www.surfguatemala.net84.net; campsites/dm/r without bathroom per person Q20/45/170), a rustic little surf camp to the east of the village. It's run by a couple of Guatemalan surfers, and board and kayak hire, surf lessons and good, simple meals (Q30 to Q50) are available. Book in advance.

Straight across the canal from Sipacate is **Rancho Carillo** (☎ 5517-1069; www.marmaya.com; r from Q375, 6-person bungalows from Q800; ✗ ⟑), a short boat ride (Q30 round trip) from town. The only trouble you'll have sleeping is from the noise of crashing waves. Call ahead and you'll probably be able to get a better price. Surfboards are available for rent here. There are a couple of cheaper, basic *hospedajes* (singles/doubles Q35/80) in town, but remember you'll be paying for the boat ride every day. Buses from Guatemala City's Centra Sur terminal (Q32, 3½ hours) pass through La Democracia en route to Sipacate every two hours.

ESCUINTLA

pop 144,720

Hot, noisy and crowded, Escuintla has good bus connections and very little else for the average traveler. Banks are located around the

plaza. There's an **ATM** (Farmacia Herdez; cnr 13a Calle & 4a Av), one block uphill from the bus terminal. Escuintla has some marginal hotels and restaurants. If stranded, try the **Hotel Costa Sur** (☎ 5295-9528; 12a Calle 4-13; s/d Q80/110; ✗), a couple of doors from Banco Reformador, which has decent, cool rooms with TV and fan. Air-con costs an extra Q20. The **Hotel Sarita** (☎ 7888-1959; Av Centro América 15-32; s/d Q380/480; ✗ ⟑ ⟑), behind the gloriously air-conditioned restaurant (mains Q40 to Q70) of the same name, provides more comfort.

All buses from the terminal pass along 1a Av, but if you really want a seat, head to the main bus station in the southern part of town, just off 4a Av. Its entrance is marked by a Scott 77 gas station. Buses depart for Antigua (Q7, one hour) about every half hour, from 5:30am to 4:30pm. Buses going to Guatemala City (Q35, 1½ hours) go about every 20 minutes from the street outside, from 5am to 6pm. There are buses all the way through to Monterrico at 12:50pm, 3:30pm and 4:50pm (Q25, one hour); otherwise catch a bus to Puerto San José or Iztapa and make a connection there. Buses coming along the Carretera al Pacífico may drop you in the north of town, necessitating a sweaty walk through the hectic town center if you want to get to the main station.

MONTERRICO

A favorite for weekending Guatemalans (and Antigua-based language students), Monterrico is a relatively pretty town that is slowly developing into a coastal resort.

On the outskirts, particularly to the south, are some very opulent weekend houses owned by Guatemala City movers and shakers. Seeing these mansions next to simple thatched-roof huts is a stark reminder of the polarity of Guatemala's economic reality.

Swimming is good here, and there's occasionally a wave worth surfing. Take care, though – a vicious undertow claims victims every year.

Weekends can be hectic. Come on a weekday and you'll find a much mellower scene (with lower hotel prices). The village has a post office (on Calle Principal) but no bank. Internet access is available from the optimistically named **Speed Internet** (per hr Q12) on the main street near the ferry dock. Even if you're not studying at the Proyecto Lingüístico Monterrico (p162), the school is the best source of tourist information in town.

Behind the beach, on the other side of town, is a large network of mangrove swamps and canals, part of the 190km Canal de Chiquimulilla. Also in the area is a large wildlife reserve and a center for the hatching and release of sea turtles and caimans (crocodilians similar to alligators).

Sights & Activities

A big attraction is the **Biotopo Monterrico-Hawaii**, a 20km-long nature reserve of coastal mangrove swamps filled with bird and aquatic life. The reserve is a breeding area for endangered leatherback and olive ridley turtles, who lay their eggs on the beach in many places along the coast.

Canals lace the swamps, connecting 25 lagoons hidden among the mangroves. **Boat tours** of the reserve, passing through the mangrove swamps and visiting several lagoons, take around 1½ to two hours and cost Q75 for one person, Q50 for additional people. Sunrise is the best time for wildlife. If you have binoculars, bring them for bird-watching, which is best in January and February. Locals will approach you on the street (some with very impressive-looking ID cards), offering tours, but if you want to support the Tortugario (who, incidentally, have the most environmentally knowledgeable guides), arrange a tour directly through the Cecon-run Tortugario Monterrico.

Tortugario Monterrico visitors center (admission Q40; ☺ 8am-noon & 2-5pm) is just a short walk east down the beach and back a block from the Monterrico hotels (left, if you're facing the sea). Several endangered species of animals are raised here, including leatherback, olive ridley and green sea turtles, caimans and iguanas. There's an interesting interpretative trail and a little museum with pickled displays in bottles. The staff offer lagoon trips (see Boat tours, above), night walks (Q25) from September to February to look for turtle eggs, and will accept volunteers.

Proyecto Lingüístico Monterrico (☎ 5475-1265; espanolmonterrico@yahoo.com; Calle Principal) is a recommended Spanish school based in central Monterrico; 20 hours of study per week costs Q750/1150/1250 tuition only/with homestay/in self-catering accommodations.

The Arcas-run **Reserva Natural Hawaii** (☎ 4144-2142; www.arcasguatemala.com) comprises a sea-turtle hatchery with some caimans 8km east along the beach from Monterrico. It is separate from and rivals Cecon's work in the same field.

Volunteers are welcome year-round, but the real sea-turtle-nesting season is from June to November, with August and September being the peak months. Volunteers are charged Q580 a week for a room, with meals extra and homestay options. A bus (Q5, 30 minutes) leaves the Monterrico jetty every couple of hours during the week and every hour on weekends for the bumpy ride to the reserve. Pick-ups (Q30 per person) also operate on this route. Check out the Arcas website for more information.

Guatemala City–based **Productos Mundiales** (☎ 2366-1026; www.productos-mundiales.com; 3a Av 17-05, Zona 14, Guatemala City) offers marine wildlife-watching tours (from Q1250 per person, six hours), leaving from nearby Puerto Iztapa. Throughout the year you stand a pretty good chance of seeing pilot whales, bottlenose dolphins, spinner dolphins, olive ridley turtles, leatherback turtles, giant manta rays and whale sharks. From December to May, humpback and sperm whales can also be seen. Reservations (five days in advance via bank account deposit) are essential – see its website for details.

Sleeping & Eating

All hotels listed here are on the beach, unless otherwise stated. To save a difficult, hot walk along the beach, take the last road to the left before you hit the sand. All these hotels either front or back onto it – except for Hostel El Gecko. The majority have restaurants serving whatever is fresh from the sea that day. Many accommodations offer discounts for stays of three nights or more. Reserve for weekends if you want to avoid a long hot walk while you cruise around asking for vacancies. Weekend prices are given here. Midweek, you'll have plenty more bargaining power.

Johnny's Place (☎ 5812-0409; www.johnnysplacehotel.com; dm Q45, r Q160, 4-person bungalows Q350; P ☺) The first place you come to turning left on the beach, Johnny's is one of the biggest operations in town. Rooms could be better – some are run-down and others lack light. It has a decent atmosphere though, and attracts a good mix of backpackers and family groups.

Hostel El Gecko (dm with/without kitchen use Q50/35) Going in the opposite direction from most of the hotels (ie heading right from Calle Principal), the first place you'll come to is this very basic hostel run by a couple of young Guatemalans. There are very few frills here, but it's a backpackers' favorite, for the cheap beds and friendly atmosphere.

Brisas del Mar (☎ 5517-1142; s/d Q60/120; P ☒) Behind Johnny's, one block back from the beach, this popular newcomer offers good-sized rooms and a 2nd-floor dining hall with excellent sea views.

El Mangle (☎ 5514-6517; r with fan/air-con Q125/250; P ☒ ☒) Eclectic decorations fill the grounds of this friendly little place 300m further along the beach. Rooms are decent-sized, with hammocks strung on individual porches. The restaurant here pumps out some very tasty wood-fired pizza.

Hotel Pez de Oro (☎ 2368-3684; www.pezdeoro.com; s/d Q350/390; P ☒) This is the funkiest looking place in town, with comfortable little huts and bungalows scattered around a shady property. The color scheme is a cheery blue and yellow and the rooms have some tasteful decorations and big overhead fans. The excellent restaurant, with big sea views, serves great Italian cuisine and seafood dishes. Pastas cost from Q50, whole fish from Q60.

Taberna El Pelicano (mains Q60-120; ☙ lunch & dinner Wed-Sat) By far the best place to eat in town, with the widest menu and most interesting food, such as seafood risotto (Q70), beef carpaccio (Q55) and a range of jumbo shrimp dishes (Q120).

There are many simple seafood restaurants on Calle Principal. For the best cheap eats, hit either of the two nameless *comedores* on the last road to the right before the beach, where you can pick up an excellent plate of garlic shrimp, rice tortillas, fries and salad for Q40.

Drinking & Entertainment

Las Mañanitas (mains Q50-80; ☙ lunch-late) On the beachfront at the end of the main street, this little beach bar is what Monterrico really needed – plenty of hammock chairs looking out over the beach, a good range of drinks and low-key music playing in the background.

Playa Club (Johnny's Place; ☎ 5812-0409; www.johnnys placehotel.com) This club heats up on weekends, with plenty of reggaetón, house music and drinks specials keeping the crowd moving.

Getting There & Away

There are two ways to get to Monterrico. Coming from Guatemala City or Antigua, it's most logical to catch a bus which, with the new bridge at Pueblo Viejo, goes right through to Monterrico. The Pueblo Viejo–Monterrico stretch makes for a pretty journey, revealing local life at a sane pace.

The other option is to head to La Avellana, where *lanchas* and car ferries depart for Monterrico. The Cubanita company runs a handful of direct buses to and from Guatemala City (Q40, four hours, 124km). Alternatively, you reach La Avellana by changing buses at Taxisco on Hwy CA-2. Buses operate half-hourly from 5am to 4pm between Guatemala City and Taxisco (Q35, 3½ hours) and roughly hourly from 7am to 4:30pm between Taxisco and La Avellana (Q5, 40 minutes), although taxi drivers will tell you that you've missed the last bus, regardless of what time you arrive. A taxi between Taxisco and La Avellana costs around Q60.

From La Avellana catch a *lancha* or car ferry to Monterrico. The collective *lanchas* charge Q5 per passenger for the half-hour trip along the Canal de Chiquimulilla, a long mangrove canal. They start at 4:30am and run more or less every half hour or hour until late afternoon. You can always pay more and charter your own boat. The car ferry costs Q80 per vehicle.

Shuttle buses also serve Monterrico. **Mario's Tours** (☎ 7762-6040; www.mariostours.net; Calle Principal, Panajachel) goes to Panajachel (Q370 per person). **Adrenalina Tours** (www.adrenalinatours.com) covers Antigua (Q125), Panajachel (Q415) and San Pedro la Laguna (Q330). The services listed here may not leave every day, but there is a daily shuttle that runs from outside the Proyecto Lingüístico Monterrico at 1pm and 4pm, which charges Q60/130 to Antigua/Guatemala City. Book tickets at the school.

CENTRAL GUATEMALA

This region holds some of the best, most rewarding opportunities for getting off the beaten track. While the tour buses are all whizzing between the capital and Tikal, independent travelers are finding a wealth of undiscovered gems.

Semuc Champey and Grutas de Lanquín are on everybody's list if you're in Guatemala, but there are literally hundreds more caves, waterfalls and other natural attractions to check out, mostly scattered around the well-established travelers' hub of Cobán. Check www.cobanav.net for a little inspiration.

SALAMÁ
pop 30,100 / elev 940m
A wonderful introduction to the Baja Verapaz department's not-too-hot, not-too-cold

climate, Salamá is a town with a couple of attractions. Excellent information on the area is available at www.laverapaz.com.

Hwy 17, also marked as CA-14 on maps, leaves the Carretera al Atlántico at El Rancho, 84km from Guatemala City. It heads west through dry, desertlike lowlands, then turns north and ascends into the forested hills. The turnoff for Salamá is 47km from Guatemala City.

Banrural (9am-5pm Mon-Fri, to 1pm Sat) on the south side of the plaza (opposite the church) changes cash and traveler's checks, and has a Visa and MasterCard ATM. Internet access (Q6 per hour) is available at Telgua, just east of the plaza. A police station is one block west of the plaza.

Sights

Attractive Salamá has some reminders of colonial rule. The main plaza boasts an ornate **colonial church** with gold-encrusted altars and a carved pulpit (look for it to the left before the altar). Be sure to check out Jesus lying in a glass coffin with cotton bunting in his stigmata and droplets of blood seeping from his hairline. Thick mascara and the silver lamé pillow on which he rests his head complete the scene. The Salamá **market** is impressive for its colorful, local bustle, particularly on Sunday.

Tours

EcoVerapaz (5722-9095; ecoverapaz@hotmail.com; 8a Av 7-12, Zona 1) has local, trained naturalists offering interesting tours throughout Baja Verapaz, including caving, bird-watching, hiking, horseback-riding and orchid trips. The company also goes to Rabinal to check out its museum and crafts, and arranges trips to see

the famous rodeos of Baja Verapaz. Guides speak some English. One-day tours are Q350 per person and group discounts are offered.

Sleeping

Turicentro Las Orquídeas (7940-1622; Carretera a Salamá Km 147; campsites Q30) Travelers with camping gear may want to check out this place. Here, a few kilometers east of Salamá out on Hwy 17, the Turicentro has a grassy area for camping plus a cafe, pool and open spaces hung with hammocks. You can use the pool (Q20 per person per day) even if you're not camping here.

Hotel Rosa de Sharon (5774-8650; 5a Calle 6-39; s/d Q80/130; P) The neat, bright rooms here loom over the busy market area, but they're set back from the road, so remain peaceful. They're big and clean, with whacky decorations such as wrought-iron hat stands made to look like trees.

Posada de Don Maco (7940-0083; 3a Calle 8-26; s/d Q110/140; P) This clean, family-run place has simple but spacious rooms with fan and good bathrooms. The courtyard includes a collection of caged squirrels.

Eating

You don't have to step far from the plaza to eat well, but don't plan a late dinner – restaurants close early here, with the exception being on Pollo Campero on the plaza.

Café Deli-Donas (15a Calle 6-61; cakes Q15, sandwiches Q25, licuados Q15; 8am-6pm Mon-Sat) This exceedingly pleasant little cafe (where even the bathrooms smell good) is like an oasis in Salama's busy market zone. Excellent coffee, homemade cakes and light meals are the go here.

EXPLORE MORE OF BAJA VERAPAZ

The countryside around Salamá has some wonderful, little-visited attractions.

The village of **San Jerónimo**, between the highway and Salamá has a beautiful **church**, and a former sugar mill that is now a **museum** (admission free; 8am-4pm Mon-Fri, 10am-noon & 1-4pm Sat & Sun). On the town plaza are some large stones that were carved in ancient times.

Nine kilometers west of Salamá is **San Miguel Chicaj**, known for its traditional **fiesta** (September 25–29) and weaving.

Past San Miguel, the colonial town of **Rabinal** is famous for its ceramics, citrus plantations and adherence to pre-Columbian traditions. The annual **fiesta of St Peter** (January 19–25) is a good time to be in town.

On the eastern side of the highway, the **Salto de Chalisco** (www.chilasco.net.ms; admission Q15) is reportedly Central America's highest waterfall. You can stay here as part of a community-run tourism initiative. See the website for details.

Antojitos Zacapanecos (cnr 6a Calle & 8a Av; mains Q20; ☼ lunch & dinner) For something a little different in the fast-food vein, check out the huge flour tortillas filled with pork, chicken or beef from this place. Better yet, grab one to go and have a picnic in the plaza.

Cafetería Central (cnr 15a Calle & 9a Av; lunches Q30; ☼ breakfast & lunch) Try the savory, filling lunches at this place a few doors back toward the plaza from Cafe Deli-Donas. The chicken broth followed by grilled chicken, rice and salad, with perhaps a mango to finish, is a worthy feast.

Getting There & Away

Buses going to Guatemala City (Q30 to Q40, three hours, 151km) depart hourly between 3am and 8pm from the northeast corner of the park. There is a scheduled Pullman at 3am, with others sometimes rolling through unannounced. Arrive early for a seat. Buses coming from Guatemala City continue west from Salamá to Rabinal (Q5, 40 minutes, 19km) and then 15km further along to Cubulco. Buses for San Jerónimo (Q4, 25 minutes), La Cumbre (Q3, 25 minutes) and Cobán (Q20, 1½ to two hours) all leave from the northwest corner of the park in front of Antojitos Zacapanecos, about every half hour from early morning to 4pm.

BIOTOPO DEL QUETZAL

Along the main highway (CA-14) 34km north of the turnoff for Salamá is the Biotopo Mario Dary Rivera reserve, commonly called the **Biotopo del Quetzal** (admission Q35; ☼ 7am-4pm); it's at Km 161, near the village of Purulhá (no services). The ride along here is sobering: entire hillsides are deforested and covered in huge sheets of black plastic meant to optimize growing conditions for *xate,* a low-growing green palm exported for use in floral arrangements.

If you intend on seeing a quetzal, Guatemala's national bird, you'll likely be disappointed – the birds are rare and elusive, and their habitat is almost destroyed. The best time to see them is between February and September. However, it's still worth a visit to explore their lush, high-altitude cloud-forest habitat.

Two well-maintained trails wind through the reserve past several waterfalls, most of which cascade into swimmable pools. Deep in the forest is **Xiu Ua Li Che** (Grandfather Tree), some 450 years old, which was alive when the conquistadors fought the Rabinals in these mountains.

SPLURGE IN THE BIOTOPO DEL QUETZAL

Quite likely the most beautiful hotel in the Verapaz region, the **Hotel Restaurant Ram Tzul** (☎ 2355-1904; www.m-y-c.com.ar/ramtzul; Hwy 14 Km 158; s/d Q245/355; P) is 3km from the *biotopo* entrance. The restaurant/sitting area is in a tall, thatched-roof structure with fire pits and plenty of atmosphere. The rustic, upmarket theme extends to the rooms and bungalows, which are spacious and elegantly decorated and the hotel property includes waterfalls and swimming spots.

The reserve has a visitors center, a little shop for drinks and snacks, and a camping and barbecue area. The ruling on camping changes often. Check by contacting **Cecon** (☎ 2331-0904; www.usac.edu.gt/cecon, in Spanish; Av La Reforma 0-63, Zona 10, Guatemala City), which administers this and other *biotopos*. Trail guide maps in English and Spanish (Q5) are sometimes available at the visitors center. They contain a checklist of 87 birds commonly seen here. Other animals include spider monkeys and *tigrillos,* similar to ocelots. Good luck.

Services in the area include the **Parque Ecológico Gucumatz** (☎ 5368-6397; s/d old building Q100/140, new building Q130/170; P), carved out of the jungle on a hillside 200m away from the *biotopo* entrance, has good-sized, simple rooms with cold showers in the older wooden building and hot showers in the newer concrete one. Reasonably priced, simple meals (mains around Q30) are served, and there are vegetarian options.

Any bus to/from Guatemala City will set you down at the park entrance. Heading in the other direction, it's best to flag down a bus or microbus to El Rancho and change there for your next destination. The road between the *biotopo* and Cobán is good – smooth and fast (although curvy). As you ascend into the evergreen forests, you'll still see tropical flowers here and there.

COBÁN

pop 67,000 / elev 1320m

Not so much an attraction in itself, but an excellent jumping-off point for the natural wonders of Alta Verapaz, Cobán is a prosperous city with an upbeat air. Return visitors will marvel at how much (and how tastefully) the town has developed since their last visit.

This was once a stronghold of the Rabinal Maya. In the 19th century, German immigrants moved in, founding vast coffee and cardamom *fincas* and giving Cobán the look and feel of a German mountain town. The era of German cultural and economic domination ended during WWII, when the US prevailed upon the Guatemalan government to deport the powerful *finca* owners, many of whom supported the Nazis.

Guatemala's most impressive indigenous festival, the folkloric festival of **Rabin Ajau**, takes place in late July or early August.

Orientation & Information

Most services of interest to travelers are within a few blocks of the plaza. Most buses will drop you out of town at the Campo Dos bus terminal north of town. It's a 15-minute walk (2km) or Q10 taxi ride to the plaza from there. The heart of Cobán is built on a rise, so unless what you're looking for is in the dead center, you'll be trudging uphill and downhill.

Along with the offices listed here, the Casa D'Acuña (p168) can also give you loads of information.

Banco G&T (1a Calle) Opposite Casa Blanc Hostel, has a MasterCard ATM. Good for changing US dollars and traveler's checks.

Banco Industrial (cnr 1a Calle & 7a Av, Zona 1) Has a Visa ATM. Can change US dollars and traveler's checks.

Cybercobán (3a Av 1-11, Zona 4; per hr Q5) East of the plaza.

Inguat (☎ 7951-0216; 7a Av 1-17, Zona 1; ⏰ 8am-4pm Mon-Fri, 9am-1pm Sat)

Lavandería Econo Express (7a Av 2-32, Zona 1; wash & dry Q30) Laundry facilities.

Mayan Internet (6a Av 2-28; per hr Q5) West of the plaza.

Municipalidad (1a Calle, Zona 1; ☎ 7952-1305, 7951-1148) Some switched-on young staff work in an office behind the police office.

Post office (crn 2a Av &3a Calle) A block southeast of the plaza. There are plenty of card phones outside Telgua on the plaza.

Sights & Activities
TEMPLO EL CALVARIO

You'll get a fine view over town from this church atop a long flight of stairs at the north end of 7a Av Zona 1. Indigenous people leave offerings at shrines and crosses in front of the church.

PARQUE NACIONAL LAS VICTORIAS

This forested 82-hectare **national park** (admission Q10; ⏰ 8am-4:30pm, walking trails 9am-3pm), right in town, has ponds, barbecue, picnic areas, campgrounds, children's play areas, a lookout point and extensive trails. The entrance is near the corner of 3a Calle and 9a Av, Zona 1. It's an isolated spot – consider hiking in a group.

VIVERO VERAPAZ

Orchid lovers mustn't miss a chance to see the many thousands of species at this famous **nursery** (☎ 7952-1133; Carretera Antigua de Entrada a Cobán; admission Q10; ⏰ 9am-noon & 2-4pm). The rare *monja blanca*, or white nun orchid (Guatemala's national flower), grows here, as do hundreds of miniature orchid species. The national orchid show is held here each December.

Vivero Verapaz is on the Carretera Antigua de Entrada a Cobán, about 2km from the town center – a 40-minute walk southwest from the plaza. You can hire a taxi for around Q20.

FINCA SANTA MARGARITA

This working **coffee farm** (☎ 7952-1586; 3a Calle 4-12, Zona 2; admission Q30; ⏰ guided tours 8am-12:30pm & 1:30-5pm Mon-Fri, 8am-noon Sat) offers guided tours of its operation. From propagation and planting to roasting and exporting, the 45-minute tour will tell you all you ever wanted to know about these powerful beans. At tour's end, you're treated to a cup of coffee and can purchase beans straight from the roaster for Q25 to Q40 per 500g. The talented guide speaks English and Spanish.

MUSEO EL PRÍNCIPE MAYA

This private **museum** (☎ 7952-1541; 6a Av 4-26, Zona 3; admission Q10; ⏰ 9am-6pm Mon-Sat) features a collection of pre-Columbian artifacts, with an emphasis on jewelry, other body adornments and pottery. The displays are well designed and maintained.

ASK A LOCAL

I'm always surprised when people come to Cobán and they don't visit the Parque Nacional Las Victorias (see above). We have a beautiful national park, right next to the center of the city – where else are you going to see that?

Encarnación Morán, Cobán

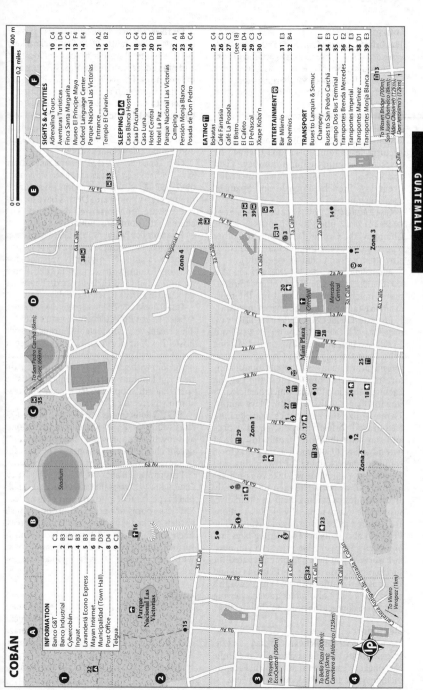

COBÁN

GUATEMALA

INFORMATION
Banco G&T	1	C3
Banco Industrial	2	B3
Cybercobán	3	E3
Inguat	4	B3
Lavandería Econo Express	5	B3
Mayan Internet	6	B3
Municipalidad (Town Hall)	7	D3
Post Office	8	D4
Telgua	9	C3

SIGHTS & ACTIVITIES
Adrenalina Tours	10	C4
Aventuras Turísticas	11	D4
Finca Santa Margarita	12	C4
Museo El Príncipe Maya	13	F4
Oxford Language Center	14	E4
Parque Nacional Las Victorias Entrance	15	A2
Templo El Calvario	16	B2

SLEEPING
Casa Blanca Hostel	17	C3
Casa D'Acuña	18	C4
Casa Luna	19	C3
Hotel Central	20	D3
Hotel La Paz	21	B3
Parque Nacional Las Victorias Camping	22	A1
Pensión Monja Blanca	23	B4
Posada de Don Pedro	24	C4

EATING
Bokatas	25	C4
Café Fantasia	26	C3
Café La Posada	27	C3
El Bistro	(see 18)	
El Cafeto	28	D4
El Peñascal	29	C3
Xkape Kob'n	30	C4

ENTERTAINMENT
Bar Milenio	31	E3
Bohemios	32	B4

TRANSPORT
Buses to Lanquín & Semuc Champey	33	E1
Buses to San Pedro Carchá	34	E3
Campo Dos Bus Terminal	35	C1
Transportes Brenda Mercedes	36	E2
Transportes Imperial	37	E3
Transportes Martínez	38	D1
Transportes Monja Blanca	39	E3

Courses

The **Oxford Language Center** (☎ 5892-7718; www.olc english.com; 4a Av 2-16, Zona 3) charges around Q1400 for 20 hours of Spanish lessons, with discounts for groups. Its rationale for charging more than the competition is that it pays its teachers better.

Tours

Aventuras Turísticas (☎ 7951-4213; www.aventuras turisticas.com; 3a Calle 2-38, Zona 3), in Hostal de Doña Victoria, leads tours to Laguna Lachuá, the caves of Lanquín, Semuc Champey, Tikal and Ceibal, and will customize itineraries. It employs French-, English- and Spanish-speaking guides.

Casa D'Acuña (☎ 7951-0484; casadacuna@yahoo.com; 4a Calle 3-11, Zona 2) offers its own tours to Semuc Champey, the Grutas de Lanquín and other places further afield. Its guides are excellent. It also offers accommodation (see right).

Adrenalina Tours (☎ 7951-2200; www.adrenalina tours.com; Diagonal 4, 3-36, Zona 2) offers tours to pretty much everywhere, and has the most extensive range of shuttle services in town.

Proyecto EcoQuetzal (☎ /fax 7952-1047; www. ecoquetzal.org; 2a Calle 14-36, Zona 1; ☿ 8:30am-1pm & 2-5:30pm Mon-Fri) is an innovative project offering 'ethnotourism' trips to the Chicacnab cloud forests (near Cobán) and the subtropical rain-forests of Rocjá Pomtilá (near the Laguna Lachuá; see also p170) in which participants stay in villages with a Q'eqchi' Maya family. To maximize the experience, travelers are encouraged to learn some Q'eqchi' words and stay with their host family for at least two days. For Q300 you'll get a guide for a couple of days, lodging for two nights, and four meals. Your guide will take you on hikes to interesting spots. The men of the family are the guides, providing them an alternative, sustainable way to make a living. Reservations are required at least one day in advance. The Proyecto also rents boots, sleeping bags and binoculars at reasonable prices, so you need not worry if you haven't come prepared for such a rugged experience. Participants should speak at least a little Spanish. With a month's notice, this outfit also offers quetzal-viewing platforms; contact the office for full details.

Sleeping

Parque Nacional Las Victorias Camping (campsites per person Q20) Camping is available at Parque Nacional Las Victorias, right in town. Facilities include water and toilets, but no showers.

Casa Blanca Hostel (☎ 4034-9291; 1a Calle 3-25, Zona 1; dm/s/d without bathroom Q35/50/100) This backpackers' favorite is a total winner in terms of location, and offers decent shared rooms, sleeping four in two bunks. The patio has a good simple cafe and the young staff are full of info and tips.

Hotel La Paz (☎ 7952-1358; 6a Av 2-19, Zona 1; s/d Q40/75; P) This cheerful, clean hotel, 1½ blocks north and two blocks west of the plaza, is an excellent deal. It has many flowerbeds, and a good cafetería next door.

Casa Luna (☎ 7951-3528; www.cobantravels.com; 5a Av 2-28, Zona 1; dm/s/d without bathroom incl breakfast Q50/75/150; ▯ ☎) Modern rooms set around a pretty, grassy courtyard. Dorms have lockers and private rooms are well decorated. The shared bathrooms are spotless.

Posada de Don Pedro (☎ 7951-0562; cobnposadadon pedro@hotmail.com; 3a Calle 3-12, Zona 2; r per person with/ without bathroom Q75/40) This family-run place has spacious rooms with terracotta-tiled floors around a happy little courtyard. There are good sitting areas to while the day away.

Casa D'Acuña (☎ 7951-0482; casadacuna@yahoo.com; 4a Calle 3-11, Zona 2; dm/d without bathroom Q50/100; ☎) This clean, very comfortable European-style hostel has four dormitories (each with four beds) and two private doubles, all with shared bathroom with good hot-water showers. Also here is a fabulous restaurant called El Bistro (p169), a gift shop, laundry service and rea-sonably priced local tours.

ourpick Hotel Central (☎ 7952-1442; 1a Calle 1-79, Zona 1; s/d Q120/160; P ☎) Reasonable-sized rooms and lovely outdoor sitting areas make this a decent choice. Try for a room at the back for better ventilation and views out over the town.

Pensión Monja Blanca (☎ 7952-1712; 2a Calle 6-30, Zona 2; s/d Q170/225, without bathroom Q120/150; P) This place is peaceful despite being on a busy street. Spotless rooms are arranged around a lush garden packed with fruit and hibiscus trees. Each room has an old-time feel to it and is furnished with two good-quality single beds with folksy covers. This is a good place for solo women travelers.

Eating

Most of the hotels in Cobán come with their own restaurant. In the evening, food trucks (kitchens on wheels) park around the plaza and offer some of the cheapest dining in town. As always, the one to go for has the largest crowd of locals hanging around and chomp-ing down.

Xkape Koba'n (2a Calle 5-13, Zona 2; snacks Q15, mains Q30; 🕑 10am-7pm) The perfect place to take a breather or while away a whole afternoon, this beautiful, artsy little cafe has a lush garden out back. Some interesting indigenous-inspired dishes are on the small menu. The cakes are homemade, the coffee delectable and there are some interesting handicrafts for sale.

Café Fantasia (Oficinas Profesionales Fray Bartolomé de las Casas, 1a Calle 3-13; breakfast Q20-30; 🕑 Mon-Sat) Another good central cafe, this one offers several types of hot chocolate. It's a cozy little place in which to enjoy breakfasts, pastries and coffee or light meals, with a pleasant terrace away from the traffic.

Café La Posada (1a Calle 4-12, Zona 2; snacks under Q35; 🕑 11am-7pm) This cafe has tables on a veranda overlooking the square, and a comfortable sitting room inside with couches, coffee tables and a fireplace. All the usual cafe fare is served. Snacks comprise nachos, tortillas, sandwiches, burgers, tacos, *tostadas* (toasted corn), fruit salad and more.

El Peñascal (5a Av 2-61; mains Q55-90; 🕑 lunch & dinner) Probably Cobán's finest stand-alone restaurant, this one has plenty of regional specialties, Guatemalan classics, mixed meat platters, seafood and snacks in a relaxed, upmarket setting.

our pick El Bistro (4a Calle 3-11, Zona 2; mains Q60-120; 🕑 from 7am) Casa D'Acuña's restaurant offers authentic Italian and other European-style dishes served in an attractive oasis of tranquility to background classical music. In addition to protein-oriented mains, there is a range of pastas (Q40 to Q65), salads, homemade breads, cakes and outstanding desserts.

Cobán offers more good eats:

El Cafeto (2a Calle 1-36 B, Zona 2; mains Q25-40; 🕑 breakfast, lunch & dinner) Cute little plaza-side cafe offering good set lunches, a half-decent wine selection and delicious coffee.

Bella Pizza (2a Calle 13-47, Zona 1; mains Q40-60; 🕑 lunch & dinner) Good range of pizzas, pastas and salads.

Bokatas (4a Calle 2-34, Zona 2; mains Q40-80; 🕑 dinner) Outdoor eatery pumping out big steaks and loud music in equal portions.

Entertainment

Cobán has several places where you can get down and boogie.

Bar Milenio (3a Av 1-11, Zona 4) Has a bar, food, a pool table and mixed music disco.

Bohemios (cnr 8a Av & 2 Calle, Zona 2; admission Q10-25; 🕑 Thu-Sat) A mega-disco with balcony seating and bow-tied staff.

Getting There & Away

The CA-14/Carretera al Atlántico route is the most traveled circuit between Cobán and the outside world, but buses also serve other off-the-beaten-track routes. There is a phenomenal route between Cobán and Huehuetenango, but see Road Out (p138) before deciding to go that way. Or head from Cobán to El Estor, on Lago de Izabal, or to Poptún in El Petén on the backdoor route via Fray Bartolomé de Las Casas.

Minibuses, known as microbuses, are replacing, or are additional to, chicken buses on many routes. Many buses leave from Cobán's Campo Dos bus terminal, east of the stadium.

The boxed table, below, lists bus services leaving from the bus terminal.

Destinations not served by the Campo Dos bus terminal include the following:

Cahabón (Q40; 4½hr; 85km) Same buses as to Lanquín.

El Estor (Q45; 5hr; 166km) Two minibuses daily leave from Transportes Imperial, behind the Transportes Monja Blanca terminal at 9:30am and 11:30pm. This road gets washed out in heavy rains – check at the office to see if the bus is running. There are additional departures from Transportes Brenda Mercedes (3a Av and 3a Calle, Zona 4) at 9:30am, 11:30am and 1:30pm.

Guatemala City (Q40-55; 4-5hr; 213km) Transportes Monja Blanca (🕿 7951-3571; www.tmb.com.gt; 2a Calle 3-77, Zona 4) has buses leaving for Guatemala City every 30 minutes from 2am to 6am, then hourly until 4pm.

Lanquín (Q30; 2½-3hr; 61km) Transportes Martínez (6a Calle 2-40, Zona 4) has multiple departures throughout the day. Minibuses also depart from the corner of 5a Calle and 3a Av, in Zona 4, from 7am to 4pm, some continuing

BUSES FROM COBÁN (CAMPO DOS BUS TERMINAL)		
Destination	**Cost (Q)**	**Duration (hr)**
Biotopo del Quetzal	10	1¼
Chisec	15	2
Fray Bartolomé de Las Casas	35	4
Nebaj	55	5½-7
Playa Grande (for Laguna Lachuá)	50	4
Raxruhá	25	2½-3
Salamá	20	1½
Sayaxché	60	4
Tactic	6	40min
Uspantán	30	4½

DIY: PARQUE NACIONAL LAGUNA LACHUÁ

You'll see many Cobán tour operators offering trips to the **Laguna Lachuá** (☎ 4084-1706; www.lachua.org; park admission Q40, campsites Q25, bunk with mosquito net Q50), a beautiful lagoon set in a national park and surrounded by thick jungle. It's not that hard to organize yourself, though buses from Cobán pass the entrance to the park and there's a lovely lagoon-side eco-*albergue* where you can stay and cook (bring food with you). The community of **Rocjá Pomtilá** (☎ 5381-1970; rocapon@yahoo.com), on the eastern edge of the park, also offers homestays and tours of the area.

---

to Semuc Champey. Do check these times, though, as they seem to be fluid.

San Pedro Carchá (Q3; 20min; 6km) Buses every 10 minutes, from 6am to 7pm, from the lot in front of the Transportes Monja Blanca terminal.

AROUND COBÁN

Cobán (indeed all of Alta Verapaz) is becoming a hot destination for adventure travel. Not only does the area hold scores of villages where you can find traditional Maya culture in some of its purest extant form, it also harbors caves, waterfalls, pristine lagoons and many other natural wonders.

San Juan Chamelco

About 12km southeast of Cobán is the village of San Juan Chamelco, with swimming at **Balneario Chio**. The **church** here, which dates back to the colonial period and may have been the first church in Alta Verapaz, sits atop a small rise and has awesome views of the villages below. Mass is still held here in Spanish (5pm Sunday) and Q'eqchi' (7am and 9:30am Sunday).

The best place to stay in the area is in nearby Aldea Chajaneb, 4km from San Juan Chamelco, where **Don Jerónimo's** (☎ 5301-3191; www.dearbrutus.com/donjeronimo; s/d Q210/375; **V**) rents comfortable, simple bungalows. The price includes three ample, delicious vegetarian meals fresh from the garden. He also offers many activities, including tours to caves and the mountains, and inner tubing on the Río Sotzil. The **Grutas Rey Marcos** (www.grutasdelreymarcos.com; admission Q25; ☻ 9am-5pm) are just down the road from Don Jerónimo's.

The caves go for more than 1km into the earth, although chances are you won't get taken that far. A river runs through the cave (you have to wade through it at one point) and there are some impressive stalactites and stalagmites.

Buses to San Juan Chamelco (Q3, 20 minutes) leave from the Wasen Bridge (Diagonal 15, Zona 7) at the eastern edge of Cobán. To reach Don Jerónimo's, take a bus or pick-up (Q2, 15 minutes) from San Juan Chamelco toward Chamil and ask the driver to let you off at Don Jerónimo's. Alternatively, hire a taxi from Cobán (Q80).

Grutas de Lanquín

The best excursion from Cobán is to the caves near Lanquín, a pretty village 61km east. If you get this far, be sure to visit Semuc Champey as well.

The **Grutas de Lanquín** (admission Q30; ☻ 7am-6pm) are a short distance northwest of the town and extend several kilometers into the earth. You must first stop at the police station in the *municipalidad* in Lanquín, pay the admission and ask them to open the caves; there is no attendant at the caves. The caves have lights, but bring a powerful flashlight anyway. You'll also need shoes with good traction, as it's slippery inside.

Although the first few hundred meters of cavern has been equipped with a walkway and electric lights, most of this subterranean system is untouched. If you're a neophyte spelunker, think twice about wandering too far – the entire extent of this cave has yet to be explored, let alone mapped. Aside from funky stalactites and stalagmites, these caves are crammed with bats; at sunset, they fly out of the mouth of the cave in dense, sky-obscuring formations. The river here gushes from the cave in clean, cool and delicious torrents; search out the hot pockets near the shore.

Just downhill from the entrance to the caves, you'll see the entry to **Parque Natural Guayaja** (☎ 4154-4010; www.guayaja.com; admission Q10, campsites Q50), the area's latest attraction. Here you'll find the near-obligatory canopy tour (Q100), plus rappelling (Q75) and hiking trails (Q10). If you don't have a tent, you can rent one from the park office for Q75 per night.

The sublimely located **El Retiro** (☎ 4513-6396; www.elretirolanquin.com; hammocks/dm Q20/35, r with/without bathroom Q190/70, cabins without bathroom Q120; 🖥 🛜) is about 500m along the road beyond Rabin Itzam. Be warned – it's the sort of place you could lose yourself for months (and it looks like some have). *Palapas* look down over green fields to a beautiful wide river, the same one that flows out from the Lanquín caves. It's safe to swim, even inner tube if you're a confident swimmer. Attention to detail in every respect makes this a backpackers' paradise. Excellent vegetarian food (three-course dinner Q35) is available in the bar-restaurant.

In Lanquín, **Rabin Itzam** (☎ 7983-0076; s/d Q80/120, without bathroom Q60/80) has big rooms with balconies and good views. The wooden doors are carved with Maya symbols. This place is quiet and private. **El Recreo** (☎ 7983-0057; hotel_el_recreo@hotmail.com; s/d Q255/320, without bathroom Q35/70; P 🔊), between the town and the caves, is more attractive. It has large gardens, two swimming pools and a restaurant.

The large outdoor eatery, **La Estancia de Alfaro** (mains Q20-50; 🕙 breakfast, lunch & dinner), halfway between town and El Retiro, serves good-sized plates of steak, eggs and rice, and gets rowdy and beerish at night.

Buses operate several times daily between Cobán and Lanquín, continuing to Cahabón. At least one bus per day passes through en route to El Estor. There are eight buses to Cobán (Q30, three hours) between 6am and 5:30pm. There are scheduled departures for Semuc Champey at 1pm and 3pm (Q10, 30 minutes), tourist shuttles (Q15) at 9:30am (book at your hotel) and pick-ups (Q10) leaving whenever they are full half a block from the main square.

Semuc Champey

Eleven kilometers south of Lanquín, along a rough, bumpy, slow road, is **Semuc Champey** (admission Q50), famed for its great natural limestone 300m-long bridge, on top of which is a stepped series of pools of cool, flowing river water that's good for **swimming**.

The water is from the Río Cahabón, and much more of it passes underground, beneath the bridge. Although this bit of paradise is difficult to reach, the beauty of its setting and the perfection of the pools, which range from turquoise to emerald green, make it all worthwhile.

If you're visiting on a tour, some guides will take you down a rope ladder from the lowest pool to the river, which gushes out from the rocks below.

It's possible to camp (Q50 per tent) at Semuc Champey, but be sure to pitch a tent only in the upper areas, as flash floods are common. It's risky to leave anything unattended, as it might get stolen. The place now

has 24-ho
potential
everything
the parking
Cacki'ik; Q
pools. It's a

Just befo
Champey, y
for the **Gruta**
which many
ing than the .... a flashlight
for the two-hour tour of the caves, or you'll be stumbling around by candlelight. A half hour of river tubing is generally included in the price.

There are two very good places to stay near Semuc Champey:

Posada El Zapote (☎ 5568-8600; dm Q25, s/d Q75/125, without bathroom Q40/70) is about 3km before Semuc Champey and has good, simple rooms set on ample grounds. Also has a reasonable Italian restaurant onsite.

El Portal (☎ 7983-0016; dm Q35, r with/without bathroom Q150/80) is just 100m short of the entrance to Semuc Champey, and has well-spaced wooden huts dotted around the bank sloping down to the river. There's no electricity, but meals and tours are available. Bookings are advised.

COBÁN TO POPTÚN

The Cobán to Poptún route via Fray Bartolomé de Las Casas used to be a desolate dirt road. Nowadays, plenty of buses and pick-ups ply the decent roads. This route is a great opportunity for you to get off the Gringo Trail and into the heart of Guatemala.

The hospitable town of **Fray Bartolomé de Las Casas**, often referred to as 'Fray' (pronounced fry), is sizable for the middle of nowhere. You can't make it from Cobán to Poptún in one shot, so you'll be spending the night here. Banrural, just off the plaza, changes US dollars and traveler's checks and has an ATM. The post office and police station are nearby. The *municipalidad* is on the plaza.

The friendly **Hotel La Cabaña** (☎ 7952-0352; 2a Calle 1-92 Zona 3; s/d Q70/140, without bathroom Q35/75) has the best accommodations in town. Eating options are limited here – try Comedor Jireh and Restaurante Doris on the main street. Otherwise grab a steak (with tortillas and beans; Q10) at the informal barbecue shacks that open along the main street at night.

At least one daily bus departs from the plaza at 4am for Poptún (Q80, seven hours, 100km). Buses for Cobán leave hourly between 4am and 4pm. Some go via Chisec

ers take the slower route
chá.

A & CHIQUIMULA

he hot, dry hill-studded flatlands that run
own to the southern border, cowboy culture lives on in the Zacapa and Chiquimula
departments. Packing a pistol is not uncommon here – indeed, it goes well with the big
hat and boots. Most travelers use the area
as a gateway to El Salvador and Honduras,
but others come for the religious pilgrimage
to Esquipulas or to check out the dinosaur
museum at Estanzuela.

Capital of the department of the same
name, Zacapa is just east of Hwy 10 a few
kilometers south of Estanzuela. This town
offers little to travelers, though the locals do
make cheese, cigars and superb rum.

ESTANZUELA
pop 10,500

En route to Chiquimula, you turn off the
Carretera al Atlántico onto the CA-10 and
into the Río Motagua valley, a hot, 'dry tropic'
area that once supported a great number and
variety of dinosaurs. Three kilometers south
of the Carretera al Atlántico you'll see a small
monument on the right (west) side of the road
commemorating the terrible earthquake of
February 4, 1976.

Less than 2km south of the monument is
the small town of Estanzuela, with its **Museo
de Paleontología, Arqueología y Geología Ingeniero
Roberto Woolfolk Sarvia** (8am-5pm Mon-Fri). This
interesting museum holds bones of dinosaurs,
a giant ground sloth some 30,000 years old
and a prehistoric whale. Also on display are
early Maya artifacts. To get here, go 1km west
from the highway directly through town, following the small *museo* signs.

CHIQUIMULA
pop 50,700 / elev 370m

Capital of its namesake department,
Chiquimula lies in a mining and tobacco-
growing region on CA-10, 32km south of the
Carretera al Atlántico. Although small, it's a
major market town for eastern Guatemala.
It's also a transportation point and overnight
stop for those en route to Copán in Honduras
(the reason most travelers stop here). Among
other things, Chiquimula is known for its

sweltering climate, decent budget hotels and
the flower-packed central plaza.

Orientation & Information

Chiquimula is easy to get around on foot
and the busy market is right by Telgua. Many
banks will change US dollars and traveler's
checks, including those listed here.

Banco G&T (7a Av 4-75, Zona 1; 9am-8pm Mon-Fri,
10am-2pm Sat) Half a block south of the plaza, changes
both and also gives cash advances on Visa and MasterCard.

Banrural (cnr 2a Calle & 10a Av, Zona 1) Has a Visa ATM.

Biblioteca El Centro (cnr 4a Calle & 8a Av; per hr Q5;
8am-7pm Mon-Fri, 8am-6pm Sat & Sun) Check email
here.

Post office (10a Av btwn 1a & 2a Calles) Is in an alley
around the side of the building opposite the bus station.

Telgua (3a Calle) Is a few doors downhill from Parque
Ismael Cerna.

Viajes Tivoli (7942-4933; 8a Av 4-71, Zona 1) Can
help with travel arrangements.

Sleeping

Hotel Hernández (7942-0708; 3a Calle 7-41, Zona 1;
s/d without bathroom Q40/80, with fan Q80/120, with air-
con Q120/180; P ⊠ 🛜 🖭) It's hard to beat the
Hernández – it's been a favorite for years,
and keeps going strong, with its central position, spacious, simple rooms and good-sized
swimming pool.

Posada Doña Eva (7942-4956; 2a Calle 9-61, Zona 1;
s/d Q50/60) Set way back from the busy streets,
the cool clean rooms here offer a minimalist
approach to comfort, with TV and fans.

Hotel Victoria (7942-2732; cnr 2a Calle & 10a Av,
Zona 1; s/d Q50/70) If you're just looking for somewhere to crash close to the bus terminal, these
rooms are a pretty good bet. Clean and not
too cramped, with TV and a decent *comedor*
downstairs. Get one at the back – the street
noise can be insane.

Posada Perla de Oriente (7942-0014; 2a Calle 11-50,
Zona 1; r per person with fan/air-con Q80/125; P ⊠ 🖭)
Surprisingly tranquil for its location just around
the corner from the bus terminal, with some of
the best-value rooms in town. They're large and
unadorned, but the grounds are quiet and leafy
and the big swimming pool is a bonus.

Hostal Maria Teresa (7942-0177; 5a Calle 6-21,
Zona 1; s/d Q190/350; ⊠ 🛜) Set around a gorgeous
colonial courtyard with wide shady passage-
ways. The single rooms are a bit poky, but
the doubles are generous and all the comforts are here: cable TV, hot showers and
air-conditioning.

Eating & Drinking

There's a string of cheap *comedores* on 8a Av behind the market. At night, snack vendors and taco carts set up along 7a Av opposite the Parque Ismael Cerna, selling the cheapest eats in town.

Anda Picate (8a Av 2-34, Zona 1; mains Q25-40; lunch & dinner) For that late-night (until 11pm) Tex-Mex munchout, this is the place to be – big burritos, tacos three for Q10 and cheap beer in a relaxed, clean environment.

Corner Coffee (6a Calle 6-70, Zona 1; bagels Q30, breakfast Q25-30; 7am-10pm) You could argue with the syntax, but this air-con haven right on the lovely Parque Calvario serves the best range of sandwiches, burgers and bagels in town.

Peccato Café (cnr 5a Calle & 6a Av; mains Q30-60; 7pm-1am) About the only place you'd want to go drinking in town, this is a friendly and stylish little bar-restaurant. Drinks are well-priced, TVs are huge and the food is OK if nothing mind-blowing.

Charli's (7a Av 5-55; mains Q40-90; 8am-9pm) Chiquimula's 'fine dining' option (table-cloths!) has a wide menu, featuring pasta, pizza, seafood and steaks, all served amid chilly air-con, with relaxed and friendly service.

Parillada de Calero (7a Av 4-83; mains Q45-90; breakfast, lunch & dinner) An open-air steakhouse, serving the juiciest flame-grilled cuts in town. This is also the breakfast hot spot – the Tropical Breakfast (pancakes with a mound of fresh fruit; Q40) goes down well in this climate.

Getting There & Away

Several companies operate buses and microbuses, arriving and departing from the bus station area on 11a Av, between 1a and 2a Calles. **Litegua** (7942-2064; 1a Calle btwn 10a & 11a Avs), which operates buses to El Florido (the border crossing on the way to Copán) has its own bus station a half block north. For the Honduran border crossing at Agua Caliente take a minibus to Esquipulas and change there. If you're headed to Jalapa, you'll need to go to Ipala to make the connection. For Río Dulce, take a Flores bus, or a Puerto Barrios bus to La Ruidosa junction and change there. If you're going to Esquipulas, sit on the left for the best views of the basilica. See the table on the following page for sample fares and destinations.

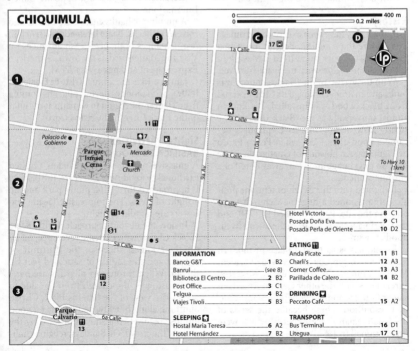

BUSES FROM CHIQUIMULA

Destination	Cost (Q)	Duration	Departures
Anguiatú (Salvadoran border)	25	1hr	5am-5:30pm
El Florido (Honduran border)	25	1½hr	5:30am-4:30pm
Esquipulas	10	45min	5am-9pm
Flores	100	7-8hr	6am, 10am & 3pm
Guatemala City	50	3hr	3am-3.30pm
Ipala	6	1½hr	5am-7pm
Puerto Barrios	40	4½hr	3:30am-4pm
Quiriguá	25	2hr	3:30am-4pm
Río Hondo	15	35min	5am-6pm

ESQUIPULAS

From Chiquimula, CA-10 goes south into the mountains, where it's cooler and a bit more comfortable. After an hour's ride through pretty country, the highway descends into a valley ringed by mountains. Halfway down the slope, about 1km from town, a *mirador* provides a good view. As soon as you catch sight of the place, you'll see the reason for coming: the great Basílica de Esquipulas that towers above the town, its whiteness shining in the sun.

History

This town may have been a place of pilgrimage even before the conquest. Legend has it that Esquipulas takes its name from a Maya lord who ruled this region when the Spanish arrived.

With the arrival of the friars, a church was built, and in 1595 an image of Christ carved from black wood was installed. It's known almost universally as the 'Black Christ.' The steady flow of pilgrims to Esquipulas became a flood after 1737, when Pedro Pardo de Figueroa, Archbishop of Guatemala, came here on pilgrimage and went away cured of a chronic ailment.

Delighted with this development, the prelate commissioned a huge new church to be built on the site. It was finished in 1758, and the pilgrimage trade has been the town's livelihood ever since.

Esquipulas is assured a place in modern history, too. Beginning here in 1986, President Marco Vinicio Cerezo Arévalo brokered agreements with the other Central American leaders on economic cooperation and conflict resolution. These became the seeds of the Guatemalan Peace Accords, which were finally signed in 1996.

Orientation & Information

The basilica is the center of everything. Most of the good cheap hotels are within a block or two, as are numerous small restaurants. The highway does not enter town; 11a Calle, also sometimes called Doble Vía Quirio Cataño, comes in from the highway and is the town's 'main drag.'

The **post office** (6a Av 2-15) is about 10 blocks north of the center. **Telgua** (cnr 5a Av & 9a Calle) has plenty of card phones. Check your email at **Global.com** (3a Av; per hr Q5), opposite Banco Internacional.

A number of banks change US dollars and traveler's checks. **Banco Internacional** (3a Av 8-87, Zona 1) changes both, gives cash advances on Visa and MasterCard, is the town's American Express agent and has a Visa ATM.

January 15 is the annual **Cristo de Esquipulas festival**, with mobs of devout pilgrims coming from all over the region to worship at the altar of the Black Christ (El Cristo Negro).

Sights & Activities

BASÍLICA DE ESQUIPULAS

A massive pile of stones that has resisted earthquakes for almost 250 years, the basilica is approached through a pretty park and up a flight of steps. The impressive facade and towers are floodlit at night.

Inside, the devout approach **El Cristo Negro** (Black Christ) with extreme reverence, many on their knees. Incense, the murmur of prayers and the scuffle of sandaled feet fill the air. When throngs of pilgrims are here, you must enter the church from the side to get a close view of the famous Black Christ. Shuffling along quickly, you may get a good glimpse before being shoved onward by the press of the crowd. On Sundays, religious holidays and (especially) during the festival, the press of devotees is intense. Otherwise, you may have the place to yourself.

OTHER SIGHTS

The **Centro Turístico Cueva de las Minas** (admission Q15; 6:30am-4pm) has a 50m-deep cave (bring your own flashlight), grassy picnic areas and the Río El Milagro, where people come for a dip and say it's miraculous. The cave and river are 500m from the entrance gate, which is behind the basilica's cemetery, 300m south of the turnoff into town on the road heading toward Honduras. Refreshments are available.

If you've got kids along (or even if you don't), **Parque Chatún** (7873-0909; www.parque chatun.com; adult/child Q65/55; 9am-6pm Tue-Sat), a fun park 3km out of town, should provide some light relief from all the religious business. There are swimming pools, a climbing wall, campgrounds, a petting zoo, canopy tour and a mini bungee jump. Entry includes the use of all these, except the canopy tour. If you don't have a vehicle, look for the minibus doing rounds of the town, or get your hotel to call it – it will take you out there for Q3.

Sleeping

Esquipulas has an abundance of accommodations. On holidays and during the annual festival, every hotel in town is filled, whatever the price; weekends are busy as well, with prices substantially higher. On nonfestival weekdays, ask for a *descuento* (discount). For cheap rooms, look in the streets immediately north of the towering basilica.

Hospedaje Esquipulas (7943-2298; cnr 1a Av & 11 Calle 'A,' Zona 1; s/d Q80/130) A reasonable little no-nonsense budget hotel. Rooms are clean enough and on the small side, but bathrooms are spacious.

Hotel La Favorita (7943-1175; 2a Av 10-15, Zona 1; s/d Q150/200, without bathroom Q40/70; P) The real budget-watcher's choice, the rooms with shared bathroom here are a bit grim, but those with bathrooms are good enough.

Hotel Monte Cristo (7943-1453; 3a Av 9-12, Zona 1; s/d Q180/250, without bathroom Q80/100; P) Good-sized rooms with a bit of furniture and super-hot showers. A policy of not letting the upstairs rooms until the downstairs ones are full might see you on the ground floor.

Hotel Portal de la Fe (7943-4261; www.portaldelafe. com; 11 Calle 1-70, Zona 1; s/d Q250/450; P) One of the few hotels with any real style in

town. Subterranean rooms are predictably gloomy, but upstairs the situation improves considerably.

Eating

Esquipulas' budget restaurants are clustered around the north end of the park, where hungry pilgrims can find them readily. Most eateries open from 6:30am until 9pm or 10pm.

The street running north opposite the church – 3a Av – has several eateries.

Restaurante Calle Real (3a Av; breakfast Q20-30, mains Q30-60; breakfast, lunch & dinner) Typical of many restaurants here, this big eating barn turns out cheap meals for the pilgrims. There's a wide menu, strip lighting and loud TV.

La Rotonda (11a Calle; breakfast from Q25, large pizza Q100; breakfast, lunch & dinner) Opposite Rutas Orientales bus station, this is a round building with chairs arranged around a circular open-air counter under a big awning. It's a welcoming place, clean and fresh. There are plenty of selections to choose from, including pizza, pasta and burgers.

Restaurante Payaquí (breakfast Q30, mains Q50-90; breakfast, lunch & dinner) On the west side of the park in the hotel of the same name, this is a bright and clean cafetería with big windows looking out onto the park. Prices are reasonable, and there's a good selection.

La Hacienda (cnr 2a Av & 10a Calle, Zona 1; mains Q70-130; breakfast, lunch & dinner) The best steakhouse in town also serves some decent seafood and pasta dishes. There's a cafe-bakery attached and the breakfasts (Q45) are a good (but slightly pricey) bet.

Getting There & Away

Buses to Guatemala City arrive and depart from the **Rutas Orientales bus station** (7943-1366; cnr 11a Calle & 1a Av), near the entrance to town. Minibuses to Agua Caliente arrive and depart across the street; taxis also wait here, charging the same as the minibuses, once they have five passengers.

Minibuses to Chiquimula and to Anguiatú depart from the east end of 11a Calle; you'll probably see them hawking for passengers along the main street.

Agua Caliente (Honduran border) (Q20; 30min) Minibuses every 30 minutes, from 5am to 5pm.

Anguiatú (Salvadoran border) (Q15; 1hr) Minibuses every 30 minutes, from 6am to 6pm.

Chiquimula (Q10; 45min) Minibuses every 15 minutes, from 5am to 6pm.

Flores/Santa Elena (Q110; 8hr) Transportes María Elena (☎ 7943-0448; 11 Calle 0-54, Zona 1) buses depart at 6am, 10am and 2pm, passing Quirguá (Q45, two hours), Río Dulce (Q60, four hours) and Poptún (Q90, six hours).
Guatemala City (Q50; 4hr) Rutas Orientales (☎ 7943-1366; 11 Calle 1-82, Zona 1) has hourly departures from 2am to 5pm.

IZABAL

This lush little corner of the country really packs in the attractions. The Río Dulce–Lago de Izabal area is gorgeous and largely untouched. The Garífuna enclave of Lívingston shows a whole other side to Guatemala and the little-visited ruins at Quiriguá have some of the finest carvings in the country.

QUIRIGUÁ

pop 4600

Quiriguá's archaeological zone is famed for its intricately carved stelae – gigantic sandstone monoliths up to 10.5m tall – that rise like ancient sentinels in a quiet tropical park. From the Río Hondo junction it's 68km along the Carretera al Atlántico to the village of Quiriguá. See opposite page for details of how to get to the archaeological site from here.

History

Quiriguá's history parallels that of Copán, of which it was a dependency during much of the Classic period. The location lent itself to the carving of giant stelae. Beds of brown sandstone in the nearby Río Motagua had cleavage planes suitable for cutting large pieces. Although soft when first cut, the sandstone dried hard. With Copán's expert artisans nearby for guidance, Quiriguá's stone carvers were ready for greatness. All they needed was a leader to inspire them – and pay for the carving.

That leader was Cauac Sky (AD 725–84), who sought Quiriguá's independence from Copán. In a war with his former suzerain, Cauac Sky took Copán's King 18 Rabbit prisoner in 737 and beheaded him soon after. Independent at last, Cauac Sky called up the stonecutters and for the next 38 years they turned out giant stelae and zoomorphs dedicated to his glory.

In the early 20th century the United Fruit Company bought all the land around Quiriguá and turned it into banana groves. The company is gone, but the bananas and Quiriguá remain. In 1981, Unesco declared Quiriguá a World Heritage Site.

Sights

It's hot and there are mosquitoes everywhere, but the parklike **archaeological zone** (admission Q80; ☾ 8am-4:30pm) is unforgettable. The giant stelae on the Great Plaza are awe-inspiring despite their worn condition.

Stelae A, C, D, E, F, H and J were built during the reign of Cauac Sky and carved with his image. **Stela E** is the largest Maya stela known, standing 8m above ground, with about an-

---

GETTING TO EL SALVADOR

To Santa Ana via Anguiatú

Thirty-five kilometers from Chiquimula and 14km from Esquipulas, Padre Miguel junction is the turnoff for **Anguiatú**, the border of El Salvador, which is 19km (one hour) away. Minibuses pass frequently, coming from Chiquimula, Quezaltepeque and Esquipulas.

The border at Anguiatú is open 24 hours. Plenty of trucks cross here. From Angiatú, microbuses run every half hour to Metapan where you'll find onward connections to Santa Ana and other Salvadoran destinations.

To Santa Ana via San Cristóbal

Hourly buses (Q25, one hour) connect El Progreso on the Guatemalan side with the border crossing at **San Cristóbal**.

To Las Chinamas

Frequent minibuses connect Guatemala City, Cuilapa and Valle Nuevo (the border crossing for **Las Chinamas** in El Salvador). Note that there's nowhere you'd want to stay between Cuilapa and the border.

For details on crossing the border from El Salvador, see p300.

other 3m buried in the earth. It weighs almost 60 tons. Note the elaborate head-dresses; the beards on some figures (an oddity in Maya art and life); the staffs of office held in the kings' hands; and the glyphs on the stelae's sides.

At the far end of the plaza is the **Acropolis**. At its base are several zoomorphs, blocks of stone carved to resemble real and mythic creatures; frogs, tortoises, jaguars and serpents were favorite subjects. The low zoomorphs can't compete with the towering stelae in impressiveness, but are superb as works of art, imagination and mythic significance.

A small museum just past the entrance has a few information displays and a model of how the site (much of it unexcavated) would have looked in its heyday. A *tienda* (small shop) near the entrance sells cold drinks and snacks.

Sleeping & Eating

Both of the hotels listed here have restaurants. To get to the Royal, walk down the main street, veering right at the first fork and then follow the road around to the left at the bend. The Posada is further around, past the football field and very badly signposted – ask plenty of directions, or hire a tuk-tuk (Q5 per person) from the highway.

Hotel y Restaurante Royal (☎ 7947-3639; s/d Q60/85; P) Of the budget options in town, this is by far the better choice with spacious, clean rooms and a restaurant serving simple meals. Prices are heavily negotiable.

Posada de Quiriguá (☎ 7934-2448; www.posada dequiriqua.com; s/d from Q130/300) By far the finest place to stay in town is this Japanese-run inn, enjoying a lovely hilltop location set in a lush tropical garden. Rooms are simple but comfortable and the menu (mains Q40 to Q70) features a couple of Japanese dishes.

Getting There & Away

Buses running along the routes Guatemala City–Puerto Barrios, Guatemala City–Flores, Esquipulas–Flores or Chiquimula–Flores will stop at the turnoff to Quiriguá town. Drivers will drop you at the turnoff to the archaeological site if you ask.

The transportation center in this area is Morales, about 40km northeast of Quiriguá. It's not pretty, but it's where the bus for Río Dulce originates. If a seat isn't important, skip Morales and wait at the La Ruidosa junction for the Río Dulce bus.

Getting Around

From the turnoff on the highway (1.5km from Quiriguá town) it's 3.4km to the archaeological site. Buses and pick-ups provide transportation between the turnoff and the site for Q5 each way. If you don't see one, don't fret; it's a nice walk on a new road (complete with dedicated bicycle/tuk-tuk lane) through banana plantations to get there.

If you're staying in Quiriguá and walking to and from the archaeological site, take the shortcut along the railway line from the village through the banana fields, crossing the access road near the site entrance. A tuk-tuk from Quiriguá village to the site should cost around Q15.

LAGO DE IZABAL

Guatemala's largest lake is earning its place on travelers' radars. Many visitors stay at Río Dulce village, north of the bridge where Hwy CA-13, the road leading north to Flores and Tikal, crosses the lake. East of this bridge is the beautiful Río Dulce, which opens into El Golfete lake before flowing into the Caribbean at Lívingston; a river trip is one of the highlights of a visit to eastern Guatemala.

Other lake highlights include El Castillo de San Felipe (an old Spanish fortress) and the Bocas del Polochic river delta. Many quiet and secluded spots in this area await your exploration.

Río Dulce

At the east end of the Lago de Izabal where it empties into the Río Dulce, this town still gets referred to as Fronteras. It's a hangover from the days when the only way across the river was by ferry, and this was the last piece of civilization before entering the wilds of El Petén.

Times have changed. A huge bridge now spans the water and the Petén roads are some of the best in the country. The town sees most tourist traffic from yachties – the US coast guard says this is the safest place on the western Caribbean for boats during hurricane season. The rest of the foreigners here are either coming or going on the spectacular river trip down to Lívingston (see p188).

ORIENTATION & INFORMATION

The places listed here – except for Hotel Backpacker's – are on the north side of the bridge. Get off near Río Bravo Restaurante. Otherwise you'll be walking the length of what may be Central America's longest bridge – a steamy 30-minute walk.

Many businesses in the area use radio to communicate. You can make calls at Cap't Nemo's Communications.

The town's most complete tour operator is **Otitrans** (☎ 7930-5223; otitours@hotmail.com), located under the bridge on the road to the dock. You can book *lanchas*, tours, sailing trips and shuttles here.

Four banks in town, all on the main road, change cash or traveler's checks. **Banco Industrial** (☼ 9am-5pm) has a Visa ATM. Banrural has Visa and MasterCard ATMs. Banco Agromercantil will give cash advances on credit cards.

Cap't Nemo's Communications (☼ 7am-8pm Mon-Sat, 9am-2pm Sun), beside Bruno's on the river, offers email (Q8 per hour) and international phone and radiophone calls.

The websites www.mayaparadise.com and www.riodulcechisme.com have loads of information about Río Dulce. Bruno's has an excellent notice board, advertising everything from boats for sale to captains looking for crew.

TOURS
Check the noticeboard at Bruno's or ask around at any of the marinas for the latest on which sailboats are offering charter tours.

Aventuras Vacacionales (☎ 7873-9221; www.sailing-diving-guatemala.com) runs fun sailing trips on the sailboat *Las Sirenas* from Río Dulce to the Belize reefs and islands (from Q3200, seven days) and Lago Izabal (from Q1450, four days). The office is in Antigua but you can also hook up with this outfit in Río Dulce.

SLEEPING
By the Water
The following four places are out of town on the water, which is the best place to be. You can call or radio them from Cap't Nemo's and they'll come and pick you up.

Hotel Backpacker's (☎ 7930-55480; www.hotelbackpackers.com; dm Q40, s/d Q80/150, without bathroom Q60/120) Across the bridge, this is a business run by Casa Guatemala and the orphans it serves. It's an old (with the emphasis on old) backpacker favorite, set in a rickety building with very basic rooms. The bar kicks on here at night. If you're coming by *lancha* or bus, ask the driver to let you off here to spare yourself the walk across the bridge.

Casa Perico (☎ 7930-5666; dm Q45, bungalows Q200, s/d without bathroom Q60/120) One of the more low-

key options in the area, set on a little inlet about 200m from the main river. Cabins are well built and connected by boardwalks. The Swiss guys who run it offer river tours and put on an excellent buffet dinner (Q60), or you can choose from the menu (mains Q30 to 40).

El Tortugal (☎ 7742-8847; www.tortugal.com; Q75, r without bathroom Q250, bungalows from Q350; ☎) The best-looking bungalows on the river are located here, a five-minute *lancha* ride east from town. There are plenty of hammocks, seriously hot showers and free kayaks for guests.

Hacienda Tijax (☎ 7930-5505/7; www.tijax.com; s Q160-560, d Q240-610; P ☎) This 200-hectare hacienda (estate), a two-minute boat ride across the cove from Bruno's, is a special place to stay. Activities include horseback riding, hiking, bird-watching, sailboat trips and walking and canopy tours around the rubber plantation. Accommodations is in lovely little cabins connected by a boardwalk. Most cabins face the water and there's a very relaxing pool/bar area.

In Town
Bruno's (☎ 7930-5721; www.mayaparadise.com/bruno.htm; dm Q35, s Q170-220, d Q250-300; P ☎ ☎ ☎) A path leads down from the northeast end of the bridge to this riverside hangout for yachties. The dorms are clean and spacious and the new building offers some of the most comfortable rooms in town, with air-con, and balconies overlooking the river. They're well set up for families and sleep up to six.

Las Brisas Hotel (☎ 7930-5124; s/d Q70/130; ☎) This hotel is opposite the Fuentes del Norte office. All rooms are clean enough and have three beds and fans. Three rooms upstairs have private bathroom and air-con (Q200). It's central and good enough for a night, but there are much better places around.

EATING
All of the hotels listed above have restaurants. Bruno's serves good breakfasts, gringo comfort food and has a full bar. The Hacienda Tijax is a popular lunch spot – give them a call and they'll come pick you up.

ourpick Sundog Café (sandwiches Q25, meals from Q35; ☼ breakfast, lunch & dinner; Ⓥ) Down the hill a bit from Tijax express, this open-air bar-restaurant makes great sandwiches on homemade bread, a good selection of vegetarian dishes and fresh juices. It's also the place to come for unbiased information about the area.

Restaurante Río Bravo (breakfast Q30, mains Q60-100; ☺ breakfast, lunch & dinner) With an open-air deck over the lake, this place has some good eats and a very local flavor. It doesn't get too fancy, but there is a good range of steaks, pasta and seafood on offer in a relaxed environment.

Ricky's Pizza (pizza from Q50; ☺ lunch & dinner) Upstairs in the main part of town, offering surprisingly good pizzas. The set lunches (Q20) are excellent value.

GETTING THERE & AWAY
Boat
Colectivo lanchas go down the Río Dulce (from the new dock) to Lívingston, usually requiring eight to 10 people, charging Q125/200 per person one-way/round-trip. The trip is a beautiful one and the morning departure makes a 'tour' of it, with several halts along the way (see p188). Boats usually leave from 9am to about 2pm. There are regular, scheduled departures at 9:30am and 1:30pm. Pretty much everyone in town can organize *lancha* service to Lívingston and most other places you'd care to go, but they charge more.

Bus
Beginning at 7am, 14 Fuente del Norte buses a day head north along a paved road to Poptún (Q30, two hours) and Flores (Q60, four hours). The 12:30pm bus continues all the way to Melchor de Mencos (Q90) on the Belize border. With good connections you can get to Tikal in a snappy six hours. There are also services to San Salvador (El Salvador; Q125) and San Pedro Sula (Honduras; Q135), both leaving at 10am.

At least 17 buses daily go to Guatemala City (Q55, six hours) with Fuente del Norte and Litegua. Línea Dorada has 1st-class buses departing at 1:30pm for Guatemala City (Q120) and at 3:30pm for Flores (Q100). This shaves up to an hour off the journey times.

Minibuses leave for Puerto Barrios (Q20, two hours) when full, from the roadside in front of Las Brisas Hotel.

Otitrans (☎ 7930-5223; otitours@hotmail.com) has shuttles to Antigua and Cobán (both Q330), Copán and Flores (both Q290).

Dilapidated Fuente del Norte buses and better-looking minibuses leave for El Estor (Q20, 1½ hours) from the San Felipe and El Estor turnoff in the middle of town, hourly from 7am to 6pm. The road is paved about halfway, and smooth dirt for the remainder.

Río Dulce to Flores
North across the bridge is the road into El Petén, Guatemala's vast jungle province. It's 208km to Santa Elena and Flores, and another 71km to Tikal.

The entire stretch of road from the Carretera al Atlántico to Santa Elena has been paved, so it's a smooth ride all the way from Río Dulce to the Tikal ruins.

The forest here is disappearing at an alarming rate, falling to the machetes of subsistence farmers. As the UN's Food and Agriculture Organization has repeatedly reported, sections are felled and burned off, crops are grown for a few seasons until the fragile jungle soil is exhausted, then the farmer moves deeper into the forest to slash and burn anew. Cattle ranchers have contributed to the damage, as has the migration of Guatemalans from the cities to El Petén.

El Castillo de San Felipe
The fortress and **castle** (admission Q20; ☺ 8am-5pm) of San Felipe de Lara, about 3km west of the bridge, was built in 1652 to keep pirates from looting the villages and commercial caravans of Izabal. Although it deterred the buccaneers a bit, a pirate force captured and burned the fortress in 1686. By the end of the next century, pirates had disappeared from the Caribbean and the fort's sturdy walls served as a prison. Eventually, the fortress was abandoned and became a ruin. The present fort was reconstructed in 1956.

Today, the castle is protected as a park and is one of the lake's principal tourist attractions. In addition to the fort, the site has a large park, with barbecue/picnic areas, and you can swim in the lake.

Near the *castillo*, **Hotel Don Humberto** (☎ 7930-5051; s/d Q50/85; ☐) has basic rooms with big beds and good mosquito netting. It's nothing fancy, but more than adequate for a cheap sleep.

San Felipe is on the lakeshore, 3km west of Río Dulce. It's a beautiful 45-minute walk between the two, or minibuses provide transportation for Q8, running about every half hour. In Río Dulce they stop at the corner of the highway and the road to El Estor; in San Felipe they stop in front of Hotel Don Humberto, at the entrance to El Castillo.

Boats coming from Lívingston will drop you in San Felipe if you ask them. The Río Dulce boat trips usually cruise by El Castillo. Some will let you get out and visit the castle.

EXPLORE MORE OF IZABAL

While Río Dulce town is OK, the best places to stay around here are much further off the beaten track. Here's a sampling:

Finca Tatin (☎ 5902-0831; www.fincatatin.com; dm Q45, s/d Q125/160, without bathroom Q65/110) About 10km upstream from Lívingston, this wonderful forest retreat offers accommodations in individually decorated wood-and-thatch cabins scattered through the jungle. There are plenty of walks and kayak tours to do in the area. Lanchas (small motorboats) traveling between Río Dulce and Lívingston (or vice versa) will drop you here. See the website for more transportation options.

Hotelito Perdido (☎ 5725-1576; www.hotelitoperdido.com; dm Q45, bungalows with/without bathroom Q180/130) Just across the river from the Finca Tatin, this beautiful new place is run by a couple of young travelers. The ambience is superb and the whole place is solar powered and constructed in such a way as to cause minimal impact on the environment. It's a small, intimate place, so it's a good idea to book ahead. Call to get picked up from Lívingston (Q40) or get dropped off by any boat going between there and Río Dulce.

Hotel Kangaroo (☎ 5363-6716; www.hotelkangaroo.com; dm Q70, r Q150-180, cabins with/without bathroom Q220/180; 🖳 🛜) On the Río La Colocha, just across the water from El Castillo de San Felipe, this beautiful, simple Australian-run place is built up on stilts in the mangroves. Wildlife is particularly abundant around here, with blue warblers, pelicans, a 7-foot iguana and turtles making the surrounds their home. Call from Río Dulce or San Felipe and they'll come and pick you up for free, even if you're just dropping in for lunch.

Denny's Beach (☎ 4636-6516; www.dennysbeach.com; dm Q75, s/d from Q240/375; 🍴 🖳) Outside of Mariscos, on Lago de Izabal's south side, this is a great place to get away from it all. Hiking, swimming and wakeboarding are all on offer here, alongside delicious, reasonably priced meals. There's free boat transportation from Mariscos – see the website for details.

Ten kilometers inland on the Río Sarstún (which forms the border between Belize and Guatemala) is **Lagunita Creek** (☎ 5241-9342), where a community-tourism project offers lodging in a simple **ecolodge** (per person Q80). Simple meals (Q50 to Q65) are available, or you can bring your own food to cook. Highlights include kayaking through the beautiful, turquoise river waters and guided nature walks/bird-watching tours. Transportation can be expensive – lanchas from Lívingston charge Q1200 per boatload (up to eight people), with a small discount for smaller groups.

Or you can come over from Río Dulce by private launch for Q80.

Finca El Paraíso

On the lake's north side, between San Felipe and El Estor, the **Finca El Paraíso** (☎ 7949-7122; admission Q10, cabins Q350) is a popular day trip from Río Dulce and other places around the lake. At the *finca*, which is a working ranch, you can walk to an incredibly beautiful spot in the jungle where a wide, hot waterfall drops about 12m into a clear, deep pool. You can bathe in the hot water, swim in the cool pool or duck under an overhanging promontory and enjoy a jungle-style sauna. Also on the *finca* are several interesting caves and good hiking. Next door to the farmhouse is the more humble but better-value **Brisas del Lago** (cabins per person Q75).

The *finca* is on the Río Dulce–El Estor bus route, about one hour (Q9) from Río Dulce and 30 minutes (Q6) from El Estor. To get

to the waterfall, head north from the road. Head south for the farmhouse and lake. The last bus in either direction passes at around 4:30pm to 5pm.

El Estor

Gorgeously sited and rarely visited, this small town looks over the Lago de Izabal to the Sierra de las Minas. It's most often used as a staging point for visits to the **Refugio de Vida Silvestre Bocas del Polochic**, a highly biodiverse wildlife reserve at the west end of the lake, but is also a gateway for the difficult, but possible, back route to Lanquín and Cobán.

ORIENTATION & INFORMATION

El Estor is an easily negotiable town. Buses from Río Dulce terminate at Parque Central, on whose east side is **Café Portal** (🕒 6:30am-10pm), which provides excellent information, tours and transportation. **Banrural** (cnr 3a Calle & 6a Av; 🕒 8:30am-5pm Mon-Fri, 9am-1pm Sat) changes US dollars and

American Express traveler's checks and has an ATM. The **municipal police** (cnr 1a Calle & 5a Av) are near the lakeshore. There are some excellent ecotourism options on offer in the nearby Bocas del Polochic wildlife reserve – contact the **Fundación Defensores de la Naturaleza** (☎ 7949-7130; www.defensores.org.gt; cnr 5a Av & 2a Calle) for details.

The Asociación Feminina Q'eqchi' sells clothes, blankets and accessories made from traditional cloth woven by the association's members. To find it go two blocks north along 5a Av from Parque Central, then two blocks west. All profits benefit the women involved in the program.

SLEEPING & EATING

Restaurante Típico Chaabil (☎ 7949-7272; 3a Calle; r per person Q75; P) Although they go a bit heavy on the log-cabin feel, the rooms at this place, at the west end of 3a Calle, are the best deal in town. Get one upstairs for plenty of light and good views. The restaurant here, on a lovely lakeside terrace, cooks up delicious food, such as *tapado* (the Garífuna seafood and coconut stew; Q60). The water here is crystal clear and you can swim right off the hotel's dock.

Hotel Vista al Lago (☎ 7949-7205; 6a Av 1-13; s/d Q90/150) Set in a classic, historic building down on the waterfront, this place has plenty of style, although the rooms themselves are fairly ordinary. Views from the upstairs balcony are superb.

Hotel Ecológico (☎ 7949-7245; www.ecohotelcabanas dellago.blogspot.com; s/d Q125/175) Carved into a lush jungly setting 2km east of El Estor, the cabins here are pleasing, rustic affairs, but the lakefront setting is the real winner. The good-value, open-air restaurant has great views.

The Chaabil apart, the best place to look for food is around the Parque Central, where **Café Portal** (mains Q25-45; ☼ breakfast, lunch & dinner) serves a broad range of fare with some vegetarian options. On the other side of the park, **Restaurante del Lago** (mains Q40-80; ☼ breakfast, lunch & dinner), on the 2nd floor, catches some good breezes and a bit of a lake view – it has the widest menu in town.

GETTING THERE & AWAY

See Río Dulce (p177) for information on buses from there. The schedule from El Estor to Río Dulce (Q20, 1½ hours) is hourly, from 6am to 4pm.

The road west from El Estor via Panzós and Tucurú to Tactic, south of Cobán, has had a bad reputation for highway holdups and robberies in the past, especially around Tucurú – ask around for current conditions. It's also prone to getting flooded out during the wet season – another reason to inquire. You can get to Lanquín by taking the truck that leaves El Estor's Parque Central at 9am for Cahabón (Q30, four to five hours), and then a bus or pick-up straight on from Cahabón to Lanquín the same day. Four buses go direct to Cobán (Q45, six hours) on this route, leaving at the very unfriendly times of 1am, 2am, 4am and 6am from El Estor's Parque Central.

PUERTO BARRIOS

pop 76,450

The country becomes even more lush, tropical and humid heading east from La Ruidosa junction toward Puerto Barrios. Port towns have always had a reputation for being slightly dodgy, and those acting as international borders doubly so. Perhaps the town council wants to pay homage to that here. Or perhaps the edgy, slightly sleazy feel is authentic. Either way, for foreign visitors, Puerto Barrios is mainly a jumping-off point for boats to Punta Gorda (Belize) or Lívingston, and you probably won't be hanging around.

The powerful United Fruit Company owned vast plantations in the Río Motagua valley. It built railways (whose tracks still run through the middle of town) to ship produce to the coast. Puerto Barrios was built early in the 20th century to put that produce onto ships sailing for New Orleans and New York. Laid out as a company town, Puerto Barrios has long, wide streets arranged neatly on a grid. Many of its Caribbean-style wood-frame houses are on stilts.

Orientation & Information

Its spacious layout means you must walk or ride further in Puerto Barrios to get from place to place. It's 800m from the bus terminals in the town center to the Muelle Municipal (Municipal Boat Dock) at the end of 12a Calle, from which passenger boats depart. **El Muñecon** (cnr 8a Av, 14a Calle & Calz Justo Rufino Barrios) is a statue of a dock worker; it's a favorite landmark and monument in the town.

Banco Industrial (7a Av btwn 7a & 8a Calles) Changes US dollars and traveler's checks and has a Visa ATM.

Banco Reformador (8a Av btwn 9a & 10a Calles) Changes US dollars only and has a MasterCard ATM.

GUATEMALA

GUATEMALA

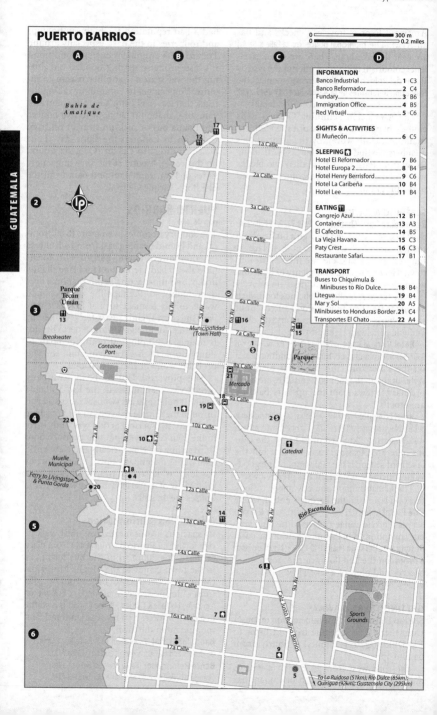

PUERTO BARRIOS

0		300 m
0		0.2 miles

INFORMATION
Banco Industrial **1** C3
Banco Reformador **2** C4
Fundary... **3** B6
Immigration Office............................ **4** B5
Red Virtu@l... **5** C6

SIGHTS & ACTIVITIES
El Muñecón **6** C5

SLEEPING
Hotel El Reformador **7** B6
Hotel Europa 2 ....**8** B4
Hotel Henry Berrisford **9** C6
Hotel La Caribeña **10** B4
Hotel Lee **11** B4

EATING
Cangrejo Azul.....................................**12** B1
Container..**13** A3
El Cafecito **14** B5
La Vieja Havana **15** C3
Paty Crest..**16** C3
Restaurante Safari............................**17** B1

TRANSPORT
Buses to Chiquimula &
    Minibuses to Río Dulce............**18** B4
Litegua **19** B4
Mar y Sol..**20** A5
Minibuses to Honduras Border .**21** C4
Transportes El Chato **22** A4

*Bahía de
Amatique*

1a Calle

2a Calle

3a Calle

4a Calle

5a Calle

6a Calle

Parque
Tecún
Umán

Breakwater

4a Av
5a Av
6a Av
7a Av
8a Av

Container
Port

Municipalidad
(Town Hall)

7a Calle

8a Calle

Mercado

9a Calle

10a Calle

11a Calle

12a Calle

13a Calle

14a Calle

15a Calle

16a Calle

17a Calle

Parque

Catedral

Río Escondido

Sports
Grounds

Muelle
Municipal

*Ferry to Livingston
& Punta Gorda*

2a Av
3a Av
4a Av
5a Av
6a Av
7a Av
8a Av

6a Av

Calz Justo Rufino Barrios

*To La Ruidosa (51km); Río Dulce (85km);
Quiriguá (92km); Guatemala City (295km)*

Immigration office (cnr 12a Calle & 3a Av; ☺ 24hr) A block from the Muelle Municipal. Come here for your entry or exit stamp if you're arriving from or leaving for Belize. If you're heading to Honduras, you get your exit stamp at another immigration office on the road to the border.

Red Virtu@l (cnr 17a Calle & Calz Justo Rufino Barrios; per hr Q6; ☺ 8am-9:30pm) You can go online here.

Sleeping

Hotel Lee (☎ 7948-0685; 5a Av; s/d Q60/90) This is a friendly, family-owned place, between 9a and 10a Calles, close to the bus terminals. Typical of Puerto Barrios' budget hotels, it offers straightforward, vaguely clean rooms. The little balcony out front catches the odd breeze.

Hotel La Caribeña (☎ 7948-0384; 4a Av; s/d Q70/100) Good little budget rooms in a quiet location. The restaurant has been repeatedly recommended for its seafood dishes, particularly the 'super sopa' seafood stew.

Hotel Europa 2 (☎ 7948-1292; 3a Av; s/d Q100/150, with air-con Q150/200; [P] [⊗]) The best of the budget options in the port area, this hotel, between 11a and 12a Calles, just 1½ blocks from the Muelle Municipal, is run by a friendly family and has clean rooms with TV, arranged around a parking courtyard.

Hotel Henry Berrisford (☎ 7948-7289; cnr 9a Av & 17a Calle; s/d Q80/160) A big four-story modern concrete construction offering decent-sized, slightly shabby rooms with cable TV. The lobby is an impressive sight and there are plenty of sitting areas scattered around.

Hotel El Reformador (☎ 7948-0533; reformador@ intelnet.net.gt; cnr 7a Av & 16a Calle; s/d with fan Q100/160, with air-con Q150/200; [P] [⊗] [♥]) Like a little haven away from the hot busy streets outside, the Reformador offers big, cool rooms set around leafy patios. Air-con rooms lead onto wide interior balconies. There is a restaurant (meals Q50 to Q80) here.

Eating

Container (7a Calle; snacks Q20; ☺ lunch & dinner) The oddest cafe in town – made from two shipping containers, at the west end of 7a Calle, with fine bay views, thatched huts out over the water and plenty of cold, cold beer.

La Vieja Havana (8a Av; mains Q30-60; ☺ lunch & dinner) This laid-back little place does good Cuban dishes (including *ropa vieja* – a shredded beef stew) and has excellent-value set lunches for Q20.

Paty Crest (cnr 6a Av & 7a Calle; mains Q40-60; ☺ lunch & dinner) With one of the widest menus in town,

stretching from pizza to lasagna to steaks (the T-Bone comes heartily recommended; Q65). Also features one of the best-looking bars in town, a long, wooden affair, decorated with nautical paraphernalia and offering a very complete selection of drinks.

our pick **El Cafecito** (13a Calle 6-22; mains Q40-90; ☺ breakfast, lunch & dinner Mon-Sat) This sweet little air-conditioned spot whips up some of the most interesting food in town. Portuguese dishes such as *feijoada* (stewed beans, pork, beef, chicken and other stuff; Q55) and a good range of seafood, sandwiches and breakfasts. There's draft beer on tap, too.

Restaurante Safari (☎ 7948-0563; cnr 1a Calle & 5a Av; seafood Q60-100; ☺ 10am-9pm) The town's most enjoyable restaurant is on a thatched-roof, open-air platform right over the water about 1km north of the town center. Locals and visitors alike love to eat and catch the sea breezes here. Excellent seafood of all kinds including the specialty *tapado* – that great Garífuna casserole (Q100); chicken and meat dishes are less expensive (Q40 to Q80). There's live music most nights. If the Safari is full, the Cangrejo Azul next door offers pretty much the same deal, in a more relaxed environment.

Getting There & Away

BOAT

Boats depart from the Muelle Municipal at the end of 12a Calle.

GETTING TO PUNTA GORDA, BELIZE

A **Transportes El Chato** (☎ 7948-5525; www.transporteselchato.com.gt; 1a Av) *lancha* (small motorboat) departs from the Muelle Municipal in Puerto Barrios at 10am daily for Punta Gorda (Belize; Q200, one hour), arriving in time for the noon bus from Punta Gorda to Belize City. Tickets are sold at El Chato's office, which is 1½ blocks from the *muelle* (pier).

Mar y Sol (☎ 7942-9156) at the Muelle Municipal also has *lanchas* for Punta Gorda (Q175 to Q200, one hour), leaving at 10am and 1pm.

There are also departures for Punta Gorda from Lívingston – see p188 for details.

Before boarding you also need to get your exit stamp at the nearby immigration office (see above left).

Regular *lanchas* depart for Lívingston (Q30, 30 minutes) every day at 6:30am, 7:30am, 9am and 11am. For departure times from Lívingston, see p188. Buy your ticket as early as you can on the day (you can't book before your day of departure) – spaces are limited and sometimes sell out.

Outside of these regular times, *lanchas* depart whenever they have five people ready to go and cost Q50.

Most of the movement from Lívingston to Puerto Barrios is in the morning, returning in the afternoon. From Lívingston, your last chance of the day may be the 5pm *lancha*, especially during the low season when fewer travelers are shuttling back and forth.

BUS & MINIBUS

Litegua (☎ 7948-1172; cnr 6a Av & 9a Calle) leaves for Guatemala City (Q60 to Q90, five to six hours, 295km), via Quiriguá and Río Hondo, 19 times between 1am and noon, and also at 4pm. *Directo* services avoid a half-hour detour into Morales.

Buses for Chiquimula (Q40, 4½ hours, 192km), also via Quiriguá, leave every half hour, from 3am to 4pm, from the corner of 6a Av and 9a Calle. Minibuses to Río Dulce (Q20, two hours) leave from the same location.

TAXI

Most cabs charge around Q20 for longish rides around town.

PUNTA DE MANABIQUE

This promontory to the north of Puerto Barrios is being slowly and carefully developed for ecotourism by the conservation group, **Fundary** (☎ 7948-0944; www.fundary. org; 17a Calle, Puerto Barrios). As well as sporting Guatemala's best Caribbean beaches, the area offers endless bird-watching, hiking, sportfishing and other nature-based activities. The community of Estero Lagarto offers accommodations in their **ecolodge** (☎ 4433-4930; per person Q50) where good, simple meals are available. You can arrange tours of the area from here. For transportation information and to make reservations, contact Fundary.

LÍVINGSTON

pop 25,400

Quite unlike anywhere else in Guatemala, this largely Garífuna town is fascinating in itself, but also an attraction for a couple of good beaches, and its location at the end of the river journey from Río Dulce.

Unconnected by road from the rest of the country (the town is called 'Buga' – mouth – in Garífuna, for its position at the river mouth), boat transportation is (logically) quite good here, and you can get to Belize, the cayes, Honduras and Puerto Barrios with a minimum of fuss.

The Garífuna (Garinagu, or Black Carib) people of Lívingston and southern Belize are the descendants of Africans brought to the New World as slaves. They trace their roots to the Honduran island of Roatán, where they were forcibly settled by the British after the Garífuna revolt on the Caribbean island of St Vincent in 1795. From Roatán, the Garífuna people spread out along the Caribbean Coast, from Belize to Nicaragua. Intermarrying with the Carib people, as well as with Maya and shipwrecked sailors of other races, they've developed a distinct culture and language incorporating African, *indígena* and European elements.

Town beaches are largely disappointing, as the jungle comes to the water's edge. Those beaches that do exist are often clogged with vegetation and unsafe for swimming, thanks to contaminated water. Safe swimming is possible at Los Siete Altares (p186) and Playa Blanca (see opposite).

Orientation & Information

After half an hour you'll know where everything is. For more on Lívingston, check out its community website, www.livingston.com.gt.

GETTING TO HONDURAS

Minibuses leave Puerto Barrios for the Honduran border (Q15, 1¼ hours) every 20 minutes, from 5am to 5pm, from 6a Av outside the market. The road to the border turns off the CA-9 at **Entre Ríos**, 13km south of Puerto Barrios. Buses and minibuses going in all directions wait for passengers at Entre Ríos, making the trip from the border fairly easily, whichever direction you are traveling in. Minibuses from Puerto Barrios stop en route to the border at Guatemalan immigration, where you might have to pay Q10 for an exit stamp. Think of it as one last tip to Guatemalan officialdom.

For information on crossing from Honduras, see p389.

Banrural (Calle Principal; 🕑 9am-5pm Mon-Fri, to 1pm Sat) Changes US dollars and traveler's checks and has an ATM.

Happy Fish (Calle Principal; per hr Q8) This restaurant offers email services.

Immigration office (Calle Principal; 🕑 6am-7pm) Issues entry and exit stamps for travelers arriving directly from or going directly to Belize or Honduras. Outside its normal hours, you can knock at any time.

Laundry (☎ 7947-0303; www.hotelcasarosada.com; Hotel Casa Rosada, Calle Marcos Sánchez Díaz) Laundry service.

Sights & Activities

The **Museo Multicultural de Lívingston** (admission Q20; 🕑 9am-6pm), upstairs on the municipal park in front of the public dock, has some excellent displays on the history and culture of the area, focusing on the ethnic diversity, with Garífuna,

Q'eqchi' (Kekch[...] represented. Wh[...] open-air alligato[...]

The best bea[...] **Quehueche** – reach[...] minutes and **Play**[...] 12km from Líving[...] and you need a b[...]

Use mosquito [...] cautions, especially in the jungle; mosquitoes near the coast carry malaria and dengue fever.

Rasta Mesa (☎ 4200-4371; www.site.rastamesa.com; Barrio Nevago; 🕑 10am-2pm & 7-10pm) Offers classes in Garífuna cooking (per person Q50) and drumming (per person Q100) as well as massages (Q150) and can hook you up with volunteer work in the area.

Dangers & An[...]
Lívingston h[...]
tlers opera[...]
into 'le[...]
tou[...]

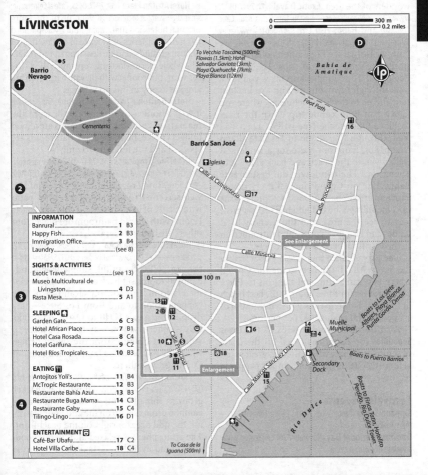

LÍVINGSTON

INFORMATION		
Banrural	**1**	B3
Happy Fish	**2**	B3
Immigration Office	**3**	B4
Laundry		(see 8)

SIGHTS & ACTIVITIES		
Exotic Travel		(see 13)
Museo Multicultural de Livingston	**4**	D3
Rasta Mesa	**5**	A1

SLEEPING		
Garden Gate	**6**	C3
Hotel African Place	**7**	B1
Hotel Casa Rosada	**8**	C4
Hotel Garífuna	**9**	C2
Hotel Ríos Tropicales	**10**	B3

EATING		
Antojitos Yoli's	**11**	B4
McTropic Restaurante	**12**	B3
Restaurante Bahía Azul	**13**	B3
Restaurante Buga Mama	**14**	C3
Restaurante Gaby	**15**	C4
Tilingo-Lingo	**16**	D1

ENTERTAINMENT		
Café-Bar Ubafu	**17**	C2
Hotel Villa Caribe	**18**	C4

...oyances

...as its edgy aspects and a few hus-
...te here, trying to sweet-talk tourists
...nding' money and paying up front for
...s that don't happen. Take care with anyone
who strikes up a conversation for no obvious
reason on the street or elsewhere.

Like many coastal places in Guatemala,
Lívingston is a *puente* (bridge) for northbound
drug traffic. There's little in the way of turf
wars – the industry is fairly stable – but there
are some big-time players around and a lot
of money at stake. Keep your wits about you.

Tours

A few outfits in Lívingston offer tours that
let you get out and experience the natural
wonders of the area. **Exotic Travel** (☎ 7947-0133;
www.bluecaribbeanbay.com; Restaurante Bahía Azul, Calle
Principal) and **Happy Fish** (☎ 7947-0661; www.happy
fishtravel.com; Restaurante Happy Fish, Calle Principal) are
both well-organized operations offering basically the same range of trips. The popular
Ecological Tour/Jungle Trip takes you for a
walk through town, out west up to a lookout
spot and on to the Río Quehueche, where you
take a half-hour canoe trip down the river
to Playa Quehueche (see p185). Then you
walk through the jungle to **Los Siete Altares**
(see p188), hang out there for a while and
walk down to the beach and back along it to
Lívingston. The trip leaves the Restaurante
Bahía Azul on Calle Principal every day at
9am and arrives back around 4:30pm; it costs
Q75 including a boxed lunch. This is a great
way to see the area, and the friendly local
guides can also give you a good introduction
to the Garífuna people who live here.

The Playa Blanca tour goes by boat first to
the Seven Altars, then on to the Río Cocolí,
where you can swim, and then on to Playa
Blanca for two or three hours at the best beach
in the area. This trip runs with a minimum of
six people and costs Q100 per person.

Also on offer are day trips to the **Cayos
Sapodillas** (or Zapotillas), well off the coast
of southern Belize, where there is great snorkeling (Q400). A minimum of six people is
required.

Festivals & Events

Semana Santa (Easter week) Packs Lívingston with
merrymakers.
Garífuna National Day (November 26) Celebrated with
a variety of cultural events.

Virgin of Guadalupe (December 12) Celebrations
dedicated to Mexico's patron saint.

Sleeping

Prices in Lívingston hit their peak from July
to December – outside of these months many
midrange and top-end places listed here halve
their rates.

Casa de la Iguana (☎ 7947-0064; Calle Marcos Sánchez
Díaz; dm Q40, cabin with/without bathroom Q150/110; ☎)
Five minutes' walk from the main dock, this
party hostel offers good-value cabins. They're
clean, wooden affairs, with simple but elegant
decoration. Happy hour here rocks on and
you can camp or crash in a hammock for Q20
per person. Spanish classes are available for
Q570 per 20 hours.

Hotel African Place (☎ 7947-0435; Calle al Cementario;
s/d Q50/80, without bathroom Q40/70) One of the more
original hotels in Guatemala, built by a Spaniard
to resemble a series of Moroccan castles. It is set
on lush grounds, and turtles swim in the 'moat.'
The whole place is looking very much the worse
for wear, but rooms with private bathroom are
as good as any in this price range.

Hotel Garífuna (☎ 7947-0183; Barrio San José; s/d
Q50/75) About a five-minute walk from the
main street, these big breezy rooms are a solid
budget choice. Beds are good, bathrooms are
spotless and the folks are friendly.

Hotel Ríos Tropicales (☎ 7947-0158; www.mctropic.
com; Calle Principal; s/d Q100/150, without bathroom Q50/100;
☎) The Ríos Tropicales has a variety of big,
well-screened rooms facing a central patio
with plenty of hammocks and chill-out space.
Rooms with shared bathroom are bigger, but
others are better decorated.

Hotel Salvador Gaviota (☎ 7947-0874; www.hotel
salvadorgaviota.es.tl; Playa Quehueche; s/d Q125/250, without
bathroom Q50/100) Beautiful, simple wood-and-
bamboo rooms set back a couple of hundred
meters from a reasonably clean beach. Day
trippers going to and from Los Siete Altars
drop in for meals (Q40 to Q80) and drinks
here – otherwise you may have the place to
yourself. It's 500m from the swing bridge
where the road ends – a taxi will charge about
Q15 to get you there.

Flowas (☎ 7947-0376; infoflowas@gmail.com; dm/s/d
Q75/100/200) A rightly popular little backpacker
getaway, this place offers rustic wood-and-
bamboo cabins set up on the 2nd floor (catching the odd breeze) right on the beachfront.
The atmosphere is relaxed and there's good,
cheap food available. A taxi (Q10 from the

dock) will drop you within 150m of the front gate.

Garden Gate (☎ 7947-9272; www.gardengate-guest house.com; s/d without bathroom Q120/150; 🛜) Just putting on the finishing touches at the time of research, this lush hilltop property offers three spotless rooms with a simple, pleasing decor. Maria, the founder of Tilingo-Lingo (see below) runs the place, so you know the food is good. There's a big garden, plenty of hammocking opportunities and bicycle rental for guests.

Vecchia Toscana (☎ 7947-0884; www.vecchiatoscana -livingston.com; Barrio Paris; r with fan/air-con Q420/670; 🍽 🖳) This beautiful new Italian-run place down on the beach has some of the best rooms in town. Fan-cooled ones are a bit squishy, but the more expensive numbers are spacious enough and the grounds and common areas are immaculate. There's a good Italian restaurant with sea views out the front.

Eating

Food in Lívingston is relatively expensive because most of it (except fish and coconuts) must be brought in by boat. There's fine seafood here and some unusual flavors for Guatemala, including coconut and also curry. *Tapado*, a rich stew made from fish, shrimp, shellfish, coconut milk and plantain, spiced with coriander, is the delicious local specialty. Calle Principal is dotted with many open-air eateries.

Antojitos Yoli's (Calle Principal; items Q10-30; 🕒 8am-5pm) This is the place to come for baked goods. Especially recommended are the coconut bread and pineapple pie.

Restaurante Gaby (Calle Marcos Sánchez Díaz; mains Q30-50; 🕒 breakfast, lunch & dinner) For a good honest feed in humble surrounds, you can't go past Gaby's. She serves the good stuff: lobster, *tapado*, rice and beans and good breakfasts at reasonable prices. The *telenovelas* (soap operas) come free.

ourpick Tilingo-Lingo (Calle Principal; mains Q40-80; 🕒 breakfast, lunch & dinner) An intimate little place down near the beach. It advertises food from 10 countries, and makes a pretty good job of it, with the Italian and East Indian dishes being the standouts.

McTropic Restaurante (Calle Principal; mains Q40-100; 🕒 breakfast, lunch & dinner) Some of the best-value seafood dishes in town are on offer at this laid-back little place. Grab a table streetside for people-watching and sample some of the good Thai cooking.

Restaurante Buga Mama (☎ mains Q40-100; 🕒 breakfast, lunch & place enjoys the best location of rant in town, and profits go to the A Ak Tenemit. There's a wide range of se homemade pasta, curries and other dis on the menu, including a very good *tapado* (Q100). Most of the waiters here are trainees in a community sustainable tourism development scheme, so service can be sketchy, but forgivable.

Restaurante Bahía Azul (Calle Principal; mains Q60-100; 🕒 breakfast, lunch & dinner) The Bahía's central location, happy decor and good fresh food keep it popular. The menu selection is wide, with a good mix of Caribbean, Guatemalan and Asian influences. It opens early for breakfast.

Drinking

Adventurous drinkers should try *guifiti*, a local concoction made from coconut rum, often infused with herbs. It's said to have medicinal as well as recreational properties.

A handful of bars down on the beach to the left of the end of Calle Principal pull in travelers and locals at night (after about 10pm or 11pm). It's very dark down here, so take care. The bars are within five minutes' walk from each other, so you should go for a wander and see what's happening. Music ranges from *punta* to salsa, merengue and electronica. On Fridays things warm up but Saturday is party night – often going till 5am or 6am.

Happy hour is pretty much an institution along the main street, with every restaurant getting in on the act. One of the best is at **Casa de la Iguana** (see opposite page).

Entertainment

A traditional Garífuna band is composed of three large drums, a turtle shell, some maracas and a big conch shell, producing throbbing, haunting rhythms and melodies. The chanted words are like a litany, with responses often taken up by the audience. *Punta* is the Garífuna dance; it's got a lot of gyrating hip movements.

Quite often a roaming band will play a few songs for diners along the Calle Principal around dinnertime. If you like the music, make sure to sling them a few bucks. Several places around town have live Garífuna music, although schedules are unpredictable:

Café-Bar Ubafu (Calle al Cementerio) Probably the most dependable. Supposedly has music and dancing nightly, but liveliest on weekends.

rs can enjoy a

...lle Marcos Sánchez Díaz;
...inner; 🕑) This
...any restau-
...ociación
...food,
...hes

...ver from Río
...Puerto Barrios.
...ats from Belize.
...ates combined
...eiba (the cheap-
est gateway, ...ay Islands) for
Q400 per person, with a minimum of six people. Leaving Lívingston at 7:30am or earlier
will get you to La Ceiba in time for the boat to
the islands, making it a one-day trip, which is
nearly impossible to do independently.

There's also a boat that goes direct to Punta
Gorda on Tuesday and Friday at 7am (Q200,
1½ hours), leaving from the public dock. In
Punta Gorda, the boat connects with a bus to
Placencia and Belize City. The boat waits for
this bus to arrive from Placencia before it sets
off back for Lívingston from Punta Gorda at
about 10:30am.

If you are taking one of these early international departures, get your exit stamp from
immigration in Lívingston (see p191) the day
before. Leaving Guatemala by boat, travelers
pay Q85 exit tax.

AROUND LÍVINGSTON
Río Dulce Cruises

Tour agencies in town offer day trips up the
Río Dulce to Río Dulce town, as do most
local boatmen at the Lívingston dock. Many
travelers use these tours as one-way transportation to Río Dulce, paying Q125/180 one
way/round trip. It's a beautiful ride through
tropical jungle scenery, with several places
to stop on the way. Be aware that of the two
departures per day, only the 9:30am one does
the following tour. The 2:30pm boat goes direct to Río Dulce.

Shortly after you leave Lívingston heading upriver, you'll enter a steep-walled gorge
called **Cueva de la Vaca**, its walls hung with
great tangles of jungle foliage and bromeliads.
Tropical birdcalls fill the air. Just beyond is **La
Pintada**, a graffiti-covered rock escarpment.
Further on, a thermal spring forces sulfurous
water out at the base of the cliff, providing a
delightful place for a swim.

Emerging from the gorge, the river eventually widens into **El Golfete**, a lakelike body of
water that presages the even more vast Lago
de Izabal.

On the north shore of El Golfete is the
Biotopo Chocón Machacas, a 7600-hectare reserve
established to protect the river, mangrove
swamps and the manatees that inhabit the waters. A network of 'water trails' provides ways
to see the reserve's flora and fauna. A nature
trail begins at the visitors center (Q25), winding its way through forests of mahogany, palms
and rich tropical foliage. Jaguars and tapirs live
in the reserve, although seeing one is unlikely.
The walrus-like manatees are even more elusive. These huge mammals can weigh up to
a ton, yet glide effortlessly beneath the river.

From El Golfete, the boats continue upriver, passing increasing numbers of expensive
villas and boathouses, to the village of Río
Dulce, where the road into El Petén crosses
the river, and to El Castillo de San Felipe on
Lago de Izabal (p179).

Los Siete Altares

The 'Seven Altars' is a series of freshwater
falls and pools about 5km (1½-hours' walk)
northwest of Lívingston along the shore of
Bahía de Amatique. It's a pleasant goal for a
beach walk and a good place for a picnic and
swim. Follow the shore northward to the river
mouth and walk along the beach until it meets
the path into the woods (about 30 minutes).
Follow this path all the way to the falls.

Boat trips go to the Seven Altars, but locals
say it's better to walk there to experience the
natural beauty and the Garífuna people along
the way. About halfway along, just past the
swinging bridge is Hotel Salvador Gaviota (see
p186), whose attached **restaurant** (mains Q40-80;
🕑 lunch & dinner) serves decent food, ice-cold
beers and soft drinks.

EL PETÉN

Once synonymous with bad roads and impas-
sible jungle, this region has been tamed over
the years. Ever since the Maya exodus in the
9th century AD, this has been Guatemala's
least-populated region, but continued government efforts to populate it have been hugely
successful. In 1950 barely 15,000 people lived
here. Now the number is well over 500,000.
It's no surprise that most people you meet
were born elsewhere.

The regional superstar is, of course, Tikal,
but many visitors are far more blown away
by 'lesser' ruins such as Yaxhá and the mas-

sive, largely unexcavated sites at El Mirador and Nakbé.

In 1990 the Guatemalan government established the one-million-hectare Maya Biosphere Reserve, which includes most of northern El Petén. The Guatemalan reserve adjoins the vast Calakmul Biosphere Reserve in Mexico and the Río Bravo Conservation Area in Belize, forming a reserve of over two million hectares.

Many visitors linger in Poptún, a small town 113km southeast of Santa Elena that has been a popular backpacker layover for years.

GETTING THERE & AROUND

The roads leading into El Petén have now all been paved, so travel is fast and smooth. Unfortunately, improved access has encour-

aged the migration of farmers and ranchers from other areas, increasing the pressure on resources and leading to even more deforestation in a region where forests were already disappearing at an alarming rate.

The Guatemalan government has developed the adjoining towns of Flores, Santa Elena and San Benito, on the shores of Lago de Petén Itzá, into the region's tourism base. Here you'll find an airport, hotels and other services. A few small hotels and restaurants are at Tikal, but other services there are limited.

POPTÚN

pop 24,600 / elev 540m

Poptún is about halfway between Río Dulce and Flores, and makes a good stopover en

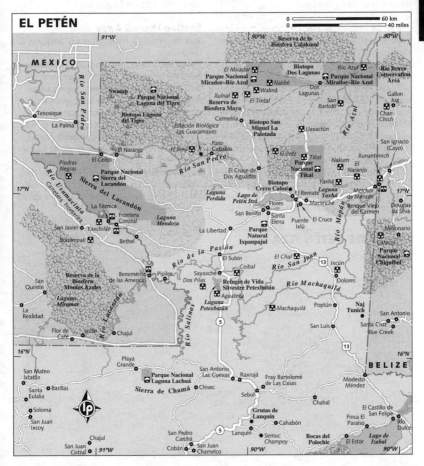

EL PETÉN

route to Tikal, especially if you're coming via Fray Bartolomé de Las Casas.

Most buses and minibuses stop on the main road through town: Fuente del Norte buses stop by the Shell station; minibuses to San Luís, 16km south, go from the next corner south, and minibuses to Flores start half a block further along. **Banco Industrial** (Av 15 de Septiembre 7-27) and **Banrural** (Av 15 de Septiembre & Calle del Parque) have ATMs and change US dollars and American Express traveler's checks.

Sleeping & Eating

Finca Ixobel (☎ 5892-3188; www.fincaixobel.com; campsites per person Q25, dm Q35, tree houses s/d Q60/90, s/d Q125/250, without bathroom Q75/110, bungalows s/d 150/275; Ⓟ 🖵 ⚲ Ⓥ) This friendly, relaxed 160-hectare spot offers tent sites, *palapas*, beds and good homemade meals with veggie options galore. Swimming, horseback riding, camping trips, inner-tubing on the river and a famous, thrilling cave trip (which even includes body-surfing rapids) are all organized on a daily basis, for a reasonable charge.

Meals here are excellent, including the all-you-can-eat buffet dinner for Q60. After 9pm many people move on to the pool bar, where reasonably priced cocktails and other drinks are served. Volunteer opportunities exist for bilingual English-Spanish speakers; volunteers get free room and board.

The turnoff for the *finca* is marked on Hwy 13. In the daytime ask the bus or minibus driver to let you off there; it's a 15-minute walk to the *finca*. After hours, or to skip the

hike in, get off the bus in Poptún and take a taxi (Q30) or tuk-tuk (Q20). When leaving Finca Ixobel, most buses will stop on the highway to pick you up, but not after dark. The *finca* also offers shuttles to/from Flores for Q50. Shuttles coming from Flores should drop you at the gate, but check first.

The following two hotels are in Poptún town:

Hotel Izalco (☎ 7927-7372; 4a Calle 7-11; s/d Q92/153, without bathroom Q60/75; Ⓟ) Small but clean rooms with TV and good mosquito netting. Some of those with bathroom don't have a fan. And you'll need a fan.

Tropical Inn (☎ 7927-7533; Av 15 de Septiembre 5-54; s/d with fan Q158/219, with air-con Q183/244; Ⓟ ⚲ ⚲) The designers of this lodging on Poptún's main drag had the good sense to place rooms well away from the noisy street, facing a tropical patio with a small pool.

Getting There & Away

Bus departures from Poptún include the following:

Flores/Santa Elena Línea Dorada offers 1st-class service at 4:30am, 5am and 5pm. Less comfortable Fuente del Norte buses (Q25; two hours; 113km) go every hour or two almost around the clock. The best option is to take a minibus (Q30; about every 10 minutes; 6am to 6pm).

Fray Bartolomé de Las Casas (Q65; five hours; 100km) A bus departs at 10:30am daily from opposite Banrural a block south of Av 15 de Septiembre; the journey takes up to seven hours in the rainy season.

Guatemala City (seven hours; 387km) First-class Línea Dorada buses (Q115 to Q160) depart at 11:30am, 11pm and 11:30pm. Fuente del Norte buses (Q80) leave approximately every hour from 5:30am to midnight.

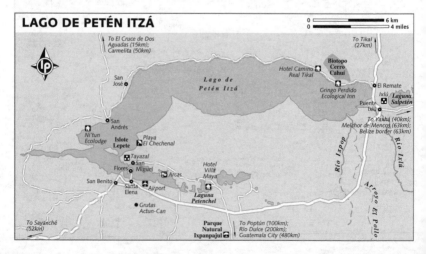

LAGO DE PETÉN ITZÁ

0 — 6 km
0 — 4 miles

To El Cruce de Dos Aguadas (15km); Carmelita (50km)

To Tikal (27km)

San José

Lago de Petén Itzá

Hotel Camino Real Tikal

Biotopo Cerro Cahuí

El Remate

Gringo Perdido Ecological Inn

Ixlú · Laguna Salpetén

Puente Ixlú

San Andrés

To Yaxhá (40km); Melchor de Mencos (63km); Belize border (63km)

Ni'tun Ecolodge

Islote Lepete

Playa El Chechenal

Tayazal

San Miguel

Arcas

Flores

San Benito

Santa Elena

Airport

Hotel Villa Maya

Río Ixpop

Río Ixlú

Grutas Actun-Can

Laguna Petenchel

To Sayaxché (52km)

Parque Natural Ixpanpajul

To Poptún (100km); Río Dulce (200km); Guatemala City (480km)

Arroyo El Pollo

GUATEMALA

Río Dulce (Q50; two hours; 99km) All Guatemala City–bound buses make a stop in Río Dulce.

FLORES & SANTA ELENA

pop Flores 30,600, Santa Elena 29,000 / elev 110m

Flores is spectacularly located on an island in Lago de Petén Itzá. Small hotels and restaurants line the lakeside streets, meaning you don't have to shell out the big bucks to get a room with some awesome views. It does have a slightly twee, built-up edge to it, though, and many Tikal-bound shoestringers opt for the natural surrounds and tranquility of El Remate (p197), just down the road.

A 500m causeway connects Flores to the lakeshore town of Santa Elena, where you'll find banks, supermarkets and buses. Adjoining Santa Elena to the west is San Benito (population 46,300). There's not really much for the average traveler here, unless you're up for a night of slumming it in one of the town's numerous cantinas. The three towns form one large settlement that is usually referred to simply as 'Flores.'

History

Flores was founded on a *petén* (island) by the Itzáes after their expulsion from Chichén Itzá. They named the place Tayasal. Hernán Cortés peaceably dropped in on King Canek of Tayasal in 1524 on his way to Honduras. Only in March 1697 did the Spaniards finally bring Tayasal's Maya forcibly under their control.

At the time of conquest, Flores was perhaps the last major functioning Maya ceremonial center; it was covered in pyramids and temples, with idols everywhere. The God-fearing Spanish soldiers destroyed these buildings, and no trace remains.

Tayasal's Maya fled into the jungle and may have started anew, giving rise to stories of a 'lost' Maya city; some believe this is El Mirador, near the Guatemala–Mexico border.

Orientation

The airport is on the eastern outskirts of Santa Elena, 2km from the causeway connecting Santa Elena and Flores. Most buses arrive and depart from the new bus terminal 1km south of the causeway.

Information

EMERGENCY

Asistur (Tourist Assistance; ☎ 5414-3594)

Hospital San Benito (☎ 7926-1333; Calz de San Benito)

> ### ASK A LOCAL
>
> The best place to kick back and read a book is the northern shore of Lago de Petén Itzá, east of San José. I can hang in a hammock by the shore, with the murmur of the waves and breezes rustling through trees… Add to that the delight of the Petén region sun and air, and best of all, after I've read a bunch and want a break, I can dive into the lake, then I can forget about the world and realize that, yes, perfection does exist.
>
> *Estuardo Lira, Guatemala City*

INTERNET ACCESS

Petén Net (Map p194; Calle Centro América, Flores; per hr Q10; ☺ 8am-10pm Mon-Sat, 9am-9pm Sun)

Tayasal Net (Map p194; Calle Unión; per hr Q8; ☺ 8am-10pm Mon-Sat, 1-10pm Sun) Inside Hotel Posada Tayasal.

LAUNDRY

Lavandería San Miguel (Map p194; Calle Fraternidad, Flores; ☺ 8:30am-6pm Mon-Sat) Charges Q35 to wash and dry a load.

MONEY

If you just need an ATM and aren't going to Santa Elena, there's one in front of the Hotel Petén Espléndido on Calle 30 de Junio (Map p194).

Other banks are on 4a Calle in Santa Elena. The following all change at least American Express US-dollar traveler's checks and have ATMs:

Banco Agromercantil (Map p193; ☺ 9am-6pm Mon-Fri, 9am-1pm Sat) Also changes euros.

Banco Continental (Map p193; ☺ 9am-5pm Mon-Fri, 9am-1pm Sat)

Banrural (Map p193; ☺ 8:30am-7pm Mon-Fri, 8:30am-1pm Sat) Also changes euros.

The bus terminal in Santa Elena also has a Cajero 5B ATM. Many travel agencies and places to stay will change US dollars, and sometimes traveler's checks, at poor rates.

POST

Post office Flores (Map p194; Av Barrios); Santa Elena (Map p193; inside Centro Comercial Karossi, 4a Calle & 2a Av)

TOURIST INFORMATION

Inguat (Map p194; ☎ 7867-5334; ciudadfloresinfo center@gmail.com; Av Santa Ana; ☺ 8am-4pm Mon-Fri) The official tourist office has town maps and brochures though reliable information may be harder to obtain. Inguat also maintains information kiosks on the Playa Sur, open 7am to 11am and 2pm to 6pm daily, and at the Aeropuerto Internacional Mundo Maya.

TRAVEL AGENCIES

Several travel agencies in Flores and Santa Elena offer trips to archaeological sites, shuttle minibuses and other services.

Aventuras Turísticas (Map p194; ☎ 4034-9550; www.aventurasturisticas.com; Av Barrios) Shuttles to Cobán, tours to Tikal, bicycle rentals.

Martsam Travel (Map p194; ☎ 7867-5093; www.martsam.com; Calle 30 de Junio, Flores)

Sights & Activities

The limestone caves of **Grutas Actun-Can** (admission Q20; ☼ 8am-5pm), also called La Cueva de la Serpiente (Cave of the Serpent), holds no serpents, but the cavekeeper may give you the rundown on the cave formations, which suggest animals, humans and various scenes. Bring a flashlight and adequate shoes – it can be slippery. Explorations take 30 to 45 minutes. At the cave entrance is a shady picnic area.

Actun-Can is a good goal for a long walk from Santa Elena. Head south on 6a Av past the Telgua office. About 1km from the center of Santa Elena, turn left, go 300m and turn right at the electricity generating plant. Go another 1km to the site. A taxi from Flores should cost Q30 to Q40 one way, or Q100 to Q150 round trip with waiting time.

Sleeping

FLORES

Hostel los Amigos (Map p194; ☎ 7867-5075; www.amigoshostel.com; Calle Central; dm Q30, r with bathroom per person Q80; 🖳) Flores' one true hostel, with a 10-bed dorm, hammocks and even a tree house, offers all the global traveler's perks: nightly bonfires, happy hours, heaped helpings of organic food, yoga and cut-rate jungle tours.

Hospedaje Doña Goya (Map p194; ☎ 7867-5513; hospedajedonagoya@yahoo.com; Calle Unión; dm/s/d Q30/70/110, s/d without bathroom Q60/80) One of the best budget choices in town with comfortable beds and a roof terrace with a palm-thatched shelter and hammocks for enjoying lake views. Dorms are spacious and spotless.

Hotel Mirador del Lago (Map p194; s/d Q50/80, r with view Q100; Calle 15 de Septiembre; 🖳) Though minimally maintained, this holds a good position just up from the causeway, with a terrace fac-

ing the lake. Upstairs units catch good afternoon breezes.

Hotel La Unión (Map p194; ☎ 5908-1037; Calle Unión; s/d Q50/90, r with view Q110; 🖳) Considering the location beside the waterfront promenade, this well-maintained property is quite a deal, with relatively stylish decor in fan-cooled rooms. Enjoy a cocktail on the lakeside terrace.

Hotel Santa Rita (Map p194; Calle 30 de Junio; s/d/tr Q60/80/120) It's never going to be beautiful, but the Santa Rita is cheap and central, with smallish, institutional green rooms along shared balconies.

Hospedaje Doña Goya 2 (Map p194; ☎ 7867-5516; hospedajedonagoya@yahoo.com; Calle Unión; s/d Q70/140, r with balcony Q140; 🖳 🖳) Doña Goya's other place has plain, airy and well-scrubbed rooms with screened windows, and most give some kind of view.

Hotel Casablanca (Map p194; ☎ 5699-1371; Playa Sur; s/d Q70/100) The first hotel you reach coming off the causeway, is family-run with simple, spacious rooms and a terrace for lake-gazing. Catches a bit of street noise.

Hotel Petenchel (Map p194; ☎ 7867-5450; Playa Sur; s/d Q100/120, with air-con Q150/170; 🖳) Eight spacious rooms, with firm beds and high-arched ceilings, set around a lush courtyard.

Hotel Casa Amelia (Map p194; ☎ 7867-5430; Calle Unión; www.hotelcasamelia.com; s/d incl breakfast Q180/280; 🖳 🖳 🛜) A newcomer on the Flores scene, offering bright, stylish chambers with excellent lake views. There are good views from the roof terrace.

Three more budget hotels with respectable rooms:

VOLUNTEERING IN EL PETÉN

There are some volunteer positions on offer around these parts.

The **Estación Biológica Las Guacamayas** (☎ 7867-5098; www.asociacionbalam.org), in the Parque Nacional Laguna del Tigre (p207), and the rehabilitation center at **Arcas** (☎ 5476-6001; www.arcasguatemala.com) offer the chance to work with wildlife. Each charges around Q1000 per month for food and board.

Project Ix-Canaan (www.ixcanaan.com), based in El Remate (p197) runs a community clinic, women's center, library and research center. Volunteers work in the clinic, build and maintain infrastructure and lead workshops or teach local children.

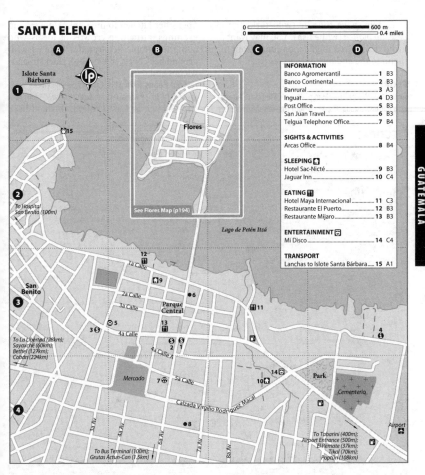

SANTA ELENA

0 _____ 600 m
0 _____ 0.4 miles

GUATEMALA

INFORMATION
Banco Agromercantil **1** B3
Banco Continental **2** B3
Banrural **3** A3
Inguat **4** D3
Post Office **5** B3
San Juan Travel **6** B3
Telgua Telephone Office...............**7** B4

SIGHTS & ACTIVITIES
Arcas Office **8** B4

SLEEPING
Hotel Sac-Nicté **9** B3
Jaguar Inn **10** C4

EATING
Hotel Maya Internacional **11** C3
Restaurante El Puerto...................**12** B3
Restaurante Mijaro.......................**13** B3

ENTERTAINMENT
Mi Disco **14** C4

TRANSPORT
Lanchas to Islote Santa Bárbara.....**15** A1

Hotel Casa del Lacandón (Map p194; ☎ 7867-5594; Calle Unión; s/d/tr Q60/100/140) Makes the most of its lakeside setting, with a lookout terrace and cafe. The rooms at the rear have fantastic views.

Hotel El Peregrino (Map p194; ☎ 7867-5115; peregrino@itelgua.com; Calle La Reforma; s/d Q100/150, with air-con Q175/300) Large rooms feature tiled floors, powerful overhead fans and window screens.

Mayab Hotel (Map p194; ☎ 7867-5469; mayabhotel@gmail.com; Calle 30 de Junio; s/d Q125/175; 🖳) Decent-sized, low-lit rooms – No 8, with its rear balcony, is by far the best. An upstairs terrace overlooks the lake.

SANTA ELENA

Hotel Sac-Nicté (Map p193; ☎ 7926-2356; 1a Calle; s/d/tr from Q50/80/100; 🅿) The best budget option on this side of the causeway, a block up from the

waterfront, with views wiped out by the glitzy Esplendido hotel. Rooms have ceiling fans and cold showers. The quality varies – try to get one of the triples on the south side, with dusty balconies facing the interior gardens.

Jaguar Inn (Map p193; ☎ 7926-0002; Calz Virgilio Rodríguez Macal 8-79; s/d Q125/180, with air-con Q170/225; 🅿 🍴) Comfortable without being fancy, with wood-paneled, faded rooms along a leafy patio. It's a decent deal, though its out-of-the-way location may only appeal to travelers with vehicles.

Eating

On the menu at many places is a variety of local game, including *tepezcuintle* (paca, a rabbit-sized jungle rodent), *venado* (venison), armadillo, *pavo silvestre* (wild turkey) and *pescado blanco* (white fish). You may want to avoid dishes that might soon jump from the menu to the endangered species list.

FLORES

Antojitos Mamelina (Map p194; cnr Calle Centro América & Av Barrios; tostadas Q3; 5-9pm Thu-Sun) Mamelina

opens her kitchen to the public on weekend evenings, attracting crowds of locals who come to sample her *tostadas* (topped with ground beef, beets or avocado), chicken sandwiches and flan.

Cool Beans (Map p194; Calle 15 de Septiembre; sandwiches Q18-30; breakfast, lunch & dinner Wed-Mon;) Also known as Café Chilero, this laid-back

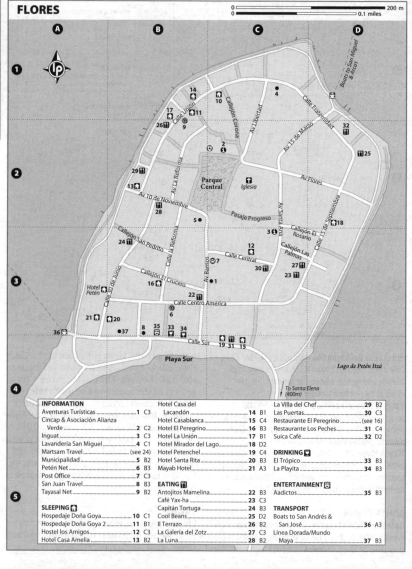

FLORES

0   200 m
0   0.1 miles

INFORMATION		Hotel Casa del		La Villa del Chef 29 B2
Aventuras Turísticas 1 C3		Lacandón 14 B1		Las Puertas 30 C3
Cincap & Asociación Alianza		Hotel Casablanca 15 C4		Restaurante El Peregrino .... (see 16)
Verde 2 C2		Hotel El Peregrino 16 B3		Restaurante Los Peches 31 C4
Inguat 3 C3		Hotel La Unión 17 B1		Suica Café 32 D2
Lavandería San Miguel 4 C1		Hotel Mirador del Lago 18 D2		
Martsam Travel .... (see 24)		Hotel Petenchel 19 C4		DRINKING
Municipalidad 5 B2		Hotel Santa Rita 20 B3		El Trópico 33 B3
Petén Net 6 B3		Mayab Hotel 21 A3		La Playita 34 B3
Post Office 7 C3				
San Juan Travel 8 B3		EATING		ENTERTAINMENT
Tayasal Net 9 B2		Antojitos Mamelina 22 B3		Aadictos 35 B3
		Café Yax-ha 23 C3		
SLEEPING		Capitán Tortuga 24 B3		TRANSPORT
Hospedaje Doña Goya 10 C1		Cool Beans 25 D2		Boats to San Andrés &
Hospedaje Doña Goya 2 .... 11 B1		Il Terrazo 26 B2		San José 36 A3
Hostel los Amigos 12 C3		La Galería del Zotz 27 C3		Línea Dorada/Mundo
Hotel Casa Amelia 13 B2		La Luna 28 B2		Maya 37 B3

locale features salons for chatting, watching videos or laptop browsing. The lush garden with glimpses of the lake makes a *tranquilo* spot for breakfast or veggie burgers. Be warned – the kitchen closes at 9:01pm sharp.

Café Yax-ha (Map p194; ☎ 5830-2060; Calle 15 de Septiembre; mains Q30-60; ⏱ breakfast, lunch & dinner Wed-Mon) Wallpapered with photos and articles relating to local Maya sites, this cafe-restaurant is home base for an archaeological tour outfit. What's special here is the pre-Hispanic and Itzá items featured on the menu – pancakes with ramón seeds, yucca scrambled with mora herbs, chicken in *chaya* (a spinach-like leafy vegetable) sauce.

La Villa del Chef (Map p194; Calle Unión; salads Q34, mains Q59-95; ⏱ lunch & dinner) Go out back to reach the rustic deck built over the water at this casual, German-run restaurant emphasizing natural ingredients. Choose from a selection of Middle Eastern salads and Guatemalan favorites. Don't miss happy hour, from 5pm to 8pm.

La Galería del Zotz (Map p194; Calle 15 de Septiembre; ⏱ breakfast, lunch & dinner) An exhaustive survey of Flores' eateries concluded that this unassuming gallery-cum-natural-foods-cafe serves the town's finest cappuccinos and lattes, along with healthful breakfasts, pizzas, pastas and curries.

Las Puertas (Map p194; cnr Calle Central & Av Santa Ana; pasta & salads Q40-50; ⏱ 8am-midnight Mon-Sat) An airy, atmospheric salon where overhead fans whirr from wood beams and sweet-natured Q'eqchi' women work the bar, Las Puertas prepares an eclectic choice of dishes highlighted by pasta variations and abundant salads. There's live jazz or reggae most nights.

our pick **Il Terrazo** (Map p194; Calle Unión; pasta Q48-72; ⏱ breakfast, lunch & dinner Mon-Sat) An Italian gourmet restaurant set on a rooftop terrace underneath a thatched canopy. The fettuccine, tortellini and taglioni are all produced in house, and they'll prepare panini to go. The fruit smoothies are unbelievable.

Capitán Tortuga (Map p194; Calle 30 de Junio; mains Q55-105; ⏱ breakfast, lunch & dinner) A barnlike locale with a pair of lakeside terraces serving heapings of comfort food – especially pizzas – at medium prices. Beer-quaffing groups should opt for the *cubetazos* – five bottles in a bucket for Q75.

La Luna (Map p194; cnr Calle 30 de Junio & Av 10 de Noviembre; mains Q63-115; ⏱ noon-midnight Mon-Sat) In a class by itself, this popular restaurant cultivates a classic tropical ambience, with innovative chicken, fish and beef dishes

surpassing similar dishes anywhere else in Guatemala. There are also good pasta and vegetarian options.

More cheap eats in Flores? No problem.

Food stalls (Parque Central; tacos & burritos Q10) A good place to dine cheap on *antojitos* (snacks).

Restaurante Los Peches (Map p194; Playa Sur; mains Q25; ⏱ 7am-10pm) Inexpensive plates of meat, rice, tortillas and salad.

Suica Café (Map p194; Calle Fraternidad; mains Q40-60; ⏱ lunch & dinner Mon-Sat) Japanese food in El Petén? The Japanese owners take a fair stab at your faves (miso soup, tempura, sushi).

Restaurante El Peregrino (Map p194; Av La Reforma; mains Q50; ⏱ 7am-10pm) Serving generous helpings of home-cooked fare, such as pork-belly stew and breaded tongue. Daily lunch specials (Q20) are a bargain.

SANTA ELENA

Restaurante Mijaro (Map p193; 4a Calle; mains Q35-45; ⏱ breakfast, lunch & dinner) You'll find good home cooking at both branches of this friendly, locally popular *comedor*, one on the main street and the other round the corner on 4a Av. The latter features a thatch-roofed garden area. Besides the grub, they do good long *limonadas* (lime-juice drink).

Restaurante El Puerto (Map p193; 1a Calle 2-15; mains Q100; ⏱ 11am-11pm) Seafood is the star attraction at this breezy, open-air hall by the lakefront with a well-stocked bar at the front. Enjoy shellfish stews, *ceviches* or the famous *pescado blanco* – white fish from the lake.

For a splurge with style, try the waterfront restaurant at the Hotel Maya Internacional.

Drinking

Flores doesn't exactly jive at night but there are a couple of places to hang out. Flores' little Zona Viva is a strip of bars along Playa Sur, and nearly all the lakeside restaurants in Santa Elena have afternoon happy hours, a great way to unwind and watch the sunset.

El Trópico (Map p194; Playa Sur; ⏱ 5:30pm-1am Mon-Sat) This is a nice spot to start the night: the candlelit terrace is good for gazing at the lights of Santa Elena reflected across the lake while enjoying an icy *cerveza* (beer).

La Playita (Map p194; Playa Sur) A mostly male gathering place (though they'll let girls in their playhouse), this waterfront drinking barn has been a Flores fixture for decades. Don Rafael, who spent his career building Johnson outboard motors, still works the bar. Sol beer by the liter for Q20, Gallos are Q10.

GUATEMALA

Entertainment

Locals gather in the cool of the evening for long drinks, snacks and relaxation in the Parque Central, where a marimba ensemble plays some nights.

For cinematic options, Cool Beans (p194) has a video lounge, and Hostel Los Amigos (p192) shows documentaries on Guatemala.

Aadictos (Map p194; Playa Sur) If you're up for dancing, join the raucous throngs on the raised floor of Aadictos, where DJs pump out merengue, rock and reggaetón each weekend.

Mi Disco (Map p193; 4a Calle, cnr Rodríguez Macal; cover Fri & Sat Q25) 'El Mi' is Santa Elena's major disco, a cavernous hall with a big stage for salsa combos. If you'd rather croon than dance, Monday to Wednesday evenings are reserved for karaoke.

Getting There & Away

AIR

Aeropuerto Internacional Mundo Maya, sometimes called Petén International Airport, is just east of Santa Elena. **Grupo TACA** (☎ 7926-0650; www.taca.com) has at least three flights daily between here and the capital (Q1330/2245 one way/round trip); it also flies to Cancún, Mexico. The Belizean airline **Tropic Air** (☎ 7926-0348) flies twice a day from and to Belize City, charging Q945 each way for the one-hour trip.

BUS & MINIBUS

The Terminal Nuevo de Autobuses is on 6a Avenida, about 1km south of the causeway to Flores. The following lines use the terminal:

Autobuses del Norte (☎ 7924-8131; www.adnauto busesdelnorte.com)
Fuente del Norte (☎ 7926-2999)
Línea Dorada (☎ 7924-8535)
Transportes María Elena (☎ 5850-4190)

Santa Elena's terminal is also used by a slew of microbuses, with frequent service to numerous destinations. The cooperative **ACTEP** (☎ 7924-8215), with an office on the left side of the terminal, runs micros to Poptún, Melchor de Mencos, San Andrés, Bethel–La Técnica, Paso Caballos and elsewhere, while others offer service to Sayaxché, El Remate and Tikal.

Going to Belize City, it's cheaper but slower to take microbuses to the border and on from there. Going to Flores, it's cheaper to catch a bus to Sayaxché, from where connecting micros leave for Cobán at 11am and 3pm. To get to Puerto Barrios, take a Guatemala City–bound Fuente del Norte bus and change at La Ruidosa junction, south of Río Dulce.

Services include those listed in the table below (as always, schedules are changeable and should be confirmed before heading out).

SHUTTLE MINIBUS

Aventuras Turísticas (see p192) offers daily shuttles to Cobán (Q125, four hours), Lanquín, Semuc Champey and Antigua. **San Juan Travel** (☎ 5461-6010; sanjuant@hotmail.com) Flores (Map p194; Playa Sur) Santa Elena (Map p193, 2a Calle) operates shuttle minibuses to Tikal (Q60, 1¼ hours each way). They leave hourly from 5am to 10am. Most hotels and

BUSES FROM FLORES & SANTA ELENA

Destination	Cost (Q)	Duration (hr)	Departures	Frequency
Belize City	160	4-5	7am	1 daily
Bethel (Mexican border)	35	4½	11am-4pm	5 daily
Chetumal (Mexico)	225	8	7am	1 daily
El Ceibo/La Palma (Mexican border)	30	4	4:40am-6pm	11 daily
El Remate	20	40min	5am-6pm	every 30min
Esquipulas	110	8	6am-2pm	every 4hr
Guatemala City	from 110	8-9	3am-11pm	hourly
Melchor de Mencos (Belizean border)	25	2	5:45am-6pm	hourly
Poptún	25	1¾	5am-6:30pm	every 10min
Río Dulce	from 60	4	3am-11pm	hourly
Sayaxché	20	1½	5:45am-6pm	every 15min
Tikal	50	1¼	5am-1pm	every 2hr

GETTING TO CHIAPAS, MEXICO

The only route with regular transportation connections is via **Bethel** or **La Técnica** o[...]
(Guatemalan) bank of the Río Usumacinta and **Frontera Corozal** on the Mexican bank[...]
posite page for details of bus services to and from Bethel and La Técnica and shuttle m[...]
services all the way through to **Palenque**. Guatemalan immigration is in Bethel; bus drivers t[...]
La Técnica will normally stop and wait for you to do the formalities in Bethel.

It's cheaper and quicker from La Técnica than from Bethel, but crossing at La Técnica means a longer bus journey on the Guatemalan side. See p47 for details on transportation between the border and Palenque.

You can also cross the border at a new crossing from the Mexican state of Tabasco to El Ceibo, a village on the Río San Pedro. See opposite page for details on microbus service from Flores. Immigration posts operate on both sides of the border from 9am to 5pm. From the Mexican side, vans and buses proceed to Tenosique, Tabasco (M$35, one hour, hourly 6am to 5pm), from where minibuses leave for Palenque up to 7pm (M$50, two hours).

See p47 for information on crossing from Mexico.

---

travel agencies can book these shuttles and they will pick you up where you're staying. Returns leave Tikal at 12:30pm, 2pm, 3pm, 4pm and 5pm. If you know which round trip you plan to be on, ask your driver to hold a seat for you or arrange one in another minibus. If you stay overnight in Tikal and want to return to Flores by minibus, it's a good idea to reserve a seat with a driver when they arrive in the morning.

Getting Around

A taxi from the airport to Santa Elena or Flores costs Q20. Tuk-tuks will take you anywhere between or within Flores and Santa Elena for Q5. Aventuras Turísticas (see p192) rents mountain bikes for Q30 per day.

EL REMATE

The closest decent accommodations to Tikal can be found in this enchanting village on the shores of Lago de Petén Itzá. It's a mellow little place – two roads, basically – much more relaxed and less built up than Flores. Most hotels here are set up for swimming in (and watching the sun set over) the lake.

El Remate is known for its wood carving. Several handicrafts shops on the lakeshore opposite La Mansión del Pájaro Serpiente sell local handicrafts and rent canoes, rafts and kayaks.

From El Remate an unpaved road snakes around the lake's northeast shore to the Biotopo Cerro Cahuí, the luxury Hotel Camino Real Tikal and on to the villages of San José and San Andrés, on the northwest side of the lake. It's possible to go all the way around the lake by road.

With their newfound prosperity, Rematecos have built a *balneario municipal* (municipal beach) just off the highway; several cheap pensions and small hotels have opened here as well.

Sights & Activities

At the northeast end of Lago de Petén Itzá, about 3km from the Flores–Tikal road, the **Biotopo Cerro Cahuí** (admission Q40; ⏰ 7am-4pm) covers 651 hectares of subtropical forest. Within are mahogany, cedar, ramón, broom, sapodilla and cohune palm trees, as well as many species of lianas and epiphytes, these last including bromeliads, ferns and orchids. The hard wood of the sapodilla was used in Maya temple-door lintels, some of which have survived from the Classic period to our own time. Chicle is still sapped from the trees' innards.

Among the many animals within the reserve are spider and howler monkeys, ocelots, white-tailed deer, raccoons, armadillos, numerous species of fish, turtle and snake, and the Petén crocodile. Depending upon the season and migration patterns, you might see kingfishers, ducks, herons, hawks, parrots, toucans, woodpeckers and the beautiful ocellated (Petén) turkey, which resembles a peacock.

A network of loop trails starts at the road and goes uphill, affording a view of the lake and Lagunas Salpetén and Petenchel. A trail map is at the entrance.

The admission fee includes the right to camp or sling your hammock under small thatched shelters inside the entrance. There are toilets and showers.

Flores –
...ges out
...

...ition 1350)
...200), on the
...zá both have
...nools and vol-
...has a lakefront
waters.........d buses run from
Flores/Santa Elena...........these villages.

The **Museo Regional del Sureste de Petén** (☉ 8am-5pm) at Dolores, 25km north of Poptún is reason enough to go there – it displays some of the most significant finds from the southern Petén sites. An hour's walk to the north is the little-visited site of **Ixcún** (admission Q30), where you'll see the second-largest stela in the Maya world.

The dock opposite the entrance is the best place to swim along the generally muddy shore of the lake.

Most El Remate accommodations can book five-hour **horseback rides** to Laguna Salpetén and a small archaeological site there (Q150 per person) or two-hour boat trips for **bird-watching** or nocturnal **crocodile-spotting** (each Q100 per person). Try Casa de Ernesto or Hotel Mon Ami (see above right); the latter also offers sunset lake tours with detours up the Ixlu and Ixpop rivers (Q150 per person).

Ascunción, next door to the Sak-Luk Hostel, rents kayaks (Q35 per hour), bicycles (per hour/day Q10/60) and horses (Q150 for 2½ hours).

Sleeping & Eating

Most hotels have their own restaurants and there are simple *comedores* scattered along the main road. The following two places are on the main road:

Hotel Sun Breeze (☎ 7928-8044; sunbreezehotel@gmail.com; s/d Q75/100, without bathroom Q40/60) Down the lane toward the lake, nearly at the junction, is this excellent-value homey guesthouse. Rear units are best, with lake views through well-screened windows. It's a short stroll to El Remate's public beach.

Hostal Hermano Pedro (☎ 2261-4419; www.hhpedro.com; s/d Q75/150) Set in a two-story wood-and-stone house, 20m off to the right from the main road, the spacious rooms are refreshingly simple and comfortable, with a few frills like lacy curtains, big fans and balcony porches. Guests can use the kitchen or grab a hammock in the common room.

The following places are on the north-shore road:

Casa de Ernesto (☎ 5750-8375; casadeernesto@ymail.com; s/d Q100/200, without bathroom Q40/70; 🛇) Ernesto and his clan offer cool and comfortable adobe huts in the woods with thatched roofs, tiled floors, and good rustic-style beds. Add Q50 for air-con. Canoe rentals, horseback riding to Laguna Salpetén and expeditions for the great white fish are among the activities offered.

Hotel Mon Ami (☎ 7928-8413; www.hotelmonami.com; dm Q57, s/d Q125/205, without bathroom Q85/165; 🛜) A 15-minute walk from the Tikal road and a stone's throw from the Biotopo Cerro Cahui, this maintains a good balance between jungle wildness and Euro sophistication. Quirkily furnished cabins and dorms with hammocks are reached along candlelit paths through gardens bursting with local plant life, though the bathhouse needs a feng-shui overhaul. Fans of French cuisine will appreciate the open-air restaurant (mains Q50 to Q80; open for breakfast, lunch and dinner).

Las Orquideas (pasta Q55, mains Q65; ☉ lunch & dinner Mon-Sat) Almost next door to Doña Tonita, Las Orquideas has a genial Italian owner-chef cooking up genuine Mediterranean fare, with tempting desserts too.

Getting There & Around

El Remate is linked to Flores by a frequent microbus service (see p196).

For Tikal, collective shuttles leave El Remate at 5:30am, 6:45am, 7:45am and 8:45am, starting back at 2pm, 3pm, 4pm and 6pm (Q50 round trip). Any El Remate accommodations can make reservations. You can also catch one of the hourly shuttles (Q30) or regular microbuses (Q15) passing through from Santa Elena to Tikal.

For Melchor de Mencos on the Belizean border, get a minibus or bus from Puente Ixlú, 2km south of El Remate.

TIKAL

Towering pyramids poke above the jungle's green canopy to catch the sun. Howler monkeys swing noisily through the branches of ancient trees as brightly colored parrots and toucans dart from perch to perch in a cacophony of squawks. When the complex warbling song of some mysterious jungle bird tapers

---

GETTING TO SAN IGNACIO, BELIZE

It's 100km from Flores to **Melchor de Mencos**, the Guatemalan town on the border with Belize. See p196 for information on bus services to the border and also on more expensive services going right through to **Belize City** and **Chetumal, Mexico**.

The road to the border diverges from the Flores–Tikal road at **Puente Ixlú** (also called El Cruce), 27km from Flores. It continues paved until about 25km short of the border.

There should be no fees at the border for entering or leaving Guatemala, and none for entering Belize. There are moneychangers at the border with whom you can change sufficient funds for immediate needs.

See p250 for information on crossing the border from Belize.

---

off, the buzz of tree frogs fills the background and it will dawn on you that this is, indeed, hallowed ground.

Certainly the most striking feature of **Tikal** (☎ 2367-2837; www.parque-tikal.com; admission Q150; ☙ 6am-6pm) is its steep-sided temples, rising to heights of more than 61m. But Tikal is different from Copán, Chichén Itzá, Uxmal and most other great Maya sites because it is deep in the jungle. Its many plazas have been cleared of trees and vines, its temples uncovered and partially restored, but as you walk from one building to another you pass beneath the dense rainforest canopy. Rich, loamy smells of earth and vegetation, a peaceful air and animal noises all contribute to an experience not offered by other Maya sites.

You can, if you wish, visit Tikal in a day trip from Flores or El Remate. You can even make a (literal) flying visit from Guatemala City in one day, using the daily flights between there and Flores airport. But you'll get more out of Tikal if you spend a night here, enabling you to visit the ruins twice and to be here in the late afternoon and early morning, when other tourists are rare and wildlife more active.

History

Tikal is set on a low hill above the surrounding swampy ground – which might be why the Maya settled here around 700 BC. Another reason was the abundance of flint, used to make clubs, spearheads, arrowheads and knives. Flint could also be exported in exchange for other

goods. Within 200 years, the Maya of Tikal had begun to build stone ceremonial structures, and by 200 BC a complex of buildings stood on the site of the North Acropolis.

CLASSIC PERIOD

The Great Plaza was beginning to assume its present shape and extent 2000 years ago. By the dawn of the early Classic period, about AD 250, Tikal had become an important, heavily populated religious, cultural and commercial city. King Yax Moch Xoc, whose reign began around AD 230, founded the ruling dynasty.

Under King Great Jaguar Paw (who ruled in the mid-4th century), Tikal adopted a new, brutal method of warfare used by the rulers of Teotihuacán in central Mexico. Rather than meeting their adversaries in hand-to-hand combat, the army of Tikal encircled their enemy and killed them by throwing spears. This first use of 'air power' among the Maya of Petén enabled Tikal to conquer Uaxactún and become the dominant kingdom in the region.

By the middle of the Classic period, during the mid-6th century, Tikal sprawled over 30 sq km and had a population of perhaps 100,000. In 553 Lord Water ascended to the throne of Caracol (in southwestern Belize), and by 562, using the same warfare methods learned from Tikal, conquered and sacrificed Tikal's king. Tikal and other Petén kingdoms suffered under Caracol's rule until the late 7th century.

TIKAL'S RENAISSANCE

Around 700 a powerful king named Moon Double Comb (682–734), also called Ah Cacau (Lord Chocolate), 26th successor of Yax Moch Xoc, ascended Tikal's throne. He restored not only its military strength, but also its primacy as the Maya world's most resplendent city. He and his successors were responsible for building most of the surviving temples around the Great Plaza. He was buried beneath the staggering height of Temple I.

Tikal's greatness waned around 900, part of the mysterious general collapse of lowland Maya civilization.

No doubt the Itzáes, who occupied Tayasal (now Flores), knew of Tikal in the late Postclassic period (1200–1530). Perhaps they even came to worship at the shrines of their old gods. Spanish missionary friars left brief references to these jungle-covered structures, but these writings moldered in libraries for centuries.

REDISCOVERY

It wasn't until 1848 that the Guatemalan government sent an expedition, under Modesto Méndez and Ambrosio Tut, to visit the site. In 1877 Dr Gustav Bernoulli of Switzerland visited Tikal and removed lintels from Temples I and IV to Basel, where they are still on view in the Museum für Völkerkunde.

Scientific exploration at Tikal began with the arrival of English archaeologist Alfred P Maudslay in 1881; others who continued his work include Teobert Maler, Alfred M Tozzer and RE Merwin. Tozzer worked at Tikal from the beginning of the century until his death in 1954. Tikal's inscriptions were studied and deciphered by Sylvanus G Morley.

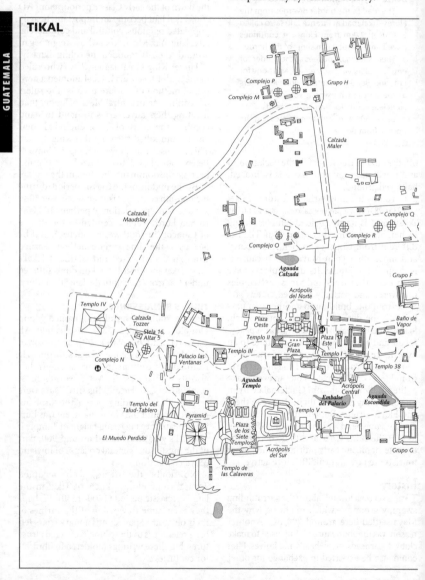

TIKAL

Complejo P
Grupo H
Complejo M
Calzada Maler
Calzada Maudslay
Complejo Q
Complejo O
Complejo R
Aguada Calzada
Grupo F
Acrópolis del Norte
Templo IV
Baño de Vapor
Plaza Oeste
Calzada Tozzer
Stela 16, Altar 5
Templo II
Plaza Este
Gran Plaza
Complejo N
Palacio las Ventanas
Templo III
Templo I
Templo 38
Aguada Templo
Acrópolis Central
Templo del Talud-Tablero
Embalse del Palacio
Aguada Escondida
Pyramid
Templo V
El Mundo Perdido
Plaza de los Siete Templos
Acrópolis del Sur
Grupo G
Templo de las Calaveras

Since 1956 archaeological research and restoration has been carried out by the University of Pennsylvania and the Guatemalan Instituto de Antropología e Historia. In the mid-1950s an airstrip was built to make access easier. In the early 1980s the road between Tikal and Flores was paved, and direct flights abandoned. Tikal National Park was declared a Unesco World Heritage Site in 1979.

Orientation & Information

The 550-sq-km Parque Nacional Tikal contains thousands of separate ruined structures. The central area of the city occupied about 16 sq km, with more than 4000 structures.

GUATEMALA

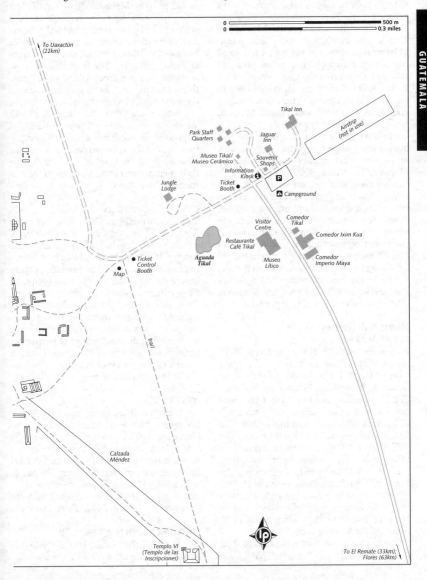

The road from Flores enters the national park 17km south of the ruins. The gate opens at 6am. Multilingual guides are available at the information kiosk. These authorized guides always display their accreditation carnet, listing the languages they speak. Before 7am, the charge for a half-day tour is Q100 per person. After that you pay Q450 for a group of up to eight people; or ask if you can join a private group.

Near the visitors center is the ticket booth, Tikal's three hotels, a camping area, a **tourist information center** (8am-4pm), a few small *comedores,* a post office, a police post and two museums. From the visitors center it's a 1.5km walk (20 to 30 minutes) southwest to the Gran Plaza. To visit all the major building complexes, you must walk at least 10km, so wear comfortable shoes. Guards at the ticket booth will try to sell you an 'official' site map but it's fairly useless. A better map, available at the visitor center shops, is published by Mapas de Guatemala (Q20).

It's a good idea to wear shoes with good rubber treads that grip well. The ruins here can be very slick from rain and organic material, especially during the wet season. Bring plenty of water, as dehydration is a real danger if you're walking around in the heat. Please don't feed the *pisotes* (coatis; a tropical mammal related to a raccoon) that wander about the site.

The Jaguar Inn will exchange US dollars and traveler's checks at a poor rate and offers internet access for a cool Q50 per hour.

Sights & Activities
GREAT PLAZA

Follow the signs to reach the Great Plaza (Gran Plaza). The path enters the plaza around **Temple I**, the Temple of the Grand Jaguar, built for King Moon Double Comb. The king might have worked out the plans himself, but it was erected above his tomb by his son, who succeeded to the throne in 734. Burial goods included 180 beautiful jade objects, 90 pieces of bone carved with hieroglyphs, and pearls and stingray spines, used for ritual bloodletting. At the top of the 44m-high temple is a small enclosure of three rooms covered by a corbeled arch. The lofty roof comb was originally adorned with reliefs and bright paint, perhaps symbolizing the 13 realms of the Maya heaven.

Since at least two people tumbled to their deaths, the stairs up Temple I have been closed. Don't fret: the views from **Temple II** just across the way are nearly as awe-inspiring. Temple II was once almost as high as Temple I, but now measures 38m without its roof comb.

The **North Acropolis** (Acrópolis del Norte), while not as impressive as the twin temples, is of great significance. Archaeologists have uncovered about 100 structures dating as far back as 400 BC. The Maya rebuilt on top of older structures, and the many layers, combined with the elaborate burials, added sanctity and power to their temples. Look for the two huge, powerful wall masks, uncovered from an earlier structure. The final version of the Acropolis, as it was around AD 800, had more than 12 temples atop a vast platform, many of them the work of King Moon Double Comb.

On the plaza side of the North Acropolis are two rows of stelae. Although hardly as impressive as those at Copán or Quiriguá, these served the same purpose: to record the great deeds of the kings of Tikal, to sanctify their memory and to add 'power' to the surrounding structures.

CENTRAL ACROPOLIS

On the south side of the Great Plaza, the Central Acropolis (Acrópolis Central) is made up of a maze of courtyards, little rooms and small temples. It is thought by some to have been a residential palace for Tikal's nobility. Others believe the tiny rooms might have been used for sacred rites, as graffiti found within suggests. Over the centuries the room configuration was repeatedly changed, indicating perhaps that this 'palace' was in fact a residence changed to accommodate different groups of relatives. A century ago, one part of the acropolis, called Maler's Palace, provided lodgings for archaeologist Teobert Maler when he worked at Tikal.

WEST PLAZA

The West Plaza (Plaza Oeste) is north of Temple II. On its north side is a large late-Classic temple. To the south, across the Tozzer Causeway, is Temple III, 55m high. Yet to be uncovered, it allows you to see a temple the way the last Tikal Maya and first explorers saw them. The causeway leading to Temple IV was one of several sacred ways built among the complexes, no doubt for astronomical as well as aesthetic reasons.

SOUTH ACROPOLIS & TEMPLE V

Due south of the Great Plaza is the South Acropolis (Acrópolis del Sur). Excavation has just begun on this 2-hectare mass of masonry. The palaces on top are from late-Classic times, but earlier constructions probably go back 1000 years.

Temple V, just east of the South Acropolis, is 58m high and was built around AD 700. Unlike the other great temples, this one has rounded corners and one tiny room at the top. The room is less than a meter deep, but its walls are up to 4.5m thick. Restoration of this temple started in 1991.

PLAZA OF THE SEVEN TEMPLES

This plaza (Plaza de los Siete Templos) is on the other side of the South Acropolis. The little temples, clustered together, were built in late-Classic times, though the structures beneath go back at least a millennium. Note the skull and crossbones on the central temple (the one with the stela and altar in front). On the plaza's north side is an unusual triple ball court; another, larger version of the same design stands just south of Temple I.

EL MUNDO PERDIDO

About 400m southwest of the Great Plaza is El Mundo Perdido (The Lost World), a complex of 38 structures surrounding a huge pyramid. Unlike the rest of Tikal, where late-Classic construction overlays earlier work, El Mundo Perdido holds buildings of many different periods. The large pyramid is thought to be Preclassic with some later repairs and renovations, the Talud-Tablero Temple (or Temple of the Three Rooms) is an early Classic structure, and the Temple of the Skulls is late-Classic.

The pyramid, 32m high and 80m along its base, had huge masks flanking each stairway but no temple structure at the top. Each side displays a slightly different architectural style. Tunnels dug by archaeologists reveal four similar pyramids beneath the outer face; the earliest (Structure 5C-54 Sub 2B) dates from 700 BC, making the pyramid the oldest Maya structure in Tikal.

TEMPLE IV & COMPLEX N

Complex N, near Temple IV, is an example of the 'twin-temple' complexes popular during the late-Classic period. These complexes are thought to have commemorated the completion of a *katun*, or 20-year cycle in the Maya calendar. This one was built in 711 by King Moon Double Comb to mark the 14th *katun* of *baktun* 9. (A *baktun* is about 394

years.) The king is portrayed on Stela 16, one of Tikal's finest.

Temple IV, at 64m, is Tikal's highest building. It was completed about 741, in the reign of King Moon Double Comb's son. A series of steep wooden steps and ladders takes you to the top.

TEMPLE OF THE INSCRIPTIONS (TEMPLE VI)

Compared to Copán or Quiriguá, Tikal sports relatively few inscriptions. The exception is this temple (Templo de las Inscripciones), 1.2km southeast of the Great Plaza. On the rear of the 12m-high roof comb is a long inscription; the sides and cornice of the roof comb bear glyphs as well. The inscriptions give us the date AD 766. Stela 21 and Altar 9, standing before the temple, date from 736. Badly damaged, the stela has now been repaired.

NORTHERN COMPLEXES

About 1km north of the Great Plaza is **Complex P**. Like Complex N, it's a late-Classic twin-temple complex that probably commemorated the end of a *katun*. **Complex M**, next to it, was partially torn down by late-Classic Maya to provide material for the causeway – now named after Alfred Maudslay, who is most widely known for his photographs of Central American ruins – that runs southwest to Temple IV.

Complexes Q and R, about 300m due north of the Great Plaza, are late-Classic twin-pyramid complexes. Complex Q is perhaps the best example of the twin-temple type, as it has been mostly restored. Stela 22 and Altar 10 are excellent examples of late-Classic Tikal relief carving, dated 771.

Complex O, due west of these complexes on the west side of the Maler Causeway, has an uncarved stela and altar in its north enclosure. The point of stelae was to record happenings – why did this one remain uncarved?

MUSEUMS

Tikal has two museums. The **Museo Lítico** (Museum of Stone; admission Q10; ⏱ 8am-4:30pm Mon-Fri, to 4pm Sat & Sun), the larger of the two, is in the visitors center. It houses a number of stelae and carved stones from the ruins. Outside is a large model showing how Tikal looked around AD 800. The photographs taken by Alfred P Maudslay and Teobert Maler of the jungle-covered temples in various stages of discovery in the late 19th century are particularly striking.

The **Museo Tikal** or **Museo Cerámico** (Museum of Ceramics; admission Q10, free with Tikal site ticket; ☺ 9am-5pm Mon-Fri, 9am-4pm Sat & Sun) is near the Jaguar Inn. It has some fascinating exhibits, including the burial goods of King Moon Double Comb, carved jade, inscribed bones, shells, stelae, ceramics and other items recovered from the excavations.

BIRD-WATCHING

Around 300 bird species (migratory and endemic) have been recorded at Tikal. Early morning is the best time to go; even amateurs will have their share of sightings. Ask at the visitors center about early-morning and late-afternoon tours. Bring binoculars, tread quietly and be patient and you'll probably see some of the following birds:

- tody motmots, four trogon species and royal flycatchers around the Temple of the Inscriptions
- two oriole species, collared aracaris, and keel-billed toucans in El Mundo Perdido
- great curassows, three species of woodpecker, crested guans, plain chachalacas and three species of tanager around Complex P
- three kingfisher species, jacanas, blue herons, two sandpiper species and great kiskadees at the Tikal Reservoir near the entrance; tiger herons in the huge ceiba tree along the entrance path
- red-capped and white-collared manakins near Complex Q; emerald toucanets near Complex R

HIKING

The Sendero Benilj'a'a, a 3km trail with three sections, begins in front of the Jungle Lodge. Ruta Monte Medio and Ruta Monte Medio Alto (both one hour) are accessible year-round. Ruta Monte Bajo (35 minutes) is accessible only in summer. A short interpretive trail called El Misterio de la Vida Maya (The Mystery of Maya Life) leads to the Great Plaza.

TIKAL CANOPY TOUR

At the national park entrance, you can take a fairly expensive one-hour treetop tour through the forest by harness attached to a series of cables linking trees up to 300m apart, with **Tikal Canopy Tour** (☎ 5819-7766; www.canopy tikal.com; tour Q248; ☺ 7am-5pm).

Tours

All the hotels can arrange guided tours of the ruins, as well as tours to other places in the region. Day tours from Flores/Santa Elena can be arranged through Martsam Travel (p192).

Sleeping

The days of bribing a guard and sleeping on top of Temple IV are gone – if you are caught in the ruins after hours, you'll be escorted out, for security reasons. Nowadays, the best way to catch solitude and get an early glimpse of the wildlife is to camp at the entrance.

Other than camping, there are a few places to stay at Tikal. Most are booked in advance by tour groups. It may be best to stay in Flores or El Remate and visit Tikal on day trips.

On the other hand, staying at Tikal enables you to relax and savor the dawn and dusk, when most of the jungle fauna can be observed.

There's no need to make reservations if you want to stay at Tikal's **campground** (campsites per person Q30) opposite the visitors center. This is a large, grassy area with a clean bathroom block, plenty of space for tents and *palapa* shelters for hanging hammocks.

Jaguar Inn (☎ 7926-0002; www.jaguartikal.com; campsites per person Q25, with tent Q75, s/d Q346/504; [P] [X] [□]) Although the little duplex bungalows here are kind of jammed together and the walls are thin, it still makes a decent, relatively cheap sleep in the park. Hammocks on the little porches are a bonus. Its attractive little restaurant serves pastas and salads.

Jungle Lodge (☎ 7861-0446, 2476-8775; www.jungle lodgetikal.com; s/d Q562/710, without bathroom Q290/314; [P] [□] [🐕]) The largest and loveliest of the hotels was originally built to house archaeologists working at Tikal. Self-contained bungalows are well spaced throughout rambling, jungle-like grounds where ocellated turkeys and agoutis roam. The restaurant-bar is the classiest around these parts, serving veggie pastas, crepes, pepper steak and other international dishes in a tropical ambience (mains Q80 to Q100).

As you arrive in Tikal, look on the right-hand side of the road to find the little *comedores:* Comedor Imperio Maya, Comedor Ixim Kua (the most appealing), and Comedor Tikal. These *comedores* offer dining in rustic surroundings with generally unimaginative fare like grilled chicken or grilled steak (Q40 to Q50); some serve veggie plates consisting of boiled *güisquil* (squash), carrots, beans and plantains. All are open from 5am to 9pm daily.

In the visitors center, **Restaurante Café Tikal** has a more upmarket attitude, though prices are only slightly higher than at the *comedores*, with pastas and hamburgers among the offerings. Among the hotel restaurants the Jungle Lodge (see left) is best.

Picnic tables beneath shelters are located just off Tikal's Gran Plaza, with soft-drink and water vendors standing by, but no food is sold. If you want to spend all day at the ruins without having to make the 20- to 30-minute walk back to the *comedores,* carry food and water with you.

Getting There & Away

For details of transportation to and from Flores and Santa Elena, see p196. From Belize, you could hire an Asetur microbus, for Q575/660 one way/round trip for up to four persons from Melchor de Mencos to Tikal; additional passengers are Q60 each. To go to Tikal and continue onward to Flores, the cost is Q905, plus Q85 for additional passengers. Otherwise, get a bus to Puente Ixlú, sometimes called El Cruce, and switch there to a northbound minibus or bus for the remaining 36km to Tikal. Note that there is little northbound traffic after lunch. Heading from Tikal to Belize, start early and get off at Puente Ixlú to catch a bus or minibus eastward. Be wary of shuttles to Belize advertised at Tikal: these have been known to detour to Flores to pick up passengers!

UAXACTÚN

pop 700

Uaxactún (wah-shahk-*toon*), 23km north of Tikal along a poor, unpaved road through the jungle, was Tikal's political and military rival in late Preclassic times. It was eventually conquered by Tikal's King Great Jaguar Paw in the mid-4th century, and was subservient to its great southern sister for centuries thereafter.

Villagers in Uaxactún live in houses lined up along the airstrip. They make a living by collecting chicle, *pimienta* (allspice) and *xate* (*sha*-tay; a frond exported for floral arrangements) from the surrounding forest.

Sights

The pyramids at Uaxactún were uncovered and stabilized to prevent further deterioration; they were not restored. White mortar is the mark of the repair crews, who patched cracks to keep out water and roots. Much of the work on the famous **Temple E-VII-Sub** was done by Earthwatch volunteers in 1974.

Turn right from the airstrip to reach Groups E and H, a 15-minute walk. Perhaps the most significant temple here is E-VII-Sub, among the earliest intact temples excavated, with foundations going back perhaps to 2000 BC. It lay beneath much larger structures, which have been stripped away. On its flat top are sockets for poles that would have supported a wood-and-thatch temple.

About 20 minutes' walk to the northwest of the runway you'll find Groups A and B. At **Group A** early excavators, sponsored by Andrew Carnegie, cut into the temple sides indiscriminately, looking for graves, occasionally using dynamite. This process destroyed many temples, which are now being reconstructed.

Although officially there's a Q30 admission fee to enter the site, there's seldom anyone around to collect it.

Tours to Uaxactún can be arranged in Flores or at the hotels in El Remate and Tikal. Jungle Lodge (see opposite) has a trip departing daily at 8am and returning at 3pm, costing Q625 per person, including guide and lunch.

Both of the sleeping options that follow offer tours to more remote Maya sites such as El Mirador (see p207), El Zotz (see p207), Río Azul, Xultún, Nakbé and San Bartolo.

Sleeping & Eating

To reach anyone in Uaxactún call ☎ 7783-3931, then wait a few minutes for them to fetch your party. There is currently no cell phone coverage, though that may well have changed by the time you read this.

Aldana's Lodge (posadaaldana@gmail.com; campsites per person Q15, s/d Q25/40) To the right off the street leading to Grupos B and A, the Aldana family offers half a dozen clapboard cabins, with thin mattresses on pallets. Father and son Alfido and Hector Aldaña lead tours to jungle sites, and Amparo prepares good meals. Camping using Aldana's equipment costs Q20 per person.

Campamento, Hotel & Restaurante El Chiclero (campamentoelchiclero@gmail.com; campsites per person Q25, r Q100) On the north side of the airstrip, El Chiclero has 10 spartan, institutional green rooms underneath a thatched roof, with decent mattresses and mosquito-netted ceilings and windows. Clean showers and toilets are in an adjacent outbuilding; lights out at 10pm. Perky owner Neria does the best food in town (Q50 for soup and a main course with rice). Accommodations prices are very negotiable.

A few basic comedores also provide food: Comedor Uaxactún and Comedor Imperial Okan Arin.

Getting There & Away

A Pinita bus leaves Santa Elena for Uaxactún (Q35) at 2pm, passing through El Remate around 3pm, Tikal by 4pm, and starting back for Santa Elena from Uaxactún between 6am and 7am the following day. This means you'll need to spend two nights in Uaxactún to see the ruins. During the rainy season (from May to October, sometimes extending into November), the road from Tikal to Uaxactún can become pretty muddy: locals say it is always passable but a 4WD vehicle might be needed during the wet.

If you're driving, the last chance to fill your fuel tank as you come from the south is at Puente Ixlú, just south of El Remate. From Uaxactún, unpaved roads lead to other ruins at El Zotz (about 30km southwest), Xultún (35km northeast) and Río Azul (100km northeast).

SAYAXCHÉ & CEIBAL

Sayaxché, on the south bank of the Río de la Pasión, 61km southwest of Flores, is the closest town to nine or 10 scattered Maya archaeological sites, including Ceibal, Aguateca, Dos Pilas, Tamarindito and Altar de Sacrificios. Otherwise, for travelers it's little more than a transportation halt between Flores and Cobán.

Minibuses and buses from Santa Elena stop on the north bank of the Río de la Pasión. Frequent ferries (Q2 for pedestrians, Q25 for cars) carry you across to the town.

Banrural, just up the main street from Hotel Guayacán, has an ATM and changes euros and American Express travelers checks.

Hospedaje Yaxkín Chen (☎ 4053-3484; bungalows per person Q50) is a bit east of the center with 10 cheery bungalows amid an impressive variety of plants and trees. A big, open-air restaurant serves tacos, river fish and chicken cacciatore. It's four blocks east and a block south of the church. The hospitable owners will pick you up at the dock if you phone ahead.

Café del Río (mains Q40; ❤ breakfast, lunch & dinner) is the most atmospheric place to eat in town and is actually across the river on the big wooden dock built out over the water. Forget about the Q4 round trip and enjoy the wholesome food, sweet breezes and icy beer.

Restaurante Yaxkin, a couple of doors from Hotel Mayapán, is typical of the few other eateries in town: basic, family run and inexpensive.

Ceibal

Unimportant during the Classic period, Ceibal grew rapidly thereafter, attaining a population of perhaps 10,000 by AD 900. Much of the growth might have been due to immigration from what is now Chiapas, in Mexico, because the art and culture of Ceibal seems to have changed markedly during this period. The Postclassic period saw the decline of Ceibal, after which its low ruined temples were quickly covered by thick jungle.

Ceibal is not one of the most impressive Maya sites, but the journey to Ceibal is among the most memorable. A two-hour voyage on the jungle-bound Río de la Pasión brings you to a primitive dock. After landing you clamber up a rocky path beneath gigantic trees and vines to reach the archaeological zone.

Smallish temples, many still (or again) covered with jungle, surround two principal plazas. In front of a few temples, and standing seemingly alone on jungle paths, are magnificent, intact stelae. Exploring the site takes about two hours.

See p192 for travel agents who offer tours to Ceibal from Flores. From Sayaxché, Café del Río, runs lanchas here (Q450 for up to three people). **Viajes Don Pedro** (see opposite page) charges Q500 for up to five passengers. The fee should include a guide to the site, who may actually be the boatman. In high season, ask the lancheros about joining a tour group.

If you wish, you can get to Ceibal cheaper by land: get any bus, minibus or pick-up heading south from Sayaxché on Hwy 5 (toward Raxruhá and Chisec) and get off after 9km at Paraíso, from which a dirt track leads 8km east to Ceibal. You may have to walk this last 8km. In the rainy season check first that this stretch is passable.

See p196 for details of minibuses and buses from Flores. The round-trip schedule is similar.

Southbound from Sayaxché, buses and microbuses leave at 5am, 11am and 3pm for Cobán (Q60, three hours). More frequent micros go as far as Raxruhá (Q25, two hours), about hourly from 5:30am to 4pm, from where there are frequent departures for Cobán. For Chisec, you can change in Raxruhá or at San Antonio Las Cuevas. Vehicles depart from a lot behind the Hotel Guayacán. From the north side, micros leave for Santa Elena every 15 minutes, from 5:45am to 6pm (Q20, 1½ hours).

For river transportation, inquire at **Viajes Don Pedro** (☎ 4580-9389; servlanchasdonpedro@hotmail.com), next door to Restaurante Yaxkín. A trip all the way down the Río de la Pasión to Benemérito de las Américas (Mexico), with stops at the ruins of Altar de Sacrificios, should not cost more than Q3000 (3½ hours to ruins, up to four passengers). Alternatively, you could ride on one of the freight ferries passing through a few times a week for around Q150.

REMOTE MAYA SITES

Several sites of interest to archaeology buffs and adventurous travelers are open for limited tourism. Outfits like Martsam Travel and Aventuras Turísticas (p192) work with the local Comités Comunitarios de Ecoturismo (Community Ecotourism Committees) in the remote villages that serve as starting points for these treks. By choosing them, you'll be participating in a considered program of low-impact, sustainable tourism and you will have a guide who is highly knowledgeable about local conditions.

Few of these tours offer anything approaching comfort, and you should be prepared for buggy, basic conditions. For some good descriptions on how to get to these and other remote sites, have a look at www.mostlymaya.com.

The ceremonial site of **Yaxhá**, on the lake of the same name, is about 48km east of El Remate. Scholars believe it may have been a vacation spot for Maya nobility during the Classic period. The ruins here include a large plaza and two temples. A ruined observatory sits on Topoxté island in the middle of the lake.

El Zotz is about 25km west of Tikal. Zotz means 'bat,' and you'll encounter plenty on a trek here. Among the many unexcavated mounds and ruins is Devil's Pyramid, which is so tall that you can see the temples of Tikal from its summit. Trips to El Zotz can be extended to include a trek to Tikal.

El Perú, 62km northwest from Flores in the **Parque Nacional Laguna del Tigre**, lies along the Scarlet Macaw Trail. The trek starts in Paso Caballos and continues by boat along the Río San Juan. Several important structures here have been dated to between AD 300 and 900. Archaeologists believe El Perú was an important commercial center.

Another destination in Parque Nacional Laguna del Tigre that is sometimes combined with El Perú trips is the **Estación Biológica Las Guacamayas** (Scarlet Macaw Biological Station; www.lasguacamayasbiologicalstation.com) on the Río San Juan. This is a scientific station surrounded by rainforest, where among other things scarlet macaws and white tortoises are observed.

El Mirador (www.miradorbasin.com) is buried within the furthest reaches of El Petén's jungle, just 7km from the Mexican border. A trip here involves an arduous 60km trek in primitive conditions. The metropolis at El Mirador flourished between 150 BC and AD 150, when it was abandoned for mysterious reasons. The site holds the tallest pyramid ever built in the Maya world: El Tigre is over 60m high, and its base covers 18,000 sq meters. Its twin, La Danta (Tapir), although technically smaller, soars higher because it's built on a rise. There are hundreds of buildings at El Mirador, but almost everything is still hidden beneath the jungle.

This trip is not for the faint of heart, but if expense is not a concern, you can go the easy way: by helicopter. **Tikal Park** (www.tikalpark.com) offers one- and two-day 'heli-tours' to El Mirador from Flores, arriving in just half an hour at the site.

GUATEMALA DIRECTORY

ACCOMMODATIONS

This chapter's accommodations coverage includes places where a typical double (room for two people) costs Q150 or less. Doubles under about Q90 are generally small, dark and not particularly clean. A typical Q150 double should be clean, sizable and airy, with a bathroom, TV and, in hot parts of the country, a fan. Unless otherwise specified, the rooms listed here have private bathrooms.

Room rates often go up in touristy places during Semana Santa (Easter week), Christmas to New Year's and July to August. Semana Santa is the major Guatemalan holiday week of the year, and prices can rise by anything from 30% to 100% on the coast, in the countryside – anywhere Guatemalans go to relax – as well as in such international-tourism destinations as Antigua. At this time advance reservations are a must. Room prices listed here are for high (but not absolute peak) season. Off-season you can expect prices to drop around 20% and owners to be much more willing to negotiate discounts.

Be aware that room rates are subject to two large taxes – 12% IVA (value-added tax) and

10% to pay for the activities of the Guatemalan Tourism Institute (Inguat), although there is discussion about eliminating this second tax. All prices in this book include both taxes.

Camping can be a hit-or-miss affair, as there are few designated campgrounds, and safety is rarely guaranteed. Where campsites are available, expect to pay from Q20 to Q50 per night. Prices for campsites in this chapter are for the entire site unless otherwise noted.

Travelers attending Spanish school have the option of living with a Guatemalan family. This is usually a pretty good bargain – expect to pay between Q250 and Q500 per week for your own room, shared bathroom, and three meals daily except Sunday. It's important to find a homestay that gels with your goals. Some families host several students at a time, creating more of an international hostel atmosphere than a family environment.

ACTIVITIES

Caving

Guatemala attracts cavers from all over the world. The limestone area around Cobán is particularly riddled with cave systems whose true extents are far from known. The caves of Lanquín (p170) and Rey Marcos (p170) are open for tourist visits. There are also exciting caves to visit from Finca Ixobel (p190), near Poptún and Flores (p192).

Climbing & Hiking

Guatemala's volcanoes are irresistible challenges, and many of them can be climbed in one day from Antigua (p108) or Quetzaltenango (p142). There's further great hill country in the Ixil Triangle and the Cuchumatanes mountains north of Huehuetenango, especially around Nebaj (p136) and Todos Santos Cuchumatán (p153).

The Lago de Atitlán is surrounded by spectacular trails (p120), although robberies here have made some routes inadvisable. Hikes of several days are perfectly feasible, and agencies in Antigua, Quetzaltenango and Nebaj can guide you. In El Petén's jungles, hikes to remote archaeological sites such as El Mirador and El Perú (p207) offer an exciting challenge.

Cycling

There's probably no better way to experience the highlands than by bicycle. Panajachel (p117), Quetzaltenango (p143) and Antigua (p109), in particular, are the best launch points, with agencies offering trips and/or equipment.

Horseback Riding

There are stables in Antigua (p109), Santiago Atitlán (p124), Quetzaltenango (p139), El Remate (p197) and San Pedro La Laguna (p125).

Paragliding

Paragliding is an obvious sport in Guatemala – the mountains and volcanoes make excellent launch points and the views are superb. There are reliable, experienced operators in Panajachel (p120) and San Marcos La Laguna (p128).

Water Sports

You can dive inside a volcanic caldera at Lago de Atitlán (p130), raft the white water of the Río Cahabón near Lanquín (p170), sail from the yachtie haven of Río Dulce (p177), and canoe or kayak the waterways of Monterrico (p161), Lívingston (p184), the Bocas del Polochic (p180) or Punta de Manabique (p184). Surfing is a relatively young sport in Guatemala, but there are a couple of places where you might catch a wave, the best-established being Sipacate (p161).

Wildlife-Watching & Bird-Watching

Few national parks and reserves have many tourist facilities, but they do have lots of wildlife- and bird-watching.

Fine bird-watching locations in El Petén's jungles include Tikal (p198), El Mirador (p207), Biotopo Cerro Cahuí (p197), Laguna Petexbatún and (for scarlet macaws) Estación Biológica Las Guacamayas (p207).

Elsewhere, the wetlands of Bocas del Polochic, Punta de Manabique and Monterrico, the Río Dulce and Laguna Lachuá national parks and the Biotopo del Quetzal (p165) also provide lots of avian variety.

Mammals are more elusive but you should see several species at Tikal. Monkey fans will also be happy at the Reserva Natural Atitlán (Panajachel; p120), the Bocas del Polochic (p180) and Biotopo Cerro Cahuí (p197).

Zip Lining/Canopy Tours

Zip lining has taken off in a big way in Guatemala. New courses spring up all the time, but some that were happening at the time of writing include the following: Reserva Natural Atitlán outside of Panajachel (p120), Parque

Natural Guayaja (p170), Parque Chatún (p175) and the Tikal National Park (p204).

BOOKS

For more in-depth information, grab a copy of Lonely Planet's *Guatemala* guide.

Guatemalan Journey, by Stephen Benz, is another one to enjoy while you're in Guatemala. It casts an honest and funny modern traveler's eye on the country. So does Anthony Daniels' *Sweet Waist of America,* also published as *South of the Border: Guatemalan Days,* where the medic author pinpoints some of the country's quirky contradictions.

In *Sacred Monkey River,* Christopher Shaw explores by canoe the jungle-clad basin of the Río Usumacinta, a cradle of ancient Maya civilization along the Mexico–Guatemala border. A great read.

Bird of Life, Bird of Death, by Jonathan Evan Maslow, subtitled 'A naturalist's journey through a land of political turmoil,' tells of the author's searches for the resplendent quetzal ('bird of life') – which he found increasingly endangered, while the zopilote (vulture; 'bird of death') flourished.

See p32 for suggested books on the Maya and p713 for travel literature selections that cover Guatemala and surrounding countries.

BUSINESS HOURS

Guatemalan shops and businesses are generally open from 8am to noon and 2pm to 6pm, Monday to Saturday, but there are many variations.

Restaurant hours are typically 7am to 9pm Monday to Saturday (some close on Sunday), but can vary by up to two hours either way. Most bars open from 10am or 11am to about midnight. The *Ley Seca* (dry law) stipulates that bars and *discotecas* must close by 1am, except on nights before public holidays. It is rigidly adhered to in large cities and universally laughed at in smaller towns and villages. Antigua has a municipal law on the books that may soon be enforced, stating that no alcohol is to be served after 10pm – you can imagine how the majority of the tourist industry feels about it.

Banks typically open 9am to 5pm Monday to Friday (again with variations), and 9am to 1pm Saturday. In some towns banks are open on Sundays; these are specified in individual listings where relevant. Government offices usually open 8am to 4pm, Monday to Friday.

Official business is always best conducted in the morning.

CLIMATE

Although Guatemala is officially the 'Land of Eternal Spring,' temperatures can be freezing at night in the highlands, especially in the dry season – from late October to May – this is a good time to be on the coast or in El Petén.

Guatemala's coasts are tropical, rainy, hot and humid. Temperatures often reach 32°C to 38°C (90°F to 100°F), and the humidity abates only slightly in the dry season. On the Caribbean side, rain is possible any time. Cobán has about one month of dry weather (April), though you can catch some less-than-soggy spells between November and March.

The vast jungle lowland of El Petén has a tropical climate that is seasonally hot and humid or hot and dry. December and January are the coolest months, while March and April are like hell on earth.

DANGERS & ANNOYANCES

Drunk, alone, lost, late at night and loaded with cash is the stupidest way to walk around Guatemala. And pretty much any combination of the above is kind of stupid. A lot of people do things here they would never do back home. Sometimes they get away with it. Sometimes it backfires. Use your intuition and chances are you'll stay out of trouble.

That said, no one could pretend that Guatemala is a very safe country. The daily papers are full of gory stuff that Guatemalans do to each other. Thankfully for travelers, a lot of it is gang violence and they keep it to themselves.

Rapes and murders of tourists do happen occasionally, but robberies on remote walking trails is by far the most frequently reported incident involving tourists. For a scary litany of recent incidents, visit the website of Guatemala City's **US embassy** (http://guatemala.usembassy.gov) and click on 'Recent Crime Incidents Involving Foreigners.' Be aware that when they talk about crime statistics involving US citizens, they include Guatemalans who have gone to the US, obtained citizenship and returned home, not just tourists. This bloats the figures quite substantially.

Further, marginally less alarming, information is on the website of the **US Department of State** (http://travel.state.gov) and the website of the **UK Foreign and Commonwealth Office** (www.fco.gov.uk).

Robberies against tourists on walking trails tend to occur in isolated spots on well-known walks. Some trails around the Lago de Atitlán (see p115) and on the volcanoes outside Antigua are particularly notorious.

Other potential dangers are pickpocketing, bag-snatching, bag-slitting and the like in crowded bus stations, buses, streets and markets, but also in empty, dark city streets.

It's best to travel and arrive in daylight hours. If that's not possible, travel at night using 1st-class buses and catch a taxi to your hotel once you arrive. For a warning on solo female travelers traveling on intercity buses, see p89.

Kidnapping is not unknown in Guatemala and in a few rare instances, foreigners have been the culprits. Please exercise caution when talking to or photographing children, especially in rural areas. A misunderstanding here can lead to quite serious consequences.

Any crowd can be volatile, especially when drunk or at times of political tension. For more information on dangers and annoyances, see p715.

Scams

One common scenario is for someone to spray some sticky liquid like ketchup on your clothes. An accomplice then appears to help you clean up the mess and robs you in the process. Other methods of distraction, such as dropping a purse or coins, or someone appearing to faint, are also used by pickpockets and bag-snatchers.

Regrettably, ATM-card cloners have moved into Guatemala, targeting Guatemalans and foreigners alike. They operate by attaching a card-reading device to the ATM (often inside the slot where you insert your card) and once they have your data, proceed to drain your account. There have been reports of card cloning in all the major tourist destinations. The only way to avoid it is to use ATMs that cannot be tampered with easily (inside supermarkets or shopping malls) or by going into the bank and getting a cash advance there. The ATMs most prone to tampering are the ones in the little unlocked room at the front of a bank.

You should *never* have to enter your PIN number to gain access to an ATM room.

Reporting a Robbery or Theft

After a theft you may need a statement from the police for your insurance company. Tell them: *'Yo quisiera poner una acta de un robo'*

(I'd like to report a robbery). This should make it clear that you merely want a piece of paper and aren't going to ask the police to do anything active. Specially trained tourist police (often English-speaking) operate in some major tourist areas – you can call them in Antigua (☎ 5978-3586) and Guatemala City (☎ 2251-4897).

Outside of those areas (and normal office hours) your best bet is to call **Asistur** (☎ 1500), which operates a 24-hour nationwide toll-free hotline in English and Spanish. It can give you information and assistance, help deal with the police and even arrange a lawyer if need be.

EMBASSIES & CONSULATES

New Zealand and Australia do not have embassies in Guatemala, although New Zealand has an Honorary Consulate. The Canadian embassy can be of some assistance, but otherwise you'll have to go to Mexico City. The following embassies are in Guatemala City.

Belize (off Map p92; ☎ 2367-3883; embelguate@yahoo.com; Office 1502, Europlaza 2, 5a Av 5-55, Zona 14)

Canada (Map p92; ☎ 2363-4348; www.guatemala.gc.ca; 8th fl, Edificio Edyma Plaza, 13a Calle 8-44, Zona 10)

Cuba (off Map p92; ☎ 2332-4066; http://embacu.cubaminrex.cu; Av Las Américas 20-72, Zona 13)

El Salvador (off Map p92; ☎ 2360-7660; emsalva@intel.net.gt; Av Las Américas 16-46, Zona 13)

France (off Map p92; ☎ 2421-7370; www.ambafrance.org.gt; 5a Av 8-59, Zona 14)

Germany (off Map p92; ☎ 2364-6700; www.guatemala.diplo.de; Edificio Plaza Marítima, 20a Calle 6-20, Zona 10)

Honduras (off Map p92; ☎ 2366-5640; embhond@intelnet.net.gt; 19a Av 'A' 20-19, Zona 10)

Ireland (Map p92; ☎ 2384-9446; irelandgua@gmail.com; Edificio La Galería Office 15A, 7a Av 14-44, Zona 9)

Israel (Map p92; ☎ 2333-4624; 13 Av 14-07, Zona 10)

Japan (Map p92; ☎ 2382-7300; Av La Reforma 16-85, Zona 10)

Mexico (Map p92; ☎ 2420-3400; embamexguat@itelgua.com; 2a Av 7-57, Zona 10)

Nederlands (Map p92; ☎ 2381-4300; www.mfa.nl/gua; 13th fl, Torre Internacional, 16a Calle 0-55, Zona 10)

Nicaragua (Map p92; ☎ 2368-2284; embaguat@terra.com.gt; 13 Av 14-54, Zona 10)

New Zealand (Map p92; ☎ 2363-1848;13 Calle 7-71, Zona 10)

Spain (Map p92; ☎ 2379-3530; 6a Calle 6-48, Zona 9)

UK (Map p92; ☎ 2380-7300; www.ukinguatemala.fco.gov.uk; 11th fl, Torre Internacional, 16a Calle 0-55, Zona 10)

USA (Map p92; ☎ 2326-4000; http://guatemala.usembassy.gov; Av La Reforma 7-01, Zona 10)

FESTIVALS & EVENTS

Events of national significance include the following:

El Cristo de Esquipulas (January 15) This superdevout festival in Esquipulas brings pilgrims from all over Central America to catch a glimpse of the Black Christ housed in the Basilica.

Semana Santa (March/April; Holy Week, the week leading up to Easter Sunday) Statues of Jesus and Mary are carried round the streets of towns all round the country, followed by devout crowds, to mark Christ's crucifixion. The processions walk over and destroy *alfombras* (elaborate carpets of colored sawdust and flower petals). The week peaks on Good Friday.

Fiesta de la Virgen de la Asunción (August) Peaking on August 15, this is celebrated with folk dances and parades in Tactic, Sololá, Guatemala City and Jocotenango.

Día de Todos los Santos (All Saints' Day; November 1) Sees giant kite festivals in Santiago Sacatepéquez and Sumpango, near Antigua, and the renowned horse races in Todos Santos.

Quema del Diablo (The Burning of the Devil; December 7) Starts at around 6pm throughout the country when everyone takes to the streets with their old garbage, physical and psychic, to stoke huge bonfires of trash. This is followed by impressive fireworks displays.

FOOD & DRINK
Food

Desayuno chapín, or Guatemalan breakfast, is a large affair involving eggs, beans, fried plantains, tortillas and coffee. Breakfast is usually eaten between 6am and 10am.

Lunch is the biggest meal of the day and is eaten between about noon and 2pm. Eateries usually offer a fixed-price meal (*almuerzo* or *menú del día*) – consisting of soup and a main course featuring meat with rice or potatoes and a little salad or vegetables – or just a *plato típico*: meat or chicken, rice, beans, cheese, salad and tortillas.

La cena (dinner) is, for Guatemalans, a lighter version of lunch, usually eaten between about 7pm and 9pm. Even in cities, few restaurants will serve much after 10pm. In rural areas, sit down no later than 8pm to avoid disappointment.

On the coast, seafood is the go. In Livingston try the delicious coconut and seafood stew called *tapado*. Elsewhere, your fish or shrimp is generally fried, but can also be cooked *con ajo* (with garlic). These plates generally come with salad, fries and tortillas. Also good is *caldo de mariscos*, a seafood stew with fish, shrimp and mussels.

You can expect the average cost of a main dish to be anything from Q20 in a small *comedor* to Q70 in a decent restaurant.

Drinks

Ron (rum) is one of Guatemala's favorite strong drinks, and though most is cheap in price and taste, some local products are exceptionally fine. It should be sipped slowly, like fine cognac. Cheaper rums are often mixed with soft drinks. *Aguardiente* is a sugarcane firewater that flows in *cantinas* and on the streets, and gets you drunk hard and fast.

Jugos (fresh fruit and vegetable juices), *licuados* (milkshakes) and *aguas de frutas* (long, cool, fruit-flavored water drinks) are wildly popular and with good reason. Many eateries offer them, and almost every village market and bus terminal has a stand with a battalion of blenders. The basic *licuado* is a blend of fruit or juice with water and sugar. A *licuado con leche* uses milk instead of water. Soft drinks as a whole are known as *aguas* (waters). If you want straight, unflavored water, say '*agua pura.*'

On the coast, the most refreshing nonalcoholic option is a green coconut – you'll see them piled up roadside. The vendor simply slices the top off with a machete and sticks a straw in.

GAY & LESBIAN TRAVELERS

Few places in Latin America are outwardly gay-friendly, and Guatemala is no different. Technically, homosexuality is legal for persons 18 years and older, but the reality can be another story, with harassment and violence against gays too often the norm. Guatemala City and Quetzaltenango have a small community of transvestite streetwalkers who are often the victims of violent assault. Don't even consider testing the tolerance for homosexual public displays of affection here.

Although Antigua has a palatable – if subdued – scene, affection and action are still kept behind closed doors; the chief exception is the gay-friendly club La Casbah (p114). In Guatemala City, Genetic and the Black & White Lounge are the current faves (see p98). Mostly, though, gays traveling in Guatemala will find themselves keeping it low-key and pushing the twin beds together.

The **Gully** (www.thegully.com) usually has some articles and information relevant to Guatemala. The best site, **Gay Guatemala** (www.gayguatemala.com), is in Spanish.

HOLIDAYS

The main Guatemalan holiday periods are Semana Santa (Easter), Christmas–New Year and July and August. During Semana Santa room prices rise in many places and it's advisable to book accommodations and transportation in advance.

Guatemalan public holidays:

New Year's Day January 1
Easter (Holy Thursday to Easter Sunday inclusive) March/April
Labor Day May 1
Army Day June 30
Assumption Day (Día de la Asunción) August 15
Independence Day September 15
Revolution Day October 20
All Saints' Day November 1
Christmas Eve afternoon December 24
Christmas Day December 25
New Year's Eve afternoon December 31

INTERNET ACCESS

Most medium-sized towns have cybercafes, with fairly reliable connections. Internet cafes typically charge less than Q8 per hour.

Wi-fi is becoming readily available across the country, but can only really be counted on in large and/or tourist towns. Most (but not all) hostels offer wi-fi, as do many hotels in the midrange and up categories. The best reliable source of wi-fi around the country is at Pollo Campero restaurants – they're in pretty much every town of any size and all offer free, unsecured access.

INTERNET RESOURCES

Guatemala (www.visitguatemala.com) Moderately interesting official site of Inguat, the national tourism institute.
Guatemala Times (www.guatemala-times.com) The best English-language news source focusing on Guatemala.
Lanic Guatemala (http://lanic.utexas.edu/la/ca/guatemala) The University of Texas' magnificent set of Guatemala links.
Lonely Planet (www.lonelyplanet.com) Succinct summaries on Guatemala travel; the popular Thorn Tree forum; and links to the most useful travel resources elsewhere on the web.
Mostly Maya (www.mostlymaya.com) Extensive, practical information on visiting remote Maya sites, plus plenty more.
Xela Pages (www.xelapages.com) Good information on the highlands and coast and an excellent forum where you can get answers to even your most obscure questions.

LANGUAGE

Guatemala has some great slang, and various books have been written on the subject (the best being ¿Qué onda vos? by Juan Carlos Martínez). Here's a small selection to get you started:

canche – blonde or light-skinned person
chapín – Guatemalan
chavo/a – guy/girl
de huevos – cool
ishto/a – young boy/girl
papichulo/mamichula – attractive man/woman
pisto – money

LEGAL MATTERS

Police officers in Guatemala are sometimes part of the problem rather than the solution. The less you have to do with the law, the better.

Whatever you do, don't get involved in any way with illegal drugs: don't buy or sell, use or carry, or associate with people who do – even if the locals seem to do so freely. As a foreigner you are at a distinct disadvantage, and you may be set up by others. Drug laws in Guatemala are strict and, although enforcement may be uneven, penalties are severe.

MAPS

The best overall country map for travelers is International Travel Maps' *Guatemala* (1:500,000), costing around Q100 in Guatemala. The cheaper *Mapa Turístico Guatemala,* produced locally by Intelimapas, tends to be the most up-to-date on the state of Guatemala's roads, many of which have been newly paved in recent years. It also includes plans of many cities. Inguat's *Mapa Vial Turístico* is another worthwhile map. Guatemala City, Antigua, Panajachel and Quetzaltenango all have bookstores selling some of these maps: see city sections. For 1:50,000 and 1:250,000 topographical sheets of all parts of Guatemala, head to the Instituto Geográfico Nacional (p90).

MEDIA

The most respected of Guatemala's many newspapers are *La Prensa Libre* (www.prensalibre.com), *Siglo Veintiuno* (www.sigloxxi.com), *La Hora* (www.lahora.com.gt) and *El Periódico* (www.elperiodico.com.gt). *El Quetzalteco* (www.elquetzalteco.com.gt) is Quetzaltenango's thrice-weekly newspaper. Some of the best investigative journalism in the country can be found in the magazine *Revista...Y Qué?* (www.revistayque.com).

MONEY

Guatemala's currency, the quetzal (ket-*sahl*, abbreviated to Q), was fairly stable at around Q7.5=US$1 for years, but currency manipulation by the Guatemalan central bank has seen it hovering around Q8 at the time of writing. The quetzal is divided into 100 centavos.

You'll find ATMs (cash machines, *cajeros automáticos*) for Visa/Plus System cards in all but the smallest towns, and there are MasterCard/Cirrus ATMs in many places too, so one of these cards is the best basis for your supplies of cash in Guatemala. The 5B network is widespread and particularly useful as it works with both Visa and MasterCard cards. For a warning about ATM use, see Scams, p210.

In addition, many banks give cash advances on Visa cards, and some on MasterCard. You can pay for many purchases with these cards and with American Express cards.

If you don't have one of these cards, a combination of American Express US-dollar traveler's checks and a limited amount of US cash is the way to go. Take some of these as a backup even if you do have a card. Banks all over the country change US-dollars, and many of them change US-dollar traveler's checks too. American Express is easily the most recognized traveler's-check brand.

In many places you can make payments with US dollars, and a few places will accept traveler's checks. Currencies other than the US dollar are virtually useless in any form, although a small handful of places will now change cash euros.

Banks generally give the best exchange rates on both cash and traveler's checks. If you can't find an open bank, you can often change cash (and occasionally checks) in travel agencies, hotels or shops.

Some towns suffer from change shortages: always try to carry a stash of small bills.

A 10% tip is expected at restaurants. In small *comedores* tipping is optional, but follow the local practice of leaving some spare change. Tour guides are generally tipped around 10%, especially on longer trips.

Exchange Rates

The table shows currency exchange rates at the time this book went to press.

Country	Unit	Q
Australia	A$1	6.51
Canada	C$1	7.52
Euro zone	€1	9.53
Japan	¥100	8.79
New Zealand	NZ$1	5.30
UK	UK£1	11.56
USA	US$1	8.01

PHOTOGRAPHY

Photography is a sensitive subject in Guatemala. Always ask permission before taking portraits, especially of Maya women and children. Don't be surprised if your request is denied. Indigenous children make a habit of requesting payment (usually Q1) in return for posing. In certain places, such as the church of Santo Tomás in Chichicastenango, photography is forbidden. Maya ceremonies (should you be so lucky to witness one) are off-limits for photography unless you are given explicit permission. If local people make any sign of being offended, you should put your camera away and apologize immediately, both out of respect and for your own safety. Never take photos of army installations, men with guns or other sensitive military subjects.

POST

The Guatemalan postal service was privatized in 1999. Generally, letters take eight to 10 days to travel to the US and Canada and 10 to 12 days to reach Europe. Almost all cities and towns (but not villages) have a post office where you can buy stamps and send mail. A letter sent to North America costs around Q15 and to anywhere else around Q20.

The Guatemalan mail system no longer holds poste restante or general delivery mail. The easiest and most reliable way to receive mail is through a private address. Language schools and some hotels will be happy to do this. If you want to get a package couriered to you, make sure the courier company has an office in the town where you are staying, otherwise you will be charged some hefty 'handling fees.'

RESPONSIBLE TRAVEL

By spending money in small, local businesses, staying for extended periods, volunteering and interacting with 'everyday' people, you have the potential to have a positive effect on Guatemala.

GUATEMALA

Readers should be aware that, while Guatemala certainly uses its Maya heritage to decorate hotel rooms and as eye candy on tourism posters, there is a history of serious neglect of indigenous people. Repeated studies have shown that government spending per capita is lowest in the departments that have the highest indigenous population.

You can do your bit by buying handicrafts directly from the makers or at cooperatives. Many language schools claim to help the local population. Unfortunately, this has become something of a marketing gimmick, and there are some operators who do no such thing – make some independent inquiries before swallowing what they tell you wholesale.

There are many worthwhile NGOs working to improve the situation; see p216 for contact details.

Drugs are everywhere in Guatemala, and ridiculously cheap when compared to the prices back home. Be aware that many younger Guatemalans see travelers as role models, and don't understand that the wild behavior that they see is (sometimes) just vacation madness. The other side of it is that, sadly, selling drugs to tourists is much more profitable than just about any other profession, so by being a customer you may be contributing to somebody's decision to drop out of school and become a full-time dealer.

STUDYING

Guatemala is celebrated for its many language schools. A spot of study here is a great way not only to learn Spanish but also to meet locals and get an inside angle on the culture. Many travelers heading down through Central America to South America make Guatemala an early stop so that they can pick up the Spanish skills they need for their trip.

Guatemalan language schools are a lot cheaper than those in Mexico, but few people leave disappointed. There are so many schools to choose from that it's essential to check out a few of them before choosing. It's not hard to see whether a school is professional and well organized, or whether its teachers are qualified and experienced.

Antigua is the most popular place to study, with around 100 schools (see p109). Quetzaltenango (p143), the second-most popular, attracts a more serious type of student; Antigua has a livelier students' and travelers' social scene. San Pedro La Laguna (p126)

and Panajachel (p126) on the Lago de Atitlán both have a handful of language schools, and if you'd like to learn Spanish while hanging out in a remote mountain town, there are schools in Nebaj (p136) and Todos Santos (p154). On average, schools charge Q900 to Q1200 for four hours of one-on-one classes five days a week and accommodations with a local family.

You can start any day at many schools, any week at all of them, and study for as long as you like. Decent schools offer a variety of elective activities from salsa classes to movies to volcano hikes. Many schools offer classes in Maya languages as well as Spanish.

TELEPHONE

Guatemala has no area or city codes. Calling from other countries, dial the international access code, ☎ 00 in most countries, then the Guatemala country code, ☎ 502, then the eight-digit local number. The international access code from Guatemala is ☎ 00.

Many towns and cities frequented by tourists have privately run call offices where you can make international calls for reasonable rates. If the telephone connection is by internet, the rates can be very cheap (Q1 a minute to the USA, Europe and Australia), but line quality is unpredictable.

Many travelers use an account with a VOIP service like Skype (www.skype.com). If an internet cafe does not have Skype installed, it can usually be downloaded in a matter of minutes. Headphone and microphone equipment in Guatemala is of varying quality, if it exists at all – if you're planning on using internet cafe computers to make calls, buy earbuds with a microphone attached before you leave – they take up very little room in your pack and you can plug them into the front of most computers in the country.

Telgua street phones are found all over Guatemala. To use one, you'll need to buy a Telgua phone card (*tarjeta telefónica de Telgua*) from shops and kiosks. The cards come in denominations of 20, 30 and 50 quetzals: you slot them into a Telgua phone, dial your number, and the display will tell you how much time you have left.

Unless it's an emergency, don't use the black phones placed strategically in tourist towns that say 'Press 2 to call the United States free!' This is a bait and switch scam; you put the call on your credit card and return home to find you have paid between US$8 and US$20 per minute.

Telgua street phones bear instructions to dial ☎ 147-110 for domestic collect calls and ☎ 147-120 for international collect calls. The latter number is usually successful for the USA and Canada, less so for the rest of the world.

Cell Phones

Cell phones are widely used. It's possible to bring your cell phone, have it 'unlocked' for use in Guatemala (this costs around Q50 in Guatemala), then substitute your SIM card for a local one. This works on some phones and not others and there doesn't appear to be a logic behind it. Guatemalan phone companies work on either 850MHz, 900MHz or 1900MHz frequencies – if you have a tri- or quad-band phone you should be OK. Compatibility issues, and the possibility of theft (cell phones are a pickpocket's delight) make buying a cheap prepaid phone on arrival the most popular option.

Prepaid phones are available pretty much everywhere and cost around Q100 to Q150, often coming with Q100 or so in free calls. Cards to restock your credit are sold in nearly every corner store. Calls cost Q1.50 per minute anywhere in the country, the same for the US (depending on the company you're with) and up to five times that for the rest of the world.

At the time of writing, Movistar had the cheapest rates (with coverage limited to major cities) and Tigo and Claro had the best coverage.

TOURIST INFORMATION

Guatemala's national tourism institute, **Inguat** (www.visitguatemala.com), has information offices in Guatemala City, Antigua, Panajachel, Quetzaltenango and Flores; a few other towns have departmental, municipal or private-enterprise tourist information offices. See city sections for details. Inguat operates a free 24-hour tourist information and assistance line; call ☎ 1500. Often the best source of tourist information in town will be the front desk of your hostel.

The Guatemalan embassy in your country may provide some tourist information.

TRAVELERS WITH DISABILITIES

Guatemala is not the easiest country to negotiate with a disability. Although many sidewalks in Antigua have ramps and cute little inlaid tiles depicting a wheelchair, the streets are cobblestone, so the ramps are anything but smooth and the streets worse!

Many hotels in Guatemala are old converted houses with rooms around a courtyard that is wheelchair accessible. The most expensive hotels have facilities such as ramps, elevators and accessible toilets. Transportation is the biggest hurdle for disabled travelers: travelers in a wheelchair might consider renting a car and driver, as buses will prove especially challenging, due to lack of space.

Mobility International USA (www.miusa.org) advises disabled travelers on mobility issues, runs exchange programs (including in Guatemala) and publishes some useful books. Also worth consulting are **Access-Able Travel Source** (www.access-able.com) and **Accessible Journeys** (www.disabilitytravel.com).

Antigua-based **Transitions** (transitionsguatemala@yahoo.com) is an organization aiming to increase awareness and access for disabled persons in Guatemala.

VISAS & DOCUMENTS

Citizens of the USA, Canada, EU countries, Norway, Switzerland, Australia, New Zealand, Israel and Japan are among those who do not need visas for tourist visits to Guatemala. On entry into Guatemala you will normally be given a 90-day stay (the number 90 will be written in the stamp in your passport) – these 90 days being for the entire CA-4 region (Guatemala, Nicaragua, Honduras and El Salvador).

You can get this extended *once,* for an additional 90 days, for around Q120. The exact requirements change with each government, but just for kicks, here's how it was working at the time of writing: You needed to go to the **Departamento de Extranjería** (Foreigners' Office; ☎ 2411-2411; 6a Av 3-11, Zona 4, Guatemala City; ☺ 8am-2:30pm Mon-Fri), with *all* of the following:

- A credit card with a photocopy of both of its sides.
- Two photocopies of the first page of your passport and one of the page where your entry visa was stamped.
- A recent, passport-sized color photograph.

If you got in before noon, extensions were being issued on the afternoon of the same day. If not, they were issued the next morning

Citizens of some Eastern European countries are among those who do need visas to visit Guatemala. Inquire at a Guatemalan embassy well in advance of travel.

GUATEMALA

Visa regulations are subject to change – it's always worth checking with a Guatemalan embassy before you go.

If you have been in the CA-4 for your original 90 days plus the 90-day extension, you must leave the region for 72 hours (Belize and Mexico are the most obvious, easiest options), after which you can return to the region to start all over again. Some foreigners have been repeating this cycle for years. For more on the CA-4, see boxed text, p723.

For the latest information on visas, also check out lonelyplanet.com.

VOLUNTEERING

If you really want to get to the heart of Guatemalan matters and you've altruistic leanings, consider volunteer work. Volunteering is rewarding and exposes foreigners to the rich and varied local culture typically out of reach for the average traveler. Opportunities abound, from caring for abandoned animals and kids to tending fields. Travelers with specific skills such as nurses, doctors or teachers are particularly encouraged to investigate volunteering in Guatemala.

Most volunteer posts require basic or better Spanish skills and a minimum time commitment.

Some excellent sources of information on volunteer opportunities are Proyecto Mosaico Guatemala in Antigua (see p109), and EntreMundos, based in Quetzaltenango (see p144) – the latter has a free online database listing hundreds of volunteer opportunities.

Many language schools have close links to volunteer projects and can introduce you to the world of volunteering. The best worldwide site for volunteer positions (with many Guatemala listings) is www.idealist.org.

WOMEN TRAVELERS

Women should encounter no special problems traveling in Guatemala. In fact, solo women will be pleasantly surprised by how gracious and helpful most locals are. The primary thing you can do to make it easy for yourself while traveling here is to dress modestly. Modesty in dress is highly regarded, and if you practice it you will usually be treated with respect.

Specifically, shorts should be worn only at the beach, not in town, and especially not in the highlands. Skirts should be at or below the knee. Wear a bra, as going braless is considered provocative. Many local women swim with T-shirts over their swimsuits; in places where they do this, you might want to follow suit to avoid stares (and sunburn).

Women traveling alone can expect plenty of attempts by men to talk to them. Often they are just curious and not out for a foreign conquest. It's up to you how to respond, but there's no need to be intimidated. Consider the situation and circumstances (on a bus is one thing, on a barstool another) and stay confident. Try to sit next to women or children on the bus if that makes you more comfortable. Local women rarely initiate conversations, but usually have lots of interesting things to say once the ball is rolling.

VOLUNTEERING

There are a wealth of volunteering opportunities available in Guatemala. A lot of them center on education and environmental issues. Here are a few offbeat ones that may appeal:

- **Arcas** (www.arcasguatemala.com) Works to protect the endangered sea-turtle population on the southern coast. Also has projects in El Petén.
- **EntreMundos** (www.entremundos.org) Produces a bimonthly newspaper and acts as a bridge between volunteers and NGOs.
- **Estación Biológica Las Guacamayas** (www.lasguacamayasbiologicalstation.com) A combined research/conservation center in El Petén.
- **La Calambacha** (www.lacambalacha.org) Based in San Marcos La Laguna, fosters confidence-building, social integration and artistic formation through arts workshops for kids.
- **Proyecto Payaso** (www.proyectopayaso.org) A traveling clown troupe specializing in community AIDS awareness and education.
- **Safe Passage** (www.safepassage.org) Provides education, health care and opportunities for kids scavenging in Guatemala City garbage dumps.

Nasty rumors about Western women kidnapping Guatemalan children for a variety of sordid ends have all but died down. Still, women travelers should be cautious around children, especially indigenous kids.

Although there's no need to be paranoid, the possibility of rape and assault does exist. Use your normal traveler's caution – avoid walking alone in isolated places or through city streets late at night, and don't hitchhike. For a warning on women traveling alone on buses, see p89.

WORKING

Some travelers find work in bars, restaurants and places to stay in Antigua, Panajachel or Quetzaltenango, but the wages are just survival pay. Río Dulce is the place to go if you're looking to crew on a boat around the Caribbean or north to the US.

If you are considering working here, bear in mind that the job you take could probably go to a Guatemalan, and the argument that 'they come to my country and take our jobs' is a very weak one indeed.

GUATEMALA

Belize

Belize bumps and grinds to an entirely different groove from the rest of Central America. Creole culture is dominant here and everybody knows the words to even the most obscure Bob Marley songs. Ever wanted to hear a policeman tell you that every little thing was going to be all right? Come to Belize.

Then there are the Garífuna. Master percussionists, proud 'cause they were never slaves, still eating and speaking as they did when they arrived here 200 years ago.

And there are the Maya, *mestizos* and Latinos. Some have 'always' been here, some came more recently, fleeing nasty situations in their homelands. Nearly everybody speaks English, but Spanish speakers outnumber the rest. In some of the Maya villages down south, there are people who only speak Mopan or Q'eqchi'.

Throw in some caves to tube, some reefs to dive, white sands and turquoise waters out on the cays, some good eatin', a barefoot, beer-drinking, hammock-swinging lifestyle and much, much more trouble to get into, and you can see why you're coming to Belize.

FAST FACTS

- **Area** 22,966 sq km (8875 sq miles) – slightly larger than Wales or the US state of Massachusetts
- **Budget** US$40 to US$60 per day
- **Capital** Belmopan
- **Costs** Budget hotel in Belize City US$20, bottle of beer US$2, three-hour bus ride US$5, set lunch US$5
- **Country Code** ☎ 501
- **Languages** English, Spanish, Creole, Garífuna
- **Money** US$1 = BZ$2 (Belize dollars); US dollars accepted everywhere
- **Population** 307,899
- **Seasons** Dry (December to May), rainy (June to November)
- **Time** GMT minus six hours

TRAVEL HINTS

Keep a Belizean dollar in a separate pocket – somebody may ask you for it. And stop walking so fast.

OVERLAND ROUTES

The Mexican border town of Chetumal has good connections into Belize. The other popular entry point is Benque Viejo del Carmen on the Guatemalan border on the road from Tikal.

CURRENT EVENTS

Belize is pretty laid-back, and there's little in the way of military coups or wide-scale unrest to grab international headlines. Current topics in Belizean newspapers concern oil exploration and the distribution of oil revenues. Belize is a small-scale oil producer, and debate is pretty fierce over whether the potential benefits of exploration and shipment are worth the risks of environmental damage. The debate is made even more heated by the fact that oil revenue is largely concentrated in a few hands, whereas the consequences of environmental damage will almost certainly damage the country as a whole.

Tourism plays a huge role in Belize, and the financial downturn of the last few years hasn't been good for the country's economy. Many Belizeans are hoping that the worst of the global financial crisis is past, and some in the tourism industry are gearing up to welcome visitors interested in learning about the country's Maya heritage in the run up to the year 2012.

Drugs are still an issue: Belize is a transshipment point for the northbound drug trade, and drug-related crime, though usually not directed towards tourists, is common.

HISTORY
Belize before Columbus

Belize certainly earns its place on the Ruta Maya – ruins are everywhere and the Maya population is still thriving, particularly in the southwest. The Maya have been in Belize since the first human habitation. One of the earliest settlements in the Maya world, Cuello, was near present-day Orange Walk. Maya trade routes ran all through the country, and the New River, Río Hondo and Belize River all played an important role in early trade and commerce. Important archeological sites such

as Cahal Pech (p248), near San Ignacio and Lamanai, date from this period.

Pirate's Paradise

Lack of effective government and the onshore safety afforded by the barrier reef attracted English and Scottish pirates to Belizean waters during the 17th century. They operated freely, capturing booty-laden Spanish galleons. In 1670, however, Spain convinced the British government to clamp down on the pirates' activities. Most of the unemployed pirates went into the logwood business.

During the 1780s the British actively protected the loggers' interests, at the same time assuring Spain that Belize was indeed a Spanish possession. But this was a fiction. By this time, Belize was already British by tradition and sympathy, and it was with relief and jubilation that Belizeans received the news, on September 10, 1798, that a British force had defeated the Spanish armada off St George's Caye.

Into the 19th Century

With the diminishing importance of logging, Belize's next trade boom was in arms, ammunition and other supplies sold to the Maya rebels in the Yucatán who fought the War of the Castes during the mid-19th century. The war also brought a flood of refugees from both sides to Belize.

In 1859 Britain and Guatemala signed a treaty that gave Britain rights to the land provided that the British built a road from Guatemala to the Caribbean coast. The treaty still stands, but the road has never been built, and many Guatemalan-made maps show Guatemala – which has never formally accepted Belize as a separate territory – extending all the way through Belize to the coast.

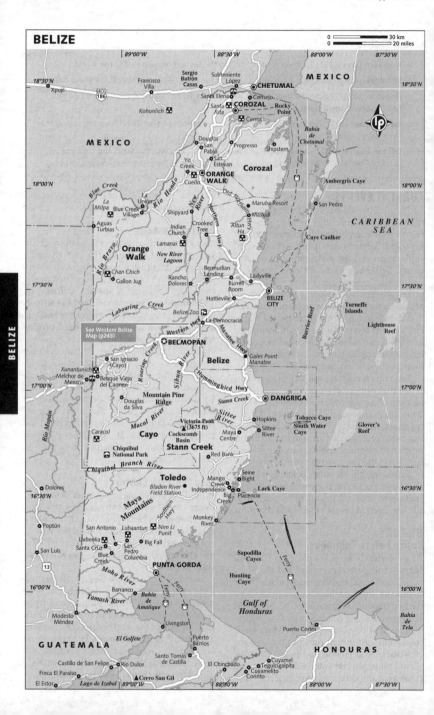

BELIZE

Independence & Beyond

The country's first general election was held in 1954, and the People's United Party (PUP) won handsomely on leader George Price's pro-independence platform. On September 21, 1981, the colony of British Honduras officially became the independent nation of Belize.

Since independence, the political landscape has been one of one-term governments (the United Democratic Party, or UDP, being the other player there), corruption scandals, power struggles and broken electoral promises. In 2003 PUP won an unprecedented second term. In 2007, the UDP again took the reigns of power after a campaign promising hope and change; many Belizeans grumble that the new government has been slow in implementing reform.

THE CULTURE
The National Psyche

Rule number one in Belize: give respect and you'll get respect. Belizeans are friendly and curious by nature, but often wait to see what you're like before deciding how they're going to be. Treat them well, they're bound to do the same for you.

Belize's long association with the UK has left some odd legacies. Perhaps because of this (and the language thing), the country is more closely aligned with the USA than with other Central American countries.

Many Belizeans identify more closely with the Caribbean than they do with Central American culture. For this reason, your bus driver is more likely to be blasting reggae than Latino music, even if the route you're on is going through Maya villages on the Guatemalan border in the Toledo district and there's nary a dreadlock in sight.

People

But don't let the prevalence of reggae music fool you into thinking that Belize's cultural mix is solely Caribbean. While Creoles – descendants of the African slaves and British pirates – make up the country's largest ethnic group, a full one-third of Belize's people are *mestizos* (persons of mixed European and Central American indigenous ancestry), some of whose ancestors immigrated from the Yucatán during the 19th century.

The Maya people of Belize make up about 10% of the population and are divided into three linguistic groups. The Yucatec live in the north near the Yucatán border, the Mopan live in western Belize around the border town of Benque Viejo del Carmen, and the Q'eqchi' inhabit far southern Belize in and around Punta Gorda. In recent years, political refugees coming in from Guatemala and El Salvador have added to Belize's Maya population.

Southern Belize is the home of the Garífuna (or Garinagus, also called Black Caribs). The Garífuna are of South American indigenous and African descent. They look more African, but they speak a language that's much more indigenous and their unique culture combines aspects of both peoples.

Other ethnic groups in Belize include small populations of Europeans, North Americans and East Indians. Though small in percentage, Belize's Mennonite community is considered the backbone of the country's agricultural sector, and much of the dairy and produce you're likely to consume on your travels will have come from a Mennonite farm. Immigration from Taiwan and China is also on the rise.

ARTS
Music

Music is by far the most popular art form in Belize, from the reggae-soaked cays and the ribcage-rattling tunes pumped out on every bus in the country. Styles are much more Caribbean than Latin – after a few weeks you'll be an expert on calypso, soca, steel drums and, quite possibly, reggae.

Punta rock is the official musical style of Belize. Its origins are from the music of the Garífuna – drum heavy with plenty of call and response. This music is designed to get your hips moving. Probably the most famous *punta* rocker is Pen Cayetano (who has collaborated with various artists), who plays in Belize regularly when not touring internationally.

The blending of Garífuna rhythms with reggae dance hall and soca has produced a new generation of *punta* rockers who often rely on electronic accompaniment instead of live musicians. If you want to catch one of these lively shows, keep an eye out for Super G and the Griga Boyz or Poots 'Titiman' Flores.

The *parranda* style, which owes its roots to more traditional Garífuna arrangements with acoustic guitar, drums and shakers is most widely associated with artists such as Paul Nabor and the late Andy Palacio.

Brukdown, another Belizean style, was developed by Creoles working in logging camps during the 18th and 19th centuries. It

BELIZE

ANDY PALACIO

On January 19th, 2008, musician Andy Palacio died of coronary complications. Though only 47, Palacio was considered the most influential musician in Belize and the nation's musical ambassador. His memorial, held at the Baron Bliss Center for the Performing Arts in Belize City the following Friday, drew record numbers. The next day, his body was brought back to the village of Barranco (p261) where a traditional Garifuna wake was held.

It is said that on that day towns emptied out from Belize City to Punta Gorda, and the Southern Highway was thronged as mourners headed to the tiny village where Andy was born – and finally, laid to rest – to pay their last respects.

involves an accordion, banjo, harmonica and a percussion instrument – traditionally a pig's jawbone is used, the teeth rattled with a stick. Wilfred Peters' Boom and Chime band is perhaps the best known of the *brukdown* artists.

The Maya of Belize are off on their own tangent when it comes to music. Most notable here is the flute music of Pablo Collado and the traditional marimba (played with large wooden xylophones, double bass and drum kit) of Alma Beliceña.

ENVIRONMENT
The Land
Belize is mostly tropical lowland, typically hot and humid for most of the year. Rainfall is lightest in the north, heaviest in the south. The southern rainforests receive almost 4m of precipitation annually, making the south the country's most humid region.

An exception to Belize's low-lying topography and hot, sticky climate can be found in the Maya Mountains, which traverse western and southern Belize at elevations approaching 1000m. The mountains enjoy a more pleasant climate than the lowlands – comfortably warm during the day, cooling off a bit at night. The country's coastline and northern coastal plain are largely covered in mangrove swamp, which indistinctly defines the line between land and sea. Offshore, the limestone bedrock extends eastward into the Caribbean for several kilometers at a depth of about 16.5ft (5m). At the eastern extent of this shelf

is the second-longest barrier reef in the world (after Australia's Great Barrier Reef).

Wildlife
The lush tropical forests contain huge ceiba trees as well as mahogany, guanacaste and cohune palms, all festooned with orchids, bromeliads and other epiphytes and liana vines. Much of the shorelines of both the mainland and the islands are cloaked in dense mangrove.

Baird's tapir is Belize's national animal. The *gibnut* or *tepezcuintle* (paca), a rabbit-size burrowing rodent, is abundant. Other tropical animals include the jaguar, ocelot, howler monkey, spider monkey, peccary, vulture, stork and anteater.

There are 60 species of snake in the forests and waters of Belize, but only a handful are poisonous: The fer-de-lance, the coral snake and the tropical rattlesnake are especially dangerous.

Two types of crocodile call Belize home – the American crocodile, which lives in fresh- and saltwater, and Morelet's croc, which only lives in freshwater and doesn't eat people.

Belize's birdlife is varied and abundant, with hummingbirds, keel-billed toucans, woodpeckers and many kinds of parrots and macaws.

In the seas live turtles, lobsters, manatees and a great variety of fish.

National Parks & Protected Areas
Nearly 40% of land in Belize is protected, either by national organizations or private trusts. Much of the Maya Mountain forest south of San Ignacio is protected as the Mountain Pine Ridge Forest Reserve and Chiquibul National Park. There are smaller parks and reserves, including marine reserves, throughout the country.

Environmental Issues
Belize takes environmental issues quite seriously, and much has been done to protect the endangered species that live within its borders. Species under threat include the hawksbill, green and leatherback sea turtles, the Morlet's and American crocodiles, the scarlet macaw, the jabiru stork and the manatee. Deforestation for farmland is becoming a concern, leading to loss of habitat, soil erosion and salination of waterways. Continuing oil drilling in the Cayo district, as well as new exploration in other parts of the country, is an environmental concern.

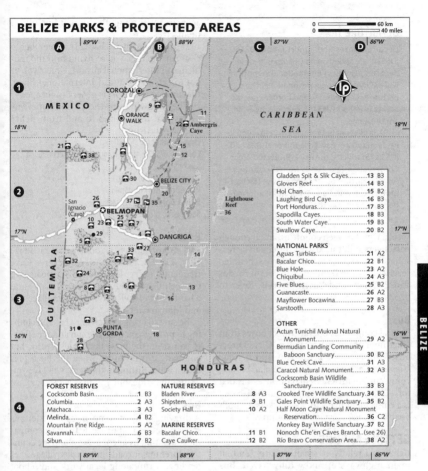

BELIZE PARKS & PROTECTED AREAS

0   60 km
0   40 miles

Gladden Spit & Slik Cayes	13	B3
Glovers Reef	14	B3
Hol Chan	15	B2
Laughing Bird Caye	16	B3
Port Honduras	17	B3
Sapodilla Cayes	18	B3
South Water Caye	19	B3
Swallow Caye	20	B2

NATIONAL PARKS

Aguas Turbias	21	A2
Bacalar Chico	22	B1
Blue Hole	23	A2
Chiquibul	24	A3
Five Blues	25	B2
Guanacaste	26	A3
Mayflower Bocawina	27	B3
Sarstooth	28	A3

OTHER

Actun Tunichil Muknal Natural Monument	29	A2
Bermudian Landing Community Baboon Sanctuary	30	B2
Blue Creek Cave	31	A3
Caracol Natural Monument	32	A3
Cockscomb Basin Wildlife Sanctuary	33	B3
Crooked Tree Wildlife Sanctuary	34	B2
Gales Point Wildlife Sanctuary	35	B2
Half Moon Caye Natural Monument Reservation	36	C2
Monkey Bay Wildlife Sanctuary	37	B2
Nonoch Che'en Caves Branch	(see 26)	
Río Bravo Conservation Area	38	A2

FOREST RESERVES

Cockscomb Basin	1	B3
Columbia	2	A3
Machaca	3	A3
Melinda	4	B2
Mountain Pine Ridge	5	A2
Savannah	6	B3
Sibun	7	B2

NATURE RESERVES

Bladen River	8	A3
Shipstem	9	B1
Society Hall	10	A2

MARINE RESERVES

Bacalar Chico	11	B1
Caye Caulker	12	B2

BELIZE

TRANSPORTATION

GETTING THERE & AWAY
Air

Belize City has two airports. All international flights use Philip SW Goldson International Airport (BZE), 9 miles (16km) northwest of the city center.

Major airlines serving Belize include American (from Miami and Dallas), Continental (from Houston), Delta (from Atlanta) and Grupo TACA (from Los Angeles). Most international air routes to Belize City go via these gateways.

Grupo TACA also offers direct flights between Belize City and Guatemala City (Guatemala), San Salvador (El Salvador), and San Pedro Sula (Honduras), as well as connecting flights from Nicaragua, Costa Rica and Panama. Belize's two national airlines are Maya Island Air and Tropics Air. Though primarily domestic airlines, both also run flights to Belize City, Tikal, and occasionally Guatemala City.

At the time of writing, a second international airport on the Placencia peninsula was still unfinished.

Boat

Scheduled boats and occasional small passenger boats ply the waters between Punta Gorda in southern Belize and Lívingston and Puerto Barrios in eastern Guatemala. See p259 for details. These boats can usually be hired for

DEPARTURE TAX

Departure taxes and airport fees of BZ$60 (US$30) are levied on non-Belizean travelers departing Goldson International Airport in Belize City for foreign destinations. The departure tax at Belizean land border-crossing points is BZ$30 (US$15). Exit fees by water are the same.

Regardless of how you leave Belize, you'll be required to pay an additional BZ$7.50 (US$3.75) which is the PACT (Protected Areas Conservation Tax). Funds from this tax help to maintain the country's impressive tracts of protected natural areas. For more information, see www.pactbelize.org.

special trips between countries, and if enough passengers split the cost, the price can be reasonable. There are also regularly scheduled services between Dangriga and Puerto Barrios and Placencia and Puerto Barrios. Refer to p252 for details.

Bus

Several companies operate direct buses from Chetumal (Mexico) to Belize City. Direct buses run between Belize City and Benque Viejo del Carmen on the Guatemalan border, connecting with Guatemalan buses headed for Flores. The ferry terminal in Belize city is a convenient place to book tickets for both boats and buses leaving the country.

GETTING AROUND

Belize is a relatively small country, and all main highways are now fully paved. Bus is the mode of transportation for most Belizeans, so departures are frequent – there's no real need to book ahead, apart from around public holidays, but it *is* wise to turn up early and snag yourself a seat. See right for specific details.

Air

Belize's two domestic airlines are **Maya Island Air** (☎ 223-1140; www.mayaregional.com) and **Tropic Air** (☎ 226-2012, in USA 800-422-3435; www.tropicair.com). Both airlines service two principal domestic air routes: Belize City–Caye Caulker–San Pedro–Corozal; and Belize City–Dangriga–Placencia–Punta Gorda, and both have offices in each municipal airport. Tickets for both airlines can be booked through hotels, tour

agencies, or through the local airline offices themselves.

When flying into Belize City, remember to confirm whether you're flying into the municipal or international airport. Unless you've got to catch an onward international flight, the municipal airport is generally cheaper.

The following are the current one-way prices and flight times to and from Belize Municipal Airport.

Caye Caulker (BZ$52; 20min)

Corozal (BZ$120; 45min flying time, connect through San Pedro)

Dangriga (BZ$60; 15min)

Placencia (BZ$118; 35min)

Punta Gorda (BZ$152; 1hr)

San Pedro (BZ$52; 20min)

Boat

Fast motor launches zoom between Belize City, Caye Caulker and Ambergris Caye frequently every day. Even faster boats run between Corozal and Ambergris Caye, and a handy ferry service runs between Placencia and Mango Creek.

Be sure to bring sunscreen, a hat and clothing to protect you from the sun and the spray. If you sit in the bow, there's less spray, but you bang down harder when the boat goes over a wave. Sitting in the stern will give you a smoother ride, but you may get soaked.

Bus

A dizzying array of companies now offer bus services throughout Belize, with larger companies operating frequent buses along the country's three major roads and smaller village lines tending to run along local work and school schedules. Though it may seem chaotic, in actuality getting around in Belize by bus is fairly simple; nowadays most of the bus companies tend to congregate around central terminals or market areas (in the past this wasn't the case).

Outside Belize City, bus drivers will usually pick up and drop off passengers at undesignated stops – either tell the driver's helper where you want to get off or flag them down on the roadside to get on. Express buses generally only stop at designated stops.

Car & Motorcycle

If you plan to drive in Belize, you'll need to bring a valid driver's license from your home country. Hiring cars can be expensive, and you must be 25 years or older and pay with credit

---

BELIZE BY BOAT

Traveling between mainland Belize, Caye Caulker and Ambergris is a snap thanks to the services of Belize's water taxis. **Caye Caulker Water Taxi Association** (☎ 226-0992; www.cayecaulkerwatertaxi. com) and **San Pedro Water Taxi** (☎ 226-2194; www.sanpedrowatertaxi.com) both run boats between Belize City and San Pedro with a stop at Caye Caulker. Boats run more or less hourly from Belize City to San Pedro from 8am to 5:30pm. One-way fares are BZ$20. From San Pedro to Belize City boats run from 7am until 4:30pm. From Belize City to Caye Caulker boats run from 8am to 5:30pm, and from 7:30am to 5pm going the other direction. One-way fares are BZ$15. Boats between Caye Caulker and San Pedro run on a similar schedule. One-way fares are BZ$15.

Against the wind, the trip from Belize City to Caulker takes 30 to 45 minutes. The San Pedro ride takes 45 minutes to an hour. Water taxis also run to St George's Caye and Caye Chapel.

The Belize Marine Terminal (Map p228), at the north end of the Swing Bridge, is the main dock for boats to the northern cays in Belize City.

Thunderbolt Travels (☎ 226-2904) has boats that depart San Pedro at 3pm daily for Corozal. One-way fares are BZ$45. During high season a second boat is sometimes added.

---

card. Depending on the season, rental rates can hit US$80 per day, and hammering out a deal with a taxi driver can get you a much better deal.

Taxi
Except for in Belize City, you're never really going to need a taxi inside of towns. In Belize City, the fixed fare is BZ$6 in the daytime, within the city. At night, the price gets a bit more flexible (in an upwards direction).

BELIZE CITY

pop 70,800

While no longer the capital, Belize City retains its importance. It's got the shops, the schools and the population there's a buzz on the streets that the actual capital (Belmopan) can only dream about.

Sitting right on the coast and straddling the Haulover Creek, the city should be a picturesque place. It has its moments, but many of the old wooden houses have fallen victim to hurricanes or fire and the modern construction is of the fairly bland concrete-block style.

Still, there's no better place to see Belize in action. The bars and discos pack out almost nightly, Albert St comes alive during the day and the northern neighborhoods around Fort George and Newton Barracks boast kilometers of seaside parks, which fill up in the afternoons with locals catching a breeze.

ORIENTATION
Haulover Creek, a branch of the Belize River, runs through the middle of the city, sepa-

rating the commercial center (bounded by Albert, Regent, King and Orange Sts) from the slightly more genteel residential and hotel district of Fort George to the northeast.

Just south of the Swing Bridge and Haulover Creek is the old part of town, which can be slightly seedy and best explored during the day.

The Swing Bridge joins Albert St with Queen St, which runs through the Fort George district and its pleasant King's Park neighborhood. The bridge, a product of Liverpool's ironworks, was built in 1923 and is the only known working bridge of its type in the world. Its operators manually rotate the bridge open at 5:30am and 5:30pm daily, just long enough to let tall boats pass and to bring most of the traffic in the city center to a halt.

At the bridge's northern end is the Belize Marine Terminal (Map p228), which is used by motor launches traveling to Caye Caulker and Ambergris Caye.

INFORMATION
Bookstores
Image Factory Art Foundation (Map p228; 91 N Front St; www.imagefactory.bz) The best selection of books by Belizean writers, plus many art-oriented titles.

Emergency
Ambulance (☎ 90)
Fire department (☎ 90)
General emergency/police (☎ 911)
Tourist police (☎ 227-6082, 1-800-898-000)

Internet Access
KGs Cyber Café (Map p228; 60 King St; per hr BZ$6; ☽ 9am-6pm)

Turton Library (Map p228; 156 N Front St; per hr BZ$4; ☉ 9am-5pm Mon-Fri, 9am-noon Sat; 🔀) Cheapest internet access in town, fast connections and air-con.

Laundry

G's Laundry (Map p228; 22 Dean St)
North Front Street Laundry (Map p228; 22 North Front St)

Medical Services

Karl Heusner Memorial Hospital (Map p226; ☎ 223-1548; Princess Margaret Dr) In the northern part of town.

Money

There are several international ATMs throughout the city, including one next to the Marine Terminal Building.

Belize Bank (Map p228; 60 Market Sq)
First Caribbean International Bank (Map p228; 21 Albert St)

Post

Post office (Map p228; N Front St; ☉ 8am-noon & 1-5pm Mon-Sat) Facing the Marine Terminal building.

Telephone

BTL (Map p228; cnr Albert & Church Sts; ☉ Mon-Sat) Sells phone cards and has private cabins with air-con where you can make local and international calls.

Tourist Information

Belize Audubon Society (Map p228; ☎ 223-5004; www.belizeaudubon.org; 12 Fort St) Offers information on national parks and wildlife reserves throughout the country.

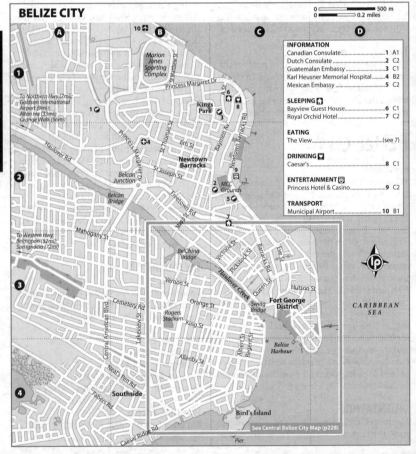

BELIZE CITY

INFORMATION
Canadian Consulate.................................1 A1
Dutch Consulate 2 C2
Guatemalan Embassy 3 C1
Karl Heusner Memorial Hospital..........4 B2
Mexican Embassy 5 C2

SLEEPING 🛏
Bayview Guest House................................6 C1
Royal Orchid Hotel 7 C2

EATING
The View..(see 7)

DRINKING 🍷
Caesar's..8 C1

ENTERTAINMENT ☺
Princess Hotel & Casino..........................9 C2

TRANSPORT
Municipal Airport....................................10 B1

GETTING INTO TOWN

From the Airport

The taxi fare to or from the international airport is BZ$40. It's a half-hour (1.8 miles; 3km) walk from the air terminal out along the access road to the Northern Hwy, where it's easy to catch a bus going either north or south.

From the Bus Station

The bus station (Map p228) is on the west bank of the Collet Canal, about five-minutes' walk from the Swing Bridge. As you exit the terminal, turn left, then take the first right along Orange St. This is a dodgy area – if you arrive at night, it's worth paying the BZ$6 for a taxi to your hotel.

Belize Tourism Board (BTB; ☎ 227-2420; www.belizetourism.org; 🕒 8am-noon & 1-5pm Mon-Fri, to 4pm Fri) international airport (☎ 225-3412); tourist village (☎ 223-5623) The newly built central office is at the corner of Regent and South Sts.

DANGERS & ANNOYANCES

Yes, there is petty crime in Belize City, but it's not as bad as some doomsayers will tell you. Take the same commonsense precautions that you would in any major city. Don't flash wads of cash, expensive camera equipment or other signs of wealth. Don't leave valuables in your hotel room. Don't use or deal in illicit drugs. Don't walk alone at night, and avoid deserted streets, even in daylight.

It's always better to walk in pairs or groups and to stick to major streets in the city center, Fort George and King's Park. Especially avoid walking along Front St south and east of the Swing Bridge; this is a favorite area for muggers.

Report any incidents or hassles to the BTB or the Tourist Police so staff will be aware of trouble spots and patterns.

SIGHTS & ACTIVITIES

In just a few hours it's possible to take in many of the city's major sights and sounds by foot.

Starting from the Swing Bridge, walk south along Regent St, one block inland from the shore. The large, modern **Commercial Center** to the left, just off the Swing Bridge, replaced a ramshackle market dating from 1820. The ground floor holds a food market; offices and shops are above.

As you continue down Regent St, you can't miss the prominent **Court House**, built in 1926 as the headquarters for Belize's colonial administrators. It still serves administrative and judicial functions.

Battlefield Park is on the right across from the Court House. Always busy with vendors, loungers, con artists and other slice-of-life segments of Belize City society, the park offers welcome shade in the midday heat.

Turn left just past the Court House and walk one block to the waterfront street, called Southern Foreshore, to find the **Bliss Institute** (www.nichbelize.org). Belize City's prime cultural institution, it's home to the National Institute for Culture and History, which stages periodic exhibits, concerts and theatrical works.

Continue walking south to the end of Southern Foreshore, then south on Regent St to the **House of Culture** (☎ 227-3050; admission BZ$10; 🕒 8:30am-4:30pm Mon-Fri), built in 1814.

Down beyond the House of Culture you come to **Albert Park**, which gets nice sea breezes and has a well-maintained playground, and **Bird's Island**, a recreation area with a basketball court and an open-air restaurant that serves snacks and cool drinks.

Inland from the House of Culture, at the corner of Albert and Regent Sts, is **St John's Cathedral**, the oldest Anglican church in Central America, dating from 1847.

A block southwest of the cathedral is **Yarborough Cemetery**, whose gravestones outline the turbulent history of Belize going back to 1781.

Walk back to the Swing Bridge northward along Albert St, the city's main commercial thoroughfare. Note the unlikely little **Hindu temple** between South and Dean Sts.

SLEEPING

Budget accommodations are mainly clustered around the Marine Terminal, and the area a little to the north. Prices listed here (and throughout this chapter) include tax and service charge. In low season, you may be able to bargain.

The following are in Central Belize City (Map p228) except where noted.

BELIZE

CENTRAL BELIZE CITY

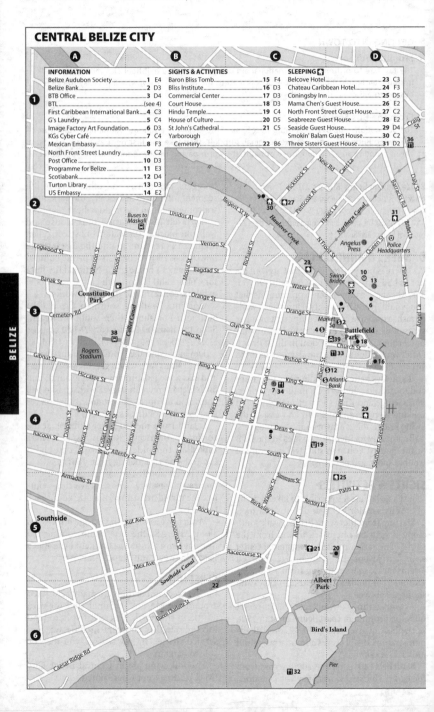

INFORMATION
Belize Audubon Society	**1** E4
Belize Bank	**2** D3
BTB Office	**3** D4
BTL	(see 4)
First Caribbean International Bank	**4** C3
G's Laundry	**5** C4
Image Factory Art Foundation	**6** D3
KGs Cyber Café	**7** C4
Mexican Embassy	**8** F3
North Front Street Laundry	**9** C2
Post Office	**10** D3
Programme for Belize	**11** E3
Scotiabank	**12** D4
Turton Library	**13** D3
US Embassy	**14** E2

SIGHTS & ACTIVITIES
Baron Bliss Tomb	**15** F4
Bliss Institute	**16** D3
Commercial Center	**17** D3
Court House	**18** D3
Hindu Temple	**19** C4
House of Culture	**20** D5
St John's Cathedral	**21** C5
Yarborough Cemetery	**22** B6

SLEEPING
Belcove Hotel	**23** C3
Chateau Caribbean Hotel	**24** F3
Coningsby Inn	**25** D5
Mama Chen's Guest House	**26** C3
North Front Street Guest House	**27** C2
Seabreeze Guest House	**28** E2
Seaside Guest House	**29** D4
Smokin' Balam Guest House	**30** C2
Three Sisters Guest House	**31** D2

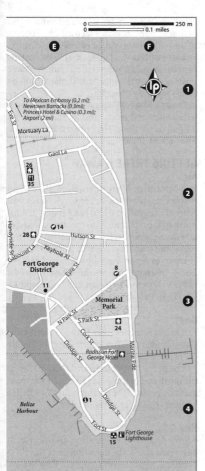

```
0                    250 m
0              0.1 miles
```

To Mexican Embassy (0.2 mi);
Newtown Barracks (0.3mil);
Princess Hotel & Casino (0.3 mi);
Airport (2 mi)

Eve St.
Mortuary La

Gaol La

Handyside St.

Gabourel La

Keyhole Al
Hutson St

Fort George District

Eyre St

Memorial Park

N Park St
S Park St

Cork St

Dredge St

Radisson Fort George Hotel

Marine Pde

Belize Harbour

Dredge St

Fort St

Fort George Lighthouse

CARIBBEAN SEA

BELIZE

North Front Street Guest House (☎ 227-7595; 124 N Front St; s/d/tr BZ$20/30/40; 🖥 🛜) Basic, safe and clean haven with front and rear verandas for chilling out. Proprietor Melanie Speer lives on the spot and runs a tight ship, so guests are in good hands.

Smokin' Balam Guest House (☎ 601-4510; 628-2003; smokin balam2@yahoo.com; 59 N Front St; r with/without bathroom BZ$45/30; 🖥) With a tiny deck overlooking the river, this hotel-giftshop-internet cafe has a range of spacious-enough, basic rooms. A small cafe downstairs serves breakfasts starting at BZ$4.

Seaside Guest House (☎ 227-8339; 3 Prince St; dm BZ$40, s/d BZ$55/110, s/d without bathroom BZ$50/100; 🖥 🛜) A long-time favorite with the backpacker crowd, the Seaside Guest House is set in a wooden Caribbean style house up on the 2nd floor, so there is plenty of breeze. The place attracts an interesting crowd, and group, weekly and monthly discounts are available.

Seabreeze Guest House (☎ 223-6798; 18 Gabourel Lane; r BZ$45-75; 🖥 🐾) One of the old backpacker standbys, the Seabreeze has comfortable rooms with new beds and a breezy upstairs communal area.

Three Sisters Guest House (☎ 203-5729; 36 Queen St; s/d with bathroom BZ$54/60) This old favorite still has homey, spacious rooms and a friendly family atmosphere.

Belcove Hotel (☎ 227-3054; www.belcove.com; 9 Regent St W; s/d BZ$67/80, s/d without bathroom BZ$55/65; 🛜) Simple, clean rooms with fan. Out back, there's a lovely communal balcony overlooking the river. Pay an extra BZ$20 for air-con and TV.

Coningsby Inn (☎ 227-3726; 76 Regent St; coningsby _inn@btl.net; s/d with bathroom BZ$120/130; 🛜) Clean, secure and well positioned for a midpriced Belize city stay; the restaurant serves tasty and economical meals.

Also recommended:

Mama Chen's Guest House (☎ 223-2057; 5 Eve St; r with/without bathroom BZ$60/40) Small rooms located close to downtown.

Bayview Guest House (Map p226; ☎ 223-4179; 58 Baymen Av; r from BZ$50; 🎮 🛜) Clean and quiet Taiwanese-owned guesthouse in the serene north end of town.

Royal Orchid (Map p226; ☎ 203-2783; 153 Douglas Jones St; r from BZ$110; 🛜) Large four-story hotel three blocks north of the Swing Bridge with a top-floor restaurant boasting a 360-degree view.

Chateau Caribbean (☎ 223-0800; 6 Marine Parade; www.chataucaribbean.com; s/d/tr BZ$158/178/198; 🛜)

The grand dame of Belize's old-school colonial hotels. The restaurant-bar boasts a harbor view.

EATING

Belize City's restaurants present a well-rounded introduction to Belizean cuisine.

The following are in Central Belize City (Map p228) except where noted.

Cenie's Diner (2nd fl, Commercial Center; breakfast from BZ$6, lunch BZ$6-10) Formerly known as Big Daddies, while management has changed, the food is still much the same. Lunch is served cafeteria-style from 11am and lasts until the food is gone. Still one of the cheaper places in town; head upstairs for river views.

Dit's (☎ 227-2230; 50 King St; mains BZ$10, burgers BZ$5) A homey place with a loyal local clientele, Dit's offers huge portions at low prices and serves up the stew chicken you'll be dreaming about long after you've returned home.

The View (Map p226; ☎ 203-2783; top of Royal Orchid Hotel, 153 Douglas Jones St; mains from BZ$12; ⊙ 7am-10pm) If it's a view your after, you won't get one finer than from this 4th-floor bar and restaurant. Menu includes Belizean, American and Mexican favorites.

Bird's Isle Restaurant (☎ 207-6500; Bird's Island; mains US$8-12; ⊙ lunch & dinner Mon-Sat) Down at the south end of town, this place serves up good burgers and reasonably priced meals in a shady, open-air location.

Brodie's (2 Albert St; ⊙ 8:30am-6pm Mon-Fri, until 5pm Sat, until 1pm Sun) This department store has the best downtown grocery supplies for picnics and long bus trips. A bigger one is on the Northern Highway (☎ 223-5687; 2½ mile, Northern Highway)

Also recommended:

Moon Clusters Coffee House (☎ 203-0139; 25 Daly St) The coolest cafe in town, serving up six types of espresso, frappuccino and donuts and pastries.

Mama Chen's Restaurant (☎ 223-2057; 5 Eve St; meals from BZ$6; Ⓥ) Vegetarian Chinese food.

DRINKING & ENTERTAINMENT

Weekends are your best bet to party in Belize City. There are a few places to have a beer in the center, but the real action takes place 1.2 miles (2km) north, about a BZ$6 taxi ride.

Bird's Isle (☎ 207-6500; Map p228) Down at the south end of town. Open-air restaurant by day, chill-out spot by night. Thursday is karaoke night, and Saturday is 'ole-skool' dance. BZ$4 Belikins.

Princess Hotel & Casino (Map p226; Newtown Barracks Rd) This is the only cinema in Belize City;

check daily papers for what's showing. Also here are a bowling alley/video arcade, a couple of upmarket bars and, of course, the casino.

Bliss Institute (Map p228; ☎ 227-2458; Southern Foreshore) Belize's fanciest entertainment venue hosts occasional concerts and plays. Stop by for its monthly program.

Caesar's (Map p226; Newtown Barracks Rd) Catch Latino-flavored music and all the action on a small dance floor. The crowd starts turning up at about 10:30pm.

GETTING THERE & AWAY

Air

For information on international travel to Belize City, see p223. Belize City's Municipal Airport (TZA; Map p226) is 1.5 miles (2.5km) north of the city center, on the shore. You can take domestic flights from the international terminal, but it's always cheaper (sometimes way cheaper) to depart from the Municipal Airport. Local Belizean airlines are **Maya Island Air** (☎ 223-1140; www.mayaairways.com) and **Tropic Air** (☎ 223-5671; www.tropicair.com).

Boat

Fast motor launches zoom between Belize City, Caye Caulker and Ambergris Caye frequently every day. See Belize by Boat (p225) for details.

The Belize Marine Terminal (Map p228), at the north end of the Swing Bridge, is the main dock for boats to the northern cays. See Belize by Boat (p225) for more details.

Bus

All roads lead to Belize City, and nearly all buses now stop at the main (formerly Novelo's) Terminal, regardless of company. Easy to find, it's the large building painted Rasta red, gold and green. Local buses make stops along the highways; express buses generally don't.

Belmopan (local/express BZ$6/9; 1-1¼hr; half-hourly departures)

Benque Viejo del Carmen (local/express BZ$8/12; 3hr; half-hourly departures)

Chetumal (Mexico) (local/express BZ$10/14; 3hr)

Corozal (local/express BZ$9/12; 2-3hr; hourly departures)

Dangriga (local/express BZ$10/14; 3-4hr; regular departures)

Orange Walk (local/express BZ$5/7; 2hr; hourly departures)

Placencia (local/express BZ$20/26; 4hr; regular departures)

Punta Gorda (local/express BZ$20/22; 6-7hr; regular departures)

San Ignacio (local/express BZ$7/11; 2-3hr; half-hourly departures)

GETTING AROUND

Trips by taxi within Belize City (including to/from Municipal Airport) cost BZ$6 for one or two people. Prices go up at night, and haggling is possible.

THE NORTHERN CAYS

Belize's go-to place for water-based fun are two tiny cays to the northeast of Belize City. Diving, snorkeling, windsurfing, sailing – it's all here. Protected sea grass along the shoreline doesn't really encourage swimmers, and most people swim off docks that jut into deeper water. If you just want to laze around on the beach, southern towns such as Hopkins (p253) or Placencia (p255) might be a better bet.

See p255 for details on the cays further south.

CAYE CAULKER
pop 1300

A short hop from Belize City, Caye Caulker remains a backpacker favorite. A tiny place, you could make a tour of it in less than two hours. Many travelers head to Caulker for a couple of days before heading to more developed Ambergris.

The village is located on the southern portion of the island. Actually, Caulker is two islands, since Hurricane Hattie split the island just north of the village. The split is called, simply, the Split (or the Cut). It has a tiny beach, with swift currents running through it. North of the Split is mostly undeveloped land, and part of it has been declared a nature reserve.

The water is good for swimming here, but sea grass is the problem. Jump off a dock, or head north to the Split.

Orientation & Information

The village has two principal streets: Front St to the east and Back St to the west. The distance from the Split in the north to the village's southern edge is little more than a half mile (0.8km).

South of the village is the **Belize Tourism Industry Association** (☎ 226-2251) where you can get information on what to see and do on the island. Cash is available at **Atlantic Bank** (Middle Street), and you can check your email at **Cayeboard Connection** (Front St; per hr BZ$12). Caye Caulker's website (www.gocayecaulker.com) is a great source for pretrip research.

> **BEER! BEER! BEER!**
>
> Fan's of Belize's favorite libation won't want to miss a tour at the **Belikin factory** (☎ 225-2058; Old Airport Rd, Ladyville; ☼ 8am-3pm Mon-Fri). The tour includes a 15-minute tour of the brewery, followed by 45 minutes of no-holds-barred all-you-can-drink Belikin beer, stout and lager. Fruit juices and soda available for teetotalers.

Activities

The surf breaks on the barrier reef, easily visible from the eastern shore of Caye Caulker. However, don't attempt to swim out to it – the local boaters are completely heedless of swimmers. Swim only in protected areas.

A short boat ride takes you out to the reef to enjoy some of the world's most exciting **snorkeling**, **diving** (including the shark-filled Blue Hole) and **fishing**.

Several places in town rent water-sports equipment. Snorkeling gear and beach floats each cost around BZ$10 per day and sea kayaks are BZ$15 per hour.

With their calm waters protected by the reef, near constant onshore winds and sweet water temperature, the cays are making a name for themselves as a kitesurfing location. **Kitexplorer** (☎ 623-8403; www.kitexplorer.com; off Front St; ☼ Nov-Jul) offers introductory, refresher and advanced courses, as well as renting equipment to licensed, experienced kitesurfers. Courses start from BZ$260.

Belize Diving Services (☎ 226-0143) does certification, and leads dive tours to Turniffe Atoll and the local reef.

Tours

A variety of inland and sea trips can be arranged from Caulker.

Raggamuffin Tours (☎ 226-0348; www.raggamuffintours.com) offers a three-day, two-night sailing trip (BZ$600), camping on Tobacco and Rendezvous cays. There are plenty of opportunities for snorkeling and fishing along the way to Placencia. If you're heading south, not interested in the mainland and want to see some more of the cays, this is the trip for you.

A great one-stop tour shop that pretty much does everything is **Tsunami Adventures** (☎ 226-0462; www.tsunamiadventures.com) located right on Front St by the Split. Tsunami can arrange three-hour night snorkeling trips (BZ$65),

BELIZE

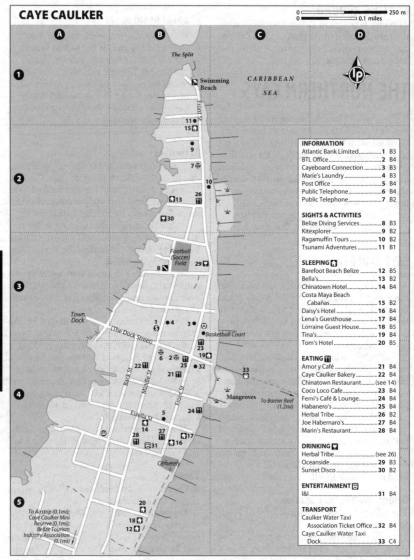

CAYE CAULKER

0 — 250 m
0 — 0.1 miles

INFORMATION
Atlantic Bank Limited............**1**	B3
BTL Office...........................**2**	B4
Cayeboard Connection..........**3**	B3
Marie's Laundry..................**4**	B3
Post Office.........................**5**	B4
Public Telephone.................**6**	B4
Public Telephone.................**7**	B2

SIGHTS & ACTIVITIES
Belize Diving Services...........**8**	B3
Kitexplorer.........................**9**	B2
Ragamuffin Tours...............**10**	B2
Tsunami Adventures............**11**	B1

SLEEPING
Barefoot Beach Belize.........**12**	B5
Bella's..............................**13**	B2
Chinatown Hotel.................**14**	B4
Costa Maya Beach Cabañas...**15**	B2
Daisy's Hotel.....................**16**	B4
Lena's Guesthouse..............**17**	B4
Lorraine Guest House...........**18**	B4
Tina's..............................**19**	B4
Tom's Hotel.......................**20**	B5

EATING
Amor y Café.......................**21**	B4
Caye Caulker Bakery............**22**	B4
Chinatown Restaurant........(see **14**)	
Coco Loco Cafe...................**23**	B4
Femi's Café & Lounge..........**24**	B4
Habanero's........................**25**	B4
Herbal Tribe......................**26**	B2
Joe Habernaro's..................**27**	B4
Marin's Restaurant..............**28**	B4

DRINKING
Herbal Tribe....................(see **26**)	
Oceanside..........................**29**	B3
Sunset Disco......................**30**	B2

ENTERTAINMENT
I&I...................................**31**	B4

TRANSPORT
Caulker Water Taxi Association Ticket Office...**32**	B4
Caye Caulker Water Taxi Dock..................**33**	C4

one-day trips to Turniffe Atoll (BZ$140) and two-hour boat tours of Caulker (BZ$50). All prices are per person. Tsunami also rent snorkels (BZ$10) and canoes (BZ$50) by the day.

Sleeping

Bellas (☎ 226-0360; monkeybite38@yahoo.com; dm BZ$20, r without bathroom BZ$35, campsites per person BZ$12) A low-key little place with a serious backpacker vibe. Rooms are set in the main wooden building or rustic cabins in the yard. Free kitchen and kayak use for guests.

Daisy's Hotel (☎ 226-0150; s/d/tr BZ$25/38/48) Some of the cheapest rooms on the island, and not a bad deal, either – spacious and airy, but basic. Get one upstairs where the ventilation's better.

DIVING THE BLUE HOLE

If you've ever seen a tourism poster for Belize, you probably know what the Blue Hole looks like – a lot of people come to Belize just to dive it. Situated in the middle of Lighthouse Reef, it's a sinkhole of startling blue water about 400ft (122m) deep and 1000ft (305m) wide.

After a fast descent to 130ft (40m), you swim beneath a stalactite-laden overhang and among a variety of reef sharks (black tips, bulls, lemons and maybe hammerheads or tiger sharks).

The dive can be undertaken with an open-water diving license, and can be arranged with nearly every dive shop on the cays. Prices are around BZ$380 for a day trip (which involves three dives).

Lena's Guest House (☎ 226-0106; r BZ$60) Right down on the beachfront, Lena's offers a decent deal – big, clean rooms with beds and overhead fans. The wide communal balconies have excellent views.

Costa Maya Beach Cabañas (☎ 226-0432; cabañas s/d/tr BZ$100/130/140; ☞) Traditional Belizean beachfront *cabañas* (cabins), all units are beautifully furnished. Complimentary bicycles and canoes and a private dock make this a great base in Caulker.

Barefoot Beach Belize (☎ 226-0205; d BZ$138, ste BZ$258, cottage BZ$290; ☞) This pretty little pink-and-turquoise beachfront hotel has rooms with king- or queen-sized beds, fridges, air-con and private patios. Suites have full kitchens. Cottages are stand-alone houses that fit a family of four.

Also recommended:

Tina's (☎ 226-0351; dm BZ$22, r BZ$40) Still a backpacker favorite, though rooms may not be clean enough for more fastidious guests.

Lorraine Guest House (☎ 206-0162; d with bathroom BZ$35) Cheap beachside bungalows. A bargain for the location.

Tom's Hotel (☎ 226-0102; toms@btl.net; s/d BZ$50/65) Reasonably clean rooms with a nice open courtyard area.

Chinatown Hotel (☎ 226-0228; Estella St; www.china townhotelbelize.com; r BZ$80-100; ☞) Clean rooms with cable TV.

Eating

There are plenty of places for Belizean food ranging from grilled seafood to stewed chicken and rice and beans. Any given evening you'll find half a dozen or so small grill and picnic table set-ups along the beach; any are a good bet for a fine – and usually cheaper – meal.

Do your part to avoid illegal fishing: don't order lobster outside its mid-June to mid-February season or conch outside of October to July.

Marin's Restaurant (meals around BZ$9) Up on the 2nd floor among the treetops, this place serves up hearty Belizean fare and seafood dishes. Breakfasts are cheap and good.

Coco Loco Cafe (sandwiches BZ$10) The best range of sandwiches, bagels and cakes come out of this friendly little cafe out the back of a gift shop/art gallery. There's good coffee, too.

Chinatown Restaurant (☎ 226-0368; meals BZ$10-20) Under the Chinatown Hotel, this is one of the more upscale Chinese restaurants on Caye Caulker. Most typical Sino-Belizean fusion dish: conch chowmein (BZ$11).

Habanero's (☎ 226-0487; mains BZ$20-30) Dine by the light of a hurricane lamp and enjoy the seafood kebabs in coconut sauce (BZ$35) while gazing through the extensive cocktail list. Budget travelers should check out Joe Habanero's, a more relaxed bar and grill just down the block.

Femi's Café & Lounge (Front St; mains from BZ$10) Set out on a deck over the water, Femi's has great food and the best smoothies in town.

Herbal Tribe (Front St; mains from BZ$15) Serving some of the best grilled lobster in town, Herbal Tribe is a long-time Caye Caulker mainstay for both cuisine and libations.

Drinking & Entertainment

Caye Caulker is such a pleasant place that much of the nightlife takes place in a mixture of indoor and outdoor (ie the beach) venues. **Herbal Tribe** (Front St) is a breezy place with mellow grooves and two rum drinks for BZ$5 from 6pm to 8pm. The **Oceanside** (☎ 226-0233; Front St) often hosts live bands and is open past midnight, and Hotel Beyond the Sea has a cool ocean-facing bar. All of these are on Front Street. On the south end of town, **I&I Bar** is the happening reggae spot.

Getting There & Away

Caye Caulker is serviced by regular flights between Belize City and Ambergris by Maya Island Air and Tropic Air. Caulker is also the midpoint for water taxis between Belize City and Ambergris. See Belize By Boat (p225) for details.

BELIZE

Getting Around

Caulker is so small that most people walk. If need be, you can rent a bicycle (BZ$20 per day) or golf cart (BZ$100 per day) or use the golf-cart taxi service, which costs around BZ$5 for a one-way trip anywhere on the island.

AMBERGRIS CAYE & SAN PEDRO
pop 8500

Belize's prime tourist location and the most developed of the cays, Ambergris is still fairly laid-back. San Pedro is a true town, but there are enough sandy streets and beachside bars to maintain the impression of a tropical paradise. The far northern part of the island is still largely undeveloped, and many are those who'd prefer to keep it this way.

Outside of town, especially to the south and directly to the north, large resorts and gated retirement villages are springing up with frightening regularity. Even so, there are still a surprising number of budget-friendly establishments in the downtown area.

Most of the island's population lives in the town of San Pedro, near the southern tip. The barrier reef is only a half mile (800m) east of San Pedro.

Orientation

San Pedro has three main north–south streets, which used to be called Front St (to the east), Middle St and Back St (to the west). Now these streets have tourist names – Barrier Reef Dr, Pescador Dr and Angel Coral Dr – but some islanders still use the old names.

Once you hit the river at the end of Pescador Dr you'll cross a small metal bridge; a BZ$2 toll is sometimes asked for. From there, a single dirt road runs north for close to 15 miles (25km). Pass through the condos and new developments just over the bridge; you'll find some outstanding beaches, as well as several laid-back eating and drinking venues.

Information

Various private roadside **tourist kiosks** (10am-9pm) are scattered around town – they're tour consolidators and make commissions by gathering groups together for tours. Otherwise they can be reasonably helpful with general enquiries. Tourist information is also available on the caye's own website (www.ambergriscaye.com). **Lime Tour Center** (☎ 226-4152; www.limetours.com; opposite Tropic Air) is also a convenient spot for information and meeting other travelers and locals.

Full Chevere (Tarpon St; per hr BZ$5), **Caribbean Connection** (Barrier Reef Dr; per hr BZ$10) and **Pelican Internet** (Barrier Reef Dr; per hr BZ$12) all offer internet, coffee and fresh juices. Several laundromats lie at the southern end of Pescador Dr, among them **Nellie's Laundromat** (per pound BZ$2).

You can change money easily in San Pedro, and US dollars and traveler's checks are accepted in most establishments. **Atlantic Bank** (Barrier Reef Dr) and **Belize Bank** (Barrier Reef Dr) have 24-hour ATMs.

For medical services, head to the **Lion's Club Medical Clinic** (☎ 226-2851; Lion St), located across the street from the Maya Island Air terminal at the airport. **San Carlos Medical Clinic** (☎ 226-2918; Pescador Dr) treats ailments and does blood tests. There is also a pharmacy and pathology lab onsite.

Activities

Ambergris is good for all water sports: scuba diving, snorkeling, sailboarding, boating, surfing, parasailing, swimming, deep-sea fishing and sunbathing. Many island hotels have their own dive shops, which rent equipment, provide instruction and organize diving excursions. In fact, just about any local can put you in touch with someone organizing water-sports trips.

Snorkeling and picnicking excursions cost from BZ$60. The going rental rate for a snorkel, mask and fins is BZ$15. Manatee-watching off Goff's Caye can be added to a snorkeling trip (BZ$210).

Sailsports Belize (☎ 226-4488; www.sailsportsbelize.com) rents windsurfers for US$22 per hour and sailboats for US$22 to US$48 per hour; lessons are available. Kitesurfing courses are available from US$165.

All beaches are public, and most waterside hotels and resorts are generous with their lounge chairs on slow days. While sandy beaches are plentiful, protected sea grass at the waterline makes entry from the shore not terribly pleasant, so you'll be swimming from piers. The beaches north of San Pedro tend to be the quietest.

Tours

The *Reef Runner* glass-bottom boat, found on Barrier Reef Dr, makes daily reef trips for BZ$70 per person. The aptly named *Rum Punch II*, a wooden sailboat, runs sunset cocktail cruises for BZ$50 (book at tour agents in town). *La Gaviota* is a sailing boat; go to Lily's Hotel (Barrier Reef) across from Belize Bank.

Tours are available to the Maya ruins at Altun Ha (BZ$180) and Lamanai (BZ$310) or beyond to the Belize Zoo, Xunantunich, Crooked Tree Bird Sanctuary, the Community Baboon Sanctuary, Mountain Pine Ridge and Tikal (Guatemala). Any hotel, travel agency or dive shop can fill you in on tours, or contact **Seaduced by Belize** (☎ 226-2254) or **Bottom Time Dive Shop** (☎ 226-3788/39) at Banyan Bay Resort.

Sleeping

Pedro's Inn (☎ 226-3825; Seagrape Dr; r BZ$110, s/d without bathroom BZ$25/40; 🛜 🖳) Out on the southern side of town, Pedro's has both good budget and midrange accommodations, and daily bike rentals (BZ$12). Long-term rentals are available.

Ruby's Hotel (☎ 226-2063; Barrier Reef Dr; s/d BZ$50) Set in a classic wooden beachfront building, Ruby's has long been a backpacker favorite.

Tomas Hotel (☎ 226-2061; Barrier Reef Dr; r with fan/air-con BZ$65/85) Large clean rooms with refrigerator, TV and private bath. A good deal for the middle of San Pedro.

our pick **Ak'bol Yoga Retreat & Eco Resort** (☎ 226-2073; www.akbol.com; s/d BZ$70/100, cabañas BZ$270) Yoga in Paradise? Ak'bol is a yoga retreat and family-friendly ecoresort on the tranquil north side of Ambergris Caye with seven thatch-roofed *cabañas* with private outdoor showers and a large hotel-style building with communal bathrooms and showers. Check the website for retreat dates, workshops and specials. Drop in classes at its yoga studio over the sea are BZ$30.

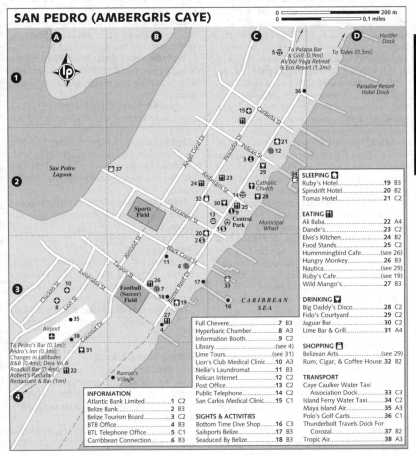

SAN PEDRO (AMBERGRIS CAYE)

BELIZE

Spindrift Hotel (☎ 226-2174; www.ambergriscaye. com/spindrift; Barrier Reef Dr; r BZ$106-220; 🖥 🛜 🦟) A good midpriced place on the waterfront; deluxe rooms are slightly larger and have beach views.

Changes in Latitudes B&B (☎ 226-2986, in USA 800-631-9834; www.ambergriscaye.com/latitudes; Coconut Dr; r from BZ$170-250; 🔌 🛜) This charming little gay-friendly bed and breakfast in the south side of town features individually themed rooms.

Also recommended is **Tides** (☎ 226-2283; www. ambergriscaye.com/tides; 57 Boca del Río Dr; r from BZ$150; 🖥 🛜 🦟), which has big, clean rooms and a poolside bar.

Eating

Several small cafes in the center of town serve cheap, simple meals. The best places for low-budget feasting are the stands in front of Central Park, where you can pick up a plate of stewed chicken with beans and rice, barbecue and other delicacies for about BZ$6. Budget snackers take note: a small home-front stand on Ambergris St, between Pescador and the lagoon, serves up freshly cut fruit, nuts and baked goods daily.

Hummingbird CAFE (Vilma Linda Plaza, Tarpon St; burgers BZ$8) Formerly Tabu, this hip little cafe serves up healthy breakfasts, bagels and burgers. There's a mouthwatering selection of homemade cakes and excellent coffee.

Palapa Bar & Grill (☎ 226-3111; 1 mile north of Bridge; meals BZ$15-20) This is the real deal, a *palapa* (shelter with a thatched, palm-leaf roof and open sides) on stilts at the end of a 50-yard pier in the Caribbean. Excellent American and Belizean specialties and beer and spirits. Off-restaurant swimming and inner tubing free of charge. Come for a meal; stay for a float.

Elvi's Kitchen (☎ 226-2176; cnr Pescador Dr & Ambergris St; meals BZ$17-50) A long-standing San Pedro favorite, Elvi's all you can eat Grand Maya Buffet Dinner (Friday; BZ$50) may be the best meal splurge on the island.

Ali Baba (Coconut Dr; mains BZ$20-30) The Ali Baba serves some good Middle Eastern and Mediterranean food, and even has Egyptian-style *shisha* pipes (BZ$20).

Wild Mango's (☎ 226-2859; Barrier Reef Dr; mains BZ$25-50; 🕒 Tue-Sun) Offers creative, carefully prepared food by an award-winning chef. Lunches are gourmet sandwiches, dinner features international fare such as Argentine steaks and Guatemalan chicken and a range of seafood dishes.

Nautica (Upstairs, Fido's Courtyard, Barrier Reef Dr; meals BZ$32-60) This upscale bar and grill of-

fers a fusion of Belizean, Caribbean and Mediterranean seafood dishes in a lovely setting. A good place to splurge on a great meal.

Also recommended:

Dande's (Pescador Dr) San Pedro's only premium ice cream, custard and sorbet.

Hungry Monkey (Pescador Dr; subs from BZ$10-14) Subs that hit the spot made from fresh local ingredients.

Robert's RasSafari Restaurant & Bar (☎ 666-0450; past mile marker 5.5) Ice-cold beers, reggae music and the best Jamaican jerk chicken in Belize.

Ruby's Cafe (☎ 226-0063; Barrier Reef Dr; snacks from BZ$6) Tiny place with good cakes and pastries.

Drinking & Entertainment

Lime Bar and Grill (☎ 226-4152; Coconut Dr; drinks from BZ$5) Opposite Tropic Air, this relative newcomer to the San Pedro scene has a full bar, kitchen and free wi-fi.

Fido's Courtyard (☎ 226-3019; Barrier Reef Dr) This bar, near Pelican St, is the landlubbers' favorite, with live music most nights.

Big Daddy's Disco (Barrier Reef Dr) Right next to San Pedro's church, this is a hot nightspot, often featuring live reggae, especially during winter.

Jaguar Bar (Barrier Reef Dr) Near Big Daddy's, this jungle-themed bar is often closed off-season, but it rocks in winter.

Deja Vu (Coconut Dr) A big air-conditioned disco south of town. Friday is the night to be here.

Roadkill Bar (Coconut Dr) Out front of the Deja Vu, this laid-back open-air bar often has live music.

Pedro's Bar (Seagrape Dr) Next to Pedro's Inn, the bar boasts a pool table, foosball and video games.

Shopping

Belizean Arts (☎ 226-3019; Fido's Courtyard) One of the best shopping spots, it sells ceramics, woodcarvings and paintings alongside affordable and tasteful knick-knacks.

Rum, Cigar and Coffee House (☎ 226-2020; Pescador Dr) The three staples of a great Belize vacation. Come in for coffee and rum samples!

Getting There & Away

Maya Island Air (☎ 226-2435; mayaairways.com) and **Tropic Air** (☎ 226-2012; www.tropicair.com) offer several flights daily between San Pedro and the Belize City airports, as well as flights to Corozal. See p223 for details.

Regular boats go from Ambergris to Belize City via Caye Caulker, and there is currently one boat daily from Ambergris to Corozal. See p225 for details.

Getting Around

You can walk to town from the airport in 10 minutes or less, and the walk from the boat docks is even shorter. A taxi from the airport costs BZ$5 to any place in town, BZ$10 to the hotels south of town. Nearly all hotels have bicycles for rent.

Joe's Bike Rental (Caribena Dr) rents bikes for BZ$20/80 per day/week.

Polo's Golf Carts (☎ 226-3542; Barrier Reef Dr) rents carts for BZ$130/500 per day/week. You'll need a valid driver's license.

For something a little different, **Segway of Belize** (☎ 620-9345; Coconut Dr) rents all-terrain Segways by the hour (BZ$56 per hour). They also do Segway tours of the island (BZ$150 and up).

Minivan taxis cost BZ$5 for a one-way trip anywhere. The far north resorts are accessed by water taxi.

NORTHERN BELIZE

Much more Latino than the rest of the country, you'll find whatever Spanish you have useful here. The landscape is flat and lush, mostly given over to farming, although there are a couple of interesting and easily accessible wildlife reserves.

Some important Maya sites can be found here, too. The most popular, Lamanai, is reached by a riverboat ride that is a joy in itself, but the national favorite must be Altun Ha, whose image has been immortalized on banknotes and beer-bottle labels.

BERMUDIAN LANDING COMMUNITY BABOON SANCTUARY

In 1985 local farmers organized to help preserve the endangered black howler monkey and its habitat. Care is taken to maintain the forests along the banks of the Belize River, where the black howler, found only in Belize, feeds, sleeps and – at dawn and dusk – howls (loudly and unmistakably).

At the **Community Baboon Sanctuary** (☎ 220-2181; www.howlermonkeys.org; admission BZ$14; ☉ 8am-5pm), in the village of Bermudian Landing, you can learn all about the black howler and the 200 other species of wildlife found in the reserve. A one-hour guided nature walk is included with your admission, arranged at the visitors center. Horseback riding is available for BZ$50, as are three-hour canoe trips (BZ$56) and 1½-hour night hikes (BZ$24). Crocodile-viewing night tours are BZ$110.

Sleeping & Eating

Rustic accommodations are available at the reserve but are best arranged in advance. **Village homestays** (d incl 2 meals BZ$50) can be arranged here, too.

Howler Monkey Resort (☎ 220-2158; www.howlermonkeyresort.com; cabañas from BZ$65; 🐒) Set on a bend in the river, this well-laid-out place offers a beautiful setting and decent accommodations from which to explore the jungles and listen to the howlers howl. Owners Ed and Melissa offer various packages including meals, jungle tours and canoe rentals.

Nature Resort (☎ 610-1378, 607-5448; naturer@btl.net; cabañas from BZ$130) Adjacent to the visitors center, Nature Resort has 10 beautiful newly renovated and well-maintained family-sized thatched-roof *cabañas* complete with fridge, coffee maker and microwave. The resort can also arrange meals for visitors.

Getting There & Away

The Community Baboon Sanctuary is in Bermudian Landing, 26 miles (42km) west of Belize City – an easy day trip from Belize City or the cays.

If you're driving, turn west off the Northern Hwy at the Burrell Boom turnoff (Mile 13). From there it's another 12 miles (20km) of dirt road to the sanctuary.

National operates buses to Bermudian Landing (BZ$4, one hour). Some travelers catch one of the frequent Northern Hwy buses heading north, get off at Burrell Boom and hitch the 13 miles (8km) to the sanctuary. If you hitch, take the usual precautions.

ALTUN HA

Northern Belize's most famous Maya ruin is **Altun Ha** (admission BZ$10; ☉ 9am-5pm), 34 miles (55km) north of Belize City along the Old Northern Hwy. The site is near Rockstone Pond village, south of Maskall.

Altun Ha (Maya for 'Rockstone Pond') was undoubtedly a small but rich and important Maya trading town, with agriculture also playing an essential role in its economy. Altun Ha had formed as a community by at least 600 BC, perhaps several centuries earlier, and the

BELIZE

town flourished until the mysterious collapse of Classic Maya civilization around AD 900.

Highlights of the grass-covered temples arranged around the two plazas are the **Temple of the Masonry Altars** (Structure B-4) in Plaza B and the **Temple of the Green Tomb** in Plaza A.

Modern toilets and a drinks shop are onsite.

Sleeping & Eating

Camping, though not strictly legal, is sometimes permitted; ask at the site.

Mayan Wells (☎ 225-5505; www.mayanwells.com; cabins BZ$50, campsites per person BZ$10) About 1.25 miles (2km) before reaching Altun Ha, this is a popular stop for lunch or refreshments. The one cabin is simple but adequate and camping is allowed on the premises; bathroom and shower facilities are available.

Getting There & Away

The easiest way to visit Altun Ha is on one of the many tours running daily from Belize City (BZ$80, half day including admission); most travel agents can line you up with one. To get here by public transportation, catch an afternoon bus departing the Main Bus Terminal (Map p228) for the town of Maskall, north of Altun Ha. Get off at Lucky Strike, from where it's a 2 mile (3.5km) walk/hitch (on a very lightly trafficked road) to Altun Ha.

LAMANAI

By far the most impressive site in this part of the country is Lamanai, in its own archaeological reserve on the New River Lagoon near the settlement of Indian Church. Though much of the site remains unexcavated and unrestored, the trip to Lamanai, by motorboat up the New River, is an adventure in itself.

Take along a sun hat, sunblock, insect repellent, shoes (rather than sandals), lunch and water.

As with most sites in northern Belize, Lamanai ('Submerged Crocodile,' the original Maya name) was occupied as early as 1500 BC, with the first stone buildings appearing between 800 and 600 BC. Lamanai flourished in late Preclassic times, growing into a major ceremonial center with immense temples long before most other Maya sites.

Unlike at many other sites, the Maya lived here until the coming of the Spanish in the 16th century. British interests later built a sugar mill, now in ruins, at Indian Church. The archaeo-logical site was excavated by Canadian David Pendergast in the 1970s and 1980s.

Most visitors opt to reach Lamanai by taking a spectacular boat ride up the New River from the Tower Hill toll bridge south of Orange Walk. The operators might tell you something different, but most tours are roughly the same. One reliable outfit is **Jungle River Tours** (☎ 302-2293; lamanaimayatour@btl.net; 20 Lovers' Lane, Orange Walk). River trips to Lamanai are BZ$90 per person for a tour including lunch, guide, fruit and admission fees.

If you're really keen, you may be able to get a good deal for the boat trip only by going down to the boat landing at the toll bridge and negotiating with the fishermen there.

Though the river voyage is much more convenient and enjoyable, Lamanai can be reached by road (36 miles/58km) from Orange Walk via Yo Creek and San Felipe. A bus service from Orange Walk is available but limited, making a day trip impossible. Hitching a ride with farmers is always an option.

ORANGE WALK
pop 18,000

Nestled on a bend in the New River, Orange Walk is a medium-sized Belizean town best known as a place where farmers from the surrounding district come to trade and socialize. The country's biggest rum distillery is here, and the town itself can get pretty lively in the evenings. Most tourists use the town as a base for boat trips to the ruins at Lamanai (see left) and other trips into the jungles of the Orange Walk district.

The Northern Hwy, called Queen Victoria Ave in town, serves as the main road. The center of town is shady Central Park, on the east side of Queen Victoria Ave. The town hospital is in the northern outskirts, readily visible on the west side of Northern Hwy.

Orientation & Information

It's easy to find your way around Orange Walk. Queen Victoria Ave is the main thoroughfare. Central Park is in the center of town, on the east side of Queen Victoria Ave. Orange Walk lacks an official tourism information center, though hotels can provide local information.

Orange Walk has a **Scotia Bank** (cnr Main St & Park Lane) and a **Belize Bank** (cnr Main St & Market Lane), both are on Main Street one block east of Central Park. You can check your email at **Cyberwalk**

WORTH THE TRIP: CROOKED TREE WILDLIFE SANCTUARY

Midway between Belize City and Orange Walk, 3.5 miles (5.5km) west of the Northern Hwy, lies the fishing and farming village of Crooked Tree. In 1984 the Belize Audubon Society succeeded in having 5 sq miles around the village declared a **wildlife sanctuary** (admission BZ$8; ☉ 8am-4pm) principally because of the area's wealth of birdlife. The best time of year for wildlife-watching is from January to mid-May, when the water in the lagoon drops to its lowest level and the animals must come further out into the open to reach their food.

Day trips to Crooked Tree are possible, but it's best to stay the night so you can be here at dawn, when the birds are most active. A guided tour costs BZ$160 for groups of four (less per person for larger groups). Arrangements can be made through the visitors center or from the **Belize Audubon Society** (Map p228; ☎ 223-5004; www.belizeaudubon.org; 12 Fort St, Belize City).

There are a number of guesthouses at Crooked Tree, and a few small eateries as well. **Carrie's Restaurant** (☎ 663-8148; ☉ lunch & dinner) serves great local food from a breezy shack on her family land and allows camping for BZ$10 per person.

The village is 3½ miles (5km) west of the northern highway. Jex Bus offers daily services departing from Belize City at Regent St West for Crooked Tree village at 10:50am daily; return trips leave Crooked Tree at 6:00am and 6:50am. If you start early from Belize City or Corozal, you can bus to Crooked Tree Junction and walk or hitch the 3½ miles (5.5km) to the village.

(☎ 322-3024; 115 Otre Benque; per hr BZ$4; ☉ 9am-9pm Mon-Fri, 2-8pm Sat & Sun) at the north end of town, and clean jungle-dirty clothes at **Mary's Laundry** (☎ 322-3454; Progresso St; per pound BZ$1).

Sleeping

Akihito Hotel (☎ 302-0185; 22 Belize Corozal Rd; r BZ$30-70, dm BZ$15; 🖳 🛜) Offering the best budget deals in town, the Akihito's cheaper rooms are serviceable concrete boxes with spotless shared bathrooms. The more expensive rooms have air-con, private bathrooms and cable TV. There are dorm rooms on the 3rd floor, and even a room with a spa bath.

Orchid Palm Inn (☎ 322-0719; www.orchidpalminn.com; 22 Queen Victoria Ave; s/d with fan BZ$55/70, with air-con BZ$70/80; 🖳 🛜) Across from the bus stop, beds in this lovely family-run hotel are big and some of the furnishings surprisingly hip. Winner of the Belize Tourism Board 'Small Hotel of the Year' for 2007.

Hotel de la Fuente (☎ 322-2290; www.hoteldelafuente.com; 14 Main St; s/d BZ$70/98; 🖳 🛜) A nice little midpriced hotel on the north side of town with clean rooms in a variety of arrangements. All rooms have air-con (knock BZ$15 off the price if you don't intend to use it) cable TV and full wireless coverage. There's free coffee in the morning, and owners can arrange tours and point visitors in the right direction during their stay in Orange Walk.

Lamanai Riverside Retreat (☎ 302-3955; Lamanai Alley; r BZ$80) It offers good-value cabins with air-con and cable TV in a lovely setting down by the river, a five-minute walk south of town. The restaurant here is deservedly popular. The Retreat also does trips to Lamanai for BZ$90, all inclusive.

Eating

Orange Walk is the best place in Belize for street food. Surrounding the town square are tiny cafes, snack stalls, fruit stands and pushcarts offering a veritable smorgasbord of northern Belizean and Mexican foods, including rice and beans, tacos, enchiladas, stewed chicken, ice cream and more. Everything is supercheap, between BZ$1 and BZ$5, and hygiene standards are generally pretty good.

our pick **Panificadora La Popular** (☎ 322-3229; Belize Rd; ☉ 6:30am-8pm Mon-Sat, 7:30am-noon & 3-6pm Sun) The best bakery in Belize. Trust us on this one.

Juanita's (8 Santa Ana St; meals from BZ$8) Opposite the Shell fuel station, this is a simple place with tasty local fare at low prices.

Carlos Restaurante & Pizza (1 B Teat St; pizza from BZ$15, meals from BZ$8) Around the corner from Cyberwalk is Orange Walk's finest pizza, served by French-Canadian Carlos. Salads are excellent as well.

Lamanai Riverside Retreat (☎ 302-3955; Lamanai Alley; meals BZ$9-25) This riverside restaurant gives the feeling of calm and isolation, even though it's only a short walk from town. The bar is especially popular in the evenings.

Nahil Mayab (☎ 322-0631; cnr Guadalaupe & Santa Anna Sts; meals from BZ$12) A fairly upscale restaurant in a working-class town, Nahil Mayab

BELIZE

serves delicious steak and seafood meals for around BZ$30. Cheaper Mexican and Maya fare available.

Getting There & Away

Buses run hourly for Belize City (BZ$5, two hours) and Corozal (BZ$4, one hour), and points in between, with additional southbound runs in the early morning and northbound runs in the late afternoon to accommodate work and school schedules. All services use the bus stop on the corner of Queen Victoria Ave and St Peter St.

COROZAL

pop 9000

This gateway to Mexico (and the northern cays) is far enough from the border to have the best of both worlds – that fascinating mix of cultures that border towns have, without the associated sleaze and hassle.

Corozal is a pretty place, with many parks and seaside promenades. South of town, retirees from the USA are moving in fast, attracted by the climate and easy-going lifestyle.

Orientation & Information

Corozal is arranged around a town square in the Mexican style. You can walk easily to any place in town.

The main road is 7th Ave, which briefly skirts the sea before veering inland through town. Corozal has a number of beautiful homes (in various states, from crumbling to fully restored) with a lovely Spanish Colonial feel, and even the remains of the **Maya temple** (admission free) of Santa Rita just north on the main highway. Corozal boasts the usual banking trifurcate of **Belize Bank** (cnr 5th Ave & 1st St N), **Scotia Bank** (cnr 4th Ave & 1st St S) and **Atlantic Bank** (cnr 4th Ave & 3rd St N). Internet services are provided at **Gamma Computer Center** (cnr 4th Ave & 4th St N).

Sights

CERROS ARCHAEOLOGICAL SITE

Cerros (admission BZ$10; ☼ 8am-5pm) flourished as a coastal trading center in late Preclassic times. Unlike at other Maya sites, little subsequent construction from the Classic and Postclassic periods covers the original structures here because, at around AD 150, Cerros reverted rapidly to a small, unimportant village. Thus the site has given archaeologists important insights into Maya Preclassic architecture.

Climb **Structure 4**, a temple more than 65ft (20m) high, for stunning panoramic views.

This small site is located on a peninsula 3.5 miles (5.6km) south of Corozal across the bay. Most people catch a boat to the site, but you can drive there on a rough dirt road. Tours (approximately BZ$50 per person including guide) can be arranged through your hotel. You can also charter a boat (BZ$120) or arrange for a fisherman to take you over to the site to explore independently. The boat trip takes about 15 minutes; then you walk 10 minutes to the site. Cerros is one of the buggiest places in Belize, so use plenty of mosquito repellent.

Sleeping

ourpick **Sea Breeze Hotel** (☎ 422-3051, 605-9341; www.theseabreezehotel.com; 23 1st Ave; r BZ$40-60; ☜) Reminiscent of the kind of cheap and pleasant Key West hotel where Hemingway might have spent his last years drinking and writing. The 2nd floor has a bar with a stunning view of Corozal Bay. Good food and strong coffee are available on request.

Maya World Guest House (☎ 666-3577; byron chuster@gmail.com; 16 2nd St N; s/d BZ$45/55) An offbeat and artistically done guesthouse, Maya World consists of two houses and an enclosed garden-filled courtyard. The front house is a restored two-story colonial home with a wraparound veranda complete with hammock; the one out back is a two-story building with four simple but functional rooms.

Hotel Maya (☎ 422-2082; www.hotelmaya.net; 7th Ave; r BZ$65-126) Clean and colorful rooms featuring local artwork. The attached restaurant serves good food, and owner Rosita is a great source of local information.

Las Palmas (☎ 422-0196; www.laspalmashotelbelize. com; 123 5th Ave S; r BZ$90-140) Clean rooms with floral bedspreads and big bathrooms make this a long-standing Corozal favorite.

Corozal Bay Inn (☎ 422-2691; www.corozalbayinn.com; Almond Dr; cabañas from BZ$120; ☜ ☒) Fronting the sea at the far south end of town, this relaxed, family-run place has cozy, tiled, mosquito-netted, air-con cabañas set around a broad sandy area.

Eating & Drinking

Though Corozal isn't a street-food mecca like Orange Walk, the **Corozal Market** (6th Ave; ☼ 6:30am-5:30pm Mon-Sat, to 3pm Sun) is a good place get cheap Mexican snacks and fresh vegetables. In addition to the usual array of Belizean

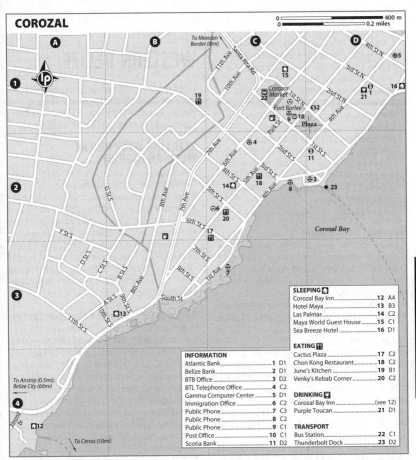

COROZAL

To Mexican Border (8mi)

0   400 m
0   0.2 miles

Santa Rita Rd

Corozal Market

Fort Barlee

Plaza

Corozal Bay

To Airstrip (0.5mi);
Belize City (60mi)

To Cerros (10mi)

BELIZE

snack shacks and Chinese restaurants, these places serve pretty decent food.

Venky's Kabab Corner (☎ 402-0546; 5th St S; dishes BZ$8-15; 🕙 10:30am-9:30pm) The place is not much to look at on the inside, but the Indian food served by Chef Venky is excellent and filling. Two main dishes and a few sides easily serve three people.

Cactus Plaza (☎ 422-0394; 6 6th St S; mains BZ$10-20; 🕙 dinner Wed-Sun) This place serves some excellent, authentic Mexican dishes, such as tacos, *salbutes* (stuffed tortilla) and *panuchos* (fried tortilla spread with black-bean paste and toppings) in a bright, clean environment. The disco at this unique-looking restaurant features a DJ on Saturdays and karaoke on Fridays and Sundays.

Chon Kong Restaurant (☎ 422-0169, 5th Ave; mains US$6-15; 🕙 lunch & dinner) Of the many Chinese restaurants in Corozal, locals say this one, with a long menu and pleasant decorations is the best.

Corozal Bay Inn (☎ 422-2691; Almond Dr; 🕙 7am-11pm) With a fully stocked bar beneath a lovely enclosed and air-conditioned *palapa* offering outdoor oceanfront seating as well, the Corozal Bay Inn's bar is a very chilled spot in which to eat and drink.

Also recommended:

June's Kitchen (☎ 422-2559; 26 3rd St S; meals from BZ$10; 🕙 breakfast & lunch) A bit off the beaten trail but worth it.

Purple Toucan (☎ 622-9200; 52 4th Ave; 🕙 noon-midnight) Good Mexican dishes, and their homemade hot sauce will melt your tongue clean off.

GETTING TO MEXICO

Corozal is 8 miles (13km) south of the border crossing at Santa Elena–Subteniente López. Most of the frequent buses that travel between Chetumal (Mexico) and Belize City stop at Corozal. Otherwise, hitch a ride or hire a taxi (BZ$20) to get to **Santa Elena**. Buses running between Corozal and Chetumal will wait for you to complete border formalities. You'll have to pay a tourist fee of BZ$38 (US$19) to leave Belize.

San Pedro Water Taxi runs boats from San Pedro to Chetumal, Mexico for BZ$80.

See p71 for information on crossing the border from Mexico.

Getting There & Away

Corozal has its own airstrip, about 1 mile (1.6km) south of the town center, reached by taxi (BZ$10). Maya Island Air's newly built terminal provides shelter, and taxis meet all incoming flights.

Maya Island Air (☎ 422-2333; mayaairways.com) and **Tropic Air** (☎ 422-0356; www.tropicair.com) each have three flights daily between Corozal and San Pedro on Ambergris Caye (BZ$76 to BZ$100 one way, 20 minutes). From San Pedro you connect with flights to Belize City and beyond.

Boats operated by **Thunderbolt Travels** (☎ 422-0026) depart Corozal at 7am for San Pedro. During high season, a 3pm boat is often added. One-way fares are BZ$45. The Thunderbolt will also stop at Sarteneja (BZ$25) for pickups and drop-offs if requested.

Buses leave Corozal and head south via Orange Walk (BZ$4, one hour) to Belize City (BZ$12, three hours) at least every hour from 4am to 7:30pm, with extra buses in the morning.

WESTERN BELIZE

Out here, the largely unspoilt landscape is dotted with caves, mountain peaks rising to over 3000ft (900m), waterfalls and Maya sites. There are plenty of opportunities for exploration.

STARTING WEST ON THE WESTERN HIGHWAY

Heading west from Belize City along Cemetery Rd, you'll pass right through Lords Ridge Cemetery and soon find yourself on the Western Hwy. In 15 miles (25km) you'll pass Hattieville, founded in 1961 after Hurricane Hattie wreaked destruction on Belize City, and in another 13 miles (21km) you'll come to the Belize Zoo. Buses run at least hourly along the Western Hwy and upon request will drop you anywhere between Belize City and Belmopan.

Belize Zoo & Tropical Education Center

In natural surroundings on 29 acres (12 hectares), the **Belize Zoo & Tropical Education Center** (☎ 220-8004; www.belizezoo.org; Mile 29, Western Hwy; adult/child BZ$20/10; ☼ 8:30am-5pm, closed major holidays) is a wonderful zoo, the inhabitants of which are nearly all animals rescued from unscrupulous collectors. On a self-guided tour (45 to 60 minutes) you'll see over 125 native animals, including jaguars, ocelots, howler monkeys, peccaries, vultures, storks, crocodiles, tapirs and *gibnuts*. The zoo is on the north side of the highway (a sign marks the turnoff). The zoo also offers night tours, a rare treat as many of

EXPLORE SARTENEJA

Sarteneja (sar-ten-*eh*-ha) is a fishing village near the northeast tip of the Belizean mainland, and a hidden gem for those looking for a beautiful and inexpensive place from which to explore both the nautical and jungle treasures of the region.

The village spreads just a few blocks back from its long, grassy seafront, and its from this lovely seaside setting that visitors can head out to the Shipstern Nature Reserve and take bird-watching, snorkeling, fishing and manatee-watching trips all along the fabulous coast of Northern Belize.

Sarteneja is also where you'll find **Backpacker's Paradise** (☎ 423-2016; http://backpackers.bluegreen belize.com; cabins from BZ$25, campsites BZ$6.50), an idyllic 27-acre (11-hectare) patch of unspoiled jungle and tropical farmland where you can spend days exploring the jungle, eating tropical fruit and swimming in the nearby ocean. *Cabañas* are screened-in huts with thatched roofs and king-sized beds, and there's a communal kitchen, a screened-in chill-out spot, and a small onsite restaurant serving a number of French and Belizean favorites. Horses and bicycles are available for rent.

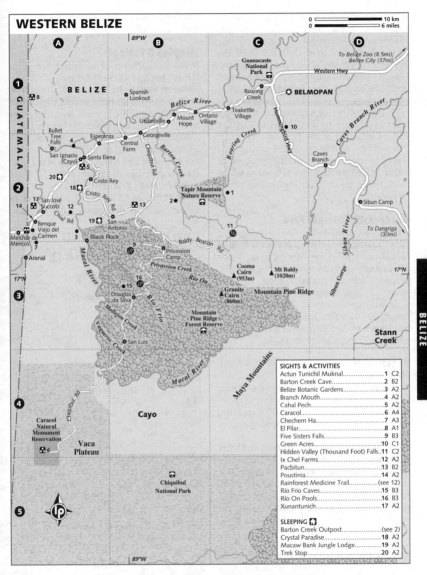

WESTERN BELIZE

SIGHTS & ACTIVITIES

Actun Tunichil Muknal	1 C2
Barton Creek Cave	2 B2
Belize Botanic Gardens	3 A2
Branch Mouth	4 A2
Cahal Pech	5 A2
Caracol	6 A4
Chechem Ha	7 A3
El Pilar	8 A1
Five Sisters Falls	9 B3
Green Acres	10 C1
Hidden Valley (Thousand Foot) Falls	11 C2
Ix Chel Farms	12 A2
Pacbitun	13 B2
Poustinia	14 A2
Rainforest Medicine Trail	(see 12)
Río Frio Caves	15 B3
Río On Pools	16 B3
Xunantunich	17 A2

SLEEPING

Barton Creek Outpost	(see 2)
Crystal Paradise	18 A2
Macaw Bank Jungle Lodge	19 A2
Trek Stop	20 A2

the occupants are nocturnal. To arrange a night tour, call or contact the zoo before closing time.

Competing for customers just west of the zoo on the Western Hwy are Cheers and Amigo's, both at Mile 31 of the Western Highway. Each serves Belizean, Mexican and American dishes accompanied by ice-cold Belikins, all at moderate prices.

Monkey Bay Wildlife Sanctuary

This **Wildlife Sanctuary** (☎ 820-3032; www.mon keybaybelize.org; Mile 31½, Western Hwy; campsites per person BZ$15, tent rental BZ$6, bunkhouses per person BZ$25, cabañas BZ$35; 📶) and environmental education center offers lodging and activities for casual travelers, as well as the opportunity to do an internship with the organization for those with a more long-term interest in Belize. Established in the 1980s by conservationists Matthew and Marga Miller, the 1.7-sq-mile (4.4-sq-km) sanctuary stretches from the Western Hwy to the Sibun River, encompassing areas of tropical forest and savannah and providing an important link in the biological corridor between coastal and inland Belize.

Casual visitors should contact the sanctuary in advance to find out what activities will be available at the time of their visit. Possibilities include canoe and caving trips and dry-season trips to Cox Lagoon, about 12 miles (19km) north, which is home to jabiru storks, deer, tapir, black howlers and lots of crocodiles.

Guanacaste National Park

Further west down the highway, at the junction with Hummingbird Hwy, is **Guanacaste National Park** (admission BZ$10; ☻ 8am-4:30pm), a small 52-acre (21-hectare) nature reserve at the confluence of Roaring Creek and the Belize River.

A hike along the park's 2 miles (3km) of trails will introduce you to the abundant and colorful local birdlife. After your hike, you can head down to the Belize River for a dip in the park's good, deep swimming hole.

BELMOPAN

pop 16,400

Travelers arriving in Belize's capital are faced with that most basic of all existential questions: what am I doing here? Thankfully, the town provides a ready answer: changing buses.

Founded in 1961 after Hurricane Hattie wiped out much of Belize City, the idea (hey – let's all pack up and move to the middle of nowhere with a bunch of public servants) hasn't really caught on yet. There are embassies, government buildings and, if you do get stuck, enough services to satisfy your basic needs.

Belmopan, just under 2.5 miles (4km) south of the Western Hwy and about a mile east of Hummingbird Hwy, is a small place easily negotiated on foot. The regional bus lines all stop at Market Sq, which is near the post office, police station, market, **Belize Bank** (Constitution Dr), **Scotia Bank** (Constitution Dr) and the **BTL telephone office** (Bliss Pde).

Being the capital, Belmopan naturally has the usual array of banking facilities, and an **internet cafe** (per hr BZ$5; ☻ 8am-8pm) inside the

bus station is as good a place as any to while away your time.

Sleeping & Eating

Belmopan is a town for bureaucrats and diplomats, not one for budget travelers.

Eastern Guest House (☎ 625-9018; Constitution Dr; s/d BZ$38/49; ☎) This is the budget choice, in a very budget-unfriendly town. Rooms are very basic, fan-cooled and tolerable for a night.

Hibiscus Hotel (☎ 822-1418; hibiscus@btl.net; off Constitution Dr; r from BZ$95, f BZ$110) There's nothing to get excited about here, so it matches the mood of the town pretty well.

Bull Frog Inn (☎ 822-2111; 25 Half Moon Ave; www.bullfroginn.com; s/d BZ$100/115; ☎) If you're in Belmopan, why not splurge? A fine place,

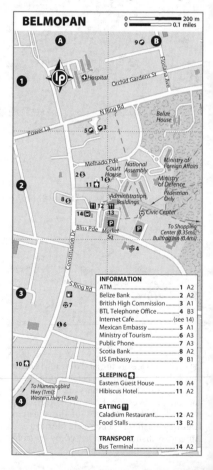

BELMOPAN

0   200 m
0   0.1 miles

INFORMATION	
ATM	**1** A2
Belize Bank	**2** A2
British High Commission	**3** A1
BTL Telephone Office	**4** B3
Internet Cafe	(see 14)
Mexican Embassy	**5** A1
Ministry of Tourism	**6** A3
Public Phone	**7** A3
Scotia Bank	**8** A2
US Embassy	**9** B1

SLEEPING	
Eastern Guest House	**10** A4
Hibiscus Hotel	**11** A2

EATING	
Caladium Restaurant	**12** A2
Food Stalls	**13** B2

TRANSPORT	
Bus Terminal	**14** A2

BELIZE

EXPLORE MORE OF WESTERN BELIZE

Western Belize has plenty of opportunities for getting off the beaten track. Here are just a few:

- **Branch Mouth** is a local swimming spot 20 minutes' walk from San Ignacio (Cayo), where the Macal and Mopan Rivers meet.
- Take a mellow canoe ride from San Ignacio to the **Belize Botanic Gardens**, a sanctuary, boasting 400 tree species and over 160 types of orchid,
- The outdoor sculpture park of **Poustinia** has works by international and local artists,

---

good-sized rooms and a fully stocked wi-fi-ready bar.

Caladium Restaurant (☎ 822-2754; Market Sq; mains BZ$10-30) Just opposite the bus station, this restaurant offers daily special plates for BZ$8, plus standard Belizean dishes and snacks.

Another option for food is the **market food stalls** (Market Sq), which feature plenty of snack carts selling tasty, low-cost munchies.

Getting There & Away

Thanks to its location near a major highway intersection, Belmopan is a stop for virtually all buses operating along the Western and Hummingbird Hwys.

Buses to and from Belize City (local/express BZ$6/9, one/1¼ hour) depart half-hourly.

SAN IGNACIO (CAYO)

pop 17,000

Way out near the western border, San Ignacio offers a plethora of archaeological and natural attractions in the surrounding hills. Together with Santa Elena across the river, this is the chief population center of the Cayo District and the town has a prosperous, upbeat feel. That said, it's still small, and during the day, quiet. At night the quiet disappears and the jungle rocks to music from the town's bars and restaurants.

San Ignacio's Saturday **market** is the biggest in Belize, drawing farmers, craftspeople and merchants from all over the Cayo district and beyond. Beginning before dawn and continuing to mid-afternoon, the market is a great place to buy clothing, jewelry, vegetables and cooked food, or just to watch the intricate tapestry of Belizean culture come to life.

Orientation

San Ignacio is west of the river; Santa Elena is to the east. Two bridges join the towns and are usually both one way – the newer, northernmost bridge leads traffic into San Ignacio, and the Hawkesworth Bridge, San Ignacio's landmark suspension bridge, leads traffic out of town. During the rainy season, however, the new bridge often floods, and traffic is diverted to the Hawkesworth Bridge. Burns Ave is the town's main street. Almost everything in town is accessible on foot.

Information

The Review (West St; www.aguallos.com) has its main office in town, and offers free tourist information and copies of the bimonthly directory *The Review*. Look for the red, gold and green letters 'Don't Watch Me, Watch Yourself' over the door.

Belize Bank and Atlantic Bank are both on Burns Ave and have 24-hour ATMs. The **post office** (Missiah St) is on the upper floor of Government House, near the bridge.

Trade Winds Internet (☎ 824-2396, West Street; per hr BZ$5) offers internet access on new computers, DVD burning, printing, scanning and...free coffee. It also sells new camping gear for those looking to head out into the bush.

Amber Mystic Books (West St) is a wonderful shop for books, art and music that welcomes trade-ins.

The basic San Ignacio Hospital is up the hill off Waight's Ave, west of the center. Across the river in Santa Elena is Hospital La Loma Luz.

Sights & Activities

Two Maya archaeological sites make good excursions from San Ignacio. Cahal Pech is right on the edge of town, and El Pilar is a short distance to the northwest.

Maya for 'Tick City,' **Cahal Pech** (admission BZ$10; ⌚ 6am-6pm), not its original name, was a city of some importance from around 900 BC to AD 800. There are 34 buildings spread over 6 acres (2.4 hectares) and grouped around seven plazas. **Plaza B**, about 500ft (150m) from the museum building and parking area, is the site's largest plaza and also the most impressive. It's surrounded by some of the site's most significant buildings. Off Plaza A, **Structure A-1** is the site's tallest pyramid.

Cahal Pech is about a mile (1.6km) from Hawkesworth Bridge off Buena Vista Rd. You can walk or catch a taxi (about BZ$6).

BELIZE

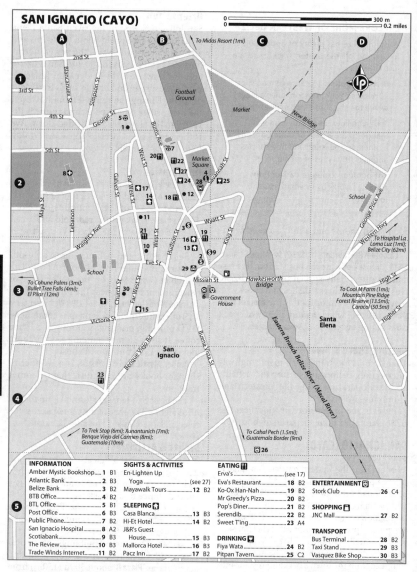

SAN IGNACIO (CAYO)

INFORMATION		SIGHTS & ACTIVITIES		EATING		
Amber Mystic Bookshop..... 1	B1	En-Lighten Up		Erva's .... (see 17)		
Atlantic Bank 2	B3	Yoga .... (see 27)		Eva's Restaurant.............. 18	B2	
Belize Bank 3	B2	Mayawalk Tours 12	B2	Ko-Ox Han-Nah 19	B2	ENTERTAINMENT
BTB Office............................ 4	B2			Mr Greedy's Pizza 20	B2	Stork Club 26 C4
BTL Office............................ 5	B1	SLEEPING		Pop's Diner...................... 21	B2	
Post Office........................... 6	B3	Casa Blanca................... 13	B3	Serendib.......................... 22	B2	SHOPPING
Public Phone....................... 7	B2	Hi-Et Hotel 14	B2	Sweet T'ing 23	A4	JNC Mall 27 B2
San Ignacio Hospital......... 8	A2	J&R's Guest				
Scotiabank.......................... 9	B3	House........................ 15	B3	DRINKING		TRANSPORT
The Review........................ 10	B3	Mallorca Hotel 16	B3	Fiya Wata 24	B2	Bus Terminal 28 B2
Trade Winds Internet....... 11	B2	Pacz Inn 17	B2	Pitpan Tavern................. 25	C2	Taxi Stand 29 B3
						Vasquez Bike Shop 30 B3

About 12 miles (19km) northwest of San Ignacio, beyond Bullet Tree Falls, **El Pilar** is perched almost 900ft (275m) above the Belize River. El Pilar has been left largely uncleared, and five archaeological and nature trails meander among the jungle-covered mounds.

En-lighten Up (3rd fl, JNC Mall, Burns Ave; enlighten upyogabelize@gmail.com) is a yoga studio on the main drag that has daily classes and a drop-in rate of BZ$12. The schedule is posted on the door. Yoga instructor Melissa also operates a hilltop retreat outside of town; inquire at the studio for details.

Vasquez Bike Shop (☎ 662-5599; shanevasquez2003@ yahoo.com; Church St, across from Sacred Heart Hospital) is the only shop of its kind in San Ignacio that sells, repairs and rents high-end mountain bikes (Schwinn, Treks and Specialized). Rentals are BZ$52 per day, BZ$25 per day for a week or more.

Tours

Several operators offer a range of tours in the surrounding area and as far afield as the cays and Tikal, Guatemala. Cayo native **Carlos Panti** (669-5552; carlos.caveguide@yahoo.com) specializes in small-group spiritually themed journeys into the Actun Tunichil Muknal cave for BZ$150 per person. **Mayawalk Tours** (824-3070; www.mayawalk.com; 19 Burns Ave) offers tours to the cave (BZ$160 per person) and Tikal (BZ$360 per person). **Pacz Tours** (824-0536; www.pacztours. net) also employs knowledgeable guides.

Sleeping

Hi-Et Hotel (824-2828; thehiet@yahoo.com; 12 West St; s/d BZ$40/50, without bathroom BZ$20/25) The one saving grace of the little rooms with a shared bathroom upstairs here are their small balconies – otherwise things would get very close. Rooms with bathroom are much better.

J&R's Guest House (626-3604; 20 Far West St; s/d/tr BZ$25/30/35) This is a modern home up the hill from the main drag, with a family atmosphere, and a porch out front that is a great place for breakfast (complimentary) and to watch the hummingbirds flit.

Pacz Inn (824-2821, 670-3812; paczinn@gmail.com; 4 Far West St; s/d BZ$50/60, s/tr without bathroom BZ$40/60)

The big, clean rooms here are a refreshing sight in San Ignacio's budget-hotel scene.

Casa Blanca (824-2080; http://casablancaguesthouse. com; 10 Burns Ave; s/d with fan BZ$45/55, with air-con BZ$75/95) Set in a family-style home, the rooms at Casa Blanca are well appointed and very homey.

Mallorca Hotel (824-2960; mallorcahotel@ gmail.com; Burns Ave; s/d/tr BZ$45/55/75, with air-con BZ$75/95/115) Another family-run place on the main drag, the 10-room Mallorca is clean and centrally located.

Cahal Pech Village Resort (824-3740; www.cahal pech.com; standard r/cabañas BZ$158, family ste BZ$198;) Overlooking San Ignacio, Cahal Pech, and Xunantunich, the views at this Belizean family-owned resort are beautiful. Rooms are colorful, bright and appointed with locally made Maya handicrafts. Nonguests can use the pool for BZ$10

Eating

Mr Greedy's Pizza (804-4648; Burns Ave; burgers from BZ$7, pizzas from BZ$13;) A great little pizzeria, bar and burger joint on the main drag that uses homemade ingredients, makes cocktails and milkshakes, and even sells slices (BZ$4).

Erva's (824-2821; 4 Far West Street; mains from BZ$8) Great local food downstairs from Pacz Inn.

Cahal Pech Village Resort (824-3740; breakfast/ lunch/dinner from BZ$8/10/12) With two chefs and a 360-degree view, the restaurant at the Cahal Pech Village resort is a great place to start, end, or even the spend the day. It also has a full bar.

BELIZE

GET OUTTA TOWN!

Just outside of San Ignacio are a number of beautiful and low-key campsites, ecoresorts and family homestays.

Midas Resort (824-3172; www.midasbelize.com; Branch Mouth Rd; campsites per person BZ$16, d cabins from BZ$108) A little slice of nature right on the edge of town. Cabins have porches, air-con and cable TV. There's a restaurant and bar, and you can swim in the river at the back of the property.

Trek Stop (823-2265; www.thetrekstop.com; Km 114, Western Hwy; campsites BZ$10, s/d cabins BZ$30/56) Laid out on a jungly hillside about 6 miles (10km) west of San Ignacio, this place is ideal for backpackers. Cabins are simple but well spaced, giving you the feeling of seclusion. There's a butterfly house and Frisbee golf course onsite. Kitchen facilities are available. From town, catch the bus to Melchor or Benque and ask the driver to let you off at Trek Stop.

Cohune Palms (600-7508; www.cohunepalms.com; cabins BZ$70-110) About 3 miles (5km) northwest of San Ignacio, near Bullet Tree Falls, Cohune Palms is set on riverbank grounds and offers kitchen access. The site is beautiful. Bicycles and inner tubes are available and staff can usually pick you up in San Ignacio.

Cool M Farm (824-2276; cool.m.farm@gmail.com; cabañas BZ$80/90) A 75-acre (30-hectare) garden-filled dairy farm 20 minutes' walking distance from San Ignacio with two lovely fan-cooled *cabañas* with comfortable double beds, desks, modern bathrooms and a sun porch overlooking the valley. Breakfast of organic eggs, yogurt, granola and bread (all from the farm) for two is included in the price.

ourpick **Ko-Ox Han-Nah** (☎ 824-3014; 5 Burns Ave; mains BZ$8-18; ⏰ breakfast, lunch & dinner) This bright, open eatery on the main drag is quickly turning into the place to be for locals and visitors alike, and with good reason; the food. With nearly all locally produced ingredients, Ko-Ox serves stunning dishes like grilled eggplant with locally made cheese (BZ$12) and locally raised chicken, pork and lamb dishes.

Serendib (☎ 824-2302; Burns Ave; mains from BZ$15; ⏰ lunch & dinner) San Ignacio's only Sri Lankan restaurant has great food and a peaceful courtyard dining area.

Also recommended:

Sweet T'ing (Benque Viejo Rd; cakes from BZ$3, coffee from BZ$3; ⏰ noon-9pm) A tiny bakery at the top of the hill; definitely worth the walk up.

Eva's Restaurant(☎ 804-2267; 22 Burns Ave; mains BZ$5-12; ⏰ breakfast, lunch & dinner) A Cayo institution for food, drinks and information. Happy hour from 3pm to 7pm, BZ$2 rum-and-cokes, and BZ$4 beers.

Pop's Diner (Far West St; mains from BZ$8; ⏰ breakfast & lunch) Friendly old-school-style hole-in-the-wall diner serving all-day breakfast and bottomless coffee.

Drinking & Entertainment

Pitpan Tavern (across from Market Sq) The name may have changed, but the deal remains the same – a happy hour from 5pm to 7pm, reggae bands, drunk locals and drunker foreigners.

Fiya Wata (Burns Ave) On the main drag, Fiya Wata has cheap drinks, a pool table, and endless diversion for locals and visitors alike.

Stork Club (18 Buena Vista St; admission BZ$10; ⏰ Thu-Sat) Inside the supersnazzy San Ignacio Resort Hotel, this disco consistently comes to life when the bars empty out.

Getting There & Away

Buses from San Ignacio's Market Sq run to and from Belize City (local/express BZ$10/14, two/three hours) and Belmopan (local/express BZ$4/6, 1½ hours/45 minutes) nearly every half hour.

See boxed text (p250) for travel to Benque Viejo del Carmen and onwards to Guatemala.

The taxi stand is located on the traffic circle opposite Government House. Rates can be surprisingly high for short trips (a trip of a few miles can easily cost BZ$10 to BZ$20).

MOUNTAIN PINE RIDGE AREA

South of the Western Hwy, between Belmopan and the Guatemalan border, the land begins to climb toward the heights of the Maya Mountains, which separate the Cayo District from the Stann Creek District to the east and the Toledo district to the south.

In the heart of this highland area – a land of macaws, mahogany, mangoes and jaguars – over 300 sq miles (777 sq km) of tropical pine forest has been set aside as the Mountain Pine Ridge Forest Reserve. The reserve and its surrounding area are full of rivers, pools, waterfalls and caves to explore.

Sights
RAINFOREST MEDICINE TRAIL

This herbal-cure research center is at **Ix Chel Farms** (admission BZ$10; ⏰ 8am-noon & 1-5pm), 8 miles (13km) southwest of San Ignacio up Chial Rd.

Dr Eligio Pantí, who died in 1996 at age 103, was a healer in San Antonio village who used traditional Maya herb cures. Dr Rosita Arvigo, an American, studied medicinal plants with Dr Pantí, then began several projects to spread the wisdom of traditional healing methods and to preserve the rainforest habitats, which harbor an incredible 4000 plant species.

One of her projects was the establishment of the **Rainforest Medicine Trail**, a self-guiding path among the jungle's natural cures.

CAVES

If you want to visit any of the following caves you'll have to join a tour. Ask at your hotel or check out some of the suggested Cayo guides (p247).

The **Río Frio Caves** are the region's most-visited and famous caverns, but gaining in popularity is **Barton Creek Cave** (full-day tours around BZ$130 per person, including meals). One of the more popular day trips offered out of San Ignacio, the cave holds spooky skulls and bones, and pottery shards from the ancient Maya. To see them you'll have to negotiate some very narrow passages.

Attracting the most raving recommendations is **Actun Tunichil Muknal** (BZ$160 per person). In an effort to prevent looting of the Maya bones and artifacts within, and to keep general wear and tear to a minimum, only a couple of tour operators are allowed to run tours here at this point.

POOLS & WATERFALLS

At **Río On Pools**, small waterfalls connect a series of pools that the river has carved out of granite boulders. Some of the falls double as water slides. The pools at tranquil **Five Sisters Falls**, accessible by an outdoor-elevator ride (small charge, usually BZ$5) at Five Sisters Lodge, are connected by five falls cascading over a short drop-off.

The region's aquatic highlight is **Hidden Valley (Thousand Foot) Falls**, southeast of San Antonio. Hiking trails surround the falls and a viewing platform at the top of the cascade is a great spot for catching a Mountain Pine Ridge vista. The falls actually are around 1500ft (450m) high, but they aren't spectacular in the dry season.

ARCHAEOLOGICAL SITES

The highlands here hold two Maya ruins of interest, one small and one huge.

Pacbitun, a small site, 12 miles (20km) south of San Ignacio via Cristo Rey Rd, near San Antonio, seems to have been occupied continuously through most of Maya history, from 900 BC to AD 900. Today only lofty **Plaza A** has been uncovered and partially consolidated. **Structures 1 and 2**, on the east and west sides of the plaza, respectively, are worth a look.

Some 53 miles (86km) south of San Ignacio via Chiquibul Rd lies **Caracol** (admission BZ$10, full-day tours BZ$150; ☺ 8am-5pm) a vast Maya city hidden in the jungle. The site encompasses some 35 sq miles (88 sq km), with 36,000 structures marked so far.

Sleeping

The forests and mountains of the greater Mountain Pine Ridge area are dotted with small inns, lodges and ranches offering accommodations, meals, hiking, horseback trips, caving, swimming, bird-watching and similar outdoor activities.

Barton Creek Outpost (☎ 662-4797; www.barton creekoutpost.com; per person BZ$10) In a country full of gorgeous places, this one shines. Nestled in a river bend about 200m from the Barton Creek Cave (see opposite page), it's the sort of place you come for a day and stay for a week. Good simple meals are available.

Macaw Bank Jungle Lodge (☎ 608-4825; www.macaw bankjunglelodge.com; cabañas BZ$170-250) Beautiful, off the grid and off the beaten path, Macaw Bank is 8 miles (13km) from San Ignacio nature reserve and has jungle trails, and an onsite restaurant, and even its own unexcavated Maya ruin. The lodge offers river access to the Belize Botanical Garden and river tubing.

Crystal Paradise (☎ 820-4014; www.crystalparadise. com; 1st person incl breakfast & dinner BZ$190, each additional person BZ$70) Beautiful thatched-roof double, triple and family-sized *palapas* are spread out across 21 lush acres (8.5 hectares) filled with tropical fruit trees. Paradise offers canoeing, horseback riding, marked trails and bird-watching platforms.

WEST TO GUATEMALA

From San Ignacio it's another 10 miles (16km) southwest down Western Hwy to the Guatemalan border.

San Jose Succotz

This small town sits on the Mopan river at the crossing point to Xunantunich. A pretty little town, SJC is home to the St Joseph's Church and Benny's Kitchen. The town comes alive every year during the annual Succotz festival on the weekend of the second week of April for a three-day festival featuring dances, football, greasy-pole climbs, greased-pigs chasing marimba music, and of course, local food. The festival takes place on the weekend following Easter.

Benny's Kitchen (☎ 823-2541; meals from B$6) is a local institution that serves excellent Guatemalan and Belizean meals, attracting locals and travelers alike.

Xunantunich

Belize's most accessible Maya site of significance, **Xunantunich** (admission BZ$10; ☺ 7:30am-4pm), pronounced soo-*nahn*-too-neech, is reached via a free ferry crossing at San José Succotz, about 7 miles (12km) west of San Ignacio. From the ferry it's a 1-mile walk (2km) uphill to the ruins.

The site's dominant structure, **El Castillo** (Structure A-6), rises 130ft (40m) above the jungle floor. The stairway on its northern side – the side you approach from the courtyard – goes only as far as the temple building. To climb to the **roof comb** you must go around to the southern side and use a separate set of steps. On the temple's east side, a few of the masks that once surrounded the structure have been restored. Structure A-11 and Plaza A-3, formed a residential 'palace' area for the ruling family.

Buses on their way between San Ignacio and Benque Viejo del Carmen will drop you at the crank-powered ferry. Ferry hours are 8am to noon and 1pm to 5pm; crossing is on demand and free for both foot passengers and cars.

GETTING TO GUATEMALA

Buses run from San Ignacio to **Benque Viejo del Carmen**, the border town for crossing into Guatemala, nearly every half hour. From the bus station, it's another 3km to the border. A taxi will cost BZ$10.

Cross early in the morning to have the best chance of catching buses onward. Get your passport (and, if applicable, your car papers) stamped at the Belizean station, then cross into Guatemala. The border station is supposedly open 24 hours a day, but try to cross during daylight hours. If you need a Guatemalan visa or tourist card (see p215), obtain it before you reach the border.

A bank at either side of the border changes money, but the itinerant money changers often give you a better deal – for US cash. The rates for exchanging Belizean dollars to Guatemalan quetzals and vice versa are sometimes poor.

Both Transportes Pinita and Transportes Rosalita buses westward to **Santa Elena–Flores (Guatemala)** depart town the Guatemalan side early in the morning. More comfortable minibuses are sometimes available for BZ$12 per person.

To go on to **Tikal**, get off the bus at El Cruce (Puente Ixlú), 22 miles (36km) east of Flores, and wait for another bus, minibus or obliging car or truck to take you the final 21 miles (35km) north to Tikal.

See p199 for information on crossing the border from Guatemala.

Benque Viejo del Carmen

A sleepy town 2 miles (3km) east of the Guatemalan border, Benque Viejo del Carmen has few services for travelers, and you're better off staying in San Ignacio. The town stirs from its normal tropical somnolence in mid-July, when the **Benque Viejo Festival** brings three days of revelry. Buses run to and from Belize City nearly every 30 minutes (local/express BZ$8/12, 2½/three hours), passing through San Ignacio.

Chechem Ha

This **Maya cave** (☎ 820-4063; per person BZ$40; ✆ tours 9:30am & 1:30pm) comes complete with ancient ceremonial pots. Members of the Morales family, who discovered the cave, act as guides, leading you up the steep slope to the cave mouth, then down inside to see what the Maya left. Call ahead to reserve a space and inquire about getting a ride here from San Ignacio. Bring strong shoes, take water and a flashlight.

You can camp at Chechem Ha or sleep in one of the simple **bunks** (per person incl meals BZ$80).

SOUTHERN BELIZE

Often overlooked by travelers, the south has its fair share of charms. Well worth a look are the Garífuna towns of Dangriga and Hopkins, as are the remote but budget-friendly cays at Tobacco Caye and Glover's Reef, which is great for diving and snorkeling.

Down south, Placencia draws the crowds, but remains low-key in all but absolute peak season. Punta Gorda is the jumping-off point for the little visited Toledo district, home of unrestored ruins, natural wonders and traditional villages.

HUMMINGBIRD HIGHWAY

Heading southeast from Belmopan, the Hummingbird Hwy stretches 49 miles (79km) to the junction of the Southern Hwy and the turnoff to Dangriga. It is almost entirely paved, but be prepared to slow for roadwork or sudden transitions to dirt road.

Blue Hole National Park

The **Blue Hole** – focus of the like-named **national park** (admission US$4; ✆ 8am-4pm) – is a cenote (se-noh-tay; water-filled limestone sinkhole) some 328ft (100m) in diameter and 108ft (33m) deep. Fed by underground tributaries of the Sibun River, it's deliciously cool on the hottest days and makes an excellent swimming hole.

The park visitors center is about 11 miles (18km) south of Belmopan on Hummingbird Hwy. At the center is the trailhead to **St Herman's Cave**, a large cavern once used by the Maya during the Classic period. This is one of the few caves in Belize you can visit independently, although a guide is required if you wish to venture in further than 150 yards. Also here are a series of nature trails and an observation tower.

DANGRIGA

pop 11,500

Dangriga is the largest town in southern Belize. Much smaller than Belize City, it's friendlier and quieter and a great place to get amid the Garífuna culture. The best time to do this is November 19, which is **Garífuna Settlement Day**, a frenzy of dancing, drinking and celebration of the Garífuna's heritage. For the rest of the year you'll find the folks here a bit more laid-back, but equally welcoming.

Orientation & Information

Stann Creek empties into the Gulf of Honduras at the center of town. Dangriga's main street is called St Vincent St south of the creek and Commerce St to the north. The bus station is at the southern end of Havana St just north of the Shell fuel station. The airstrip is a mile (2km) north of the center, near the Pelican Beach Resort. The Riverside Café

serves as the unofficial water-taxi terminal where you can arrange trips out to the southern cays with local fishermen or trades people.

Belize Bank and **Scotia Bank** are both on the main drag south of the creek. You can get your clothes washed and check your email at the same time at **Val's Laundry** (1 Sharp St), where a load costs BZ$2 per pound, and an hour on the internet costs BZ$4 per hour.

Sights

Eight miles (13km) northwest of town on Melinda Rd is **Marie Sharp's Factory** (☎ 520-2087; ☼ 7am-noon & 1-4pm), the source of Belize's beloved hot sauce. Casual tours, often led by Marie herself, are offered during business hours. There is also a gift shop. In 2008 a

DANGRIGA

BELIZE

GREEN ACRES

This is *the* place to be for equestrians! The **jungle ranch**, located at Mile 36 on the Hummingbird Hwy (which is about 17miles/20 minutes from Belmopan en route to Dangriga) offers guided horseback riding (for beginners to advanced levels) for BZ$70 per person, and extreme jungle and cave adventures by horseback for BZ$100 per person. Rides are typically half-day affairs, and are definitely not your average pony ride. The ranch also offers camping for BZ$30, with tent rental for an additional BZ$20. Group rates and other guiding services are available. The site, though primitive, is absolutely lovely and has restrooms, cold-water showers, and an area for food preparation. Contact **Kimberlee Chanona** (☎ 670-5698; kchanona@email.com) at Green Acres Ranch for more details.

female British traveler was assaulted while walking solo on the road to the factory. Although the perpetrators were caught and punished, the Sharp family now advises against walking the road from the main highway, and offers transportation with advanced notice.

The **Gulisi Garífuna Museum** (Stann Creek Valley Rd; admission BZ$10; ☽ noon-7pm Tue-Fri, 8am-2pm Sat) provides an excellent overview of the vibrant Garífuna culture in photographs, film and music. Workshops and language courses are held here. It's about 1.2 miles inland from the bus station – any bus leaving town can drop you here.

Sleeping & Eating

Val's (☎ 502-3324; www.valsbackpackerhostel.com; 1 Sharp St; dm BZ$22; ▣) Val's had fans from all over the world back when she just had a laundry. Then she put in internet access and dorm rooms with lockers, fans galore and big, clean, shared bathrooms. Now she's a backpacking institution.

Chaleanor Hotel (☎ 522-2587; www.toucantrail.com/chaleanor-hotel.html; 35 Magoon St; s/d BZ$63/101, without bathroom BZ$22/36; ☜) The budget rooms here are pretty much wooden boxes with windows. The saving grace being the shady rooftop terrace, strung with hammocks and offering sea views. All rooms come with fans; for air-con add BZ$30.

Ruthie's Seaside Cabañas (☎ 502-3184; cnr Magoon St & Yemeri Rd; d BZ$55) Clean and comfy cabins,

right by the seaside, all rooms can fit four with double bed and a bunk bed. Each extra person over two is BZ$12. There's cable TV and hot showers.

Jungle Huts (☎ 522-0185; 4 Ecumenical Blvd; r from BZ$58, cabañas BZ$58, tr BZ$98; ☜) Clean and comfy cabins, right by the seaside. There's cable TV and hot showers, three *cabañas* and 13 rooms. All rooms have hot and cold water, and some have TV. Add BZ$20 for air-con.

Red Lobster (N Riverside Dr; mains BZ$4-10; ☽ lunch & dinner Mon-Sat) No relation to the US chain of the same name, this small riverside shack just up from the Dangriga morning market serves fried fish, *panades* (fried corn shells with fish or chicken), *garnaches* (fried corn chips with beans and cheese) and other Belizean faves on the cheap. They even have lobster on the weekends for between BZ$10 and BZ$20.

Roots Kitchen (☎ 601-2519; 2246 Ecumenical Dr; dishes BZ$5-10) Belizean standards and Wednesday, Friday and Saturday Garífuna feasts of fish stewed in coconut milk, served with *hudut*, a paste made from plantain.

Riverside Café (☎ 669-1473, S Riverside Dr; mains from BZ$9; ☜) Just east of the North Stann Creek Bridge, this long-time favorite cafe serves tasty meals at budget to moderate prices. Right on the river, this is a good place to ask about fishing and snorkeling trips out to the cays or treks inland.

Also recommended is **Alexies** (mains from BZ$4; ☽ lunch & dinner Mon-Sat), a little hole in the wall up from Habets, with Belizean faves, cakes and pies.

Drinking

Local Motion Bar & Pool (Commerce St) Loud music, cold beer, dodgy characters…what more could you want?

Riverside Tavern (St Vincent St) Just south of the bridge, this club (known locally as 'the club') gets a bit of a crowd for midweek karaoke sessions, but things really start jumping on the weekends.

The *palapa* next to Austin Rodriguez's drum studio is a pretty and popular spot for evening libations.

Getting There & Away

Maya Island Air (☎ 522-2659) and **Tropic Air** (☎ 226-2012) serve Dangriga on flights also stopping at Placencia, Punta Gorda and Belize City.

Boats to the southern cays can be charted in front of the Riverside Cafe. Carlos Noel

> **MEET DANGRIGA'S ESTEEMED DRUM MAKER**
>
> As the heartland of Garífuna culture and the home of Austin Rodriguez, Dangriga is one of the best places in Belize to shop for drums. Drum-making duty of the venerable master (who is pushing 80) has largely passed to his daughter Norielee, who crafts the Rodriguez drums of the same mahogany, mayflower, cedar deer, goat, cow and sheepskin as her father. Small drums begin around BZ$70, and can go up from there. The Rodriguez workshop is located on a breezy patch of beach just east of the Dangriga morning market.

Reyes, captain of the **Nesymein Neydy** (☎ 522-0062, 604-4738) arranges trips into the cays around Dangriga for BZ$500 for a group of up to six for the day.

Buses to Belize City (local/express BZ$10/14, three to four hours) via Belmopan leave regularly from 5am to 7pm. All Belize-bound buses pass through Belmopan, from which transfer to Cayo is available. Buses to Punta Gorda (local/express BZ$10/13, 4½ hours) leave from 5:30am to 6:15pm. There are currently three buses per day to Hopkins (BZ$5, 45 minutes) at 11:30am, 12:30pm and 6:15pm, and five per day to Placencia (BZ$10, 2½ hours) beginning at 9am and running until 6pm.

SOUTHERN HIGHWAY

South of Dangriga are some great opportunities for experiencing off-the-beaten-track Belize.

Hopkins

pop 1800

This Garífuna fishing village stretches over a mile along the coast and is dotted with accommodation and eating options. Though once a backpacker haven, Hopkins has seen a steady rise in higher-end places, which in turn has led to higher prices at the restaurants in town, and even in some of the low-to-midrange accommodations. This said, Hopkins is still a far cry from Placencia, and both midrange and budget accommodations and eats are available.

ORIENTATION & INFORMATION

The still-unpaved Hopkins road leads 4 miles (6.5km) through savannah from the southern highway, ending in a T-junction in Hopkins Village. At the junction sits a privately run information booth, a grocery store, and King Cassava Restaurant. This is where buses leaving Hopkins stop, and there are restaurants and accommodations to the north and south of this junction.

As the time of writing, there are no banks or ATMs in Hopkins.

SLEEPING

Yagudah Inn (☎ 503-7089; s/d BZ$20/30) Four basic and airy fan-cooled rooms on the south side of town with shared bathroom in a traditional Belizean beach house, with a good restaurant at the side serving tasty seafood dishes. You can set up your tent on the beachfront for BZ$15 a person.

our pick **Lebeha Drumming Center & Cabañas** (☎ 666-6658; www.lebeha.com; r with/without bathroom BZ$50/30, beachfront cabañas from BZ$98; wi-fi) On the northern end of town and home of Garífuna drummer Jabbar, Lebeha has beautiful beachfront cabins that sleep up to five, and more Caribbean-style jungle huts next to the drumming center. Drumming performances and lessons are available. Inquire about longer term low-season discounts.

Windschief (☎ 523-7249; www.windschief.com; big/small cabins BZ$50/90; internet; wi-fi) The in place for windsurfing in Hopkins, Windschief has big, wooden cabin-style rooms with sea views, a cocktail bar, hammocks and windsurfers for rent (BZ$60 per day).

Palmento Grove (☎ 523-7311; palmentogrove@gmail.com; cabañas from BZ$60) Set on a 25-acre (10-hectare) patch of land on the northwest side of town, Palmento is a Garifuna ecocultural resort with four *cabañas*, a restaurant and bar and conference room.

Tipple Tree Beya (☎ 520-7006; www.tippletree.com; beachfront r BZ$60-80, cabañas BZ$100) On the south side; well-cared beach house with a spacious porch filled with brightly colored hammocks.

> **BELIZE TO HONDURAS BY BOAT**
>
> The **Nesymein Neydy** (☎ 522-0062, 604-4738; BZ$110 one-way) travels between Dangriga to Porto Cortés, Honduras, leaving Friday at 10:30am and returning on Monday at 11am from Cortés. Passengers are requested to show up 90 minutes before departure time to deal with immigration procedures. See p389 for crossing from Honduras.

ASK A LOCAL

We have nice places in Belize for families, but we Belizeans tend to leave the country for vacations. I just went to Hopkins for the first time and I am fascinated with the place. I have to come back with my kids. The beach is nice and the town is surrounded by nature. It's really relaxing.

Minerva Varela, Ladyville

Tipple's fan-cooled rooms have sea views, ocean breezes, coffee makers and fridges.

EATING & DRINKING

Most restaurants serve good, inexpensive seafood and Belizean dishes, including *gibnut* from around BZ$12.

King Cassava (☎ 502-2277; mains BZ$8-20; ☯ 11am-midnight) Excellent meat and seafood dishes, and naturally, there's no shortage of Belizean standards such as stewed chicken, fried fish, and rice and beans.

Yugadah Café (☎ 503-7255; mains BZ$10-20; ☯ Thu-Tue) Serves Belizean fare, burgers and burritos and a variety of world-class homemade sauces.

Thongs Café (☎ 662-0110; mains BZ$12-20; ☜) Hopkin's newest eatery serves an esoteric variety of moderately priced meals and the best coffee drinks in town.

TOURS

Closer to the Barrier Reef than Placencia by 10 miles (16km), Hopkins is a good place to be based for the budget-minded ocean voyager. **See More Adventures** (☎ 667-6626; seemoreadventures@gmail.com) and **Bullfrog Tours** (☎ 669-0046; issymcm@yahoo.com) are both independent tour operators based in town that do land and sea trips around the region.

GETTING THERE & AWAY

Buses pass four times a day in either direction to Placencia (BZ$6, two hours) and Dangriga (BZ$6, one hour). **Tina's Bicycle Rental** (☎ 668-3321; south side of Hopkins) rents bikes for BZ$20 per day.

Sittee River

Another small coastal village where you can get away from it all is Sittee River, a few miles down from Hopkins. Probably the most budget-friendly place in the area is **Glover's Atoll Bunkhouse** (☎ 509-7099; dm BZ$18, r BZ$24, cabañas BZ$67). A few shacks on stilts, some hammocks

slung between trees, and a breezy little riverside restaurant to boot, the Bunkhouse is the epitome of what you'd expect at backpacker-friendly prices. Camping is available for BZ$8 per person, and free kayaks and canoes are available for guests. Glover's Atoll Bunkhouse is also where the boat to Glover's Reef picks up passengers.

A quick walk down the road is **Sittee River Internet** (☎ 670-8358; www.sitteeriver.net; per hr BZ$10.50, wi-fi BZ$8) where you can check your email and get an espresso, iced coffee or smoothie. They also share space with **Barefoot Yoga Studio** (drop-in classes BZ$30).

A couple of buses a day that travel the Dangriga–Hopkins–Placencia route stop at Sittee River. The road from Hopkins to Sittee River runs through some beautiful jungle terrain.

Cockscomb Basin Wildlife Sanctuary

Almost halfway between Dangriga and Independence is the village of Maya Center, where a track goes 6 miles (10km) west to the **Cockscomb Basin Wildlife Sanctuary** (admission BZ$10; ☯ 7:30am-4:30pm). The varied topography and lush tropical forest within the 98,000-acre (39,000-hectare) sanctuary make it an ideal habitat for a wide variety of native Belizean fauna.

SPLURGE

The road stretching south out of Hopkins is home to high-end resorts such as Jaguar Reef and Hamanasi, and not in general thought to be fertile grounds for those shopping for midrange resort options. However, **Parrot Cove Lodge** (☎ 523-7225; www.parrotcovelodge.com; r from BZ$200; ☜ ☲) nicely fits that small niche between backpacker and high end with high-quality accommodations at midrange prices. The small beachfront lodge has eight beautifully appointed rooms with air-con, full bathrooms with hot showers, DVD-equipped TVs and even coffee makers supplied with local beans. The lodge has its own dock, a courtyard pool with small waterfall, and an excellent beachfront bar and restaurant serving meals made with organic local vegetables and freshly caught seafood. Rates can go as low as BZ$150 in the low season, and management offers deeper discounts for longer stays.

BELIZE

Visitor facilities at the reserve include a campsite (BZ$5 per person), several dorm-style rental cabins with solar electricity (BZ$36 per person), a visitors center and numerous hiking trails. A taxi from Maya Center will cost about BZ$20.

For information, or to book a cabin, contact the **Belize Audubon Society** (Map p228; ☎ 223-5004; www.belizeaudubon.org; 12 Fort St, Belize City).

PLACENCIA
pop 1200

Perched at the southern tip of a long, narrow, sandy peninsula, Placencia is 'the cay you can drive to.' Not too long ago, the only practical way to get here was by boat from the mainland. Now a road runs all the way down the peninsula and an airstrip lies just north of town. The palm-lined beaches on its east side attract an international crowd looking for sun and sand, and they make low-key pastimes such as swimming, sunbathing and lazing about the preferred 'activities' for many visitors.

High season in Placencia begins the week before Christmas and lasts until late April. During the full moons of May and June the town hops as whale sharks come to spawn in the waters off Placencia. The three big events in Placencia are Lobsterfest, on the last weekend of June, the Mistletoe Ball, in mid-December, and the Placencia Arts Festival in February.

Try to time your trip to hit one of these. Check www.placencia.com for more details.

Bargain hunters should be able to get discounted rates during the low season.

Orientation & Information

The village's main north–south 'street' is actually a narrow concrete footpath that threads its way among simple wood-frame houses (some on stilts) and beachfront lodges. An unpaved road skirts the town to the west, ending at the peninsula's southern tip, which is the bus stop.

An easy walk takes you anywhere in town. The airstrip is about half a mile (0.8km) from the start of the village.

At the south end of town you'll find the wharf, fuel station and bus stop. Your cash needs can be met at Belize Bank and Scotia Bank. Check your email at **Purple Space Monkey Café** (internet for customers free; ☘ 8am-midnight; ☎). Another spot for internet checking, laundry and strong coffee amid a sea breeze is the **Bosun's Chair** (laundry BZ$8, internet per hr BZ$8; ☘ 7am-7pm). **Placencia Office Supply** (☎ 523-3205; internet per hr BZ$10; ☘ 8:30am-7pm) has high-speed internet, CD burning and digital card readers. There's also a small tourist center, but it's often closed.

Tours

Vying to sign up customers for tours of the region are **Ocean Motion Guide Service** (☎ 523-3162)

BELIZE

CAYS OF SOUTHERN BELIZE

Tobacco Caye, South Water Caye and the resorts of Glover's Reef are all accessed by boat from Dangriga, Hopkins and Sittee River. Their distance from Belize City has kept casual visitors away, protecting the reef from much human impact. Dolphins, manta rays and manatees are commonly sighted, and the quantity and variety of coral that is on display is incredible. Good snorkeling and diving can be had right off the shore from the cays.

Tobacco Caye is a 5-acre (2-hectare) island catering to travelers on a low-to-moderate budget. Diving, fishing, snorkeling and hammocking are the favorite pastimes here. Lodging possibilities include **Lana's** (☎ 520-5036; d without bathroom incl 3 meals per person BZ$60), which has 10 spartan rooms; and **Gaviota's** (☎ 509-5032) with rooms for about the same price.

Passage to Tobacco Caye can be arranged along the river near the Riverside Café in Dangriga. The cost is around BZ$50 one way.

Probably the best deal for the money is **Glover's Atoll Resort** (☎ 520-5016, 509-7099; www.glovers. com.bz; campsites/dm/cabins per week BZ$298/398/498). Located on Glover Reef's Northeast Caye, the resort offers budget accommodations on a 9-acre (3.6-hectare) atoll about 20 miles (32km) from the mainland. Facilities at the resort are rustic, but the 360-degree Caribbean view can't be beat. It's a great deal for budget travelers, especially if you plan ahead and bring your own water, food and other supplies (though meals are available at the resort for between BZ$18 and BZ$24) Boats to the reef leave from Glover's Guest House (Southern Belize/Sittee River), and are included in the price of the accommodation. Daily rates are also available. The folks who run the resort offer all sorts of activities, from snorkeling to sailing to dive training. Check the website for more details.

and **Nite Wind Guide Service** (☎ 503-3487), both operating out of small offices near the wharf. **Trip and Travel** (☎ 523-3205; ⊙ Mon-Sat) operates out of Placencia Office Supply and mainly focuses of fly-fishing tours up Monkey River. Its shop also functions as a full-fledged copy and internet shop.

On a pier in the main part of the village is **Sea Horse Dive Shop** (☎ 523-3166; www.belizescuba.com), doing certification courses and dives for certified divers. Egbert Cabral is the owner of Permit Angling (☎ 523-3132; permit@btl.net) and runs fishing tours off his motor boat for BZ$600.

Operating from a red-and-green shack **Lost in Paradise** (☎ 628-0911; www.placenciavillageguide.com) offers land and sea tours all over the area, as well as operating its own dive school offer-

ing three-day open-water PADI certification courses for BZ$800.

For inland tours, including kayaking expeditions, check what's on offer with **Toadal Adventure** (☎ 523-3207; www.toadaladventure.com), which operates out of Deb and Dave's Last Resort.

Sleeping

Placencia has lodgings in all price ranges.

Omar's Guesthouse (☎ 624-7168; dm BZ$25; r with/without bathroom BZ$50/40) Rooms are simple but comfortable, and the dorm area has a shared kitchenette. Hammocks on the porch, and a beach view makes Omar's a good, cheap choice.

Travelers Inn (☎ 523-3190; s/d BZ$35/40, without bathroom BZ$25/30) A classic beachside no-frills joint, the Inn keeps it real with linoleum

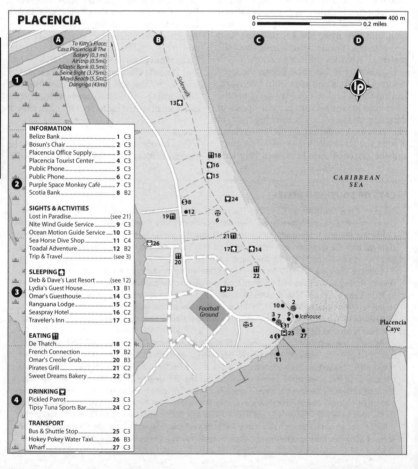

PLACENCIA

0 — 400 m
0 — 0.2 miles

To Kitty's Place;
Casa Placencia & The
Bakery (0.3 mi);
Airstrip (0.5mi);
Atlantic Bank (0.5mi);
Seine Bight (3.75mi);
Maya Beach (5.5mi);
Dangriga (43mi)

CARIBBEAN SEA

Placencia
Caye

Football
Ground

Icehouse

BELIZE

floors, mostly mosquito-proof windows and creaky fans.

Lydia's Guest House (☎ 523-3117; lydias@btl.net; s/d BZ$35/40; 🛜) Small but clean no-frills rooms in a quiet part of the village are nothing to write home about, but views from the upstairs balcony are lovely.

Deb & Dave's Last Resort (☎ 523-3207; www.toadaladventure.com; r BZ$40-50) Basic, fan-cooled wooden rooms are set around a leafy garden and there are good screened sitting areas. It's in a quiet but central location.

Seaspray Hotel (☎ 523-3148; www.seasprayhotel.com; r BZ$50-150; 🛜) The 'economy' rooms are fairly ordinary, but they have bathroom, fan and fridge. The more expensive rooms are larger and have porches and sea views.

Casa Placencia (☎ 503-3143; www.casaplacencia.com; r BZ$90-390; 🛜) On the north end of town, with beautifully decorated rooms with kitchenettes, cable and wi-fi. Long-term rentals available, and all guests are plied with freshly baked brownies and pastries.

Ranguana Lodge (☎ 523-3112; www.ranguabelize.com; cabañas BZ$170-178; 🍴 🛜) Five beautiful and colorfully painted *cabañas* set amid a garden-filled courtyard and a gorgeous stretch of beach. All *cabañas* have full kitchens, hot- and cold-water showers, big windows and porches with hammocks.

Eating

our pick **Omar's Creole Grub** (mains BZ$12-30) How does Omar serve simultaneously the best and cheapest seafood dishes in Placencia? By cutting out the middle man and catching it all himself. Crab, lobster, conch, shrimp and fish of all description, all trapped, speared or otherwise caught by Omar and grilled to perfection. The only way to get it fresher would be catching it yourself (fishing and lobstering trips available from BZ$110 per person; inquire at the restaurant).

De Thatch (☎ 503-3385; mains from BZ$18; 🖥) Food here is pricey for this part of town, but the setting – in a wood-floored *palapa* right on the beach – and the mounds of fresh seafood on the menu make it worthwhile. Burritos, burgers and breakfasts are more reasonably priced.

French Connection (☎ 523-3656; mains from BZ$40; 🕐 dinner Mon-Wed, Fri & Sat, lunch Sun) This is the place for a romantic splurge. Modern French cuisine and Belize fusion is the go here, with a big emphasis on seafood. Reservations are recommended. Check the board between 5pm

and 6pm for the early-bird special, a three-course meal for BZ$35.

Sweet Dreams Bakery (snacks from BZ$3) Home-baked personal pizza, multigrain breads, baked goods of all sorts and freshly brewed local coffee.

Pirates Grill (mains from BZ$15) A small shack with a bar and tour shop on the sidewalk by the beach serving crepes (BZ$8) and excellent curries as well as more traditional Belizean fare.

The Bakery (☎ 503-3143; Thu-Mon) Serves what may well be the most decadent cherry fudge brownies and coconut *blondies* on the planet. Try a 'manwish,' an ice-cream/brownie sandwich that will push your glucose levels into orbit. Located north of town just past the water tower.

Drinking

Most bars and many restaurants have sun-down happy hours, usually featuring rum and juice for BZ$2. The **Pickled Parrot** (www.pickledparrotbelize.com; 🕐 noon-midnight or later) on the main street always has a good crowd, and the **Tipsy Tuna** (🕐 7pm-midnight Sun-Wed, to 2am Thu-Sat), a towering 'sports bar' with occasional live music and a happening little beachfront bar, is usually more hit than miss.

Getting There & Around

Ritchie's (☎ 523-3806) runs a regular bus service from Placencia to Dangriga (BZ$10, 2½ hours) with three runs daily. From Placencia, buses leave from the tip of the peninsula at 6:20am, 7:00am and 1pm. From Dangriga station, buses leave at 11am, 2pm and 4:30pm. On Sundays the earliest buses do not run.

Maya Island Air (☎ 523-3475; www.mayaairways.com) and **Tropic Air** (☎ 523-3410; www.tropicair.com) offer daily flights linking Placencia with Belize City and Dangriga to the north and Punta Gorda to the south. Taxis meet most flights and will bring you anywhere in town for BZ$5. At the time of research, a new airport was being constructed on the northern end of the peninsula.

The quickest way out of town is on the **Hokey Pokey Water Taxi** (BZ$10), which departs Placencia five times between 10am and 6pm for **Mango Creek**. At Mango Creek, walk five minutes up the main street, turn left at the gas station and wait in front of Sherl's Restaurant. Buses to Punta Gorda (BZ$10, two hours) and Belize City (BZ$20, 4½ hours) roll in every hour or so.

BELIZE

Bikes can be rented at the **Seabreeze Restaurant** (per hr/day BZ$4/BZ$20).

PUNTA GORDA
pop 5300

'Sleepy' is an understatement for this southern seafront town. People here are so laid-back they can't even be bothered calling the town by its full name – all over Belize it's known simply as PG.

Rainfall and humidity are at their highest, and the jungle at its lushest, here in the Toledo district. Prepare yourself for at least a short downpour almost daily and some sultry weather in-between.

PG was founded for the Garífuna who emigrated from Honduras in 1832. Though it's still predominantly Garífuna, it's also home to the usual bewildering variety of Belizean citizenry: Creoles, Q'eqchi' Maya, expat Americans, Brits, Canadians, Chinese and people from eastern India.

Orientation & Information

The town center is a triangular park with a bandstand and a distinctive blue-and-white clock tower. Saturday is market day, when area villagers come to town to buy, sell and barbecue. It's a fascinating and colorful mix-up.

The BTB office and **Toledo Visitors' Information Center** (☎ 722-2531; ☽ 8am-noon & 1-5pm Tue-Fri, 8am-noon Sat) share office space. **Belize Bank** (cnr Main & Queen Sts) and **Scotia Bank** (cnr Main & Prince Sts) both have ATMs.

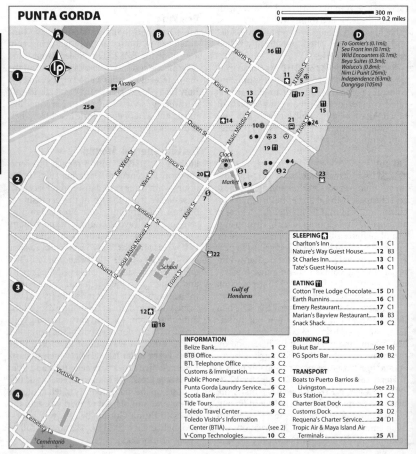

PUNTA GORDA

0 ——— 300 m
0 ——— 0.2 miles

To Gomier's (0.1mi);
Sea Front Inn (0.1mi);
Wild Encounters (0.1mi);
Beya Suites (0.3mi);
Waluco's (0.8mi);
Nim Li Punit (26mi);
Independence (63mi);
Dangriga (105mi)

Airstrip

North St

King St

N Main St

Queen St

Main Middle St

Front St

Clock Tower

Market

Prince St

Far West St

West St

Main St

Clements St

Jose Maria Nunez St

Church St

Front St

School

Victoria St

Cemetery La

Cementario

Gulf of Honduras

SLEEPING 🛏
Charlton's Inn **11** C1
Nature's Way Guest House **12** B3
St Charles Inn **13** C1
Tate's Guest House **14** C1

EATING 🍴
Cotton Tree Lodge Chocolate **15** D1
Earth Runnins **16** C1
Emery Restaurant **17** C1
Marian's Bayview Restaurant **18** B3
Snack Shack **19** C2

INFORMATION
Belize Bank **1** C2
BTB Office **2** C2
BTL Telephone Office **3** C2
Customs & Immigration **4** C2
Public Phone **5** C1
Punta Gorda Laundry Service **6** B2
Scotia Bank **7** B2
Tide Tours **8** C2
Toledo Travel Center **9** C2
Toledo Visitor's Information
Center (BTIA) .... (see 2)
V-Comp Technologies **10** C2

DRINKING 🍸
Bukut Bar .... (see 16)
PG Sports Bar **20** B2

TRANSPORT
Boats to Puerto Barrios &
Livingston .... (see 23)
Bus Station **21** C2
Charter Boat Dock **22** C3
Customs Dock **23** D2
Requena's Charter Service **24** D1
Tropic Air & Maya Island Air
Terminals **25** A1

GETTING TO HONDURAS

On Fridays you can head directly to Honduras from Placencia by hopping aboard the **Gulf Cruza** (☎ 523-4045). The boat leaves Placencia at 9:30am and arrives at Puerto Cortés at 2pm. The trip costs BZ$100, and the boat makes a quick stop at Big Creek.

The **Punta Gorda Laundry Service** (Main St) charges BZ$2 per pound.

V-Comp (Main St; per hr BZ$5; ☺ 8am-8pm Mon-Sat) provides internet access.

Sleeping

Nature's Way Guest House (☎ 702-2119; 65 Front St; s/d/tr/q BZ$26/36/56/66; ☐) One of the better budget hotels in Belize. There's a shady courtyard with plenty of hammock action and excellent breakfasts for BZ$8.

Tate's Guesthouse (☎ 722-0007; 34 Jose Maria Nunez St; s/d BZ$35/45; ☐ ☏) Tate's has tidy little rooms in a family-run guesthouse. Rooms have bathroom, shower, cable TV and wi-fi. Add BZ$15 for air-con.

Charlton's Inn (☎ 722-2197; 9 Main St; s/d BZ$65/70) On the north side of town, Charlton's is a dependable and clean hotel with attached restaurant. All rooms come with cable, hot showers and air-con. Some rooms have wi-fi.

Also recommended:

St Charles Inn (☎ 722-2149; 23 King St; s/d BZ$30/44) Rooms come with cable TV and have some good balcony areas for hanging out.

Sea Front Inn (☎ 722-2300; 4 Front St; s/d BZ$130/150; ☏) Its fully furnished penthouse boasts jungle and sea views.

Eating & Drinking

Punta Gorda has a number of stalls and restaurants serving traditional Belizean fare. You'll find most of these along the main street on either side of the town square. Best bet for lunch is easily one of the sidewalk stands serving grilled chicken, beans and slaw for around BZ$5.

Gomier's Restaurant (Alejandro Vernon St; from BZ$7; ☑) In a town where coleslaw constitutes a vegetable and shacks serving fried fish and stewed chicken mark the culinary landscape, Gomier's consciously crafted vegetarian dishes, herbal tonics and seaweed-based energy shakes stand out like a Hare Krishna at a Texas BBQ. Across from the Sea Front Inn.

Marian's Bayview Restaurant (☎ 722-0129; Front St; meals from BZ$10) Across from Nature's Way Guest House, Marian's serves Belizean and East Indian dishes made with organic produce and locally farmed meats. Marian's has the best bay view in PG.

ourpick Earth Runnins & Bukut Bar (☎ 702-2007; www.earthrunnins.com; 13 Main Middle St; meals from BZ$12; ☺ Wed-Mon) The in spot for fine cuisine and cool tunes in PG. Check out its website for specials and upcoming music.

Emery Restaurant (Main St; meals BZ$12-20) Serves fresh-fish specials daily, good Mexican food and quite possibly the best fried chicken to be had in all of Belize.

Also recommended:

Snack Shack (Main St; mains BZ$10-20;) A popular outdoor venue serving burgers, burritos, sandwiches and pastries.

PG Sports Bar (cnr Main & Prince Sts) A good bet for live music on weekends. It's a good-sized, fairly standard bar, incongruously enhanced by a staggering collection of US sports photos and posters.

Cotton Tree Lodge Chocolate (Front St; ☺ 8am-noon & 1:30-5pm Mon-Fri, 8am-noon Sat) Hands down the best chocolate confections available in the country. Chocolate-covered mangos are out of this world, and the Belizean coffee is the strongest around. Try one chocolate barrel: a chocolate barrel filled with one barrel (rum). Free tours daily.

Getting There & Away

Punta Gorda is served daily by **Maya Island Air** (☎ 722-2856; www.mayaairways.com) and **Tropic Air** (☎ 722-2008; www.tropicair.com). Ticket offices are located at the airport. Flights to Belize City are between BZ$164 and BZ$204.

Requena's Charter Services (☎ 722-2070; 12 Front St) operates the *Mariestela*, with boats departing Punta Gorda at 10am daily for Puerto Barrios (Guatemala). Tickets cost BZ$40 one way. **Memos boat service** (☎ 625-0464) runs the same route but leaves at 12:45pm and charges BZ$50. A few other services in town offer

---

THE TOLEDO HOWLER

A community-based newspaper with calendars of events, current affairs, restaurant guides, maps, and plenty of other useful information for traveling around the deep south. Best of all, The *Howler* is available in print and in downloadable pdf format at http://belizenews.com/howler.

BELIZE

regular and chartered services to Guatemala. Check the BTIA office for more information. Both services offer return trips.

One boat goes to Lívingston, Guatemala (BZ$50) at 10am on Tuesdays and Fridays.

Buses depart regularly for Belize City (local/express BZ$20/22, six/seven hours) via Dangriga and Belmopan.

Local village buses run daily between PG and villages throughout the Toledo district. Buses leave from around the town square, and schedules can be obtained through TEA or at the Toledo Visitor's Information Center.

AROUND PUNTA GORDA
Villages of Toledo
SAN PEDRO COLUMBIA
Around 20 miles (32km) northwest of Punta Gorda is the village of San Pedro Columbia, the largest Q'eqchi' Maya community outside of Guatemala. In addition to having a few stores and restaurants, the village is close to the source of the Columbia branch of the Río Grande, a lovely river great for swimming and tubing. Behind the village, up into the hills, you'll find the **Columbia Forest Reserve**, which has thousands of acres of forest, sinkholes, caves and ruins hidden in the valleys.

Maya Mountain Research Farm (p265) is just a few miles upriver from the village. Columbia is also close to Lubaantun (see opposite page) and 20 minutes by bus from Nim Li Punit (see opposite page), making the village an ideal place from which to explore two of the area's most complex and amazing ruins.

AMERICAN CROCODILE EDUCATION SANCTUARY

Wildlife biologists and herpetologists Cherie and Vince Rose operate ACES (American Crocodile Education Sanctuary), a 36-acre (14.5 hectare) solar- and wind-powered crocodile sanctuary about 5 miles (8km) out of PG with two beautiful and luxurious jungle *cabañas* complete with full kitchens, sleeping and living areas. All income generated goes back into croc research, rescue and care. Rates vary by season, but usually range around BZ$220 per day per *cabaña*. Check www.americancrocodilesanctuary. org or call ☎ 665-2762 for full details.

SAN MIGUEL
This Q'eqchi' village of 400 people is on the road close to the Lubaantun ruins and the Southern Hwy. You can walk to Lubaantun or make a little expedition to **Tiger Cave**, 1½ hours' walk away, returning by canoe along the Río Grande.

LAGUNA
About 13 miles (21km) northwest of Punta Gorda, Laguna is just 2 miles (3km) off the Southern Hwy and quick and easy to get to. It's home to about 300 Q'eqchi' Maya villagers. The lagoon the village is named for, about a two-hour walk away, is at the heart of the 8.6-sq-mile (22-sq-km) **Aguacaliente Wildlife Sanctuary**, an extensive wetland area.

SAN ANTONIO
The largest Mopan Maya community in Belize (population about 2500), San Antonio is home to a beautiful **stone church** with wonderful stained-glass windows. The **Feast of San Luis**, a harvest festival where the famous Deer Dance is performed, is celebrated in town from about August 15 to 25.

SANTA ELENA
Santa Elena is another Mopan village, 6 miles (10km) west of San Antonio, with about 300 people. Just east is the little **Río Blanco National Park**, containing the spectacular **Río Blanco Falls** and one of the country's best swimming holes.

PUEBLO VIEJO
Three miles (5km) beyond Santa Elena, the name Pueblo Viejo is Spanish for 'Old Town,' which is appropriate as this was the first settled Mopan village in Belize. Today it is home to about 550 people. It's still an isolated place, without electricity. There are beautiful **waterfalls** close by and you can take **jungle hikes** or go **horseback riding**.

SAN JOSE
Also known as Hawaii (a Mopan word, pronounced ha-wee-ah), this Mopan village of 700, known for practicing organic farming, is located in the foothills of the Maya Mountains. The rainforest surrounding it is among the most pristine in Toledo. You can make jungle hikes to **Gibnut Cave** and a 200ft **sinkhole**. The village honors its patron saint with three days of eating and dancing to marimba and harp music around March 19.

TRAVELS WITH TEA

The **Toledo Ecotourism Association** (TEA; ☎ 702-2119; 65 Front St, Punta Gorda), runs a Village Guesthouse and Ecotrail Program that takes participants to any of 20 traditional Mopan Maya, Q'eqchi' Maya, Creole and Garífuna villages.

Accommodation is offered in specially built, rustic but comfortable guesthouses and costs BZ$21 per person per night, plus a one-off BZ$10 administrative fee. Meals in family homes cost BZ$8 and activities on offer, such as nature tours, music, dancing and storytelling, cost around BZ$8 per hour. The tours don't include transportation; check with the TEA for village bus schedules.

More than 85% of the tour fee stays in the village with the villagers, helping them achieve a sustainable, ecofriendly economy as an alternative to traditional slash-and-burn agriculture.

Visits and accommodations in the villages listed below can be arranged through TEA. More adventurous travelers should be able to find accommodations with locals, meals and guides through village stores, which generally double as social hubs and ad-hoc meeting places.

BLUE CREEK
This village of some 250 people, part Q'eqchi' and part Mopan, does indeed have a pretty, blue-tinted river running through the middle. Howler monkeys inhabit the surrounding hilly jungles, otters live along the creek and green iguanas are plentiful. Blue Creek is a tourist stop for the **Blue Creek Cave** (Hokeb Ha Cave; admission BZ$2) and some excellent hiking around a hill known as **Jungle Height**.

BARRANCO
An anomaly, Barranco is a Garífuna community surrounded by Maya villages. It is a major spiritual homeland of the Garífuna, and a great base from which to explore **Temash-Sarstoon National Park**, an amazing and remote 64-sq-mile (166-sq-km) protected reserve of rainforest, wetlands, estuaries and rivers lined by towering mangroves and stretching all the way to Guatemala. Other activities available at Barranco include **drumming** and **dory building** (a dory is a traditional Belizean canoe).

Maya Ruins of Toledo
The Toledo district boasts two major Maya ruins. **Lubaantun** (Fallen Stones; admission BZ$10; ☺ 8am-5pm), 1 mile (1.6km) northwest of the village of San Pedro Columbia have been excavated to some extent but not restored. The many temples are still mostly covered with jungle, so you will have to use your imagination to envisage the great city that once thrived here.

Somewhat more restored is **Nim Li Punit** (Big Hat; admission BZ$10; ☺ 9am-5pm). Named after the headgear worn by the richly clad figure on Stela 14, Nim Li Punit may have been a tributary city to the larger, more powerful Lubaantun.

Both ruins are an easy trip from Punta Gorda, and can be seen together in a day.

BELIZE DIRECTORY

ACCOMMODATIONS
Lodgings in Belize vary from very basic to charming to downright decadent. There are plenty of beachfront *cabañas* on the cays and in seafront towns, jungle huts down south, and hotels ranging from grim to opulent in towns.

Some lodgings offer separate prices for rooms with or without air-con; these are generally the same rooms, but the extra BZ$15 to BZ$30 gets you the air-con remote. Hotels without air-con options are noted in text. Nearly all hotels discourage in-room smoking.

The HI (Hostelling International) is non-existent in Belize, but there are a few places around offering dorm-style accommodations costing from around BZ$20. This is a good way to save money and meet people.

During the peak seasons (mid-December to April, and June to August) prices can be higher and lodging harder to find. However, during low season, bargaining is possible.

ACTIVITIES
Snorkeling and diving are best on the cays. Boats depart Ambergris (p234) and Caulker (p231) cays on day and overnight voyages to the best spots.

Inland, horseback riding, canoeing and kayaking, cave-tubing, hiking, bird-watching and archaeology are all possibilities.

BELIZE

BOOKS

Belizean historian Assad Shoman's *13 Chapters in the History of Belize* is a detailed account of the history of the country and tends not to glamorize the colonial past as some other studies do.

Warlords and Maize Men: A Guide to the Maya Sites of Belize, by Byron Foster, is recommended for its descriptions of the lives of the Maya.

Snapshots of Belize: An Anthology of Short Fiction, published in Belize by Cubola Productions, features short stories of past and present Belize.

BUSINESS HOURS

Most restaurants in Belize are open from around 8am until 8pm, though some stay open well into the night. Some restaurants cater mostly to workers, and will thus open earlier for breakfast and lunch only. Exceptions – those only open for breakfast and lunch, for example – are noted. Most banks are open 8am to 1:30pm Monday to Thursday and 8am to 4:30pm Friday. Most banks and many businesses and shops close on Wednesday afternoon. Shops are usually open 8am to noon Monday to Saturday and 1pm to 4pm Monday, Tuesday, Thursday and Friday. Some shops have evening hours from 7pm to 9pm on those days as well.

Most businesses, offices and many restaurants close on Sunday.

CLIMATE

The busy winter season runs from mid-December to April, with a second peak from June to August. The dry season (November to May) is the best time to travel (although prices can be higher and lodging harder to find). If you do visit in summer (July to November), be aware this is hurricane season. Belize City was badly damaged by hurricanes, with heavy loss of life, in 1931, 1961 and 1978.

For climate charts, see p714.

DANGERS & ANNOYANCES

Petty theft is the greatest danger (and annoyance) to travelers in Belize. Take care not to show obvious signs of wealth. Keep a close eye on camera equipment, don't leave valuables in plain view in cars and try to watch your bags when you're on a bus. Belize City has a bad reputation, mostly a hangover from the past, but you should still exercise normal precautions.

Assaults have been known to happen and it is strongly advised that single travelers avoid walking on secondary roads.

If you're driving, be extra careful – Belize is renowned for road accidents. Wear your seat belt, and be aware of what's going on in front and behind you.

EMBASSIES & CONSULATES

Canada (Map p226; ☎ 223-1060; cdncon.bze@btl.net; 80 Princess Margaret Dr, Belize City)

Germany (☎ 222-4369; seni@cisco.com.bz; 3½ miles Western Highway, Belize City)

Guatemala (Map p226; ☎ 223-3150; 8 A St, Kings Park, Belize City)

Honduras (☎ 224-5889; 114 Bella Vista, Belize City)

Mexico (Map p228; ☎ 223-0193/0194; cnr Wilson Street/Newton Barracks Belize City)

Netherlands (Map p226; ☎ 223-2953; cnr Baymen Av & Calle Al Mar, Belize City)

UK (Map p244; ☎ 822-2146; Embassy Sq, Belmopan)

USA (Map p244; ☎ 822-4011; 4 Floral Park Rd, Belmopan)

FESTIVALS & EVENTS

On major holidays, banks, offices and other services are closed. National holidays are denoted with an asterisk.

The following list describes the major holidays and festivals; they may well be celebrated for several days around the actual date:

New Year's Day* (January 1)

Fiesta de Carnival (February; Sunday to Tuesday before the beginning of Lent) Celebrated in northern Belize.

Baron Bliss Day* (March 9) Honors the memory of one of the great benefactors of Belize.

Holy Week (April; held in the week leading up to Easter Sunday) Various services and processions.

Labor Day* (May 1)

Commonwealth Day* (May 25)

Feast of San Pedro (June; date varies) San Pedro, Ambergris Caye.

Lobster Season opens (successive weekends in June and early July, after the season officially opens, usually early June) Placencia, Caye Caulker and San Pedro.

Costa Maya Festival (August; dates vary) San Pedro, Ambergris Caye – a celebration of Maya coastal culture with participants from Belize and the Yucatán.

National Day* (St George's Caye Day; September 10)

Independence Day* (September 21)

Pan American Day* (Columbus Day; October 12)

Garífuna Settlement Day* (November 19) Hopkins and particularly in Dangriga (p250).

Christmas Day* (December 25)

Boxing Day* (December 26)

FOOD & DRINK

Belize has never developed an elaborate native cuisine. Recipes are mostly borrowed – from the UK, the Caribbean, Mexico and the USA. Each community has its own local favorites, but Garífuna and Maya dishes and traditional favorites, such as boil-up, rarely appear on restaurant menus. Even so, there is some good food to be had, especially the fresh fish options near the sea.

Rice and beans prevail on Belizean menus and plates. They're usually served with other ingredients – chicken, pork, beef, fish, vegetables, even lobster – plus some spices and condiments, such as coconut milk. 'Stew beans with rice' is stewed beans on one side of the plate, boiled rice on the other side and chicken, beef or pork on top.

Meals are not usually spicy, but the popular Marie Sharp's hot sauces are on virtually every table to liven things up if you need it.

Local beer is good and inexpensive. Belikin is about the only brand you're ever likely to see (except in fancy bars), so get used to it. It comes in regular, light, stout and premium. Opinion is divided on whether tap water is safe to drink – bottled water is cheap and readily available, anyway.

GAY & LESBIAN TRAVELERS

Unfortunately, the rules for gay and lesbian travelers in Belize seem to be the same as those in most Central American countries – keep it low key, and look but don't touch. While it's an incredibly tolerant society, underlying Latino machismo and traditional religious beliefs combine to make public displays of same-sex affection a pretty bad idea.

See p718 for general information about traveling in the region.

INTERNET ACCESS

All but the smallest of towns have cybercafes, and nowadays even many budget hotels boast wireless access. Expect to pay between BZ$4 to BZ$10 for internet access. Note that Belize is one of a handful of countries that not only blocks Skype, but also several other text-chat programs as well.

INTERNET RESOURCES

Belize by Naturalight (www.belizenet.com) Covers just about everything visitors might want to know.
Belize First Magazine (www.belizefirst.com) Information of interest to travelers and expats. Especially helpful

---

> ### ASK A LOCAL
>
> My three favorite Garífuna dishes are *tapuw*, a stew made from plantains, coco, okra and fish; *hudut*, which is mashed plantain, coconut milk, fresh vegetables and fish; and *budaga*, a stew of grated green banana, seasoned coconut water and fried snapper. Hopkins is the best place to find genuine Garífuna food.
> *Celine Castillo, Sittee Point*

---

are reader recommendations on lodgings, restaurants and tours.
Belize Forums (www.belizeforum.com/cgi-bin/ultimatebb.cgi) An excellent bulletin board with mostly reliable information.
Belize Tourism Board (www.travelbelize.org) Has comprehensive tourist information.

LANGUAGE

Belize is officially English-speaking, and most of its citizens, with the exception of new arrivals from Guatemala, Honduras and Mexico, read and speak English fluently. Creole people speak their own colorful dialect as well as standard English, flavored with the Caribbean's musical lilt. You'll hear Garífuna in the south. Spanish is the first language in the north and in some towns in the west. Other languages in the mix are Maya, Chinese, Mennonite German and Hindi.

MAPS

If you're driving, pick up a copy of Emory King's annual *Driver's Guide to Beautiful Belize*, sold in bookstores and gift shops in Belize City. The guide has basic maps and detailed route descriptions – which is helpful since road markers in Belize are few and far between.

For more detail, the 1:350,000 *Belize*, published by International Travel Maps and Books of Vancouver is widely available throughout the country.

MEDIA
Newspapers & Magazines

Most Belizean newspapers are supported by one political party or another, and as a consequence, much space is devoted to political diatribe. The left-leaning *Amandala* (www.amandala.com.bz) has the largest circulation in the country. The *Belize Times* (www.belizetimes.bz) represents the PUP perspective, while the *Guardian* (www.guardian.bz) goes in to bat

BELIZE

for the UDP. The *Reporter* (www.reporter.bz) appears to present the most neutral coverage.

Belize News (www.belizenews.com) has links to most of the country's media. Run out of San Ignacio, *The Review* (www.aguallo. com) is a bimonthly directory for tourism and promotional news widely available throughout the country.

Radio

LOVE-FM (www.lovefm.com) is the most widely broadcast radio station in Belize, with spots at 95.1 and 98.1 on the dial. It's a beguiling mix of local news, public-service announcements ('Belizeans! Be kind to tourists!') and the world's best (and worst) love songs. KREM at 96.5 plays a more modern selection of music.

MONEY

The Belizean dollar (BZ$) is divided into 100 cents. Coins come in denominations of one, five, 10, 25 and 50 cents, and one dollar; bills (notes) are all of the same size but differ in color and come in denominations of two, five, 10, 20, 50 and 100 dollars. Be sure to carry small denominations if you're heading off the tourist trail.

Prices in the country are generally quoted in Belizean dollars, written as '$30 BZE,' though you will also occasionally see '$15 US.' To avoid surprises, be sure to confirm with service providers whether they are quoting prices in US or Belizean dollars.

For general information on costs and money in Central America see p20.

ATMs

Belize Bank, Scotia Bank and Atlantic Bank have the most reliable ATMs; nearly all of which accept international cards and are open 24/7. Corozal, Orange Walk, Belize City, Belmopan, San Ignacio, Dangriga, Placencia and Punta Gorda all have banks with ATMs.

Credit Cards

Credit cards are useful, particularly when buying cash from a bank. Visa and MasterCard are the most widely accepted. Some tour operators and many midrange and high-end hotels and restaurants accept cards.

Exchanging Money

Most businesses accept US currency in cash without question. They usually give change in Belizean dollars, though they may return US change if you ask for it. Many also accept US-dollar traveler's checks.

Canadian dollars and UK pounds sterling are exchangeable at any bank, although non-US-dollar traveler's checks are not consistently accepted by Belizean banks. It is difficult if not impossible to exchange other foreign currencies in Belize.

Money changers at border-crossing points will change your US cash for Belizean dollars legally at the standard rate of BZ$2 for US$1. If you change money or traveler's checks at a bank, you may get only BZ$1.97 for US$1; they may also charge a fee of BZ$5 (US$2.50) to change a traveler's check.

The exchange rates at press time are given below; for daily conversion rates check out www.xe.com.

Country	Unit	BZ$
Australia	A$1	1.65
Canada	C$1	1.88
Euro zone	€1	2.39
Japan	¥100	2.12
New Zealand	NZ$1	1.33
UK	£1	2.87
USA	US$1	1.95

International Transfers

The fastest way to have money transferred from abroad is with Western Union. It has offices all over the country and charges US$85 for a US$1000 transfer.

POST

A postcard sent by airmail to Canada or the USA costs BZ$0.30; a letter BZ$0.60. To Europe it's BZ$0.40 for a postcard and BZ$0.80 for a letter. Address poste restante (general delivery) mail to: (name), c/o General Delivery, (town), (district), Belize, Central America. To claim poste restante mail, present a passport or other identification; there's no charge. Post offices in Belize are open from 8am until 5pm, Monday to Friday, and from 8am until 1pm on Saturday. Most branches close for lunch between noon and 1pm.

RESPONSIBLE TRAVEL

Many people come to Belize to appreciate the natural beauty of the country. Belizeans are quite conscientious about maintaining their environment, and visitors should show the same respect.

Don't remove coral or shells from the sea, and mind your fins when snorkeling or diving; coral is fragile and endangered. Avoid buying items made from turtle shell or coral. Don't swim with manatees or attempt to piggyback a sea turtle. You may like it, but they find it very stressful.

Don't take or buy Maya artifacts – it's illegal, and some say you'll be hexed!

Use air-con sparingly. It's expensive and places an enormous strain on local energy reserves. Instead, move more slowly than normal and use fans (or hang out in the lobby of fancy hotels); you'll find that you adjust to the heat after a few days.

When in the jungle, stay on trails to avoid trampling plants. Appreciate wildlife from a distance. Never feed wild animals, including those in the sea.

STUDYING

Educational opportunities in Belize are as varied and laid-back as the Belizean people themselves. Head to Gale's Point Manatee (a charming little village 1½ hours south of Belize City) to learn both Creole drumming and drum making at the **Maroon Creole Drum School** (methos_drums@hotmail.com). If getting your hands dirty learning sustainable agriculture and solar engineering are more your thing, medium and long-term live–work opportunities are offered at the breathtakingly beautiful **Maya Mountain Research Farm** (www.mmrfbz.org) in the mountains west of the town of San Pedro Colombia in the toledo district. And down in Punta Gorda, master vegetarian chef **Gomier** (☎ 620-1719; gomier@hotmail.com) teaches tofu-making and vegetarian cooking classes at his restaurant on the north end of town.

TELEPHONE

Formerly privately owned, the country's telephone system **Belize Telemedia Ltd** (BTL; www.belizetelemedia.net/) was nationalized in 2009, and is now controlled by the Belizean government. BTL has offices in major cities. Telephones are generally very reliable (and inexpensive) when calling within the country. International calls are sometimes a different story. BTL has an online directory.

Local calls cost BZ$0.25 (US$0.13). Telephone debit cards are sold in denominations of BZ$10, BZ$20 and BZ$50. In some stores you can choose your amount and they just print out a docket with your pin number on it.

Travelers with cell phones can purchase stored-value SIM cards with local numbers for BZ$50 from any BTL shop. This will allow you to make and receive calls, as well as send text messages within Belize. Stored-value phones can be recharged at nearly any shop.

Users of Skype should note that Belize is one of a handful of countries that block this and most other voice-over-internet software. Some internet cafes get around this by using a non-Belize-based satellite provider.

TOURIST INFORMATION

The government-run **BTB** (www.travelbelize.org) maintains tourist offices in Belize City, Punta Gorda and Corozal. They're generally underfunded, but staffed by friendly folks who usually do what they can to answer your questions.

TOURS

A variety of companies offer tailored and themed travel packages for individuals and groups.

Vitalino Reyes (☎ 602-8975; www.cavetubing.bz) is both a cave-tubing pioneer and tour guide specializing in package tours combining popular destinations such as Tikal, Altun Ha and the Belize Zoo with cave-tubing expeditions. His tours range throughout the country, and are a great way to get from one end of Belize to the other. **Up Close Belize** (☎ in US 832-426-2385, 670-5698; www.upclosebelize.com) has custom-built tours geared towards individuals and small groups throughout Belize.

TRAVELERS WITH DISABILITIES

Unfortunately, Belize's infrastructure for travelers with a disability is virtually nonexistent. See p723 for general advice about traveling in the region.

VISAS & DOCUMENTS

Citizens of the EU and many countries (among them Australia, Canada, Mexico, New Zealand, the USA and many Caribbean nations) do not need to obtain a Belizean visa in advance, provided you have a valid passport and an onward or round-trip airline ticket (with a departure from Belize, or any other country in the region). A visitor's permit valid for 30 days will be stamped in your passport at a border crossing or at the airport. One

BELIZE

month extensions are easily obtainable from immigration offices in Belize City, Corozal, Orange Walk, Dangriga, Belmopan, Placencia and Punta Gorda. Visa offices are open from 8am until noon and 1pm to 5pm Monday to Friday. The price of an extension is BZ$50; after six months, the price increases to BZ$100.

Also check out www.lonelyplanet.com for up-to-date visa information, or the Belizean government website (www.belize.gov.bz).

VOLUNTEERING

Belize is full of volunteer opportunities; not surprisingly, many of them are environmentally based. Most programs expect volunteers to pay, and costs can vary wildly.

Help for Progress (www.progressbelize.org) Belizean NGO that works with grass-roots organizations in fields such as education, gender issues, citizen participation and environment.

Teachers for a Better Belize (www.tfabb.org) US-based organization that sends volunteers to schools in the Toledo district to train local teachers.

Plenty International (www.plenty.org) Has opportunities to work with community groups and cooperatives in the Toledo district.

WOMEN TRAVELERS

Men in Belize can be forward and at times aggressive with comments about women's appearance. This can be uncomfortable and embarrassing, but shouldn't be considered threatening. The more modestly you're dressed, the less attention you'll receive.

WORK

Officially you need a resident's visa to get a job in Belize. You might, however, pick up some work on the cays or in Placencia working in bars.

El Salvador

El Salvador is Central America's smallest, most densely populated country, with the region's largest economy and its fewest foreign tourists. Once only a trickle of headstrong surfers and foreign correspondents passed through its rigorous border posts, but now a new breed of traveler is pushing through in search of an authentic experience in an undervisited land.

El Salvador is a perennial tease. Glimpses of tropical paradise, lush tracts of pre-industrial national park lands, colonial splendor astride pristine volcanic lakes, searing colors and a fierce creative vision sit quietly in the shadows of an indomitable local pride. Here you'll find a glorious coastline, a buzzing culture-clad capital, hard-core war tourism and small-town charm by the plaza-load.

Salvadorans themselves are increasingly content to return home from prolonged stints abroad, the once enviable rite of passage now cut short by global economics and a growing sentiment that home might just be where the fresh start is.

FAST FACTS

- **Area** 21,040 sq km (smallest in Central America)
- **Budget** US$25 to US$30 per day
- **Capital** San Salvador
- **Costs** Budget hotel US$10, bottle of beer US$1.50, three-hour bus ride US$1.60, bean-and-cheese *pupusa* US$0.30, surfboard rental US$10 per day
- **Country Code** ☎ 503
- **Languages** Spanish, Nahuat
- **Money** US dollar (US$)
- **Population** 6.7 million (most populated in Central America)
- **Seasons** Dry (November to April), wet (May to October)
- **Time** GMT minus six hours, no daylight saving time

TRAVEL HINTS

If you want to blend in with locals, travel with a duffel bag and wear neat clothes and long pants. A simple, '*Buenos días/buenas tardes. ¿Como va?*' (Good morning/afternoon. How's it going?) launches any encounter (in the market, a hotel or elsewhere) the right way. It might open doors.

OVERLAND ROUTES

From Guatemala, enter through Anguiatú, San Cristóbal or La Hachadura. From Honduras, El Poy or El Amatillo are best; you can exit El Salvador via Perquín, but you cannot enter there.

HIGHLIGHTS

- **Ruta de las Flores** (p303) Charge the western highlands: hiking *fincas* (plantations), stepping into hot springs and chowing at the weekend food fairs.

- **La Costa del Bálsamo** (p293) Ride great breaks, string a hammock under the palms and soak up the lax atmosphere.

- **Parque Nacional Imposible** (p306) Steal stunning ridgetop views and splash in river pools, while hiking from the park's remote backdoor.

- **Suchitoto** (p319) Scope the weekend arts scene with the hip *capitalinos* in El Salvador's unofficial cultural capital.

- **San Salvador** (p277) Put your hands in the air for Central America's finest nightlife and museums.

- **Off the beaten track** (p317) Put your trust in an ex-guerrilla guide while exploring the rugged territory of the former FMLN stronghold of Perquín.

CURRENT EVENTS

Political change hit El Salvador in March 2009 when the left-wing Frente Farabundo Martí para la Liberación Nacional (FMLN) party – led by former TV journalist Mauricio Funes – rose to power for the first time since its inception as a guerrilla resistance movement. This represented a major victory for democratic process and reconciliation in the country, but whether the Funes administration can live up to its promises of political transparency and widespread social change remains to be seen. A late-2009 split within the opposition Alianza Republicana Nacionalista (Arena) party ensured the short-term future of the new government looks steady. A January 2010 formal apology for the government's role in past atrocities – and full compliance in external investigations – is a step in the right direction.

Despite a 10% slump in 2009, the economy is still too reliant on remittances from abroad (one fifth of the national economy) – rising interest rates have made it more difficult for the American dream to be replicated further south. Microfinance institutions are set to play a bigger role in enabling Salvadorans to better invest their hard-earned overseas capital.

Natural disasters continue to plague the country. In 2005, Hurricane Stan left thousands homeless and killed 69, only days after Volcán Santa Ana erupted, triggering landslides and ruining coffee and other crops. Then in November 2009 the remnants of Hurricane Ida saw 14in of rain drop on central El Salvador in under 24 hours. Two hundred people were killed in the floods, and the re-sulting loss of homes and farmland illustrated the vulnerability of the nation's poor.

HISTORY
Traders & Raiders

Paleo-Indian peoples populated El Salvador as early as 10,000 years ago, literally leaving their mark with cave paintings in modern Morazán. Around 2000 BC the Olmecs followed, leaving as their legacy the Olmec Boulder, a giant head sculpture similar to those from Mexico, found near Casa Blanca.

El Salvador was once a key regional trading center. Archaeological remains reveal diverse influences, from Pipil, Teotihuacan and Maya in the west to Lenca, Chorti and Pok'omama in the east. The step pyramid ruins at Tazumal, San Andrés and Casa Blanca show 3000 years of nearly constant pre-Hispanic habitation.

When Spanish conquistador Pedro de Alvarado arrived in 1524, he saw a country dominated by Pipils, descendants of Toltecs and Aztecs. These northern peoples (from modern-day Mexico) dubbed their home Cuscatlán, 'Land of Jewels.' Their maize-based farming economy flourished enough to support several cities and a sophisticated culture with pursuits that included hieroglyphics, astronomy and mathematics. Their dialect is related to modern Nahuat.

From Indigo to Independence

Spanish rule started with a year-long struggle against the Pipil. The Spaniards prevailed and laid claim to the land, transforming it into plantations of cotton, balsam and indigo. Agriculture boomed throughout the 1700s, with indigo the number-one export. A small group of Europeans, known as the 'fourteen families,' controlled virtually all of the colony's wealth and agriculture, enslaving indigenous peoples and Africans to work the land.

Conflict simmered under this gross imbalance of power. A revolt against Spain in 1811 was led by Padre (Father) José Delgado. While it failed, it planted a seed of discontent. Independence was gained 10 years later, on September 15, 1821, when El Salvador became part of the Central American Federation.

Pushing for land reform, Anastasio Aquino led an indigenous rebellion in 1883. Though it was subdued and Aquino executed, he became a national hero. El Salvador withdrew from the Central American Federation in 1841, but Independence Day continues to be celebrated on September 15.

In Comes Coffee

In the late 19th century, synthetic dyes undermined the indigo market, and coffee took the main stage. A handful of wealthy landowners expanded their properties, displacing more indigenous people. Coffee became the most important cash crop and *cafetaleros* (coffee growers) earned purses full of money that was neither taxed nor redistributed at reasonable wages to the workers. By the 20th century, 95% of El Salvador's income derived from coffee exports, but only 2% of Salvadorans controlled that wealth.

The 20th Century

The vindictive government vigorously eradicated union activity in the coffee industry during the 1920s. In January 1932, Augustín Farabundo Martí, a founder of the Central American Socialist Party, led an uprising of peasants and indigenous people. The military responded brutally by systematically killing anyone who looked indigenous or supported the uprising. La Matanza (the Massacre) resulted in the death of 30,000 individuals, including Martí, who was killed by firing squad. The FMLN (Frente Farabundo Martí para la Liberación Nacional) revolutionary army would later take up his name in his honor.

Over the course of the 1970s, landlessness, poverty, unemployment and overpopulation became serious problems. In government, the polarized left and right tangled for power through coups and electoral fraud. In 1972, José Napoleon Duarte, cofounder of the Christian Democrat Party (Partido Democrático Cristiano; PDC), ran for president supported by a broad coalition of reform groups. When his victory was denied amid allegations of fraud, protests followed. The military averted an attempted coup, and the right responded to increasing guerrilla activity by creating 'death squads.' Thousands of Salvadorans were kidnapped, tortured and murdered.

In 1979 a junta of military and civilians overthrew President Carlos Humberto Romero and promised reforms. When promises were not met, opposition parties banded together as the Frente Democrático Revolucionario (FDR) and allied with the FMLN, a revolutionary army composed of five guerrilla groups for whom armed struggle appeared as the only means of change. The successful revolution in Nicaragua in 1979 had encouraged many Salvadorans to demand reforms. One of them was Monsignor Oscar A Romero, a formerly conservative priest who took up the cause of the people.

On March 24, 1980, outspoken Archbishop Romero was assassinated while saying Mass in the chapel of the San Salvador Divine Providence Cancer Hospital. His murder ignited an armed insurrection that same year that was to turn into a civil war.

Civil War

The rape and murder in late 1980 of four US nuns performing relief work in El Salvador prompted the Carter administration to suspend military aid. But in 1981, the newly elected Reagan administration, bristling from the threat of Nicaragua's socialist revolution, pumped huge sums into the moribund Salvadoran military. Uncle Sam's support would effectively prolong the conflict. When guerrillas gained control of areas in the north and east, the Salvadoran military retaliated by decimating villages. In 1981, the US-trained elite Atlacatl Battalion killed more than 700 men, women and children in El Mozote, Morazán. As many as 300,000 citizens fled the country.

In 1982 Major Roberto D'Aubisson, founder of the extreme-right Arena party, became president of the legislative assembly and enacted a law granting the legislative body power over the president. D'Aubisson created death squads targeting, among others, trade unionists and agrarian reformers. In response, the FMLN offensive blew up bridges, cut power lines and destroyed coffee plantations

EL SALVADOR

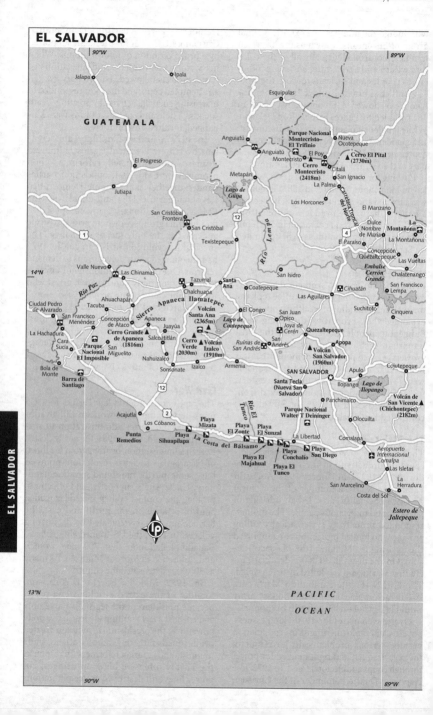

EL SALVADOR

EL SALVADOR

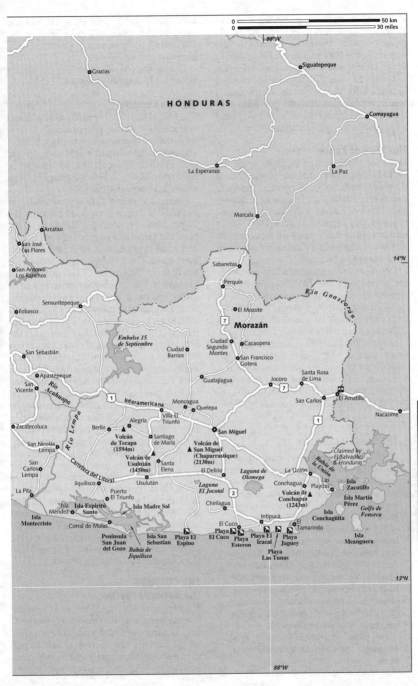

and livestock – anything to stifle the economy. When the government ignored an FMLN peace proposal, the rebels refused to participate in the 1984 presidential elections, in which Duarte won over D'Aubisson. For the next few years the PDC and FMLN engaged in peace talks unsuccessfully. Death squads continued pillaging, and the guerrillas continued to undermine the military powers and jeopardize municipal elections.

The Price of Peace

Hope for peace neared in 1989, when the FMLN offered to participate in elections if the government agreed to a postponement to ensure democratic polls. Its calls were ignored and Alfredo Cristiani, a wealthy Arena businessman, was elected president. The FMLN's response was a major attack on the capital. In retaliation, the military killed an estimated 4000 'leftist sympathizers.'

UN-mediated negotiations began between the government and FMLN in April 1990. Among the first agreements was a human-rights accord signed by both parties. Yet, violent deaths actually increased in 1991 when a UN mission arrived to monitor human rights.

On January 16, 1992, a compromise was finally signed. The FMLN became an opposition party, and the government agreed to various reforms, including dismantling paramilitary groups and death squads, replacing them with a national civil police force.

THE SEARCH GOES ON

When government forces razed villages during the civil war, they didn't always kill everyone. Some children, taken from their mothers' arms or found helpless on the killing field, were spared. Those survivors were given up for adoption and displaced.

The organization Pro-Búsqueda was formed to find displaced children and reconnect them to their original families. Through a combination of DNA tests, family accounts, adoption files and newspaper reports, Pro-Búsqueda has managed to reunite hundreds of families. An estimated 5000 children were displaced by the war, hence Pro-Búsqueda has many cases still pending.

For more information, contact **Pro-Búsqueda** (☎ 2235-1039; www.probusqueda.org.sv).

Land was to be distributed to citizens and human-rights violations to be investigated. But instead, the government gave amnesty to human-rights abusers.

During the course of the 12-year war, an estimated 75,000 people were killed.

Modern Currents

The FMLN has mostly proven to be a model example of a former guerrilla organization transitioning to mainstream politics. Sceptics argued that Salvadorans would always prefer conservatives. However this all changed in 2009 when Mauricio Funes led the FMLN to power in a popular victory.

Gangs are still a national obsession in El Salvador. Funes is expected to revise the 'Super Mano Dura' (Super Hard Hand) approach of his predecessor in tackling the issue, and a jaded public will be scrutinizing his every move. Gang violence again topped the headlines in 2009 when Christian Poveda, a prominent French photographer and filmmaker, was murdered by four members of the notorious, heavily tattooed Mara Salvatrucha (M-18) gang. His documentary, *La vida loca* (Crazy Life), was the result of four years living closely with the gang. Poveda's death was emblematic of a year in which 4365 murders were committed, up a staggering 35% from 2008. President Funes reacted with increased military presence in the most violent gang areas, none of which travelers are likely to see.

The ongoing test for the new administration will be whether or not it can curb the actions of the Mara Salvatrucha (*mara* means 'gang', *trucha* means 'clever trout'). Also known as M-13 and M-18, these gangs of roughly 100,000 across Central America were formed in the US in response to orchestrated attacks by Mexicans. Deported en masse between 2000 and 2004, the *maras* became heavily involved in drug cartels, guns, the sex trade and illegal immigration. Despite countless arrests, the previous government's policy of Super Mano Dura failed to have a lasting impact.

THE CULTURE
The National Psyche

Most travelers who have been to El Salvador rate its people as the best part. Straight-talking, strong-minded and hard-working, Salvadorans are also extremely helpful and almost universally friendly (even gang members can rustle up charm when interviewed).

Salvadorans have a powerful sense of justice and freely express their opinion. The civil war still looms large in the national psyche, as it must – not only are the memories too searing to forget, but many ex-combatants (and their disciples) remain in positions of power. At the same time, Salvadorans are genuinely dismayed to learn that many foreigners know little about El Salvador beyond the war. They will eagerly volunteer information and assistance.

Lifestyle

With a strong work ethic, Salvadorans have quickly raised their country from the wreckage of civil war to nearly the top of Central America's economic ladder. Remittances sent home from Salvadorans living abroad, which annually total US$3 billion (20% of national GDP), provide a significant boost and are changing the way Salvadorans live and work. Poverty and unemployment persist, with 30% of the population below the poverty line, mostly in rural areas. That said, El Salvador enjoys the highest minimum wage in Central America (about US$150 per week) and is notably more prosperous than neighboring countries.

People

Salvadorans show more European physical traits than other Central Americans, due largely to the brutal repression of indigenous people and minor Afro-Caribbean influence. Roughly 94% of the population is *mestizo* (a mixture of Spanish and indigenous) but fair features are not uncommon. Indigenous people are descended from the Pipils, with Toltec and Aztec roots. Government brutality against them has taken its toll, and they now represent only 1% to 5% of the population. Few speak Nahuat or wear traditional dress.

RELIGION

El Salvador, like the rest of Latin America, is experiencing an explosive growth of evangelical churches. Their fiery services seem to have brought fresh energy to faith. Town-square services with booming speakers are becoming an all-too-typical way of spreading 'the word.' Protestant churches now account for 50% of believers, which speaks of frustration with the traditional Catholic Church. Before and during the war, priests and missionaries were often outspoken critics of government repression – many, such as Archbishop Oscar Romero, were killed for their stands.

ARTS

El Salvador's artisan products can be innovative and high-quality. Fernando Llort's Naïve Art (see boxed text, p274) inspired an industry of brightly painted crafts in childlike motifs in the community of La Palma (p323). Guatajiagua (p317) in Morazán produces unique black pottery with a Lenca influence and Ilobasco (p308) is known for its *sorpresas,* intricate miniatures hidden in ceramic shells (see boxed text, p310).

Poetry is beloved in El Salvador. Iconoclast poet Roque Dalton was exiled for radical politics. He eventually returned home to aid the guerrilla cause but was executed by his own side under suspicion that he was a CIA operative. Notable works include *Taberna y otros lugares* (1969), a political vision in verse, and *Miguel Marmol.* Progressive poet Claudia Lars wrote spare, bold erotic poetry and is considered one of the country's foremost writers.

Using the pen name Salarrué, lauded writer Salvador Efraín Salazar Arrué's *Cuentos de barro* (Tales of Mud), published in 1933, marks the beginning of Central America's modern short-story genre. Likewise Manlio Argueta's *One Day of Life* (1980), a tale of a rural famly in the backdrop of the civil war, is considered a modern classic. One of the more interesting contemporary Salvadoran novelists is Horacio Casellanos Moya. His recently translated *Senselessness* (2004) is a burning black comedy about government-sponsored violence. For further information about these and other modern writers, see **Concultura** (www. dpi.gob.sv, in Spanish), the country's official arts and culture board, which has a bibliography of Salvadoran authors.

Films *Romero,* produced by Ellwood Kieser in 1988, and *Salvador,* directed by Oliver Stone, offer Hollywood versions of the civil war.

ENVIRONMENT
The Land

The Land of Volcanoes, El Salvador has two volcanic ranges spanning east to west, spicing the views, as well as daily life, with a little drama. Much of the land is deforested but mountains in the far north are blanketed in pine and oak, jagged rock formations and cloud forests. The Río Lempa bisects the country with a fertile swath of land. While El Salvador is the only Central American country not to have a Caribbean coast, there is over 300km of Pacific coastline bordering mangroves, estuaries and tropical dry forest.

EL SALVADOR

Lakes and freshwater lagoons provide drinking water and recreation.

Wildlife

El Salvador was drastically deforested over the 20th century. As a result, many species of plants and animals ceased to exist in the country. However, national parks and protected lands still maintain good biodiversity.

The country has over 800 animal species. Almost half are butterflies, with bird species second in number, with about 330 resident species (and 170 migratory), including quetzals, toucans, herons, kingfishers, brown pelicans, egrets, parakeets and sandpipers. The remaining mammal species number around 200 and can be seen mostly in reserves. They include opossums, anteaters, porcupines, agoutis, ocelots, spider monkeys and white-tailed deers. In all, about 90 species are in danger of extinction, including marine turtles, armadillos and over 15 types of hummingbird.

With so much of the land cultivated, few original plants still exist. Small stands of balsam trees survive along the western Pacific coast (dubbed the Costa del Bálsamo) and mangroves line many estuaries. Bosque Montecristo and El Imposible offer the widest variety of indigenous plants, and Parque Nacional los Volcanes offers good vegetation. Plants in these areas include mountain pines, oaks, figs, magueys, ferns and orchids.

National Parks & Reserves

El Salvador has only four official national parks, but there are a number of locally or privately administered reserves.

Barra de Santiago A remote bar of mangrove-fringed estuaries and beaches on the Pacific coast. See p305.

Cerro El Pital El Salvador's highest peak. *Torogoz* (blue-crowned motmots) and quetzals can be observed on its piney slopes. See p324.

La Laguna de Alegría An emerald-green lake fed by hot springs, in the crater of dormant Volcán de Tecapa. Ocelots and coatis are among wildlife inhabiting primary growth forest surrounding the lake. See p309.

Laguna El Jocotal This freshwater lagoon east of Usulután is an important sanctuary for migratory birds from October to March. See p309.

Parque Nacional El Imposible Near El Salvador's western limit; one of the last remnants of original tropical forest with waterfalls, views and numerous endangered plant and animal species. See p306.

Parque Nacional Los Volcanes (Cerro Verde) A volcano-crater forest with amazing views of nearby Izalco and Santa Ana volcanoes. Highlights include emerald toucanets, motmots and hummingbirds. See p295.

Parque Nacional Montecristo–El Trifinio A mountainous cloud-forest reserve at the borders of El Salvador, Honduras and Guatemala. Wildlife includes pumas, spider monkeys and agoutis. Giant ferns, orchids and bromeliads are abundant. See p299.

Parque Nacional Walter T Deininger This dry tropical forest on the Pacific coast is the habitat for 87 bird species, deer and pacas. See p291.

Environmental Issues

Overpopulation and the exploitation of the land for export agricultural crops (such as coffee, sugar and cotton) continue to propel El Salvador's massive deforestation. High population density remains the principal obstacle to the regeneration of ecosystems. Today, a mere 17% of the country is forested, with only a minuscule 2% to 5% of that primary forest.

BEHIND THE SCENES OF NAÏVE ART

Holy scenes, strange birds, unabashed rainbow colors: the childlike images of Fernando Llort Choussy have come to symbolize hope in a war-torn Central America. Compared to Miró and Picasso, Llort differs with earnest iconography and flat tropical hues in a style dubbed as primitive modern.

Ironically, this strong Latin American identity was forged when he went to France to study architecture and then theology. Religious symbols are recurring motifs in his artwork. He prefers the rough and everyday to the exalted.

When Llort returned to El Salvador in the early 1970s, he arrived to the tensions and violence leading up to the civil war. Llort moved to La Palma, a distant mountain town in the north, to take refuge. The apparent simplicity of a life in harmony with nature further informed his style. He started La Semilla de Dios (God's seed; p323), a workshop to teach others his craft and professionalize local artisans.

Llort has since lived in San Salvador and abroad, but the workshop is still going strong in his former studio. You can find his work on the face of the Catedral Metropolitana (p280) in San Salvador as well as in the White House, MoMA and the Vatican.

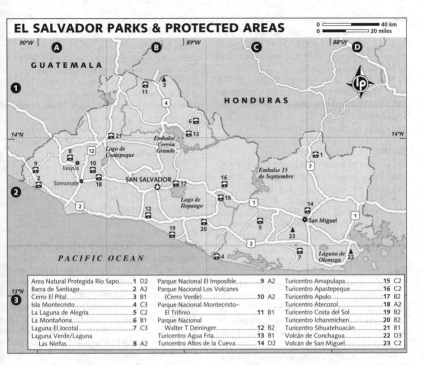

EL SALVADOR PARKS & PROTECTED AREAS

Area Natural Protegida Río Sapo.......**1** D2	Parque Nacional El Imposible..............**9** A2	Turicentro Amapulapa....................**15** C2
Barra de Santiago.............................**2** A2	Parque Nacional Los Volcanes	Turicentro Apastepeque.................**16** C2
Cerro El Pital....................................**3** B1	(Cerro Verde).............................**10** A2	Turicentro Apulo..............................**17** B2
Isla Montecristo................................**4** C3	Parque Nacional Montecristo–	Turicentro Atecozol........................**18** A2
La Laguna de Alegría.......................**5** C2	El Trifinio.................................**11** B1	Turicentro Costa del Sol................**19** B2
La Montañona..................................**6** B1	Parque Nacional	Turicentro Ichanmichen................**20** B2
Laguna El Jocotal.............................**7** C3	Walter T Deininger.....................**12** B2	Turicentro Sihuatehuacán.............**21** B1
Laguna Verde/Laguna	Turicentro Agua Fría.......................**13** B1	Volcán de Conchagua....................**22** D3
Las Ninfas....................................**8** A2	Turicentro Altos de la Cueva...........**14** D2	Volcán de San Miguel.....................**23** C2

As a result, many native species have become endangered or extinct.

Deforestation and unplanned urban sprawl intensify the effects of natural disasters. In recent years El Salvador has been repeatedly pummeled by Mother Nature, producing a laundry list of disasters. In 1998, floods caused by Hurricane Mitch produced 200 fatalities and left 70,000 homeless, acutely damaging the lower Río Lempa. Earthquakes in 2001 brought on landslides and destroyed buildings, killing 1159 people and destroying or damaging almost 300,000 homes.

Before the earthquakes, environmental groups had issued increasingly dire warnings about those very issues for a house-filled hillside in the wealthy neighborhood of Santa Tecla. When the earthquake hit, the slope collapsed, burying dozens of houses and untold numbers of people in a suffocating wall of mud.

The eruption of Santa Ana volcano in October 2005, coupled with Hurricane Stan's torrential rains, unleashed scores of landslides, with the largest loss of life in poor areas built on steep slopes or riverbeds. Likewise in 2009, massive floods killed 200 people and devastated large tracts of land and housing within 50km of the capital.

Río Lempa, a crucial watershed, suffers from pollution, as do many other rivers and lakes. Meanwhile, uncontrolled vehicle emissions challenge urbanites' respiratory functions in any metropolitan area. In 2006, the government vowed to take on the most visible problem – trash. The lack of proper disposal sites means gangs of vultures circling roadside dumps are a common sight.

Violence reached the environmental sector in late 2009 when a third activist was murdered in Cabañas district for trying to block a proposed Pacific Rim gold mine.

TRANSPORTATION

GETTING THERE & AWAY

El Salvador's discerning immigration officials scrutinize entry and exit stamps, so avoid cutting corners. Request a 90-day visa in advance if you'd like one, otherwise you may be given less time.

EL SALVADOR

Air

The **Aeropuerto Internacional Comalpa** (☎ 2339-8264) is located 44km south of San Salvador. A major Latin American hub, it is also a gateway to North American cities.

TACA (☎ 2267-8222), **American Airlines** (☎ 2298-0777), **United Airlines** (☎ 2279-3900), **Continental** (☎ 2207-2040), **Delta Air Lines** (☎ 2275-9292) and **Copa Airlines** (☎ 2209-2672) are among others providing services to El Salvador.

Boat

El Salvador shares the Golfo de Fonseca with Honduras and Nicaragua. Boats occasionally ferry passengers between La Unión (El Salvador), Coyolito, Amapala or San Lorenzo (Honduras), and Potosí (Nicaragua). Going by sea does not save time since there are no scheduled passenger boats and land crossings are relatively close.

Bus

Border crossings to Guatemala are La Hachadura, Las Chinamas, San Cristóbal and Anguiatú. Ordinary buses to the borders leave San Salvador from the Terminal de Occidente, usually connecting through Sonsonate, Santa Ana, Ahuachapán or Metapán.

Border crossings to Honduras include El Poy, El Amatillo and Sabanetas/Perquín. Note that there is no Salvadoran immigration post at Sabanetas/Perquín. It is OK to leave the country here only if you don't plan on returning. Ordinary buses to the border leave from the Terminal de Oriente in San Salvador.

See p288 for more information on international buses leaving from the hotels and Terminal Puerto Bus.

Car & Motorcycle

If you drive into El Salvador, you must show a driver's license (an international driving permit is accepted) and proof that you own the vehicle. You must also fill out extensive forms. Car insurance is available and advisable but not required. Vehicles may remain in El Salvador for 30 days. If you wish to stay longer, it's best to leave the country and drive back in rather than attempt to deal with the Transport Ministry.

GETTING AROUND
Boat

You'll need to use a boat to get around the Bahía de Jiquilisco (p311) in eastern El

---

ENTRY & DEPARTURE TAXES

US citizens and some other nationalities may be required to pay for a US$10 tourist card upon arrival to El Salvador's airport. There's a US$32 departure tax to fly out of the airport, often already included in the cost of your plane ticket. The Central America-4 agreement allows for travel between the borders of Guatemala, Honduras, El Salvador and Nicaragua with one entry fee; for details see p329.

Salvador and for any trips in the Golfo de Fonseca (p316), near La Unión. Otherwise, water transportation is rare.

Bus

Hypercolored American school buses run frequently to points throughout the country and are very cheap (US$0.40 to US$4). Some weekend fares increase up to 25%. Routes to some eastern destinations have different categories: *ordinario, especial* and *super especial*. The latter two options cost more, but they are faster and more comfortable. Most intercity bus services begin between 4am and 5am and end between 6pm and 7pm.

Car & Motorcycle

Most roads in El Salvador are paved, but traffic is not easy to negotiate and roads are not particularly well signed. Gas is not cheap either. A gallon of regular unleaded is about US$3.20.

Police set up checkpoints, especially on roads to border crossings. Carjacking is a problem, as is getting parts stolen off your parked car. Don't drive alone in areas of ill repute and park in safe places. Car insurance is a good idea, but not required.

Rental cars are available in San Salvador and San Miguel. The following are in San Salvador:

Alamo Uno Rent a Car (Map p286; ☎ 2211-2111; Blvd del Hipódromo 426)

Avis (Map p286; ☎ 2261-1212, airport 2339-9268; www.avis.com.sv, in Spanish; 43a Av Sur 127; per day US$40)

Budget (Map p286; ☎ 2260-4333; www.budget.com.sv, in Spanish; 1a Calle Poniente 2765; per day US$35)

Quick Rent a Car (☎ 2229-6959; www.quickrentacar.com.sv, in Spanish) Offers hotel or airport pick up/drop off.

Hitchhiking

Buses or collective pickups go just about anywhere you could want to go, so hitching isn't usually necessary. Both men or women usually hop in the back of pickup trucks, but women might think twice before climbing into a car of only men.

SAN SALVADOR

pop 1.8 million (metropolitan area)

At first glance San Salvador feels like any mid-sized American city, with its wide boulevards prey to chain stores, gas-guzzling 4WDs and endless fast-food joints. But lift your head above the consumerist, smog-filled haze, and you'll find a lush volcanic skyline, the finest nightlife in Central America, a vibrant arts scene leaning hard left, and an *el centro* crackling with friendly, market-driven chaos.

Delaying your jaunt to the countryside will ensure encounters by the barload with straight-talking, hard-working locals who practice a unique blend of reconciliation, resilience and civic pride. This is an open-hearted city: the taxi driver talks of his two decades in Melbourne; the guerrilla-turned-barber is obsessed with *telenovelas;* the poets, painters and engineers dance all night to heavy metal, reggaetón and *cumbia,* and gossip all morning in a tree-lined city park, fine museum, mall or restaurant. There's enough going on here to extend a trip a day or two – like day trips to the festive Pipil neighborhood of Panchimalco or to El Boqueron – especially if you befriend a few *guanacos* (nickname for *salvadoreños*).

Known as *la ciudad de las dos caras de la moneda* (the city of two sides of the coin), San Salvador's huge wealth gap means that crime is a reality. But the hard-core violence is limited to a few neighborhoods east of town, like Soyopango, which is of no interest to most travelers. Follow the lead of locals and move with purpose, which won't be hard when your next brightly painted microbus whizzes around the corner at full throttle.

HISTORY

San Salvador was founded in 1525 by the Spanish conqueror Pedro de Alvarado, about 30km northeast of where it now stands, near Suchitoto. It was moved to its present site three years later, and declared a city in 1546. It was here in San Salvador in 1811 that Father José Matías Delgado first called for Central American independence. Once this was achieved, San Salvador became the capital of the united Provinces of Central America from 1834 to 1839 when El Salvador gained its own independence. It has since been the capital of El Salvador.

Natural disasters have beleaguered the city, including more than a dozen major earthquakes (and hundreds of smaller ones). San Salvador was destroyed by tremors in 1854 and 1873, by the eruption of Volcán San Salvador in 1917 and yet again by floods in 1934. The earthquake of October 10, 1986 caused considerable damage, and the most recent on January 13, 2001 contributed its share.

From assassinations to student protests, San Salvador served as a flashpoint in El Salvador's long civil war. In November 1989, the FMLN's 'final offensive' brought bitter fighting into the city streets. To quell the attack, government forces bombed neighborhoods thought to harbor guerrillas and their supporters. Hundreds of civilians and soldiers on both sides died. After a 26-month stalemate, peace accords were signed in 1992.

Today over a quarter of the population of El Salvador inhabits the metropolitan area of the capital. Though San Salvador produces nearly 65% of the national GDP, unemployment is high and people do whatever they can to get by – vendors of all ages ply the streets and major intersections, selling everything from candy to cell-phone chargers. On buses, vitamins and other supplements are marketed with vigor and creativity.

ORIENTATION

San Salvador follows the same grid pattern as most Central American cities. Unfortunately, signage is sparse in the central area (check for names on the street curbs). From the zero point at the cathedral, Av España goes north and Av Cuscatlán south; Calle Arce runs to the west and Calle Delgado to the east.

Avenidas (avenues) run north–south, and change from Sur (South) to Norte (North) when they cross the major east–west artery (Calles Arce and Delgado). Likewise, avenues are odd- or even-numbered depending on whether they are east or west of the north–south artery (Avs Cuscatlán and España). So, 5a Av Sur is south of Calle Arce and west of Av Cuscatlán (because it's odd-numbered). Calles (streets) are similarly ordered, only using Oriente (East; abbreviated 'Ote') and Poniente (West; abbreviated 'Pun' or 'Pte'). It's confusing to the visitor at first, but you'll quickly learn the orderliness of it. The odd/even thing can be tricky, ie 25a Av is one block from 27a Av, but it is more than 25 blocks from 26a Av!

From the city center, 1a Calle Poniente and Calle Rubén Darío, to the north and south of Arce respectively, are the main roads to the wealthier west.

INFORMATION
Bookstores
Bookmarks (Map p286; www.bookmarks.com.sv; Centro Commercial Basilea, Blvd del Hipódromo) Good range of English-language fiction and guidebooks (including Lonely Planet).

Centro de Intercambio y Solidaridad (CIS; off Map p284; Colonia Libertad, Av Bolivar No 103) This center for peace and social justice has a good library for students and volunteers.

La Ceiba Libros (Map p284; Metrocentro, 1st fl, Blvd de los Héroes) Stock up on Salvadoran history and literature in Spanish here.

Emergency
Police (Map p284; ☎ 2261-0630; Calle Berlin; ☺ 24hr)

Immigration
Immigration office (Direccíon General de Migracíon y Extranjería; Map p281; ☎ 2202-9650, 2221-2111; Paseo General Escalón; ☺ 9am- 5pm Mon-Fri, 9am-1pm Sat) For visa renewal and other immigration matters.

Internet Access
Internet cafes are plentiful along Calle Arce, near the Universidad Tecnológica. Around Blvd de los Héroes check out the following:

Cybercafé Genus (Map p284; Av Izalco 102-A; per hr US$1; ☺ 9am-11pm Mon-Fri, 10am-8pm Sat & Sun)
PC Station (Map p284; MetroSur, Blvd de los Héroes; per hr US$1; ☺ 7am-10pm Mon-Sat, 9am-7pm Sun) Offers web-based international calling.

Near the center:
Ciber Snack (Map p281; cnr 2a Av Sur & 4a Calle Oriente; per hr US$1; ☺ 7:30am-6:30pm Mon-Sat)

Laundry
Lavapronto (Map p284; Calle Los Sisimiles 2944; ☺ 7am-6pm Mon-Fri, 7am-5pm Sat)

Medical Services
Hospital Bloom (off Map p284; ☎ 2225-4114; cnr Blvd de los Héroes & Av Gustavo Guerrero) Public hospital with long lines. Specializes in children's treatment.
Hospital Diagnóstico Escalón (Map p286; ☎ 2264-4422; 3a Calle Poniente) Recommended by the US embassy.

Money
Banks and 24-hour ATMs are found throughout the capital, issuing US dollars.
Banco Credomatic (Map p281 & p284) Branches located in the *centro* and next to the Super Selectos supermarket, in the Centro Comercial San Luis, off Calle San Antonio Abad. Changes traveler's checks or gives cash advances on MasterCard.
Casas de Cambio (Map p281) Changes foreign currency.
Citibank (Map p281) ATMs that accept all cards are located in Metrocentro Mall and Galerías Mall. Branches change traveler's checks and can give cash advances on Visa cards.
Dispensa de Don Juan (Map p281) Near Plaza Barrios, has several ATMs and is probably the most secure place to withdraw money in the *centro*.

GETTING INTO TOWN FROM THE AIRPORT
Shuttles operated by **Taxis Acacya** (Map p281; ☎ airport 2339-9282, in town 2271-4937; cnr 19a Av Norte & 3a Calle Poniente) offer the best way to/from the airport. The trip costs US$5 and takes 45 minutes. In San Salvador, shuttles leave from Taxis Acacya behind the Puerto bus terminal, at 6am, 7am, 10am and 2pm. From the airport, they depart at 9am, 1pm and 5:30pm.

Microbus 138 (US$0.60, 45 minutes to one hour, every 10 minutes) passes the airport – if you remind the driver – traveling to and from the city center. Pick it up just south of Plaza Barrios in town. If heading into town, cut through the parking lot to reach the highway (a 75m walk) and a bus shelter. Once downtown, a taxi costs US$5 to US$8. Bus 30 goes to Metrocentro and Blvd de los Héroes (from Plaza Barrios walk two blocks north, turn right one block to Parque Libertad).

You can also go directly from the airport to La Libertad – it's about the same distance as San Salvador. Take bus 133 to the *puente a Comalapa* (Comalapa overpass) a few minutes away. A path leads up onto the intersecting road; from there it's 100m to the town of Comalapa, where bus 187 or 495 goes every 20 minutes to La Libertad (US$0.35).

A taxi between San Salvador or La Libertad and the airport costs US$25 – don't bother trying to bargain.

SAN SALVADOR

EL SALVADOR

SIGHTS & ACTIVITIES		
Centro Monseñor Romero	**1**	B4
Hospital La Divina Providencia (El Hospitalito)	**2**	C2
Jardín Botánico La Laguna	**3**	B4
Melida Anaya Montes/Spanish Language School	**4**	D1
TRANSPORT		
Terminal de Oriente	**5**	F2

Post

Correos Central (Map p281; Centro Gobierno; 🕑 7:30am-5pm Mon-Fri, 8am-noon Sat) A smaller branch is in Metro-centro by the Blvd de los Héroes entrance (Map p284).

Tourist Information

Corsatur (off Map p279; ☎ 2243-7835; www.elsalvador. travel; 🕑 8am-12:30pm, 1:30-5:30pm) Inconveniently located outside the city; luckily it has an excellent new website.

Instituto Salvadoreño de Turismo (ISTU; Map p281; ☎ 2222-8000; istu@mh.gob.sv; Calle Rubén Darío 619; 🕑 8:30am-noon, 1-4pm Mon-Sat) General information about El Salvador's national parks and *turicentros*.

Ministerio de Trabajo's Auxiliary Office (Map p286; ☎ 2209-3700; Paseo General Escalón 19; 🕑 8am-12:30pm, 1:30-4pm Mon-Fri) Issues permits to stay at the four government-run workers' vacation centers in Lago de Coatepeque, El Tamarindo, La Palma and La Libertad. Apply here in person with your passport and the number of people in your group. Plan your stay between Wednesday and Saturday (the centers are closed other days), and workers get weekend preference.

Peace Corps (Map p286; ☎ 2208-2911; www.peacecorps. gov; Calle Las Dalias 3; 🕑 9am-4.30pm Mon-Fri) If you want to get off the beaten track, this US-based organisation may be a good resource. Volunteers are very receptive to visitors.

SalvaNatura (Map p286; ☎ 2279-1515; www.salva natura.org, in Spanish; 33 Av Sur 640; 🕑 8am-12:30pm, 2-5:30pm Mon-Fri) Friendly and helpful staff manage Parque Nacional El Imposible and Parque Nacional los Volcanes. Call before visiting either park.

Tourist police (☎ 2298-9983)

DANGERS & ANNOYANCES

Crime is still a serious problem in San Salvador. Travel light, avoid wearing flashy jewelry and watches, and stay aware of your belongings, especially on buses, in market areas and among street crowds. If you are robbed, just hand over the goods. Always take taxis after 8pm. The center is off-limits for walking around at night, along with Parque Cuscatlán. Ample nightlife lines Calle San Antonio Abad and Blvd de los Héroes, but take a cab to get to your hotel, even if it's just around the corner.

Pollution is a consistent pest, seemingly set in place by the surrounding mountains. Thick vehicle exhaust, especially from buses, can leave you with runny eyes and a sore throat.

Accidents between cars and pedestrians are frequent and frightening. Be extra-careful crossing the street. Pedestrians don't have the right of way and no car will chivalrously cede it to you.

PEOPLE PACKING HEAT

Enter El Salvador and you'll wonder if you've stumbled onto an National Rifle Association convention. Banks, hotels and even bikini boutiques are patrolled by clean-shaven guards packing M16s and 9mm pistols. While the war is long over, this security-obsessed country employs over 18,000 security guards. In addition, there are countless private citizens accessorizing with arms, easily purchased in gun shops at the mall among the boutiques.

Of the estimated 500,000 firearms in El Salvador, 60% are illegal. The stricter measures of President Saca's Super Mano Dura (Super Hard Hand) policy created more arrests but few convictions. The pressure is on incumbent Mauricio Funes to come up with a new strategy, such as a nationwide amnesty on illegal weapons.

SIGHTS
City Center

El centro overloads the senses with blaring beats, sputtering traffic and crowds squeezing through the artery of busy markets. It is far more interesting than the sterile suburbs, and long-term makeovers are finally starting to bear fruit. The main plaza is **Plaza Barrios**, where local protests usually begin or end. Two blocks east is **Parque Libertad**, where a winged statue of Liberty holds court.

CATEDRAL METROPOLITANA

Fernando Llort painted the colorful *campesino* motif facade of this beige stucco building (Map p281). Its blue-and-yellow-checked dome faces Plaza Barrios and marks the center of the city's street grid. More or less completed in 1999 after years of renovation, the cathedral stands on the site of an earlier version that burned in 1956. Archbishop Oscar A Romero's tomb is underneath, visited by Pope John Paul II in March 1993.

IGLESIA EL ROSARIO

If you only see one church (Map p281) in El Salvador – and there are *plenty* to choose from – check out this rare non-colonial structure with a rainbow of colored glass across its belly. The soaring arched roof covers a unique interior adorned with scrap-metal figures. More stone and metal statues stand on the side across from the entrance. The father of Central American independence, Padre Delgado, is buried here.

OTHER HISTORIC BUILDINGS

Government headquarters before the devastating 1986 earthquake, the ornate **Palacio Nacional** (Map p281) occupies the west side of Plaza Barrios. Built in the early 20th century of Italian marble, the palace displays the classical style fashionable at the time. The imposing **Biblioteca Nacional** (Map p281) is on the plaza's south end. The **Teatro Nacional** (Map p281), east from the cathedral along Delgado, was erected in 1917 and functioned as a movie house for 50-odd years before an opulent renovation added ornate gilt boxes, sensuous ceiling mural and red velvet galore. West down 6a

Calle Poniente, you'll see the Gothic towers of the decaying **Iglesia El Calvario** (Map p281).

West of the Center

Calle Rubén Darío heads west from the center, changing names a couple of times along the way. Bus 52 rumbles down the entire length of this road. When the street is Alameda Roosevelt, it passes pleasant **Parque Cuscatlán** (Map p286), where women sell *pupusas* and kids kick soccer balls. Further along, it passes **Estadio Flor Blanca** (Map p286), the national stadium, where soccer matches and the occasional rock concert are held. At 65a Av, you come to **Plaza Las Américas** (Map p286), with the statue **El Salvador del Mundo** (Map p286). Continuing west the road becomes Paseo

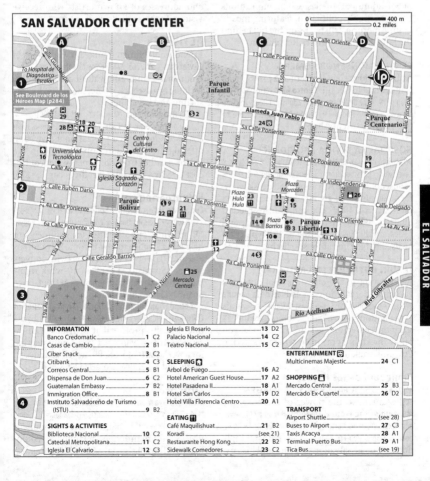

SAN SALVADOR CITY CENTER

EL SALVADOR

Gral Escalón, going through the fashionable Colonia Escalón. Further west you hit Plaza Masferrer.

MUSEO NACIONAL DE ANTROPOLOGÍA DAVID J GUZMÁN

This outstanding anthropology **museum** (Map p286; Av La Revolución; admission US$3; 9:30am-5pm Tue-Sun) has two floors of well-presented exhibits on the Maya and Salvadoran history, arts and economy. The ceremonial pottery is a highlight, as are the prehistoric rock carvings outside. All explanations are in Spanish.

MUSEO DE ARTE DE EL SALVADOR (MARTE)

The modern-art **museum** (Map p286; adult/student US$3/1; 10am-6pm Tue-Sun) is a good overview of Salvadoran aesthetics. Changing exhibits are often highly politicized, featuring mostly Latin American artists. It's up the hill behind the large Monumento a la Revolución.

CENTRO MONSEÑOR ROMERO

At Universidad Centroamericana José Simeón Cañas (La UCA), the **Centro Monseñor Romero** (Map p279; Calle de Mediterraneo; admission free; 8am-noon & 2-6pm Mon-Fri, 8-11:30am Sat) pays homage to the martyred archbishop.

HOSPITAL LA DIVINA PROVIDENCIA

Also known as **El Hospitalito** (Map p279; cnr Av 'B' & Calle Toluca; admission free; usually 8am-noon & 2-5pm) Monseñor Romero was assassinated by government agents while giving mass in this chapel on March 24, 1980. You can tour his modest quarters, where his blood-soaked shirt and robes are displayed, as well as the typewriter he used to type his famously stirring homilies.

JARDÍN BOTÁNICO LA LAGUNA

A revelation in the city, this cool botanical garden, otherwise known as **Plan de la Laguna** (Map p279; admission US$1; 9am-5:30pm Tue-Sun) sits at the bottom of a volcanic crater. Take bus 44 from the center, and ask the driver to let you off at the right spot, from where it's a 1km downhill walk to the garden.

Boulevard de los Héroes

MUSEO DE LA PALABRA Y LA IMAGEN

A testament to the power of memory, the **Museum of the Word & Image** (off Map p284; www.museo.com.sv; 27 Av Norte 1140; admission US$1; 8am-noon & 2-5pm Mon-Fri, 8am-noon Sat) painstakingly documents El Salvador's culture and history.

Modern-art installations and black-and-white war photos sit alongside portraits of indigenous groups and women in history. Director Carlos Henríquez Consalvi, a Venezuelan-born journalist, was the founder and front voice for the pro-guerrilla Radio Venceremos.

MUSEO DE ARTE POPULAR

A little gem of a **museum** (Map p284; Av San José 125; admission US$1; 10am-5pm Tue-Sat) dedicated to El Salvador's quirky folk art. Discover weaving techniques and the history of *sorpresas*, miniature scenes of life hidden under carved forms of eggs or fruit (see p310). *Cuadros* (paintings) depict village life, more recently including humorous takes on illegal immigration or marriage and sex. Ask for the names and addresses of known artists who receive visitors to their village workshops.

ACTIVITIES

Friendly and bilingual Julio and Gabi Vega of **Akwaterra** (2263-2211; www.akwaterra.com) offer tailor-made land- and water-based ecotours, including horseback riding, mountain biking, surfing and kayaking.

El Salvador Divers (Map p286; 2264-0961; www.elsalvadordivers.com; 3A Calle Poniente; 9am-6.30pm Mon-Fri, 9am-1pm Sat) is a professional dive shop offering dives in Lago Ilopango and in the Pacific near Los Cóbanos. Open-water courses cost US$365, two-tank fun dives cost US$75.

Volunteering

Centro de Intercambio y Solidaridad (CIS; 2235-1330; www.cis-elsalvador.org; Colonia Libertad, Av Bolivar 103) provides opportunities for volunteers to help teach English to low-income Salvadorans (see p329) or observe elections (with conversational Spanish). There's a 10-week minimum commitment and teachers get half-price Spanish classes in return.

Foundation for International Medical Relief of Children (FIMRC; www.fimrc.org; Las Delicias) is a US-based micro-health project that provides medical services in disadvantaged areas. Volunteering for a week starts at US$500, which includes all meals and lodging at Posada Del Rey I.

COURSES

Mélida Anaya Montes Spanish Language School (CIS; Map p279; 2235-1330; www.cis-elsalvador.org; Colonia Libertad, Av Bolivar 103), named after a prominent FMLN commander, is a language school that incorporates social and political themes.

Language classes meet for four hours daily and cost US$115 per week, plus a one-time US$25 application fee and a US$10 administration fee. Homestays for US$80 a week, including two meals per day, are available.

SLEEPING

Zona Rosa and Colonia Escalón have the city's best hotels and nightlife. Safe and convenient, the Blvd de los Héroes area offers reasonable lodgings close to the Universidad Nacional and some good eating options. The shady streets around the Universidad Tecnológica (south of the Puerto bus terminal) offer easy access to the airport shuttle and international buses. The city center is convenient for markets but not much else.

City Center

With most rooms let by the hour and the sketch-factor high at night, the *centro* (Map p281) is the preference of few travelers.

Hotel San Carlos (☎ 2222-4603; Calle Concepción 121; r per person US$15) You'd probably stay here due to its proximity to the Tica bus terminal. This dive sports pancake-thin mattresses in cramped rooms – at least they're decently clean and have private bathrooms.

Near Universidad Tecnológica

This area west of *el centro* (Map p281) is safer and more relaxed than downtown, with lots of cheap eats and internet cafes. It's convenient to the Terminal Puerto Bus for international buses. Take taxis at night.

Hotel Pasadena II (☎ 2221-4786; 3a Calle Poniente 1037; s/d with fan US$12/17) Pasadena II is an affordable choice with friendly service and an array of abodes ranging from cramped and noisy to spacious and quiet. Look around for the better rooms. There's a reasonable restaurant facing the street.

Hotel Villa Florencia Centro (☎ 2221-1706; www.hotelvillaflorencia.com, in Spanish; 3a Calle Poniente 1023; s/d/tr US$13/19/21) Undoubtedly the best place to stay around the center, the friendly management at this bargain colonial hotel ensures the small rooms with terracotta tiles are freshly presented. The sunny courtyard is decked with antique bits and bobs, while the upstairs restaurant serves cheap meals (*carne asada,* or roasted beef, is US$2) and plays the evening *telenovelas.*

Hotel American Guest House (☎ 271-0224; 17 Av Norte 119; s/d US$15/17, with bathroom US$20/25) This vintage cheap sleep is run by a lovely elderly couple who take full responsibility for the floral wallpaper and post-period furniture. Rooms are very big for the price, and the leafy balcony restaurant is a good place to chill.

Arbol de Fuego (☎ 2275-7065; www.arboldefuego.com; Av Antiguo Cuscatlan, Colonia La Sultana; s US$45-55, d US$55-65, all incl breakfast; 🍴 🖳) The 'Fire Tree' is a great choice if you need to recharge the travel batteries. The rooms are brightly painted and well decked out with locally sourced linens and artwork, and loads of fresh flowers. The shared balconies are green and inviting.

Boulevard de los Héroes

You can easily walk to bars and restaurants on Calle San Antonio Abad or Blvd Universitario, or down to Metrocentro mall. Buses to the bus terminals, Zona Rosa and the center (and from there, the airport) all pass here. All listings are on Map p284.

La Estancia (☎ 2275-3381; Av Cortés 216; dm/d US$8/20; 🖳) A Peace Corps favorite with a more welcoming feel than your average hostel, La Estancia is run by the energetic Doña Ana. This unmarked lilac-trim house is accommodating to shoestringers – free coffee, communal kitchen, plus a relaxed patio and TV room. Private rooms with TV, bathrooms

---

A DAY IN THE ART OF A CITY

Aside from the usual museums and galleries, visit the cathedral (p280) downtown for the image of the Madre del Salvador, a 17th-century polychrome wooden sculpture that was a gift of Queen Sofia of Spain, and an extraordinary tabernacle with images taken from the first engravings done in America. If you visit the Jardín Botánico La Laguna (p282) in Antiguo Cuscatlán you can walk up to the charming town plaza, which has a nice church and famous *pupuserias*. The **Sala Nacional de Arte** is at Parque Cuscatlán – it always has interesting exhibitions. Finally, if you're a bit adventurous, then visit sculptor **Guillermo Perdomo's studio** in Santo Tomas on the ridge of Lago Ilopango's crater. You will be personally received by the artist and his wife Bettina (bettina deperdomo@hotmail.com). It's an unforgettable view of the lake, the Pacific Ocean and the city.

and faux-wood paneling are excellent value for couples. Dorms are very cramped.

Casa de Huéspedes Tazumal (☎ 2235-0156; www.hoteltazumalhouse.com; 35a Av Norte 3; s/d US$23/30, with air-con US$25/33, with bathroom US$25/30, with bathroom & air-con US$30/40; 💻) In a safe neighborhood with a handful of good sleeping options, Tazumal stands out for its professional, friendly service

and spotless rooms. Beds are firm and new, and the bathrooms befit a far more expensive hotel. Guests get free internet and water bottle refills, yummy breakfast in a cute courtyard and unofficial updates on San Salvador's social scene.

Hostal San José (☎ 2235-0156; www.sanjosehostal.com; Blvd Universitario 2212; s/d US$32/42; 💻) This fine

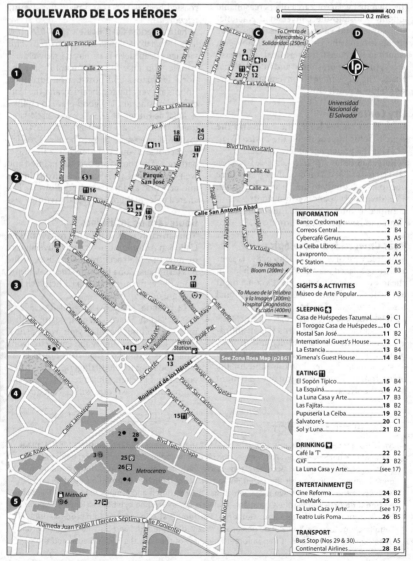

BOULEVARD DE LOS HÉROES

0 ——— 400 m
0 ——— 0.2 miles

INFORMATION	
Banco Credomatic	**1** A2
Correos Central	**2** B4
Cybercafé Genus	**3** A5
La Ceiba Libros	**4** B5
Lavapronto	**5** A4
PC Station	**6** A5
Police	**7** B3

SIGHTS & ACTIVITIES	
Museo de Arte Popular	**8** A3

SLEEPING 🏠	
Casa de Huéspedes Tazumal	**9** C1
El Torogoz Casa de Huéspedes	**10** C1
Hostal San José	**11** B2
International Guest's House	**12** C1
La Estancia	**13** B4
Ximena's Guest House	**14** B4

EATING 🍴	
El Sopón Típico	**15** B4
La Esquina	**16** A2
La Luna Casa y Arte	**17** B3
Las Fajitas	**18** B2
Pupusería La Ceiba	**19** B2
Salvatore's	**20** C1
Sol y Luna	**21** B2

DRINKING 🍷	
Café la 'T'	**22** B2
GXF	**23** B2
La Luna Casa y Arte	(see 17)

ENTERTAINMENT 🎭	
Cine Reforma	**24** B2
CineMark	**25** B5
La Luna Casa y Arte	(see 17)
Teatro Luis Poma	**26** B5

TRANSPORT	
Bus Stop (Nos 29 & 30)	**27** A5
Continental Airlines	**28** B4

EL SALVADOR

hostel, located in a quiet, well-loved house on a quiet, leafy street, is popular with locals and travelers alike. The rooms are neat and moderately stylish with firm beds and big windows. Bathrooms are spotless, breakfast is delicious and there's a free bus pick-up service.

Also recommended:

Ximena's Guest House (☎ 260-2481; www.ximenas guesthouse.com; Calle San Salvador 202; dm US$8-10, d US$35; 🖳) Old stalwart of indie travel scene, struggling to age gracefully.

International Guest's House (☎ 2226-7343; i_guest house@hotmail.com; 35a Av Norte 9 Bis; s/d US$23/40; 🖳) Across the road from Tazumal; popular with groups.

El Torogoz Casa de Huéspedes (☎ 2235-4172; eltoro goz@telsal.net; 35a Av Norte 7B; s/d incl breakfast US$28/45; 🖳 🖳) Relaxed family hotel next to the International.

Zona Rosa & Colonia Escalón

Casa Huéspedes de Australia (Map p286; ☎ 223-7905; Blvd Venezuela 3093; s US$20, s/d with air-con US$30/35; 🅿 🖳) María Lidia oversees this consistently popular hostel in a relaxed and convenient neighborhood. The communal hallways are bright and loungy. Breakfast (US$2) is huge.

Hotel Villa Florencia Zona Rosa (Map p286; ☎ 2257-0236; www.hotelvillaflorencia.com, in Spanish; Av La Revolución; s/d/tr incl breakfast US$41/53/73; 🅿 ✂ 🖳) The fancier Villa Florencia – the other is located downtown (see p283) – is one of the best midrange hotels in San Salvador. The rooms are pokey but well conceived, with gold decor and fancy fittings, plus there's a lovely stone courtyard and tasty cafeteria. Service is astute.

La Posada del Rey I (Map p286; ☎ 2264-5245; www. posadadelreyprimero.com, in Spanish; Pasaje Dordelly, Colonia Escalón; s/d/tr US$47/70/93; ✂ 🖳) The 'King' makes no appearance at this secluded hotel fitted with landscape paintings that mirror the gorgeous 2nd-floor views. Rooms are busy with carved furniture, blue-washed walls and ornate, comfortable bedding. The pretty courtyard restaurant is sluggish with service.

Suites Las Palmas (Map p286; ☎ 2250-0800; www. hotelsuiteslaspalmas.com.sv; Blvd El Hipódromo, Colonia San Benito; r/ste incl breakfast US$55/75; ✂ 🖳 🖳) These swanky suites are a bargain for groups spending a night on the Zona Rosa tiles. King-sized beds, plus a generous living area with fold-out sofas and flashy bathrooms. Views from the rooftop pool are outstanding.

Hotel Vista Marella (Map p286; ☎ 2263-4931; www. hotel-vista-marella.123.com.sv; Calle San Juan José Canas, Colonia Escalón; s/d incl breakfast US$55/65; 🖳 🖳) The midrange choice of seasoned expats.

EATING

City Center & Around

The center has plenty of eateries but few standouts. For a quick bite check out the **sidewalk comedores** (Map p281; mains US$1-3) a block west of Plaza Barrios dishing up *panes de pollo* (big chicken sandwiches) and *bistec encebollada* (onion grilled beef).

Café Maquilishuat (Map p281; Simáu Centro, 1st fl; mains US$2-6; ☯ 7:30am-7pm) The pick of the inner-city eateries is this super busy, pristine *típica* joint with a steady flow of diners enjoying daily meat and dessert specials and huge glasses of *horchata* (malted milk) and *atole* (cinnamon rice milk).

Koradi (Map p281; ☎ 2221-2545; 9a Av Sur; mains US$2-4; ☯ 11am-7pm) A little streetside vegetarian gem, with delicious *carne asada de soya* (soy-bean 'meat,' US$3) and a counterful of fresh tamales and salads. It's easy to miss.

Típicos Margoth (Map p286; ☎ 2278-6632; Paseo Escalón; mains US$3-5; ☯ 11am-10pm) An assembly line of smiling cooks churns out local fare to local folk seated in brightly lit cafe-style booths. It's a fun way to initiate yourself in Salvadoran cuisine.

Shen Zhuan (Map p286; ☎ 2243-0424; 5 Av La Revolucion; mains US$4-7; ☯ 11am-10pm Tue-Sun) This fresh and tasty Taiwanese vegetarian restaurant next door to the Villa Florencia Zona Rosa is so soulful you can catch the good vibrations from the front door. The *fideo ulong* (udon noodles) are the star, as is the handmade tofu.

Restaurante Hong Kong (Map p281; 9a Av Sur; mains US$4-9; ☯ lunch & dinner) Negotiate the sticky floor and the 100-capacity seating plan to find 10 bored waitresses, blaring televisions and a long tradition of no-fuss universal Chinese food. The vegetable chow mein (US$5) is pretty good, as are the *licuados* (fruit shakes).

Barrukada (Map p286; ☎ 2264-8547; 3 Calle Poniente Colonia Escalón; mains US$6-12; ☯ noon-1am Tue-Sun) A new American-style sports bar under an open-air thatched roof where staff bounce around serving big plates of barbecued ribs, fresh fish and ice-cold beer. Big screens show basketball, baseball and long-lost music videos.

Also recommended:

Le Croissant (Map p286; 1a Calle Poniente 3883; Colonia Escalón; pastries US$1-3; ☯ 7:30am-6:30pm) Chain patisserie worth following.

Deli Crepe (Map p286; ☎ 2102-4959; Blvd Hipódromo; mains US$2-4; ☯ 9am-4pm Mon-Sat) Tiny, cheap *típico* place in Zona Rosa.

EL SALVADOR

EL SALVADOR

ZONA ROSA

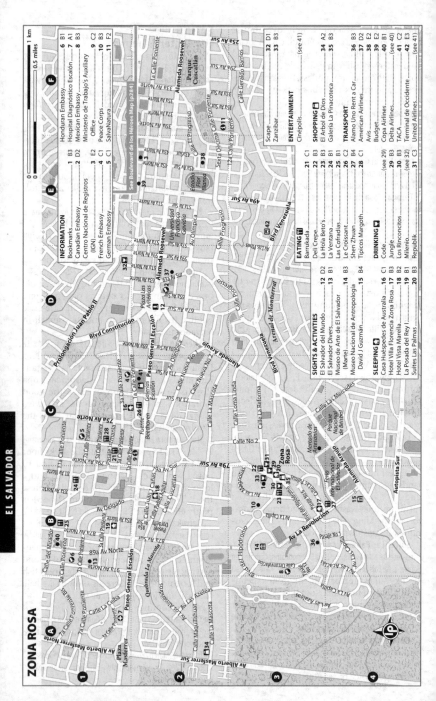

0   0.5 miles
0   1 km

See Boulevard de los Héroes Map (p284)

La Ventana (Map p286; ☎ 2264-4885; 83 Av Norte; mains US$5-12; ☽ 8-1am Tue-Sat, 10-1am Sun) American breakfasts and German sausages at this happening bar-restaurant.

Las Cofradías (Map p286; ☎ 2264-6148; Calle de Mirador, Colonia Escalón; buffet US$7; ☽ dinner) *Tradición del campo* and other Salvadoran specialities.

La Hola Beto's (Map p286; Blvd del Hipódromo; mains US$8-20; ☽ lunch & dinner) Great new location for this booming sushi and *marisco* (seafood) bar.

Boulevard de los Héroes

Calle San Antonio Abad has the best dining options but the many spots in and around the Metrocentro mall are clean and convenient. All listings are on Map p284.

Pupusería La Ceiba (Calle San Antonio Abad; mains US$1-3; ☽ Mon-Sat) Whether you're grabbing a dollar breakfast of tamales, coffee and eggs or downing a few hot *pupusas*, this corner cafe is a bargain.

Sol y Luna (cnr Blvd Universitario & Av C; mains US$2-4; ☽ 8am-5:30pm) Enjoy rare vegetarian fare served cafeteria-style. Loaves of cashew-almond bread, salads and fruit shakes round out the options. You can also purchase hard-to-find health supplements.

La Esquiná (Calle San Antonio Abad; mains US$2-5; ☽ 7:30am-5pm Mon-Sat) A cross-section of San Salvador enjoys the welcoming atmosphere and top-notch *comida a la vista* at this breezy 'corner' restaurant. The black-and-white cement floor keeps the place cool, as do the cruisy jazz tunes.

La Luna Casa y Arte (☎ 2260-2921; www.lalunacasayarte.com; Calle Berlín 228; mains US$2-7; ☽ noon-2am Mon-Fri, 4:30pm-2am Sat) The city's coolest arts venue (see below) also prepares sublime bar food, including thick toasted sandwiches and a superb *plato de bocas mixtas* featuring sausages, quail eggs, hearts of palm and chunks of cheese.

El Sopón Típico (cnr Pasajes las Palmeras & los Almendros; mains US$5; ☽ 10:30am-9pm) Taxi drivers, teenagers and families fill up the wooden benches at this revered corner restaurant where friendly staff slave behind an open grill. Anything with meat in it – rabbit, rooster, goat – is to kill for.

Also recommended:

Las Fajitas (Blvd Universitario; mains US$4-8; ☽ lunch & dinner) Popular Tex-Mex with an open kitchen.

Salvatore's (35a Av Norte; mains US$4-7; ☽ lunch & dinner) Quality pizza and pasta.

DRINKING
Bars & Clubs

La Luna Casa y Arte (Map p284; ☎ 2260-2921; www.lalunacasayarte.com; Calle Berlín 228; ☽ noon-2am Mon-Fri, 4:30pm-2am Sat) Get out of your hotel room, put on your finest beret and pointy shoes and get your conservative backside to the hippest bar in town. As the patrons say, '*no importa como llegues, la onda es llegar*' (who cares how you get here, the vibe is to arrive). Check out the website for the weekly rotation of live music, as well as free films and live poetry. The food (see left) is good too.

Café La 'T' (Map p284; Calle San Antonio Abad 2233; ☽ 10am-9:30pm Mon-Wed, 10am-11pm Thu-Sat) This is a little lefty cafe with live music (jazz or folk) on some Fridays (US$2) and free films on Wednesday and Thursday at 7:30pm. There's light food, beer and wine, and fine coffee.

La Ventana (Map p286; ☎ 2264-4885; 83 Av Norte 510; mains US$5-12; ☽ noon-midnight Mon-Thu, noon-1am Fri & Sat, 8am-10pm Sun) Lively and upmarket, this social hive continues to be a perennial local favorite with cheap Belgian ales and German beers. At 9a Calle Poniente.

Los Rinconcitos (Map p286; Blvd del Hipódromo 310; 6pm-1am Wed-Sat) A sophisticated party set stew over stiff drinks and tapas at this former karaoke bar that sees Latin rock steal the stage on weekends. Head out back for some intimate outdoor entertainment.

Jungle (Map p286; ☎ 2124-7341; Blvd del Hipódromo; ☽ 10pm-7am Thu-Sat) When only the dirtiest nightclub will do. It opens late and closes in time for *desayuno* (breakfast).

Also recommended:

Zanzibar (Map p286; ☎ 2279-0833; Centro Commercial Basilea; ☽ 11am-1am) Latin fusion, mostly.

Republik (Map p286; ☽ 2pm-1am Wed-Sun) Brass knobs and faux-oak panels. Good *mojitos* (US$5) too.

Code (Map p286; Blvd del Hipódromo; ☽ 10pm-7am Thu-Sat) Next to Jungle, though more classy. Sort of.

GXF (Map p284; Calle San Antonio Abad 2249; ☽ 10pm-5am Thu-Sat) A new reggaetón bar on the San Antonio strip.

Gay & Lesbian Venues

Scape & Milenio (Map p286; Condominios Juan Pablo II; ☽ 9:30pm-1am Thu-Sat) Two gay bar-discos in the same building. On Prolongación Juan Pablo II.

ENTERTAINMENT

Look for *Diario de Hoy*'s Thursday pullout section *Planeta Alternativa* for weekly concert and event listings.

Cinemas

Hollywood films with Spanish subtitles dominate the theaters while some bars listed earlier have alternative movie nights. Major

EL SALVADOR

ASK A LOCAL

Live music in San Salvador rocks! Right now the coolest bands in the country are REDD (traditional rock), Friguey (new wave ska), Esquina Opuesta (progressive rock), Los Remedios (reggae), Edicion Limitada (pop rock) and Los Tachos (new wave ska).

Letty, San Salvador

newspapers have schedules, as does www. multicinema.com.sv. Wednesday is half price.

Cine Reforma (Map p284; ☎ 2225-9588; Blvd Universitario) Discounts on random Tuesdays.

CineMark (Map p284; ☎ 2261-2001; Metrocentro, 3rd fl, Blvd de los Héroes; admission US$3)

Cinépolis (Map p286; Galerías Escalóon) An 11-screen megaplex.

La Luna Casa y Arte (Map p284; ☎ 2260-2921; www. lalunacasayarte.com, in Spanish; Calle Berlín 228; admission free) Screenings at 8pm Wednesday.

Multicinemas Majestic (Map p281; ☎ 2222-5965; Av España; admission US$1.75)

Theater

Teatro Luis Poma (Map p284; ☎ 2261-1029; Metrocentro; admission US$5) A modern playhouse with great offerings, strangely set at the mall.

SHOPPING

The country's most definitive artist is La Palma painter Fernando Llort (see boxed text, p274). His gallery **El Arbol de Dios** (Map p286; Calle la Mascota; admission free; ⏰ 9am-9:30pm Mon-Sat) houses an extensive collection of his work, including sophisticated pieces that differ from his simpler, better-known wood paintings. It's four long blocks south of Plaza Masferrer.

Galería La Pinacoteca (Map p286; ☎ 2223-2808; www.lapinacoteca.net; Blvd El Hipódromo 305, Zona Rosa) The best independent gallery in the city, featuring both rising and established Salvadoran painters and sculptors, and the irrepressible curator, Ana Lynn de Lima.

The former army barracks is now the **Mercado Ex-Cuartel** (Map p281; Calle Delgado; ⏰ 7:30am-6pm Mon-Sat, 7:30am-2pm Sun) where *artesaños* from across the country hawk their wares – hammocks and embroidered fabrics are the go. The nearby **Mercado Central** (Map p281; Calle Delgado; ⏰ 7:30am-6pm Mon-Sat, 7:30am-2pm Sun) is the locals' favorite for clothes and electronics.

The newest 'lifestyle center,' **La Gran Vía** (off Map p279), is actually a very pleasant

mall experience, with good nightclubs and restaurants.

GETTING THERE & AWAY
Air
Aeropuerto Internacional Comalpa (off Map p279), 50km southeast of San Salvador, is a major Central American hub. Airline offices in San Salvador include the following:

American Airlines (Map p286; ☎ 2298-0777; Edificio La Centroamericana, Alameda Roosevelt)

Continental Airlines (Map p284; ☎ 2207-2040; Metrocentro, 2nd fl)

Copa Airlines (Map p286; ☎ 2209-2672; World Trade Center I, cnr 89a Av Norte & Calle del Mirador)

Delta Airlines (Map p286; ☎ 2275-9292; World Trade Center I, cnr 89a Av Norte & Calle del Mirador)

TACA (Map p286; ☎ 2267-8222; Galerías Escalón, street level)

United Airlines (Map p286; ☎ 2279-3900; Galerías Escalón, street level)

Bus
In San Salvador international buses leave from **Terminal Puerto Bus** (Map p281; cnr Alameda Juan Pablo II & 19a Av Norte). Take city bus 29, 101D, 7C or 52 to get there.

King Quality (☎ 2271-1361; www.kingqualityca. com) offers deluxe service to Guatemala City from the Terminal Puerto Bus, featuring aircon, movies and a meal (US$33 one way, five hours), departing at 6am and 3:30pm. It also has daily services to San José (US$62, 18 hours) leaving at 3:30am. For Honduras, air-conditioned buses leave every day for Tegucigalpa at 6am and 3pm (US$28, six hours) and San Pedro Sula at 5am and 12:30pm (one way/round trip US$28/41, six hours).

Tica Bus (☎ 2222-4808; www.ticabus.com; ⏰ 8am-4:30pm) has service to Guatemala City at 6am (one way/round trip US$15/30, five hours) from the Hotel San Carlos (p283). Reserve one to two days in advance and arrive at the San Carlos a half-hour early. Tica Bus is inside the hotel. From Guatemala City it continues to the Mexican border at Tapachula, Chiapas. From San Salvador, the trip takes 12 hours and costs US$30.

Tica Bus leaves the Hotel San Carlos at 5:30am and arrives in Managua, Nicaragua, at 3:30pm (US$30 one way). The bus arrives in San José, Costa Rica, between 3pm and 4pm (US$50 one way from San Salvador). It then leaves at 10pm for Panama (US$75 one way from San Salvador), where you arrive between 3pm and 4pm on the third day.

San Salvador has three main terminals for national long-distance buses.

TERMINAL DE ORIENTE

Buses serving all points east and a few northern destinations arrive and depart from the **Terminal de Oriente** (Map p279; Alameda Juan Pablo II), on the eastern side of the city. To get to the terminal, take bus 9, 29 or 34 from the city center; bus 29 or 52 from Blvd de los Héroes; bus 7C or 34 from Terminal de Occidente; or bus 21 from Terminal de Sur. Frequent departures:

Chalatenango Bus 125 (US$1; 2hr)
El Poy (Honduran border) Bus 119 (US$1.70; 3hr)
Ilobasco Bus 111 (US$0.70; 1½hr)
La Palma Bus 119 (US$1.60; 2¾hr)
La Unión Bus 304 (US$3; 4hr) Faster *especial* service available.
San Miguel Bus 301 (US$1.25-2.50; 3hr) Faster *especial* service available.
San Vicente Bus 116 (US$0.90; 1½hr)
Suchitoto Bus 129 (US$0.80; 1½hr)

TERMINAL DE OCCIDENTE

Buses serving all points west, including the Guatemalan border, arrive and depart from the **Terminal de Occidente** (Map p286; Blvd Venezuela near 49a Av Sur). To get here, take bus 34 from the city center; bus 44 from Blvd de los Héroes (get off at Blvd Venezuela and walk a few blocks west to the terminal); or bus 7C or 34 from Terminal de Oriente. Frequent departures:

Ahuachapán Bus 202 (US$1; 2¼hr)
Cerro Verde Santa Ana bus to El Congo (US$0.80; 40min), then bus 248.
Joya de Cerén Bus 108 to San Juan Opico (US$0.65; 1¾hr)
La Hachadura Bus 205 to Sonsonate (US$1.55; 3½hr), then bus 259.
La Libertad Bus 102 (US$0.60; 1hr); catch it at its terminal behind Parque Bolivar or at Terminal de Occidente.
Lago de Coatepeque Santa Ana bus to El Congo (US$0.90; 40min), then bus 248.
Las Chinamas Bus 202 to Ahuachapán (US$1.55; 2½hr), then bus 263.
Los Cóbanos Bus 205 to Sonsonate (US$1.30; 2½hr), then bus 257.
Metapán Bus 201A (US$2.50; 1¾hr)
Ruinas de San Andrés Santa Ana bus 201 (US$0.80; 40min) to the turnoff to ruins.
San Cristóbal Bus 498 (US$1.25; 3hr)
Santa Ana Bus 201 (US$0.80; 1¼hr)
Sonsonate Bus 205 (US$0.80 *directo*, US$1 *especial*; 1¼hr)

TERMINAL DE SUR (TERMINAL SAN MARCOS)

In the south of the city, **Terminal de Sur** (off Map p279; Autopista a Comalapa), also called Terminal San Marcos, serves destinations to the south and southeast. To get here take bus 26 or microbus 11B from the city center; or bus 21 from Terminal de Oriente. Departures:

Costa del Sol Bus 495 (US$1.20; 2½hr)
Puerto El Triunfo Bus 185 (US$1.50; 2hr)
Usulután Bus 302 (US$1.60; 2½hr) Faster *especial* service available.

GETTING AROUND
Bus

San Salvador's bus network is extensive, from large smoke-spewing monsters to zippy microbuses. Fares are US$0.20 to US$0.30.

Buses run frequently from 5am to 7:30pm daily; fewer buses run on Sunday. Services stop between 7:30pm and 8:30pm; microbuses run later, until around 9pm. After 9pm you'll have to take a taxi.

In the center, it is fastest to walk a few blocks away from Plaza Barrios to catch your bus. Key routes include the following:

Bus 9 Goes down 29a Av Norte alongside the Universidad de El Salvador. Then it turns east toward the city center, heading past the cathedral and up Independencia past Terminal de Oriente.
Bus 26 Passes Plaza Barrios and Parque Zoológico on its way to Terminal del Sur.
Bus 29 Goes to Terminal de Oriente via the center. Buses stop between Metrocentro and MetroSur.
Bus 30 Heads downtown and is the best way to get to and from bus 138 to the airport. Pick it up on behind Metrocentro or at Parque Libertad in the center.
Bus 30B A very useful route, especially from Blvd de los Héroes. The bus goes east on Blvd Universitario, then southwest down Blvd de los Héroes to Metrocentro. From there, it goes west along Alameda Roosevelt. It then turns south at 79a Av and continues along Blvd del Hipódromo to Av Revolución, then returns on Alameda Araujo, Roosevelt, and 49a Av Sur back to Metrocentro.
Bus 34 Runs from Terminal de Oriente to Metrocentro then down to the Zona Rosa, turning around right in front of Marte art museum. Passes Terminal de Occidente on return.
Bus 42 The bus goes west along Calle Arce from the cathedral and continues along Alameda Roosevelt. At El Salvador del Mundo, it heads southwest along Alameda Araujo, passing the Mercado de Artesanías and Museo Nacional de Antropología David J Guzmán, and continues down the Carretera Interamericana, passing La Ceiba de Guadalupe.

EL SALVADOR

Bus 101 Goes from Plaza Barrios in the center, past Metro-Sur, the anthropology museum, La Ceiba de Guadalupe and on to Santa Tecla.

Car & Motorcycle

Avoid driving through the city center. The traffic gets snarled in daytime and the area is unsafe at night. It's quickest to take major thoroughfares. One-way streets have an arrow painted on the pavement or signage. For details on car hire, see p276.

Taxi

Taxis are plentiful but unmetered so negotiate a price in advance. A ride in town should cost between US$5 and US$8 during daytime. Rates go up a few dollars late at night. License plates beginning with 'A' indicate a registered taxi; in theory they can be held accountable for problems. If you don't spot a passing taxi, call **Taxis Acacya** (Map p281; ☎ 2271-4937) or **Acontaxis** (☎ 2270-1176).

AROUND SAN SALVADOR

San Salvador's perimeter is a profane mix of shantytowns and ancient ruins. Further out, cool volcano-top towns offer respite from the heat, while La Libertad is the gritty gateway to the Western Pacific coast and a plethora of world-class surfing options.

CIHUATÁN

The modest ruins of **Cihuatán** (admission US$3; ☼ 9am-4pm Tue-Sun) were once an immense urban area alongside the Río Guazapa, possibly the largest pre-Columbian city between Guatemala and Peru. The city thrived for 100 years before being sacked and burned by unknown invaders in the 10th century AD. It was likely occupied by Maya, Lenca and other groups joined together for commerce during an unstable period.

From the Terminal de Oriente, take bus 119 toward Chalatenango and get off about 4km beyond Las Aguilares; ask the driver to let you off at the ruins. It's a 900m walk to the site.

EL BOQUERÓN

Quezalatepeque (Volcán San Salvador) has two peaks. The higher peak, at 1960m, is called Picacho. The other, Boquerón (Big Mouth), is 1893m high and has a second cone within its crater – 45m high and perfectly symmetrical – formed in 1917. A paved road to the top affords an easy climb with unbelievable views as your reward. Bring a bag to pick up litter if you're so inspired. **El Boquerón Canopy Tours** (☎ 2508-0398; canopy ride US$27; ☼ 9am-5pm) can provide a not-so-cheap thrill.

Get an early start as busing from San Salvador takes a couple of hours. From Parque Cuscatlán, take bus 101A or B to Santa Tecla. From there, bus 103 departs from 6a Av Sur to the village of Boquerón. The bus comes sporadically, but pickups depart from the same place. The summit is 1km beyond the village.

RUINAS DE SAN ANDRÉS

In 1977 a step pyramid and a large courtyard with a subterranean section were unearthed at this **site** (admission US$3; ☼ 9am-5pm Tue-Sun), inhabited by Maya between AD 600–900. Experts believe that up to 12,000 people lived here. The city once dominated the Valle de Zapotitán and possibly the neighboring Valle de las Hamacas where San Salvador is now situated.

The peaceful ruins are 300m north of the highway and 33km west of San Salvador in the Valle de Zapotitán. Take the Santa Ana bus 201 from San Salvador's Terminal de Occidente and get off at km 33, at a small black sign for the ruins. If combining this with a visit to Joya de Cerén, visit Joya de Cerén first, then catch any bus on the highway for the short distance to San Andrés.

JOYA DE CERÉN

Called the Pompeii of America, Unesco World Heritage Site **Joya de Cerén** (www.cihuatan.org; admission US$3; ☼ 9am-5pm Tue-Sun) was a small Maya settlement buried under volcanic ash when the Laguna Caldera Volcano erupted in AD 595. Fleeing residents left behind a wealth of everyday items that provide clues into ancient planting, home building and food storage.

The remodeled museum offers a good collection of artifacts and models of the villages. One compelling piece is a small dish showing fingerprints smeared in the remains of an interrupted meal.

The site is 36km west of San Salvador – take bus 108 from Terminal de Occidente and get off after crossing the bridge over the Río Sucio.

LOS PLANES DE RENDEROS

This hillside district, 12km to the south of San Salvador, is famous for **Puerta del Diablo** (Devil's Door). Two towering boulders, reputedly one single stone split in two, form

EL SALVADOR

a lookout with fantastic views, minus those of garbage strewn about. During the war this place was an execution point, the cliffs offering easy disposal of the bodies.

The boulders are 2km past the family-friendly **Parque Balboa** (admission US$0.80). Take bus 12 'Mil Cumbres' from the east side of the Mercado Central, at 12a Calle Poniente. If you're driving, head down Av Cuscatlán until you see the signs.

PANCHIMALCO

Set on the green slopes of Cerro Chulo, Panchimalco is a small town renowned for its religious festivals, particularly Palm Sunday, when residents march through the streets bearing decorated palm fronds. Early May's **Fería de Cultura de las Flores y las Palmas** features palm artistry, folk dancing and fireworks. Inhabited by descendants of the Pipils, Panchimalco has reinvented itself as an artist enclave.

Bus 17 departs for Panchimalco from Av 29 de Agosto on the south side of the Mercado Central in San Salvador.

LA LIBERTAD

pop 20,100

El Salvador's most infamous port still sports an uneasy mix of drugs, crime and surfing, however there is change in the salty air. From the fabulous, sticky fish market on the pier to the sunset barrels on famed Punta Roca point, local authorities have poured money into gentrifying an otherwise sketchy patch of prime coastal real estate. Police abound; cool cafes, bars and restaurants hawk for passing custom; and an amphitheatre, skate park and convention center invite corporate and community events.

Off the beach La Libertad is still a stinking-hot, working-class city with far more energy, souped-up buses and loud-mouthed touting than you'd expect for a town of such modest proportions. Most travelers bypass it for the more chilled-out beaches to the west, but it's an ideal stop for banks and other amenities, or for a steady dose of seaside grit.

Information

Banco Agrícola Branches are located east of the market in Barrios or in El Faro mall. Changes traveler's checks; there's a new 24-hour ATM at El Faro mall.

Cyber Fenix (2a Calle Poniente; per hr US$1; ⏰ 8am-8pm)

Post office (2a Calle Oriente) Near 2a Av Norte.

Dangers & Annoyances

La Libertad has a dangerous reputation thanks to its long-standing drug trade. Avoid the area southeast of the plaza at night (there's better nightlife at the restaurants east of the Lighthouse mall). Surfers should go accompanied to the point at Punta Roca and not bring valuables; potential threats are both human and canine.

Strong rip currents proliferate throughout the coast. Lifeguards only work weekends in La Libertad and Playa San Diego. Black clams raised in the estuary hold a high concentration of toxins; avoid eating them if you want to keep catching waves.

Sights & Activities

BEACHES

La Libertad fills up with city dwellers on weekends. The beach is rocky and covered with large black boulders, and the riptide, along with sewage, makes the water uninviting in the rainy season (May to October). If you just want to frolic in waves, hit the Costa del Bálsamo or go 4km east to sandy Playa San Diego.

SURFING

You'll find world-class surfing at **Punta Roca**, a lively right-hand break smack in front of town. Scenes from classic surf flick *Big Wednesday* were filmed here. Beginners launch at Playa La Paz (November to February), El Zonte or El Sunzal. Top surf spots with accommodations are found on the Costa Bálsamo (p293).

Surf Doctor Saul has expanded **Hospital de Tablas de Surf** (☎ 2335-3214; 3a Av Norte 28-7) into the neighboring premises, meaning even more space for repairing, renting and selling boards, in addition to offering surfing lessons. Just knock if it appears closed.

WILDLIFE-WATCHING

About 4km east of La Libertad, along the Comalapa road, **Parque Nacional Walter T Deininger** (admission US$1, guide US$12; ⏰ 7am-noon & 1-5pm) is named for the German settler who donated the land. It includes two types of forest: *caducifolio*, which sheds its leaves in summer, and *galería*, which retains its foliage year-round. A well-maintained 18km trail skirts the park; you must be accompanied by a ranger. Signs mark trails to Río Amayo, 'the Mystery Cave' and a lookout showing the forest cascading to the sea. Deer, raccoon and the endangered *tepezcuintle* (paca) can be spotted, in addition to many bird

EL SALVADOR

species, including the *torogoz* (blue-crowned motmot), El Salvador's national bird.

To visit Parque Deininger, you supposedly must obtain a permit from **ISTU** (☎ 2222-8000) in San Salvador (p280) five days prior to arrival. You might just try showing up and talking with the guard. It's a 15-minute ride from La Libertad – catch bus 187.

Sleeping

Posada Margoth (cnr 3a Av Sur btwn 2a & 4a Calles Poniente; s/d without bathroom US$7/14) A rough trailer-park feel, the Margoth has stuffy, though not unclean rooms, facing a dying garden. There's no phone number or toilet paper.

Hostal El Roble (☎ 7252-8498; http://elrobleelsalvador. blogspot.com; Playa San Diego; dm/r US$8/20) This super-chilled little hostel on low-key San Diego offers all manner of ocean endeavors. Dorm beds are clean and spacious, and the doubles represent excellent value. A shuttle runs to/from the airport and the border for around US$10.

La Posada Familiar (☎ 2335-3252; cnr 3a Av Sur & 4a Calle Poniente; s/d US$10/12, s/d with bathroom US$12/15) Clean but cave-like rooms around a raked dirt courtyard. The plain singles are sad cells; check your fan before settling in.

Hotel Rick (☎ 2335-3542; 5a Av Sur; d US$25; ⚡) Still a fine choice for surfers and transient folk is this orange, two-story motel facing a central car park. The keen owners fastidiously prepare the small rooms and have recently renovated some bathrooms. The 2nd floor is brighter and airier.

La Hacienda de Don Rodrigo (☎ 2335-3166; 5a Av Sur; r US$42-57; ⚡) The last hotel on the famous point is a reliable family choice, with big, breezy rooms, a huge 2nd-floor balcony, a compact swimming pool facing the beach and a neat bar.

Also recommended:

Hotel Pacific Sunrise (☎ 2346-2000; www.hotel elsalvador.com; cnr Calle El Obispo & Carretera Litoral; s/d US$45/57; ⚡ 🖵 ⚡) Best Western at best.

Eating

Los Asados JC (3a Av Norte btwn Calle El Calvario & 2a Calle Poniente; mains US$3-4; ⌚ 7am-9:30pm) Trendy fast-food joint packed with surfers snacking on *pupusas*, frijoles in all shapes and wonderfully sloppy tacos.

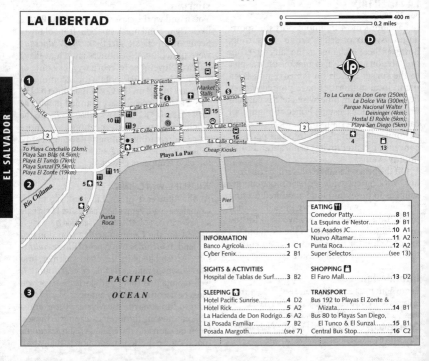

LA LIBERTAD

| 0 | 400 m |
| 0 | 0.2 miles |

EL SALVADOR

La Calle Poniente
1a Calle Poniente
Market Stalls
Calle El Calvario
Calle Gdo Barrios
Calle El Calvario
2a Calle Poniente
2a Calle Oriente
4a Calle Poniente
4a Calle Oriente
Cheap Kiosks
Playa La Paz
Av Bolívar
Av Luz
7a Av Norte
5a Av Norte
3a Av Norte
2a Av Norte
1a Av Norte
4a Av Norte
El Av Norte
5a AV Sur

To Playa Conchalío (2km);
Playa San Blas (4.5km);
Playa El Tunco (7km);
Playa Sunzal (9.5km);
Playa El Zonte (19km)

To La Curva de Don Gere (250m);
La Dolce Vita (300m);
Parque Nacional Walter T
Deininger (4km);
Hostal El Roble (5km);
Playa San Diego (5km)

Río Chilama
Punta Roca
Pier

PACIFIC OCEAN

INFORMATION	
Banco Agrícola	1 C1
Cyber Fenix	2 B1

| **SIGHTS & ACTIVITIES** | |
| Hospital de Tablas de Surf | 3 B2 |

SLEEPING 🛏	
Hotel Pacific Sunrise	4 D2
Hotel Rick	5 A2
La Hacienda de Don Rodrigo	6 A2
La Posada Familiar	7 B2
Posada Margoth	(see 7)

EATING 🍴	
Comedor Patty	8 B1
La Esquina de Nestor	9 B1
Los Asados JC	10 A1
Nuevo Altamar	11 A2
Punta Roca	12 A2
Super Selectos	(see 13)

| **SHOPPING 🛍** | |
| El Faro Mall | 13 D2 |

TRANSPORT	
Bus 192 to Playas El Zonte & Mizata	14 B1
Bus 80 to Playas San Diego, El Tunco & El Sunzal	15 B1
Central Bus Stop	16 C2

EL SALVADOR'S TOP FIVE SURF SPOTS

With 16 right-hand point breaks and 28°C (82°F) water swarming with sea turtles, what's not to love? Bad luck for lovers of the left-hand – Playa El Tunco is pretty much your only bet. Our favorites:

Punta Roca Iconic for a reason. Central America's best wave is often compared to South Africa's J Bay. A rocky bottom makes it fast and strong. Bring just your board – theft is common on the walk to the point (see p291).

Las Flores A fast sandy point break best at low tide. Picture a hollow take off ending on a black sand beach. A 300m ride is possible – welcome to the Wild East.

Punta Mango Short, strong and vertical, this aggressive Indo-men Hawaiian-style break is best reached by boat from Las Flores beach or via bus from El Cuco. A pretty tightly held wave so don't drop in!

Playa El Sunzal The most popular wave in El Salvador; fun, consistently big right-hander with a seasoned surf crowd of friendly locals and fly-ins.

'Secret Spot' Surfers love their secrets, however poorly kept. Temperamental at times, but fast and hollow when cranking, it's named after a distance between 58km and 60km…

Comedor Paty (Calle El Calvario; mains US$2-5; ☺ lunch & dinner) The friendly female proprietor returns workers to their jobs well fed on *comida a la vista*. It's around the corner from the surf doctor.

La Esquina de Nestor (cnr 2a Calle Poniente & 3a Av Norte; mains US$3-4; ☺ 10am-10pm) This tiny *taquería* (taco cafe) dishes up authentic Mexican tacos stuffed with shrimp, beef or pork.

our pick Nuevo Altamar (4a Calle Poniente; www.nuevoaltamar.com; mains US$5-15; ☺ 11am-11pm) A team of brisk, old-school waiters serves highly recommended *cazuela* (seafood soup) and other pescatarian delights to in-the-know locals at the pick of the restaurants opposite Punta Roca.

Punta Roca (cnr 5a Av Sur & 4a Calle Poniente; mains US$4-10; ☺ 8am-8pm, later on weekends) This is a local institution, with a expat surf family at the helm. The cook serves up superb *mariscadas* (seafood soup) and shrimp cocktails on the beachfront. Stay for at least one sunset beverage.

Self-caterers can stock up at **Super Selectos** (El Faro Mall; ☺ 7:30am-8pm).

Other options near Playa San Diego:

La Curva de Don Jere (☎ 2335-3436; Calle San Diego; mains US$8-10; ☺ 9am-10pm) 200m south of Shell.

La Dolce Vita (☎ 2335-3592; Calle San Diego; mains US$11; ☺ 9am-10pm) Next to Don Jere.

Getting There & Away
There is no bus terminal. Bus 102 goes to and from San Salvador (US$0.60, one hour). In San Salvador, catch it at its terminal behind Parque Bolivar or at Terminal de Occidente. In La Libertad, buses leave from the corner of 4a Av Norte and Calle Gerardo Barros.

See p278 for details of how to get to La Libertad from the airport.

To Sonsonate, take bus 287 (US$1.25, 2½ hours, 1:45pm only) from the bus stop at 2a Calle Poniente or bus 192 to Playa Mizata and change.

Getting Around
Surfers can take boards on all buses. Bus 80 goes west from La Libertad to Playa El Tunco and Playa El Sunzal (US$0.25, every 15 minutes from 4:30am to 6pm) or east to Playa San Diego (US$0.30, every 15 minutes from 5:40am to 6pm). Buses leave from 4a Av Norte at 2a Calle Oriente.

For Playa El Zonte or Playa Mizata take bus 192 (US$0.50, every 30 minutes from 7am to 5:30pm).

LA COSTA DEL BÁLSAMO
This spectacular coast stretches from La Libertad westward to Sihuapilapa. The region takes its name from the valuable aromatic oil extracted here by burning the bark of live balsam trees. Today only a handful of trees remain and cotton has become the main cash crop.

From La Libertad, the road west twists around rocky headlands, giving glimpses of sheltered coves and sandy beaches (mostly private). The western sections of this route are especially raw and beautiful. Skip the weekend hordes and parking lots at Playas Conchalío and El Majahual and press on for a whole 50km of uninterrupted beaches.

Bus 80 goes as far as Playa El Sunzal. Beyond that, take the less frequent bus 192.

Sleeping & Eating
PLAYA CONCHALÍO
Centro Obrero Dr Humberto Romero Alvergue (Ruta 2; free with permit) This workers' center has plain

EL SALVADOR

rooms and flimsy cots, fronting a rocky beach. Shacks by the beach gate serve food. Guests must obtain prior written permission from the Ministerio de Trabajo in San Salvador (p280).

PLAYA EL TUNCO

In many parts of the world, little El Tunco would heave year-round with indie travelers and beach bums. But this is El Salvador, so it's cruisey for now.

Sombra (☎ 7729-5628; www.surflibre.com; dm/d US$6/14, dm/d/tr with bathroom US$7/14/21) Otherwise known as José's place, La Sombra is a mecca for budget surfers who compare scars on the wooden deck and crash out under towering cathedral ceilings. There's free Zona Rosa bus pick-up in San Salvador.

Papaya's Lodge (☎ 2389-6231; www.papaya surfing.com; s/d US$8/14) The mainstay of Tunco backpacking is the domain of surfing pioneer Jamie Delgado. Small, clean rooms with shared bathroom have cement block walls and step out onto a shady river deck backed by mangroves. The surf shop offers repairs and lessons.

Hotel Mopelia (☎ 2389-6225; www.hotelmopelia-salv ador.com; dm US$10, r with/without air-con US$30/15) The savvy travel community heads for Mopelia, a small recently renovated haven for lounge gurus, surf rats and straight-up party people. Only eight rooms – all spotless and well maintained – means that service is personal and your privacy assured. There's a popular pizza joint, Tunco Veloz, and a hopping little bar that plays smooth electronica.

La Guitarra (☎ 2389-6388; www.surfingeltunco.com; r US$35-45, with air-con US$65-75; ☒ ☐ ☒) Reason enough to visit Tunco, an incongruous rock 'n' roll 'path of fame' leads you to spotless, freshly painted thatched rooms, each with private bathroom and perfect beds. Very public private landings ensure everyone knows everyone in no time, which is probably exactly what you want. The front bar is kitted out with political pop art, a big pool table, TV lounge and free internet. The beach bar is *the* sunset hot spot.

Dare Dare Cafe (☎ 7080-0263) Killer chai lattes (among other exotic blends), American breakfasts and house smoothies in a smartly decorated deli with full magazine racks and a hammock-strewn gazebo on the river mouth.

La Bocana (mains $6-16) This reliable seafood restaurant turns into a popular nightspot once the fish digests.

Near La Guitarra is **Super Tunco**, a friendly convenience store and unofficial info booth run by ex-American Corey.

Other sleeping options:

Eco Del Mar (☎ 7852-2124; www.ecosurfelsalvador. com; r US$25-30, with air-con US$40-50; ☒) Five sustainably designed apartments.

Tekuani Kal (☎ 2389-6388; www.tekuanikal.com; s/d incl breakfast US$50/65; ☒ ☒) Ultra stylish, faux-indigenous vibe.

PLAYA EL SUNZAL

This relaxed surf spot is just down the beach from El Tunco.

Sunzal Point Surf Lodge (☎ 2389-6070; www. surfsunzal.com; Carretera Litoral Km 44; dm/r US$7/15; ☐) Formerly known as El Hostel, this friendly place run by three ex-backpackers is right on the famed Sunzal break. The grounds are spacious, the shared bathrooms are brand new and there's full use of kitchen facilities. Nonsurfers can choose from a range of land-based tours.

PLAYA EL ZONTE & BEYOND

The ultimate *playa* for chilling – and learning to surf – on the Costa del Bálsamo. Life has changed sharply for this tiny community; show respect by traveling sustainably.

Esencia Nativa (☎ 2302-6258; esencianativa@yahoo. com; s/d/t with fan US$12/20/25, r with bathroom & air-con US$35; ☒ ☒ ☒) Locally owned and operated by lovable Alex and Amelia, this community-minded, casual retreat is a hit with the backpack shufflers and the odd surfer. The sizable double rooms have comfy beds and clean bathrooms. The pool is flanked by a cool bar/restaurant, table-tennis table, indoor lounge and a shaded loft.

Horizonte Surf Resort (☎ 2323-0099; saburosurfcamp@ hotmail.com; s/d/t with air-con US$35/40/50; ☒ ☒ ☒) The heart of Zonte surf culture (Esencia Nativa has the soul) has comfortable rooms (the best are upstairs), a manicured garden and inviting pool. It also runs a very popular beachside restaurant across the sand street.

A string of more secluded hotels is found across the river. The pick is **El Dorado** (☎ 7226-6166; www.surfeldrado.com; dm/s/d $16/35/58; ☒ ☒ ☒), a French-Canadian surf venture with beautiful, breezy rooms fitted with bamboo art.

Playa Mizata sits 35km beyond El Zonte, home to some lovely and lesser-known right and left breaks. The next spot of interest is Los Cóbanos, a series of small coves with El Salvador's best diving. A fabulous bargain beach house, **Kalindigo** (☎ 7306-0193; kalindigo.info@gmail.com; dm US$10, d/tr US$30/40;), recently opened here, with a friendly local travel vibe. To get here take the half-hourly bus 257 from Sonsonate (US$0.55, 40 minutes).

WESTERN EL SALVADOR

El Salvador's coffee stronghold offers a heady blend of adventure and old money, gastronomy and lush national parks. It's here that the Ruta de las Flores winds its charms through artesan, cobblestone villages, where stumbling across running waterfalls and bubbling hot springs is as easy as finding a good espresso and a thriving marketplace. Meanwhile Santa Ana, the provincial capital, is a confident, colonial town with a mesmerising lake at its doorstep and some grand ruins out back. But western El Salvador is also an exercise in inequality. On baking hot, volcanic precipes, *campesinos* struggle to subsist on the weight of coffee sacks, stuck deep beneath the poverty line as dynasties hold on to the good life. When El Salvador finally enjoys the destination status of its neighbors, you'll see its impact here first.

PARQUE NACIONAL LOS VOLCANES

This **park** (admission US$1; 8am-5pm) is a natural treasure, encompassing three major volcanoes (Cerro Verde, Volcán Santa Ana and Volcán Izalco) and thousands of hectares. It's a major bird sanctuary, with many migratory species passing through, including emerald toucanets, jays, woodpeckers, motmots and 17 species of hummingbird.

Active Volcán Izalco is the youngest in the group. Its cone began forming in 1770 from a belching hole of sulfuric smoke and today stands 1910m high. Izalco erupted throughout the 20th century, spewing smoke, boulders and flames and earning its reputation as 'the lighthouse of the Pacific.' Today, this bare, perfect cone stands devoid of life in an otherwise fertile land.

Without Izalco's stark drama but 400m higher, Santa Ana (also known as Ilamatepec) is El Salvador's third-highest point. Its eruption in October 2005 triggered landslides that killed two coffee pickers and forced the evacuation of thousands. The barren and windy summit affords spectacular views of a steep drop into the crater on one side and Lago de Coatepeque on the other.

SPLURGE

La Cocotera (☎ 2245-3691; www.lacocoteraresort.com; Barra de Santiago; d incl meals from US$150;) is an amazing new resort on the undervisited Barra de Santiago that doesn't wear its 'eco' tag lightly. Oceanfront rooms featuring clean lines, minimalist decor and wonderful king-sized beds open onto a long, empty beach surrounded by coconut and mango trees. Estuary and nature tours are first class, as are the inclusive meals and gigantic swimming pool. Only natural materials are used – palm fronds, handwoven fabrics, plant vines – sourced locally and crafted with local hands. Central America needs more places like this.

Tourist police are posted along the trails and at the summits. Crime has dropped dramatically in recent years, but you should not hike solo. More useful park information is at www.complejolosvolcanes.com.

Four-hour guided hikes to either volcano (Izalco US$1; Santa Ana US$1.80) begin at 11am *only*, so don't arrive late! This also means you can't do both in one day. Wear sturdy shoes. A short alternative is a 40-minute nature trail which offers views of the lake and Volcán Santa Ana. It starts in the parking lot.

Sleeping & Eating

San Blas has two camping complexes in the shadow of Volcán Santa Ana. **Campo Bello** (☎ 2271-0853) offers round cement dwellings that sleep four. **Casa de Cristal** (☎ 2483-4713) has rustic *cabañas*. Call ahead for prices, camping possibilities and availability.

A local cooperative manages a rustic **campground** (☎ 2483-4713/4679; 2 adults US$35), 13km from San Blas heading toward Los Andes. Los Andes has a ranger who can also guide Santa Ana hikes. For information, contact SalvaNatura in San Salvador (see p280).

Getting There & Away

Arrive by 11am since the guided hikes leave just once a day. The easiest, surest route is to come from Santa Ana, where bus 248 goes all the way to the entrance (see p298). The last bus leaves the park at 5pm but verify times with the driver who drops you off.

Leave early from San Salvador to make connections. Take any bus to Santa Ana and disembark at El Congo on the Carretera Panamericana; walk uphill to the overpass and catch bus 248. Ask to be sure you're in the right place.

If you're driving, Parque Nacional Los Volcanes is 67km from San Salvador via Sonsonate or 77km by the more scenic route toward Santa Ana.

LAGO DE COATEPEQUE

Unlike more famous lakes in Central America (hint, hint, Guatemala) you can happily swim in this 6km-wide sparkling blue volcanic puddle while above you broods the dramatic peaks of Cerro Verde, Izalco and Santa Ana. Ah, El Salvador!

A handful of cheap hotels dot the lake's edge, but most accommodation is the preserve of San Salvador's elite – one ex-president even owns an island here. For around US$5 you can relax and enjoy lake access at one of the hotels on the northeast shore. For US$20 you can rent a boat for a couple of hours.

Sleeping & Eating

Hostal 3er Mundo (☎ 2441-6239; s/d US$12/20;) An overhaul of the Amacuilco Guesthouse has given backpackers another reason to return to the lake. There's a variety of well-presented rooms, a book exchange, a small pool and sauna, kayak and canoe rental, a lakeside restaurant and and cable TV. A small shop sells interesting works by local artists.

Hotel Torremolinos (☎ 2441-6037; www.torremolinoslagocoatepeque.com; r per person US$15-30; mains US$5-20;) Brave the long rickety bridge and giant wooden stilts for the best seafood on Coatepeque. There's live music most weekends but most folk depart by sunset. The rooms are decent enough if you can't get home. There's also a nice swimming pool and a relaxing open terrace.

El Gran Mirador (☎ 2411-3754; r incl breakfast US$25) Eat fresh *mojarro* fish from the lake at the slick upstairs seafood restaurant then sleep in one of three small, cement rooms with the lake in your lap. It's on your left, about halfway down the road from Santa Ana.

Hostal Nantal (☎ 2319-6792; Carretera al Cerro Verde Km 53.5; d incl breakfast US$30;) A smart option for exploring Cerro Verde, this garden retreat has recently reopened its four rooms with private bathrooms (some with lake views). The friendly owner Claudia can arrange tours.

To get here take the Parque Nacional de los Volcanes bus from Santa Ana.

Comedor Patricar (mains US$2-5; 7:30am-8pm) Enjoy the no-frills *típica* and seafood. It's around the curve past Hotel Torremolinos with no lake view.

Also recommended:

Centro de Obreros Constitución (free with permit; Wed-Sun) Basic, government-run lodging.

Rancho Alegra (☎ 7888-0223; Carretera al Cerro Verde Km 53.5; d incl breakfast US$30;) Next door to Torremolinos, with a younger vibe.

Getting There & Away

Buses 220 and 242 depart Santa Ana for the lake every half-hour. They pass El Congo and descend to the shoreline, passing the Centro de Obreros, Amacuilco and Hotel Torremolinos in that order. The last return bus to Santa Ana leaves at 6pm.

SANTA ANA
pop 178,600

Hints of a wealthy yesteryear linger in the colonial backstreets of Santa Ana, a socially conservative major city, and long home to the country's largest coffee plantations. Santa Ana is also the closest thing to a university town outside San Salvador, reflected in the lively nightlife and proud entrepreneurial spirit. The plaza is among the grandest in El Salvador, making it more than a handy departure point for Lago de Coatepeque, the Maya ruins at Tazumal or the Ruta de las Flores.

Information

Ciberworld (Av Independencia Sur btwn 9a & 11a Calle Poniente; per hr US$1; 8am-7:30pm Mon-Sat, 9am-6pm Sun) Friendly service.

Citibank (cnr Independencia Sur & 3a Calle Oriente) Has an ATM.

Red Cross (☎ 441-2645, 447-7213; cnr 1a Av Sur & 3a Calle Oriente; 24hr)

Virtu@l Center (cnr 3a Av Sur & 7a Calle Oriente; per hr US$0.60; 8am-7pm Mon-Fri, 8:30am-6pm Sat, 9am-1pm Sun)

Sights

Santa Ana's biggest attraction is its large neo-Gothic **cathedral**. Ornate moldings cover the front, and interior archways and pillars are painted in slate and pink stripes (consider it preppy-neo-Gothic). On the square west of the cathedral is the **Teatro de Santa Ana**, with an impressive, ornate interior.

Sleeping

Casa Frolaz (☎ 2440-5302; www.casafrolaz.com; 29 Calle Poniente; dm US$7) This beautiful home in a quiet part of town offers fabulous value and local expertise to independent travelers. Javier Díaz runs a tight operation, and the dorm rooms are huge and dust-free, with private balcony for guests. You can use the bright kitchen and living area, or just doss in the garden of a real life *salvadoreño*. There's plenty of street parking.

Casa Verde (☎ 7540-4896; 7a Calle Poniente; s/d/tr incl breakfast US$8/16/24; 🕸 🖳) Near the historic district of Santa Ana is this hole-in-the-wall restored house – it's the pick of the budget places in town. The recent remodelling includes two 'stately rooms' and a 'tanning area.'

Call if unattended as Carlos works across the road in the hardware store.

Hotel Livingston (☎ 2441-1801; 10a Av Sur; d US$10, with cable TV US$15; 🕸) A cement block complex off the street, Livingston offers well-kept if cavernous rooms. Beds have mirrored headboards and the hodgepodge of sofas and chairs pass for decor. A good choice for quick access to the bus terminals.

Hotel Tazumal (☎ 2440-2830; 11a Calle Poniente; r US$15) Across the road from Santa Ana's finest transvestite bars is this quiet little budget place set inside an old house. A cool, spacious hallway leads to four large rooms and a groomed garden facing a tiled terrace. The bathrooms are tired though, and the mattresses are worn thin.

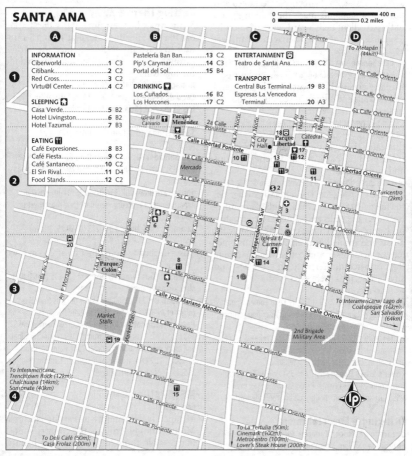

EL SALVADOR

Eating

Hit the row of **food stands** (1a Av Norte; US$1-2) on the plaza for enormous chicken sandwiches in soft bread, burgers and greasy fries.

El Sin Rival (Av Independencia Sur; cones US$0.50-1; 9am-9pm) This popular chain makes natural sorbets so good it's outrageous. Try the tart *arrayán* (a bittersweet local fruit) or *mora* (blackberry).

Pastelería Ban Ban (Av Independencia Sur; pastries US$0.50-2.50; 8am-7pm) One of Santa Ana's charms is that the whole population breaks for coffee and cake mid-afternoon. It's likely that you'll find them here enjoying simple sandwiches and pastries in an air-conditioned setting.

Deli Café (cnr 10a Av Sur & 25 Calle Poniente; smoothies US$1-2; 9am-6:30pm) Green picnic tables and floral arrangements mask the true intention of this excellent deli: award-worthy smoothies, juices and cakes. It's between the market and Casa Frolaz.

Cafe Santaneco (2447-8431; Calle Libertad Poniente; mains US$2-4; breakfast & lunch) Cheap and particularly cheerful city eatery with green and yellow walls and a knowing clientele enjoying fresh *comida a la vista*.

Pip's Carymar (cnr Av Independencia & 9a Calle Oriente; mains US$2-10; 8am-9:30pm) Locals seem to love this cafeteria-style diner serving everything from pizza to pasta to sandwiches. Indoor and outdoor seating.

Café Expresiones (Calle 11 Poniente btwn 6a & 8a Av Sur; meals US$3-6; Mon-Sat) The scholarly owner ran the full palette – plus a thick daub of gray matter – over the walls and courtyard to create a bookstore-cafe and inner-city retreat. Students, artists and young lovers enjoy delicious omelettes, cheesecakes and coffee while penning that one-act masterpiece. It's booze- and smoke-free, plus there's free wi-fi.

Also recommended:

Portal del Sol (7747-1036; 17 Calle Poniente; mains US$5-12; lunch & dinner) Pan-American pop setting and cuisine. Next to a metal art shop.

La Tertulia (2440-2144; cnr Av Fray Felipe & 33 Calle Poniente; mains US$7-17; lunch & dinner) Best service and food in town; near football stadium.

Lover's Steak House (2484-7511; www.loverssteak house.com; 21 Calle Oriente, Barrio San Miguelito; mains US$8-20) New location, though still busy and tiki-torch-lit.

Drinking & Entertainment

Trenchtown Rock (Carretera Panamericana desvío a Chalchuapa 7pm-late Wed-Sat) Test your capacity for spontaneous fits of joy in this electric roadside Rasta club outside Chalchuapa.

Los Horcones (2484-7511; 1a Av Norte; 10am-2am) For the perfect place to tipple a beer, consider this offbeat open-air spot overlooking the cathedral. Tree-trunk pillars and hand-hewn benches provide a rustic setting.

Los Cuñados (cnr Calle Libertad Poniente & 10 Av Sur 25; mains US$2-10; 8am-9:30pm) Drink tall glasses of freezing beer at this downtown watering hole with sticky floors and big-screen TVs.

Teatro de Santa Ana (2447-6268; 2a Calle Poniente) Stop by for the current program of concerts, plays and dance performances.

Cinemark (Av Independencia at 35a Av Poniente; admission US$3) For Hollywood action flicks and the occasional tear-jerker.

Getting There & Away

Santa Ana's bus terminal abuts the market on 10a Av Sur. Buses take at least 15 minutes to leave the terminal since they crawl through market stalls. Destinations include the following:

Ahuachapán Bus 210 (US$0.45; 1¼hr)

Lago de Coatepeque Buses 220, 242 (US$0.40; 1¼hr)

Las Chinamas (Guatemalan border) Take any Ahuachapán bus and transfer.

San Cristóbal (Guatemalan border) Bus 236 (US$0.50; 1hr)

San Salvador Bus 201 (*directo* US$0.80, 1½hr; *especial* US$1.25; 1¼hr) All buses also stop at Metrocentro in San Salvador.

Sonsonate Buses 209, 216 (US$0.55; 1½hr) Bus 216 departs from La Vencedora terminal (one block west of Parque Colón).

Tazumal, Chalchuapa Bus 218 (US$0.25; 30min)

Buses departing from other locations in town include these ones:

Anguiatú (Guatemalan border) Bus 235 (US$1.10) to Metapán and transfer.

Metapán Bus 235 (US$0.90; 1½hr) departs from the corner of Av F Moraga Sur and 13a Calle Poniente.

Parque Nacional los Volcanes (Cerro Verde) Bus 248 (US$0.90; 1¾hr) departs from La Vencedora Terminal one block west of Parque Colón at 7am, 8am, 10:15am, 11:20am, 12:20pm, 1:40pm and 3:30pm. Last bus returns at 5pm. Confirm departure times.

METAPÁN

pop 18,500

Metapán is the gateway to Parque Nacional Montecristo–El Trifinio, the country's most inaccessible though perhaps most beautiful national park. It's closed from May to November to let the wildlife breed in peace. When it is open you need a 4WD vehicle to get there. While Metapán is mostly what a border town should be – hot, hectic and dead after dark – the town square (10 blocks off the main drag) has been thoughtfully renovated and the old town is still largely intact.

Information

Fusión Ciber Café (2 Av Sur at 15 de Septiembre; per hr US$0.60)

Scotiabank (Av Ignacio Gómez) Exchanges traveler's checks and has a 24-hour ATM.

Sights & Activities

On the El Salvador–Guatemala border, lesser-known Lago de Güija is a beautiful fishing and bird-watching wetland. In the dry season you can hike to archaeological sites and find rock carvings along the shore. Swimming is not recommended due to the deceptively pretty blue-green algae. It's several kilometers south of Metapán and 30km north of Santa Ana along CA12. To get there, take a Santa Ana–bound bus and get dropped off at the junction to the lake. It is a 2km walk from there.

Rafting El Salvador (☎ 2440-5130; combo trips US$50 per person) offers a good-value rafting/canopy package at Apuzunga Waterpark outside Metapán. Its main office is at Metrocentro in Santa Ana.

Sleeping & Eating

Hotel California (☎ 2442-0561; s/d US$12/20) An ideal roadside sleepover if the trip to/from Guatemala has taken its toll. The best of the large rooms have views of El Trifinio. It's a five-minute walk out of town, 500m north of the terminal. Across the road is a fancy new, nameless Mexican restaurant that serves bargain 'family' meals (US$10 for a three-person feast) and all-day drink specials.

For those who want to stay 'in town,' **Hotel Christina** (☎ 2442-0044; 4a Av Sur btwn Calle 15 de Septiembre & 2a Calle; s/d US$12/15, with air-con US$18/23; ☒) is downhill from the terminal. The upstairs terrace is great for people-watching and there's a handy general store downstairs.

The town plaza, with regulation church, hall, grassy patch and market stalls, also features a string of bright cafes in beautiful old facades. The best is **Kikes Coffee** (Parque Central; iced coffee US$1).

Getting There & Away

The bus terminal sits on the highway facing the entrance to town. For Santa Ana, take bus 235 (US$0.90, 1½ hours) or a *directo* (US$2.50, one hour). San Salvador bus 201A (US$2.50, 1¾ hours) departs seven times daily. Bus 235 and microbuses go to the Guatemalan border at Anguiatú (US$0.50, 30 minutes); the last leaves at 6:30pm. Bus 463 departs 5:30am and noon daily for the gorgeous and also hair-raising haul over the mountains to Citalá (US$2, three hours), close to the Honduran border crossing at El Poy.

PARQUE NACIONAL MONTECRISTO–EL TRIFINIO

Isolated and pristine, this borderland park boasts thick cloud-forest canopy, exotic orchids and abundant wildlife. The borders of El Salvador, Honduras and Guatemala converge at the highest point (2418m), referred to as El Trifinio. Oak and laurel trees grow to 30m, and leaves intertwine to form a canopy impenetrable to sunlight. The forest floor provides a habitat for abundant exotic plant life including mushrooms, lichens and mosses, and tree ferns up to 8m tall. The temperature averages between 10°C (50°F) and 15°C (59°F). This is the most humid region in the country, with 2000mm annual precipitation and 100% average relative humidity.

Animals seen (albeit rarely) include spider monkeys, two-fingered anteaters, porcupines, spotted and hooded skunks, pumas, red and gray squirrels, wild pigs, opossums, coyotes and agoutis. The forest is also home to at least 87 bird species, including quetzals, green toucans, woodpeckers, hummingbirds, nightingales, white-faced quails and striped owls.

There is no place to stay here – you must camp. Ask trail directions from the owner of the small shop here. You have a few options but none of the trails are well marked. Several

---

GETTING TO GUATEMALA

To El Progreso

The **San Cristóbal–El Progreso** border is open 24 hours but cross during daylight hours. From Santa Ana, take bus 236 to San Cristóbal (US$0.50, one hour, every 20 minutes from 5:30am to 9pm). Buses on the other side of the border go to El Progreso. The last bus back from San Cristóbal is at 6pm.

To Guatemala City via Las Chinamas

Agencia Puerto Bus (☎ 2440-1608; 25a Calle Poniente) offers ordinary and *especial* service to Guatemala City via **Las Chinamas–Valle Nuevo**. Ordinary buses (US$9, four hours) leave hourly from 5am to 4pm, except 7am. *Especial* buses (a well-spent US$11.50, 3½ hours) leave at 7am and 5:30pm. Another option is to catch a 1st-class bus at Las Chinamas.

To Chiquimula

From Metapán, microbuses run every half-hour to the **Anguiatú–Chiquimula** border (open 24 hours but more reliably from 6am to 7pm). On the Guatemalan side, buses run frequently to Chiquimula (one hour, last bus at 5:30pm) and onward to Guatemala City (three hours, last bus from Chiquimula at 3:30pm). This is the quickest route to Nuevo Ocotopeque or Copán Ruínas, Honduras. In El Salvador, the last bus from the border to Metapán is at 6:30pm.

See p176 for information on crossing the border from Guatemala.

---

hiking trails begin from Los Planes (about 1900m), a grassy clearing in a bowl at the foot of Cerro Montecristo. Two trails lead about 1km each to wooden observation towers with views of the park and surrounding area. The trail you are probably looking for is the one to the top. The park highlight, it is a tough 7km climb through dense, misty cloud forest. At the summit a plaque marks the borders of the three countries. The views and the photo opportunities are outstanding.

Information

The area above Los Planes is closed from May to November, the breeding season of the local fauna. To take full advantage of the park, you'll need to spend the night. Camping is free at Los Planes – bring all your own equipment, food and water. Get advance permission from the National Parks and Wildlife Service at the **Ministerio de Medio Ambiente** (☎ 2267-6259/6276; www.marn.gov.sv, in Spanish; Alameda Araujo/Carretera Santa Tecla Km 5.5; ☑ 7:30am-4:30pm Mon-Fri) in San Salvador. Admission is US$6 per day for foreigners plus US$1.15 per vehicle, required for taxis as well.

Getting There & Away

Unfortunately, getting to Los Planes is a challenge, and not a cheap one. If you have a 4WD, you can drive there (22km from Metapán). **Francisco Monterrosa** (☎ 2402-2805) charges US$45 for day trips or US$85 to drop you off and return a day or two later. If he isn't

available, look for other drivers in Metapán near the park turnoff.

If you wait at the road in early morning, you may be able to catch a ride with the rangers or residents of a small village in the park; but there are no guarantees and the trip back remains unresolved. You can walk to the gate (5km), but you can't walk beyond that without a private vehicle – that's the rule.

RUINAS DE TAZUMAL

The Maya ruins of **Tazumal** (admission US$3; ☑ 9am-5pm Tue-Sun), the most important and impressive in El Salvador, are in the pre-Columbian town of **Chalchuapa**, 13km west of Santa Ana on the way to Ahuachapán. In the K'iche' language Tazumal means 'pyramid where the victims were burned.'

Archaeologists estimate that the area was first settled around 5000 BC. Part of a 10-sq-km zone, much is still buried under Chalchuapa's more basic housing. Theft of the ruins – and the resale of precious artifacts – is an ongoing concern. The excavated areas span a period of over 1000 years. While these ruins are very important for El Salvador, they pale in comparison to those in neighboring countries. The latest restoration, inaugurated in December 2006, restored the original stone-and-mortar construction in much of the ruins. Don't expect to get too close – a chain-link enclosure prevents visitors walking on the pyramids.

EL SALVADOR

The **museum** displays artifacts showing active trade as far away as Panama and Mexico, with explanations in detailed English. Other finds, including the Estela de Tazumal, a 2.65m-high basalt monolith inscribed with hieroglyphics, are at the Museo Nacional de Antropología David J Guzmán in San Salvador (see p282). Across the highway is **Casa Blanca** (admission US$3; ☼ 9am-5pm Tue-Sun), home to some Preclassic ruins and an indigo worshop where you can dye your own fabrics.

Bus 218 comes from Santa Ana, 14km (45 minutes) away. A sign on the main road through Chalchuapa points toward the ruins, about a five-minute walk from the highway. If driving from Santa Ana, stay right at the fork in the road, continuing toward Ahuachapán, then turn left at the Texaco station in Chalchuapa. The ruins are at the end of the road.

AHUACHAPÁN
pop 38,630

Regardless of how you tackle the Ruta de Las Flores, you'll probably pass through Ahuachapán, an elevated regional center 16km short of Guatemala. As a commercial hub for coffee, you'd expect a bit more, well, perk, however the real action in Ahuachapán bubbles deep underground – its geothermal energy supplies over 15% of the country's electrical power.

The hubs of Plaza Concordia and Parque Menéndez are five blocks apart, connected by the busy commercial street Av Menéndez, which runs north–south. The road to Tacuba is poorly marked; ask a local.

Information

Most services and restaurants are near Plaza Concordia.

Ciber Café Cetcomp (2a Av Sur at 1a Calle Poniente; per hr US$0.60; ☼ 9am-8pm Mon-Fri, 9:30am-8:30pm Sat, 10am-9pm Sun)
Scotiabank (Av Menendez at 4 Calle Poniente) Changes Amex and Visa traveler's checks.

Sights & Activities

Green gardens and palms make **Plaza Concordia** an agreeable stop to catch a breeze. The kiosk occasionally holds concerts and free events. East of the plaza is **Nuestra Señora de Asunción**, with pretty *azuelo* floors and a stained-glass Virgin.

Ahuachapán bubbles with geothermal activity, evidenced in the steaming mud pits found about. To visit **Los Ausoles**, aka *los infernillos* (the little hells), contact guide **Carlos Alvarado Martínez** (☎ 2413-3360).

Sleeping & Eating

Budget hotels here have all but disappeared. Head for Tacuba or the Ruta de Las Flores for a cheap bed.

Hotel Casa Blanca (☎ 2443-1505; cnr 2a Av Norte & Calle Barrios; s/d with fan US$20/30, with air-con US$35/59; P ⊠ ⊡ ⊠) An indefatigable matriarch welcomes business conventions and stray tourists to this elegant home in a preserved colonial street. Rooms are out-of-the-box B&B, showers are hot and steamy, and the pool is fit only for a kid.

La Estancia (1a Av Sur btwn Calle Barrios & 1a Calle Oriente; mains US$2-4; ☼ 7am-6pm Mon-Sat) This airy mansion-turned-restaurant is ideal for breakfast or lunch, serving buffet-style *típica*.

Restaurant Mixta 'S' (2a Av Sur at 1a Calle Poniente; mains US$4-5; ☼ 8am-9pm) Definitely stop at this shiny, happy diner if you're after fresh *mixtas* – pitas stuffed with pickled veggies, salsa and

---

DETOUR: CHALCHUAPA

Most visitors leave Chalchuapa after an hour at Tazumal – what a shame! This pre-Columbian town is a great snapshot of everyday Salvadoran life. Laguna Cuzcachapa is a natural sulfur pond located in the suburbs, a very mystical place of great significance in Maya culture. Locals suggest coming here when faced with difficult decisions, but beware the *siguanaba* (a mythical creature that poses as a beautiful woman to lure solo male travelers)! You can swim in natural spring-water pools at **El Trapiche** (location of the first Maya settlement in 2000 BC) or jump into a waterfall in **Salto El Espino**.

Our favorite coffee in El Salvador is at a cool cafe called **Mountain Coffee** (7 Calle Oriente & 3 Av Sur). Also the yummiest *chilate*, a nourishing drink made of corn served with *camote* (sweet potato) and sugary *buñuelos* (cassava), is found at **Chilate & Crafts** (5 Av Sur 6). Opposite Tazumal is a famous *yuqateria* serving *yuka* (yam) with roasted pork – a national delicacy. You can find beautiful, cheap jade and quartz jewelry nearby too.

There's a good guesthouse too called **Hostal Las Flores** (☎ 2408-1098; Av 2 de Abril; r US$25; ⊠).

meat or cheese. Add an extra straw to your overflowing *licuado* (fruit shake) for the full date experience.

Getting There & Away

Buses line the market-choked Av Menéndez at 10a Calle Oriente, one block north of the Parque Central. Buses for the Guatemalan border at Las Chinamas leave from 8a Calle Poniente, at the northwest corner of Parque Menéndez. The following buses travel to and from Ahuachapán:

Las Chinamas Bus 263 or Ruta 11 (US$0.50; 40min; 5am-7:30pm)

San Salvador Bus 202 (US$1.10; 2½hr; *especial* US$2; 1¼hr)

Santa Ana Bus 210 (US$0.50; 1hr) Alternatively, take the faster San Salvador bus, get off at Metrocentro and catch a local bus into town.

Sonsonate (via Apaneca & Juayúa) Bus 249 (US$0.85; 2hr), bus 23 (*directo* US$1.20; 1½hr)

Tacuba Bus 264 or Ruta 15 (US$0.60; 40min; 5:30am-7pm)

TACUBA

The Americas' first communist revolution took place here in 1932, but time – and government – has long forgotten this poor mountain outpost on the back doorstep of spectacular Parque Nacional El Imposible. A freshly paved road has increased to a trickle Tacuba's fee-paying adventurers. Sustainable tourism is almost assured here, and Tacuba's end-of-the-road location means that your small effort still brings a large reward.

Sights & Activities

Parque Nacional El Imposible (p306) is a tropical treasure edging Guatemala and oddly absent from most itineraries. The mostly primary forest here runs deep with rivers and beautiful waterfalls. Patient wildlife spotters can eye

GETTING TO GUATEMALA CITY

The **Las Chinamas–Valle Nuevo** border is open 24 hours but it's best to cross in daylight. Buses leave Ahuachapán from Parque Menéndez every 15 minutes (US$0.50, 5am to 7:30pm) for the Guatemala border. Cross the border 300m to the bus stop for service to Guatemala City via Cuilapa. Tica bus (US$3) passes every half-hour and is safer than 2nd-class service. The last bus from the border to Ahuachapán is at 5:45pm.

pumas and black-crested eagles, but it's the misty peaks and gleaming Pacific Ocean vistas that capture most visitors' attention.

The park is run by **SalvaNatura** (☎ 2279-1515; www.salvanatura.org, in Spanish; admission US$6). In theory you need to visit the San Salvador office to pay the entry fee, but on weekends there's usually someone around.

The vast majority of travelers in Tacuba hook up with the insatiable Manolo from **Imposible Tours** (☎ 2417-4268; www.imposibletours.com; Hostal de Mamá y Papá; tours US$15), a passionate operator committed to improving the lot of the locals. His popular four-hour **waterfall tour** (US$25) is a series of adventurous plunges (or assisted abseils) into icy pools. Among other tours is a **mountain bike ride** to the Pacific Ocean – which can include an overnight stay at a cool beach house in **Barria de Santiago** (2-day tour incl food & drink US$55) and a swim with cayman crocodiles. More gentle tours include a hike to the seven hot pools at **Termas Santa Teresa** (US$15).

It's safe to go it alone in Parque Nacional Imposible – best enter the park from the north and end at the visitors center.

Sleeping & Eating

Hostal de Mamá y Papá (☎ 2417-4268; www.imposibletours.com; dm/d US$7/14, meals extra US$4) The Imposible Tours *hostal* is truly a family affair. Mamá exudes warmth and runs a wonderful kitchen, while Papá strums his guitar. The ground-floor rooms are spacious and include private hot showers, while those beyond the bird-filled garden are more secluded. The upstairs chill-out area has great views. Call ahead for directions. Ask about the new medical volunteer project.

Sol de Media Noche (mains US$2-4; 6:30am-5pm Mon-Sat) Soy lasagna, leafy salads and carrot *tortas* were on offer when we visited this informal vegetarian cafe run by a Salvadoran Hindu sect. Menu changes daily. It's two blocks past the plaza.

Midrange options:

Rancho La Flores (☎ 7899-2396; Colonia Bella Vista; s/d US$14/28;) Three rooms with good views.

La Cabaña (☎ 2417-4332; r US$30;) Big grounds; downhill from the square.

Getting There & Away

Bus 264 and Ruta 15 (US$0.60, 40 minutes, 5:30am to 7pm) go to Ahuachapán from the main plaza.

RUTA DE LAS FLORES

The wildflower of Salvadoran tourism is a 36km-long winding trip through brightly colored colonial towns famed for lazy weekends of gastronomy and gallery-hopping, as well as more adventurous pursuits like mountain biking, horseback riding and hiking to hidden waterfalls scattered throughout the glorious Cordillera Apaneca. Home to the country's first coffee plantations, some of its finest indigenous artisans and a world-famous weekly food festival, the 'Flower Route' anticipates El Salvador's return to the traveler's map.

Bus 249 runs frequently between Sonsonate and Ahuachapán, stopping in all the towns along the way, including Juayúa, Apaneca and Ataco.

Juayúa
pop 10,100

'Why-*ooh*-ah' is famed for its weekend **fería gastronómica** (food fair) where crowds from across the country sample the region's best cuisine and dance to live music on the plaza. Barbecued iguana, guinea pig and frog skewers headline an ambitious menu; less risky fare includes *riguas de coco* (fried coconut and cornmeal) and *elote loco* (crazy corn) lathered with parmesan cheese and mustard.

During the week, Juayúa returns to its relaxed roots, as travelers stroll the warm, cobblestone streets, venture into the surrounding hills to explore hot springs and waterfalls, or just catch their breath by *Cristo Negro*, an important religious statue carved by Quirio Cataño in the late 16th century and housed in the church.

Juayúa has a tumultuous past. Indigenous uprisings in the region ignited the revolutionary movement of 1932. Backed by the coffee elite, government forces brutally quelled the ill-organized insurrection.

ORIENTATION & INFORMATION

Ideal for wandering, Juayúa is small and its streets follow a standard grid. The church is on the west side of the plaza and behind it is the market.

Cyber & Equipment (1a Av Norte; per hr US$0.75; 8:30am-9pm)

Juayutur (9am-5pm Sat & Sun) Juayúa's tourist agency dispenses information about the town and area excursions at its kiosk on the east side of the plaza.

Scotiabank (Calle Monseñor Óscar Romero) Exchanges traveler's checks, gives Visa advances and is adding an ATM.

ACTIVITIES

A recommended hike and swim is to **Los Chorros de Calera**, a series of falls spewing from fractured cliffs to form large, cold pools. The **Ruta de las Seite Cascadas** follows the Río Bebedero over seven scenic drops. Consult Hotel Anáhuac or Casa Mazeta for directions. Occasional thefts mean that certain activities are better undertaken with guides. Other guided excursions include lake visits, coffee tours and waterfall rappels.

SLEEPING & EATING

Hotel Anáhuac (2469-2401; www.tikal.dk/elsalvador; dm/s/d US$7/12.50/25;) The Anáhuac remains Juayúa's unofficial *ministerio de turismo*. The red-tile colonial building offers large, airy rooms and a grassy courtyard. Guests enjoy cooking and internet privileges. César's hikes to hot springs and horseback tours are well worthwhile, as is a night listening to Jenne perform at El Cadejo. Both Danish and English are spoken.

Casa Mazeta Hostal (2406-3403; alex.721@hotmail.fr; dm/s/d US$7/12.50/25;) Run by Alex, a cool young Frenchman, this corner house has been lovingly converted into a brand new, first-class backpackers. Dorms are impeccably presented, with excellent storage and hot-water bathrooms. The large communal areas have great natural light, eclectic furnishings and beautiful tiled floors. Go for the double room with the water fountain.

Casa de Huespedes Doña Mercedes (2452-2287; cnr 2a Av Sur & 6a Calle Oriente; d with/without bathroom US$25/23) A quiet home with large, quality rooms featuring firm beds and spanking-clean shared bathrooms. It's two blocks east and one block south of the plaza.

Taquería la Guadalupana (2a Calle Oriente; mains US$2-5; lunch & dinner Tue-Sun) Irresistible Mexican – evidenced by the chicken in *mole poblano* and *nopal* (cactus) salads, served at cozy benches or in a shaded courtyard.

Tienda San José (main plaza; mains US$2-8; 8:30am-11pm) A mini-mart hides a surprisingly hip dining area, great for the late-night munchies.

El Cadejo (3a Avenida Norte; mains US$3-6; 3pm-late Thu-Sat) An exciting addition to Juayúa's nightlife is this new bar with a guaranteed *buena vibra*. Smoke water pipes while listening to local singer-songwriters, including Jenne from Hotel Anáhuac. Aside from the usual short and tall drinks on offer, you can eat tasty pastas, nachos and wraps.

EL SALVADOR

RR (Calle Mercedes Caceres 1-4 Poniente; mains US$6-16; ☺ lunch & dinner Tue-Sun) Chef Carlos will cook practically whatever you desire, but is a wizard at preparing sizzling-stone hot plates of *revolotijo vegetariano* ('vegetarian revolution,' or mixed vegetables), lean, tender steaks and the finest, freshest salads in El Salvador. The dimly lit courtyard setting is very *capitalino*, and travelers continually rave about the place.

SHOPPING

Canchis Canchis (☎ 2469-2730) The pick of the town's *tiendas* is this colorful shop on the main plaza run by artists Jorge and Veronica who make or sell everything from handpainted coasters to wooden fish and pencil drawings.

GETTING THERE & AWAY

Bus 249 has services northwest to Apaneca (US$0.40, 20 minutes), Ataco (US$0.50, 30 minutes) and Ahuachapán (US$0.80, one hour) and also south to Sonsonate (US$0.55, 45 minutes) during daylight. Buses leave every 15 minutes from the park, or from four blocks west on weekends. For Santa Ana, bus 238 (US$0.50, 40 minutes) goes direct, leaving a few blocks west of Parque Central six times daily.

Apaneca
pop 8600

There's a slight chill in the air in this unearthly quiet mountain town – at 1450m, Apaneca is the second-highest in El Salvador, which largely explains why its coffee is so highly sought after. Cruising the cobblestone streets and the odd nursery aside, there's not much happening in town. Hunt out some locally crafted furniture, or do what the active travelers do, and use it as a base for more high-octane pursuits in the surrounding Sierra Apaneca Ilamatepec.

The beautiful Iglesia San Andres was one of the oldest churches in the country until the 2001 earthquake reduced it to rubble. Restorations are near completion.

ORIENTATION & INFORMATION

The market is west of the park and the church is to the south. Buses drop off and pick up on the main street, right in front of the market. A tourist information booth operates on the plaza on weekends.

Cybercafé Apaneca (3a Av Sur; per hr US$0.75; ☺ 8am-11pm) is behind the former church. There are no banks.

SIGHTS & ACTIVITIES

The crater lakes **Laguna de las Ninfas** and **Laguna Verde**, north and northeast of town, are within hiking distance. The former is swampy, reedy and rife with lily pads; the latter is deep and cold. You can camp at **Chichicastepeque** (aka Cerro Grande), which at 1816m affords outstanding views of the region, although the antennae make it look a lot less wild. For directions or a guide stop by the tourist kiosk.

Apaneca Canopy Tours (☎ 2433-0554; US$30) offers a 2.5km zip-line ride through mountain forest. Tours leave daily at 9:30am, 11:30am, 2pm and 4pm.

A convoy of dirt buggies now leaves **Apaneca Aventura** (☎ 2433-0470/7136-5851; www.apanecaaventura.com; 4a Avenida Norte; 2hr tour for 2 people US$65) daily for Laguna Verde. It's a novel way of getting around and getting dirty.

Vivero (nursery) tours make for a relaxed afternoon of strawberries, strong coffee and rare plants. **Vivero Alejandra** (☺ 7am-4pm Wed-Sun) is a short walk from the center (toward Juayúa). Other *viveros* include **Vivero Santa Clara**, across from Alejandra, and **Las Flores de Eloisa** (☎ 2433-0415), a small cafe 2km toward Ahuachapán.

Finca Santa Leticia (☎ 2433-0357; www.hotelsantaleticia.com; km 86.5; d incl breakfast US$75; 🌀 🖳 🖭) is a hotel, restaurant and coffee farm just south of Apaneca, ideal for families and groups. The highlight of the small onsite **archaeological park** (admission US$5) is two pot-bellied figures carved from huge basalt boulders, weighing between 6350kg and 11,000kg. Experts speculate that these 2000-year-old chubbies were created by early Maya in deference to their rulers.

SLEEPING & EATING

The best restaurants only open weekends when San Salvadorans come day tripping.

Hostal la Magaña (☎ 2433-0268; Av Central btwn 4 & 6 Calles Sur; s/d US$12/24) Quiet and hospitable, this home has two large rooms steeped in burgundy and varnish, as well as impeccable bathrooms. Guests can cook, or relax on the billowy living-room sofas.

Hostal Colonial (☎ 2433-0662; hostalcolonial_apaneca@hotmail.com; cnr 1a Av Sur & 6a Calle Poniente; r US$20-30) Colorful rooms face onto a peaceful courtyard. The owners are very private.

Mercado Saludable (mains US$1.50-3; ☺ 6:30am-8pm) Cheap eats deluxe, this market facing the park offers good little eateries serving ham,

EL SALVADOR

eggs and beans, and *atole* as well as chicken dishes and *pupusas*.

La Cocina de Mi Abuela (☎ 2433-0100; cnr 1a Av Norte & 4a Calle Oriente; mains US$7-15; ☯ 11am-7pm Sat & Sun) Considered one of El Salvador's best restaurants, serving national fare and magnificent desserts.

For more options, check out resort lodges near Apaneca on the highway. Their upmarket restaurants offer the inevitable *buena vista* and a relaxed atmosphere to dally in.

GETTING THERE & AWAY

Bus 249 plies the route between Ahuachapán and Sonsonate, stopping in Apaneca every half-hour. The last bus runs between 7pm and 8pm. Ask a local to be sure.

Ataco

With a small indigenous presence, and many locals involved in the town's thriving textile trade, pastel-colored Ataco is earmarked for bigger crowds. More intimate than Juayúa, it has seen a surge in sleeping and dining options. The town seems commited to keeping its colonial charms intact – though it could keep an eye on protecting its water source – and recent excavations have revealed good ruins nearby.

The **tourist information kiosk** (☯ 7am-7pm Sat & Sun) sits at the entrance to town. You can pick up a handy street map here. Ask about guide services (US$5 to US$10 per person). Options to explore include **Salto de Chacala**, a 50m waterfall on the Río Matala, and **Chorros del Limo**, a spring which forms a broad pool ideal for a dip.

Diconte-Axul (2a Av Sur at Calle Central; ☯ 8am-6pm) is popular for its homemade textiles, tie-dyes and hand-painted objects. The rambling **market** (2a Av Sur) makes for a fascinating walkabout.

SLEEPING & EATING

Cipi Hostel (☎ 2416-5122; www.cipihostels.com; 1a Calle Poniente; dm US$7, r US$20-30; ☒ ☐) This brilliant new backpacker joint is the passion project of Elena, a cheerful manager who studied tourism in Melbourne. Soft linens, fresh flowers, hot showers and spacious grounds make this the best value in town. A Spanish language school should be open when you read this. Elena leads recommended hikes to, among other places, Cerro de la Empalizada.

Casa de Bambú (☎ 2450-5175; 8a Av Sur at 2a Calle Oriente; r without bathroom US$15; ☐) Some basic rooms are available upstairs at this place, which is run by a local doctor.

Villa Santo Domingo (☎ 2450-5442; r US$25; ☐) Beautiful gardens and a spread of local antiques and artworks round out a very pleasant hotel experience hidden inside this red-brick building.

La Caretta (☎ 2450-5369; cnr Av Central & 4a Calle Poniente; mains $3-9) A fine *comida típica* place that also trades in colorful *artesanías*. The *gallo en chicha* (rooster in corn liquor) is the best in town.

Café Tayua (1a Calle Poniente; meals US$3-10) Another hip, art-laden Ataco institution, serving good coffee and *rico* paninis such as the 'hula-hula,' with grilled chicken, pineapple and mozzarella.

House of Coffee (☎ 2450-5353; Av Central; meals US$2-10; ☯ 9am-7pm Mon-Fri, 9am-10pm Sat & Sun) Our favorite coffee in Ataco, and sourced from the owner's nearby plantation. You'll be satisfied by the crepes.

Bus 249 stops on the corner of 2a Calle Oriente and 4a Av Sur. One heads north to Ahuachapán (US$0.35, 15 minutes), and south to Apaneca (US$0.25, 10 minutes), Juayúa (US$0.45, 30 minutes) and Sonsonate (US$0.70, one hour). Frequency is every 15 minutes.

Founded by the pre-Columbian Pipils, the next town along is **Salcoatitán**, which has lots of tiny art galleries down cobblestone streets.

SONSONATE

pop 65,100

The southern end of the flower route is a bustling, sweaty commercial town nicknamed 'Cincinnati.' Home to some of El Salvador's most notorious gangs, it mostly makes a living from coffee and cattle. It's also an important transport hub, so chances are you'll find yourself at the swanky new bus terminal. One thing Sonsonate does do well is party – the city's vivid **Semana Santa** celebration is a national highlight.

The artisan village of **Izalco**, 8km northeast at the foot of Volcán Izalco, was the site of a major indigenous revolt in 1932. Nearby is **Atecozol**, a *turicentro* with swimming holes, kiosks and gardens. The grounds feature stone sculptures by Agustín Estrada – one commemorates Atonatl, a feisty indigenous warrior who pegged conquistador Pedro de Alvarado with an arrow in 1524.

There's easy access to the coastal points of **Los Cóbanos**, a prime Pacific Ocean diving destination, and **Barra de Santiago**, a protected mangrove forest reserve where you can swim

EL SALVADOR

EXPLORE MORE OF WESTERN EL SALVADOR

If you've a sense of adventure and an interest in how indigenous forms have transformed through time, check out the following:

- View local artisans crafting basketry and furniture in **Nahuizalco**, but the real trip is to the night market, with indigenous treats such as grilled *garrobo* (lizard) and snake. There's no lodging – day trip it from Sonsonate. Take bus 249 from Juayúa (to the highway turnoff, 500m away) or bus 53D from Sonsonate.

- The ancient Nahual community of **Izalco** has famed religious wood carvings parading in both Catholic and indigenous rites. Access via Sonsonate bus 53A.

---

with cayman crocodiles, canoe with local fishers and fossick for ancient ruins in the muddy shores. To stay on the huge, unspoilt ocean beach, contact Ximena's Guest House (p285) in San Salvador or Hostal de Mamá y Papá (p302) in Tacuba.

Orientation & Information

The bus terminal is 2km east of the city center. The main north–south street is Av Morazán/Av Rafael Campos. To orient yourself in town, the church is on the east side of the Parque Central.

Citibank (cnr Calle Marroquín & 4a Av Norte) Has a 24-hour ATM.

Post office (1a Av Norte btwn 1 & 3 Calles Poniente)

Sleeping & Eating

Dirt-cheap hotels are in the rough area by the old bus terminal – 'dirt' being the operative word here. Better options are in town.

Hotel Orbe (☎ 2451-1517; cnr 4a Calle Oriente & 2a Av Flavian Muchi; s/d with bathroom US$14/18, s/d with air-con US$20/24; ❄) The long-standing Orbe is still the best value pick in the center. Service is good, and it's close to amenities.

Hotel Plaza (☎ 2451-6626; www.hotelplazasonsonate.com; 9a Calle Oriente at 8a Av Norte; s/d US$35/45; P ❄ ❄) So what if it's stuck in the '80s? The Plaza's rooms are Alaska-cool with firm beds and cable TV. You can rest your traveling bones at the pool and the restaurant is worth trying too.

Hotel Agape (☎ 2451-2667; Km 63 Carretera de San Salvador; s/d US$35/45; P ❄ ❄) Located out on

the highway, and is recommended by travelers for its swimming pool and friendly service.

La Casona (3 Calle Poniente btwn 1 & 3 Av Norte; mains US$1.50-4; ❄ breakfast & lunch Mon-Sat) *Comida a la vista* is dished up fresh and *pupusas* sizzle and steam in the city's best bargain restaurant, located in an antiquated building.

For junk-food feasting, try the **food stands** (7a Calle Oriente at 10a Av Norte; ❄ 5-10pm) where you can grab burgers, sandwiches, fries and *pupusas*.

Getting There & Away

Take a taxi or bus 53C from the central park to the bus station. Buses to San Salvador leave from outside the terminal. Destinations include the following:

Ahuachapán (via Juayúa, Apaneca & Ataco) Bus 249 (US$0.95; 2hr)

Barra de Santiago Bus 285 (US$1; 1¼hr; 10:30am & 4:30pm), or take bus 259 to turnoff and catch a pickup.

La Hachadura Bus 259 (US$0.85; 1¾hr)

La Libertad Bus 287 (US$1.25; 2½hr)

La Perla Bus 261 (US$0.80; 1½hr)

Los Cóbanos Bus 257 (US$0.50; 40min)

Parque Nacional El Imposible Any La Hachadura bus to Puente Ahuachapío or Cara Sucia (US$0.45; 30min).

San Salvador Bus 205 (*directo* US$0.80; 1½ hr; *especial* US$1.50; 1½hr)

Santa Ana Bus 216 (US$0.65; 1¼hr)

The terminal also serves Izalco (bus 53A), Nahuizalco (bus 53D) and Acajutla (bus 252).

PARQUE NACIONAL EL IMPOSIBLE

Tropical mountain forest Parque Nacional El Imposible was named for the perilous gorge that claimed the lives of farmers and pack mules transporting coffee to the Pacific port. Decreed a national park in 1989, it sits in the Apaneca Ilamatepec mountain range between 300m and 1450m above sea level, and includes eight rivers which feed the watershed for Barra de Santiago and the mangrove forests along the coast.

This original forest – the remains of a threatened ecosystem – is still home to an extraordinary variety of plant and animal life, including pumas, tigrillos, wild boars, king hawks and black-crested eagles. Hiking can get muddy and steep but offers grand vistas of misty peaks and the gleaming Pacific Ocean.

Information

The main San Benito entrance is on the southeast side, beyond the hamlet of San Miguelito. The park is run by **SalvaNatura** (☎ 2279-1515; www.

salvanatura.org, in Spanish; entry US$6); in theory you need to visit the San Salvador office (p280) to pay the entry fee and arrange for guide service (there is no guide fee but a US$5 tip is customary). The best time to visit is October to February, as the rainy season hinders travel.

The solar-powered visitors center has a modest museum and lookout tower with ocean views.

Major hikes:

Cerro El Leon A tough 8km circuit topping out on one of the park's highest peaks (1113m), starting in a lush, humid gorge and climbing through dense forest. This trail offers terrific panoramic views. From the visitors center the trail descends steeply 1km to the Río Ixcanal. Crossing the river you climb the other side, known as Montaña de los Águilares, to the summit. Return by a different route, along the narrow ridge between the Ixcanal and Guayapa river valleys. Allow several hours and bring plenty of water.

Los Enganches An ideal picnic spot, this big swimming hole is reached by a trail (3.5km one way), which passes Mirador El Mulo and descends steeply. Along the way you'll pass Mirador Madre Cacao, with views of the southeastern part of the park. Look for agoutis and coatis.

Piedra Sellada A 4km trail to a swimming spot and a stone etched with Maya writings. Take the Los Enganches trail; just before the end another trail cuts upriver 1km to Piedra Sellada.

Sleeping & Eating

Hostal El Imposible (☎ 2411-5484; d US$30, extra person US$10; 🏊) About 1km from the park entrance is this smart eco-resort featuring five A-frame cabins. The views from the patios are gorgeous, plus there's a delicious organic restaurant.

Three large camping areas with toilets and grills are within walking distance of the visitors center; the furthest one (20-minute walk) is the least crowded. Camp free with your entrance fee; the visitors center rents gear

(tents US$5 to US$7, bring bedding). Small fires are allowed and potable water is available.

Getting There & Away

From Sonsonate catch bus 259 toward La Hachadura and get off at Cara Sucia. From there, a bus leaves at 11am and a pickup at 2pm (both US$2, one hour) for the main entrance. The trucks return to Cara Sucia every morning at 5:30am and 7:30am. If you think you might miss the pickups in Cara Sucia, you may be able to cut them off at Puente Ahuachapío (bridge), a few kilometers short of Cara Sucia. If the pickups have already passed, you may be able to hitch a ride (13.5km).

You can also visit the park from the northern side via Tacuba.

EASTERN EL SALVADOR

Eastern El Salvador may not possess the star attractions of elsewhere in the country, but with timeless mountain villages such as Alegría, the devastating war around Morazán, and its long, deserted golden beaches, even the most worldly traveler will be pleasantly surprised.

Prior to the war, subsistence farming was long the primary means of survival here. The inevitable demand for nationwide land reform resonated throughout the poorer communities, and the northeast in particular became a fierce guerrilla stronghold. Far from the capital, these mountainous areas witnessed horrific atrocities – none worse than El Mozote – but barely a village was spared from the fighting, and the resilience of the locals will stir visitors for generations to come.

Remittances continue to pour in from relatives working abroad – whether this is a long-term economic solution is still to be seen – but new money is nonetheless providing opportunities to a generation bristling with positive intent. However, stalled construction of a deluxe port at La Unión is a reminder that development takes time in the 'Wild East.'

Further south run beautiful sand beaches, especially around El Cuco and Las Flores. Better yet, they only see fleeting traffic from nearby cities such as San Miguel, the working-class capital with a distinctly cavalier attitude. Real off-the-beaten-track coastal adventure is found at Golfo de Fonseca and Bahía de Jiquilisco, where tiny fishing villages pay little attention to the big, bad outside world.

EL SALVADOR

There are two ways to travel east – along the Carretera Interamericana or along the Carreteradel Litoral (CA2); the latter accesses the beaches, and the former the northern reaches. The Ruta de La Paz (peace route) runs north from San Miguel.

EAST ALONG THE INTERAMERICANA

The Carretera Interamericana goes east from San Salvador to San Miguel, on to La Unión and up again to the El Salvador–Honduras border at El Amatillo.

A few towns of interest lie between San Salvador and San Vicente on the Interamericana. **Cojutepeque**, 32km east of San Salvador, is a small town best known for the Cerro las Pavas (Hill of the Turkeys), featuring an outdoor shrine to the Virgen de Fátima, brought here from Portugal in 1949. Religious pilgrims come on Sunday and on May 13, **El Día de la Virgen**. In San Salvador, catch bus 113 from the Reloj de Flores, just west of the Terminal de Oriente; it's about a 45-minute ride.

Further along the highway (54km from San Salvador or 22km from Cojutepeque) is the turnoff to **Ilobasco**, a town famous for ceramics known as *sorpresas* (see the boxed text, p310). Upon entering the town a string of *artesanía* shops lines Av Carlo Bonilla. The annual **crafts fair** runs September 24 to 29. Take bus 111 or 142 from the Terminal de Oriente or from Cojutepeque.

Another 8.5km heading east along the Interamericana is the road to **San Sebastián**, known for woven hammocks and textiles, and unique as most of the weavers are male. The fair takes place at the end of January. Take bus 111 or catch a bus in Cojutepeque.

SAN VICENTE

pop 34,600

One of the prettiest towns in the east, San Vicente is dwarfed by pointy Volcán Chichontepec in the Jiboa Valley. Look out for the equally dramatic, though manmade, behemoth of Torre Kiosko, an otherwordly clock tower that juts from the farmland like some Disneyland ride gone haywire. Home to many musicians, San Vicente is also very gay-friendly – the annual Miss Gay San Vicente draws quite the crowd (and the contestants!).

El Pilar, a beautiful colonial church built in the 1760s, was badly damaged by an earthquake; despite renovations, it remains closed.

Orientation & Information

The cathedral sits on the east side of the park. A large army barracks takes up the entire block southwest of the park. The main drag, 1a Av, runs north–south, passing a block west of the park.

Citibank (2a Av Sur) Cashes traveler's checks and has a 24-hour ATM.

Fast Line Ciber Café (2a Calle Oriente; per hr US$1; ☺ 9am-9pm)

Police (☎ 2303-7300, 2396-3353; cnr 1a Av Norte & 3a Calle Poniente) Can arrange for an escort up the volcano.

Activities

The double-peaked **Chichontepec** (also known as Volcán San Vicente) offers a moderate climb through coffee plantations. This eight-hour round-trip is relatively safe but it's best to go in a group or get a police escort from Nuevo Tepetitán or San Vicente. Wear sturdy boots and bring a sweatshirt, lots of water and food for you and your escorts. Take bus 191 (US$0.25, 20 minutes) to Nuevo Tepetitán, where the trail begins. Buses leave from the corner of Calle Alvaro Quiñonez de Osorio and 9a Av every half-hour from 6:30am; last return bus is at 7:15pm.

Sleeping & Eating

Hotel Central Park (☎ 2393-0383; s with fan/air-con US$10/15; ❄) Come for the 2nd-floor terrace, stay for a bed if you really must – only the sheets resemble anything fresh or clean. The small bar is popular among the gay community, and the restaurant (open 6:30am to 10pm) below the hotel serves decent *típica*. Doors are locked at 8pm.

Casa de Huespedes El Turista (☎ 2393-0323; 4a Calle Poniente 15 at 1 Av Sur; d US$10-15) San Vicente's best bargain offers ultratidy rooms (early arrivals pay more) which are a bit dated and small. Enjoy the hammock, leafy courtyard and roof with a view.

Comedor Rivolí (1 Av Sur; mains US$2-4; ☺ 7am-8:30pm) The most popular place in town, and justly so – check out the baked chicken, salads and roasted veggies, all fresh and homemade. This *comida a la vista* is served in a spotless dining room alongside rose gardens. Don't miss the delicious dollar *licuados*.

Getting There & Away

All buses pass by the Parque Central after leaving the bus terminal up the hill on 6a Calle and 15 Av. Beat the crowds at the park without hoofing it to the terminal by catching buses at 6a Calle and 2a Av. Departures include the following:

Alegría Catch an eastward bus from the Carretera Interamericana and transfer at Villa El Triunfo.

Ilobasco Bus 530 (US$0.60; 1hr) Departures at 6:50am, 11am and 4pm.

San Miguel Bus 301 from the turnoff at the highway (US$1.50; 1½hr). Last bus at 6pm.

San Salvador Bus 116 (US$0.85; 1½hr) Last bus at 6pm.

Zacatecoluca Bus 177 (US$0.60; 50min).

ALEGRÍA

Alegría is a beautiful mountain town enjoying a renaissance with domestic visitors. Its lofty location, near-spotless streets and windowsills overflowing with rose bushes, sunflowers and orchids give it a fairytale feel quite unlike the rest of El Salvador. Young artists and new businesses are infusing energy here. A few lazy days and nights hiking by the lake and serenading the town square could well prove a highlight of your travels.

The friendly **tourist agency** (☎ 2628-1087; 1a Av Norte at 1a Calle Poniente) has a municipal office and a booth on the Parque Central. It also offers some worthy guided hikes (US$10 to US$15 per half-day) to coffee plantations, geothermal plants and sites related to philosopher and native Alegrían, Alberto Masferrer. The scenic crater lake **La Laguna de Alegría** (admission US$0.25) is a 2km downhill walk from town. Its icy waters are said to be medicinal. Don't miss the beautiful view from the **Mirador de las Cien Grados** – a vista point at the top of 100 steps. Take the road toward **Berlín**, another pretty mountain village.

Sleeping & Eating

Casa Alegre (☎ 7201-8641; www.lacasaalegre.zoomblog.com; Av Camilo Campos; d/tw US$10/20) Primarily a 'creative residence,' the passion of local artists Memo and Paola is best seen on the 1st-floor gallery where recycled art and contemporary pieces jostle for your attention. There's a worthy volunteer program that runs art classes for local kids. The few rooms are clean and basic, and the tiled bath is invariably cold.

Casa de Huéspedes la Palma (☎ 2628-1131; 1a Av Norte near Calle Alberto Masferrer; dm US$10; 💻) Big rickety rooms with worn tiles and firm beds characterize this family guesthouse which also has a curious clutter of photos, carvings and religious dioramas. A plus is the onsite internet cafe serving coffee on the plaza.

Entre Piedras Hotel (☎ 2313-2812; entrepiedras.alegria@hotmail.com; Av Camilo Campus; s/d US$16/32; 💥 🚫 💻) This beautiful, small hotel on the edge of the town square is the ideal resting place 'between walks.' It boasts original stone foundations and breezy rooms with wooden panelling throughout. Firm beds have high-quality linens and there's a charming courtyard cafe (paninis US$5). Book ahead on weekends.

La Casa Mia (☎ 2634-0608; www.berlinlacasamia.com; 2a Av Norte, Berlín; d US$33) Nearby Berlín is a copycat cute village. If Alegría is full, or you just want some real mountain beauty, stay at this intimate family hotel that opened more than 70 years ago.

Merendero Mi Pueblito (mains US$1-5; 🕙 7am-7pm) Alegría's best-value food is at this worn cafe where beans simmer in cast-iron pots over an open flame and the whole family chips in. It's south of the park.

El Portal (🕙 11am-9pm) The pick of the park cafes for an evening beer (US$1).

Getting There & Away

Alegría sits between the Interamericana and Litoral highways and is accessible from either side. From Carretera Interamericana, catch a minibus from Villa El Triunfo to Santiago de María (US$0.30, 15 minutes), where buses leaves hourly for Alegría (US$0.60, 45 minutes). See Usulután (p310) for transportation from the Carretera del Litoral side.

CARRETERA DEL LITORAL

The Carretera del Litoral (Hwy CA2) runs from San Salvador southeast through Zacatecoluca and Usulután, eventually coming to a crossroads with routes heading north to San Miguel and south to the Pacific coast.

The first town of any size southeast of San Salvador is **Zacatecoluca** (57km), near *turicentro* Ichanmichen. From there, the Litoral is a well-marked four-lane highway with shoulders, until you get to the Río Lempa. Beyond the bridge, the road narrows but maintains decent shape. Another 27km to the east is the departmental capital of Usulután.

The highway then skirts a rugged range to the south. The turnoff for one of El Salvador's best beaches, **Playa El Espino**, is just past El Tránsito, 10km east of Usulután. The newly paved road has cut the trip to 20 minutes. Further east, **Laguna El Jocotal** is an important migratory bird sanctuary, sadly littered with trash. Your best bet is to tour the lagoon via canoe with a local.

EL SALVADOR

¿TÍPICA OR PÍCARA?

Sorpresas (surprises) are little scenes and figures hidden in egg-sized shells, pioneered by folk artist Dominga Herrera of Ilobasco. Underneath a bulbous papaya or white chapel you'll find a charming microsized scene of village life – usually. One local artist got sassy and sculpted a couple in the giddy throes of sex. The illicit art was condemned by the town priest and briefly removed from stores. But prosperity may have beat out piety. '*Pícara*' (sinful) *sorpresas*, now available as matchbox copulation scenes, continue selling strong. Expect yours to come discreetly wrapped.

The road then winds up into lava hills until the roundabout at El Delirio. From there, it's a straight shot north to San Miguel or south to Playa El Cuco and the eastern beaches.

ISLA MONTECRISTO

A steamy, pristine sanctuary for hundreds of pelicans and egrets, this island and estuary sit where the Río Lempa meets the Pacific Ocean. During the war, the island and its cashew plantation were abandoned and taken over by the FMLN. After 1992, it was resettled by local farmers taking advantage of the postwar land transfer program. These days there are about 25 families growing organic cashews as an export crop.

ourpick Hostal Lempa Mar (☎ 2310-9901; www.gbajolempa.net; La Pita; r US$25), operated by a local development group, is highly recommended. Simple cabins offer basic rooms with shared bathrooms and a comfortable terrace, and there are meals available in the restaurant. **Boat tours** travel through narrow corridors in the mangroves; some visit the cashew plantations as well. A fishing cooperative in Estero Jaltepeque can arrange **fishing trips** or the rental of traditional **canoes**.

La Pita and Montecristo are at the end of a 22km road which connects the Carretera Litoral to the coast. The road can be rough in rainy season. Take bus 155 (US$0.70, 40 minutes) or a pickup from the Texaco in San Nicolas Lempa, with departures between 6am and 5:30pm.

From La Pita, *lanchas* (small motorboats; US$20 round trip) or canoes (US$4 one way) can take you out to the island.

USULUTÁN

pop 45,300

Tented market stands choke the streets of this chaotic departmental capital at the foot of 1450m Volcán de Usulután. Middle Eastern immigrants exert a strong influence over the town's commerce. But for travelers Usulután will probably serve as a way station to Bahía de Jiquilisco and the lovely Playa El Espino. You can also reach the mountain hamlet of Alegría from here.

Information

Citibank (2a Calle Oriente near Av Dr Guandiquil) On the Parque Central, it cashes traveler's checks and has a 24-hour ATM.

Cyber Planet (4a Calle Oriente btwn 2a & 4a Avs Norte; per hr US$0.50; ⏰ 8:30am-6pm Mon-Sat, 8:30am-noon Sun; 🖥)

Sleeping & Eating

La Posada de Don Quijote (☎ 2635-9792; cnr 1a Calle Poniente & 1a Av Sur; s/d US$12/24; 🖥) This new hotel inside a small shopping complex has spacious rooms with freshly unpacked mattresses, piping hot showers and a pleasant 1st-floor terrace.

Pastelería Trigo Puro (Calle Dr Penado; mains US$2-3; ⏰ 7am-5pm Mon-Sat) Fat cinnamon rolls, doughnuts and coconut cookies beckon from the glass case of this popular bakery, also serving cafeteria-style *típico*. It's one block west of the park.

L'Azteca (Calle Dr Federíco Penado at 1a Av Norte; mains US$2-3; ⏰ 10am-8pm) Large Mexican place with open windows, long wooden benches and a sizzling barbecue out front. The *tortas* cooked out front are delicious, as are the sizable tacos and the icy cold *licuados*.

The **Mercado Central** (4a Av Norte btwn 2a & 4a) is a hit with street-food aficionados.

Getting There & Away

Usulután's main bus terminal is 1.5km east of the Parque Central (taxi US$2). The San Miguel terminal is west of town, but passengers can board along 1a Calle Oriente, a block south of the Parque Central. Buses to Alegría, Puerto Triunfo and San Salvador all take 4a Calle west through the center of town. Since most buses travel this way through town you don't necessarily have to go to the terminal (unless you want a seat).

Alegría; Bus 348 to Berlín (US$1; 1hr)

Playa El Cuco Bus 373 to El Delirio (US$0.80; 2hr)

Playa El Espino Buses 351 & 358 (US$1.20; 1½hr) Catch them from a small lot 100m west of main terminal, across from a supermarket.

Puerto El Triunfo Bus 363 (US$0.50; 1hr) Leaves from a lot along the highway.

Puerto Parada Bus 350 (US$0.30; 30 min)

San Miguel Bus 373 (US$0.80; 1½hr) Take this bus to connect to La Unión.

San Salvador Bus 302 (*directo* US$1.50; 2½hr; *especial* US$2; 1½hr)

Zacatecoluca Bus 302 (US$0.70; 1½hr)

BAHÍA DE JIQUILISCO

With kilometer after kilometer of white sand pounded by surf, and inland mangroves facing the volcanoes, the Península San Juan del Gozo beckons. The inland sector is a habitat for gray egrets, pelicans and other waterbirds. Fishing towns include **Corral de Mulas** and **Isla Méndez**. Other less-accessible beaches are at **Punta San Juan** on the peninsula's east end and **Isla Madre Sal**. Also called Isla Jobal, **Isla Espíritu Santo** has endless coconut groves and a coconut-oil processing plant, but the beaches are no big deal. The Pacific side has strong and powerful surf, so be careful.

The gateway to Bahía de Jiquilisco, seedy **Puerto El Triunfo** is best sped through. If you're desperate, Hotel El Jardín has doubles for US$12. The pier eateries overlooking the bay offer fresh fish, *pupusas* and *licuados*.

Corral de Mulas & Isla Méndez

Passenger boats to **Corral de Mulas** (US$2) leave in the early morning from the dock. El Icaco is a better option to *Corral II*. Once there, cut through town on sandy – sometimes flooded – roads to the beach (30 minutes). The last boat back is at 4pm; if you miss it, ask for a lodging recommendation at the *alcaldía*.

Isla Méndez offers a bay beach with calm, shallow waters and a palm-frocked ocean beach with crashing surf. Due to bus schedules, travelers are obliged to stay the night. It could be interesting, however. Local community development group **Adesco** (☎ 7727-3453) can arrange US$10 overnight family homestays. It also arranges boat trips around the bay (US$35 per group) that travel through mangroves and Palacio de las Aves, home to hundreds of waterfowl.

Popular with sportfishing families from San Salvador, the **Barillas Marine Club** (☎ 2263-3650; www.barillasmarina.com; family bungalows US$115; 🚻 🖳 🖭) rents comfortable houses on a private marina.

OFF-THE-BEATEN-TRACK: ISLA SAN SEBASTIAN

Isla San Sebastian is the largest island on the Bahía de Jiquilisco. To get here, take the 350 bus to Puerto Parada from Usulután. The road ends at an estuary; there are a couple of cheap fish restaurants here and a few boats bobbing about (US$25 round trip). If the empty beaches convince you to stay in the pretty little archipelago, ask for **La Familia Flores** (r US$15) and you'll be shown to a unique family home made entirely from coconut husks, a potentially lucrative building material. You might just be the second foreigner to stay here!

Bus 368 (US$1, 1¼ hours) goes to Isla Méndez from San Marcos Lempa (30km away on the Carretera Litoral) at 1pm and 2pm, returning at 5:30am and 6:30am. From San Marcos Lempa buses go to Puerto El Triunfo (11km) frequently.

See Usulután (opposite page) for bus information; the last bus to Puerto El Triunfo is at 4:40pm, the last one back to Usulután is at 5:30pm. From the highway turnoff, take bus 377 to San Miguel (US$1.35, 2½ hours, last bus 2:50pm) or bus 185 to San Salvador (US$1.55, two hours, every 30 minutes, last bus 2:50pm).

SAN MIGUEL
pop 218,400

The ugly stepsister to San Salvador, San Miguel is an intense working-class city, its sticky heat rising up from calamitous streets. It's also a brashly confident place with a commercial energy to rival the capital and locals who relish the seedy, sexy nightlife.

Founded in 1530, organised crime long held sway over politicians and police. It's hoped the new government will draw vigilantes into the fold, but with remittances still pouring in – and unemployment still high – it's as likely to change face as iconic Volcan Chaparrastique is to erupt anytime soon.

Parque David J Guzmán is Parque Central, with the cathedral to the east. The area is choked with traffic by day and dodgy by night. The area west of central park is quieter and more secure. Av Roosevelt (Carretera Interamericana) skirts the southwestern edge of town, where you'll find the majority of nightclubs and a large Metrocentro mall.

Information

Banco Cuscatlán (4a Calle Oriente & Av Barrios) Exchanges traveler's checks and foreign currency and has a 24-hour ATM.

Banco Salvadoreño (cnr Av Barrios & 2a Calle Poniente) Cashes traveler's checks, does Visa cash advances and has a 24-hour ATM.

Immigration office (Migración; ☎ 2660-0957; cnr 15a Calle Oriente & 8a Av Sur; ◷ 8am-4pm Mon-Fri)

Post office (cnr 4a Av Sur & 3a Calle Oriente)

Dangers & Annoyances

Although gang violence has quietened with new security measures, the city center is still the wrong place to be once the sun sets.

Sights & Activities

CENTRO

Facing Parque David J Guzmán, San Miguel's cathedral, **Catedral Nuestra Señora de la Paz**, dates from the 18th century. Around the corner, on 2a Calle Oriente, is the **Antiguo Teatro Nacional**, a neoclassical gem which functioned as a cinema during the silent-film era and later as the Telecom headquarters and a public hospital. The **Museo Regional del Oriente** is in the same building on the 2nd floor. The collection of pottery and photos is meager but it's free.

AROUND TOWN

Archaeology buffs will appreciate the **Ruinas de Quelepa**, grassy mounds covering 40 terraced ceremonial platforms, largely unexcavated.

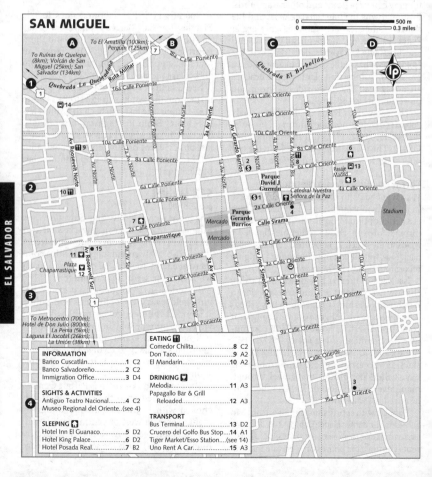

SAN MIGUEL

0   500 m
0   0.3 miles

Lenca inhabited the site between the 2nd and 7th centuries AD, trading with Copán in Honduras as well as Mexico. Stone sculptures uncovered here are on display in the Museo Regional del Oriente. The ruins are 8km west of San Miguel off the Interamericana. From the cathedral, bus 90 to Moncagua (US$0.40, 30 minutes) passes them.

If you're game for a steep nine-hour slog, consider climbing 2130m **Volcano Chaparrastique**, aka Volcán de San Miguel, a towering cone southwest of San Miguel. Arrange police escorts through the **Chinameca Police Station** (☎ 2665-0074; fax 2665-1014). Request with two weeks' notice, if possible. The top affords gaping views of the coast and a patchwork of rolling farmland. The crater is hundreds of meters deep, with a jumble of boulders and Virgins at the bottom. Get there with a rental car or take the Placitas bus from San Miguel at the corner of Calle Chaparrastique and 7a Av Sur and then arrange a taxi.

Festivals

Every November San Miguel honors the Virgen de la Paz with **Fiestas Patronales**, marking the occasion with holy processions and enormous, colorful sawdust carpets. Save yourself for its blowout finale, **Carnaval**, a city-wide party held the last Saturday of November.

Sleeping

The cheapest places to stay are by the bus terminal, a gritty area unsafe after dark.

ourpick Hotel de Don Julio (☎ 2661-4113; 14 Calle Elizabeth; s/d without bathroom US$8/12, d US$25; P ⊠ ⬚) Highly recommended for all types is this ultra-modern hotel with clean double bedrooms, superb bathrooms and volcano views. Extras include cable TV, minibar, small gym and internet cafe. It's in one of San Miguel's better neighborhoods.

Hotel Inn El Guanaco (☎ 2261-5029; 8a Av Norte at Pasaje Madrid; s/d US$20/30; ⊠) Small and welcoming, El Guanaco has enormous spotless rooms with hot-water bathrooms and cable TV. For something quiet and removed, choose the 3rd floor. There's a pool table and promising smells wafting up from its ground-level restaurant.

Hotel King Palace (☎ 2661-1086; www.hotelking palace.com, in Spanish; 6a Calle Oriente 609; s US$22-28, deluxe d US$28-35; ⊠ ⬚ ⬚) Right across from the bus station, this business hotel's greatest asset is the helpful and professional staff. Spacious

renovated rooms have flat-screen TVs; the cheapies are small but fine.

Hotel Posada Real (☎ 2261-7174; cnr 7a Av & 2a Calle Poniente; s/d US$23/30; ⊠) In the safer and sub-dued neighborhood west of the market, this well-kept pink two-story hotel offers bland but amenable rooms, with good beds, air-con and TV. Take an upstairs room; those downstairs smell of mildew.

Eating

The best value is *comida a la vista* for breakfast and lunch at a *comedor;* show up early when the trays are full and the food is fresh.

Pastelería Lorena (3a Calle Poniente 21; cakes US$0.20-3; ⓨ 7am-7pm) El Salvador's most famous bakery started here. A glass of *horchata* and a slice of *Maria Luisa* (jam cake) are the business.

Comedor Chilita (cnr 8a Calle Oriente & 6a Av Norte Bis; mains US$2-3; ⓨ 7am-10pm) This buzzing cafeteria spoons up a happy, huge variety that includes steamed veggies, spaghetti and roasted pepper chicken. After 4pm, it's all *pupusas* – use the side entrance on 8a Calle Oriente.

El Mandarín (Av Roosevelt Norte 407; mains US$4-10; ⓨ 10am-9pm) Authentic Chinese cuisine in an immaculate, heavily air-conditioned restaurant. The sweet-and-sour chicken and vegetable chow mein are both seriously satisfying.

La Pema (mains US$5-12; ⓨ 10:30am-4:30pm) One of the country's most famous restaurants; get the *mariscada* (creamy seafood soup), served up with a mallet and thick cheese tortillas. It's 5km on the road to Playa El Cuco.

Good, cheap Mexican is found at **Don Taco** (Av Roosevelt Norte 320; mains US$2-3; ⓨ noon-10pm).

Drinking

The notorious party district *el triángulo* (intersection of Av Roosevelt and the highway) doesn't get going until 11pm, when the mariachis congregate at the intersection gas station to await a prized gig. Be sure to ask your taxi driver for a *discoteca*, and not a 'nightclub,' unless of course you're looking for strippers. Robberies have been committed by men posing as taxi drivers outside nightspots.

Papagallo Bar & Grill Reloaded (Plaza Chaparrastique, Av Roosevelt Sur) The new venue in the Pizza Hut compound has diminished the crowds somewhat, but management assured us the Latin and pop-music dance floor 'really gets going' after midnight. Decent food is served all night.

Melodia (Plaza Chaparrastique, Av Roosevelt Sur) They should make all *discotecas* like this – booming,

EL SALVADOR

cheesy, high-heeled and high-octane Latin pop paradise where large contingents of well-heeled students compete for each other's attention. Drinks are cheapest before midnight, but of course it's empty till 1am.

Getting There & Away

BUS

San Miguel's bus terminal has clearly marked bus lanes but ask around for schedules. Taxi to your hotel if you arrive at night. Destinations include the following:

El Amatillo (Honduran border) Bus 330 (US$1.90; 1½hr) At 10 minute intervals from 4am to 6pm.
El Cuco Bus 320 (US$1; 1½hr)
La Unión Bus 324 (US$1; 1¼hr)
Marcala, Honduras Bus 426 (US$3.50; 5½hr) Departs 4:40am and 11:40am.
Perquín Bus 332 (US$1.35; 3hr) Leaves at 6:20am, 9:50am, 10:20am, 12:40pm and 3:20pm. Alternately, take 328 to San Francisco Gotera and transfer to a pickup.
Puerto El Triunfo Bus 377 (US$1.60; 2hr)
San Salvador Bus 301 (US$2.20; 3hr; *especial* US$3.20; 2hr)
Usulután Bus 373 (US$1; 1½hr)

CAR

Hire a car through **Uno Rent A Car** (☎ 2661-0344; Av Roosevelt Sur).

LA UNIÓN

pop 23,600

While some pockets retain a salt-crusted colonial charm, La Unión is the kind of town Popeye would look over his shoulder in. It's hot and downright dirty, with little to keep you here but an overdue boat headed for the horizon. The heat is brutal; even dogs whimper at noon. Locals hope that the new deep-sea port will generate more prospects, but two years since construction it still sits ominously quiet, awaiting clearance from the captains of industry. Till then, chow down on dried squid and ready your beach bum for the remote islands in the Golfo de Fonseca (p316).

Playa Las Tunas and Playa Jaguey are good beaches on the coast west of La Unión, while beaches near Playa El Cuco and El Tamarindo are excellent.

For some respite from the heat, and views of the gulf, head to **Conchagua**, at the base of the imposing volcano of the same name.

Information

Cyber Café (3a Av Norte btwn 3a & 7a Calles Oriente; per hr US$0.70) High speeds and newish computers.

Immigration office (☎ 2604-4375; cnr Av General Cabañas & 7a Calle Poniente; 6am-10pm Mon-Sat) Next door to the post office, the sign says *Control Migración*. You must stop by here if you're arriving or departing by boat from Nicaragua or Honduras.
Plaza Médica Vida (☎ 2604-2065; Calle General Menéndez btwn 7a & 9a Avs Sur; 24hr) A decent hospital near the center.
Scotiabank (3a Calle Oriente btwn 1a Calle Sur & Av General Cabañas) Changes traveler's checks and has a 24-hour ATM.

Sleeping & Eating

Casa de Huéspedes El Dorado (cnr Calle San Carlos & 2a Av Norte; s/d US$8/12;) The mango trees in the courtyard are the redeeming feature of this grim guesthouse in the heart of the marketplace. The tiny rooms are crammed with old beds and rusty fans. Management is nonchalant.

Hotel San Francisco (☎ 2604-4159; Calle General Menéndez btwn 9a & 11a Avs Sur; s/d with air-con US$32/40;) Fernando is the eccentric barefooted owner of this colonial structure that is more impressive from the outside. Rooms are pricey given the old beds and leaky bathrooms, but it's located in a decent street and guests can store their belongings if headed for the islands.

Comfort Inn (☎ 2665-6565; km 2.8 Calle a Playitas Carretera Panamericana; r US$69;) This fairly new out-of-the-box hotel has decent-sized rooms and a swimming pool. You can sleep four people for the room price. It's on the way into town.

Pupusería Mayra (Calle General Menéndez; mains US$1-2; 5-10pm) Across the road from San Francisco and heaving with a post-gospel crowd, this local insitution is the best bet for *panes de pollo* (chicken sandwiches) and fresh *pupusas*. Don't be shy or they'll run out.

Cappucino's (1 Calle Poniente 2-2; coffee US$2, snacks US$2-4; 8am-7pm) Like a mirage in a desert of dodgy street food, Cappucino's is a flash new cafe with ice-cold air-con and plush vinyl lounges run by a recently returned ex-Californian. The coffee is clearly the star, but try the breakfast sandwiches (US$4).

For fine seafood dining check out the waterfront east of the center. Nearby **Las Lunas** (3a Av Norte, Playa Los Coquitos; 2pm-2am) offers nightlife in the form of karaoke and occasional Saturday concerts under a thatched bar.

Getting There & Away

The bus terminal is on 3a Calle Poniente between 4a and 6a Avs Norte. Services include the following:

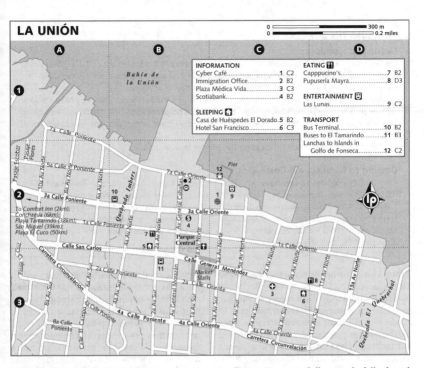

LA UNIÓN

0 _____ 300 m
0 _____ 0.2 miles

INFORMATION
Cyber Café.....................1 C2
Immigration Office..........2 B2
Plaza Médica Vida...........3 C3
Scotiabank....................4 B2

SLEEPING
Casa de Huéspedes El Dorado.5 B2
Hotel San Francisco..........6 C3

EATING
Capppucino's..................7 B2
Pupusería Mayra.............8 D3

ENTERTAINMENT
Las Lunas......................9 C2

TRANSPORT
Bus Terminal.................10 B2
Buses to El Tamarindo.......11 B3
Lanchas to Islands in Golfo de Fonseca.............12 C2

Conchagua Bus 382A (US$0.25; 15min)

El Amatillo (Honduran border) Santa Rosa de Lima bus 342 (US$0.95; 1hr) to San Carlos, transfer to bus 330 at the turnoff.

El Tamarindo Bus 383 (US$0.95; 1¾hr)

Las Playitas Bus 418 (US$0.90; 1hr)

San Miguel Bus 324 (US$0.90; 1¼hr; *especial* US$1.10; 1hr)

San Salvador Bus 304 (US$3; 4hr; *especial* US$5; 3hr)

Santa Rosa de Lima Bus 342 (US$0.90; 1½hr)

BEACHES NEAR LA UNIÓN

These long, sweeping stretches of golden sand are often overlooked by international beach-combers. The preserve of San Miguel elite, **Playa Esteron** is the pick, partly due to its small, clean surf and endless expanses of empty shore.

La Tortuga Verde (☎ 7774-4855; Playa Esteron; d US$20; ⊠ ☎) is the inspired vision of entrepreneurial *el gringo*, Tom Poliak. 'The Green Turtle' is one man's organic fantasy – superlative beach-front rooms constructed from recycled wood and found stone. Soft, indirect lighting adjusts your eyes to the billion stars above your flywire ceiling. Old cheese presses and canoe paddles complement a conceptual garden and ultra-cool swimming pool. Other features include

a village restaurant, dollar *tienda* full of used Manhattan fashions, expert surf trips with Tom and a small day-spa. Yoga retreats are planned, as are monthly music festivals and a permanent turtle hatchery (10,000 eggs were saved in 2009 alone). The primary school next door is run by Tom's sister and welcomes volunteers. La Tortuga Verde is 3km east of El Cuco.

About 3km west of Esteron is the more prominent **Playa El Cuco**, which is overrun with weekenders from San Miguel. Be aware of potential jellyfish and manta rays – shuffle while walking out. There are plenty of good, cheap seafood restaurants in the sandy town square. **Azul Surf Club** (☎ 2612-6820; www.azulsurfclub.com; Playa El Cuco; cabins US$50; ⊠ ⬜ ☎) is a beautiful new high-end surf resort that runs admirable service projects in the area. Specialising in package stays, passing travelers can get a pretty good deal too.

Further west, **Las Flores** is a prime surfing point suitable for beginners from December to February. The rest of the time it's best left to pros. Mama Cata at **Familia Segovia** (☎ 2619-9173; casacata1@hotmail.com; Playa Las Flores; r US$15) will sort you out. You can access the famed Punta

---

CROSSING THE BORDER

Getting to Honduras

For Tegucigalpa (US$27, five hours), 1st-class **King Quality** (☎ in San Salvador 2271-1361) buses stop at San Miguel's **Esso gas station** (Av Roosevelt at Ruta Militar) at around 8am and 3:30pm daily – be early just in case. Buy tickets at the gas station one day in advance.

Otherwise, bus 330 drops you 50m from El Amatillo on the Salvadoran border where a bridge crosses into Honduras. Honduran buses then go to **Choluteca** (US$2.10, 1½ hours) and on to **Tegucigalpa** (US$2, 3½ hours); the last bus for both leaves at 5:30pm. The last bus from El Amatillo to San Miguel goes at 6:30pm.

See p433 for information on crossing the border from Honduras.

Getting to Nicaragua & Costa Rica

King Quality operates to **Managua** (US$27, nine hours), continuing on to **San José, Costa Rica** (US$47, 19 hours). It stops at San Miguel's Esso gas station at about 7:30am and 1:30pm.

From El Amatillo microbuses run from 5:30am to 5pm across the southern tip of Honduras to the Nicaraguan border town of **Guasaule** (US$5 depending on number of passengers, two hours). Walk 200m for the connections which reach **León** and **Managua**. Note that Americans must pay US$7 to enter Nicargaua.

Mango break by boat from either Las Flores or El Cuco.

Broad and sandy **Playa Jaguey** is another good beach between El Tamarindo and El Cuco, with moderate surf. Private homes front the beach but you can still use it. There are no facilities. **Playa Las Tunas** is also pleasant enough, with a wide, flat beach reaching 100m to an estuary. The seafood restaurants get rowdy on weekends.

From La Unión, bus 383 takes a circular route to El Tamarindo; it passes Las Tunas and Jaguey on the way. For a breezy shortcut, take the same bus only as far as Buenavista and catch a *lancha* across the inlet to El Tamarindo (US$0.30) and hop on bus 383 returning to La Unión via Jaguey and Las Tunas.

ISLANDS IN GOLFO DE FONSECA

About as remote as it gets in tiny El Salvador, these lush, volcanic gulf islands are not quite tourist brochure material. Once the playground of 17th-century pirates, they remind us that tropical paradise is more than a developer's dream away. Isolated fishing villages, bored locals, and trash-strewn black-sand beaches jar against cinematic bird sanctuaries, pretty pepper-colored coves and warm, abundant waters.

The nearest island, **Isla Zacatillo**, has the largest community, and numerous coves with sandy beaches can be explored here. The principal village has a few stores and lodgings in a wooden shack over the bay. For solitary beaches, head for **Isla Martín Pérez**, just south of Zacatillo. More mountainous, **Isla Conchagüita** offers hiking opportunities. Fishing boats are neatly lined up under *enramadas* (arbors or protective awnings, typically made of wood or branches) along the beachfront of the main village. Locals say there are prehistoric rock carvings on the way out to Playa Brava, a black-sand beach an hour's walk from the village.

The pick of the islands is, of course, the furthest from the mainland. **Isla Meanguera** was long the subject of territorial disputes with Honduras and Nicaragua, until an international court declared it part of El Salvador in 1992. Aside from a small, friendly village, the island boasts **Playa Majahual**, a spectacular beach when clean. It's a 45-minute walk from the ferry landing; shuttles (US$1) depend on availability.

Nestled in a picturesque bay, **Hotel La Joya del Golfo** (☎ 2648-0072; www.hotellajoyadelgolfo.com; Isla Meanguera; d US$79, extra person US$10; ⊠ ⊡) is a wonderful place to stay, which is lucky because it's your only option on the island. The rooms are large, with grandiose beds and luxuriant, gilt-edged bathrooms, cable TV and clear views of 'Bird Island.' Rina, the friendly owner, is also a tremendous chef, while her two helpful English-speaking sons can arrange fishing, hiking and diving trips. Call before arriving or to arrange pick-up.

La Unión has services to Zacatillo (US$2, 20 minutes) and Meanguera (US$2.50, 1½ hours) from the pier. Departure times vary, but are generally from 10:30am, returning at

5am the next day. Day trippers have to arrange a private pick-up.

A private 'express' *lancha* costs US$60 round trip to Meanguera. Agree on a price before the journey starts, and pay only half up front to ensure your return trip. Ferries for the islands also depart from Las Playitas further down the coast.

Boat service from La Unión to Coyolitos, Honduras, and the port of Potosí, Nicaragua, is very infrequent. Ask a navy officer at the pier. You could also try calling Hotel La Joya del Golfo on Isla Meanguera to see if it has a trip planned. Prices vary widely. The land route may not be too exciting, but neither is hanging out in La Unión.

MORAZÁN

The rugged northeastern Morazán Department is a predominantly poor farming region that is generating a quiet buzz for its sustainable, community-based nature and war tourism. The museum in Perquín and a memorial in El Mozote are powerful displays of reconciliation and remembrance. The cool climate attracts an increasing number of city-slicking nationals, as does the country's cleanest river, the Río Sapo, and the countless hikes to waterfalls and war hideouts.

Indigenous traditions survive in villages around San Francisco Gotera, the department capital. The village of **Cacaopera** (bus 337 from San Francisco Gotera) has a small ethnographic **museum** (admission US$1; ✆ 9am-noon & 2-5pm Mon-Fri) with photo exhibits and artifacts from the local Kakawira indigenous community. Miguel Ayala of the museum is

a good contact. Through the museum you can also arrange guided hikes in the dry season (December to April) to pre-Columbian petroglyphs (US$15 per group). The museum maintains a rustic **hostel** (✆ 2651-0251; dm US$5), without electricity or running water. You can bathe in the nearby Río Torola and cook on the wood-burning stove. Sure, it's roughing it, but the experience is undoubtedly unique.

The community at **Guatajiagua** produces quality black pottery in the Lenca tradition. Visit **Cedart** (Calle Principal; ✆ 8am-5pm Mon-Fri, 8am-noon Sat) crafts shop or ask the clerk to point you in the direction of local artist workshops.

Perquín
pop 5500

A visit to the former FMLN headquarters in the mountain town of Perquín is paramount to understanding El Salvador's brutal civil war. It was in these hills that the opposition garnered its most loyal support, and despite vigorous bombing campaigns, the military was unable to dislodge the guerrilla forces. The town itself isn't beautiful but the cool mountain climate and excellent war museum make a trip here the highlight of El Salvador for many visitors.

INFORMATION
Cyberspace (per hr US$1; ✆ 8am-9pm Sat-Thu, 8am-6pm Fri)
Prodetur (✆ 2680-4086; Parque Central; ✆ 8am-5pm Mon-Fri, 8am-2pm Sat) Perquín's helpful tour office organizes guided tours and hikes (US$15) with a few days' notice. Early August commemorates the signing of the peace accords with various guided trips available.

OFF-THE-BEATEN-TRACK

Morazán is opening itself up to community-based tourism. Peace Corps volunteer Ari Borinsky has some cool suggestions for getting out and about in his designated patch:

▪ Visit the **aguas termales** (hot springs) in Canton El Progreso where you can bathe in a beautiful *pila* perfectly made for two. It's an hour-long bus ride from Perquín, then a one-hour hike to the Rio Araute. Pass the small school (wave to the students) then follow an old sign pointing the way.

▪ **El Salto** waterfall is only for the true *aventureros*. To get here you must walk along the slippery banks of the Rio Araute. Local guides and brothers, **Edwin and Carlos** (✆ 7490-8082/7219-5750; tours US$10-20), can happily assist.

▪ Near San Fernando, **La Cascada del Chorreron** is the most impressive and most accessible waterfall in the region. The water comes from a permanent, natural spring and saw one of the bloodiest battles of the civil war, La Batalla del Moscardon. From San Fernando, you can hike for 2km through a *reserva natural* along smooth terrain. The 40m-high waterfall falls into a beautiful crater which is perfect for swimming.

SIGHTS

A few blocks north of the park, the **Museo de la Revolución Salvadoreña** (Calle Los Héroes; admission US$1.20; ⏰ 8:30am-4:30pm Tue-Sun) charts the causes and progress of the armed struggle. Highlights include the collection of anti-war posters from throughout the world, the stark color photos of life inside guerrilla camps, the incredible assortment of Soviet weapons and some histories of those who died in action. It's a somber, stirring visit.

The newly opened **El Campamento Guerrillero Simulado** (Calle Los Héroes; admission US$0.50; ⏰ 8:30am-4:30pm Tue-Sun) is a reconstructed guerrilla camp connected by swing bridges and dirt tracks in a patch of partially cleared woodland. Sites include the remains of the downed helicopter that carried Lieutenant Colonel Domingo Monterrosa, head of the notorious Atlacatl Battalion, to his death. You'll see the studios of the FMLN's clandestine station Radio Venceremos ('We Will Win Radio'), part of an elaborate hoax that used a radio transmitter rigged with explosives to bring Monterrosa's helicopter down.

The museum is also the contact point for ex-guerrilla guides who can take visitors on fascinating **guided trips** (groups US$20) throughout the war zone. The most popular destination is El Mozote (see opposite page).

ACTIVITIES

Mountainous Perquín offers excellent hiking and river swimming. An abundance of orchids and butterflies make it a prime bird-watching zone – 12 varieties of oriole have been spotted along with the rare chestnut-headed oropendola. The **Río Sapo** is one of three rivers cutting through the forest – you can swim or camp here after visiting El Mozote. It's about a 45-minute walk and well worth the effort. The beautiful upper watershed has lots of friendly communities such as **Cumaro**. Local guide Don Santos can arrange visits to the local swimming hole and extremely welcome guest appearances at the local school. Likewise local farmers will show you a day on the pick in coffee, corn and sugar plantations. You can stay at **Cabaña las Veraneras** (☎ 7733-4493; Caserío Cumaro; campsites/r per person US$2/6, meals US$1.50). Guests of Niña Nilda become one more member of the family. You can also contact the Prodetur office (p317) in Perquín for reservations.

Quebrada de Perquín is a smaller, craggier creek, also good for swimming. **Cerro de Perquín** is a 10-minute hike from town, while **Cerro el Pericón** is a longer haul. Both offer gorgeous views. For guides consult Prodetur or the museum.

Tours Ciclista de Montaña is a major cycling race held in November, while **Festival de Montaña** is a new weeklong cultural festival in late December.

SLEEPING & EATING

Eco Albergue Río Sapo (☎ 2680-4086/7; campsites/dm per person US$4/7) Access to a swimming hole and a dozen hikes is the best reason for staying at these rustic dorm-style cabins at Area Natural Protegida Río Sapo. There's no electricity and limited water; bring your own food and flashlights. You can rent a tent (US$3) or sleeping bag (US$1) if you don't have your own. It's operated by Prodetur.

La Posada de Don Manuel (☎ 2680-4037; s/d US$8/16) This converted lumber mill has very basic concrete rooms, but the installation of hot water is a nice touch, as is the high-speed wi-fi. The restaurant – the domain of highly skilled Corina – is rather gloomy, but the food comes highly recommended. Manuel offers all kinds of guide services. It's 500m before town.

Hotel Perkin Lenca (☎ /fax 2680-4046; www.perkinlenca.com; r per person incl breakfast US$20, 1-4 person cabins incl breakfast US$40-74) The pride of Ronald Brenneman, an American with extensive experience building low-income housing in Honduras, the Lenca looks and feels like an authentic mountain lodge, handcrafted from pine and oak. The cabins are perfect for families, and the double rooms are great value, all with hot water. Tours are readily available. The onsite restaurant and bakery, La Cocina de Ma'Anita, is worth the trip itself. The produce is mostly organic and always delicious. Try the preserves, ice creams and meat dishes.

La Cocina de la Abuela (mains US$2-4) The pick of the cheap *comedores* on the town square.

GETTING THERE & AWAY

The CA7 north of San Miguel to the Honduran border is in good shape. Bus 332 runs from San Miguel to Perquín (US$1.50, 2½ hours) at 6am, 7am, 9:50am and 12:40pm. Alternatively, there's the more frequent bus 328 to San Francisco Gotera (US$0.70, 1½ hours) from where pickups go on to Perquín (US$0.50, one hour). The last bus back to San

Miguel is at 4pm; the last pickup to Gotera leaves at 5:40pm, but you have to catch the 5pm to make the last Gotera–San Miguel bus.

El Mozote

On December 11, 1981, government soldiers terrorized and executed the residents of this northern hill village. It's estimated that 757 people died: of the 143 victims uncovered, 131 were children. El Mozote is now a destination for those paying homage to the massacre. A tribute includes bright murals painted on the church, depicting the town as it was back then and as its children hope it to someday be again. There is also a plaque with the names of those who had died and a rose garden planted over the collective grave of the massacred children. This modest village has no lodgings and few services.

It's important to remain sensitive to the seriousness of the site. Locals are accustomed to an international presence; they've even set up snack bars and children tag behind visitors asking for handouts. As tempting as it is to give, it's best if you donate directly to the box inside the tour office.

From Perquín walk or take a pickup 3km south to a fork in the highway. El Mozote is 10km from the paved road; Jateca-bound buses pass here at 8am. On the way you'll pass Arambala, once decimated by air raids. The same bus returns from El Mozote at 12:45pm and can drop you at the turnoff. Combine this trip with a visit to Río Sapo, a 30-minute walk from El Mozote.

Prodetur and the Museo de la Revolución Salvadoreña (see opposite) in Perquín can do trips here, but show respect by using local Spanish-speaking El Mozote guides once in the village.

GETTING TO HONDURAS

Bus 426 goes from Perquín to Marcala, Honduras (US$2.50, three hours) daily at 6:30am and 11:40am. It stops at Honduran immigration, where a US$3 tax is charged on your 90-day CA-4 visa. This is due to a border dispute, as previously there was no Salvadoran immigration or customs post at **Sabanetas–Marcala**. Travelers can now re-enter El Salvador without any problems here. For information on crossing from Honduras, see p361.

NORTHERN EL SALVADOR

Timeless, charming Suchitoto – an immaculate colonial town just 47km from the capital – is the star of northern El Salvador, a mostly mountainous farming region enjoyed by trekkers. Travelers en route to Honduras will find themselves high above the world here, on a musical bus slowly traversing craggy hills and pine forests, with time no longer of the essence and other travelers a whole countryside away.

Detours too are well rewarded. La Palma is a unique artist hangout where *arte naif* continues to capture the world's imagination. Hiking trips from San Ignacio and Miramundo, among other bucolic hamlets, are the equal of any in Central America. The commercial hub of Chalatenango – now the center of El Salvador's safest province – is set to enjoy stronger economic prospects if a new national highway development goes ahead as planned.

The Chalatenango district bore the brunt of the military's *tierra arrasada* (scorched land) tactics, which burned fields and killed livestock as a form of combat.

The main provider of water and hydro-electric power for El Salvador, Chalatenango Department faces a serious deforestation problem.

SUCHITOTO

Seemingly lifted from a magic realism novel, Suchitoto has held firm – nay, prospered – against the weight of history just as its weekend arts fest turns the quintessential town square into one giant production of *guanaco* pride. None of this is new, however; when indigo ruled the marketplace and the beautiful Spanish church was packed to the brimstone daily, Suchitoto was the country's unabashed cultural capital. It retains its title with ease.

For those not fussed by the gallery and bar scene – much of it not open during the week – countless hikes to waterfalls, caves and beautiful Lago Suchitlán begin and end just meters from town. Suchitoto is also a bird migration zone with over 200 species. Thousands of hawks and falcons fill the skies as the seasons change, and birds of all sorts nest in the relative safety of the lake islands.

It is presumed that Yaquis and Pipils settled in the area some 1000 years ago. El Salvador's capital was established near here in the early 16th century. More recently, some of the earliest fighting of the civil war began in Suchitoto, accompanied by much destruction and emigration. Today the town has rebounded to become the highland seat of national tourism.

Orientation & Information

La Iglesia Santa Lucía stands on the east side of the Parque Centenario, the town center. Signs to the lake lead you a block east of the park, left onto 3a Av Sur, then down steeply to the water (about 1km). You can also follow the street that forms the park's western edge (Av 15 de Septiembre); it merges with 3a Av Sur several blocks down. Parque San Martin is two blocks west and two blocks north of the town center.

A 24-hour **HSBC ATM** is found on the town square; **Banco ProCredit** (cnr 2a Av Norte & 2a Calle Poniente) can change some foreign currency and cash travelers' checks.

Internet cafes abound; try **X-Streme Speed Cyber Cafe** (☎ 2235-1722; 1a Calle Poniente; per hr US$1; ☼ 8am-8pm). Suchitoto's **tourism office** (☎ 2335-1739; www.suchitoto-elsalvador.com; Calle San Martin 2; ☼ 8am-4pm) rents bikes (per hour US$1) and informs about hikes, activities and cultural events. For more up-to-date information, visit www.gaesuchitoto.com or the restaurant of Robert Broz Moran, aka *el gringo*.

Sights & Activities

Geologic oddity **Cascada los Tercios** tumbles over a cliff of tightly packed hexagonal stone spires. The waterfall underwhelms when water is low (often), but the rock formation and the trip there are interesting enough. It's 1.5km to the left on the main road, but don't hike alone as some robberies have been reported.

It's a 1½-hour hike to **Salto El Cubo**, a 15m waterfall cascading into a pair of pools. You can climb from the lower one to the upper, hemmed in by rocks with the water crashing down from above. To get there, take Calle Francisco Morazán west out of town to a rocky trailhead, a narrow path descending steeply to the falls.

Suchitoto Adventure Outfitters (☎ 2250-0800/113; www.suchitotooutfitters.com) is the premier travel company in Suchitoto thanks to the expertise and enthusiasm of René Barbon. Brilliant tailormade tours include the usual Suchitoto and El Salvador routes, plus more obscure adventures such as kayaking trips to the Pacific Ocean and moving tours to nearby **Cinquera**, a former FMLN stronghold where ex-guerrillas willingly retell real-life horror stories. An excellent new **hostel** (☎ 2389-5732; ardmcqr@

yahoo.es; cabins US$30) run by the Association for Reconstruction and Municipal Development (ARDM) has just opened in Cinqeura on the edge of a beautiful national park. A war museum here is nearly finished. ARDM is seeking volunteers for community and ecotourism projects. Call the hostel for details.

Southwest of town, the former FMLN hideout of Volcán Guazapa is a popular **horseback riding** (six-hour trip US$25) destination operated by an independent cooperative. Visitors can check out *tatús*, clever dugout hideouts, as well as craters and bomb shells. Book trips through the tourism office, La Casona or El Gringo.

The regional tourism office arranges city tours that include some 30 historic buildings. Also, browsing the **art galleries** can make an agreeable afternoon. Check out **Casa del Escultor** (☎ 2335-1836; www.miguelmartino.com; 2a Av Sur; ☼ Sat & Sun), the studio of acclaimed Argentine sculptor Miguel Martino, and **Shanay** (☎ 2335-1836; www.miguelmartino.com; 3a Av Norte; ☼ Sat & Sun), home of Víctor Manuel Sanabria.

The **Centro Arte para la Paz** (☎ 2335-1080; www.capsuchitoto.org; 2a Calle Poniente 5) organises a range of cultural activities from its premises in an old Dominican convent. Free films are screened on Fridays at 5pm.

Pajaro Flor Spanish School (☎ 2335-1509; www.pajaroflor.com; 4a Calle Poniente 22) offers 20 hours of accomplished private instruction for US$160; homestays can be arranged for U$4 to US$10 per day. Also, **Global Platform** (☎ 7655-8997; www.globalplatform.org.sv; 2a Calle Poniente 9) is a Danish NGO that offers Spanish lessons in conjunction with grassroots development projects around Suchitoto. Non-Danes are welcome to apply; a month costs roughly US$400, which includes basic lodging, food and various excursions.

To escape the heat, swim for US$3 in the huge pool with a view at **El Tejado** (☎ 2335-1769; 3a Av Norte 58; d $60; ☒ ☐ ☒).

For listings of local festivals see p326.

Sleeping & Eating

El Gringo (☎ 2327-2351; www.elgringosuchitoto.com; ☐) Run by newly inducted chief of tourism and long-term expat Robert Broz Morán, this is a new hostel in a quiet part of town. The cheap, authentic *comedor* comes highly recommended.

Hostal Vista Lago (☎ 2335-1357; 2a Av Norte 18; r per person US$8) Another good cheapie, with one of the best views in town. The friendly owner prepares pokey, colorful rooms.

EL SALVADOR

La Casona (☎ 2335-1969; www.lacasonasuchitoto.com; 4ta Calle Oriente No 9; r US$12) Part of ex-guerrilla tourism current bar owner Jerry's alternative tourism is this leftist-run lodging with large cement rooms with bathrooms. Some travelers might not love bunking in what's essentially a bar but the large spaces make it fairly quiet.

La Villa Balanza (☎ 2335-1408; Parque San Martín; s/d US$15/20) A backyard of reassembled war junk in a cool, stone courtyard greets a steady stream of backpackers at this parkside cheap sleep. The brand new adjoining house (US$20) is the best value by a mile, but all rooms with lake views are a good deal. It faces Parque San Martín.

Las Puertas (☎ 2393-9200; www.laspuertassuchitoto. com; cnr 2a Av Norte & Av 15 de Septiembre; r US$75-95; ✷ ▯) Lidby is the bubbly, kind-hearted manager of this stylish new hotel situated on the town square. Handcrafted artworks abound in lavish rooms with views in two directions – the open balcony facing the square or the shared landing for spectacular mountain sunsets. The convivial downstairs bar feels like a Central American film noir set. Check for cheap rates in quiet times.

Pupusería Niña Melita (6a Calle Oriente btwn Calle al Lago & 3a Av Norte; pupusas US$0.25) How's this for hometown flavor? Melita hits the sidewalk nightly, frying up bean-, zucchini- or meat-filled *pupusas*, while her 96-year-old mother (nostalgic for mud ovens) decries the modernized recipe to passersby. Don't listen – they're delicious.

La Lupita del Portal (☎ 2335-1429; mains US$3-8) Run by Lorena, the wife of René from Suchitoto Adventure Outfitters, this is the most popular cheap restaurant in town, situated on the south side of the square. Service is brisk and smiley, and good-value meat and

---

SPLURGE

Los Almendros de San Lorenzo (☎ 2335-1200; www.hotelsalvador.com; 4a Calle Poniente; d US$120; ✷ ▯) is the most elegant hotel in El Salvador. Owned by the former French ambassador, the converted hacienda is decorated by works from leading national artists and retains its mountain village charm. Rooms appear lifted from European fashion magazines, with standing bathtubs and decadent headboards. A superb glass-encased restaurant and stone swimming pool offset the temperamental service.

---

vegetarian dishes are accompanied by fresh salads, sandwiches and gigantic juices.

On weekends food vendors fill the plaza selling *riguas* (sweet buttery corn tortillas wrapped in a corn husk) and *fogonazo* (sugarcane juice), spiked with the strong stuff on request. The two top hotels, **La Posada Suchitlan** (☎ 2335-1064; Barrio San José) and **Los Almendros de San Lorenzo**, are busy with weekend diners.

Other options:

Luna Blanca (☎ 2335-1661; 1a Calle Oriente; r per person US$7) Great budget choice with big communal balcony.

El Obraje (☎ 2335-1173; 2a Calle Oriente 3; r per person US$11) Tiny rooms named after famous writers.

Xela's Pizza (☎ 2335-1397; pizzas US$6-10) Delicious pizza under the trees. Follow the signs from the plaza.

Drinking

You won't find a more authentic leftist bar than **El Necio** (4a Calle Oriente No 9; ☽ 6pm-1am), a low-lit drinking den run by Jerry, an amiable ex-guerrilla. Che posters and revolutionary posturing have never been so apt.

The town's go-to nightspot is **Harlequín** (☽ 7pm-1am Fri-Sun), with eclectic tunes playing in a trellised garden with twinkling lights. Thursday night is salsa night at **Dos Gardenias** (☎ 2335-1868; 3a Av Norte 48; ☽ 11am-10pm Wed-Sun), a chic bar, restaurant and gallery in a new location that retains the same in-the-know clientele and elegant proprietress.

Getting There & Away

From San Salvador's Terminal de Oriente take bus 129. To return, the same bus departs from the corner of 1a Calle Poniente and 4a Av Sur, a block west of Parque Centenario. By car, go toward Cojutepeque on the Interamericana. When you get to San Martín, turn left at the Texaco sign.

If you're headed north, catch bus 163 to Las Aguilares (US$0.80, one hour), where buses pass for Chalatenango, Las Palmas and the El Salvador–Honduras border. A slower but more scenic option is to take a boat (per person US$6, 20 minutes) or car ferry (per person US$1, per car US$4) across Lago de Suchitlán to San Francisco Lempa and from there catch a bus to Chalatenango. The last one leaves at 3pm.

CHALATENANGO
pop 16,200

The sleepy Chalatenango province comes momentarily to life each morning in the capital, 'Chalate,' the business headquarters of northern El Salvador. Honking trucks navigate the narrow streets, overflowing with pineapples, sugarcane, indigo and coffee, while colorful buses are stacked with friendly locals selling DVDs, toiletries and glittery sequined dresses. As the commerical center for small rural mountain villages, there's a real contrast between the ambitious, city-bound youth and a generation of leather-skinned subsistence farmers, recounting tales of FMLN might. The large military garrison on the plaza was built during wartime to rein in revolutionary activity in this FMLN stronghold.

Orientation & Information
The Parque Central is divided by 3a Av, with the church on the east (uphill) side and the main park on the west (downhill) side. The market extends up the main east–west street, Calle San Martín-Calle Morazán. A huge army barracks stands north of the main park; most buses pick up and drop off on 3a Av, south of the park. Exceptions are the buses to Arcatao and Las Vueltas, which leave at the top of Calle Morazán, near the turnoff to the *turicentro*.

There's a 24-hour ATM at **Citibank** (4a Calle Poniente near 6a Av Sur), and it also changes traveler's checks. Try **Cibercafé@halate Online** (1a Calle Oriente at 5a Av Norte; per hr US$0.80; 8am-9:30pm Mon-Sat, 9am-1pm Sun) for internet access.

A cacophonous market is held on Tuesday and Sunday in the town center.

Sights
The **Iglesia de Chalatenango**, with its squat bell tower and bright chalky facade, sits on the east side of the Parque Central, a stone's throw from the military garrison.

A 20-minute walk from the Parque Central, **Turicentro Agua Fría** (admission US$0.80; 8am-5pm) has a lush park with picnic tables, but the main draw is the pools set with an artificial rock island topped by a waterslide. Dry season means water shortages – expect an overdose of chlorine. A cafeteria serves beer and meals. To get here, go up Calle Morazán (east) about 400m, and turn left at the big sign.

For panoramic views of the Cerrón Grande reservoir, climb **Cerro La Peña**, a 1½-hour hike starting at a trailhead before the *turicentro*. A number of roads and paths reach the top; ask passersby for directions.

Sleeping & Eating
Hotel la Ceiba (2301-1080; d US$12) A rough-and-tumble hotel behind the military garrison. The neighborhood is not so good, so stay in your musty room after dark.

La Posada del Jefe (2335-2450; Calle el Instituto, Barrio El Calvario; s/d US$16/25;) Up the hill 10 blocks to the east you'll find the only decent place in town, with bone-white concrete rooms filled with ex-office furniture. There's a little convenience store out front. To get here take a little red mototaxi (US$1). It's kind of fun.

Cafe Colombia (4a Calle Poniente; coffee US$1) Cruisy locals play chess beneath a ceiling made from continental coffee bags. Aerobics and techno blare through the open gym window. Tasty ham sandwiches are served.

Comedor Carmary (3a Av; mains US$2-3; 7am-2pm Mon-Sat) This tidy cafeteria packed with bus-stop patrons serves tasty *comida a la vista*, which might include stewed chicken in tomatoes, plantains and the ubiquitous beans and rice, alongside tall glasses of fresh juice.

The open-air **market** (5am-1pm) offers a visual feast of veggies, fruits and grains, as well as stock to replenish your toiletries. It's just east of Av Fajardo.

Getting There & Away
Bus 125 runs regularly from San Salvador (US$0.90, two hours) and terminates on 3a Av Sur, a few blocks south of the church. To La Palma and El Poy, take bus 125 toward El Amayo (the highway intersection) and transfer to bus 119 (1½ hours) heading north.

See opposite page for details on taking buses to local villages.

AROUND CHALATENANGO
The countryside around Chalate climbs into dry forest studded with toothy peaks and rugged tawny hills. The small villages in this remote area have stunning landscapes and interesting histories.

Beyond the Río Sumpul, **Arcatao** is a beautiful village in the mountains bordering Honduras. Ask in the municipal office about tours of the *tatus* (cave hideouts), which attest to Arcatao's former role as an FMLN stronghold. The local **Jesuit order** (2354-8009; bartolome2408@yahoo.com) receives guests and can set up guided tours of the area. Call ahead.

Northwest of Chalate, **Concepción Quezaltepeque** is a hammock-making center. You'll see women threading them along the side of the road. Prices range from US$30 to US$120, depending on size, length, thickness and material. Shops line the main street; browse a few first to compare quality.

La Montañona is a pine-forest reserve at 1600m with prime views and pre-Columbian rock carvings. The civil war left several *tatus*, including one used by clandestine guerrilla radio station Radio Farabundo, as well as an underground guerrilla hospital. You can stay in the small village – a rustic cabin has beds and shared bathroom (US$5 per night). Teresa Avilar cooks up basic meals. Call **Cesar Alas** (☎ 7723-6283) before going; he oversees the lodging and acts as a guide to the area.

A strenuous climb passing Dulce Nombre de María travels cobbled roads through pastel villages. Enjoy views of flat valleys sprung with volcanoes and the mountainous Honduran border beyond. North is **El Manzano**, a cooperative of ex-FMLN combatants. Its trails cross forest and coffee farms, and destinations include historic war sites and waterfalls. The top of El Pilón offers more incredible views. The *tienda* in the middle of town has information on lodging, meals and guides.

Getting There & Around
The following bus departures originate in Chalatenango:

Aracatao Bus 508 (US$1.15; 2hr) Departs hourly from 7am to 5:30pm from the top of Calle Morazán.

Concepción Quezaltepeque Bus 300B (US$0.35; 20min) At 3a Av Sur terminal in Chalate.

El Manzano No direct service. Take 125 to the *desvío* (turnoff) for Dulce Nombre de María to pick up bus 124 from San Salvador to Dulce Nombre de María. Take a pickup to El Manzano.

La Montañona Buses 295 or 542 (US$1; 2hr) pass by the turnoff to Montañona, departing at 11:15am and 12:15pm from 3a Av Sur between 1a and 3a Calles Poniente. From the turnoff it's a steep 6km climb to the village – pickups often make the trip.

LA PALMA
A collective exercise in street art en masse, La Palma must have more public murals per capita than anywhere else on earth. This cool mountain village 84km north of San Salvador is literally splashed with loud, tutti-frutti tones. Everything from street signs to market stalls gives off an inner-child vibe, á la *Sesame Street* in the '70s. It's an antidote to drab town planning, and hikers will enjoy the contrast between the surrounding verdant,

GETTING TO SAN PEDRO SULA OR COPÁN RUINAS, HONDURAS

The bus from La Palma drops you about 100m from the El Salvador–Honduras border (open 24 hours), where you pay US$2 to enter Honduras. From **El Poy**, you can take a bus or *colectivo* taxi to Nueva Ocotepeque, Honduras. From there buses leave hourly for San Pedro Sula. For Copán Ruinas, transfer at La Entrada.

The last bus to El Poy from La Palma (bus 119, US$0.50, 30 minutes) leaves at 7pm. The last bus south from El Poy to San Salvador leaves around 4:15pm.

See p385 for information on crossing the border from Honduras.

challenging peaks and the apricot, mauve and lemon-colored homes. Locals are adept at handling tourists.

Painter Fernando Llort moved here in 1972, founding Naïve Art, a trend that still represents El Salvador around the world (p274). These bright, primitive images of mountain villages, *campesinos* or Christ are synonomous with the modern Salvadoran art movement. He taught local residents how to create the same images and started a successful cooperative. Today 75% of the village makes a living by mass-producing these bright motifs.

Hikers often prefer lodging in the neighboring village of **San Ignacio** as it's closer to the trails.

Information
Citibank (cnr Calle Barrios & 1a Calle Poniente) 24-hour ATM on the northeast corner of Parque Centro.

Palma City Online (Calle Principal; per hr US$0.80; ☺ 8am-7pm)

Tourist office (☎ 2335-9076; Parque Municipal; ☺ 8am-4pm Mon-Fri, 9am-1pm Sat & Sun) Very helpful. Spanish only.

Sights
Visitors are welcome to peek into workshops to see families painting away. Local cooperative **La Semilla de Dios** (3a Calle Poniente at 5a Av Norte), founded in 1977 by Fernando Llort himself (see boxed text, p274), crafts quality products in workshops behind the store. If you ask permission you can wander through the workshops and watch the painters and woodworkers at work. **Copapase** is the most

established cooperative in the area – it even has a small **museum** (☎ 2305-9376; ✆ 8am-5pm Mon-Fri, 8am-noon Sat & Sun).

Activities

Cerro El Pital (2730m) is the highest peak in El Salvador, but thanks to an access road, it is also one of the easiest to hike. From nearby San Ignacio, bus 509 to Las Pilas leaves you at Río Chiquito near the trail. It's about 1½ hours to the top, where spectacular views await. You will know you've reached the summit when you find the cement block marking it. It is private property, so bring US$2 to cover admission.

Once there, ask for directions to **Piedra Rajada**, a huge cloven rock a half-hour walk from the summit, accessed by a nerve-wracking log bridge spanning a 25m drop. Don't try this one in wet weather.

The pinnacle of awesome forest views is in **Miramundo**, a small, aptly named community perched on a steep hillside. Back at Río Chiquito, follow the right-hand fork for about an hour to Miramundo. Right on the trail, the ridgetop **Hostal Miramundo** (☎ 2230-0437; www.hotelmiramundo.com; 4-person cabins US$50) has cosy new cabins, with nice wooden touches and great beds. Highly recommended tours are available, including a horseback ride to Casa Grande.

San Ignacio is a great base for hard-core hiking enthusiasts. For a guide, contact José Samuel Hernández, the owner of **Comedor y Artesanías El Manzana** (☎ 2305-8379; Carretera La Palma–El Poy km 85), outside La Palma, or **Humberto Regalado** (☎ 2352-9138), who owns and maintains the trail to Peña Cayaguanca.

Buses to Las Pilas, passing through Río Chiquito, leave San Ignacio at 7am, 9:30am, 12:30pm, 2:30pm and 4:30pm and return at the same times.

Sleeping & Eating

Five kilometers south of town, Centro Obrero Dr Mario Zamora Rivas offers 15 remodeled cabins and a couple of pools, and is free with permission from the Ministerio de Trabajo in San Salvador (p280). Trails crisscross the forested grounds.

Hotel Posada Real (☎ 2335-9009; r per person with bathroom US$9) A nice location and a cute little snack bar, but there's not much character in these cinderblock rooms. The price is good though, plus they have hot water.

Hotel de Montaña El Pital (☎ 2335-9344; r per person with bathroom US$15, with air-con US$35; ✖ ✆) The brand-spanking tiled rooms upstairs are expensive by La Palma standards, but the older rooms are fine, the pool is seasonally open and the shiny new restaurant seats 100.

Cafe de Cafe (☎ 2335-9190; Calle El Principal) The closest thing to a city cafe, with leather lounges, fine coffee (US$1) and *licuados* (US$1.50 to US$2), and free wi-fi. It's popular with teenagers.

Restaurante del Pueblo (mains US$1-5; ✆ 7am-9pm) If a dollar buys you a sandwich in thick bread, going all out means a good *plato típico* (grilled meat, bananas, beans, cheese and cream).

Cartagena Pizza (☎ 2305-9475; Barrio el Centro; pizzas US$3-12) These delicious thin-based pizzas make a welcome change from the standard Central American fare.

The village of San Ignacio has additional sleeping and eating options, including the top-value **Posada de Reyes** (☎ 2335-9318; www.hotelposada dereyes.com; r US$25-35; ✖ ✆ ☎). Get room No 15.

Alternatively, **Hotel La Palma** (☎ 2305-9344; www.hotellapalma.com; r per person US$15; ✆ ☎) is a quiet mountain getaway bordered by the Río La Palma. Ask for the newer chalets. It's a short taxi ride from San Ignacio.

Getting There & Away

Bus 119 runs every half-hour from San Salvador's Terminal de Oriente to the El Salvador–Honduras border at El Poy, stopping at La Palma (US$1.60, 2¾ hours). Some enter San Ignacio, 3km to the north, others drop you off at the entrance.

From San Ignacio you can catch the bus to El Pital and its environs.

EL SALVADOR DIRECTORY

ACCOMMODATIONS

El Salvador has a decent selection of hotels and improved backpacker infrastructure. The cheapest places are often in seedy areas near bus terminals; paying a bit more is worthwhile for personal security. In many areas, prostitution outranks tourism and travelers might find their only options are room-per-hour lodgings. This book attempts to include the safest and most secure options for travelers.

Camping and *eco-albergues* (ecohostels; basic shared cabins, some with modest kitchen facilities) are appearing around popular outdoor destinations. Bring your own camping equipment, as the selection here is scant.

You can stay for free at *centros de obreros* (government workers' centers), which are huge compounds designed to give workers and their families a place to relax on the weekend. The main locations are Lago de Coatepeque, El Tamarindo, La Palma and outside La Libertad. You must reserve them in advance at the appropriate office in San Salvador; see p280 for details.

Room rates are stable season to season, except during the summer holidays (first week of August), when hotels in popular towns fill up fast. The average rate for dorms is around US$8, and for doubles US$25.

ACTIVITIES
Diving
Diving in El Salvador is more expensive and admittedly inferior to nearby Honduras or Belize. That said, it does offer one of the few coral reefs on the American side of the Pacific, as well as a chance to dive in crater lakes. The best time for diving is from October to February, especially December and January. One five-star operator is **El Salvador Divers** (Map p286; ☎ 2264-0961; www.elsalvadordivers.com; 3a Calle Poniente 5020, Colonia Escalón, San Salvador), offering open-water and advanced certification courses for around US$300.

Hiking
El Salvador has some excellent hiking, in spite of serious deforestation. Parque Nacional El Imposible (p306), near the border with Guatemala, offers the best combination of easy access and rewarding primary-forest hikes. The Ruta de las Flores offers waterfall and hot springs hikes; find guides for hire in Juayúa (p303). Further north, the pristinely beautiful Parque Nacional Montecristo–El Trifinio (p299) is renowned for wildlife. Access is difficult and it's closed during the May–November mating season. Parque Nacional los Volcanes (p295), with two climbable volcanoes, is a beautiful, if sometimes crowded, destination. Hikes from the northwestern towns of La Palma and San Ignacio offer stunning vistas. You can access El Salvador's highest peak (Cerro El Pital, 2730m; see opposite) from here. The northeastern state of Morazán, in particular Perquín, has a cool climate and fine hiking. As a longtime stronghold of the FMLN, it also has interesting and sobering sites related to the civil war.

Surfing
El Salvador is a world-class surf destination, with kilometers of empty right-hand breaks. Punta Roca, the country's finest wave, is at the scruffy port of La Libertad (p291), which is readily accessible from the capital. Several beaches west of here also have excellent waves and all-service surf lodges. Your best bets for lessons are at Esencia Nativa in Playa El Zonte (p294), or a number of places in Playa El Tunco (p294). Peak season is March to December.

BOOKS
Major Salvadoran authors (see p273) are available in translation. Joan Didion's *Salvador* is a moving account of the early days of the war. Nonfiction about the civil war includes *Massacre at El Mozote* by Mark Danner, *Witness to War: An American Doctor in El Salvador* by Charles Clements MD, and *Rebel Radio,* a fascinating, firsthand account of clandestine radio stations operated by FMLN guerrillas.

Óscar Romero: Memories in Mosaic by María López Vigil, is a recommended account of the clergyman's life and political conversion told by those who knew him. *When the Dogs Ate Candles* by Bill Hutchinson, is an anecdotal history of the conflict based on interviews with refugees. Archaeology buffs can read about Central America's Pompeii in *Before the Volcano Erupted: The Ancient Ceréen Village in Central America* by Payton Sheets.

BUSINESS HOURS
Businesses generally operate 9am to 6pm weekdays, while government offices are open 8am to 4pm. Some offices and stores close at lunchtime, between noon and 2pm, but this practice is fading. Banks are open 8am to 4pm or 5pm weekdays, and most open Saturday morning as well. Restaurants serve dinner early, and 4pm is *pupusa* hour.

CLIMATE
The *invierno* (wet season) is from May to October, and the *verano* (dry season) is from November to April. During the rainy season, it usually only rains at night.

In San Salvador, the maximum temperature varies from 27°C (80°F) in November to 30°C (86°F) in March and April; the minimum temperatures range from 16°C (61°F) in January and February to 20°C (68°F) in March. The coastal lowlands are the hottest region. For climate charts see p714.

EL SALVADOR

CUSTOMS

Salvadoran border officials are among the most scrutinizing in the region. They check for previous entry and exit stamps. If you're entering on an international bus, your bags may well be searched. Carry your passport with you in all border regions, regardless of whether you're leaving the country, since there are a lot of police checkpoints (mostly searching for drugs).

DANGERS & ANNOYANCES

Crime shouldn't deter travelers from El Salvador any more than it does from the rest of Central America. Despite the country's reputation for violence, attacks on tourists are rare.

Take common-sense precautions: carry as little as possible on day trips, be aware of your bags on buses and avoid toting expensive items. Before traveling, make copies of your credit cards and important documents; carry a copy with you and leave one with someone at home who could fax you them in a pinch. After dark it's best to take a taxi, even if the rates can be a little steep. This is particularly important in San Salvador, San Miguel, Sonsonate, La Unión and La Libertad.

Most volcano climbs are best done with a police escort, partly for your safety and partly so you won't get lost on unmarked and intersecting trails. The service is free, but you must request it by phone or in person a day in advance (and preferably more). Officers are friendly and trustworthy.

Of course, violence does occur. Two major *maras* (gangs) operate in the country. Travelers are unlikely to have encounters with a gang member as groups concentrate in neighborhoods with no outside appeal, and also because the police control most tourist areas. Still, visitors should avoid traveling at night. Weapons are widespread, so never resist a robbery – it's not worth it.

EMBASSIES & CONSULATES

Australia, New Zealand and the UK do not have consular representation in El Salvador. Australians can get assistance at the Canadian embassy. Except for the US embassy, the following are in San Salvador.

Canada (Map p286; ☎ 2279-4655; Alameda Roosevelt, 63a Av Sur, Torre A)

France (Map p286; ☎ 2279-4016; www.embafrancia.com.sv; 1a Calle Poniente 3718)

Germany (Map p286; ☎ 2247-0000; www.san-salvador.diplo.de; 7a Calle 3972)

Guatemala (Map p281; ☎ 2271-2225; 15a Av Norte btwn Calles Arce & 1a Calle Poniente, Colonia Escalón)

Honduras (Map p286; ☎ 2263-2808; 89a Av Norte btwn 7a & 9a Calle Poniente, Colonia Escalón)

Mexico (Map p286; ☎ 2243-0445; cnr Calle Circunvalación & Pasaje 12, Colonia San Benito)

Nicaragua (☎ 2263-8789; Calle El Mirador btwn 93a & 95a Av Norte, Colonia Escalón)

USA (off Map p279; ☎ 2278-4444 ext 2628; www.sansalvador.usembassy.gov; Blvd Santa Elena Final, Antiguo Cuscatlán, La Libertad)

FESTIVALS & EVENTS

Fería Gastronómica A wonderful food fair (p303) held every weekend in Juayúa.

Festival de El Salvador (August 1-6) Celebrates El Salvador's patron saint; all cities have festivities with San Salvador's the biggest.

Festival del Invierno (August) Perquín's art and music festival popular with the boho crowd and college students.

Festival de Maíz (August) Suchitoto's corn harvest festival with religious processions and street parties.

Bolas de Fuego (August 31) To commemorate an eruption of Volcán San Salvador that destroyed the original town, Nejapa residents spar by throwing balls of fire then dance till dawn around street bonfires.

Festival de Hamacas (mid-November) Hammocks fill the streets of Concepción Quezaltepeque (p322) during this street fair.

FOOD & DRINK

A typical breakfast includes eggs, beans or *casamiento* (rice and beans mixed together), fried plantains, cheese, tortillas and coffee or juice. *Panaderías* usually offer a selection of morning cakes and coffee. *Almuerzo* (lunch) is the largest meal of the day and often the most expensive.

El Salvador street food is all about *pupusas*, round cornmeal dough stuffed with a combination of cheese, refried beans, *chicharrón* (pork rinds), or *revuelta* (all three), and grilled. *Curtido*, a mixture of pickled cabbage and vegetables, provides the final topping. Most *pupuserías* open at around 4pm and some work the same sidewalk space for years. Also popular in the evening are *panes*, French breads sliced open and stuffed with chicken, salsa, salad and pickled vegetables.

Licuados (fruit drinks made with water or milk), *gaseosas* (soft drinks) and coffee are easily had in El Salvador. Note that *refresco*, which means soft drink in many countries, here means lemonade, *horchata* (rice milk and cinnamon) and other water-based drinks. A *refresco de ensalada* is not coleslaw puree, but a mixed fruit juice served with a spoon for the fruit salad floating on top, sangria style. Water can be bought in either bottles or half-liter bags.

Local beers include Pilsener [sic], the most popular, and Golden, a lighter brew.

GAY & LESBIAN TRAVELERS

Gay people receive little tolerance. Some hotels refuse to rent a room with one bed to two men; women will encounter less scrutiny. In San Salvador, the area around Blvd de los Héroes has cultural centers and clubs that, being more bohemian, are also more gay-friendly. Gay organization **Entre Amigos** (☎ 2225-4213; entreamigos@ salnet.net; Av Santa Victoria No 50, near Blvd de los Héroes) is the most established in the country, dedicated mostly to HIV/AIDS outreach.

INTERNET ACCESS

Internet access is easily found across the country, though speeds vary considerably. Expect to pay between US$0.50 to $1 per hour.

INTERNET RESOURCES

www.elsalvador.travel ISTU's new, largely incomplete website.

www.elsalvadorturismo.gob.sv Corsatur's official website is mildly better than reading a brochure.

www.lanic.utexas.edu/la/ca/salvador An excellent resource of Salvadoran websites, arranged by topic.

www.laprensa.com.sv Spanish-language website for one of El Salvador's major daily newspapers.

www.puntamango.com Website of Mango's Lounge surf shop in La Libertad; it tells you where to find the best waves in El Salvador.

www.salvanatura.org For reservations or information on Parque Nacional El Imposible and Parque Nacional Los Volcanes.

www.search-beat.com/elsalvador.htm Topic-based lists of Salvadoran websites.

www.surfer.com.sv Shows off the west Pacific surf scene; links in English.

LANGUAGE

Spanish is the national language. In a few indigenous villages a handful of people still speak the Nahuat language of the Pipil, but there is academic interest in preserving it. Many Salvadorans pick up some English working in the USA, Australia and elsewhere, and English speakers pop up in the unlikeliest places.

LEGAL MATTERS

Law enforcement is strict and effective, from beat cops to border officials. Police are entitled to stop buses and search people and bags, and do so with some frequency, often helped by army soldiers. Bribes are generally not expected or accepted. If arrested, cooperate and call your embassy, although if you have committed a crime there's little your embassy can do. Even minor offences require jail time.

MAPS

Corsatur (see p280) and the Ministry of Tourism offer glossy maps of El Salvador and the capital, available at some hotels and tour offices. Map addicts should hit the **Centro Nacional de Registros** (IGN; Map p286; www.cnr.gob; 1a Calle Poniente, San Salvador, 2nd fl; ⏰ 8am-12:30pm & 2-5pm Mon-Fri), behind MetroSur, for high-quality city and country maps. Simple maps of hiking trails are sometimes available at respective visitors centers.

MEDIA

San Salvador's main newspapers are *La Prensa Gráfica* and the conservative *El Diario de Hoy*; check them for domestic and international news, plus entertainment listings. *El Mundo* and *El Latino* are thinner afternoon papers.

MONEY

On January 2001, El Salvador adopted the US dollar as its official currency. The previous currency (the colón) technically still exists, but you'll probably never see one.

ATMs

ATMs are found in most cities and towns, with the exception of Perquín. Citibank, Scotiabank and Banco Atlántida have the largest network of ATMs. Plus/Visa and Cirrus/MasterCard cards generally work well. Look for safer locking cabins to withdraw money and avoid taking out cash at night.

Bargaining & Tipping

Bargaining is less common here than in other Central American countries. A little back-and-forth is common with taxi drivers and market shopkeepers, but hard bargaining can seem a bit rude. Tip 10% in restaurants; it is not customary to tip taxi drivers, though rounding up the amount is appreciated.

EL SALVADOR

Cash

Bring US dollars, preferably in US$20 bills and smaller. There is no need to buy, carry or use the old currency as ATMs have dollars. Only Banco Cuscatlán exchanges non-US currency. The border crossings have moneychangers.

Credit Cards

Credit cards are accepted in modern malls, high-end hotels and upmarket stores. Smaller establishments add a 6% to 12% surcharge. Visa cards encounter the least resistance. MasterCard is becoming more widely accepted while American Express is less common.

Exchange Rates

The table shows currency exchange rates at the time this book went to press.

Country	Unit	US$
Australia	A$1	0.87
Canada	C$1	0.97
Euro zone	€1	1.22
Japan	¥100	1.10
New Zealand	NZ$1	0.70
UK	UK£1	1.48

Traveler's Checks

Most Citibank, Scotiabank and Banco Atlántida branches change traveler's checks (passport and purchase receipt required). American Express checks are best. There are also Western Union offices in most towns.

POST

There are two rates for sending international mail: airmail and express mail. Letters sent by airmail to the USA should arrive in 10 days (US$0.50), to Europe and Asia up to 15 days (US$0.65). Letters sent express to the USA should take five days (US$1), to Europe and Australia 10 days (US$1.20). FedEx and DHL have offices in large cities.

RESPONSIBLE TRAVEL

Many travelers come to El Salvador with a notion of which 'side' they supported in the civil war (usually the FMLN). In fact, both sides committed terrible atrocities and in 12 years of war, neither came to fully represent (or betray) the ideals of the majority of Salvadorans. Visitors should not be hesitant to discuss the war, but should honor the personal experiences of everyday Salvadorans.

The country is fairly new to tourism and Salvadorans remain relatively unjaded toward backpackers. Hard bargaining, whether in taxis or in markets, is rare. It may be too late to reverse the unpleasant wheeling and dealing of Guatemala and elsewhere, but in El Salvador, an honest price and a friendly transaction are still the norm.

STUDYING

Options are few but some English institutes offer Spanish classes. The best is the **Centro de Intercambio y Solidaridad** (CIS; off Map p284; ☎ 2226-2623; www.cis-elsalvador.org), which offers Spanish classes with progressive sensibilities. Homestays are available. Suchitoto has two excellent new schools (p320).

TELEPHONE

The country code when calling El Salvador from abroad is ☎ 503. Phone numbers usually have eight digits; there are no internal area codes. Telecom and Telefónica payphones accept their respective phone cards. Buy prepaid phone cards (in US$3, US$5 and US$10 denominations) at pharmacies and corner stores. Phone booths post local and international dialing instructions in English and Spanish. Some internet cafes offer web-based calling.

TOURIST INFORMATION

El Salvador has few tourist information offices, and even fewer that provide more than fluff. Offices with friendly and informed staff include those in Perquín and Suchitoto. Juayúa and Apaneca have information kiosks open on weekends. Friendly hotel owners can be very helpful resources. In the capital you'll find the office of **Corporación Salvadoreña de Turismo** (Corsatur; off Map p279; ☎ 2243-7835; corsatur@salnet.net; Blvd Santa Elena, San Salvador; ☉ 8am-12:30pm & 1:30-5:30pm), offering brochures and fliers. The **Instituto Salvadoreño de Turismo** (ISTU; Map p281; ☎ 222-8000; istu@mh.gob.sv; 719 Calle Rubén Darío btwn 9a & 11a Avs Sur, San Salvador; ☉ 8:30am-12:30pm & 1:30-4pm Mon-Sat) has very general information about El Salvador's national parks and *turicentros*.

TRAVELERS WITH DISABILITIES

There are many disabled people in El Salvador – most victims of war-related violence – but there are few services or amenities to make their lives easier. There are few well-maintained ramps and handrails or services for the visually and hearing impaired.

However, disabled travelers (and all travelers) will find Salvadorans extremely friendly and eager to help.

VISAS & DOCUMENTS

Citizens of the USA, Canada, Australia, New Zealand, South Africa, Switzerland, Norway, Japan, Taiwan, Brazil, Argentina, Mexico, other Central American countries, Israel and EU member countries do not need a visa, but must purchase a single-entry tourist card for US$10 when entering the country. For those who do need a prearranged visa, the cost is US$30. The standard length of stay is 30 days, but you can request up to 90 days – do so quickly before the official stamps your passport! If you leave and return within the allotted time, you can use the same tourist card.

The Central America-4 agreement allows for travel between the borders of Guatemala, Honduras, El Salvador and Nicaragua with one entry fee and one passport stamp (in this case, be sure you ask for the 90-day option). If you are traveling overland, please note the change; it's possible you will have to 'remind' some border guards about the agreement.

For up-to-date visa information visit http://www.lonelyplanet.com/el-salvador/practical-information/visas.

No vaccinations are required unless you are coming from an area infected by yellow fever (some are recommended, however; see p735).

VOLUNTEERING

In San Salvador's Blvd de los Héroes area, **Centro de Intercambio y Solidaridad** (CIS; off Map p284; ☎ 2235-1330; www.cis-elsalvador.org; Colonia Libertad, Av Bolivar 103) offers Spanish classes to tourists and English classes to low-income and activist Salvadorans, always with a strong emphasis on progressive politics. A friendly place to visit, the CIS has positions for volunteer English teachers (10-week minimum), and information about NGOs working on various issues, including community development, gang intervention, the environment and more. CIS cannot arrange an actual volunteer position, but can point you in the right direction. During national elections, you can volunteer with CIS's well-respected international election-observer mission.

Global Platform (☎ 7655-8997; globalplatform-elsalvador@ms.dk; 2a Calle Poniente, Barrio San José) is a Danish NGO based in Suchitoto that offers Spanish lessons and lodging in return for assistance on community projects in the surrounding area. A month costs roughly US$400 all-inclusive.

WOMEN TRAVELERS

Foreign women spark interest, there is no doubt. Men will hiss or catcall but for many it's harmless hormonal babble, as much about male bonding as the female passerby. Nearly all the men you actually meet are extremely courteous and polite. Solo women are unlikely to encounter dangerous situations if they take ordinary precautions. On long bus rides, sitting next to a woman or kids avoids painful, 'Do you have a boyfriend?' conversations. At least, enjoy Latin culture's chivalric aspects while you're here.

EL SALVADOR

Honduras

Tourism in Honduras crashed and burned in late 2009. When former President Manuel Zelaya was exiled to Costa Rica, all of the tourists went with him. Insurance companies pulled the plug and occupancy rates plummeted countrywide. But the little country that could, where Columbus cast his eyes starboard and spotted the lush tropical shores near Trujillo; where the Maya built a monumental citadel at Copán Ruinas that flourished for some five centuries; where laid-back Afro-Caribbean vibes permeate life on the north coast and the reef-rich Bay Islands; and where cobblestone colonial mountain towns flourish below misty mountaintops, has taken its worst year for tourism in the country's history and used it as an opportunity to reset. In the meantime, you can jungle-hop through the intriguing and wild Mosquito Coast, bathe in the crystalline waters of tranquil Utila and Roatán, bird-watch until your eyes bulge out in verdant cloud forests and wander forgotten colonial capitals like Gracias and Comayagua without a soul to share it all with. Go on. Honduras is waiting.

FAST FACTS

- **Area** 112,090 sq km (about the size of England)
- **Budget** US$25 to US$30 per day, more on the Bay Islands
- **Capital** Tegucigalpa
- **Costs** Budget hotel room US$7 to US$20, meal U$2 to US$7, open-water diving course on Utila or Roatán US$240
- **Country Code** ☎ 504
- **Languages** Spanish; also English on Bay Islands
- **Money** US$1 = L18.90 (lempiras); US dollars accepted on Bay Islands
- **Population** 7.79 million
- **Seasons** Rainy season (September to February, especially on the coast), dry season (December to May)
- **Time** GMT plus eight hours

TRAVEL HINTS

Antimalarial medication should be seriously considered if traveling on the north coast or Bay Islands. Chloroquine – sold as 'Aralen' in most pharmacies – is the drug of choice. See p737 for dosage.

OVERLAND ROUTES

Border crossings include Corinto and El Florido (Guatemala), El Amatillo and El Poy (El Salvador), and Guasaule (Nicaragua). There are twice-weekly ferries to Belize, and occasional hitchhiker possibilities to Nicaragua and Jamaica. There is no fee to leave Honduras, but entering is L60 (US$3).

HIGHLIGHTS

■ **Bay Islands** (p408) Immerse yourself in this diver's paradise, both for its prices and the rich underwater world that makes up part of the Earth's second-largest reef system.

■ **Copán Ruinas** (p369) Marvel at intricate stone carvings and epic ancient structures tracing back to an extraordinary Maya empire.

■ **Gracias** (p381) Explore the sleepy former capital of Central America, now a cobblestoned refuge of colonial days gone by.

■ **Lago de Yojoa** (p360) Discover misty cloud forests soaring above postcard-blue waters flush with birds and homebrews near the Pulhapanzak waterfalls.

■ **Best journey** (p358) Buckle up for a bone-rattling ride through La Ruta Lenca, a series of little-visited highland communities with proud indigenous hearts.

■ **Off the beaten track** (p427) Go into the wild on an upriver adventure into Central America's last untamed wilderness, the Reserva de la Biosfera del Río Plátano.

CURRENT EVENTS

Little Honduras took the global center stage on June 28, 2009, when then-President Manuel Zelaya was ousted in a dramatic twilight raid on his home in the suburbs of Tegucigalpa. While Zelaya was forcefully expatriated to Costa Rica, international media and foreign heads of state jumped all over Honduras, calling it a military coup and condemning Honduran powers-that-be as totalitarian powermongers. But the 'coup' in Honduras may not have been a coup at all.

In the months leading up to the constitutional crisis, Zelaya was accused of abusing power, allegedly attempting to rewrite the constitution and moving forward with an illegal re-election campaign and plans to establish a National Constituent Assembly. Invoking its own constitutional law, the supreme court issued a court order for the armed forces to detain and remove Zelaya from office, with President of Congress, Roberto Micheletti, taking over as interim president with the support of the military, the judicial and executive branches of government and the Catholic church.

According to the Honduran Constitution it was a legal move. However, the armed forces made a crucial mistake: deporting Zelaya rather than holding him for trial (there's a list of crimes he is accused of, including treason and abuse of office) was not only illegal but allowed Zelaya to stand by defiantly, vowing to return to Honduras and reclaim the presidency. Three months after his removal, Zelaya made good on his promise, clandestinely entering the country and making his way to the Brazilian embassy in Tegucigalpa. Meanwhile, Honduras held transparent democratic elections in November 2009, electing Nationalist party candidate Porfirio 'Pepe' Lobo, a center-right conservative (the polar opposite of Zelaya). In a controversial move, Lobo signed a letter of safe passage for Zelaya days before his inauguration, allowing the ousted president to travel hassle-free to the Dominican Republic as a 'distinguished guest,' ending a three-month standoff at the Brazilian embassy. The day before Zelaya's departure, Congress approved an amnesty decree for all political offenses committed during the crisis, effectively giving the country internal closure on the matter.

All was not contentious, however, as Los Catrachos, the Honduran national soccer team – as if on cue – earned a trip to the 2010 World Cup after a dramatic last-minute US goal against Costa Rica sent them through. Honduras' first appearance at the big dance since 1982 breathed new life into a wounded country drowning in a wholly controversial year, but it was short-lived. Los Catrachos were sent packing in the group stage after failing to score a single goal.

HISTORY
Pre-Columbian History

More than 3000 years ago, pre-Columbian settlers made their homes and farms in the fertile Copán, Sula and Comayagua valleys – although humans are thought to have roamed these lands from about 10,000 BC. Recovered pottery fragments suggest separate settlements and groups traded with each other.

At around the same time as the European Dark Ages, Copán Ruinas, the southeasterly

HONDURAS

HONDURAS

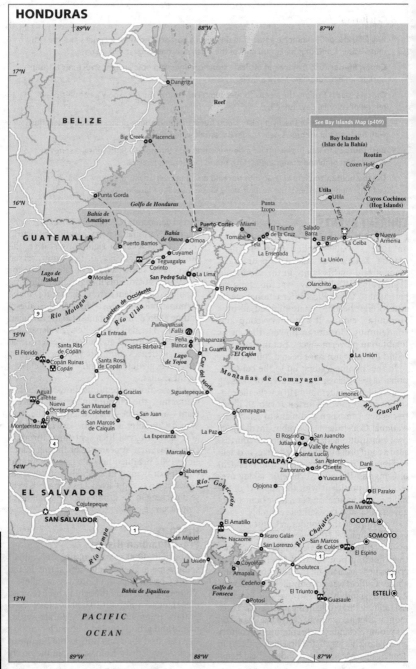

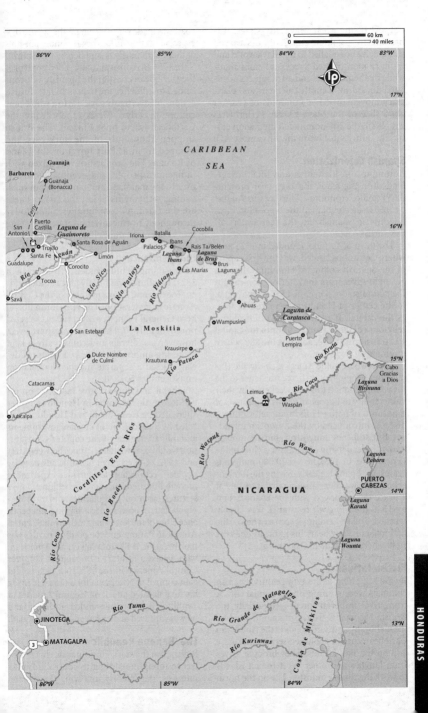

outpost of the great Maya city-states, was basking in a golden era. Sculptors carved stone stelae unequalled in the Maya world and military men plotted successful campaigns, while mathematicians and astronomers calculated uncannily accurate calendars and planetary movements. For hundreds of years, a good slice of the Maya Classic Period (AD 250–900), the city dominated the region culturally, until its decline in the 9th century AD.

Spanish Colonization

Columbus, on his fourth and final voyage, landed on the tropical shores near present-day Trujillo, Honduras. The day was August 14, 1502, and he named the place Honduras ('depths' in Spanish) for the deep waters off the north coast.

The town of Trujillo, founded in 1525 near where Columbus landed, was the first capital of the Spanish colony of Honduras, but the gleam of silver from the interior soon caught the conquistadors' eye. In 1537 Comayagua, in the center of Honduras, replaced Trujillo as the capital. It remained the political and religious center of Honduras until the capital was transferred to Tegucigalpa in 1880, where it remains today.

As elsewhere in the Americas, *indígenas* (indigenous people) put up fierce resistance to the invasion, although this was weakened by their vulnerability to European germs. Hundreds of thousands of native Hondurans fell victim to diseases introduced by the European intruders. But still they fought on, most famously under the leadership of Lempira, a chief of the Lenca tribe. In 1537 he led 30,000 *indígenas* against the Spanish, nearly driving the foreigners out. He was later assassinated, possibly at a peace talk arranged with the Spanish, and by 1539 the *indígena* resistance was largely crushed. Today, Lempira is seen as a hero – the national currency bears his name as does the state where he made his last stand.

British Influence

By the beginning of the 17th century, Spanish colonists were coming under regular attack from rival imperial forces – especially the British. Merchants from Britain, attracted by the mahogany and hardwoods of the Honduran Caribbean coast, established settlements there and on the Bay Islands. They brought slaves from Jamaica and other West Indian islands to work the timber industry. Life on the north coast was made very difficult for the Spaniards – especially as the Mískito began aiming potshots at them with muskets supplied by the British.

In 1786 Britain eventually ceded control of the Caribbean coast to the Spanish, but continued to influence the region. In fact, British actions inadvertently gave rise to a whole new culture. In early 1797, slaves rebelled on the Caribbean island of St Vincent. The British shipped thousands of the survivors and dumped them at Port Royal on the island of Roatán. The group survived, mixed with indigenous people, and eventually crossed over to the mainland and fanned out in small fishing settlements along the coast. These are the Garífuna communities found today throughout northern Honduras, stretching into Guatemala and Belize.

Independence

After gaining its independence from Spain in 1821, Honduras was briefly part of independent Mexico and then a member of the Central American Federation. The Honduran liberal hero General Francisco Morazán was elected president in 1830. The union was short-lived, however, as liberals and conservatives kept bickering among themselves. Honduras declared itself a separate independent nation on November 5, 1838.

Liberal and conservative factions continued to wrestle for power in Honduras. Power alternated between them, and Honduras was ruled by a succession of civilian governments and military regimes. (The country's constitution would be rewritten 17 times between 1821 and 1982.) Government has officially been by popular election, but Honduras has experienced literally hundreds of coups, rebellions, power seizures, electoral 'irregularities' and other manipulations of power since achieving independence. One of the few things to unify the Central American nations and the political parties was the threat of William Walker, an American, who waged a military campaign to conquer Central America in the 1850s. In fact, he did gain control of Nicaragua for a time. He made his final ill-fated attack on Central America at Trujillo. His campaign ended in defeat, and he was captured and executed by firing squad.

The 'Banana Republic'

Right from the start, Honduras has been subject to foreign meddling to control business interests, particularly involving the banana industry – hence the phrase 'banana republic.' Around the end of the 19th century, US traders marveled at the rapid growth of bananas on the fertile north coast just a short sail from southern USA. With the development of refrigeration the banana industry boomed. US entrepreneurs bought land for growing bananas utilizing generous incentives by a succession of Honduran governments. The three major companies were the Vaccaro brothers (later to become Standard Fruit), which operated around La Ceiba; the Cuyamel Fruit Company near the Río Cuyamel and Tela; and after 1912, United Fruit, to the east, which by 1929 had swallowed up Cuyamel. The three companies owned a large part of northern Honduras, and by 1918, 75% of all Honduran banana lands were held by US companies.

Bananas provided 11% of Honduras' exports in 1892, 42% in 1903 and 66% in 1913. The success of the industry made the banana companies extremely powerful within Honduras, with policy and politicians controlled by their interests. Cuyamel Fruit Company allied itself with the Liberal Party, United Fruit with the National Party, and the rivalries between banana companies shaped Honduran politics.

20th-Century Politics

The USA increasingly came to influence Honduran affairs. In 1911 and 1912, when it appeared that banana interests were threatened by Honduran political developments, US president William Howard Taft sent the US Marines into Honduras to 'protect US investments.'

During the worldwide economic depression of the 1930s, in the midst of civil unrest, General Tiburcio Carías Andino was elected president, establishing a virtual dictatorship that lasted from 1932 until 1949, when US pressure forced him to cede power.

A two-month strike in 1954 – which became known as 'the Banana Strike' in which as many as 25,000 banana workers and sympathizers participated – remains a seminal moment in Honduran labor history. Unions were recognized, and workers gained rights that were unheard of in neighboring Central American countries.

A military coup in 1956 marked an important shift in Honduras politics. Although civilian rule returned in 1957, a new constitution put the military officially out of the control of civilian government. The military now had a much more important role in the country's politics, the legacy of which continues to this day.

In 1963 Colonel Osvaldo López Arrellano led another military coup and ruled as president until 1975, apart from a brief return to democracy in 1971 to 1972. He was forced to resign because of a scandal involving a L1.25 million bribe from a US company, United Brands. Colonel Juan Alberto Melgar Castro, who slowed agrarian reform, replaced him in a military coup. He in turn was ousted by yet another military coup in 1978. This was led by General Policarpo Paz García, who eventually instigated democratic presidential elections in 1981. Military rule was finally over.

The 1980s

During the 1980s Honduras was surrounded by revolutions and conflict. In July 1979 the revolutionary Sandinista movement in Nicaragua overthrew the Somoza dictatorship, and Somoza's national guardsmen fled into Honduras. Civil war broke out in El Salvador in 1980 and internal conflict worsened in Guatemala.

With revolutions erupting on every side, and especially with the success of the Nicaraguan revolution in 1979, Honduras became the focus of US policy and strategic operations in the region. After the USA pressured the government to hold elections, a civilian, Dr Roberto Suazo Córdova, was elected president. Real power arguably rested with the commander-in-chief of the armed forces, General Gustavo Álvarez, who supported an increasing US military presence in Central America. US military involvement in Central America had increased dramatically following Ronald Reagan's election as US president. The USA funneled huge sums of money and thousands of US troops into Honduras as it conducted provocative maneuvers clearly designed to threaten Nicaragua. Refugee camps of Nicaraguans in Honduras were used as bases for a US-sponsored covert war against the Nicaraguan Sandinista government, known as the Contra war. At the same time the USA was training the Salvadoran military at Salvadoran refugee camps inside Honduras.

General Gustavo Álvarez was also responsible for the formation of the notorious Battalion 3-16, which targeted and 'disappeared' hundreds of political enemies. Although the repression was small-scale when compared with El Salvador and Guatemala, public alarm grew.

HONDURAS

Local opposition to the US militarization of Honduras also increased, creating problems for the Honduran government. In March 1984 General Álvarez was exiled by fellow officers, and General Walter López Reyes was appointed his successor. The Honduran government promptly announced it would re-examine US military presence in the country and in August suspended US training of the Salvadoran military within its borders.

The 1985 presidential election, beset by serious irregularities, was won by the Liberal Party candidate José Simeón Azcona del Hoyo, who had obtained only 27% of the votes. Rafael Leonardo Callejas Romero of the National Party, who had obtained 42% of the votes, lost.

In Washington, the Reagan administration was rocked by revelations it had illegally used money from arms sales to Iran to support anti-Sandinista Contras in Honduras. Large demonstrations followed in Tegucigalpa, and in November 1988 the Honduran government refused to sign a new military agreement with the USA. President Azcona Hoyo said the Contras would have to leave. With the election of Violeta Chamorro as president of Nicaragua in 1990, the Contra war ended and the Contras were finally out of Honduras.

Modern Currents & 'Coups'

Through the presidential administrations of Rafael Leonardo Callejas Romero (1990–94) and Carlos Roberto Reina Idiaquez (1994–98), Honduras struggled economically, with the unstable lempira on a downward spiral against the dollar. Things started to turn around after the election of the Liberal Party's Carlos Roberto Flores Facusse (1998–2002), but Honduras was dealt an unfortunate economic blow: the devastating Hurricane Mitch in November 1998. The storms caused damage estimated at US$3 billion. According to some analysts, it set the country's economic development back by decades.

In 2001, Ricardo Maduro from the National Party was elected president, largely on the back of his promises to reduce crime. Maduro was no doubt committed to the cause – his son was kidnapped and murdered in 1997. Despite pouring huge resources into the problem, crime continued largely unabated. In January 2006, Maduro was succeeded by a cowboy-hat-wearing rancher from Olancho named José Manuel Zelaya Rosales. Zelaya's early administration was smudged by widespread allegations of corruption – in the first year of his presidency alone, as many as 11 ministers resigned amid corruption charges.

During his tenure, Zelaya aligned himself closely with other Latin American left-wing leaders such as Venezuela's Hugo Chávez, and similarly allied organizations like ALBA (Bolivarian Alliance for the Peoples of Our America) – a sea change for a nation that had long been Central America's strongest US ally. But it was Zelaya's plan to hold a referendum to rewrite Honduras' 38-year-old constitution that got him into hot water with the supreme court. The so-called *cuarta urna* – the fourth ballot box – was a proposed government-run poll that would have allowed Hondurans to vote on the possibility of Zelaya to rewrite the constitution and make himself eligible for a second term, something the Honduran constitution forbids.

The supreme court, which declared the proposed referendum illegal, went into action, ordering Zelaya removed from office and detained in June 2009 (see p331). But the armed forces, in an effort to avert widespread rioting and perhaps civil war, flew Zelaya to Costa Rica rather then placing him under arrest. While the world cried foul, the Honduran government stood its ground, standing up to the USA, Brazil and other world powers, calling the event a 'constitutional transition' all the while its country teetered precariously on the precipice of becoming a failed state. President of Congress, Roberto Micheletti, assumed interim presidential duties. With Zelaya on the sidelines, Honduras moved forward with transparent elections in November 2009, electing National Party member Porfirio 'Pepe' Lobo. Though no single country in the world recognized the de facto government as lawful, several recognized the legitimacy of Porfirio Lobo's election.

Meanwhile, Lobo allowed Zelaya to travel hassle-free to the Dominican Republic, where he was expected to remain in the exclusive Casa de Campo resort complex in La Romana, 100km from Santo Domingo, for up to one year while deciding his future. It was a win of sorts for Zelaya, who got to maintain his dignity (in his eyes) and depart the country he governed for three and a half years amid a sea of supporters at Aeropuerto Internacional Toncontín with his held head high. He boarded a plane for the Dominican Republic and flew away into the history books. *Maybe.*

THE CULTURE
The National Psyche

Generalizations don't – and shouldn't – come easily for a country with such wide-ranging cultures. The *ladino* businessman will have a different outlook to the Garífuna fisherman, who may not have much in common with a Lencan subsistence farmer. However, Hondurans are less likely to reach a collective flashpoint than their neighbors, at least historically. While Guatemala, El Salvador and Nicaragua all fought fierce civil wars in the 1980s, Honduras remained relatively conflict-free; US intervention certainly played a role, but so, perhaps, did the go-with-the-flow nature of the people. Most visitors find Hondurans intensely proud of their country and will be taken aback by their friendliness and hospitality – although some feel that masks a reserve that makes many Hondurans difficult to get to know.

Lifestyle

Lifestyles in Honduras vary as widely as the country's shockingly unequal social spectrum. The fortunate economic elite often lead an Americanized lifestyle, driving SUVs and shopping at the latest air-conditioned malls. Far more commonly, Hondurans are forced to scratch a living. Poverty is perhaps at its most shocking in urban areas, where poor conditions are accompanied by the constant threat of violence.

In rural and coastal areas, the pressures are different but still intense. Many are being forced to give up their traditional lifestyles, and move to the city or look for seasonal work – on coffee plantations for example. Lack of opportunities at home have also forced many Hondurans to seek jobs in the USA. An estimated one million Hondurans are living and working in that country, at least half of them illegally.

Hondurans are hugely family-oriented, as is common in Central America. They often have a wider family network than many Europeans or North Americans are used to – aunts, uncles, grandparents, cousins and even more distant relatives often play a significant role in family life.

Another attitude in Honduran society is machismo. Women are often still treated as second-class citizens. Wages are much lower (women can expect to earn a third of the average male wage, according to a UN Development Program report) and reported levels of domestic abuse are disturbing. Stories of men who do a runner when their partner becomes pregnant are commonplace.

The same macho tendencies mean that gay culture is very much in the closet.

People

Honduras is experiencing the most rapid urbanization in Central America: the urban population was 44% in 1990 and around 48% in 2008, with a predicted annual growth rate of 2.9%. Up to 90% of Hondurans are *mestizo*, a mixture of Spanish and *indígena*.

The Tolupanes (also called Jicaque or Xicaque) live in small villages dotting the departments of Yoro and Francisco Morazán. They are thought to be one of the oldest indigenous communities in Honduras.

The Maya-Ch'orti' people live near the Guatemalan border, in the department of Copán, while the Lenca live in southwestern Honduras. They are notable for their colorful traditional clothing and head scarves.

Arguably the most ethnically diverse region of Honduras is La Moskitia. It is home to the Mískito people and the Pech (who are generally less outgoing than the Mískitos). The Pech also live along the highway from San Esteban to Tocoa. In the interior of La Moskitia, the Tawahka inhabit the area around the Río Patuca – now designated as the Tawahka Asangni Biosphere Reserve. Numbering fewer than 1000, they still have their own language. The Garífuna live on Honduras' north coast, from La Moskitia all the way across to Belize. Other people with African ancestry – descended from Caribbean immigrants who came to work on the banana plantations – live on the north coast and Bay Islands.

RELIGION

Honduras is nominally a Roman Catholic country, but that has changed rapidly in the last couple of decades with the rise of the evangelical movement. Just how many Roman Catholics have converted to evangelical Christianity is difficult to tell – figures are unreliable. The *CIA World Factbook* states that 97% of Hondurans are Roman Catholic, though Roman Catholic analysis estimates that over 100,000 Hondurans are Protestants. Unlike neighboring Guatemala, few indigenous customs or beliefs have been integrated into Christian worship. However, a belief in witchcraft and superstition is common in some parts of Hondurans.

THE FOOTBALL WAR

Legendary football manager Bill Shankly once said: 'Some people believe football is a matter of life and death…it is much more important than that.' Even Mr Shankly might have balked at Honduras' and El Salvador's sporting rivalry, which spilled off the pitch and onto the battlefield in the 1969 Guerra de Fútbol – the notorious Football (Soccer) War.

Tensions did not suddenly break out on the stadium terraces. In the 1950s and 1960s, a flagging economy forced 300,000 Salvadorans to seek better conditions in Honduras. However, the Honduran economy was itself ailing, and Salvadorans began to be targeted as scapegoats. In June 1969, Honduran authorities started throwing Salvadoran immigrants out of the country. A stream of Salvadoran refugees followed, alleging Honduran brutality.

In the same month, the two countries were playing World Cup qualifying matches against each other. At the San Salvador game, Salvadorans attacked Honduran fans, defiling the Honduran flag and mocking the anthem. Across the border, angry Hondurans then turned on Salvadoran immigrants. Tempers frayed further and the El Salvador army invaded Honduran territory on July 14, capturing Nueva Ocotepeque. Honduras retaliated with air strikes. A ceasefire was called after only six days, but around 2000 Hondurans lost their lives, while thousands of Salvadorans fled home.

ARTS

Although not as well known for its art as Guatemala, Honduras does have some notable *artesanías*. Lenca pottery, with its black-and-white designs and glossy finish, can be of high quality and there are some skilful replica Maya carvings and glyphs in Copán Ruinas.

Honduras has a thriving visual arts scene. The 'primitivist' movement – often depicting scenes of mountain villages – is famous. José Antonio Velásquez (1906–83) is its most renowned exponent.

Musically, Honduran airwaves are usually filled with imported rhythms, but the country does have homegrown talent, including Guillermo Anderson, who combines folk with salsa, *punta* and rock. Karla Lara is another singer-songwriter whose folksy strumming is winning fans. And most recently, Aurelio Martínez has taken off as one of the stars of the new *punta*-rock rage, a fusion of traditional Garífuna *punta* with an electric sound. Honduras also contributes significantly to the reggaetón movement, with artists like Raggamofin Killas, El Pueblo and DJ Sy.

On the literary scene, Lucila Gamero de Medina (1873–1964) was one of the first Central American female writers. Rafael Heliodoro del Valle (1891–1959) was a respected journalist whose ideas had a lot of clout regionally. Ramón Amaya-Amador (1916–66) was a political writer who published *Prisión verde* (1945) about life on a banana plantation. Juan Ramón Molina (1875–1908) is perhaps the country's best-loved poet while Roberto Quesada is one of Honduras' top living authors.

Dance is another popular art form – the Garífuna people of the north coast are known for their distinctive *punta* music and dance. If you get a chance to see a performance by the Ballet Folklórico Garífuna, don't miss it.

A film industry is virtually nonexistent, but Honduras has been the fictional setting in some films, most recently *Sin nombre* (2009), a Sundance prizewinner about gangs and illegal immigration that opens in Honduras (though shot in Mexico). *The Sounds of La Mosquitia,* an independent film depicting the sights and sounds of the feral jungle region, including insight into the Tawahka, Misquita, Garífuna and Sumo people who live there, won a National Environmental prize in 2009. Actress America Ferrera of *Ugly Betty* fame is ethnically Honduran.

ENVIRONMENT

Honduras is a country of breathtaking natural beauty, with a huge range of bird, mammal, reptile and plant species. However, illegal logging, underresourced authorities and crass development projects are putting this under threat. While the environment has plenty of defenders, they face a tough struggle against developers, corruption and plain ignorance.

The Land

Countries don't come that big in Central America but, on the isthmus, Honduras weighs in as the second-largest (after Nicaragua), with an area of 112,090 sq km. It has coast on the Caribbean Sea (644km), and on the Pacific along the Golfo de Fonseca (124km). Guatemala is to the west, on the southwest is El Salvador and the Golfo de Fonseca, and to the southeast is Nicaragua. The fertile north is by far the most developed – its banana plantations have long been a mainstay of the economy. Honduras' many islands include the Bay Islands and Hog Islands in the Caribbean and several in the Golfo de Fonseca.

Much of the Honduran interior is mountainous with peaks from 300m to 2849m high. There are many fertile highland valleys, but, unlike in Guatemala, there are no active volcanoes. Lowlands exist along both coasts and in several river valleys.

Wildlife
There is a dazzling array of flora and fauna in Honduras. Jaguars, tapirs, crocodiles and the mighty Ceiba tree are found in tropical zones; in the cloud forests are quetzals, rare butterflies, orchids and magnificent pine trees; while whale sharks, coral and seahorses thrive in the country's turquoise Caribbean waters. It is the sheer variety of habitats that allows so many different species to thrive. Honduras has mangrove swamps, freshwater lakes, oceans, lagoons, cloud forests, pine forests and tropical rainforests (considerably more than Costa Rica, which somehow manages to hog the ecotourism limelight).

Much of the habitat is under threat from deforestation. Endangered species include the scarlet macaw (the national bird), Utilan iguana, manatee, quetzal, jaguar, whale shark and tapir. Their future depends on just how much protection Honduras' so-called protected areas can really offer.

National Parks & Protected Areas
Honduras has many ecologically protected areas, including parques nacionales (national parks), refugios de vida (wildlife refuges), biological reserves and biosphere reserves. More than one-fifth of Honduras qualifies as an existing or proposed protected area, but the effect of that is debatable. All too often the government lacks the resources – or the political will – to stop development and deforestation.

These are some of the more important protected areas, including marine reserves:
Lancetilla Jardín Botánnico It has more than 700 plant species and 365 species of bird. See p393.

Parque Nacional Cusuco A cloud forest, with a large population of quetzals. See p367.
Parque Nacional Jeannette Kawas (Punta Sal) Habitats include mangrove swamps, a small tropical forest, offshore reefs, several coves and a rocky point. The park has a large number of migratory and coastal birds. See p393.
Parque Nacional La Tigra Near Tegucigalpa, this protects a beautiful cloud forest set in former mining country. See p354.
Parque Nacional Maritimo Cayos Cochinos The Cayos Cochinos (Hog Islands) are a protected reserve and proposed national marine park. Thirteen cays, two of them large, with beautiful coral reefs, well-preserved forests and fishing villages make up the reserve. See p401.
Parque Nacional Montaña de Celaque An elevated plateau, with four peaks more than 2800m above sea level, including Honduras' highest peak. See p384.
Parque Nacional Pico Bonito The park has high biodiversity and many waterfalls. Pico Bonito is the highest peak here, at 2436m. See p403.
Refugio de Vida Laguna de Guaimoreto Has mangrove forest and a great variety of wildlife, including birds, manatees and dolphins. See p407.
Refugio de Vida Punta Izopo Made up of tropical wet forest, mangrove forest and wetlands. It has many migratory birds, a beautiful rocky point and white-sand beaches. See p394.
Refugio de Vida Silvestre Cuero y Salado The largest manatee reserve in Central America (although that's no guarantee of seeing one). Monkeys and birdlife also abound. See p402.
Reserva de la Biosfera del Río Plátano A World Heritage Site and the first biosphere reserve in Central America, the Río Plátano is 5251 sq km of lowland tropical rainforest with remarkable natural, archaeological and cultural resources. See p427.
Sandy Bay/West End Marine Reserve On the northwestern end of Roatán in the Bay Islands, this marine reserve has some of the most colorful coral reefs around. See p418.
Tawahka Asangni Biosphere Reserve A tropical rainforest on the ancestral lands of the Tawahka people, a very threatened indigenous group. Access is by plane to Ahuas or Wampusirpi then by boat upstream to Krausirpe and Krautara, or by a multiday rafting trip down the Río Patuca from Juticalpa.
Turtle Harbor On the northwestern side of Utila in the Bay Islands, Turtle Harbor is another marine reserve and proposed national marine park visited frequently by divers.

Environmental Issues
Deforestation is the most pressing environmental issue facing Honduras today. Reliable reports suggest up to 85% of Honduran timber

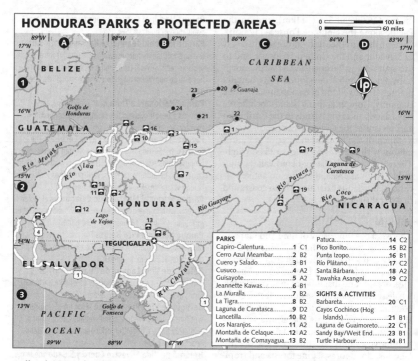

HONDURAS PARKS & PROTECTED AREAS

PARKS	
Capiro-Calentura	1 C1
Cerro Azul Meambar	2 B2
Cuero y Salado	3 B1
Cusuco	4 A2
Guisayote	5 A2
Jeannette Kawas	6 B1
La Muralla	7 B2
La Tigra	8 B2
Laguna de Caratasca	9 D2
Lancetilla	10 B2
Los Naranjos	11 A2
Montaña de Celaque	12 A2
Montaña de Comayagua	13 B2

Patuca	14 C2
Pico Bonito	15 B2
Punta Izopo	16 B1
Río Plátano	17 C2
Santa Bárbara	18 A2
Tawahka Asangni	19 C2
SIGHTS & ACTIVITIES	
Barbareta	20 C1
Cayos Cochinos (Hog Islands)	21 B1
Laguna de Guaimoreto	22 C1
Sandy Bay/West End	23 B1
Turtle Harbour	24 B1

is illegal (38% of which ends up in the US). Every year, around 2% of the country's forest cover is chopped to the ground – roughly four times the combined area of the Bay Islands.

Even Honduras' most treasured nature reserve, the Reserva de la Biosfera del Río Plátano, is under threat. Loggers and livestock landowners clear the land there with little resistance; in 1996, Unesco escalated the area into the 'at risk' category.

In late 2008, the Honduran government hired a Norwegian company to begin petroleum exploration off the coast (it was confirmed in 1999 that Honduras sits on 4 to 5 billion tons of untapped oil reserves) but large-scale drilling would take around US$250 million in initial outlay, which Honduras does not have, so it still sits in the relatively distant future.

According to environmental reports, mining activity is polluting the Lago de Yojoa (the largest source of freshwater in the country) with heavy metals. Meanwhile, overfishing (and illegal catches) in the Bay Islands are putting its magnificent reef ecosystem in danger.

TRANSPORTATION

GETTING THERE & AWAY
Air

Frequent direct flights connect Honduras with other Central American capitals and many destinations in North America, the Caribbean, South America and Europe. Most international flights arrive and depart from the airports at San Pedro Sula and Tegucigalpa. By far the busiest and largest airport is at San Pedro Sula. There are also direct flights between the USA and Roatán, coming from Houston and Atlanta.

Boat

The only regularly scheduled passenger boat service between Honduras and another country is two small boats that run once weekly from Puerto Cortés to Belize. Otherwise, it might be possible to arrange passage with cargo or fishing vessels if you pay your way. On the Caribbean coast, you can try to find a boat around Puerto Cortés, Tela, La Ceiba, Trujillo, Palacios or the Bay Islands. The most common international destinations for these boats are Puerto Barrios (Guatemala), Belize and Puerto Cabezas (Nicaragua).

On the Pacific side, you might be able to get a ride on boats sailing between countries. But the land crossings are so close it might not be worth the effort. San Lorenzo and Coyolito are the main Honduran port towns in the gulf.

If you arrive or depart from Honduras by sea, be sure to clear your paperwork (entry and exit stamps, if necessary) immediately with the nearest immigration office.

Bus

To Guatemala, the main crossings are at El Florido (Guatemala), Agua Caliente and Corinto. To El Salvador, the main crossings are El Poy and El Amatillo; there is also a crossing at Sabanetas, across the highlands from Marcala. Only Honduras has an immigration post here because of a border dispute, although this may change. The crossings to Nicaragua are at Las Manos (Honduras), El Espino and Guasaule (Nicaragua).

Frequent buses serve all of these border crossings. Most buses do not cross the border. You cross on foot and pick up another bus on the other side. The exceptions are international buses; the following provide services to San Salvador (El Salvador), Guatemala City, Antigua (Guatemala), Managua (Nicaragua), San José (Costa Rica) and Panama City (though not all go to each):

King Quality (www.king-qualityca.com)
Tica Bus (www.ticabus.com)
Transportes Hedman Alas (www.hedmanalas.com)

GETTING AROUND
Air

Domestic air routes have proliferated in Honduras recently; it's now easy to fly to any of the Bay Islands from La Ceiba, Tegucigalpa and San Pedro Sula, and to fly between these three major cities. (Flights to the Bay Islands from Tegucigalpa and San Pedro Sula connect through La Ceiba.) Air routes into the Moskitia are also making that remote area more accessible.

DEPARTURE TAX

If you fly out of Honduras, you must pay L691 (US$37) departure tax at the airport. The domestic departure tax is L36 (US$2).

Airlines include the following:

Aerolíneas Sosa (☎ in San Pedro Sula 550-6545, in Tegucigalpa 233-5107, in La Ceiba 443-1894, in Roatán 445-1658; www.aerolineasosa.com) Based in La Ceiba.

SAMI (☎ in Brus Laguna 433-8031, in La Ceiba 442-2565, in Puerto Lempira 433-6016)

TACA/Isleña (☎ in San Pedro Sula 516-1061, in Tegucigalpa 236-8222, in La Ceiba 441-3191, in Roatán 445-1088; www.taca.com, www.flyislena.com)

Boat

Two passenger ferries, the luxury catamaran *Galaxy Wave* and the *Utila Princess II*, operate between La Ceiba and the Bay Islands. The *Galaxy Wave* goes to Roatán (1¾ hours), while the smaller, less fancy *Utila Princess II* goes to Utila. There is no ferry service between the two islands. There is also a less reliable ferry between Trujillo and Guanaja.

In the Moskitia, almost all transportation is along the waterways. There are also water taxis on Roatán from West End to West Bay, and from Coyolito on the Golfo de Fonseca over to the Isla del Tigre.

Bus

Buses are a cheap and easy way to get around in Honduras. The first buses of the day often start very early in the morning; the last bus usually departs in the late afternoon. Buses between Tegucigalpa and San Pedro Sula run until later.

On major bus routes, you'll often have a choice between taking a *directo* (direct) or *ordinario* (ordinary), which is also known as *parando* or *servicio a escala*. The *directo* is much faster and almost always worth the extra money, even on short trips.

Deluxe buses offer faster service between Tegucigalpa, San Pedro Sula, Copán Ruinas, Tela and also La Ceiba, using modern aircon buses (sometimes with movies and soft drinks). *Ejecutivo* (executive) or *servicio de lujo* (luxury service) buses are more expensive than *directo* buses, often double the price. They can be a worthwhile splurge for long trips.

Microbuses or *rapiditos* are smaller minivan-like buses that cover some routes, and tend to go faster and leave more frequently than regular buses.

Chicken buses operate between major towns and their satellite villages.

Car & Motorcycle

The main highways are paved roads, mostly in reasonable condition. Away from the highways, roads tend to be unpaved. Conditions can vary wildly according to rainfall and the time of year, ranging from acceptable to impassable.

Rental cars are available in Tegucigalpa, San Pedro Sula, La Ceiba and on Roatán. Prices vary between L482 to L896 a day for an economy car with a hefty deductible (L38,500).

Taxi

Taxis are everywhere in Honduran towns. They don't have meters but most towns have a fixed about-town fare, starting at L20 in smaller places and going up to L50. Taxis in San Pedro Sula and Tegucigalpa are more expensive. Expect to pay L50 and L60 respectively for a ride about town. Taxi fares increase at night. In the major cities, *colectivos* (shared taxis) ply a number of prescribed routes, costing around L10 to L15 per passenger. Always confirm the fare before you leave. If it seems a rip off, negotiate or wait for another.

Three-wheeled mototaxis have flooded into Honduras in the past few years. They are usually cheaper than taxis.

TEGUCIGALPA

pop 1.08 million

In many ways Tegucigalpa is a typical, sprawling Central American metropolis. The streets are often snarled with fume-belching traffic, while the crowds are thick and the pace is frenetic. However, the setting is spectacular – the city is nestled in a valley surrounded by a ring of mountains, and it has a certain chaotic charm.

You may even feel a bit of affection for it when you glimpse a 16th-century church or the view across the precipitous city landscape, or perhaps after a fine meal at a restaurant. Expect this feeling to last until around the time you get stuck in the next traffic jam (not long).

At an altitude of 975m, Tegucigalpa has a fresher and milder climate than the country's coasts – although long-term residents report a steady temperature rise, as in many other areas of the world. The city is also struggling to cope with huge migration to its bright lights – you will see shantytowns clinging to the mountainsides in the upper reaches of the urban sprawl.

The name Tegucigalpa (teh-goos-ee-*gal*-pa) is a bit of a mouthful; Hondurans often call the city Tegus (*teh*-goos) for short. The name, meaning 'silver hill' in the original local Nahuatl dialect, was given when the Spanish founded the city as a silver and gold mining center in 1578, on the slopes of Picacho. Tegucigalpa became the capital of Honduras in 1880, when the government seat was moved from Comayagua, 82km to the northwest.

ORIENTATION

The city is divided by the Río Choluteca. On the east side of the river is Tegucigalpa, including downtown and more affluent districts such as Colonia Palmira. Plaza Morazán, often still called Parque Central, with the city's cathedral, is in the heart of the city. West of this, Av Miguel Paz Barahona is a pedestrian shopping street, extending four blocks from the plaza to Calle El Telégrafo; this section has been renamed Calle Peatonal, and it's a busy thoroughfare with many shops, restaurants and banks.

Across the river from Tegucigalpa is Comayagüela, which is poorer and dirtier, with a sprawling market, long-distance bus stations, budget hotels and *comedores* (cheap eating places). Several bridges connect the two areas.

Maps

Instituto Geográfico Nacional (3 Av Barrio La Bolsa; 🕓 8am-4pm Mon-Fri) sells detailed Honduran road and topographical maps.

INFORMATION
Bookstores

Metromedia Av San Carlos (☎ 221-0770; Av San Carlos; 🕓 10am-8pm Mon-Sat, noon-6pm Sun); Multiplaza Mall (☎ 231-2294; Blvr Juan Pablo II; 🕓 8am-8pm) Sells English-language books, magazines, music and more, including day-old copies of the *New York Times*. Has a cafe.

Emergency & Medical Services

Ambulance (☎ 195; 🕓 24hr) Red Cross.
Honduras Medical Center (☎ 280-1500; Av Juan Lindo; 🕓 24hr) One of the best hospitals in the country.
Police (☎ 199, 222-8736; 5a Av; 🕓 24hr)

Immigration

Immigration office (☎ 238-5613; Anillo Periférico near Universidad Technólogica de Honduras; 🕓 8:30am-4:30pm Mon-Fri) Extends visas and handles immigration matters.

Internet Access

Hondutel (☎ 222-8107; cnr Av Cristóbal Colón & Calle El Telégrafo; 🕓 7am-8:30pm Mon-Sat)
Multinet Colonia Palmira (Centro Comercial Plaza Criolla, Blvr Morazán; per hr L30; 🕓 8am-7pm Mon-Sat); Centro (Calle Peatonal; per hr L18; 🕓 8:30am-8pm) Reliable chain internet cafe and call center.

Mundo Virtual (☎ 238-0062; Calle Salvador Mendieta; per hr L25; ⏱ 8am-9pm Mon-Sat, 9am-8pm Sun) Professional staff, lots of flat screens.

Laundry

Dry Cleaning Lavandería Maya (☎ 232-5923; Av Maipú, Colonia Palmira; per 4.5kg L140; ⏱ 7am-6pm Mon-Fri, 8am-4pm Sat)

Su-perc Jet (☎ 237-4155; Av Máximo Jérez/Juan Gutemberg, Barrio Guanacaste; per 500g L12; ⏱ 8am-5pm Mon-Sat)

Money

Unibanc ATMs are dotted about the city, including the airport, on the northeast corner of Parque Central, in the Hedman Alas bus terminal and in the shopping malls.

BAC/Bamer (Blvr Morazán; ⏱ 9:30am-5:30pm Mon-Fri)

Banco Atlántida (Parque Central; ⏱ 9am-4pm Mon-Fri, 9am-2pm Sat) Changes Amex traveler's checks and has a 24-hour ATM.

Citibank (Centro Comercial Plaza Criolla, Blvr Morazán) One of several banks here.

HSBC (Blvr Morazán) 24-hour ATM.

Post

There's a DHL office near Mailboxes, Etc.

Comayagüela post office (6a Av btwn 7a & 8a Calles; ⏱ 8am-3:30pm Mon-Fri, to noon Sat) In the same building as the Hondutel office.

Downtown post office (☎ 237-8453; cnr Av Miguel Paz Barahona & Calle El Telégrafo; ⏱ 7:30am-5pm Mon-Fri, 8am-1pm Sat)

Mailboxes, Etc (☎ 235-9750; Blvr Morazán 2301; ⏱ 8am-6pm Mon-Fri, 9am-1pm Sat) Has Federal Express, UPS and DHL for international deliveries and Viana for domestic.

Telephone

Most internet cafes have much cheaper rates for international calls than Hondutel.

Hondutel (☎ 222-1120; cnr Av Cristóbal Colón & Calle El Telégrafo; ⏱ 7:30am-9pm Mon-Sat) Pricey state-run call center.

Tourist Information

Amitigra (☎ 231-3641; www.amitigra.org; 2a Calle Nunciatura Apostolica 210, Colonia Palmira; ⏱ 8am-noon & 1-5pm Mon-Fri) Manages, and has information on, Parque Nacional La Tigra.

Corporación Hondureña de Desarrollo Forestal (Cohdefor; ☎ 223-4346; Colonia El Carrizal; ⏱ 7:30am-3:30pm Mon-Fri) The national office; you can get information on Honduras' national parks, wildlife refuges and other protected areas.

Instituto Hondureño de Turismo (☎ 222-2124; www.letsgohonduras.com; 2nd fl, Edificio Europa, cnr Av Ramón Ernesto Cruz & Calle República de México; ⏱ 9am-5pm Mon-Fri) Has some information on national parks and wildlife refuges. Not well-geared to handle walk-in travelers, though very helpful and friendly.

Tourist Info booth (☎ 234-0292; ⏱ 7am-5pm) Airport arrivals hall tourism booth co-run by city hall, Instituto Hondureño de Turismo and Canaturh, the national tourist board.

Travel Agencies

Several reliable travel agencies are clustered in front of and nearby Hotel Honduras Maya. There are others on Calle Peatonal, near Parque Central. Be aware that some agencies charge just for the *cotización* (pricing out an itinerary).

Mundirama Travel (☎ 232-3909; Edificio Ciicsa, cnr Avs República de Panamá & República de Chile; ⏱ 8am-5pm Mon-Fri, 8am-noon Sat) Can help with travel planning, and is the local American Express rep.

DANGERS & ANNOYANCES

Like most developing-world cities, Tegucigalpa is dangerous and the crime is palpable. However, with common sense, you should be able to enjoy the city without putting yourself at undue risk. During the day, downtown Tegucigalpa and Colonia Palmira are usually fine to walk around – although beware of pickpockets around Plaza Morazán (Parque Central). Be especially alert and careful in and around the bus terminals and markets of Comayagüela, which is very rough-and-tumble and not a place to linger day or night. San Isidro Market is a particular hot spot for petty theft. Take taxis at night. In Colonia Palmira, gangs of transvestites have also been known to mug tourists (you won't be spreading that news across your Facebook status update, will you?). Steer clear.

As for dress code: shorts and sandals quickly give you away as a foreign traveler. This should go without saying, but here goes anyway: keep your cash and valuables well hidden. Finally, seek advice from your hotel or locals before hopping on a local city bus. Some are prone to theft and 'taxing' carried out by gang members.

SIGHTS

At the center of the city is the fine white-washed **cathedral** – although its faded exterior needs restoration – and, in front of it, the **Plaza Morazán**, often called Parque Central. The domed 18th-century cathedral (built between 1765 and 1782) has an intricate baroque altar

TEGUCIGALPA

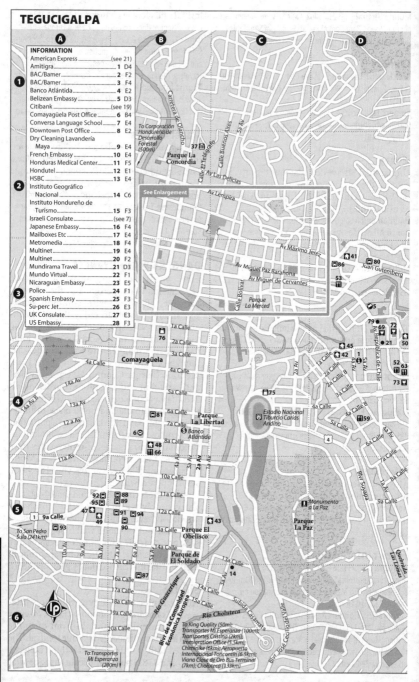

INFORMATION
American Express	(see 21)	
Amitigra	1	D4
BAC/Bamer	2	F2
BAC/Bamer	3	F4
Banco Atlántida	4	E2
Belizean Embassy	5	D3
Citibank	(see 19)	
Comayagüela Post Office	6	B4
Conversa Language School	7	E4
Downtown Post Office	8	E2
Dry Cleaning Lavandería Maya	9	E4
French Embassy	10	E4
Honduras Medical Center	11	F5
Hondutel	12	E1
HSBC	13	E4
Instituto Geográfico Nacional	14	C6
Instituto Hondureño de Turismo	15	F3
Israeli Consulate	(see 7)	
Japanese Embassy	16	F4
Mailboxes Etc	17	E4
Metromedia	18	E4
Multinet	19	E4
Multinet	20	F2
Mundirama Travel	21	D3
Mundo Virtual	22	F1
Nicaraguan Embassy	23	E5
Police	24	F1
Spanish Embassy	25	F3
Su-perc Jet	26	E3
UK Consulate	27	E3
US Embassy	28	F3

HONDURAS

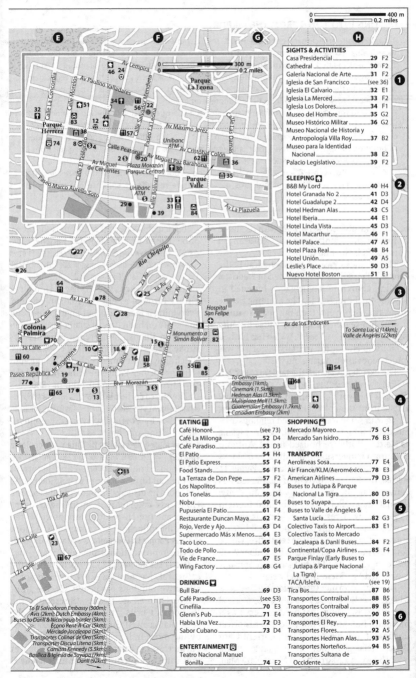

SIGHTS & ACTIVITIES

Casa Presidencial	**29**	F2
Cathedral	**30**	F2
Galería Nacional de Arte	**31**	F2
Iglesia de San Francisco	(see 36)	
Iglesia El Calvario	**32**	E1
Iglesia La Merced	**33**	F2
Iglesia Los Dolores	**34**	F1
Museo del Hombre	**35**	G2
Museo Histórico Militar	**36**	G2
Museo Nacional de Historia y Antropología Villa Roy	**37**	B2
Museo para la Identidad Nacional	**38**	E2
Palacio Legislativo	**39**	F2

SLEEPING

B&B My Lord	**40**	H4
Hotel Granada No 2	**41**	D3
Hotel Guadalupe 2	**42**	D4
Hotel Hedman Alas	**43**	C5
Hotel Iberia	**44**	E1
Hotel Linda Vista	**45**	D3
Hotel Macarthur	**46**	F1
Hotel Palace	**47**	A5
Hotel Plaza Real	**48**	B4
Hotel Unión	**49**	A5
Leslie's Place	**50**	D3
Nuevo Hotel Boston	**51**	E1

EATING

Café Honoré	(see 73)	
Café La Milonga	**52**	D4
Café Paradiso	**53**	D3
El Patio	**54**	H4
El Patio Express	**55**	F4
Food Stands	**56**	F1
La Terraza de Don Pepe	**57**	F2
Los Napolitos	**58**	F4
Los Tonelas	**59**	D4
Nobu	**60**	E4
Pupusería El Patio	**61**	F4
Restaurante Duncan Maya	**62**	F2
Rojo, Verde y Ajo	**63**	D4
Supermercado Más x Menos	**64**	E3
Taco Loco	**65**	E4
Todo de Pollo	**66**	B4
Vie de France	**67**	E5
Wing Factory	**68**	G4

DRINKING

Bull Bar	**69**	D3
Café Paradiso	(see 53)	
Cinefilia	**70**	E3
Glenn's Pub	**71**	E4
Había Una Vez	**72**	D3
Sabor Cubano	**73**	D4

ENTERTAINMENT

Teatro Nacional Manuel Bonilla	**74**	E2

SHOPPING

Mercado Mayoreo	**75**	C4
Mercado San Isidro	**76**	B3

TRANSPORT

Aerolíneas Sosa	**77**	E4
Air France/KLM/Aeroméxico	**78**	E3
American Airlines	**79**	D3
Buses to Jutiapa & Parque Nacional La Tigra	**80**	D3
Buses to Suyapa	**81**	B4
Buses to Valle de Ángeles & Santa Lucía	**82**	G3
Colectivo Taxis to Airport	**83**	E1
Colectivo Taxis to Mercado Jacaleapa & Danlí Buses	**84**	F2
Continental/Copa Airlines	**85**	F4
Parque Finlay (Early Buses to Jutiapa & Parque Nacional La Tigra)	**86**	D3
TACA/Isleña	(see 19)	
Tica Bus	**87**	B6
Transportes Contraibal	**88**	B5
Transportes Contraibal	**89**	B5
Transportes Discovery	**90**	B5
Transportes El Rey	**91**	B5
Transportes Flores	**92**	A5
Transportes Hedman Alas	**93**	A5
Transportes Norteños	**94**	B5
Transportes Sultana de Occidente	**95**	A5

of gold and silver. The *parque*, with its statue of former president Francisco Morazán on horseback, is the hub of the city.

Three blocks east of the cathedral is the **Parque Valle**, with the **Iglesia de San Francisco**, the first church in Tegucigalpa, founded in 1592 by the Franciscans. The building beside it was first a convent, then the Spanish mint; it now houses the lackluster **Museo Histórico Militar** (☽ 7:30am-4pm Mon-Fri), which has limited exhibits on Honduras' military history. It was under renovation during our visit.

The excellent **Galería Nacional de Arte** (☎ 237-9884; admission L30; ☽ 9am-4pm Mon-Sat, 9am-2pm Sun) displays the work of Honduras' finest visual artists from the colonial era to the modern, along with some well-preserved religious artifacts. Just alongside is the 18th-century **Iglesia La Merced**. Both are housed in the Antiguo Paraninfo Universitario building, two blocks south of the cathedral and facing **Parque La Merced**. In 1847 the convent of La Merced was converted to house Honduras' first university; the national gallery was established there in 1996. The well-restored building is itself a work of art. The unusual modern building on stilts next door is the **Palacio Legislativo**, where congress meets. It was here in December 2009 that congress voted 111 to 14 against reinstating ousted President Manuel Zelaya.

The nearby former **Casa Presidencial** (Presidential Palace; cnr Paseo Marco Aurelio Soto & Calle Salvador Mendieta) is a grand building that used to serve as a museum, but now is home to the historical document archive. Honduras' current Casa Presidencial is in new Tegucigalpa, sitting oddly between a Marriott and Metroplaza Mall.

Tegucigalpa's newest museum is the nicely done **Museo para la Identidad Nacional** (MIN; ☎ 238-7412; www.min.hn; Av Miguel Paz Barahona btwn Calles Morelos & El Telégrafo; admission adult/child L60/30; ☽ 9am-5pm Tue-Sat, 10am-4pm Sun) – the place to go for a comprehensive overview of Honduran history through a series of colorful exhibits. Everything is in Spanish, but English-speaking guides are on hand (free of charge) as are audio guides in English and French. The masterstroke here is a 3-D film tour of Copán ruins, which shows four times per day. The museum is in the former Palace of Ministries and the city's first general hospital, built in 1880.

The **Museo del Hombre** (☎ 220-1678; Av Miguel de Cervantes btwn Calles Salvador Corleto & Las Damas; admission L20; ☽ 9am-3pm Mon-Fri) displays mostly contemporary Honduran art.

The **Museo Nacional de Historia y Antropología Villa Roy** (☎ 222-0608; admission L20; ☽ 8am-4pm Mon-Sat) is housed on a hill overlooking the city, in the opulent former home of ex-president Julio Lozano. The displays chronologically recreate Honduras' colorful past, including archaeological and pre-Hispanic history, as well as the rise of the influential fruit companies. A block west is **Parque La Concordia**, a sedate park with carving reproductions from the Copán ruins.

Iglesia Los Dolores (1732), northwest of the cathedral, has a plaza out front and some attractive religious art inside. On the front of Los Dolores are figures representing the Passion of Christ – his unseamed cloak, the cock that crowed three times – all crowned by the more indigenous symbol of the sun. Further west is **Parque Herrera**, where you can pop into a peaceful 18th-century **Iglesia El**

HONDURAS

Calvario, and the striking **Teatro Nacional Manuel Bonilla**, dating from 1912, with an interior inspired by the Athens Theatre of Paris.

Chiminike (☎ 291-0339; www.chiminike.com; Blvr Fuerzas Armadas de Honduras; admission L50; ☽ 9am-noon & 2-5pm Tue-Fri, 10am-1pm & 2-5pm Sat & Sun) is Tegucigalpa's popular new children's museum. About 7km south of central Tegus, its exhibits (Spanish only) range from a display on the human body to an outline of Maya history. Kids should like the *casa de equilibrio* (equilibrium house) – a small tilted house designed to highlight your sense of balance (admission L15).

COURSES

Conversa Language School (☎ 232-2809; aerohond@cable color.hn; Paseo República de Argentina 257; ☽ 8am-5:30pm Mon-Sat) offers intensive courses (120 hours, L22,920). Homestays can also be arranged (per month, including two meals per day, L5730).

SLEEPING

Downtown Tegucigalpa is safe-ish during the day, although not at night. Comayagüela is an even dodgier part of town but closer to the bus terminals. Wandering around here day or night is not recommended. Colonia Palmira is away from downtown, in a good neighborhood. Accommodations there are noticeably pricier. For upper-midrange accommodations and beyond, check out the Sector Hotelero surrounding Leslie's Place.

Downtown

Hotel Iberia (☎ 237-9267; Calle Los Dolores; s without bathroom L150, d with/without bathroom L240/220, tr without bathroom L330) Easily the best cheapie downtown. Run by a nice family, it is an oasis of calm away from the hurly-burly of the street outside. Rooms are clean and the shared bathroom is fine (although hot water only runs from 6am to 8am). There is an upstairs common room with a TV – also good for an afternoon card game.

Nuevo Hotel Boston (☎ 238-0510; Av Máximo Jérez 321; s/d/tr from L275/400/800) A very good budget downtown hotel, if you can get past the rules and regulations (shirt and shoes at all times, no visitors) and the shock-green bathrooms. There is good news for giants – spick-and-span rooms, all set around a leafy courtyard, have large doorways and high ceilings. Another perk is the free coffee and cookies. Rooms facing the street are large, but noisy and not worth the extra charge for a small balcony.

Hotel Granada No 2 (☎ 237-7079; Subida Casamata 1326; s/d/tr L350/400/480; P ⬜) Comfortable bed: check. Secure: check. Clean: check. Free purified water and coffee: check. Just forget about any flourishes in this '70s concrete block of a building. Rooms have TVs and guests have 10 minutes' free internet.

Hotel MacArthur (☎ 237-9839; homacart@datum.hn; Av Lempira 454; s/d/tr with fan L741/931/1121, with air-con L931/1121/1311; P ⊠ ⬛) The most professional cheapish hotel downtown offers somewhat inconsistent rooms: some are sparsely decorated and lack charm; others are cozy with views over nearby Iglesia Los Dolores. All are comfortable and good value. Rooms at the front have more character but are noisier. There is an inexpensive cafeteria serving breakfast and dinner, as well as an attractive pool that nobody seems to use.

Colonia Palmira

Hotel Guadalupe 2 (☎ 238-5009; hotelguadalupe2@cable color.hn; 1a Calle; s/d/tr L390/440/530; P ☎) Safe and comfortable, this has just one drawback: its Stalinist-style box-rooms let in little light and can make you feel trapped in a Cold War spy movie – with rambunctious street noise as its soundtrack. Many volunteers stay here for the security and the good neighborhood.

Hotel Linda Vista (☎ 238-2099; Calle Las Acacias 1438; s/d/tr L932/1237/1580; P ⊠ ☎) This almost annoyingly secure small hotel has six rooms with mahogany furnishings, big closets and spacious bathrooms. The jungly thatch of green in front is well tended and boasts pretty views, while the rear garden has a truly lovely view of the Tegucigalpa sprawl. Continental breakfast is included.

B&B My Lord (☎ 221-0780; www.hotelmylord.com; 3a Calle 20; s with fan L1205, d with air-con L1314; P ⊠ ⬜) Another charming newcomer in a cozy, colonial-like home on a quieter residential street just one block from American chain restaurant Hell. That's the downside. The upside is it's also close to good espresso cafes and clubs; the large rooms all come with an extra sofa/pullout bed; and there's a tranquil, bird-filled courtyard.

Leslie's Place (☎ 220-5325; www.dormir.com; Calzada San Martin 452; s/d/tr incl breakfast L1342/1673/2007; P ⊠ ☎) Even smaller and more intimate thanks to the political turmoil's toll on tourism, Leslie closed 13 rooms due to horrid occupancy rates. The seven remaining are cozy enough to almost call this spot a boutique hotel. If you fancy treating yourself, it's a charming, English-speaking hotel with Guillermo Yuscarán landscape paintings on the walls, and tasteful, authentic Honduran decor. The owner plans on bringing the room inventory back up to at least 14, eventually.

Comayagüela

Hotel Plaza Real (☎ 237-0084; 6a Av btwn 8a & 9a Calles; r without bathroom from L200, d/tr L275/390) Set back from the street, a lush green courtyard area defines this hotel. Rooms are not bad, although overdue for a paint job. Hot water is on tap, as is purified water and coffee. Scuzzy jeans beware – there's a laundry station (hand-wash).

Hotel Unión (☎ 237-4313; 8a Av btwn 12a & 13a Calles; s/d/tr L225/350/375; ☐) Rooms here have beds and very little space for anything else. But it's fine if all you want is just to crash out before a morning bus.

Hotel Hedman Alas (☎ 237-9333; 4a Av btwn 8a & 9a Calles; s/d/tr L398/406/755) Though preciously short on natural light, this is a good secure option in bus stations-ville, even though a tourism attendant told us it was 'a horrible place.' Really, it's fine – clean rooms include brass-based lamp shades and impressionist prints. Breakfast (L50) is served between 8am and 10am.

Hotel Palace (☎ 237-6660; 12a Calle btwn 8a & 9a Avs; d with fan L450, d with air-con L600; P ✗) A hefty grille door marks the inner entrance to the rooms here – enter the Fort Knox of Tegucigalpa hotels. Rooms are surprisingly pricey for what you get – a prison-cell ambience right up to the barred windows, and curtains branded with the hotel name. But you do get a friendly front desk and cable TV. There is also parking and a whole bunch of conveniently close bus stations.

EATING

Tegucigalpa's eating options range from street food to sophisticated candlelit restaurants serving refined global cuisine. The best coffee comes courtesy of lively chains Espresso Americano and Cafemania.

Downtown

La Terraza de Don Pepe (Av Cristóbal Colón 2062; mains L75-250; ☺ 8am-10pm Tue-Sat, 8am-7pm Sun) Down-at-heel charm abounds in this famous, good-value central restaurant. Its daily specials (L80) are a steal and the tasty Cuban sandwiches are even cheaper. What really makes this place unique is an upstairs alcove formerly known as the men's restroom. In 1986 a statue of the Virgin of Suyapa was stolen from

the Basílica de Suyapa. After a nationwide hunt, it turned up here.

Café Paradiso (Av Miguel Paz Barahona 1351; mains L80-195; ☺ 9am-9pm Mon-Sat) Though it's lost some luster due to declining safety in its surroundings, bohemians still gather here, arguably Tegus' most cultured hangout, where European and Latin American dishes are served on cute round tables draped in kaleidoscopic tablecloths. The service can leave something to be desired. There are often temporary art exhibitions decorating the walls. English-language movies are shown at 7pm Tuesday; poetry readings at 7pm Thursday.

Restaurante Duncan Maya (cnr Av Cristóbal Colón & Calle Adolfo Zuniga; mains L105-200; ☺ 8am-10pm Mon-Sat, to 9:30pm Sun) In a new atmospheric location with low-slung archways and colossal wooden columns, this downtown mainstay buzzes with people, running the sky-blue-clad waitresses off their feet (you may need to wait a while to get served). Easily the best cheapie downtown.

Some other options:

Supermercado Más x Menos (cnr Avs La Paz & 4a; ☺ 7:30am-9pm Mon-Sat, 8am-8:30pm Sun) An exceptional market for self-caterers and day trippers.

Food stands At the side of Iglesia Los Dolores, these stands offer a variety of tempting cheapie lunchtime street-food dishes from *pupusas* (cornmeal mass stuffed with cheese or refried beans) and *baleadas* (flour tortilla filled with beans and cheese) to beef and chicken grills and seafood soups.

Colonia Palmira

Food is pricier in this district, but eye candy and relative safety are free of charge.

Pupusería El Patio (Blvr Morazán; pupusas L23-28; ☺ 11am-1:30am) One of the most raucous, lively places in the city at the weekend, this beer-hall of a place heaves with middle-class revelers. Tables fill with bottles, and the karaoke gets more full-blooded as the night goes on. Dads, mums and kids join in the fun. Tacos and typical Honduran dishes are the main items on the menu – groups should go for the Plato de Variedad (L188), which introduces all of the Honduran staples and serves three to four people.

Vie de France (Calle Las Minitas, Colonia Tepeyuc; items L58-255; ☺ 8am-9pm Mon-Fri, noon-8:30pm Sun) Nice French bakery with croissants, *pain au chocolat* and good panini, located on the road that bridges old Tegus and new Tegus.

Taco Loco (Blvr Morazán; tacos L63-90; ☺ 11am-11pm) A definite dive in pricey surroundings, Taco Loco dishes up tasty tacos (choose from beef, chicken, pork and others) that are big on flavor and small on the bottom line. Get a side of grilled *cebollas lloronas* (cry-baby onions) to juice up your order, and don't leave out that smoky hot sauce.

Café la Milonga (Paseo República de Argentina 1802; mains L80-233; 11:30am-8:30pm Mon-Thu, to 7pm Fri & Sat) Though it looks dead from outside, this strangely sophisticated hot spot opens up into a back courtyard, where a well-heeled crowd with an edge gathers over unpretentious Argentine steaks and cocktails. Its early closing time is reflective of the neighborhood, the political turmoil and the plethora of late-night venues in the area, but it's well worth an early stop. Tango and live music also make appearances.

our pick Café Honoré (Paseo República de Argentina 1941; sandwiches L103-285; 8:30am-9pm Mon-Sat, to 6pm Sun) This smart picnic deli/wine shop is a godsend, serving up the best sandwiches between southern Texas and northern Brazil. There are 41 gourmet hot and cold combinations to choose from. It's not cheap for a sandwich by Central American standards, but it's money well spent.

Nobu (Paseo República de Peru 2002; mains L120-200, sushi L160-199; 11am-3pm & 6-10pm Mon-Sat, noon-8pm Sun) The burnt-orange Asian atmosphere and backyard Buddha garden attract some of Tegus' hip and beautiful, which is a better draw then the distinctly average Thai curries and odd sushi (blue cheese roll?). Still, it fulfills the craving if you're tired of *pupusas*, and the tranquil and trendy environment help make up for it.

El Patio (Blvr Morazán; mains L179-414; 11am-11pm) The posh-restaurant branch of the city's three famous El Patio venues (there's a *pupusaría* and

an express location inside the new Los Próceres shopping complex). Waitresses dash between tables in traditional Honduran dress, while a mariachi band serenades diners in the vast open dining space. The meals are not cheap but the portions are enormous. Try the *pincho grande de res*, a succulent *carne asada* kebab grilled to perfection and served with a load of fixings.

Comayagüela

There are low-end eateries and street food strewn about Comayagüela, but it is not a place to wander aimlessly with a bulky backpack.

Todo de Pollo (6a Av near 8a Calle; half-chicken L65; breakfast, lunch & dinner) The name means 'everything chicken.' Guess what's on the menu?

DRINKING

Colonia Palmira hogs the best of Tegucigalpa's nightlife. There are also several bars and nightclubs along Blvr Morazán and around Plaza San Martín in the Sector Hotelero in Colonia Palmira. You won't be able to party 'til dawn in this city. There's a controversial 2am curfew on the city's clubs and bars in a bid to clamp down on the nighttime violence. Most establishments enforce it quite abruptly.

Había Una Vez (Plaza San Martín 501, Colonia Palmira; 6pm-midnight Tue-Thu, to 2am Fri & Sat) This artsy bar/club is perfect for low-key clubbers, who want to mingle with a sexy alt-intellectual crowd without epileptic strobe lights and pounding reggaetón. DJs spin the gamut from acid jazz to electronica on weekends, but there's cool music otherwise throughout the week. Revolving local art exhibitions dot the

---

ASK A LOCAL: TEGUCIGALPA'S FIVE BEST LOCAL DISHES

- **Tortilla Soup, Los Napolitos** (Calle República de Uruguay, Colonia San Carlos; mains L165-299; 11:30am-10pm Tue-Sat, 9:30am-5pm Sun) It's the original recipe – everything at this Mexican/Honduran restaurant is very authentic.

- **Los Patilitos de Carne, Los Tonelas** (Av Tiburcio Carias, Barrio Guadalupe; mains L12-20; 9am-7pm Mon-Sat) The typical flavor of Honduras.

- **Pupusas Bravos, Pupusería El Patio** (Blvr Morazán; pupusas L23-28; 11am-1:30am) These *pupusas*, with cheese, beans and *chicharrónes*, have a spicy kick with jalapeños!

- **BBQ Wings, Wing Factory** (Level 1, Centro Comercial El Dorado, Blvr Morazán; 12 wings L135; 10am-midnight Mon-Sat, 11am-4pm Sun) These aren't buffalo wings – they are Honduran-style with a salsa *criolla*.

- **Plato Mixto, Carnitas Kennedy** (3a Entrada Kennedy, Colonia Kennedy; mains L50-95; 9:30am-9pm Mon-Sat, 10am-8pm Sun) There's beef, pork, chicken, chorizo, *frijolitos*, *chismoll* and *cuajada* for only L60 or so. It's the best cheap meal in Tegucigalpa!

Marlon Sobalvarro, executive chef, Hotel Clarion

walls and there's an expensive but great Med-Latin-Peruvian fusion restaurant before 10pm.

Glenn's Pub (Colonia Palmira; ☉ 6pm-2am Mon-Sat) A long-standing 'secret' among *capitalinos* – during the day you can't even find it – this small dive caters to a mix of free-spirited 20-somethings and hardened local drinkers, and spills out onto the sidewalk on weekend nights. Cheap beers flow and the tunes are Purple Hazy, kept at a respectable volume.

Cinefilia (Calle Principle de las Naciones Unidas, Colonia Palmira; ☉ from 5pm Wed-Sat) This bohemian bar draws an alternative crowd for over 20 bottled beers (hey, this *is* Honduras!) from nine countries on offer. Cleaveland is a Honduran attempt at an English stout (you be the judge). Art-house DVDs are also on sale.

Sabor Cubano (Paseo República de Argentina 1933, Colonia Palmira; ☉ 11am-2am Tue-Sat, 11:30am-3pm Sun) Head here if your hips don't lie – this is Tegucigalpa's dance hot spot. There's no cover charge. It's just a pleasant, relaxed atmosphere with couples, some more elegant than others, moving the night away to the *una-dos-tres* of a salsa beat. It doubles as a solid Cuban restaurant. Friday is the night, after 11pm.

Bull Bar (☎ 3190-6325; República de Chile, Colonia Palmira; ☉ 6pm-2am Tue-Sat) The door is a royal pain, but this boisterous lounge/rock club packs in a lot of sexiness within its high-octane walls. It's all dressed in sensual reds and blacks, with hanging cymbals and disco balls hovering over a trendy crowd who can't hear a word any of their co-trendsetters are saying. It's both brash and beautiful.

SPLURGE

Models mingle amid other Honduran high society and a chunk of expats at the stylish **Rojo, Verde y Ajo** (☎ 232-3398; Paseo República de Argentina 1930; mains L157-448; ☉ noon-2am Mon-Sat), one of Tegus' top gastro destinations. It's too rowdy to be romantic, but the excellent menu proves that Honduran-slanted cuisine leaves more than *pupusas* to be desired. Go for the chicken with *loroco*, a herbaceous vine, if it's in season; otherwise the chicken in creamy sun-dried tomato sauce and the octopus carpaccio are both knockouts as well. And do not skip dessert: the owner nicked the recipe for the *dulce de leche* volcano from Uruguay – a decadent caramel dream you'll thank for its appearance in Central America.

ENTERTAINMENT

Grab an *Agendarte* pamphlet from the library at the Galería Nacional de Arte for a monthly rundown on cultural events and attractions.

Café Paradiso (Av Miguel Paz Barahona 1351; ☉ 9am-8pm Mon-Sat, to 9:30pm Tue & Thu) Shows English-language movies every Tuesday night at 7pm and has poetry readings on Thursday at 7pm.

Teatro Nacional Manuel Bonilla (☎ 222-4366; www.teatromanuelbonilla.hn; Av Miguel Paz Barahona) This characterful place hosts a variety of performing arts.

Cinemark (☎ 231-2044; www.cinemark.hn; Multiplaza Mall, Blvr Juan Pablo II; tickets L63) A modern multiscreen cineplex showing recent Hollywood fare.

SHOPPING

Honduran handicrafts are sold at many places around town.

Mercado Mayoreo (☎ 8am-5pm Fri, 6am-3pm Sat) Every Friday and Saturday, this colorful cheap market sets up shop near the Estadio Nacional. There's a dazzling array of produce and stalls, hawking everything from birdcages to vegetables and some great little *pupusa* cafes too.

Mercado San Isidro (☉ 7am-5pm) Located in Comayagüela, you can find just about anything for sale in this sprawling market, from vegetables to secondhand clothing to some excellent leatherwork and other crafts. Be alert for pickpockets.

Multiplaza Mall (Blvr Juan Pablo II; ☉ 10am-8pm Mon-Sat, noon-6pm Sun) When *capitalinos* talk about 'the mall,' they mean here. The most convenient shopping complex for travelers, it's southwest of Colonia Palmira, with ATMs, bookstores, internet and a cinema.

GETTING THERE & AWAY
Air

The airport is 6.5km south of Tegucigalpa. See p346 for information on getting into town. Note that Honduras' main airport is in San Pedro Sula, not Tegucigalpa. Travelers looking for international flights should consider flying from there.

Aerolíneas Sosa (☎ 233-5107, airport 234-0137; www.aerolineasosa.com; Centro Comercial Galleries Maya, Blvr Morazán; ☉ 8am-noon & 1-5pm Mon-Fri, 8am-noon Sat)

Air France (☎ 236-0029; www.airfrance.com; 2nd fl, Edif Galerías La Paz; ☉ 9am-5pm Mon-Fri, 9am-noon Sat) Also home to KLM and Aeroméxico.

American Airlines (☎ toll free 800 220-1414, in Honduras 216-4800; Edif Palmira; ☉ 8am-5:30pm Mon-Fri, 9am-noon Sat) Across from Hotel Honduras Maya.

Continental Airlines (☎ 269-4441, airport 233-3676; www.continental.com; Edif Los Próceres 3, Blvr Morazán; ⏱ 8am-5:30pm Mon-Fri, 8am-noon Sat) Also home to Copa Airlines.

Delta (☎ airport 238-2827)

TACA/Isleña (☎ 234-2422; www.taca.com; Blvr Morazán; ⏱ 8am-5pm Mon-Fri, 9am-5pm Sat, 9am-2pm Sun)

Destination	Cost (L)
La Ceiba	1678
Roatán (via La Ceiba)	2515
San Pedro Sula	1924
Utila (via La Ceiba)	2506

Bus

Excellent bus services connect Tegucigalpa with other parts of Honduras; unfortunately, each bus line has its own station. Most are clustered in Comayagüela. See Map p344 for locations. Keep a wary eye on your belongings in this part of town. See boxed table, p352, for sample services from Tegucigalpa.

If you are staying in Colonia Palmira, **Transportes Hedman Alas** (☎ 239-1764; Edif Florencia Plaza, Blvr Suyapa) has a far nicer and safer departure office then its Comayagüela main terminal located behind Multiplaza Mall, offering one departure daily at 5:45am to San Pedro Sula (for connections to Copán Ruinas or La Ceiba).

The free magazine *Honduras Tips* has a very useful bus routes section, though be wary of the schedules.

INTERNATIONAL & LONG-DISTANCE BUSES

Tica Bus (☎ 220-0579; 16a Calle btwn 5a & 6a Avs, Comayagüela) goes to El Salvador, Guatemala and Nicaragua and the Mexican border, and has connections to Costa Rica and Panama.

King Quality (☎ 225-5415; Blvr Commanded Economical European near 6a Av, Comayagüela) goes to El Salvador, Guatemala, Nicaragua and Costa Rica. The latter has two classes: 'Quality' is 1st class and 'King' is even more deluxe. Make sure you arrive 45 minutes before taking any international departures.

For more information, see table on p352.

GETTING AROUND
Bus

City buses are cheap (L3), loud, dirty and can be dangerous. Theft is common and gangs sometimes target buses. Unless you are confident about the areas you are going through, stick to the *colectivos* or taxis.

For getting to the airport, see boxed text, p346.

Car & Motorcycle

Before hiring a vehicle be sure to ask about the deductible (the amount you pay before insurance kicks in) – it can be as high as L38,500. Hire rates range between L482 and L866 per day (the local companies are cheaper).

Rental companies:

Avis (☎ 239-5712; www.avis.com.hn; Blvr Suyapa; ⏱ 8am-6pm)

Econo Rent-a-Car (☎ 235-2105, airport 291-0108; www.econorentacarhn.com; Calle Principle, Col El Trapiche; ⏱ 7am-7pm Mon-Fri, 7am-5pm Sat & Sun)

Hertz (☎ 238-3772, airport 234-3784; hertz@multi visionhn.net; Centro Comercio Villa Real; ⏱ 8am-6pm Mon-Sat)

National/Alamo (☎ 250-1362, airport 233-4962; Residencia Modelo; ⏱ 8am-6pm Mon-Sat)

Taxi

Taxis cruise all over town and honk to advertise when they are available. A ride in town costs around L50.

Street taxis to the airport cost L50 to L60.

There are a couple of useful downtown taxi *colectivo* stops, particularly helpful for the airport, and Mercado Jacaleapa terminal (where buses depart for El Paraíso and Danlí). They charge L11.

You will have to wait for them to fill up. *Colectivos* to the airport also leave from the stop on Calle Morelos, five blocks west of Parque Central (L10).

AROUND TEGUCIGALPA

SUYAPA

The huge gothic **Basílica de Suyapa**, the most important church in Honduras, dominates the landscape on the Suyapa hillside, about 7km south of the center of Tegucigalpa.

The construction of the basilica, which is famous for its large, brilliant stained-glass windows, was begun in 1954, and finishing touches are still being added.

La Virgen de Suyapa is the patron saint of Honduras; in 1982 a papal decree made her the patron saint of all Central America. She is represented by a tiny painted wooden statue, only 6cm tall. Many believe she has performed hundreds of miracles. The statue is brought to the large basilica on holidays, especially for the

HONDURAS

BUSES FROM TEGUCIGALPA
International Buses

Destination	Cost (L)	Duration (One Way)	Bus Line	Phone	Departure
Guatemala City (Guatemala)	580-1694	22hr (with overnight in San Salvador)	Tica Bus	220-0579	6am
		15hr (with layover in San Salvador)	King Quality	225-5415	5:30am 5:15am & 10am
		14hr	Hedman Alas	237-7143	
Managua (Nicaragua)	380-724	8hr	Tica Bus	220-0579	9:30am
		7-8hr	King Quality	225-5415	5:30am & 2pm
San José (Costa Rica)	760	2 days (with overnight in Managua)	Tica Bus	220-0579	9:30am
San Salvador (El Salvador)	285-952	6½hr	Tica Bus	220-0579	6am
		6-7hr	King Quality	225-5415	5:30am & 2pm
Tapachula (Mexico)	855	40hr (overnight in San Salvador, transfer in Guatamala City)	Tica Bus	220-0579	6am

Long-Distance Buses

Destination	Cost (L)	Duration (One Way)	Bus Line	Phone	Departure
Agua Caliente	311	9-10hr	Sultana de Occidente	237-8101	Hourly 6am-1:30pm
Catacamas	108	3½hr	Hedman Alas Discovery	222-4256	6:30am, 8:30am, 9:30am, 10:30am, 12:15pm, 2:15pm, 3:30pm, 5pm
Choluteca	44-58	3hr	Mi Esperanza	225-2901	Hourly 6am-4pm
Comayagua	37	2hr	Norteños	237-0706	6:30am, 7:30am, 9am, 10am, noon, 2pm
Copán Ruinas	475-570	7hr	Hedman Alas	237-7143	5:45am & 10am
El Paraíso	65	2hr	Colinas de Oro	9523-1637	Hourly 6am-6pm, to 4pm Sun
Juticalpa	86	2½hr	Discovery	222-4256	6:30am, 8:30am, 9:30am,10:30am, 12:15pm, 2:15pm, 3:30pm, 5pm
La Ceiba	217-570	7½hr	Hedman Alas	237-7143	5:45am, 10am, 1:30pm
			Cristina	225-1446	5:30am, 6:15am, 7:30am, 8:30am, 9:30am, 11am, 12:30pm, 2pm
La Entrada	186	6hr	Sultana de Occidente	237-8101	Hourly 6am-1:30pm
La Paz	38	2hr	Flores	237-3032	Hourly 6:30am-5pm
Las Manos*	76	2½hr	Colinas de Oro	9523-1637	6am & noon
San Pedro Sula	210-450	4hr	Hedman Alas	237-7143	5:45am, 7am, 9am, 10am, 12:30pm, 3pm, 5:30pm
			Viana Clase de Oro	225-6583	6:30am, 9:30am, 1:30pm, 3:30pm (Sun-Fri), 6:15pm
Santa Rosa de Copán	248	7hr	Sultana de Occidente	237-8101	Hourly 6am-1:30pm
Tela	217	5hr	Cristina	225-1446	5:30am, 6:15am, 7:30am, 8:30am, 9:30am, 11am, 12:30pm, 2pm
Trujillo	280	10hr	Contraibel	237-1666	6:30am & 8:30am

*Nicaraguan border; last bus from border to Ocotal (Nicaragua) at 4pm

HONDURAS

annual **Feria de Suyapa** beginning on the saint's day (February 3), and continuing for a week; the celebrations attract pilgrims from all over Central America. Most of the time, however, the little statue is kept on the altar of the very simple old **Iglesia de Suyapa**, built in the late 18th and early 19th centuries. It's on the plaza a few hundred meters behind the newer basilica.

Buses for Suyapa (L3, 30 minutes) leave from the corner of 6a Av and 7 Calle in Comayagüela; see Map p344. Get off at the university and walk the short distance from there.

SANTA LUCÍA
pop 9300

Perched among pine-covered hills, Santa Lucía is a charming old colonial mining town with a spectacular vista over the Tegucigalpa sprawl in the valley below. It is less obviously touristy than nearby Valle de Ángeles, which is part of its appeal.

Within its enchanting 18th-century *iglesia* are old Spanish paintings and a **statue of Christ of Las Mercedes**, donated to Santa Lucía by King Philip II in 1572. If the high arched wooden doors of the church are closed, walk around to the office at the rear and ask to have them opened for you. Apart from a few hikes, and one or two restaurants, there is very little to do in the town, apart from meandering along its tranquil streets and getting a feel for a Honduras that time forgot.

There are few restaurants in Santa Lucia. Try Restaurant Jambalaya for food or a late tipple – it's on the main road leading into town just past the lake.

For accommodations, try **La Posada de Doña Estefana** (☎ 779-0441; meeb8@yahoo.com; Barrio El Centro; r from L475; P X), in a beautifully tranquil setting with a fine panorama of the church. Its rooms are pretty good too, done out in a colonial style with stained-glass windows. When you consider the location, it is a bargain. Santa Lucía is such a low-key little place you may have to knock on the door or the garden gate a few times before anyone answers the door.

Getting There & Away
Santa Lucía is 14km east of Tegucigalpa, 2km uphill from the road leading to Valle de Ángeles and San Juancito. Buses leave every 45 to 60 minutes from 7:30am to 8pm (L8.50, 45 minutes) from an Esso station off Av la Paz, near Hospital San Felipe (see Map

p344). Return buses leave Santa Lucía every 30 minutes from 5:15am.

Another option is to take the Valle de Ángeles bus from the same Hospital San Felipe stop, get off at the crossroads and walk the 2.5km into town.

VALLE DE ÁNGELES
pop 14,300

Eight kilometers past Santa Lucía, Valle de Ángeles is another beautiful, former colonial mining town. An official tourist zone, the town has been restored to its original 16th-century appearance in parts, especially around the attractive Parque Central, where there is a handsome old church. The annual **fair** takes place on October 4.

Artisan souvenir shops line the streets, selling Honduran *artesanías,* including wood carvings, basketry, ceramics, leatherwork, paintings, dolls, wicker and wood furniture. Prices are usually less than in Tegucigalpa. One of the most distinctive artists' displays is one block south of the Parque Central in a flamboyantly pink and blue building. **Galeria Sixtina** (☎ 766-2375; ☺ 10am-6pm) is the brainchild of a classically trained artist who has gathered artworks and contributed personally to this richly colorful collection. Angels, appropriately enough, are the central theme.

Valle de Ángeles is an easy day trip from Tegucigalpa, but it is also a quiet, relaxing place to stay. It gets busy on weekends and holidays; otherwise, the town is usually quiet.

Sleeping & Eating
Posada del Ángel (☎ 766-2233; hotelposadadelangel@ yahoo.com; s/d/tr from L475/760/950; P X X) Rooms wrap around a large area, with a pool and lush gardens as the centerpiece. Older rooms aren't as warm as the common areas, but five newer rooms are nearly double the price. It is two blocks north of the *iglesia*.

Villas del Valle (☎ 766-2534; www.villasdelvalle.com; Carr a San Juancito; s/d/tr L650/700/780; ☺) These simple, neat brick-built cabins a short walk from the center are your best bet for lodging in Valle de Ángeles. The onsite restaurant is open until 7pm on weekends (6pm otherwise), and stays open later as a bar when the place is busier. Wi-fi across the premises is an added bonus.

Restaurante Turístico (Carr a San Juancito; mains L99-250; ☺ 8am-6pm) The most memorable eating option in town is a short walk above the main turnoff to Valle de Ángeles. It is a classic colonial-style restaurant with an attractive terrace and an even better view over the town and valley below. Meals are simple meat and fish dishes but tasty. Walk past the Posada del Ángel and keep walking uphill for 1km.

On the central park:

Restaurante Jalapeño (☾ lunch & dinner Tue-Sun) Has good veggie options.

El Anafre (☎ 766-2942; mains L150-300, pizza L280-450; ☾ 10am-8pm) Serves up reasonable Italian fare.

Getting There & Away

Colectivo minibuses for Valle de Ángeles (L17.50, 30 minutes, 6:45am to 7pm, every 45 minutes) depart from the Esso gas station stop near the Hospital San Felipe in Tegucigalpa. There are also cheaper, slower school buses from the same spot (L13, one hour, hourly). The last return minibus leaves from Valle de Ángeles at 5:30pm.

PARQUE NACIONAL LA TIGRA

A beautiful national park just a short hop from the capital city, **La Tigra** (adult/child L192/95; ☾ 8am-4pm Tue-Sun, last entrance 2pm) has a lush cloud forest in former mining country belonging to the Rosario Mining Company. The mining scars can still be seen. In 1980 this became Honduras' first national park – it is an essential water supply for the city. It has a great abundance of (elusive) wildlife, from pumas to peccaries, and is a botanist's delight, with lush trees, vines, lichens and large ferns, colorful mushrooms, bromeliads and orchids.

The climate at La Tigra is fresh and brisk; in fact it's often quite cold – bring plenty of warm clothes with you. Long pants and long sleeves are best, as the forest has many mosquitoes.

Amitigra (☎ 231-3641; Calle Nunciatura Apostolica 210, Colonia Palmira, Tegucigalpa; ☾ 8am-noon & 1-5pm Mon-Fri) has information and manages overnight visits to the park. You can pay park/lodging fees here or at the park entrances. La Tigra has two entrances, Jutiapa and El Rosario. There are visitors centers at both entrances, where rangers are always on duty.

Hiking

There are eight trails, all well maintained and easy to follow. It is a rugged, mountainous area – people have been lost for days in the dense forest after they wandered off the trails. Both the Amitigra office and the visitors center have maps of the trails.

The **Sendero Principal** is the busiest and most direct route through the park. It is actually the old disused road leading from Tegucigalpa to the mines and runs 6km from Jutiapa to El Rosario. From Jutiapa, you descend past abandoned mines, small rivers and views over the San Juancito valley before reaching El Rosario. A more appealing trail is to **Sendero La Cascada**, which leads to a 40m waterfall. Coming from Jutiapa, follow the Sendero Principal over 1km to the Sendero La Cascada cut-off, located at a sharp bend in the trail. Descend the steep stone steps and continue another 2km past smaller falls and abandoned mines to a T-intersection: go straight to reach the falls (10 to 20 minutes), or left to reach El Rosario via Sendero La Mina. From El Rosario, **Sendero La Mina** leads you past abandoned mining buildings. Later, there is also a left turnoff to the falls (10 to 20 minutes).

Guides (not really needed) are available to take you along the trails. They are used especially for large groups (per group L100 to L300).

Sleeping & Eating

Camping is L95 per person.

Eco-Albergue El Rosario (☎ 9865-7016; r per adult/child L475/135) This visitors center has eight rustic rooms with fresh sheets. It is at the park entrance.

Cabañas & Eco-Albergue Jutiapa (per adult/child L475/135) This newer Jutiapa visitors center offers basic rooms, with capacity for 20 people.

Cabaña Mirador El Rosario (☎ 767-2141; r L600) This spot is perched on the mountainside and offers great views, lovely rooms, laundry, homemade jams and chutneys and easy access to the national park. The catch: there are only two rooms, so call ahead. Vegetarian meals are served (breakfast L50, dinner L90). They will pick you up in San Juancito for L200 (no arrivals after 10pm).

Both visitors centers have basic **comedores** (meals L40-90; ☾ Jutiapa 8am-5pm Sat & Sun or with advanced notice, El Rosario 6am-10pm daily).

Getting There & Away

The western entrance to the park, above Jutiapa, is the closest to Tegucigalpa, 22km away. In Tegus, take a bus (L17) at 7am and 7:30am from Parque Finlay on Av Máximo Jérez; or at 9:30am and 2pm (L20) from the Gasolinera Dippsa on Av Máximo Jérez at Av la Plazuela, across from a Banco Atlántida branch. Other buses (every 45 minutes, from 6am) toward El Hatillo from the same place

HONDURAS

can usually drop you at Los Planes, a soccer field 2km before the visitors center. On the return trip, buses leave from Los Planes; the first is at 5:30am, the last around 3:40pm. After that you'll need to walk 4km to the next town (Los Limones), where buses run later. A taxi to this entrance from Tegus costs about L400.

The eastern park entrance is at El Rosario, overlooking San Juancito, an atmospheric former mining town. From Tegucigalpa, buses to San Juancito (L18, 1½ hours) leave from Mercado San Pablo (3pm Monday to Friday; 8am, 12:40pm and 3pm Saturday; 8am and 12:40pm Sunday), Valle de Ángeles bus stop, opposite Hospital San Felipe (3pm and 5:30pm Monday to Friday with an extra 5pm ride on Sunday), and Supermercado Más x Menos (4:30pm Saturday). From San Juancito, you'll need to leg the steep last 4km to the park entrance, flag down a local truck (L200) or make arrangements with Cabaña Mirador El Rosario.

Buses to Tegus from San Juancito leave from the yellow bridge in town (at around 5:15am and 6:15am) and from the kiosk on the main road (several departures between 7:15am and 5:30pm).

WESTERN HONDURAS

People have lived here for millennia, making their marks on the landscape in spectacular ways – most strikingly at the captivating Copán archaeological ruins. Travelers usually whizz from the ruins to the coast via San Pedro Sula, the underappreciated dynamo of the Honduran economy. Yet those who stay rarely regret it. The Montaña de Celaque cloud forests, dazzling Lago Yojoa birdlife, colonial charms of Santa Rosa de Copán and Gracias, and the slow-changing, colorful Ruta de Lenca communities are all excellent reasons to linger.

The newly improved road between San Pedro Sula and Tegucigalpa is probably the most traveled in Honduras; it's 241km along Honduras' Carretera del Norte (Hwy 1), about a four-hour bus trip. The route passes Comayagua, Siguatepeque, the Lago de Yojoa and the beautiful Pulhapanzak waterfall (about 45 minutes west of the highway by bus).

This region, called the Valle de Comayagua, was well settled in pre-Columbian times, and agriculture has been practiced here for at least 3000 years. Fourteen archaeological sites have been identified in the department of Comayagua, and ancient pottery, jewelry and stone carvings have all been unearthed.

COMAYAGUA
pop 114,500

Comayagua, 84km northwest of Tegucigalpa, is the historical first capital of Honduras and was a religious and political center for over three centuries, until power shifted to Tegucigalpa in 1880. The town's colonial past is evident in its several fine old *iglesias* (churches), an impressive cathedral, colonial plazas and two interesting museums. A very Catholic city, it's also considered the best place in Honduras for visitors to witness Easter celebrations.

An important source of income for the town is Soto Cano, an air base used by the US military. Better known as La Palmerola, it formed a base for 2000 US soldiers during the 1980s when the Contra war was raging in Nicaragua. Since then, it's been converted to a Honduran base with about 550 American military personnel stationed there holding the Central American fort.

The base's strategic importance received a boost in 1999 when US bases were closed in Panama.

Orientation
Like most Honduran towns, life centers around the Parque Central, which has been tastefully refurbished with gardens, benches and piped-in music. Comayagua is walkable, though the area between the Parque Central and the hotels can feel lonely after dark. Solo travelers should consider taking a cab home if it's late.

Streets are also defined according to the compass: ie: NO for *noroeste* (northwest), NE for *noreste* (northeast), SO for *suroeste* (southwest), SE for *sureste* (southeast).

Information
Banco Atlántida (Parque Central) Has a Visa/Plus ATM machine.

Banco de Occidente (Parque Central) Changes Visa and Amex traveler's checks.

Centro Médico Comayagua Colonial (☎ 772-1126/4026; 3a Calle NE; ☼ 24hr)

Ecosimco (Ecosistema Montaña de Comayagua; ☎ 772-4681; ecosimco@hondutel.hn; Camara de Comercio; ☼ 9am-noon & 1-5pm Mon-Fri) Manages the Montaña de Comayagua National Park; 500m north of town. Look for the big green gates.

HONDURAS

Hondutel (1a Av NE btwn 4a & 5a Calles NO; ⏱ 8am-6pm) Telephone needs.

L@Red (☎ 772-4162; Parque Central; per hr L25; ⏱ 9am-7pm) Convenient internet access.

Neon Macro.net (☎ 772-2418; 1a Calle NO; per hr L22; ⏱ 8am-9pm Mon-Sat, 2-8pm Sun)

Police (☎ 772-0080)

Post office (1a Av NE btwn 4a & 5a Calles NO; ⏱ 8am-3:30pm Mon-Fri, to noon Sat)

Red Cross (☎ 195, 772-0290)

Sights

The **cathedral** (Parque Central; ⏱ 7am-8pm) in the center of town is the largest colonial-era place of worship in Honduras. It was built from 1685 to 1715 and is adorned with intricate wooden carvings and gold-plated altars. The main altar

is similar to that of the Tegucigalpa cathedral; both were made by the same (unknown) artist. The clock in the cathedral tower is the oldest in the Americas and one of the oldest in the world. The Moors built it over 800 years ago for the palace of Alhambra in Granada. In 1620 it was donated to the town by King Phillip III of Spain. Look out for the older Roman-style IIII rather than IV on the clock face.

Other fine *iglesias*, all generally open from 7am to 8pm, include **San Francisco** (founded 1560); **San Sebastián** (1580), on the south end of town; and the much remodeled **Nuestra Señora de la Caridad** (7a Calle NO at 3a Av NO; ⏱ 7am-8pm), built at the end of the 16th century and used as a place of worship for the local indigenous community. Comayagua's first *iglesia* was **La**

COMAYAGUA

0 _____ 400 m
0 _____ 0.2 miles

INFORMATION
Banco Atlántida.....................1 B2
Banco de Occidente................2 B2
Centro Médico Comayagua
  Colonial.............................3 C2
Hondutel.............................4 B2
L@ Red 5 B2
Neon Macro.net....................6 A3
Police..................................7 B2
Post Office...........................8 B2

SIGHTS & ACTIVITIES
Cathedral.............................9 B2
Iglesia La Merced..................10 B3
Iglesia San Francisco.............11 B2
Iglesia San Sebastián.............12 C4
Museo Colonial de Arte
  Religioso...........................13 B2
Museo Regional de
  Arqueología........................14 B2
Nuestra Señora de la Caridad.15 A1

SLEEPING
Hotel America Inc..................16 B3
Hotel Maru..........................17 B3
Hotel Norimax......................18 B3

EATING
La Gota de Limón...................19 B2
Repostería y Cafetería La
  Económica..........................20 B3
Restaurante Plaza Colonial....21 B2
Restaurante Mang Ying.........22 A1
Villa Real.............................23 B2

TRANSPORT
Buses to San Pedro Sula........24 B3
Buses to Tegucigalpa............25 B3
Main Bus Stop.......................26 B4
Pickups to Río Negro/Parque
  Nacional Montaña de
  Comayagua........................27 B3

To Ecosimco
(500m)

Río Chiquito

7a Calle NO

6a Calle NO

5a Calle NO

4a Calle NO

3a Calle NO

Parque
Central

2a Calle NO

HSBC
ATM

Parque
La Merced

Mercado

1a Calle NO

El Bulevar

3 1a Av NO

2 1a Av NO

1a Av NE

2a Av NE

Av 2a de Julio

Calle Manuel Bonilla/
Calle Barrio Toron Dón

1a Calle SO

To San Pedro
Sula (157km)

Carretera del Norte

To Soto Cano (15km);
Tegucigalpa (84km)

HONDURAS

Merced. Building started in 1550 and it was consecrated as a cathedral in 1561; the plaza in front is very pretty. Another colonial *iglesia*, San Juan de Dios (1590), was destroyed by an earthquake in 1750, but samples of its artwork are on display in the Museo Colonial. If you read Spanish, look for a small book entitled *Las Iglesias Coloniales de la Ciudad de Comayagua*, which contains an interesting history of Comayagua and its churches. It's available at both museums.

Opened in 1962 the **Museo Colonial de Arte Religioso** (☎ 772-0169; Av 2a de Julio near 3a Calle NO; admission L25; ♥ 8am-noon & 2-4:30pm Tue-Sun) was once the site of the first university in Central America, founded in 1632, and in operation for almost 200 years. Priests have occupied the building even longer, since 1558. Totally renovated in 2005, the museum contains artwork and religious paraphernalia from all five churches of Comayagua, spanning the 16th to the 18th centuries.

A block north of the cathedral, the **Museo Regional de Arqueología** (☎ 772-0386; admission L76; ♥ 8:30am-4pm) displays some fine ancient Lenca artifacts, including pottery, *metates* (stone on which grain is ground), stone carvings and petroglyphs. Descriptions are in Spanish only. It is housed in a former presidential palace.

Sleeping

Hotel Maru (☎ 772-1311; cnr Calle Manuel Bonilla & 1a Av NO; r with/without bathroom L150/120) Facing a long and sad courtyard, rooms here are for lempira pinchers only. Shared bathrooms are not pretty – shell out the extra lemps for a private one, but don't expect anything apart from an open pipe for your shower. Owners were friendly, though.

Hotel America Inc (☎ 772-0530; cnr 1a Av NO & 1a Calle NO; s/d with fan from L292/402, with air-con from 361/641; ✖ ♥ ♨) Still probably the best value for money (despite that murky pool), this friendly hotel is really two hotels in one: old but renovated rooms on the pink side (perfectly great for the price, just don't clothesline yourself on those shower doors); and fancy new digs with refurbished *baños*, freshly laid tiles and wood furnishing on the yellow side. The lobby-only wi-fi is a bummer, though.

Hotel Norimax (☎ 772-1210; cnr Calle Manuel Bonilla & El Bulevar; s/d/tr with air-con L300/350/450; ℗ ✖) The three floors of enthusiastically average rooms are a reasonable deal here, though the bathrooms are cramped. All rooms have cable TV, and purified water is free.

Eating & Drinking

Repostería y Cafétería La Económica (1a Av NE, Parque la Merced; items L10-30; ♥ 8am-7pm Mon-Sat) Cakes, pastries and lovely slushes are the order of the day at this cafe in an old colonial building. It's in a prize location overlooking the charming Plaza Merced.

Restaurante Plaza Colonial (Parque Central; mains L63-225; ♥ 7:30am-9pm) Whether a coffee break or a quick bite, this plaza cafe is an atmospheric spot to watch Comayagua go about its business. There's *comida típica* (typical lunch) and a few gringo staples (hamburgers, club sandwiches, spaghetti), a bang-up *limonada* and plenty of character throughout its various rooms.

La Gota de Limón (5a Calle NO; mains L90-130; ♥ 11am-3pm & 6pm-2am Tue-Sun) This pleasant spot tucked around the corner from Parque Central offers a lovely interior courtyard as ambience, a few Mexican dishes (fajitas, for example) and the Honduran carnivore rundown of various beef, chicken and pork dishes.

Villa Real (1a Av NE btwn 4a & 3a Calles NO; mains L90-180; ♥ 6pm-10pm Mon-Sat, disco to 3am) Extenuating circumstances on the restaurant's part have prevented us from trying the food here for two editions now. However, it has a reputation for dishing up some of the finest Honduran cuisine around in a fine colonial setting; and for turning into a raucous disco Thursday to Saturday.

Restaurante Mang Ying (cnr 7a Calle NO & El Bulevar; mains L115-335; ♥ 9:30am-10:30pm) Cure your *pupusa* blues in a heartbeat: this authentic spot dishes up extra-tasty Westernized Chinese and looks out for your lempiras in the meantime (dishes can easily feed two). Considering this ain't China (or San Francisco), we were shocked at how good it was.

Getting There & Away

Comayagua is about 1km east of the highway, serviced to and from Tegucigalpa (L38, two hours, every 30 minutes) by **Transportes Catrachos** (☎ 772-0260; cnr 1a Calle SO & 1a Av NO), which has a downtown terminal, although its station in Tegucigalpa is away from the center in a sketchy area. Transportes El Rey, at the entrance to town, drops you in a more welcoming part of Tegucigalpa.

Transportes Rivera (☎ 772-1208; cnr 2a Calle SO & 1a Av NO) runs to San Pedro Sula (L72, three hours, hourly 6am to 4pm). Buses to Marcala (L50, 1½ hours) leave just outside the Rivera

HONDURAS

DETOUR

Spanning more than 300 sq km of primary and secondary forest, **Parque Nacional Montaña de Comayagua** (Panacoma; admission L35) has two main trails leading through the cloud forest, from near the small village of Río Negro, 42km north of Comayagua, to waterfalls (no bathing). The park is managed by **Ecosimco** (p355).

The first trail is to **Cascada de los Ensueños**, a 75m waterfall about an hour's hike away through mostly secondary forest. The second trail veers off the first just before reaching Los Ensueños, and leads to another waterfall, **El Gavilán**.

Simple **accommodation** (☎ 990-0802; r L60-120) in bunks is available at the house of Don Velásquez in Río Negro. You can hire a guide (recommended) in Río Negro. Pickup trucks to Río Negro (L35, four hours) leave from the south side of the Comayagua market at 11am, noon and 1pm.

---

terminal, departing at 6am, 8:35am, 10am, 11:30am and 3pm.

Any Tegucigalpa–San Pedro bus will pick you up or drop you off at the turnoff, although you may have to pay the full fare. Check beforehand.

SIGUATEPEQUE

pop 81,600

Siguatepeque is an unremarkable town about halfway between Tegucigalpa (117km) and San Pedro Sula (124km), roughly two hours from both. It is known for its pleasant climate. You may want to stop at Siguatepeque to break your journey, but that would be odd – Comayagua is far more interesting.

Orientation & Information

There are two squares in town. From the main highway 2km away, the first one you get to is dusty Plaza San Pablo, with basketball courts and the market. Three blocks east is the much more attractive Parque Central.

Banco Atlántida (Plaza San Pablo) Changes American Express traveler's checks.

Banco del Occidente (Plaza San Pablo) Near the plaza's southeast corner and now has an ATM.

Plaz@net (Plaza San Pablo; per hr L16; 🕑 8am-8pm) You can also make international calls.

Police (☎ 773-0042)

Sleeping & Eating

Hotel Gómez (☎ 773-0868; Calle 21 de Junio; s/d with fan L200/280, d with air-con L400; P 🗙 🛜) This motor-court-style hotel sits right between the two plazas; the walls are a little scruffy but it's otherwise clean and good value. The newer higher-floor rooms offer more space to stretch your beaten kicks.

Hotel Plaza San Pablo (☎ 773-4020; www.hotelplaza sanpablo.com; Calle 21 de Junio; s/d with fan L345/470, with air-con L455/500; P 🗙 🛜) A very friendly midrange. Ignore the King Arthur facade – the rooms here are well kept and comfortable and there's wi-fi throughout. You'll have to fork over L45 for breakfast, but the condoms are free.

Pizzería Venezia (Calle 21 de Junio; pizza L90-200; 🕑 9am-9pm) As well as excellent authentic pizzas, this venue dishes up good sandwiches with all the trimmings. It has outdoor seating and a simple interior with classic red-check tablecloths. Pizza sold by the slice as well.

Getting There & Away

Most buses going between Tegucigalpa and San Pedro Sula will drop you on the main highway. A taxi into town costs L25 or you can walk the 2km to the center.

Buses depart from an open lot a block west of Plaza San Pablo. Frequent departures run to San Pedro Sula from 4:50am to 4:15pm (L55); direct buses leave for Tegucigalpa every hour or even more often, from 4:15am to 4:15pm (L55, 2½ hours). Buses to Comayagua (L25, one hour) depart every 15 minutes from 5am to 5:30pm.

There are also buses to La Esperanza (L50 to L55) every hour from 5am to 4pm, which leave half a block west of the plaza in front of the Hospedaje Central (the owners operate the service).

LA ESPERANZA

pop 9000

Up in the highlands, slow-paced La Esperanza is known for its markets. The Lenca influence is strong here – you will see many women wearing the distinctive, colorful Lenca headdress. For these reasons – and not those muddy streets – it is a more interesting stopover than Marcala. The highest town in Honduras at 1600m, it can get a little chilly, too.

La Esperanza is the capital of the Intibucá department, one of the poorest in Honduras, and attracts a large number of foreign volunteers.

The **Global Volunteer Network** (☎ in USA 800-032-5035; www.globalvolunteernetwork.org) places volunteers in La Esperanza – teaching English and building homes and schools.

Orientation & Information

La Esperanza sits on a subtle incline and uphill is west in this town. There are few street names or numbers, but just about everything is on the main street (Av Morazon) or on the parallel street (Av Los Proceres). The bus terminal is on the main road near the bottom of the hill, the Parque Central at the top. An old, slightly dilapidated church is on the east side. Hondutel, the police and post office are on Parque Central. For cash, there's a **Banco Atlántida** (Av Los Proceres) one block north of Parque Central. Check your email at **Cyber Mania** (per hr L20; ⊙ 8am-9pm) in the same building half a block north of Parque Central, across from the jail. On the hill at the far western end of town is **La Gruta**, a small cave now converted into a chapel.

Sleeping & Eating

Hotel Mejia Batres (☎ 783-4189; s without bathroom L150, s/d/tr L300/450/500; **P**) Very convenient (just one block west of the Parque Central), this hotel has simple, clean rooms. There's internet across the street, which adds convenience to the value.

Casa Mia Hostal (☎ 783-3778; Av Los Próceres; s/d L200/350) The four rooms here above a little downstairs *comedor* (called Delis House) are bigger, shinier and cleaner than anything you'll find for this price. That said, the room we checked out smelled like sewage, which is unfortunate, because it's otherwise the perfect little cheapie.

El Fogón (mains L65-145; ⊙ 9am-9:30pm, to 12:30am Fri & Sat) Well, if typical *comida típica* were this good, you'd be complaining a lot less. This atmospheric spot is punching above La Esperanza's weight class and is your best bet for a good meal and a drink to boot, under a thatched palapa roof and among walls adorned with Lencan pottery and masks. World sports are shown around the two bars and there's a great patio out back. One of our co-authors swears by the breakfast. It's one block from Parque Central between Avs Morazon and Los Próceres.

Opalaca's (mains L80-175; ⊙ 10:30am-9:30pm) This place, just west of Parque Central, specializes in grills, which arrive sizzling in front of you. It's the classiest spot in town, with a colonial setting and a calming fountain.

Getting There & Away

The bus situation in La Esperanza is confusing, with buses leaving from various spots all over town and no residents that can agree on who goes where from what point. We know this much: the **Transportes Carolina** (☎ 783-0521) terminal at the eastern end of town beyond the bridge is your best bet to get out of town. It services Tegucigalpa (L100, 3½ hours) hourly from 4:15am to 3pm and San Pedro Sula (L100, 3½ hours) hourly from 4:30am to 3:30pm. Also departing from here, which locals call Punta Carolina, is a direct bus to Santa Rosa de Cópan at 6am (L100, 2½ hours) which can also drop you in San Juan (L35, one hour) or Gracias (L70, two hours). Direct buses to San Juan and Gracias also depart from here throughout the morning, including 9:30am, 11am, 11:40am and 2:30pm (at least). Buses to Marcala (L40) depart from in front of Hotel Mina, four blocks east of Parque Central, at a few unreliable times even unbeknownst to the front desk at Hotel Mina throughout the day. Other local buses leave from the *mercado quemado* (burned market), a couple of blocks down from the central park. A ride around town to the terminals costs L12. Pickups to San Juan and Gracias are also an option.

If you are driving, the road between Marcala and La Esperanza is 4WD-only due to a few hairy spots. If you are coming from Marcala, there is a clandestinely marked detour to the right about 1km before the pavement ends. If you miss it, you will drive 8km into the mountains – to a narrow dead end where turning around is a skill reserved for those that were champions at the board game Operation. The road on to San Juan is passable year-round in any car.

MARCALA
pop 30,900

Marcala is a highland town with a strong indigenous heritage – it lies at the southern end of Honduras' Ruta Lenca. Although it looks unremarkable, the town is in prime coffee country – and there are several opportunities to see the world's favorite bean being harvested and prepared. Several hikes in the surrounding area take in picturesque waterfalls and caves.

Orientation & Information

There are no street names in Marcala. Orient yourself at the Parque Central. The town hall is on the west side, while there is a small church to the north. One block northeast of the park are the post office and Hondutel. Just along from them is BanhCafé bank, which changes small amounts of American cash.

Banco Atlántida ATM and banking needs at the entrance to town.

Cooperativa RAOS (☎ 764-5181) At this place, Miriam Elizabeth Pérez (Betty) is a mine of information on local sights.

Police (☎ 764-5715)

TIC (☎ 764-4132; per hr L18; ☺ 8am-9pm, to 7pm Sun) Internet access, two blocks west of and half a block north of the basketball courts.

Tourist office (Parque Central; ☺ 8am-noon & 1-4pm, closed Wed) Suspiciously closed kiosk supposedly with helpful staff offering information, brochures and maps on area sights.

Activities

La Estanzuela is one of several hikes in the area, going to a pretty waterfall and a cavern, **La Cueva del Gigante**, which has prehistoric paintings. It is on the way to La Esperanza. Ask how to get there at the tourist office.

Cooperativa RAOS (☎ 764-5181; cooperativaraos@ yahoo.com; ☺ 8am-noon & 1-4pm Mon-Fri, 8am-noon Sat) on the road toward La Esperanza, is Honduras' first organic farming cooperative. *Finca* tours (per person L100 to L300) include visiting two to three plantations, learning about organic farming and talking to the farmers.

Sleeping & Eating

Hotel San Miguel (☎ 764-5793; r L200; Ⓟ) A family-run guesthouse with bare rooms, electric showers and a cheap little *comedor* that fires up strong regional coffee. The family is friendly, but the dogs are a royal pain in the ass. It's two blocks north then two-and-a-half blocks east of the Parque Central, just beyond a whitewashed church.

Hotel Jerusalén Medina (☎ 764-5909; s/d L220/270; Ⓟ) Curiously closed when we came through, this simple, three-story motel went unchecked. Normally, its well-kept rooms offer thick bedspreads and private bathrooms facing a concrete parking lot – all it takes to win the honor of town's best digs. It is one block north and two blocks east of the Parque Central and may also be called Hotel Nueva Jerusalén.

Casa Gloria (meals L50-90; ☺ 8am-8pm) At the southwestern corner of the park, this stately terracotta-colored spot offers buffet meals and service with a smile, in an old colonial-style house decorated with some fine Lenca ceramics.

Getting There & Away

Buses leave from various points, but all pass the Texaco gas station at the east end of the main road in and out of town, making it a good de facto bus stop.

To get to Tegucigalpa, **Transportes Lila** (☎ 764-5799), one-and-a-half blocks east of the park, has several departures between 4am and 2pm (L68). The 8am and 9am service is *ejecutivo* (luxury class) and costs L83. For San Pedro Sula, Transportes Vanessa has one departure from Parque Central at 5am (L120, five hours).

Buses to La Esperanza (L40) leave at 6:30am and 8:30am (plus 7:30am Saturday and Sunday) from the basketball court across from BanhCafé, although this bus can be unreliable. Buses to Comayagua (L50, 2½ hours, seven departures between 6:45am and 3:15pm) and La Paz (L35, 1¾ hours, eight departures from 7:30am to 3:45pm) also leave from here.

CUEVAS DE TAULABÉ

On the highway about 25km north of Siguatepeque and 20km south of the Lago de Yojoa is the entrance to the **Cuevas de Taulabé** (CA-5 Hwy, Km 140; admission L35; ☺ 8am-5pm), a network of underground caves with unusual stalactite and stalagmite formations. The entrance fee includes a guide. A tip may get you to some of the less-visited areas. So far, the caves have been explored to a depth of 12km with no end in sight.

The first section of the caves has lights and a cement pathway; the pathway can be slippery, so wear appropriate shoes.

LAGO DE YOJOA

This picturesque lake lies 157km north of Tegucigalpa and 84km south of San Pedro Sula. It is a popular beauty spot with abundant birdlife. There are some spectacular wildlife-spotting opportunities, especially on the less-developed west side, where there is also an excellent place to stay with its own microbrewery. Around 440 different bird species – over half the total in Honduras – have been spotted around the lake. One bird-watcher counted 37 different species in a single tree while sitting on his hotel terrace in the morning. Quetzals are also regularly sighted around here. If you are coming for bird-watching, look out for *Field Guide to the Birds of Lake Yajoa* by Robert and Irma Gallardo, a unique guide sold only in this country (mostly in Copán Ruinas).

GETTING TO EL SALVADOR

Buses bound for San Miguel, El Salvador (L90, 5½ hours), via Perquín (L60, three hours), leave from Marcala one block west of the park next to Mercadito Diana No 2 at 5:30am and noon.

There is no fee to leave Honduras, nor is there a border post due to a long-standing border dispute. However, an immigration officer should board your bus near Pasamonos, 30 minutes from the border, and check passports etc (tourists pass freely between the CA-4 treaty countries, so no stamps are necessary). There is now a border post on the El Salvador side, so crossing here is easier than it has been in the past (see p319).

Fishing on the lake is good, especially black bass. Bring your own tackle, as it might not be available locally. Hotels around the lake can arrange boat trips.

The **Asociación de Municipios del Lago de Yojoa y su Área de Influencia** (Amuprolago; ☎ 9988-2300; CA-5 Hwy; ☺ 8am-4pm Mon-Fri) may be a mouthful, but it is useful, with detailed current information about the lake and surrounding areas. It is just south of the town of Monte Verde.

Sleeping & Eating

our pick **D&D Brewery** (☎ 9994-9719; Los Naranjos; www. dd-brewery.com; campsites per person L40, s/d L180/260, cabins from L500; P ☒ ☎ ☒) Oregonian brewmaster Robert Dale set up this highly original place to stay, 4km from Peña Blanca, where accommodations vary from camping to sparse but well done cabins with spas. The lush gardens have over 200 different orchid species, while the onsite microbrewery produces some of Honduras' best beers – and purified water for all on premises. The good outdoor restaurant has home-grown coffee from the surrounding mountains, killer burgers and spectacular blueberry pancakes. Serious bird-watching tours (L225 to L450) – either to the lake or spectacular Parque Nacional Montaña Santa Bárbara – can also be organized. The Mochito bus from the main San Pedro Sula terminal drops you at the entrance. A rustic cloud-forest lodge near San Luis Planes (see boxed text, p362) is on the way.

El Cortijo del Lago (☎ 608-5527; www.hotellakeyajoa. com; dm L150, r from L200, cabañas from L300; P ☒ ☒) In a lovely setting right on the lake, this American/Honduran option has a restau-rant that can whip up veggie options as well as canoes and rowboats for rent. The dorms are unflashy, but tidy and well-kept. Make sure you check out the sunroom upstairs. El Cortijo is 2km from the La Guama turnoff.

Finca Paradise (☎ 9819-3080; Los Naranjos; r/cabañas L500/1000) No red carpets are rolled out to visi-tors, but the setting on a working coffee planta-tion next to a gurgling river is a winner. Rooms feature good beds and spiffy sheets while the two raised *cabañas* are nearly five-star and sleep six. It's 800m down the same road from D&D and a good alternative when the brewery is full – you can walk over for brews.

Getting There & Away

The easiest access to the lake is from San Pedro Sula. Get a bus to El Mochito from the main terminal (L45, 1½ hours, every 30 minutes) to San Buenaventura (where the Pulhapanzak Falls are located; see p362) and Los Naranjos. The bus can drop you right at D&D.

The last bus back to San Pedro Sula leaves at about 4:30pm. For the north side of the lake, change in Peña Blanca. From Tegucigalpa, get a San Pedro Sula–bound bus to La Guama. From there, take a bus or pickup from the left-hand turnoff toward Peña Blanca (L13, every 25 minutes) where you can make your connection.

SANTA BÁRBARA
pop 36,800

About 53km west of Lago de Yojoa, Santa Bárbara, capital of the department of the same name, is a medium-sized colonial-era town with a striking cathedral. The large **Hotel Boarding House Moderno** (☎ 643-2203; Calle El Progresso; s/d with fan L250/350, with air-con L500/600; P ☒) has spacious but slightly dated rooms. All have cable TV.

You will have your most memorable meal at **Mesón Casa Blanca** (☎ 643-2839; Av La Constitucion; meals L75-85; ☺ 7:30am-8:30pm). It is like eating in a family home in a time warp, with stuffed deer heads and old photos on the wall. Typical Honduran dishes are served.

Roads connect Santa Bárbara with the Tegucigalpa–San Pedro Sula and the San Pedro Sula–Nueva Ocotepeque highways. **Los Junqueños** (☎ 643-2113) buses to Tegucigalpa leave from one-and-a-half blocks north of the plaza, past Banco Atlántida, twice a day. All other buses leave from or near the main termi-nal, a block west of Parque Central. From the main terminal, one block west of the Parque

EXPLORE MORE AROUND LAGO DE YOJOA

Pulhapanzak is a short (17.5km) hop from Lago de Yojoa. With a little more effort, you can get to more remote but rewarding ruins and mountainous wildlife refuges.

■ **Pulhapanzak** (☽ 6am-6pm), a magnificent 43m waterfall on the Río Lindo, is an easy day trip from San Pedro Sula (60km away), surrounded by some lush, well-preserved forest. It's a popular spot for swimming and can be crowded on weekends and holidays. You can camp here if you have your own gear. Entry to the area costs L40. From San Pedro, take a bus to Mochito (L45, one hour) and ask the driver to let you off at San Buenaventura. From there it is a well-marked 15-minute walk; or take the less frequent but more convenient Pulhapanzak Express bus directly to the entrance. The last bus back passes through San Buenaventura around 4pm.

■ **Parque Eco-Arqueológico Los Naranjos** (☎ 9654-0040; admission L114; ☽ 8am-4pm), northwest of the lake, was first occupied around 1300 BC, and is thought to be the largest Preclassic-era Lenca archaeological site. Excavation is still in its initial stages. The park includes trails for viewing semiexcavated ruins and to observe plants and wildlife, particularly birds. The D&D Brewery (p361) is close to the park and can arrange guided tours.

■ East of the lake (and across the highway), **Parque Nacional Cerro Azulmeambar** (☎ 9865-9082; www.paghonduras.org/pancam.html; admission L20) is a well-equipped park with kilometers of trails leading to waterfalls, caves with ancient artifacts and untouched cloud forest. There is also a **visitors center** (☎ 608-5510, in Tegucigalpa 773-2027) and lodge that sleeps 10, a restaurant and small store. The park entrance is down a turnoff from La Guama on the main CA-5 highway. Frequent pickups head to Santa Elena. From there, walking to the park's PANACAM Lodge takes about one hour. Contact Mesoamérica Travel (p364) in San Pedro Sula to arrange tours.

■ West of the lake, isolated **Parque Nacional Santa Bárbara** contains Honduras' second-highest peak, **Montaña de Santa Bárbara** (2744m). You will need a guide to visit the park, which is only minimally developed. To visit, head to the town of San Luis Planes; a bus to San Luis Planes leaves Peña Blanca at 10:30am daily, retuning at 6am (you'll need to spend the night or hitchhike). Once there, ask for **Edán Teruel** (☎ 674-3304), who is known as the best guide in the area (L200 per day). He can sort out lodging too. You can also arrange tours at D&D Brewery (see p361).

Central, buses run every half hour to San Pedro Sula until 5pm (L56, 1½ to two hours). To move on to Copá Ruinas, take an *ordinario* toward San Pedro Sula and transfer at La Ceibita.

SAN PEDRO SULA
pop 710,000

San Pedro Sula might play second fiddle to Tegucigalpa in terms of population and political matters, but when it comes to business and industry, it calls the shots. Often simply called San Pedro, the city is Honduras' economic engine room, generating almost two-thirds of the country's GDP. Its airport is the country's most modern. Its restaurants and nightlife arguably outstrip those of the capital. Unfortunately, its gangland crime is also on a par, though it still wins the Best Big City in Honduras competition.

Part of San Pedro's economic success is geographical: exports are handled easily with the port of Puerto Cortés under an hour away.

San Pedro originally made its wealth from bananas or *oro verde* (green gold) as locals call it. However, in 1998 flooding caused by Hurricane Mitch wiped out many of the plantations. Currently San Pedro makes its readies from the *maquila* (clothes-weaving) factories. The industry is not without controversy – high-profile cases in the US have highlighted some dubious sweatshop practices. There is little doubt, however, that the business is a vital source of income for many *sanpedranos* (residents of San Pedro).

San Pedro is extremely hot and humid from around April to September. The rainy season runs from May to November.

Orientation

Downtown San Pedro is circled by a highway bypass, the Circunvalación, which is lined with shopping malls, restaurants and banks. Within that circle, central San Pedro is flat with avenidas (avenues) running north–south and calles running east–west. The numbering begins

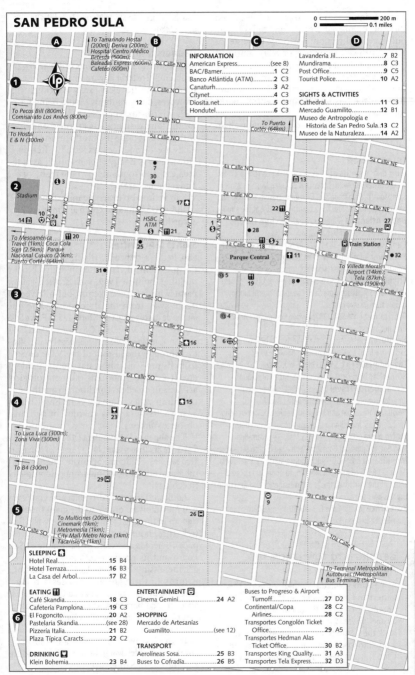

SAN PEDRO SULA

0 —————— 200 m
0 —————— 0.1 miles

INFORMATION
American Express.................(see 8)
BAC/Bamer..............................**1** C2
Banco Atlántida (ATM)...........**2** C3
Canaturh.................................**3** A2
Citynet...................................**4** C3
Diosita.net.............................**5** C3
Hondutel.................................**6** C3
Lavandería Jil..........................**7** B2
Mundirama................................**8** C3
Post Office..............................**9** C5
Tourist Police.........................**10** A2

SIGHTS & ACTIVITIES
Cathedral................................**11** C3
Mercado Guamilito.................**12** B1
Museo de Antropología e
  Historia de San Pedro Sula..**13** C2
Museo de la Naturaleza.........**14** A2

To Tamarindo Hostal
(200m); Deriva (200m);
Hospital Centro Médico
Betesda (500m);
Baleadas Express (600m);
Cafeteo (600m)

To Pecos Bill (800m);
Comisariato Los Andes (800m)

To Hostal
E & N (300m)

To Puerto
Cortés (64km)

To Mesoamérica
Travel (1km); Coca Cola
Sign (2.5km); Parque
Nacional Cusuco (20km);
Puerto Cortés (64km)

Parque Central

To Villeda Morales
Airport (14km);
Tela (87km);
La Ceiba (190km)

Train Station

To Luca Luca (300m);
Zona Viva (300m)

To B4 (300m)

To Multicines (200m);
Cinemark (1km);
Metromedia (1km);
City Mall/Metro Nova (1km);
Taca/Isleña (1km)

To Terminal Metropolitana
Autobuses (Metropolitan
Bus Terminal) (5km)

SLEEPING 🛏
Hotel Real...............................**15** B4
Hotel Terraza..........................**16** B3
La Casa del Arbol....................**17** B2

EATING 🍴
Café Skandia...........................**18** C3
Cafetería Pamplona...............**19** C3
El Fogoncito...........................**20** A2
Pastelaria Skandia.................(see 28)
Pizzería Italia..........................**21** B2
Plaza Tipica Caracts...............**22** C2

DRINKING 🍷
Klein Bohemia.........................**23** B4

ENTERTAINMENT 🎭
Cinema Gemini........................**24** A2

SHOPPING
Mercado de Artesanías
  Guamilito..........................(see 12)

TRANSPORT
Aerolíneas Sosa.....................**25** B3
Buses to Cofradía..................**26** B5
Buses to Progreso & Airport
  Turnoff...............................**27** D2
Continental/Copa
  Airlines..............................**28** C2
Transportes Congolón Ticket
  Office.................................**29** A5
Transportes Hedman Alas
  Ticket Office.....................**30** B2
Transportes King Quality.....**31** A3
Transportes Tela Express.....**32** D3

HONDURAS

where Primera (1a) Av crosses 1a Calle. From there the numbered avenidas and calles extend out in every direction: northeast (noreste, or NE), northwest (noroeste, or NO), southeast (sureste, or SE) or southwest (suroeste, or SO).

Every address has a numbered calle or avenida and is further specified by its quadrant. As ever, the bustling Parque Central marks the hub of the city.

The spectacular Merendón mountain chain looms to the west.

Information

The city's malls also have banks with ATMs.

BAC/Bamer (5a Av NO btwn 1a & 2a Calles NO; 9am-5pm Mon-Fri, 9am-noon Sat) Exchanges traveler's checks and has a Unibanc ATM. Also has a branch with ATM at the airport.

Banco Atlántida (Parque Central) This bank changes traveler's checks and has an ATM.

Canaturh (521-3814; 12a Av NO btwn 2a & 3a Calle NO) Tourist information and the best place to pick up information on Parque Nacional Cusuco.

Citynet (cnr 3a Calle SO & 5a Av SO; per hr L10; 8am-8pm Mon-Sat, 10am-8pm Sun) Cheapest internet in town is up a narrow staircase.

Diosita.net (550-1307; Parque Central; per hr L25) Internet access.

Hondutel (cnr 4a Av SO & 4a Calle SO; 7am-8:30pm) Expensive local and international phone service.

Lavandería Jil (557-0334; 8a Av NO btwn 2a & 3a Calles NO; per load L80; 7am-6pm Mon-Sat, to noon Sun)

Mesoamérica Travel (557-8447; www.meso america-travel.com; cnr 8a Calle & 32a Avenida NO) Helpful, professional and knowledgeable; does interesting upscale tours, including a trip to a banana plantation.

Metro Nova (580-1149; City Mall; 10am-8pm Mon-Sat, to 6pm Sun) Bookstore with a big English section.

Mundirama (550-7400; Edificio Martinez Valenzuela, 2a Calle SE; 8am-5pm Mon-Fri, to noon Sat) Located south of the cathedral, this is a travel agency and American Express agent.

Post office (cnr 9a Calle & 3a Av SO; 7:30am-5pm Mon-Fri, 8am-noon Sat)

GETTING INTO TOWN FROM THE AIRPORT

San Pedro's Villeda Morales Airport, the largest and most modern in the country, is about 14km east of town. Coming from the airport, there is no direct bus but you can walk the 2.5km to the main road and catch a bus into town. Otherwise, taxis cost about L200 to L300 depending on time of day.

Tourist police (550-0001; cnr 12a Av NO & 1a Calle 0; 24hr)

Dangers & Annoyances

San Pedro Sula has a serious crime and gang problem. Mostly it is gang member on gang member and travelers rarely get caught up. However, do be cautious. Avoid being flashy with your belongings (save the MP3 player for the long-distance bus journey) and dress with restraint (save the shorts for the beach). Taxis are a good idea, especially after dark. Downtown is dodgy after nightfall, as is the area east and south of it (where many of the budget hotels are).

San Pedro also bears the unfortunate label of the AIDS capital of Central America. Plan accordingly.

Sights & Activities

San Pedro's **cathedral**, which overlooks the Parque Central, is quite an ugly, blocky building, built in 1949, with scuffed yellow paint within. It is unkempt but a haven of peace away from the street noise. The fine **Museo de Antropología e Historia de San Pedro Sula** (557-1874; cnr 3a Av NO & 4a Calle NO; adult/child L38/20; 9am-4pm Mon & Wed-Sat, 9am-3pm Sun) walks visitors through the history of the Valle de Sula from its pre-Columbian days to the modern era. It exhibits hundreds of archaeological artifacts in excellent condition, from the surrounding valley. Signage is in English and Spanish. Its entrance is 'guarded' by two large obsolete cannons.

The **Museo de la Naturaleza** (557-6598; 1a Calle 0 near 12a Av NO; admission L20; 8am-4pm Mon-Fri, to noon Sat) has academic Spanish-language exhibits covering everything from paleontology to ecology.

Look west in San Pedro Sula, and your eyes will inevitably be drawn to the giant **Coca-Cola sign** up in the hills. Walking up there is a fine trek (three hours there and back at a leisurely pace). There is an excellent panorama of San Pedro and its green streets as a reward. To get there, simply follow 1a Calle west until it turns to the right and crosses a bridge. After the bridge, turn left at 2a Calle, go past an entrance barrier and carry on climbing. Your surroundings swiftly change from city to jungle.

In the last week of June, San Pedro celebrates a large **festival** in honor of its founding and the day of San Pedro.

Sleeping

San Pedro's budget options are mostly in the downtown area south of 1a Calle O, near the former cluster of bus stations. The area gets dodgy after dark and now that most of the buses depart from the main terminal, there isn't such a compelling reason to stay there. You'll be happier in neighborhoods to the north.

Tamarindo Hostal (☎ 557-0123; www.tamarindo hostel.com; 9a Calle A btwn 10a & 11a Avs NO; dm L220, s/d/ tr with air-con L500/700/900; P ⊠ 🛜) The 5am rooster wake-up call is definitely not cool but otherwise this great hostel in a relatively safe neighborhood gets most things right. Unfortunately, the owner, Angela Bendeck, a famous rock/jazz singer in Honduras, was away when we came though, so we didn't get to see the normal vibe, but there are schnauzers; funky, bright murals, and impromptu unplugged sessions. There is a 2nd-floor deck with hammocks, a large common room and a well-equipped kitchen. Dorm rooms are upscale for Honduras and come with clean linen and cable TV. English and Spanish are spoken.

Hotel Terraza (☎ 550-3108; 6a Av SO btwn 4a & 5a Calles SO; s/d L250/300, s/d/tr with air-con L350/400/500; ⊠) There are some missing lamp shades and some eyebrow-raising decor choices, but this typical cheapie does the job with hot water, cable TV, desks and fairly spacious rooms. There is also a lempira-friendly restaurant off the lobby.

our pick **Hotel Real** (☎ 550-7929; www.realhn.com; 6a Av btwn 6a & 7a Calle SO; s with fan L300, s/d with air-con L450/500; ⊠ 💻) This is the best nonhostel budget hotel in Honduras. Faux adobe walls and a plethora of small touches – hand-carved furnishings, Lencan pottery and lots of hanging plants – keeps this central option oozing with charm; all rooms, with cable TV but no hot water, look out onto an open courtyard with a *palapa* kiosk that serves *baleadas* (flour tortilla filled with beans and cheese) and *comida típica* for breakfast. Enjoy it while you're here – your lempiras won't stretch this far elsewhere.

Hostal E&N (☎ 552-5731; www.hostaleyn.com; cnr 5a Calle & 15a Av NO; s/d/tr incl breakfast L856/951/1046; P ⊠ 💻) This is a reasonable option if Tamarindo Hostal is full – it is a little further west in the same good part of town. Rooms can feel a bit small (they pack the beds in) but it includes air-con and hot water and the hardwood floors are nice. It is a lot better value if you are in a group.

La Casa de Arbol (☎ 504-1616; www.hotelcasadearbol. com; 6a Av NO btwn 2a & 3a Calles NW; s/d/tr incl breakfast L1542/1873/2204; P ⊠ 🛜) In the one-time home of (and started by) one of San Pedro Sula's most important former mayors, this discerning boutique hotel is where to drop extra cash for splurge-worthy comforts. The *árbol* in question is a mango tree that juts straight up the through the center of the building. The 13 well-appointed rooms feature snuggle-up duvets, bathtubs and flat-screen LCD TVs and there is a calming cascading rock wall off the lobby.

Eating

San Pedro Sula has a wide range of culinary choices catering to all budgets and a surprisingly broad range of cuisines. Many more upmarket places, as well as US fast-food franchises, are on Circunvalación. There is a whole bunch of cheap and cheerful *comedores* at Mercado Guimilito and a great, open-air food court of *comida típica* called Plaza Típica Coracts that's always packed for lunch.

Baleadas Express (13a Calle NO btwn 11a & 12a Avs NO; baleadas L15-38; ⏱ 6am-10pm) This addictive and exceptionally good-value Honduran fast-food joint will renew your faith in *baleadas*. Pick your filling (eggs with chorizo, chicken, avocado, plantains and more) and sit back and enjoy the deluxe version of this Honduran breakfast staple. You'll be back.

Cafetería Pamplona (Parque Central; mains L42-195; ⏱ 7am-8pm Mon-Sat, 8am-8pm Sun) A bit of a San Pedro institution, this is a diner with a Honduran twist. It is good value although service can be offhand. Serves tasty, generously portioned *típica*.

El Fogoncito (1a Calle O at 11a Av NO; mains L47-389; ⏱ 11am-11pm Sun-Wed, to 2am Thu-Sat) Almost feels like Texas in here. Yummy Tex-Mex is dished up at this popular Mexican restaurant. Its cantina style includes all the usual suspects from tacos to fajitas, as well as some more adventurous options. The bar makes it a good drinking option too. Four *tacos al pastor* for L94 is a good way to go.

Café Skandia (Gran Hotel Sula, Parque Central; mains L48-285; ⏱ 24hr) This place is so cool you might mistake it for a hip LA diner trying to be retro. It is cheap, bright and central, service is fast and pleasant, and you can have a waffle by an outdoor pool lined with palm trees. And, as a cafe that never sleeps, you get all sorts of characters passing through, from tourists and businessmen to diplomats and sugar daddies with their 'companions.' The menu is loaded with previously MIA items (milk shakes, onion rings, apple pie). Also don't miss its pastry shop (Pastelaria Skandia) next to the Continental Airlines office.

our pick **Pecos Bill** (cnr 6a-7a Calles NO & 14 Av NO; mains L95-250; ☺ 10am-10pm) Whoever's idea this was surely had some screws loose, but the endearing, strange, only-in-Honduras combination of a car wash and a restaurant is a winner. The breezy, open-air restaurant serves up succulent grills. Choose your meat (or shrimp – but why?), dabble it with chimichurri, *pico de gallo*, and hot sauce then throw it into the warm tortillas under a layer of some of the best refried beans in the country: pure carnivore heaven. Try the *churrasco*. And, by the way, did you need your car washed?

Deriva (☎ 516-1012; 9a Calle btwn 10a & 11a Avs NO; mains L190-350; ☺ noon-2:30pm & 6-10pm Mon-Sat) Oenophiles take heart: there's real wine here, some 10 by the glass and many more on the Argentine/Chilean-heavy wine list (though the reds are served entirely too cold). Yes, this is one of the classiest restaurants in Honduras, a place to come for a blowout if you are flying home tomorrow. With a specialist wine shop next door, grape is definitely the way to wash down the excellent Peruvian cuisine. Feels nice to put down that Salva Vida, doesn't it?

Also check out:

Cafetéo (13a Calle NO btwn 11a & 12a Avs NO; items L18-85; ☺ 7am-10pm Mon-Sat, 8am-8:45pm Sun) This excellent coffee stop is the spot to grab a caramel macchiato, green tea latte or just a plain cup of excellent coffee. There are muffins and panini as well. It's next door to Baleadas Express.

Pizzería Italia (cnr 1a Calle O & 7a Av NO; pizza L125-190; ☺ 10am-10pm) It's a dingy dive, but this long-standing pizzeria has survived recessions and explosive population growth since opening its doors in 1976. Pizzas are a luxury in Honduras – these are quite good, but not particularly cheap.

Comisariato Los Andes (6a Calle NO; ☺ 8am-9pm Mon-Sat, to 8pm Sun) A good supermarket for self-caterers.

Drinking

The Zona Viva, which hugs the inside of the Circunvalación between 7a Calle SO and 11a Calle SO, is home to the main concentration of bars and clubs. Unfortunately, they are often spread too far apart to get in a good pub crawl.

Klein Bohemia (cnr 7a Calle SO & 8a Av SO; ☺ 4:30pm-midnight Wed, Thu & Sat, to 1am Fri) Set up by Swiss expats who have since moved on, this central boho oasis is still going strong. Its bleak downtown setting is not promising, but appearances are deceptive. Venture to the upstairs bar, and you will find a cultured, young crowd. There

are regular live bands and showings of independent films.

Luca Luca (15 Av SO btwn 8 & 9 Calles SO, Zona Viva; ☺ 9:30pm-late Thu-Sat) Named after Luca Brasi from *The Godfather*, this trendier bar is set up in ultralounge style, but not quite so Vegas-y. It's smaller and more intimate and features DJs spinning the gamut nightly, though the gamut involves more merengue and salsa than Eminem or Shakira.

B4 (cnr 9a Calle SO & 16a Av SO, Zona Viva; admission L100; ☺ 9:30pm-late Thu-Sat) An open-air, 2nd-floor disco, which does wonders for overheating. Live bands belt out the salsa and rock, DJs pick up the slack on everything else. It was one of the hot spots at time of research, but if the norm is any indication, probably closed by now.

Entertainment

There are many places around town, including Klein Bohemia (see below left), that show films. **Cinema Gemini** (☎ 550-9060; 1a Calle O at 12a Av NO) shows current Hollywood fare for L50 (L25 on Tuesday, L80 per couple on Thursday), but be sure to check if the movie is dubbed.

Mall theaters include **Cinemark** (City Mall) and **Multicines** (Multiplaza Mall) with tickets for around L65.

Shopping

Mercado Guamilito (cnr 8a & 9a Avs & 6a & 7a Calles NO; ☺ 7am-5pm Mon-Sat, to noon Sun) is a huge market that runs the gamut of stalls from fruits and vegetables to household goods, tailors, and shoe repairers. At the front, it also houses the **Mercado de Artesanías Guamilito**, with a wide selection of arts, handicrafts and gifts from all over Honduras, Guatemala and El Salvador.

Getting There & Away

AIR

Aeropuerto Internacional Ramón Villeda Morales (☎ 6689-3261) is 14km east of San Pedro Sula (about a L200 to L300 taxi ride). It is a larger, busier airport than the one serving Tegucigalpa. It is served by daily direct flights to all major cities in Central America; and several to US cities. Domestically it has flights to Tegucigalpa, La Ceiba, Puerto Lempira and the Bay Islands (usually via La Ceiba).

International airlines:

Aeroméxico (☎ airport 668-4039; www.aeromexico.com)
American Airlines (☎ 553-3506, airport 668-3244; www.aa.com; Edificio Banco Ficohsa, Av Circunvalación at 5a Calle SO)

Continental/Copa (☎ 552-9770, airport 668-3212; www.continental.com; 4a Av NO btwn 1 & 2 Calles NO)
Delta (☎ 550-1616; www.delta.com)
Maya Island Air (☎ 668-0569; www.mayaislandair. com) Flies to Belize.
Spirit Airlines (☎ in the US 1-800-772-7117; www. spiritair.com)
TACA (☎ 550-8222; www.taca.com; Colonia Trejo, Av Circunvalación, Edif Yude Canahuati)

Domestic airlines:
Aerolíneas Sosa (☎ 550-6545, airport 668-3128; www.aerolineasosa.com; 1a Calle 0 btwn 7a & 8a Av SO)
Central American airways (☎ airport 233-1614; www.central-american-airways.com)
CM Airlines (☎ airport 547-2425; www.cmairlines.com)
Isleña (☎ 550-8222; Colonia Trejo, Av Circunvalación, Edif Yude Canahuati)

BUS
In San Pedro Sula, with a few exceptions, bus companies depart from the main **Terminal Gran Central Metropolitana** (☎ 516-1616; www.grancentralhn. com) 6km south of Parque Central, the largest bus station in Central America. A few companies maintain ticket offices in their old terminals in the center but do not depart from there; see the map for locations. There is a handy directory at the terminal's entrance, which is nice, because the ticket offices seem scrunched among all the shopping. The free magazine *Honduras Tips* has a useful bus routes section, as does the *El Heraldo* newspaper. If you do need to get to the terminal, take any bus down 2a Av SE (L0.20) or take a taxi for around L60 to L80. See the table, p368, for sample bus services and fares from San Pedro Sula.

International Buses
International bus line **Transportes Hedman Alas** (☎ 516-2273; ticket office 3a Calle NO btwn 7a & 8a Avs NO) is an expensive luxury line with services to Guatemala City and Antigua. In addition to its shiny new terminal attached to Gran Central Metropolitana, it maintains ticket offices in town as well as in the arrivals hall of the airport next to the car-rental agencies. **Transportes King Quality** (☎ 553-4547; cnr 2a Calle SO & 9a Av SO; ☒ 8am-5pm Mon-Fri, 8am-2pm Sat) has high-end service that is less harsh on the wallet. It departs direct to San Salvador with a connection to Guatemala City. **Transportes La Sultana** (☎ 516-2048) goes to San Salvador; it's less expensive but less comfortable. **Tica Bus** (☎ 516-2022) offers deluxe services to Nicaragua, Costa Rica and Panama via Tegucigalpa. **Frente del Norte** (☎ 9843-0507) also goes to Guatemala with connections to Belize and Mexico.

Getting Around
BUS
It's best to limit your use of local buses. They are subject to frequent robberies. There is no direct bus to the airport, but you can get on any El Progreso bus and ask the driver to let you off at the airport turnoff (L21). From there, it's a 2.5km walk with no shade; if you have bags, consider a taxi – is it really worth the trouble to save L200?

CAR & MOTORCYCLE
Car-rental agencies in San Pedro Sula:
Avis (☎ airport 668-3164)
Budget (☎ airport 668-4421)
Econo Rent-A-Car (☎ airport 668-1881)
Thrifty (☎ airport 668-2427)

TAXI
Average fares in town are L40 to L50. Taxis cost about L200 to L250 to the airport, L60 to L80 to the bus terminal. All fares rise substantially between the hours of 10pm and 7am.

PARQUE NACIONAL CUSUCO
Parque Nacional Cusuco (admission L190; ☒ 8am-4:30pm), 45km west of San Pedro Sula in the impressive Merendón mountain range, is a cloud-forest park. Its highest peak is **Cerro Jilinco** (2242m). Bird-watchers have spotted toucans and parrots, and quetzals are sometimes seen, mostly from April to June. There are also monkeys, reptiles and amphibians (a new species of toad was discovered here in 1981).

Five different trails are marked. The trails marked Quetzal and Las Minas lead up to **waterfalls** and **swimming holes**.

The best place to go for information on the park is the Tourism Commission at the community of **Buenos Aires**, located a few kilometers short of the park entrance and visitors center. Contact **Carlos Alvarenga** (☎ 9914-5775) who can arrange guides as well as transport from Cofradia. Alvarenga also runs the **Ecoalbergue** (☎ 9914-5775; r per person L190), which offers five rooms, a kitchen and negotiable camping. Getting there by public transportation is a challenge, but it can be done. In San Pedro, catch a bus at the Central Metropolitana (L25, every 20 minutes). From Cofradia, pickups

HONDURAS

BUSES FROM SAN PEDRO SULA
International Buses

Destination	Cost (L)	Duration (One Way)	Bus Line	Phone	Departure
Antigua, Guatemala	970	9hr	Hedman Alas	516-2273	10:25am & 3pm
Guatemala City, Guatemala	550	8hr	Congolón	553-1174	2am
	600	8hr	Frente del Norte	9843-0507	6am
Managua, Nicaragua	608	12hr	Tica Bus	516-2022	5am
Panama City, Panama	1976	3 days	Tica Bus	516-2022	5am
San Jose, Costa Rica	988	2 days	Tica Bus	516-2022	5am
San Salvador, El Salvador	393	7hr	Sultana	516-2048	6:15am
	500	7hr	Frente del Norte	9843-0507	6am
	800	7hr	King Quality	553-4547	7am

Long-Distance Buses

Destination	Cost (L)	Duration (One Way)	Bus Line	Phone	Departure
Agua Caliente	165-213	5hr	Congolón	553-1174	Every 2hr 5:30am-11pm
Comayagua	70	2hr	Diaz	505-9955	6:30am, 7:30am, 9:30am, 10:30am, 12:30pm, 1:30pm, 2:30pm, 3:30pm
Copán Ruinas	110	3hr	Casasola	516-2031	7am (Fri-Sun only), 8am, 11am, 1pm, 2pm, 3pm, 7pm
	323-380	3hr	Hedman Alas	516-2273	11am & 3pm
El Mochito	45	2hr	Tima	659-3161	Every 30min 5:40am-5:40pm
La Ceiba	90	3hr	Contraibal	9908-1509	6am, 7:30am, 9am, 10:30am, noon, 1:20pm, 2:40pm, 4pm
	90	3hr	Cotuc	520-7497	*5:15am, 6:45am, 8:15am, 9:45am
	323-380	2½hr	Hedman Alas	516-2273	6am, 10:30am, 3:20pm, 6:20pm
Puerto Cortés	42	1hr	Impala	665-0606	Every 15min 5:30am-6:30pm
Pulhapanzak & Lago de Yojoa	14	2hr	Etul	516-2011	Every 20min 4:45am-4:30pm
	27	2hr	Pulhapanzak Express	No phone	8:30am, 10am, 11am, noon, 2pm, 4:20pm, 5pm, 5:40pm, 6:20pm
Santa Rosa de Copán	86	3hr	San José	653-3256	Hourly 5am-12:30pm
Siguatepeque	55	3hr	Etul	516-2011	Every 20min 4:45am-4:30pm
Tegucigalpa	141	4hr	El Rey Express	516-2014	Hourly 5am-6pm
	220-437	5hr	Hedman Alas	516-2273	10 per day 5:45am-6:10pm
Tela	70	1½hr	**Tela Express	No tel	Every 2hr 7am-4:30pm
	304-361	2hr	Hedman Alas	516-2273	10:25am & 6:30pm
Trujillo	165	6hr	Cotuc	520-7497	5:15am, 6:45am, 8:15am, 9:45am
	165	6hr	Contraibal	9908-1509	6am, 7:30am, 9am, 10:30am, noon, 1:20pm, 2:40pm, 4pm

*If you are aiming to catch the morning ferry to Roatán or Utila in La Ceiba, you must be on the 5:15am departure.

**Departs from city center.

go up to the village of Buenos Aires (L20, one hour). The pick-up times are irregular but they are most frequent in the morning. Making an early start is strongly recommended. The Cusuco National Park offers magnificent biodiversity as cloud forest. With some luck you may spot a variety of wildlife such as toucans, monkeys, tapirs or the resplendent quetzal. Huge tree ferns – of up to 20m, the highest in all of Central America – are typical for Cusuco and give you the impression of being in a *Jurassic Park* world. From March to May one of the typical early morning sounds of Cusuco National Park is the monotonous call of the resplendent quetzal, the mystic and holy bird of the Aztecs and Mayas. The charm of Cusuco does not only come from the nature, but also from the quiet and harmonic life in the 38 surrounding coffee towns, of which Buenos Aires is a good example.

The park can be reached all year with 4WD vehicle; it is about two to three hours' drive from San Pedro Sula.

LA ENTRADA

La Entrada is an unattractive crossroads town with a reputation for narcotrafficking. Lots of buses and traffic pass through on the way northeast to San Pedro Sula, south to Santa Rosa de Copán and Nueva Ocotepeque, and southwest to Copán Ruinas. You won't be here otherwise.

The intersection at the south end of town is a good place to catch a bus. Buses to Copán Ruinas, however, stop at a small kiosk under an almond tree about 75m past the Hotel San Carlos, on the turnoff toward the ruins. Destinations include the following:

Copán Ruinas (L45, two hours, every 40 minutes 6am to 4pm)

Nueva Ocotepeque (L80, 2½ to three hours, every 45 minutes 6am to 4pm)

San Pedro Sula (*ordinario* L53, one to 1½ hours, every 30 minutes 5:30am to 6pm; *directo* (direct) L82, one hour, 8:10am, 10:10am and 3:10pm)

Santa Rosa de Copán (*ordinario* L20, 1¼ hours, every 30 minutes 6am to 7pm; *directo* L35, 45 minutes, every one to 1½ hours 7am to 3pm)

COPÁN RUINAS

pop 38,600

The beautiful, tranquil little town of Copán Ruinas, often simply called Copán, is the most traveler-oriented – and pleasant – town in Honduras. It's a 700m stroll from the famous Maya ruins of the same name. Sloping cobblestone streets, white adobe buildings with red-tile roofs and an attractive colonial church give it an aura of timeless peace. Most travelers stop in Copán just for the ruins, but that's a mistake: Copán's collection of excellent bars and restaurants, beautiful attractions in the surrounding countryside and friendly population are all reasons to linger.

Orientation

The renovated Parque Central, with the church on one side, is at the heart of town. The ruins are 700m outside of town, a pleasant 15-minute stroll along a footpath to one side of the highway to La Entrada. Las Sepulturas archaeological site is 2km further along.

Information

BAC/Bamer (Parque Central) Has a Unibanc ATM that accepts Visa and MasterCard.

Banco Atlántida (Parque Central) Changes US dollars and traveler's checks. It also has an ATM.

Canaturh (☎ 651-3829; www.copanhonduras.org; ☽ 8am-5pm Mon-Fri, to noon Sat) Good for free tourism info and maps throughout Honduras, though keep in mind it's member-based.

Copán Connections (☎ 651-4182; www.copanconnections.com; ☽ 2-7pm) Below Twisted Tanya's, this is a good source of free tourist information, especially with regards to the Bay Islands and Guatemala. And Copán, too.

Hondutel (☽ 7am-9pm)

La Casa de Todo (☎ 651-4185) Food, internet (per hour L20) and laundry services (wash, dry and fold L20 per lb) are all provided at this aptly named place.

Maya Connections (per hr L20; ☽ 9am-7pm) Also does laundry (per lb L20).

Post office (☽ 8am-4pm Mon-Fri, 8am-noon Sat).

Sights

The fascinating Copán archaeological site, 1km outside of town, is the area's big draw. It and other fine places to visit in the area are covered on p374.

Museo de Arqueología Maya (☎ 651-4437; admission foreigners/Central Americans L285/80; ☽ 9am-5pm), on Parque Central, is a little dated but still worth a visit. The exhibits include excavated ceramics, fragments from the altars and the supports of the Maya ruins, an insight into the Maya's sophisticated use of calendars and a re-creation of a female shaman's tomb. Some descriptions have English translations.

HONDURAS

Memorias Frágiles (☎ 651-3900; admission free; ⏱ 8am-5pm Mon-Fri) This permanent photo exhibition was a gift from Harvard University's Peabody Museum and features a worthwhile collection of rare photos detailing the first archeological expeditions to Copán at the turn of the 20th century. It's located inside the Palacio Municipal on Parque Central.

Enchanted Wings Butterfly House & Nature Center (☎ 651-4133; www.copannaturecenter.com; adult/child L115/50; ⏱ 8am-4:30pm) is the brainchild of Robert Gallardo, a former Peace Corps volunteer and a renowned nature expert. There's something hypnotic about the butterflies and the spectacular tropical flora with around 150 species of orchids (which bloom from February to June). It is on the outskirts of town, walkable in about 20 minutes – or a short hop on mototaxi. You can also organize bird-watching tours from here.

Casa K'inich (☎ 651-4105; admission L20; ⏱ 8am-noon & 1-5pm Tue-Sun) includes an interactive recreation of the ancient football game practiced by the Copán residents more than a millennia ago. Displays are in three languages – English, Spanish and Ch'orti'. Kids might get a kick out of the stela with a cutout hole to poke their heads through. It's located at the *mirador*.

Mirador El Cuartel is a lookout, from the atmospheric ruins of an old jail, with a fine view of the town and surrounding countryside. Worth the climb.

The **Copán Ruinas fair** is celebrated from March 15 to 20.

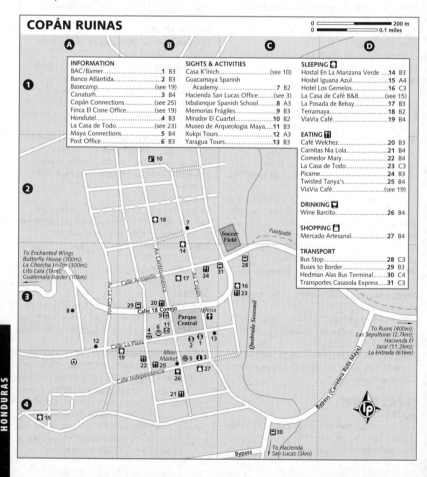

COPÁN RUINAS

0 —————— 200 m
0 —————— 0.1 miles

INFORMATION	
BAC/Bamer	1 B3
Banco Atlántida	2 B3
Basecamp	(see 19)
Canaturh	3 B4
Copán Connections	(see 25)
Finca El Cisne Office	(see 19)
Hondutel	4 B3
La Casa de Todo	(see 23)
Maya Connections	5 B4
Post Office	6 B3

SIGHTS & ACTIVITIES	
Casa K'inich	(see 10)
Guacamaya Spanish Academy	7 B2
Hacienda San Lucas Office	(see 3)
Ixbalanque Spanish School	8 A3
Memorias Frágiles	9 B3
Mirador El Cuartel	10 B2
Museo de Arqueología Maya	11 B3
Xukpi Tours	12 A3
Yaragua Tours	13 B3

SLEEPING 🛏	
Hostal En La Manzana Verde	14 B3
Hostel Iguana Azul	15 A4
Hotel Los Gemelos	16 C3
La Casa de Café B&B	(see 15)
La Posada de Belssy	17 B3
Terramaya	18 B2
ViaVia Café	19 B3

EATING 🍴	
Café Welchez	20 B3
Carnitas Nia Lola	21 B4
Comedor Mary	22 B4
La Casa de Todo	23 C3
Picame	24 B3
Twisted Tanya's	25 B4
ViaVia Café	(see 19)

DRINKING 🍷	
Wine Barcito	26 B4

SHOPPING 🛍	
Mercado Artesanal	27 B4

TRANSPORT	
Bus Stop	28 C3
Buses to Border	29 B3
Hedman Alas Bus Terminal	30 C4
Transportes Casasola Express	31 C3

Activities

Tour companies will also organize activities for you; see below.

HORSEBACK RIDING

There is some fine horseback-riding country around Copán Ruinas. It should be obvious, but don't hire a horse from a random kid on the street.

Hacienda San Lucas (☎ 651-4495; www.hacienda sanlucas.com) arranges excellent, hassle-free horseback riding. Your view from the saddle could take in Los Sapos, a local archaeological site. Three-hour rides cost around L1500. See boxed text, p374, for more on the hacienda.

Scenic, professional horseback-riding tours, usually part of a day-long or overnight trip (see p374) are run by **Finca El Cisne** (☎ 651-4695; www.fincaelcisne.com).

BIRD-WATCHING

Rugged countryside around town means plenty of chances to spot hundreds of species of birds. Former Peace Corps volunteer Robert Gallardo, at Enchanted Wings Butterfly House, is one of the country's foremost experts on wildlife, and has personally added 13 species to the list of birds found in Honduras. He organizes tours locally (per person per day L25) and further afield.

Courses

Both the Spanish schools in Copán get very positive feedback. Prices listed here include a tour such as horseback riding or a trip to the Agua Caliente hot springs.

Guacamaya Spanish Academy (☎ 651-4360; www. guacamaya.com) Offers a package of 20 hours of one-on-one tuition for L2660. For L1650 more you can have full board and lodging with a local family. Its location is slightly more central than Ixbalanque's.

Ixbalanque Spanish School (☎ 651-4432; www. ixbalanque.com) In a swanky new location with terrific views, at the west end of town. It offers 20 hours of one-on-one instruction in Spanish for L4465 per week, including a homestay with a local family that provides three meals a day. Instruction only, for 20 hours per week, costs L2565.

Tours

A huge number of tours can be organized from Copán Ruinas. You can cave, visit a Maya village, make tortillas or manufacture ceramics, plunge into hot springs, visit a coffee plantation or head off into the wilds.

Basecamp (☎ 651-4695; www.basecamphonduras.

com; 🕙 7am-9pm) Run by the hip trio from ViaVia Café, Basecamp are the go-to folks for nature hikes, horseback rides and an engaging alternative hike that lifts the lid on what life is really like for local residents (half of the profits from this tour buys school books for local children). It's the only place to offer motorbike tours around the neighboring mountains and is the official booker for tours to Finca El Cisne (p374). It's located inside ViaVia Café.

Xukpi Tours (☎ 651-4684; www.xukpitourscopan.com) Formerly operated by the ebullient and extremely knowledgeable Jorge Barraza and now by his cousin Yobani Peraza (Barraza lives Stateside and comes only in for large groups) who runs several ecological tours locally and further afield. The ruins and bird-watching tours are justly famous, and they'll do trips to all parts of Honduras and to Quiriguá (Guatemala).

Yaragua Tours (☎ 651-4147; www.yaragua.com; 🕙 8am-9pm) Leads hikes, horseback-riding trips, excursions to Lago de Yojoa and even some outings to nearby caves. Ask for Samuel, a well-respected and trusted local guide.

Sleeping

Hostal En La Manzana Verde (☎ 651-4695; dm L95; P) This remains the most traveler-friendly gathering point in Copán. There are 18 beds that coordinate with very neat (but welcomed) personalized kitchen shelves and a hilarious list of sarcastic rules that should have you in stitches (No dorm sex unless we can film it, etc).

Hostel Iguana Azul (☎ 651-4620; www.iguanaazulco pan.com; dm/s/d L120/220/270; P 🛜) This characterful place keeps its standards just as high as when it set up over a decade ago, boasting a funky-colonial motif and an impeccably clean mantra. It has two dormitories and three private rooms in a low-key ranch home. There's a small tropical garden, and the common area has books, magazines, travel guides and lots of handy travel tips. As far as backpacker accommodations go, you aren't likely to be more comfortable at too many other spots in Central America.

Hotel Los Gemelos (☎ 651-4077; info@casadetodo. com; s/d without bathroom L150/200; P) Copán's original backpackers isn't what it used to be, though if you are looking for a threadbare cheapie, it still provides that. Compact rooms surround a well-tended courtyard flower bed. If nobody is around, pop into Casa de Todo on the corner.

ViaVia Café (☎ 651-4652; www.viaviacafe.com; s/d L230/300; 🛜) Run by a trio of friendly Belgians, this hotel has spotless rooms with private bathroom, tiled floors and comfy beds donned with colorful Guatemalan bedspreads. There are only five rooms – best to email a booking if you can. The covered patio, great bar – often with live DJ – and restaurant make this a traveler focal point. English, French, German, Dutch and, of course, Spanish are spoken.

La Posada de Belssy (☎ 651-4680; s/d/tr L250/300/380; **P**) You get an excellent deal at this very friendly family-run place with a heap more character than average. Bedrooms are spick-and-span, but the formerly excellent terrace seemed a bit neglected on our visit (though it has wi-fi). Breakfast is available for L50 and there's free purified water and coffee; guests are also welcome to whip up their own meal in the kitchen.

our pick La Casa de Café B&B (☎ 651-4620; www.casadecafecopan.com; s/d incl breakfast L875/1100; **P** ✶ ✈) This impeccably decorated B&B has rooms that are adorned with carved wooden doors and Guatemalan masks. The setting is stunning – the view over breakfast is of morning mists rising around the Guatemalan mountains. There is also an upscale house and townhouse available (L1700 to L2200 a night, negotiable for longer stays).

Terramaya (☎ 651-4623; www.terramayacopan.com; s/d with breakfast L1200/1500; ✶ ✈) For comforts and style approaching upper midrange, this 2010 newcomer hovers somewhere between a B&B and boutique hotel, offering six smartly appointed rooms, a lovely backyard garden and candlelit terrace with misty-eyed mountain views. Two upstairs rooms offer spectacular balconies with vistas out to the ruins and the mountains beyond.

La Chorcha Lodge (☎ 651-3657; www.lachorchalodge.com; s/d with breakfast L1645/2190) It's out of shoestring range, but naturalists will want to check out these new *cabañas* on the forested hillside above the Enchanted Wings Butterfly House, inaugurated the week of our visit. Each of the six pine cabins features a custom stained-glass bird or butterfly fashioned from Swarovski digiscopes of well-known naturalist Robert Gallardo's personal photos. There are around 130 species of birds on the property as well as a soothing aquatic plant pond and waterfall. The best rooms have views towards a water treatment plant – a bit of an architectural flaw – but it's a peaceful escape above town nonetheless.

Eating

Comedor Mary (mains L34-130) Expats and locals alike rave about this simple restaurant for good reason: a recent World Bank grant win turned this into the nicest and best *comedor* in Honduras. *Comida típica* is redefined here

(try the *lomito de res a la plancha*), service is uncharacteristically friendly and the atmosphere is upscale (for a *comedor*). Sit on the sundeck, sip an excellent *licuado,* and wonder in awe that you can eat this well for L90.

Café Welchez (breakfast L40-77; ☺ 6:45am-9:45pm) Whoa Nelly! What's that Banoffee pie doing in this tranquil Honduran *pueblo*? God only knows, but it's insanely good. The best coffee is still Espresso Americano (also on the square) but this dessert and caffeine shop is more of a local tradition. Breakfast is cheap and there's always a fresh selection of delectable cakes and pies (L20 to L35). It's part of the Hotel Marina Copán complex.

La Casa de Todo (mains L64-118; **V**) Homemade bread, yoghurt and organic coffee are dished up in this cafe's verdant garden; veggie options, including salads, are good. The service can be slow. Mainly light meals and snacks are served.

ViaVia Café (mains L65-110; ☺ 6:30am-midnight) This inventive restaurant specializes in meat-optional, vegetarian-slanted global cuisine. The adjoining bar – Copán's liveliest – keeps the atmosphere frenzied in the evenings, usually at the hands of DJ Diego. Or, if you fancy a slower pace, take a seat on the outdoor terrace during the day and watch Copán amble by. Current pirated Hollywood fare is screened Sunday, Monday and Tuesday at 7pm (L20).

Picame (mains L70-125) A great-value hole-in-the-wall with the hardest-working chefs in town (a Dutch-Honduran partnership). The burgers are freshly prepared, and the *baleadas* are big and filling. Order a day in advance from a laundry list of sandwiches for box lunches to go. CNN – what many Hondurans now refer to as the Chavez News Network for its supposed biased coverage of the Zelaya affair – is often on the tube if you need to check what is happening in the world.

Carnitas Nia Lola (main L105-355; ☺ 7am-10pm) You could deal a poker hand in a straitjacket faster then the service here, but stiff daiquiris ensure you soon won't care. It's a bit of a theme bar, all saloon doors, faux antique clutter and paraphernalia, but this remains a bustling, open-air meeting and eating place two blocks south of the plaza. The *anafres* (free with meals) are quite a production here, heated by fiery coals from the grill, but not as Hollywood as the waitresses and their impressive platter-balancing skills – on their heads. There are a few veggie choices but really it's all about the *carne* – and the interesting ménage à trois of tourists, families and local drunks.

our pick Twisted Tanya's (2-/3-course meals L380/420; 10am-10pm Mon-Sat) If you have traveled in Honduras longer than about 12 hours, you will have heard of Tanya. She is the larger-than-life personality who runs this funky restaurant/bar that is so easy to love. From spicy curries to jalapeño filet mignon to house-made bagels, you can't go wrong here and Tanya does nothing half-assed. The cocktail menu is one of the most extensive in the country and there are L120 backpacker specials nightly from 3pm to 6pm to offset the upscale prices of the main menu. Tanya used to run the Twisted Toucan in Roatán and is a good source of information on the Bay Islands, where her husband, the bartender, is from.

Drinking

ViaVia Café is the most popular bar in town and Twisted Tanya's is also a good spot for a night of imbibing.

Wine Barcito (5pm-midnight Sun-Thu, to 2am Fri & Sat) This breezy 2nd-floor bar dishes up cocktails (L60 to L80) and several Argentine/Chilean reds by the glass. The improvised lounge cushions, set upon Cervecería Hondureña beer crates, are an interesting design touch, as is the line of tables bucking up against some menacing power lines.

Shopping

Items to look out for are leatherwear, woven baskets, textiles from Guatemala and tobacco. Check out La Casa de Todo east of the park, and the **Mercado Artesanal**, a block south of the park. Perhaps the most enticing souvenirs are replica Maya carvings made by a local man called **Lito Lara** (651-4980). He keeps a few

wares in his home in town, but has moved his main operation and shop 1km out of town on the road to the Guatemalan border.

Getting There & Away

Minibuses and pickups to and from Copán Ruinas to the Guatemalan border depart every 25 minutes (or when full), 6am to 4pm, and charge around L20. On the Guatemala side, buses to Esquipulas and Chiquimula leave the border regularly until about 5pm.

Transportes Casasola (651-4078) is a cheaper way of getting to San Pedro Sula (L110, three hours, departs 5am, 6am, 7am and 2pm) with connections on to Tela and La Ceiba. Its luxury coaches run at a fraction of the Hedman Alas prices – although they do pack in the passengers. The office is next door to the Hotel Clásico Copán, east of the Parque Central, though had plans to relocate to the nearby Calle Acropolis caddy corner from the soccer field. It also runs to Santa Rosa de Copán (L80, 2½ hours) once daily at 6:40am.

Hedman Alas (651-4037) has its terminal just outside of town. It offers luxury service to San Pedro Sula (L323 to L380, three hours), Tegucigalpa (L485 to L580, seven hours) and La Ceiba (L485 to L580, seven hours); departures at 5:15am, 10:30am and 2:30pm daily. It also goes to Antigua, Guatemala (L708 to L1008, six hours) at 2:20pm each day.

If you want to leave at another time, you can easily take a bus to La Entrada (L45, two hours) and transfer there to San Pedro Sula, or to Santa Rosa de Copán. Buses to La Entrada depart every 40 minutes from 5am to 5pm.

Getting Around

Little three-wheeled mototaxis whizz around the cobbled streets. The going rate for a ride

GETTING TO ANTIGUA, GUATEMALA

Several operators, including **Basecamp** (651-4695; www.basecamphonduras.com; 7am-9pm), run shuttles between Guatemala and Copán Ruinas (L247, six hours, twice daily). Scheduled shuttles leave Copán and can drop you in Guatemala City (five hours) en route.

Moneychangers will approach you on both sides of the **El Florido** (24hr) border anxious to change Guatemalan quetzals for Honduran lempiras, or either for US dollars. Usually they're offering a decent rate because there's a Guatemalan bank right there and the current exchange rate is posted in the Honduran immigration office – look for it. There's no bank on the Honduran side of the border. US dollars may be accepted at some establishments in Copán Ruinas, but it's best to change some money into lempiras.

Legally speaking, there is no charge to leave Honduras, though border guards here try to charge a small fee (L20). Ask for a receipt or to see the law in writing. There is a Q10 charge to enter Guatemala.

around town is L8 to L10 for locals. Double that for foreign tourists. You don't have to pay gringo rates – it just depends on negotiation skills (in Spanish) and persistence.

AROUND COPÁN RUINAS

Macaw Mountain (☎ 651-4245; www.macawmountain. com; admission L190; ☺ 9am-5pm) is a beautifully landscaped bird sanctuary about 2.5km outside of the town center. It is the brainchild of a former Roatán resident whose flock of rescued, abandoned and endangered birds started at 90 and has grown to 170. The birds, which include macaws, parrots, toucans and some raptors, are treated with real care. Some are allowed out of their cages at feeding time, squawking and interacting with visitors. The entrance fee is valid for three days. A restaurant and cafe are onsite. A mototaxi from town costs around L20 but you can walk it in 30 minutes. Be sure to ask about day trips to Finca Miramundo, its certified eco-sustainable coffee plantation located at 1300m in the cloud forest up the mountain, where an overnight lodge is also in the works.

Visiting the **Finca El Cisne** (☎ 651-4695, www. fincaelcisne.com; r per person incl 3 meals, horseback tour & admission to thermal baths L1460) highlands coffee and cardamom plantation, 24km from Copán Ruinas, is more a privileged invitation into a traditional hacienda family home than a tour. Founded in the 1920s and still operating, the *finca* (plantation) raises cattle and grows coffee and cardamom, but also produces corn, avocado, breadfruit, plantain, beans, oranges, star fruit and even some wood trees. Day tours include guided horseback riding through the forests and pastures (sometimes with a stop to swim in the nearby Rió Blanco) and tours of the coffee and cardamom fields and processing facilities. If you come during February or October, you can help out with the harvest. Carlos Castejón, a friendly, English-speaking, US-trained agronomist whose family owns the *finca*, leads most tours. Lodging is in a homey cabin; meals (cooked in a traditional wood-fired stove) and a visit to nearby hot springs are included. See Basecamp (p371) in Copán Ruinas for booking.

Day tours (per person L1120) include transportation to and from Copán Ruinas and lunch.

A set of well-done hot springs, **aguas termales** (admission L200; ☺ 10am-10pm), are 24km north of Copán Ruinas, a lovely hour's drive through fertile mountains and coffee plantations. On one side of the river are cheaper, less developed springs, while across the way you'll find the 'spa,' a set of nicer springs amid a Maya motif.

COPÁN ARCHAEOLOGICAL SITE

One of the most important of all Maya civilizations lived, prospered then mysteriously crumbled around the **Copán archaeological site** (☎ 651-4108; www.ihah.hn; general admission L285, museum L133, tunnels L285; ☺ 8am-4pm), now a Unesco World Heritage Site. During the Classic period (AD 250–900), the city at Copán Ruinas culturally dominated the region for centuries. The architecture is not as grand as Tikal's but the city produced remarkable sculptures and hieroglyphics. Its culture was so developed, it is often labeled the 'Paris of the Maya world.' For a fuller understanding, be sure to visit the excellent Museum of Sculpture at the site.

The ruins are a pleasant 1km stroll outside of Copán. A visitors center, the museum and a cafe-gift shop are at the main entrance. A larger gift shop and a good cheap *comedor* are nearby. The **Asociación Guís Copán** (☎ 651-4108; guiascopan@yahoo.com) has a small kiosk at the entrance, where certified guides wait politely for hire – no accosting tourists! Guides are recommended and English, German, Italian and French are spoken. They are pricey but you can offset by grouping up. Prices for

---

SPLURGE

Hacienda San Lucas (☎ 651-4495; www.haciendasanlucas.com; s/d incl breakfast L2612/2992; P ⏰) is a beautifully restored traditional hacienda on the tranquil outskirts of Copán. You have to dig deep to stay here…but there are other ways to get the flavor of the place. There is a terrifically atmospheric restaurant serving local extrovert Flavia Cueva's justifiably famous 'Maya restoration cuisine,' a five-course culinary journey not to be missed (limited seating – call ahead). Horseback riding (L1500) and hiking (entrance L60) are popular here too, for the beautiful views of town. A new yoga pavilion overlooks Copán's Acropolis (call for classes). The grounds include Los Sapos (the Toads), a Maya archaeological site believed to be related to fertility rites. Cueva has won ecological awards for the efforts here, including its 50% reliance on solar power.

groups up to nine people for the ruins alone are L475, for 10 to 19 people, L570 and so on. It is cheaper to hire guides onsite, but they are less specialized. In town, you can find pricier options with specializations. A gaggle of beautiful wild (though nearly domesticated) macaws greet visitors as you enter the site.

The booklet *History Carved in Stone: A Guide to the Archaeological Park of the Ruins of Copán* by William L Fash and Ricardo Agurcia Fasquelle, is usually available from the visitors center. For further reading see *Scribes, Warriors and Kings* by William Fash (2001), a smooth and comprehensible overview with less archaeological-ese; and *Chronical of the Maya Kings and Queens, 2nd Edition* (2008) by Simon Martin and Nikolai Grube, whose Copán chapter is the best guide yet published to the ruins.

History
PRE-COLUMBIAN HISTORY
From dating pottery discovered in the area, scientists believe people have lived in the Copán valley for more than two millennia – since at least 1200 BC. Craft and trade seemed to thrive early on – excavated artifacts show influences from as far afield as central Mexico.

Around AD 426, one royal family came to rule Copán, led by a mysterious king named K'inich Yax K'uk' Mo' (Great Sun Lord Quetzal Macaw). He was associated with the massive urban state in Mexico known today as Teotihuacan, but probably hailed from the city of Caracol in modern Belize. He ruled from 426 to 435. Archaeological evidence indicates that he was a great shaman and warrior; 16 later kings revered him as the semidivine founder of the city. His dynasty ruled throughout Copán's golden age.

The early kings (from 435–628) mostly remain shrouded in mystery – only a few names have come to light: K'inich Popol Hol, the second king; Ku Ix, the fourth king; Waterlily Jaguar, the seventh; Moon Jaguar, the 10th; and Butz' Chan, the 11th.

Under the great Smoke Imix (Smoke Jaguar), the 12th king, Copán's military and trading might grew stronger. For more than half a century (628–695), Smoke Imix consolidated and expanded power, and the city grew. He might have even taken over the nearby princedom of Quiriguá, as one of the famous stelae there bears his name and image. During his rule, some of the city's most magnificent temples and monuments were built. By the time he died, many more people had come to live in thriving Copán.

The warlike 13th king, Waxaklajuun Ub'aah K'awiil (popularly known as 18 Rabbit), began his rule in 695. Under him, the intricate, skillful craftsmen and sculptors for which the city became famed really began to flourish. 18 Rabbit also wasted no time seeking further military conquests – but little good it did him in the end. In a battle with the forces of neighboring Quirigua and their King K'ak Tiliw Chan Yoaat (Cauac Sky), 18 Rabbit's life came to a grisly end when he was captured and beheaded in 738. Perhaps his gruesome demise marked the beginning of the end of Copán's heyday. Certainly, his successor, K'ak' Joplaj Chan K'awiil (Smoke Monkey), the 14th king (738–749), left little mark on Copán.

Possibly in a bid to record or restore the city's former glories, Smoke Monkey's son, K'ak' Yipyaj Chan K'awiil (Smoke Shell; 749–763), commissioned some of Copán's most famous buildings and completed the city's most important monument, the great Hieroglyphic Stairway. This immortalizes the achievements of the dynasty from its establishment until 755, when the stairway was dedicated. It bears the longest such ancient inscription ever discovered in the Maya region, and the longest pre-Columbian indigenous inscription in the entire world.

Yax Pasaj (Sunrise or First Dawn; 763–820), Smoke Shell's successor and the 16th king of Copán, continued to build and renovate Copán throughout his long reign. However, the dynasty's power was now clearly declining and its subjects had fallen on hard times. The final ruler of the dynasty, U Cit Tok', came to power around 822. His reign was mysteriously cut short, indicating that one single event – perhaps a military defeat – caused the end of a dynasty that spanned four centuries.

Archaeologists are still working out what happened to the Maya at the end of the Classic period; what caused the collapse and abandonment of so many cities? The best evidence at present points to a series of major 8th-century droughts from which dozens of kingdoms never recovered. The integration that characterized Classic Maya society, and that supported the institution of divine kingship, was probably not sustainable after that time.

HONDURAS

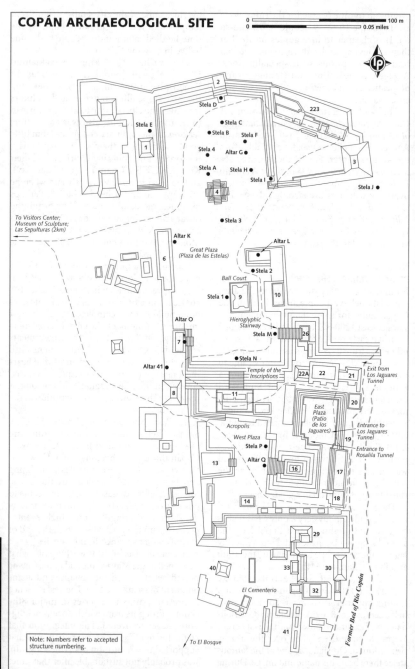

COPÁN ARCHAEOLOGICAL SITE

0 ——————————— 100 m
0 ——————————— 0.05 miles

2

Stela D

223

Stela E

Stela C
Stela B
Stela F

1

Stela 4
Altar G

3

Stela A
Stela H
Stela I

4

Stela J

To Visitors Center;
Museum of Sculpture;
Las Sepulturas (2km)

Stela 3

Altar K

Altar L

Great Plaza
(Plaza de las Estelas)

6

Stela 2

Ball Court

Stela 1
9
10

Hieroglyphic
Stairway

Altar O

Stela M
26

7

Stela N

Exit from
Los Jaguares
Tunnel

Altar 41

Temple of the
Inscriptions

22A   22   21

8

11

20

East
Plaza
(Patio
de los
Jaguares)

Entrance to
Los Jaguares
Tunnel

Acropolis

West Plaza

Stela P

19

Entrance to
Rosalila Tunnel

13

Altar Q

16

17

14

18

29

40

33

30

El Cementerio

32

41

To El Bosque

Former Bed of Río Copán

Note: Numbers refer to accepted
structure numbering.

HONDURAS

EUROPEAN DISCOVERY

The first known European to see the ruins was Diego García de Palacio, a representative of Spanish King Philip II, who lived in Guatemala and traveled through the region. On March 8, 1576, he wrote to the king about the ruins he found here. Only about five families were living here then, and they knew nothing of the history of the ruins. The discovery was not pursued, and almost three centuries went by until another Spaniard, Colonel Juan Galindo, visited the ruins and made the first map of them.

Galindo's report stimulated Americans John L Stephens and Frederick Catherwood to come to Copán on their Central American journey in 1839. When Stephens published the book *Incidents of Travel in Central America, Chiapas, and Yucatán* in 1841, illustrated by Catherwood, the ruins first became known to the world at large.

TODAY

The history of the ruins still unfolds today, as archaeologists continue to probe the site. The remains of thousands of structures have been found in the 27 sq km surrounding the Principal Group, most of them within about 1km of the Principal Group. In a wider zone, thousands more structures have been detected in hundreds of sites in the 135 sq km surrounding the ruins. These discoveries indicate that at the peak of Maya civilization here, around the end of the 8th century, the valley of Copán had over a minimum of 20,000 inhabitants – a population not reached again until the 1980s.

In addition to examining the area around the Principal Group, archaeologists are continuing to explore and make new discoveries at the Principal Group itself. Five separate phases of building on this site have been identified; the final phase, dating from AD 650 to 820, is what we see today. But buried underneath the visible ruins are layers of other ruins, which archaeologists are exploring by means of underground tunnels. This is how the Rosalila temple was found, a replica of which is now in the Museum of Sculpture; below Rosalila are other earlier temples such as Margarita, and even earlier, Hunal, which contains the tomb of the founder of the dynasty, Yax K'uk' Mo'.

Occasionally the ruins are a stage for more controversial, political actions. In September 2005, 1500 indigenous Maya Ch'orti', descendants of the original builders of Copán, occupied the ruins and barred visitors. Their five-day occupation of the site was in protest at stalled government land reforms, aimed at giving indigenous communities a way of lifting themselves out of poverty. At least one Maya Ch'orti' leader has been killed in the past decade. While the protests have subsided recently, the difficult social conditions for many of the 8000 Maya Ch'orti' in the area remains a major, unresolved issue.

Museum of Sculpture

While Tikal is celebrated for its tall temple pyramids and Palenque is renowned for its limestone relief panels, Copán is unique in the Maya world for its sculpture. Some of the finest examples are on display at this impressive museum, opened in August 1996. Entering the museum is an experience by itself: You go through the mouth of a serpent and wind through the entrails of the beast before suddenly emerging into a fantastic world of sculpture and light.

The highlight of the museum is a full-scale replica of the Rosalila temple, which was discovered in nearly perfect condition by archaeologists in 1989 by means of a tunnel dug into Structure 16, the central building of the Acropolis. Rosalila, dedicated in AD 571 by Copán's 10th ruler, Moon Jaguar, was apparently so sacred that when Structure 16 was built over it, Rosalila was not destroyed but was left completely intact. The original Rosalila temple is inside the core of Structure 16.

The Principal Group

The Principal Group is a group of ruins about 400m beyond the visitors center, across well-kept lawns, through a gate in a strong fence and down shady avenues of trees.

STELAE OF THE GREAT PLAZA

The path leads to the Great Plaza and the huge, intricately carved stone stelae portraying the rulers of Copán. Most of Copán's best stelae date from AD 613 to 738, especially from the reigns of Smoke Imix (628–95) and 18 Rabbit (695–738). All seem to have originally been painted; a few traces of red paint survive on Stela C. Many stelae had vaults beneath or beside them in which sacrifices and offerings could be placed.

Many of the stelae on the Great Plaza portray King 18 Rabbit, including Stelae A, B, C, D, F, H and 4, and are remarkable in the Maya area for being carved in high relief. Perhaps the most beautiful stela in the Great Plaza is Stela A (731); the original has been moved inside the Museum of Sculpture, and the one outdoors is a reproduction. Nearby, and almost equal in beauty, are Stela 4 (731); Stela B (731), depicting 18 Rabbit upon his accession to the throne; and Stela C (AD 782), with a turtle-shaped altar in front. This last stela has figures on both sides.

At the northern end of the Great Plaza, at the base of Structure 2, Stela D (736) also portrays King 18 Rabbit. On its back are two columns of hieroglyphs; at its base is an altar with fearsome representations of Chac, the rain god. In front of the altar is the burial place of Dr John Owens, an archaeologist with an expedition from Harvard's Peabody Museum, who died during work in 1893.

On the eastern side is Stela F (721), arguably the most beautiful of 18 Rabbit's sculptures. It has a more lyrical design, with the robes of the main figure flowing around to the other side of the stone, where there are glyphs. Stela H (730) might depict a queen or princess rather than a king. Stela J, further off to the east and probably the earliest of 18 Rabbit's stelae, resembles the stelae of Quiriguá in that it is covered in glyphs forming an intriguing mat design, the symbol for kingship, instead of human figures.

Stela E (614), erected on top of Structure 1 on the west side of the Great Plaza, is among the oldest stelae. Stela 1 (692), on the structure that runs along the east side of the plaza, is of a person wearing a mask. Altar G (800), commissioned by Yax Pasaj and showing twin serpent heads, is among the last monuments carved at Copán.

BALL COURT & HIEROGLYPHIC STAIRWAY

South of the Great Plaza, across what is known as the Central Plaza, is the ball court (Juego de Pelota; AD 731), the second-largest in Central America. It is not exactly clear how this game was played, although participants probably kept a hard rubber ball in the air without using their hands; Casa K'inich (p370) has a video reconstruction. The one you see is the third or fourth ball court built in this spot; the other two smaller ones were buried by this construction. Note the macaw heads carved at the top of the sloping walls. The central marker in the court was the work of King 18 Rabbit.

South of the ball court is Copán's most famous monument, the Hieroglyphic Stairway, the work of 18 Rabbit. Today it's protected from the elements by a massive tarp. This lessens the impact of its beauty, but you can still get an idea of how it looked. The flight of 63 steps bears a history – in several thousand glyphs – of the royal house of Copán; the steps are bordered by ramps inscribed with more reliefs and glyphs. The story inscribed on the steps begins by noting the death and burial inside the stairway of the 12th king and goes on to discuss the history of the later dynasty but is still not completely understood, because the stairway was partially ruined and the stones jumbled.

At the base of the Hieroglyphic Stairway is Stela M (AD 756), bearing a figure (probably King Smoke Shell) in a feathered cloak; glyphs tell of the solar eclipse in that year. The altar in front shows a plumed serpent with a human head emerging from its jaws.

Beside the stairway, a tunnel leads to the tomb of a nobleman, a royal scribe who might have been the son of King Smoke Imix. The tomb, discovered in 1989, held a trove of painted pottery and beautiful carved jade objects that are now in Honduran museums.

ACROPOLIS

The lofty flight of steps to the south of the Hieroglyphic Stairway is called the **Temple of the Inscriptions**. On top of the stairway, the walls are carved with groups of hieroglyphs. South of the stairway are the most secluded areas of the Acropolis. These are organized into the **East Plaza** and the **West Plaza**. The West Plaza is bordered on the east by temple 16 dedicated by Yax Pasaj. At the base rests a replica of his famed Altar q (AD 776), among the most famous sculptures here; the original is inside the Museum of Sculpture. Around its sides, carved in superb relief, are the 16 great kings of Copán, ending with the altar's creator, Yax Pasaj. Beneath the altar was a sacrificial vault in which archaeologists discovered the bones of 15 jaguars and several macaws that were probably sacrificed to the glory of Yax Pasaj, and his that were probably sacrificed to Yax Pasaj's predecessors. On the north side of the East Plaza sits the throne building of 18 Rabbit, with its serpent-mouth doorway and interior sculpture.

TUNNELS

In 1999, archaeologists opened up to the public two tunnels that allow visitors to get a glimpse of pre-existing structures below the visible surface structures. The first, **Rosalila tunnel**, is very short and takes only a few visitors at a time. The famous temple is only barely exposed, and behind thick glass. The other tunnel, **Los Jaguares**, was originally 700m in length, but a large section has been closed, reducing it to about 80m, running along the foundations of Temple 22. This tunnel exits on the outside of the main site, so you must walk around the base and rear of the main site to get back in again. While fascinating, it's hard to justify the L285 extra you pay to get in.

Las Sepulturas

Often overlooked by visitors, Las Sepulturas is a tranquil escape from the crowds at the main ruins. Although not as grand, the excavations here have shed light on the daily life of the Maya of Copán during its golden age.

Las Sepulturas, once connected to the Great Plaza by a 1km causeway, was possibly the residential area of rich, powerful nobles and religious leaders. One huge, luxurious compound seems to have housed some 250 people in 40 or 50 buildings arranged around 11 courtyards. The principal structure, called the House of the Bakabs (officials), had outer walls carved with full-size figures of 10 males in fancy feathered headdresses; inside was a massive hieroglyphic bench.

To get to the site, you have to walk out of the parking lot entrance to the main ruins, turn right, and follow the pleasant white flagstone walking path, then right again at the sign.

SANTA ROSA DE COPÁN
pop 48,000

Santa Rosa de Copán is a cool mountain town with cobbled streets and some lovely, restored colonial buildings. Its size and hustle-bustle atmosphere definitely steal some of the colonial thunder – it's far less tranquil than Gracias, for example – but it also has more to offer, including some great bars and restaurants and far better preserved architecture. However, it doesn't have any world-class sights like Copán Ruinas and, consequently, not as many tourists, which is part of its charm. It's actually a perfect place for extended stays.

The annual **festival day** is August 30. The town is also renowned for its colorful **Semana Santa** celebrations.

The town is up on a hill, 1.5km from the bus terminal on the highway. Most hotels are a short walk from the Parque Central, which has the police station to the north side, a lovely cathedral to the east and Hondutel to the west.

Information

Banco Atlántida (1a Calle NO at 3a Av NO) Changes traveler's checks and gives cash advances on Visa cards. No ATM.
Banco del Occidente (Parque Central) In the same building as Western Union, it changes traveler's checks and gives cash advances on Visa cards.
Banet/Unibanc ATM (1a Calle) Just down from Banco del Occidente, takes Visa, Cirrus, MasterCard and American Express.
Bonsai Cyber Café (Calle Real Centenario btwn 2a Av & 3a Av NO; per hr L16; 9am-10pm) Fancy equipment and *cabinas*, slow internet connection.
Hondutel (Parque Central; 7am-9pm) Telephone services.
Police (662-0214)
Post office (Parque Central; 8am-4pm Mon-Fri, 8am-noon Sat)
Tourist office (662-2234; www.visitesantarosedeco pan.org; 8am-6pm Mon-Fri, 9am-5pm Sat) In a kiosk in the central park, it has plenty of suggestions for places to eat and stay within Santa Rosa, as well as details on the town's cultural significance and historic buildings; and arranges tours. Internet access is L15 per hour with fast connection.

Sights

La Flor de Copán Cigar Factory (662-0185; tours L40; 10am & 2pm Mon-Fri), 2km out of town, shows visitors the craft behind making hand-rolled cigars. A taxi from town costs L40. Tours are available in English. If you just want to smoke some, there's a store on Calle Real Centenario at 3a Av NO.

Those who love a good cup of coffee can see how their favorite bean is prepared at **Beneficio Maya** (662-1665; www.cafecopan.com; Colonia San Martín; 7am-noon & 1:30-5pm Mon-Sat), a coffee-processing plant. Tours to nearby *fincas* run during the coffee harvest season (November to February). Call a day in advance.

Tours

Lenca Land Trails (662-1128; lencatours@gmail.com; Calle Real Centenario near 3a Av NO; 8am-noon) is run by Max Elvir, a well-known local guide, who operates out of Hotel Elvir and offers highly recommended tours to nearby indigenous Lenca villages and Parque Nacional Montaña de Celaque. Max speaks English.

Sleeping

Hotel El Rosario (662-0211; 3a Av NE btwn 1a & 2a Calles; r per person without bathroom L150, with bathroom L200) Two blocks east of the park, next door to a dodgy by-the-hour place, this hotel is impeccably kept with no-frills rooms off a

HONDURAS

long corridor. Beds are a bit soft but skylights add some natural brightness. It is managed by the *señora* who runs the pharmacy next door.

Hotel Alondra's (☎ 662-1194; 3a Av SO btwn 1a & 2a Calles SE; s/d/tr L300/500/700) One of the new options in town, this is a wholesome, family-run place, kept scrupulously tidy. The one drawback is the slightly gloomy rooms, but the private bathrooms all have hot water.

Hotel VIP Copán (☎ 662-0265; hotelvipcopan@hotmail.com; cnr 1a Calle NE & 3a Av NE; s/d with fan L445/695, s/d with air-con L645/845; P ⬚ ⬚ ⬚) This central option has very comfortable albeit totally lifeless rooms with uncreased bedspreads and shiny-tiled bathrooms. Some do not let much natural light in, which might be good if you don't fancy waking up at 5am with the roosters. Its adjoining Restaurante Mundo Maya (mains L40 to L220) has a good reputation locally.

Posada de Carlos y Blanca (☎ 662-1028; astrid_ixel@hotmail.com; Calle Real Centenario near 4a Av SO; s/d incl breakfast L440/661; P ⬚) There's a warm family setting at this comfy midrange in a converted home. The English-speaking daughter, Astrid, is a lifesaver here, helping and hosting where most of the day help can't, and the breakfast is wonderful. Reservations are hard to come by.

Eating

Ten Napel Café (1a Calle NO btwn 2a & 3a Avs NO; items L16-60; ⬚ 8:30am-noon & 2-7pm Mon-Sat) A fitting coffeehouse for cafe country, this cozy spot churns out excellent lattes and cappuccinos, *licuados* (L30) for non-caffeine junkies and even wine by the glass. There's a great garden patio as well.

Pizza Pizza (Calle Real Centenario near 6a Av NE; pizza L38-260; ⬚ 11:30am-9pm Thu-Tue) This appealing pizzeria concentrates on delivering the finest brick-oven pizza in town as well as hunger-killing doorstopper sandwiches. There's also an English-language book exchange here.

Tío Kike (1a Av SE near 1a Calle SE; mains L65-120; ⬚ 9am-7pm Mon-Thu, to 10pm Fri & Sat) An unexpectedly appealing hole-in-the-wall that serves up good *típica*. The roasted chicken and fruit smoothies are particularly good.

Zotz (Calle Real Centenario btwn 2a & 3a Av; mains L75-220; ⬚ noon-midnight) From John Travolta albums and an upright bass to antique sewing machines, the walls in this always-crowded bar/restaurant are cluttered with so much kitsch Americana paraphernalia, it looks like a garage sale turned home-makeover show. The bar-food menu is all over the place, like an Applebee's on Honduran acid, and the bar itself is one of Honduras' best. It's the kind of place that when you walk through the doors, you know everything's gonna be alright.

El Rodeo (1a Av SE btwn 1a & 2a Calles SE; mains L125-230; ⬚ 10am-10pm Mon-Thu, to 4am Fri & Sat) This Southwestern-themed steakhouse doubles as a surprisingly good boho bar Thursday to Saturday nights with live music from 9pm. The food is definitely carnivore territory, with a wealth of well-prepared gaucho cuts to choose from.

Drinking & Entertainment

The View (cnr Calle Real Centenario & 4a Av NE; cover L50-100; ⬚ 7:30pm-7am Wed-Sat) This is where you'll find the well-to-do and hot to trot – and door security that must think it's in a city like the logo, not little old Santa Rosa. It's a trendy upstairs dance bar and terrace that goes until sunrise. Leave the flip-flops and Tevas at home.

Flamingos (1a Av SE near 1a Calle SE; ⬚ 10am-11pm Mon-Wed, to 3am Thu-Sat) A flamingo-themed resto-bar seems a tad Palm Springs-ish, but this spot hops, both for its good seafood, and the crowd that comes to drink and dance after 10pm on Thursdays and weekends. But if you have a flamingo phobia, this is definitely not your bag.

Cinema Don Quijote (☎ 662-2625; Plaza Saavedra, 1a Calle NE at 3a Av NE; L40) Shows late-release Hollywood films at 7pm nightly.

Getting There & Away

Most Santa Rosa de Copán buses come and go from the Terminal de Transporte on the main highway, 1.5km from town. A *colectivo* into town costs L40.

Sultana de Occidente (☎ 662-0940) buses to Tegucigalpa, San Pedro Sula and Agua Caliente (Guatemala) depart from a separate terminal next door. **Congolón** (☎ 662-3834) has a terminal further up the highway nearer town and is another option for San Pedro Sula and Nueva Ocotepeque.

If you're going to San Pedro Sula, best catch a direct bus, which stops only once (at La Entrada). The regular buses are more frequent but slower.

Destinations from Santa Rosa:

Copán Ruinas (L80; 3hr) One *directo* bus at 2pm (Casasola Espress); otherwise best to go direct to La Entrada and transfer.

Gracias (L40; 1½hr; every 30min)

La Entrada (L35; 1¼hr; every 30min from 6am-6pm) Same buses as to San Pedro Sula; or direct microbuses.

Nueva Ocotepeque Sultana buses (L70; 1½hr; hourly from 12:30pm-7pm) It's L90 to continue on to the border at Agua Caliente (2½ hours).

San Juan/La Esperanza One direct bus daily to San Juan (L70; 3hr) and La Esperanza (L100; 4hr) at 11am.

San Pedro Sula Sultana (L90; 2½hr; hourly from 4am-1pm); Congolón (L90; 3½hr; 1:30pm, 3pm, 3:30pm & 4pm)

San Salvador Several companies take turns heading to San Salvador via El Poy (L266; 4hr). Departures are at 8:30am from Restaurant JM at the Terminal.

Tegucigalpa Sultana (L198; 7hr; hourly from 4am-1pm)

GRACIAS
pop 43,600

Gracias is a small, tranquil cobblestone town 47km southeast of Santa Rosa de Copán. For a brief time in the 16th century, it was the capital of all Spanish-conquered Central America. Traces of its former grandeur remain in its centuries-old buildings and various colonial churches. The pace of life along its cobblestone streets rarely moves much faster than walking.

Gracias was founded in 1526 by Spanish Captain Juan de Chavez; its original name was Gracias a Dios (Thanks to God). The Audiencia de los Confines, the governing council for Central America, was established here on April 16, 1544; the buildings that the council occupied are still here. Eventually the town's importance was eclipsed by Antigua (Guatemala) and Comayagua.

The area around Gracias is mountainous and beautiful. Much of it is forested. The town makes a good base for exploring Parque Nacional Celaque.

Orientation & Information

Gracias is a small town and everything is within walking distance except an ATM – you'll need to go to Santa Rosa de Copán for that. The post office and Hondutel are side by side, a block south of the shiny new Parque Central, renovated in 2009 with seemingly a new park bench for each of its citizens. The police are also in the park. Oddly, street numbering here is some of the best in Honduras, but still no names.

Banco de Occidente (Parque Central) Exchanges traveler's checks and US dollars.

Ecolem (per hr L16; ☼ 8am-8pm) Internet access.

El Jarrón crafts shop (☎ 9870-8821; guiamarco lencas@yahoo.com) On the road to La Esperanza, here you'll find Marco Aurelio, who can arrange/guide hikes in Celaque (L250 to L800), trips to La Campa and San Manuel De Colohete (L450 to L800), three-hour horseback-riding

trips (L300 per person), bike rental (per hour L30) and tent rental (per night L70 to L80).

Hospital Dr Juan Manuel Galvez (☎ 656-1100; Carretera a Santa Rosa de Copán; ☼ 24hr)

Lavandería La Estrella (per lb L10; ☼ 8am-5pm Mon-Sat)

Tourist office (Parque Central kiosk; ☼ 8am-noon & 1:30-4:30pm Mon-Fri) Has some useful information binders. You'll need to speak Spanish.

Sights & Activities

High on a hill west of the Parque Central, **Castillo San Cristóbal** (☼ 7am-5pm) is worth the walk for its excellent views of the town. Gracias has several colonial *iglesias:* **San Marcos**, **Las Mercedes** and **San Sebastián**. Next door to the Iglesia de San Marcos, the **Sede de la Audiencia de los Confines**, important in the town's history, is now the *casa parroquial*, the residence for the parish priest. This church is one of the few you will find on a central park with an entrance facing elsewhere.

Casa Galeano (☎ 625-5407; admission L30; ☼ 9am-6pm) is in a beautiful restored colonial house with extensive gardens; this new museum does not fulfill its potential. There is beautiful flooring, an interesting local history and summary of the Lenca culture but signage is in Spanish only.

Most of the area's other attractions, including fine hot springs and the Parque Nacional Montaña de Celaque, are a few kilometers out of town (see p383).

Sleeping

Hotel Erick (☎ 656-1066; r L150; Ⓟ) A perennial favorite among the budget-traveler crowd, this is a clean, family-run hotel. Beds are on the saggy side, but this is the best cheapie option in town, if you can cope with bare cement as a design scheme. All rooms have a cold-water bathroom. You can ask about tours and transport to the national park here, although you will need some Spanish.

Finca Bavaria (☎ 656-1372; s/d/tr L200/250/400) Set on a neglected 35,000-sq-m *finca de café* (coffee plantation), this once was probably a tranquil and interesting budget option Now the whole thing just seems to be deteriorating.

our pick Hotel y Restaurante Guancascos (☎ 656-1219; www.guancascos.com; s/d/tr from L350/420/600; Ⓟ ⓦ) The comfortable rooms here are the most tastefully decorated in Gracias, while the top rooms (12, 13 and 14) have fine views over town, as does the terrace restaurant, a good place for meeting fellow travelers.

Hotel Tres Piedras (☎ 656-0880; trespiedras@yahoo. es; s/d/tr L430/624/825; P 🛜) A welcome addition on the scene in 2009, this smart hotel is almost boutique. The 16 rooms are well appointed with elegant bedspreads. There's also an interesting open-air courtyard featuring chains to catch the rain and deliver it to the gardens and not the hallways and common areas (the owner is an engineer).

Posada de Don Juan (☎ 656-1020; www.posadade donjuan.com; s/d/tr from L771/991/1432; P 🛇 💻 📶) Though this definitely has more style than other places in town (draping bougainvillea, artsy black-and-white photographs of town), the rooms are modern and clean but too simple for the price, and it all seems out of context with the town's general price point. But it has a wonderful pool and a good restaurant.

Eating & Drinking

For good, cheap street eats, head to the area known as Calle 8, which has become somewhat of a hangout.

`ourpick` **Rinconcito Graciano** (mains L40-70; ⏲ 10-11:30am & 7-9pm) Though the restaurant now plays second fiddle to owner Lizeth Perdomo's newborn (hence the limited hours, subject to normalization by 2011), don't miss a meal here if you can help it. Perdomo serves traditional Lencan dishes, prepared with organic ingredients, on lovely wooden tables in a bohemian setting. Dishes and drinks are served in traditional Lencan pottery, which changes the

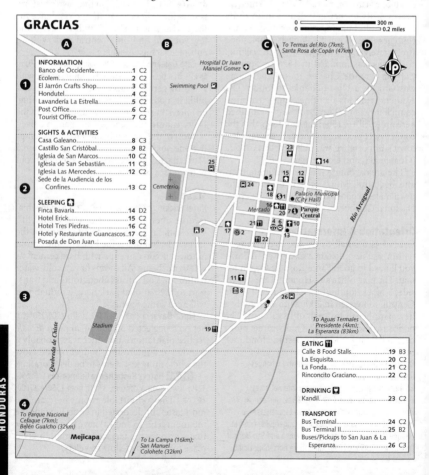

GRACIAS

0 ────── 300 m
0 ────── 0.2 miles

To Termas del Río (7km);
Santa Rosa de Copán (47km)

Hospital Dr Juan Manuel Gomez

Swimming Pool

Cemeterio

Palacio Municipal (City Hall)

Mercado

Parque Central

Río Arcagual

To Aguas Termales Presidente (4km);
La Esperanza (83km)

Quebrada de Chiste

Stadium

To Parque Nacional Celaque (7km);
Belén Gualcho (32km)

Mejicapa

To La Campa (16km);
San Manuel Colohete (32km)

HONDURAS

flavor dynamic. It's one of the most interesting and authentic restaurants in the country.

La Esquisita (mains L50-80; 7am-9pm, to 8pm Sun) Just a few simple home-cooked buffet meals are available here daily and it's always swarmed with locals. The food is quite tasty and filling – like you might get at grandma's house if your grandma were Honduran.

La Fonda (mains L70-90; 10am-10pm) The verbal menu at this inexpensive spot for good *comida típica* varies nightly and is served on tableclothed plastic tables in a salmon-colored house blasting U2 and Men at Work. Weird. But good.

Kandil (7-10pm Tue-Thu, to 1am Fri & Sat) Owned by a young painter/photographer, this culturally aware bar is the only tourist-friendly spot for drinks in Gracias. The candlelit space is beautiful, with rotating exhibitions from local artists. Good sandwiches and quesadillas (L20 to L50) are served, as is the most popular drink, frozen mojitos. The loungy tunes do not include reggaetón or *ranchera*. Where anyone drank in La Ruta Lenca east of Santa Rosa before this, we have no idea.

Getting There & Away

Little mototaxis zip around town, charging L10 for a ride.

The winding mountain road between Gracias and Santa Rosa de Copán is very scenic. Lempira Express buses to Santa Rosa de Copán (L40, 1½ hours) leave the bus terminal every 40 minutes from 5:30am to 5:00pm. See p380 for details on buses coming from Santa Rosa to Gracias.

Three direct services go to San Pedro Sula (L110, three hours, 6am, 8:30am and 9am).

There is no direct service to Copán Ruinas. Catch a bus to La Entrada, then change for Copán Ruinas. It takes around four hours and should cost around L125.

There is some beautiful highland countryside along the road that connects to towns in the southeast, including San Juan (L40, one hour) and La Esperanza (L70, two hours). These buses might sometimes depart from the Terminal II in the morning; but you are better off heading to the improvised stop in front of ENEE (near El Jarrón) on the road out of town to La Esperanza. Departures from there include 5am, 7:15am and 9am and they all must pass here, anyway. The road was still being paved (and widened) during time of research, when the pavement

stretched about halfway to La Esperanza. Catch buses to San Juan and La Esperanza from the last bridge out of town. Pickups are also a tried-and-tested option for these destinations. Catch them from the same place. From San Juan, pickups connect to La Esperanza until the early afternoon.

AROUND GRACIAS

Bathing in the public **Aguas Termales Presidente** (admission L50; 6am-11:30pm) is a memorable experience. It is a roughshod tourist attraction but the setting, practically within a forest, makes it special – where else can you watch wisps of steam rise from natural springs, as lush foliage sways above you? Four kilometers southeast of town, the hot springs have several pools at various temperatures. Go to the baths higher up where the water is warmer. There is a restaurant, bar and grubby changing rooms onsite. It's walkable in an hour or so, but a lot of people hitch rides there and back. On weekends and holidays, this can be way too crowded; consider trying the private **Termas del Río** (656-1304; admission L60; 7:30am-9pm), 7km north of Gracias. These are just as beautiful, better maintained and less crowded, but harder to get to on public transport because mototaxis are not allowed on the main road. Inquire about transport options at Hotel Guancascos.

Several small towns near Gracias are also worth a visit. The Lenca people in this area produce some distinctive handicrafts. **La Campa**, a scenic little town 16km south of Gracias, is particularly known for its excellent black-and-white pottery seen throughout the country. It has two hotels and workshops where you can see craftsmen and women shaping their art.

San Manuel Colohete, 16km past La Campa, is another attractive little mountain town with a beautiful, recently restored, colonial church, famous for its 400-year-old fresco paintings. There is one hotel in town.

A once-daily direct bus to La Campa (L20) leaves from Terminal II in Gracias at noon. You can also catch a 1pm San Manuel Colohete (L40, one hour) bus that passes La Campa on the way. It departs San Manuel back to Gracias about 6am the next morning, so you will need to spend the night and catch a ride back. Travel times can be considerably longer in the rainy season. Hitching is also possible around here.

PARQUE NACIONAL MONTAÑA DE CELAQUE

Celaque (which means, oddly, 'box of water' in the local Lenca dialect) is one of Honduras' most impressive national parks. It boasts **El Cerro de las Minas**, the country's highest peak at 2849m above sea level. Its slopes are covered by lush forest, which evolves in fascinating steps the higher you climb. The park contains the headwaters of several rivers, a majestic waterfall visible from the entire valley, and very steep slopes, including some vertical cliffs, totally inaccessible because of the dense forest.

The park is rich in plant and animal life. Pumas, ocelots and quetzals live here, but they are rarely seen. More common are beautiful butterflies, monkeys, black squirrels and reptiles, but you have to be very quiet and up very early to see much wildlife.

Information

The entrance fee (L50) was payable at the visitors center at the time of research, but there was talk of the money exchange moving into town. Information on hiking in the park is available from Hotel Guancascos or the tourist office in Gracias' central park. A visitors center at 1400m above sea level marks the entrance to the park.

Hiking & Camping

The visitors center no longer offered bunks and a kitchen at time of research, but camping was still allowed (L15 per person). Near the visitors center is a river, which is mighty tempting after a long grueling hike; however,

the river provides drinking water, and so swimming here is strictly prohibited.

The next shelter, Campamento Don Tomás, is 2000m above sea level and a three-hour uphill walk along a well-marked forest trail. You'll pass several small streams where you can collect water. Bring purification tablets or a filter. The camp is nothing more than three walls, a concrete floor and corrugated roof. Bring your own tent or hammock and a mosquito net. There's a small latrine and no running water.

A second campground, El Narajo, is only a few kilometers away, but the trail is very steep (one to two hours). It's a pretty camp – just inside the cloud forest – but consider leaving your tent and bags at Don Tomás and climbing the summit as a day trip until a new shelter here (proposed at the time of research) is up and running. From the second camp, it's another two or three hours on a beautiful rolling trail through the cloud forest to the summit. Because of clouds and tree cover, you might not see anything from the top, but there's a sign there all the same.

Many people misjudge the time they need for the climb. It takes two days to go to the top of the mountain. Get an early start and make it to one of the campsites, then summit; the next day walk all the way down. The trail is somewhat unclear in places – look for the colored ribbons. Do not wander off the trail; the forest is so dense it can be hard, or impossible, to find the trail again. A Dutch hiker disappeared here in 1998.

Bring some warm clothes and adequate hiking boots – temperatures in the park are much chillier than in Gracias. It is also often damp and rainy.

You can arrange guides in the village just before the entrance. Look for **Luis Melgar** (☎ 9971-5114) or one of his brothers. Guides charge L350 for short trips and L500 per day for overnight trips. There are no English-speaking guides.

Another option is to organize a tour through the **Asociación de Guías** (☎ 656-0627).

Getting There & Away

The main entrance to the park is about 7km uphill from Gracias. Another entrance is at Belén Gualcho (see boxed text, left), on the western side, but access is better from the Gracias side, which has more facilities and more pristine forest.

DETOUR TO BELÉN GUALCHO

Belén Gualcho is a picturesque colonial town clinging to the side of a mountain at 1600m above sea level, on the other side of Parque Nacional Montaña de Celaque from Gracias. Road access is from Santa Rosa de Copán. Attractions include an interesting *iglesia* and a Lenca market on Sunday. There's an entrance to Parque Nacional Celaque here, and a rural trail leading to San Manuel Colohete, but no checkpoint, and no services.

A few buses go between here and Santa Rosa each day. There are a couple of basic places to stay and to eat, and there's even an internet cafe.

GETTING TO GUATEMALA & EL SALVADOR

Getting to Esquipulas, Guatemala

The Honduras–Guatemala border at **Agua Caliente** (24hr) is a half hour's drive from Nueva Ocotepeque; go through Honduran immigration first, then catch a ride (Q10, 2km) up the hill to the Guatemalan post. From there buses go frequently to **Esquipulas** (10km, 30 minutes), where you can connect to **Guatemala City** or **Flores**. There are no accommodations in Agua Caliente; the last bus from Agua Caliente to Nueva Ocotepeque is at 5:30pm.

Getting to La Palma, El Salvador

The Honduras–El Salvador border at **El Poy** (24hr) is 15-minute drive from Nueva Ocotepeque; on both sides, the bus drops you about 100m from the border, where you can walk across and catch a bus onward.

There should be no fee to leave Honduras or to enter El Salvador. If Honduran authorities ask for an exit fee, ask for a receipt or to see the law in writing – that should suddenly make the fee go away. Likewise, there should be no fee to leave El Salvador. There is a posted, official L60 fee to enter Honduras. On the Salvadoran side, buses leave frequently for **San Salvador** and **La Palma**. The last one to San Salvador leaves El Poy around 4pm to 4:30pm. On the Honduran side, the last bus from El Poy to Nueva Ocotepeque leaves at 4:30pm.

For information on crossing the border from El Salvador see p323.

You can go on foot from Gracias to the park entrance – it takes about two hours. Look for the well-marked shortcut for those *a pie* (on foot). From the house where you pay your fees, it's about another half hour uphill to the park visitors center. However, we recommend saving your energy for hiking in the park. A bumpy mototaxi ride will take you there for about L100 to L150.

Alternatively, you arrange a lift through Hotel Erick or Hotel Guancascos in Gracias.

SAN JUAN

A slowly improving highway and the dogged efforts of Peace Corps volunteers have put this tiny, traditional mountain town on the tourist map. It is well worth a stop if you are looking for an opportunity to meet locals and learn about the lifestyle of this remote, undervisited part of the country.

Local guides and accommodation can be arranged through the local tourism cooperative. Look for **Gladys Nolasco** (754-7150), the president of the cooperative, next door to Los Jarritos restaurant. Excursions include a trek to **La Cascada de los Duendes**, which goes through cloud forest and a series of waterfalls, ending with a coffee *finca* tour; and **El Cañon Encantado**, a tour of local beauty spots with the guide telling legends of the ghosts who inhabit it (Spanish only). Horseback riding, visits to traditional artisans, and coffee roasting and tasting tours can also be arranged.

All buses and pickups going between Gracias (see p383) and La Esperanza (see p359) stop here.

NUEVA OCOTEPEQUE

pop 19,100

In the southwest corner of Honduras, dust-blown Nueva Ocotepeque is a crossroads town, with a lot of traffic to and from the nearby borders at Agua Caliente (Guatemala) and El Poy (El Salvador). There's not much to the town, but it's a surprisingly quiet place to stay overnight before or after crossing the border. To check emails, head to **Cyber.com** (per hr L20; 8am-noon & 2-7pm) in a lavender house one block west behind Parque Central. For cash, there's a Banet ATM one block north of the park.

The **Reserva del Guisayote** is a biological reserve that is the easiest to access of any cloud forest in Honduras. It is 16km north of Nueva Ocotepeque via a paved road.

Sleeping & Eating

All the places to stay and eat in Nueva Ocotepeque are on or near Calle Intermedio, which runs through town.

Hotel Turista (653-3639; Av General Francisco Morazán; d without bathroom L230, s/d L230/360; P) Freshly decked out in pastel-hued glory, this is the best of the cheapies around the bus stations. It's surprisingly nice and clean for the price.

Servi Pollo (combos L45-78; 🕑 6am-9pm) Well, you weren't expecting to get haute cuisine here, were you? This fast-food joint has fried and roast chicken, as well as burgers. From the bus stop go south, left at the Banco Occidente, then take the second right.

Getting There & Away

Two long-distance bus companies serve Nueva Ocotepeque: **Congolón** (☎ 653-3064) is half a block south of the Parque Central while **Sultana** (☎ 653-2405) is two blocks north of the park. Destinations:

Agua Caliente (L20; 30 min; every 30min from 6am-6pm) Buses leave from the Transporte San José terminal two blocks north of the park.

El Poy/Salvadoran border (L15; 15 min) Buses leave every 20 minutes from 6:30am to 7pm, departing from the same place as the Agua Caliente buses from 7am to 4pm.

La Entrada (L90-100; 2½hr) Take any San Pedro Sula bus.

San Pedro Sula (L140-180; 4½hr) Sultana departs hourly from 4am to 4pm (with the exception of noon and 1pm), while Congolón has five departures daily: first at midnight, last at noon.

Santa Rosa de Copán (L65-70; 2hr) Take any San Pedro Sula bus.

Tegucigalpa (L250-280; 9hr) Sultana departs hourly between 4am and 11am or take the San Pedro Sula bus and transfer. One Congolón direct bus leaves at midnight (L280).

NORTHERN HONDURAS

The lush, tropical northern region of Honduras has seduced visitors for centuries – its natural wonders and easy Caribbean vibe make it difficult to resist.

Tangled among the beaches are mangrove swamps and tropical vegetation; beyond them lie virgin jungle, slopes and rivers that just scream out to adventure travelers. Whether it is the howler monkeys of Parque Nacional Jeannette Kawas, or the manatees of the wildlife refuge at Cuero y Salado, nature stands strong in this part of the country. All this despite the huge agricultural development on the fertile, narrow coastal plains, which have yielded enough bananas to float an entire economy.

La Ceiba is the region's party town, and a jumping-off point for the Bay Islands. Its *zona viva* (party zone) has kept many a good-time gringo under its spell for longer than planned. Beyond its urban core are 1001 outdoor adventures: rafting down the Río Cangrejal, hiking in Pico Bonito or whizzing on a canopy tour in the coastal jungle. Stretching right along the coast are Garífuna villages, bastions of a culture rich with African and Carib heritage. The Garífuna are descendants of slaves abandoned by the British on Roatán at the end of the 18th century.

Most people (rightly) quickly skip through port town of Puerto Cortés, but the two other main towns, Tela and Trujillo, both have their charms – beaches, plentiful seafood and laidback people to name but a few.

The coast fills with tourists during **Semana Santa** when Hondurans enjoy a week of holidaying and making merry. Book in advance at this time and beware the prices – they can double. Most places are quiet the rest of the time.

DANGERS & ANNOYANCES

Travelers have been accosted and robbed on lonely stretches of beach outside La Ceiba, Tela (especially) and Trujillo, mostly by groups of youths. Some people have had belongings swiped from the beach while they were in the water. Be vigilant. Do not walk along these beaches without company, and never after dark.

The north coast has a very high rate of HIV infection: plan accordingly.

PUERTO CORTÉS

pop 118,100

Puerto Cortés, 64km north of San Pedro Sula, is the westernmost of Honduras' major Caribbean towns. It is one of Honduras' principal deepwater ports, and over half of the country's export shipping trade, mostly bananas, pineapples and other produce, passes through here. However, there's not a lot of interest to travelers beyond the ferry to Belize. If you're waiting around for it, stay in Omoa or Travesía/Baja Mar.

Information

In addition to the banks below, there is an **HSBC** (3a Av btwn 1a & 2a Calles E) and a **Citibank** (2a Av btwn 6a & 7a Calles E).

BAC/Bamer (Parque Central) This bank has a Unibanc ATM.

Banco de Occidente (2a Av at 4a Calle) On the corner of Parque Central; changes traveler's checks and gives cash advances on Visa cards.

Multinet Internet Café (Parque Central; per hr L20; 🕑 8am-7pm Mon-Sat) The most convenient internet/telephone café in town.

Sights

Playa de Cieneguita, a few kilometers toward Omoa, is the most pleasant beach in the area and has a couple of beachside restaurants and upscale hotels. Other beaches at Travesía and Baja Mar (p388) are accessible by local bus. The proximity to San Pedro Sula means the beaches here can get crowded on weekends and holidays.

The **annual fair** in Puerto Cortés is held on August 15.

The main reason for coming to Puerto Cortés is its weekly boat service to Belize.

Sleeping & Eating

There are plenty of places to stay in Puerto Cortés, although few nice ones. There are loads of common restaurants around Parque Central, and American fast-food chains, too.

Hotel El Centro (☎ 665-1160; 3a Av btwn 2a & 3a Calles E; s/d with fan L325/455, with air-con L442/577; ⓟ ⓧ) Cramped but secure rooms are well kept and have clean bedding, making this the best cheapie in the center. It is convenient to the bus stations, Parque Central and lots of restaurants and banks.

Hotel Costa Azul (☎ 665-5215; www.hotelcostaazul. net; Playa Muncipales; s/d/tr incl breakfast from L800/900/1000; ⓟ ⓧ ⓦ ⓡ) This pricier midrange outside the center has its advantages: the pool is wonderful and modern rooms include all expected amenities. There's a good restaurant and it all sits just across the street from the popular and vaguely pleasant grassy beach, Playa Municipales. But the real coup is that you can walk to the Belize ferry – it's 600m away, so springing for a room here eliminates costly taxis.

Parrilladas Hareb (3a Av at 10a Calle E; mains L55-65; ⏲ 8am-10pm) This popular BBQ place serves grilled meat and chicken. Seating is on the front patio of a private home. Arrive early

for a seat on weekends – it's hopping with customers at peak hours.

Getting There & Away

BOAT

Two different companies run crossings to Belize. The crossings are not always on time, and the schedule has changed several times recently. The **D-Express** (☎ 9991-0778; www.belizeferry. com) leaves next door to Restaurant El Delfin in Barra la Laguna, 3km southeast of Puerto Cortés, at 11:30am Monday to Big Creek and Placencia. For those on a visa run, the boat returns on Fridays from the Placencia Shell Gas Dock at 9:30am or from Big Creek/Mango Creek at 11:30am (BZ$110), unless there are enough of you to book a private charter return. Another company, **Water Taxi Nesymein Neydy** (☎ 3396-1380), goes to Belize from the same spot at noon on Monday, calling at Dangriga (closer to Belize City). Tickets to each destination cost L1000, whichever boat you take. You need to be there by 10am to sign up, with your passport, on the day of travel. To get to the ferries, take any San Pedro–Omoa bus and get off at La Laguna and follow signs to Restaurant Delfin. You can also change lempiras to Belizean dollars at the dock.

Note that it may be cheaper and easier for you to get to Belize via the Guatemalan port of Puerto Barrios (see p183).

BUS

The two bus companies that service San Pedro Sula have terminals side by side on 4a Av between 3a and 4a Calles, one block north and half a block west of the Parque Central. Both **Impala** (☎ 665-0606) and **Caribe** (☎ 665-0606) service

---

DIG THAT BEAT: INSIDE GARÍFUNA DANCING

Shaking to live Garífuna music is a highlight of the north coast. Musicians create a throbbing pared-down sound using large drums, a turtle shell, maracas and a big conch shell. Words are chanted, the audience responds and dancers begin to move their hips in physics-defying loops to the *punta*, a traditional Garífuna dance.

During mid-July every year, the **national Garífuna dance festival** takes place in the small town of Baja Mar (p388), near Puerto Cortés. All towns and villages have annual fiestas, and cultural events and gatherings of one kind or another happen throughout the year. **Garífuna Day** (April 12), a big holiday for all the Garífuna communities, commemorates the day in 1797 when the Garífunas arrived in Honduras. Often you can arrange for dances if you ask around at Garífuna villages.

Near Trujillo, the towns of Santa Fe and Santa Rosa de Aguán (p407) have their festivals on July 15 to 30 and August 22 to 29, respectively. The last three days are usually the most frenetic.

The National Ballet Folklórico Garífuna, based in Tegucigalpa, is a first-rate dance troupe that has performed around the world; if you get a chance to attend a performance, don't miss it.

Puerto Cortés from a shared terminal on 2a Av between 4a and 5a Av. Between them, buses leave for San Pedro Sula every five to 10 minutes from 4:20am to 6pm (L35 to L42).

From separate side-by-side terminals, **Transportes Citral Costeños** (☎ 655-0888; 3a Calle Este) has buses to the Corinto border with Guatemala every 20 minutes (L44 to L50, two hours). Along the way, you can hop off in Omoa (L14). The former has one direct bus daily at 2:10pm (L55). Last bus leaves at 4:30pm.

See the Travesía & Baja Mar (see below) and Omoa (see right) sections for information on buses to those areas.

TRAIN

A passenger train that used to operate between Puerto Cortés and Tela has now stopped permanently.

TRAVESÍA & BAJA MAR

Just to the east of Puerto Cortés, Travesía and Baja Mar are two seaside Garífuna villages. The beach at Travesía is cleaner than the one at Baja Mar. The road from Puerto Cortés runs along the sea, first through Travesía and on to Baja Mar; the two villages form a continuous row of wooden houses beside the sea, with small fishing boats lining the shore.

There are one or two restaurants in each village. Baja Mar is best known as the home of the Garífuna national dance festival (see boxed text, p387), held here every year between July 9 and 24. Members of all three dozen or so Garífuna communities in Honduras attend, sometimes dancing right through the night.

Sleeping & Eating

Hotel Frontera del Caribe (☎ 665-5001; r L350; P) Right on the (trash-strewn) beach in Travesía, this is a vaguely pleasant place to stay near Puerto Cortés if you're on a budget. Seven upstairs rooms (sleeping up to three people), all with private bathroom and ceiling fan, are simple, clean and often have a pleasant sea breeze. Downstairs is a somewhat pricey beachside restaurant that serves breakfast, lunch and dinner.

The bus coming from Puerto Cortés stops just outside the door.

Getting There & Away

The bus to Travesía and Baja Mar departs from a vacant lot next door to Restaurant Glorieta Los Amigos near the Citral terminal in Puerto Cortés at 7am, 9:30am, 10:30am, 12:15pm, 2pm,

4pm and 5:30pm; the last bus back leaves Baja Mar around 3:45pm, passing Travesía around 4pm. The bus runs less frequently on Sunday.

A taxi will take you between Puerto Cortés and Travesía in about 10 minutes for L100.

OMOA

pop 37,300

The small, snail-paced village of Omoa lies 18km west of Puerto Cortés on a broad, curving bay that makes for great sunsets. It's a bit of a tragic story. Once a longtime weekend getaway for San Pedro Sula residents as well as a magnet for a steady stream of backpackers heading to or coming from nearby Guatemala, Omoa these days is suffering under the weight of some heavy bad luck. The highway to the border is now paved, so not so many folks stop. But worse are the controversial Gas del Caribe liquid-gas spheres in town. Not only an eyesore, but the gas company has installed wave breakers that shifted currents and Omoa is slowly watching helpless as its football-field-length sands slowly disappear. Then, to add insult to injury, a 7.3 earthquake struck in 2009, further sweeping away large swaths of beach. That all said, it's still not a bad place to break up a journey; it's safe, with one good hostel, an historic fort and a clutch of seafood restaurants along the seafront. The beach certainly isn't postcard-worthy but the vibe is addictive.

Omoa's **annual festival** is held on May 30.

Information

Buses to Puerto Cortés leave every 40 minutes from the beach between 5:45am and 8:15pm. If you're in a hurry, walk the 1km to the highway for more regular buses. Banco de Occidente changes traveler's checks but there are no ATMs in Omoa. Bring cash. Check your email at Roosternet on the main road nearer to the highway.

Sights

Omoa's claim to historical fame is its Spanish fortress (now with a museum), the **Fortaleza de San Fernando de Omoa** (adult/child L76/10; ⏰ 8am-4pm Mon-Fri, 9am-5pm Sat & Sun). Built between 1759 and 1777 under orders from King Fernando VII of Spain to protect the coast from rampant piracy, in 1779 the fortress was captured by the British after only a four-day battle. Still in good shape, the fort is maintained by the Instituto Hondureño de Antropología e Historia.

Sleeping & Eating

Omoa has a slew of beachfront restaurants, but all are pricier than they should be. You'll save money if you head away from the beach, not towards it. That said, we like Escapate.

Roli's Place (☎ 658-9082; www.yaxpactours.com; campsites per person L60, hammock L60, dm L80, s/d without bathroom L150/180, s/d without air-con L220/250, d/tr with air-con L330/380; ☒) A well-equipped hostel with a communal kitchen and free use of kayaks and bicycles. The well-furnished double rooms are a steal at these prices, complete with LCD TVs with international channels, and sit alongside dormitories, double rooms with shared showers, a terrace for hammocks and a tent area. There is purified water on tap. Watch out for the (numerous) hostel rules, including a 10pm noise curfew, no candles except for Christmas and no liquor – the Swiss-German owner has little patience with rule-breakers. He operates a shuttle to La Ceiba and Puerto Barrios.

Hotel Fisherman (☎ 658-9224; r with fan L200, with air-con L300; ☒) and **Hotel Tatiana** (☎ 658-9787; r with fan L300, with air-con L600; ☒) are basic budget options across from the beach.

Burgers & Mariscos (Carretera a Guatemala; mains L50-150) It's a haul on foot (about a 15-minute walk from Roli's) but shoestringers flock to this excellent option on the main highway just near the Omoa turnoff for its cleanliness (real soap and real hand towels in the bathroom), good food and good prices. The L50 burger and fries is tough to beat. The *tamarindo* is lovely as is the setting – on a breezy colonial-style porch with a big flat-screen TV.

Sueños del Mar (☎ 658-9047; www.suenosdelmar. com; beachside; mains L75-120; ☺ 8am-5pm; ☒ 🖳) Located on the far western end of the beach, this hotel/restaurant does bang-up breakfasts that you miss (bacon, sausage, hash browns, bangers etc) and healthy sandwiches and salads for lunch. Breakfast is served until 5pm, making this by far the most ideal and cleanest option in town. The rooms – nicest in town – are L660 for a double and sit on a somewhat secluded stretch of beach in town.

Getting There & Away

Buses to Omoa depart from Puerto Cortés every 20 minutes from 5am to 5:40pm (L20, 30 minutes) from the **Citral Costeños terminal** (☎ 655-0888; 3a Calle Este). Most will take the turnoff on the highway, and drop passengers off on the beach. From Omoa to Puerto Cortés, buses depart every half hour from 5:45am to 8:15pm. From Puerto Cortés, buses leave frequently for San Pedro Sula, a transport hub.

Roli's Place runs shuttles to La Ceiba (L360, minimum six people) or to Puerto Barrios in Guatemala (L270).

TELA
pop 88,100

Tela is a hot mess with a sinister appeal. You know it ain't right to love it, but you sorta do, anyway. On the surface it's not much to look at. It is warm and humid, and the center is just another Honduran town – maybe moving at a slower pace. But after a day or so checking out its beaches, chatting to the locals and sampling the seafood, many find themselves falling for its languid, laid-back vibe. After all, these are the most welcoming beaches on the Honduran north coast (though they could still use a clean up).

Tela is sleepy most of the year, but it's another story during **Semana Santa** (Holy Week

---

GETTING TO GUATEMALA & BELIZE

Getting to Puerto Barrios, Guatemala

The Guatemalan border is 51km southwest of Omoa in **Corinto** (☺ 6am-6pm). Buses to the border leave from the main highway (L40, every hour) and will drop you at the first set of *comedores* near the border. From there, walk through immigration procedures and to the Guatemalan microbuses waiting on the Guatemalan side and connect to **Puerto Barrios** (Q15, 1¼ hours).

There is no regular passenger boat service from Honduras to Guatemala.

See p184 for information on crossing the border from Guatemala.

Getting to Placencia, Belize

Boats to Belize leave from **Barra La Laguna** next to Restaurant Delfin near Puerto Cortés every Monday for Placencia/Mango Creek and Dangriga. Tickets (L1000) need to be purchased several hours in advance. See p387. For crossing from Belize, see p259.

before Easter), when the town fills up with Honduran vacationers. During Semana Santa, hotel room rates can double, and advance bookings are essential if you want to get a bed. In July and August, the number of travelers skyrockets, although room rates are unchanged.

The town is a good base for excursions to several wildlife and beauty hot spots nearby.

Orientation

Tela is divided into two sections: Tela Vieja, the 'old town,' on the east bank of Río Tela where the river meets the sea; and Tela Nueva, on the west side of the river, where Hotel Villas Telamar hugs the best stretch of beach.

Information

Banco Atlántida (4a Av at 9a Calle NE) Changes traveler's checks and gives cash advances on Visa or international MasterCards.

Banco de Occidente (Parque Central) Northeast corner of Parque Central. Cash advances on Visa and MasterCard.

Fundación Prolansate (☎ 448-2042; www. prolansate.org; 7a Av at 8a Calle NE; ☺ 7am-5:30pm Mon-Thu, to 4:30pm Fri) Promotes sustainable tourism in Tela and has information on Lancetilla Botanical Gardens and Punta Sal and can organize educational visits.

Garífuna Tours (☎ 448-2904; www.garifunatours.com; 9a Calle NE at 5a Ave NE; ☺ 7:30am-6pm Mon-Sat, to 5pm Sun) Local, well-established tour operation.

Hondutel (☎ 448-2004; 4a Av; ☺ 8am-4pm)

Hospital Tela Integrado (☎ 442-3176; ☺ 24hr) Medical services.

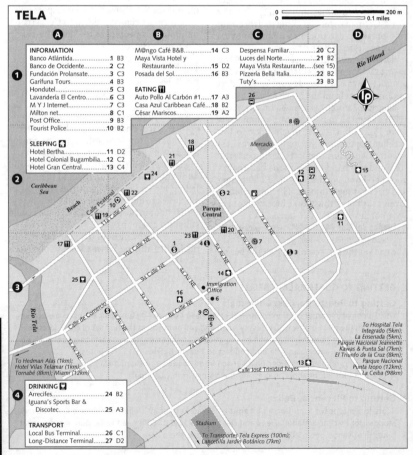

TELA

0 ——— 200 m
0 ——— 0.1 miles

INFORMATION	
Banco Atlántida	1 B3
Banco de Occidente	2 C2
Fundación Prolansate	3 C3
Garífuna Tours	4 B3
Hondutel	5 C3
Lavandería El Centro	6 C3
M Y J Internet	7 C3
Milton net	8 C1
Post Office	9 B3
Tourist Police	10 B2

SLEEPING	
Hotel Bertha	11 D2
Hotel Colonial Bugambilia	12 C2
Hotel Gran Central	13 C4
M@ngo Café B&B	14 C3
Maya Vista Hotel y Restaurante	15 D2
Posada del Sol	16 B3

EATING	
Auto Pollo Al Carbón #1	17 A3
Casa Azul Caribbean Café	18 B2
César Mariscos	19 A2
Despensa Familiar	20 C2
Luces del Norte	21 B2
Maya Vista Restaurante	(see 15)
Pizzería Bella Italia	22 B2
Tuty's	23 B3

DRINKING	
Arrecifes	24 B2
Iguana's Sports Bar & Discotec	25 A3

TRANSPORT	
Local Bus Terminal	26 C1
Long-Distance Terminal	27 D2

Río Hiland

Caribbean Sea

Mercado

Parque Central

Beach

Immigration Office

Río Tela

To Hedman Alas (1km);
Hotel Vilas Telamar (1km);
Tornabé (8km); Miami (12km)

To Hospital Tela
Integrado (5km);
La Ensenada (5km);
Parque Nacional Jeannette
Kawas & Punta Sal (7km);
El Triunfo de la Cruz (8km);
Parque Nacional
Punta Izopo (12km);
La Ceiba (98km)

Calle José Trinidad Reyes

Stadium

To Transportes Tela Express (100m);
Lancetilla Jardín Botánico (7km)

HONDURAS

M Y J Internet (☎ 448-1596; 6a Av NE; per hr L15; 🕑 7:30am-5pm Mon-Sat)

Milton.net (☎ 9646-8641; 10a Calle at 9a Ave NE; per hr L10; 🕑 8am-9pm Mon-Sat) Ramshackle little internet cafe and call center.

Lavandería El Centro (☎ 448-0568; 4a Av NE; 🕑 7:30am-5:30pm Mon-Sat) Charges L70 to wash, dry and fold one load of clothes.

Post office (4a Av; 🕑 8am-4pm Mon-Fri, 8am-noon Sat)

Tourist police (☎ 9713-6731; 11a Calle NE at 4a Av NE; 🕑 24hr)

Dangers & Annoyances

An onslaught of brazen assaults and robberies were occurring in 2009 in Tela, and travelers report the tourist police – once believed to be curtailing the problem – have offered little help or sympathy (there are only six of them, after all). Don't take anything of value to the beach, nor should you walk around alone on the boardwalk or beach after 6pm. During the day, also avoid walking alone beyond the Hotel Villas Telamar Resort on the western end of the beach and the La Ensenada Beach Resort pier on the eastern end. Also be weary of 'sleeping' homeless in Parque Central – they like to pop up and hijack you. That said, the 2009 elections saw a new term beginning January 2010 for an old Minister of Security in town, who's said to be a hardliner on tourist crime.

Sights & Activities

Tela's main attraction is its **beaches**, which stretch around the bay for several kilometers on either side of the town. The beach in front of the town is sandy, but can be littered. The beach just over the bridge in Tela Nueva, in front of Hotel Villas Telamar, is much better; its pale, powdery sand and shady grove of coconut trees are kept impeccably clean. Beach chairs and tents can be rented by nonguests (each L35), but only when occupancy is low at the resort. Beaches further afield, while much better, can be risky for solo travelers or after dusk.

Just outside of Tela there is some prime bird-watching and nature-spotting territory (see p393).

Tela's annual **fiesta day** is June 13.

Tours

Garifuna Tours (☎ 448-2904; www.garifunatours.com; 9a Calle NE at 5a Ave NE; 🕑 7:30am-6:30pm Mon-Sat, to 5pm Sun) Offers all-day boat excursions (from L456), as well as bird-watching excursions to Los Micos Lagoon and kayak excursions to the Parque Nacional Punta Izopo.

Bilingual tours (English and Spanish) are available. Some travelers report that the guides are not very informative.

Honduras Caribbean Tours (☎ 448-2623; www. honduras-caribbean.com; cnr 11a Calle & 6a Av NE) Friendly tour agency inside Casa Azul cafe, offering the usual suspects in the area as well as sport-fishing from L5491 for up to four people. English, Italian and German are spoken.

Sleeping

Hotel Bertha (☎ 448-1009; 8a Calle NE btwn 8a & 9a Avs NE; s/d/tr L200/250/450; 🛜) This is a great deal, especially for a solo traveler. Rooms are unexpectedly nice for the price and it's a mere skip from the main Tela bus terminal. If there were only a small cafe or fountain in the courtyard, it'd be perfect, though rumor has it some travelers' things occasionally go missing from the rooms here.

Posada del Sol (☎ 448-3201; 8a Calle NE btwn 3a & 4a Avs NE; r/tr L250/350) Though a tad dreary, this easy-come, easy-go little family-run *posada* (pension) has well-scrubbed basic rooms. The family, who live onsite, are relaxed and friendly and will chat to you as you lounge in the communal courtyard.

M@ngo Café B&B (☎ 448-0388; www.mangocafe.net; cnr 5a Av & 8a Calle NE; s/d/tr with fan L250/280/350, with air-con L280/340/440; 🛜) A lot of backpackers end up here so it's not a bad place to meet people. It is fairly ordinary – you get basic, clean rooms with hot water and an absolutely blaring soundtrack from the TelCell store across the street. It is operated by Garífuna Tours. You can also rent bikes here (per day L95).

our pick **Maya Vista Hotel y Restaurante** (☎ 448-1497; www.mayavista.com; Barrio Lempira; s/d with fan L551/661, with air-con L841/998; P 🛜 💻) Still one of the town's big traveler gathering spots and with good reason, even though it is pricier than most places. Most rooms have tasteful indigenous-inspired decor and a superb panorama of the bay. The stack-em-high design evokes MC Escher and means you should have a floor (and therefore the view) to yourself. There is also a very good restaurant onsite. English and French are spoken.

Hotel Colonial Bugambilia (☎ 448-3222; www.hotel colonialtela.com; cnr 8a Av NE & 9a Calle NE; s/d L550/650, ste from L1450; P 🛜) This young hotel is a great deal if you don't mind not being beachfront. It's pert and clean, but lacks a bit of character save a few art pieces. The interior rooms are dark, but quieter than those looking onto the street. Suites are spacious but cramped with extra couches and kitchenettes.

HONDURAS

Hotel Gran Central (☎ 448-1099; www.hotelgrancentral. com; Av Honduras; s/d L760/950; P ✗ ☐) If you fancy splashing out, this is the place to do it. The renovated colonial building has been beautifully decorated by the well-traveled, engaging French owners, with small design touches in the common areas previously unseen on the Honduran coast. The high-ceilinged rooms are painted in earth colors and lead out to a bougainvillea-draped balcony with views over the abandoned train station – 'a genuine Central American view,' according to the owners. There is a small bar, and breakfast is available. Note that the hotel is 200m from the beach, but it's a straight shot.

Eating

Seafood is plentiful, delicious and cheap in Tela. Seafood soups are a particular delicacy of the town; fish, shrimp, lobster and *caracol* (conch) are found in many restaurants. Another specialty of the town is *pan de coco* (coconut bread); you'll see Garífuna women or their children walking around town selling it. Try it – it's delicious.

Tuty's (9a Calle NE at 5a Av NE; mains L32-65; ☽ 8am-5pm Mon-Sat, 7am-3pm Sun) You'll find simple Formica tables, a reliable, bustling kitchen and friendly service (although you may have to wait for it) at this place just off Parque Central. There are generously stuffed omelette breakfasts if you are bored of *baleadas*, as well as pancakes, pastries, juices and delicious *licuados* (try banana). Lunchtime options include sandwiches, tacos and quesadillas.

Luces del Norte (11a Calle NE at 5a Av NE; breakfast L45-89, mains L60-250; ☽ 7am-10pm) With its rustic, wooden setting and sea-salt faded paint, this remains as popular as ever among both backpackers and locals – it has some real devotees. Excellent seafood is dished up among the tropical plants that sway throughout the restaurant. Pick your own seafood style – the menu runs the gamut from pasta to paella – or grab a read from the book exchange.

Auto Pollo Al Carbón #1 (11a Calle NE at 2a Av NE; half chicken L60; ☽ 7am-11pm) Not a frill to be seen here: just simple roast-chicken platters served under a corrugated-iron roof in an open-air shack, a wishbone's throw away from the Caribbean Sea. You can smell it from considerable distance.

Casa Azul Caribbean Café (cnr 11a Calle & 6a Av NE; mains L75-95; ☽ 11am-11pm) This remains one of the most traveler-friendly spots in town. Belly-up to the welcoming bar for happy-hour two-for-one cocktails (6:30pm to 7:30pm), or nosh on the meat and seafood-heavy menu. The *anafres* with housemade tortillas are particularly well done. Most staff speak English.

Pizzería Bella Italia (☎ 448-1055; 4a Av NE at Calle Peatonal; mains L80-300; ☽ lunch & dinner Tue-Sun) The friendly Italian owners spent almost a decade in Santa Rosa de Copán before moving to Tela to be near the beach. Pizza here is terrific – from personal to 16-piece *gigantes* (extra large) – but the specialty is the *panzerotti*, a variation of calzone stuffed with salami, ham, mushrooms and more.

Maya Vista Restaurante (☎ 448-1497; Barrio Lempira; mains L120-225) The view over Tela's bay is spectacular from this well-established travelers' favorite – it is quite something to eat the house specialty, garlic spaghetti and *camarones* (prawns), with the waves crashing below. The French-Canadian chef also does spicy homemade sausages and surf and turf, among others. Afternoon coffee and cake is also a good option.

César Mariscos (☎ 448-2083; 3a Av NE; mains L120-300; ☽ 7am-10pm) Overlooking a shady area of the beach, this extremely reliable boardwalk seafooder breads, flambées, and grills all manner of seafood, namely shrimp, conch, fish and lobster. For something that bites you back, try the fish fillet in creamy jalapeño sauce.

Despensa Familiar (Parque Central; ☽ 7am-7pm Mon-Sat, to 6pm Sun) For self-caterers.

Drinking

The outdoor bar at the Maya Vista restaurant, with its fine ocean views, is about as good as it gets for an evening beer or frozen margarita and is a good way to mingle with sexy locals.

Arrecifes (☎ 448-1021; Calle Peatonal; ☽ 8am-late) A good spot for a beachfront tipple. Domestic beers run L27 and cocktails L40 to L60.

Iguana's Sports Bar & Discotec (10a Calle NE near 2a Av NE) The only true *discoteca* in town, but it was shut for Christmas when we rolled through.

Getting There & Away

Slower normal buses leave Tela every 20 minutes for La Ceiba (L38, 2½ hours, 4:15am to 6pm) from the long-distance terminal at the corner of 9a Calle NE and 9a Av NE, three blocks northeast of the square. For quicker direct buses, you can take a taxi to the Dippsa gas station on the highway, where buses headed to La Ceiba from San Pedro Sula pass regularly.

Transportes Tela Express (2a Av NE) operates direct buses to San Pedro Sula (L$70, two hours) from its terminal a block past the train tracks. There are eight departures from 6am to 5pm Monday to Saturday and from 7am to 5:30pm on Sunday. **Hedman Alas** (☎ 448-3075; Hotel Villa Telemar; 🕑 10:30am-2pm & 3-5pm 5:30-8pm) operates two buses to San Pedro Sula daily at 6am and 1:05pm (L304 to L361, two hours), from where you can make a hassle-free connection to Copán (L456 to L551) and elsewhere.

Local buses to the Garífuna villages near Tela depart from a dirt lot on the corner of 11a Calle and 8a Av (see p395 for times and schedules).

Getting Around

Tela has many taxis; a ride in town costs L20. A taxi to Triunfo de la Cruz, La Ensenada or Tornabé is around L100 to L120. Mountain bikes can be rented at the **M@ngo Café B&B** (☎ 448-2856; cnr 8a Calle NE & 5a Av NE) for L95 for a full day.

AROUND TELA
Lancetilla Jardín Botánico

The second-largest tropical garden in the world, the **Lancetilla Botanical Garden & Research Center** (www.lancetilla.org; admission L115; 🕑 7am-4pm) was founded by the United Fruit Company in 1926 to experiment with the cultivation of various tropical plants in Central America. Although it is still an active research center, the public can now wander through this tropical wonderland of plant species from all corners of the globe. It has the largest collection of Asiatic fruit trees in the western hemisphere.

Admission includes an introductory tour, then you are free to roam the well-marked trails through the arboretum and main garden area. The bottom of the garden leads to a swimming hole.

Birdlife also thrives at Lancetilla – hundreds of species have been spotted, and this is a popular and accessible spot for birdwatchers. Each year on December 14 and 15 the Audubon Society conducts a 24-hour bird count; you can participate if you're here at that time. Migratory species are present from November to February. Bird-watching is best in the early morning or late afternoon.

There's a **visitor information office** (☎ 408-8806; 🕑 7am-4pm) where the park begins, and an explanatory map is available. Guides are available for tours (per hour L100) through the exotic plants in the arboretum. You can arrange bird-watching tours (per hour L100) in advance by calling the information office ahead of time. Expect a very early morning start. Some information is also available from **Fundación Prolansate** (☎ 448-2042; www.prolansate.org; 7a Av at 8a Calle NE; 🕑 7am- 5:30pm Mon-Thu, to 4:30pm Fri).

Accommodation is available, including **cabins** (L500; 🛏) with three individual beds and private bathrooms. You need to call the visitor information office to book in advance.

GETTING THERE & AWAY

Lancetilla is 7km southwest of the center of Tela. A good way to get here is by bike, which you can rent in Tela. Five kilometers from town there is a turnoff from the highway that leads to the main gardens. You pay at a ticket office here. Alternatively, a taxi will take you there for around L100.

Parque Nacional Jeannette Kawas

Standing on the beach at Tela, you can look out and see a long arc of land curving out to the west to a point almost in front of you. This point, **Punta Sal**, is part of the Parque Nacional Jeannette Kawas.

The park has several white-sand beaches, including the pretty **Playa Cocalito**. Offshore coral reefs make for fine **snorkeling**, and howler monkeys live in the forest. The park used to be known as Parque Nacional Marino Punta Sal. It was renamed for Jeannette Kawas, an environmental campaigner and former director of Prolansate, who was murdered in 1995 following her tireless work to protect the park from developers. There is a L95 fee to enter.

On the park's east side is the **Laguna de los Micos** (Lagoon of the Monkeys) with mangrove forests, which harbors hundreds of bird species (especially from November to February, when migratory species flock here).

You can arrange day trips, which include hiking, snorkeling and hanging out on Playa Cocalito. Garífuna Tours runs here (see p391).

GETTING THERE & AWAY

Aside from day trips with the Tela tour companies, you can negotiate a trip with one of the boatmen who tie up under the bridge between old and new Tela. You can also make the trip from the town of Miami. From there you can do a day trip by boat or even walk to Punta Sal and camp there – although there have been assaults on this deserted stretch of beach.

Refugio de Vida Punta Izopo

Standing on the beach at Tela and looking to the east, you can see another point: **Punta Izopo**, part of the Punta Izopo Wildlife Refuge. Rivers entering the wildlife refuge spread out into a network of canals that channel through the tangle of mangrove forest. Monkeys, turtles and even crocodiles live here as well as many species of birds, including toucans and parrots.

You can arrange kayak trips through the Tela tour agencies (see p391). Gliding silently through the mangrove canals in a kayak, you can get close to wildlife without disturbing it. It's 16km by road from Tela to El Triunfo de la Cruz (see right), a one-hour walk on the beach or a one-hour canoe ride. Entrance fee is L60.

Garífuna Villages

Several Garífuna villages are within easy reach of Tela. All of them are on the coast, with rustic houses right on the beach, fishing canoes resting on the sand and tiny restaurants serving delicious Garífuna food; the specialties are seafood soups and fish cooked in coconut. Although you can, in theory, quite easily walk to all these villages along the beaches, it is not always safe. They are mostly tranquil little places, although thefts and the occasional assault have been reported. A tour or public transport is a safer option.

All villages have places to stay and at least a couple of restaurants beside the beach specializing in seafood (of course).

The closest village is attractive little **La Ensenada**, 3km east along the arc of the beach from Tela, just before you reach the point, Punta Triunfo, crowned by the Cerro El Triunfo de la Cruz. **Hotel Laguna Mar** (☎ 9811-5558; d L600; P ❄), toward the western edge of town and just 100m from the beach, is the cleanest, nicest spot to stay with meticulously maintained gardens and neat little rooms. There is a good beach just in front. There are seafood restaurants in La Ensenada (although most are only open on the weekend) and places to drink along the beach.

The larger village of **El Triunfo de la Cruz** can be reached by regular buses from Tela, departing from the corner on the east side of the market. It is the largest, most developed of the Garífuna villages, and doesn't have the same peaceful feeling of the other villages. There are a couple of reasonable places to stay. **Cabañas y Restaurante Colón** (☎ 9989-5622; s/d/tr L200/300/450; P ❄) is in the center, with a bunch of rustic *cabañas* a few footsteps away from the sand. There is a seafood restaurant (mains L60 to L200) onsite (and another a sand-blown click away), open for all meals. The upmarket choice here is the **Caribbean Coral Inn** (☎ 9994-9806; www.caribbeancoralinns.com; s/d incl breakfast L969/1168), offering rustic but well-appointed beachside cabins with hammocks and hot-water bathrooms, market-fresh meals and wines from Chile, Argentina and Italy. Both La Ensenada and Triunfo de la Cruz are now accessible by a newly paved road.

On the other side of Tela, to the west, is **Tornabé**, another Garífuna village, 8km away. It is a largish village, with little to offer travelers.

Past Tornabé, the beach road becomes rougher and can only be negotiated by 4WD. It continues for several more kilometers to **Miami**, a beautiful but basic village on a narrow sandbar between the Caribbean Sea and the Laguna de los Micos. This area may well change beyond recognition. The Inter-American Development Bank has approved a controversial 'soft' loan for a giant hotel complex and golf club to be built in the area –

GUIFITI: MOONSHINE SECRETS

The local moonshine on the north coast of Honduras is a mysterious concoction known as Guifiti (sometimes spelt Gifiti or Güfiti). Legend has it that it is a natural aphrodisiac, and aficionados claim all sorts of medicinal qualities, from helping diabetes to cleaning arteries. The exact recipe varies from brewer to brewer, although most versions will contain a base of *aguardiente* (a potent local gut-rot), as well as a blend of herbs and spices. In fact, there are rumors that in some versions not all of the ingredients are entirely legal. Perhaps that is why you cannot pick up a bottle from supermarket shelves. However, make a few discreet enquiries in most north-coast towns and villages, and it won't be long before you track down a dram – even in surprisingly upmarket locations. It's pretty powerful stuff so don't throw too many glasses down your throat too quickly. If you are keen to spread the love and take some home, you can buy a legal version of it in the Mercado Guamilito in San Pedro Sula (p366).

hardly a big step towards ecologically and culturally sensitive tourism. Infrastructure was still being laid at time of research, including paving the main road through town.

GETTING THERE & AWAY

Although you can walk along the beach from Tela to any of the villages, the walk is not always safe and should not be done alone or at night.

Buses to the Garífuna villages depart from the local bus terminal in Tela. There are two routes: one heading west to Tornabé, another heading east to Triunfo de la Cruz. Buses on both routes depart hourly from around 7am to 5pm Monday to Saturday; the fare ranges from L12 to L17, and it takes about 30 to 45 minutes to reach the villages.

If you're driving or cycling, you can get to Tornabé by the beach road heading west from Tela. Be careful where you cross the sandbar at the Laguna de los Micos between San Juan and Tornabé; vehicles regularly get stuck in the sand here. You may need a 4WD vehicle to get past Tornabé to Miami. You can also get to Tornabé from the highway; the turnoff, 5km west of Tela, is marked by a sign to 'The Last Resort.' To drive to La Ensenada or Triunfo de la Cruz, take the highway to the turnoff for Triunfo de la Cruz, 5km east of Tela. After 1km the road forks. Go left to La Ensenada, right to Triunfo de la Cruz.

LA CEIBA
pop 178,300

It is known as Honduras' party town – Tegucigalpa thinks, San Pedro Sula works and La Ceiba has fun, the saying goes. There is certainly a full and vibrant nightlife, which makes this port city, set beneath the magnificent Pico Bonito mountain, more than just a jumping-off point to the Bay Islands or La Moskitia. Certainly, *ceibeños*, as the locals are known, are proud of their city, Honduras' third largest. It is not a particularly attractive place at first glance. The beaches are just average, and the buildings are not much to write home about either. But with some fine bars and restaurants, and excellent adventure tourism just a short hop away, it's small wonder that many visitors linger longer than planned.

Orientation

The heart of La Ceiba is its attractive, shady Parque Central. Av San Isidro, running from the east side of the plaza to the sea, is

La Ceiba's main drag. A block or two over, Av 14 de Julio is another major commercial street. Av La República, running to the sea from the opposite side of the plaza, has train tracks down its center that used to transport Standard Fruit Company cargo to the pier.

Over the estuary is Barrio La Isla, the city's *zona viva*, or party zone. There's a large Garífuna community on this side.

Information

Tour companies (p397) are your best bet for booking travel services. All the banks in the Mall Megaplaza have ATMs.

BAC/Bamer (☎ 443-0668; Av San Isidro) Use Visa and MasterCard here.

Banco Atlántida (Av San Isidro) Changes traveler's checks and has an ATM.

Europanet (☎ 440-2951; Parque Central; per hr L20; ☼ 8am-6pm Mon-Sat) Centrally located internet cafe next to Gran Hotel París.

Fundación Cuero y Salado (☎ /fax 443-0329; www. cueroysalado.org; Av Ramón Rosa at 15a Calle; ☼ 8am-noon & 1-5pm Mon-Fri, 8-11am Sat) Tourist information that also manages the Cuero y Salado Wildlife Reserve.

Hondutel (Av Ramón Rosa btwn Calles 5a & 6a; ☼ 8am-4pm) Domestic and international phone calls.

Hospital Eurohonduras (☎ 440-0927; Av Atlántida; ☼ 24hr)

Immigration office (☎ 442-0638; 1a Calle near Av 14 de Julio; ☼ 7:30am-3:30pm)

Lavandería Express (per 4.5kg L90; ☼ 7:30am-noon & 1-5:30pm) Laundry services.

Lavandería Wash & Dry (per 4.5kg L2.65; ☼ 8am-noon & 1-5pm Mon-Sat) Laundry services.

Post office (Av Morazán at 14a Calle; ☼ 8am-4pm Mon-Fri, 8am-noon Sat) A bit of a trek from the center.

Tourist office (☎ 440-3044; 8a Calle; ☼ 8am-4:30pm Mon-Fri)

Tourist police (☎ 441-0860; Residencial El Toronjal; ☼ 24hr)

Sights

Parque Swinford (Av La República btwn 7a & 8a Calles) is a lush, tropical botanical oasis in the heart of La Ceiba, complete with a restored railway carriage from the area's track heyday. You will probably have to share it with a few smooching couples.

Museum of Butterflies & Other Insects (☎ 442-2874; www.hondurasbutterfly.com; Calle Escuela Internacional G-12, Colonia El Sauce; adult/child L60/30; ☼ 8am-5pm Mon-Sat) is a remarkable collection of over 13,000 butterflies, moths and other insects. Most of them were collected in Honduras by schoolteacher Robert Lehman, and all are displayed in cases covering the walls. Highlights include the largest moth in the world, with a 30cm (1ft) wingspan, and a gigantic quarter-pound beetle, the heaviest in the world.

The city reaches its good-time peak at **Carnaval**, when it gets very busy. It's celebrated here during the third week in May; Saturday is the biggest day, with parades, costumes, music and celebrations in the streets.

Activities

La Ceiba is, quite rightly, the adventure and ecotourism capital of Honduras. See opposite page for details of tour operators offering the following activities.

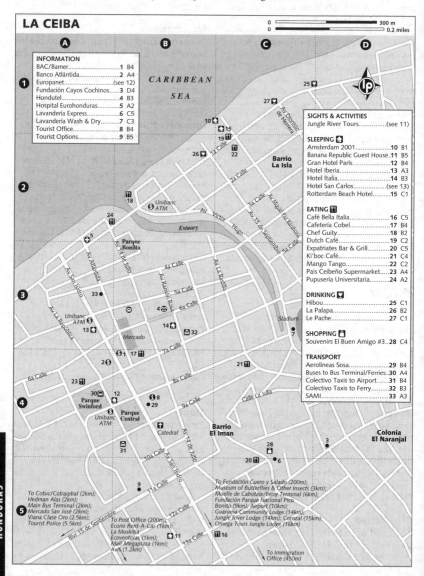

LA CEIBA

0 — 300 m
0 — 0.2 miles

INFORMATION
BAC/Bamer.............................1 B4
Banco Atlántida.....................2 A4
Europanet.............................(see 12)
Fundación Cayos Cochinos.....3 D4
Hondutel.............................4 B3
Hospital Eurohonduras..........5 A2
Lavandería Express................6 C5
Lavandería Wash & Dry..........7 C3
Tourist Office........................8 B4
Tourist Options......................9 B5

CARIBBEAN
SEA

Barrio
La Isla

Unibanc
ATM

Estuary

Parque
Bonilla

Mercado

Parque
Swinford

Unibanc
ATM

Parque
Central

Catedral

Barrio
El Iman

Stadium

Colonia
El Naranjal

SIGHTS & ACTIVITIES
Jungle River Tours................(see 11)

SLEEPING
Amsterdam 2001....................10 B1
Banana Republic Guest House.11 B5
Gran Hotel París....................12 B4
Hotel Iberia..........................13 A3
Hotel Italia...........................14 B3
Hotel San Carlos................(see 13)
Rotterdam Beach Hotel..........15 C1

EATING
Café Bella Italia.....................16 C5
Cafetería Cobel.....................17 B4
Chef Guity............................18 B2
Dutch Café...........................19 C2
Expatriates Bar & Grill...........20 C5
Ki'boc Café...........................21 C4
Mango Tango.........................22 C2
Pais Ceibeño Supermarket......23 A4
Pupusería Universitaria..........24 A2

DRINKING
Hibou..................................25 C1
La Palapa..............................26 B2
Le Pache..............................27 C1

SHOPPING
Souvenirs El Buen Amigo #3...28 C4

TRANSPORT
Aerolíneas Sosa.....................29 B4
Buses to Bus Terminal/Ferries.30 A4
Colectivo Taxis to Airport......31 B4
Colectivo Taxis to Ferry.........32 B3
SAMI...................................33 A3

To Cotuc/Cotraipbal (2km);
Hedman Alas (2km);
Main Bus Terminal (2km);
Mercado San José (2km);
Viana Clase Oro (2.5km);
Tourist Police (5.5km)

To Post Office (200m);
Econo Rent-A-Car (1km);
La Moskitia
Ecoventuras (1km);
Mall Megaplaza (1km);
Avis (1.2km)

To Fundación Cuero y Salado (200m);
Museum of Butterflies & Other Insects (3km);
Muelle de Cabotaje/Ferry Terminal (6km);
Fundación Parque Nacional Pico
Bonito (9km); Airport (10km);
Guaruma Community Lodge (14km);
Jungle River Lodge (14km); Corozal (15km);
Omega Tours Jungle Lodge (16km)

To Immigration
Office (450m)

GETTING INTO TOWN

To & From the Airport

La Ceiba's airport, the Aeropuerto Internacional Golosón, is 10km west of La Ceiba along the highway to Tela. Any bus heading west from the main bus terminal could drop you there. Taxis from Colectivo Taxensa leave from the southwest corner of Parque Central and pass the airport (L15 to 6pm, L20 to 11pm); you have to wait for the taxi to fill up. A normal taxi costs between L60 and L80.

Coming from the airport, don't take one of the taxis right at the airport door, which charge about L190 per person for the ride into town; walk out to the main road and flag down a *colectivo* which will take you into town for around L15 to L20 per person.

From the Bus Terminal

The main bus terminal is at Mercado San José, about 1.5km west of central La Ceiba. The **Viana Clase Oro** (☎ 441-2330; www.vianatransportes.com) express bus terminal is another 500m further west along the same street, at the Servicentro Esso Miramar. A local bus runs between the main bus terminal and the central plaza (L5.50), or you can take a taxi (L20). Buses marked 'Terminal' head to the station from the bus stop at Av La República between 7a & 8a Calles (L5.50).

To & From the Pier

Ferries to the **Bay Islands** operate from the Muelle de Cabotaje, about 8km (20 minutes) east of town. From the bus terminal or from town, taxis should take you there for L45 to L60 per carload (up to four people); from the pier back to either location should be the same price. A *colectivo* goes from the town center from 7a Calle, a good lempira-saving option if you are traveling alone (L20). There is no *colectivo* on the way back. Buses marked 'Muelle de Cabotaje' head to the ferries from the bus stop at Av La República between 7a & 8a Calles (L5.50).

WHITE-WATER RAFTING & CANOEING

The **Río Cangrejal** offers some of the best white-water rafting in Central America. Both Jungle River Tours and Omega Tours offer trips. You will likely have fun on both. Omega Tours cost more, but its trips are better received. Canoe or kayak trips in nearby, less-visited lagoons such as **Cacao Lagoon** often turn up more monkey and bird sightings than trips to Cuero y Salado. Find out how long you'll be on the water and if lunch or excursions (like short hikes into Parque Nacional Pico Bonito) are included.

HIKING

Independent travelers can visit Cuero y Salado wildlife refuge and hike in the Pico Bonito National Park without joining an expensive tour group (see p403 for more on how to go it alone). Some of the more complicated trips are better done with a guide, including trips to area waterfalls and Garífuna villages. Guaruma Servicios is a good option for the Río Cangrejal side of Pico Bonito, while on the El Pino side, get in touch with the tourism committee at **Vivero Natural View** (☎ 368-8343).

CANOPY TOURS

Jungle River Tours operates an eight-cable circuit that lasts two hours and includes a 200m slide across the river (per person L771, reservation required). Like all Jungle River tours, a free night at the river lodge is included. There is now an even longer canopy tour about 500m past Sambo Creek, east of La Ceiba (see p402).

Festivals & Events

Visitors from far and wide descend on La Ceiba for its annual **Carnaval**, held during the week of May 15, which is the day of San Isidro, the town's patron saint. People dress up in costumes and masks and dance themselves silly; it's a great time.

Tours

Guaruma Servicios (☎ 442-2673; www.guaruma.org) A worthwhile operation dedicated to boosting opportunities for the local community through sustainable tourism. It's based at the small village of Las Mangas in Río Cangrejal.

Jungle River Tours (☎ 440-1282/68; www.jungleriver lodge.com) At Banana Republic Guest House, organizes white-water rafting trips (from L771), canopy tours and hiking; rappelling and bouldering also available. Trips can

HONDURAS

include a free night at its jungle lodge. Warning: though very popular, numerous accidents and two deaths have been reported to LP and elsewhere regarding this operator.

La Moskitia Ecoaventuras (☎ 441-3279; www.lamoskitia.hn; Colonia El Toronjal) Jorge Salaverri is the pioneer of tours to La Moskitia (five days from L18,886). He also offers white-water rafting, tours of Pico Bonito and Cuero y Salado, and there's a guesthouse on the Río Cangrejal on the way. Clients snag a free room in his La Ceiba guesthouse near Mall Megaplaza per tour booked.

Omega Tours (☎ 9631-0295; www.omegatours.info; Omega Tours Jungle Lodge, road to Yaruca Km 9) Set up by a former international kayaker, it offers white-water rafting (from L930), swimming, kayak and canoe trips, horseback riding, and jungle- and river-hiking tours. All trips include a free night at its jungle lodge. Slightly pricier but slicker than rival Jungle River Tours.

Tourist Options (☎ 9982-7534; www.hondurastouristoptions.com; Blvr 15 de Septiembre) Friendly agency, arranging trips to Garífuna villages, Pico Bonito, Cuero y Salado and Cayos Cochinos. Located in the Viajes Atlántida travel agency. Ask for Francis, an English-speaking agent.

Sleeping

Accommodations are fairly uninspired in La Ceiba. Staying in the center is convenient, although it is eerily quiet at night. Barrio La Isla is nearer the nightlife. There is now one decent hostel, which has improved things. More interesting accommodation is outside the city amid the tropical jungle by the Río Cangrejal.

DOWNTOWN

Banana Republic Guest House (☎ 440-1268; www.jungleriverlodge.com; Av La República; dm L135, r with/without bathroom L340/285; P 💻) This is a welcome addition to La Ceiba's accommodation scene, which was short on good hostels, but though it's an established travelers' scene in a charmingly aged clapboard home, the priority is as a filter for the Jungle River Lodge and its tours.

Hotel San Carlos (☎ 443-0330; Av San Isidro btwn 5a & 6a Calle; s/d L150/200; P) Upstairs rooms are jail-bare with cold cement floors but sufficiently clean linen. It has the same owner as the midrange Hotel Iberia next door. You do not have to go far for bread – it is set behind a bakery.

Hotel Italia (☎ 443-0150; hotel@carrion.hn; Av Ramón Rosa near 6a Calle; s/d/tr L418/528/550; P 💥 🍴) Owned by the Carrion department store, this solid midrange has a brightly lit courtyard and a well-manicured garden and pool area but the in-room furniture is in seriously need of upgrading. The main concern is its location

right in the middle of the market chaos – fine during the day, super sketchy at night.

Hotel Iberia (☎ 443-0401; www.hoteliberia.com; Av San Isidro btwn 5a & 6a Calles; s/d L580/696; P 💥 🛜) Not the best deal for what you pay (the rooms are past their overhaul date) but the service is friendly, the hotel is secure and there's wi-fi. It's centrally (and noisily) located with rooms surrounding a depressing courtyard that is luckily also home to commercial businesses, including a psychologist. Rooms have private hot-water bathrooms and the doubles are quite spacious. It's popular with Bay Islanders.

Gran Hotel París (☎ 443-2391; www.granhotelparishn.com; Parque Central; s/d/tr L819/972/1318; P 💥 🛜 🍴) The Left Bank it ain't, but this superbly located midrange is a bit nicer than the facade would have you believe. There's a nice pool, wi-fi, safe deposit boxes and an overall Best Western feel to the whole shebang. Service is friendly and it's right on Parque Central.

BARRIO LA ISLA

These two options are a good 15-minute walk from downtown, but a mere stumble away from the nightlife.

Amsterdam 2001 (☎ 443-2311; Av Miguel Paz Barahona off 1a Calle; r from L150, tr L200) A palpable step down from her brother's place next door, this spot offers five musty rooms, unwelcoming cement floors and paint-peeling walls; but it *is* cheaper, and rightfully so.

Rotterdam Beach Hotel (☎ 440-0321; Av Miguel Paz Barahona off 1a Calle; r from L250, t L350; P) This eight-room option offers simple but clean rooms and a lush courtyard area 100m from the beach. Dorms are on the way if tourism rebounds and you can use the internet for free next door at the Quinta Real Hotel.

RÍO CANGREJAL

Jungle River Lodge (☎ 440-1268; www.jungleriverlodge.com; road to Yaruca Km 7; dm L198, d from L617) The rooms are rustic but the setting is a winner. On a hillside, the lodge overlooks the roaring Río Cangrejal. Sitting in the outdoor restaurant will be one of your more memorable Honduran experiences (meals L114). More aggressive canopy tours start here (see warning, above left); swimming, hiking and white-water rafting options are nearby. To get here, take a Yaruca bus from the main terminal and look for a sign on your right, or call and organize it with Banana Republic Guest House. You stay in the dorm room for free if you take an organized trip.

Omega Tours Jungle Lodge (☎ 440-0334; www.omegatours.info; road to Yaruca Km 9; s/d without bathroom L190/380, cabins L665-1900; 🛜) Set in the mountainside a little up from the river, Omega Lodge is a study in tasteful development. A trip with Omega Tours includes a clean, basic room at the bottom of the complex. A lot more pricey but very memorable are the cabins at the top – beautifully done out in a style best described as modernist German meets tropical tree cabin, and with superb views. The simpler Creek Cabin is elevated over running water. Outdoor showers are solar heated, no chemicals are used in the swimming pool, and waste is managed with an ecofriendly, self-contained system (in a Latin American first, the sign asks you to throw toilet paper *in* the toilet!). Among the tropical gardens is a bar and restaurant serving excellent and varied dishes with some German and vegetarian selections (breakfast L40 to L90, mains L80 to L220). Take the Yaruca bus from the main terminal and look for a sign on your left, just beyond the Jungle River Lodge; or contact Omega to arrange a transfer (L285 up to four people).

Guaruma Community Lodge (☎ 9917-5325; www.guaruma.org; d/tr/q L285/335/385) Set high in the mountainside community of Las Mangas, beyond the two jungle lodges, these hillside cabins were built by a local workforce. They are basic but well-constructed and clean, and include hot water. Profits are channeled back into the community. There's a restaurant with good-value meals (L60 to L80) for guests. You can organize walks with local guides through the surrounding jungle, including to the lovely El Bejuco waterfall. The one downer is that there is not much in the way of organized transfers. You'll have to make your own way by bus to Yaruca (see p401) or flag a pickup.

Casa Cangrejal (☎ 408-2760; www.casacangrejal.com; road to Yaruca Km 9; s/d/tr L1653/1983/2534; Ⓟ 🛜) For a splurge-worthy change of pace, this quaint B&B is fashioned from Río Cangrejal stone and set off from the river just a tad from Omega Tours. Rooms are large and stylish, with indigenous tapestries, solid, built-in cement bed frames, spacious baths and wi-fi. A full breakfast is included.

Eating

DOWNTOWN

Pupusaría Universitaria (1a Calle near Av 14 de Julio; pupusas L16, mains L85-90; 🕑 10am-11pm) *Pupusas, Pinchos y Taco* – could be the next Gael García

Bernal film, but it's merely the advertised specialties (*pinchos* are kebabs) of this excellent budget haunt, housed in a clapboard-and-bamboo building.

Ki'boc Café (4a Av btwn Calle 8 & 9; breakfast L45-85; 🕑 7am-7pm Mon-Fri, 8am-7pm Sat, 8am-noon Sun) This adorable artsy cafe serves organic coffee and a host of excellent breakfasts (the Occidente-style *chilaquiles* are a real treat). It's the 'in' gathering spot of the moment and also offers a massive book exchange for travelers.

Cafetería Cobel (7a Calle at Av Atlántida; meals L52; 🕑 6:30am-6pm Mon-Sat) Packed little eatery where you can get your *comida típica* (typical lunch) for a pittance, including grilled meat or chicken with rice. The bustle means you may take a while to attract the attention of the neatly uniformed waitresses. There is air-con in the back room – or you can order a *licuado* (L21) to cool down.

Café Bella Italia (cnr Av San Isidro & 13a Calle; mains L100-220; 🕑 11:30am-2pm & 5-10pm) Take your pick from the outside terrace shaded by arching palm leaves or the cute little Tuscan-flavored inside dining area at this upper-scale European-style cafe. There's good espresso and simple but tasty Italian pastas and desserts.

our pick **Expatriates Bar & Grill** (12a Calle, Barrio El Imán; mains L109-259; 🕑 4pm-midnight Mon-Thu, 4pm-2am Fri, 11am-2am Sat, 11am-11pm Sun) This is a slice of home under a thatched roof in the tropics. Big games are often screened here; the BBQ chicken wings and burgers are rightfully famous and vegetarian options are reasonable too (with hydroponically grown organic lettuce). The L40 Guinness Pub drafts go down all too easy. Free calls to the US and Canada and wi-fi.

Pais Ceibeño Supermarket (7a Calle; 🕑 7am-8pm Mon-Sat, to 7pm Sun) For self-caterers.

BARRIO LA ISLA

Dutch Café (Av Miguel Paz Barahona off 1a Calle; breakfast L40-55, mains L65-100; 🕑 7am-10pm) Next to Rotterdam Beach Hotel and Amsterdam 2001 – and run by the same family – this serves simple, good-value dishes such as chicken tacos, French toast and spaghetti.

Mango Tango (🕑 dinner Wed-Sun; mains L90-265) A mainstay on the main strip, often packed with diners and drinkers enjoying the open-air ambience. Go for the signature pork chop – it's huge! Cocktails (Tom Collins, Sex on the Beach) go for about L70 and beers here live just on the edge of freezing.

Chef Guity (off 1a Calle; mains L90-280; ◷ 11am-10pm Tue-Sun) This is a simple open-air Garífuna restaurant. The service is friendly but as laid-back as a Sunday morning – don't go if your time is tight. However, the specialty is the excellent *tapado* (a fish stew in coconut sauce) but there's lobster, fish and shrimp, too.

Drinking & Entertainment

Most of La Ceiba's nightlife centers in and around 1a Calle in Barrio La Isla, known as the *zona viva*.

La Palapa (Av 15 de Septiembre off 1a Calle; ◷ 11:30am-late) The food won't thrill you, but this massive, two-story thatched-roof bar/restaurant gets rowdy with locals and tourists, here to imbibe hard in the open-air atmosphere. DJs play nightly and there's live music (merengue, rock, *bacheta*) on weekends.

Hibou (☎ 1a Calle at Av Manuel Bonilla; cover from L100; ◷ 9:30pm-late Thu-Sat) This club caters mostly to 20-somethings, mostly with money to burn, mostly pretty attractive. That's what you're looking for, right? Dress to impress.

Le Pache (1a Calle btwn Avs Dionisio de Herrera & Miguel Paz Barahona; cover from L100; ◷ 10pm-late Thu-Sat) The hot newcomer on the scene, Le Pache caters to a well-heeled crowd hell-bent on modeling contracts and out to steal the next guy's thunder. There's a beachfront dance floor and pool deck; and a late-night *parrilla* that serves food after midnight – a rarity. Leave the flip-flops, the board shorts and the Yankees hats at the hotel.

Cines Millenium (Mall Megaplaza; L60) Two-screen theater with recent Hollywood fare.

Shopping

Mall Megaplaza (22a Calle at Av Morazán; ◷ 10am-9pm) A modern mall with a cinema, food court, internet cafes, banks and ATMs as well as an airline office.

Souvenirs El Buen Amigo #3 (☎ 440-1085; 12a Calle, Barrio El Iman; ◷ 8am-6:30pm Mon-Sat) Has a good choice of Honduran *artesanías*, although it is a bit out of the way. It includes everything from Lencan pottery to Maya replicas and colorful hammocks.

Cigar buffs can get a wide range of local and imported cigars at the Expatriates Bar & Grill (p399).

Getting There & Away

La Ceiba's Aeropuerto Golosón is 10km west of downtown. Flights leave frequently for San Pedro Sula, Tegucigalpa, the Bay Islands and La Moskitia.

AIR

Aerolíneas Sosa (☎ 443-1399, at airport 440-0692; www.aerolineasosa.com; Av San Isidro btwn 8a & 9a Calles) Flies to Roatán four times daily; Utila Monday, Wednesday and Friday; and Puerto Lempira Monday to Saturday, among others.

SAMI (☎ 442-2565; Av Atlantida btwn 4a & 5a Calles; ◷ 7am-7pm) Representative inside Hotel Tropical.

TACA/Isleña (☎ 441-3191, airport 443-2683; www.fly islena.com; Mall Megaplaza, 1st fl, 22a Calle at Av Morazán)

Destination	One-Way Cost (L)
Guanaja	1392
Puerto Lempira	2470
Roatán	1056
San Pedro Sula	1392
Tegucigalpa	1684

BOAT

Ferries to the Bay Islands operate from the Muelle de Cabotaje, about 8km east of town. *Colectivos* will take you there for L20 per person; coming back from the pier, it *should* be L30 to L40 per person. Tickets are available either on the day of travel or one day before only.

Boats ply the waters between La Ceiba and the Bay Islands. The **Galaxy Wave** (☎ in La Ceiba 414-5739, in Roatán 445-1795) sails twice daily to Roatán; the smaller **Utila Princess II** (☎ La Ceiba pier 408-5163; ◷ ticket office 7am-4pm) goes between La Ceiba and Utila, also twice daily. Departures for Roatán are at 9:30am and 4:30pm (one way 1st class/normal class L524/624, 1¾ hours). From Roatán, the boats leave Terminal Nueva, Dixon's Cove (between Coxen Hole and French Harbor) at 7am and 2pm. Those inclined to seasickness will want to take precautions heading to Roatán – the *Galaxy Wave* is design-prone to roll in such a way that makes many passengers sick.

For Utila (one way L425, one hour), there are departures at 9:30am and 4pm, returning from the island at 6:20am and 2pm. Same seasickness warning here – this is colloquially known as the Vomit Comet. For Guanaja, see p406.

Note that these times are particularly prone to change. Check before you depart.

You could ask around the Muelle de Cabotaje about boats to other destinations. Captains of cargo and fishing boats might be persuaded to take along a passenger, but the practice is officially discouraged so don't count on it.

BUS

Most bus traffic goes through the bus terminal at Mercado San José, about 1.5km west of the center of La Ceiba – but there are some important exceptions. A local bus runs between the bus terminal and the central plaza (L5.50), or you can take a taxi (L20). **Diana Express** (☎ 441-6460), **Catisa-Tupsa** (☎ 441-2539) and **Kamaldy** (☎ 441-2028) all have offices there. The **Viana Clase de Oro** (☎ 441-2230) express bus terminal is another 500m further west along the same road, at the Esso gas station. **Cotuc** (☎ 441-2199), for Trujillo, shares its terminal with Cotraibal further down the main highway, while luxury bus company **Hedman Alas** (☎ 441-5347; www.hedmanalas.com) has its terminal on the main highway just east of the center.

Getting Around

CAR

There are numerous rental agencies in La Ceiba: **Avis** (☎ 441-2802; www.avis.com.hn; Entrada Principal a La Ceiba; ☺ 7:30am-6pm)
Econo Rent-A-Car (☎ 442-8686; www.econorentacarhn.com; Carretera a Tela; ☺ 8am-5pm) Located near Megaplaza Mall.

TAXI

Taxis in La Ceiba are easy to find – they will normally find you – and a ride anywhere in town costs L20, going up a bit after 8pm.

AROUND LA CEIBA
Cayos Cochinos

Cayos Cochinos (the Hog Islands), 29km from La Ceiba and just 17km from the shore, can be visited as a day trip or camping trip from La Ceiba. Access is by motorized canoe

BUSES FROM LA CEIBA

Destination	Cost (L)	Duration (One Way)	Bus Line	Phone	Departure
Copán Ruinas	N/A	N/A	N/A	N/A	Take any early bus to San Pedro Sula & transfer
El Porvenir	12	45min	Main Terminal	N/A	Every 45min 6:30am-6pm Mon-Sat, hourly 8am-5pm Sun
La Unión-Cuero y Salado	16	1½hr	Main Terminal	N/A	Every 45min 6:30am-6pm Mon-Sat, hourly 8am-5pm Sun
Nueva Armenia	26	1½hr	Main Terminal	N/A	9:30am, 10:30am, 12:30pm, 2:30pm, 4:30pm
Sambo Creek/Corazal	12	1hr	Main Terminal	N/A	Every 35min 6:15am-7:10pm
San Pedro Sula	90	3hr	Diana Express	449-0388	8:30am, 9:30am, 12:30pm, 3:30pm, 4:30pm
	90	3hr	Catisa-Tupsa	441-9539	Hourly 5am-6pm
	323-380	3hr	Hedman Alas	441-5347	6:30am, 10:30am, 3pm
	280-467	3hr	Viana Clase Oro	441-2330	6:30am, 10:30am, 3pm
Tegucigalpa	217	7hr	Kalmaldy	441-2028	3:10am, 7am, 9:10am
	550-950	6½hr	Viana Clase Oro	441-2330	6:30am, 10:30am, 3pm
	475-580	6½hr	Hedman Alas	441-5347	5am, 10am, 2:20pm
Tela	57	2hr	Kamaldy	441-2028	3:10am, 7am, 9:10am
	38	2hr	Main Terminal	N/A	Every 25min 4:15am-6pm
Trujillo	100	3hr	Cotuc/Cotraipbal	441-2129	Hourly 6:15am-7pm
Yaruca/Río Cangrejal	13	20min	Main Terminal	N/A	9am, 11am, noon, 2:30pm, 4pm or any Las Mangas bus

from the town of Nueva Armenia or Sambo Creek, east of La Ceiba.

The Hog Islands and the waters and reefs around them are a designated biological marine reserve – it is illegal to anchor on the reef, and commercial fishing is prohibited. Consequently, the reefs are pristine and fish-abundant. Diving and snorkeling are excellent around the islands, with black coral reefs, wall diving, cave diving, seamounts and a plane wreck. The islands are also known for their unique pink boas.

It is possible to go independently to the cays, although you will not save much money, and local boatmen are unlikely to have a radio or life jackets. Day trips start at around L665 per person if you are already in Sambo Creek or L741 for pick-ups in La Ceiba. Tourist Options (p398) in La Ceiba is the specialist for tours here. It is worth contacting the foundation that campaigned for the marine park, **Fundación Cayos Cochinos** (☎ 442-2670; www.cayoscochinos.org; Av Victor Hugo, 13a Calle 1175, Barrio Colonia El Naranjal, La Ceiba), for more information.

Rustic accommodations are available on some of the cays.

Garífuna Villages

Two seaside fishing villages are easy to reach from La Ceiba: **Corozal**, 15km east of La Ceiba, and **Sambo Creek**, 6km further east. Both places have thriving Garífuna communities, and you will see women in the striking traditional attire and headdresses. However, poverty here is tangible. There are also some good-value restaurants. You can arrange to see local musical groups in both villages. Sambo Creek is far more tourist-friendly than Corozol, and the beach is more inviting as well.

If you are out this way, don't miss the awesome **Sambo Creek Canopy Tour and Spa** (☎ 3355-6481; canopy tour & spa L855), which whizzes you through the treetops for more than an hour, and includes as long as you want in the hillside thermal springs, a spectacular series of natural cold and hot springs and waterfalls set amid the rainforest (a day pass for the springs is L475 – more than worth it!). You can order food for delivery from the beachfront restaurants. The turnoff to the canopy is to the left, about 500m further along from the Sambo Creek turnoff on the main highway to Trujillo.

At Sambo Creek, **Centro Turístico Sambo Creek** (☎ 9587-0874; mauricioelvir@yahoo.com; s/d without bathroom L150/250), owned by Tourist Options in La Ceiba, offers five large rooms with clapboard

flooring and double beds, right on the beach. There's a breezy hammock patio and seafood restaurants. There are five boats on premises to whisk you off to Cayo Cochinos, which you can see off in the distance.

Just out of town, at the bottom of a dirt-track turnoff 200m past the main Sambo Creek entrance (walkable along the beach from Sambo Creek in the dry season), are several great options that beat La Ceiba itself for places to lose a day or two. All three of the following are cash only. The new **Paradise Found** (☎ 9861-1335; http://paradisefoundlaceiba.com; r L740; P X ▣) offers two smallish but well-appointed rooms (with microwaves, minibars, cable TV and coffee machines) and a windswept tiki bar and restaurant. Dante, a trained chef, focuses on the food, which is a godsend. There's always Yankee pot roast, spinach/eggplant lasagna, and his 'Best Burger Ever' (nothing short of astonishing), all of which backpackers can nab for a special price of L100. If you don't stay here, you must eat here. There are two mountain-view rooms on the way.

Helen's Hotel & Restaurant (☎ 441-2017; www.villa helen.com; s/d L600/700, cabins L800-1600; P X ▣ ☒) has options to suit most budgets (although those on a serious shoestring have to sleep several to a bed). The outdoor restaurant is also appealing. Lush gardens, two swimming pools, and a spa bath are other pluses. A day pass here costs L30.

Right next door and Québécois-owned you'll find **Hotel Canadien** (☎ 408-9927; www.hotelcanadien.com; d/tr/q L800/913/1026; P X ▣ ☒), a big whitewashed building with tastefully decorated rooms, all of which have a separate living space with an additional pull-out futon and table area. The restaurant has some spectacular views of the Caribbean Sea, which laps just outside the hotel. Evangelical church groups often stay here. It was for sale when we came through, though, so there could be changes by the time you read this.

Motorboat rides (per person around L660) can be arranged to Cayos Cochinos from here. However, going on organized trips is generally not much more expensive and you have a bit more peace of mind (onboard radios for example).

REFUGIO DE VIDA SILVESTRE CUERO Y SALADO

On the coast about 30km west of La Ceiba, the Cuero y Salado Wildlife Refuge takes its name from two rivers, the Cuero and Salado that meet at the coast in a large estuary. This estuary, now a reserve, protects varied and abundant wildlife; manatees are the most famous (and the hardest to see), but there are also howler and white-faced monkeys, sloths, agoutis (rabbit-sized rodents), iguanas, caimans and hundreds of bird species. Migratory birds are here from around August/September to April/May.

The small town of **La Unión** is the gateway to the reserve. From there, you catch a train to its entrance. At the end of the railroad track is a new **visitors center** (☎ 443-0329; adult/child L189/65) in Salado Barra, with a small but informative exhibition on the refuge. You can organize tours from here. For further information on the refuge, contact La Ceiba–based **Fundación Cuero y Salado** (☎ 443-0329; www.cueroysalado.org; 19 Av at Av 14 de Julio, La Ceiba; ☼ 8-11:30am & 1-5:30pm Mon-Fri).

By far the best way to get around and see the reserve is by water. Canoe tours (L120 for two people plus L200 for guide) can be arranged at the visitors center.

A well-maintained **dorm** (per person L150) is a short walk away, and simple meals are available at the visitors center cafe. **Camping** (per person L80) is also permitted.

Getting There & Away

To get to the reserve, take a bus to La Unión from La Ceiba's main terminal (L16, 1½ hours, every 45 minutes from 6:30am to 6pm). From La Unión, jump on the *trencito* (a railcar) for the 9.5km ride on the old banana railroad to the visitors center in Salado Barra (one or two people L250, three or more people L125 each, 45 minutes, every 1½ hours, 7am to 3pm). Between trains, you can take a *burra*, a railcar basket pushed gondola-style by a couple of men with poles (one person L200, L50 additional per person, one hour). Tell the *trencito* or *burra* drivers when you'd like to return; the last bus from La Unión to La Ceiba is at 4pm. If you walk along the railway tracks, it takes 1½ hours to reach the visitors center at a brisk pace (it's about 9.5km). When you reach the reserve, hire a boat (one to two people L300, L125 per extra person) and guide (L125, up to seven people) for a two-hour trip through the reserve.

PARQUE NACIONAL PICO BONITO

Pico Bonito is the lush, forested area that climbs steeply behind La Ceiba. It is one of Honduras' best-known national parks, with an unexplored core area of 500 sq km. It has magnificent, varied forests at different elevations as well as rivers, waterfalls and abundant wildlife, including jaguars, armadillos, monkeys and toucans.

Pico Bonito itself is one of the highest peaks in Honduras at 2436m (and very difficult to climb). The original entrance to the park is at El Pino; from La Ceiba it is on the way to Tela. In El Pino, you can arrange tours or accommodations at the **Vivero Natural View tourist office** (☎ 368-8343).

The other entrance is at Río Cangrejal, where a new **visitors center** (☼ 7am-4pm) has been built, along with a suspension bridge that has become a tourist attraction in itself (for locals). You can pay the park entrance fees here, or just L20 to cross the bridge. A small insect museum is located upstairs. It's up in the hills on the other side of La Ceiba, where the Río Cangrejal river lodges are located (see p398).

Almost every tour agency in La Ceiba offers Pico Bonito tours, mostly to the El Pino side. For additional information about the park, contact the **Fundación Parque Nacional Pico Bonito** (Funapib; ☎ 442-3044; www.picobonito.org; Carretera a Tela, Colonia Palmira, La Ceiba; ☼ 8am-4pm Mon-Fri).

You can also see the park on horseback; see p397.

Entrance to Pico Bonito National Park is adult/child L133/76.

Hiking

The park's first trail is still a favorite. It is a moderately difficult three-hour hike to **Cascada Zacate** (per person incl guide, transport & park entrance fee L210). You'll hear the falls before you see them – in fact, they are also known as Cascada Ruidoso (Noisy Falls). You can organize this hike at the Vivero Natural View.

On the Río Cangrejal side, there is a lovely trail threading through some lush mountainside jungle to **El Bejuco** waterfall. Contact Guaruma Servicios (p397) to arrange a guide. Several of the lodges have their own trails, which are worth investigating.

Sleeping

For lodging on the Río Cangrejal side, see p398.

Centro Ecoturístico Natural View (☎ 368-8343; r L220) A couple of simple rooms sleep two here. It is a few kilometers north of the highway. Camping is possible on the large grassy plot. This is also a good place to eat and relax après-hiking, with *palapa*-covered tables and shady hammocks.

Getting There & Away

Any bus headed toward Tela or San Pedro Sula can drop you at El Pino. To get to **Vivero Natural View** (☎ 368-8343) look for the purple tourist information sign on your right.

To get to the Río Cangrejal side of the park, take a Yaruca- or Las Mangas–bound bus from the main terminal in La Ceiba; see p401 for times.

TRUJILLO
pop 60,000

Sleepy, tropical Trujillo sits above the wide arc of the Bahía de Trujillo, an expanse of water that has seen the sails of Columbus and many a famous buccaneer. It burns a serene crystal blue when the weather cooperates.

As it's the end of the road to a certain extent, few travelers end up in Trujillo, but rather come with a purpose. A place to lose yourself for a spell? Perhaps. But things move at their own pace here. Whether you sample some of the excellent seafood or take in the town's nightlife, don't plan to do it in a rush.

Shrimp and the nearby port of Puerto Castilla play an important role in the local economy. Trujillo is the capital of the department of Colón.

History

For a small town, Trujillo has had an important part in the history of Central America. It was near Trujillo, on August 14, 1502, that Columbus first set foot on the American mainland, having sailed from Jamaica on his fourth (and final) voyage. The first Catholic Mass on American mainland soil was said on the spot where he and his crew landed.

Founded on May 18, 1525, Trujillo was one of the earliest Spanish settlements in Central America. The first Spanish town in the colonial province of Honduras, it was the provincial capital until the seat was shifted to Comayagua in 1537. The Catholic bishop's seat remained in Trujillo until 1561, when it too was moved to Comayagua.

The Spanish used the port at Trujillo to ship out gold and silver from the interior of Honduras – and inevitably pirates soon came sniffing around. The Bahía de Trujillo was the scene of several great battles when the town was attacked by pirates, including Henry Morgan.

The Spanish built several fortresses, the ruins of which are still visible; the ruins of the fort of Santa Bárbara lie near the plaza in town. Despite the fortifications, the buccaneers prevailed, and after a sacking by Dutch pirates in 1643, the town lay in ruins for over a century until it was resettled in 1787. Trujillo was also the stage for William Walker's bid to take over Central America. It was doomed to failure – he was captured and executed by firing squad. His grave is now in the town center.

Information

The hostel Casa Kiwi has a folder full of local information and bus timetables. There is also a Fundación Capiro-Calentura Guaimoreto (Fucagua) office, although staff offer limited help.

Banco Atlántida (Parque Central) Changes cash and traveler's checks, and has a 24-hour ATM.

Cyber Net Café (per hr L20; ⏰ 8am-10pm) For internet access.

Hondutel (3a Calle; ⏰ 8am-4pm Mon-Fri) Telephone services.

Lavandería Colón (2a Calle; per load L85; ⏰ Mon-Sat) Laundry services.

Police (☎ 434-4054; Parque Central)

Post office (4a Calle; ⏰ 8am-noon & 2-4pm Mon-Fri, 8-11am Sat)

Tourist office (☎ 434-3140; Parque Central; ⏰ 9am-5pm Mon-Fri) Local character Nelson runs this as his pet project.

Sights

The ruins of a 17th-century Spanish fortress, the **Fortaleza Santa Bárbara de Trujillo** (☎ 434-4535; admission L57; ⏰ 9am-noon & 1-5pm), are in the center of town near the plaza, overlooking the sea. The fort has recently undergone a makeover and now includes a small museum. It houses several old cannons and other historic relics. A plaque marks the place where North American adventurer/would-be conqueror William Walker was executed and there's an excellent view along the coast. The museum also has colonial and Garífuna artifacts on display, and it has occasional temporary displays.

There are several **beaches** in and around Trujillo, including one at the front edge of town. Ask if it is safe to swim. The water is not always the cleanest, especially in rainy season. There are also beachside open-air thatched-roof restaurant-bars near the airstrip, a 20-minute walk east along the beach from town. Casa Kiwi has a good stretch of beach away from any town pollution.

Near the Río Cristales, the **Museo y Piscinas Naturales Riveras del Pedegral** (admission L35; 7am-5pm, hours vary) is a fascinating, eclectic and disorganized collection of exhibits. You'll find jade jewelry arranged higgledy-piggledy alongside ancient pre-Columbian archaeological relics as well as Pech and Mískito artifacts. There are also a whole bunch of other random objects – check out the piece of a plane that crashed in the bay in 1985 for example. The museum admission includes entry to the gardens at the rear of the museum, with a couple of open-air swimming pools, and picnic and children's play areas.

Just west of town, where the Río Cristales flows into the sea, there is the largely Garífuna

district of Barrio Cristales. You can see the **grave of William Walker** who was buried in the town's cemetery following an ill-fated bid to conquer Central America. Other good places to visit (including Parque Nacional Capiro-Calentura) are a short distance from town.

Visitors descend upon Trujillo for the **Semana Santa** celebrations and it also gets busy for the **annual fair** of the town's patron saint, San Juan Bautista, in the last week of June (the exact day is June 24, but the festival goes on for a week).

Sleeping

Trujillo has a number of good places to stay. Most of the good ones are out of town. You should book ahead during Semana Santa.

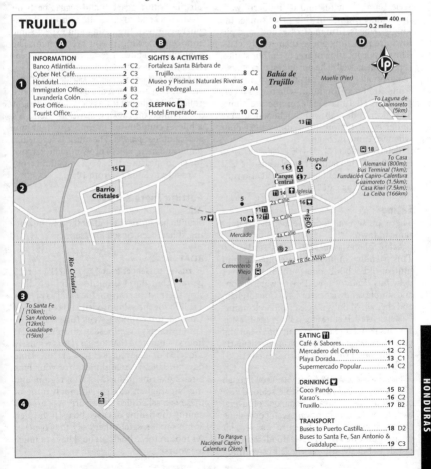

TRUJILLO

INFORMATION		
Banco Atlántida	1	C2
Cyber Net Café	2	C3
Hondutel	3	C2
Immigration Office	4	B3
Lavandería Colón	5	C2
Post Office	6	C2
Tourist Office	7	C2

SIGHTS & ACTIVITIES		
Fortaleza Santa Bárbara de Trujillo	8	C2
Museo y Piscinas Naturales Riveras del Pedregal	9	A4

SLEEPING		
Hotel Emperador	10	C2

EATING		
Café & Sabores	11	C2
Mercadero del Centro	12	C2
Playa Dorada	13	C1
Supermercado Popular	14	C2

DRINKING		
Coco Pando	15	B2
Karao's	16	C2
Trujillo	17	B2

TRANSPORT		
Buses to Puerto Castilla	18	D2
Buses to Santa Fe, San Antonio & Guadalupe	19	C3

Bahía de Trujillo

Muelle (Pier)

To Laguna de Guaimoreto (5km)

To Casa Alemania (800m); Bus Terminal (1km); Fundación Capiro-Calentura Guaimoreto (1.5km); Casa Kiwi (7.5km); La Ceiba (166km)

Barrio Cristales

Parque Central

Hospital

Iglesia

2a Calle

3a Calle

Mercado

4a Calle

Calle 18 de Mayo

Cementerio Viejo

Río Cristales

To Santa Fe (10km); San Antonio (12km); Guadalupe (15km)

To Parque Nacional Capiro-Calentura (2km)

HONDURAS

Casa Kiwi (☎ 9967-2052; dm/s/d L100/160/180, s/d cabins with air-con L600/700; [P] [✗] [▣]) This beach-side hostel has justifiably become a magnet for backpackers. It's 7.5km out of town but that's no bad thing – most guests find everything they need at the restaurant and bar, not to mention its isolated stretch of beach and miraculous sunsets. It is the kind of place where travelers find one- or two-night stays gently slipping into one or two weeks. Smart seaview cabins with pristine, blue-tiled bathrooms have broadened the appeal beyond the budget crew. A taxi from town *should* cost L100.

Casa Alemania (☎ 434-4466; campsites with/without electricity L200/100, d from L300; [P] [✗] [▣]) A consummate German host, owner Gunter Wassmus reigns over his distinctive, steep European-style Casa Alemania and its modern, well-appointed rooms. In this price range, the king-size beds, firm mattresses and solid pillows are punching above their weight class. The seaside location nearer to the bus station is pleasant as well. The onsite restaurant does bang-up all-you-can-eat breakfasts for L80 while Gunter's Honduran wife runs a nicer-than-expected massage/acupuncture clinic. Ten nicer suites, all with kitchenettes, were under construction in an annex next door when we came through.

Hotel Emperador (☎ 434-4446; r with/without air-con L500/200; [✗]) This family-run place is the best of the downtown budget options. It also runs a little adjoining cafeteria.

Eating

There are several good inexpensive restaurants in town.

Café & Sabores (mains L60-80; ⏲ 6am-8pm Mon-Sat) This friendly counter-top cafe offers a faint hint of old-school soda fountain. It serves delicious *licuados* for L25 (try watermelon) and simple sandwiches for L40 (Cubans, ham and cheese). Mainly, it's clean and welcoming.

Merendero del Centro (meals L35; ⏲ 7am-3pm Mon-Sat) This popular place serves up *típico* hot and fast. The *baleadas* and pastels are particularly tasty although the daily lunch specials (L35) are hard to resist.

Playa Dorada (mains L60-420; ⏲ 8am-10pm) Though it's touted as the most reliable seafood restaurant in town, Playa Dorada, one of several back-to-back, straightforward seafooders along the beach just down from *centro*, was very hit or miss on our visit. The seafood soup was excellent, but the fish *ceviche* left us yearning

for Peru. Like most of its neighbors, it offers pleasant, breeze-blown seating on the sand.

Supermercado Popular (Parque Central; ⏲ 7:30am-7:30pm Mon-Sat, 8am-noon Sun) For self-caterers.

Drinking & Entertainment

Truxillo (2a Calle; cover L40; ⏲ 8pm-late Thu-Sat) A recent makeover turned this club into something somewhat unexpected: three ambiences (dance floor, VIP lounge and moonlit outdoor terrace) are a tad flash for a town of this size. Reggaetón, merengue and Latin rock keep the locals moving from 8pm until the early morning hours. Thursday night is karaoke night.

Coco Pando (Barrio Cristales; cover L20; ⏲ from 9pm Fri-Sun) In the mainly Garífuna neighborhood, discos are held Friday to Sunday nights. The air fills with reggaetón and reggae beats on lively weekend nights – though the atmosphere can be intimidating and expect some innocent hassling if you are foreign. The nightclub is above a restaurant with exceptionally good-value Garífuna dishes.

Karao's (2a Calle; cover L30; ⏲ 9pm-late Thu-Sat) This was the best and safest disco in town when we rolled through, but it was closed up the night we planned on causing a ruckus there. It's a bilevel club doused in timber with an upstairs outdoor *palapa*. The music is reggaetón, *punta* and merengue. Throw in some karaoke for good measure. It's also a restaurant from Tuesdays to Sundays from 10am.

Getting There & Away

AIR

Trujillo has an airport but, at the time of writing, it had been closed for years.

BOAT

A rustic **passenger boat** (☎ 9600-2235) for 25 people (but don't think for a minute they stop there) departs from the *muelle* (pier) at Trujillo for the seldom-visited Bay Island of Guanaja three times a week (one way L150, 1pm, Monday, Wednesday and Friday, 2½ hours) – but note that the service is regularly canceled or delayed. Returns are the same days at 9am. You could also try your luck hitching a ride to the Moskitia region, and the Nicaraguan coast – although none of these is a scheduled departure. Ask around among the fishing or cargo boats at the pier. Some say it's safe, others say they'd never set foot in these boats – you'll have to judge for yourself.

BUS

The two main bus companies, **Contraibal** (☎ 434-4932) and **Cotuc** (☎ 444-2181), operate from the large main bus terminal 1km from town, with direct and ordinary services. Be sure to get the direct – the ordinary ones tend to stop if a gecko blinks on the roadside, and can take hours longer.

There is another smaller terminal closer to town, where the local chicken buses and the services through Olancho depart.

Buses for San Pedro Sula (L164, six hours) – making a stop in La Ceiba (L110, three hours) – leave the terminal every 45 minutes from 1:45am to 3pm. Three direct buses go to Tegucigalpa at 12:30am, 2am and 4:45am daily from the main terminal (L280, 10 hours), going via La Ceiba and El Progreso; or transfer in La Ceiba or San Pedro Sula.

Local buses go from Trujillo to day-trip Garífuna villages of Santa Fe, San Antonio and Guadalupe, leaving from in front of the old cemetery. Buses to Puerto Castilla (L15) across the bay (going past Casa Kiwi for L10) leave from the gas-station terminal at 6am, 9:30am, 11am, 11:45am, 2pm, 3:30pm, 4:30pm and 5:40pm. There are nine return buses from Puerto Castilla (three on Sunday).

Getting Around

Taxis abound in the center of Trujillo. Fares around town are L20. The taxi fare out of town is usually L120 to L150, although you will usually be quoted more.

AROUND TRUJILLO
Santa Rosa de Aguán

Paul Theroux's novel *The Mosquito Coast*, which was later made into a movie starring Harrison Ford, featured this small tropical town. Just 40km from Trujillo, Santa Rosa de Aguán is a good place to get a taste of the Moskitia if you don't have the time or the money to go all the way out there. The town was severely damaged during Hurricane Mitch – 44 people drowned – and it hasn't fully recovered. Still, it has an engaging, frontier-like atmosphere, and you can hire boats to take you up the Río Aguán, where you might catch sight of 3m alligators.

There's an annual **Garífuna festival** here from August 22 to 29. Two very basic hotels charge around L70. Five buses to Santa Rosa de Aguán (L36) leave Trujillo from the gas-station terminal each day at 6:45am, 10am,

1pm, 3pm and 4:45pm. There are four return buses at 5am, 6am, 10am and 3pm.

Parque Nacional Capiro-Calentura

The mountain behind Trujillo, called **Cerro Calentura**, 1235m above sea level at the summit, is part of the Capiro-Calentura National Park. You can get there simply by heading straight up the hill from town, though a recent string of robberies has worn a bit of the shine off that adventure. The unpaved road goes right up to the summit, which is 10km from town. It is badly eroded in places and a 4WD is essential. You could also walk it in about three and a half hours.

On the way up the hill, you pass through a couple of distinct vegetation zones. At around 600m to 700m the vegetation changes from tropical rainforest to subtropical low-mountain rainforest, and you find yourself in a zone of giant tree ferns, with lush forest, large trees, vines and flowering plants. There's plenty of wildlife in the park, too, including many species of tropical birds and butterflies, reptiles and monkeys.

About a third of the way up, a couple of trails take off from the road to the left, leading to a waterfall and a tiny reservoir; they're not marked, but you can see them distinctly from the road. It can be sunny, clear and warm in Trujillo, and cloudy and much cooler at the top of the hill. If you're lucky, you can get a superb view from the top over the beautiful Valle de Aguán, along the coast as far as Limón, and across the bay. There is a radar station at the summit.

Information about the park is from the tourist office, or from the **Fundación Capiro-Calentura Guaimoreto** (Fucagua; ☎ 434-4294; Barrio Jérico; ☉ 7am-5pm) – its office is out past the airport – although info can be quite vague.

You're best off doing this in a group or with a guide. Although it is generally a safe walk, occasional attacks have been reported.

Laguna de Guaimoreto

Five kilometers east of Trujillo, past the airstrip and the Río Negro, is Laguna de Guaimoreto, a large lagoon with a natural passageway onto the bay. About 6km by 9km, the lagoon is a protected wildlife refuge; its complex system of canals and mangrove forests provide shelter to abundant animal, bird and plant life, including thousands of migratory birds between November and February, and the elusive manatee. There have even been reported panther sightings.

You can also hire **rowing boats** or **canoes** (and even someone to paddle for you) if you turn left down the road marked by the sign 'Refugio de Vida Laguna Guaimoreto' and call out when you get to the old bridge between Trujillo and Puerto Castilla. If your bargaining skills are up to it, you can rent canoes for around L300.

Shipwreck

Just off the coast 2km east of Casa Kiwi on the road to Puerto Castillo is the wreck of a sunken ship that is good for **snorkeling**. It is close to the shore, and is easily accessible from the beach. Ask at Casa Kiwi for more details.

BAY ISLANDS

Spectacular diving and snorkeling draws visitors from around the world to the three Bay Islands (Islas de la Bahía) – Roatán, Utila and Guanaja – about 50km off the north coast of Honduras. Their reefs are part of the second-largest barrier reef in the world after Australia's Great Barrier Reef, and teem with fish, coral, sponges, rays, sea turtles and even whale sharks. Divers come year round, although the rainy season (November to February) puts a dampener on things – it makes diving trickier and some dive sites difficult to access. Diving here is very affordable.

Lodging and food (more expensive than on the mainland on all three islands) are easily cheapest on Utila, so the majority of backpackers go there. On the other hand, Roatán has better beaches and more non-diving things to do. Both islands have many aficionados. Diving is also good on Guanaja, though the prices on this island are prohibitive to most backpackers.

The island economy is based mostly on tourism and fishing, and shrimp and lobster catching.

HISTORY

Ruins on all three Bay Islands indicate that they were inhabited well before the Europeans arrived. Apparently human habitation began around AD 600, although the evidence is slim until after around AD 1000. The early settlers might have been Maya; there are also caves that perhaps provided shelter for groups of Pech (Paya), and Nahuatl-speaking people

seem to have been here (Nahuatl was the language of the Aztecs in Mexico).

Christopher Columbus, on his fourth and final voyage to the New World, landed on the island of Guanaja on July 30, 1502. He encountered a fairly large population of *indígenas,* whom he believed to be cannibals. The Spanish enslaved many islanders and sent them to work in the plantations of Cuba and in the gold and silver mines of Mexico.

English, French and Dutch pirates turned their attention to the islands, establishing settlements and raiding the gold-laden Spanish cargo vessels. The English buccaneer Henry Morgan established his base at Port Royal on Roatán in the mid-17th century; at that time, as many as 5000 pirates were ensconced on the island.

In March 1782, after many vain attempts, the Spanish waged a successful land attack against Port Royal, either killing or selling the pirates off as slaves.

One of the most influential events occurred on April 12, 1797. Thousands of Black Caribs were dumped by the British on Roatán, following a rebellion on the Caribbean island of St Vincent. This group settled at Punta Gorda, survived and mixed with the natives. Migrant groups reached the mainland, setting up small fishing and agricultural villages along the coast from Belize to Nicaragua. And the Garífuna were born.

The Bay Islands, along with the Moskitia in northeastern Honduras, remained in the hands of the British until 1859, when Great Britain signed a treaty ceding the Bay Islands and the Moskitia to Honduras. Only in the last few decades, however, when Honduran education officials decided that Spanish must be spoken in all the country's schools, did the islanders begin to speak Spanish. English, spoken with a broad Caribbean accent, remains the preferred language of most islanders, although more and more migrants from the mainland are shifting the balance.

The orientation of the islands is still, in many ways, more toward the UK and the USA than toward the Honduran mainland just 50km away; many islanders are more likely to have visited the US than their own capital, Tegucigalpa, and many have relatives in the US. The government focuses much of its tourism development efforts on the islands. Recently the Bay Islands were declared a Free Trade Zone, which means that businesses are exempt from the sales taxes applied on the mainland.

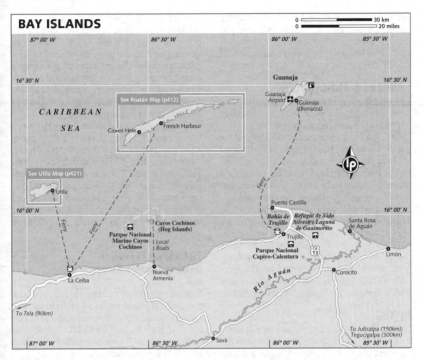

PEOPLE

The population of the Bay Islands is very diverse. *Isleñas* have heritage that includes African and Carib, European and other ancestry. English is the dominant spoken language, and Spanish is a second language. On Roatán there is a Garífuna settlement at Punta Gorda.

There are still some white descendants of early British settlers, especially on Utila. You might meet people who look like they just got off the boat from England, Scotland or Ireland, though actually their ancestors came here over a century ago.

Many islanders are strongly religious (you will quickly spot the number of churches). Be mindful of this in the way you dress – men going into shops without a shirt on can be taken as a sign of disrespect.

Recently, many Ladinos have come from the mainland, especially to Roatán, where taxi drivers and security guards are in high demand. The migration is changing the island's language; you hear much more Spanish here than just a few years ago.

There is also a significant population of foreigners, working for dive shops and other tourist-oriented businesses; in dive shops you often hear a variety of languages, including English, Spanish, German, Italian, French and Hebrew.

CLIMATE

The rainy season on the islands runs roughly from October or November to February. March and August are the hottest months; at other times the sea breezes temper the heat. Tropical storms are possible in September.

COSTS

The Bay Islands are much more expensive than the mainland. Guanaja is the most expensive of the three, and well out of backpacker range. Roatán is less expensive, but still a steep hike up – it's not cheap if you are a lone traveler. If you're in a group, you can minimize your food and accommodation costs – especially if you get a shared place with a kitchen. Internet costs are still sky high in West End. Utila easily has the cheapest places to stay and eat. There is little to choose between diving prices (see p410) on Roatán and Utila.

Visiting the islands will inevitably eat into your budget, but if you want to dive, it doesn't get much more affordable (or better) in the Caribbean than here. If you can only afford to dive a few times, or not at all, you can snorkel and kayak cheaply, or swim and sunbathe free of charge.

DANGERS & ANNOYANCES

The islands are generally safer than the mainland, although the occasional assault does happen on Roatán. When swimming or snorkeling, don't leave unattended valuables on the beach. There have been reports of thefts from West Bay in Roatán and occasionally in Utila.

The main things likely to affect visitors are the mosquitoes and sand flies, which are voracious, especially during the rainy season. You'll need plenty of repellent, which you can bring along or buy on the islands. It's very important that you to consider antimalarial medication – five different strains of the disease have been identified on Roatán alone. Mosquitoes also carry dengue fever. The recommended dose is 500mg of chloroquine once a week; ask for 'Aralen' in any pharmacy.

DIVING

Diving is by far the most popular tourist activity on the Bay Islands, and it's still one of the cheapest places in the world to get a diving certification. Note that diving is more difficult and not as rewarding during the islands' rainy season (November to February). Dive shops usually offer an introductory courses (basic instruction plus a couple of dives) and full PADI-certification courses qualifying you to dive worldwide. Though most dive shops are affiliated with PADI, NAWI and SSI courses are also available. An open-water diving certification course typically lasts three to four days and includes two confined-water and four open-water dives. Advanced diving courses are also available. Despite the low cost, safety and equipment standards are usually reasonable – accidents are rare, despite the high volume of divers.

Utila used to have the lowest certification and fun-diving prices of the three Bay Islands, but prices on Roatán are about the same now. (Food and lodging are still cheaper on Utila, however.) Guanaja is not a budget destination. PADI-certification dive packages on Utila and Roatán work out to at around L5890 (including materials) but can fluctuate several hundred lempiras in either direction. You can save close to L600 by skipping the printed materials and handling the course study online before departure. Single-tank dives are generally L665 to L855 each, with prices dropping the more dives you book.

Don't make the mistake of selecting a diving course purely on the basis of price – you'll find the differences are small, anyway. Instead, find a shop that has a good record and where you feel comfortable.

Qualified divers also have plenty of options, including fun dives, 10-dive packages, night dives, deep dives, wreck diving, customized dive charters and dives to coral walls and caves. There is a great variety of fish and marine life present, and the visibility is great. The waters between Roatán and Utila are among the best places in the world to view whale sharks, usually from May to September.

TRANSPORTATION
Getting There & Away
AIR

Several companies operate flights from the mainland of Honduras (La Ceiba) to the Bay Islands. Some flights originate at San Pedro Sula. Airlines include **Isleña/TACA** (☎ 445-1088, reservations 443-0179; www.flyislena.com) and **Sosa** (☎ 445-1658; www.aerolineassosa.com).

Delta and Continental both have flights to Roatán from the USA (see p419).

BOAT

There are regular boat services from La Ceiba to Roatán and Utila. A less-reliable boat service runs from Trujillo to Guanaja (see p406). See each island for relevant times. Make sure you check the times as they are prone to change. Ferry companies still do not offer direct services between these islands – you have to go via La Ceiba. More private boat owners are now making the trip.

Ask around, you will quickly find out what is going on.

There are occasional ad hoc yachts from Utila to Belize, or Lívingston in Guatemala, but these are subject to the whims of yacht owners. Normally yacht owners advise a dive shop in Utila beforehand if they are planning a visit.

Getting Around
BOAT

Water taxis are used on Roatán between West End and the beach at West Bay, as well as at the

DON'T TOUCH THE CORAL!

The coral and sponge formations in the Bay Islands (and throughout the region's entire barrier reef) are the result of centuries of growth. However, they are under pressure from pollution produced by humans and pumped into the water. In fact, a recent World Resources Institute report estimates that more than 80% of the sediment and more than half of all nutrients that damage the reefs come from Honduras, where large rivers drain agricultural runoff (one of the main causes of reef deterioration) into the Caribbean. Only with careful management will the wonderful underwater reef that skirts the coast of Central America be preserved.

For the most part, the magnificent reefs around the Bay Islands remain healthy and pristine, thanks to the historically low number of divers. But those numbers have risen dramatically in recent years, especially among beginners, and the coral is already beginning to show signs of damage. With even more divers expected to come (not to mention legions of snorkeler-toting cruise ships), it is crucial for everyone to help preserve the reef. Coral is fascinating and beautiful, and many beginning (and experienced) divers are tempted to touch it, but avoiding contact is extremely important. 'Don't touch the coral' is a refrain you will often hear in the Bay Islands.

community of Oak Ridge, where many of the houses are on stilts above the water. Water taxis are also common on Guanaja, where you'll need a boat to go between the main village, which is on a small cay, and the main island.

CAR & MOTORCYCLE
You can rent cars on Roatán and motorcycles on all three islands. However, renting vehicles here is not cheap (from about L808 a day), especially if fuel isn't included.

TAXI
Taxis ferry people all around Roatán, and to a lesser degree on Utila. *Colectivo* fares are reasonable (L30 to L70), but private rates are high (L120 to L200).

ROATÁN
pop 28,400
Roatán is the largest and best known of the Bay Islands. It is about 50km off the coast of Honduras from La Ceiba. Long and thin (50km in length by 2km to 4km wide), the island is a real diving and snorkeling mecca, surrounded by over 100km of living reef. Its beaches are picture-postcard idyllic, especially stretches along West End and West Bay, with clear turquoise water, colorful tropical fish, powdery white sand and coconut palms.

A new US$62-million Mahogany Bay Cruise Center in Dixon's Cove, built by Carnival Cruise Lines (complete with a chairlift!) opened in 2009, further enabling mass tourism but also, with its retail center, bars and restaurants, easing the pressure on the West End, where cruise passengers previously congregated.

Dangers & Annoyances
Occasional assaults have occurred on the beach between West End and West Bay; this attractive beachside walk is fine during the day, but best avoided after sunset. Coxen Hole can get sketchy after nightfall and you should avoid hitching or waiting for taxis on the main roads outside of the towns after dark – robberies are not uncommon.

Roatán is sometimes used as a drugs thoroughfare. Be aware of that if you stumble across any particularly desolated coves.

West End
Curled around two small turquoise bays and laced with coconut palms, West End is a busy but pleasant village on the west end of the island. This is where virtually all backpackers and divers come, and the town's one sandy road is packed with restaurants, hotels and dive shops. Most accommodations are midrange to expensive, but a few cheaper options exist, and more are being built.

ORIENTATION
It's impossible to get lost in West End, though some hotels and shops can be hard to find. The road from Coxen Hole intersects with the town's main sandy road at the eastern side of Half Moon Bay, the first of West End's two small bays. Buses and taxis to Coxen Hole wait at this intersection. Immediately to the right (north) are a few hotels, restaurants, bars and dive shops; further down are a few additional lodging options.

Left (south) from the intersection, the road curls around Half Moon Bay, passes a Baptist church and turns into 'the strip,' where you'll find most of West End's restaurants, bars and dive shops. You can walk end to end in five to 10 minutes. *Colectivo* water taxis to West Bay leave from a pier across from Pura Vida dive shop (L50).

INFORMATION
There are three ATMs in West End – an HSBC outlet by the Coconut Tree supermarket, a Unibanc option next to Tyll's Dive, and the most dependable, 200m up the main road beyond Casa del Sol at Banco Lafise, next to Woody's. Internet connection on Roatán can be frustratingly sporadic and frequently drops out. Prices are just as painful. For medical attention, Anthony's Key Resort operates the best clinic in town.

Bamboo Hut Laundry (8am-4pm Mon-Sat) On the main road, beyond most of the main restaurants and shops, this will wash, dry and fold up to 5lb of dirty clothes for L75.

Barefoot Charlie's (9am-9pm; per hr L120) Weekly internet rates and a two-for-one book exchange are also available.

Paradise Computers (West End/French Harbour; per hr L120; 8am-9:30pm Mon-Sat, noon-8pm Sun) Cheaper prepaid internet accounts available (one hour/10 hours L95/570).

Roatán Online (www.roatanonline.com) A charmless but comprehensive guide to all things Roatán.

Tourist police (9994-9240; 24hr) Just off the main drag north of Argentinean Grill.

ACTIVITIES
Diving
The entire coastline of Roatán, especially the western tip, is dotted with dozens of dive sites, many just meters off the shore. With names such as Hole in the Wall, Sponge Emporium, Black Rock and Texas, Roatán is truly a diver's paradise, with endless variety and near-perfect diving conditions. Diving in Roatán used to cost more than on Utila, but the difference is now negligible. Roatán tends to have smaller classes than on Utila, and the reef is in slightly better shape. Most sites are nearby, so shops typically offer three to four one-tank dives per day, as opposed to two two-tank dives common on Utila. Prices are pretty standard among the shops: a four-day PADI open-water diving certification course costs around L5890 including instruc-

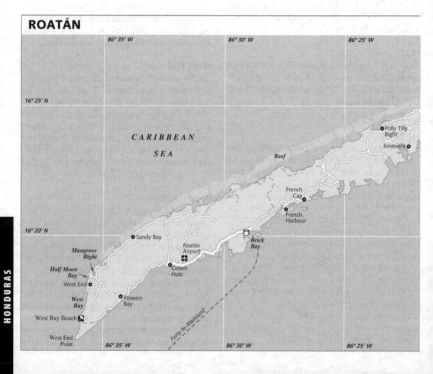

ROATÁN

tion book and marine park fee; an advanced course is usually the same; single-tank dives run from L665 to L855 per dive, less the more dives you buy. Most dive shops depart three times per day.

Prices for courses are now supposed to be standard among most of the dive outfits on the island, although not all adhere. But remember that price isn't everything.

Make sure you sign up with a diving outfit that belongs to the **West End & Sandy Bay Marine Park** (www.roatanmarinepark.com). The reef is under enormous pressure, both from the building works and the amount of visitors, and this organization is campaigning strongly to conserve its beauty. Most shops have joined and voluntarily charge all divers a park fee (annual/daily L190/57). Please only use shops that are part of this effort – there's a list of member shops at the marine park's website. All of the following dive shops are members.

Run by Alvin Jackson, a local instructor with almost three decades of experience, **Native Sons** (☎ 445-4003; www.nativesonsroatan.com) has a good reputation. All dives are led by instructors, not dive masters. Native Sons has

fast, well-maintained boats that easily go to the more distant dive sites.

Ocean Connections (☎ 327-0935; www.ocean -connections.com) has small classes and a friendly, noncompetitive atmosphere, catering to a slightly older crowd. It also has a dive shop and a second location in West Bay. Packages are available with Sea Breeze Inn.

Pura Vida (☎ 445-4110; www.puravidaresort.com) is a Cuban-run resort/dive shop with a good reputation. The instructors are multilingual and organize dives according to high or low season. English, German and French are spoken. There is also a fine Italian restaurant next door. Higher-end dive/lodgings packages are offered.

Capably managed by a young British couple, **Reef Gliders** (☎ 8413-5099; www.reefgliders.com; next to Purple Turtle) has two modern Panga boats; it is very safety and conservation conscious. It offers dawn and night dives and free accommodations for backpackers and dive/lodging packages with Valerie's.

Sueño del Mar (☎ 445-4343; www.suenodelmar.com) is an upscale option with a well-equipped retail shop and beautifully kept accommodations – some include a balcony with sea view.

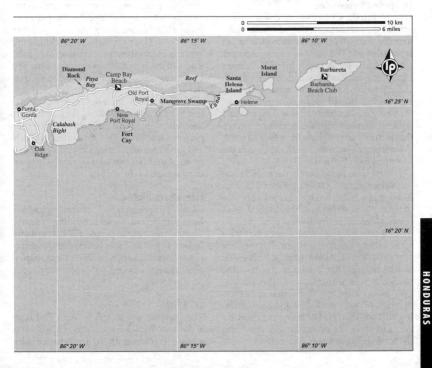

HONDURAS

GETTING INTO TOWN

From the Airport

Colectivo taxis charge L70 to West End, L200 if you want to go direct on your own. It's worth making a little more effort: walk out the airport gates, cross the road and taxis are a third of the price or less (agree on a fare before getting in). Even cheaper, take a *colectivo* taxi to Coxen Hole (L35) then a minibus (L20) or another *colectivo* (L35) to West End.

From the Pier

Taxis are the quick, easy and expensive way to get to West End. Drivers have a price-sharking system in operation from the pier – the going rate is quoted at L70 a ride. If you haven't got much stuff, walk 150m to the main road (wait on the far side) and flag a *colectivo* (L35 to Coxen Hole, then L35 from Coxen Hole to West End) or a minibus (L20). Minibuses don't run on Sunday.

It is geared toward the luxury end of the market (four-day open-water course with lodging L11,673). Eight new rooms and a shiny new office and shop were being constructed when we passed through.

A relaxed, friendly dive shop on the main drag is **Tyll's Dive** (☎ 9698-0416; www.tyllsdive.com). **West End Divers** (☎ 445-4289; www.westenddivers. com), a small dive shop opposite the water-taxi pier, caters to a younger crowd.

Deep-Sea Submarine

One of Roatán's most unusual activities is offered by Karl Stanley, the man behind the grandly named **Roatán Institute of Deep Sea Exploration** (☎ 3359-2887; www.stanleysubmarines. com; dives from L7500). A highly inventive, driven history major, Stanley became obsessed with submarines when he was nine years old. Now he has turned his passion into a commercially viable reality, having designed and built his own submersible. He is the subject of the documentary, *A View from Below* (www. aviewfrombelow.com), which debuted at the Montréal Film Festival in 2009.

Stanley takes passengers in the small yellow submarine, named *Idabel* after the Oklahoma location in which it was constructed, to depths of up to 300m, 450m or 600m. Light doesn't penetrate to those depths and those who do dare to take the ride come face to face with some extraordinary marine life that very few ever get to see, including the elusive six-gilled sharks. Stanley freely admits you take the plunge at your own risk, and takes passengers' money after they dive (but don't worry, Stanley's piloted over 15,000 dives and counting without injury). The above is priced for two and more can pile in for free providing the total weight remains under 205kg.

Beaches & Snorkeling

Half Moon Bay has a small, nice beach and decent snorkeling, although there is some sea grass to wade through. Watch the currents here, sometimes they get unruly – people have drowned. Hire your snorkel equipment from the Marine Park office that overlooks the beach (L95) – the money goes to help protect the reef. The beach at **West Bay**, about 4km southwest of West End village, is the most beautiful beach on Roatán – although more and more high-end resorts are lining the beach; you can rent beach chairs (per person L93, or try just 'tipping' the guard) or bring a blanket and set up under the palms at the far end. There's fantastic snorkeling at the western end, and buoys to ward off the boats. You can easily rent snorkel equipment. Try Las Rocas at the beginning of the beach (per day L190).

You can walk to West Bay from West End – just keep heading west along the beach – but the walk is not safe at night. Water taxis (per person each way L50, 10 minutes) go back and forth regularly. Plan on returning by 5pm or so. A normal private taxi there costs an extortionate L120.

Horseback Riding

Roatán's surprisingly lush, undulating interior has some decent horseback-riding country. The friendly, helpful people at **El Rancho Barrio Dorcas** (☎ 9687-1067; www.barriodorcasranch.com) arrange horseback trips for L760 a head. They also organize rides on full-moon nights (per person L950).

SLEEPING

The cheapest way to stay in West End is in a dorm room with access to a communal kitchen. If you're not keen on dorms, couples and groups have better and cheaper options. Accommodations fills up fast, especially during the high season (July to August, November to January and Easter). Unfortunately, few hotels take reservations, and then only with a credit card or bank deposit. Many taxi drivers will try to shepherd you to hotels where they get a commission – not all hotels play that game, so insist on stopping at your choice.

Valerie's (dm L150, r without bathroom L300, cottages L500) Valerie's mad, ramshackle tumble of wooden rooms and dormitories has been on the market for several years but nobody is buying. Perhaps for good reason; her place charms some and repels others. The shared kitchen for the bottom dorm is nothing short of grim, but the upstairs dorms are a big step up. A new sky deck at least offers good sunset views with your brews. But really, it's for lempira-pinchers only.

Milka's Rooms (☎ 445-4005; per person r L190) This is a good cheapie, with four rudimentary but functioning kitchens. The three newer cabins with hot water are the best deal, but all the rooms are adequate, if a little tight on space. It's tucked away just behind Pura Vida.

Georphi's Tropical Hideaway (☎ 445-1794; www. georphi.com; dm L192, d L480, cabins with shared kitchen from L480, q with kitchen L1152; **P** ✕ 🖳) Perhaps the best-value backpacker accommodations on the island, especially if you're with others. This is a sprawling collection of hexagonal cabins in lush, sloping grounds. All the cabins are sturdy-but-basic pine structures, some have a kitchen, and all have a private patio with hammocks. Shared kitchens are miniscule but functional. Check its Facebook page for details on individual rooms. From the intersection, turn left and walk along the beach toward the end of the sandy road. It is on the same site as Rudy's eatery.

Chillies (☎ 445-4003; www.nativesonsroatan.com/chillies.htm; d/tr L380/513, cabins with shared kitchen & without bathroom L456, with bathroom L570) This place is an ever-popular budget-traveler choice and it's with good reason. The shared bathrooms are unusually pleasant, while the landscaped gardens are lush. Cabins are a good option for couples. Shared kitchens are not great, but they serve their purpose well enough. It is affiliated with the Native Sons dive shop.

Sea Breeze Inn (☎ 445-4026; www.seabreezeroatan. com; r with/without air-con L550/456, studio with/without air-con L850/750, ste with/without air-con L1227/1038; **P** ✕) This is a good option for families or groups. Rooms are neat, with plenty of character but not much space. The suites, however, are spacious, and are great places to chill out. Each has a fridge and microwave, and hammocks draped on the porch in front. Ask for the ocean-view suites up top if you can – lest you be stuck with a cemetery view. It is a three-story wood building behind the Cannibal Café.

Mariposa Lodge (☎ 445-4450; www.mariposa-lodge. com; d without bathroom L500, apt with/without air-con L1000/800; ✕ 🖳) A short way behind the main sandy road and set in tropical gardens, this place is one of Roatán's most attractive lodgings. The apartments – fully kitted out with gas cookers and fridges – are a great place to kick back after a day's diving. Each has a deck with hammocks, some with fine sea views.

Casa del Sol (☎ 445-4218; www.casadelsolroatan.com; r from L500, q with air-con L1190; ✕ 🖳) A newer set-up, this is right by the entrance to West End where the road forks off to West Bay. Billed as Mexican Riviera meets tropical island, it is a very good-value midrange option. Rooms have a Mexican-style color wash, there are big ceramic floor tiles and the bathroom sinks are hand-painted porcelain from El Salvador. All rooms have kitchenettes and air-con ability (for L190 extra). The studios sleep four and have big bathtubs.

Posada Arco Iris (☎ 445-4264; www.roatanposada.com; s/d/tr with fan L798/912/1026, with air-con L1083/1197/1311, apt from L1254; **P** ✕ 🖳) Guatemalan and Argentine tapestries and carvings, impeccably varnished floors, and an extended leafy, shady setting are some of the stylish touches that make this classy midscale choice stand out. Rooms and apartments are available – for groups it can work out reasonably cheaply. You do get free internet, use of a full kitchen (with the apartment), as well as beach chair and kayak use.

Half Moon Resort (☎ 445-4442; www.roatanhalfmoonresort.com; s/d/tr L869/1096/1315; **P** ✕ 🖳) This is down at the bottom of a shaded cul-de-sac. Its location is a winner. The pine-constructed rooms are nothing fancy (you might expect fancier for the price), but when you tumble out of bed to the sun lounges right by the reef (prime snorkeling territory), you won't care. Snorkeling gear, kayaks and coffee are included in the room.

Posada Las Orquideas (☎ 445-4387; www.posadalasorquideas.com; s/d with air-con L1083/1197, with kitchen L1311/1425; **P** ✕ 🖳) Run by the same people who manage Posada Arco Iris, with similar amenities and tasteful decor. This is more secluded and has a jetty that is just for guests, jutting out over the pretty Gibson Bay. Go past Arco Iris and follow the signs.

Las Rocas Resort (☎ 408-5760; www.lasrocasresort.com; r incl breakfast L1770-2700; P ⌘ ⌂ ⌦) On West Bay with just 13 units, Las Rocas is the sort of upper midrange where guests really get to know each other: over breakfast, on the dive boat, at the bar. Bungalows are simply but comfortably appointed, with polished wood floors, air-con and firm beds; superior rooms have peaked ceilings, king-size beds and (in some cases) awesome ocean views. True to its name, Las Rocas is built on a rocky outcrop and doesn't have a beach of its own. West Bay beach is a short walk away, and the hotel has a tiny saltwater pool and a waterfront wooden deck for sunbathing.

EATING

Food in West End is pricey. A few basic places have reasonable prices. Staying in a place with a kitchen will cut costs, especially if you are in a group. Supermarket prices are lowest at Sun in French Harbour, but it can be a pain to go there and back. If practical, shop in La Ceiba before getting on the ferry.

Rudy's (mains L58-221; ☺ 6am-5pm Sun-Fri) The banana pancakes (L76) are renowned at this pleasant open-air cafe. Service can drag a bit, but it just gives you more time to watch the waves washing in across the sandy main road. It also has reasonably priced lunch dishes, including spaghetti dishes, and generous mugs of coffee go for L24.

Cream of the Trop (ice cream L60, breakfast L80-100; ☺ 9am-5pm) The island's only homemade ice cream, offering several yummy flavors of tropical gelato, one of Roatán's few espresso machines, and crepes and egg/tortilla combos for breakfast.

Creole's Rotisserie Chicken (half chicken L100; ☺ 2-11pm Mon-Sat, to 10pm Sun) Easily the biggest bang for your buck this side of the mainland, this classic open-air budget option dishes up some genuinely tasty fare. Its few tables are often full to overflowing as tourists and locals queue for the roast chicken dishes, with healthily portioned sides of rice, beans, potato salad or coleslaw. According to locals, it's the only consistent meal on the island. Get there early.

Cannibal Café (mains L50-225; ☺ 7am-10pm Mon-Sat) Seriously large tacos are a specialty here at this relaxed Mexican-food eatery attached to Sea Breeze Inn. Thick, square-shaped tortillas are served warm, but are a little greasy. Everything on the menu can be made vegetarian.

Lighthouse Restaurant (mains L80-300; ☺ 7:30am-10pm) Simple waterside restaurant serves good seafood in the evening – including grilled fish, shrimp salad and lobster. There are different, cheaper menus for breakfast and lunch.

our pick Tong's (mains L260-480; ☺ noon-3:30pm & 5:30-9:30pm) Chef Tong's classic curries are remarkable and the island herbed beef will transport you across to Thailand. The atmosphere is memorable as well, with a string of candlelit tables jutting out over the water along the dock.

Argentinean Grill (mains L270-450; ☺ 10am-10pm Fri-Wed) Carnivores should head here for a splurge. As you would expect, steaks are the order of the day – prepped by an Argentine chef who knows how to turn a filet mignon into a juicy beast – and there's malbec by the glass to wash it down. It's in front of Posada Arco Iris.

Three good street-food options include **Keith's BBQ** (mains L80-90; ☺ 7am-6pm Thu & Sun), on the north end of Half Moon Bay beach, dishing out local-style BBQ chicken, pork and beef, including BBQ sausage *baleadas* for breakfast; **Tacos Al Pastor** (mains L100; ☎ 6pm-midnight Mon-Thu, to 3am Fri & Sat), across from the Baptist church; and **Jerk Stop** (mains L120; ☎ 9am-midnight Tue-Fri & Sun), next to Paradise Computers, serving up jerk chicken, pork and sides of fritters or plantains.

There are four supermarkets in West End, with roughly the same high prices. **Coconut Tree Market** (☺ 7am-8pm) is at the intersection, dead center along the strip. Watch out for the pickup trucks that pass through, laden with cheap fresh fruits. As with all produce in Honduras, wash it before you eat – crops here are usually sprayed with DDT.

DRINKING & ENTERTAINMENT

The West End drag is lined with bars dishing out live music, DJs or reggaetón to keep the island party vibe alive deep into the night. Follow your eyes and ears. Foster's (local ruffians), Nova (video quizzes), Twisted Toucan (older) and the Dive (games) are all popular.

Earth Mamas (☺ 7:30am-5pm Mon-Sat) This eco-boutique and juice bar serves up organic smoothies, the only wheatgrass within miles, and also sells organic clothing and cosmetics, including natural insect repellent. There is also yoga three to four times per day. It's tucked away behind Paradise Computers.

Sundowners (☺ 11am-9:30pm) A classic across from Native Sons and Posada Arco Iris, this is a beachside bar, at its liveliest in the early evening when off-duty divers gather to watch the horizon turn brilliant shades of red.

Blue Marlin (noon-midnight Mon-Thu, to 2am Fri & Sat, to 10pm Sun) This new hot spot was the place to be during our visit, mainly due to its lovely location oceanside with superb sunset views. It's understandably popular at sunset but into the evening as well. There's live music on Fridays with hopes of expanding to Wednesdays as well.

Coxen Hole

Coxen Hole is the largest town on Roatán, and home to government offices, banks, the post office and Hondutel. The airport is just outside town. People come here on business errands or to stock up at the supermarket, HB Warren (cheaper than the West End). It's hot, humid and there are no good beaches. Avoid walking around at night, as discos and bars can get rowdy.

ORIENTATION

The commercial section of Coxen Hole is a few short blocks. The HB Warren supermarket, with the tiny city park beside it, is at the center of town; everything of interest is nearby or on the road leading into town. Buses and taxis arrive and depart from in front of the city park. The airport is a five-minute drive east. The main through road in town is one way (west to east) – be careful if you are driving a rented car, as there are no signs telling you this.

INFORMATION

BAC/Bamer (Front St) Has an ATM.

Banco Atlántida (Front St; 9am-4pm Mon-Fri, 8:30am-noon Sat) Has an ATM; gives advances on Visa cards and changes traveler's checks. Queues are often long.

HSBC (Front St) Changes American Express traveler's checks. Also has an ATM.

Martinez Cyber Center (445-1432; per hr L40; 8am-7pm Mon-Sat) Internet and international phone calls; behind HSBC.

Police (445-3439)

Post office (8am-4pm Mon-Fri) Just opposite the HSBC bank on the same side of the street as the HB Warren supermarket.

Yaba Ding Ding (9am-5pm Mon-Sat) Postcard and souvenir store located off the main street down a precinct toward the water.

EATING

Try **Comedor Jaylin** (Front St; mains L65-250; 6am-7pm), a locally recommended, little hole-in-

the-wall that is cheap and clean, with good local fare. Go for a *baleada* for just L65. It's adjacent to the Wood Medical Center. Stock up on groceries at **HB Warren supermarket** (445-1208; 7am-7pm Mon-Sat).

French Harbour

French Harbour is the second-largest town on Roatán. An important port, it's home to a large fishing, shrimp and lobster fleet. With no decent budget hotels and restaurants, the area's main attraction for backpackers is the impressive **Arch's Iguana Farm** (455-7743; admission L150; 9am-4pm) in French Cay, just outside of town. It is a worthwhile stop, save the depressing caged animals (monkeys, coatimundi). Less a farm than the house of a serious iguanaphile, everywhere you look you see iguanas – on the driveway, in the trees, under bushes, everywhere. In all around 3000 iguanas live here, some as long as 5ft (1.5m). Noon is feeding time, and the best time to visit. When the sun is out, they all come down and are easier to spot.

For self-caterers, **Sun Supermarket** (7am-8pm Mon-Sat, 8am-2pm Sun) is far and away the biggest and best supermarket on the island.

Oak Ridge

Oak Ridge is another port town on Roatán's eastern side, but it's less appealing than French Harbour and perhaps barely a leg up on Coxen Hole. It's known officially as José Santos Guardiola, but almost no one calls it by its Spanish name. The tiny town hugs a protected harbor, with wooden houses on stilts all along the shore and colorful boats plying the waters. More homes and shops are on a small cay just a two-minute motorboat ride from shore. Water taxis take passengers around the harbor and across to the cay for L30; they dock in front of the bus stop.

Water taxis can also take you on a pleasant tour through mangrove canals to Jonesville, a small town on a nearby bight. A 45- to 60-minute boat tour costs L200 for up to eight people (the price drops to L100 each with six or more). For another L100, you can stop and eat at the locally famous Hole in the Wall restaurant.

SLEEPING & EATING

The Hole in the Wall is a popular place with a sunny terrace, and all-you-can-eat fresh shrimp for around L10 on Friday and Sunday. West of Jonesville, you have to take a water

HONDURAS

ASK A LOCAL: ROATÁN BEST DIVE SPOTS

■ **Green Outhouse** – Great for a first deep dive of the day. Lots of marine life. Two walls, first from 15ft (4.5m) to 50ft (15m) and then the main wall from 60ft (18m) down.

■ **West End Wall** – Dramatic vertical wall starting at 20ft (6m) and going straight down. Good marine life. Healthy gorgonians with lots of creole wrasse.

■ **Herbie's Place** – Now called Texas but originally named after my brother over 30 years ago. Huge barrel sponges and deep water gorgonians, usually lots of current and plenty of barracudas, groupers and marine life.

■ **Mary's Place** – Lots of deep swim-throughs and an amazing main crack where a peninsula of coral broke away from the wall. Gorgeous coral, schools of Atlantic spadefish in the crack.

■ **The Aguilar Wreck** – Something for everyone. Reef, wall, sand bottom, garden eels, lots of blue parrot fish, huge groupers, a resident moray eel and then ending the dive in the shallow reef with lots of marine life.

Alvin Jackson, Roatán dive legend and owner of Native Sons dive shop

---

taxi from Oak Ridge to get here, or combine it with a tour of the mangrove forest (up to eight people around L300).

Reef House Resort (☎ 445-2297; www.reefhouse resort.com; 7-night all-inclusive dive package s/d per person L19,855/17,000) This is an excellent, relaxed resort, favored by those who want to concentrate on diving. There is an unspoiled reef just in front, and dive masters instinctively know how to spot the wildlife. The resort is like being at a large family gathering – you talk about your latest underwater adventure over a hearty lunch and dinner in a central dining hall. Most guests come on seven-night packages, which include a room, meals, three dives a day, unlimited shore diving, a night dive and transport to or from the airport.

Sandy Bay

About 4km before you reach West End is Sandy Bay, a quiet little community strung out along the seashore. It's not as developed as West End and it doesn't have a village center as such – it's just a long settlement along several kilometers of beach.

Anthony's Key Resort, long one of Roatán's best dive resorts, is not for budget travelers, but offers several dolphin attractions. It has the **Institute for Marine Sciences**, a research and educational facility working with dolphins. There is a **dolphin show** (admission free; ⏰ 4pm daily). You can also come face-to-face with a resident dolphin with the **Dolphin Beach Encounter** (per person L1172) or go on a **dolphin dive** (per person L2590) or **snorkel** (L1947). However, if you have seen *The Cove*, you'll want to skip this attraction. The

resort also houses the small but interesting **Roatán Museum** (☎ 9556-0212; admission L20; ⏰ 8am-5pm), with reasonable displays on the island's archaeology, history, geology and wildlife. It includes what locals call *yaba ding ding* (pre-Columbian artifacts).

Across the road from Anthony's Key Resort, the lush **Carambola Botanical Gardens** (☎ 445-3117; admission L120; ⏰ 7am-5pm) covers 40 acres of protected hillside, with several nature trails filled with orchids, spice plants and an 'iguana wall.' It won't be long before you spot a wandering agouti (rodentlike animal). A lookout has views to Utila and, at the right time, into the dolphin show at Anthony's Key Resort.

The in-the-know spot around here is the **Oasis Lounge** (mains L125-180; ⏰ noon-midnight) located high on a hill just off the main road. It draws loads of expat locals for its varied menu, which pleases travelers from the US (with Black Angus burgers and buffalo chicken sandwiches), Britain (with Guinness, Newcastle, Boddingtons) and everywhere else (with 25oz Honduras beers L50). There is a lounge and bar area with cool tunes and a pool, where drunk folks have been known to lose their clothes. It's run by a young couple who also do loads for the community by way of food drives and benefits.

Be on the lookout for **Fish House Gallery** (☎ 9947-8975; www.ilovepaintingfish.com; paintings from L950), the home gallery of British artist Adam Hunt, whose paintings and souvenirs are fashioned from recycled metal and wood as well as the island's discarded trash. Call ahead.

Getting There & Away

AIR

Roatán's **Aeropuerto Juan Ramón Galvez** (☎ 445-1880) is a short distance east of Coxen Hole.

Isleña/TACA (☎ 445-1088; www.flyislena.com) and **Sosa** (☎ 445-1154; www.aerolineassosa.com) have offices in Roatán's airport; they offer daily flights between Roatán and La Ceiba (all charge around L1056 each way), with domestic and international connections. At the time of research, **Continental** (☎ 445-0224; www.continental.com) operated nonstop flights year-round from Houston to Roatán and up to seven per day from Houston and Newark (high season only); **Delta** (☎ 445-2181; www.delta.com) had flights from Atlanta on Saturday only.

The only airline flying direct between Roatán and Tegucigalpa is **CM Airlines** (☎ 9522-5304; www.cmairlines.com), which departs on Fridays and Sundays at 2:15pm.

BOAT

The **Galaxy Wave** (☎ 445-2265; one way 1st-class/normal class L525/624; ☒ ticket office 5:30am-3:30pm) is a sleek, comfortable catamaran ferry service that zips between the island and the mainland in about one and a half hours. The boat leaves Roatán from a new terminal in Dixon's Cove (between Coxen Hole and French Harbour) at 7am and 2pm, and leaves from La Ceiba at 9:30am and 4:30pm. The swells can be bumpy – ask for the anti-seasickness tablets if your tummy is sensitive. There is no direct service from Roatán to Utila – you have to go to La Ceiba first. Tickets are available only one day prior to travel or on day of travel.

Captain Vern (☎ 3346-2600, 9910-8040; vfine@hotmail.com) offers daily catamaran sailboat trips between Roatán's West End (the pier in front of Coconut Divers) and the Alton's Dive Center and Driftwood Café piers in Utila (L1100 one way, four to five hours), leaving Roatán at 1pm and Utila at 6:30am. Call ahead.

Getting Around

BICYCLE

Captain Van's (☎ 445-4076; ☒ 9am-4pm), across from the church in West End, rents bicycles for L198 per day.

BOAT

Many towns – Oak Ridge, West End, West Bay – have regular water-taxi services. Anywhere else, you can fairly easily hire someone to take you wherever you want to go. In West End,

colectivo boats to West Bay (per person L50, last one from either end around 5pm) leave across from Pura Vida dive shop. You have to wait until they fill up.

BUS

Roatán has two bus routes, both originating in Coxen Hole. Bus 2 (Ruta 2) is the one most visitors use. It travels west from Coxen Hole past Sandy Bay (L13) and on to West End. Minibuses depart from both ends and take about 25 minutes in each direction (L20, every 10 minutes from 6am to 6pm).

Bus 1 travels east from Coxen Hole past the airport, past Polly Tilly Bight, through Punta Gorda and on to Oak Ridge (L20 to L40, every 30 minutes from 6am to 5:30pm); the cost depends on the destination. Travel time varies by driver, taking up to one hour to get to Oak Ridge.

CAR & MOTORCYCLE

Some car rental agencies on Roatán:

Avis (☎ 445-0122; www.avis.com.hn; airport; ☒ 7am-5pm)

Captain Van's (☎ 445-4076; www.captainvans.com; ☒ 8am-4pm) Across from the church in West End, this rents motorcycles (L992 to L1212 per day) and scooters (L860 per day), as well as mountain bikes (L198). It has the best reputation for safety and maintenance.

Econo Rent-A-Car (☎ 445-2265; www.econorenta carhn.com; ☒ 8am-6pm) Outside the airport.

HITCHHIKING

Although Lonely Planet cannot recommend hitching, it is easy on Roatán in the daytime, and usually safe. It's much more difficult – and risky – to get a ride at night.

TAXI

Taxis operate around the island. Many are *colectivos* during the day and don't charge much more than buses; from West End to Coxen Hole or Coxen Hole to French Harbour, a *colectivo* is L30 to L35 per person. Again, if you are the first passenger, let the driver know you want to go *colectivo*. As everywhere in Honduras, always clarify the price of the ride before you start. Robbery of tourists traveling in taxis has been reported – keep your wits about you.

UTILA

pop 2800

It's not hard to imagine Utila was once as a slow and welcoming place, an idyllic

Caribbean hideaway for the British elite – its distinct architecture and charming Main St whisper hints of lazy days gone by. Today, Utila is still a lethargic aquatic Eden, but the introduction of motorcycles and all-terrain vehicles have turned what should be a pleasant pedestrianized walkway – Main St – into a game of tourism Frogger. But Utila remains a world away from its aquabrother to the east, Roatán, from the British twang in the local English dialect to the petiteness of it all. It doesn't take long for Utila to grow on you.

Dive courses and individual dives cost about the same here as on Roatán – maybe slightly less – but food and lodging is noticeably cheaper – although more expensive than on the mainland. Utila's shops focus on certification courses, and classes can be larger than on Roatán. Utila does not have the beaches that Roatán does, and the snorkeling isn't as good, but the strong local presence and culture make for a unique, refreshing island experience. The party scene is stronger here, which appeals to younger backpackers. In reality, it feels like a cool college town revolving around a small diving university.

Utila is a small island, about 13km long and 5km wide, with tiny cays dotted on the south side. It is the closest island to the mainland, just 29km away. Utila is mostly flat, with only one small hill. The population lives almost entirely in one settlement on a curving bay; another small settlement is on a cay about a 20-minute boat ride away.

Orientation

Utila is very easy to find your way around. East Harbour (known as Utila Town) is the only town on the island, with one main road and a smaller one, known generally as Cola de Mico road that intersects with the road in front of the pier. At the east end of the main road is the old airport, just a few hundred meters from the main intersection and a good place for snorkeling. At the western end of the road is Chepes beach, also good for snorkeling.

The public jetty, where the ferries arrive and depart, is at the intersection of the town's two main roads. There, you can turn left, right or go straight; several dive shops send people to meet the boat and hand out maps with the location of competing shops mysteriously absent. There used to be a notion that shops and restaurants were better or worse depending on the direction you turned from the pier,

but that is completely irrelevant now – you'll find good (and not so good) places in all directions. Besides, the town is so small, you can check out literally every shop and hotel in less than an hour. Captain Morgan's Dive Center, right at the intersection, will watch your backpack while you go to look for a place to stay.

Supermarkets, the post office, Hondutel and a Spanish school are on the main road.

Information

The website www.aboututila.com has general info and news about Utila. Most dive shops and many hotels accept lempira, US dollars, traveler's checks and credit cards (usually with service fee). There are Unibanc and Banco Atlántida ATMs side by side each other just east of the intersection. The post office is right by the public dock. There's an immigration office on the 1st floor of the Palacio de Municipio building next to the public jetty. Utila has numerous internet centers, and some dive shops also offer internet access to students. Several local homes offer laundry service along Main St – just look for signs.

Alice's Laundry (☎ 425-3785; ☒ 7am-8pm; medium load L100)

Captain Morgan's Dive Centre (☎ 425-3349; www.divingutila.com; Main St; ☒ 8am-7pm) Across from the pier, Captain Morgan's offers straightforward tourist information and advice, and you can even leave your backpack there while you look for a hotel.

Caye Caulker Cyber Café (East Main St; per hr L40; ☒ 8am-8pm) Offers a low-cost connection, as well as cheap international calls.

Dave Restaurant (☎ 425-2057) Has a decent selection of books in English and other languages.

Deposito Henderson (☎ 425-3148; West Main St; ☒ 7am-noon & 2-6pm Mon-Fri) Exchanges dollars, euros and traveler's checks.

Morgan's Travel (☎ 425-3161; utilamorganstravel@yahoo.com; at pier opposite ferry office; ☒ 8am-noon & 2-5:30pm Mon-Fri, 8am-noon & 2-5pm Sat) Arranges plane tickets off the island and taxis to and from the airport.

Police (☎ 425-3145)

Utila Community Clinic (☎ 425-3137; West Main St; ☒ 10am-3:30pm Mon-Fri) Run by Dr John McVay, a well-regarded US doctor. There's also a pharmacy onsite.

Sights & Activities
WILDLIFE-WATCHING

The **Iguana Research & Breeding Station** (☎ 425-3946; www.utila-iguana.de; admission L40; ☒ 2-5pm Mon, Wed & Fri), east of Mamey Lane, studies and protects the endangered Utila iguana. The island's

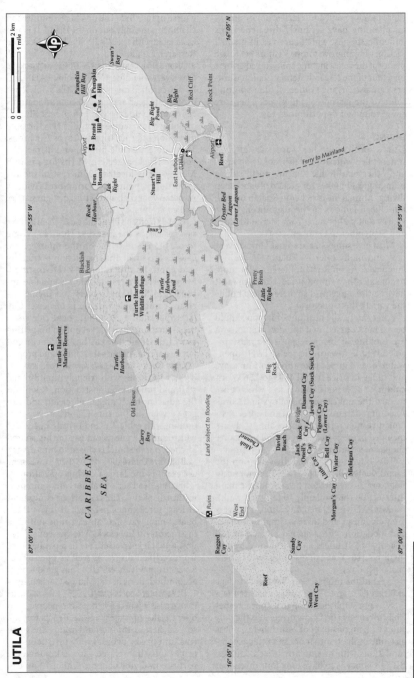

UTILA

rapid development and a lack of environmental planning have seriously threatened this endemic species, which survives in a small section of mangrove forest. Visitors get to see plenty of these fascinating, spiny-tailed critters on a tour of the research station. Station workers can also arrange other wildlife-spotting tours to the far side of the island. There are some volunteer opportunities, too.

DIVING
Utila's south shore has warm crystal-clear waters filled with tropical fish, corals, sponges and other marine life. On the north side, a plunging wall makes for great drift and deep diving. Animal life is richer in Roatán overall, but Utila is famous for the magnificent whale sharks that gather here from March to April and September to October.

Most dive shops start a course almost every day, and many offer instruction in various languages. As on Roatán, there is a lot more to consider than simply price (although most have a price agreement so there should not be the variety there once was).

After safety, the next question you should be asking yourself is if the dive school you are looking at has a responsible, sustainable attitude toward the reefs? PADI openwater dive courses take three to four days and range in price from L4793 to L5635, including a L58-per-day reef fee, which goes toward the upkeep of the buoys and coral. Accommodations, breakfast, and a free two-tank dive after certification are almost always included in the price. All of the following dive shops are members of UDSEC.

The longest-established dive shop on the island, **Gunter's Dive Shop** (☎ 425-3350; www.ecomar ineutila.com) is the furthest away from the main intersection (but still only 10 minutes' walk). It has a PADI-registered dive shop, the divers are welcoming, and there is simple, clean accommodation with a shared kitchen or full apartments. It offers an instructor development course. You can also hire kayaks here (L300 per day).

West of the intersection, **Bay Islands College of Diving** (BICD; ☎ 425-3291; www.dive-utila.com) is a busy, well-established shop that appeals especially to nervous first-time divers. It is the only shop with an onsite pool, which helps, but is also one of the few that doesn't offer accommodations with its similarly priced courses. BICD's policy is to have only four divers per

course or fun dive. The onsite recompression chamber is the only one on the island. It is also associated with the Whale Shark and Oceanic Research Center.

Alton's Dive Center (☎ 425-3704; www.diveinutila. com), a very friendly and welcoming PADI- and NAUI-certified dive school (Utila's only), has up-to-date gear and cheap accommodations right on the dock – you can practically roll out of bed into a dive boat. It is also the only dive shop offering trips to Cayos Cochinos. They are a sociable bunch, and attract the younger backpacker crowd (its logo is Bob Marley). It is located 300m east of the intersection. Upping the spring-break vibe is in-ocean volleyball and Saturday night parties and cook-outs.

Captain Morgan's Dive Centre (☎ 425-3349; www. divingutila.com) is the first dive shop you come to on the island, right on the intersection. Classes are small and instruction is friendly and good. Its dive shop is PADI-certified. Managers take a responsible, sustainable approach to the island's reefs and diving. Its clean, comfortable lodging is on Jewel Cay (see opposite), a 20-minute boat ride from the main island, and a great option for getting away from it all. The cay has no cars or golf buggies and fewer bugs than the island proper.

Cross Creek (☎ 425-3397; www.crosscreekutila.com; East Main St) comes with friendly multilingual staff and professional instruction. Rooms at the adjacent hotel are small, clean, and can get very hot in the sun. Cabins are a better option, with cable TV and private hot-water bathrooms. All guests can use the big shared kitchen, but the hotel is closed to non-divers.

Utila Dive Centre (UDC; ☎ 425-3326; www.utiladive centre.com) is the largest diving operation in Utila. It is dead serious about safety and professionalism and replaces various equipment at least three times per year. It owns three boats and always has at least nine full-time instructors on the clock. Another consideration is that it keeps students in separate boats from certified divers, as well as open-water divers from advanced. UDC has good, cheap accommodations at the Mango Garden Inn.

Utila Water Sports (☎ 425-3264; www.utilawater sports.com) is owned by the same people who operate the upscale Laguna Beach Resort, so gear here is top-notch. Groups are small (maximum six people) and instruction is professional but relaxed – lower key than the party-central vibe of some schools. You can use kayaks for free if diving here. East of the intersection.

SNORKELING

There's snorkeling on both ends of the main road. Manmade **Bando Beach** (☎ 425-3190; East Main St; admission L60; ☺ 9am-5pm) is at the old airport at the east end of town. You can also rent kayaks (L3) and old snorkeling gear (L5) there. **Chepes Beach** is at the opposite (west) end of the road, and is a pleasant, albeit small, spot, with palm trees, white sand and some basic beachside bars and snack joints.

Many dive shops rent snorkel gear to students and nonstudents (per day around L150).

The **Whale Shark & Oceanic Research Center** (☎ 425-3760; www.wsorc.com; West Main St; ☺ 9am-noon & 2-5pm Mon-Fri, 2-5pm Sun) offers free seminars on whale sharks as well as snorkeling outings to view them on Mondays, Wednesdays and Fridays (L1026).

KAYAKING & CANOEING

You can kayak to **Rock Harbour** by going into Oyster Bed Lagoon and then into Lower Lagoon and along the mangrove canal. There's a good beach at Rock Harbour, and it's very private, since the only way to get there is by boat or by hiking across the island. A round trip from town, with time at the beach, takes a full day. Another option is to kayak under the bridge separating the town from the airport, into the lagoon and then up the channel to Big Bight Pond. You can rent kayaks at Gunter's Dive Shop.

BOAT TRIPS

Many local fishermen and families have signs in their windows for boat tours. They can take you to Water Cay, to Rock Harbour via the mangrove canal, though the lagoon etc.

HIKING

For a complete escape from town, walk 3km across the island to the caves of **Pumpkin Hill Bay**. You will get an idea of what the island used to be like before the tourism boom. One of the caves was allegedly a hideout for the pirate Henry Morgan.

THE CAYS

Several cays on Utila's southwest shore make good day trips. **Jewel** and **Pigeon Cays**, connected by a small bridge, are home to a charming village and the best fish burgers on the north coast. Captain Morgan's Dive Centre operates from here, and loans kayaks and snorkel gear to students.

Water Cay, just beyond Pigeon and Jewel Cays, is a beautiful, uninhabited little island covered with palm trees. In high season, a caretaker keeps things clean and collects L39 per visitor for the upkeep of the island. Utila's annual **Sun Jam party** is usually held here, often in August, when hundreds of locals and visitors pack the island for a fun night of dancing, drinking and general mayhem. The best snorkeling is off the southeastern corner, but watch for boat traffic.

There are several ways of traveling to the cays – you will quickly spot the signs around town. Trips run about L100 per person to Jewel Cay or Pigeon Cay, from where you can organize further transport to Water Cay; or find a sailor in town to take you direct to Water Cay for L800 (round trip) for up to four people.

Courses

Utila is not a natural spot for learning Spanish as many of its residents speak English. However, there are a couple of language schools, and opportunities to speak Spanish are increasing with the large number of mainland migrants.

Utila Spanish School (☎ 9710-5775), far west of the intersection, offers Spanish classes at all levels. One-on-one classes cost L95 per hour. Intensive, 20-hour weeks cost L1900 and meet for four hours per day.

Sleeping

Utila has a bunch of good cheap places to stay, and several midrange ones. It doesn't take long to walk around and find something that suits you (you can leave your backpack at Captain Morgan's, near the pier). Many dive shops, including Captain Morgan's Dive Center, Utila Water Sports and Utila Dive Center, have good, cheap (or free) accommodations for students. Only hotels open to walk-ins are listed here.

Note that it can be hard to get a good room during the busy tourist seasons (July to August and mid-December to Easter), and also during the Sun Jam festival (usually in August). Reservations are advisable at these times.

MAIN ROAD

Mango Inn (☎ 425-3326; www.mango-inn.com; Cola de Mico; dm from L59, d/tr from L1073/1170, cabins from L1658; ☒ ☒) Straight up the hill from the pier, the

Mango Inn sits on lush grounds with two sundecks and a great three-tiered pool with hot tub. It offers rooms for all budgets, from backpacker dorms (nondivers in the dorm pay L195 from the second night on) to simple standard rooms to very well-appointed cabins. Shared bathrooms are nicer than average, though some of the private baths are cramped. Overall, it's a solid midrange option, often full of divers from Utila Dive Centre. Travelers also flock to the attached pizzeria.

Rubi's Inn (☎ 425-3240; rubisinn@yahoo.com; s/d/tr from L285/380/475; ☒ ▢) Probably the best deal on the island, Rubi's Inn has spotless rooms with polished floors, white bedspreads, and compact, neatly tiled bathrooms (even with attractive shower curtains). The property has a delightful little jetty that juts out onto the waters of Utila harbor. It is no secret, however, and books up fast – just don't expect it to answer any reservation inquires via email.

Margaritaville Beach Hotel (☎ 425-3366; margarita villehotel@yahoo.com; West Main St, Sandy Bay; r with fan/air-con L380/760, cabins with air-con L1330; ☒) Just under 100 yards from Chepes Beach, Margaritaville is a two-story Caribbean-style house with porches. Rooms are simple – two beds, a fan and a bathroom – while across the street, the roomy cabins are a slight step up – updated furnishings, private porches, and on the bay.

Bayview Hotel (☎ 425-3114; bayviewinternet@ yahoo.com; d with fan L475, with air-con L665; ☒ 🤶) Reasonable rooms are spacious, include wi-fi and all have bathrooms with hot water. For the same price, ask for one of the four newer rooms with seaviews and small balconies. It lies well west of the intersection.

Freddy's Place (☎ 9621-9471; www.bayislands connection.com; East Main St; r with shared kitchen from L475; ☒) The eight reasonable rooms – all freshly painted – featured at this British-run spot are basically two-bedroom apartments, with a common kitchen to share between the two rooms. It's a very good long-term option. The hammocks on the outside porch apparently catch 'the best breeze in Utila.' Located east of the intersection over the bridge.

our pick **The Lighthouse** (☎ 425-3164; www. utilalighthouse.com; East Main St; r with/without bay view; L1228/944.50; ☒ 🤶) Easily the best option on the island and likely out of the range of most shoestringers, though it's high value when you consider its puritanical cleanliness, its striking Bostonian framework that sits beautifully over the water with a wraparound porch for all rooms, and the homespun hospitality of its owners, who are direct descendants of the island's original British colonists.

INLAND

From the pier, go straight across the main road for a number of good budget lodging options. The advantage to sleeping inland is that it's ever so slightly quieter.

Tony's Place (☎ 425-3376; s/d L100/175) These basic but neat wooden box rooms, stacked on two floors, all have shared bathrooms and nicer sheets than expected. They are on the same site as the owner's house, and are a reasonable long-term rent option. Look out for the white-and-green building around the corner from the Mango Inn.

Rose's Inn (☎ 425-3283; Mamey's Lane; r with/without bathroom L285/189) This countryside house on stilts about five minutes' walk up the hill from the fire station (west of the intersection) is a cheap deal, with hot water included. Guests in the clean, military-barrack-simple rooms share a kitchen. Arrange your stay at Rose's supermarket at the bottom of the hill.

Hotel Bavaria (☎ 425-3809; petrawhite3@hotmail. com; Cola de Mico; s/d L250/300, with hot water L300/350) Rooms are located above a family house with lively children. The six rooms are impeccably kept, right down to the polished floorboards, all with bathrooms (cold water only in all but one). It is perched on the hill, just a short way up from the Mango Inn.

Eating

There's a good selection of eating options for such a small settlement. Several places to stay also have kitchens where you can cook. There are several minimarkets along Main St and fresh produce comes in on Tuesday afternoons and Friday evenings. Get there quick.

Thompson's Bakery (Cola de Mico; items L40-100; ⏰ 6am-8pm Mon-Sat, to 2pm Sun) This might be the best cheap breakfast in Honduras. Sink your teeth into a piping-hot homemade biscuit (known as Jonnycakes), plain or stuffed with ham, eggs and cheese. For fat bagels stuffed with Nutella, try 'Bakery' on East Main St.

Mango Café (pizza L78-220; ⏰ 6am-2pm & 6pm-2am) In a lush courtyard at the Mango Inn (though independent), this pizzeria also known as La Dolce Vita boasts an Italian owner who built the massive brick oven here himself – out of it churns tasty thin-crust pizza. There's also an authentic Italian espresso machine (hard to come by in these parts). Not bad for drinks, either.

RJ's BBQ (East Main St; mains L85-205; ☺ 5:30-11pm Wed, Fri & Sun) In a fresh new pine box, this joint has legions of fans that clamor for anything from the BBQ pit, from burgers to barracuda, pork to lobster. It's only open three days a week, which we are quite sure other restaurants around town are quite thankful for.

Dave's Restaurant (East Main St; mains L95-115; ☺ 11am-3pm & 6:30-9:30pm Mon-Sat) This is a massively popular spot serving grilled chicken or pork with your choice of sauces, from peach BBQ to jalapeño cream, as well as Thai curries and veggie enchiladas. All mains come with mashed potatoes, rice and an edible fresh salad. Good bang for the buck.

Wooden Spoon (mains L100-110; ☺ 6:30-9pm Sat-Thu) You'll have to jockey for dinner with dive instructors, who pre-order the one meat or veggie meal available each night from this hot secret early in the day to ensure service after 7:30pm. It's that popular.

Jade Seahorse Restaurant (dishes L100-300; ☺ 7:30am-2pm & 6-10pm; **V**) The colorfully chaotic interior, including plastic iguanas poised on columns, is the island's most distinctive restaurant setting. Just picture the fruits of a one-night stand between Gaudí and *Alice in Wonderland* and you have an idea of the quirky decor here. It was closed due to the political crisis when we came though, but was expected to reopen in 2010. Dishes are creative and mostly vegetarian. The attached bar, Treetanic, is equally LSD-ish.

El Picante (Cola de Mico; mains L110-251; ☺ 11am-10pm Sun-Thu, 11am-5pm Fri, 5-10pm Sat) Utila's first Mexican restaurant is in a charming house that is over 100 years old. Try the killer chips and salsa.

Driftwood Café (mains L130-220; ☺ 11am-11pm Tue-Sun) This delightful option is a little way west, offering respite from the pumping tunes that blast out in the center of town. The seafood soup is a classic, but these Texans belt out a 10-hour smoked brisket and glorious grills as well. It's very popular with 'yachties' and local expats, as it's tucked away on the far end of the main drag.

La Piccola (West Main St; mains L140-300; ☺ 5-10pm Wed-Mon & 11:30am-3pm Dec, Apr-Aug) A spunky Italiana runs this classier choice, with excellent homemade ravioli, imported beef, fresh fish and an actual wine list. The chicken scallopine and gorgonzola-walnut ravioli are favorites. There are six pennes and spaghettis to choose from on the L95 backpacker menu.

Bush's Supermarket (☺ 6:30am-6pm Mon-Sat, 6:30-10:30am Sun) Opens early so you can get your day's supplies before you hop on a dive boat. The attached cafeteria run by Carmela is famous for its cinnamon rolls.

Drinking

Past the Mango Inn, the Bar in the Bush is popular, but can get rowdy. It usually is just open on Wednesday and Friday nights. Lone travelers should take care at night, since the pathway to the bar is unlit.

Treetanic (☺ 8pm-midnight, to 1am Wed & Fri) Drinking at this psychedelic mango treetop bar feels a bit guilty, like drinking inside a children's pop-up book, if the pop-up book was *The Electric Kool-Aid Acid Test,* of course. You half expect to find Willy Wonka tending bar. It ranked number four in Singha and Lonely Planet's 2009 Great Bars of the World.

Tranquila Bar (☺ 4pm-1am Sun-Thu, to 3am Fri & Sat) Jutting out on a small jetty, this is a relaxed place to swap dive tales and travel stories. An eclectic music mix on the sound system adds to the easygoing vibe, but these days the new Wii sees most of the action. Eventually, the party moves next door to equally popular though rowdier Coco Loco.

La Cueva (☺ 11am-midnight) This divey little newcomer packs 'em in, even on rainy nights.

RENT YOUR OWN ISLAND!

It is not every day you have the chance to step out your front door and let the sands of your own Caribbean island run between your toes. But that's exactly what you can do just off Utila for surprisingly little money. You can choose between two different cays, both of which have cabins and facilities – as well as the essential crystal-clear waters lapping at the edge. If you do it in a group, it can even work out reasonably cheap. **Sandy Cay** is available for L1950 a night, (two-night minimum). It has a butane fridge and solar power and sleeps six. The slightly more luxurious **Little Cay** goes for L2437 a night. It has its own generator. To arrange your own private getaway, contact George Jackson on **Pigeon Cay** (☎ 425-2005) or ask at Captain Morgan's Dive Centre (p420).

It's an odd mix: Utilans, dive instructors, aged alcoholics and cute open-water wannabes. It's run by a young hip French-Argentine who has lived in at least 10 countries. The banana-infused rum is deadly.

Entertainment

Reef Video & Cinema (☎ 425-3754; ☼ 9:30am-7pm Mon-Sat) Rents DVDs (L40), and shows different films each night at 7:30pm in a cute little upstairs 60-seater cinema (L45). It is east of the intersection.

Shopping

Gunter's Driftwood Gallery (☎ 425-3113; west of Cola de Mico; ☼ hours vary) A quirky workshop a couple of blocks inland, where the eponymous Gunter carves and displays sculptures (lots of sharks) made from driftwood. Turn left just before Mango Inn; you'll see the sign on your right. It is more likely to be open all afternoons except Sunday.

Getting There & Away

AIR

Flights between Utila and La Ceiba cost about L1056 and take about 15 minutes.

Aerolíneas Sosa (☎ 452-3161; www.aerolineassosa.com; ☼ 8am-noon & 2-5:30pm Mon-Fri, 8am-noon & 2-5pm Sat) flies to Utila from La Ceiba on Monday, Wednesday and Friday at 3:30pm and direct from San Pedro Sula on Saturday. It returns to La Ceiba Tuesday, Thursday and Saturday at 6am. It's on-island representative is Morgan's Travel (p420).

BOAT

The **Utila Princess II** (☎ 425-3390; ☼ ticket office 8-11am & 2-4:30pm) runs from La Ceiba to Utila at 9:30am and 4pm. Crossings take one hour. Prepare for a fun but wet ride if you sit up front! The same boat returns from Utila to La Ceiba at 6:20am and 2pm. Tickets are L425 to Utila, L400 to La Ceiba; arrive half an hour in advance. Occasional charter boats go to the mainland or to Roatán, but they can be expensive and don't run to a set schedule. Don't depend on them.

Captain Vern (☎ 3346-2600, 9910-8040; vfine@hotmail.com) offers daily catamaran sailboat trips between the Alton's Dive Center and Driftwood Café piers in Utila to Roatán's West End (the pier in front of Coconut Divers), leaving Utila at 6:30am (L$1100 one way, four to five hours). Call ahead.

When seas are calm, the smaller **Ramon Express** (☎ 9928-4936; one way L300) boat leaves from Frank Morgan's pier Monday, Wednesday and Friday at 7am to La Ceiba for L100 less than the ferry. The dock is just before the ferry dock on the east side. Same-day returns to Utila run L340.

Getting Around

Tuk-tuks zip up and down the main road and charge a standard L30 for any distance. You can also rent scooters, golf carts and ATVs but you can walk the entirety of Utila's main road in all of 20 minutes. Try a bike.

Utila Bike Rental (☼ 7am-noon & 1-6pm Sun-Fri) rents out bikes hourly/daily/weekly for L25/100/500.

THE MOSKITIA & EASTERN HONDURAS

The eastern part of Honduras, including the entire department of Gracias a Dios and the eastern sides of Olancho and Colón, is a vast, sparsely inhabited area of rivers and forests. The largely untamed tropical, easternmost part of Honduras is known as the Moskitia. The area abounds in animal and birdlife.

Only two major roads traverse the area northeast of Tegucigalpa. Both run between Tegucigalpa and Trujillo, and are traveled by bus routes. One goes via Tocoa, Savá, Olanchito, La Unión and Limones; it climbs the mountains west of Juticalpa and can be driven in about 10 or 11 hours. The other, longer, route goes via Juticalpa (three hours). These areas are little visited by tourists.

LA MOSKITIA

The Moskitia, that vast part of Honduras you see on maps, with very few roads, is unlike anything else you will experience in the country. It is one of Central America's last frontiers of untamed wilderness. Huge expanses of land are virtually untouched jungle, where people and animals are living much as they would have lived two centuries ago. It is sometimes referred to as Central America's Amazon, and the description is apt, both in that its natural beauty is just as awe-inspiring – and also that it is under threat.

Manatees, tapirs and jaguars all still thrive here – they have learnt to be circumspect around man, and they may not be easy to spot.

Crocodiles can be seen in the waters, while birdlife is raucous. Toucans, macaws, parrots, egrets and herons are among the many species that keep ornithologists coming back again and again.

The different human cultures here are fascinating too. There are five different groups, with isolated pockets of Pech and Tawahka in the interior, as well as Mískito, Garífuna and *ladino* populations.

A visit to the region is not for the faint-hearted. Conditions are rustic at best, and you will find little air-conditioned comfort. A bit of Spanish will come in handy too. Expect your traveling expenses to go up significantly here. Its isolation means prices are noticeably higher. But the intrepid few that make the effort are often thrilled by what they find and the memories they take back. How this unspoiled paradise is developed and protected is crucial. Environmentalists say that La Moskitia offers one last chance to get it right. And gliding down the river in a dugout canoe, past mud houses backed by vine-heavy trees, you can't help but hope they – we – do.

Dangers & Annoyances

This is wild country and needs to be treated with respect. Crucially, never venture into the rainforest without a guide. Trails are faint and overgrown, and hikers can quickly become hopelessly lost.

Avoid crossing the bigger lagoons late in the day – afternoon winds can create swampingly large waves. From November to March, sudden squalls wreak havoc any time of day.

Malaria occurs here: bring insect repellent and mull over the pros and cons of antimalarial pills. A water purification kit (a filter or iodine tablets) is also a good idea. Most lodging options are equipped with mosquito nets.

Finally, the Moskitia is known to be used by drug-runners. The chances of it affecting you are slim, but note that smuggling is often done at certain times of year (the rainy season in particular) when the chances of detection are smaller. Ask around to minimize your chances of being caught in the crossfire.

Tours

Several travel companies undertake tours into the Moskitia region, providing an easier (and not necessarily much more expensive) way to get a taste of the Moskitia. All of the following ones have been recommended: Basecamp (p371) in Copán Ruinas; Omega Tours (p398) and La Moskitia Ecoaventuras (p398) in La Ceiba; and Mesoamérica Travel (p364) in San Pedro Sula.

When planning your trip, **La Moskitia Ecoaventuras** (☎ 441-3279; www.lamoskitia.hn; Colonia El Toronjal, La Ceiba) is an excellent resource for both DIY advice and planned itineraries.

Laguna de Ibans

The small traditional coastal communities around Laguna de Ibans are likely to be your first overnight stop if you come the overland route. The quiet Mískito village of **Raista** has wooden houses on stilts and narrow dirt paths beneath a high leafy canopy. **Raista Eco Lodge** (☎ 8926-5635; s/d/tr without bathroom L200/360/450) has sturdy, rustic and surprisingly nice wooden rooms with modern toilets, mosquito nets, and family-friendly hospitality. Large, filling meals (around L70) are prepared here.

Belén is practically an extension of the same settlement. It also has lodging and the airstrip, but there is really no compelling reason to sleep there over Raista.

Colectivo boats headed to Palacios pass Raista and Belén at around 3am to 3:30am (L200, two hours). There is an airport between the two towns – arrange flights at the SAMI office in Raista. You can also arrange transport to Las Marías, for the Río Plátano Biosphere Reserve, from here; the trip takes five to six hours (round trip L4000). An early-morning *colectivo* boat takes passengers from Raista to Palacios in time to catch the first speedboat to Iriona.

For Río Plátano, irregular *colectivo* pickup trucks pass, mostly during lobster-diving season (August to May) every hour (L60, 45 minutes); another passes in the other direction at the same frequency, making stops in Cocobila, Ibans and Plaplaya. Inquire at Raista.

Reserva de la Biosfera del Río Plátano

The Río Plátano Biosphere Reserve is a magnificent nature reserve, declared a World Heritage Site in 1980. A vast unspoiled, untamed wilderness, it is home to extraordinary animal life, including a number of endangered species. The best time of year to visit is from November to July, and the best time for seeing birds is during February and March, when many migratory birds are here.

One of the best places to organize tours is in **Las Marías**, a one-phone town at the heart

HONDURAS

of the reserve, with around 100 Mískito and Pech families. There is no running water or electricity, though there are a few generators. There are several basic lodgings there, which will also cook you simple meals. Clean, airy **Hospedaje Doña Justa** (☎ 9966-9234; center of town; r without bathroom per person L80, meals L50) with a large flower garden, and the sprawling **Hospedaje Doña Rutilia** (☎ 8911-2090; r without bathroom per person L150, meals L60), on the river, are good options. You can leave messages at the above phones (in Spanish only).

A head guide assigns guides, according to your requirements, for a fee of L100 per group. Trips vary from a twilight crocodile tour to one-day excursions to a nearby petroglyph to amazing, but arduous, three-day trips through primary rainforest (Pico Dama), which require more guides. Head guides cost L220 to L250 a day, while secondary guides are paid L150. Neither prices nor number of guides are negotiable and a 10% tip is voluntary for good service. Bring camping equipment and your own food. Get an early start for your best chance to see the wildlife. It's best to arrange tours through your *hospedaje*, not any average José trying to sell you something along the riverbanks.

An *expreso* from Raista to Las Marías has a hefty fixed price of L4000 for up to three people (five to six hours). See opposite page for how to get to Raista. Hook up with other travelers to spread the costs. The fare is for a round trip and the boatman waits in Las Marías for two nights, so after the second night it'll cost you an extra L250 per night. You can save money by crossing the Laguna de Ibans by boat (L600, 25 minutes), hiking with a local guide on the Liwaraya trail that connects Laguna Ibans with the Río Plátano (L150, two hours), and then grabbing another boat on to Las Marías (L1200, three hours). You can coordinate all of this at Raista.

The super intrepid can also access the biosphere by a multiday raft ride down the river from Dulce Nombre de Culmí. Contact Omega Tours or La Moskitia Ecoventuras (see p398) for more information.

Palacios

Many travelers will have to pass through Palacios, a tense, rather lawless place known as a drug-courier corridor. It is not recommended. But overland travelers who miss the *colectivo* boat connections further downriver

might get stuck here. If you do, the new and peachy-looking **Hotel Moskitia** (☎ 9996-5648, 442-8059 in La Ceiba; www.hotelmoskitia.com; r L500) offers modern rooms with private baths and breezy balconies, right on the Laguna de Bacalar (though locals swear it was built with narco-trafficking lempiras).

Dugout canoes will run you across from Batalla (L50, five minutes).

Brus Laguna
pop 13,900

Beside the lagoon of the same name at the mouth of the Río Patuca, Brus Laguna is an accessible entry point to La Moskitia, as flights come here. You can head to Raista or even straight to Las Marías from here. A good backpacker crash pad is **Villa Biosfera** (☎ 9919-9925; s/d without bathroom L180/350), a stilted wooden cabin on the lagoon with eight rooms and mosquito nets. For substantially more comfort, **Hotel Ciudad Blanca** (☎ 9553-8766; s/d/tr L350/550/750; ⊠ ▣) is the newest and best in town, with an internet cafe next door (L50 per hour). **Aerolíneas Sosa** (☎ 443-1399; www.aerolineas sosa.com) normally has flights from La Ceiba to Brus Laguna but those had been suspended at time of writing.

From Batalla, direct *colectivos* head to Brus Laguna between 3pm and 5pm (L400, four hours).

Wampusirpi

This appealingly rustic place is a good base for exploring the Tawahka region upriver (see opposite). Locals, mainly Mískito people, survive on small plots of rice, beans, bananas and yucca, and by fishing the Patuca River. Houses are mostly on stilts as this area is prone to flooding. There are basic unmarked accommodations if you ask around, and you can do the same to arrange somewhere to eat.

SAMI (☎ Brus Laguna 433-8031, Puerto Lempira 433-6016) has air service to Wampusirpi.

Puerto Lempira
pop 35,700

Puerto Lempira, the largest town in the Moskitia, is situated on the inland side of the Laguna de Caratasca. It has good airlines, which is the main reason for visiting, although the town does have a few modern conveniences such as restaurants and internet.

Puerto Lempira has several sleeping options. The best is **Hotel Yu Baiwan** (☎ 433-6348; s/d/

EXPLORE MORE AROUND THE MOSKITIA

For intrepid eyes, the vast expanse of La Moskitia conceals fascinating insights into indigenous cultures and a finely balanced jungle ecosystem.

- One of the most isolated and fragile of Honduras' indigenous peoples is the Tawahka, found deep in La Moskitia. To visit these communities you need to venture a long way up Río Patuca, to the towns of **Krausirpe** and **Krautara**, using Wampusirpi (see opposite page) as a base. Krautara is smaller and more isolated, and remains 100% Tawahka.

- If you get the chance, take in **Plaplaya**, a lovely traditional Garífuna village a short boat ride from Raista (see p427), where giant leatherback sea turtles nest and are released by volunteers April to July.

- One of the most rewarding trips is a three-day hike up **Pico Dama** into the heart of the Reserva de la Biosfera del Río Plátano. Go to Las Marías to arrange it; see p427.

---

tr L450/500/600;), which has friendly service, fresh linen and cable TV.

SAMI/Air Honduras (☎ 433-6016) flies to/from Puerto Lempira, and has an office in the turquoise building at the end of the airstrip. You can also buy tickets at an ice-cream shop (open 8am to 6pm) a block and a half from the pier.

It is possible to do the entire route overland to Puerto Lempira from Batalla; after arriving in Brus Laguna from Batalla (see opposite page), an 8am *colectivo* boat departs for Ahuas (L365, three hours) where you connect to a bus for Ribra Creek (price included, 30 minutes). Then catch a speedboat from Ribra Creek to Puerto Lempira (L365, two hours). Canvassing La Moskitia this way takes two days and will save you a bit of money over flying, but it's really about the adventure.

Getting There & Away

AIR

All flights to the Moskitia depart from La Ceiba. Scheduled flights go to Brus Laguna and Puerto Lempira. These change regularly, so check beforehand.

Aerolíneas Sosa (☎ in La Ceiba 443-1894, in Puerto Lempira 433-6432, in Brus Laguna 433-8042; www.aerolineassosa.com; Av San Isidro btwn 8a & 9a Calles, La Ceiba; ⏰ 7am-5pm Mon-Fri)

SAMI (☎ in La Ceiba 442-2565, in Brus Laguna 433-8031) Covers internal Moskitia routes. Prices range from L803 (Belén–Brus Laguna) to L1280 (Belén–Wampusirpi).

OVERLAND

Going overland via the north coast is an increasingly popular and accessible entry point to the Moskitia. You will need to start while the roosters are still dozing to make it happen in a day. From La Ceiba, take an early Trujillo bus (no later than 6:15am, preferably earlier) to Tocoa (L80). La Ceiba departures from 6:15am onwards let passengers out at the *punta de taxi* El Porvenir in Tocoa. Grab one to the marketplace (L20), where you catch *pailas* (pickup trucks) to Batalla (L500, four to six hours), a small Garífuna town (the earliest departures from La Ceiba go directly to the bus terminal). *Pailas* leave stuffed with passengers and cargo – dangerously so – between 9am and 10am daily (prepare to be mobbed by drivers demanding your business and be aware of drinking and driving). From Batalla *colectivo* boats make many stops – tell the driver you want to go to Raista (L200, two hours). Depending on weather and traffic, this should get you into Belén and Raista before dark – these villages are a good jumping-off point for your Moskitia adventure. Coming from Trujillo, you can catch the same trucks at the Corocito turnoff (again, with an eye-rubbingly early start – any bus going from Trujillo to La Ceiba will drop you off here).

Occasionally storms wash out the roads to Batalla. In that case, you can go via Iriona. The bus leaves Tocoa from the terminal hourly between 7am and 2pm (L130, seven hours). Again, if you're coming from Trujillo, stop at Corocito (taking the 5:45am bus) where the bus passes through. From Iriona you can get the next speedboat to Belén (L19, two hours). To continue on to Puerto Lempira overland, see above left.

To return, take the 3am to 4am boat in Belén, Raista, Cocobila and Ibans daily to Batalla (L200, one to two hours), for a 5am to 6am truck to Tocoa, which will drop you outside town at **Mirna Express** (☎ 444-3512), where you can continue on to La Ceiba, San Pedro

HONDURAS

Sula or Tegucigalpa; or to Palacios (L200, one to two hours) and get a 6am speedboat to Iriona, where a bus goes to Tocoa.

Getting Around

Different seasons present different challenges in terms of getting around the Moskitia. The rainy reason (November to January) is the most difficult.

AIR

SAMI (☎ in Brus Laguna 433-8031, in Puerto Lempira 433-6016) has irregular flights between the main towns, averaging from L803 to L1280.

BOAT

Most transportation in Moskitia is by boat. Upriver, the most common boat is a *pipantes,* a flat-bottomed boat made from a single tree trunk that's propelled by a pole or paddle. A *cayuco* is a wood-planked boat with an outboard motor that is commonly used on longer trips, either as an *expreso* (private taxi) or a cheaper set-route *colectivo.* Trips include Las Marías to Raista (L4000, 1½ hours) or Batalla to Raista (L200, one to two hours).

PICKUPS

Irregular pickup trucks ply the single dirt road along the Laguna de Ibans from the town of Ibans west through Cocobila, Raista and Belén, and east to the town of Río Plátano, though less so than in the past as most folks now have motorcycles.

SOUTHERN HONDURAS

Honduras touches the Pacific with a 124km coastline on the Golfo de Fonseca. Bordered by the gulf on the seaward side and by hills on the land side, the strip of land here is part of the hot coastal plain that extends down the Pacific side of Central America through several countries. It's a fertile agricultural and fishing region; much of Tegucigalpa's fish, shrimp, rice, sugarcane and hot-weather fruits (like watermelon) come from this area. Honduras' Pacific port is at San Lorenzo.

Southern Honduras is much traveled; it is where the Interamericana crosses Honduras, carrying all the north- and southbound traffic of Central America, and also where the highway branches north from the Interamericana toward the rest of Honduras.

TEGUCIGALPA TO THE NICARAGUAN BORDER

Between Tegucigalpa and the border post of Las Manos (the quickest route to Nicaragua), there are several interesting stops. Notice the scars of clear-cutting in this area, a legacy of indiscriminate logging. Many Hondurans fear they are headed down the same path as El Salvador, the most deforested country in Central America.

About 40km east of the capital, at Zamorano, there's a turnoff for **San Antonio de Oriente**, an attractive Spanish colonial mining village about 5km north of the highway. This is the village immortalized by Honduran primitivist painter José Antonio Velásquez.

Further east is a turnoff south to **Yuscarán**, 66km from Tegucigalpa. Capital of the department of El Paraíso, it is a picture-postcard colonial mining town. Its **annual fair** is on December 8.

A large town 92km east of Tegucigalpa and 19km from El Paraíso, **Danlí** (population 126,000) is the biggest town on this route and the center of a sugarcane- and tobacco-producing region. There are also several **cigar factories** where you can buy good hand-rolled cigars. The annual festival at Danlí, the **Festival del Maíz** in the last weekend in August, is a big event and attracts people from far and wide. The **Laguna de San Julian**, 18km north of Danlí, is a manmade lake popular for outings.

In Danlí, the central **Hotel La Esperanza** (☎ 763-2106; s/d without bathroom L178/280, s/d with fan L280/448, s/d with air-con L392/662; P ✖) is easily the best budget option in town, with rooms that stretch alongside a long, green patio. All rooms have cable TVs. Just off the central park, the cavernous **Rancho Mexicano** (☎ 763-4528; mains L40-100; ⏱ 11am-10pm) is good for a bite.

In El Paraíso, the **Hotel Isis** (☎ 793-4251; Parque Central; s/d L160/240; P) will do just fine for a night at the border – rooms are dead simple but there's hot water, private bathrooms and secure parking. The bus to the border leaves nearby.

TEGUCIGALPA TO THE PACIFIC

Highway CA-5 heads south about 95km from Tegucigalpa until it meets the Interamericana at **Jícaro Galán**, winding down from the pine-covered hills around the capital to the hot coastal plain. From the crossroads at Jícaro Galán, it's 40km west to the border with El Salvador at **El Amatillo**, passing through the town of **Nacaome** 6km west of Jícaro Galán, or it's 115km east to the Nicaraguan border

---

GETTING TO NICARAGUA

Only 122km from Tegucigalpa is the border crossing at **Las Manos** (🕐 24hr). You can make it in a day if you get an early start.

    Transportes Colinas de Oro (☎ 9523-1637) in Tegucigalpa runs two direct buses from Tegucigalpa to the border at 6am and noon; otherwise, take a bus to El Paraíso or Danlí and transfer. Buses to Danlí depart from the **Discua Litena bus terminal** (☎ 9523-1800) at Mercado Jacaleapa in Tegucigalpa. Buses to Las Manos and El Paraíso leave from Transportes Colinas de Oro across the street at Centro Comercial El Alhambra. You can take a *colectivo* from the post a block east of Parque La Merced (L11). Actual taxis should cost you L60. There are several routes, so be sure you're on one that passes the Danlí bus terminal.

    The routes: Danlí (direct L58, 1½ hours, many departures from 6am to 6pm); El Paraíso (direct L65, two hours); Las Manos (L76, three hours, two direct departures at 6am and noon; or connect in Danlí or El Paraíso).

    The last bus from El Paraíso to the border is at 4pm, and the last bus from Las Manos to El Paraíso at 5pm. The first bus departs at 6:30am, and from the border to El Paraíso the first bus leaves at 7am. Once you cross, catch a bus to Ocotal and transfer to Managua.

    See boxed text, p474, for information on crossing from Nicaragua.

---

at **El Espino**, passing through **Choluteca** 50km from Jícaro Galán.

If you're traveling along the Interamericana, crossing only this part of Honduras in transit between El Salvador and Nicaragua, you can easily make the crossing in a day; from border to border it's only 150km (three hours by bus). If, however, you want to stop off, there are a few possibilities. The border stations are nominally open 24 hours, though have been known to shut up shop at 5pm, so if you can't make it by that time, you may have to spend the night.

GOLFO DE FONSECA

The shores of Honduras, El Salvador and Nicaragua all touch the Golfo de Fonseca; Honduras has the middle and largest share, with 124km of coastline and jurisdiction over nearly all of the 30-plus islands in the gulf. In September 1992 the International Court of Justice eased previous disputes by ruling that sovereignty in the gulf must be shared by the three nations, barring a 5km maritime belt around the coast. Of the islands in the gulf, sovereignty was disputed by Honduras and El Salvador in three cases. The court found in favor of Honduras regarding the island of El Tigre, but El Salvador prevailed on Meanguera and Meanguerita. Tensions remain over the islands and the Honduran press regularly print unabashedly patriotic articles articulating Honduras' ownership rights.

The European discovery of the Golfo de Fonseca was made in 1522 by Andrés Niño, who named the gulf in honor of his benefactor,

Bishop Juan Rodríguez de Fonseca. In 1578 the buccaneer Sir Francis Drake occupied the gulf, using El Tigre as a base, as he made raids as far afield as Peru and Baja California. There are still rumors that Drake left a hidden treasure, but it has never been found.

El Salvador has a major town on the gulf (La Unión), but Honduras doesn't; on the Honduran part of the coastline, there are only small settlements, and the highway never meets the sea except on the outskirts of San Lorenzo. The Golfo de Fonseca is an extremely hot region.

Isla El Tigre
pop 2400

The inactive volcanic island of El Tigre, with a 783m peak, is a ferociously hot place with a kind of untouched charm – there are few cars here and nobody is in a rush. Its main town is **Amapala**, a scruffy fishing village founded in 1833 with picturesque crumbling clapboard architecture. It was once Honduras' Pacific port town, before the port was moved to mainland San Lorenzo. A lot of visitors descend on the island for the **Semana Santa** holidays – otherwise there is a trickle of backpackers, who come for an off-the-beaten-track trip and the island's fine seafood.

There is a **tourist office** (🕐 8am-noon & 2-5pm Mon-Fri, 8am-noon Sat) on the dock with a complete list of all the accommodations options and a map of the island's many beaches. Check out the back of a two-lempira note for a view of Amapala.

ACTIVITIES

You can hike up **El Vijía**, about 100m up, where there's a good view of the gulf and its islands. El Tigre also has several beaches of dubious quality: **Playa Grande** is the biggest and most popular, with questionable quality sands but beautiful views out to sea. There are also views right over to El Salvador from the black-sand **Playa Negra** to the north of the island. Rays can be a painful danger at low tide – ask people whether it is safe before you go for a dip.

SLEEPING & EATING

Accommodations are more expensive than on the mainland. Playa Grande offers a plethora of dodgy eateries, with Dignita being the most popular.

Hotel Veleros (☎ 795-8040; Playa El Mora; r with fan/air-con L400/600) The island's best value has clean, comfortable rooms (cold-water bathroom only). Right next door is the well-known Veleros beachfront restaurant, with good seafood dishes (mains L50 to L395). Maritza Grande, the owner, is well versed on tourist activities on the island, and can sort out alternative lodging if her place is full. It is on Playa El Mora (also known as Playa el Burro), a L50 taxi ride from Amapala.

Mirador de Amapala (☎ 795-0407; www.mirador deamapala.com; s/d/tr L850/1200/1400; ☒) Though top dog here, the neglect is palpable, despite the fact that there is a nice swimming pool and a big-screen TV. Rooms are fine, but should be better than that at this price.

Restaurant El Faro (mains L60-300; ☒ 10am-11pm) A good seafood option right on the waterfront, overlooking the pier. Shrimp and lobster can get pricey, but we had a nice ceviche that didn't make us sick for L90, washed down with an excellent homemade *limonada*. Nice spot for *cervezas*, too.

GETTING THERE & AROUND

Small *colectivo* boats (L15 to L20, 20 minutes) depart from Coyolito, 30km from the Interamericana. You have to wait until the boat fills up with 10 passengers. Otherwise you can pay L80 for a private boat trip, the preferred, hassle-free choice. If going to Veleros, ask to be dropped there instead and save the taxi fare. Buses go to Coyolito from San Lorenzo (L19, one hour, every 40 minutes until 5:30pm) from the terminal behind San Lorenzo's prefabricated market or from

a dusty turnoff 2km north of town. Note that there are no overnight facilities at Coyolito.

To get around town, minibuses leave from the Parque Central, generally doing semicircle circuits half-way around the island and returning the same way (L10). A few buses go all the way around. Mototaxis charge around L10 for a *colectivo* trip.

CHOLUTECA

pop 157,600

Choluteca, capital of the department of the same name, is the largest town in southern Honduras. The town is built near Río Choluteca, the same river that runs through Tegucigalpa. The first thing you will notice is the heat, which has even long-term residents mopping sweat from their brow before morning tea. There is an old, somewhat neglected historic quarter (with nicely patterned streets) and no real reason to linger.

The **annual festival day** is December 8.

Orientation & Information

Though streets in Choluteca follow a standard grid, with calles running east–west, and avenidas north–south, it is a very confusing city, least of which to do with the lack of street signage. The city is divided into four zones: NO (*noroeste*, northwest), NE (*noreste*, northeast), SO (*suroeste*, southwest) and SE (*sureste*, southeast). The Parque Central is in the middle. Good luck!

The bus terminal is in the southeast zone, on the corner of Blvr Carranza and 3a Av SE. The Mi Esperanza bus terminal is one and a half blocks north. The old market (Mercado Viejo San Antonio) is nine long blocks west and two blocks north – best to take a cab (L0.80).

The **post office** (cnr 2a Calle NO & 3a Av NO) is three blocks east of the old market. The state phone company, Hondutel, is next door.

Sleeping & Eating

Choluteca has several good-value hotels near the bus terminal and in the city center.

Hotel Mi Esperanza (☎ 782-0885; 2a Calle NO; s/d with fan L130/190, with air-con L190/290; P ☒) You've hit rock bottom here, a bare-bones basic option close to the market. For the shower, a Hazmat suit wouldn't be uncalled for, though rooms do open out onto a vaguely pleasant concrete courtyard and the affiliated *comedor* is a step up. You are better off closer to Blvr Enrique Weddle.

Hotel Pacifica (☎ 782-3249; just off Blvr Enrique Weddle; s/d with fan L200/270, with air-con L300/400; P ☒) Located half a block south from the Wendy's on Blvr Enrique Weddle, this place has distinctly average rooms with air-con, squishy beds, cold-water spigot-showers and secure parking. It's a much better cheapie than Mi Esperanza and is in basically the same location as Hotel Rivera.

Hotel Rivera (☎ 782-0828; hotelriverach@yahoo.com; Blvr Enrique Weddle; s/d/tr L500/600/700; P ☒ ☎ ☒) It's more expensive, but this well-equipped hotel is very comfortable – some newer apartments even include laundry machines – and located a bit out of the chaos of *centro*, near a wealth of fast-good restaurants on the road to Nicaragua. Your money buys extra peace, friendlier streets and a pool but not necessarily hot water. Another benefit is the tourism office is next door at Hotel Internacional, if you're so inclined.

Comedor Mi Esperanza (meals L47-50; ☒ 6:15am-8:30pm) This exceptionally good-value cafe is infinitely more welcoming than the hotel of the same name a half block away. It's often frequented by local workers and serves three menu-less meals per day.

Fusiones Gourmet (combos L80-120; ☒ 11:30am-3pm & 6-11pm) Attached to the Hotel Rivera, this is one-part upscale restaurant, one-part fast-food drive-thru. The benefit is there is one chef for both. The entrées are pretty fancy (especially for a town like Choluteca) but the burger, rib and shrimp combos are a steal, especially considering all the beef is imported from Argentina.

Getting There & Away

Several companies share a bus terminal on Blvr Carranza, at the corner of 3a Av NE. Some buses swing by the market after leaving the station. For details about crossing the various borders, see the boxed text, below, and the boxed text, p431.

San Marcos de Colón, near Nicaraguan border (L23; 1½hr; every hour from 6:30am to 6pm) From there take a *colectivo* to border at El Espino (L13; 15min). Last bus from San Marcos to Choluteca at 4pm.

Tegucigalpa (L60; 4hr; every 30 minutes from 4:35am to 5:50pm)

Mi Esperanza has its own **bus terminal** (☎ 782-0841; 3a Av NE), one and a half blocks north of the other station. It runs the Tegucigalpa–Choluteca–San Marcos de Colón route and the buses are usually more direct and comfortable. Destinations include the following:

San Marcos de Colón, near Nicaraguan border (L25; one to 1½hr; 7 buses daily at 7am, 10:15am, 12:15pm, 1:45pm, 3:30pm, 5pm & 6pm)

Tegucigalpa (normal L60; 3hr; 7 buses daily at 5am, 6:15am, 7:30am, 9am, 11:30am, 1:30pm & 3:30pm)

Rey Express (☎ 782-2712) and 1st-class **Saenz** (☎ 782-0712) also make runs out of Choluteca and have terminals around the block from the main terminal. Both are good additional but pricier options for Tegus and beyond.

GETTING TO NICARAGUA & EL SALVADOR

Choluteca is within striking distance of three border crossings: El Amatillo for entering El Salvador, and Guasaule and La Fraternidad/El Espino for entering Nicaragua.

El Amatillo (El Salvador): from the Choluteca terminal, buses (L41, 2¼ hours, 3:30am to 6pm) leave every 25 minutes. Entering Honduras, you can take the same bus to Choluteca, or another for Tegucigalpa (L60, three hours, every 30 minutes 4:35am to 5:50pm).

Guasaule (Nicaragua) feels distinctly dodgy and you should stay alert for pickpockets or be wary of anyone being overly 'helpful.' From the Choluteca terminal, the *directos* (L27, 45 minutes, 6am to 6pm) leave every 25 minutes and return until 5pm.

La Fraternidad/El Espino (Nicaragua): from San Marcos de Colón *colectivo* taxis (marked Fraternidad/Chinchayote) and microbuses operate between 8:30am and 4:30pm and charge around L13 for the 15-minute ride. Both wait until they fill up before leaving; they line up in front of Mi Esperanza bus terminal. There's identical service from the border until about 5:30pm. There are no direct buses from Choluteca to El Espino. **Blanquita Express** (☎ 782-3972) has buses from San Marcos to Tegucigalpa (L98, 3½ hours, 6:30am, 8am, 11:15am, 1pm, 3:15pm).

There is no fee on the books to exit Honduras – ask for a receipt or to see the law in writing. Entering Honduras has an official charge of L60. See p316 for information on crossing the border from El Salvador, and p474 and p481 for crossing from Nicaragua.

SAN MARCOS DE COLÓN

If it is getting late and you are heading for the El Espino border, stop off for the night at the pretty town of San Marcos de Colón. It is surprisingly tranquil for somewhere so close to a border and is very well kept – some would even say manicured. **Hotel Colonial** (☎ 788-3822; s/d/tr L250/275/300; P), two blocks south of the Parque Central, is excellent value, with comfortable rooms including etched wooden headboards, high ceilings and cable TV. **La Esquisita** (mains L20-70; ☯ 8am-8pm) is short on options but long on taste. It serves cheap and tasty *comida típica* all day.

HONDURAS DIRECTORY

ACCOMMODATIONS

Economical accommodations are available just about everywhere in Honduras. The cheapest places have a shared cold-water bathroom, but can range from the truly awful to not-so-bad. A fair number of innocent-looking hotels are in fact used by the hourly crowd, so look at a room or two and get a sense of the place before staying there. Prices range from L120 to L220 for a budget room.

A room with a private cold-water bathroom is a step up, and hot water a step beyond that (be weary of any hotel claiming hot water for less than L500 – your definition of hot is sure to differ from theirs). You'll usually pay more for two beds than for one – save money and sleep with a friend. The same goes for air-con, only more so. Electricity costs are high, so it's an expensive luxury – sometimes doubling the price of the room. Most budget travelers will stick with fans.

Camping is not a vacation activity followed by many Hondurans, and organized campsites such as those in the USA or Europe do not exist. That said, camping is allowed in several national parks and reserves and is mentioned in the text wherever it is relevant. Water and toilets or latrines are sometimes available, and occasionally even kitchens, but generally you should bring your own gear.

If you are in one of the more touristy areas and are thinking about improving your Spanish, consider a homestay with a local family, which you can organize through a language school. Starting from around L1250 a week, often including full board, these are often a very economical and culturally rewarding option.

ACTIVITIES

Honduras' national parks are great places for hiking. Several of the parks offer trails that are well-maintained, visitors centers for information and orientation, and even guides. Guides are sometimes necessary, but the majority do not speak English. Having a guide will often allow you to learn more about the environment you're in and to see more wildlife. The north coast and the Bay Islands have great beaches and several excellent parks, plus, of course, some of the best snorkeling and diving in the world.

Bird-Watching

Bird-watching is becoming a popular activity in Honduras, where you can spot hundreds of species. It's difficult to name the most impressive birds, as there are so many: quetzals, toucans, scarlet macaws (Honduras' national bird) and the brilliant green and green-and-yellow parrots are all contenders. National parks and wildlife refuges have been established to protect many environments good for seeing birds – for example, cloud forests, tropical rainforests and coastal wetlands. Quetzals are seen in many of the cloud forest national parks, including Cusuco (p367), Celaque (p384) and La Tigra (p354).

Migratory birds are present along the north coast during the northern winter months from November to February. Good places for bird-watchers to see them are in the lagoons, national parks and wildlife refuges, and at Lancetilla Botanical Gardens (p393) near Tela. Each December 14 and 15, the Audubon Society does a 24-hour bird count at Lancetilla and other nearby places. Contact the office of **Fundación Prolansate** (☎ 448-2042; www.prolansate. org; 7a Av at 8a Calle NE, Tela; ☯ 7am- 5:30pm Mon-Thu, to 4:30pm Fri) if you'd like to participate.

The Lago de Yojoa (p360) is another excellent place for bird-watching – more than half of Honduras' species have been counted here so far.

In some places you can head out on bird-watching tours. A couple of companies in Copán Ruinas offer bird-watching tours (p371) in the local area and further afield, including La Moskitia.

Diving & Snorkeling

The Bay Islands reef is magnificent, and you can learn to dive here for less money than anywhere else in the Caribbean. Dozens of dive shops offer all levels of courses, from beginner to instructor. Snorkeling gear can be rented or bought, or you can bring your own – all three islands have great snorkeling right from shore. The Cayos Cochinos (Hog Islands) also have turquoise seas and kaleidoscopic marine life.

Horseback Riding

Horseback riding is a popular activity at Copán Ruinas (p371). Horseback tours are also conducted into Parque Nacional Pico Bonito (p403) near La Ceiba and at West End (p414) on Roatán Island.

Kayaking, Canoeing & Small-Boat Tours

Small-boat tours are a good way to visit a number of national parks, wildlife refuges and nature reserves along the north coast, including Punta Sal (p393) and Laguna de los Micos (p393) near Tela, Cuero y Salado (p402) near La Ceiba and the Laguna de Guaimoreto (p407) near Trujillo. Kayaking tours of the Refugio de Vida Punta Izopo (p394) near Tela let you slip silently among the canals of the mangrove forests, where you'll see lots of wildlife.

The Moskitia region, though more remote, is accessible by airplane and bus and offers many more possibilities for canoe and boat trips on rivers and lagoons, especially via the Río Patuca.

White-Water Rafting

White-water rafting is popular on the Río Cangrejal near La Ceiba; several companies in La Ceiba offer rafting tours on this river (see p397).

BOOKS

Topics such as the Copán archaeological site, the banana industry and the Contra war have been well studied, while others, like non-Maya indigenous communities and environmental issues, have not.

Gangs are currently a hot topic and have received extensive newspaper and magazine coverage.

Honduras: A Country Guide by Tom Barry and Kent Norsworthy (1991) and *Honduras: A Country Study* (1990) by the US Federal Research Division are oldish but have concise historical information.

The United States, Honduras, and the Crisis in Central America by Donald E Schultz and Deborah Sundloff Schulz (1994) discusses the role of the US in Central America during the region's tumultuous civil wars.

Don't be Afraid, Gringo (1987) is the intriguing first-hand story of peasant Elvia Alvarado's reluctant rise as a labor leader, and of the Honduran labor movement, flaws and all.

Bitter Fruit by Stephen C Schlesinger is mostly about the United Fruit Company in Guatemala, but provides insight on the banana giant's impact on Honduras as well. *The Banana Men: American Mercenaries and Entrepreneurs in Central America, 1880–1930* (1995) and *The Banana Wars: United States Intervention in the Caribbean, 1898-1934* (2002), both by Lester D Langley, are incisive accounts of the banana companies' political and economic influence in Central America and the Caribbean.

Los barcos (The Ships; 1992), *El humano y la diosa* (The Human and the Goddess; 1996) and *The Big Banana* (1999) are all by Roberto Quesada, one of Honduras' best known living novelists. *Gringos in Honduras: The Good, the Bad, and the Ugly* (1995) and *Velasquez: The Man and His Art*, are two of many books by Guillermo Yuscarán, aka William Lewis, an American writer and painter living in Honduras. *Around the Edge* (1991) by English journalist Peter Ford relates Ford's journey along the Caribbean coast from Belize to Panama, especially in La Moskitia.

Love Paul Theroux or hate him, his *The Mosquito Coast* is a vivid fictional account of life in the jungle and the characters it attracts. O Henry also wrote an evocative novel *Cabbages and Kings* loosely based on Trujillo.

The Spanish-only *Honduras hoy: el golpe, la resistencia* by Argentine journalist Mariano Saravia (www.marianosaravia.com.ar) was the only book published at press time on the political crisis in Honduras.

BUSINESS HOURS

Businesses are open during the following hours; exceptions are noted in specific listings.

Banks 8:30am to 4:30pm Monday to Friday and 8:30 to 11:30am Saturday

Restaurants 7am to 9pm daily

Shops 9am to 6pm Monday to Saturday and 9am to 1pm or 5pm Sunday

CLIMATE

The mountainous interior is much cooler than the coastal lowlands. Tegucigalpa, at 975m, has a temperate climate, with maximum/minimum temperatures varying from 25/14°C (77/57°F)

HONDURAS

in January to 30/18°C (86/64°F) in May. The coastal lowlands are much warmer and more humid year-round; the Pacific coastal plain near the Golfo de Fonseca is hot indeed. December and January are the coolest months.

The rainfall also varies in different parts of the country. The rainy season runs from around May to October. On the Pacific side and in the interior, this means a relatively dry season from around November to April. However, the amount of rain, and when it falls, varies considerably from year to year.

On the Caribbean coast, it rains year-round, but the wettest months are from September to January or February. During this time floods can occur on the north coast, impeding travel and occasionally causing severe damage (400 people died in floods in November 1993).

Hurricane season is June to November. For climate charts see p714.

DANGERS & ANNOYANCES

Most travelers enjoy their time in Honduras and their trips pass without unpleasant incidents. That said, Honduras does have a crime problem, as many developing countries do. The country's ingrained gun culture may unsettle visitors, but the chances of a firearms assault are slim – petty theft is a far more likely risk. You should be cautious – but not paranoid – in the cities, especially San Pedro Sula and Tegucigalpa, which both have gang problems (again, travelers are rarely targeted). Walking in the center in the daytime is usually fine – although don't flash your belongings about. Spring for a cab at night if you are downtown. Violence against women is on the rise (2009 saw an alarming 37% rise in femicide incidents).

In general, small towns are much safer than the big cities. Watch yourself on the north coast, especially on the beach. Avoid leaving items unattended and do not walk on the beach alone or at night. Although still rare, thefts, muggings and even rapes have occurred on the beaches here. Avoid travel (especially driving) at night, when *banditos* and drug runners do their dirty work, and stay vigilant of your surroundings night or day on the mainland.

Malaria-carrying mosquitoes and biting sand flies on the north coast, the Bay Islands and the Moskitia are an annoyance and, along with unpurified water, can be the greatest threat to your well-being. Also watch out for jellyfish and stingrays, which are present on both the Caribbean and Pacific coasts.

If you go hiking through wild places, beware of poisonous snakes, especially the fer-de-lance (known locally as *barba amarilla*); the coral snake is also present. Crocodiles and caimans live in the waterways of the Moskitia, as do the peaceful manatee and much other wildlife. Honduras also has scorpions (not lethal), black widow spiders, wasps and other stinging insects. You probably will never see a dangerous animal, but be aware that they exist.

EMBASSIES & CONSULATES

The following are in Tegucigalpa. For a full list, see Lonely Planet's *Honduras* guide:

Belize (Map p344; ☎ 238-4614; embajadabelizehond@yahoo.com; Centro Comercial Hotel Honduras Maya, Av República de Chile; ☽ 9am-noon & 2:30-4pm Mon-Fri)

Canada (off Map p344; ☎ 232-4551; www.canadainternational.gc.ca/costa_rica; Centro Financiero Banexpo, Local 3, Blvr San Juan Bosco; ☽ 7:30am-4pm Mon-Thu, to 1pm Fri)

El Salvador (off Map p344; ☎ 239-7017/909; Diagonal Aguán 2952; ☽ 8am-4pm Mon-Fri)

France (Map p344; ☎ 236-6800; www.ambafrance-hn.org/france_honduras; Av Juan Lindo 337)

Germany (off Map p344; ☎ 232-3161; www.tegucigalpa.diplo.de; Av República Dominicana 925)

Guatemala (off Map p344; ☎ 232-1580; embhonduras@minex.gob; Calle Arturo López Rodezno 2421, Colonia Las Minitas; ☽ 9am-1pm Mon-Fri)

Israel (Map p344; ☎ 232-0776; rosario_losk@hotmail.com; inside Conversa Language School/Aerocasillas Postal Service, Paseo República de Argentina 257; ☽ 8:15am-5:30pm Mon-Fri)

Japan (Map p344; ☎ 236-5511; www.hn.emb-japan.go.jp; Calzada República de Paraguay btwn 4a & 5a Calles; ☽ 8:30am-12:15pm & 1:30-5pm Mon-Fri)

Netherlands (off Map p344; ☎ 239-8090; 3a Av 2315; ☽ 9am-noon Mon-Fri)

Nicaragua (Map p344; ☎ 232-7224; Calle Las Minitas, Colonia Lomas de Tepeyac; ☽ 8am-noon Mon-Fri)

Spain (Map p344; ☎ 236-6865; www.mae.es/embajadas/tegucigalpa; Calle Santander 801; ☽ 9am-1pm Mon-Fri)

UK (Map p344; ☎ 237-6577; www.ukinguatemala.fco.gov.uk/en/working-with-honduras; Calle Principal 2402, Colonia La Reforma; ☽ 9am-noon Mon-Fri)

USA (Map p344; ☎ 236-9320; www.honduras.usembassy.gov; Av La Paz; ☽ 8am-11:30am Mon-Fri)

FESTIVALS & EVENTS

Just about every city, town and village in Honduras has a patron saint and celebrates an annual festival or fair in the days around their saint's day. Some are big events, attracting crowds from far and wide. These are mentioned in the various town sections, where relevant.

Feria de Suyapa The patron saint of Honduras is celebrated in Suyapa, near Tegucigalpa, from around February 2 to 11. February 3 is the saint's day. The services and festivities bring pilgrims and celebrants from all over Central America.

Carnaval at La Ceiba Celebrated during the third week in May, the third Saturday is the biggest day, with parades, costumes, music and celebrations in the streets.

San Pedro Sula Held in the last week of June, this is another popular celebration.

Feria Centroamericana de Turismo y Artesanía (Fecatai) Every year, from December 6 to 16, this all–Central American international tourism and crafts fair is held in Tegucigalpa.

Artisans' & Cultural Fair An annual all-Honduras artisans' and cultural fair held in the town of Copán Ruinas from December 15 to 21.

The fairs at Tela (June 13), Trujillo (June 24), Danlí (last weekend in August) and Copán Ruinas (March 15 to 20) are also good, and there are many others.

Several Garífuna music and dance troupes give presentations throughout the country, including the excellent Ballet Folklórico Garífuna. April 12, the anniversary of the arrival of the Garífuna people in Honduras in 1797, is a joyful occasion celebrated in all Garífuna communities.

FOOD & DRINK

Honduras does not have the wealth of local cuisine that Mexico or Guatemala has, but a few dishes are distinctive. Garífuna communities are famous for coconut bread and *casabe* (a crispy flat bread common throughout the Caribbean) – both are quite tasty. Seafood, especially fish, crab and lobster, is ubiquitous on the north coast, while fried chicken is a street-food staple nationwide. Another staple is *anafres,* a bean and *quesillo* cheese dip, served up in a heated clay pot and eaten like nachos. Ubiquitous *baleadas,* a breakfast staple involving beans and *quesillo* wrapped in a flour tortilla, are a tasty but easily worn-out treat (even Wendy's makes them!). Honduras has several beers on offer – Salva Vida and Port Royal are the favorite among travelers, then there is Imperial (popular in Olancho) and the lighter Barena. They are all produced by the same brewery, Cervecería Hondureña (owned by the SAB Miller multinational). All are cheap but nothing to write home about.

For excellent, home-brewed beers, visit D&D Brewery in Lago de Yojoa (p361).

In all but the most basic restaurants, expect to pay taxes of 12% (food) and 15% (alcohol), which may or may not be included in the posted menu prices; as well as a 10% tip – some restaurants will automatically add the service to the bill.

GAY & LESBIAN TRAVELERS

Honduras is very much 'in the closet,' and open displays of affection between gay or lesbian couples are often frowned upon. Discreet homosexual behavior was tolerated more before the advent of HIV/AIDS in Honduras around 1985. Since then anti-gay incidents have increased, along with stricter legislation. Organizations serving the gay, lesbian and transsexual/transgender communities include **Asociación LGTB Arcoiris de Honduras** (☎ 206-2408; arcoirisghn@yahoo.com), **Colectiva Violeta** (☎ 237-4905; colectivo_violeta@yahoo.com) and **Asociación Kukulcán** (☎ 239-7326; kukulcan@amnettgu.com).

HOLIDAYS

New Year's Day January 1

Day of the Americas April 14

Semana Santa (Holy Week) Thursday, Friday and Saturday before Easter Sunday.

Labor Day May 1

Independence Day September 15

Francisco Morazán Day October 3

Día de la Raza (Columbus Day) October 12

Army Day October 21

Christmas Day December 25

INTERNET ACCESS

Every city and most towns and villages usually have at least one internet cafe. Connections tend to be reasonable, and cost L18 to L20 per hour. Access on the Bay Islands has improved thanks to satellite connection, but is still the country's most expensive at around L120 per hour.

INTERNET RESOURCES

A quick search on any decent internet search engine will bring you a host of hits on Honduras.

http://lanic.utexas.edu/la/ca/honduras Extensive list of links to articles and websites on everything from politics to sports to tourism.

www.hondurasnews.com Translations of the latest big news issues to hit Honduras.

www.hondurastips.honduras.com The website of the free tourist magazine *Honduras Tips*.

HONDURAS

www.hondurasweekly.com The former official site of *Honduras This Week,* Honduras' only English-language newspaper, now independently operating as *Honduras Weekly*.

www.letsgohonduras.com Honduras' ministry of tourism website.

www.lonelyplanet.com/worldguide The source of updated Lonely Planet coverage.

www.sidewalkmystic.com Private website with practical info on travel in Honduras.

www.travel-to-honduras.com Links to various services, including volunteer organizations.

LANGUAGE

Spanish is spoken throughout the mainland, although it is a second language for some indigenous communities in the Moskitia and Garífuna towns on the north coast. On the Bay Islands, Spanish is gaining ground on English and Garífuna, especially on Roatán.

LEGAL MATTERS

Police officers in Honduras aren't immune to corruption. If you plan to rent a car, for example, be aware that transit police are not above looking for infractions to get a little money for gas. Tourist police are fairly new to Honduras – you should be seeing more of them, especially in places like Tela and La Ceiba – and they are generally trustworthy. While travelers should not hesitate to contact the nearest police officer or station in emergencies, look for tourist police for less urgent matters.

MAPS

Good maps are hard to find in Honduras. Tourist offices and visitors centers are the best places for them. Bookstores occasionally carry maps.

The Instituto Geográfico Nacional in Tegucigalpa (p342) publishes high-quality maps of the various departments (states), both political and topographic. It sells a few city and municipal maps as well.

MEDIA

Honduras Tips is a bilingual (English and Spanish) magazine-directory indispensable for travelers. It gives lots of information on things to see and do and places to stay and eat, with maps and photos. The magazine is published twice a year and is available for free in many hotels, travel agencies, tourist information offices and other places frequented by travelers.

Honduras Weekly (www.hondurasweekly.com) is an online English-language newspaper updated daily by an international team of journalists and analysts who closely track events in Honduras. Honduras has four national newspapers: **El Heraldo** (www.elheraldo.hn) and **La Tribuna** (www.latribuna.hn) are published in Tegucigalpa, **La Prensa** (www.laprensahn.com) and **El Tiempo** (www.tiempo.hn) in San Pedro Sula, all prone to varying degrees of sensationalism.

MONEY

The unit of currency in Honduras is the lempira. Notes are of one, two, five, 10, 20, 50, 100 and 500 lempiras. There are 100 centavos in a lempira; coins are of one, two, five, 10, 20 and 50 centavos. Centavos are virtually worthless, except for occasional use on urban bus routes.

ATMs

There are cash machines in all cities and towns throughout the country. ATMs operated by HSBC, BAC/Bamer, Banco Atlántida and Unibanc are the most reliable, and most likely to accept out-of-country debit cards. Always be alert when withdrawing cash; whenever possible, take out money during the day, and at a machine that's in a lockable cabin or inside the bank itself.

ATMs typically spit out 500-lempira bills, which can be a hassle to break – get in the habit of using big bills at hotels and larger restaurants, and saving the small bills for taxis, small eateries, street stands, markets and so forth.

Bargaining

Crafts are fairly rare in Honduras, so you won't find many opportunities to bargain while shopping. Prices for many services are fixed, so there shouldn't be any need to bargain. In large cities, for example, both *colectivos* and private taxis have a single fixed price for rides around town.

Ask at your hotel what taxis should cost; if you get in knowing what the price should be, most drivers won't argue. In La Moskitia, prices are fixed (and high); bargaining isn't too fruitful.

Cash

Banks will exchange US dollars and occasionally euros. Bring your passport and go in the morning. Your hotel may let you pay in US dollars (worth doing to avoid the bank queues), or exchange them for you, as may some places in the more touristy areas.

Credit Cards

Visa and MasterCard are widely accepted, including at major supermarkets, retail stores, hotels and car rental agencies. Expect a 6% to 12% surcharge at some hotels and restaurants, especially in the Bay Islands.

Cash advances on Visa cards are available at most banks, including BAC/Bamer, Banco Atlántida and Banco de Occidente. BAC/Bamer can usually process advances on MasterCard too. There's typically no transaction charge on the Honduran end for Visa or MasterCard cash advances, but of course the interest rates charged tend to be astronomical.

Exchange Rates

The US dollar and (to a lesser extent) the euro are the only foreign currencies that are easily exchanged in Honduras; away from the borders you will even find it difficult to change the currencies of Guatemala, El Salvador or Nicaragua.

The table below shows currency exchange rates at the time this book went to press.

Country	Unit	L
Australia	A$1	15.87
Canada	C$1	17.75
Euro zone	€1	23.07
Japan	¥100	21.35
New Zealand	NZ$1	12.95
UK	UK£1	28.23
USA	US$	18.90

Traveler's Checks

Though American Express traveler's checks can be changed in all major towns (Banco Atlántida and BAC/Bamer are the best banks to use), they are a dying breed and not worth the hassle. The daily limit is US$100 and hotels and other retailers want nothing to do with them.

POST

Post offices in most Honduran towns typically are open Monday to Friday 8am to 5pm (often with a couple of hours off for lunch between noon and 2pm) and on Saturday from 8am to noon. Postcards/letters cost L15/25 to the US, L25/35 to Europe and L30/40 to Australia. Delivery takes 10 to 14 days, longer for Australia. Despite the apparently long delivery times for postal items, Honducor, the Honduran postal service, is considered relatively reliable. In fact, travelers from Nicaragua or Guatemala often hang on to their postcards and mail them from Honduras.

For more secure delivery try FedEx, DHL, Express Mail Service (EMS), or Urgent Express; all have offices in Tegucigalpa, San Pedro Sula and other major cities.

RESPONSIBLE TRAVEL

Travelers should not buy anything made of coral – the reefs are widely protected and the items, like coral necklaces or bracelets, probably come from illegal harvests. On the Bay Islands, particularly Utila, fresh water, energy and landfill space are in short supply. Have short showers, and refill your water bottles, rather than buying new ones. If you go diving, make sure you go with a dive outfit that is fully signed up to protecting the environment.

Be very aware of the cultural differences in indigenous communities. Tread sensitively – taking lots of photos in an indigenous area can rouse suspicion.

STUDYING

Spanish courses are popular in Copán Ruinas and the Bay Islands. As well as open-water and advanced open-water certifications, shops on the Bay Islands offer most or all upper-level dive courses and specialties, including nitrox, dive master and instructor.

TELEPHONE

Many internet cafes offer clear, inexpensive phone service using high-speed internet connections. Calls to the US typically cost L1 to L2 per minute. Expect to pay a bit more to call Europe: per minute L2 to L3.

PRICE WARNING!

The prices in this chapter are particularly susceptible to increases, due to the timing of our research period shortly after the political crisis in 2009. Many businesses, operators and hotels saw occupancy and reservations drop to 0% during the crisis, and slashed prices in late 2009 in an effort to stimulate tourism again. By the time you read this, travelers are expected to have returned and prices consequently increased to normal levels.

HONDURAS

Hondutel (www.hondutel.hn) has call centers at its offices throughout the country. Rates to the US are competitive at just L2 per minute, but prices to Europe are an outrageous and unrealistic L43.85 per minute. Calls to the rest of the world are higher as well. Call centers are usually open from 7am until around 9pm every day.

Some Hondutel offices and internet cafes with phone service have fax services. Prices vary widely, but are usually per page, as opposed to per minute. You can receive faxes as well, with a minimal per-page fee. Fax service typically has more limited hours, usually 8am to 4pm Monday to Friday.

Honduran carriers Digicel and Claro use GSM 1900 protocols, while Tigo uses GSM 850. These are generally compatible with North American carriers Cingular, T-Mobile, Fido and others, but will be incompatible with GSM 900/1800 phones common in Europe, Australia, New Zealand and many Asian countries.

Honduras' country code is ☎ 504. There are no area codes beyond the country code; when dialing Honduras from abroad simply dial the international access code plus the Honduran country code plus the local number. For domestic long-distance calls within Honduras, there is no need to dial an area code.

To reach a domestic long-distance operator dial ☎ 191; for local directory assistance dial ☎ 192; for directory assistance for government telephone numbers dial ☎ 193; for an international operator dial ☎ 197. A direct connection to an operator in the USA is available by dialing ☎ 800-0121 for Sprint, ☎ 800-0122 for MCI WorldCom and ☎ 800-0123 for AT&T.

Hondutel offices sell 'Telecards' which have a code on the back. Simply follow the instructions on the back to make a call from any pay phone.

TOILETS

Public toilets are few and far between in Honduras – stop at your hotel or at restaurants. Western-style flush toilets are the norm in most places although toilet paper goes in the wastepaper basket, not down the hatch. The exception to the rule is La Moskitia, where running water is rare and latrines are typical.

TOURIST INFORMATION

The national tourist office is the **Instituto Hondureño de Turismo** (IHT; ☎ 222-2124, toll-free 800-222-8687; www.letsgohonduras.com) in Tegucigalpa. IHT also maintains a **US office** (☎ toll-free 800-410- 9608; Suite 305, 2828 Coral Way, Miami, FL 33145). Around the country, tourist information offices are run by the municipal government and public agencies (listed in the Information section of each destination).

TRAVELERS WITH DISABILITIES

Honduras has few facilities for disabled travelers, other than in upmarket hotels and resorts. Wheelchair-bound visitors will find it difficult to negotiate Tegucigalpa and San Pedro Sula because of street congestion and generally poor road or sidewalk surfaces. Even smaller towns are difficult to negotiate as roads surfaces are often unpaved or made up of cobblestones. Public transport is often crowded, dirty and inefficient, and rarely geared to less-able travelers. Toilets for the disabled are virtually nonexistent, other than in four- or five-star hotels.

VISAS & DOCUMENTS

Citizens of most western European countries, Australia, Canada, Japan, New Zealand and the United States normally receive 90-day tourist cards when entering the country. This applies to the countries signed up to the CA-4 border agreement – Guatemala, Nicaragua, Honduras and El Salvador. You do not receive a stamp on your passport when passing between these countries.

Upon arrival you will fill out a short immigration form, the yellow portion of which will be stapled into your passport. Do not lose it! This form will be collected when you depart, and it will be stamped if you seek an extension of your stay. Once inside Honduras you can apply for a one-time 30-day extension at any immigration office (called a *prórroga* and costing L386 or US$20); after that, you'll need to take a trip to Belize or Costa Rica for at least three days.

As visa information is always changing, see www.lonelyplanet.com for the latest information.

VOLUNTEERING

A number of organizations offer volunteer opportunities in Honduras, on projects in many parts of the country and ranging from building homes to teaching English to involving school children in environmental programs. The website www.travel-to-honduras.com has a long list of groups that run volunteer programs in Honduras, from large operations like Casa Alianza, Houses for Humanity and i-to-i, to smaller ones like the Cofradía Bilingual School and the Utila Iguana Conservation Project.

A good short-term option is **Global Brigades** (☎ in US 866-276-4077, in Honduras 9518-2627; www. globalbrigades.org), the world's largest student-led global health and sustainable development organization, which offers weeklong programs for travelers.

WOMEN TRAVELERS

Honduras is basically a good country for women travelers. As elsewhere, you'll proba-bly attract less attention if you dress modestly. On the Bay Islands, where lots of beach-going foreign tourists tend to congregate, standards of modesty in dress are much more relaxed, though topless bathing is most definitely frowned upon.

Cases of rape against foreign tourists have been reported in a few places along the north coast. As peaceful and idyllic as the coast looks – and usually is – be wary of going to isolated stretches of beach alone, and don't walk on the beach at night.

Nicaragua

To the new generation of travelers, Nicaragua represents booming beach breaks, volcano hiking, thrilling island paradises and laid-back colonial towns, so it seems that the message – 'the civil war finished decades ago, people!' – has finally gotten across to an audience who had it pegged as a trouble spot. In fact, it's now the safest country in Central America, and a surprisingly easy place to travel around.

Yet the iconic images of idealistic young people giving their lives for a dream of liberty have never quite disappeared, and Nicaragua remains a land where people, whatever their beliefs, tend to go beyond cheap chatter. A place of poets and artists, of opinions both well-informed and cheerily imparted. Despite the landscape being extra well-endowed with natural beauty, it is the Nicaraguans themselves who remain their country's chief asset.

Nicaragua boasts both a Pacific and a Caribbean coast, and these two sides of the country differ in myriad ways. In the west of the country you can zip between colonial cities on good paved roads, while in the east is an enormous wilderness that, a couple of golden Caribbean paradises apart, won't be touristy any time this century.

FAST FACTS

- **Area** 129,494 sq km (approximately the size of Greece or New York State)
- **Budget** US$20 to US$30 per day
- **Capital** Managua
- **Costs** Hostel in León US$6 to US$8, bottle of beer US$0.70, three-hour bus ride US$3.50, lunch US$3
- **Country Code** ☎ 505
- **Languages** Spanish, English
- **Money** US$1 = C$21.00 (córdobas)
- **Population** 5.5 million
- **Seasons** Dry (November to April), wet (May to October)
- **Time** GMT minus six hours, no daylight saving

TRAVEL HINTS

Shared taxis often cost little more than buses. A lightweight hammock is great for boat trips and can save you heaps on accommodations.

OVERLAND ROUTES

Nicaragua's border with Honduras can be crossed at Las Manos, El Espino or Guasaule. From Costa Rica, you can enter by road at Peñas Blancas or by boat via Los Chiles.

HIGHLIGHTS

- **Isla de Ometepe** (p500) Scramble to the summits of the two volcanoes that join to make this majestic island.
- **Corn Islands** (p513) Snack on coconuts and swim crystal-clear waters in this unspoiled Caribbean getaway.
- **Granada & León** (p484) and (p476) Savor the delights of these cultured colonial towns, easily reached from Managua.
- **Río San Juan** (p507) Board a riverboat to explore this picturesque watercourse, home to abundant birdlife and an unexpected fortress.
- **Matagalpa & Estelí** (p465) and (p470) Discover the hard-working highlands in these earthy, open cities, coffee and cowboy country respectively.
- **Off the beaten track** (p512) Bargain with local fishermen to take you boating in the intriguing Mískito area of Laguna de Perlas.

CURRENT EVENTS

After 16 years on the sidelines, the return of President Daniel Ortega was always going to be eventful. The Frente Sandinista de Liberación Nacional (FSLN; Sandinista National Liberation Front) leader got off to a positive start, resolving the energy crisis that had crippled the country for years and reintroducing free health care and education. But municipal elections in late 2008 brought a real sense of crisis to the country, with the opposition claiming widespread fraud. Both the US and EU agreed with them and froze large amounts of aid to Nicaragua.

Ortega threw more fuel on the fire by pushing for constitutional changes to allow him to stand for re-election when his current term expires in 2011. After failing to get the votes necessary in the parliament, the FSLN rushed a bill through a court stacked with judges loyal to the party. This brought the usually divided opposition onto the streets in mass protest, but whether the unity lasts long enough to curtail the president's ambitions remains to be seen.

While the politicians have been concentrating on their power plays, the world economic crisis has battered the country, particularly those many Nicaraguans that live hand to mouth. Foreign manufacturing companies have cut staff, tourist numbers have dropped, and, most importantly of all, the international remittances from family and friends that many depend upon have dried up. With no money coming in and little faith in their leaders to resolve things, more young Nicaraguans than ever are packing up and heading abroad, most as undocumented immigrants, in search of a way out of poverty.

HISTORY
Early History

Fascinatingly, the earliest traces of human habitation in Nicaragua are some 6000-year-old footprints found near the banks of Lago de Managua, within the area occupied by the present-day capital.

Nicaragua was home to several indigenous groups, including the ancestors of today's Rama who live on the Caribbean coast, and the Chorotegas and Nicaraos, on the Pacific side. The latter spoke a form of Nahuatl, the language of the Aztecs. Many Nicaraguan places retain their Nahuatl names.

European Arrival

The indigenous inhabitants' first contact with Europeans was in 1502, when Columbus sailed down Nicaragua's Caribbean coast.

The next exploratory mission, led by Gil González de Ávila, came north from the Sp......settlement at Panama, arriving in 152.. It found a chieftain, Cacique Nicarao, governing the southern shores of Lago de Nicaragua and the tribe of the same name. The Spaniards thus named the region Nicaragua.

Two years later the Spanish were back to colonize, led this time by Francisco Hernández de Córdoba, who founded the cities of Granada and León in 1524. Both were established near indigenous settlements whose inhabitants were subjugated and put to work. Attempts at founding a similar city near

Managua were resisted; the indigenous settlement was destroyed as punishment.

Colonial Settlement

The gold that had initially attracted the Spaniards soon gave out, but Granada and León remained. Granada, with a direct connection to the Caribbean and Europe via Lago de Nicaragua, became a comparatively rich colonial trading centre. With its wealthy business class, the city was the natural center for the Conservative Party, favoring traditional values of monarchy and ecclesiastical authority.

Originally founded on Lago de Managua, León was hit by a series of disasters culminating in a major earthquake in 1610, which convinced the authorities to pack up and establish a new city some 30km northwest. It was poorer than Granada, but the Spanish made it the capital of the colonial province. León in time became the center for radical clerics and intellectuals, who formed the Liberal Party and supported the unification of Central America and reforms based on those of the French and American revolutions.

The difference in wealth between the two cities, and the political supremacy of León, led to conflicts that raged until the 1850s, at times erupting into outright civil war. The continual fighting between them stopped only when the capital was moved to the neutral location of Managua.

While the Spanish were settling the Pacific lowlands, the English were the dominant influence on the Caribbean side of Nicaragua. English, French and Dutch pirates plying the Caribbean established settlements and attacked the east coast in the 17th century, at times even penetrating to Granada via the Río San Juan.

Early Independence

Along with the rest of Central America, Nicaragua gained independence from Spain in 1821, was briefly part of Mexico, was then incorporated into the new Central American Federation and finally achieved complete independence in 1838. The cities of León and Granada continued to feud.

After independence, the Liberals and Conservatives weren't the only groups vying for power. With the Spanish out of the picture, Britain and the USA both became interested in Nicaragua and its strategically important passage from Lago de Nicaragua to the Caribbean. Both countries wanted to build an interoceanic canal through Central America, and Nicaragua looked the likeliest spot.

In 1848 the British seized the Caribbean port of San Juan del Norte, at the mouth of the Río San Juan, and renamed it Greytown. Meanwhile, the California gold rush had added fire to the quest for an Atlantic–Pacific passage, and prospectors were transported to America's west coast via the Río San Juan and a Pacific steamer service.

The Late 19th Century

In 1857 the Liberals, disgraced after inviting William Walker (see boxed text, right) into the country, lost power to the Conservatives and were unable to regain it for the next 36 years. The new government set up shop in Managua, then little more than a village, which had been nominated as capital in 1852 in an attempt to quell the rivalry between Granada and León.

In 1860 the British signed a treaty ceding the Caribbean region to the now-independent governments of Honduras and Nicaragua. The Nicaraguan section remained an autonomous region until the 1890s.

Zelaya's Coup & US Intervention

In 1893 a Liberal general named José Santos Zelaya deposed the Conservative president and became president. Zelaya soon antagonized the US by seeking a canal deal with Germany and Japan. Encouraged by Washington, which sought to monopolize a transisthmian canal in Panama, the Conservatives rebelled in 1909. After Zelaya ordered the execution of two US mercenaries accused of aiding the Conservatives, the American government forced his resignation. In 1912 the US responded to another rebellion, this time against the corrupt Conservative administration, by sending 2500 marines to Nicaragua.

For most of the next two decades the US dominated politics in Nicaragua, installing presidents it favored and ousting those it didn't, using its marines as persuasion. In 1914 the Bryan-Chamorro Treaty was signed, granting the US exclusive canal rights in Nicaragua; America actually had no intention of building such a canal, but wanted to ensure that no one else did.

In 1925 a new cycle of violence began with a Conservative coup. The marines were with-

DOING THINGS THE WILLIAM WALKER WAY

Latin America's turbulent history is littered with colorful characters, but there were few messiah complexes bigger than that of William Walker, an American adventurer who directed and starred in *Conquistador 2*, more than three centuries after Cortéz took the New World by storm with the original hit. He started his one-man mission in 1853, leading a small party to attack Mexico, where he declared himself president of 'independent' Sonora before being ignominiously driven out.

In 1855 the Liberals of León asked Walker to help them seize power from Granada's Conservatives. Walker entered Nicaragua with 56 followers, attacked Granada and prevailed. Instead of ceding it to his employers, he soon had himself elected president of Nicaragua (in 'free and fair elections' no doubt), and the US recognized his government. He then reinstituted slavery, declared English the country's official language, mortgaged the entire nation to fund personal borrowing, and invaded Costa Rica, announcing his intention to control the whole of Central America. This was a step too far, and those nations united to drive him out. Walker fled Granada, leaving the city alight, and was forced to return to the USA.

Not easily put off, he landed with a small army at Greytown six months later, only to be arrested and deported by the US Navy. He tried again in 1860; this time the British Navy captured him and turned him over to the Hondurans, who ended his adventures with a volley of rifle fire in 1860. His grave is in Trujillo's old cemetery (see p405).

drawn, but as political turmoil ensued, they returned the following year.

Sandino & the Somoza Era

The Conservative regime was opposed by a group of Liberal rebels including Augusto C Sandino, who eventually became leader of a long-term guerrilla campaign resisting US involvement. The marines headed home in 1933 after handing over military power to the US-trained Guardia Nacional, led by Anastasio Somoza García.

In February 1934, Somoza engineered the assassination of Sandino, who was abducted and gunned down after being summoned to dinner at the presidental palace to discuss disarmament. Somoza, with his main enemy out of the way, then set his sights on supreme power. Overthrowing Liberal president Sacasa a couple of years later, he established himself as president in 1937, founding a family dynasty that was to rule for four decades.

After creating a new constitution to grant himself more power, Somoza García ruled Nicaragua as an internationally notorious dictator for the next 20 years, sometimes as president, at other times behind a puppet president. He amassed huge personal wealth by corrupt means (the Somoza landholdings attained were the size of El Salvador). Of course, the majority of Nicaraguans remained entrenched in poverty.

Somoza supported the USA (the CIA used Nicaragua as a launchpad for both the 1954 overthrow of Guatemalan leader Colon Jacobo Arbenz Guzmán and the 1961 invasion of Cuba) and was in turn supported by the US government.

After his assassination in León in 1956 (see boxed text, p479), Somoza was succeeded by his elder son, Luis Somoza Debayle, and the Somoza family, with the help of the Guardia Nacional, continued to rule Nicaragua. In 1967 Luis died, and his younger brother, Anastasio Somoza Debayle, assumed control.

Rising Opposition

In 1961 Carlos Fonseca Amador, a prominent figure in the student movement that had opposed the Somoza regime in the 1950s, joined forces with Colonel Santos López (an old fighting partner of Sandino's) and other activists to form the Frente Sandinista de Liberación Nacional (Sandinista National Liberation Front), or FSLN.

On December 23, 1972, at around midnight, an earthquake devastated Managua, leveling over 250 city blocks, killing over 6000 people and leaving 300,000 homeless. As international aid poured in, the money was diverted to Anastasio Somoza and his associates, while the people who needed it suffered and died. This obvious abuse dramatically increased opposition to Somoza among all classes of society. Wealthy businesspeople also

NICARAGUA

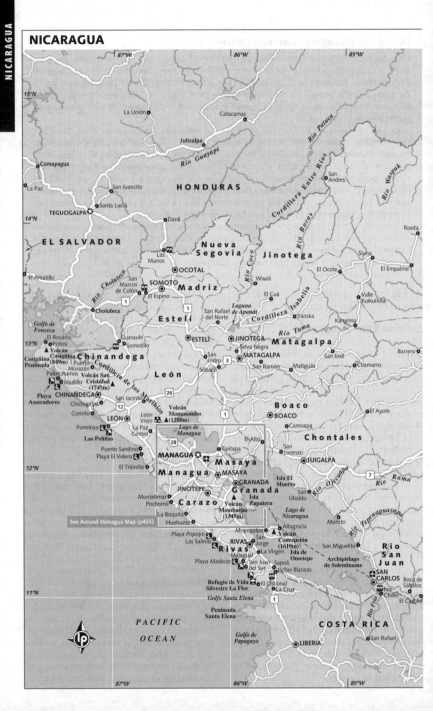

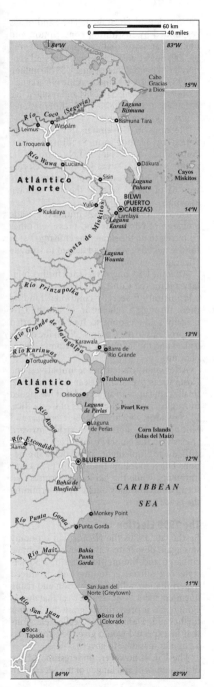

turned against Somoza as they saw their own ventures being eclipsed by the Somoza family's corrupt empire.

By 1974 opposition was widespread. Two groups were widely recognized – the FSLN (Sandinistas), led by Carlos Fonseca, and the Unión Democrática de Liberación, led by Pedro Joaquín Chamorro, popular owner and editor of the Managua newspaper *La Prensa*, which had long printed articles critical of the Somoza regime.

In December 1974 the FSLN kidnapped several leading members of the Somoza regime, gaining ransoms and the freeing of political prisoners in exchange for the release of the hostages. The Somoza government responded with a campaign of systematic killings over the following 2½ years. Fonseca was killed in a skirmish in 1976.

Revolution & the FSLN

The last straw for the Nicaraguan public was the assassination in January 1978 of Chamorro. Violence erupted and a general strike was declared. Business interests united with moderate factions in the Frente Amplio Opositor (FAO; Broad Opposition Front) and unsuccessfully attempted to negotiate an end to the Somoza dictatorship.

In August 1978 the FSLN occupied the Palacio Nacional and took over 2000 hostages, demanding freedom for 60 imprisoned Sandinistas. The government acceded, and the hostages were released. Nevertheless, the revolt spread, with spontaneous uprisings in many major towns. The Guardia Nacional responded swiftly and ruthlessly, shelling those cities and killing thousands.

The FAO, having exhausted its negotiating efforts, threw in its lot with the Sandinistas, whom they now perceived as the only viable means to oust the dictatorship. This broad alliance formed a revolutionary government provisionally based in San José, Costa Rica, which gained recognition from some Latin American and European governments and military support in the form of arms shipments. Thus the FSLN was well prepared to launch its final offensive in June 1979. The revolutionary forces took city after city, with the support of thousands of civilians. On July 17, as the Sandinistas were preparing to enter Managua, Somoza resigned the presidency and fled the country. (He was assassinated by Sandinista agents a year later in Asunción,

Paraguay.) The Sandinistas marched victoriously into Managua on July 19, 1979.

They inherited a shambles. Poverty, homelessness, illiteracy and staggeringly inadequate health care were just a few of the widespread problems. An estimated 50,000 people had been killed in the revolutionary struggle, and perhaps 150,000 more left homeless.

The FSLN and prominent anti-Somoza moderates (including Violeta Barrios de Chamorro, widow of the martyred Pedro Joaquín Chamorro) set up a five-member junta to administer the country. The constitution was suspended, the national congress dissolved and the Guardia Nacional replaced by the Sandinista People's Army.

However, the alliance between moderates and the FSLN didn't last long. In April 1980 Chamorro and the one other moderate resigned from the ruling junta when it became clear that the FSLN intended to dominate the council of state, which was being set up to serve as the nation's interim legislature. The junta thus was reduced from five members to three, with revolutionary commander Daniel Ortega Saavedra appointed coordinator.

Trying to salvage what it could of its influence over the country, the US (under President Jimmy Carter) authorized US$75 million in emergency aid to the Sandinista-led government. However, by late 1980 it was becoming concerned about the increasing numbers of Soviet and Cuban advisors in Nicaragua and allegations that the Sandinistas were beginning to provide arms to leftist rebels in El Salvador.

The Contra War

After Ronald Reagan became US president in January 1981, relations between Nicaragua and the US took a turn for the worse. Reagan suspended all aid to Nicaragua and began funding the counterrevolutionary military groups known as Contras, operating out of Honduras and eventually out of Costa Rica as well. Most of the original Contras were ex-soldiers of Somoza's Guardia Nacional, but as time passed, their ranks filled with disaffected local people.

The Contra war escalated throughout the 1980s. As US money flowed to the Contras, their numbers grew to over 15,000 fighters. Honduras was heavily militarized, with large-scale US-Honduran maneuvers threatening

an invasion of Nicaragua. The Sandinistas responded by instituting conscription and building an army that eventually numbered 95,000. Soviet and Cuban military and economic aid poured in, reaching US$700 million in 1987. A CIA scheme to mine Nicaragua's harbors was revealed in 1984 and resulted in a judgment against the US by the International Court of Justice.

Elections in November 1984 were boycotted by leading non-Sandinistas, who complained of sweeping FSLN control of the nation's media. Daniel Ortega was elected president with 63% of the vote, and the FSLN won 61 of the 96 seats in the new national assembly.

In May 1985 the USA initiated a trade embargo of Nicaragua and pressured other countries to do the same. The embargo lasted for the next five years and helped to strangle Nicaragua's economy.

After the US Congress rejected further military aid for the Contras in 1985, the Reagan administration secretly continued funding them through a scheme in which the CIA illegally sold weapons to Iran and diverted the proceeds to the Contras. When the details leaked out, the infamous 'Iran-Contra Affair' blew up.

After many failed peace initiatives, the Costa Rican president, Oscar Arias Sánchez, finally came up with an accord that was signed in August 1987 by the leaders of Costa Rica, El Salvador, Nicaragua, Guatemala and Honduras. Though a great stride forward (Arias won the Nobel Peace Prize), it proved difficult to implement, as participating nations failed to follow through on their commitments, while the US took measures that seemed intentionally aimed at undermining the peace process.

The 1990 Election

By the late 1980s the Nicaraguan economy was again desperate. Civil war, the US trade embargo and the inefficiencies of a Soviet-style centralized economy had produced hyperinflation, falling production and rising unemployment. As it became clear that the US Congress was preparing to grant the Contras further aid, Daniel Ortega called elections that he expected would give the Sandinistas a popular mandate to govern.

The FSLN, however, underestimated the disillusionment and fatigue of the Nicaraguan people. Economic problems and the daily grind had eclipsed the dramatic accomplishments of the Sandinistas' early years: redistributing Somoza lands to small farming cooperatives, reducing illiteracy from 50% to 13%, eliminating polio through a massive immunization program and reducing the rate of infant mortality by a third.

The Unión Nacional Opositora (UNO), a broad coalition of 14 political parties opposing the Sandinista government, was formed in 1989. UNO presidential candidate Violeta Barrios de Chamorro had the backing and financing of the US, which had promised to lift the embargo and give hundreds of millions of dollars in economic aid to Nicaragua if UNO won. With such bribes in place, the UNO handily took the elections of February 25, 1990, gaining 55% of the presidential votes and 51 of the 110 seats in the national assembly, compared with the FSLN's 39. Ortega had plenty of grounds for complaint, but, to his credit, in the end he went quietly, perhaps avoiding further conflict.

Politics in the '90s

Chamorro took office in April 1990. The Contras stopped fighting at the end of June with a symbolic and heavily publicized turning-in of their weapons. The US trade embargo was lifted, and US and other foreign aid began to pour in.

She faced a tricky balancing act in trying to reunify the country and satisfy all interests. The promised economic recovery was slow in coming; growth was sluggish, and unemployment remained stubbornly high. Nevertheless, in 1996, when Nicaragua went to the polls again, the people rejected the FSLN's Ortega and opted for former Managua mayor Arnoldo Alemán of the PLC, a center-right liberal alliance.

Alemán's achievements included investing heavily in infrastructure and reducing the size of the army by a factor of 10, but his administration was plagued by scandal, as corruption soared and Alemán amassed a personal fortune from the state's coffers. Meanwhile, however, the Sandinistas had their own image problems, as the ever-present Ortega was accused by his stepdaughter of sexual abuse. In a gesture of mutual self-preservation, Ortega and Alemán struck a deal, popularly known as *el pacto* (the pact), aimed at nullifying the threat of the opposition, pulling the teeth of anticorruption watchdogs and guaranteeing Alemán immunity from further investigation.

Currents in the New Millennium

With scandals gripping the country, the 2001 elections were heavily monitored. Ortega reinvented himself and declared his the party of 'peace and love,' complete with pink posters and flower-covered banners, but voters turned out in record numbers (96%) to elect Alemán's former vice-president, Enrique Bolaños, to the top job.

Bolaños took office pledging to clean up the country's corrupt government, a policy at odds with his party. Although he managed to have Alemán stripped of his immunity and sentenced to 20 years in prison, Alemán has since had the conviction overturned by supreme court judges installed under *el pacto*, and is freely roaming the country talking himself up for a presidential run in 2011.

By the end of the Bolaños term, the right was deeply divided and the stage was set for a return of the FSLN in the November 2006 elections. After three failed attempts, Ortega was finally able to regain his prize. He received just 38% of the popular vote but was able to claim the presidency without a runoff thanks to changes to electoral rules he made under Alemán. Upon taking office in January 2007, he proclaimed a new era of leftist Latin American unity, forging close ties with Venezuelan leader Hugo Chávez, and leaving the USA and some international investors a little jumpy. However, anti-imperialist rhetoric aside, so far the new Ortega government has not made the radical change some of his supporters were waiting for.

THE CULTURE
The National Psyche

Nicaraguans are a proud people and vocal about their views. Opinions differ over whether the Sandinista years were a failure or a success, but Nicas (Nicaraguans) love to debate, and if you spend time chatting you'll learn more about the current political scene than you ever would reading a paper (or guidebook!). Nicaraguans rightly have a lot of respect for their artistic, literary and cultural history, and are never afraid to cheerily big-up local achievements.

While there are plenty of regional attitudes – on the Caribbean coast many feel little affinity with the rest of the country – Nicaraguans get

NICARAGUA

on surprisingly well with each other given their turbulent recent history. One thing they all seem to have in common is an unshakable suspicion of their southern neighbor Costa Rica.

Lifestyle

It's not easy to generalize about Nicaraguan lifestyle. Observing the well-dressed crowds in Managua's trendy shopping malls, you might assume they are a Westernized, urban, wealthy elite. Some are, but probing a little more you'll find that a good number are impoverished single parents from the country on a once-a-year trip to buy their children toys that they can barely afford.

Some 50% of Nicaraguans live below the poverty line, and huge numbers move to Nicaragua's capital of Managua, Costa Rica or the US in order to get work. This has put a great strain on the traditional family structure; it's common for young parents to leave their children to be brought up by relatives while they send money home for their upbringing and education.

While traditional conservative values are still strong in some areas, these were shattered by the revolution in other parts of the country. The Sandinista ideal considered women as absolute equals in all aspects of society, and Nicaragua is still well ahead of the game in this respect. Predictably, attitudes to homosexuality differ according to where and whom you ask.

People

Of Nicaragua's 5.5 million inhabitants, Mestizos, of mixed Spanish and indigenous ancestry, form the majority, with 69%; Spanish and other whites comprise 17%, blacks 9% and indigenous people 5%.

The great majority of Nicaraguans live in the Pacific lowland belt. The Caribbean region is sparsely populated; it makes up half the country's land area but has only 12% of its population. This zone includes the Sumos and Ramas, and the Mískitos, all of whom have their own language. English is also spoken on this coast.

Nicaragua is a nation of young people: almost 70% of the population is under 30 years old. The population is 57% urban.

RELIGION

Catholicism is the dominant religion in Nicaragua, claiming almost 60% of the population, but large bites of the theological cake

---

FEVER PITCH

When you hear someone talk about 'El Presidente,' they may not be referring to the country's leader, but to former Montreal Expos pitcher Denis Martínez, a Nicaraguan legend in the national sport, beisbol, which pushes soccer into a distant second place. The sport was first played competitively in Bluefields in the late 19th century, but it didn't really take off until the arrival of US marines in the country a couple of decades later. Since then, Nicaraguans have been fanatical about it, with games played everywhere from dusty city lots to cattle fields. There is a professional league too; in Managua crowds of 20,000 or more gather to see its Bóer club play against the three other major league teams: Granada, León and Chinandega (teams vary depending on who can raise the annual registration fee). Check www.lnpb.com.ni for fixtures.

---

have been taken in recent years by evangelical Protestant sects, who make up 22% of the population these days. The importance of religious issues is high – a recent ban on abortion (even to save the mother's life) was ratified by most of parliament, including Daniel Ortega, an avowed atheist who has now found God (some say for votes).

ARTS

Nicaragua is a bright star in the firmament of Latin American literature, and poetry is the country's most important and beloved art. Rubén Darío (1867–1916), a poet who lived in León, is one of the most renowned authors in the Spanish language, and his writings have inspired literary movements and trends throughout the Latin world.

Three outstanding writers emerged soon after Darío, and their works are still popular: Azarías Pallais (1884–1954), Salomón de la Selva (1893–1959) and Alfonso Cortés (1893–1969). In the 1930s the experimental 'Vanguardia' movement came on the scene, led by José Coronel Urtecho, Pablo Antonio Cuadra, Joaquín Cuadra Pasos and Manolo Cuadra. A number of leading personalities in the Sandinista leadership, including Sergio Ramírez, Rosario Murillo and Ernesto Cardenal, made literary contributions as well as political ones.

Cardenal, in fact, was responsible for a whole new style of Nicaraguan art when he harnessed the talents of the local population of the Solentiname archipelago. The result, a distinctive, colorful, primitivist style of painting, is famous worldwide.

The Caribbean coast, with its distinct culture, has its own art forms, too. In Bluefields, the calypso-influenced *palo de mayo* (maypole) is a widely popular musical genre.

ENVIRONMENT
The Land
Nicaragua, comprising 129,494 sq km, is the largest country in Central America. It is bordered on the north by Honduras, the south by Costa Rica, the east by the Caribbean Sea and the west by the Pacific Ocean.

The country has three distinct geographical regions.

PACIFIC LOWLANDS
The western coastal region is a broad, hot, fertile lowland plain broken by 11 major volcanoes. Some of the tallest are San Cristóbal (1745m), northeast of Chinandega; Concepción (1610m), on Isla de Ometepe in Lago de Nicaragua; and Mombacho (1345m), near Granada.

The fertile volcanic soil and the hot climate, with its distinct rainy and dry seasons, make this the most productive agricultural area in the country. It holds the country's major population centers.

Also in the area are Lago de Nicaragua (also known by its indigenous name, Cocibolca), the largest lake in Central America, studded with over 400 islands, and the smaller Lago de Managua (Xolotlán).

NORTH-CENTRAL MOUNTAINS
The north-central region, with its high mountains and valleys, is cooler than the Pacific lowlands and also very fertile. About 25% of the country's agriculture is concentrated here, including most coffee production. The highest point in the country, Pico Mogotón (2438m), is near the Honduran border, in the region around Ocotal.

CARIBBEAN COAST
The Caribbean ('Atlantic') region occupies about half of Nicaragua's area. The 541km coastline is broken by many large lagoons and deltas. Twenty-three rivers flow from the central mountains into the Caribbean, including the Río Coco (685km), Nicaragua's longest river, and the Río San Juan (199km), which flows from Lago de Nicaragua. These define much of the borders with Honduras and Costa Rica respectively. The Caribbean region gets an immense amount of rainfall. It is sparsely populated and covered by tropical rainforest. The largest towns are Bluefields and Bilwi (Puerto Cabezas), both coastal ports. Several small islands, including the much-visited Corn Islands (Islas del Maíz), lie off the Caribbean coast, surrounded by coral reefs.

Wildlife
Boasting some of the largest forest reserves in the region and one of the lowest population densities, Nicaragua's incredible biodiversity is appreciated by scientists and tourists alike.

ANIMALS
Three species of sea turtle make their annual nesting grounds along the extensive undeveloped beaches of Nicaragua's Pacific coast and on islands off the Caribbean coast. Other reptiles and amphibians found in Nicaragua include green iguanas, black iguanas, and numerous species of lizards and caimans.

The country has a wealth of birdlife, from tropical species resident in a variety of forest environments to waterbirds on the lakes and rivers, and migrants passing between North and South America. Urracas (white-throated magpie jays) are found throughout the country, but scissor-tailed flycatchers, scarlet macaws and the colorful national bird, the guardabarranco (blue-crowned motmot), may be more difficult to spot.

Mantled howler monkeys are perhaps the easiest primates to find, as their mighty roar gives their location away, but Nicaragua also hosts Geoffroy's spider monkeys and white-faced capuchin monkeys, both of which are also common.

Among the more curious aquatic species are the sharks of Lago de Nicaragua. A member of the bull shark family, *Carcharhinus leucas* is the world's only known shark species that can pass between saltwater and freshwater. These were once in great abundance in the lake; today, owing to massive overfishing, they are rarely seen.

PLANTS
Nicaragua's plant life is at least as diverse as its animal life. The various ecosystems,

NICARAGUA

ranging from dry tropical forest to cloud forest to rainforest, provide fertile territory for botanical exploration. Tree varieties include tamarind, kapok, frangipani and *palo de sal*, which adapts to its high-salinity coastal environment by excreting salt crystals. Orchids, including the nocturnally blooming *huele de noche*, flourish in the cloud forests of Mombacho and Miraflor.

National Parks & Protected Areas

The government has assigned protected status to approximately 18% of Nicaraguan territory, comprising 76 different areas whose level of protection varies significantly. Enforcement is a tough task, but Marena (Ministry of Environment and Natural Resources) does a sterling job and has offices in most towns that can provide some level of information for the visitor. The following is just a small sample of the country's biodiversity:

Parque Nacional Volcán Masaya This active volcano near Masaya also has 20km of hiking trails. See p494.

Refugio de Vida Silvestre La Flor A beach south of San Juan del Sur that's one of the best places to observe nesting sea turtles. See p499.

Reserva Biológica Río Indio Maíz A reserve near El Castillo in the south with 2640 sq km of virgin tropical humid forest. See boxed text, p508.

Reserva de Biosfera Bosawás Unexplored and rather inaccessible, this vast expanse of virgin cloud forest lies in the northeast. See boxed text, p470.

Reserva Natural Isla Juan Venado A long, narrow barrier island near León with an ecosystem rich in amphibians, reptiles and migratory birdlife. See p482.

Reserva Natural Volcán Mombacho A wildlife-rich volcano not far from Granada. See p490.

Environmental Issues

Like its neighbors on the Central American isthmus, Nicaragua is beset by grave environmental problems. High on the list is the rapid loss of its forests, which is being chopped at some 700 sq km a year, leading to erosion, loss of soil quality and disappearance of species. Pesticides from the resultant ranches then invade the water table and ultimately the food chain. Nicaragua's two major lakes are also both polluted, with Lake Managua being particularly toxic.

Nevertheless, there is some hope. Environmental awareness is slowly growing around the country and organic farming methods are becoming increasingly popular. Meanwhile, the FSLN government, fully aware of the potential of ecotourism in the country, has taken a real interest in environmental issues, even calling in the army to back up the nation's underresourced park rangers.

TRANSPORTATION

GETTING THERE & AWAY
Air

Nicaragua's main airport is Augusto C Sandino in Managua (MGA; p462). There are daily direct flights to a number of US cities, including Miami, Atlanta and Houston, while low-cost carrier Spirit airlines has a late-night service to Fort Lauderdale, Florida. There are also direct regional services to San Salvador, San José, Tegucigalpa, and Panama, with connecting services to other Latin American destinations.

It's always worth checking flight prices to neighboring Costa Rica, a smooth bus ride away, as they can be substantially cheaper.

Boat

The Costa Rican border station at Los Chiles is only reachable by boat from San Carlos up the Río Frío (see p506). It's an easy, straightforward crossing.

Bus

There are extensive international bus services from Managua to the other Central American nations. See p463 for details. Although more time-consuming, it's cheaper to take a local bus to the border, cross and take an onward bus on the other side. There are land borders at Guasaule (p481), El Espino and Las Manos (p474) for Honduras, and Peñas Blancas (p495) for Costa Rica.

Car & Motorcycle

You can drive over any of Nicaragua's land borders but you will need registration papers in your name, insurance, your passport and a driver's license. You will get a 30-day permit and a special stamp in your passport. If you leave without the vehicle, you will be charged a (hefty) import duty. Your home driver's license is valid for 90 days after entering the country, after which you technically need to apply for a Nicaraguan license. In reality, this is rarely an issue.

GETTING AROUND
Air

Nicaragua's national carrier **La Costeña** (☎ 2263-2142; www.lacostena.com.ni) has daily flights from a small terminal in Managua airport to the Caribbean coast and San Carlos. Flights are often full, so be sure to book in advance.

Boat

Boats are the only form of transport in some parts of Nicaragua, particularly on the Caribbean side of the country, where rivers are the main highways. There are several scheduled routes on Lago de Nicaragua, including one from Granada to Ometepe and on to San Carlos. From San Carlos, public boats

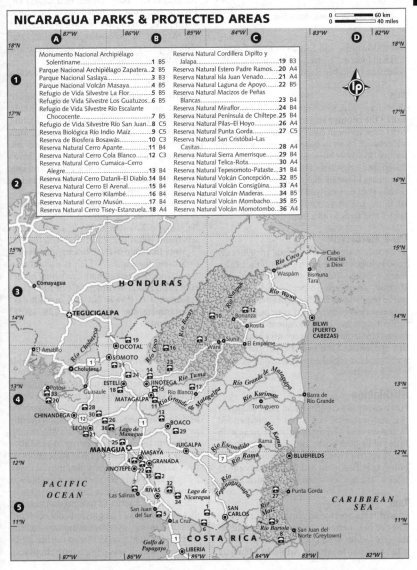

NICARAGUA PARKS & PROTECTED AREAS

0 — 60 km
0 — 40 miles

Monumento Nacional Archipiélago
  Solentiname....................................1 B5
Parque Nacional Archipiélago Zapatera..2 B5
Parque Nacional Saslaya........................3 B3
Parque Nacional Volcán Masaya...........4 B5
Refugio de Vida Silvestre La Flor............5 B5
Refugio de Vida Silvestre Los Guatuzos..6 B5
Refugio de Vida Silvestre Río Escalante
  Chococente.....................................7 B5
Refugio de Vida Silvestre Río San Juan..8 C5
Reserva Biológica Río Indio Maíz.........9 C5
Reserva de Biosfera Bosawás...............10 C3
Reserva Natural Cerro Apante.............11 B4
Reserva Natural Cerro Cola Blanco.......12 C3
Reserva Natural Cerro Cumaica–Cerro
  Alegre..13 B4
Reserva Natural Cerro Datanlí–El Diablo.14 B4
Reserva Natural Cerro El Arenal...........15 B4
Reserva Natural Cerro Kilambé............16 B4
Reserva Natural Cerro Musún..............17 B4
Reserva Natural Cerro Tisey-Estanzuela..18 A4

Reserva Natural Cordillera Dipilto y
  Jalapa..19 B3
Reserva Natural Estero Padre Ramos....20 A4
Reserva Natural Isla Juan Venado.........21 A4
Reserva Natural Laguna de Apoyo.......22 B5
Reserva Natural Macizos de Peñas
  Blancas..23 B4
Reserva Natural Miraflor.....................24 B4
Reserva Natural Península de Chiltepe..25 B4
Reserva Natural Pilas–El Hoyo.............26 A4
Reserva Natural Punta Gorda..............27 C5
Reserva Natural San Cristóbal–Las
  Casitas...28 A4
Reserva Natural Sierra Amerrisque.......29 B4
Reserva Natural Telica-Rota.................30 A4
Reserva Natural Tepesomoto-Pataste...31 B4
Reserva Natural Volcán Concepción......32 B5
Reserva Natural Volcán Consigüina.......33 A4
Reserva Natural Volcán Maderas.........34 B5
Reserva Natural Volcán Mombacho......35 B5
Reserva Natural Volcán Momotombo....36 B4

ENTRY FEES & DEPARTURE TAX

On entering the country, visitors are required to purchase a tourist card for US$5. Entering by land attracts an additional migration fee of US$2. Anyone flying out of the country must pay US$32 international departure tax, usually included in your ticket price. Leaving the country by land costs US$2. Domestic departure tax is US$2.

travel down the Río San Juan to El Castillo and San Juan del Norte, and also across to the Solentiname archipelago.

Bus

Buses travel to destinations all over the western half of the country and to some points east as well (the Caribbean coast generally lacks accessible roads). Intercity buses – most of which are former US school buses – are reliable, frequent, cheap and crowded. There are also express minibuses between major cities. Bus services usually start very early in the morning and finish in the late afternoon. See p463 for specific routes and fares to and from the capital.

Car & Motorcycle

The roads in western Nicaragua are generally good between major towns. Get off the beaten track a little, and the quality deteriorates sharply. There are no particularly unusual traffic regulations, and Managua driving is the only experience likely to get your pulse racing.

Renting a car is an excellent way to see more remote parts of the country and is neither complicated nor overly expensive. There are several car-rental agencies in Managua; see p464 for details.

Hitchhiking

Hitchhiking is a common and accepted practice in Nicaragua, but is not recommended in and around Managua. In rural areas with little public transportation, most drivers with a pickup truck will stop. Jump in the back unless specifically invited inside. It's polite to offer a little money when you're given a ride.

Taxi

Shared taxis operate in all the major towns. They're not metered, so be sure to settle on the fare before getting in. Most towns have a flat fare per passenger, while in Managua

it varies according to distance. You can also negotiate quite a fair price to use taxis to travel between cities.

MANAGUA

pop 927,197 (Managua city)

Nicaragua's lakeside capital and largest city literally had its heart ripped out in 1972 by an earthquake that destroyed its old center, leaving Managua as a sprawling series of suburbs, with shopping malls rather than central plazas as centers of community life.

But it's only heartless in a geographical sense. While it lacks the colonial charms of León or Granada, it's a pulsating, occasionally chaotic medley of rich and poor, traditional and westernized, and can be truly fascinating. Plus, its spread-out nature (best glimpsed while speeding around corners, chatty cab driver gesticulating with both hands) means that there's plenty of drooping tropical greenery and little crowding. There are also a couple of standout sights, and plenty of big-city amenities.

Managua spreads across the southern shore of Lago de Managua, known to indigenous inhabitants as Xolotlán. Other lakes fill the craters of old volcanoes within and near the city.

More than one in five Nicaraguans lives in or around the capital, which is the national center for commerce, manufacturing, higher education and government. Only 50m above sea level, it is always hot and humid: daytime temperatures hover around 32°C (90°F) year-round.

HISTORY

At the time of the Spanish conquest, Managua was an indigenous lakeside settlement whose inhabitants practiced agriculture, hunting and fishing. These early Managuans put up a vigorous resistance to the Spanish, who responded by destroying their city. Managua subsequently remained a village until the mid-19th century.

The city rose out of obscurity in 1852 after conflicts between liberal León and conservative Granada repeatedly erupted into civil war. Lying midway between the two, Managua was chosen as a compromise capital.

Since then, a series of natural disasters has thrashed the city. The gracious old center of the city was destroyed by earthquake and the ensuing fire in March 1931, and burned again five years later. It was completely rebuilt into

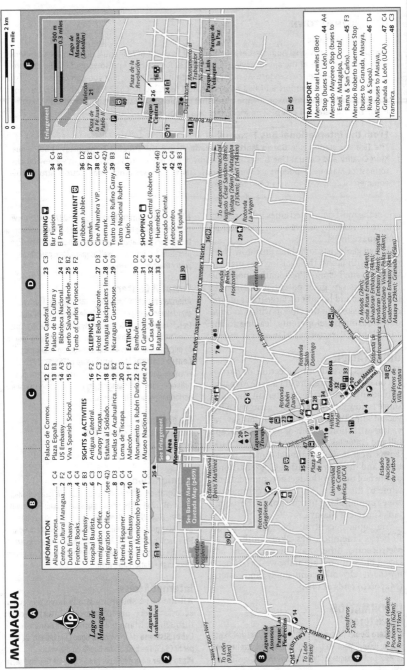

NICARAGUA

GETTING INTO TOWN

From the Airport

Aeropuerto Internacional Augusto César Sandino is 11km east of Managua, right on the Carretera Panamericana. Taxis at the airport charge up to US$20 for the ride into town and go direct without picking up other passengers. At night it is worth it, but in the day you can cross the busy road in front of the airport and hail a *colectivo* taxi for C$80 to C$120. Even cheaper, but not recommended with large bags, are the buses that run along the same road to Mercado Huembes (C$5), from where you can pick up a city bus or a cheaper taxi.

From the International Bus Terminals

The Tica Bus station is in **Barrio Martha Quezada**. Across the street is Transportes El Sol, while King Quality and Central Line buses arrive nearby. From any of these locations, it's a few blocks to most of Managua's budget accommodations. Transnica buses arrive near Metrocentro, in the commercial center of town, a C$40 taxi away.

---

one of the most developed cities in the region, only to be razed by an even more devastating earthquake in 1972.

When geologists found the downtown area riddled with faults, the decision was made to leave the site behind. President Somoza and his partners saw great potential for profit in the disaster and bought up large tracts of land on the outskirts of the city on which to build new housing developments, leading to the sprawl that characterizes Managua of today.

ORIENTATION

Managua's spread-out collection of *barrios* sits on the southern shore of Lago de Managua (Xolotlán). The former center on the lakeshore is now largely derelict, having been left vacant after the 1972 quake, but has several visitor attractions. South of here, the Tiscapa hill and crater lake is the city's main landmark. To its west is the pyramidal Hotel Crowne Plaza and the Barrio Martha Quezada, home of much of the city's budget accommodations, while to the south is a thriving commercial zone running along the city's main thoroughfare, Carretera Masaya.

Managua's central market, Mercado Roberto Huembes, lies 2km southeast of Metrocentro; other major markets (and adjacent bus stations) are at the western (Bóer), northern (Oriental, confusingly) and eastern (Mayoreo) ends of town.

INFORMATION
Bookstores

Frontera Books (Map p455; ☎ 2270-2345; Hospital Monte España, 100m N) Managua's only real bilingual bookstore has thousands of English-language titles. Also buys and sells used books.

Librería Hispamer (Map p455; ☎ 2278-3923; www.hispamer.com.ni; UCA, 1c E, 1c N) The biggest bookstore in town offers the nation's best selection of Latin American literature and history as well as many local periodicals, pretty much all in Spanish.

Cultural Centers

Alianza Francesa (Map p455; ☎ 2267-2811; www.alianzafrancesa.org.ni; Embajada de México, ½c N) This French-funded venue is particularly active on the local arts scene with regular exhibitions, film nights and lively concerts by international artists and up-and-coming local bands.

Centro Cultural Managua (Map p455; ☎ 2222-5291; www.inc.gob.ni; Parque Central, 1c S) Government-run cultural center with changing art exhibits, concerts, dance performances and film events.

Emergency

Ambulance (Red Cross; ☎ 128)
Fire (☎ 115)
Police (☎ 118)

Immigration

Immigration office Ciudad Jardín area (Migración; Map p455; ☎ 2244-3989; www.migracion.gob.ni; Semáforos Tenderí, 200m N; ☼ 8am-1pm Mon-Fri); Metrocentro mall (Map p455; www.migracion.gob.ni; ☼ 10am-6pm Mon-Fri, 10am-1pm Sat & Sun) The main office is located near the Ciudad Jardín area but there is a more convenient office in the Metrocentro mall.

Internet Access

All the large shopping malls have free wi-fi access. There are numerous internet cafes throughout Managua. Convenient ones:

Cyber Sistema (Map p459; Antiguo Cine Dorado, 2c N; per hr C$15) The best of the bunch on this strip.
Plaza Inter (Map p459; per hr C$30) Inside the food court.

Medical Services

Pharmacies, found all over Managua, are usually open until 10pm.

Hospital Bautista (Map p455; ☎ 2249-7070; www. hospitalbautistanicaragua.com; Barrio Largaespada) Professional and reasonably priced emergency and outpatient services. Some staff speak English.

Hospital Metropolitano Vivian Pellas (off Map p455; ☎ 2255-6900; www.metropolitano.com.ni; Carretera Masaya Km 9.5) Located south of the city, this is the most advanced (and expensive) hospital in the country.

Money

There are numerous ATMs in Managua. Many are Visa/Plus only, but those operated by Banco de América Central (BAC) also take MasterCard/Cirrus and dispense both córdobas and US dollars. Handy locations include the airport, Plaza Inter, and Metrocentro, as well as Esso service stations on the eastern edge of Barrio Martha Quezada and elsewhere.

All banks in Managua will change US dollars, while most will also change euros. If you don't fancy waiting in long lines, street-corner money changers, or 'coyotes,' usually change dollars at a slightly better rate than the banks. They are mostly honest traders, but research the current rate and double check the amount before you walk away. Look for them at Plaza España (Map p455) and around the main markets.

Post

Palacio de Correos (Map p455; ☎ 2222-2048; Plaza de la Revolución, 2c O) The main post office has poste restante services (mail is kept for up to 45 days).

Telephone

Enitel calling cards, available in Claro stores and some *pulperias,* can be used with landline, cellular and public phones. It is easier and cheaper to make international calls from internet cafes or the dedicated calling shops dotted around the city.

Tourist Information

Intur (Nicaraguan Institute of Tourism; Map p459; ☎ 2222-3333; www.visitanicaragua.com; Crowne Plaza, 1c S, 1c O) Has helpful maps and can recommend hotels and attractions in Managua and beyond. There is another office in the airport.

DANGERS & ANNOYANCES

Managua is nowhere near as dangerous as it seems, and a vast majority of visits to the capital are incident free. That said, crime has risen here in recent years, and like in any large city in the region, it pays to take some basic precautions. Keep your camera and iPod hidden, look at your map before you set out and only carry as much money as you realistically are going to need during the day. Except in the upmarket areas, always take a taxi after dark, and to the Área Monumental even during daylight hours. Barrio Martha Quezada has its share of incidents, mostly on its northern edge and between it and Plaza Inter; take a taxi through here, even if it's just a couple of blocks.

SIGHTS & ACTIVITIES
Área Monumental

What was once the heart of Nicaragua's capital is an eerie, evocative zone of monuments and ruined buildings (Map p455) that have largely

---

WHERE THE STREETS HAVE NO NAME – NAVIGATING MANAGUA

Like other Nicaraguan cities and towns, Managua has few street signs, and only the major roads are named. Large buildings, *rotondas* (traffic circles) and traffic lights serve as de facto points of reference, and locations are described in terms of their direction and distance, usually in *cuadras* (blocks), from these points. Just to complicate matters, many of these references no longer exist, so you may get addresses that begin with something like *'de donde fue Sandy's'* (from where Sandy's used to be…).

In addition, in Managua a special system is used for the cardinal points, whereby *al lago* (to the lake) means 'north' while *arriba* (up) is 'east' and *abajo* (down) is 'west,' the latter expressions derived from the sun's movement. South is just plain old *sur.* Thus you might hear: *'del antiguo Cine Dorado, una cuadra al lago, dos cuadras arriba,'* meaning from the old Dorado Cinema, one block north, two blocks to the east.

Confused? You get used to it. Listings in this section give the address in Spanish – but we use the cardinal points N (norte), S (sur), E (este) and O (oeste) – so you can ask locals or just let the cab driver figure it out. *Cuadra* is abbreviated to 'c' in addresses for listings.

been untouched since an earthquake leveled the area in 1972. Bits are being rehabilitated, but funds are still too short (and the likelihood of another quake too high) to comprehensively restore the area. It's an intriguing spot to visit, but take care when walking around here, and use taxis if you don't feel safe.

Marked by a single towering flagpole, the **Plaza de la Revolución** denotes the center of the zone. On its eastern side is the area's most emotive ruin, the **Antigua Catedral** (old cathedral). Built in 1929, the imposing shell of the neoclassical edifice is still beautiful, especially in the late-afternoon light, but it is unstable and is closed to the public. Check out the clock on the southern tower, which still shows the hour the earthquake hit in 1972. Across the plaza, the tomb of Sandinista commander Carlos Fonseca lies within the **Parque Central**, a pretty plaza dotted with mango trees and flamboyanes.

Inside the grandiose Palacio Nacional is the **Museo Nacional** (Map p455; ☎ 2222-2905; admission US$4; ◷ 9am-4pm). Set around two leafy courtyards, the museum is well presented, and includes an excellent selection of pre-Hispanic ceramics, a geological overview, some fine contemporary Nicaraguan art and an excellent collection of pre-Columbian statues. Admission includes an optional guided tour.

Directly south of the park is the old Grand Hotel, now the **Centro Cultural Managua** (see p456). On the lake side of the park, the **Monumento a Rubén Darío** pays homage to Nicaragua's foremost poet. Toward the lake is the oblong **Teatro Nacional Rubén Darío** (see p462).

The theater faces the **Malecón**, a promenade lined with run-down bars and restaurants looking over the heavily polluted (don't swim) Lago de Managua. It's a lively drinking (and fighting) spot on weekends, but during the week it feels abandoned. Far more pleasant is the government-run **Puerto Salvador Allende**, just to the west, where you can chill in tiny thatched gazebos overlooking the water or grab a beer at one of a number of pleasant bars. Cruises across the lake to nearby Isla del Amor (lower/upper deck C$70/100) depart from here every couple of hours from Tuesday to Sunday. Nearby, the funky Concha Acústica (Acoustic Shell) overlooks the huge **Plaza de la Fé Juan Pablo II**, scene of notable public ceremonies including those marking the anniversary of the revolution.

The unabashedly political **Estatua al Soldado** stands on the west side of Av Bolívar, diagonally across from the Centro Cultural.

'Workers and *campesinos* onward till the end,' reads the inscription below a bronze giant, who holds a pickax and an assault rifle bearing the Sandinista colors. As if in response, **Parque de la Paz** three blocks east proclaims an end to conflict. It was here that the weapons from the 1980s conflict were gathered to be destroyed and buried, and it is still possible to glimpse twisted gun barrels sticking out of the concrete that encircles a burned-out tank. Ironically, the peace park is notorious for muggings, so make a beeline to the security office, from where the guards will gladly escort you around for a small tip.

Huellas de Acahualinca

These ancient **footprints** (Map p455; ☎ 2266-5774; admission US$4, photography fee US$1; ◷ 9am-4pm) are Managua's most fascinating attraction, and highly recommended for the glimpse of a long-vanished human past that it affords. Buried 4m deep under compacted volcanic material, the tracks were discovered by quarrying workmen in 1874. There are 10 sets of human footprints (men, women and children) that have been dated to some 6000 years ago; they pace in one direction, toward the lake. There are also tracks of deer and *mapache* (a type of raccoon) present. An additional area excavated in 1978 shows the prints continuing nearby, and it is thought there could be many more in the surrounding area. The entry fee includes an optional guided tour in Spanish.

The neighborhood around here is a little sketchy, and you are well advised to take a taxi to the door.

Loma de Tiscapa

It's well worth climbing this **hill** (Map p455; admission US$1; ◷ 8am-6pm) that rises behind the Hotel Crowne Plaza. It's a short stroll up the road, and perfectly safe, as the path is guarded. There are great views down over the Tiscapa crater lake below, as well as over the rest of the city. Here too is the lugubrious silhouette of Sandino, visible from all around town. The hilltop was the site of the former presidential palace destroyed by the 1972 earthquake. The area that looks like a wrecked car park was actually a notoriously brutal prison during the Somoza dictatorship. There is also **Canopy Tiscapa** (☎ 8805-6213; www.canopytoursnicaragua.com; per person US$15; ◷ 9am-6pm), a short but spectacular 1.2km, 25-minute zip-line tour around the crater.

BARRIO MARTHA QUEZADA

INFORMATION	
ATM	(see 29)
Cyber Sistema	1 B2
Esso (ATM)	2 D2
French Embassy	3 A2
Intur	4 D3
Plaza Inter	(see 29)

SIGHTS & ACTIVITIES	
Casa del Obero	(see 25)

SLEEPING	
Apartahotel Yenros	5 C3
Casa Vanegas	6 C3
Guest House Santos	7 B3
Hospedaje Dulce Sueño	8 C3
Hospedaje El Dorado	9 B3
Hospedaje El Ensueño	10 C3
Hotel Los Felipe	11 B3
Hotel Los Cisneros	12 B3

Hotel Jardin de Italia	13 C3
La Posada del Angel	14 C3

EATING	
Cafetín Mirna	15 B3
Cafetín Tonalli	16 C3
Comida a la Vista	17 B3
Comidas Sara	18 B3
Doña Pilar	19 B3
Flora's Buffet	20 C3
Licuados Ananda	21 A2
Tacos Lalo	22 B3

DRINKING	
Caramanchel	23 D3
El Grillo	24 D3

ENTERTAINMENT	
Central Sandinista de Trabajadores	25 B2
Cinema Plaza Inter	(see 29)
Estadio Nacional Denis Martínez	26 B2
La Casa de los Mejía Godoy	27 D3
Q	28 C2

SHOPPING	
Plaza Inter	29 D3

TRANSPORT	
Dollar	30 D3
King Quality	31 D3
Lugo	32 A3
Tica Bus Station	33 C3
Transportes El Sol	34 C3

Nueva Catedral

South of Tiscapa along the road to the Rotonda Rubén Darío is another Managua landmark, the **cathedral** (Map p455; ☎ 2278-4232) inaugurated in 1993. It's a curious building studded with dozens of domes that help provide structural support during earthquakes and represent the 63 churches in the Managua diocese. Inside the monumental entrance is a strikingly colorful postmodern interior with a nice shrine on the northwest side.

COURSES

Viva Spanish School (Map p455; ☎ 2270-2339; www.vivaspanishschool.com; Edificio FNI, 2c S) This school offers intensive Spanish courses for US$175 a week (US$225 for a couple) and can arrange flexible homestays. It's just east of Metrocentro.

FESTIVALS & EVENTS

The **Festival de Santo Domingo**, Managua's main fiesta, kicks off on August 1, when a tiny model of the saint is brought from its home in the hills south of Managua into the city. The diminutive figure is followed by crowds of noisy fans, the most hard-core of whom cover themselves in motor oil to show their devotion. There is also traditional music, fireworks and a horse parade. The party continues for 10 days until the saint is marched back up to the hills.

Sandinista supporters from all over the country descend on the old center for the **anniversary of the 1979 Sandinista revolution** (July 19), a massive open-air party involving plenty of singing and booze.

SLEEPING
Barrio Martha Quezada

Barrio Martha Quezada, better known to *taxistas* as 'Ticabus,' is a compact residential district west of Hotel Crowne Plaza with many cheap guesthouses and places to eat. Budget travelers have always tended to congregate here, not least for its proximity to international bus terminals.

Don't believe touts at the Tica Bus station who will lead you to some dive, insisting that it is, in fact, one of the places listed here! These places are all on Map p459.

Hospedaje El Ensueño (☎ 2228-1078; Tica Bus, 1c N; r per person US$6) The small rooms in this family-run cheapie lack ventilation and the beds sag, but they have cable TV and private bathrooms and the price is hard to beat.

Guest House Santos (☎ 2222-3713; www.casade huespedessantos.com.ni; Tica Bus, 1c N, ½c O; r per person US$7; **P**) While the basic rooms with their loud paint jobs and poky bathrooms are not particularly well maintained, this legendary backpacker spot has a laid-back vibe and plenty of character. Airy common areas with rocking chairs, funky vintage furniture, amateur artwork and *Return of the Jedi* sheets all add to its charm.

Hospedaje Dulce Sueño (☎ 2228-4215; Tica Bus, 20m E; s/d US$8/16; ☎) Just a couple of doors from the Tica Bus terminal, this appealing new place is throwing out a challenge to the more established budget options in the area. It has comfortable rooms with good tiled bathrooms, firm beds and cable TV. There is also wi-fi access, an open kitchen and a rooftop hammock area.

Casa Vanegas (☎ 2222-4043; casavanegas@cablenet.com. ni; Tica Bus, 1c E; s/d US$10/16; ☒ ☐) At the east end of the Tica Bus block, this excellent choice is run by a welcoming family and has spotless rooms with cable TV, a small patio, kitchen access and a lounge with internet service (per hour C$20).

Apartahotel Yenros (☎ 2222-5221; Tica Bus, 75m N; r with/without air-con US$30/15; ☒) The three quiet rooms behind the family home are spacious and comfortable with big TVs and firm beds. Discounts are available for long-term guests.

OUR PICK Hotel Los Felipe (☎ 2222-6501; www.hotel losfelipe.com.ni; Tica Bus, 1½c O; s/d with fan US$15/20, with air-con US$25/30; **P** ☒ ☐ ☎) Hands down the best value in town, this popular hotel has clean and comfortable rooms running alongside a lush garden with a large pool and a thatch-roofed bar/restaurant.

Hotel Los Cisneros (☎ 2222-7273; www.hotellos cisneros.com; Tica Bus, 1c N, 1½c O; s/d with fan US$25/30, with air-con US$41/46, apt from US$40; **P** ☒ ☐ ☎) Something of a retreat from any Managua cares, this colorful option has comfortable rooms with hot-water bathrooms surrounding a courtyard full of plants. Upgrade to an apartment for a kitchenette, an airy lounge room with rocking chairs and your own hammock.

La Posada del Angel (☎ 2268-7228; frente Iglesia San Francisco; s/d US$55/65; **P** ☒ ☎) From the wrought-iron bed frames to the handcrafted wood furniture, there is no shortage of class in this elegant boutique hotel in a more upmarket area. Breakfast is served in the garden by the decent-sized pool.

Other options:

Hospedaje El Dorado (☎ 2222-6012; Tica Bus, 1½c O; r per person US$7; **P**) Has smallish, dark rooms but you'll enjoy the welcome and the rocking chairs.

Hotel Jardín de Italia (☎ 2222-7967; Tica Bus, 1c E, ½c N; s/d with fan US$15/30, with air-con US$25/40; ☒ ☐) The spacious rooms are tidy and homey, and have decent bathrooms.

Elsewhere in Managua

Managua Backpackers Inn (Map p455; ☎ 2267-0006; www. managuahostel.com; Antiguo Chamán, 75m S; dm with fan/air-con US$8/11, s/d US$20/30; ☒ ☐ ☎ ☎) Managua's only real backpackers hostel has a relaxed vibe with a great location a short walk from bars, shops and restaurants. The rooms are basic but comfortable and there are plenty of amenities including a DVD room, well-equipped kitchen and pleasant pool area. The fan dorm is sweltering – pay the extra for the air-con option.

Nicaragua Guesthouse (Map p455; ☎ 2249-8963; www.3dp.ch/nicaragua; Rotonda La Virgen, 2c S, 2½c O; s/d US$15/20, with air-con US$28/35; ☒) In a tranquil leafy *barrio* in the eastern part of the city, this peaceful spot has attentive owners and basic but comfortable rooms with private bathrooms. It would be a great deal but the 11pm curfew is lame.

Hotel Bello Horizonte (Map p455; ☎ 2249-0435; Rotonda Bello Horizonte, 1c N, 1c E, 1c N, ½c E; s/d US$35/40; ☒ ☐) Close to the bustling nightlife of Bello Horizonte, this hotel offers clean, unadorned rooms with cable TV, air-con and hot water on a quiet residential street. For US$5 more you get your own balcony.

EATING
Barrio Martha Quezada & Around

With an abundance of cheap eateries catering to local office workers, this area is a great place to get a taste for Nicaraguan cuisine.

Cafetín Mirna (Map p459; Tica Bus, 1c O, 1c S; breakfast C$30-50; ☼ 6:30am-2pm) The spot for breakfast on this side of town with fresh juices, tasty *gallo pinto* and fluffy pancakes. There's also a decent lunch buffet.

Flora's Buffet (Map p459; Tica Bus, 1c E, 1½c N; meals C$40-60) Located in a renovated mechanic's workshop, this no-frills *comedor* has a tempting buffet with all your Nica favorites, but what really pulls the crowds are the filling bowls of delicious soup. Come on a Friday for the outrageously good seafood special.

Doña Pilar (Map p459; meals C$45-60; ☼ 6-9pm Mon-Sat) Get mouthwatering regional fare at this popular evening *fritanga*. Chicken, beef or pork are served with *gallo pinto*, chopped pickled cabbage and plantain chips. For vegetarians there is fried cheese, potato cakes and *manuelitas* (savoury pancakes with cheese and cinnamon).

Licuados Ananda (Map p459; frente estatua Montoya; meals C$45-60; **V**) This open-air vegetarian restaurant overlooks pleasant gardens and has a fabulous array of *licuados* (sweet fruit-juice blends), as well as a healthy lunch buffet.

Comida a la Vista (Map p459; frente antiguo Cine Dorado; meals C$40-80) While the line seems to take forever, when you finally get to the front at this busy lunch buffet you will find that you have very little time to choose. Fortunately everything is great, including the prices.

ourpick Comidas Sara (Map p459; Tica Bus, 1c N, 1½c O; dishes C$60-80; ☺ 4pm-late) Super cheap and oh so tasty, this humble *comedor* serves up delicious homestyle pastas, curries and other international favorites at plastic tables on the sidewalk outside the family home. Stick around for beers and you will get to repeatedly run the gauntlet through the living room, under the washing and over granddad's bed to the bathroom out the back.

Other food options:

Cafetín Tonalli (Map p459; Tica Bus, 2c E, ½c S; lunch C$45; ☺ 7am-3pm Mon-Sat) Yogurt, herbal tea and inviting lunches are served in the lovely garden at the back of this cafe run by a women's co-op. There's also an attached bakery.

Tacos Lalo (Map p459; Parque El Carmen, 1c S, 20m E; mains C$60-80) Chow down on authentic Mexican dishes served in the owner's front yard. Take note: the sauces have plenty of bite.

Elsewhere in Managua

Most of Managua's popular restaurants are located around Carretera Masaya to the south of the Metrocentro mall.

El Garabato (Map p455; Seminole Plaza, 3½c S; dishes C$60-140; **V**) Grab a table in the elegant garden out the back of this chilled cafe-restaurant and pick from a full menu of delicately prepared Nicaraguan specialties that includes heaps of vegetarian options.

Bambule (Map p455; semáforos El Nuevo Diario, 6c N, ½c E; mains C$90-130) If you are not going to make it to the Atlantic coast this trip, make sure you get to this funky *costeño* restaurant. The big portions of seafood are delicious, but for the full experience, order the house specialty – *rondon* (coconut-based stew). The neighborhood is rough, so it's best to call a taxi.

Ratatouille (Map p455; frente Iglesia San Agustin; dishes C$90-120) Lunchtime crowds cram into this tiny French-run bistro tucked away in a small shopping centre for tasty light meals, superb salads and the best desserts in the city.

La Casa del Café (Map p455; Lacmiel, 1c E, ½c S; light meals C$120-160; ☎) With a breezy upstairs balcony, wi-fi access and all your favorite caffeinated beverages, this upmarket cafe is the perfect place to escape the chaos of the city. The food is overpriced, but no one will hurry you along if you sip frozen mochaccinos all day.

DRINKING

Managua is far and away the country's nightlife capital. There are three particularly interesting zones: the Zona Rosa around Carretera Masaya, the area around the Intur office, and Bello Horizonte, where there's a cluster of lively bars.

Bar Fussion (Map p455; Monte de Los Olivos, 1c N) Hidden behind a large concrete wall, the vibe at this indoor/outdoor hipster hangout is more house party than city bar. Some of the country's best bands regularly play here.

Caramanchel (Map p459; Crowne Plaza, 1c S, ½c O) Everyone seems to know everyone else in this unpretentious bar in Bolonia. The ambience is extremely casual, as is the dress code, and there is a small dance floor where you groove to salsa, reggae and samba.

El Panal (Map p455; UNI, 100m O) Popular with local artists, poets and other goatee strokers, this intimate open-air bar tucked away down a dirt path near the UCA is a local bohemian institution. It gets packed on Wednesday nights for jazz and *trova* concerts.

El Grillo (Map p459; frente Intur) A no-nonsense late-night drinking spot with a pleasant beer garden overlooking the street and a jukebox full of rock ballads. An entertaining crowd descends on the place once everywhere else has closed.

ENTERTAINMENT
Discotecas

Chamán (Map p455; Restaurante Tiscapa, 200m S; cover C$50-150) That garish concrete pyramid in the middle of some fields is not some monument to an ancient civilization, it is Managua's favorite disco. Inside it is your classic meat market with drunk girls dancing on tables while equally smashed guys look on in awe.

Moods (off Map p455; Galerías Santo Domingo; cover C$60-200) Easily the most upmarket club in town, with polished chrome, laser lighting and visiting DJs playing through a massive sound

NICARAGUA

system. Pull those dress shoes and nice slacks from the bottom of your pack; the doormen are serious about their dress code.

Caribbean Jubilee (Map p455; cover C$30) If you prefer dancehall to reggaetón and soca to *bachata*, it's worth the long hike across town to reach this lively club popular with the local Creole community.

Q (Map p459; cover C$50) Managua's biggest and most popular gay and lesbian club has lively dance music and an excellent dance floor that gets pretty wild later on. The area is not so great – take a taxi.

Live Music
La Casa de los Mejía Godoy (Map p459; ☎ 2222-6110; www.losmejiagodoy.com; costado oeste Plaza Inter; cover US$4-10) Revolutionary-era singers Carlos and Luis Enrique Mejía Godoy and other artists perform their famous Nicaraguan folk songs at this appealing, thatched space with friendly staff. There's live music from Thursday to Saturday; for the bigger-name concerts, it's wise to drop in the day before to buy your ticket.

Central Sandinista de Trabajadores (Map p459; Edificio CST; cover C$60; ☻ 2-8pm Sun) Every Sunday, senior citizens from all over town unbutton their shirts, put on their gold chains and arm their suspenders before hitting the dance floor and carving it up to live *cumbia* and salsa at this atmospheric party in the Sandinista Workers Center. This is one event photographers will not want to miss.

Theater & Cinema
Cine Alhambra VIP (Map p455; Camino de Oriente; tickets C$140) Check out the latest blockbusters in wide leather armchairs. Come before 4pm and pay C$60.
Cinema Plaza Inter (Map p459; Plaza Inter; tickets C$68) Multiscreen cinema complex with ice-cold air-conditioning.
Cinemark (Map p455; Metrocentro; tickets C$65) Upstairs at Metrocentro, this cinema scores top marks on the comfort/price index.

Teatro Justo Rufino Garay (Map p455; ☎ 2266-3714; www.rufinos.org; Estatua Montoya, 3c O, 20m N) A small, alternative theater hosting experimental and contemporary works. Art-house films are shown on Wednesdays.
Teatro Nacional Rubén Darío (Map p455; ☎ 2222-7426; www.tnrubendario.gob.ni; Área Monumental) This impressive theater hosts high-quality plays, concerts, and exhibitions by national and visiting artists.

Sport
Managua's Bóer baseball team faces its rivals in the professional league (October–January) and national championship (February–July) at the **Estadio Nacional Denis Martínez** (Map p459; tickets C$40-150), just northwest of Barrio Martha Quezada. Check www.lnbp.com.ni and www.beisbolnica.com for schedules.

At the time of going to press, professional soccer games were being played at the rustic Estadio Olímpico IND, but by the time you read this, the 25,000-seat Estadio Nacional de Fútbol on the grounds of the UNAN should be fully operational.

SHOPPING
By far the easiest to manage of Managua's markets is the centrally located **Mercado Roberto Huembes** (Map p455; ☻ 8am-6pm), a fairly laid-back place selling food, clothes and shoes as well as the best selection of *artesanías* (handicrafts) in the country after Masaya. In addition to quality hammocks, leather bags and pottery, you will also find heaps of cheap, cheesy souvenirs and T-shirts.

If are looking for clothes, prices are much better in the chaotic **Mercado Oriental** (Map p455; ☻ 8am-5pm), the biggest market in Central America. While the Oriental definitely has an image problem – wealthier Nicaraguans will tell you that you are sure to be scammed, robbed and beaten – in reality it isn't that dangerous and shopping here is definitely an experience. Only bring as much money as you are likely to need and be ready to fight off flirtatious shop assistants who will grab you by the hand and physically pull you into their stores.

GETTING THERE & AWAY
Air
The airport is small and manageable, with a modern international section and a quainter domestic terminal alongside. In the international section there's a couple of all-card ATMs, car hire, and free wi-fi. There is also an

Intur (🕑 8am-10pm) office by the customs area with English-speaking staff that can make hotel reservations. See boxed text, p456, for transportation details.

La Costeña (☎ 2263-2142; www.lacostena.com.ni) has an office in the airport and has flights from Managua to Bluefields (US$127 round trip), Corn Islands (US$164), Puerto Cabezas (US$149) and San Carlos (US$116). One-way fares are 60% to 65% of the return fare. It is sometimes possible to show up and book a flight out for the same afternoon, but it's wise to call ahead and make a reservation (no credit card needed).

Bus

INTERNATIONAL

International buses are run by **Tica Bus** (Map p459; ☎ 2222-6094; www.ticabus.com), **King Quality** (Map p459; ☎ 2222-3065; www.kingqualityca.com; frente Plaza Inter), **Transnica** (Map p455; ☎ 2270-3133; www.transnica.com) and **Transportes El Sol** (Map p459; ☎ 2222-7785; frente Tica Bus), all with daily departures to other Central American destinations.

Principal international bus departures:

Guatemala City King Quality (US$70; 17hr; 2:30am, 3:30am) Also, Tica Bus' 5am service to San Salvador continues on the next day to Guatemala City (US$52; 5hr).

Panama City Tica Bus (US$52; 27hr; noon) Via San José, Costa Rica.

San José, Costa Rica King Quality (US$36; 8hr; 2:30pm); Tica Bus (US$23; 9hr; 6am, 7am, noon); Transnica (US$23; 9hr; 5:30am, 7am, 10am; US$35 *ejecutivo*; 8hr; noon)

San Salvador, El Salvador King Quality (US$33; 10hr; 3:30am, 11:30am); Tica Bus (US$35; 11hr; 5am); Transportes El Sol (US$35; 11hr; 5:30am)

Tegucigalpa, Honduras King Quality (US$41; 8hr; 3:30am,11:30am); Tica Bus (US$23; 8hr; 5am) Tica Bus' morning service continues to San Pedro Sula (US$37).

DOMESTIC

Intercity buses depart from the city's major markets: buses heading for southwestern destinations and the Costa Rican border depart from **Mercado Roberto Huembes**; for León and the border with Honduras from **Mercado Israel Lewites** (Bóer; ☎ 2265-2152); and for Matagalpa, Estelí and other northern destinations, including the Honduran border, as well as El Rama, for the Caribbean coast, and San Carlos, from **Mercado Mayoreo**.

Particularly at Mercado Roberto Huembes, aggressive touts will push you towards the bus to your destination, make sure it is the *expreso* and not the *ordinario*, which takes far longer.

See boxed text, below, for destinations serviced from Managua.

Quicker and more comfortable microbuses depart from opposite the UCA university.

Granada (C$20; 1hr; every 20min)

León (C$40; 1½hr; depart when full)

Masaya (C$15; 45min; every 20min)

GETTING AROUND
Bus

Local buses are frequent and crowded; watch your pockets. Buses do not generally stop en route – look for the nearest bus shelter. The fare is C$2.50.

Useful routes include the following:

102 Acahualinca to Mayoreo via Montoya, Bolonia, UCA, Mercado Oriental and Bello Horizonte.

110 Mercado Bóer to Mercado Mayoreo, via the UCA, Metrocentro, Mercado Huembes and Mercado Iván Montenegro.

BUSES FROM MANAGUA

Destination	Cost (C$)	Duration (hr)	Frequency
El Rama	150	6	6 daily
Estelí	60	2¼	every 30min
Granada	20	45min	every 20min
León	35	1½	hourly
Masaya	10	1	every 25min
Matagalpa	60	2¼	hourly
Ocotal	75	3½	hourly
Peñas Blancas	65	3	hourly
Rivas	55	2	10 daily
San Carlos	150	10	6 daily
San Juan del Sur	70	2¾	10am & 4pm daily

119 From Linda Vista to Mercado Huembes, with stops at Rotonda El Güegüense, the UCA and Carretera Masaya.
195 Area Monumental to Huembes via Bolonia, UCA and Mercado Oriental.
MR 4 Mercado Bóer to La Virgen via Bolonia, Mercado Oriental and Mercado Huembes.

Car

The usual car-rental multinationals compete with a few local operators. Note that advertised rates rarely include insurance, which costs around US$15 per day for the most basic cover. Lower-priced operators:
Dollar (Map p459; ☎ 2222-2269; www.dollar.com.ni; inside Hotel Crowne Plaza) Weekly rates start at US$135/72 in high/low season.
Lugo (Map p459; ☎ 2266-5240; www.lugorentacar.com.ni; Canal 2, 2c N, 3c O) High-season rates from US$19 per day.

Taxi

Finding a cab in Managua is never a problem; drivers honk as they pass to signal their availability. Drivers pick up additional passengers along the way, so you can hail a taxi even if it's occupied, but for a bit extra you can ask them to go direct. Taxis are not metered and fares should be agreed on before you get in. The standard rate for a short ride is around C$30 to C$40 per person; longer journeys right across town should not exceed C$60 per person. Fares go up a little after dark.

If you are traveling with valuables or at night, consider forking out a little extra for a **radio taxi** (☎ 2263-1838).

AROUND MANAGUA

LAGUNAS DE XILOÁ & APOYEQUE

Half a dozen *lagunas*, or volcanic crater lakes, lie near Managua's city limits. Of these, the best for swimming is **Laguna de Xiloá**, on the Península de Chiltepe, about 20km northwest of Managua off the road to León. Xiloá is also suitable for diving; its clear waters provide the habitat for at least 15 endemic aquatic species. There are a few kiosks selling food and some bars dotted around the lakeshore. Though crowded on weekends, the *laguna* remains quite peaceful during the week.

A contrast to developed Xiloá is the wild, inaccessible **Laguna de Apoyeque**, set deep within a steep 500m-high volcanic crater. It is usually only visited by scientists, however adventurous travelers can find a guide (US$10)

to take them down to the lake in the village of Alfonso Gonzalez, off the main Xiloá road. It is a hard slog along an unmarked trail that will take the best part of a day.

To get here, take bus 110 from Managua's UCA bus station to Ciudad Sandino, where you can catch an onward bus or a taxi to the lagoons.

POCHOMIL & PACIFIC BEACHES

A famous Nicaraguan vacation spot, **Pochomil** is a gorgeous swimming beach on the Pacific coast 62km from Managua. The promenade is stocked with bars, restaurants and a few hotels which, the place having been eclipsed by San Juan del Sur in recent years, are usually fairly empty (Easter apart). The restaurant owners fight (sometimes literally) for your custom. The beach is wide, sandy and good for swimming or sunning; the sunsets are fabulous.

If you want to stay, **Hotel Altamar** (☎ 269-9204; r with fan/air-con US$20/40; P ☒) is a bright, cheery place with hammocks and a variety of mediocre rooms that accommodate up to three people. The restaurant, with lovely views, has moderate prices and tasty seafood.

The fishing village of **Masachapa** is just 2km north of Pochomil. While the beach here isn't as inviting, it feels more real and is significantly cheaper. **Hotel Vista del Mar** (☎ 2269-0115; r US$30-40; P ☒ ☒) has clean, modern rooms, some with water views, and a fine restaurant from where you can watch the local fishers hauling their *pangas* (fibreglass skiffs) up onto the beach.

There's excellent surfing in these parts; there is a left point break just north of Montelimar (where the resort complex has a Visa ATM) and a right reef break just to the south. Closer to Masachapa is Quizala, a decent beach break.

Buses from Managua's Mercado Israel Lewites go to Masachapa and Pochomil (C$25, 1½ hours) every half hour from 6am to 5pm.

NORTHERN NICARAGUA

Cooler than the coastal lowlands, the mountainous region just south of Honduras is cowboy country, with luminous cloud formations and crisp, chilly nights. The departments of Matagalpa, Estelí, Jinotega and Madriz compose this highland region, rich with coffee, tobacco and livestock.

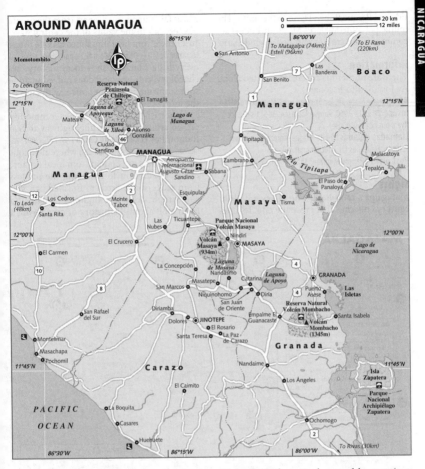

AROUND MANAGUA

Esteli is the principal town between Managua and the Honduran border, and the Miraflor and Tisey nature reserves are located in the mountains surrounding the city. South of Esteli, a turnoff at Sébaco leads to the pleasant towns of Matagalpa and Jinotega, and several private reserves and coffee plantations that make for intriguing visits.

MATAGALPA
pop 89,132 / elev 682m

The coffee capital of Matagalpa is blessed with a refreshing climate that comes as a delicious relief after the sweaty lowlands. Surrounded by lovely green mountains, it's a bustling, unkempt but prosperous town spread unevenly over hilly terrain. Though tiny here, the Río Grande de

Matagalpa is the nation's second-longest river, flowing all the way to the Caribbean.

Spanish conquistadors found several indigenous communities coexisting here, including the Molagüina, whose tongue-twisting Nahuatl name for the town, Matlatlcallipan (House of Nets), became Matagalpa.

Matagalpa makes a good destination with its down-to-earth ways, friendly people, proximity to cloud-forest reserves and selection of great places to stay.

Orientation

Bordered on its western edge by the river, Matagalpa's central zone is concentrated around two one-way streets that link the city's principal plazas, Parque Morazán on the north side and Parque Rubén Darío to the south. The municipal cathedral faces Morazán; budget accommodations are concentrated around Darío.

Information

There are numerous cybercafes located along Av José Beníto Escobar.

BAC (Parque Morazán, ½c S) Visa/Cirrus/MasterCard ATM.

Intur (☎ 2612-7060; Parque Morazán, 3c S) Useful for flyers but not much else.

Llamadas Heladas (frente Parque Morazán; 🕑 8am-9:30pm) Best lines for international calls.

Post office (Parque Morazán, 1c S)

Sights

Matagalpa's **cathedral** is one of several 19th-century churches that grace the city. Its inte-rior is fairly unadorned, apart from the ornate plasterwork in the vaults of the central nave. Just down from here, the **Museo del Café** (Parque Morazán, 1c S; 🕑 9am-12:30pm & 2-6pm) has a bit of everything Matagalpan – local history, archaeology, culture – and does indeed include some information about coffee, with cups of the local brew to try.

Coffee isn't the only valuable commodity grown around here. On the highway to San Ramon lies **El Castillo de Cacao** (☎ 2772-2002; admission US$5; 🕑 9am-4pm Mon-Sat) where delicious chocolate bars are crafted from local organic cacao. In addition to following the process from sacks of raw seeds to finished bar, you will sample delectable liquid chocolate and learn a bit about the history of cacao, which

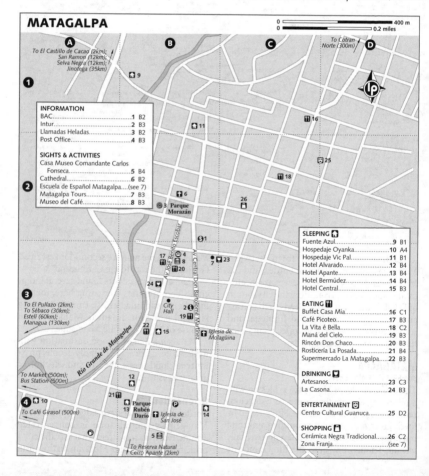

MATAGALPA

0 — 400 m
0 — 0.2 miles

To El Castillo de Cacao (2km);
San Ramon (12km);
Selva Negra (12km);
Jinotega (35km)

To Cotran
Norte (300km)

Parque
Morazán

City
Hall

Iglesia de
Molagüina

To El Pullazo (2km);
To Sébaco (30km);
Estelí (60km);
Managua (130km)

Río Grande de Matagalpa

Av Central Don Bartolomé Martínez

Av José Benito Escobar

To Market (500m);
Bus Station (500m)

To Café Girasol (500m)

Parque
Rubén
Darío

Iglesia de
San José

To Reserva Natural
Cerro Apante (2km)

CAFFEINATED ADVENTURES IN THE NORTHERN HIGHLANDS

For a glimpse into the life of Nicaragua's hard-working *campesinos* (farmers), head to the small town of **San Ramón**, 12km east of Matagalpa, where local agricultural co-operative **UCA San Ramon** (☎ 2772-5247; www.agroecoturismorural.com; guides per day US$15) has developed a tempting menu of fantastic activities in four nearby rural villages: La Pita, La Reina, La Corona and El Roblar. In addition to trying your hand picking and sorting organic coffee, you can descend into a spooky abandoned gold mine, scale some amazing lookouts or swim beneath waterfalls surrounded by forest. Also on offer are courses in Nicaraguan cooking and traditional medicine.

It is possible to visit the attractions on a day trip from Matagalpa – set out early to give yourself plenty of time – but it is highly recommended to spend the night in one of the villages to fully experience rural life. You can sleep in newly constructed rooms (US$7 per person) next to family homes in all the villages or in the charming mud-brick guesthouse (US$20) in La Pita offering comfortable rooms with private bathroom and amazing mountain views. Traditional meals (US$3.50) are available in all the communities.

Buses to San Ramón (C$10) leave every half hour from Cotran Norte in Matagalpa, but it is much faster to take a shared taxi (C$20). From San Ramón you can hike to the communities or hire a bicycle (US$10 per day).

---

was once the official currency of the region. It's a C$30 taxi ride from town.

Matagalpa is known throughout Nicaragua as the birthplace of Carlos Fonseca, the inspirational leader of the Sandinista revolution killed in a National Guard ambush in 1976, three years before the fall of Somoza. The small but informative **Casa Museo Comandante Carlos Fonseca** (☎ 8655-6304; Parque Rubén Darío, 1c E; ☾ 8am-5:30pm Mon-Fri) is located in the revolutionary's humble childhood home where he grew up in desperate poverty with his mother and four siblings despite the fact that his father was a local coffee baron.

For excellent views over the city, hike up into the **Reserva Natural Cerro Apante** (admission US$1.50) on the south side of town. To find the trail, walk south from the western edge of Parque Rubén Darío until you reach Finca San Luis.

Activities & Tours

There's heaps to do in the surrounding area. A charitable setup that accepts volunteers, **Café Girasol** (☎ 2772-6030; ☾ 6:30am-10pm) sells detailed leaflets (C$25) for a number of self-guided walks in the Matagalpa area that vary in length from four to eight hours. It is located by the main bridge a couple of blocks southwest of the market.

Matagalpa Tours (☎ 2772-0108; www.matagalpa tours.com; Parque Morazán, 1c S, ½c E; ☾ 8am-6pm Mon-Sat) is a well-run, English-speaking setup that offers a wide range of excursions in Matagalpa and the surrounding hills. Excursions are cheaper if more people go. For two, think

US$15 each for a couple of hours, US$25 for a half-day and US$50 for a whole day.

Courses

Escuela de Español Matagalpa (☎ 2772-0108; www. matagalpa.info) Run out of the same office as Matagalpa Tours, this language center has a flexible program of classes for different abilities and requirements. Packages including homestay or hotel accommodations cost from US$182 for a 15-hour week.

Festivals & Events

No valentine? No problem. In Matagalpa everyone gets to party on February 14 as a host of musical groups accompany residents in a march between the two main parks to celebrate the anniversary of achieving city status.

The biggest event of the year is the city's **annual festival**, held during the week of September 24, in honor of its patron saint La Virgen de la Merced (Our Lady of Mercy). The **Festival de Polkas, Mazurcas y Jamaquellos** livens up the closing weekend celebration with traditional dances from Nicaragua's five northern departments.

Sleeping

Hospedaje Vic Pal (☎ 2772-6735; catedral, 3c N; s/d without bathroom US$2.50/5, d US$6) Super cheap, clean and friendly, this family-run guesthouse has very basic rooms and mountain views from its laundry-filled courtyard.

Hotel Bermúdez (☎ 2772-6744; Parque Rubén Darío, 2c E; s/d US$4/8) This friendly local institution offers a motherly welcome and rooms that are clean and decent, if a little run-down. Most have their own cold-water bathroom; all are different, with those at the front quite a bit lighter. The mattresses also vary substantially in quality.

Hospedaje Oyanka (☎ 2772-0057; Parque Rubén Darío, 4c O; s/d US$6/8) At the back of a cafe halfway between the bus station and Parque Rubén Darío, this small hotel is excellent value with real mattresses and private bathrooms in well-finished rooms.

Hotel Apante (☎ 2772-6890; frente Parque Rubén Darío; s/d US$8/12) Bang on Parque Rubén Darío and with plenty of bang for your buck; with a wide choice of value-packed rooms, this place is tops. If you've been traveling a while, you'll weep at how good the showers are. Avoid the upstairs rooms, which are regularly bombarded with disco noise. The doorbell is around the corner to your left.

Hotel Alvarado (☎ 2772-2830; Parque Rubén Darío, ½c N; s/d without bathroom US$8/10, s/d US$12/15) This courteous central pad has a number of very appealing rooms with cable TV, hot water and wonderful mountain views as well as some rather ordinary budget options. They are all different so ask to see a few before making a choice.

ourpick **Hotel Central** (☎ 2772-3140; Parque Rubén Darío, 2½c N; s/d US$12/15) It's tough to beat this spotless, friendly and professional place on the main street. The modern rooms at the back are brighter and more comfortable, but all feature new mattresses, plump pillows and cable TV.

Fuente Azul (☎ 2772-2733; Parque Morazán, 4c N, 3c O; d with/without bathroom US$19/12, P 🛜) Another heartwarmingly good Matagalpa sleep-spot, with modern, comfortable rooms with big beds, cable TV and wi-fi.

Eating

For a cheap, filling snack it's hard to beat the regional specialty güirílas con cuajada (sweet corn pancake with soft salty cheese) that are sold hot off the grill in the evening on the sidewalk a couple of blocks north of the cathedral. For self caterers, **Supermercado La Matagalpa** (Parque Rubén Darío, 3c N) stocks local coffee, chocolate and cheeses as well as producing its own line of pickles and hot sauce.

Buffet Casa Mia (Parque Morazán, 3c E, 4c N; meals C$50) This popular buffet on the northern side of town prepares tasty breakfasts and lunches at rock-bottom prices.

Rincón Don Chaco (Parque Morazán, 2c S; juices C$25, dishes C$50-60; 🕑 Sun-Fri; V) It looks like a regular greasy diner from the outside, but Don Chaco

is in fact one of the healthiest pit stops in town. The vitamin-boosting batidos (fruit shakes) are absolutely delicious and there are also cheap meals and a soy-based vegetarian plate.

Café Picoteo (Parque Morazán, 2c S; dishes C$50-110) A popular meeting spot that is a bit like a school bus – the front is a respectable cafe serving coffee and cakes while the back bar area is where the cool folk hang, drinking liters of beer and munching on tacos, burgers and fajitas.

Maná del Cielo (Parque Morazán, 3c S; meals C$60-80) Matagalpa's favorite buffet is busy from morning to evening, which means the juicy chicken kebabs, jalapeño beef and other great dishes are always fresh.

Rosticeria La Posada (Parque Rubén Darío, ½c O; dishes C$60-100) Dose up on calories and then burn them right off at this unpretentious fried-chicken joint which morphs into a disco on weekend nights.

ourpick **La Vita é Bella** (Parque Morazán, 2c E, 1½c N; dishes C$60-130; V) Difficult to find but worth the search, this hidden gem serves up tasty Italian specialties in an intimate setting. There are plenty of vegetarian options and the spinach ravioli and penne con pesto are both excellent, but the real highlight is the thin-crust pizzas (C$65 to C$160). It's halfway down the alley in front of 'Bar Piraña.'

El Pullazo (☎ 2775-4449; Carretera Managua; dishes C$110-150) The huge portions at this popular steakhouse about 2km south of town are a challenge to even the strongest appetite. While the menu is not extensive – choose from beef, chicken or pork together with starchy sides – it's delicious and remarkably good value for the high quality involved. A C$30 taxi will get you there.

Drinking & Entertainment

Centro Cultural Guanuca (☎ 2772-3562; www.grupo venancia.org; Guadalupe 1½c S) Run by a nonprofit women's organization, this great venue shows art-house and regional movies on Friday evenings and hosts concerts and live events ranging from theater to break-dancing competitions on Saturdays. Check the website or call for upcoming events.

Artesanos (Parque Morazán, 1c S, ½c E) A relaxing cafe-bar by day, in the evenings Artesanos is Matagalpa's hottest drinking destination. Hip locals flock to its earthy front bar and leafy courtyard to sip cocktails, down ice-cold beers or smoke a hookah accompanied by the sounds of electronica and world music.

La Casona (Parque Morazán, 3c S) This normally sleepy restaurant bursts into party mode on Thursday and Friday nights when crowds pack into its basement patio to groove to local bands and down large amounts of rum.

Shopping

Matagalpa is known for its fine black pottery, and some pieces are small enough to easily stow in a backpack.

Cerámica Negra Tradicional (☎ 2772-2464; catedral, 2c E) displays the work of Doña Ernestina Rodríguez, including jewelry and tiny tea sets. A small shop in the centre of Parque Rubén Darío showcases the work of a number of other local artists.

Zona Franja (☎ 2772-4581; Parque Morazán, 1c S, ½c E), inside the Matagalpa Tours building, sells a variety of local handicrafts including colorful bags weaved in the indigenous community of El Chile.

Getting There & Away

The main **bus station** (☎ 2772-4659), known as Cotran Sur, is about 1km west of Parque Rubén Darío. Another minor bus station, Cotran Norte, lies at the other end of town and serves rural destinations in the north.

Buses departing from Cotran Sur:

Estelí (C$25; 1½hr; every 30min)
Jinotega (C$25; 1½hr; every 30min)
León (C$60; 2½hr; 6am, 3pm & 4pm daily)
Managua (C$60; 2hr; hourly)
Masaya (C$60; 3hr; 2pm & 3:30pm daily)

For León, you can also take any Estelí-bound bus and transfer at San Isidro.

JINOTEGA

pop 45,580 / elev 1000m

Aptly nicknamed City of Mists, Jinotega is a quiet town in a fertile valley high in a mountainous coffee-growing region. Rarely visited by tourists and enclosed on all sides by towering peaks, the town has a raw, frontier feel to it and is a great base from which to visit the surrounding cloud-covered wilderness or try your hand picking coffee. The highest of Nicaragua's major cities, it can also be decidedly chilly at times.

The steep drive up the old highway from Matagalpa is one of the most scenic in the country and reason enough for a visit to Jinotega. Colorful roadside stands along the potholed highway sell flowers and big bundles of carrots, beets and cabbages.

There's an **Intur office** (☎ 2782-6551; Parque Central, 2c S, 3c E) that has information on activities in the surrounding mountains. A couple of blocks north of the park, BAC has an all-card ATM.

Sights

Though unremarkable from the outside, the **Catedral San Juan** (c 1805) has a fine white interior bristling with beautifully sculpted saints; it's an impressive collection of religious art. Across the street, a monument to Sandinista leader Carlos Fonseca rests amid the tall trees of Jinotega's charming **Parque Central**. Unfortunately, the council has recently 'restored' the **murals** on the east side of town and the freshly painted versions lack the charm of the originals, but they are still worth a look for an insight into the culture of the revolution.

And don't leave town without hiking your way to the top of **Cerro la Cruz**, where the cross that appears to float over the town at night is embedded in a boulder-crusted ridge. The views from the top are phenomenal. The steep one-hour hike begins from the cemetery.

Activities & Tours

SOPPEXCCA (Society of Small Coffee Producers, Exporters & Buyers; ☎ 2782-2617; www.soppexcca.org/en; Cotran Norte, 1½c N) organizes visits to the farms of some of its members including Finca La Estrella, where you can take part in the harvest or hike in pristine cloud forest, and Finca Mirador El Dorado, which offers horseback riding and boating trips. Guides to both places cost US$8 while homestay accommodation is available from US$5 per person. At the cooperative's Café Flor de Jinotega you can sample a cup of its delicious brew and discuss the options.

Sleeping

Alojamiento Mendoza (☎ 2782-2062; Parque Central, 1c E; r per person US$4) Right in the middle of town, this friendly guesthouse has dark, basic rooms that are fine for just crashing the night. The cheap *comedor* out the front is an added bonus.

Hotel Primavera (☎ 2782-2400; Parque Central, 5c N; s/d without bathroom US$5/10, r with bathroom US$12) On the northern side of town, this family-run cheapie has superclean rooms with decent mattresses set around a pleasant courtyard.

Hotel Central (☎ 2782-2063; contiguo Esso; r US$12) Easily the best value for money in town, this recently renovated spot has comfortable rooms with hot water and cable TV. Upstairs rooms are brighter.

DIY: BOSAWÁS

If you are the kind of traveler that relishes dropping off the radar, then the **Reserva de Biosfera Bosawás** is the place for you. The largest rainforest in the Americas after the Amazon, it's a magical place of spectacular forested peaks and fast-flowing rivers that rush past tiny indigenous villages. With no roads, no hotels and no electricity, it's a tough place to visit, but the potential for adventure is enormous.

The easiest way into the reserve is via the town of **Wiwili** on the Río Coco on northern Jinotega department. There is no public transport on the river, but if you're not in a hurry, it is possible to travel all the way to the Caribbean using the boats of local traders and organizations. You can hire local guides to take you deep into the reserve in any of the communities along the way.

Another option is to travel from Jinotega to the village of **Ayapal**, from where boats leave irregularly for the trip down the narrow Río Bocay, past the mysterious caves of Tunawalan, to the Mískito village of San Andrés on the Río Coco.

Once you get into the reserve proper, the only places to stay are in indigenous Mayanga and Mískito villages, where you can often arrange some sort of accommodation or at the very least tie up your hammock. It can get cold in the night, so bring warm clothes as well as plenty of food, water purification tablets and a flashlight.

Hotel Sollentuna Hem (☎ 2782-2334; sollentuna hem@gmail.com; Parque Central, 2c E, 4c N; s/d US$18/20; (P)) A favorite among travelers, this pleasant hotel has hospitable management, and rooms that range from cozy singles to roomier doubles, all with decent beds, cable TV and hot water.

Eating & Drinking

There are a few street-food stalls around the park, and *fritangas* fire up around town in the evenings.

our pick Casa de Don Colocho (Parque Central, 3c S, 3c E; pastries C$10-20) Escape the weather and down a couple of cups of piping-hot local coffee as you work your way through the selection of delicious pastries at this excellent bakery.

No name Fritanga (Parque Central, 1c E, 20m S; meals C$50) Branding gurus would despair, but this unsigned, no-name eatery has built up quite a following. Must have something to do with the cheap and delicious barbecued chicken and beef kebabs. Look for it next to Farmacia Vargas.

Soda El Tico (Parque Central, 1c E, ½c S; buffet C$60-80; ☉ 7:30am-10pm) This gleaming spot wipes all the buffet competitors off the map. Some days it seems that the whole town comes here for lunch. Get there early to take your pick from the variety of well-prepared plates.

La Taberna (Parque Central, 2c O; ☉ 1pm-1am) With handcrafted tables, mud-brick walls and a dark wood interior, Jinotega's best bar is a bit like a cross between a Wild-West saloon and a Kalahari game lodge. The cool crowd comes late.

Getting There & Away

There are two bus stations. Northbound buses depart from the main market beside the highway east of town. The bus station for Matagalpa, Estelí and Managua sits near the town's southern entrance.

Estelí (C$46; 2hr; 7am, 9am, 1pm, 2:45pm & 3:30pm)
Managua (C$80; 3½hr; 10 daily)
Matagalpa (C$25; 1½hr; every 30 minutes 5am-5:30pm)

ESTELÍ

pop 97,488

Big on cowboy bravado but with a solid progressive streak, Estelí is a complex yet unpretentious city sitting at the centre of an agriculturally rich highland valley. It is the kind of place where oversized belt buckles are sold right alongside organic lettuce, and firing shotguns and yoga are both common pastimes.

Partly because of its strategic location on the road to Honduras, Estelí saw heavy fighting during the revolution – it was bombarded in April 1979 and severely damaged – and the town has remained a Sandinista stronghold ever since.

These days, the city is best known for its world-class cigar industry and as a gateway to the spectacular community-based tourism projects in the surrounding mountains.

Orientation

The Carretera Panamericana runs north–south along the eastern side of the town; both bus stations are on the highway.

Atypically, Estelí uses a street numbering system, and every block is clearly signed. The intersection of Av Central and Calle Transversal is the center of the system. Calles (streets) ascend in number north and south of Calle Transversal; avenidas (avenues) ascend east and west of Av Central. Streets and avenues are suffixed 'NE' (northeast), 'SO' (southwest) etc, according to which quadrant of town they belong to.

Information

BAC (cnr Av 1a SO & Calle Transversal) All-card-friendly ATM.

Estelínet (BAC, ½c S; per hr C$15) One of the fastest internet connections in town.

Fider (☎ 2713-3918; fiderest@ibw.com.ni; Petronic, 1½c E) Manages Reserva Natural Cerro Tisey-Estanzuela. Stop by for information and a great map.

Intur (☎ 2713-6799; esteli@intur.gob.ni; parque, ½c S) Plenty of brochures but limited expertise.

Post office (parque, 8c S)

UCA Miraflor (☎ 2713-2971; Calle 1a, ½c N) Information and booking for Reserva Natural Miraflor.

Sights & Activities

Galería de Héroes y Mártires (☎ 8419-3519; catedral, ½c S; entry by donation; 🕑 9am-5pm Mon-Sat) is an emotive place to visit, with photos of the young men and women who gave their lives during the revolution displayed around the large room along with some weaponry and personal belongings. The gallery is run by mothers of the martyrs, and they are the ones who make a visit here so compelling. They are more than willing to share their own stories, providing insight into the struggles that many Nicaraguans experienced.

The 1823 **cathedral** is worth a wander, while a number of interesting murals can be seen in the surrounding blocks. Get up early for the organic market at the **Parque Central** on Friday mornings for homemade yogurt, fresh fruits and other delights.

About 1km south of town is **Cecalli** (☎ 2713-7078; Carretera Panamericana; 🕑 9am-5pm Mon-Fri), an organic farming cooperative that specializes in medicinal plants. In addition to producing over 150 elixirs, lotions, teas and creams, the centre also offers acupuncture and massage.

Courses

Estelí has a large selection of Spanish language schools, a holdover from its days as a haven for international volunteers during the revolution.

Cenac Spanish School (☎ 2713-5437; www.spanish schoolcenac.com; Carretera Panamericana; per week incl homestay US$165) Well-established school that offers varied cultural activities and can organize volunteer placements.

Escuela de Héroes y Mártires (☎ 8419-3519; inside Galería de Héroes y Mártires; per week incl homestay US$160) More low-key than the competition, the Escuela de Héroes y Mártires offers classes right in the middle of town.

Los Pipitos (☎ 2713-5511; www.lospipitosesteli.org. ni; Petronic Salida Sur, 100m S, 100m E, 50m S; per week incl homestay US$170) Professionally run nonprofit school in a vibrant vocational training centre for disabled and impoverished youth.

Tours

Estelí is internationally acclaimed for producing some of the best cigars going round. It is possible to visit a number of the local factories to meet the skilled artisans who rapidly convert piles of cured tobacco leaves into perfectly rolled stogies with their bare hands. **Tabacalera Cubanica** (☎ 2713-2383; Carretera Panamericana), creator of the award-winning Padrón brand, can organize tours with advanced notice, however as a tax-exempted business it is unable to sell cigars onsite. Alternatively, Hospedaje Luna (below) organizes guided tours to smaller producers where you can make purchases.

Sleeping

Several inexpensive, basic guesthouses lie along Av Central, several blocks south of the center, in a characterful shopping district.

Hospedaje San Francisco (☎ 2713-3787; Parque Infantil, ½c N; s/d without bathroom US$2.50/5) These stable-like, narrow rooms with trippy wallpaper are a steal if you're not big on ventilation or natural light.

Hospedaje Chepito (☎ 2713-3784; Parque Infantil, ½c S; s/d without bathroom US$3.50/5) The best of the cheapies, this friendly place is cleaner than the competition and has basic but adequate rooms arranged around a simple courtyard. It's still not one to show your parents photos of, though.

our pick Hospedaje Luna (☎ 8441-8466; www.cafe luzyluna.com; catedral, 1c N, 1c E; dm/s/d without bathroom US$8/10/17, s/d with bathroom US$12/20; 🛜) With spotless rooms, hot showers, free organic coffee and a wealth of information on Estelí and the surrounding area, this new hostel checks all the boxes. Profits are donated to community projects in Miraflor.

Hotel Miraflor (☎ 2713-2003; Parque Central, 1c N; s/d US$12/18) A welcoming family-run operation with basic, clean rooms and hot water just half a block from the Parque Central.

Hostal Tomabú (☎ 2713-3783; hostaltomabu.esteli@ gmail.com; costado sur Parque Infantil; s/d US$12/22; P) Friendly and welcoming, this unsigned hotel on the south side of the Parque Infantil offers brightly painted rooms, some offering mountain views, with hot water and cable TV.

Hotel El Mesón (☎ 2713-2655; catedral, 1cN; s/d with fan US$15/23; P) This spot has reasonable

rooms, with warm showers and cable TV, set around a leafy courtyard. The rooms at the far end of the garden get less traffic noise.

Eating

For cheap meals, there are a number of steam table buffet restaurants in town offering similar options for breakfast and lunch.

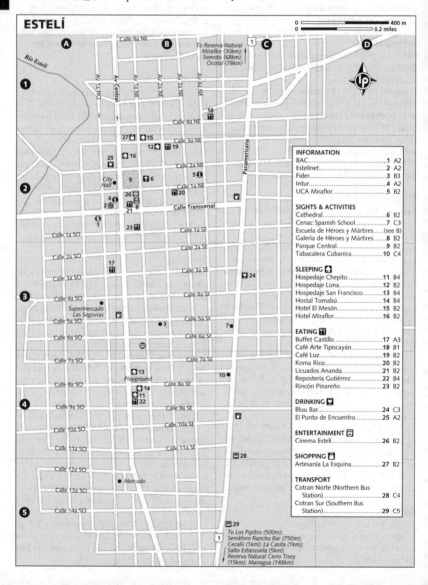

ESTELÍ

0 ——— 400 m
0 ——— 0.2 miles

INFORMATION	
BAC	1 A2
Estelinet	2 A2
Fider	3 B3
Intur	4 A2
UCA Miraflor	5 B2

SIGHTS & ACTIVITIES	
Cathedral	6 B2
Cenac Spanish School	7 C3
Escuela de Héroes y Mártires	(see 8)
Galería de Héroes y Mártires	8 B2
Parque Central	9 B2
Tabacalera Cubanica	10 C4

SLEEPING	
Hospedaje Chepito	11 B4
Hospedaje Luna	12 B2
Hospedaje San Francisco	13 B4
Hostal Tomabú	14 B4
Hotel El Mesón	15 B2
Hotel Miraflor	16 B2

EATING	
Buffet Castillo	17 A3
Café Arte Tipiscayán	18 B1
Café Luz	19 B2
Koma Rico	20 B2
Licuados Ananda	21 B2
Repostería Gutiérrez	22 B4
Rincón Pinareño	23 B2

DRINKING	
Bluu Bar	24 C3
El Punto de Encuentro	25 A2

ENTERTAINMENT	
Cinema Estelí	26 B2

SHOPPING	
Artesanía La Esquina	27 B2

TRANSPORT	
Cotran Norte (Northern Bus Station)	28 C4
Cotran Sur (Southern Bus Station)	29 C5

To Reserva Natural
Miraflor (30km);
Somoto (68km);
Ocotal (78km)

To Los Pipitos (500m);
Semáforo Rancho Bar (750m);
Cecalli (1km); La Casita (1km);
Salto Estanzuela (5km);
Reserva Natural Cerro Tisey
(15km); Managua (148km)

Reposteria Gutiérrez (☎ 2714-1774; Parque Infantil, ½c S; pastries C$5-20) Sip real coffee or hot chocolate in this cozy bakery as you sample its selection of delicious cookies, cakes, doughnuts and pastries. A great place to stock up on munchies before that trip to the mountains.

Licuados Ananda (Parque Central, 1c S, ½c E; juices C$15; ☺ 8am-5pm Mon-Fri, 8am-2pm Sat; (V)) Set in a garden around an empty swimming pool, this guru-inspired setup has excellent juices and vegetarian snacks including burgers and soy tacos. Ask about early morning yoga classes.

La Casita (Carretera Panamericana; snacks C$20-60; ☺ 9am-7pm Tue-Sun, 2-7pm Mon) About 1km south of town, just past Cecalli (C$15 in a cab), unsigned La Casita sits on the lush grounds of Finca Las Nubes. In addition to the best coffee in town, the menu includes freshly baked breads, local cheeses, homemade yogurt and juices. Be sure to take a walk around the grounds and greet the geese. Closed first Monday of the month.

Koma Rico (cine, 2c E; meals C$40-60; ☺ Sat-Thu) Stack your plate high at this popular *fritanga* that's based upon the tried-and-tested marriage of tasty barbecued meats and ice-cold beer.

Buffet Castillo (☎ 2713-0337; Parque Central, 4c S, ½c O; meals C$50; ☺ 7am-3pm Mon-Sat) Often packed at lunchtime, this neat diner offers up restaurant-quality meals, including ribs, fried fish and jalapeño chicken, at a budget price.

Café Luz (☎ 8441-8466; catedral, 1c N, 1c E; dishes C$60-150; ☺ (V)) Over *gallo pinto*? The menu at this chilled cafe features great curries, lasagna and plenty of interesting vegetarian options. And for those rainy Estelí days there is organic coffee and free wi-fi.

our pick Rincón Pinareño (☎ 2713-4369; catedral, 1½c S; dishes C$60-150; ☺ Tue-Sun) Run by an expat Cuban family, this popular bistro serves up juicy pressed sandwiches, delicious pork chops and the best desserts in town.

Café Arte Tispiscayán (☎ 2713-7303; catedral, 2c N, 3c E; mains C$130-150) Part gallery, part cafe this attractive spot serves rich traditional dishes at handcrafted wooden tables surrounded by the impressive soapstone sculptures of owner Freddy Moreno.

Drinking & Entertainment

El Punto del Encuentro (Parque Central, ½c O; ☺ 11:30am-10:30pm) Ignore the dingy front bar and walk straight on through to the leafy garden full of terracotta-tiled huts where locals meet to down cocktails and cold beers.

Semáforo Rancho Bar (Carretera Panamericana; cover C$40-60; ☺ 8pm-5am Thu-Sun) Estelí's most popular nightspot, Semáforo attracts an all-ages, fun-loving crowd with one single mission – to shake and groove to live music until the early hours of the morning. Bands come from all over the country to play under the giant thatched roof.

Bluu Bar (Carretera Panamericana; cover C$40-60; ☺ 8pm-5am Thu-Sun) Frequented by a young, hip and hard-partying clientele, this neon-lit dance bar squeezes plenty of action into a small storefront.

Cinema Estelí (Parque Central; admission C$30) On the south side of the park, this quaint single-screener shows a semi-recent Hollywood hit nightly.

Shopping

Artesanía La Esquina (catedral, 1c N) Look for the wonderful local pottery and handcrafted wooden toys among the many offerings in this artisans' cooperative.

For custom-made cowboy boots (around US$80) and other leather goods check out the workshops to the south of Supermercado Las Segovias on Av 1a SO.

Getting There & Away

Near each other in the south of town on the Panamericana, Estelí's two bus terminals, **Cotran Norte** (☎ 2713-2529) and **Cotran Sur** (☎ 2713-6162) serve destinations to the north and south respectively.

Buses from Cotran Norte:

Jinotega (C$46; 3hr; 5 daily 7:30am-4pm)

León (C$60; 3hr; 3:10pm)

Ocotal (C$25; 2½hr; hourly 4am-5:30pm) For border crossing at Las Manos.

Somoto (C$25; 2hr; every 30min 5:30am-6pm) For border crossing at El Espino.

From Cotran Sur:

León (C$60; 3hr; 5:45am & 6:45am) Alternatively, take any southbound bus and change at San Isidro.

Managua (C$60; 2¼hr; 10 daily from 4:45am-3:20pm)

Matagalpa (C$25; 1¾hr; every 30min 5:20am-4:50pm)

RESERVA NATURAL MIRAFLOR

Enticing Miraflor, located some 30km northeast of Estelí, is a vast expanse of private land that is managed by the community and has been declared a nature reserve. It's

---

GETTING TO HONDURAS

Getting to Tegucigalpa

The most popular route into Honduras passes through **Ocotal**, a hardworking rural town at the base of Nicaragua's highest mountain range. While most travelers just come here to change buses, it is worth taking a taxi into town to check out the lovely botanical garden in the **Parque Central** and the faded facade of the baroque neo-classical **church**. Right by the park, **Llamarada del Bosque** (Parque Central; meals C$40-60) is an excellent buffet restaurant with a fresh courtyard. If you miss the last bus to the border, **Casa Lejos** (☎ 2732-0554; parque, 2c S, ½c O; r per person C$80) offers basic, clean lodgings in the center of town.

The bus terminal is on the Panamericana, 1km south of the park. Buses (C$10, one hour) leave every hour for the border crossing at **Las Manos**, from where it's 132km (2½ hours by bus) to Tegucigalpa. Las Manos is a major crossing, open 24 hours, although there's only bus service from 5am to 4:30pm.

Getting to Choluteca & Southern Honduras

The alternative route is through the town of Somoto to **Choluteca** (p432) via the border crossing at El Espino and the Honduran town of San Marcos de Colón. Going this way, you could reach the Salvadoran border in three hours (plus waiting time for connection). Buses for **El Espino** (C$10, 30 minutes) leave the Somoto terminal every hour from 4:15am to 5:15pm. The border is open from 8am to about 5pm daily.

See p431 and p433 for information on crossing the border from Honduras.

---

predominantly farmland, covering three climatic zones from dry to wet, stretching from 800m to 1450m.

Miraflor is a great place to get away from it all, immerse yourself in the lifestyle of traditional coffee-growing communities, and do some low-key walking, bird-watching or horseback riding. There are also several volunteer projects that you can get involved with. There is no central town; *fincas* are scattered widely across the area, and around several small community hubs.

As there's no tourist information available once you're there, it's highly advisable to visit the reserve office in Estelí before you head out. **UCA Miraflor** (see p471) promotes sustainable agriculture among the resident communities as well as managing the grassroots tourism framework in the area.

Sights & Activities

This isn't the place for epic hiking, but there are several interesting walks in the area, which appeal more for the chance to chat to local farmers than for the likelihood of spotting rare fauna, although birds are in great supply. There are also plenty of swimming holes and waterfalls (blessed relief from the sometimes intense heat). Locals sometimes charge a small fee for visiting their land.

Guides (US$15 per day for up to three people, US$5 per person for larger groups) can be arranged at UCA Miraflor in Estelí or at the homestays. They can take you around on foot or horseback (horses US$7 per person per day); be firm about what you want to see, whether it be birds, forest, coffee plantations or archaeological sights. You can read more about the area's attractions at www.miraflor.org

Sleeping & Eating

There are many accommodation options in Miraflor, most involve staying with local families. It is recommended to book with UCA Miraflor in advance (it'll give you a voucher), however many places also accept walk-ins. Accommodations are divided into two categories: homestays (US$15 per person including meals), which offer the chance for greater interaction with local residents, and *cabañas* (US$20 per person), which are more private. In many places conditions are very basic – be prepared for bucket showers and latrines. Camping is available throughout the reserve for US$2 per day.

Among the best places to stay are the rustic cabins and tree house at **Posada la Soñada** (Cebollal), the colorful and comfortable **Finca Fuente de Vida** (Cebollal), **Posada La Perla**

(La Perla) in the orchid belt and any of the authentic family accommodations in the friendly village of Sontule.

Getting There & Away

There are bus services from Estelí's Cotran Norte to various parts of the reserve (around C$20 for all destinations). Buses to El Coyolito (one hour), in the lower southwestern zone, and La Pita leave from the Pulperia Miraflor in the northern outskirts of Estelí. Swing by the UCA Miraflor office in Estelí to find out the best bus for your destination.

RESERVA NATURAL CERRO TISEY-ESTANZUELA

Smaller and less populated than Miraflor but every bit as beautiful, the Reserva Natural Cerro Tisey-Estanzuela offers phenomenal vistas, hidden caves and refreshing waterfalls just a stone's throw from Estelí. While it is possible to visit Tisey on a day trip, it is worth taking the time to explore the area fully with an overnight stay.

Don't miss the magnificent **Mirador Segoviano**, a 360-degree lookout point that is a strong contender for the most spectacular view in the country. On a clear day you can make out Lago de Managua, around a dozen volcanoes and even the Gulf of Fonseca and El Salvador.

Nearby is perhaps Tisey's most endearing attraction, Alberto Gutiérrez's wonderful **Galería del Arte El Jalacate** (entry by donation). After being inspired by a dream, Don Alberto has spent the past four decades carving figures and landscapes from both ancient and modern times into a 40m cliff face. Despite being almost 70, the eccentric artist skips through his beautifully landscaped garden, shimmies along steep mountain paths and leaps up fruit trees as he explains the inspiration behind his work.

A further 2km down the road is the entrance to **La Garnacha**, one seriously switched-on mountain community. In addition to growing organic vegetables and coffee, residents of this tiny village also produce artisanal goat's cheese, make handicrafts and offer trips (US$5 per guide) to nearby attractions, including the tough trek to the bat-filled **Cuevas de Cerro Apaguaji**. Bring a torch and watch your step, local legend has it that the caves are inhabited by hobgoblins.

In the lower elevations of the reserve, only 5km from Estelí, lies the region's most refreshing attraction, **Salto Estanzuela** (admission US$0.75), an impressive 36m waterfall that feeds a superb swimming hole complete with pebble beach. On the weekend it gets packed with picnickers, but during the week you may well have the place to yourself. It is a 20-minute walk from the signed gate on the main road just before the community of Estanzuela.

Sleeping & Eating

Eco-Posada (☎ 2713-6213; r without bathroom US$4, cabins US$12) Located at the highest point on the mountain near the entrance to the Mirador Segoviano, this friendly lodge on a family-run organic farm offers basic rooms as well as more comfortable cabins with private bathrooms surrounded by lush gardens. Reasonably priced meals (C$40 to C$70) are also available.

La Garnacha Cabins (☎ 2713-7785; cabins US$15-40) Overlooking a small lake, these community-run cabins have hot water and can sleep two to 10 guests. Basic rooms (US$3) in local homes can also be organized from here.

The *comedor* in La Garnacha prepares excellent meals (C$60 to C$100) using local organic produce.

Getting There & Away

There are two buses a day serving Tisey from Estelí's Cotran Sur, at 6:30am and 1:30pm, passing by the entrance to Salto Estanzuela before continuing onto the Eco-Posada and the La Garnacha turnoff, from where it is a 2km walk to the community. Buses return from the La Garnacha turnoff at 8am and 4pm. It is possible to take a taxi to the entrance of Salto Estanzuela from Estelí for around C$100.

SOMOTO
pop 19,730

Somoto was once a sleepy highland town best known for its donkeys and *rosquillas* (baked corn biscuits). However, all this changed in 2003 when the **Cañon de Somoto** hit the news, a mere 75 million years after its formation. While locals had long known about the existence of the magnificent gorge, it took its 'discovery' by a couple of European scientists to elevate its status and thrust tiny Somoto into the spotlight

The canyon, within which lies the origin of the mighty Río Coco, has been declared a national monument and protected as part of the surrounding **Reserva Natural Tepesomoto-Pataste** (admission US$0.50). It is a spectacular spot, where the nascent river has carved a 3km-long gorge in the solid rock, leaving towering granite ridges that at times are less than 10m apart.

It is possible to hike up into the lower reaches of the canyon on your own, however taking a local guide (per person half/full day US$10/20) is highly recommended to fully experience the attractions of the area. The guides offer a number of different routes that take visitors along the top of the ridge before descending at the far end of the canyon and hiking, leaping and swimming your way back along the river. They can also arrange camping and accommodations in the local community for those serious about exploring the zone.

The main entrance to the park is 15km north of Somoto on the road to the Honduran border; either hop on any El Espino bus and ask to be let off at 'el cañon' (C$6) or take a taxi from town (C$50). You can also wait on the highway for a shared taxi (C$10 per person).

Somoto town is a quiet rural center with little to hold visitors, however the charming colonial church on the plaza is one of the nation's oldest, dating from 1671.

There are many places to stay in town, but it's tough to beat **Hotel Panamericano** (☎ 2722-2355; Parque Central; r per person with/without bathroom US$10/8), on the plaza. It has very basic cells with shared hot-water bathrooms or pretty decent en suite rooms with TV. Look at a few, as they are all different.

Somoto's bus station is located on the Panamericana, a short walk from the center of town. Buses depart hourly for the border at El Espino (C$8, 40 minutes) and Ocotal (C$16, one hour), and every 40 minutes for Estelí (C$22, two hours). Express buses for Managua (C$78, 3½ hours) leave at 5am, 6:15am, 7:30am, 2pm, 3:15pm and 3:45pm.

LEÓN & NORTHWESTERN NICARAGUA

The most volcanic region in Central America, northwestern Nicaragua is dominated by the Cordillera de los Maribios, a chain of 10 volcanoes, some active, paralleling the Pacific coast from the northwestern shores of Lago de Managua to the Gulf of Fonseca. These volcanoes rise out of hot, agriculturally rich lowlands, where maize, sugarcane, rice and cotton are grown. The region has also proved fertile ground for independent thought and radicalism over the centuries from the push for Central American independence to the Sandinista revolution.

LEÓN
pop 144,179

Long Nicaragua's capital and still principal totem of its artistic, religious, and revolutionary history, proud León is one of Nicaragua's two legendary colonial jewels. A faded romance pervades its eave-shaded streets, where, as the evening approaches, the city's sociable residents pull rocking chairs onto the sidewalk to chew the fat. León's favorite son is Rubén Darío, the famed national poet, who is buried here in the city's centerpiece, the noble 18th-century cathedral, the largest in Central America. Although León's charms are more subtle than its perennial rival Granada, its youthful energy, pumping nightlife and excellent accommodations options have made it the hot destination among independent travelers looking to get a full-flavored taste of Nicaraguan culture.

History

León was originally founded in 1524 by Francisco Hernández de Córdoba near the foot of Volcán Momotombo. After a series of natural disasters, the Spanish abandoned the site in 1610 to rebuild the city near the important indigenous settlement of Subtiava, where it remains.

León served as the nation's capital for most of the colonial period and also served as the ecclesiastical center for the entire region, resulting in an impressive legacy of many fine churches and colonial buildings. The Universidad Autónoma de Nicaragua (UNAN), Nicaragua's first university, was founded here in 1912.

Traditionally León has been the most politically progressive of Nicaraguan cities. During the revolution, virtually the entire town fought against Somoza. Dramatic murals around town serve as reminders of that period and the city remains a strong Sandinista heartland.

Orientation

Av Central and Calle Central Rubén Darío intersect at the northeast corner of Parque Central, forming northeast, northwest, southeast and southwest quadrants. Calles ascend numerically as they go north or south of Calle Central; avenidas ascend east or west of Av

Central. However, the Leonese rarely use this system when giving directions; instead, they prefer the old reliable '2½ blocks east of the Shell station.' The bus station is on the northeastern outskirts of town. The old indigenous town of Subtiava is a western suburb.

Information

Internet cafes are all over town. Most budget hotels have laundry service or a place to wash clothes.

BAC (esquina de los bancos) Visa/MasterCard ATM that dispenses US dollars and córdobas.

BanPro (Iglesia Recolección, ½c S) Another all-network ATM.

Clínica San José (☎ 2311-3319; frente Iglesia San José) Private clinic that offers outpatient and 24-hour emergency services.

Fevernov@ (contiguo Plaza Siglo Nuevo; per hr C$15) Next to the cinema; fast service.

Intur (☎ 2311-3682; Parque Rubén Darío, 1½c N) Busy staff can arrange hookups with local guides but are not really traveler focused.

Lavamatic (☎ 2315-2396; hospital, ½c O; ☼ 7am-9pm) Has self-service machines and will do pricey service washes (C$160 to C$230).

Llamadas Heladas (Parque Central, ½c N; ☼ 9am-9pm) Best international phone connections.

Oficina de Información Turística (☎ 2311-3528; catedral, ½c N; ☼ 8:30am-noon & 2-6pm Mon-Fri, 9am-5pm Sat & Sun) Run by enthusiastic university students, this office can book accommodations and arrange city tours.

Post office (Iglesia San Francisco, 3½ c N)

Sights

CHURCHES & PLAZAS

León's **cathedral** is the largest in Central America. Construction began in 1747 and went on for over 100 years. According to local legend, the city's leaders feared their original grandiose design for the structure would be turned down by Spanish imperial authorities, so they submitted a more modest but bogus set of plans.

The fairly sober facade – more triumph-of-the-will neoclassicism than fluttering cherubs – fronts a high-vaulted, light and unornamented interior. The tomb of Rubén Darío is on one side of the altar, guarded by a sorrowful lion.

Around the church, you'll find the Stations of the Cross by Antonio Sarría, considered masterpieces of colonial art, as well as El Cristo Negro de Pedrarias, brought here in 1528 and possibly the oldest catholic image in the Americas. Make sure to take the **roof-top**

tour (admission US$1; ☼ 8am-noon & 2-4pm Mon-Sat) for spectacular views over the city's terra-cotta tile rooftops to the surrounding volcanic peaks. You can also visit the basements to see the entrances to subterranean tunnels that once linked the cathedral with other major churches in the city.

Three blocks north of the cathedral, the 18th-century **Iglesia de La Recolección** (1a Av NE) has a magnificent yellow baroque facade, with carved vines wound around stone pillars, and symbols in bas-relief medallions depicting the Passion. The **Iglesia El Calvario** (Calle Central), another 18th-century building, stands at the east end of Calle Central. Its facade, between a pair of red-brick bell towers, displays biblical scenes; enter the building to admire its slender wood columns and ceiling decorated with harvest motifs. Other colonial churches worth visiting include **Iglesia La Merced** (1a Calle NE) and **Iglesia San Juan** (3a Av SE).

MUSEUMS & MONUMENTS

Rubén Darío is esteemed worldwide as one of Latin America's greatest poets. The house where he grew up, three blocks west of the plaza, is now the **Museo Rubén Darío** (Calle Central; admision free; ☼ 8am-noon & 2-5pm Tue-Sat, 8am-noon Sun), with a selection of his possessions and writings that succeeds in bringing the man to life.

Nearby, **Fundación Ortiz** (☎ 2277-2627; Iglesia San Francisco, ½c S; admission US$1; ☼ 10:30am-6:30pm Tue-Sat, 9am-5pm Sun) is an artistic treasure trove set in two attractive colonial buildings on opposite sides of the street. There's an impressive selection of European masters and a quite stunning assembly of Latin American art, including pre-Columbian ceramics and contemporary Nicaraguan painting. This is Nicaragua's finest art gallery by a huge margin.

Located inside La XXI, a former jail for political prisoners under the Somoza regime, the **Museo de Leyendas y Tradiciones** (frente ruinas San Sebastián; admission US$1; ☼ 8am-noon & 2-5pm Tue-Sat, 8am-noon Sun) is a curious mix of life-sized models of local folk heroes and murals detailing the hard-core torture methods the National Guard favored in these very cells. It is both great fun and disturbing.

Another worthwhile visit is to the moving **Galería de Héroes y Mártires** (Parque La Merced, 20m O; admission US$1; ☼ 8am-5pm Mon-Sat). Run by mothers of FSLN veterans and fallen heroes, the gallery has photos of over 300 young men and women from the León area who died fighting

NICARAGUA

the Somoza dictatorship and the US-backed Contras.

For great views over the city, climb the hill to the former National Guard stronghold of **El Fortín de Acososco** on the southern outskirts of town. The building is located in a somewhat sketchy area next to the municipal garbage dump so leave your valuables in the hotel and travel in a group.

EL BARRIO SUBTIAVA

About 1km west of the cathedral, in the neighborhood of Subtiava, lies the recently restored **Iglesia de San Juan Bautista de Subtiava**, the oldest intact church in the city. Built in the first decade of the 18th century, it features a typical arched timber roof upon which is affixed an

extraordinary sun icon, said to have been a device to attract the indigenous community to worship.

A short walk from here stands **El Tamarindón** (Iglesia Subtiava, 3c S, 2c O), the ancient tree from which the Spanish hung Subtiava *cacique* (chief) Adiáct in 1614. The tree has become a symbol of indigenous resistance and is marked by a simple plaque.

Courses

A number of hostels including Vía Vía, La Tortuga Booluda and Bigfoot Hostel can organize private Spanish tuition onsite for about US$6 per hour.

Casa de Cultura (☎ 2311-2116; Parque La Merced, 2c O) Decorated with elaborate murals, this relaxed cultural

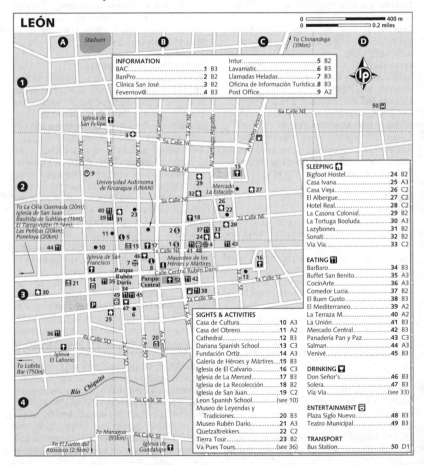

LEÓN

0   400 m
0   0.2 miles

To Chinandega (39km)

INFORMATION	
BAC	1 B3
BanPro	2 B2
Clínica San José	3 B2
Fevernov@	4 B3
Intur	5 B2
Lavamatic	6 B3
Llamadas Heladas	7 B3
Oficina de Información Turística	8 B3
Post Office	9 A2

SLEEPING	
Bigfoot Hostel	24 B2
Casa Ivana	25 A3
Casa Vieja	26 C2
El Albergue	27 C2
Hotel Real	28 C2
La Casona Colonial	29 B2
La Tortuga Booluda	30 A3
Lazybones	31 B2
Sonati	32 B2
Vía Vía	33 C2

EATING	
BarBaro	34 B3
Buffet San Benito	35 A3
CocinArte	36 A3
Comedor Lucía	37 B2
El Buen Gusto	38 B3
El Mediterraneo	39 A2
La Terraza M	40 A2
La Unión	41 B3
Mercado Central	42 B3
Panadería Pan y Paz	43 C3
Salman	44 A3
Venivé	45 B3

SIGHTS & ACTIVITIES	
Casa de Cultura	10 A3
Casa del Obrero	11 A2
Cathedral	12 B3
Dariana Spanish School	13 C3
Fundación Ortiz	14 A3
Galería de Héroes y Mártires	15 B3
Iglesia de El Calvario	16 C3
Iglesia de La Merced	17 B3
Iglesia de La Recolección	18 C2
Iglesia de San Juan	19 C2
Leon Spanish School	(see 10)
Museo de Leyendas y Tradiciones	20 B3
Museo Rubén Darío	21 A3
Quetzaltrekkers	22 C2
Tierra Tour	23 B2
Va Pues Tours	(see 36)

DRINKING	
Don Señor's	46 B3
Solera	47 B3
Vía Vía	(see 33)

ENTERTAINMENT	
Plaza Siglo Nuevo	48 B3
Teatro Municipal	49 B3

TRANSPORT	
Bus Station	50 D1

Stadium

Iglesia de San Felipe

Av Central

Av Santiago Argüello

Av Pedro Araúz

6a Calle NE

5a Calle NE

4a Calle NE

Universidad Autónoma de Nicaragua (UNAN)

3a Calle NE

Mercado La Estación

2a Calle NE

1a Calle NE

To La Olla Quemada (20m); Iglesia de San Juan Bautista de Subtiava (1km); El Tamarindón (1.5km); Las Peñitas (20km); Poneloya (20km)

Iglesia de San Francisco

Parque Rubén Darío

Parque Central

Mausoleo de los Héroes y Mártires

Calle Central Rubén Darío

2a Calle SE

To Lobito Bar (750m)

Iglesia El Laborio

4a Calle SO

Río Chiquito

5a Calle SE

To Managua (93km)

6a Calle SE

To El Fortín del Asososco (2.5km)

Iglesia de Guadalupe

center offers cheap art, dance, music and, for those tiring of machismo, kung fu classes.

Dariana Spanish School (☎ 2311-1235; www.dss-spanishschool.com; Iglesia El Calvario, ½c O; 20hr with/without homestay US$210/115) This locally run school gets consistently good reviews from travelers and includes free cultural activities and tours in its program.

León Spanish School (☎ 2311-2116; www.leonspanishschool.org; inside Casa de Cultura; 20hr with/without homestay US$224/140) Professional setup that can hook up students with volunteer opportunities.

Tours

Many thrill seekers make the trip to León for a single purpose – to 'surf' Cerro Negro, one of the most active volcanoes in the Americas. Volcano boarding involves hauling yourself up the hot black gravel slope (45 minutes) and then hurtling down at full speed standing on a 'sandboard' or sitting on a toboggan (about 45 seconds). Wipeouts, grazes and bruises are common, but it you are sufficiently deranged to want to try, Bigfoot Hostel, Va Pues Tours and Tierra Tours all offer the trip for around US$28 per person.

NicAsi (☎ 8414-1192; www.nicasitours.com) Specializes in historical and cultural tours. Popular options include cooking workshops (US$20) and the cowboy-for-a-day tour (US$45) where you can test your cattle herding and lasso skills on a local farm. There is no office but sign-up sheets can be found in most hostels.

Quetzaltrekkers (☎ 2311-6695; www.quetzaltrekkers.com; Iglesia Recolección, 1½c O) Fantastic nonprofit organization that offers fun multiday volcano hikes for US$25

to US$65, including public transport, meals and camping. Your fees are used to fund social projects in local communities. Volunteers are welcome.

Tierra Tour (☎ 2315-4278; www.tierratour.com; Iglesia Merced, 1½c N) Well-established operator that offers trips to León Viejo (US$35), the hot springs of San Jacinto (US$20) and the wetlands of Isla Juan Venado (US$50) among others.

Va Pues Tours (☎ 2315-4099; www.vapues.com; frente Iglesia Laborio) As well as volcano hikes and trips to Isla Juan Venado, this professionally run outfit in CocinArte restaurant offers interesting cultural tours around León including a journey through indigenous Subtiava lands with a community elder (US$25).

Festivals & Events

León is famous for its fiestas:

La Gritería Chiquita (August 14) Dates back to 1947 when an erupting Cerro Negro threatened to bury the city in ash only to stop suddenly when a local priest vowed to initiate a preliminary *gritería* (shouting), similar to December's Día de la Purísima but changing the response to ¡La asunción de María! ('The ascension of Mary!').

Día de la Virgen de Merced (September 24) León's saint's day, solemnly observed with religious processions through the streets of the city. The preceding day is more festive: revelers don a bull-shaped armature lined with fireworks, called the *toro encohetado*, then charge at panic-stricken onlookers as the rockets fly.

Día de la Purísima Concepción (December 7) A warm-up for the Día de la Concepción de María (December 8), celebrated throughout Nicaragua. It is the occasion for the *gritería*, in which groups wander around calling on any house that displays an altar and shouting, ¿Quién causa tanta alegría? ('Who causes so much joy?') to receive the response, ¡La concepción de María! ('The conception of Mary!'). The household then offers the callers traditional treats such as honey-dipped plantain slices and seasonal fruits.

Sleeping

Casa Vieja (☎ 2311-4235; Iglesia Recolección, 1c E, ½c N; dm/r without bathroom US$3.50/9) More than a little run down, Casa Vieja offers the cheapest beds in town in a great central location. While the rooms downstairs are dark and musty, if you are lucky enough to nab the room at the top you will enjoy phenomenal views over the tiled rooftops right from your saggy mattress.

El Albergue (☎ 8894-1787; hostalelalbergue@yahoo.es; Petronic, ½c O; dm/d without bathroom US$4/14; ☐) A relaxed hostel offering a tranquil, no-frills atmosphere. The spacious rooms have comfy mattresses; the dorms are less appealing, with narrow beds and foam pads. There's use of a simple kitchen, a bar, free bikes and plenty of rocking chairs to chill out. Discounts offered to volunteers.

Vía Vía (☎ 2311-6142; Iglesia Recolección, 1c E, ½c S; dm/r US$5/15) The original León backpacker spot and still one of the best deals in town. Built around a lush tropical garden, the rooms are elegantly finished and have great bathrooms while the dormitories are spacious and comfortable (no bunk beds). There is an atmospheric bar up front which attracts a good mix of locals and tourists.

Sonati (☎ 2311-4251; www.sonati.org; Iglesia Recolección 1c N, ½c E; dm/s/d US$5/11/20; 🖳 🛜) Brand new at the time of research and already very popular, Sonati has clean and comfortable rooms set around a pleasant garden, a guest kitchen and an extremely laid-back vibe. Guests and non-guests alike can refill their large water bottles here for just C$2. Profits from the hostel fund local environmental education programs.

our pick La Tortuga Booluda (☎ 2311-4653; www.tortugabooluda.com; catedral, 4½c O; dm US$6, s/d from US$17/24; 🖳 🛜) Quiet yet sociable and boasting value-adding extras such as a free pancake breakfast, a top-notch kitchen, organic coffee and the best book exchange in town, the 'Lazy Turtle' immediately feels like a home away from home. Rooms are simple but stylish, the dorms are spacious and there is a chilled lounge area.

Bigfoot Hostel (☎ 8917-8832; Iglesia Recolección, 1c E, ½c S; www.bigfootnicaragua.com; dm/r without bathroom US$6/13; 🛜 🖳) This popular place right opposite Vía Vía has a young, party-orientated backpacker vibe. The dorms are dark and susceptible to noise from the common areas while the shared bathrooms could be better. On the plus side, there is a solid guest kitchen and great *mojitos* at the bar. Don't expect to fit more than one (big) foot at a time in the so-called swimming pool.

Casa Ivana (☎ 2311-4423; Teatro Municipal, 20m O; s/d US$7/8) Centrally located in a typical Leonese home, the rooms here are neat, simple and good value, however the owners can be a little prickly.

Lazybones (☎ 2311-3472; www.lazybonesleon.com; Parque Rubén Darío, 2½c N; dm US$8, r with/without bathroom US$28/19; 🖳 🛜 🖳) This quiet backpacker palace is a real treat on the eyes, set around a lengthy courtyard with murals and hammocks. The dorms are clean and comfortable and the rooms are generally appealing, but what sets Lazybones apart is the lovely pool area out the back – a real bonus in a city this hot.

La Casona Colonial (☎ 2311-3178; Parque San Juan, ½c O; s/d US$20/30; 🗙) The dark, fan-cooled rooms at this family-run hotel have noble old furnishings, including beds you have to clamber up on to. There are also gardens, books, soft chairs, sympathetic management, and total peace and quiet.

Hotel Real (☎ 2311-2606; hotel.real@gmail.com; Iglesia Recolección, 1½c E; s/d incl breakfast US$35/45; 🔀 🛜 🖳) If the big, comfortable air-con rooms at this professionally run place have you tempted, then the amazing sunsets from the rooftop terrace are likely to seal the deal.

Eating

Hit the makeshift stands that set up outside Colegio La Salle in the evening for León's favorite fast food, chicken tacos with cabbage and cream. Other cheap plates can be found at the excellent pair of *fritangas* that set up behind the cathedral of a night. Self-caterers can find great fresh fruit and veggies at the **mercado central**, while León's main supermarkets, **La Unión** (1a Calle NE) and **Salman** (1a Calle NO), are six blocks apart.

Panadería Pan y Paz (frente Amocsa; pastries C$12-30; ⏰ 7am-5pm Mon-Sat) This small French bakery has the best bread in town as well as real croissants and great sandwiches.

our pick La Terraza M (Parque Rubén Darío, 2½c N; breakfast C$50, dishes C$80-120) Set in a shady garden, this relaxed cafe is a great place to escape from the heat and enjoy a light and fresh meal. In addition to healthy breakfasts, there are also quality sandwiches and more substantial plates on offer.

CocinArte (frente Iglesia Laborio; mains C$80-130; 🅥) In a city that has never quite outgrown its not-eating-veg stage, CocinArte is a real gem. There are delicious vegetarian versions of typical Nicaraguan dishes as well as international plates such as falafel and chana masala.

BarBaro (Parque Rubén Darío, 1c S; mains C$85-145) This popular new bar-restaurant boasts the most extensive menu in town, full of international favorites like satay chicken and Caesar salads. The drinks list is equally varied with a great selection of cocktails.

Venivé (Catedral, 2c O; tapas C$25-40, mains C$110-170) A classy bar/restaurant, Venivé offers a full menu but is famed for its delicious tapas. Try the rich paté or delicious *albóndigas* (meatballs).

Lobito Bar (Iglesia Subtiava, 2c S, 4½c E; mains C$115-130) A Subtiava institution, Lobito Bar serves tasty barbecued meats and the best ribs in town in a pleasant open dining area. Bring a healthy appetite as the portions are huge.

El Mediterraneo (Parque Rubén Darío, 2½c N; dishes C$120-200) León's most romantic dining experience, El Mediterraneo has a graceful yet relaxed ambience, chilled music and well-prepared pastas, seafood, meats and curries. It also has a decent wine list and great pizzas.

As a student town, León has a number of cheap and filling steam table buffets. Get in early as the best stuff goes quick.

Buffet San Benito (frente Iglesia San Francisco) The cheapest sit-down meal in town.

El Buen Gusto (catedral, ½c E) Another seriously cheap option.

Comedor Lucía (Iglesia Recolección, 1c E, ½c S; 🕑 7am-3pm Mon-Sat) Slightly more expensive, but a step up in quality.

Drinking

With scores of bars and numerous discos there is always a party somewhere in León. Vía Vía is an easygoing destination for a drink except on Friday nights when its free concerts draw a boisterous crowd.

La Olla Quemada (Parque Rubén Darío, 4c O) A cracking bohemian bar with live music, salsa nights and independent films that pulls in crowds of travelers and locals alike.

Solera (frente Teatro Municipal) Popular with a more mellow crowd, this sociable sit-down bar is a great place to share a bottle of rum and chat into the early hours. There is live music a couple of times a week.

Don Señor's (frente Parque La Merced; disco cover C$30) This place is more than just a hot nightspot – it's three. There's a disco upstairs, a relaxed bar with tables overlooking the street downstairs and a restaurant-pub called El Alamo around the corner.

Entertainment

Teatro Municipal (2a Av SO) The impressively preserved Teatro Municipal is León's premier venue for music, dance and theater, and most touring ensembles perform here. Check the notice board for upcoming events.

Plaza Siglo Nuevo (1a Calle NE; tickets C$60) León's cinema shows mostly big-budget American films.

Getting There & Around

León's chaotic **bus station** (☎ 2311-3909; 6a Calle NE) is 1km northeast of the center. You can take a microbus to Managua (C$40, 1¼ hours) or Chinandega (C$25, 45 minutes). These depart continuously from the left side of the main platform, as they fill up. Regular buses:

Chinandega, via Chichigalpa (C$20; 1½hr; every 15min 4:30am-6pm)

Estelí (C$60; 3hr; 5:20am, 12:45pm, 2:15pm & 3:15pm) Alternatively, take bus to San Isidro (departures every 30 minutes) and change there.

Managua (Mercado Bóer) expresos (C$35; 1½hr; every 30min); ordinarios (C$30; 2¼hr; every 20min 5am-6:30pm)

Matagalpa (C$60; 2½hr; 4:20am, 7:30am & 2:45pm) Alternatively take bus to San Isidro (departures every 30 minutes) and change there.

Local buses and pickup trucks (C$4) leave from the Mercado Central for Subtiava, the bus terminal and the Managua highway. Taxis around town are C$15 per person, more at night.

AROUND LEÓN
Poneloya & Las Peñitas Beaches

Long, inviting beaches lie just 20km west of León. **Poneloya** and its southern extension, **Las Peñitas**, are separated by a rock formation that offers a fine vantage point. Swimming is good – safest at the southern end of Las Peñitas – but be very wary of the currents, which have claimed many lives over the years. When the swell picks up, surfers can take their pick from a number of decent waves. Crowds descend here on weekends and holidays, but during the week these darkish sand beaches are practically deserted, apart from the glorious coasting pelicans. You can easily visit as a day trip from León, but the relaxed atmosphere will likely entice you to stay.

GETTING TO CHOLUTECA, HONDURAS

The **Guasaule** border, 60km northeast of Chinandega, is the principal road crossing between Nicaragua and southern Honduras. It's open 24 hours, but buses only run 6am to 6pm. It is a hot and thoroughly unpleasant place with plenty of touts hanging around, but if you are coming from León, it is by far the most direct route. After obtaining your Nicaraguan exit stamp, it is about 1km to the Honduran immigration facility. Pedicabs make the trip for around C$20.

There are buses from **Chinandega** to the border (C$30, 1¾ hours, half-hourly). On the Honduran side, buses run regularly to **Choluteca** and express minibuses dash across southern Honduras to El Amatillo on the border with El Salvador.

See p431 for information on crossing the border from Honduras.

Coco Surf School (☎ 8958-7443; www.cocosurfschool. com; Las Peñitas) offers lessons, board rental and repairs from a small hut right on the sand.

SLEEPING & EATING

The best accommodations lie along Las Peñitas beach. Perched above a rocky outcrop and one of Las Peñitas' best breaks, **Playa Roca** (☎ 8428-8903; www.playaroca.com; dm US$6, r with/ without bathroom US$35/20) is a scenic spot with a vibrant atmosphere. The rooms are nothing special, and there are no beach views, but they are reasonable value considering the prime location. The bar is popular with day trippers.

A couple of hundred meters further south, **Oasis** (☎ 8839-5344; www.oasislaspenitas.com; dm/s/d cabins US$6/12/15/20) is a favorite among backpackers and surfers with a lazy vibe and top-value beachfront accommodations. The two beachside cabins are spitting distance from the breakers. It also rents surfboards (US$8 per day) and body boards (US$5 per day).

Barca de Oro (☎ 2317-8109; www.barcadeoro.com; dm/s/d US$6/15/20) is at the end of the road. It's on the estuary rather than the ocean, but it's a great place with a lovely garden and clean, attractive rooms. There are also kayaks and well-priced meals at its outdoor restaurant.

For outstanding food, visit local landmark **Hotel Suyapa Beach** (dishes C$130-240). The large beachside restaurant gets packed with wealthy day trippers from Managua, but the delicious meals are worth the wait. Give the musty rooms a miss.

Poneloya, 2km north, has a couple of places to crash. Possibly the most rickety place you will ever stay, **Hotel Lacayo** (☎ 8946-0418; s/d US$5/10) has been standing for almost a century but looks highly unlikely to see out the next big storm. Still, it is cheap, full of character and right on the beach. The currents are very dangerous just here.

Across the road, away from the beach, is **Hotel La Posada** (☎ 2317-0378; r US$25; ⊠), where the rooms are significantly better, although no bargain. For inexpensive seafood and cheap *comida corriente*, head to the thatched-roof shacks by the water's edge at **La Bocanita** (snacks C$40-80, meals C$60-200), about 1km further north.

GETTING THERE & AWAY

Buses leave hourly from El Mercadito in Subtiava, one block north and one block west of Iglesia de San Juan Bautista. They stop first in Poneloya, then head down to Las Peñitas (C$15, 45 minutes). Day trippers take note: the last bus returns at 6:40pm. A taxi from León should cost around US$12.

Reserva Natural Isla Juan Venado

This reserve, south of Las Peñitas, is a long, narrow barrier island extending 22km to Salinas Grandes. The island encloses a network of mangrove-lined estuaries, forming an ecosystem that sustains a variety of migratory birds, reptiles and amphibians, as well as vast squadrons of mosquitoes. It is a nesting area for olive ridley and leatherback turtles between July and January. Hotels in Las Peñitas organize tours, but you can arrange them yourself at the visitors center, where rangers

---

EXPLORE MORE AROUND LEÓN

The area around León is fertile ground for exploration.

- In the heart of the volcano corridor, **San Jacinto** is base camp for assaults on three volcanoes: Telica, Rota and Santa Clara. Nearby, **Los Hervideros de San Jacinto** are a network of hot springs and boiling mud pools. Local kids will show you around for a few córdobas. To get there take any Estelí- or San Isidro–bound bus and exit at San Jacinto – about 25km from León.

- Up the main highway from León, you reach **Chichigalpa**, home of the Flor de Caña rum distillery. The facility is not usually open to the public, but if you get a group together, it is possible to arrange a tour through the **Commission of Culture** (☎ 2343-2456; alchichi@ibw.com. ni) at the *alcaldía* (mayor's office).

- Around 35km south of León lies the turnoff to Nicaragua's most recognizable landmark, the near-perfect cone of **Volcán Momotombo**. It is a hot, arduous full-day hike to the summit and visitors must first get a permit from the offices of the **Ormat Momotombo Power Company** (Map p455; ☎ 2270-5622; Centre Finarca, Carretera Masaya) in Managua. It is far more convenient to go with a tour from León (p479).

DIY: COSIGÜINA PENINSULA

With charming fishing villages nestled on lovely beaches, vibrant wetlands and fantastic surfing, the Cosigüina Peninsula can't stay undiscovered for long, but right now it's sublime, a natural playground free of crowds and gated communities where you can have the beach to yourself during the day and immerse yourself in village life in the evening.

On the southernmost part of the peninsula, **Playa Asseradores** is a long stretch of prime beach with an excellent beach break called 'Boom Wavos.'

Heading north, you will come to the turnoff to **Jiquilillo**, a pretty fishing village on a rocky point at the end of a long gray-sand beach. The sea here is calm and ideal for swimming and there are a couple of great budget accommodation options in the village.

A couple of kilometers north, the community of Padre Ramos is located inside the boundaries of the **Reserva Natural Estero Padre Ramos**, one of the most important wetlands in Central America. Olive ridley and other sea turtles nest here from July to December. Swing by the ranger's office for information on boat tours with local guides or you can hire a dugout canoe and explore the reserve on your own. Cheap accommodations and meals are available in the community as well as in Venecia, a short boat ride across the inlet.

Dominating the skyline at the end of the peninsula is **Volcán Cosigüina**, once Central America's tallest volcano. A massive eruption in 1835 obliterated its peak and these days it takes about three hours to climb what is left of the mountain for spectacular views over the Golfo de Fonseca to Honduras and El Salvador. Trails begin at the ranger station in the community of El Rosario or from the small town of Potosí.

Buses to all destinations on the peninsula depart from the chaotic Mercadito in Chinandega. From Potosí, collective boats leave occasionally for the islands of the Golfo de Fonseca and La Union in El Salvador – get an exit stamp from *migración* in Potosí.

---

will put you in touch with local guides who can show you the island by boat for US$40 to US$60 per group.

León Viejo

At the foot of Volcán Momotombo are the remains of the original colonial provincial capital, **León Viejo** (admission US$2, photography US$2; ⏰ 8am-5pm). Founded in 1524, Old León was abandoned less than a century later after being hit by a series of earthquakes. The settlement was subsequently completely buried under layers of ash from Momotombo.

It was not until 1967 that its location was finally discovered on the shore of Lago de Managua. Excavations have revealed a large plaza, a cathedral, church, and monastery, as well as private dwellings.

The headless remains of Francisco Hernández de Córdoba, founder of both León and Granada, were found buried alongside those of the jealous first governor, Pedrarias Dávila, who had him beheaded. The skeleton of the bishop Antonio de Valdivieso, assassinated in 1550 for his defense of indigenous rights, has also been identified here.

While the ruins and discoveries are archaeologically fascinating, many visitors are disappointed. All that remains of most buildings is a foundation wall about 0.3m high. The highlight, though, is the fabulous volcano view from what was once the city's fortress.

You can take a tour here from León, but it is easy to visit by yourself. Regular buses run from León to La Paz Centro (C$18, 45 minutes) meeting buses to Puerto Momotombo (C$10), less than 1km from the site.

GRANADA & THE MASAYA REGION

This geographically rich area boasts a number of Nicaragua's most vaunted attractions, including the spellbinding colonial town of Granada and the handicraft center of Masaya. The area is also rich in biodiversity. Wildlife abounds on the flanks of Volcán Mombacho, and Parque Nacional Volcán Masaya is one of the country's most visibly active craters. Lush tropical forest surrounds the banks of the crystalline Laguna de Apoyo, and Las Isletas on Lago de Nicaragua make for another fine swim setting.

Just west of Granada, the Pueblos Blancos (White Villages) stand amid a highland coffee-growing region rich in pre-Columbian traditions. These charming towns are an excellent place to observe some of Nicaragua's most beautiful craftwork in the making.

GRANADA
pop 107,000

The goose that laid Nicaraguan tourism's golden egg is beguiling Granada, whose restored colonial glories render it a high point of many travelers' time in Central America. The carved colonial portals, elegant churches, and fine plaza, as well as its location on Lago de Nicaragua, have enchanted visitors since the city was founded in 1524.

With the sun-dappled colors of its adobe buildings making the streets an absolute joy to stroll, and Nicaragua's best selection of places to stay and eat, Granada is the sort of place where you can while away a lot of time, and its proximity to sprinkled islets on Lago de Nicaragua and to two major volcanoes only increases your options.

Tourism is having a significant impact here, both positive and negative. Expats buying up colonial homes are driving prices out of reach of locals, who are forced further out, leaving the picturesque center a little lifeless. Try to be conscious of spreading your money around here, patronizing local- and not just foreign-owned businesses.

History

Nicknamed 'the Great Sultan' in reference to its Moorish namesake across the Atlantic, Granada is Nicaragua's oldest colonial city. Founded in 1524 by Francisco Hernández de Córdoba, it stands at the foot of Volcán Mombacho on the northwestern shore of Lago de Nicaragua. With access to the Caribbean Sea via the lake and the Río San Juan, Granada soon became a rich and important trade center and remained so into the 19th century. This same Caribbean passage made Granada an easy target for English and French buccaneers, who sacked the city three times between its founding and 1685.

Conservative Granada was ever-locked in bitter rivalry with liberal León, which erupted into full-blown civil war in the 1850s. To gain the upper hand, the Leonese contracted filibuster William Walker (see boxed text, p445), who conquered Granada

and ruled from here. Fleeing in 1856, he had the city torched, leaving only the infamous placard, 'Here was Granada.' In more recent times, an expensive restoration program has given a new glow to its bright colonial charms.

Orientation

The cathedral and plaza Parque Central in front of it form the center of the city, built on a grid pattern. The neoclassical market, built in 1890, is three blocks to the south.

Calle La Calzada, one of Granada's prettiest and most touristy streets, runs eastward from the plaza for 1km to the city dock, where boats leave for Ometepe and San Carlos. South of the dock, a lakefront park area extends 2km toward a small port from where day cruises depart to the Las Isletas.

Information

INTERNET ACCESS

There are internet places all over town. Most charge C$15 to C$20 per hour.

Kablenet (Parque Central, 1½c O) One of the best, with a fast connection, air-con and cheap international calls.

LAUNDRY

Several of the sleeping options will do your laundry; there are also numerous drop-off services around town.

La Lavandería (☎ 2552-0018; Parque Central, 2c E; washer/dryer C$60 per cycle; ☺ 8am-6pm) Has plenty of self-service machines as well as a wash-dry-fold service for C$10 per pound.

MONEY

BAC (Calle Atravesada) Has a number of all-card-friendly ATMs.

POST

Post office (Convento San Francisco, ½c O)

TELEPHONE

Llamadas Heladas (Parque Central; ☺ 9am-9pm) For local and international calls

TOURIST INFORMATION

Intur (☎ 2552-6858; Calle Arsenal, frente Iglesia San Francisco) Up-to-date transport information, a passable city map and heaps of flyers.

UCA (Union of Agricultural Co-operatives; ☎ 2552-0238; www.ucatierrayagua.org; Shell Palmira, 75m O; ☺ 8am-2pm Mon, Wed & Fri) Organizes community-based tours to rural villages.

GRANADA

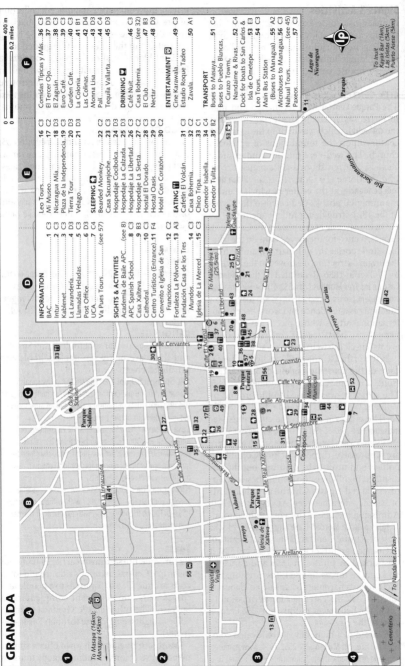

Sights & Activities

Granada has some excellent attractions, but perhaps its greatest joy is to be found in simply strolling around, admiring the restored colonial buildings lining its streets. It's a photographers' paradise, particularly at dawn and dusk.

CITY CENTER

The **Parque Central** with its mango and malinche trees is a pleasant shady spot, bossed by the **cathedral**, which was built in the early 20th century upon the foundations of an earlier church. The well-kept interior contains four chapels; a dozen stained-glass panels are set into the dome. To its north is the **Plaza de la Independencia**, at the center of which stands a monumental obelisk dedicated to the heroes of the 1821 struggle for independence.

On the east side of this plaza is the Casa de los Leones, named for the carved lions on the fabulous stone portal, the only part remaining from the original structure, destroyed in the blaze set by Walker in 1856. Renovated by the **Fundación Casa de los Tres Mundos** (☎ 2552-4176; www.c3mundos.org; Casa de los Leones; admission US$2; ☼ 8am-6pm), it now functions as a residence and workspace for international artists whose pieces are presented here. It also hosts regular concerts and other events; check the website for details.

Just northeast, the striking light-blue facade of the **Convento e Iglesia de San Francisco** fronts a complex that was initiated in 1585. The structure was burned to the ground by William Walker in 1856 and rebuilt in 1867–68. These days it houses the city's must-see **museum** (☎ 2552-5535; Calle Cervantes; admission US$2; ☼ 8:30am-5:30pm Mon-Fri, 9am-4pm Sat & Sun). There are impressive displays of pre-Columbian pottery and primitivist painting, but the undisputed highlight is the sombre basalt sculptures carved by the Chorotega inhabitants of Isla Zapatera between AD 800 and 1200. Admission includes a bilingual guided tour.

Iglesia de La Merced (Calle Xalteva), four blocks west of Parque Central, is the most beautiful of Granada's churches. Completed in 1539, it was sacked by pirates in 1655 and damaged by Leonese forces in 1854, then restored in 1862. It has a baroque facade and an elaborate interior. Ask the caretaker for permission to climb the bell tower (admission US$1) for a view of the city.

Housed in a meticulously renovated colonial home, **Mi Museo** (☎ 2552-7614; www.mimuseo.org; Calle Atravesada, frente Bancentro; ☼ 8am-5pm) is a private museum with a magnificent collection of pre-Columbian ceramics dating back to 2000 BC. There is almost no labeling going on, so take up the offer of a free guided tour.

Eight blocks west of the plaza, **Fortaleza La Pólvora** (☼ 8am-5pm), a military garrison built in 1749, was used by Somoza forces to interrogate and execute opponents. The view over the tiled rooftops to Lago de Nicaragua is exceptional.

LAGO DE NICARAGUA

On the lake, the **Centro Turístico** (admission US$0.25) is a 2km stretch of restaurants, picnic areas and playgrounds, all shaded by mango trees. Though people do swim here, the water is polluted. Boats depart for day trips to Las Isletas from restaurants at the southern end of the beach, or from the Puerto Asese dock (see p489).

Courses

DANCE

Academia de Baile APC (☎ 2552-4203; Parque Central; group/private classes per hr US$5/7) Group and individual instruction in *bachata*, salsa and merengue. Ask for Martin in the APC Spanish School.

LANGUAGE

Granada is a popular spot for learning Spanish and there are many reputable schools and private teachers.

APC Spanish School (☎ 2552-4203; www.spanishgranada.com; Parque Central; 20hr with/without homestay US$195/100) Offers one-on-one classes in an atmospheric old mansion right on the park.

Casa Xalteva (☎ 2552-2436; www.casaxalteva.org; Iglesia Xalteva, 30m N; 20hr with/without homestay US$240/150) Energetic not-for-profit setup that funds nutrition and education programs for local children. Also organizes volunteer placements.

Nicaragua Mía (☎ 8966-5385; www.nicaraguamiaspanish.com; alcadía, 3½c E; 20hr with/without homestay US$190/100) A friendly option with experienced teachers and many cultural activities.

Tours

Picturesque horse-drawn carriages hang out in Parque Central; an hour's ride around town costs around US$20 for up to five people and comes with some eloquent commentary in Spanish. The other classic Granada tour involves a sightseeing cruise through Las Isletas (p489).

Most tour operators in town offer a similar menu of excursions including canopy tours on

Volcán Mombacho (around US$35 per person), kayaking in Las Isletas (US$25 to US$35), night trips to Volcán Masaya (US$25 to US$30) and tours of Granada itself (US$20 to US$25).

Operators include the following:

Leo Tours (☎ 8829-4372; Parque Central, 1½c E) Enthusiastic locally owned business that offers all the usual options as well as some interesting visits to local communities.

Tierra Tour (☎ 2552-8723; www.tierratour.com; catedral, 2c E) Recommended operator offering a wide a range of well-organized tours.

Va Pues Tours (☎ 2552-8291; www.vapues.com; Parque Central) Friendly setup with trips to destinations as far afield as the Río San Juan.

Velago (☎ 8459-4699; www.sailinglakenicaragua.com; catedral, 3½c E) Offers sailing classes and trips on the lake in small sailboats.

Festivals & Events

International Poetry Festival (February; www.festival poesianicaragua.com) Local and international poets take over the town for this event that also includes concerts by some of Nicaragua's best musicians.

Fiestas de Agosto (third week of August) Granada celebrates the Assumption of Mary, with fireworks, concerts, rodeos and horse parades by the lakefront.

Sleeping

Granada has a huge choice of inviting accommodations, although it's not so cheap.

Bearded Monkey (☎ 2552-4028; www.the-bearded -monkey.com; bomberos, ½c S; dm US$6, s/d without bathroom US$11/15; 🖳 🛜) Busy and perennially popular, this is the center of Granada's backpacker social scene. Set around a pleasant garden, which functions as a cafe-bar, the hostel offers OK dorms and plenty of facilities – free internet, nightly films and tours, but no kitchen. If it is full, crash on a hammock (US$4), but you won't get much privacy.

Hospedaje La Libertad (☎ 2552-4087; www.la-libertad. net; bomberos, ½c S; dm US$6, r with/without bathroom US$20/15; 🖳 🛜) In a recently renovated colonial building, this comfortable hostel has large dormitories surrounding a grassed courtyard and a kitchen for guest use.

Hospedaje La Calzada (☎ 2552-7486; Parque Central, 3½c E; s/d without bathroom US$8/10, s/d with bathroom US$10/12) While the small, simple rooms have thin mattresses are nothing special, this friendly place has a guest kitchen, a top location and prices that are hard to beat.

Hostal Oasis (☎ 2552-8006; www.nicaraguahostel.com; mercado, ½c O; dm US$8, r with/without bathroom US$28/19; 🏊 🖳 🎱) This popular hostel has top-notch

facilities, with a petite but pretty swimming pool, free internet access and a free phone call home (unless you're Danish) each day. The airy dorms are pretty good value, but the private rooms are small and cramped.

Hospedaje La Siesta (☎ 2552-3292; www.lasiesta granada.com; bomberos, 1c N, 20m E; s/d without bathroom US$12/20, s/d with bathroom US$15/25; 🛜) Tucked away in a quiet residential area, this laid-back family-run place is the perfect base for those looking to keep their distance from the hectic La Calzada tourist scene. The rooms are spotless, there is a fully equipped guest kitchen and the attentive owners can recommend plenty of activities with a local flavor.

Hospedaje Cocibolca (☎ 2552-7223; www.hospedaje cocibolca.com; Parque Central, 3c E; s/d US$15/18; 🖳 🛜) This long-time traveler favorite has clean and well-maintained rooms with fans and basic private bathrooms – go for an upstairs room for breezes and gazing over the rooftops. Guests can use the kitchen and there is a decent lobby area, but what really seals the deal is the killer location in the middle of the bar and restaurant zone.

Hostal El Dorado (☎ 2552-6932; www.hostaldorado. com; Parque Central, 1½c O; s/d US$17/28; 🖳 🛜) Located in a busy shopping area, this solid choice has a variety of comfortable rooms and a peaceful garden and common area. The hostel supports a number of social projects including the onsite workshop where you can buy quality handmade hammocks or even learn to make your own.

our pick **Casa Sacuanjoche** (☎ 2552-6151; www. casasacuanjoche.com; alcaldía, 1c E, 1½c S; r with/without bathroom US$25/20; 🛜) This choice setup above a centrally located family home has modern, spacious rooms that let in plenty of light and a breezy open kitchen/dining area overlooking the rooftops. There are free international phone calls to many destinations and the amiable owners are a great source of information.

Hotel Con Corazón (☎ 2552-8852; www.hotel concorazon.com; Iglesia San Francisco, 2c N; s/d US$55/67; 🔲 🛜 🎱) All profits from this well-run hotel fund local development projects, but you don't need an excuse to stay here. The comfortable rooms are modern and stylish, there is a sunny pool area and the service is courteous and professional.

Eating

Stop by the Parque Central for icy fruit juices and *vigorón* (yucca steamed and topped with *chicharrón* – fried pork rind – and cabbage salad; C$35), a Granada specialty. *Fritangas* set up on sidewalks around town and in the park in the early evening. For self-caterers, there are a couple of grocery stores. **Palí** (Calle Atravesada, frente mercado; ☼ 8am-8pm), by the market, is the cheapest; while **La Colonia** (Parque Sandino, 4c O; ☼ 8am-9pm), on the road to Managua, has the best selection.

Euro Café (Parque Central; snacks C$25-80) At one corner of Parque Central, this popular cafe has really excellent coffee, an airy patio, salads, hummus, and a sizable collection of books for sale (they'll buy yours if they are decent).

Comedor Tulita (bomberos, 20m O, 10m N; lunch incl fresco C$40) Locals flock to this unsigned lunch spot hidden down an alleyway for cheap plates of honest Nica grub. The cheerful staff serve up three or four mains and the usual sides – get there early as your choices will rapidly diminish.

ourpick Garden Cafe (Parque Central, 1c E; light meals C$50-90; ☜) Lacking vitamins? Head to this tranquil spot for wonderfully fresh salads and gourmet sandwiches as well as delicious smoothies and juices. There is also excellent coffee and a full breakfast menu.

Comidas Típicas y Más (catedral, 1c E; dishes C$50-90) An antidote to Granada's surplus of international restaurants, this laid-back establishment offers a complete introduction to Nicaraguan cooking with a wide variety of local plates cooked just as they should be.

Chico Tripa (Monisa, 3c N; meals C$70) Part *fritanga*, part karaoke bar, the outrageously named 'Guts Boy' is where ordinary *granadinos* head when they want to celebrate. The barbecue is one of the city's best, as evidenced by the long line of locals waiting for take-out, but the real reason to come is for the first-class people-watching in the mural-covered dining room.

Casa Bohemia (bomberos, 20m E; dishes C$80-100; ☼ dinner; **V**) In a charming colonial house this laid-back cafe serves up some of the tastiest plates in town, including several vegetarian options. Grab a table in the atmospheric courtyard.

El Tercer Ojo (☎ 2552-6541; Calle Arsenal, frente Iglesia San Francisco; dishes C$100-240; **V**) Relax in comfort at this popular new-agey hangout by the San Francisco church. With an eclectic range of cuisine including flavorful curries, great salads and many vegetarian choices, there's something for everyone. Try the sublime beef carpaccio.

Las Colinas (Shell Palmira, 1c S, 1km E; mains C$170-250) This legendary local spot is a no-frills kind of place with a packed dirt floor and unpretentious fittings. There is ample menu of tasty barbecued meats, but most come for its

delicious fried *guapote*, drawn straight from the lake, and stick around well after the plates are cleared to down a bottle or two of rum. It's easiest reached by taxi.

Other worthwhile eat spots include the following:

Cafetín El Volcán (Iglesia La Merced, 1c S; quesillos C$12-24) For the best quesillos in town.

Comedor Isabella (mercado, ½c O; lunch C$55) Economic lunch buffet with plenty of choice near the market.

Tequila Vallarta (Parque Central, 1½c E; mains C$65-185) The portions are generous and the sauces spicy at this authentic Mexican bar/restaurant.

Monna Lisa (Parque Central, 3c E; pizzas C$120-160) Pretty much the best of the pizza options.

Drinking

A popular way to start the night is at one of the bars along Calle La Calzada. If you are after a bit more intimacy, Casa Bohemia (p488) is a great place for a relaxed drink or to shoot some pool. By the lake, there are some *discotecas*, packed with young locals at weekends, and a couple of dancing ranches, frequented by an older crowd. They are fun but volatile, and you should definitely get a cab down here at night.

Nectar (Parque Central, 1½c E) One of the most atmospheric offerings on the main strip, this cozy bar has a full cocktail list, comfortable low seating and a delicious selection of snacks and light meals.

Café Nuit (Parque Central, 2½c O; admission C$20; ☼ Wed-Sun) Featuring live music nightly, Café Nuit is set back from the street in a lush outdoor courtyard, with round tables beneath the palms. It is frequented by a mellow crowd of Nicas and foreigners who take their dancing seriously – practice your moves in advance if you want to impress.

El Club (Parque Central, 3c O; ☼ 10am-midnight, until 2am Fri & Sat) Contemporary but comfortable, this popular drinking spot has a modish front bar and an appealing courtyard where smart food is served. The place really takes off on Friday and Saturday nights, when decent DJs take over and plenty of tequila is guzzled.

Inuit Kayak Bar (entrada Centro Turístico, 1km S; 🕐 24hr Fri & Sat) You know it's been a big night if you end up here. This late-night beachfront lounge inside the Centro Turístico doesn't get kicking till everywhere else starts winding down and is frequented by a very mixed crowd – it seems the only criteria for entry is being blind drunk.

Entertainment

Estadio Roque Tadeo Zavala (Calle La Inmaculada; tickets C$10-50) Watch Granada's Tiburones and Oriental baseball teams take on their rivals from around the country.

Cine Karawala (Calle Atravesada; tickets C$40) Shows semirecent films on weekends.

Getting There & Away

BOAT

Boats leave from the **dock** (🕾 ticket office 2552-2966) at the east end of Calle La Calzada at 2pm on Monday and Thursday for Altagracia on Isla de Ometepe (lower/upper deck C$40/90, three hours) and San Carlos at the southern end of Lago de Nicaragua (C$80/190, 14 hours). Seats fill up fast, so get there early or bring a hammock to string up outside unless you want to sleep on the cold metal floor. There is also a less crowded tourist-class service (lower/upper deck C$250/400) that makes the run to San Carlos in 10 hours, leaving at 7pm on Fridays.

BUS

Microbuses to Managua (C$20, one hour, every 15 minutes 5am to 7:30pm) depart half a block south of the park from 5am to 7pm, arriving at the UCA terminal. Buses depart from the main bus station on the west side of town and go to the generally less convenient Mercado Roberto Huembes (C$15, 1½ hours, every 20 minutes 5am to 7pm).

Either mode of transportation will also stop on the highway at the entrance to Masaya; buses for Masaya itself (C$10, 30 minutes) leave from a point two blocks west of the market.

From one block south of the market, buses depart for the following destinations:

Carazo towns & Pueblos Blancos (C$8-15; 45min; every 30min until 6pm)

Nandaime (C$9; 45min; every 30min)

Rivas (C$24; 1½hr; 8 daily until 3:10pm) Take the 1:30pm bus to catch the last boat to Ometepe.

TAXI & TRANSFERS

Taxis to other destinations are relatively cheap if you bargain a little. Sample fares include Masaya (US$12), Managua (US$25) and San Jorge (for Ometepe; US$30).

Paxeos (🕾 2552-8291; www.paxeos.com; Parque Central) runs an air-con minibus shuttle service to and from Managua airport. It costs US$18 per person; if you are two or more, you can beat this price in a taxi.

Getting Around

Both **Leo Tours** (🕾 8829-4372; Parque Central, 1½c E) and nearby **Nahual Tours** (🕾 8988-2461; www.nahaul tours.com; Parque Central, 1½c E) rent bikes (per hour/ half-day/day US$1/5/7) as do various hotels around town.

A taxi ride anywhere in central Granada costs C$10 per person; expect to pay double at night.

AROUND GRANADA

Las Isletas & Isla Zapatera

Just offshore from Granada, Las Isletas are a group of some 350 diminutive islands formed 10,000 years ago by an erupting Volcán Mombacho. Divided by narrow channels, they are memorably scenic and easily reached by motorboat. Many are inhabited (by traditional fishing families and now by Nicaragua's superwealthy), and some have hotels and restaurants. There's a proliferation of birdlife throughout, with egrets, herons and cranes particularly numerous around sunrise and sunset.

Among the highlights is the **Castillo de San Pablo**, a small fort built in 1784 to guard against British incursions which affords great views of both Granada and Mombacho, and **Isla de Monos** (Monkey Island) whose cheeky residents have been known to jump into boats that pass too close.

Most tour companies run daily trips to the islets, or you can arrange it yourself at the southern end of the Centro Turístico in Granada, or from Puerto Asese, 2km further south. A covered boat holding up to 12 people costs about US$15 per hour. You can arrange to be dropped off on an island and picked up later. At **Puerto Asese** itself, there are a couple of restaurants by the harbor from which you can watch birds flitting among lilies or gaze at distant volcanic peaks. Also here, **Nicaragua Dulce** (🕾 2552-6351; www.nicaraguadulce.com; Marina Cocibolca) rents kayaks and small boats with ecofriendly electric motors for those that want to explore the area on their own.

Beyond Las Isletas is the much larger **Isla Zapatera**, centerpiece of the national park of the same name. Two hours away by motorboat from Granada, this island is one of Nicaragua's most important archaeological areas, though the giant pre-Columbian stone statues have been moved to museums. Tombs and rock carvings remain on adjacent Isla El Muerto. The local community runs a basic **lodge** (☎ 2462-2363; www.sonzapote.org; dm incl all meals US$20) and a restaurant. You can camp on the island for US$3 per person. Public boats (US$8) leave from Puerto Asese on Tuesday, Friday and Sunday.

Reserva Natural Volcán Mombacho

Mombacho's jagged peaks – the highest is 1345m – stand guard over Granada. The slopes of the volcano form an island of biodiversity; vegetation and wildlife vary with altitude, and above 800m the volcano becomes a cloud forest where ferns, mosses and bromeliads cling to the trees. Still higher, the landscape transforms to dwarf forest. The moisture-rich environment of the lower slopes is perfect for the cultivation of coffee.

The last recorded major activity was in 1570, when a massive tremor caused the wall of Mombacho's crater to collapse, draining the lagoon it held and washing away an indigenous village of 400 inhabitants. The volcano is still active as evidenced by the fumaroles that push out hot air and smoke.

The reserve is managed by **Fundación Cocibolca** (☎ 2248-8234; www.mombacho.org; admission with/without transport US$12.50/2.50; ☒ 8am-5pm), which maintains trails and runs an 'eco-mobile' (old army trucks with rows of seats in the back) to the biological research station at 1100m. The ride up the steep, narrow access road is an adventure in itself. From the station, where there's also a cafe, a 1.5km self-guided trail traverses the cloud forest. Much tougher and much more interesting is the 4km, four-hour Sendero El Puma, which climbs sharply and runs along the edge of the crater for a while. A guide (US$15 per group) is mandatory for this walk.

For US$40 per person (prebooking essential), you can stay at the research station, sleeping in a clean, communal dorm. The price includes dinner, breakfast, transport and a spooky guided night walk where you'll spot crawlies galore. The money helps maintain the reserve, and it's a highly recommended experience.

From Granada, any Nandaime-bound bus (C$6) can drop you at the turnoff to the reserve, from where you can walk or take a mototaxi (C$10) 1.5km to the reception area. Time your arrival with an 'eco-mobile' departure (8:30am, 10am, 1pm and 3pm). Service is greatly reduced from Monday to Wednesday, when there is just one departure at 10:30am. Otherwise, many Granada tour operators run day trips to the reserve for around US$35 per person.

Canopy Tours Miravalle (tour per person US$30), between the highway and the official reserve entrance, offers a zip-line adventure, involving 16 platforms over the 1700m course.

Laguna de Apoyo

Set in a picturesque valley brimming with wildlife, the lovely Apoyo crater lake is another one of Nicaragua's many natural wonders. Dry tropical rainforest along the surrounding slopes contains much biodiversity, including howler monkeys and many species of bats. But the real attraction is the pristine waters of the lagoon, a massive, mineral-infused pool that is without doubt the best swim in the country.

Set back on the wooded banks of the lake, the nonprofit **Estación Ecológica** (☎ 8882-3992; www.gaianicaragua.org; dm US$10, s/d without bathroom US$16/21; ☎) offers intensive Spanish courses (US$220 for a 20-hour week, including bed and board). Lodging for nonstudents is available in the basic but comfortable rooms adjoining the school. The kitchen (which you can use) prepares tasty set meals. Kayaks can be rented, and PADI-approved divers can join expeditions to research the lake's endemic fishes.

There's an increasing number of other places to stay and eat. The **Monkey Hut** (☎ 8887-3546; monkeyhutlaguna@gmail.com; dm/s/d US$12/22/28; [P]) is a lovely house overlooking the lake. Entrance for the day costs US$6 (waived for overnight guests), and includes use of kayaks, inner tubes, assorted sporting equipment and the kitchen. The onsite pizzeria serves up decent pies (C$150 to C$200) and meals (C$95 to C$200) can be ordered from a nearby *pulpería*. Shuttles depart every morning from Hospedaje La Libertad (p487) in Granada.

Hospedaje Crater's Edge (☎ 8895-3202; www.craters-edge.com; dm US$16, r US$28-40; [P] [☒] [☎]) has a variety of well-maintained rooms and a secure dorm looking out over the lake, where you'll find kayaks, tubes and a bar. All prices include an all-you-can-eat buffet breakfast while other meals (C$80 to C$160) are also available. There is a daily minibus from the affiliated Hostal Oasis (p487) in Granada and day-visit packages including entrance, lunch and transport cost US$17.

The lake is most easily accessed by public transport from Masaya. Every half-hour, buses run to the crater rim (C$8, 25 minutes), but only three (6:30am, 11:30am, 4:30pm) descend the further 2km to the lake. If you find yourself at the rim, it is possible to hitchhike to the bottom, but walking is not recommended as robberies are common along this road. Alternatively, take a taxi from Granada (US$15) or Masaya (US$10) direct to your destination.

Pueblos Blancos

This charming mountainous region a short distance from both Masaya and Granada has a refreshing climate and is dotted with pretty villages famed for their skilled craftsmen and colorful traditions. Named after the pale white stucco homes that once dominated the area, the Pueblos Blancos (White Towns) are extremely compact, with villages practically growing into one another, which makes them easy to visit on a stress-free day trip.

The gorgeous village of **Catarina** is known for its **mirador** (admission US$1), which offers sweeping views of Laguna de Apoyo, Lago de Nicaragua and the city of Granada. The area around the main entrance has a throng of restaurants and souvenir shops and can be a little frenetic, but once you get past it, the views are well worth it. If you really want to get away from the crowds, you can rent a horse (C$120 per hour) for the steep decent to the *laguna*, at least a two-hour round trip.

Nearby, sleepy **San Juan de Oriente** may be home to less than 3000 people, but it is the most important centre of artisanal pottery in Nicaragua. As well as creating inexpensive functional pieces for everyday use, the community also produces more elaborate decorative pieces. There are workshops all over town where you can watch the artists at work or stop by the Centro de Artesania Nabotiva, a cooperative market.

Rarely visited by tourists, the friendly village of **Diria** is the gateway to the Mirador el Boquete, an alternate lookout over Laguna de Apoyo. While perhaps slightly less spectacular than Catarina, the view here is still phenomenal and the ambience is much more chilled. There are a couple of low-key bar-restaurants

and a path leading down to the water used mainly by local fitness freaks.

Buses to these villages (C$8 to C$10, 30 minutes, every 20 minutes until 5pm) leave regularly from one block south of the market in Granada.

Carazo Towns

Southwest of the Pueblos Blancos, in Carazo department, **San Marcos** and the 'twin cities' of **Jinotepe** and **Diriamba** are set in a citrus- and coffee-cultivation area. The three towns celebrate a distinctive religious and folklore ritual known as 'Toro Guaco,' in which the Nicarao town of Jinotepe and Diriamba, its Chorotega rival before the European conquest, commemorate their relationship. Jinotepe's patron is Santiago (St James), whose day is July 25; Diriamba's is San Sebastián (January 20). These two towns, along with San Marcos, carry out ceremonial visits to each other, livened up with striking costumes and masks displayed in dances, mock battles and plays satirizing their Spanish invaders. The pantomime figure of 'El Güegüense' is a symbol of Nicaraguan identity.

Buses to Diriamba, Jinotepe and San Marcos depart from one block south of the market in Granada (US$0.75, 45 minutes, every hour until 6pm). There are extremely frequent departures from Masaya and Managua as well.

MASAYA
Pop 93,053

This appealing working-class city between Managua and Granada is famous across the country as being Nicaragua's epicenter of *artesanías* and is a great place to buy gifts and souvenirs. The fabulous products crafted in characterful workshops around town and in surrounding villages are united with handicrafts from all over the country in the memorable central market.

Many visit Masaya on day trips, dropping in to attend to their gift list and take a picture at its impressive lake. But Masaya is much more than a shopping layover, it is the cradle of a rich folklore born from the city's powerful indigenous roots and home to some of the most interesting and colorful festivals in the country.

Orientation & Information

Masaya is just 29km southeast of Managua, with Granada another 16km down the road. The city sits at the edge of the Masaya crater lake, beyond which rises Volcán Masaya.

NICARAGUA

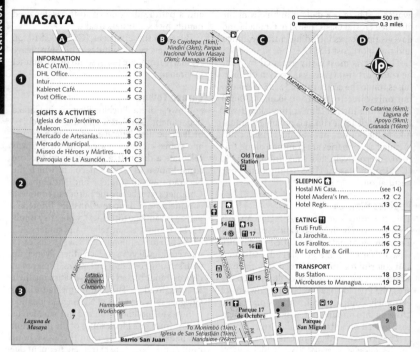

MASAYA

INFORMATION
BAC (ATM).................................**1** C3
DHL Office.................................**2** C3
Intur...**3** C3
Kablenet Café............................**4** C2
Post Office..................................**5** C3

SIGHTS & ACTIVITIES
Iglesia de San Jerónimo..............**6** C2
Malecon.....................................**7** A3
Mercado de Artesanías................**8** C3
Mercado Municipal......................**9** D3
Museo de Héroes y Mártires......**10** C3
Parroquia de La Asunción..........**11** C3

SLEEPING
Hostal Mi Casa...................(see 14)
Hotel Madera's Inn................**12** C2
Hotel Regis.........................**13** C2

EATING
Fruti Fruti..............................**14** C2
La Jarochita...........................**15** C3
Los Farolitos.........................**16** C3
Mr Lorch Bar & Grill...............**17** C2

TRANSPORT
Bus Station...........................**18** D3
Microbuses a Managua............**19** D3

To Coyotepe (1km);
Nindirí (3km); Parque
Nacional Volcán Masaya
(7km); Managua (29km)

Managua-Granada Hwy

To Catarina (6km);
Laguna de
Apoyo (9km);
Granada (16km)

Old Train Station

Estadio
Roberto
Clemente

Hammock
Workshops

Laguna de
Masaya

Barrio San Juan

To Monimbó (1km);
Iglesia de San Sebastián (1km);
Nandaime (26km)

Parque 17
de Octubre

Parque
San Miguel

BAC (Mercado Artesanías, 1c N) Has an all-card ATM.
DHL office (Mercado Artesanías) When you realize you've bought more than you can carry.
Intur (☎ 2522-7615; masaya@intur.gob.ni; Mercado Artesanías, ½c S) Has a city map and can point you to local crafts workshops.
Kablenet Café (Iglesia San Jerónimo, 1c E, 1c S; C$15 per hr) Reliable internet access.
Post office (BAC, ½c E)

Sights
MARKETS & WORKSHOPS

Masaya's famous *artesanías* can be found in many places around town. The most concentrated area is in the original market, the fabulous **Mercado de Artesanías** (Mercado Viejo), restored to its former glory after destruction in the revolution. It's quite a sight, girt by an ornate carved basalt wall punctured with numerous carved portals and complete with turrets. Here you will find a variety of stalls selling excellent-quality cotton hammocks, colorful basketry and woven mats, wood carvings, marimbas, carved and painted gourds, paintings, ceramics, jewelry and leatherwork. It's touristy, but competition keeps prices fair.

Many vendors speak English, and they're not at all pushy. Thursday nights feature live music here.

Much more local in character, the **Mercado Municipal** (Mercado Nuevo), 500m east of the old market, also has some *artesanías* for sale, as well as *comedores* and standard market goods. The market has a particularly large selection of leather sandals and tacky stuffed reptiles.

A number of modules selling *artesanías* from around the region have been built along the **malecón**, a romantic walkway that offers fabulous views over Laguna de Masaya towards the smoking Santiago crater. Nearby is **Barrio San Juan**, famous for its hammocks and *tapices* (woven straw canvases portraying rural scenes); it's fun to stroll around the workshops here. Even more interesting is the indigenous suburb of **Monimbó** which is centered around the Iglesia de San Sebastián, about 1km south of the main plaza. Here local *artesanos* will invite you into their homes to show you how the shoes, saddles, baskets, wood carvings and other crafts are made. Ask at Intur about the locations of the best workshops.

CHURCHES & PLAZAS

Many of Masaya's historic churches suffered significant damage in the earthquake of July 2000. Worst hit was the city's symbolic **Iglesia de San Jerónimo**, on the northern side of town between two plazas, though it has since been patched up and continues to serve as the centre of the city's Fiestas Patronales. On the main plaza, the early-19th-century **Parroquia de La Asunción**, has been restored to its former glory through a Spanish-funded program that makes use of the skills of local artisans.

COYOTEPE

The eerie **fortress** (admission US$1; 9am-6pm) of Coyotepe, built in 1893, stands on a hill north of town overlooking the Managua–Granada highway. It was here that Benjamín Zeledón, the 1912 hero of resistance to US intervention, made his last stand. During the Somoza dictatorship it was used as a prison for political prisoners. It is worth the climb just for the panoramic view of the region but make sure to ask for a tour of the subterranean cells, included in the admission, during which your guide will explain in detail the brutal hospitality of the Guardia Nacional. From Masaya, get a taxi (C$20) or any Managua-bound bus (C$5) to the bottom of the hill, from where it's a 1km hike to the top. If you pay extra, the taxi will to take you all the way up.

MUSEO DE HÉROES Y MÁRTIRES

This fascinating **museum** (2552-2977; Parque Central, 1½c N; 8am-5pm Mon-Fri) honors the local residents who lost their lives during the revolution and includes some interesting displays on the masks and homemade weapons used by the city's youth in the fight against the heavily armored Guardia Nacional.

Festivals & Events

The **Día de San Jerónimo** (September 30) is so popular it now encompasses nearly three months of partying. The main procession days fall on September 30 and October 7, when the patron saint, in the form of a bearded *campesino* called 'Tata Chombó' (also known as the 'Doctor of the Poor'), is carried around town on a flowery platform.

Other big festivals include the **Día de San Lázaro**, a week before Palm Sunday, which includes a procession of costumed dogs, and **Noche de Agüizotes** (last Friday in October) when the creepy characters from local horror stories come to life and parade through the street.

Sleeping

Hotel Regis (2522-2300; Av Zelaya; r per person US$4.50) Three and a half blocks north of the main plaza, likable Hotel Regis offers tidy rooms with fan alongside a pleasant courtyard, at the end of which are several spick-and-span bathrooms. Party animals beware the 10pm curfew.

Hostal Mi Casa (2522-2500; Av Zelaya; s/d without bathroom US$5/10, d with bathroom US$20) At the back of Fruti Fruti juice bar, this budget option offers great wood-paneled rooms with shared bathrooms and less appealing concrete ones with private bathroom and cable TV.

Hotel Madera's Inn (2522-5825; maderasinn@yahoo.com; Av Zelaya; d US$15-25, with air-con US$45;) This congenial, family-run hotel makes a colorful, homey base. There's a range of rooms – ask to see a few as some are far better value than others – and several pleasant areas for lounging.

Eating

The cheapest places to eat are in the Mercado Municipal, where you will find no-frills *comedors* as well as *baho* (plantain and beef stew), *vigorón* and hearty soups. In a small kiosk on the eastern side of the park, an excellent *marisquería* (seafood house) sells delicious *ceviche*.

our pick **Fruti Fruti** (Av Zelaya; smoothies C$40-50) Right among the budget accommodations is this refreshing option that serves rather excellent smoothies to beat the heat.

Los Farolitos (Av El Progreso; meals C$50-90) Value is the key word at this well-run bistro that offers flavorful meals in an intimate dining area.

La Jarochita (Av Zelaya; dishes C$65-180) A block north of the main plaza, La Jarochita prepares good Mexican fare such as tacos and *enchiladas*. It's a colorful, characterful place; grab yourself a table on the small terrace if you can.

Mr Lorch Bar & Grill (2522-7628; Av Zelaya; dishes C$100-160) Hard-core carnivores will love this friendly bar-restaurant where the steaks are juicy and there is barely a vegetable in sight.

Drinking & Entertainment

A short drive from the bustling nightlife of Managua and Granada, Masaya struggles to hold onto its own revelers, let alone attract them from outside. However, there are a number of cheerful low-key bars dotted around the park and on the weekends the *discoteca* action hots up at the *malecón* where the party continues late into the night.

Getting There & Away

Buses arrive and depart from the eastern side of the Mercado Municipal Ernesto Fernández. There are departures for Managua (C$10, 45 minutes, every 20 minutes from 4:30am to 5pm) and Granada (C$10, 40 minutes, every 25 minutes from 5am to 6pm). Microbuses to Managua (C$13.50, 30 minutes, 5am to 8pm) leave when full from the terminal in front of Parque San Miguel, one block east of the Mercado Viejo. From the highway, there are frequent microbuses and buses to both Managua and Granada. A taxi to Granada should cost around US$12.

PARQUE NACIONAL VOLCÁN MASAYA

Described by the Spaniards as the gates of hell, the craters that comprise Volcán Masaya National Park are the most easily accessible active volcanoes in the country. The park consists of a pair of volcanoes, Masaya and Nindirí, which together comprise five craters. Of these, Cráter Santiago is still quite active, often smoking and steaming and, in 2001, giving some visitors a very close shave with a light shower of superheated rocks.

The summit of Volcán Masaya (632m), the easternmost volcano, offers you a wonderful view of the surrounding countryside, including the Laguna de Masaya and the town of Masaya beyond. The park has several marked hiking trails, many of which require a guide (C$50 to C$150 per group). These include the lava tunnels of Tzinancanostoc and El Comalito, a small steam-emitting volcanic cone.

Book one day in advance for the highly recommended **night tour** (US$10 per visitor; ☻ 5-7:30pm), during which it is possible to see glowing lava deep in the crater if there is not too much smoke. In addition, you will watch thousands of *chocoyeros* (parakeets) return to their nests in the crater walls in the late afternoon and visit the lava tunnels just as the bats are heading out for their evening meals.

The **park entrance** (☎ 2522-5415; admission US$4; ☻ 9am-4:45pm) is just 6km from Masaya on the Managua highway. You can get there on any Managua-bound bus from either Masaya or Granada. The staff at the entrance will furnish you with a map; 1.5km from the entrance is the visitors center, museum, butterfly garden and camping area (C$50 per person). From

---

A FIERY PAST

According to legend, pre-Hispanic inhabitants of the area would throw young women into the boiling lava at the bottom of the crater to appease Chaciutique, the goddess of fire.

The cross overlooking Cráter Santiago is a replica of the one placed there in the 16th century by the Spanish, who hoped to exorcise the demons who dwelled within.

---

there it's 5km up to the **Plaza de Oviedo**, the main observation point for the Santiago crater.

There's no public transportation inside the reserve, but you may be able to hitch a ride; otherwise consider a round-trip taxi from Masaya (US$10) or Granada (US$18) including an hour's wait at the top. Most tour operators in Granada also make the trip.

SOUTHWESTERN NICARAGUA

Continuing south toward the Costa Rican border, the largest settlement is Rivas, from whose lake port, San Jorge, ferries head to Isla de Ometepe. Further down the Carretera Panamericana at La Virgen is the turnoff for San Juan del Sur, a popular beach town and the jumping-off point for a string of Pacific beaches as well as a major turtle-nesting zone.

This isthmus of land, only 20km wide at one point, is all that separates Lago de Nicaragua, and hence the Caribbean, from the Pacific.

RIVAS
pop 30,415

Within a stone's throw of Nicaragua's best Pacific beaches and the enchanting Isla de Ometepe, the quiet departmental capital of Rivas is never going to hold visitors' attention for long. While it possesses a number of charming colonial buildings, genuine change-your-itinerary attractions are thin on the ground and facilities for tourists are limited at best. As a result, most visitors don't venture much past the bus station and very few spend the night.

Ometepe only has a Visa/Plus ATM, so grab your cash here if that doesn't do it for you. There are oodles of cybercafes charging around C$15 per hour.

Information

BAC (Parque Central, 3c O) Has an all-card ATM.
Intur (☎ 2563-4914; rivas@intur.gob.ni; Texaco, ½c O)

Sights

Investigate the **church** on the Parque Central for its curious artworks, among which is a fresco in the cupola showing a battle at sea, with communism, Protestantism and secularism as burning hulks, and Catholicism as a victorious ship entering the harbor. Also worth visiting is the enthusiastically run **Museo de Antropología** (mercado, 1c S, 1c E; admission US$1; ◷ Mon-Sat), set in a fabulous historic mansion. Best on show is the collection of pre-Columbian ceramics and stonework found in the Rivas province.

Sleeping & Eating

Hospedaje Internacional (☎ 2563-3652; Carretera Panamericana; r with/without bathroom US$15/8) There are several cheap, basic guesthouses lining the Panamericana near the Texaco station. This is about the best of them, with accommodating staff and a variety of fan-cooled rooms – those with bathroom and TV are significantly better.

Hospedaje Lidia (☎ 2563-3477; r per person with/without bathroom US$10/8) Opposite Intur, this amiable, family-run operation offers the nicest budget lodging in town, with well-scrubbed rooms and a good attitude.

Soda Rayuela (Parque Central, 1c N, 1c E; dishes C$40-100) A step up in quality from most of the typical eating choices in town, this place has excellent local food as well as some Mexican-influenced dishes.

Vila's Rosti Pizza (Parque Central; mains C$100-200) Serves up decent steaks and burgers as well

as great people-watching from the street-side tables right on the park.

Getting There & Around

Rivas' **bus terminal** is adjacent to the market, about 10 blocks west of the Panamericana. For express services to Managua, head to the Esso station on the Panamericana on the north side of town. You can travel between the two locations by taxi or by cycle cab (C$10).

Intercity buses from Rivas include the following:

Granada (C$24; 1½hr; every 45min)
Managua (C$40; 3½hr; every 30min 3:30am-6:15pm)
San Juan del Sur (C$15; 45min; every 30min 6am-6pm)
Sapoá/Peñas Blancas (Costa Rica) (C$15; 45min; every 30min 5am-5:15pm)

If you are heading to San Juan del Sur, it is often more convenient to take a shared taxi (C$35 per person), which leave when full from the parking area of the terminal.

For San Jorge and the Ometepe ferry, there's no need to go into Rivas; shared taxis (C$10) cover the short run from the Shell station on the Panamericana.

From Rivas, there are also a couple of early morning buses north to Las Salinas, a bumpy two-hour ride (C$35). The reward: the great surfing at nearby Playa Popoyo.

SAN JORGE

This relaxed spot, 6km east of Rivas, is where most travelers head to cross over to Isla de Ometepe. The center of town is 1km from the ferry dock, where you'll find plenty of places to eat seafood with magnificent views across the lake to Ometepe, and several places to stay.

GETTING TO LIBERIA, COSTA RICA

If you are traveling in an international bus, the border between Nicaragua and Costa Rica at **Peñas Blancas** will be a piece of cake as the transport companies take care of most of the details. For everyone else, however, it can be a little hectic.

The border posts, open from 6am to 8pm daily, are a 1km walk or C$20 pedicab ride apart. On top of the normal US$2 fee for leaving Nicaragua, the municipality of Sapoá charges an additional US$1 to enter or exit the border zone.

Entering Costa Rica is free; you technically have to show an onward ticket but this is rarely enforced. If it is, you'll have to buy a San José–Managua bus ticket from one of the bus companies outside.

Express buses (C$65, three hours) for the border leave Mercado Roberto Huembes in Managua almost hourly.

From Rivas, buses (C$15, 45 minutes) make the short run to the border every half-hour. On the Costa Rican side, regular coach services connect the border with Liberia and San Jose. See p583 for information on crossing the border from Costa Rica.

See p504 for details of the boat crossing to Ometepe.

SAN JUAN DEL SUR
pop 7961

Set on a horseshoe-shaped bay framed by picturesque cliffs, San Juan del Sur is Nicaragua's main beach resort, and tourism has long replaced fishing as the town's raison d'être. The charms it offers to a burgeoning population of expats and backpackers are easy to identify: surfing, fishing and simply *being* – watching the Pacific sunset from a hammock, rum in hand is a great stress antidote. It's a fun place; travelers looking for a lively party scene or some mellow tanning-time will love it here, but if you're looking for culture or local ambience, you may find the place vacuous and gringofied.

Information

There are slowish internet places on every block (around C$15 per hour); most offer cheap international calls. Several laundry spots can be found in town charging around C$80 per load. Useful websites include www.sanjuandelsur guide.com and www.sanjuansurf.com.

BAC All-card-friendly ATM located in the Hotel Casa Blanca on the beachside strip.

El Gato Negro (www.elgatonegronica.com; Texaco, 2c O; ☼ 7am-3pm) This cafe and bookshop has an excellent selection of English-language books for sale. It's not a book exchange, although the boss might buy books from you if they're interesting and in good condition.

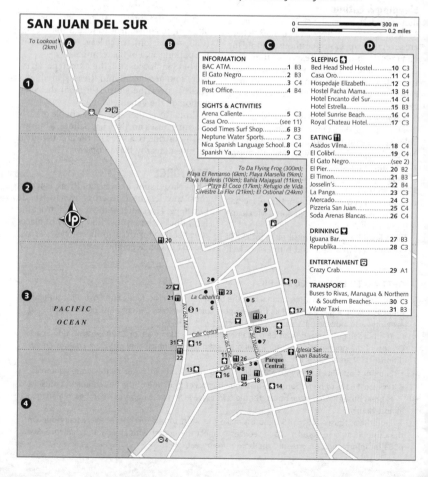

SAN JUAN DEL SUR

0 ——— 300 m
0 ——— 0.2 miles

INFORMATION
BAC ATM.............................1 B3
El Gato Negro.......................2 B3
Intur....................................3 C4
Post Office...........................4 B4

SIGHTS & ACTIVITIES
Arena Caliente......................5 C3
Casa Oro.........................(see 11)
Good Times Surf Shop............6 B3
Neptune Water Sports............7 C3
Nica Spanish Language School..8 C4
Spanish Ya............................9 C2

SLEEPING
Bed Head Shed Hostel...........10 C3
Casa Oro.............................11 C4
Hospedaje Elizabeth.............12 C3
Hostel Pacha Mama..............13 B4
Hotel Encanto del Sur...........14 C4
Hotel Estrella......................15 B3
Hotel Sunrise Beach.............16 C4
Royal Chateau Hotel............17 C3

EATING
Asados Vilma.......................18 C4
El Colibri............................19 C4
El Gato Negro..................(see 2)
El Pier................................20 B2
El Timon.............................21 B3
Josselin's............................22 B4
La Panga............................23 C3
Mercado.............................24 C3
Pizzeria San Juan.................25 C4
Soda Arenas Blancas............26 C4

DRINKING
Iguana Bar..........................27 B3
Republika............................28 C3

ENTERTAINMENT
Crazy Crab..........................29 A1

TRANSPORT
Buses to Rivas, Managua & Northern
& Southern Beaches.........30 C3
Water Taxi..........................31 B3

To Lookout (2km)

To Da Flying Frog (300m);
Playa El Remanso (6km); Playa Marsella (9km);
Playa Maderas (10km); Bahía Majagual (11km);
Playa El Coco (17km); Refugio de Vida
Silvestre La Flor (21km); El Ostional (24km)

PACIFIC OCEAN

La Cabañita

Calle Central

Av del Mar

Parque Central

Iglesia San Juan Bautista

Intur (☎ 2568-2022; frente Parque Central) Perhaps the most friendly branch in the country but a bit light on practical information.

Post office At the southern end of the beachfront drive.

Dangers & Annoyances

At the time of research, armed robberies targeting tourists had once again become an issue on the beaches surrounding the town, particularly around Remanso, Tamarindo and Hermosa. Ask around town for the latest before setting off, always travel in groups and leave your valuables in the hotel.

Sights & Activities

Apart from the attractive church on the plaza, the main sight here is the **beach**, a wide and attractive stretch of sand whose southern end is the fishing port. Even better beaches, though, are to be found nearby (p498).

There are numerous operators offering everything from deep-sea fishing to zip-line tours; this is just a selection of what's available:

Arena Caliente (☎ 8815-3247; www.arenacaliente.com; mercado, ½c N) A one-stop shop for all your surfing needs. This popular, locally run outfit offers board rental and surf lessons, plus transport to the best breaks in the region.

Casa Oro (☎ 2568-2415; www.casaeloro.com; Parque Central, 1c O) Hires surfboards for US$10 per day, runs daily shuttles to Playas Maderas and Remanso (C$80 round trip), and can arrange fishing excursions and horseback-riding trips on the southern beaches or in the hills behind town. It also offers nightly trips in season to see turtles nesting and hatching at Refugio de Vida Silvestre La Flor (see p499) for US$30 per head including park entry fee.

Da Flying Frog (☎ 2568-2351; tiguacal@ibw.com. ni; per person US$30) This canopy tour is made up of 17 platforms and 2.5km of line that passes through some forested hills on the outskirts of town. Ask your hotel to call for a pick-up.

Good Times Surf Shop (☎ 8657-1621; www. goodtimessurfshop.com; Gato Negro, 100m S) Laid-back surf center specializing in trips to less crowded beaches such as Yanqui (US$20 per person including board hire) and Colorado (US$35). Also rents bikes (US$6 per day).

Neptune Water Sports (☎ 8903-1122; www. neptunewsn.com; Parque Central, ½c N) Offers diving trips to La Flor and other local sites.

Courses

There are several low-key Spanish schools and private teachers in town offering hourly rates and weekly courses.

Nica Spanish Language School (☎ 2568-2142; www.nicaspanish.com; Parque Central, 1c O; 20hr with/ without homestay US$215/115) A popular choice with the backpacker crowd, this established school offers one-on-one tuition and comfortable homestay accommodations.

Spanish Ya (☎ 2568-3010; www.learnspanishya. com; Texaco 100m N; 20hr with/without accommodation US$220/120) Professionally run outfit set around a quiet patio overlooking the river. Onsite accommodations are available and activities such as horseback riding and beach visits are included in the price.

Sleeping

San Juan del Sur is one of the few places in Nicaragua with marked seasonal rates. At Easter and other Nicaraguan holiday times, prices can be double those listed here.

Hospedaje Elizabeth (☎ 8840-0299; mercado, 75m E; r per person US$6, d US$20) Opposite the market, this friendly guesthouse has rooms varying in size and comfort; breezy upstairs rooms are best.

Hotel Estrella (☎ 2568-2210; mercado, 2c O; r per person without bathroom US$7; 🖳) This historic hotel on the beach strip has seen a few changes in San Juan since it opened in the '20s. Many of the simple rooms have small balconies with sea views and there is an attractive common lounge area with internet access. The only downside is the hike to the shared bathrooms downstairs.

ourpick Hostel **Pacha Mama** (☎ 2568-2043; www.hostelpachamama.com; Parque Central, 1½c O; dm/d US$8/20; 🖳 🛜) Set in a bright, modern building half a block back from the beach, this new hostel is already winning over the young, party-loving crowd. Facilities available include table tennis, guest kitchen, backyard bar and free skateboards to get you around town.

Casa Oro (☎ 2568-2415; www.casaeloro.com; Parque Central, 1c O; dm US$7.50-9, r US$20; 🖳 🛜) Deservedly popular and always heavily booked, this well-run hostel has recently had a major makeover. The new dorms are excellent, with comfortable beds and spacious bathrooms, while the upgraded private rooms should be ready by the time you read this. Guests have access to a spacious kitchen.

Bed Head Shed Hostel (☎ 2568-2076; Texaco, 2c S; dm US$8; 🖳) More chilled and homey than the other hostels in town, this new place has all the usual facilities as well as a great guest barbecue area.

Hotel Sunrise Beach (☎ 8374-2172; Parque Central, 1½c O; d US$20; 🖥) This confusingly named spot feels more like a shared house than a small hotel. The rooms are bright and inviting and there is a common kitchen, TV lounge and small balcony overlooking the street.

Hotel Encanto del Sur (☎ 2568-2222; Parque Central, ½c S; s/d US$20/30; 💈 🛜) Clean, spacious rooms with cable TV, spotless bathrooms and kitchen access make this one of the best deals in town. Discounts can be arranged if you don't need air-con.

Royal Chateau Hotel (☎ 2568-2551; www.hotelroyal chateau.com; Texaco 3c S; s/d US$46/53; 🅿 💈) Spacious, freshly painted rooms set around a palm-studded parking area. If you can take the climb, the top-floor rooms offer great views.

Eating

The least expensive place to eat is the **mercado** (dishes C$40-80), with a string of neat little kitchens, all serving hearty local fare and some backpacker favorites.

There's a long row of similar restaurants along the beachfront that offer ocean breezes and fish, seafood and chicken plates for C$120 to C$255. Among the best are **Josselin's** (frente Hotel Estrella; dishes C$130-250), which has a sumptuous mixed seafood plate, and **El Timon** (frente Landmark Inn; dishes C$145-255).

Soda Arenas Blancas (frente Casa Oro; plates C$70-95) This is not your average *fritanga*. Sure you can find barbecued chicken with *gallo pinto* and *tajadas* (banana chips) but look further down the menu for the delicious a la carte dishes including the best-value seafood in town – lobster for C$95 anyone?

El Pier (Av del Mar; dishes C$70-195; 🅥) Spilling out onto the sand, El Pier is like your favorite cafe transplanted onto the beach. There is a relaxed lounge ambience and a great selection of healthy meals on the vegetarian-friendly menu. It is also a great place to throw back a few drinks in the evening.

La Panga (Texaco, 2c O, 25m S; dishes C$75-160) This hole-in-the-wall seafood cafe cooks up some pretty decent fish and chips as well as a top-notch bean burger. For health freaks, there is a choice of tasty salads and grilled fish.

El Gato Negro (Texaco 2c O; light meals C$80-125) What's that smell? It's proper coffee, organically grown, roasted on the bar in front of you, and turned out to perfection by the polished espresso machine. Fabulous. Add to that salads, sandwiches, breakfasts, and a huge selection of books for sale and it's no wonder you'll have to fight for a table.

⭑ourpick⭑ El Colibrí (☎ 8863-8612; mains C$130-220; 🅥) A little pricey but well worth it, this labor of love is tucked behind the church away from the beachfront scene. The ambience is airy and romantic, and the beautifully presented food, with many vegetarian options, is prepared using mostly organic ingredients. Call ahead to make a reservation.

Also try:

Asados Vilma (Parque Central; chicken/beef with sides C$50-90; 🕒 4-9pm) San Juan's famous Chicken Lady serves up barbecued treats and refreshing natural beverages.

Pizzeria San Juan (☎ 2568-2295; Parque Central, 20m O; pizzas C$75-145; 🕒 5-10pm) This is the best pizza place in town. No contest.

Drinking & Entertainment

Republika (mercado, ½c O) Laid-back, friendly and fun, this cozy bar feels like your local from the moment you walk in.

Iguana Bar (Av del Mar) The most consistently lively late-night option, this beachside joint fills up with a cheerful crowd of Nicaraguans and gringos banging back the rum as if prohibition started tomorrow.

Crazy Crab (Av del Mar; 🕒 Thu-Sun) San Juan del Sur's only disco is your typical tourist-town meat market, with equal numbers of locals and tourists making fools of themselves on the dance floor. Come late and half-cut and you'll have a ball. It's in a slightly dodgy area at the northern end of the main strip; take a taxi home.

Getting There & Around

Buses arrive and depart beside the market, two blocks from the beach. *Expresos* to Managua (C$75, 2½ hours) depart at 5am, 5:45am, 7am and 3:20pm daily. Buses for Rivas (C$15, 45 minutes), with connections to Managua and the border, depart every 30 minutes from 5am to 5pm. You can also get a shared taxi to Rivas (C$35) from the same place. See opposite page for routes to area beaches.

You can rent mountain bikes (US$6) to explore the town and beyond at Hospedaje Elizabeth (p497) and Good Times Surf Shop (p497).

AROUND SAN JUAN DEL SUR

There are some fabulous beaches both south and north of San Juan del Sur. It's definitely not undiscovered territory any more, but the majority of these places are still pretty unspoiled.

North of San Juan del Sur

Some 7km north of San Juan del Sur, **Playa Marsella** is a calm, beautiful beach perfect for swimming that is far less crowded than the popular surfing beaches just over the bluff. On weekends the beach is popular with day trippers and a small *rancho* sets up serving simple meals and cold drinks.

Heading north from here (back along the road; you can't walk around the headland) lies **Playa Maderas** (Los Playones), the finest surf beach in the area. With sumptuous white sand, and slowish left and right breaks that hollow out as the tide rises, it can get pretty crowded offshore, but is nevertheless one of the country's best surf spots, with something for both experts and beginners. You can stay here at the basic but well-loved **Madera Surf Camp** (campsite or hammock per person US$4, dm/d without bathroom US$7/15).

Continuing north along the beach are beautiful rocky outcrops and excellent stretches of sand for sunbathing. At the extreme northern end of the beach, the frequently recommended **Matilda's** (☎ 8456-3461; campingmatildas@gmail.com; campsite with own/permanent tents per person US$4/6, dm/s/d US$10/15/25) offers accommodations for all budgets right on the sand. Meals are available and guests can use the kitchen.

Accessible from a narrow path behind Matilda's, **Bahía Majagual** is a spectacular sheltered beach flanked by jungle-covered headlands that offers some of the best swimming in the country.

South of San Juan del Sur

The first beach to the south is **Playa El Remanso**, which has a smallish beach break ideal for beginners, and has caves and tidal pools to explore. Further south are Playas Tamarindo and Hermosa, with better and less-crowded waves. Beyond Playa Yanqui, with a gated resort community, is **Playa El Coco**, a fabulous beach ringed by postcard-pretty cliffs.

At the end of the road, and just a stone's throw from Costa Rica, the charming fishing village of **El Ostional** feels a million miles from the resorts and tour buses of San Juan. The town has a long golden beach almost completely enclosed by cliffs, jungle-covered bluffs and mountains. **Cabañas Manta Raya** (☎ 8966-7783; r per person incl breakfast US$15) rents out comfortable rooms with private bathrooms right on the beach. There are also several family-run *hospedajes* (guesthouses) in the village charging US$8 to US$15 per guest.

Refugio de Vida Silvestre La Flor

Around 20km south of San Juan del Sur, **Playa La Flor** (admission C$200) is one of the world's principal nesting areas for olive ridley and leatherback turtles. The animals lay their eggs here at night between July and January; most spectacular are the amazing *arribadas* (arrivals), when thousands of olive ridleys arrive together, packing the beaches. The eggs start hatching a month and a half after laying. Call **Marena** (☎ 2563-4264) for information on expected arrivals.

The park guards sell soft drinks and water, but bring your own insect repellent and food – it may be a long night of waiting. You can camp here for an extortionate US$30 per tent – bring the biggest tent you can find – or you might prefer to stay at El Ostional (see below left), just south of the reserve. Alternatively, Casa Oro (p497) offers popular daily trips to the reserve from San Juan del Sur.

However you arrive, make sure your visit has as little impact as possible on the performers in this amazing natural event. Keep your distance and respect the laying mothers – no camera flashes or flashlights.

Getting To/From the Beaches

Public transport to these beaches is extremely limited, often involving long walks from the bus stop to the sand. There are two daily buses heading to the northern beaches, with departures at 10:30am and 1pm (C$16). Three daily buses head south to the Remanso turnoff, Playa El Coco, Refugio la Flor and El Ostional (C$40). Check the timetables, as they vary frequently. There are fixed rates for taxi trips from San Juan to the beaches, which vary from US$20 to US$50.

If you are heading to Maderas or Remanso, it is far easier to hop on one of Casa Oro's daily shuttles (C$80 return), which gives you plenty of time to enjoy the sand and surf.

The nicest way to reach a beach is by boat. A **water taxi** (Map p496; ☎ 8877-9255) leaves San Juan daily at 11am to Majagual, stopping at the beaches along the way (US$10 return). Book your ticket at the kiosk opposite Hotel Estrella. You can also take it to the southern beaches if there's enough demand.

CHARGE IT! – NICARAGUA'S TOP SURF SPOTS

- **Playa Popoyo** has guaranteed large left and right point breaks and several surf camps. Get a bus from Rivas to Las Salinas.
- Several fine breaks can be found in the **Pochomil/Masachapa** area (p464), including a right river mouth at Quizala.
- There are both left and right beach and reef breaks within a few kilometers of **Playa El Velero** on the old León–Managua highway. Take a bus from León or Managua to Puerto Sandino, from where not-so-regular pickups complete the journey.
- **Playa Maderas** (p499) has slowish medium waves; it can get crowded but is easy to reach and reliable.
- There's a loud hollow beach break at **Playa Aserradores** (p483) and others are nearby.

ISLA DE OMETEPE

pop 29,684

Ometepe is the sort of place that belongs in fairy tales or fantasy novels; an island formed by twin volcanoes rising out of a lake. The ecological jewel that is Ometepe sees plenty of visitors these days but is still very unspoiled, a rough-and-ready sort of place with shocking roads and sleeping places whose charm lies in location and relaxation potential rather than state-of-the-art facilities. The island is a must, whether you plan to lounge on the beach, chat to plantain pickers or tackle a steep volcano climb.

The two large volcanoes are Concepción, which rises 1610m above the lake in an almost perfect cone, and Maderas (1394m). Lava flows created an isthmus between them, creating the island, whose name means 'two hills' in Nahuatl. Brooding Concepción is still active: its last major eruption was in 1957.

Ometepe is famous for its ancient **stone statues** and **petroglyphs** depicting humans, animals, birds and geometric shapes. These remnants of Chorotega settlement have been found all over the island, but they are most densely clustered along the northern side of Volcán Maderas, between Santa Cruz and La Palma.

The island's two major settlements, Altagracia and Moyogalpa, both offer accommodations and restaurants, but to experience the true charms of Ometepe, travel further out: Charco Verde, Playa Santo Domingo, Balgüe and Mérida all offer lovely settings amid the island's rich biodiversity.

The bank in Moyogalpa has a somewhat unreliable Visa ATM and some hotels accept credit cards, but it is best to bring plenty of cash from the mainland – people often stay here much longer than they planned.

ACTIVITIES

Ometepe is great for hiking, exploring and swimming. However, the terrain is rough, signage minimal and trails hard to follow. Since a number of tourists got lost and died while climbing the volcanoes, local authorities have made local guides mandatory for these trips. Guides can be hired at tour operators in Moyogalpa and Altagracia or through hotels.

Both of the volcanoes are challenging. **Volcán Maderas** is the more accessible of the two, a tough, muddy scramble through cloud forest to the crater, where there's a greenish lake below. It's about eight hours there and back. There are several routes to the top; the trails leaving from Finca Magdalena, Mérida and El Porvenir are the most used.

Volcán Concepción is a pretty serious 10- to 12-hour hike, the last bit up steep and slippery volcanic scree. Be prepared for intense heat (sun, not lava), and also for chills at the summit. The two main trails leave from points near Altagracia and Moyogalpa.

The downside is that both summits are often wreathed in cloud, but you get some great views on the way up. On the Maderas side, there are also several trails to see petroglyphs. The **petroglyphs** near the hotel of El Porvenir are a 45-minute horseback ride from Santo Domingo; ask hotel staffers for directions. Others are found at El Socorro, Finca Magdalena and El Corozal. On the south side of Maderas, an impressive 35m-high waterfall is located a couple hours' hike above San Ramón.

There are great beaches and **swimming** spots all around the island; check out Punta Jesús María, Playa Venecia and the Isla de Quiste, a beautiful islet not far from Charco Verde. The most popular beach, Playa Santo Domingo, is on the isthmus connecting the two volcanoes, and has plenty of places to stay and eat.

Many of the sleeping options have horses, bikes or kayaks to hire at reasonable rates.

TOURS

Inexpensive local guides are highly recommended for hikes, for safety, to increase your chances of spotting wildlife and for enhanced insight into the island's culture. Guides basically live off your tips, so be generous. Any hotel can arrange a guide, or stop by **UGO** (☎ 8827-7714; muelle, 50m E), a cooperative of local guides with an office by the Moyogalpa dock.

MOYOGALPA
pop 4969

Most ferries from San Jorge arrive in Moyogalpa, the larger of the island's two main villages. While it's not a pretty place, it can make a good base, with plenty of ac-commodation choices and easy access to transport and guides to explore the rest of the island.

The **Sala Arqueológica Ometepe** (☎ 2569-4225; muelle, 4½c E; admission US$2; ⊙ 8am-9pm) is worth a look. The small museum displays a decent little collection of pre-Columbian pieces, including funerary urns carved with bat, snake and frog motifs. Entry includes a guided tour.

The Sala offers slowish internet access; better is Cyber Arcía, two blocks up from the dock on the right, which also offers low-cost international calls. On the same block, Banco Pro Credit has a Visa/Plus ATM; the only cash machine on the island.

Around 5km south of Moyogalpa, and easily reached by bicycle, is the remarkable **Punta Jesús María**, a narrow sandbar that juts out into the lake, forming a natural pier perfect for swimming and picnics.

Sleeping

Hostal Ibesa (☎ 8614-1799; hostelibesa@yahoo.es; Texaco, 1c S; r per person US$4) Run by a friendly local family, the cheapest digs in town are a pretty basic affair with tin roofs, concrete floors and dodgy

ISLA DE OMETEPE

0 ————— 5 km
0 ————— 3 miles

Location of major petroglyphs; other indigenous art

ASK A LOCAL

When we want to relax we always go to swim at Punta Jesús María. I have never seen any other place like it. No matter where the wind is coming from, on one side the water is always calm.

Norvin Somarriba, Moyogalpa

wiring but are OK if you just need a place to crash before an early departure.

Hospedaje Central (☎ 2569-4262; muelle, 3c E, 1c S; dm US$4, s/d US$10/14) This popular travelers' haunt has basic but habitable rooms housing some pretty battered mattresses and a dingy dorm, but what people really come here for is the sociable vibe, colorful common areas and cheerful bar-restaurant.

Hotel Escuela Teosintal (☎ 2569-4105; muelle, 2c E, 1c S; s/d US$12/18) Run by a local nonprofit group, this great choice has comfortable rooms with cable TV and modern bathrooms in an elegantly renovated building on the southern side of town. The rooms out the back facing the garden are better than the windowless ones inside.

American Cafe and Hotel (☎ 8645-7193; muelle, 1½c E; s/d US$20/30) It doesn't look much at first, but the rooms out the back of this friendly place are absolute gems. They each have a different theme but they are all massive with wooden ceilings, big comfortable beds and spotless hot-water bathrooms. The attached cafe serves excellent breakfasts and lunches.

Eating & Drinking

La Esquinita Caliente (muelle, 3c E; snacks C$20-40, meals C$60-70) A popular hangout for locals, this *comedor* has great hotdogs and burgers as well as more substantial plates of Nica specialities.

Yogi's (muelle, 3c E, 1½c S; burgers C$80) Named after the owners' handsome black dog, this hospitable place knows how to treat a traveler, with truly excellent sandwiches, burgers and breakfasts, as well as internet access, phone calls and big-screen movies in the peaceful courtyard space. Just holler out if the front door's shut.

Los Ranchitos (muelle, 3c E, ½c S; mains C$85-150) Moyogalpa's most elegant restaurant serves up big portions of local dishes and surprisingly tasty pizza in a thatched dining area surrounded by plants. There's also a couple of comfortable rooms out the back (US$12 to US$15).

Café Bistro Cocibolca (muelle, 3c E, 1c S) Stop by this spacious bar-restaurant to shoot some pool and enjoy delicious fresh fruit juices. During the week it is chilled, but on the weekend the party gets going on the dance floor out the back.

Timbo al Tambo (muelle, 2½c E) Your best bet for action on any given night, this cozy bar has a big screen showing sporting events and a sweaty disco area upstairs where young locals gather to grind to reggaetón hits.

ALTAGRACIA

pop 7297

Not a great deal goes down in sleepy Altagracia, an attractive town at the other end of the paved road from busier Moyogalpa. It's a handy base for climbing Volcán Concepción. There's a dock 2km from town from where ferries run to Granada and San Carlos.

There's not much to see in town except for the fine ancient **stone statues** beside the church near the pretty Parque Central, and the **Museo de Ometepe** (Parque Central, 1c O; admission US$1.50; 🕑 8am-4:30pm Mon-Sat), which displays an assortment of archaeological, geological and cultural artifacts. Most interesting is a wall painting depicting the legend of Chico Largo, an angular farmer who heads a mythical community underneath Charco Verde.

Sleeping & Eating

Hospedaje Kencho (☎ 8994-4087; iglesia, ½c S; r with/without bathroom US$6/5) Shabby but welcoming, this place has bare quarters with clean shared bathrooms upstairs and more modern rooms with private bathrooms downstairs. The restaurant is decent value and a low-key spot for a cool drink and chat.

Hotel Central (☎ 2552-8770; iglesia, 2c S; r per person with/without bathroom US$6/5, cabins per person US$8) With attractive rooms, spotless bathrooms decorated with river stones and a lovely internal garden, the Central is easily the best accommodation option in town. The friendly staff can arrange tours and the restaurant serves tasty Nica meals.

Hotel Castillo (☎ 2552-8744; iglesia, 1c S, ½c O; s/d US$10/15, d with air-con US$30; ❄ 💻) A couple of blocks south of the park, the popular Castillo has quiet, airy rooms that surround a thatched, hammocked courtyard. There's a good bar/restaurant and helpful management.

There are several hearty *fritangas* and other budget eating options around Parque Central.

CHARCO VERDE & PLAYA VENECIA

On the south side of Volcán Concepción and
10km from Moyogalpa, this zone of beautiful beaches and forests of abundant wildlife
is a fine place to visit or stay. The **Reserva
Charco Verde** (admission C$10) has a hiking trail
through the woods; you'll likely see monkeys
and plenty of birds. The lovely Playa Bancón
looks across at the swimmable **Isla de Quiste**, a
prime camping spot. Ask one of the hotels for
organizing a boat service across.

There are three places to stay here, run by
members of the same family. Bookings are
often necessary. One of the most comfortable accommodations on the island, **Hotel
Finca Venecia** (☎ 8887-0191; www.fincavenecia.com;
dm/r US$7/25, cabins US$30-35; ⚇) is extremely well
run and overlooks the beach. There's a variety
of appealing cabins available (you'll pay some
US$15 more if you want to use the air-con),
simpler rooms with bathroom and a sociable
thatched restaurant. You can arrange all sorts
of activities here, and the hotel rents bikes and
can arrange horseback riding.

Right next door, the friendly **Posada Chico
Largo** (☎ 8886-4069; dm US$5, r US$15-25, with air-con
US$35; ⚇) offers budget lodging right on the
beach. The dorms and older rooms are a little
run down, but the new rooms at the back are
clean and comfortable. You can also camp on
the lawn (US$3 per person).

A couple of hundred meters east of these,
Hotel Charco Verde (☎ 8887-9302; www.charcoverde.com.
ni; r US$25, cabins US$35-55; ⚇) has modern cabins
(ask for a lake view) and characterful old rooms –
sleep upstairs. Trees surround the grounds,
and it's a short walk from there to the lagoon.

A few kilometers away, **Tesoro del Pirata**
(☎ 8927-2831; r with/without air-con US$25/15; ⚇) is
an away-from-it-all spot with functional concrete *cabañas* dotted among the trees on a
lovely sheltered beach. It's a cordial place with
a thatched restaurant that serves well-priced
meals. The owners can arrange a variety of activities including fishing trips and horseback
tours. It's 1km off the paved road some 14km
from Moyogalpa.

SANTO DOMINGO

The little community of Santo Domingo, on
the island's waist between the volcanoes, is
perhaps the most visited part of Ometepe.
While many find the gray-sand beach a tad
disappointing – it becomes seriously emaci-
ated during rainy season and the winds here

can be fierce – swimming among the freshwater waves is quite an experience.

Two kilometers west of Santo Domingo,
you'll see signs for the **Ojo de Agua** (admission US$2)
waterhole. Keep left along the muddy road
and after 20 minutes you'll reach the picturesque swimming hole, which has a kiosk selling
drinks. It's a relaxing place, and good to chat to
locals, who lug elaborate picnics down the trail.

Finca Santo Domingo (☎ 2552-8787; r with fan
US$20-25, with air-con US$35; ⚇ ▯) is a decent
midrange option, with rooms where waves
will lull you to sleep, and a great beachside
bar-restaurant. The rooms in the main building are nicer than the darkish cabins on the
other side of the road.

Also here, **Hospedaje Buena Vista** (☎ 8690-0984;
r per person US$8-10) is a great budget choice with a
genial boss, appealing fan-cooled rooms and
plenty of hammocks around to loll about in.
There's a cheap spot to eat next door.

Further south, on a less developed stretch of
beach, there are a couple of other budget options including the excellent **Casa Istiam** (☎ 8887-
9891; r per person with/without bathroom US$8/5), which
has simple, brightly painted rooms and a well-
priced restaurant that serves up tasty fish dishes.

SANTA CRUZ TO BALGÜE

Beyond Santo Domingo, the road divides
at Santa Cruz, with the left fork heading to
Balgüe, and the right to Mérida. Just down the
Balgüe road lies **Comedor Sta Cruz** (meals C$50-80),
which serves up hearty portions of delicious
typical food in an unpretentious dirt-floored
dining area.

A short walk from here you will come to
Little Morgan's (☎ 8949-7074; www.littlemorgans.com;
dm US$9, cabañas US$30), a gregarious lakeside offering popular with those that like to mix up
the relaxation with a good dose of partying.
The two cute cabins are comfortable with private open-air bathrooms, but even more impressive is the elevated open-air gazebo dorm
that offers great volcano views from your bed.

Another 1km further on is the entrance to **El
Zopilote** (☎ 8369-0644; www.ometepezopilote.com; hammocks US$2.50, dm US$5, r per person US$6-9), a laid-back
ecological farm where you can indulge your
hippie tendencies. The comfortable thatched
huts are scattered around a lush hillside and
there is an excellent lookout onsite. The Italian
owner prepares delicious pizzas three times
a week but at other times you will need to
cook for yourself. There's a small store selling

homemade bread and organic products from the farm, and there are also beekeeping and bread-making courses to keep you busy.

Travelers looking to climb Volcán Maderas might opt to stay beyond Balgüe at **Finca Magdalena** (☎ 8498-1683; www.fincamagdalena.com; dm/s/d US$3.50/5/10, cabañas US$30-40; 💻). With gorgeous views over the hillside, the old farmhouse is set on the grounds of an organic coffee cooperative and offers rustic accommodations (the dorm looks like a field hospital) as well as more modern *cabañas* and **camping** (per tent US$3) facilities. Tasty, fresh-cooked meals are available and there are various petroglyphs nearby.

MÉRIDA & SAN RAMÓN

On the other side of Maderas lies the beautiful, wind-swept shoreline of Mérida, a spread-out town with a couple of thousand inhabitants. Further south, San Ramón is a simple agricultural village, typical of the Maderas side of the island. Beyond here, the road degenerates even further but passes through some friendly and fascinatingly isolated plantain-farming communities before emerging at Balgüe.

A short walk toward Mérida from Santa Cruz, **Finca El Porvenir** (☎ 8447-9466; r per person US$8) is set in an outstandingly beautiful location on a hilltop with superb views and no noise, and is perhaps the island's supreme spot for relaxation. The simple rooms have sturdy wooden beds, private bathroom and porch that are set around a lovely flowery garden. There's a restaurant, petroglyphs just below, and walking paths, including one that ascends Maderas.

There are several appealing places to stay around Mérida. All can arrange horses or bikes to hire. The northernmost, **Caballito's Mar** (☎ 8451-2093; www.caballitosmar.com; dm US$5; 💻) is a sweet Nicaraguan-Catalan setup right on the beach with basic dormitory accomodations and a small dirt-floored cafe on the sand that is perfect for watching lakeside village life. The hostel arranges recommended kayaking trips to the nearby Río Istiam.

On the main road south of town, **Hacienda Mérida** (☎ 8868-8973; www.hmerida.com; camping per person US$3, dm US$6, r US$20-28; 💻 📶) was once a ranch of the Somoza family and is now a popular travelers' R&R spot. The dormitories are a little cramped, but the upstairs rooms are superb with wood-pannelled walls, big comfortable beds and gorgeous views from the balcony. You can rent kayaks, climb a steep path up Volcán Maderas, or swim around the

old dock. Just make sure you are around for the phenomenal sunsets.

A couple of kilometers down the road in San Ramón is Estación Biológica de Ometepe, where the trail begins to the fabulous waterfall of **Cascada San Ramón** (admission US$3), a steep four-hour round trip.

GETTING THERE & AWAY

The fastest and most popular way of reaching the island is via San Jorge near Rivas, from where boats make the 15km crossing to either Moyogalpa or San José del Sur on Ometepe.

These days, most of the crossings are made by large comfortable ferries (C$40 to C$60) but there are still a couple of less comfortable *lanchas* (small motorboats; C$30) making the trip each day. The crossing, which takes just over an hour, can be rough, particularly in the afternoon. It is possible to take vehicles on the ferries, but an advance reservation (☎ 2278-8190) is usually required.

By far the most comfortable ride is on the government-run *Rey del Cocibolca*, but it arrives in the less convenient village of San José del Sur, from where you will have to arrange onward transportation to your destination. It leaves San José for San Jorge at 7:30am and 3:20pm, returning at 9am and 5pm.

Between San Jorge and Moyogalpa, there are nine daily ferry departures each way:
Moyogalpa–San Jorge (6am, 6:45am, 9am, 10am, 11am, 12:30pm, 2pm, 4pm, 5:30pm)
San Jorge–Moyogalpa (7am, 7:45am, 8:30am, 10:30am, noon, 2:30pm, 4pm, 4:30pm, 5:45pm)

The boat from Granada to San Carlos, at the southern end of the lake, departs on Monday and Thursday at 2pm. It arrives in Altagracia (upper/lower deck C$90/40) about four hours later and takes off for the 10-hour trip to San Carlos (C$140/55) at 7pm. The returning boat departs San Carlos at 2pm Tuesday and Friday, calling at Altagracia between 11pm and 1am. Travelers are urged to buy tickets ahead of departure time at the dockside ticket offices.

GETTING AROUND

The cheapest way to get around the island is by using the rickety buses. There's an hourly service from Moyogalpa to Altagracia via the paved road (C$16, 45 minutes). This route passes the turnoff to the Volcán Maderas side of the island.

From Moyogalpa, there are three daily buses to Balgüe (C$25, two hours), leaving at

10:30am, 3:30pm and 5pm. To Mérida (C$30, two to three hours), services leave at 8:30am, 2:45pm and 4pm. Most of these services make a stop in Altagracia before backtracking to the turnoff. From Altagracia, additional buses head to Balgüe at 9am, 11:30am and 1:45pm, and to Mérida at 10:30am and 2pm. For Santo Domingo (C$20), you can catch either a Mérida or a Balgüe bus. It's also easy to hike or hitch from the turnoff from the paved road.

Taxis, either comfortable minibuses or hardier jeeps and pickups, are rare and expensive so it pays to get a group together. They wait to meet pretty much all ferry services and will take you just about anywhere on the island. From Moyogalpa, expect to pay US$20 to Altagracia or Playa Santo Domingo, US$25 to Balgüe and US$30 to Mérida.

To explore on your own, it's possible to rent a no-frills jeep in Moyogalpa at Hotel Ometepetl (US$40 for 12 hours). There are a number of motorcycle rental outfits in Moyogalpa and one in Santo Domingo charging around US$25 per day for beat-up Chinese trail bikes. Bicycles can be rented in Moyogalpa, Altagracia and Playa Santa Domingo for around US$5 per day.

SAN CARLOS & AROUND

The steamy riverside town of San Carlos is an important hub for river transport, and launchpad for a number of highly appealing attractions including the Archipiélago de Solentiname, several wildlife reserves, and the fabulously unlikely Spanish castle at El Castillo.

SAN CARLOS
pop 14,006

Despite its beautiful setting on the southeastern corner of Lago de Nicaragua, San Carlos has long been famed among travelers as the kind of destination from which to plan your departure before you even set foot in town. However, serious investment from the government through its Ruta del Agua program has given the place a major facelift, especially around the **malecón**, a lovely promenade from where you can sit and watch as the lake flows into the mighty Río San Juan. Still, as the gateway to some of the country's finest natural attractions, you probably won't spend too much time in town.

There's not a great deal to do here except explore what remains of the **old fortress** (8am-6pm), built in 1666 by the Spanish to keep invading forces from entering the lake and gaining access to Granada's wealth. The recently renovated site lies just above Parque Central and has a number of interesting displays on the history and environment of the region. The town's main fiesta, the **Carnaval Acuático**, is celebrated in early November.

There is an all-card BanPro ATM in the middle pavilion on the riverfront. In the same building, the friendly **tourist office** (10am-6pm) has transportation timetables and plenty of practical advice. If it is closed, try **Intur** (2583-0301) across the road. There are a few internet places in town, the best of which is on the eastern side of the park.

There are a couple of cheap *hospedajes* near the boat dock. Better is friendly **Hospedaje Peña** (2583-0298; Parque Central, 1c S; r per person without bathroom US$3.50), with very basic rooms with shared bathroom. Try to nab one of the breezy rooms with lake views. Up a step is gruff **Hotel Carelhys** (2583-0389; Parque Central, ½c S; r US$12), which has reasonably comfortable rooms with comfy beds, cable TV and good bathrooms. **Hotel Leyko** (2583-0354; Parque Central, 2c O; d with/without bathroom US$18/13, with air-con US$40; P) is the best hotel in town, with a variety of clean rooms and cabins, some with air-con.

A gastronomic tour-bar crawl of San Carlos should include the following:
El Granadino (lunch C$95-120, mains C$170-250) Comfortably the town's best restaurant, with high ceilings, sizzling steaks, fair prices, great service and a killer view of the lake. It's a couple of blocks east of Hospedaje Peña.
El Mirador (mains C$100-200) Set in an old Spanish bastion behind Intur, it has a terrace and real cannons at your disposal.
Kaoma (mains C$150-250) Surly service, but a great upstairs wooden deck. Lively on weekend nights. It's down the hill from the park.

Getting There & Away
The airline **La Costeña** (2583-0367) has flights from Managua (US$116 return, twice daily Monday to Friday, daily Saturday and Sunday) to San Carlos' grass strip, 3km north of town. A taxi into town costs C$15. Confirm your return flight in San Carlos as soon as you arrive; it's easy to get stranded as the planes are often block-booked by tour companies.

There are six daily direct bus services between San Carlos and Managua's Mercado

Mayoreo terminal (C$190, 10 hours). The stretch between San Carlos and Juigalpa is one of Nicaragua's worst major roads; it's a very uncomfortable ride.

A far superior way to travel is the slow but comfortable government-run boat that leaves from the municipal dock for Granada (1st/2nd class C$190/80, 16 hours, 2pm Tuesday and Friday) via Altagracia on Isla de Ometepe, San Miguelito and Morrito. A less crowded tourist-class boat (1st/2nd class C$400/250, 12 hours) leaves for Granada at 6pm Sunday and stops only in Altagracia.

San Carlos is the western terminal of the San Juan riverway. There are at least six daily departures to El Castillo (regular C$77, 2½ hours; express C$120, 1½ hours) via Boca de Sábalos (C$60, two hours). Service is reduced on weekends.

For San Juan del Norte, at the mouth of the river on the Caribbean coast, slow boats depart at 6am Tuesday, Thursday and Friday (C$286, 10 to 14 hours). They stop for bathroom stops and food along the way. Boats return at 4:30am Thursday, Saturday and Sunday. Express *pangas* (C$510, six hours) leave San Carlos at 6am Tuesday and Friday, and return Wednesday and Sunday.

ARCHIPIÉLAGO DE SOLENTINAME

Isolated Archipiélago de Solentiname (Solentiname Archipelago), in the southern part of Lago de Nicaragua, is a traditional haven for artists and a fascinating place to visit. Ernesto Cardenal, the versatile artist-poet-monk who was minister of culture during the Sandinista years, set up a communal society here for craftspeople, poets and painters, inspired by the principles of liberation theology. A distinctive school of colorful primitivist painting arose out of these revolutionary-era workshops and has become world-famous.

Solentiname comprises 36 islands; the largest are Mancarrón, San Fernando (also called Isla Elvis Chavarría) and Venada (Isla Donald Guevara). The first two have the principal facilities for travelers. **Mancarrón** also has the islands' most famous sight, the simple yet beautiful adobe **church** that was the spiritual and communal center of Cardenal's community. Near here is an interesting archaeological exhibition, while a short walk away is **El Refugio**, the main community on the island, where you can wander among the local homes watching

---

GETTING TO COSTA RICA BY BOAT

From San Carlos you can take a small boat up the jungle-clad Río Frío to the Costa Rican border station at **Los Chiles** (US$10, one hour), quite possibly the most relaxing border crossing on the continent. Boats depart from the San Carlos immigration office a block west of the dock at 10:30am, 1:30pm and 4pm Monday to Saturday, and noon and 4pm Sunday. Come half an hour before the departure time to get your exit stamp (US$2).

See p577 for information on crossing the border from Costa Rica.

---

artisans create brightly painted balsa carvings. Prices for the finished product range from C$30 to C$1000 depending on size and detail. **San Fernando** has an excellent museum, with informative displays on the pre-Columbian residents of the archipelago, as well as a gallery that showcases the work of some of the islands' best artists. There are many **petroglyphs** scattered around the islands, which make appealing destinations for hikes – there are also caves to explore on Isla Venada. Fishing is good around here, and Isla Zapote has fantastic bird-watching possibilities. Otherwise, the islands are just great for taking it easy.

Hospedaje Buen Amigo (☎ 8869-6619; r per person with/without bathroom US$10/6) on the island of Mancarrón is an appealing place to stay, with comfy and colorful rooms and local artists whittling away outside. Traditional meals (C$60) are available in the adjoining *pulpería*.

Hotel Mancarrón (☎ 2583-0083; r per person incl 3 meals US$35), near the church in Mancarrón, offers spacious rooms with bathroom and fan. Some have been recently renovated, ask to see your options.

On Isla San Fernando, **Hospedaje Mire Estrellas** (r per person without bathroom US$10) offers small wooden rooms right on the water by the dock. If you are planning on staying here, bring supplies from San Carlos or arrange meals in one of the bigger hotels on the island.

Albergue Celentiname (☎ 8893-1977; bungalows per person incl 3 meals US$40), situated on a lovely point on Isla San Fernando, has appealing *cabañas* in a lovely garden setting. Guests have access to the fine porch and canoes to explore the surrounding wilderness. Guided fishing trips are also offered.

Getting to Solentiname takes a bit of advance planning as boats don't leave every day. Boats leave Mancarrón for San Carlos via San Fernando at 4:30am on Tuesday and Friday, and return at 1pm on the same days (C$80, three hours). Otherwise you can charter a boat from San Carlos (seating at least six) for US$100. The only way between the islands is by private charter (from US$10 per trip).

RÍO SAN JUAN

The river that makes Nicaraguan hearts stir with pride flows 199km from Lago de Nicaragua to the Caribbean Sea. For much of its length, the river forms the border between Nicaragua and Costa Rica, and has been a frequent source of tension between the two nations.

A trip on the San Juan is a fabulous experience – it's a bird-watching paradise, and you may well spot caimans sunning themselves on logs. These creatures will likely face eviction should Nicaragua's grand plans of a transithmian canal ever come to fruition.

Boca de Sábalos

The friendly town of Boca de Sábalos is the first major settlement downstream from San Carlos. It's lively and sociable, always with a few people hanging around keen to strike up a conversation. You'll find a couple of cheap but decent *alojamientos* (accommodations) on the main street (ask for Katiana or Clarissa) as well as **Sábalos Lodge** (☎ 8823-5555; www.sabaloslodge.com; cabins US$30-60), which has a range of amazing *cabañas* – think Tarzan's

pad after the reality TV crew have come through – set along the river downstream from town. It has bikes and kayaks available for rent. **Hotel Sábalos** (☎ 2271-7424; www.hotelsabalos.com.ni; s/d incl breakfast US$20/36), with a wooden veranda right on the water, also appeals – it'll cost you C$1 to get rowed across here from the dock.

El Castillo
Pop 3147

About one-third of the way from the lake to the ocean is El Castillo, a fortress built by the Spanish in 1675 at a strategic bend in the river to try to halt the passage of pirates heading for the fabled gold of Granada. It's an utterly memorable spot, with the unlikely castle looking over the lively rapids below.

Bitter battles were fought at El Castillo against flotillas of assailants. In 1762 the British and their Mískito allies attacked the fort, but Spanish forces, led by the daughter of their fallen commander, managed to hold off the invaders. The **fort** (admission C$40, camera C$25; ☼ 8am-4:30pm) offers top views and has decent Spanish-language displays on its turbulent history. Admission includes a well-informed guided tour.

Right opposite the dock, a **tourist office** (☼ 8am-noon & 2-5pm) offers a well-organized system of guided excursions in the area including horseback riding, night caiman tours and visits to the Reserva Biológica Río Indio Maíz (see boxed text, p508). You can also organize similar tours through private operators including the recommended **Nena Tour** (☎ 8821-2135; www.nenalodge.com), downstream on

---

WETLAND WANDERINGS

Another great spot to visit in this vicinity is the **Refugio de Vida Silvestre Los Guatuzos**, a fabulous wetland zone that abuts the Costa Rican border and was once a minefield (it's safe now!) – a fact that ironically ensured the region remained inviolate. There are public boats to Río Papaturro on Tuesday, Wednesday and Friday from San Carlos leaving at 8am (C$80, four hours), returning Monday, Tuesday and Thursday at 6am. They dock near the **Centro Ecológico Los Guatuzos** (☎ 2270-3561; www.losguatuzos.com; dm US$11), a research station offering dorm accommodations for students and travelers. It runs walking and boating tours, including an action-packed night tour with Papaturro's very own crocodile man, Don Armando Gómez. The concentration of wildlife here is phenomenal; there are hundreds of species of birds and if you stay a while you are pretty much guaranteed to see howler, spider and white-faced monkeys as well as caimans, crocodiles, iguanas and turtles. Harder to spot, but also present, are jaguars, pumas and tapirs.

It is also possible to visit the reserve on a day trip from the nearby Archipiélago de Solentiname. A chartered boat seating at least six goes for around US$60 round trip. Wherever you arrive from, bring plenty of insect repellent!

EXPLORING THE INDIO MAÍZ

For nature lovers it doesn't get much better than this. One of Central America's most impressive rainforests, the **Reserva Biológica Río Indio Maíz** begins a few kilometers downstream from El Castillo and continues all the way to the Caribbean Sea.

There are limited access points for the casual visitor, the most popular is via Río Bartola, less than half an hour from El Castillo by boat. From the ranger station, there is a 2km walking path through towering trees that gives you a taste of what the area has to offer. A little further downstream, Aguas Frecas is less visited, making it easier to spot wild animals. You can book trips to this part of the reserve from El Castillo for US$65 to US$76 per group (maximum four people) including transport and a guide.

Continuing east, the reserve forms an impenetrable wall of forest along the Nicaraguan side of the Río San Juan (unfortunately the Costa Rican side is heavily deforested) until you reach the isolated community of **San Juan del Norte**. Surrounded by magical hidden lagoons, dense rainforest and Caribbean beaches, this rarely visited town has plenty to offer. From here you can organize multiday boat trips to indigenous communities in the heart of the reserve via the spectacular Río Indio or explore the ruins of Greytown, the once-thriving British outpost across the bay that has been completely swallowed by the jungle. There are a couple of decent places to stay in town, including **Hotel Paraíso Virgen** (muelle, 600m S; s/d US$10/20).

Adventurous travelers can take a spine-shattering speedboat (C$600, 2½ hours) over the open sea to Bluefields with departures at 8am Wednesday and Saturday. Otherwise, it is back up the river to San Carlos.

the main drag. Both Albergue El Castillo and Borders Coffee offer internet services.

SLEEPING & EATING

Of the three budget places on the main path near the dock, **Hospedaje Universal** (r per person without bathroom US$5) is the best, with small, spare rooms and tiny windows opening onto the river.

our pick **Casa del Huesped Chinandegano** (s/d US$6/10) Great value rooms in a rickety stilted house with a fantastic plant-filled porch overlooking the river a couple of hundred meters downstream from the dock. It also serves up some of the best food in town.

Albergue El Castillo (☎ 8924-5608; r per person without bathroom incl breakfast US$15) A large homely wooden building that looms over the center of town. While the price is high considering you have to share a bathroom, the rooms (which offer character but not luxury) open onto a fabulous veranda with great views.

Heading a couple of hundred meters left from the dock, you'll reach **Hotel Victoria** (☎ 2583-0188; s/d incl breakfast US$20/40; ❄), a well-run place offering wood-lined rooms with spotless bathrooms, air-con and hot water. There's also a terrace bar-restaurant.

Be sure to try *camarones* (river shrimps) while in town. These bad bastards are massive, with pincers that could castrate a bull. There are several places to eat along the riverside walk-

way. **Soda Vanessa** (mains C$120-240) has a fabulous open *comedor* right on the rapids and offers great food, including exceedingly tasty *camarones*. Overlooking the dock, **Borders Coffee** (drinks C$20-30, meals C$75-300; ❖) has funky tunes, vegetarian meals and the only real coffee in town.

Getting There & Around

There are at least six daily boats from El Castillo to San Carlos (C$77, 2½ hours) via Boca de Sábalos (C$15, 30 minutes) including three express *pangas* (C$120, 1½ hours). On Sunday, there are only services at 5am, 5:20am (express), 2pm and 3:30pm (express).

Heading downriver, boats to San Juan del Norte (C$220, eight hours) stop in El Castillo around 8:30am Tuesday, Thursday and Friday.

CARIBBEAN COAST

Nicaragua's Caribbean coast is a very distinct part of the country, and can feel like another nation. A remote rainy region scored by dozens of rivers and swathed in tropical forest, it comprises more than half the country, but much of it is virtually untouched by travelers; a veritable wilderness.

As well as being geographically and climatically distinct, the region also has a very different ethnic makeup. The Mískitos, who give their name to Moskitia (or Mosquitia), or 'the Mosquito Coast,' today number around 125,000 and live both here and in Honduras. Black Creoles brought from other parts of the Caribbean by the British are the second-largest ethnic group in the region, while indigenous Sumo and Rama people, as well as small numbers of Garífuna, also call the Atlantic coast their home.

Much of this coastline was never colonized by Spain. In the 18th century, leaders of the Moskitia area requested that it be made a British protectorate, as a defense against the Spanish. It remained British for over a century, with a capital at Bluefields, where the Mískito kings were crowned in the Protestant church.

The British signed the Moskitia over to the Nicaraguan government in 1859. The region retained its autonomy until 1894, when it was brought under direct Nicaraguan government control. The English language and the Protestant religion brought by British missionaries persist as important aspects of the regional culture. Timber, shrimp and lobster are key exports.

The steamy coast gets much more rain than the Pacific and inland regions: anywhere between 330cm and 635cm annually. Even during the March to May 'dry' season, rain is possible any time.

As well as the port of Bluefields, and the fabulous Corn Islands, there are numerous appealing destinations along this coastline, from isolated Mískito fishing communities to white-sand-fringed islets and remote rivers. If you're a fan of getting off the beaten track, this is the spot for you.

MANAGUA TO THE CARIBBEAN

While many travelers choose to fly to the Caribbean from Managua, the overland journey is no longer the grueling odyssey it once was. From Managua a good paved road leads to the important port town of **El Rama**, from where fast boats zip down the scenic Río Escondido to Bluefields. You could also schedule a stop in the delightful colonial town of **Juigalpa** along the way – check out the fine collection of pre-Columbian basalt idols in the museum.

From Managua, express buses head from the Mercado Mayoreo to El Rama (C$150, six hours) via Juigalpa (2½ hours) at 2pm, 6pm and 10pm. Ordinary buses (C$120, 6½ hours)

leave at 6am, 7am, 8:45am and 11:30am. The dock in El Rama is near the bus station, and *pangas* to Bluefields (C$200, 1¾ hours) leave first thing in the morning and then very sporadically throughout the day when full. It is possible to get to Bluefields in one day if you take the first bus. Slower boats (C$60, 4½ hours) leave from the industrial port 1km further upriver on Tuesday, Wednesday and Thursday.

El Rama isn't as seedy as it was, but it was pretty damn seedy. **Hospedaje Doña Luisa** (☎ 2517-0073; r with/without TV C$200/170) has clean, modern rooms with private bathrooms and is just steps away from the dock for early morning departures. **Casa Blanca** (Bancentro, 1c S, 1c E; meals C$60) has the best food in town and a great deck overlooking the river.

There is one bus a day from El Rama to Pearl Lagoon at 3pm, an extremely rough six-hour journey. You may prefer to travel by *panga* via Bluefields.

BLUEFIELDS
pop 40,675

The Caribbean side of Central America is very different to the Pacific side, and Bluefields, with its slow pace, ready smiles, decayed tropical charm and slightly sketchy underbelly, is quintessential. Named after the Dutch pirate, Blewfeldt, who made a base here in the mid-17th century, the town ranks in these parts as a metropolis, and is definitely worth getting to know, even if you're en route to the Corn Islands. It has a fascinating mix of ethnic groups, a lively nightlife scene and one of Nicaragua's most vibrant festivals.

Bluefields was destroyed by Hurricane Juana (Joan) in 1988 but has been rebuilt (including its beautiful bayside Moravian church). The town's economy is based on shrimp, lobster and deepwater fish; the main cargo port is across the bay at El Bluff.

Bluefields is not a particularly safe place; if you go out after dark, always take a taxi.

Orientation & Information

Most of Bluefields' commerce, *hospedajes* and restaurants are found in the blocks between Parque Reyes and the bay. Internet spots are all over the center and most offer cheap international calls. The airport is about 3km south of town.

Many of the shops in the center change dollars; look for the sign.

NICARAGUA

BanPro (frente iglesia) Has a Visa/MasterCard ATM.

Intur (☎ 2572-0221; iglesia, 1c O) A block west of the Moravian church.

Marena (☎ 2572-2324; iglesia, 1c O) National parks service office, two doors down from Intur.

Post office (iglesia, ½c S, 1c O)

Sights & Activities

The town's most striking building is the **Moravian church**, a lovely building with characteristic stained glass. Although it dated from 1849, what you see now is a concrete replica of the wooden original, flattened by Hurricane Juana (Joan).

Three blocks west of the church, **Parque Reyes** is a popular meeting point with impressive 25m trees and a monument to the six ethnic groups of the region.

Across the bay, the port **El Bluff** has a long beach that while not particularly attractive, is the only real place to swim around here. On weekends, there are a couple of huts selling food and cold beer. Boats to El Bluff (C$35) leave regularly from the dock by the market.

Around 15km south of town in the southern reaches of Bluefields Bay lies the tiny island of **Rama Key**, unofficial capital of the Rama nation. Home to over half of the remaining Rama people, it is a crowded place with groups of wooden houses jostling for space under the fruit trees. Visit the **Rama-Kriol Communal Government** (☎ 2572-1765; www.rama-territory.com; Palacio Municipal, 2½c N; ☻ 9am-5pm) for information on transportation and homestay accommodations.

Sleeping

Avoid the cheap lodgings around the market and the dock which mainly cater to prostitutes and their clients.

Hotel El Dorado (☎ 2572-1435; mercado, 2c O, ½c S; r with/without bathroom US$10/7) One of several budget lodgings on this street, there's more sleeping and less whoring done here than most. The rooms are clean and OK for the price; some are lighter and airier than others.

Hotel Kaorha View (☎ 2572-0488; parque, 3c O; s/d without bathroom US$9/15) Spotless rooms, kitchen access and a lovely balcony make this low-key place in a quiet street behind the stadium a quality choice.

Guesthouse Campbell (☎ 8827-2221; Galileo, 2½c S; s/d US$10/15) A bit out of the way but great value, this family-run guesthouse has clean, comfortable rooms with private bathrooms and cable TV.

Hotel South Atlantic (☎ 2572-1022; contiguo iglesia; r US$25; ❄) There is nothing fancy about this hospitable place next to the church, but the rooms are clean and comfortable with queen-sized beds, hot water, cable TV and air-con.

Hotel Caribbean Dream (☎ 2572-0107; mercado, 1c O, ½c S; r US$27; ❄) This professional and reliable option is set in a pretty green house two blocks south of the church. The rooms are uninteresting but clean and well-equipped, with good hot-water bathrooms. There is a great balcony overlooking the street – perfect for getting to know some of Bluefields' colorful characters.

Eating

Bluefields is a rewarding place to eat, with tasty coconut-milk-based Caribbean dishes and

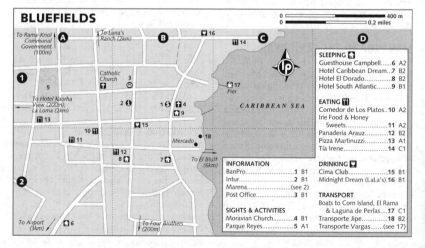

BLUEFIELDS

0 — 400 m
0 — 0.2 miles

To Rama-Kriol Communal Government (100m)

To Luna's Ranch (2km)

Catholic Church

To Hotel Kaorha View (200m); La Loma (2km)

CARIBBEAN SEA

Pier

Mercado

To El Bluff (6km)

To Airport (3km)

To Four Brothers (200m)

CELEBRATING AROUND THE MAYPOLE

Never afraid to kick up its heels on Friday night, Bluefields really pushes the boat out for its annual May fiesta, **Palo de Mayo**. Deriving in part from traditional British maypole celebrations, it's a riotous party that celebrates fertility (and, in many cases, puts it to the test).

Throughout the month, Bluefield's main *barrios* stage block parties with concerts, traditional games and plenty of dancing. But things really heat up at the end of the month when the carnival winds its way through the city's streets with gaudy floats, scantily clad dancers and marching bands. The festivities close with the boisterous 'Tulululu' in which pretty much the entire city follows the maypole through the streets, dancing through a tunnel formed by the raised hands of everyone in front of them.

---

fresh shrimp and lobster for less than you'd pay elsewhere in Nicaragua. For a cheap bite, try the coast's favorite snack, the *patí* (C$5), a crisp pastry filled with spiced minced beef; listen for the calls of the wandering salesman.

Panaderia Arauz (mercado, 2½c O; pastries C$2-30; 7:30am-noon & 2-7pm) Stock up on delicious gingerbread or indulge in the rich, moist chocolate cake at this sweet spot where everything is baked to perfection.

Comedor de Los Platos (contiguo Galileo; lunches C$40-60, frito C$40) A quiet *comedor* serving budget lunches during the day, this local institution transforms into the best *fritanga* in town in the evenings, serving up delicious *fritos* – greasy fried chicken on piles of plantain chips with pickles. Come early.

Pizza Martinuzzi (obelisco, 1c N, 1c O; pizzas C$45-200) With cartoon characters covering the walls and a team of bow-tied waiters, Bluefield's'much-loved pizzeria is just a little bizarre, but the super cheesy pies, while nothing gourmet, hit the spot nicely.

our pick **Luna's Ranch** (frente URACCAN; dishes C$55-200) There are many reasons to visit this impressive thatched ranch on the Loma Fresca hill including live concerts and the interesting collection of images of the old Bluefields, but the reason you'll come back is the generous portions of mouthwatering seafood.

Irie Food and Honey Sweets (obelisco, 20m E; dishes C$70-90) This colorful place prepares quality

meals, including many tasty regional specialties, using fresh local ingredients. The seafood soup is sensational.

Tía Irene (inside Bluefields Bay Hotel, Barrio Pointeen; dishes C$95-300) Watch fishing boats make their way to the dock from this elegant restaurant built right on the water below the Bluefields Bay Hotel. The menu is not too adventurous with beef, chicken and some fairly pricey seafood plates, but the ambience is first class.

Drinking & Entertainment

La Loma (frente Bicu) This hilltop bar/restaurant offers outstanding views over town to the bay and is a relaxing place to drink for those that actually want to hear their companions.

Midnight Dream (LaLa's) (Iglesia, 2c N) With an open-air deck that feels like it is floating on the bay and ridiculously loud reggae, country and dancehall numbers, this atmospheric spot is undeniably the coolest bar on the coast.

Cima Club (mercado, 2c O, 1c N) Don't be put off by the sketchy bar downstairs, the upmarket disco at the top is the hottest club in town, playing a mix of Latin and Caribbean pop.

Four Brothers (Barrio Cotton Tree) Dance up a storm on the wooden dance floor at this legendary disco ranch comfortable in the knowledge that your dignity is protected by the low-wattage lighting.

Getting There & Away

La Costeña (☎ 2572-2500; www.lacostena.com.ni) flies four times daily between Managua and Bluefields (US$82/126 one-way/round-trip). Flights to Corn Island (US$64/98) depart at 7:40am and 3:10pm. There's a flight from Bluefields to Puerto Cabezas (US$96/148) at 11am Monday, Wednesday and Friday. A taxi to the airport costs C$15 per person.

For El Rama, **Transporte Jipe** (☎ 2572-1871; contiguo mercado) has covered *pangas* that leave from the market dock at 5:30am and 3pm, while **Transporte Vargas** (☎ 2572-1510; muelle municipal) has open *pangas* that leave from the municipal dock at 5:30am and when full throughout the day.

There are a number of boats serving Corn Island. The *Río Escondido* (C$200, 4½ hours) leaves from the municipal dock Wednesday mornings at 9am, returning the following morning at the same time. Bigger and more comfortable, but significantly slower, the *Captain D* (C$200, six to eight hours) leaves from the same dock at 9am on Thursday, returning Saturday night at midnight. The *Island*

Express (C$200, 4½ hours) departs from El Bluff at 6am on Friday mornings – requiring either a night in Bluff or a very early *panga* from Bluefields. It comes back on Sunday night.

See Laguna de Perlas (below) for details on getting to that destination.

LAGUNA DE PERLAS

'Pearl Lagoon,' formed where the Río Kurinwas meets the sea about 80km north of Bluefields, is not only a spectacularly beautiful waterway but also one of the most ethnically diverse places in the country. The jungle-lined shores of the lagoon are home to Mískito, Garífuna and Creole communities that make fascinating places to visit. You can make pricey international calls at the Enitel office south of the dock. There are no banks here, so make sure to bring sufficient cash and count on staying a little longer than you planned.

Sights & Activities

Laguna de Perlas town is a timeless Creole community that feels a million miles from the bustle and seediness of Bluefields. Inhabited by some of the friendliest people on the coast, it is a great base from which to explore some the surrounding wetlands, forests and indigenous villages.

If you are here on the weekend, make sure to catch a baseball game at the impressive **stadium**, where half of Laguna de Perlas turns out to cheer on their side in the highly competitive local league. A 30-minute walk through the wetlands behind the town is **Awas**, a Mískito village that has the best swimming beach in the area.

A short boat ride across the lagoon from Awas, lies the laid-back village of **Kakabila**, one of the most traditional Mískito communities in the area. At present, there are no formal accommodations options here but you should be able to sling a hammock in someone's home for a small fee.

Heading north from here, **Orinoco** is the heart of the Garífuna community in Nicaragua. While similar in appearance to the other dark-skinned residents of the coast, the Garífuna have a very different history and culture. Descendants of escaped slaves and indigenous Carib who trace their origins back to the Caribbean islands of Dominica and San Vincent, the Garífuna have maintained many of their indigenous traditions as well as their unique music and dance.

Sleeping & Eating

Green Lodge B&B (☎ 2572-0507; muelle, 75m S; r per person without bathroom US$8) is more than just a pleasant guesthouse – owner Wesley is a knowledgeable source of information on local history and culture. The rooms are a little cramped but there's a peaceful patio with hammocks. Another solid budget option, **Casa Estrellas** (☎ 2572-0523; muelle, 100m S, 50m E; r without bathroom US$10) has basic but comfortable rooms with shared bathrooms and a fresh breeze off the lagoon. Moving up a level, **Casa Blanca** (☎ 2572-0508; torre, 250m O; s/d US$20/40; 🛜) is a lively household with cheery hosts. The bright double rooms have screened windows and woodwork crafted in the proprietors' own shop. Comfortable accommodations are also available at the **Hostal Garífuna** (☎ 8937-0123; www. hostalgarifuna.com; s/d US$8/10), which also serves great seafood meals.

Laguna de Perlas is blessed with a superb bakery; stop by the pink house by the dock for coconut bread and sticky pineapple rolls. For something more substantial, head to **Comedor Miss Cherry** (meals C$60-80) in front of the basketball court for *comida corriente* and delicious local dishes. **Queen Lobster** (dock, 200m N; dishes C$95-195) serves up some of the best seafood in town in a handsome thatched ranch built out over the water.

Getting There & Away

Pangas leave Bluefields for Laguna de Perlas (C$150, one hour) every morning between 7am and 8am and later as they fill. In the opposite direction, there is an early morning boat at around 6am (sign up the night before) and usually one around noon and another at 3pm, depending on demand. Every Monday and Thursday there is a *panga* from Bluefields

---

SPLURGE

The Pearl Keys, located about 30km offshore from Laguna de Perlas, are straight off the classic Caribbean postcard: tiny white-sand islands covered with coconut palms in brilliant turquoise waters. Most of the islands are uninhabited and all are surrounded by incredible marine life. A private tour for up to six people, including transport, a fresh seafood lunch and plenty of snorkeling time, can be arranged in Laguna de Perlas for around US$300.

to Orinoco via Laguna de Perlas (C$250, two hours), returning to Bluefields on Tuesday and Friday.

One bus a day leaves Laguna de Perlas at 5am for the backbreaking journey to El Rama (C$150; six hours).

CORN ISLANDS

Once a haven for buccaneers, the world-apart Corn Islands (Islas del Maíz) are now low-key vacation spots in an isolated corner of the Caribbean. The two isles – Big and Little Corn – retain all the magic associated with the Caribbean – clear turquoise water, white-sandy beaches fringed with coconut palms, excellent fishing, coral reefs and an unhurried, peaceful pace of life – without the crass development of better-known 'paradises.' Little Corn in particular lives up to this, with no cars or many other trappings of urban life.

Big Corn, 70km off the coast of Bluefields, measures about 6 sq km; its diminutive sister to the northeast is only 1.6 sq km (you can walk end to end in an hour). Most people on the islands are of British–West Indian descent and speak English. Almost all live on the larger island, making a living from fishing, particularly lobster.

Prices here are higher than elsewhere in the country, especially food, most of which is brought in by boat. Consider bringing some basic supplies with you.

The islands have somewhat of a reputation for crime, however the security situation has improved significantly in recent years and these days incidents involving travelers are very rare. Nevertheless, it still pays to take basic precautions including hiking with a guide and leaving your valuables behind when hitting remote beaches.

Big Corn Island
pop 7129

Big Corn has heaps to offer, with a wide range of accommodations, fabulous beaches, diving and hiking opportunities. The main township is Brig Bay, where boats arrive. The airport is a 15-minute walk (if you cut across the runway). There are plenty of lodging options in and around Brig Bay, but the best beaches are further south at Southwest Bay or on the east side of the island at Long Bay. Taxis are C$15 per person regardless of distance traveled. The only bank on the islands, **BanPro** (muelle, 500m S) has an all-card ATM and exchanges dollars.

For internet access, head to **Cyber Downs** (muelle, 500m N; per hr C$30).

The enthusiastically run **tourist office** (☎ 2575-5091; shereleeivel@gmail.com; inside Casa Cultura) next to the stadium has information on hikes and can hook you up with guides.

A 10-minute stroll north of the dock, **Nautilus Dive Center** (☎ 2575-5077; www.divebigcorn. com) offer all sorts of aquatic activities, including diving (US$65 for two guided dives, US$280 for the PADI open water), snorkeling (US$15) and fishing tours (US$60). It also rents bicycles for US$10 per day.

The island's biggest party is **Crab Soup** (August 27), which celebrates the abolition of slavery in the British Caribbean with colorful dances, live bands, free-flowing rum and plenty of delicious homemade soup.

SLEEPING
May Flowers (Brig Bay Beach; ☎ 8825-8146; r US$10) This clean and friendly family-run *hospedaje* offers excellent value for money right on the beach. Turn off the main road at Reggae Palace and walk along the beach for about 500m. Look for the buoys hanging from the porch.

Beach View Hotel (☎ 2575-5062; North End; r US$10-15) The concrete building looks ungainly from the outside but this great budget choice is clean, peaceful and right on the water. The rooms upstairs facing the ocean are much nicer and enjoy plenty of breezy terrace space.

Hotel Panorama (☎ 2575-5065; Brig Bay; r with/without air-con US$25/15) This aging motel-style setup 100m back from the beach is not particularly classy but the rooms are clean and the price is right.

Silver Sand (☎ 8948-1436; South End; s/d US$20/30) At a palm-studded point on the north end of lovely Long Bay, rustic cabins sit just a stone's throw from the water's edge. The friendly owners will let you camp or string up a hammock for a small fee.

our pick Yellow Tail (☎ 8659-3634; Sally Peachie; r US$25) Just east of Seva's restaurant, this relaxed place has just two cabins with fridge, cooker and private bathroom in a lovely part of the island. Even if you don't stay here, stop by for one of friendly owner Dorsey Campbell's excellent guided snorkeling trips (US$15).

Picnic Center Hotel (☎ 2575-5232; Southwest Bay; r US$40; ⚡) These bright, breezy rooms are a fine deal considering their location right on the sand of Big Corn's best beach. The thatched bar/restaurant has well-prepared lobster and shrimp dishes and is a great place for a sunset drink.

La Princesa de la Isla (☎ 8854-2403; www.laprincesa delaisla.com; Waula Point; r US$60-75; ℗) Secluded at Waula Point, this is a highly charcterful choice, with lovingly decorated stone-and-timber rooms with shell showerheads. You are paying for charisma here rather than TVs and minibars; it's better value for two people. The fabulous homestyle Italian meals are pricey but worth the splurge.

EATING

For delicious fresh-baked pineapple rolls, gooey plantain tarts and coconut bread, stop by the pink store in front of the police station. They come out hot around 1pm.

Comedor Marlene (South End; dishes C$50-150) At the entrance to the village of South End, the gregarious Miss Marlene prepares flavorful *fritos* (fried chicken with plantain chips) as well as the cheapest lobster on the island.

Art and Eat (Brig Bay; mains C$120-260) If you've finally tired of lobster and shrimp, come to this backpacker favorite for wholesome salads, thin-crust pizzas, coconut curries and other international plates.

Fisher's Cave (Brig Bay; dishes C$135-225) With a fabulous terrace right on the harbor, an excellent selection and reasonable prices, this bright restaurant is the island's favorite seafood diner.

Seva's (Sally Peachie; mains C$150-250) This local institution at the northeast tip of the island serves up tasty seafood, ice-cold beers and reggae classics on a breezy terrace overlooking the water.

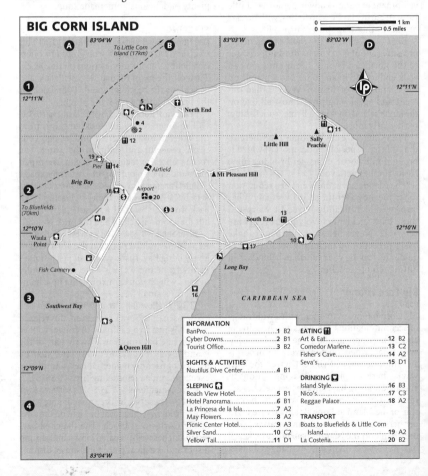

BIG CORN ISLAND

0 — 1 km
0 — 0.5 miles

DRINKING

Fishing cooperative during the week and rocking bar on the weekends, ramshackle **Nico's** (South End; ⏰ Thu-Sun) is one of a kind. Don't miss the awesome Sunday session.

Nearby, **Island Style** (Long Bay; ⏰ Fri-Sun) is a laid-back *rancho* with an open-air dance floor on the sand of a beautiful, rugged beach.

Reggae Palace (Brig Bay; ⏰ Thu-Sun), the only real disco on the island, is loud, sweaty and sleazy in equal measures, but is also a cracking night out.

Little Corn Island

pop 1200

This tiny, enchanting *isleta* is a real unspoiled gem, a rough-and-ready Caribbean paradise with deserted palm-fringed white-sand beaches interspersed with rocky coves and plenty of simple budget lodgings that'll cook you up fresh fish in their own sweet time. Take a deep breath, relax, and… has a week gone by already?

There are two dive outifts on the island. Locally owned **Dolphin Dive** (☎ 8690-0225; www. dolphindivelittlecorn.com) gets plenty of accolades from serious divers and its staff really know these waters. **Dive Little Corn** (www.divelittlecorn.com), right by the dock, is also popular and gives out a very handy map of the island. Both shops are well equipped and offer a similar menu of dives and PADI courses. Snorkel gear can be rented at the dive shops and a number of hotels.

SLEEPING & EATING

The three cheapest sleeping spots are all in a row on Cocal Beach, a 10-minute walk from the dock; just wander on over and see which of them takes your fancy.

Elsa's (☎ 8333-0971; r with/without bathroom US$25/10) A long-time favorite with backpackers, Elsa's offers comfortable thatched wooden bungalows with private bathrooms as well as some pretty basic cheaper rooms out the back. There are plenty of hammocks in which to lie back and enjoy the fresh breeze.

our pick Cool Spot/Grace's (☎ 8820-2798; r with/without bathroom US$25/10) While the colorfully painted huts are somewhat shoddy, this popular place has the liveliest atmosphere on the island and with a beach like this at your doorstep you won't be spending much time in your room anyway. The easygoing management are open to you cramming a few extra bodies into your room to bring down costs and there is a guest kitchen – a real bonus around here.

Sunrise Paradise/Carlito's (☎ 8657-0806; cabañas with/without bathroom US$35/12) More upmarket and a little quieter than its neighbors, this fine choice has clean-swept cabins with firm beds and little porches. Abundant windows ensure fine evening breezes; the beach is cleaned regularly and there's a thatched bar-restaurant serving reasonably priced food.

Ensueños (www.ensuenos-littlecornisland.com; cabañas with shared bathroom US$25-45, casitas sleeping up to 6 people US$50-70) On a good beach in the far north of the island, this quirky and charming spot has rustic grotto-like *cabañas* and more polished solar-powered *casitas* (bungalows) dotted among the forest and fruit trees. If you don't choose to partake in the delicious meals onsite bring a flashlight for the challenging walk into town.

Hotel Los Delfines (☎ 2572-9102; www.hotellosdelfines.com.ni; s/d US$40/50; ❄ 🖳) Want your creature comforts in paradise? Located in the village, this locally owned hotel has large, attractive, air-con rooms with hot showers, cable TV and a porch overlooking the pleasant gardens.

Derek's Place (www.dereksplacelittlecorn.com; huts without bathroom US$45-55) Follow the narrow jungle path to the northeastern tip of the island to find this isolated labor of love that is the perfect place to live out your Robinson Crusoe fantasies. The four beautifully crafted thatched bungalows are spread out over a breezy grassed area surrounded by coconut palms and the elegant shared bathrooms are spotless. Tasty meals are served in the intimate dining area.

Casa Iguana (www.casaiguana.net; cabañas without bathroom US$45, casitas US$75; 🖳) Set among trees with the beach just below, this popular place offers simple *cabañas* with shared bathrooms and much nicer *casitas* with private bathroom. Most have a great deck facing toward the sea. It feels overpriced, but is undeniably a lovely spot. Breakfast is available, and convivial three-course dinners (US$12 to US$16) are served at a communal table; if you want a romantic meal for two, eat elsewhere. It is usually full, so book in advance by email.

Rosas (meals C$60-200) Right by the turnoff to Casa Iguana, this open-air *comedor* has the best-value breakfasts on the island, as well as reasonably priced lunch and dinner menus.

Comedor Bridgette (meals C$120-170) This humble eatery near the dock was one of the first restaurants on the island and still offers the best value for money with big portions of delicious local fare.

Habana Libre (dishes C$180-260) Even if you have to eat coconut bread for a week to squeeze it into your budget, don't leave the island without trying the lobster at this classy Cuban restaurant. It's got Cohiba cigars too if you really want to live it up.

Getting There & Around

La Costeña (☎ 2575-5131; www.lacostena.com.ni) has two flights a day from Big Corn Island to Managua (one way/round trip US$106/164, 80 minutes) at 8:10am and 3:40pm. Both make a brief stop in Bluefields (US$64/98, 20 minutes).

From Big Corn to Little Corn, a *panga* makes the bumpy journey (US$6, 30 minutes) at 10am and 4:30pm, returning from the small island at 7am and 2pm. Boat service is conveniently coordinated with the daily flights. The crossing can be rough; for less pain, sit in the rear.

See Bluefields (p511) for details on boats to that destination.

BILWI (PUERTO CABEZAS)
pop 51,002

Bilwi, on the northeast coast of Nicaragua, is the capital of the North Atlantic region (RAAN) and still commonly known as Puerto Cabezas.

It's still an important Caribbean port, but the main interest here is the local inhabitants. It's a great place to learn about Mískito

---

> ### EXPLORE MORE OF THE CARIBBEAN COAST
>
> The Caribbean coast offers a world of opportunities for no-frills watery adventures:
>
> - Try to persuade a lobster fisherman to take you with him to the **Mískito Keys**, a biological reserve of fabulous islets, coral reefs and stilt houses 50km from Bilwi (Puerto Cabezas). Talk to Marena in town for more info.
>
> - Investigate the **Río Coco**, heart of Mískito country, which runs along the Honduran border. Waspám, the main settlement, is reachable by plane from Managua or bus from Bilwi.
>
> - Swim in secluded bays or hike through thick forest in the traditional Creole community of **Monkey Point**, 60km south of Bluefields. Arrange your trip at the Rama-Kriol Communal Government office.

---

culture; the **Asociación de Mujeres Indígenas de la Costa Atlántica** (Amica; ☎ 2792-2219; asociacionamica@yahoo.es; estadio, 1½c S; ✹ 8am-noon & 2-5:30pm Mon-Fri, 8am-noon Sat) arranges personalized excursions to traditional fishing communities, including transportation, food and lodging with local families, and opportunities to learn local crafts or do volunteer work. BanPro, a block north of the stadium, has an all-card-friendly ATM. There is an Intur office a couple of blocks west of the park and several internet places around town.

Be a little careful in Bilwi; there's plenty of cocaine smuggling going on, and some fairly shifty characters hanging out on street corners.

Sleeping & Eating

Hospedaje Rivera (☎ 2792-2471; Parque Central 1½c S; s/d without bathroom US$8/10, r US$12) A great deal for the price, these comfortable rooms (with private bathroom), above a family home by the stadium, have cable TV and views over downtown Bilwi.

Hotel Pérez (☎ 2792-2362; alcaldía, ½c S; r with/without air-con US$17/11; P ✖) This homey hotel in the center of town offers secure rooms and plenty of upstairs deck space to stretch out with a book.

ourpick Casa Museo Judith Kain (☎ 2792-2225; www.casamuseojudithkain.com; Radio Caribe, 1½c O; s/d US$12/15, with air-con US$23/27; P ✖ 🛜) Set around a lovingly renovated old home, this popular place has bright rooms with polished wood beams and a peaceful garden. There is a crafts shop showcasing the work of local artisans and the attached museum offers a glimpse into life in the old Bilwi.

There are some *comedores* in front of the park. The local favorite is **Kabu Payaska** (dishes C$120-200; ✹ 11am-midnight), about 2km north of town overlooking the area's best beach. The views and relaxed thatched ambience make it worth stopping for a beer, if not a plate of fish or lobster. Get a cab here at any time.

Getting There & Away

Take a taxi to the airport, 2km north of town. **La Costeña** (☎ 2792-2282; aeropuerto; ✹ 8am-noon & 3-6pm) has three flights a day to Managua (US$149 return, one hour and 20 minutes) and thrice weekly to Bluefields (US$148, 50 minutes).

It's a tough slog in a bus to Managua (C$420, 20 hours) – there are two daily services. The bus station is 2km west of town.

NICARAGUA DIRECTORY

ACCOMMODATIONS

Most budget options are in family-operated *hospedajes*. Usual costs are US$4 to US$8 per person for a minimally furnished room, with shared facilities and fans. You'll pay between US$8 and US$12 for your own bathroom. A room for one often costs the same as a room for two. Spending US$12 to US$18 per person will yield substantial upgrades in space and comfort; accommodations in this price category are widely available. Adding air-con usually doubles the price. In the most popular tourist destinations, especially Granada and San Juan del Sur, prices can be significantly higher. But in these places, a growing number of hostels, some quite luxurious, offer dorm-style accommodations for US$6 to US$10 per person.

In general, there are no specific seasonal rates in Nicaragua, but you can definitely ask for a discount when there is hardly anyone around. The exception is during local holidays, when prices climb exorbitantly for a week or so in major tourist destinations.

ACTIVITIES

Nicaragua is becoming an increasingly popular destination for active tourism, with kayaking on Lago de Nicaragua, volcano surfing (p479) and zip-line tours (p490) all available and well-subscribed.

Diving & Snorkeling

Reefs full of marine life near Little and Big Corn Islands (p513) offer outstanding opportunities for snorkelers and divers (with equipment rental and guided dives available on both islands). There's also diving at Laguna de Apoyo (p490) and San Juan del Sur (p496).

Hiking

There are some great hikes around Volcán Mombacho (p490), the Cañon de Somoto (p475) and the highlands around Matagalpa (p465) particularly appealing. Fit walkers will want to hike the country's many volcanoes: one of the two on Isla de Ometepe (p500), for example, or one of the several in the northwest of the country (see the boxed text, p482).

Surfing

Surfing is huge here right now, with prime spots along the Pacific coast, many only reachable by boat. San Juan del Sur (p496) is the jumping-off point for several decent beaches; check the boxed text, p500, for some other great waves. Surf camps are springing up left, right and center: keep your ear to the ground. Even remote spots are becoming more crowded – be considerate to locals anywhere you go.

BOOKS

For more in-depth coverage, check out Lonely Planet's *Nicaragua* guide. Books on Nicaragua tend to focus on its political history.

Life is Hard: Machismo, Danger, and the Intimacy of Power in Nicaragua by Roger Lancaster is a brilliant ethnographic study of the effects of political events on the Nicaraguan family. Lancaster's work explores issues of sexuality, racism and gender identity – topics often overlooked when discussing the revolution.

Culture and Politics in Nicaragua by Steven White is a fascinating look at the link between literature and revolution in Nicaragua.

The Country Under My Skin: A Memoir of Love and War by Gioconda Belli is a memoir from one of Nicaragua's most esteemed writers detailing her – at times – harrowing involvement in the revolution.

Poetry lies at the core of Nicaraguan culture and is thus worth getting to know. *Poets of Nicaragua: A Bilingual Anthology, 1918-1979* translated by Steven White gives an overview of Nicaragua's greatest 20th-century poets.

Selected Poems by Rubén Darío translated by Lysander Kemp offers a broad selection of verses from the country's celebrated poet with English translations on the facing pages.

BUSINESS HOURS

Most government offices (including Intur) and big businesses are open from 8am to noon and 2pm to 5pm weekdays. Shops, banks and businesses involved in the tourism industry tend not to close for lunch and are usually also open from 8am to noon on Saturdays. Exceptions to these hours are noted in individual listings.

CLIMATE

Nicaragua has two distinct seasons, the timing of which varies from coast to coast. The Caribbean coast is best visited from mid-January to April, when skies are more likely to be dry and sunny. Hurricane season runs from September to November. The most pleasant time to visit the Pacific or central regions is early in the dry season (December and

January), when temperatures are cooler and the foliage still lush. For climate charts see p714.

DANGERS & ANNOYANCES

Although there's less tourist crime here than in other Central American countries, it pays to be careful. Increasing violence in Managua makes it the least safe of Nicaragua's cities, while many parts of the Caribbean coast are sketchy, particularly the remote northern area.

But you're unlikely to have problems. Get taxis at night, don't make drunken scenes in public, and keep an eye on your things in buses and markets.

While crime is unlikely to affect you, poverty is a fact of life that you'll confront on a daily basis. Nicaragua is a poor country. You'll be approached regularly in some areas by street kids asking for money but they are rarely insistent.

Strong currents and riptides at Pacific beaches cause dozens of swimmers to drown each year. Lifeguards and rescue facilities are uncommon enough to warrant extreme caution when approaching the waves.

EMBASSIES & CONSULATES

The following embassies are all in Managua. Check www.cancilleria.gob.ni/acreditados for additional information.

Costa Rica (off Map p455; ☎ 2276-1352; Paseo Ecuestre No 304, Las Colinas)

El Salvador (off Map p455; ☎ 2276-0712; Av del Campo 142, Las Colinas)

France (Map p459; ☎ 2222-6210; Iglesia El Carmen, 1½c O)

Germany (Map p455; ☎ 2266-3918; Plaza España, 1½c N)

Guatemala (off Map p455; ☎ 2279-9609; Carretera Masaya Km 11.5)

Honduras (off Map p455; ☎ 2276-2406; Paseo Ecuestre No 298, Las Colinas)

Mexico (Map p455; ☎ 2278-4919; Carretera Masaya Km 4.5, 25m E)

Netherlands (Map p455; ☎ 2276-8643; Colegio Teresiano, 1c S, 1c O)

USA (Map p455; ☎ 2252-7100; Carretera Sur Km 5.5)

FESTIVALS & EVENTS

Every town and village throws an annual festival for its patron saint. Major national events include the following:

National Baseball Championship (mid-January) Nicaragua's favorite pastime comes to a head.

Semana Santa (March/April; Holy Week, the week leading up to Easter Sunday) Religious statues are dusted off and paraded through the streets in towns all over the country while the less pious go on a multiday bender.

ADDRESSES

As few streets have names and fewer houses are numbered, Nicaraguans use a unique system for addresses. They take a landmark, then give the distance from it in blocks, using cardinal points for directions; eg *catedral, 2c N* (two blocks north of the cathedral).

Abbreviations for addresses:

c	*cuadra*	block
E	*Este*	east
N	*Norte*	north
O	*Oeste*	west
S	*Sur*	south

Other landmark-based addresses, such as *detrás catedral* (behind the cathedral), are given in Spanish in the text, so that locals can point you in the right direction. See also p457.

Liberation Day (July 19) Sandinistas from all over the country descend on Managua to celebrate victory over the Somoza dictatorship.

Independence Day (September 14-15) School kids take over the streets all over the country with their marching bands.

La Gritería (December 7) Sing in honor of *La Virgen* and receive candies, fruit and, if you are lucky, tupperware.

FOOD & DRINK
Food

A variety of restaurants serving international and vegetarian cuisine can be found in Managua, León, Granada and San Juan del Sur, but the most typical (and inexpensive) fare can usually be found in street stands, market stalls and *comedores* (basic eateries). Local favorites include: *gallo pinto* (a blend of rice and beans often served with eggs for breakfast); *nacatamales* (banana-leaf-wrapped bundles of cornmeal, pork, vegetables and herbs, traditionally served on weekends); *quesillos* (soft cheese and onions folded in a tortilla); and *vigorón* (yucca steamed and topped with *chicharrón* – fried pork rind – and cabbage salad). In the evenings, *fritangas* open up on street corners, at door fronts and around the central plazas offering an artery-hardening double act of grilled meats and fried sides.

Drinks

Many restaurants serve fresh *jugos* (juices) and *refrescos naturales*, made from local fruits, herbs and seeds blended with water and sugar and poured over crushed ice. These can be a delightful treat or a sugary mess depending on how they are prepared. Look out for unusual flavors including *pithaya*, a purple cactus fruit; tamarindo, from the tamarind tree; and *chía*, a mucilaginous seed usually blended with lemon. *Tiste* is a traditional drink made from cocoa beans and corn.

In spite of the importance of coffee farming, instant is what is most commonly served outside the tourist areas. There are two major national beers. Most Nicaraguans prefer the refreshing but rather bland Toña, while many visitors opt for the slightly more flavorful Victoria.

GAY & LESBIAN TRAVELERS

While consensual homosexual activity has been decriminalized in Nicaragua, prejudices remain in sectors of society, especially with older generations. However, gay and lesbian travelers are far more likely to run into issues with conservative hotel owners than on the street.

For information on the gay community in Nicaragua contact **Cepresi** (☎ 2270-7449; www.cepresi. org.ni) a gay and lesbian advocacy group. The biggest gay scenes are in Granada and Managua.

INTERNET ACCESS

There are internet cafes absolutely everywhere, charging around C$15 per hour. Wireless internet access (wi-fi) is becoming fairly common in larger cities.

INTERNET RESOURCES

IBW Internet Gateway (www.ibw.com.ni, in Spanish) A reasonable portal site.

Intur (www.visitanicaragua.com) Official government tourism website with a nice interactive map and plenty of vague information.

Latin American Network Information Center (http://lanic.utexas.edu/la/ca/nicaragua/) University of Texas' outstanding collection of Nicaragua links.

Nicaliving (www.nicaliving.com) Expat network and forum.

ViaNica (www.vianica.com) Great resource for travelers with information on sights and activities all over the country.

LANGUAGE

Latin American Spanish vocabulary is rich in regional variations. Impress the locals with your mastery of local slang:

bacanal – party
Chele – white person
chunche – thing, small object
Nicas – Nicaraguan guys and gals

palmado – broke, penniless
tuani – cool
tuanis – right on

LEGAL MATTERS

For the most part, police in Nicaragua are professional and approachable, but there is also significant corruption.

Avoid illegal drugs, even if it seems locals are using them freely. Drug laws here make little distinction between personal use and dealing.

If you are driving and get in an accident, leave the vehicle where it is until the traffic cops arrive, even if it is blocking traffic. If someone is injured in the accident, the law permits the police to arrest all drivers until they can determine what went down. In this case, call your embassy immediately as you may need to hire a lawyer.

MAPS

Intur produces some reasonable country and regional maps covering the main tourist areas. If you need more detail, **Ineter** (Map p455; ☎ 2249-2768; www.ineter.gob.ni; frente migración) has detailed topographical maps covering the whole country that can also be downloaded free from its website.

International Travel Maps Nicaragua from ITMB publishing is a little out of date but is still the most detailed road map available.

MEDIA

To keep your finger on the pulse of Nicaraguan affairs, look for the fortnightly **Nica Times** (www.nicatimes.net), which covers the main news in the country in English. For more detailed analysis, pick up a copy of **Envío** (www. envio.org.ni), a fairly unbiased journal published by the Universidad Centroamericana (UCA). **Hecho** (www.hechomagazine.com) is a classy bilingual magazine covering Nicaraguan culture.

The leading daily newspapers are the conservative **La Prensa** (www.laprensa.com.ni) and the more centrist **El Nuevo Diario** (www.elnuevodiario. com.ni).

MONEY

The national currency is the córdoba, though you will often hear prices quoted in US dollars. The córdoba is divided into 100 centavos. Bills are in denominations of 10, 20, 50, 100, 200 and 500 córdobas. Coins are issued in 25, 50-centavo and one- and five-córdoba denominations. *Peso* is a slang term for the currency. It is often difficult to get change for

500-córdoba notes, so break them into smaller bills when you can.

US dollars are widely accepted unless they are marked or torn, however it is generally easier to use córdobas for small purchases. The Nicaraguan government devalues the córdoba by 6% annually against the US dollar in order to maintain stable relative prices despite local inflation.

In better restaurants, the 15% tax and 10% 'voluntary' tip is often added to the bill, unfortunately this is not always passed onto the staff. You should tip all guides.

In this chapter we list prices in US dollars for accommodations, sights, tours, and transportation such as international buses, car rental and flights. Meals, domestic buses, taxis and small-ticket purchase items are quoted in córdobas.

ATMs & Credit Cards

ATMs are the way to go in most of Nicaragua. There are branches of BanPro and Banco América Central (BAC) in major towns; these take Visa/Plus, MasterCard/Cirrus, Amex, and Diners debit and credit cards. There are many more ATMs that take Visa only. You'll also find ATMs in petrol stations and shopping malls.

All over Nicaragua, moderately priced hotels and restaurants will accept Visa and MasterCard. However, they will usually add about 5% to the bill for doing so. Most banks will provide cash advances on credit cards.

Traveler's checks are the way of the past. You can exchange them in many banks, but be prepared to queue and pay substantial fees.

Black Market

Street moneychangers, or *coyotes,* change money at around the same rate as banks, minus the long queues. They're generally honest, but you should know the exchange rate and do the math before completing the transaction.

Exchange Rates

The table following shows currency exchange rates at the time this book went to press.

Country	Unit	C$
Australia	A$1	17.98
Canada	C$1	20.10
Euro zone	€1	26.77
Japan	¥100	24.36
New Zealand	NZ$1	14.69
UK	UK£1	32.45
USA	US$1	21.35

POST

Postal services, handled by Correos de Nicaragua, are surprisingly reliable considering there are no real addresses. Airmail letters to the USA/Europe cost C$15/20 and take at least a week to arrive. You can receive letters at any post office by having it addressed to: (*your name*), Lista de Correo, Correo Central, (*town name*), Nicaragua. Take your passport when you go to pick it up.

RESPONSIBLE TRAVEL

The tourism industry is young in Nicaragua and visitors today have a big impact on the way it will develop in the future.

Support community-based tourism projects, most of which have their roots in collectives set up during the revolution, that generate income for many families rather than wealthy individuals.

Nicaragua's forests are under serious threat from the advancing agricultural frontier. If possible, visit at least one national park during your stay and take a guided tour. The income generated is vital for the long-term protection of these precious resources.

Watch what you eat. While turtle meat and eggs are obvious ones to avoid, also pay attention to seafood, especially lobster, and reject it if it is too small or out of season. Where possible buy fruit and vegetables in local markets rather than supermarkets to ensure more money ends up in the hands of farmers.

Local handicrafts make great souvenirs but avoid products made from endangered species and coral, both particularly prevalent on the Atlantic coast. Cigars produced in Nicaragua can be excellent, however wages and conditions in many factories are far from it. Take a tour and buy direct from the manufacturer to ensure you are not supporting some sweatshop.

STUDYING

Nicaragua is a very popular place to learn some Spanish. Granada and Estelí have the biggest choice, while there are also reputable schools in Managua, León, San Juan del Sur and Laguna de Apoyo. See individual towns for details.

Most schools charge between US$150 and US$200 per week for 20 hours of instruction (four hours per day, weekdays), including room and board with a local family. Excursions to lakes, volcanoes, beaches and cultural and historic sites, as well as meetings with community organizations, may be included in the package. The weekly price is often lower for students who commit to longer stays.

TRAVELERS WITH DISABILITIES

For those with special needs, travel in Nicaragua should be carefully planned. Where they exist, sidewalks are narrow and uneven, while the beat-up vehicles that make up the public transport system also pose a major challenge. Outside the business-class hotels of Managua, accommodations provide little if any concession to those with limited mobility and accessible toilets are few and far between. Despite all this, ordinary Nicaraguans are quick to help people with mobility issues and will come up with enterprising solutions to the difficulties that will certainly arise.

TELEPHONE

There are no area codes within Nicaragua. To call Nicaragua from abroad, use the international code (☎ 505) before the number.

The best places to make international phone calls are the dedicated calling centers, which charge around C$2 per minute to the USA and C$4 to Europe. Internet cafes are usually slightly cheaper but the lines can be scratchy.

There are a small number of coin-operated pay phones around Managua but they rarely work and it is much easier to make local calls from *pulperías,* which usually charge around C$5 per minute.

Cell phones have taken off in a big way in Nicaragua. There are two networks, Claro and Movistar, which have similar coverage and charges. A basic phone can be bought for around US$15, while a prepaid SIM card goes for US$5.

TOURIST INFORMATION

The tourist board **Intur** (www.intur.gob.ni) has an office in nearly every major town, and usually has plenty of flyers and, if you're lucky, a map. Some are excellent with detailed information on hotels, transport and guides, however most are staffed by bureaucrats with little real interest in local attractions. Backpacker hostels, many of which have information centers, are a better bet for practical information.

The environmental ministry **Marena** (www.marena.gob.ni) also has offices everywhere that can provide information on national parks and can sometimes organize guides.

In small towns, the local *alcaldía,* or mayor's office, is often a great source of information on nearby sights.

VISAS

Visitors from most countries can enter without a visa, as long as they have a passport valid for at least the next six months. You must pay US$5 to enter the country and will be granted either a 90-day (most) or 30-day stay.

If you are traveling overland it is important to note that Nicaragua is part of the CA-4 common border agreement along with Honduras, El Salvador and Guatemala. Officially, travelers can only stay for 90 days maximum in the *entire* CA-4 zone and you will only get a stamp in your passport at your initial entry point. Extensions for an additional 90 days can be organized at the immigration office in Managua (p456), after which you will need to head out of the CA-4 (most head to Costa Rica) for 72 hours and re-enter. It's not guaranteed, but travelers arriving by air from another country within the CA-4 often get a fresh 90-day entry.

For up-to-date visa information visit www.lonelyplanet.com.

VOLUNTEERING

Ever since the revolution when waves of idealistic foreign sympathizers descended on the country to lend a hand, volunteering has been very common in Nicaragua. There is no shortage of worthwhile organizations to get involved with; check at local hostels, Spanish schools or at the *alcaldía.* Among the many choices:

Building New Hope (www.buildingnewhope.org) Many Granada opportunities. Intermediate Spanish essential.

Fundación Cocibolca (www.mombacho.org) Volunteer in nature reserves including with sea turtles at La Flor (p499).

Quetzaltrekkers (www.quetzaltrekkers.com) Guide hikes and help street kids (p479).

WOMEN TRAVELERS

There are no special dangers for women traveling in Nicaragua, but the same advice applies as for the rest of Central America about dress, catcalls and so on. In fact, with the normal precautions, many women find Nicaragua to be a surprisingly pleasant country in which to travel. The Caribbean coast, however, is definitely a place to be more careful if solo.

Costa Rica

Mention Costa Rica and people think paradise. The country's Disneylike cast of creatures – ranging from howler monkeys to toucans – are populous and relatively easy to spot. The waves are prime, the beauty is staggering and the sluggish pace seductive. A peaceful oasis in a tumultuous region, this tiny nation draws 1.5 million visitors every year.

What's on tap? The question is, what isn't? Active travelers can surf, hike, snorkel and spot wildlife for starters. The incredibly varied topography means you can cruise the cloud forest one day, climb a volcano the next, and finish passed out on a hot sandy beach. Adrenaline junkies have myriad ways to make mothers worry – among them zipping through canopy lines hundreds of meters long and riding the rough surf of the Pacific.

Of course, the frenzy to snatch a piece of Shangri La has its consequences: since the boom, tourism is more chic and less cheap; classic destinations are now crowded destinations; and local culture is often lost or cast aside. But while nature here suffers its blows, like everywhere, Costa Rica's fans – ranging from international ecologists to proud Ticos (Costa Ricans) – are vocal and vigilant.

FAST FACTS

- **Area** 51,100 sq km
- **Budget** US$35 to US$50 per day
- **Capital** San José
- **Costs** Dorm bed US$10, bottle of beer US$1.50, three-hour bus ride US$4
- **Country Code** ☎ 506
- **Languages** Spanish, English on the Caribbean coast
- **Money** US$1 = ₡520 (colones), US dollars frequently accepted
- **Population** 4.5 million
- **Seasons** Dry (December to April), wet (May to November)
- **Time** GMT minus six hours ; no daylight saving time

TRAVEL HINTS

Hiking at first with a local guide will clue you into what to look for on independent hikes. The best cheap eats are *sodas* (lunch counters), offering fresh fare.

OVERLAND ROUTES

You can enter overland from Nicaragua (Peñas Blancas, Los Chiles) and Panama (Sixaola, Paso Canoas). Check visa requirements in advance.

HIGHLIGHTS

- **Parque Nacional Tortuguero** (p555) Paddling a maze of canals with growling howlers, sloths, crocs, turtles and manatees.

- **Puerto Viejo de Talamanca** (p564) Grooving to the reggae beat and rugged surf of this Caribbean beach town.

- **Montezuma** (p592) Giving in to the seductive tranquility of this terminally chilled-out Pacific beach town.

- **Parque Nacional Chirripó** (p609) Scaling Costa Rica's highest peak (3820m), where the panorama yawns from the Atlantic to Pacific.

- **Monteverde** (p569) Stalking two-toed sloths and tarantulas in a night tour of the cloud forest.

- **Off the beaten track** (p613) Blazing a trail through the pristine rainforest of Parque Nacional Corcovado, pulsing and chattering with wildlife.

COSTA RICA

CURRENT EVENTS

A huge influx of expats, US retirees and foreign travelers has ignited real-estate frenzy alongside a focus on expensive goods and services geared toward this new market. While foreigners bring much-needed investment, they also drive up property prices and displace cash-strapped locals.

It's no wonder some Ticos bristle at the thought of being in Uncle Sam's pocket. This fear was the major impetus for the resistance met by the recently passed Central American Free Trade Agreement (Cafta). Its main proponent, former President Oscar Arias Sánchez, touted its economic benefits, which include increased access to US markets and thousands of new jobs. Critics argued, albeit unsuccessfully, that Costa Rica's small farmers and domestic industries would come out the losers, unable to compete with the anticipated flood of cheap US products.

What's interesting is that this economic and cultural alignment with the USA is unique in today's Central America. While most of Latin America has elected leftist, socialist governments in a turning away from the USA, Costa Rica has placed its bets on this strategic alliance. The 2010 presidential election, which was won by Arias' former Vice President, Laura Chinchilla, served as a popular referendum of the center-right National Liberation Party.

HISTORY
Lost Civilization

Costa Rica's rainforests have been inhabited for 10,000 years. The region long served as an intersection for America's native cultures.

About 500 years ago, on the eve of European discovery, as many as 400,000 people lived in today's Costa Rica.

The Central Valley hosted roughly 20 small tribes, organized into chiefdoms, with a *cacique* (chief) leading a hierarchical society that included shaman, warriors, workers and slaves. To the east, the fierce Caribs dominated the Atlantic coastal lowlands. Adept at seafaring, they provided a conduit for trade with the South American mainland. Concentrated tribes of indigenous people in the northwest tended cornfields and were connected to the great Meso-American cultures. Aztec religious practices and Maya jade and craftsmanship are in evidence on the Península de Nicoya, while Costa Rican quetzal feathers and golden trinkets have turned up in Mexico. The three chiefdoms found in the southwest showed the influence of native Andean cultures, including coca leaves, yucca and sweet potatoes.

Heirs of Columbus

On his fourth and final voyage to the New World in 1502, Christopher Columbus was forced to drop anchor near today's Puerto Limón after a hurricane damaged his ship. Waiting for repairs, Columbus ventured into the verdant terrain and exchanged gifts with welcoming natives. He returned from this encounter claiming to have seen 'more gold in two days than in four years in Spain.' Anxious to claim its bounty, Columbus petitioned the Spanish Crown to have himself appointed governor. However, by the time he returned to Seville, his royal patron Queen Isabella was on her deathbed, and King Ferdinand awarded the prize to a rival. Columbus never returned to the New World, and worn down by ill health and court politics, he died in 1506.

To the disappointment of his conquistador heirs, the region did not abound with gold and the locals were not so affable. The pestilent swamps, volcano-topped mountains and oppressive jungles made Columbus' paradise seem more like hell for new colonies. Balboa's crossing of Panama in 1513 found a western beachhead from which to assault Costa Rica. The Spanish targeted the indigenous groups living near the Golfo de Nicoya. Intercontinental germ warfare caused outbreaks of feverish death on both sides. Scarce in mineral wealth and indigenous laborers, the Spanish eventually came to regard the region as the poorest and most miserable in all the Americas.

It was not until the 1560s that a Spanish colony was established at Cartago. This small community in the interior settled to cultivate the rich volcanic soil of the Central Valley.

Central Valley Sunday

Central America formed a loosely administered colony. Its political-military headquarters was in Guatemala and the closest bishop was in Nicaragua. Lacking strategic significance or exploitable riches, Costa Rica became a minor provincial outpost.

Costa Rica's colonial path diverged from the typical Spanish pattern in that a powerful landholding elite and slave-based economy never gained prominence. Instead of large estates, mining operations and coastal cities, modest-sized villages of small-holders developed in the interior Central Valley. Workers toiled six days a week, while Central Valley Sundays were just for prayer and rest. There were several well-connected families whose lineage went back to the founding of the colony, but anyone could acquire wealth by agricultural processing or trade. In national lore, this relative egalitarianism is touted as 'rural democracy.'

Colonial life centered on agriculture. Costa Ricans grew corn, beans and plantains for subsistence, and produced sugar, cacao and tobacco for sale. However, indigenous raids and pirate attacks kept villagers on nervous guard. When Cartago was leveled in 1723 by Volcán Irazú, new settlements sprouted in Heredia, San José and Alajuela. As the 18th century closed, the population topped 50,000.

As Spanish settlement expanded, the indigenous population plummeted. From 400,000 at the time Columbus first sailed, the number was reduced to 20,000 a century later, and to 8000 a century after that. While disease was the main source of death, the Spanish exploited native labor relentlessly. Outside the valley, several tribes managed to prolong survival under forest cover, staging occasional raids, but were eventually defeated by military campaigns.

A Sovereign Struggle

In 1821 the Americas wriggled free of Spain's imperial grip. The newly liberated colonies pondered their fate: stay together in a United States of Central America or go their separate national ways. The first solution, the Central American Federation (CAF), suffered an imbalance of power and no ability to raise taxes or have defense. Costa Rica formally withdrew in 1938.

An independent Costa Rica took shape under Juan Mora Fernandez, first head of state (1824–33). In 1824 the Nicoya-Guanacaste province seceded from Nicaragua and joined its more easygoing southern neighbor, defining the territorial borders. In 1852 Costa Rica received its first diplomatic emissaries from the USA and Great Britain.

As one empire receded, another rose. In the 19th century, the USA was in an expansive mood and Spanish America looked vulnerable. In 1856 the soldier of fortune William Walker landed in Nicaragua intending to conquer Central America, establish slavery and construct an interoceanic canal. When Walker marched on Costa Rica, he faced a hastily mobilized volunteer army of 9000 civilians. They stopped the Yankee mercenaries at Santa Rosa, chasing them back into Nicaragua. During the fight, a daring drummer boy from Alajuela, Juan Santamaría, was killed while setting fire to Walker's defenses. The battle became a national legend and Santamaría a national hero (and inspiration for an airport). You can see a memorial to this battle in Parque Nacional in San José.

Coffee Rica

In the 19th century, the introduction of the caffeinated red bean transformed the impoverished nation into the wealthiest in the region.

When an export market emerged, the government promoted coffee to farmers by providing free saplings. By the 1840s, local merchants scoped out their own overseas markets, persuading the captain of the HMS *Monarch* to transport several hundred sacks of Costa Rican coffee to London, percolating the beginning of a beautiful friendship.

Children of the 1940s learned to read with a text that stated, 'Coffee is good for me. I drink coffee every morning.' Coffee's quick fix made it popular among working-class consumers in the industrializing north. Enterprising German immigrants improved the technical and financial aspects of the business. By century's end, more than one-third of the Central Valley was dedicated to coffee cultivation, and coffee accounted for more than 90% of all exports.

The coffee industry in Costa Rica developed differently than in the rest of Central America. The coffee economy created a wide network of high-end traders and small-scale growers; in the rest of Central America, a narrow elite controlled large estates, worked by tenant laborers. However, with three-quarters of the coffee barons descended from just two colonial families, the coffee elite's economic interests became a priority in national politics. Today Costa Rica has an estimated 130,000 coffee farms.

The Banana Boom

The coffee trade unintentionally gave rise to Costa Rica's next export boom – bananas. Getting coffee out to world markets necessitated a rail link from the central highlands to the coast and Limón's deep harbor made an ideal port. But inland was dense jungle and infested swamps. The government contracted the task to Minor Keith, nephew of an American railroad tycoon.

The project was a disaster. Malaria and accidents forced a constant replenishing of workers. Tico recruits gave way to US convicts and Chinese indentured servants, who were replaced by freed Jamaican slaves. Keith's two brothers died during the arduous first decade that laid 100km of track. The government defaulted on funding and construction costs soared over budget. To entice Keith to continue, the government turned over 3240 sq km of land along the route and a 99-year lease to run the railroad. In 1890 the line was finally completed, and running at a loss.

Bananas were first grown along the railroad tracks as a cheap food source for workers. Desperate to recoup his investment, Keith shipped some to New Orleans. Consumers went, well, bananas. *Fincas* (plantations) replaced lowland forests and bananas surpassed

coffee as Costa Rica's most lucrative export by the early 20th century. Although Costa Rica became the world's leading banana exporter, the profits shipped out along with the bananas.

Joining with another American importer, Keith founded the infamous United Fruit Company, soon the largest employer in Central America. Known as *el pulpo* (the octopus) to locals, United Fruit owned huge swathes of lush lowlands, much of the transportation and communication infrastructure, and bunches of bureaucrats. The company promoted a wave of migrant laborers from Jamaica, changing the country's ethnic complexion and provoking racial tensions.

In 1913, a banana blight known as 'Panama disease' shut down many Caribbean plantations and the industry relocated to the Pacific. Eventually United Fruit lost its banana monopoly.

Unarmed Democracy

Early Costa Rican politics followed the Central American pattern of violence and dictatorship. In the 19th century, a few favored aristocrats competed to control patronage in the new state. The military, the Church and, most of all, the coffee barons were the main sources of influence. Presidents were more often removed at gunpoint than by the ballot box.

By the late 19th century, the eligible electorate expanded from 2% to 10% of the adult population. Military strongman Tomas Guardia forced higher taxes on the coffee barons to finance social reform. By the early 20th century, Costa Rica had free public education, a guaranteed minimum wage and child protection laws. Denied the right to participate, disenfranchised groups resorted to protest politics. In 1918 female schoolteachers and students staged effective strikes against the despotic displays of President Federico Tinoco Granados, who soon resigned.

Beginning in 1940, events would lead Costa Rica onto a more democratic path. At this time, President Rafael Angel Calderón Guardia defied elite expectations by championing the rights of the working class and the poor. Calderón orchestrated a powerful alliance between workers and the Church. The conservative backlash resulted in civil war after disputed elections. Armed workers battled military forces, and Nicaraguan and US forces joined in the fray. Peace was restored in under two months at the cost of 2000 deaths.

COSTA RICA

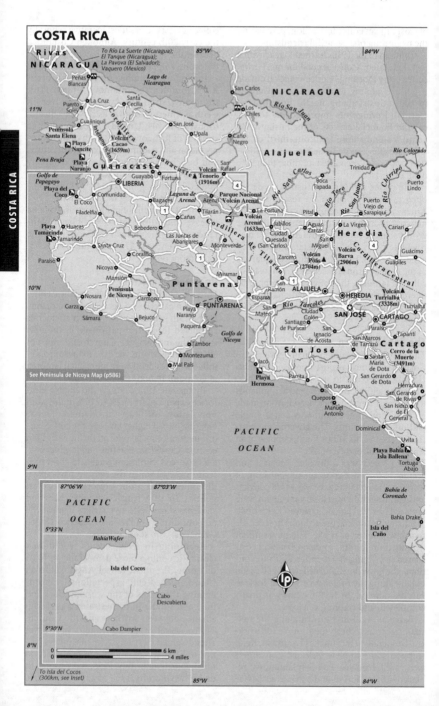

See Península de Nicoya Map (p586)

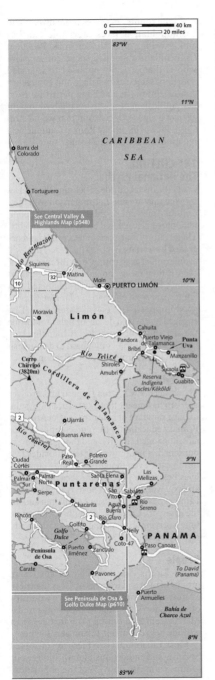

Coffee grower and utopian democrat José Figueres Ferrer became head of a temporary junta government. The 1949 constitution granted full citizenship and voting rights to women, blacks, indigenous groups and Chinese minorities. His copious decrees taxed the wealthy, nationalized banks and built a modern welfare state. Most extraordinarily, Figueres abolished the military, calling it a threat to democracy. These actions became the foundation for Costa Rica's unique and unarmed democracy.

The Contra Conflict

The sovereignty of the small nations of Central America was limited by their northern neighbor, the USA. Yankees were hostile toward leftist politics. During the 1970s, radical socialists forced the military regimes of Guatemala, El Salvador and Nicaragua onto the defensive. When they toppled the American-backed Somoza dictatorship in Nicaragua in 1979, President Ronald Reagan decided to intervene. The Cold War arrived in the hot tropics.

Under intense US pressure, politically moderate Costa Rica was reluctantly dragged in. The Contras set up camp in Costa Rica, from where they staged guerrilla raids and built a secret jungle airstrip to fly in weapons and supplies. Costa Rican authorities were bribed to keep quiet. Diplomatic relations between Costa Rica and Nicaragua grew nastier and border clashes became bloodier.

The war polarized Costa Rica. Conservatives pushed to re-establish the military and join the anticommunist crusade. On the opposing side, in May 1984, over 20,000 demonstrators marched through San José to give peace a chance. The debate peaked with the 1986 presidential election. The victor was 44-year-old Oscar Arias Sánchez, an intellectual reformer in the mold of Figueres.

Once in office, Arias affirmed his commitment to a negotiated resolution and reasserted Costa Rican national independence. He vowed to uphold neutrality and kick out the Contras. Soon, the US ambassador quit his post and a public ceremony had Costa Rican schoolchildren planting trees on the secret CIA airfield. Most notably, Arias became the driving force in uniting Central America around a peace plan, which ended the Nicaraguan war. In 1987, he was awarded the Nobel Peace Prize.

Paradise Found

Five hundred years later, the same dense rainforest that conquistadors had cursed revealed a hidden wealth: ecotourism.

An oversupply of coffee caused a crash in prices in the 1970s. The new market unpredictability brought together an unusual alliance of big business and environmentalists. If wealth could not be sustained through the country's exports, then what about imports – of tourists? Costa Rica embarked on a green revolution. By 1995, there were more than 125 government-protected sites. Almost one-third of the entire country is under some form of environmental protection.

Success encouraged private landholders to build reserves as well. It started slowly: Monteverde reserve recorded only 500 tourists in 1975; 20 years later the number surpassed 50,000. Tourism contributed more than US$750 million in 1995, passing coffee and bananas as the main source of foreign currency earnings.

Modern Currents

Costa Rica's clean-living image has proven wildly alluring, but is it really the Switzerland of Central America? Skyrocketing numbers of tourists and the accoutrements that serve them have created great stress on ecological habitats – ironic, since nature is the country's primary attraction. The market is saturated with a host of largely unregulated small hotels and services that struggle for their piece of an increasingly divided pie. Big-business developers pose another, perhaps greater threat. Costa Rica is finding that, with a fine line between economic profits and environmental conservation, sustainable tourism is difficult to execute. Communities also must face the tourism boom's nasty side effects of rampant child prostitution and drug addiction.

With economic change has come social change. Call it the hamburger effect, but the ubiquitous rice and beans has been upgraded to regular doses of American fast food. Homes are changing, divorce rates have increased and family size has shrunk. More women have entered the workforce though opportunities in the tourism and service sectors. More Ticos are entering higher education while migrant laborers from Nicaragua work the coffee plantations. Rightly or wrongly, immigrants are often blamed for increases in crime, fueling ongoing animosity between Nicas and Ticos.

As the country becomes more diverse and cosmopolitan it faces inevitable tensions and growing pains. Unlike Arias, President Chinchilla is a staunch social conservative who is diametrically opposed to legalized abortion, same-sex marriage and emergency contraception. In a striking departure from her political mentor, she has pledged to fight against proposed legislation that would strip Costa Rica of its official Roman Catholic designation, and establish a secular state.

THE CULTURE
The National Psyche

Costa Ricans take pride in defining themselves by what they are not. In comparison with their Central American neighbors, they aren't poor, illiterate or beleaguered by political instability. Their country is an oasis of peace, in a land degraded by warfare. To keep the peace, they will avoid conflict at all costs. Costa Ricans say 'yes' even if they mean 'no' and 'maybe' replaces 'I don't know.' They are well-mannered to a fault, sparing no effort to *quedar bien* (leave a good impression). You will rarely see a Tico engaged in a heated debate or fight. And while the stereotype of Costa Rican friendliness is largely true, it's sometimes hard to distinguish good manners from genuine affection.

Lifestyle

The absence of war, strong exports and stronger tourism has meant that Costa Rica enjoys the highest standard of living in Central America. Primary education is free and compulsory for all school-aged children and though it is overburdened, a nationwide system provides free health care. Even though 23% of the populace lives below the poverty line, beggars are few and you won't see abject poverty in plain view. Families have the requisite 2.4 children and for the large part, Costa Rican youths spend ample time worrying about dating, music, fashion and *fútbol* (soccer).

People

Costa Ricans call themselves Ticos (men; groups of men and women) or Ticas (females). Spanish is the dominant language. Two-thirds of the nation's 4.5 million people live in the Meseta Central, a central plain that lies at an altitude between about 1000m and 1500m.

Most inhabitants are *mestizo* (of mixed Spanish and indigenous blood). Indigenous groups comprise only 1% of the population, and include the Bribrí from the Talamanca in the southeast and the Borucas in the southern Pacific coastal areas.

Less than 3% of the population is black, concentrated on the Caribbean coast. They speak English, Spanish and a Creole dialect and trace their ancestry to immigrants from Jamaica who built railroads and worked banana plantations in the late 19th century. Chinese (1% of the population) also first arrived to work on the railroads and since then have had regular waves of immigration, particularly from Taiwan. Many of the nation's immigrants were instrumental in founding the first national parks.

With a life expectancy of 76 years, Costa Rica enjoys the highest life expectancy in Latin America after Cuba. More than 30% of the population is below the age of 15.

RELIGION

More than 75% of Ticos are Catholic (at least in principle) and 14% are evangelical Christians. The black community on the Caribbean coast is largely Protestant. While a healthy reverence for the Virgin Mary is typical, few are married to the dictates coming from Rome – apparently *pura vida* (pure life) has its concessions.

ARTS

There is little indigenous cultural influence in the nation's arts. Cultural activities of any kind are centered primarily on Western-style entertainment. San José has the lion's share of museums, in addition to a lively theater and music scene. International rock, folk and hip-hop artists visit the capital and venues around the city host live performances in a variety of musical styles.

ENVIRONMENT
The Land

Smaller than West Virginia and larger than Switzerland, Costa Rica (51,100 sq km) packs in some of the world's most diverse natural landscapes. Wedged between Nicaragua and Panama, its craggy western border is constantly pounded by Pacific surf, while the temperate Caribbean hugs tropical lowlands and swamps to the east. Costa Rica is defined by its diverse climates and topography: mangroves, swamps, sandy beaches, numerous gulfs and peninsulas, tropical dry forests, rainforests, cloud forests, temperate highlands and a variety of offshore islands. It is split in two by a series of volcanic mountain chains that run from Nicaragua in the northwest to Panama in the southeast. The highlands reach up to 3820m above sea level.

Wildlife
ANIMALS

Poison arrow frogs, giant tarantulas and spider monkeys inhabit our imagination of the tropics. In reality, few places live up to our wild expectations – except for Costa Rica. Considered the world nucleus of wildlife diversity, it has over 615 species per 10,000 sq km. Compare that to the USA's 104 species.

Bird-watching calls naturalists to Costa Rica, where there are over 850 recorded species. Because many species have restricted ranges, completely distinct populations are found region to region. Some 200-plus species of migrating birds come from as far away as Alaska and Australia, so it's not unusual to see your backyard birds feeding alongside trogons and toucans.

Spotting wild monkeys and sloths is a highlight, yet an additional 260 animal species await the patient observer. The most exotic sightings include species such as the four-eyed opossum, the jaguarundi and the elusive tapir. The prime places to spot wildlife are national parks, wildlife refuges and other protected areas (as well as their buffer zones). Early morning is the best time to see animals, as many species stay still during the hotter part of the day. Nocturnal species – such as Baird's

---

WE LOVE IT TO DEATH

Tourism may be the hidden threat to Costa Rica's environment. Some 1.5 million tourists visit every year. Not only are many parks environmentally taxed, but tourist infrastructure is strained and the local flavor is leaking out of places. What can you do?

■ Ask hotels how they dispose of waste water. Or have a look around – foul odors and pipes that empty into the street all say something.

■ Buy at markets instead of supermarkets, support small businesses and use local guides.

■ Communicate with locals. Find out what the local issues are and follow through with sensitivity toward those issues.

For more ideas, see p621.

NATIONAL PARKS & PROTECTED AREAS

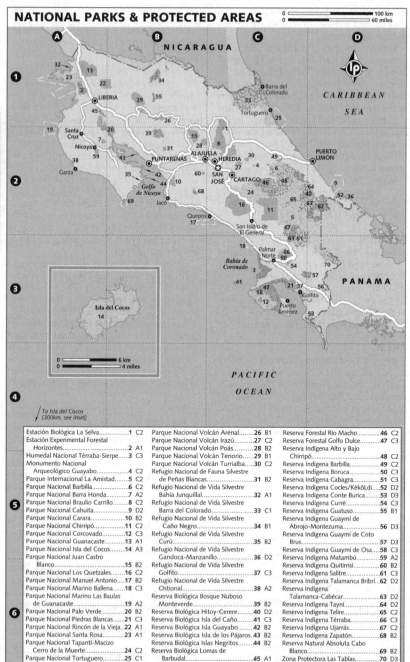

Estación Biológica La Selva................1 C2
Estación Experimental Forestal
  Horizontes....................................2 A1
Humedal Nacional Térraba-Sierpe....3 C3
Monumento Nacional
  Arqueológico Guayabo..................4 C2
Parque Internacional La Amistad......5 C2
Parque Nacional Barbilla...................6 C2
Parque Nacional Barra Honda............7 A2
Parque Nacional Braulio Carrillo........8 C2
Parque Nacional Cahuita...................9 D2
Parque Nacional Carara....................10 B2
Parque Nacional Chirripó.................11 C2
Parque Nacional Corcovado.............12 C3
Parque Nacional Guanacaste...........13 B2
Parque Nacional Isla del Cocos.........14 A3
Parque Nacional Juan Castro
  Blanco..15 B2
Parque Nacional Los Quetzales.......16 C2
Parque Nacional Manuel Antonio....17 B2
Parque Nacional Marino Ballena......18 C3
Parque Nacional Marino Las Baulas
  de Guanacaste..............................19 A2
Parque Nacional Palo Verde.............20 B2
Parque Nacional Piedras Blancas......21 C3
Parque Nacional Rincón de la Vieja..22 A1
Parque Nacional Santa Rosa............23 A1
Parque Nacional Tapantí-Macizo
  Cerro de la Muerte.......................24 C2
Parque Nacional Tortuguero...........25 C1

Parque Nacional Volcán Arenal........26 B1
Parque Nacional Volcán Irazú..........27 C2
Parque Nacional Volcán Poás...........28 B2
Parque Nacional Volcán Tenorio......29 B1
Parque Nacional Volcán Turrialba....30 C2
Refugio Nacional de Fauna Silvestre
  de Peñas Blancas...........................31 B2
Refugio Nacional de Vida Silvestre
  Bahía Junquillal............................32 A1
Refugio Nacional de Vida Silvestre
  Barra del Colorado.......................33 C1
Refugio Nacional de Vida Silvestre
  Caño Negro..................................34 B1
Refugio Nacional de Vida Silvestre
  Curú...35 B2
Refugio Nacional de Vida Silvestre
  Gandoca-Manzanilla.....................36 D2
Refugio Nacional de Vida Silvestre
  Golfito...37 C3
Refugio Nacional de Vida Silvestre
  Ostional.......................................38 A2
Reserva Biológica Bosque Nuboso
  Monteverde.................................39 B2
Reserva Biológica Hitoy-Cerere......40 D2
Reserva Biológica Isla del Caño........41 C3
Reserva Biológica Isla Guayabo.......42 B2
Reserva Biológica Isla de los Pájaros.43 B2
Reserva Biológica Islas Negritos......44 B2
Reserva Biológica Lomas de
  Barbudal......................................45 A1

Reserva Forestal Río Macho.............46 C2
Reserva Forestal Golfo Dulce...........47 C3
Reserva Indígena Alto y Bajo
  Chirripó.......................................48 C2
Reserva Indígena Barbilla.................49 C2
Reserva Indígena Boruca..................50 C3
Reserva Indígena Cabagra...............51 C3
Reserva Indígena Cocles/KéköLdi....52 D2
Reserva Indígena Conte Burica........53 D3
Reserva Indígena Curré....................54 C3
Reserva Indígena Guatuso...............55 B1
Reserva Indígena Guaymí de
  Abrojo-Montezuma......................56 D3
Reserva Indígena Guaymí de Coto
  Brus...57 D3
Reserva Indígena Guaymí de Osa....58 C3
Reserva Indígena Matambú.............59 A2
Reserva Indígena Quitirrisí..............60 B2
Reserva Indígena Salitre..................61 C3
Reserva Indígena Talamanca Bribrí..62 D2
Reserva Indígena
  Talamanca-Cabécar......................63 D2
Reserva Indígena Tayní...................64 D2
Reserva Indígena Telire...................65 C2
Reserva Indígena Térraba................66 C3
Reserva Indígena Ujarrás.................67 C2
Reserva Indígena Zapatón...............68 B2
Reserva Natural Absoluta Cabo
  Blanco...69 B2
Zona Protectora Las Tablas.............70 D3

tapir, the silky anteater and the kinkajou – require night sightings, preferably with a guide.

Working with a knowledgeable guide increases the probability of seeing wildlife and understanding its behavior. Good local guides can recognize bird calls and animal sounds. They also know where creatures tend to congregate – whether because they like the fruit of a certain tree (as the quetzal in the avocado tree), or because they fish at the mouth of the river (as the American crocodile).

ENDANGERED SPECIES

The number-one threat to most of Costa Rica's endangered species is habitat destruction, followed by hunting and trapping. Numerous species have declining populations or are in danger of extinction.

The legendary resplendent quetzal – topping every naturalist's must-see list – approaches extinction as its home forests are felled. A booming pet trade has extirpated the population of large, squawky scarlet macaws. Endangered sea turtles get a lot of attention in Costa Rica, with a wide variety of programs supporting population growth. Central America's largest land mammal, Baird's tapir, is a target for hunters, as is the placid gigantic West Indian manatee. A host of volunteer programs help visitors participate in preservation.

PLANTS

Floral biodiversity is staggering – over 10,000 species of vascular plants have been described in Costa Rica, and more join the list every year. Orchids alone account for about 1300 species. Use your visit to explore the rich variety of plant communities found in rainforests, mangrove swamps, tropical dry forests and cloud forests.

National Parks & Protected Areas

The national-park system began in the 1960s, and today 35 national parks cover 11% of the country. Scores of other protected zones include wetlands and mangroves, in addition to a slew of privately owned and operated reserves. For this reason Costa Rican authorities claim that over 25% of the country is under conservation. There are hundreds of small, privately owned lodges and reserves set up to protect the land, and many are well worth visiting.

While the national-park system appears impressive, much of the protected area is at risk. Logging, hunting and overfishing are classic problems. The government doesn't own all of this land – almost half of the areas are in private ownership – and there is no budget to buy it. Technically, the private lands are protected from development, but many landowners are finding loopholes in the restrictions and are selling or developing their properties.

Most national parks can be entered without permits, though a few limit the number they admit on a daily basis and others require advance reservations to sleep within the park's boundaries (Chirripó, Corcovado and La Amistad). The entrance fee to most parks is about US$10 per day for foreigners, plus an additional US$2 to US$5 for overnight camping where it is permitted (the camping costs are sometimes built into the admission). Some of the more isolated parks may charge higher rates.

Environmental Issues

Despite Costa Rica's national-park system, the major problem facing the nation's environment is deforestation. Originally, Costa Rica was almost all forest, but it has mostly been cleared for pasture or agriculture. Illegal logging compounds the problem. About only 5% of the lands outside of parks and reserves remains forested, while only 1% of the dry forests of northwestern Costa Rica are left.

Apart from the direct loss of tropical forests, and the plants and animals that depend on them, deforestation has led directly or indirectly to other severe environmental problems. The greatest issue is soil erosion. Forests protect the soil beneath them from the ravages of tropical rainstorms – after deforestation much of the topsoil is washed away, lowering the productivity of the land and silting up watersheds. Some deforested lands are planted with Costa Rica's main agricultural product, bananas, the production of which entails the use of pesticides and blue plastic bags to protect the fruit. Both the pesticides and the plastic bags end up polluting the environment.

Deforestation and related logging activities also create inroads into formerly inaccessible regions, leading to an influx of humans. One consequence, especially in national parks where wildlife is concentrated, is unrestrained poaching.

National parks in remote areas suffer from a lack of rangers and protection. Others are extremely popular for their world-class scenic and natural beauty, as well as their wildlife. In the once-idyllic Parque Nacional Manuel Antonio, a tiny park on the Pacific coast, annual visits

COSTA RICA

rocketed from about 36,000 visitors in 1982 to more than 150,000 by 1991. This invasion threatened to ruin the diminutive area by driving away the wildlife, polluting the beaches and replacing wilderness with hotel development.

In response, park visitors have since been 'limited' to 600 per day, and the park is closed on Monday to allow a brief respite from the onslaught. But any visitor to Manuel Antonio can tell you that, yes, the animals are plentiful but conditions (with many visitors feeding the wildlife and wildlife becoming aggressive) can be horrendous.

Costa Rica has a world-famous reputation for its national-park system – but a lack of funds, concentrated visitor use and sometimes fuzzy leadership show troubles in paradise. Earnings from the patronage of parks contribute significantly to both the national and local economies. The country has a vested interest in land preservation, and its citizens appreciate the income and jobs ecotourism generates. In spite of all this, questions remain as to how ecotourism will co-exist with expanding agricultural enterprises.

TRANSPORTATION

GETTING THERE & AWAY

Entering Costa Rica is usually hassle-free. There are no fees or taxes payable on entering the country (unless driving from North America; see p534). However, some local Tico towns have recently added their own entry/exit fees, usually US$1. Some foreign nationals will require a visa, and you may incur exit fees in the country you are departing from overland. Be aware that those who need visas cannot get them at the border. For information on visas, see p622. Travelers officially need an onward ticket out of Costa Rica before they are allowed to enter, but the rule is rarely enforced.

Air

Costa Rica is well connected by air to other Central and South American countries, as well as the USA. The national airline, Lacsa (part of the Central American Airline consortium Grupo TACA), flies to numerous points in the USA and Latin America, including Cuba. The US Federal Aviation Administration has assessed Costa Rica's aviation authorities to be in compliance with international safety

standards. Fares go up during the high season (from December through April).

Aeropuerto Internacional Juan Santamaría (p544) is about 17km outside San José, in the city of Alajuela. Aeropuerto Internacional Daniel Oduber Quirós (p581) in Liberia also receives international flights from the USA and Canada.

Bus & Boat

Costa Rica shares land borders with Nicaragua and Panama. Many travelers enter the country by bus since an extensive bus system links the Central American capitals and it's vastly cheaper than flying.

If crossing the border by bus, note that international buses may cost slightly more than taking a local bus to the border, then another onwards from the border, but they're worth it. These better-quality buses travel faster and can help you cross efficiently.

The most popular crossing point between Nicaragua and Costa Rica is on the Interamericana at Peñas Blancas (see p583). The crossing at Los Chiles (see p577), further east, is infrequently used but reportedly easy to navigate. There is a regular boat service connecting Los Chiles with San Carlos, on the southeast corner of Lago de Nicaragua.

For Panama, the main point is on the Interamericana at Paso Canoas (see p616); expect long lines. On the Caribbean side, the crossing at Sixaola (see p567) is much more sedate.

See p622 for entry requirements.

GETTING AROUND

Air

Costa Rica's domestic airlines are **NatureAir** (www.natureair.com) and **Sansa** (www.flysansa.com); the latter is linked with Grupo TACA.

NatureAir flies from Tobías Bolaños airport (p544), 8km west of the center of San José in the suburb of Pavas. Sansa operates

---

DEPARTURE TAX

There is a US$26 departure tax on all international outbound flights, payable in cash (US dollars or colones, or a mix of the two). At the Juan Santamaría airport you can pay by credit card, and Banco de Costa Rica has an ATM (on the Plus system) next to the departure-tax station.

out of Juan Santamaría airport. Both fly small passenger planes with a baggage allowance of 12kg. Space is limited and demand great during the high season, so reserve ahead.

Bicycle

The traffic may be hazardous and the roads narrow, steep and winding, but cyclists do pedal Costa Rica. Mountain bikes and beach cruisers can be rented in towns with a significant tourist presence for US$8 to US$15 per day.

Boat

Ferries cross the Golfo de Nicoya connecting the central Pacific coast with the southern tip of Península de Nicoya. The **Coonatramar ferry** (adult/child/car ₡860/515/1850, two hours) links Puntarenas with Playa Naranjo four times daily. The **Ferry Peninsular** (adult/child/car ₡810/485/1900, two hours) travels between Puntarenas and Vaqueroevery.

On the Golfo Dulce, a daily passenger ferry links Golfito with Puerto Jiménez on the Península de Osa, and a weekday water taxi travels to and from Playa Zancudo. On the western side of the Península de Osa, water taxis connect Bahía Drake with Sierpe.

On the Caribbean coast, a bus-and-boat service runs several times daily, linking Cariari and Tortuguero (p558). Canal boats travel from Moín to Tortuguero, although no regular service exists. A daily water taxi connects Puerto Viejo de Sarapiquí with Trinidad, at the border crossing with Nicaragua on the Río San Juan. Arrange boat transportation in any of these towns for Barra del Colorado.

Bus

Buses are the best way of getting around Costa Rica. They are frequent and cheap, with the longest domestic journey out of San José costing less than ₡5000.

San José is the transportation hub for the country (see p544), but there is no central terminal. Bus offices are scattered around the city: some large bus companies have big terminals that sell tickets in advance, while others have little more than a stop – sometimes unmarked. (One San José bus station consists of a guy with a clipboard sitting on a lawn chair.)

Normally there's room for everyone on the bus, and if there isn't, squeeze in. The exceptions are days before and after a major vacation, especially Easter, when buses are ridiculously full. (Note that there are no buses on the Thursday to Saturday before Easter Sunday.) There are two types of bus: *directo* and *colectivo*. *Directos* charge more and presumably make few stops. However, it goes against the instinct of Costa Rican bus drivers not to pick up every single roadside passenger.

Trips longer than four hours usually include a rest stop (buses do not have bathrooms). Space is limited on board, so periodically check that your stored luggage isn't 'accidentally' given away at intermediate stops. Keep your day pack with important documents on you at all times. Thefts from overhead racks are rampant.

Bus schedules fluctuate, so always confirm the time when you purchase your ticket. If you are catching a bus roadside, arrive early. Departure times are estimated and if the bus comes early, it will leave early.

For information on departures from San José, the master schedule is online at www.visitcostarica.com. Another more thorough but less reliable source is www.costaricabybus.com.

SHUTTLE BUS

Tourist-van shuttles are provided by **Grayline's Fantasy Bus** (www.graylinecostarica.com) and **Interbus** (www.interbusonline.com). Both run overland transportation from San José to the most popular destinations and between other destinations (see their websites for information). Fares start at US$27 for trips between San José and Jacó, and US$35 for the bumpy ride to Monteverde. These services provide hotel pick-up, air-con and are faster than public buses. Reserve online or through local travel agencies and hotels.

Car & Motorcycle

The roads vary from quite good (the Interamericana) to barely passable (just about everywhere else). Even the good ones can suffer from landslides, sudden flooding and fog. Most roads are single lane and winding, lacking hard shoulders – others are dirt-and-mud affairs that climb mountains and traverse rivers.

Speed limits are 100km per hour or less on primary roads and 60km per hour or less on others. Traffic police use radar and enforce speed limits. The wearing of seat belts is compulsory.

Most car-rental agencies can be found in San José and in popular tourist destinations on the Pacific coast (Tamarindo, Jacó, Quepos and Puerto Jiménez). Car rental is not cheap, but it is worth investing in a 4WD. Prices start at US$500 per week for a 4WD, including *kilometraje libre* (unlimited mileage). Required basic insurance costs an additional US$12 to US$20 per day. Above and beyond this, you can purchase full insurance. Alternately, your credit card may insure you for car rentals – check. As most insurance plans do not cover water damage, be extra careful when cruising through those rivers (drive slowly so as not to flood the engine).

To rent a car you need to be 21 years old or over, have a valid driver's license, a major credit card and a passport. A foreign driver's license is acceptable for up to 90 days. Carefully inspect the car and make sure any previous damage is noted on the rental agreement.

If you plan to drive from North America, you'll need all the usual insurance and ownership papers. In addition, you must buy Costa Rican insurance at the border (about US$20 a month) and pay a US$10 road tax. You are not allowed to sell the car in Costa Rica. If you need to leave the country without the car, you must leave it in a customs warehouse in San José. Note, too, that most car-rental companies in Costa Rica won't allow you to cross borders; check before you sign your contract.

Never leave valuables inside your car, even for brief periods. Always use a guarded parking lot at night and remove all luggage.

Hitchhiking

People who hitchhike will be safer if they travel in pairs and let someone know where they are planning to go. Single women should use greater discretion. Hitchhiking is never entirely safe and Lonely Planet doesn't recommend it.

Hitchhiking in Costa Rica is unusual on main roads with frequent buses. On minor rural roads, it's more common. To get picked up, most locals wave to cars in a friendly manner. Hitchhikers should offer to pay upon arrival: *¿Cuanto le debo?* (How much do I owe you?) Many will wave the offer aside, but it is polite to offer, nonetheless.

Taxi

Taxis serve urban and remote areas. They are useful for remote destinations, such as national parks, where bus services are unavailable. In small villages without clearly marked taxis, ask at the local *pulpería* (corner store) about service. If the taxi doesn't have a meter, set the fare ahead of time.

A warning – many taxi drivers are commissioned by hotels to bring in customers. In the capital, the hotel scene is so competitive that drivers say just about anything to steer you to the places they represent. They'll tell you the establishment you've chosen is a notorious drug den, it's closed down, or that, sadly, it's overbooked. Don't believe them. Be firm, and if you're still met with resistance, grab another taxi.

SAN JOSÉ

pop 350,000 / metropolitan area 1.5 million

Chepe, as it's affectionately called by Ticos, teeters between the cosmopolitan and just plain ol' commercial. On first impressions, the downtown area, thick with office towers, malls and fried-chicken chains, could be *anywhere* in today's modern world. But wander Barrio Amón and you'll find that colonial stylings still radiate. In the shifting light of dusk Parque España becomes a riot of tropical birdsong. Cool clubs and bars abound and *josefinos* (inhabitants of San José) are friendly and fast to order up another round of beers.

San José was founded in 1737, but little remains of its colonial era. Booming capitalism has left many disenfranchised and the city struggles to manage a growing crime rate so atypical of the *pura vida* spirit. For travelers, a stopover in San José is regarded as a necessary evil before heading to the 'real' Costa Rica. However, as the home of one-third of all Ticos, Chepe's complexity offers an unadulterated vista on modern-day Costa Rica.

ORIENTATION

The city is in the heart of a wide and fertile valley called the Meseta Central (Central Valley). San José's center is arranged in a grid with avenidas running east to west and calles running north to south. Av Central, the nucleus of the city, becomes a pedestrian mall between Calles 6 and 9. It turns into Paseo Colón west of Calle 14.

The center has several loosely defined *barrios* (districts). The central area is a commercial area with bus stops and cultural sights. Perhaps the most interesting district to visitors is Barrio Amón, northeast of Av 5 and Calle 1, with its concentration of landmark mansions, largely converted into hotels and fine-dining establishments. Just west of downtown is La Sabana, named after the park.

About 2km east of central San José, hoity-toity residential areas Los Yoses and San Pedro are home to a number of embassies as well as the most prestigious university in the country, La Universidad de Costa Rica (UCR). The area serves as the nightlife hub of under-30 *josefinos*, with trendy bars, restaurants and nightclubs. Much like a Latin love affair, hot spots sizzle and fizzle quickly.

While this book indicates streets and avenues, most locals instead use landmarks to guide themselves. Learn how to decipher Tico directions by turning to the boxed text, p618.

INFORMATION
Bookstores
7th Street Books (☎ 2256-8251; Calle 7 btwn Avs Central & 1; ⏰ 10am-5pm) The headquarters of all things English-language; also carries maps.

Librería Lehmann (☎ 2223-1212; www.librerialeh mann.com; Av Central btwn Calles 1 & 3; ⏰ 8am-6:30pm Mon-Fri, 9am-5pm Sat, 11am-4pm Sun) Good selection of English books and guidebooks (including Lonely Planet), as well as topographic and other maps (available upstairs).

Librería Universal (☎ 2222-2222; www.universalcr. com; Av Central btwn Calles Central & 1) On the 2nd floor, the shop has a tiny selection of English-language books, as well as a rack devoted to Costa Rican literature.

Emergency
See also p618.
Traffic police (☎ 2222-9330)

Internet Access
Checking email is easy in San José, where cybercafes are more plentiful than fruit peddlers. Rates are generally ₡300 to ₡500 per hour, though these days most hotels (even budget hostels) provide free internet access, mostly via wi-fi.

Café Internet Omni Crisval (Av 1 btwn Calle 3 & 5; per hr ₡400; ⏰ 9am-9pm Mon-Sat) A dozen terminals with speedy connections located on the main floor of the Omni Shopping Center.

Más Movil Internet (Av 5 btwn Calles Central & 1; per hr ₡300; ☎ 2221-4080) Sixteen machines, some of which are loaded with Skype for online calling.

Medical Services
Clínica Bíblica (☎ 2522-1000; www.clinicabiblica. com; Av 14 btwn Calles Central & 1) The top private clinic in the downtown area. Doctors speak English, French and German, and an emergency room is open 24 hours.

Hospital La Católica (☎ 2246-3000; www.hospital lacatolica.com; Guadalupe) A pricey private clinic located northeast of downtown. In 2009, the hospital debuted an adjacent 34-room hotel – geared at patients who arrive for treatments from abroad.

Hospital San Juan de Dios (☎ 2257-6282; cnr Paseo Colón & Calle 14; ⏰ 24hr) The free public hospital is,

---

GETTING INTO TOWN

To/From Aeropuerto Internacional Juan Santamaría

You can reserve a pick-up with **Taxi Aeropuerto** (☎ 2221-6865; www.taxiaeropuerto.com), which charges a flat rate of between US$21 and US$30 to/from most parts of San José. (These taxis are a bright orange color.) You can also take a street taxi, but the rates may vary wildly. Plan on spending at least US$20 to US$25, more in heavy traffic.

Interbus (☎ 2283-5573; www.interbusonline.com) runs an airport shuttle service that will pick you up at your hotel (US$10 per person); good value if you're traveling alone.

The cheapest option is the red **Tuasa bus** (cnr Calle 10 & Av 2; ₡400) bound for Alajuela. Be sure to tell the driver that you are getting off at the airport *(Voy al aeropuerto, por favor).*

To/From Aeropuerto Tobías Bolaños

Buses to Tobías Bolaños depart every 30 minutes from Av 1, 250m west of the Terminal Coca-Cola. A taxi to the airport from downtown starts at about US$12. **Interbus** (☎ 2283-5573; www.interbusonline.com) also has an airport shuttle service for US$10.

From the Bus Stations

International and domestic buses arrive at various bus terminals west and south of downtown. The area is perfectly walkable provided you aren't hauling a lot of luggage. If arriving at night, take a taxi to your hotel as most bus terminals are in seedy areas; taxis cost around ₡1000 within downtown.

incidentally, Costa Rica's oldest (founded 1845). It offers a wide variety of medical services and there is a children's wing. Expect long waits.

Money

Any bank will change foreign currency into colones, but US dollars are by far the most accepted currency for exchange.

Banco de Costa Rica (BCR; ☎ 2284-6600; www. bancobcr.com; cnr Calle 7 & Av 1; ⊗ 8:30am-6pm Mon-Fri) A top local bank, with ATMs that dispense colones and US dollars.

Banco de San José (☎ 2295-9797; www.bac.net; Av 2 btwn Calles Central & 1; ⊗ 8am-6pm Mon-Fri, 10am-2pm Sat) A reliable full-service bank with ATMs on the Plus and Cirrus systems.

SAN JOSÉ

INFORMATION
7th Street Books	1 F3
Banco de Costa Rica	2 F3
Café Internet Omni Crisval	3 F3
Citibank	4 E3
Correo Central	5 E3
Credomatic	6 E3
Hospital San Juan de Dios	7 C3
Instituto Costarricense de Turismo (ICT)	8 F3
Instituto Costarricense de Turismo (ICT)	(see 5)
Librería Lehmann	9 E3
Librería Universal	10 E3
Más Movil Internet	11 E2
Organismo de Investigacion Judicial	12 G4
OTEC	13 F3
Scotiabank	14 F3

SIGHTS & ACTIVITIES
Catedral Metropolitana	15 E3
Mercado Central	(see 49)
Museo de Arte y Diseño Contemporáneo	16 G3
Museo de Jade	17 F2
Museo de Oro Precolombino y Numismática	(see 8)
Museo Nacional de Costa Rica	18 G3
Parque Nacional	19 G3
Swiss Travel Service	20 F1
Teatro Nacional	(see 45)

SLEEPING
Casa Ridgway	21 G4
Cinco Hormigas Rojas	22 G2
Costa Rica Backpackers	23 H4
Hostel Casa del Parque	24 H3
Hostel Pangea	25 F2
Hotel Aranjuez	26 H2
Kabata Hostel	27 F2
Kaps Place	28 H2
Kaps Place	29 H2

EATING
Bar Morazán	30 F3
Café Mundo	31 G2
Churrería Manolo's	32 F3
Churrería Manolo's	33 F3
La Cocina de Leña	34 G1
Mercado Central	(see 49)
Restaurant Shakti	35 G4
Vishnu	36 E4
Vishnu	37 F4

DRINKING
Centro Comercial El Pueblo	(see 41)
Chelle's	38 F3
El Morazán	39 F3

ENTERTAINMENT
Bochinche	40 F4
Centro Comercial El Pueblo	41 G1
Club Oh!	42 E5
La Avispa	43 E4
Teatro Melico Salazar	44 E3
Teatro Nacional	45 F3

SHOPPING
Galería Namú	46 F2
Kiosco SJO	47 F2
Mercado Artesanal	48 G3
Mercado Central	49 D3

TRANSPORT
Buses to Alajuela, Volcán Poás & Airport (Tuasa)	50 D3
Buses to Cañas & Tilarán (Empresa Cañas)	51 C2
Buses to Cartago & Turrialba	52 G4
Buses to Changuinola/Bocas del Toro (Bocatoreños)	53 C2
Buses to Dominical & Uvita (Transportes Morales)	(see 63)
Buses to Heredia	54 E2
Buses to Jacó (Transportes Jacó)	(see 63)
Buses to Montezuma & Mal País	(see 63)
Buses to Nicaragua, Honduras & El Salvador (King Quality)	55 D2
Buses to Nicaragua, Panama, Guatemala, El Salvador & Honduras (Tica Bus)	56 F4
Buses to Nicoya, Nosara, Sámara, Santa Cruz & Tamarindo (Empresas Alfaro)	57 C2
Buses to Panama City & Managua (Panaline)	(see 53)
Buses to Peñas Blancas (Transportes Deldú)	58 D2
Buses to Puerto Jiménez (Blanco Lobo)	59 D2
Buses to Puntarenas (Empresarios Unidos)	60 C4
Buses to Quepos/Manuel Antonio (Transportes Morales)	(see 63)
Buses to Volcán Irazú	61 E3
Gran Terminal del Caribe	62 E1
Terminal Coca-Cola	63 C3
Terminal San Carlos	64 D2

Barrio México

To Interamericana (2km);
Aeropuerto Internacional
Juan Santamaría (17km);
Alajuela (18km)

Iglesia Barrio México
Plaza
Av 13
Av 11
Av 9
Av 7
Av 5
Av 3
Av 1

Paseo Colón
Av Central
Av 2
Av 4
Av 10
Av 12

To Club Vertigo (800m);
Museo de Arte Costarricense (1km);
Parque La Sabana (1km);
Estadio Nacional (1.9km);
Pavas (3.7km);
Immigration Office (5km)

Parque La Merced

Citibank (☎ 2239-9091; www.latinamerica.citibank.com/costarica/index.html; Av 1 btwn Calles Central & 1; 🕙 8:30am-6pm Mon-Fri, 9am-5pm Sat) Can cash Citibank traveler's checks, plus it has ATMs on the Cirrus, Plus and Visa systems.

Credomatic (☎ 2295-9898; www.credomatic.com; Calle Central btwn Avs 3 & 5) A subsidiary of the Banco de San José, it gives cash advances on Visa and MasterCard.

Scotiabank (☎ 2521-5680; www.scotiabankcr.com; Calle 5 btwn Avs Central & 2; 🕙 9am-5pm Mon-Fri) Good service and 24-hour ATMs on the Cirrus system that dispense US dollars and colones.

Post

Correo Central (Central Post Office; www.correos.go.cr; Calle 2 btwn Avs 1 & 3; 🕙 8am-5pm Mon-Fri, 7:30am-noon

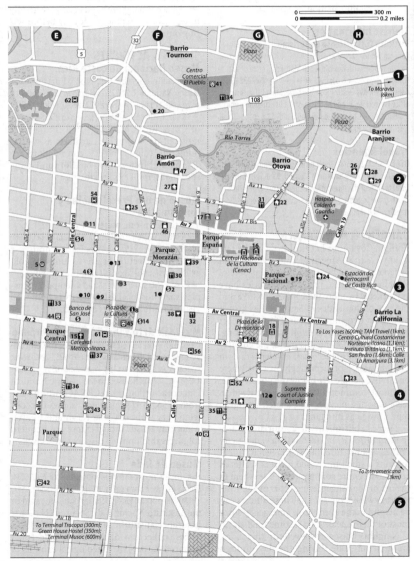

COSTA RICA

Sat) The most efficient place in Costa Rica to send and receive mail.

Telephone

Local and international calls can be made from most public phones, which are widespread. Chip and Colibrí phone cards are sold at souvenir shops, newsstands and Más X Menos supermarkets. Hotels usually have lobby phones. For general information, see p622.

Tourist Information

Instituto Costarricense de Turismo (ICT, Costa Rica Tourism Board; ☎ 2299-5800; www.visitcostarica.com; ⊙ 9am-5pm with flexible lunch Mon-Fri); Correo Central (Calle 2 btwn Avs 1 & 3); Plaza de la Cultura (☎ 2222-1090; Calle 5 btwn Avs Central & 2) The government tourism office is good for a copy of the master bus schedule (which may or may not be up to date) and handy free maps of San José and Costa Rica.

Travel Agencies

OTEC (☎ 2523-0500; www.turismojoven.com; Calle 3 btwn Avs 1 & 3; ⊙ 8am-6pm Mon-Fri, 9am-1pm Sat) Local branch of the international agency specializing in youth travel; can issue student discount cards. Long-standing and reputable.

DANGERS & ANNOYANCES

Though Costa Rica has the lowest crime rate of any Central American country, crime in urban centers such as San José is a problem. Within Costa Rica, reported robberies have skyrocketed by more than 50% since 1998 and the rate of homicides in San José has grown by almost two thirds, according to a report issued by the UN in 2009. It is worth noting, however, that despite this trend, the country still retains one of the lowest homicide rates in the Americas. Not surprisingly, in a city where one in five people live below the poverty line, the most common offense is theft. Readers have reported pickpockets, snatch-and-grab theft, as well as muggings.

The establishment of a tourism police (policía turística) in 2007 has alleviated petty crimes against foreigners somewhat, but it remains a small force: 400 officers scattered around the entire country. (You'll see them in the major tourist gathering spots in San José, wearing white polo shirts.) These officers can be helpful in the event of an emergency since most of them speak at least some English.

Neighborhoods reviewed in this book are generally safe during the day, though you should be especially careful around the Coca-Cola bus terminal and the red-light district south of Parque Central, particularly at night. The following districts are dodgy during the day and unsafe at night: Leon XIII, 15 de Septiembre, Cuba, Cristo Rey, Sagrada Familia, México, Bajo Piuses, Los Cuadros, Torremolinos, Desamparados, Pavas and La Carpio. Be advised that, like in most major cities, adjacent neighborhoods can vary greatly in terms of safety; inquire locally before setting out.

SIGHTS & ACTIVITIES
Museo Nacional de Costa Rica

Located inside the Bellavista Fortress, the **Museo Nacional** (☎ 2257-1433; www.museocostarica. go.cr; Calle 17 btwn Avs Central & 2; adult/student US$6/3; ⊙ 8:30am-4:30pm Tue-Sun) offers a quick survey of Costa Rican history. You'll find a wide range of pre-Columbian artifacts as well as numerous colonial objects and religious art. The natural-history wing has flora and fauna specimens, minerals and fossils.

Museo de Oro Precolombino y Numismática

This three-in-one **museum** (☎ 2243-4221; www.museosdelbancocentral.org; basement, Plaza de la Cultura; admission US$9; ⊙ 9am-4:45pm Tue-Sun) houses a glittering collection of pre-Columbian gold artifacts, a small exhibit detailing the history of Costa Rican currency and a temporary display space for local art. Security is tight – all visitors must leave bags at the door.

Museo de Arte y Diseño Contemporáneo

Commonly referred to as MADC, the **contemporary art and design museum** (☎ 2257-7202; www.madc.ac.cr; Av 3 btwn Calles 13 & 15; admission US$3; ⊙ 9am-4:45pm Mon-Sat) is housed in the historic National Liquor Factory building (CENAC), which dates from 1856. MADC primarily shows the contemporary work of Costa Rican and Central American artists, though there are frequent rotating exhibitions on display here as well.

Museo de Jade

San José's most famous **museum** (☎ 2287-6034; Edificio INS, Av 7 btwn Calles 9 & 11, 11th fl; adult US$7; ⊙ 8:30am-3:30pm Mon-Fri, 9am-1pm Sat) is located in the Instituto Nacional de Seguros (National Insurance Institute). It houses the world's largest collection of American jade (pronounced ha-day). Archaeological exhibits of ceramics and stonework offer insight into Costa Rica's pre-Columbian cultures.

Museo de Arte Costarricense

This sunny **museum** (☎ 2256-1281; www.musarco. go.cr; Parque La Sabana), reopening in late 2010, features Costa Rican art from the 19th and 20th centuries. Rotating exhibits feature works by Tico artists past and present. Next to this Spanish colonial-style building you'll find an impressive open-air sculpture garden.

Teatro Nacional

The **national theater** (☎ 2221-1329; www.teatronacional. go.cr; cnr Calles 3 & 5 btwn Avs Central & 2; admission US$7; ⓥ 9am-4pm Mon-Sat) is the city's most impressive public building. Built in 1897, it features a columned neoclassical facade. It is flanked by statues of Beethoven and Calderón de la Barca, a 17th-century Spanish dramatist. Paintings depicting 19th-century life line the lavish lobby and auditorium. The most famous is *Alegoría al café y el banano*, portraying idyllic coffee and banana harvests, painted by an Italian with no apparent experience in the matter (observe how the laborers hold the banana bunches).

Parks & Plazas

The shady, cobblestone-lined **Parque Nacional** (cnr Avs 1 & 3 btwn Calles 15 & 19) ranks as one of the best parks in San José. In its center is the dramatic **Monumento Nacional**, which depicts the Central American nations (with Costa Rica in the lead, of course) driving out the American filibuster William Walker.

South of the Asamblea is the stark **Plaza de la Democracia** (cnr Avs Central & 2 btwn Calles 13 & 15) which is unremarkable, except for the crafts market, the Mercado Artesanal.

Parque España (cnr Avs 3 & 7 btwn Calles 9 & 11) is surrounded by heavy traffic, but manages to become a riot of birdsong every day at sunset when the local avians come here to roost. It is also the most notorious prostitution center in the country. Tragically (or perhaps fittingly), the concrete gazebo in its center is referred to as the **Templo de Música** (Music Temple), and is regarded by many as the symbol of San José.

The heart of the city is the **Plaza de la Cultura** (cnr Avs Central & 2 btwn Calles 3 & 5), an unremarkable park that's nonetheless safe since security guards protecting the Museo de Oro Precolombino y Numismática (located underground) stroll it. The nearby **Parque Central** (cnr Avs 2 & 4 btwn Calles Central & 2) is the place to catch a

taxi or a local city bus. To the east is the modern and well-maintained **Catedral Metropolitana**.

Parque La Sabana, at the west end of Paseo Colón, is the most popular retreat from the grit and the grime. La Sabana is home to two museums, a lagoon, a fountain and a variety of sports facilities including the Estadio Nacional, where international and division-one soccer matches are played. During the daytime, it's a great place for a stroll, picnic or a relaxed jog. During the nighttime, it's a great place for getting mugged.

COURSES

The San José area has fine Spanish-language schools. Those listed here are well established or have received reader recommendations. Most also organize volunteer placements, a great way to learn Spanish while giving back to those who need it most.

Amerispan Study Abroad (☎ in the USA & Canada 800-879 6640; www.amerispan.com) A variety of educational programs, as well as volunteer placements and medical Spanish.

Centro Cultural Costarricense Norteamericano (☎ 2207-7500; www.cccncr.com; cnr Calle 37 & Calle de los Negritos, Los Yoses) A large school with Spanish courses, though it operates mainly as an English school for Ticos.

Costa Rican Language Academy (☎ 2280-1685, in the USA 866-230 6361; www.learn-spanish.com) In addition to Spanish, it offers cooking and dance.

Institute for Central American Development Studies (☎ 2225-0508; www.icads.org; Curridabat) Month-long programs, with and without homestays, are combined with lectures and activities focused on environmental and political issues.

Instituto Británico (☎ 2225-0256; www.instituto britanico.co.cr; Calle 41 btwn Avs Central & 8, Los Yoses) A good spot for teacher training and corporate instruction.

Personalized Spanish (☎ 2278-3254; www.personal izedspanish.com; Tres Ríos) Like the name implies, private classes that cater to your needs.

TOURS

The city is small and easily navigable, but if you're looking for a walking tour that will guide you to key sites, here are some recommendations:

Costa Rica Art Tour (☎ 2288-0896, 8359-5571; www. costaricaarttour.com; per person US$95) A small outfit, run by Molly Keeler, organizes a recommended day tour that visits five different artists' studios, where you can view (and buy) the work of local painters, sculptors, printmakers, ceramicists and jewelers. Lunch and hotel pick-up are included in the price. Reserve at least one week in advance.

Swiss Travel Service (☎ 2221-0944; www.swisstravelcr. com) A longtime agency offers a three-hour walking tour of San José that hits all the key sites. Its offices are inside the Radisson Europa, 250m west of Centro Comercial El Pueblo.

TAM Travel (☎ 2527-9700; www.tamtravel.com; Los Yoses Travel Center, Calle 39 btwn Av Central & 8, Los Yoses; per person US$35) This reputable agency organizes half-day walking tours of the city, along with travel throughout Costa Rica.

SLEEPING
Central San José

Most of downtown's sleeping options are located east of Calle Central, many of them in historic Victorian and art-deco mansions. Accommodations on the western side of downtown are limited: the area is commercial and crime is an issue, especially in the streets surrounding the Coca-Cola bus terminal.

Costa Rica Backpackers (☎ 2221-6191; www.costa ricabackpackers.com; Av 6 btwn Calles 21 & 23; dm US$12, d without bathroom US$28; 🖥 🛜 🐾) East of the downtown area, this extremely popular hostel has 15 dormitories and 13 private double rooms spread out over several structures that surround a nice garden with hammocks and a free-form pool. Rooms and shared bathrooms are basic, but clean, and decorated with tropical-themed murals.

Kabata Hostel (☎ 2255-0355, 2255-3264; www.kabata hostel.com; Calle 7 btwn Avs 9 & 11; dm US$12, d without bathroom US$32; 🗶) Run by a Tico family that lives onsite, this modern, no-frills spot in the district of Barrio Amón has its lobby-lounge painted in bright colors. Small, carpeted rooms are basic, but clean and share a couple of roomy bathrooms.

Hostel Pangea (☎ 2221-1992; www.hostelpangea. com; Av 7 btwn Calles 3 & 3bis; dm US$12, d with/without bathroom US$35/30, presidential ste US$60; 🖥 🛜 🐾) This industrial-strength, Tico-owned hostel – 25 dorms and 25 private rooms – has been a popular 20-something backpacker hangout in San José for years. It's not difficult to see why: it's smack in the middle of the city and comes stocked with a pool, a rooftop restaurant-lounge with stellar views and a combination bar/movie theater furnished with bean bags and a stripper pole. Needless to say, this is a party spot.

Hostel Casa del Parque (☎ 2233-3437; www.hostel casadelparque.com; cnr Calle 19 & Av 3; dm US$12, d with/without bathroom US$40/30; 🛜) A vintage art-deco manse from 1936 houses this quiet spot on the eastern edge of the Parque Nacional. Six large,

basic private rooms and one dormitory have parquet floors and simple furnishings while a private double features a vintage '30s boudoir.

Green House Hostel (☎ 2258-0102; www.green househostel.altervista.org; Calle 11 btwn Avs 16 & 18; dm/s/d/ tr US$13/21/32/43; 🛜) This attractive hostel is adorned with hanging plants, historic photographs and antiques. The rooms themselves are a bit modest, though the perk here is that they all have private bathrooms (even the dorms).

Casa Ridgway (☎ 2222-1400, 2233-6168; www. amigosparalapaz.org; cnr Calle 15 & Av 6bis; dm US$14, s/d US$22/34, without bathroom US$16/30; 🗶 🛜) This small, welcoming guesthouse, located on a quiet side street east of downtown near the Supreme Court complex, is run by the adjacent Friends' Peace Center, a Quaker organization that promotes social justice and human rights. The rooms are immaculate, as are the shared showers and communal kitchen – and the atmosphere is, well, peaceful.

Hotel Aranjuez (☎ 2256-1825; www.hotelaranjuez. com; Calle 19 btwn Avs 11 & 13; s/d/tr from US$29/42/49, s/d without bathroom US$22/25, all incl breakfast; 🖥 🛜) This rambling hotel in Barrio Aranjuez consists of several nicely maintained vintage homes that have been strung together with connecting gardens. The 35 spotless rooms come in an infinite variety of configurations and the private ones are equipped with lockboxes and cable TV.

Kaps Place (☎ 2221-1169; www.kapsplace.com; s US$25-40, d US$50-60, tr US$70, apt US$80-115; 🖥 🛜) Calle 19 (Calle 19 btwn Avs 11 & 13); Av 11 (Av 11 btwn Calle 19 & 21) A colorful little guesthouse on a residential street in Barrio Aranjuez, Kaps has 24 small, homey rooms of various configurations spread over two buildings. Run by Karla Arias, this is most decidedly a family place: expect to see kids playing in the yucca-plant-filled courtyard or hopping on the trampoline.

Cinco Hormigas Rojas (☎ 2255-3412; www.cinco hormigasrojas.com; Calle 15 btwn Avs 9 & 11; r incl breakfast US$30-58; 🗶 🛜) A one-of-a-kind B&B that is a riot of plants – literally, you have to walk through a tunnel of branches just to get to the front door – as well as a riot of everything else. Every nook and cranny of this snug, four-room inn features a piece of art or embellishments crafted out of papier-mâché.

La Sabana & Surrounds

You'll find vintage mansions in the neighborhoods that surround Parque Metropolitano La Sabana.

Galileo Hostel (☎ 2248-2094; www.hostelgalileo.com; cnr Calle 40 & Av 2; dm US$9-10, s without bathroom US$22, d without bathroom US$24-26, d US$30; ☐ ☎) In a vintage house east of Parque La Sabana, this snug little hostel has several dormitories and half a dozen private rooms of various sizes. The freshly painted dorms are tight (it's bunk to bunk), but the rooms are clean and the prices, the cheapest in town.

Gaudy's (☎ 2258-2937, 2248-0086; www.backpacker. co.cr; Av 5 btwn Calles 36 & 38; dm US$12, d with/without bathroom US$30/26; ☐ ☎) You'll find this homey hostel inside a sprawling modernist house in a residential area east of Parque La Sabana. Popular among shoestring travelers for years, it has 13 private rooms and two dormitories. The owners keep the design scheme basic and the vibe mellow. The service is professional and the rooms are well-maintained.

Mi Casa Hostel (☎ 2231-4700; www.micasahostel. com; dm US$12, r with/without bathroom US$30/28, all incl breakfast; ☐ ☎) A converted modernist home in La Sabana, it has polished wood floors, vintage furnishings and half a dozen eclectic guest rooms to choose from (two of which are dormitories). There is a pleasant garden, where a tiny bar stocks cold beer for guests, and there is a pool table, free internet and laundry service. Find it 50m west and 150m north of the ICE building.

Los Yoses & San Pedro

Both of these suburbs provide an enticing (and convenient) alternative to staying in central San José.

Hostel Bekuo (☎ 2234-1091; www.hostelbekuo.com; dm US$12, d with/without bathroom US$35/30, with bathroom & TV US$40, all incl breakfast; ☐ ☎) This restful spot feels more like a home than a hostel. This airy modernist structure has nine rooms (four of which are dormitories, one of which is reserved especially for women), as well as large tile bathrooms, an expansive TV lounge dotted with bean bags, and an interior courtyard with a pre-Columbian granite sphere right in the center. It's in Los Yoses, 325m west of Spoon.

our pick **Hostel Toruma** (☎ 2234-8186; www.hostel toruma.com; Av Central btwn Calles 29 & 31; dm/s/d US$12/35/45; ☐ ☎ 🍴) Overlooking Av Central from a small hill, this graceful neoclassical home once belonged to José Figueres Ferrer, the Costa Rican president who abolished the army and granted women the right to vote. In late 2009, the hotel completed a top-to-bottom makeover that preserved the Spanish tile floors and left the facade's decorative friezes sparkling. While the Toruma contains four dormitories, it feels much more like an inn, with 17 large private rooms, each of which is equipped with a modern bathroom, a sofa, wi-fi and flat-screen TV.

Casa Yoses (☎ 2234-5486; www.casayoses.com; dm US$12, r per person with/without bathroom US$18/15, all incl breakfast; ☐ ☎) Another mellow spot, this nine-room Spanish Revival–style house from 1949 is perched on a hill that offers lovely views of the valley from the front garden. Here you'll find 10 rooms (six of them dorms) that vary in decor and style, but all of which are spotless, with wood floors and tiled hallways.

Hotel Milvia (☎ 2225-4543; www.hotelmilvia.com; s/d/tr incl breakfast US$59/69/75; ☐ ☎) This lovely Caribbean-style plantation building once served as the home of Ricardo Fernández Peralta, an artillery colonel who fought in Costa Rica's 1948 civil war. Now owned by Brit expat Steve Longrigg and his Tica wife, Florencia Urbina, it serves as a hotel and art gallery. Nine eclectic rooms – some carpeted, others with shining wood floors, all dotted with bright pieces of art – surround a pleasant courtyard with a trickling fountain.

EATING
Central San José

Longtime neighborhood *sodas* mix effortlessly with contemporary cafes and boutique eateries in San José's eclectic downtown.

Mercado Central (cnr Avs Central & 1 btwn Calles 6 & 8) One of the cheapest places for a good lunch is at the market, where you'll find a variety of restaurants and *sodas* serving *casados*, tamales, seafood and everything in between.

Restaurant Shakti (☎ 2222-4475; cnr Av 8 & Calle 13; mains ₡2200-4500, casados ₡2700; ☺ 7:30am-7pm Mon-Fri, 8am-6pm Sat; ⓥ) This informal neighborhood health food outpost has simple, organic-focused cooking as well as fresh-baked goods.

Bar Morazán (☎ 2222-4622; 2nd fl, Calle 7 btwn Avs 1 & 3; lunch casados ₡2300; ☺ 11am-2pm) Walk through the dim, smoky lobby casino of the Hotel Costa Rica Morazán up to the 2nd floor and you will be rewarded with one of the cheapest, most-filling executive lunches (*almuerzo ejecutivo*) in San José.

Vishnu (mains ₡2400-3000, breakfast ₡1800; ☺ 8am-7pm Mon-Fri, 9am-6pm Sat & Sun; ⓥ) Calle Central (Calle Central btwn Avs 6 & 8); Av 4 (cnr Av 4 & Calle 1) You'll find a rainbow of salads, fresh vegetable stews and well-rendered soy burgers at this informal chain of vegetarian cheapies.

COSTA RICA

Churrería Manolo's (mains ₡2400-3500, casados ₡2420, churros ₡200-275; 7am-10pm) Downtown West (Av Central btwn Calles Central & 2); Downtown East (Av Central btwn Calles 9 & 11) This San José institution is famous for its cream-filled *churros* (doughnut tubes), which draw crowds of hungry *josefinos* in search of a quick sugar rush.

Café Mundo (2222-6190; cnr Av 9 & Calle 15; mains ₡2800-6500; 11am-10:30pm Mon-Thu, 5pm-12:30am Fri & Sat; V) Set on a sprawling terrace in a vintage Barrio Otoya mansion, it's a perfect spot to enjoy good pizzas and pastas within sight of a splashing outdoor fountain.

La Cocina de Leña (2222-1883/8782; Centro Comercial El Pueblo; mains ₡3500-6000; 11am-11pm Sun-Thu, to midnight Fri & Sat) 'The Wood Stove' is a charming spot with terra-cotta tiles, a wood-beam ceiling and the endearing tradition of printing its menu on brown paper bags.

La Sabana & Surrounds

The residential area around the park is dotted with long-standing family eateries.

Soda Tapia (2222-6734; www.sodatapia.com; cnr Av 2 & Calle 42; breakfast from ₡1600, casados ₡2300-3000, sandwiches from ₡1000; 6am-2am Sun-Thu, 24hr Fri & Sat) An unpretentious '50s-style diner, it's perpetually filled with couples and families noshing on grilled sandwiches and generous *casados*.

Sabores de Jeruzalem (2221-6715; cnr Paseo Colón & Calle 36; mains ₡2900-3500; 8am-7pm Mon-Thu, 8am-6pm Fri & Sun; V) A small, informal Middle Eastern shop, this sells plates of hot *shwarma* (grilled meat) and sandwiches stuffed full of fresh hummus and falafel.

ourpick Machu Picchu (2255-1717; Calle 32 btwn Av 1 & 3; mains from ₡4500; 10am-10pm Mon-Sat, 11am-6pm Sun) This locally renowned Peruvian restaurant will do you right if you have a hankering for all things Andean. A popular spot for a leisurely Sunday lunch, it has an encyclopedic menu that features tasty Peruvian classics such as *pulpo al olivo* (octopus in olive sauce), *ají de gallina* (a nutty chicken stew) and *causa* (chilled potato terrines stuffed with shrimp and avocado).

There are two good neighborhood supermarkets, namely **Más x Menos** (2248-0968; cnr Autopista General Cañas & Av 5; 7am-midnight Mon-Sat, 7am-9pm Sun) and **Palí** (2256-5887; Paseo Colón btwn Calles 24 & 26).

Los Yoses & San Pedro

There are a few gems out in the 'burbs.

Giacomin (2224-3463; Av Central east of Calle 37, Los Yoses; pastries from ₡700; 8am-noon & 2-7pm Mon-Fri, 8am-noon & 2-6:30pm Sat) Obscured by a parking lot to the east of the Automercado is this small, 1960s pastry shop which *josefinos* swear is the best in town.

Bagelmens (800-212-1314; www.bagelmenscr.com; cnr Av Central & Calle 33, Los Yoses; breakfast ₡1000-2000; 7am-9pm;) If you've been on the *gallo pinto* diet, Bagelmens offers decent bagels – as well as delicious, freshly made waffles, super-moist banana bread and surprisingly good Italian gelatos.

Comida Para Sentir (casados ₡1600-2800; 10am-6pm Mon-Fri; V) This informal, bustling student spot serves an international menu of veggie everything that includes curried rice with cashews, vegetable *casados*, whole-grain sandwiches and a mean cappuccino. It's in San Pedro, 100m north of the Iglesia de San Pedro.

Aya Sofya (2224-5050; Calle 33 at Av 1, Los Yoses; ₡2600-7900; 7am-7pm Mon-Sat; V) A hidden gem with a diminutive outdoor patio serves a variety of Turkish and Mediterranean specialties, including fresh hummus, green salads laced with feta cheese, chicken sandwiches and a rotating selection of daily specials.

DRINKING

Whatever your poison may be (ours is *guaro* sour), San José has plenty of options to keep you lubricated – from local dives to trendy lounges. The price of a beer will vary depending on the venue, but count on spending ₡1200 and up. Take your ID; some places card everyone upon entering.

Calle 3, to the north of Av Central in San Pedro, is known as the Calle La Amargura (Street of Sorrow). However, it should be called Calle de la Cruda (Street of Hangovers) because it has one of the highest concentrations of bars of any single street in town, many of which are packed with customers (mainly university students) even during daylight hours. Places come and go, but Terra U (50m north of Av Central), Caccio's (150m north of Av Central) and Tavarúa (across the street) are longtime party spots.

Chelle's (2221-1369; cnr Av Central & Calle 9; 24hr) If you're boozing the night away with Ticos, you might find yourself here at 4am, clutching a cold one and telling people you just met that you love them.

El Morazán (2256-5110; cnr Calle 9 & Av 3; cocktails ₡2500-3000; noon-midnight) Facing the Parque Morazán, this exposed-brick, Spanish tile–clad space dates back to 1904, and is a popular hangout among Chepe's young artsy set.

The Spanish Mediterranean outdoor mall, Centro Comercial El Pueblo, just northeast of the downtown, is a warren of bars, clubs and music venues. The proximity of one place to the next makes it an ideal spot for a pub crawl and there is stringent security, which keeps the atmosphere generally safe (though it can get unruly in the wee hours). Things usually get going at about 9pm and shut down by 3am.

ENTERTAINMENT

Pick up *La Nación* on Thursday for a complete listing (in Spanish) of the coming week's nightlife and cultural events. The *Tico Times* 'Weekend' section (in English) has a calendar of events. Available at the tourist office, *Guía de Ciudad*, published by *El Financiero*, features local happenings. Visit www.entreten imiento.co.cr for more up-to-date movie, bar and club listings across the San José area.

San José has a booming Spanish theatrical scene. The most revered theater is the **Teatro Nacional** (☎ 2221-5341; www.teatronacional.go.cr; cnr Calles 3 & 5 btwn Avs Central & 2), staging plays, dance, symphony and Latin music from March to November. Another major venue is the restored 1920s **Teatro Melico Salazar** (☎ 2233-5424; www.teatromelico.go.cr; Av 2 btwn Calles Central & 2).

Multicines San Pedro (☎ 2283-5715/6; www.ccm cinemas.com; 2nd fl, Mall San Pedro, San Pedro) is a popular multiplex with 10 screens showing the latest Hollywood flicks.

Jazz Café (☎ 2253-8933; www.jazzcafecostarica.com; ✷ 6pm-2am) is *the* destination in San José for live music, with a different band every night. Countless performers have taken to the stage here, including legendary Cuban bandleader Chucho Valdés and Colombian pop star Juanes.

Cover charges vary, but plan on spending about ₡4000 for local groups. It's 50m east of Antiguo Banco Popular in San Pedro.

Club Vertigo (☎ 2257-8424; www.myspace.com/ver tigocr; Paseo Colón btwn Calles 38 & 40, La Sabana), located on the ground floor of a nondescript office tower, is the city's premier club and packs in Chepe's beautiful people with a mix of house, trance and electronica. Downstairs is an 850-person-capacity sweatbox of a dance floor, while upstairs you'll find a chill-out lounge lined with red sofas. Dress to the nines and note that cover charges can skyrocket on guest-DJ nights (from ₡7000).

SHOPPING

Assuming you've dressed down and stuck a wad of extra cash in your sock, the gritty **Mercado Central** (cnr Avs Central & 1 btwn Calles 6 & 8) is the best place for hammocks *hecho en* (made in) Nicaragua and 'Pura Vida' tees (made in China). Get some export-quality coffee beans here for a fraction of the boutique price.

One of the city's best shopping experiences, the **Mercado Artesanal** (Plaza de la Democracia; cnr Avs Central & 2 btwn Calles 13 & 15; ✷ midmorning-sunset) has 100 open-air stalls hawking handcrafted jewelry, elaborate woodwork, Guatemalan sarongs and Cuban cigars.

For a quick education about local indigenous cultures, **Galería Namu** (☎ 2256-3412; www.galerianamu.com; Av 7 btwn Calles 5 & 7; ✷ 9:30am-6:30pm Mon-Sat, 9am-1:30pm Sun) does a wonderful job of bringing together artwork and crafts from a diverse population of regional ethnicities. It can also help arrange visits to remote indigenous territories in different parts of Costa Rica.

COSTA RICA

GAY & LESBIAN SAN JOSÉ

The city is home to Central America's most thriving gay and lesbian scene. As with other spots, cover prices at these venues vary depending on the night and location (from ₡2000 to ₡5000). Some clubs close on various nights of the week (usually Sunday to Tuesday) and others host women- or men-only nights; inquire ahead or check individual club websites for listings. The clubs listed below are on the south side of town, which can get rough after dark. Take taxis.

Bochinche (☎ 2221-0500; www.bochinchesanjose.com; Calle 11 btwn Avs 10 & 12) A club that features everything from classic disco to electronica, as well as special themed nights.

Club Oh! (☎ 2221-9341; www.clubohcostarica.com; Calle 2 btwn Avs 14 & 16; ✷ from 9pm Fri & Sat) A massive dance club with an attached lounge attracts a mixed crowd of gay men, lesbians and their allies. There's drinking, dancing and midnight drag shows every Friday.

La Avispa (☎ 2223-5343; www.laavispa.co.cr; Calle 1 btwn Avs 8 & 10) This is a long-standing gay establishment that has been in operation for more than three decades. La Avispa has a bar, pool tables and a boisterous dance floor that's been recommended by readers.

GETTING THERE & AWAY

Air

Aeropuerto Internacional Juan Santamaría (☎ 2437-2400; Alajuela) handles international air traffic at its main terminal. Immediately to the north of the main terminal, a diminutive blue building houses the operations of **Sansa** (☎ 2290-4100; www.flysansa.com), one of the country's two domestic airlines.

  Aeropuerto Tobías Bolaños (☎ 2232-2820; Pavas), which lies in the San José suburb of Pavas, services domestic flights on **NatureAir** (☎ 2220-3054; www.natureair.com), the country's other domestic airline.

  International carriers that have offices in San José:

Air France (☎ 2220-4111; www.airfrance.com; 7th fl, Oficentro Ejecutivo La Sabana, Edificio 6, Sabana Sur; 8am-noon & 1-5pm Mon-Fri)

American Airlines (☎ 2248-9010; www.american airlines.co.cr; Edificio Centro Cars; 8am-6pm Mon-Fri, 8am-4pm Sat) Across from the Crowne Plaza Corobicí, Sabana Este.

Continental (☎ 0800-044 00005; www.continental. com; No 2, Oficentro La Virgen, Zona Industrial, Pavas; 8am-5pm Mon-Fri, 9am-1pm Sat)

COPA (☎ 2222-6640; www.copaair.com; 1st fl, Torre Mercedes Benz, cnr Calle 24 & Paseo Colón, La Sabana; 8am-6pm Mon-Fri, 8am-4pm Sat)

Delta (☎ 2256-7909; www.delta.com; Edificio Elizabeth; 8am-5pm Mon-Fri) Located 100m east and 50m south of Toyota, Paseo Colón, La Sabana.

Grupo TACA (☎ 2299-8222; www.taca.com; cnr Calle 40 & Av Las Américas, La Sabana; 8am-8pm Mon-Fri, 8am-5pm Sat, 9am-5pm Sun) Across from the Nissan dealer.

Iberia (☎ 2431-5633; www.iberia.com; Oficentro Tical; 8am-noon & 1-5pm Mon-Fri) Located 1km east of Aeropuerto Internacional Juan Santamaría, Alajuela.

Mexicana (☎ 2295-6969; 1st fl, Torre Mercedes Benz, cnr Calle 24 & Paseo Colón, La Sabana; 8am-5pm Mon-Fri)

United Airlines (☎ 2220-4844; www.united.com; 1st fl, Oficentro Ejecutivo La Sabana, Edificio 2, Sabana Sur; 8am-10pm Mon-Fri, 9am-1pm Sat)

Bus

The **Terminal Coca-Cola** (Av 1 btwn Calles 16 & 18) is a well-known local landmark. Scores of buses leave from a four-block radius around it. Several terminals serve specific regions. Just northeast of the Coca-Cola, the **Terminal San Carlos** (cnr Av 9 & Calle 12) serves northern destinations such as Monteverde, La Fortuna and Sarapiquí. The **Gran Terminal del Caribe** (Caribe Terminal; Calle Central, north of Av 13) serves the Caribbean coast. On the south end of town,

Terminal Musoc (Av 22 btwn Calles Central & 1) caters for San Isidro de El General. Other companies have no more than a bus stop (in this case pay the driver directly); some have a tiny office with a window on the street; some operate out of a terminal.

  Buses are crowded on Friday evening and Saturday morning, even more so during Christmas and Easter. Thefts are common around the Coca-Cola terminal, so stay alert. Bus schedules change regularly and prices change with fluctuating fuel costs. Get a master bus schedule at the ICT office (p538) or online at www.visitcostarica.com.

INTERNATIONAL BUSES

International buses get booked up fast. Buy your tickets in advance – and take your passport.

Changuinola/Bocas del Toro, Panama Transportes Bocatoreños (☎ 2227-5923; cnr Av 5 & Calle 16, in front of Hotel Cocorí) US$28; six hours; departs at 9am. This bus takes the Sixaola route and passes through Changuinola, Panama, en route to Bocas del Toro.

David, Panama Tracopa (Calle 5 btwn Avs 18 & 20) US$25; nine hours; departs 7:30am.

Guatemala City, Guatemala Tica Bus (www.ticabus. com; cnr Calle 9 & Av 4) US$74; 60 hours; departs 6am, 7:30am and 12:30pm.

Managua, Nicaragua King Quality (☎ 2258-8834; Calle 12 btwn Avs 3 & 5) US$36; nine hours; departs 3am; Panaline (cnr Av 5 & Calle 16, in front of Hotel Cocorí) US$23; nine hours; departs 5am; Tica Bus (cnr Calle 9 & Av 4) Normal/executive US$21/32; nine hours; departs 6am, 7:30am and 12:30pm; Trans Nica (Calle 22 btwn Avs 3 & 5) US$21 to US$31; nine hours; departs 4am, 5am, 9am and noon.

Panama City, Panama Panaline (☎ 2256-8721; cnr Av 5 & Calle 16, in front of Hotel Cocorí) US$25; 15 hours; departs 1pm; Tica Bus (www.ticabus.com; cnr Calle 9 & Av 4) Normal/executive US$26/37; 15 hours; departs noon and 11pm.

San Salvador, El Salvador King Quality (☎ 2258-8834; Calle 12 btwn Avs 3 & 5) US$62; 48 hours; departs at 3am; Tica Bus (cnr Calle 9 & Av 4) Normal/executive US$53/58; 48 hours; departs 6am, 7:30am, 12:30pm and 11pm.

Tegucigalpa, Honduras King Quality (☎ 2258-8834; Calle 12 btwn Avs 3 & 5) US$60; 48 hours; departs 3am; Tica Bus (cnr Calle 9 & Av 4) US$42; 48 hours; departs 6am, 7:30am and 12:30pm.

DOMESTIC BUSES FROM SAN JOSÉ

For destinations within Costa Rica, consult the following.

To the Central Valley

Alajuela Tuasa (Av 2 btwn Calles 12 & 14) ₡400; 40 minutes; departs every 10 minutes from 4am to 11pm, every 30 minutes after 11pm.

Cartago (Calle 13 btwn Avs 6 & 8) ₡500; 40 minutes; departs hourly between 5:15am and 10pm.

Heredia (Calle 1 btwn Avs 7 & 9) ₡400; 20 minutes; departs every 10 minutes from 5am to 11pm.

Turrialba (Calle 13 btwn Avs 6 & 8) ₡1100; two hours; departs hourly from 5am to 10pm.

Volcán Irazú (Av 2 btwn Calles 1 & 3) Round trip ₡2500; two hours; departs 8am.

Volcán Poás Tuasa (Av 2 btwn Calles 12 & 14) Round trip ₡3400; five hours; departs 8:30am.

To Northwestern Costa Rica

La Fortuna (Terminal San Carlos) ₡2900; four hours; departs 6:15am, 8:30am and 11:30am.

Liberia Pulmitan (☎ 2666-0458; Calle 24 btwn Avs 5 & 7) ₡2800; four hours; departs hourly from 6am to 8pm.

Monteverde/Santa Elena (Calle 12 btwn Avs 7 & 9) ₡3200; 4½ hours; departs 6:30am and 2:30pm. (This bus fills up quickly – book ahead.)

Peñas Blancas, Nicaragua border crossing Transportes Deldú (☎ 2256-9072; www.transportesdeldu.com; Av 9 btwn Calles 10 & 12) ₡4400; six hours; departs 4am, 5am, 5:50am, 7:45am, 9:30am, 10:30am, 1:30pm, 4:15pm and 7pm.

To Península de Nicoya

Montezuma & Mal País (Terminal Coca-Cola, Av 1 btwn Calles 16 & 18) ₡6800; six hours; departs 6am and 2pm.

Playa del Coco Pulmitan (Calle 24 btwn Avs 5 & 7) ₡3300; five hours; departs 8am, 2pm and 4pm.

Playa Nosara Empresas Alfaro (☎ 2256-7050; Av 5 btwn Calle 14 & 16) ₡3900; six hours; departs 5am.

Playa Sámara Empresas Alfaro (☎ 2256-7050; Av 5 btwn Calle 14 & 16) ₡3600; five hours; departs noon.

Playa Tamarindo Empresas Alfaro (☎ 2256-7050; Av 5 btwn Calle 14 & 16) ₡4400; five hours; departs 11:30am and 3:30pm.

To the Central Pacific Coast

Dominical & Uvita Transportes Morales (Terminal Coca-Cola, Av 1 btwn Calles 16 & 18) ₡2500; seven hours; departs 6am and 3pm.

Jacó Transportes Jacó (☎ 2290-2922; Terminal Coca-Cola, Av 1 btwn Calles 16 & 18) ₡2000; three hours; departs 6am, 7am, 9am, 11am, 1pm, 3pm, 5pm and 7pm.

Puntarenas Empresarios Unidos (☎ 2222-8231; cnr Av 12 & Calle 16) ₡1500; 2½ hours; departs hourly from 6am to 7pm.

Quepos/Manuel Antonio Transportes Morales (Terminal Coca-Cola, Av 1 btwn Calles 16 & 18) ₡3500 to ₡3700; four hours; departs roughly every 90 minutes from 6am to 7:30pm.

To Southern Costa Rica & Península de Osa

Paso Canoas, Panama border crossing Tracopa (☎ 2221-4214; Calle 5 btwn Avs 18 & 20) ₡5000; six hours; departs 5am, 1pm, 4:30pm and 6:30pm.

Puerto Jiménez Blanco Lobo (☎ 2221-4214; Calle 5 btwn Avs 18 & 20) ₡5900; eight hours; departs 6am and noon. This bus fills up quickly in high season; buy tickets in advance.

San Isidro de El General Tracopa (☎ 2221-4214; Calle 5 btwn Avs 18 & 20) ₡2100; three hours; departs hourly from 5am to 6:30pm; Transportes Musoc (Calle Central btwn Avs 22 & 24) ₡2100; three hours; departs hourly from 5:30am to 5:30pm.

To the Caribbean Coast

All of the following buses depart from the Gran Terminal del Caribe:

Cahuita (Autotransportes Mepe) ₡3700; four hours; departs 6am, 10am, noon, 2pm and 4pm.

Cariari, for transfer to Tortuguero (Empresarios Guapileños) ₡1400; 2¼ hours; departs 6:30am, 9am, 10:30am, 1pm, 3pm, 4:30pm, 6pm and 7pm.

Guápiles (Empresarios Guapileños) ₡1100; 1½ hours; departs hourly from 5:30am to 10pm.

Puerto Viejo de Talamanca (Autotransportes Mepe) ₡4300; 4½ hours; departs 6am, 10am, noon, 2pm and 4pm.

Sixaola, Panama border crossing (Autotransportes Mepe) ₡5300; six hours; departs 6am, 10am, noon, 2pm and 4pm.

To the Northern Lowlands

Puerto Viejo de Sarapiquí Autotransportes Sarapiquí (Gran Terminal del Caribe) ₡1400; two hours; departs 6:30am, 7:30am, 10am, 11:30am, 1:30pm, 2:30pm, 3:30pm, 4:30pm, 5:30pm and 6pm.

TOURIST BUSES

Grayline's Fantasy Bus (☎ 2220-2126; www.grayline costarica.com) and **Interbus** (☎ 2283-5573; www.interbusonline.com) shuttle passengers in air-con minivans from San José to a long list of popular destinations around Costa Rica. They are more expensive than the standard bus service, but they offer door-to-door service and can get you there faster.

GETTING AROUND
Bus

Buses from Parque La Sabana head into town on Paseo Colón, then go over to Av 2 at the Hospital San Juan de Dios. They then go three different ways through town before eventually heading back to La Sabana. Buses are marked Sabana-Estadio, Sabana-Cementerio or Cementerio-Estadio. These buses are a good

COSTA RICA

bet for a cheap city tour. Buses going east to Los Yoses and San Pedro go back and forth along Av 2 and then switch over to Av Central at Calle 29. (These are easily identifiable by the big sign that says 'Mall San Pedro' on the front window.) The route starts at the corner of Av 2 and Calle 7, near Restaurante El Pollo Campesino.

Taxi

Red taxis can be hailed on the street day or night, or you can have your hotel call one for you. You can also hire taxis at the stands at the Parque Nacional, Parque Central and near the Teatro Nacional.

Marías (meters) are generally used, though a few drivers will tell you they're broken and try to charge you more – especially if you don't speak Spanish. (Not using a meter is illegal.) Make sure the *maría* is operating when you get in or negotiate the fare up front. Short rides downtown cost ₡1000 to ₡2000. A taxi to Los Yoses or San Pedro will generally cost about ₡2000. There's a 20% surcharge after 10pm that may not appear on the *maría*.

CENTRAL VALLEY & HIGHLANDS

First cultivated by indigenous people, then coffee barons and now computer companies, the fertile Central Valley is Costa Rica's quintessential heartland. With San José at its booming core, and the cities of Alajuela, Heredia and Cartago filling its perimeter, *el valle* is the country's main population center. It is also one of the world's largest microchip production centers, tapping a workforce that's young, educated and increasingly bilingual. Some quaint areas remain, but the region is mostly sprawling, savvy and modern, revealing a Costa Rica left off most tour brochures.

ALAJUELA
pop 175,000

Warm and welcoming, ordinary Alajuela has an upbeat vibe that is virtually absent in the capital. This may be Costa Rica's 'second city' but its best features seem undeniably provincial – the mango-lined plaza, old-fashioned barbershops and a soaring alabaster cathedral. It makes a convenient base for those taking early-morning flights or visiting Volcán Poás to the north.

Banks include **Scotiabank** (cnr Av 3 & Calle 2), with an ATM on the Cirrus network. Internet access is available at **BYTE** (cnr Calle 3 & Av 1, 2nd fl; per hr ₡378; ⊙ Mon-Sat). Stock up for long trips with the literary snacks at **Goodlight Books** (☎ 2430-4083; www.goodlightbooks.com; Av 3 btwn Calles 1 & 3), run by Larry, an expat with lots of helpful information.

Northwest of the parque central, **Museo Juan Santamaría** (☎ 2441-4775; www.museojuansantamaria.go.cr; cnr Av 3 & Calle 2; admission free; ⊙ 10am-5:30pm Tue-Sun) commemorates Juan Santamaría, the drummer boy martyred while torching William Walker's stronghold in the war of 1856. Once the town jail, it now houses maps, paintings and historic artifacts.

Sleeping

Hostel Trotamundos (☎ 2430-5832; www.hoteltrotamundos.com; Av 5 btwn Calles 2 & 4; dm US$12, d US$25-30, all incl breakfast; 🖳) This spot is basic, but the rooms are clean and the service is super-friendly. Three dorms and seven private units with cable TV – one of which has an outdoor balcony facing the street – are nestled into a two-story house that surrounds a tiny interior courtyard.

Hostel Maleku (☎ 2430-4304; www.malekuhostel.com; dm US$12, s/d without bathroom US$25/35; 🖳) A sweet little backpackers' abode located on the south edge of town, 50m west of the Hospital San Rafael, Maleku has tight spic-and-span rooms tucked into a vintage home on a quiet street. It's a wonderful, serene spot and the staff is very helpful.

our pick Alajuela Backpackers Boutique Hostel & Hotel (☎ 2441-7149; www.alajuelabackpackers.com; dm US$15, s/d standard US$30/45, s/d deluxe US$38/58, s/d junior ste US$48/68; 🏊 🖳 🛜) This brand new 21-room inn facing the Parque de los Niños is less a hostel than a full-blown hotel equipped with a smattering of dormitory rooms. An interior atrium is draped in plants and a 4th-floor bean-bag lounge offers a prime opportunity to sip beers while watching the planes take off at the international airport in the distance. Dormitories are wonderfully uncluttered (only four people to a room) and each comes with its own bathroom, while the private rooms are graceful, decorated in serene earth tones and equipped with cable TV and double-pane windows.

Welcome to CR B&B (☎ 2265-6563; www.welcometocr.com; d incl breakfast US$50; 🖳 🛜) This charming little place is located about 5km east of the airport on the road to San Joaquín. It's a homey spot, with three double rooms with private bathrooms and à la carte breakfast. It can book all manner of package tours.

Hotel 1915 (☎ 2441-0495; www.1915hotel.com; Calle 2 btwn Avs 5 & 7; d US$55-85; 🅿 🖳 🛜) The exteriors may not look like much, but step through the front door and you'll find yourself in a quaint 16-room inn built around a century-old home. Rooms have adobe walls, wood-beam ceilings, period-style furnishings and most are equipped with a minifridge. In addition, a graceful living room has a stained-glass window and many of the floors are clad in vintage Spanish tile.

Eating

Mercado Central (Calles 4 & 6 btwn Avs 1 & Central; ☺ 7am-6pm Mon-Sat) For the cheapest meals, head to the enclosed Mercado Central for produce stands, inexpensive lunch counters and much, much more.

Soda El Puntalito (cnr Calle 4 & Av 3; snacks ₡1000-2000) Do as the locals do and grab a stool under the old blue awning at this cheap, unassuming corner sidewalk stand.

Jalepeños Central (☎ 2430-4027; Calle 1 btwn Avs 3 & 5; dishes ₡1400-3400; ☺ 11am-9pm Mon-Sat) Run by an animated Colombian-American from New York City, this popular Tex-Mex spot will introduce some much-needed spice into your diet – as well as some super jumbo burritos.

La Mansarda (☎ 2441-4390; Calle Central btwn Avs Central & 2, 2nd fl; meals ₡2600-7500; ☺ 11am-11pm) An old standby for traditional Costa Rican fare is this casual balcony restaurant overlooking the street.

Self-caterers can stock up on groceries at the **Palí supermarket** (cnr Av 2 & Calle 10; ☺ 8am-8pm) or **Más x Menos** (Av 1 btwn Calles 4 & 6; ☺ 7am-9pm Mon-Sat, 7am-8pm Sun).

Getting There & Away

Buses to the airport and San José (₡400, 45 minutes) leave from Av 4 between Calles 2 and 4, from 5am to 11pm. Airport taxis (₡1800) leave from the parque central. The **Alajuela bus terminal** (Av 1 btwn Calles 8 & 10) has buses to Volcán Poás (see below).

PARQUE NACIONAL VOLCÁN POÁS

Ever wanted to peer into an active volcano without the drama of actually scaling it? Costa Rica's most heavily trafficked **national park** (admission US$10; ☺ 8am-3:30pm) is just 37km north of Alajuela by a winding and scenic road. The centerpiece is Volcán Poás (2704m) and its steaming, belching cauldron. The crater,

measuring 1.3km across and 300m deep, occasionally belches sulfurous mud and steaming water hundreds of meters into the air.

From the visitors center, a paved road leads directly to the crater lookout. Toxic fumes (and regulations) will keep you from going into the crater, but two trails branch out from it. To the right is **Sendero Botos**, a 30-minute round-trip hike through dwarf cloud forest nurtured by the acidic air and freezing temperatures. Bromeliads, lichen and mosses cling to the twisted trees growing in volcanic soil. Birds abound; look for the magnificent fiery-throated hummingbird, a high-altitude specialty of Costa Rica. The trail ends at **Laguna Botos**, a peculiar cold-water lake that has filled in one of the extinct craters. Going left of the crater is **Sendero Escalonia**, a slightly longer trail through taller forest. It gets significantly less traffic than the other parts of the park.

A veil of clouds envelops the mountain almost daily, appearing at around 10am. Even if it's clear, get to the park as early as possible or you won't see much. The best time to visit is during the dry season and on the less-crowded weekdays. Note that the park is also wheelchair-accessible.

From San José (₡3400, five hours), Tuasa buses depart 8:30am daily from Av 2 between Calles 12 and 14, stopping in Alajuela at about 9:15am and returning at 2:30pm. Most of these buses also make a pit stop at one of the roadside restaurants along the way.

HEREDIA
pop 100,000

Although only 11km from San José, Heredia is worlds away from the grit and grime of the capital. Its cosmopolitan bustle comes courtesy of the multinational high-tech corporations whose Central American headquarters are here. More bohemian stylings radiate from the National University. Heredia's historic center is one of the most attractive in the country, and the city serves as a convenient base for exploring the diverse attractions of the province.

Scotiabank (Av 4 btwn Calles Central & 2) changes money and has a 24-hour ATM on the Cirrus network. The university district is full of internet cafes.

Watch the older generation square off in checker tournaments at the **Parque Central**. It's also the place to soak up Heredia's colonial heritage. Built in 1798, **La Inmaculada Concepción** sits east of the park. This squat and sturdy

CENTRAL VALLEY & HIGHLANDS

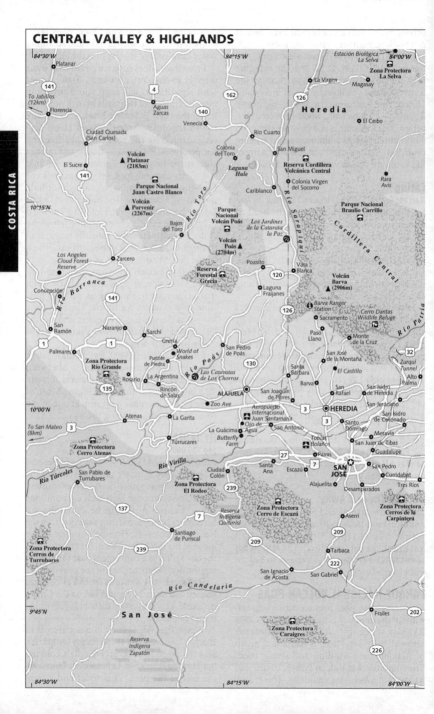

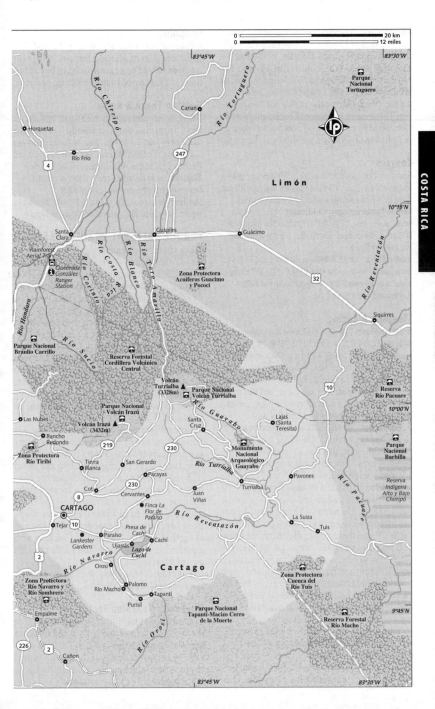

construction has survived some of the worst earthquakes in Costa Rica. North of the park, the 1867 guard tower, **El Fortín**, is the last remaining turret of a Spanish fortress and the official symbol of Heredia. You'll find the **Casa de la Cultura** (☎ 2261-4485; cnr Calle Central & Av Central; admission free; ⏰ hours vary) at the park's northeast corner. This former residence of President Alfredo González Flores (1913–17) now houses permanent historical exhibits, art shows and events.

Courses

Spanish courses are available. Prices are given for five four-hour days of classes, with/without a week's homestay, and two meals per day.

Centro Panamericano de Idiomas (☎ 2265-6306; www.cpi-edu.com; US$480/330) Based in San Joaquín de la Flores, just outside of Heredia, this popular school also has a teen program.

Intercultura (☎ 2260-8480, in the USA 800-552 2051; www.interculturacostarica.com; US$425/285) This Heredia school also arranges volunteer opportunities and offers cooking and dance classes, too.

Sleeping & Eating

Hotel Las Flores (☎ 2261-8147; www.hotel-lasflores.com; Av 12 btwn Calles 12 & 14; s/d/tr US$13/25/40; 🖥) At the southern end of town – and a bit of a walk from the action – this spotless family-run place has 29 rooms painted bright sky blue and key-lime green. The furnishings are basic, but the mattresses are thick – and all rooms have private bathrooms with hot water and TV sets.

Hotel Ceos (☎ 2262-2628; info@hotelamericacr.com; cnr Calle 4 & Av 1; s/d/tr/q US$24/33/43/53) A somewhat ramshackle spot, this has 10 large, dim, bare-bones rooms with private hot showers, cable TV and a large communal balcony.

Hotel Heredia (☎ 2238-0880; Calle 6 btwn Avs 3 & 5; s/d/tr/q US$24/33/43/53) A white-and-blue house has 12 basic ceramic-tile rooms with small, but decent bathrooms with hot-water showers. All have cable TV and there is a small garden out back.

El Testy (cnr Calle 2 & Av 2; dishes ₡1200-2800) Here it is folks: your one-stop shopping for burritos, ravioli, hamburgers, tacos, chicken and fries.

Cowboy Steakhouse (☎ 2237-8719; Calle 7 btwn Avs 3 & 5; dishes ₡1900-7400; ⏰ 5-11pm Mon-Sat) A yellow-and-red joint with two bars; it has patio seating and the best cuts of beef in town.

You can fill up for a couple of thousand colones at the **Mercado Municipal** (Calle 2 btwn Avs 6 & 8; ⏰ 6am-6pm), which has *sodas* to spare and plenty of very fresh groceries. **Más X Menos** (Av 6 btwn Calles 4 & 6; ⏰ 8:30am-9pm) has everything else.

Shopping

Artesanías Víchez (☎ 2237-9641; ⏰ Mon-Sat) The selection of crafts is crude, but you're here for one reason, and one reason only: to buy an authentic Tico cowboy hat. Saddle up and ride!

Getting There & Away

There is no central bus terminal, and buses leave from bus stops scattered around the southern part of town. For information on accessing Volcán Barva, see the section on Parque Nacional Braulio Carrillo, below.

Alajuela (cnr Av Central & Calle 9) ₡400; 20 minutes; departs every 15 minutes from 6am to 10pm.

San José (Av 8 btwn Calles Central & 1) ₡300; 20 minutes; departs every 20 to 30 minutes from 4:40am to 11pm.

PARQUE NACIONAL BRAULIO CARRILLO

Thick virgin forest, gushing waterfalls, swift rivers and deep canyons – it's hard to believe that you are only 30 minutes north of San José while walking around this underexplored **national park**. Braulio Carrillo's extraordinary biodiversity is attributed to its range in altitude, from Volcán Barva's misty cloud forest to the lush, humid lowlands reaching toward the Caribbean.

Founded in 1978, the park protects primary forest threatened when the highway between San José and Puerto Limón was built. Driving through it will give you an idea of what Costa Rica looked like prior to the 1950s – rushing rivers and rolling hills steeped in mountain rainforest.

Several rivers traverse the park: the Río Sucio (Dirty River), whose yellow waters carry volcanic minerals, and the crystal-clear Río Hondura. They intersect next to the main highway, and it's fascinating to see the contrast of colors. Volcán Barva is located at the southwestern corner of the park.

There have been many reports of thefts from cars and armed robbers on the trails or along the highway. It's best to either hike with a park ranger or arrange for a guide through any of the stations.

For more details, check the website of **Minae** (www.minae.go.cr/accvc/braulio.htm).

Quebrada González Sector

The most popular hiking area is accessed at the northern end of the park at the **Quebrada González ranger station** (☎ 2268-1038/9; admission US$8; ⏰ 7am-4pm), 22km past the Zurquí tunnel to the east of the San José–Limón highway. It has a guarded parking lot, toilets and well-marked trails. Hourly buses between San José and Guápiles can drop you off at the entrance, but it's a 2km walk back along the highway to reach the restaurant where returning buses stop. Take precautions, as muggings have been reported along this stretch.

Barva Sector

Climbing Volcán Barva is a good four- to five-hour round trip along a well-maintained trail. Begin on the western side of the park at the Sacramento entrance, north of Heredia. From there, the trail is signed and fairly obvious. It's a leisurely climb to the summit. Keep your eyes peeled for a quetzal. Near the summit there are several chilly lakes.

It is best to hike in the dry, or less-wet, season between December and April, as otherwise paths get muddy and cloud cover can disorientate hikers. Night temperatures can drop below freezing. Camping is allowed but there are no facilities.

From Heredia (Calle 1, between Avs 4 and 6) three buses a day (₡400, 6:25am, noon and 4pm on weekdays, 6:40am, 11am and 4pm on weekends) pass Paso Llano (also called Porrosatí). From there, it's a 5km walk to Sacramento and then another 3km to the **Barva ranger station** (☎ 261-2619; ☽ 7am-4pm high season), which may or may not be staffed.

CARTAGO

pop 145,000

Peace rules Cartago, where the quiet of the central plaza is only broken by rogue pigeons and the shouts of the lottery lady. Once the colonial capital, Cartago's grandeur has been somewhat diminished by Mother Nature's rumblings. Still, it retains great religious significance and a certain conservative charm. For most visitors, Cartago is the spot to catch your breath, a peaceful modern city with attractions nearby.

You can check your email at **Internet Alta Velocidad** (Calle 1 btwn Avs 1 & 3; per hr ₡300; ☽ 7:30am-7pm Mon-Fri, 8am-7pm Sat, 9am-6pm Sun), 50m east of Las Ruinas. Several banks change money – try **Banco Nacional** (cnr Av 4 & Calle 5).

Considered to be the holiest shrine in Costa Rica, **La Basílica de Nuestra Señora de los Ángeles** (cnr Av 2 & Calle 16) is the home of the revered La Negrita (see p552). Leveled by the 1926 earthquake, the church is now rebuilt in the Byzantine style. The **parque central** houses the shell of another church destroyed by the 1910 earthquake, known as **Las Ruinas de la Parroquia**

(cnr Av 2 & Calle 2). It now has a pleasant garden to visit.

The University of Costa Rica runs the exceptional **Lankester Gardens** (☎ 2552-3247; www.jardinbotanicolankester.org; adult/student US$7/5; ☽ 8:30am-4:30pm), started by a British orchid enthusiast. Orchids are the big drawcard, with 800 varieties at their showiest from February to April. A trail through the winding gardens browses tropical forest filled with bromeliads, palms and heliconias. The gardens are 6km east of Cartago, and are accessible by buses bound for Paraíso.

With its balconies overlooking the Plaza de la Basílica, **Los Ángeles Lodge** (☎ 2551-0957, 2591-4169; Av 4 btwn Calles 14 & 16; d with breakfast US$50; ☒) stands out, with spacious and comfortable rooms, hot showers and a big breakfast made to order by the cheerful owners.

Downstairs is **La Puerta del Sol** (Av 4 btwn Calles 14 & 16; casados ₡2600-3000, mains ₡2400-5000; ☽ 8am-midnight), a pleasant *soda* which has been around since 1957 and serves myriad Tico specialties, as well as burgers and sandwiches. Don't miss the vintage photos of Cartago displayed on the walls.

Getting There & Around

Most buses arrive along Av 2 and reach La Basílica de Nuestra Señora de los Ángeles before returning to the main terminal on Av 4.

Destinations include the following:

Orosi ₡400; 40 minutes; depart hourly from the corner of Calle 4 and Av 1 from 8am to 10pm Monday to Saturday. The bus will stop in front of the Orosi Mirador.

Paraíso & Lankester Gardens ₡600; 40 minutes; depart from the corner of Calle 4 and Av 1 hourly from 7am to 10pm. For the gardens, ask the driver to drop you off at the turnoff – from there, walk 750m to the entrance.

San José ₡500; 45 minutes; depart every 15 minutes from the corner of Calle 2 and Av 6, north of the Parque Central.

Turrialba ₡600; 1½ hours; depart from Av 3 between Calles 8 and 10 (in front of Tribunales de Justicia) every 45 minutes from 6am to 10pm weekdays; 8:30am, 11:30am, 1:30pm, 3pm and 5:45pm weekends.

RÍO OROSI VALLEY

Resplendent mountain vistas, crumbling churches and lazy hot springs define the appeal of this valley of coffee plantations southeast of Cartago.

Beyond Paraíso, head south 8km to the pleasant village of **Orosi**, named after a 16th-century Huetar chief. Built in 1743, the whitewashed **Iglesia de San José** is the country's oldest church still in the business of serving wafers and wine. Nearby hot springs include **Los**

COSTA RICA

LOCAL LORE: LA NEGRITA

La Negrita (The Black Virgin) is a statuette of an indigenous Virgin Mary found by a woman named Juana Pereira in Cartago on August 2, 1635. According to lore, Juana twice took the statuette home with her, though on each occasion it reappeared where she had first found it. Astounded by the miracle that transpired, the townspeople built La Basílica de Nuestra Señora de Los Ángeles (see p551) on the original spot where it was found. In 1824 La Negrita was declared Costa Rica's patron saint.

On two separate occasions, La Negrita was stolen from the basilica, though each time it later reappeared on its altar (once was by future novelist José León Sánchez, who was sentenced to Isla San Lucas for 20 years). These strange occurrences have led people to believe that the statuette has curative properties, and it's common for petitioners to offer milagrosos (metal charms) representing the body parts they hope to have healed. Even the spring that flows near the basilica is said to have curative properties, and the statuette has been credited with everything from football victories to healing toe fungus.

Each August 2, on the anniversary of the statuette's discovery, devotees walk a grueling 22km in the summer heat from San José to Cartago, arriving on their knees. It's an incredible sight, and you're more than welcome (sans kneepads) to participate.

Balnearios (☎ 2533-2156; admission US$2; ☺ 7:30am-4pm Wed-Mon), on the southwest side of town next to Orosi Lodge, and **Los Patios** ☎ 2533-3009; admission US$2; ☺ 8am-4pm Tue-Sun), 1.5km south of town. These modest pools of warm water are popular with locals and a few foreigners in the know.

Festive hostel **Montaña Linda** (☎ 2533-3640; www.montanalinda.com; campsites per person US$3.50, dm US$7.50, s/d without bathroom US$15/20, d with bathroom US$30, additional person US$5; Ⓟ 🖳) offers top-notch budget lodgings, with hot showers and kitchen privileges or home-cooked meals. In addition, it has a reader-recommended **Spanish school** (per week with homestay US$230). The hostel is located two blocks south and three blocks west of the bus stop.

Outside of **Purisil**, 8km southeast of Orosi, the private reserve **Monte Sky** (☎ 2231-3536; www.intnet.co.cr/montesky) offers excellent birdwatching (per person including meals US$45). Ask at Montaña Linda about guided walks (US$10), camping and overnight stays (per person US$25 including meals).

Almost 3km further east is the little-known **Parque Nacional Tapantí-Macizo Cerro de la Muerte** (admission US$10; ☺ 6am-4pm) where dense woods, waterfalls and over 200 bird species flourish in the wettest park in the country. About 1km before the park entrance is **Kiri Mountain Lodge** (☎ 2591-7601; www.kirilodge.net; s/d incl breakfast US$24/45), which has six rustic cabins with private hot showers resting on 50 mossy hectares of land.

Public transportation is scarce in the valley, but there are infrequent minibuses connecting the villages for a couple of hundred colones per ride.

PARQUE NACIONAL VOLCÁN IRAZÚ

Named Thunderpoint (ara-tzu) by the indigenous people, the large and looming Irazú is Costa Rica's tallest (3432m) active volcano. Its last major eruption was on March 19, 1963, welcoming the visiting US President John F Kennedy by throwing a blanket of hot volcanic ash over most of the Central Valley. Since then, activity has dissipated to a few hissing fumaroles and tremors.

There's a small **visitors center** (☎ 2551-9398, 2200-5025; park admission US$10; ☺ 8am-3:30pm) and basic cafe, but no accommodations or camping facilities. A paved road reaches the summit. From the parking lot, a 1km-long trail leads to a lookout over the bare landscape of craters and ash. When the clouds clear there are amazing views of the Pacific and Caribbean, but most days you have to employ your imagination. Clear skies are most probable in the early morning from January to April. Temperatures can drop so bring appropriate clothing.

The park is 19km north of Cartago. Most visitors arrive with an organized tour or private transportation. The only public transportation to Irazú departs from San José (₡2500) at 8am, stops in Cartago (₡2000) to pick up passengers at about 8:30am and arrives at the summit a little after 9:30am. The bus departs from Irazú at 12:30pm.

TURRIALBA
pop 27,000

Turrialba is a laid-back town near the headwaters of the Río Reventazón, a favorite of rafters and kayakers. It's also a good base for jaunts to the Monumento Nacional Arqueológico Guayabo (p554) to the north.

For river running, reputable local outfitters include **Tico's River Adventures** (☎ 2556-1231; www.ticoriver.com), 150m east of the gas station; **Río Locos** (☎ 2556-6035; www.whiteh2o.com), 500m east of town; and **Explornatura** (☎ 2556-4932; www.explor natura.com), 250m southwest of the park, which also runs a reader-recommended canyoning course. For day trips you can expect to pay anywhere from US$85 to US$120 depending on transportation, accessibility and amenities. For two-day trips, prices vary widely depending on accommodations, but expect to pay between US$195 and US$300 per person.

Agronomists the world over recognize **Centro Agronómico Tropical de Investigación y Enseñanza** (Catie; ☎ 2556-6431; www.catie.ac.cr; admission ₡500, guided tours US$15-20; ☉ 7am-4pm) as one of the most important agricultural stations in the tropics. Visitors can reserve for tours of the agricultural projects in advance, or pick up a free map for a self-guided tour. You can walk to Catie or get a taxi (₡1500) from Turrialba.

Sleeping

Whittingham's Hotel (☎ 2556-8822; Calle 4 btwn Avs 2 & Central; d with/without bathroom US$10/8) Seasoned budget travelers won't mind the seven bare-bones (but clean) concrete rooms at this long-time spot, operated by the friendly Gerald Whittingham. All come with TV and have access to warm showers. Reception closes at 5pm, so get there early.

Hotel Interamericano (☎ 2556-0142; www. hotelinteramericano.com; Av 1; s/d/tr/q with bathroom US$25/35/45/55, without bathroom US$11/20/30/40; ☎) On the south side of the old train tracks is this simple 22-room hotel, regarded as *the* meeting place in Turrialba by rafters. The

showers are immaculate, the tiled rooms are bright, the 2nd-story lounge is an ideal spot to sip beer and Luis, the bilingual manager, is a good source of local information.

Hotel Herza (☎ 2556-1097; hotelherza@gmail.com; 2nd fl, cnr Av 2 & Calle 4; d US$25; ☎) This welcome new budget spot has eight simple, very clean and airy ceramic-tile rooms with firm beds run by a helpful couple. A common terrace overlooks the street, with views of the hills in the background.

Turrialba B&B (☎ 2556-6651; www.turrialbahotel.com; Calle 1, north of Av 6; s/d/tr incl breakfast US$40/60/80; ☎ ☎) This charming and tranquil five-year-old spot has clean, bright, well-appointed rooms, a cozy living-room area, a lovely garden patio equipped with a spa bath, and a library chock full of travel guides on Latin America.

Eating

Pastelería Merayo (Calle 2 btwn Avs 2 & 4; pastries ₡350-600) Founded in 1928, this informal bakery produces made-to-order coffee that is strong and delicious, as well as some very excellent pastries. Tip: anything with *crema pastelera* (custard) is guaranteed to be good.

Restaurante Betico Mata (Hwy 10; gallos ₡600-800; ☉ 11am-midnight Mon-Fri, later Sat & Sun) This carnivore's paradise at the south end of town specializes in *gallos* (open-faced tacos on corn tortillas) piled with succulent, fresh-grilled meats, including beef, chicken, sausage or pork, all soaked in the special house marinade. All go smashingly well with an ice-cold beer.

La Feria (Calle 6, north of Av 4; casados ₡1700, mains ₡2100-5550; ☉ 11am-10pm Wed-Mon, 11am-2pm Tue; V) This unremarkable-looking spot has friendly service and excellent, inexpensive home cooking. Try the *pollo a la milanesa*, a crisp chicken cutlet served with cucumber-yogurt dipping sauce. Tasty!

A NATURAL EDUCATION

If you really want to experience the Central Valley's rural culture, pay a visit to the **Finca La Flor de Paraíso** (☎ 2534-8003; www.la-flor.org) outside of Cartago. A not-for-profit organic farm operated by the Association for the Development of Environmental and Human Consciousness (Asodecah), it has a volunteer-work program that will allow you to get your hands dirty on projects related to agriculture, reforestation, animal husbandry and even medicinal-herb cultivation. There is also an onsite Spanish school.

Prices for the volunteer-work programs, including room and board (in simple wood cabins and dormitories), are US$20 daily. Vacationers can arrange day trips (per person US$10) or overnight stays (US$50) – both of which include meals. Family rates are available. Advance reservations necessary.

The *finca* (farm) is 7km northeast of Paraíso on the road to El Yas. From Cartago, take a Paraíso bus; get off at the pink church in La Flor. The entrance to the *finca* is 100m to the south.

COSTA RICA

WHITE-WATER RAFTING IN THE TURRIALBA AREA

There are two major rivers in the Turrialba area that are popular for rafting – the Río Reventazón and the Río Pacuare. The following is a quick guide to the ins and outs (and ups and downs) of each.

Río Reventazón

This storied rock-lined river has its beginnings at the Lago de Cachí, an artificial lake created by a dam of the same name. It begins here, at 1000m above sea level, and splashes down the eastern slopes of the cordilleras to the Caribbean lowlands. It is one of the most difficult, adrenaline-pumping runs in the country – and with more than 65km of rapids, you can get as hard core as you like.

Tour operators divide the river into four sections between the dam and the take-out point in Siquirres. **Las Máquinas** (Power House) is a Class II-III float that's perfect for families, while **Florida**, the final and most popular segment, is a scenic Class III with a little more white water to keep things interesting. The **Pascua** section has 15 Class IV rapids – featuring names like 'The Abyss' – and is considered to be the classic run. The Class V **Peralta** segment is the most challenging; tours do not always run it due to safety concerns.

Water levels stay fairly constant year-round because of releases from the dam. There are no releases on Sunday, however, and although the river is runnable, it's generally considered the worst day.

Río Pacuare

The Río Pacuare is the next major river valley east of the Reventazón, and has arguably the most scenic rafting in Costa Rica, if not Central America. The river plunges down the Caribbean slope through a series of spectacular canyons clothed in virgin rainforest, through runs named for their fury and separated by calm stretches that enable you to stare at near-vertical green walls towering hundreds of meters above.

The Class III-IV **Lower Pacuare** is the more accessible run: 28km through rocky gorges and isolated canyons, past an indigenous village, untamed jungle and lots of wildlife curious as to what the screaming is all about. The **Upper Pacuare** is also classified as Class III-IV, but there are a few sections that can go to Class V depending on conditions. It's about a two-hour drive to the put-in, though it's worth it – you'll have the prettiest jungle cruise on earth all to yourself.

The Pacuare can be run year-round, though June to October are considered the best months. The highest water is from October to December, when the river runs fast with huge waves. March and April is when the river is at its lowest, though it is still challenging.

Self-caterers can find supplies at the well-stocked **MegaSuper** (cnr Calle 3 & Av 2).

Getting There & Away

A modern bus terminal is located at the western edge of town off Hwy 10.

Monumento Nacional Arqueológico Guayabo ₡400; one hour; depart 11:15am, 3:10pm and 5:30pm Monday through Saturday, 9am, 3pm and 6:30pm on Sunday.

San José via Paraíso & Cartago ₡1200; two hours; depart every 45 minutes 5am to 6:30pm.

Siquirres, for transfer to Puerto Limón ₡1000; 1¾ hours; depart every 60 to 90 minutes from 6am to 6pm.

MONUMENTO NACIONAL ARQUEOLÓGICO GUAYABO

This is the largest and most important **archaeological site** (☎ 2559-1220; admission US$7; ☺ 8am-3:30pm) in Costa Rica, though it pales alongside the Maya sites of northern Central America.

Only 19km north of Turrialba, the area was occupied from about 1000 BC to AD 1400, its peak population reaching around 10,000. Thought to be an ancient ceremonial center, it featured paved streets, an aqueduct and decorative gold. The still-functioning aqueduct is considered the most impressive find (especially considering some of the plumbing in modern-day coastal towns). Archaeologists are unsure of the site's exact significance and the reason for its abandonment. Visitors can explore its cobbled roads, stone aqueducts, mounds and petroglyphs. Much has yet to be excavated.

There's an information and exhibit center, but many of the best pieces are displayed at the Museo Nacional in San José (p538). Camping (per person US$5) is permitted, and services include latrines and running water.

Buses (₡400, one hour) from Turrialba depart at 11:15am, 3:10pm and 5:30pm Monday through Saturday and at 9am, 3pm and 6:30pm on Sunday. You can also take a taxi from Turrialba (from ₡8000).

CARIBBEAN COAST

You knew it would have something to do with seduction. Around you thick emerald forests rim sandy beaches, coconut stews simmer on gas cookers, and reggae beats drift from open doors. The heat beckons you to retreat to a hammock or float in the salty bay. Whilst the coast is hotter and wetter than the interior, the definitive difference is cultural, with over one-third of the population descended from English-speaking Jamaicans and Barbadians.

TORTUGUERO
pop 750

Located within the confines of Parque Nacional Tortuguero, accessible only by air or water, this bustling little village with strong Afro-Caribbean roots is best known for attracting hordes of sea turtles (the name Tortuguero means 'turtle place') – and the hordes of tourists who want to see them. While the peak turtle season is in July and August, the park and village have begun to attract travelers year-round. Even in October, when the turtles have pretty much returned to the sea, caravans of families and adventure travelers arrive to go on jungle hikes and to canoe the area's lush canals.

Information

A solid source of information is the town's website, **Tortuguero Village** (www.tortuguerovillage. com), which lists local businesses and provides comprehensive directions on how to get into the area. It also has a helpful map.

There are no banks or ATMs in town and only a few businesses accept credit cards, so bring all the cash you'll need. Internet connections can be iffy, especially during heavy rains.

Sights & Activities
PARQUE NACIONAL TORTUGUERO

This misty, green coastal park sits on a broad flood plain parted by a jigsaw of canals. Referred to as the 'mini-Amazon,' Parque Nacional Tortuguero's intense biodiversity includes over 400 bird species, 60 known species of frogs, 30 species of freshwater fish and three monkey species as well as the threatened West Indian manatee. Caimans and crocodiles can be seen lounging on river banks, while freshwater turtles bask on logs.

Over 50,000 visitors a year come to boat the canals and see the wildlife, particularly to watch turtles lay eggs. This is the most important Caribbean breeding site of the green sea turtle, 40,000 of which arrive every season to nest. Of the eight species of marine turtle in the world, six nest in Costa Rica, and four nest in Tortuguero. Various volunteer organizations address the problem of poaching with vigilant turtle patrols (for volunteering opportunities, see p556).

Park headquarters is at **Cuatro Esquinas** (☎ 2709-8086; admission US$10; ☽ 5:30am-6pm with breaks for breakfast & lunch), just north of Tortuguero village.

Sharks and strong currents make the beaches unsuitable for swimming.

Boating & Canoeing

A variety of guided **boat tours** (US$15, plus park-entry fee US$10) depart 6am daily from the town of Tortuguero and surrounding lodges to see the canals and spot wildlife. Canoe and kayak rental and boat tours are available in the village.

Four aquatic trails wind their way through the Parque Nacional Tortuguero. The **Río Tortuguero** acts as the entrance way to the network of trails. This wide, still river is often covered with water lilies and frequented by aquatic birds such as herons and kingfishers, as well as peacocks.

The **Caño Chiquero** is a waterway thick with vegetation, especially artichoke trees and red guacimo trees. Black turtles and green iguanas hang out here. Caño Chiqero leads to the narrow **Caño Mora** and **Caño Harold**, popular with Jesus Christ lizards and caimans.

Hiking

Behind Cuatro Esquinas station, **El Gavilan Land Trail** is the park's only public trail. The muddy, 2km-long loop traverses tropical humid forest and follows a stretch of beach. Green parrots and several species of monkeys are commonly sighted here. It is well-marked and does not require a guide.

Turtle-Watching

Visitors are allowed to check out the green-turtle rookeries at night from March to October (late July through August is prime time) and observe eggs being laid or hatching. Seeing a 180kg turtle haul itself up onto the beach, dig a nest, lay 120 eggs the size of table-tennis balls and scoot back to sea, exhausted, can be awe-inspiring. Obviously, turtle sightings are not guaranteed. A guide must accompany all visitors. Camera flashes and flashlights are prohibited by law, as they disturb the egg-laying process.

If you're unable to visit during the peak green turtle breeding season, the next best time is February to July, when leatherback turtles nest in small numbers (the peak is from mid-April to mid-May). Hawksbill turtles nest sporadically from March to October, and loggerhead turtles are also sometimes seen. Tours cost US$20 (a flat rate established by the village), which includes the purchase of a US$4 sticker that pays for the patrols that help protect the nesting sites from scavengers and looters.

Volunteering

Canadian Organization for Tropical Education and Rainforest Conservation (Coterc; ☎ 2709-8052, in Canada 905-831 8809; www.coterc.org) A reputable Canadian not-for-profit outfit that has various volunteer opportunities at its research station in Tortuguero.

Caribbean Conservation Corporation (☎ 2709-8091, in the USA 800-678 7853; www.cccturtle.org) A renowned longtime organization that has myriad volunteer options at its research station in Tortuguero.

Tours

Signs all over town advertise guide services for canal tours and turtle walks. Going rates

---

GETTING TO TORTUGUERO INDEPENDENTLY

If you want to get to Tortuguero independently, it can be done. Here is what to do:

From San José

Take the 6:30am, 9am or 10:30am bus from San José's Gran Terminal del Caribe (p544) to Cariari (₡1400, 2¼ hours). In Cariari, you will arrive at a bus station at the south end of town (known as the *estación nueva*). From here, you can walk or take a taxi 500m north to the *estación vieja* (old station), otherwise referred to as the Terminal Caribeño.

Public transportation from Cariari

The cheapest option is by public transportation on **Clic Clic** (☎ 2709-8155, 8844-0463) or **Coopetraca** (☎ 2767-7590), both of which charge ₡2600 per person for the bus-boat service from the *estación vieja* all the way to Tortuguero. For these two options, the bus service will be the same, but the boat service will be different. Buses depart Cariari at 6am, 11:30am and 3pm.

For both of these services, buy only the bus ticket to La Pavona (₡1000). After a ride through banana plantations, you will arrive at the Río La Suerte, where a number of boat companies will be waiting at the dock. (Get ready to be solicited.) We recommend Clic Clic, which is generally prompt and well-run, with experienced boat captains – but you may want to choose based on availability or on the condition of the boats. From this point, you will pay the remainder of your fare (₡1600) to the boatman. Be sure to take small change.

Ticket vendors at the *estación vieja* in Cariari may try to sell you on a combined bus-boat ticket. Note that these are only for Coopetraca, since Clic Clic does not have a sales agent in town. We recommend paying your boat fare at the dock – since it allows you to see what you're getting into – literally.

These companies will take you to the public boat dock in Tortuguero.

Private transportation from Cariari

For more expensive private service, there is **Viajes Bananero** (☎ 2709-8005), which has an office inside the San José bus terminal in Cariari. Buy your boat ticket here (US$10 per person). From this same point, you will then take a bus (₡600 per person) to its proprietary boat dock. Bus departure times are at 11:30am and 2pm. Pay the driver directly; take small change. If you are traveling in a group, Bananero can arrange custom pick-ups. For private service, you will need to reserve ahead.

The trip ends at the company's private dock on the southern edge of Tortuguero.

are about US$20 per person for a two-hour turtle tour, and US$15 for a two-hour hiking or boat excursion.

Recommended local guides:

Barbara Hartung (☎ 2709-8004; www.tinamontours. de) Offers hiking, canoe and turtle tours in German, English, French or Spanish. Also offers a unique tour about Tortuguero history, culture and medicinal plants.

Castor Hunter Thomas (☎ 8870-8634; http:// castorhunter.blogspot.com) A local who has worked as a guide for more than 20 years leads turtle tours (in season), guided hikes and wonderful canoe tours.

Chico (☎ 2709-8033) Chico's hiking and canoe tours receive rave reviews from readers.

Daryl Loth (☎ 8833-0827, 2709-8011; safari@racsa. co.cr) A personable Canadian-born naturalist (formerly of Coterc) offers excellent boat trips in a super-silent electric motorboat, as well as turtle tours (in season) and guided hikes.

Sleeping

Cabinas Tortuguero (☎ 2709-8114; cabinas_tortuguero@ yahoo.com; s/d/tr with bathroom US$20/25/30, s/d without bathroom US$10/16) Inland from Tienda Bambú, you'll find 11 brightly painted bungalows surrounding a tidy garden at this popular budget spot. Rooms are clean and there are hammocks for lounging.

Cabinas Princesa Resort (☎ 2709-8131; princesa resort08@yahoo.com; r per person with/without breakfast US$20/15; 🖭) There are three Princesa hotels scattered about town; this one, on the ocean, south of the cemetery, is best. A clapboard structure with 23 basic wood-and-concrete rooms faces an open garden with two pools.

Cabinas Miss Miriam (☎ 2709-8002, 8821-2037; s/d/ tr US$20/25/30) Spread out over two buildings (one on the north end of the soccer field, the other south of it), this solid budget option has 16 clean tiled rooms, firm foam mattresses and electric showers. Upstairs rooms in the northern building have great ocean views, while units at the southern annex are bigger.

Tropical Lodge (☎ 2709-8110/08, 8826-6246; d US$25; 🖭) Behind the Tienda Bambú food shop, this colorful Caribbean setup has 10 somewhat dark, concrete rooms, with private electric showers, four of which come with cable TV. The onsite bar is convenient, but inhibits beauty rest.

La Casona (☎ 2709-8092/47; d/tr US$25/35, d with kitchenette US$35; 🖭) Ten painted cement rooms with rustic touches surround a garden at this family-run spot on the north side of the soccer field. Three units have kitchenettes with hot plates. In addition, Jenny and her sons offer canoe rental, as well as canoe tours to a local farm on Caño Harold.

ourpick Casa Marbella (☎ 8833-0827, 2709-8011; http://casamarbella.tripod.com; d incl breakfast US$40-60; 🖭) Owned by naturalist Daryl Loth, this charming B&B opposite the Catholic church manages to be wonderfully serene while also being in the middle of it all. Ten simple whitewashed rooms have good lighting and ceiling fans, as well as super-clean bathrooms with electric showers. Hearty breakfasts (think fresh pancakes with tropical fruit) are served on an outdoor deck with views of the canal. Loth also organizes excellent area tours.

Eating

Soda Doña María (☎ 2709-8050; dishes ₡1500-3000; 🕒 7am-8pm) Recover from a hike in the park at this riverside *soda*, serving fresh *jugos* (juices), burgers and tasty fish *casados*. It's about 200m north of the park entrance.

La Casona (casados ₡3200, mains ₡3000-5600; 🕒 7:30am-11am & 1:30-8:30pm; ✔) La Casona offers a variety of Italian specialties, including a well-rendered lasagna made with hearts of palm. On the northern edge of the soccer field.

Buddha Cafe (☎ 2709-8084; pizzas ₡3200-4000, dishes ₡3500-9000; 🕒 noon-8:30pm; ✔) This riverside spot keeps a hipster vibe with ambient-club music on the sound system and Buddhist 'om' symbols stenciled onto just about everything. It's a lovely canal-side spot, with excellent pizzas, rich coffee and scumptious crepes (both savory and sweet).

Miss Miriam's (☎ 2709-8002; mains ₡4400-11,000) Run by Miss Miriam's friendly and fabulous daughter, it's so good you'll want to eat all of your meals here. Don't miss the well-spiced Caribbean chicken (the best we tasted on the entire coast), served with heaping sides of sautéed fresh veggies and Caribbean-style rice and beans.

Getting There & Away

It's not hard to get here on your own (see p558). However, if you don't care to go it alone, these package tours can take care of everything from the moment your plane lands in San José. Costs vary widely depending on accommodations and transportation.

Exploradores Outdoors (☎ 2222-6262; www. exploradoresoutdoors.com) Primarily a rafting outfit,

COSTA RICA

this company organizes overnight excursions from San José, Arenal and Puerto Viejo de Talamanca (US$169 per person).

Jungle Tom Safaris (☎ 2280-0243; www.jungle tomsafaris.com) Offers recommended one-day (US$90), overnight (from US$115) and two-night packages (from US$147) or just round-trip transportation (US$45) – useful for independent travelers who want to be free upon arrival.

Riverboat Francesca Nature Tours (☎ 2226-0986; www.tortuguerocanals.com) A highly recommended company run by Modesto and Fran Watson; it also offers sport fishing (two-day packages from US$165).

PUERTO LIMÓN
pop 85,000

A ragged port city with a faded colonial air, Puerto Limón has a deservedly rough reputation, but it is not without appeal. The birthplace of the United Fruit Company, Limón is removed from San José's sphere of influence and totally without pretension. After all, business around here still means shuffling tons of bananas, not tourists. A wacky plan to expand the port for cruise ships should help bring some investment for much-needed infrastructure. In the meanwhile, most travelers zip through town heading south to Cahuita and Puerto Viejo de Talamanca or north to Tortuguero.

Information

If traveling onward to Tortuguero, Limón will be your last opportunity to get cash.

Banco de Costa Rica (☎ 2758-3166; cnr Av 2 & Calle 1) Exchanges US dollars cash and has an ATM.

Hospital Tony Facio (☎ 2758-2222) On the coast at the northern end of town; serves the entire province.

Multiservices Pascal (☎ 2758-4090; 2nd fl, Av 2, north side of Parque Vargas; internet per hr ₡1700; ⏲ 8am-10pm) A pricey internet and international call joint with a dozen capable computers.

Post office (Calle 4 btwn Avs 1 & 2; ⏲ 9am-4pm)

Scotiabank (☎ 2798-0009; cnr Av 3 & Calle 2; ⏲ 9am-5pm Mon-Fri, 9am-1pm Sat) Exchanges cash and traveler's checks and has a 24-hour ATM on the Plus and Cirrus systems that dispenses US dollars.

Dangers & Annoyances

Theft is a problem: take precautions against pickpockets during the day, particularly in the market and along the sea wall. In addition, people do get mugged here, so stick to well-lit main streets at night, avoiding the sea wall and Parque Vargas.

Sights & Activities

The city's main attraction is the waterfront **Parque Vargas**, an incongruous expanse of bench-lined sidewalks beneath a lost little jungle of tall palms and tropical flowers, centered on an appealingly decrepit bandstand.

From here, you can head inland along Av 2, the **pedestrian mall** that caters to the cruise-ship traffic. Keep an eye out for vendors selling home-burned CDs by local bands – Limón is getting a reputation for its growing hip-hop and reggaetón scene. (A band you can definitely expect to see being hawked: Los Trinitarios, a Limón band that has been fusing calypso and salsa since the '70s.)

From the park, it's a pleasant walk north along the **sea wall**, where views of the rocky headland are set to a steady crashing of waves against the concrete jetty. After dark, this is a popular mugging and make-out spot.

The nearest beach with acceptable swimming is **Playa Bonita**, 4km northwest of town.

Sleeping

Hotels listed here are at the more wholesome end of the budget spectrum, but they can still be a little gloomy; ask to see a room and check security.

Hotel Costa del Sol (☎ 2798-0909; cnr Calle 5 & Av 5; s/d without bathroom US$9/11, d with/without air-con US$30/15; ⊗ ⏶) Limón's best budget option is this 14-room hotel toward the north end of downtown, staffed by friendly, young employees. Rooms without bathroom are grim, but the new doubles with air-con are decent, brightened up by a fresh coat of watermelon-hued paint.

Hotel Palace (☎ 2758-1068; 2nd fl, Calle 2 btwn Avs 2 & 3; d US$19) For seasoned budget travelers, this woman-owned place is a reasonably safe choice, though somewhat dilapidated – it has cracked tiles and peeling paint. The six rooms surround an interior courtyard and have built-in cold-water bathrooms in a cubicle in the corner.

Hotel Miami (☎ 2758-0490; hmiamilimon@yahoo.com; Av 2 btwn Calles 4 & 5; s/d/tr US$22/28/31, s/d/tr with air-con US$29/39/43; ⊗) A clean, secure place with a welcoming staff, the hotel has 34 tidy rooms painted mint green.

Hotel Acon (☎ 2758-1010; cnr Av 3 & Calle 3; d/tr US$45/56; ⊗) The '60s-style modernist building is in a ramshackle state, but the place is generally clean. The 39 rooms are basic: bare linoleum floors and aged wood furnishings, some with creaky air-con units, though all have hot-water baths.

COSTA RICA

PUERTO LIMÓN

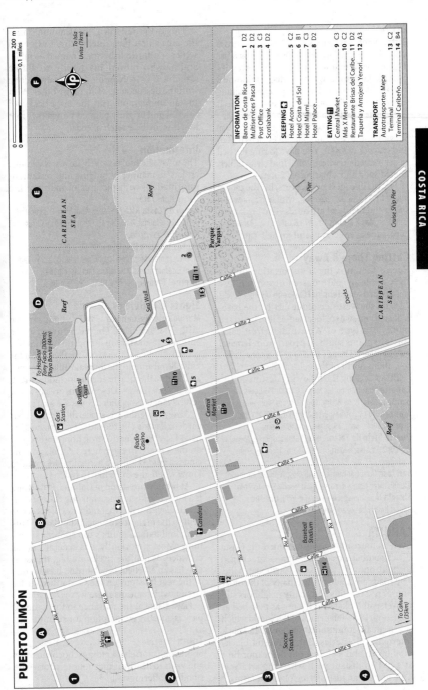

0   200 m
0   0.1 miles

To Isla
Uvita (1km)

CARIBBEAN
S E A

Reef

Reef

Reef

Parque
Vargas

Sea Wall

Calle 1

Calle 2

Calle 3

Calle 4

Calle 5

Calle 6

Calle 7

Calle 8

Calle 9

Central
Market

Radio
Casino

Basketball
Court

Gas
Station

Iglesia

Catedral

Baseball
Stadium

Soccer
Stadium

To Hospital
Tony Facio (300m);
Playa Bonita (4km)

To Cahuita
(35km)

CARIBBEAN
S E A

Docks

Pier

Cruise Ship Pier

Av. 7

Av. 6

Av. 5

Av. 4

Av. 3

Av. 2

Av. 1

INFORMATION	
Banco de Costa Rica	**1** D2
Multiservices Pascal	**2** D2
Post Office	**3** C3
Scotiabank	**4** D2
SLEEPING	
Hotel Acon	**5** C2
Hotel Costa del Sol	**6** B1
Hotel Miami	**7** C3
Hotel Palace	**8** D2
EATING	
Central Market	**9** C3
Más X Menos	**10** C2
Restaurante Brisas del Caribe	**11** D2
Taquería y Antojería Yenori	**12** A3
TRANSPORT	
Autotransportes Mepe	
Terminal	**13** C2
Terminal Caribeño	**14** B4

Eating

Restaurante Brisas del Caribe (☎ 2758-0138; Av 2; mains ₡1500-6000; ⏰ 7am-11pm Mon-Fri, 10am-11pm Sat & Sun) The best view in town isn't over the waves, it's over Parque Vargas, where outdoor tables and a breezy balcony make for good people-watching and decent Caribbean fare. Just east of Calle 1.

Taquería y Antojería Yenori (☎ 2758-8294; Calle 7 btwn Avs 3 & 4; mains ₡2000-5000; ⏰ 9am-9pm Mon-Sun) This cute little Mexican spot serves tacos (₡600) and *casados* (₡2000). You have to ring the bell to get buzzed in, where you'll find clean tables, chilled soda and a blaring air-con unit.

For the cheapest budget eats, hit the **central market** (⏰ 6am-8pm Mon-Sat), which has several *sodas* and plenty of groceries. The big supermarket **Más X Menos** (cnr Av 3 & Calle 3; ⏰ 8am-9pm), across the avenue, is useful for self-caterers.

Getting There & Away

Puerto Limón is the transportation hub of the Caribbean coast. Buses to/from San José depart/arrive at **Terminal Caribeño** (Av 2 btwn Calles 7 & 8) on the west side of the city by the baseball stadium, where local ladies line up to sell *pan bon*, a type of West Indian fruit cake. Buses to points south all depart from **Terminal Autotransportes Mepe** (☎ 2758-1572; Av 4 btwn Calles 3 & 4), 100m north of the central market.

Buses serving the following destinations:
Cahuita (Autotransportes Mepe) ₡1000; 1½ hours; depart 5am, 6am, 8am, 10am, 1pm, 2:30pm, 4pm and 6pm.
Manzanillo (Autotransportes Mepe) ₡2000; 2½ hours; depart 5:30am, 6am, 10:30am, 3pm and 6pm.
Puerto Viejo de Talamanca (Autotransportes Mepe) ₡1900; 2½ hours; depart 5:30am, 6am, 10:30am, 3pm and 6pm.
San José (Autotransportes Caribeños; Terminal Caribeño) ₡2500; three hours; depart almost hourly 5am to 7pm.
Sixaola (Autotransportes Mepe) ₡2600; three hours; depart hourly between 5am and 6pm.

CAHUITA

Even as tourism has mushroomed on Costa Rica's southern coast, Cahuita has managed to hold onto its laid-back Caribbean vibe. The roads are made of dirt, many of the older houses rest on stilts and chatty neighbors still converse in Mekatelyu. It's not as polished as Puerto Viejo de Talamanca to the south, which sports an air-conditioned strip mall and slick international eateries. But a graceful black-sand beach and a chilled-out demeanor hint at a not-so-distant past, when the area was little more than just a string of cocoa farms.

This is a proud town, too. Cahuita claims the area's first permanent Afro-Caribbean settler – a turtle fisherman named William Smith, who moved his family to Punta Cahuita in 1828. Now his descendants, along with the descendants of so many other West Indian immigrants, run the tasty backyard eateries and brightly painted bungalows that hug this idyllic stretch of coast.

Information

The town's helpful new website, www.cahuita. cr, has all manner of lodging and restaurant information, with pictures of many of the spots listed here.
Banco de Costa Rica (⏰ 9am-4pm Mon-Fri) Located at the bus terminal, it has an ATM that works on Cirrus, Plus and Visa systems.
Centro Turístico Brigitte (☎ 2755-0053; www. brigittecahuita.com; Playa Negra; per hr ₡1000; ⏰ 7am-6pm) Internet access. Also offers tours (see p562).
Internet Palmer (per hr ₡1000; ⏰ 9am-8pm)

Sights & Activities

Mariposario de Cahuita (☎ 2755-0361; admission US$10; ⏰ 8:30am-3:30pm) On the highway, at the entrance to town, you'll find this wonderful garden aflutter with lovely butterflies (great for kids). Stroll around the fountain-filled grounds and admire the local residents, including many friendly caterpillars. Descriptions are posted in several languages; guided tours are available.

A new greenhouse space filled with lush garden, **Ranario** (⏰ 8:30am-3:30pm; admission US$8) has 14 species of native frog hopping around on the loose. (No cages here.) Admission includes a guided tour – a necessity, since guides know where the frogs like to hide.

At the northwest end of Cahuita, **Playa Negra** is a long, black-sand beach flying the *bandera azul ecológica*, a flag that indicates the beach is kept to the highest ecological standards. This is undoubtedly Cahuita's top spot for swimming. Most importantly, it is generally never crowded. When the swells are big, this spot also has an excellent beach break. It is not one of the regular stops on the Costa Rica surfer circuit, which means more waves for you.

Playa Blanca at the entrance to the national park is another good option for swimming.

Tours

Snorkeling, horseback riding, chocolate tours and visits to nearby indigenous territories are standard offerings:

CAHUITA

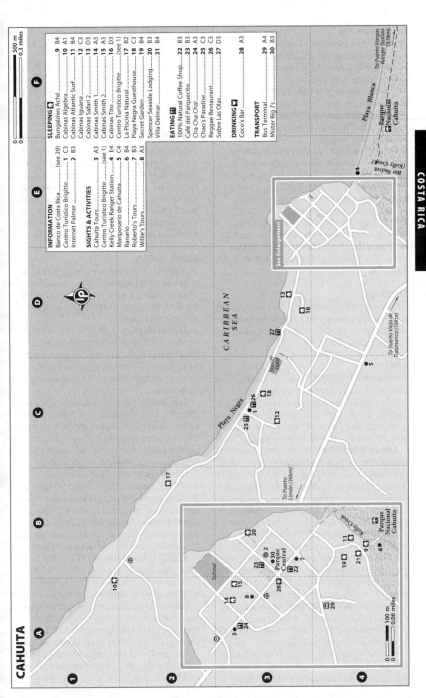

COSTA RICA

Cahuita Tours (☎ 2755-0000/232; www.cahuitatours.com) One of the most established agencies in town, this place offers snorkeling tours (US$30), boat/glass-bottom boat tours (US$25/35) and full-day trips to the Reserva Indígena Talamanca Bribrí (US$60).

Centro Turístico Brigitte (☎ 2755-0053; www.brigittecahuita.com; Playa Negra) Brigitte specializes in horseback-riding tours along the beach or to jungle waterfalls (three/five hours per person US$55/75). She also rents bikes (US$8 per day).

Roberto's Tours (☎ 2755-0117; www.robertostours.com) Arranges snorkeling trips and dolphin tours in the Parque Nacional Cahuita, but Roberto's real claim to fame is inshore/offshore sportfishing (US$75/200 per person). Bonus: after all your hard work, he'll have your haul cooked up for you at his restaurant.

Willie's Tours (☎ 8843-4700; www.willies-costarica-tours.com) Willie's signature tour takes visitors to a Bribrí family and a KéköLdi iguana farm (US$25/55). He's in a new location these days, on the main drag next to Cocorico Pizzeria Bar.

Sleeping

There are two possible areas for lodgings in Cahuita: the town center (which can be a little noisy if you're anywhere near Coco's Bar), or north of town along Playa Negra.

CENTER

Secret Garden (☎ 2755-0581; koosiecostarica@live.nl; dm US$9, s/d US$15/25) Under new management by a pair of Dutch owners, this small spot has a lush garden, as well as five tiled units with fans, mosquito nets and hot-water showers in cubicle-style bathrooms. One dormitory has five beds.

Cabinas Atlantic Surf (☎ 8919-9313; www.cabinasatlanticsurf.com; dm US$10, d with/without hot water US$25/20, extra person US$5) Recently acquired by new owners Jen and Shannon, this intimate five-room spot has clean wood *cabinas* with private bathrooms and fans, as well as patios with hammocks. A light and airy corner room upstairs is best.

Cabinas Smith 1 & 2 (☎ 2755-0068; s/d/tr older rooms US$12/16/21, s/d/tr/q newer rooms US$25/31/36/46; 🖳) A total of 11 rooms of various configurations are set on two properties that lie around the corner from each other in a quiet part of town. Newer rooms have ceramic tiled floors, cable TV, minifridges and bright mirror mosaics, while the cheaper units are far more basic.

Villa Delmar (☎ 2755-0392/75; s US$13, d US$18-25) In an out-of-the-way spot close to the national park, the Villa Delmar has 10 ramshackle *cabinas* in various configurations, some with hot-water showers and minifridges. Some of

the units are dark and a bit musty, but they are inexpensive, and the owners couldn't be more gracious.

Spencer Seaside Lodging (☎ 2755-0027; s/d US$16/30) Rooms at this longtime, locally owned spot are basic, but they are big – and the seaside setting can't be beat. Upstairs units have the better views, as well as a shared terrace strung with hammocks.

our pick Bungalows Aché (☎ 2755-0119; www.bungalowsache.com; bungalows US$40-60; 🛜) In Nigeria, *Aché* means 'Amen,' and you'll likely say the same thing when you see these spotless octagonal bungalows on a peaceful property bordering the national park. The three charming, polished wood cabins have bright red-and-white linens and come stocked with a lockbox, minifridge, kettle and private decks with hammocks.

PLAYA NEGRA

Northwest of town about 1.5km, Playa Negra is quieter and pleasant, with a limited choice of restaurants and services. If you want to bar-hop, stay in town as walking back at night is not recommended.

Cabinas Algebra (☎ 2755-0057; www.cabinasalgebra.com; d US$18, d/tr with kitchen US$25/39) Cabinas Algebra has three cabins that channel a rustic *Swiss Family Robinson* vibe. Each of the cozy units is crafted from wood and strung with hammocks.

Cabinas Tito (☎ 2755-0286; http://cahuita-cabinas-tito.com; d US$25, extra person US$8) Surrounded by extensive tropical gardens and banana plants, this charming spot offers seven clean, brightly painted cabins. Rooms are furnished in wicker, with mosquito nets and jungle accents.

Cabinas Iguana (☎ 2755-0005; www.cabinas-iguana.com; d US$25, d bungalows US$40; 🛜 🐾) Set back from the beach, several bungalows – some older, some newer – are nestled into the lushly forested grounds. Simple wood cabins of various sizes (one of which sleeps six) have ceramic-tiled floors and beds with mosquito nets.

our pick La Piscina Natural (☎ 2755-0146; d US$35) This little gem of a spot – run by inimitable Cahuita native Walter – is the top budget spot in Playa Negra. Painted cement rooms are comfortable and come with private bathrooms. But what makes this chilled-out little place so special are the lush grounds and the natural pool (great for a dip) amid the rocks. There is a huge shared kitchen, an outdoor lounge studded with intriguing driftwood sculptures and plenty of chilled beer on hand for guests.

Centro Turístico Brigitte (☎ 2755-0053; www.brigitte cahuita.com; d with/without kitchen US$35/25) A couple of basic wood *cabinas* are painted in bright colors. You can also camp on the grounds provided you have your own gear (US$3 per person per night).

Playa Negra Guesthouse (☎ 2755-0127; www.playa negra.cr; d small/big US$60/80, 2-bedroom cottages US$120; 🛜 🐕) This beautiful Caribbean-style plantation house, with several freestanding storybook cottages (equipped with full kitchens), is meticulously decorated and maintained. Guest rooms are painted sherbety colors and feature charming tropical accents – such as colorful mosaics in the bathrooms and cozy wicker lounge chairs on the private decks.

Eating
CENTER
100% Natural Coffee Shop (☎ 2755-0010; dishes ₡1700-5500; 🕐 6:30am-2pm Mon-Fri) There is no better place in Cahuita to greet the morning with a cup o' joe or unwind in the afternoon with a refreshing *jugo*.

Café del Parquecito (☎ 2775-0279; breakfast ₡2000-2900; 🕐 6am-3pm & 6pm-close) Early risers come for the coffee at this park-side spot, and you won't be disappointed if you stick to the crepes stuffed full of fresh tropical fruit.

Cha Cha Cha! (☎ 8394-4153; mains ₡2200-8000; 🕐 noon-10pm Tue-Sun; **V**) In a corner veranda of an old house, this attractive expat favorite offers everything from Jamaican jerk chicken and Cuban specialties to plenty of vegetarian options.

PLAYA NEGRA
Reggae Restaurant (☎ 2755-0269; mains ₡2000-5000; 🕐 7-11am & noon-9pm) With a friendly, laid-back vibe, this *soda* serves Caribbean-style standards.

Chao's Paradise (☎ 2755-0480; seafood mains ₡3700-7000; 🕐 11am-11pm) Follow the wafting smell of garlic and simmering sauces to this highly recommended Playa Negra outpost. It serves fresh catches cooked up in spicy 'Chao' sauce.

Sobre Las Olas (☎ 2755-0109; pastas ₡5500-6500, mains ₡5500-12,500; 🕐 noon-10pm Wed-Mon; **V**) Cahuita's top option for waterfront dining is owned by a lively Tico-Italian couple who serve a variety of Mediterranean-influenced specialties.

Drinking
This low-key town is home to one crazy loud drinking hole: **Coco's Bar** (🕐 noon-late). You can't miss it at the main intersection, painted in Rasta red, yellow and green, and cranking the reggaetón to 11. On some nights (usually on weekends) there is live music. If you're not looking to burst your eardrums, try one of the mellower drinking establishments situated right across the street.

Getting There & Away
All public buses arrive at and depart from the bus terminal about 200m southwest of Parque Central.

Puerto Limón (Autotransportes Mepe) ₡1000; 1½ hours; depart 6am, 9:30am, 10:45am, 1:45pm and 6:15pm. (These times are approximate because these buses originate in Manzanillo. Get there early just in case.)

Puerto Viejo de Talamanca/Manzanillo ₡1000; 30 minutes/one hour; depart 6:15am, 6:45am, 11:15am, 3:45pm and 6:45pm.

San José (Autotransportes Mepe) ₡3700; four hours; depart 7am, 8am, 9:30am, 11:30am and 4:30pm.

Sixaola ₡1600; two hours; depart hourly 6am to 7pm.

Getting Around
The best way to get around Cahuita – especially if you're staying out along Playa Negra – is by bicycle. In town, rent bikes at **Mister Big J's** (☎ 8887-4695; per day US$7; 🕐 7am-6pm); he also rents body boards for US$6 per day.

PARQUE NACIONAL CAHUITA
Among the country's most visited parks, Parque Nacional Cahuita is small but beautiful. Humidity nurtures a dense tropical foliage of coconut palms, mango trees and sea grapes. The forest skirts white sandy beaches on a tranquil bay. Easy to access, it attracts scads of visitors who loll in the mild surf, scan the trails for sloths and monkeys and snorkel the coral reef.

At the east end of Cahuita, **Kelly Creek ranger station** (Map p561; ☎ 2755-0461; admission by donation; 🕐 6am-5pm) sits next to **Playa Blanca** stretching 2km east. Signs for the first 500m warn not to swim, but beyond this point the waves are gentle. After the rocky Punta Cahuita you'll find Vargas Beach and **Puerto Vargas ranger station** (☎ 2755-0302; admission US$10; 🕐 8am-4pm Mon-Fri, 7am-5pm Sat & Sun). An easily navigable 7km-long **coastal trail** leads through the jungle from Kelly Creek to Puerto Vargas. Beware, Río Perezoso, near the end of the first beach, can be thigh-deep at high tide or dangerous to cross in rainy season.

Camping (US$5) is permitted at Playa Vargas, less than 1km from the Puerto Vargas ranger station. The facilities include cold outdoor showers, drinking water and pit latrines. Don't leave anything unattended. Be especially careful to store food carefully as monkeys will scarf what's left unattended.

Snorkeling conditions vary daily. In general, the drier months in the highlands (from February to April) are best for **snorkeling** on the coast, as less runoff in the rivers means less silting in the sea. To protect the reef from further damage, snorkeling is permitted only with a licensed guide.

For a good day **hike**, take the Cahuita–Puerto Viejo bus at 8am to the Puerto Vargas entrance. Walk 1km to the coast then 7km more back to Cahuita. For bird-watching or guided hikes, contact the travel agencies in Cahuita or ATEC in Puerto Viejo de Talamanca.

PUERTO VIEJO DE TALAMANCA

This burgeoning Caribbean party town is bustling with tourist activity: street vendors ply Rasta trinkets and Bob Marley T-shirts, stylish eateries serve global fusion everything, and intentionally rustic bamboo bars pump dancehall and reggaetón. The scene, in fact, can get downright hedonistic, attracting dedicated revelers who arrive to marinate in ganja and *guaro* (the local cane alcohol).

Despite the reputation for revelry, Puerto Viejo nonetheless manages to hold on to an easy charm. Stray a couple of blocks off the main commercial strip and you might find yourself on a sleepy dirt road, savoring a spicy Caribbean stew in the company of local families. Nearby, you'll find rainforest fruit farms set to a soundtrack of cackling birds and croaking frogs, and wide-open beaches where the daily itinerary revolves around surfing and snoozing.

So, chill a little. Party a little. Eat a little. You've come to just the right place.

Information

The websites Green Coast (www.greencoast.com) and Puerto Viejo (www.puertoviejocr.com) have information on lodging, eating and activities in the area.

ATEC (Asociación Talamanqueña de Ecoturismo y Conservación; ☎ 2750-0191/398; www.ateccr.org; ☺ 8am-9pm) A reliable source of information on tours and activities in the area, it also offers a number of vintage desktops with internet access (₡1200 per hour).

Banco de Costa Rica (☺ 9am-4pm Mon-Fri) The ATM here works on the Plus and Visa systems. It sometimes runs out of cash on weekends.

David's Library (☎ 2750-0232) This book exchange operates in the lobby of the Lotus Garden hotel.

Jungle Internet (☎ 2750-2086; www.junglec.com; per hr ₡1700; ☺ 8am-11pm; ☎) Decent laptops and wireless access.

Dangers & Annoyances

Unfortunately, a cottage industry of drug dealers has become a permanent part of the landscape in Puerto Viejo; in fact, in some spots, it can get quite aggressive. Be firm if you're not interested. And be aware that though the use of marijuana is common in Puerto Viejo, it is nonetheless illegal.

Sights & Activities
FINCA LA ISLA BOTANICAL GARDEN
West of town, the **botanical garden** (☎ 2750-0046; www.costaricacaribbean.com; self-guided/guided tour US$5/10; ☺ 10am-4pm Fri-Mon) is a working tropical farm and botanical garden ideal for bird-watching and wildlife observation (look for sloths and poison dart frogs).

CYCLING
The forested road to **Manzanillo** (13km) offers a scenic ride. Take the swimsuit and watch for howler monkeys and butterflies on the way.

DIVING & SNORKELING
Costa Rica's only two living reef systems form a naturally protected sanctuary from Cahuita to Manzanillo. They are home to 35 species of coral and over 400 species of fish, not to mention dolphins, sharks and, occasionally, whales. Underwater visibility is best when the sea is calm. If the surfing is bad, snorkeling is good.

Snorkel just south of **Punta Uva** (in front of the Arrecife restaurant), where you will find stunning examples of reindeer coral, sheet coral and lettuce coral. The reef at Manzanillo (p567) is also easily accessible. Rent equipment at Aquamor Talamanca Adventures (p568) in Manzanillo. Tour companies (see opposite page) offer guided trips for about US$45 per person.

Dive outfitters include **Reef Runner Divers** (☎ 2750-0480; www.reefrunnerdivers.net; 1-/2-tank dive US$65/90; ☺ 8am-6pm) and Aquamor Talamanca Adventures, in Manzanillo.

SWIMMING
Just northwest of town, **Playa Negra** offers the area's safest swimming, as well as excellent body boarding. Southeast of town the jungle

meets the sea and the waves are perfect for swimming and body surfing.

Riptides and undertows can be dangerous. Inquire at your hotel or with local tour operators about current conditions.

Tours

The highly reputable not-for-profit outfit **ATEC** (Asociación Talamanqueña de Ecoturismo y Conservación; ☎ 2750-0191/398; www.ateccr.org; 8am-9pm) promotes environmentally sensitive tourism by working with local guides and supporting local communities. Hiking, horseback riding and canoe trips involve bird-watching and visiting indigenous territories and local farms. Depending on the activity, half-day excursions start at about US$20 and go up to US$80 for overnight trips. Recommended.

Sleeping

ourpick Rocking J's (☎ 2750-0657; www.rockingjs.com; campsites per person US$4, hammocks US$5, dm US$7, d US$20-30, 3-person king ste US$60, J's Palace US$350;) Puerto Viejo's grooviest hostel and 'hammock hotel' is owned by the charismatic, mischievous 'J,' who organizes full-moon toga parties and round-the-table drinking games. If you're looking for good times, you'll find them here – along with plenty of new friends. The accommodations are basic. Tight rows of tents, hammocks, snug dorms and private doubles share rickety showers in a concrete structure that is brightened by a veritable explosion of psychedelic mosaics.

COSTA RICA

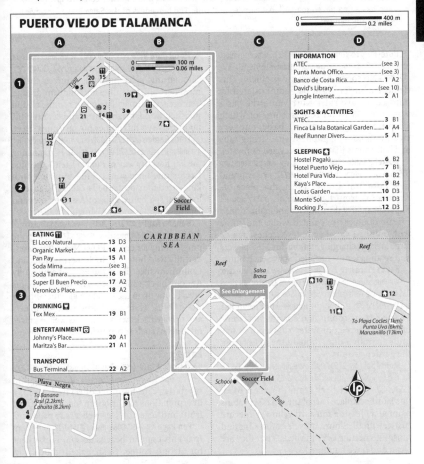

PUERTO VIEJO DE TALAMANCA

INFORMATION	
ATEC	(see 3)
Punta Mona Office	(see 3)
Banco de Costa Rica	**1** A2
David's Library	(see 10)
Jungle Internet	**2** A1

SIGHTS & ACTIVITIES	
ATEC	**3** B1
Finca La Isla Botanical Garden	**4** A4
Reef Runner Divers	**5** A1

SLEEPING	
Hostel Pagalú	**6** B2
Hotel Puerto Viejo	**7** B1
Hotel Pura Vida	**8** B2
Kaya's Place	**9** B4
Lotus Garden	**10** D3
Monte Sol	**11** D3
Rocking J's	**12** D3

EATING	
El Loco Natural	**13** D3
Organic Market	**14** A1
Pan Pay	**15** A1
Soda Mirna	(see 3)
Soda Tamara	**16** B1
Super El Buen Precio	**17** A2
Veronica's Place	**18** A2

DRINKING	
Tex Mex	**19** B1

ENTERTAINMENT	
Johnny's Place	**20** A1
Maritza's Bar	**21** A1

TRANSPORT	
Bus Terminal	**22** A2

SURFING SALSA BRAVA

One of the biggest breaks in Costa Rica, the **Salsa Brava** is named for the heaping helping of 'spicy sauce' it serves up on the sharp, shallow reef, continually collecting its debt of fun in broken skin, boards and bones. The wave makes its regular, dramatic appearance when the swells pull in from the east, pushing a wall of water against the reef, in the process, generating a thick and powerful curl. There's no gradual build up here: the water is transformed from swell to wave in a matter of seconds. Ride it out and you're golden. Wipeout and you'll rocket head-first into the reef. In his memoir, *In Search of Captain Zero*, surfer and screenwriter Allen Weisbecker describes it as 'vicious.' Some mordant locals have baptized it 'the cheese-grater.'

Interestingly, this storied wave helped turn Puerto Viejo into a destination. Thirty years ago, the town was barely accessible. But that did not dissuade dogged surfers from the bumpy bus rides and rickety canoes that hauled them and their boards on the weeklong trip from San José. They camped on the beach and shacked up with locals, carbo-loading at cheap *sodas*. Other intrepid explorers – biologists, Peace Corps volunteers, disaffected American veterans looking to escape the fallout of the Vietnam War – also materialized during this time, helping spread the word about the area's luminous sunsets, lush rainforests and monster curls. Today, Puerto Viejo has a fine paved road, global eateries and wi-fi. The fierceness of the Salsa Brava, however, remains unchanged.

Hotel Puerto Viejo (☎ 2750-0620; hotelpuertoviejocr.com; dm US$8, r per person without bathroom US$10, d US$30; 🖥 🛜) No shoes, no shirt, no problem. This dedicated surfer crash pad administered by hard-core wave rider Kurt Van Dyke has a warren of 68 wood rooms, some of which sleep up to eight. Units are basic, but very clean and come equipped with strong fans and bathrooms that run on recycled rainwater.

Hostel Pagalú (☎ 2750-1930; www.pagalu.com; dm US$10, d with/without bathroom US$28/22; 🛜) A brand new hostel on a quiet street, this place offers a break from Puerto Viejo's party scene. Superclean, airy dormitories and half a dozen private doubles are painted white and come with polished-wood accents. Niceties include large lockers, charging stations for MP3 players and reading lamps installed above each bunk.

Kaya's Place (☎ 2750-0690/060; www.kayasplace.com; s/d without bathroom US$19/27, d with/without ocean views US$40/35, s/d with garden views US$40/50, d apt/5-person apt US$70/85; 🛜) This inn just west of town has 17 snug, basic rooms and apartments (some of which share cool-water showers). A few units are rather dim, thought the ones facing the garden are airy.

Monte Sol (☎ 2750-0098; www.montesol.net; d US$20-30, d/q bungalows with kitchen US$45/65, 4-person houses US$70; 🖥 🛜) Set back from the main road, this laid-back place east of town has six cabins painted a pleasing mustard yellow. Units are rustic, with tile floors, cubicle bathrooms and mosquito netting over the beds – but they are clean and have hammocks.

Hotel Pura Vida (☎ 2750-0002; www.hotel-puravida.com; s/d/tr US$32/38/50, without bathroom US$25/30/40; 🛜) Though this place has budget prices, the atmosphere and amenities are solidly midrange. Ten breezy, immaculate guest rooms, clad in polished wood, bright linens and ceramic-tile floors make up this homey inn on a quiet street.

Lotus Garden (☎ 2750-0232; http://thelotusgarden.net; d standard US$40, ste US$70-90; 🍽 🛜 🅿) Channeling the Far East (by way of Puerto Viejo), the nine large, stone-lined suites at this inn come with king-sized four-poster beds, cable TV, air-con, lockbox, spa baths, gobs of Asian textiles and Japanese names such as 'Shogun.'

Banana Azul (☎ 2750-2035; www.bananaazul.com; d incl breakfast US$69-94, d apt US$129; 🛜 🅿) Lost in the jungle at the far end of Playa Negra, this wonderfully wild hotel run by Roberto Vreña and Colin Brownlee sits at the edge of a blissfully tranquil black-sand beach. The 13 guest rooms are all done up in the finest jungle chic: shining wood floors, white linens, frothy mosquito nets and private decks with views – as well as graceful touches such as bromeliads in the showers.

Eating

Veronica's Place (☎ 2750-0132; dishes ₡1200-3200; 🕐 7am-9pm Sun-Thu, 7am-4:30pm Fri; 🅥) A delightful vegetarian cafe, this place offers fresh, healthy interpretations of Caribbean food, using fresh fruits and vegetables, as well as soy products.

Pan Pay (☎ 2750-0081; dishes ₡1500-2800; 🕐 7am-7pm) This popular beachside spot is excellent for strong coffee, fresh baked goods and hearty wedges of fluffy Spanish omelet served with crisp tomato-bread.

Soda Tamara (☎ 2750-0148; breakfast ₡1500-2800, seafood mains ₡4200-4800; ☺ 7am-10pm) With its signature red, green and yellow paint job, this is a popular spot to grab breakfast and watch the village wake up.

Soda Mirna (mains ₡2200-3500; ☺ noon-10pm) This humble little *soda* on the main drag offers excellent people-watching and highly tasty (and inexpensive) Caribbean-style dishes.

ourpick El Loco Natural (☎ 2750-0530; meals ₡3200-9000; ☺ 5-10pm Wed-Mon; **V**) A pleasant candlelit patio cafe located 200m east of town serves up creative fusion cuisine, combining elements of Caribbean, Indian, Mexican and Thai cooking. Steamed spicy mussels in red curry sauce and tandoori chicken in coconut are just a couple of standouts. But if you really want give your taste buds a joyride, try the exquisite fish tacos – excellent with an icy *guaro* sour (₡2800) from the bar.

Get groceries at **Super El Buen Precio** (☺ 6:30am-8:30pm) or at the weekly **Organic Market** (☺ 6am-6pm Sat), with produce and typical regional snacks.

Drinking & Entertainment

Tex-Mex (☺ 6am-2am) A rowdy open-air bar on the main drag has live music, pool tables and movies on big screens playing most nights.

Maritza's Bar (☎ 2750-0003) This un-fancy local spot has regular live bands and DJs that play reggae, rock and salsa and all the funky beats in between.

Johnny's Place (☺ 1pm-3am) A Puerto Viejo institution, Johnny's Place spins reggaetón, hip-hop and salsa to a mix of locals and travelers who take up the dance floor and surround the late-night beach bonfires outside.

Getting There & Away

All public buses arrive at and depart from the bus terminal half a block southwest of Maritza's Bar. **Grayline** (☎ 2262-3681; www.grayline costarica.com) runs a private daily bus service departing Puerto Viejo at roughly 2:15pm bound for San José (US$35). Reserve ahead.

Bribrí/Sixaola ₡1100; 30 minutes/1½ hours; depart roughly every hour from 6:30am to 7:30pm.

Cahuita/Puerto Limón ₡400; 30 minutes/1½ hours; depart roughly every hour from 5:30am to 7:30pm.

Manzanillo ₡400; 30 minutes; depart 7:30am, noon, 4:30pm and 7:30pm.

San José ₡4100; five hours; depart 7:30am, 9am, 11am and 4pm.

Getting Around

Bicycle is a fine way to get around town, and pedaling out to other beaches east of Puerto Viejo is one of the highlights of this corner of Costa Rica. You'll find rentals outlets all over town (in addition to many hotels).

MANZANILLO

The 13km coastal route to Manzanillo slips past sandy beaches and dense canopy, passing through beach villages and the Reserva Indígena Cocles/Kekoldi, and ending up in Refugio Nacional de Vida Silvestre Gandoca-Manzanillo. Take a cruiser; the road is paved, but don't get too distracted spotting wildlife as the potholes are doozies. The town itself is part of **Refugio Nacional de Vida Silvestre Gandoca-Manzanillo**, a pristine remnant of wild Caribbean coastline stretching all the way to Panama.

Gandoca-Manzanillo's stunning coastal trail leads 5.5km through the rainforest and desolate beaches to Punta Mona. Wildlife includes the rare harpy eagle, monkeys and toucans.

COSTA RICA

GETTING TO GUABITO & BOCAS DEL TORO, PANAMA

One of Costa Rica's most relaxed border crossings, **Sixaola–Guabito** is popular among those traveling to the islands of Bocas del Toro.

Arrive in Sixaola early. The border is open 7am to 5pm (8am to 6pm in Guabito, Panama, which is an hour ahead of Costa Rica) – though one or both sides may close for lunch at around 1pm. Begin crossing the high metal bridge over the Río Sixaola, stopping at **Costa Rica immigration** (☎ 2754-2044) to process your paperwork.

Once over the bridge, stop in Panama immigration on the left-hand side to get your passport stamped. US citizens will have to purchase a tourist card for US$5. Personal cars can cross here (not rentals). There is no bank, but colones can be changed at the *mercado* (market) across the street. Guabito has no hotels but taxis can to take you further into Panama.

See p662 for more information on crossing the border from Panama.

The coral reef 200m offshore is 10 times the size of the Cahuita reef, with the clearest waters and best diversity of sea life in Costa Rica. The best resource on the area is the long-term resident Larkin family at **Aquamor Talamanca Adventures** (☎ 2759-9012, 8835-6041; www.greencoast.com/aquamor.htm, www.costacetacea.com; 1hr beach dive US$25, two-tank boat dive from US$59), 100m west of Maxi's Cabinas. It runs a PADI dive school, rents snorkeling gear (US$4 per hour) and kayaks, and offers dolphin-observation trips with excellent naturalist guides.

Accommodations can be found at **Punta Mona** (☎ 8321-8788; www.puntamona.org; dm incl 3 meals US$45, transportation US$10; Ⓥ), an organic farm and retreat center, 5km south of Manzanillo, which also welcomes volunteers. To arrange a stay and transportation, email ahead or visit the farm's office in Puerto Viejo, which is located behind ATEC (Map p565).

On the way into the village, **Cabinas Manzanillo** (☎ 2759-9033, 8839-8386; d/tr US$20/30) offers immaculate rooms with TV and fans in a friendly setting. Ask about discounts for extended stays.

Local matrons preside over pleasant, informal *sodas* or sell *patis* (spicy meat and plantain turnovers). The atmosphere is lively – folks stay even when the lights short out, and there's live music some weekends.

Buses to Manzanillo depart from Puerto Viejo de Talamanca (₡400, 30 minutes) at 7:30am, noon, 4:30pm and 7:30pm. They return to Puerto Viejo at 5am, 8:15am, 12:45pm and 5:15pm. These buses all continue to Puerto Limón (₡2000, 2½ hours) for onward transfers.

SIXAOLA

Falling in love in Sixaola would be tragic, as it's not the kind of place to be any length of time. Still, it has a relaxed border crossing, the fast track to Bocas del Toro, although most foreign tourists choose to travel via Paso Canoas.

Accommodations and restaurants are basic, and those in Panama are much better value. If you get stuck however, the quiet and clean **Cabinas Imperio** (☎ 2754-2289; d US$20) is right across the street from the police checkpoint.

The bus station is one block north of the border crossing. Buses go to San José (₡2600, five hours) at 6am, 8am, 10am and 3pm. Eight buses travel to and from Puerto Limón (₡5300, three hours) via Cahuita and Puerto Viejo, departing between 5am and 6pm.

NORTH CENTRAL COSTA RICA

The spark of adventure lures travelers to this sector, home of Monteverde's misty cloud forests and the smoking Volcán Arenal. Where else can you see iridescent tarantulas, careen through canopy on zip lines and top the day with a soak in bubbling hot springs? But good old-fashioned exploration (*sans* steel cables or zip-off pants) means a stop in the flat, tropical lowlands of Costa Rica's cattle country in rodeo season, or exploring the world-class wetlands at Refugio Nacional de Vida Silvestre Caño Negro. At the region's northern limit, the Río San Juan forms the border with Nicaragua. In an earlier era it served as an important link with the Caribbean coast. Today, intrepid travelers can boat across the border, or all the way to Barra del Colorado. Now that's adventure.

Most travelers short for time take the popular circuit which shortcuts around Laguna de Arenal from Monteverde with a jeep-boat-jeep (actually, minivan-boat-minivan) connection to La Fortuna, or vice versa.

TILARÁN

This ranching boomtown makes a mellow rest stop for travelers. Friendly and western, Tilarán showcases its first love – bulls – the last weekend in April with a **rodeo**, and on June 13 with a bullfight (note that the bull isn't killed in the Costa Rican version of the event) dedicated to San Antonio. It's near the southwestern end of Laguna de Arenal.

You can check email while waiting for your bus at **Cybercafé Tilarán** (☎ 2695-9010; per hr ₡600; ☻ 9am-10pm Mon-Sat), with speedy connections.

Sleeping & Eating

Hotel Tilarán 'n (☎ 2695-5043; r with/without bathroom US$11/7) On the west side of the parque central, this is an excellent budget choice as the rooms with cable TV are well cared for (and quiet if you can get one facing the rear).

Hotel Mary (☎ 2695-5479; r per person US$21) An amiable and tidy option featuring linens that grandma would love. Wooden chairs on the balcony help you survey the local scene. The downstairs restaurant (mains US$3 to US$6; open 6am to midnight) with a cool tin counter serves Tico and Chino favorites.

Hotel La Carreta (☎ 2695-6593; www.lacarretacr. com; s/d incl breakfast US$40/55; ☎) Owners Rita and Ed have beautifully refurbished these skylit rooms, installing orthopedic beds, reading lights and hand-painted murals by local artists. In addition to the indoor dining area, there's a pleasant garden terrace for sipping coffee and reading something you've picked up from the book exchange in the front room.

Getting There & Away

Buses depart from the terminal just west of the parque central. The route between Tilarán and San José goes via the Interamericana, not La Fortuna. Sunday afternoon buses to San José are often sold out by Saturday.

Ciudad Quesada, via La Fortuna ₡1550; four hours; depart 7am and 12:30pm.

Monteverde/Santa Elena ₡1200; 2½ hours; depart 7am and 4pm.

Puntarenas ₡1530; two hours; depart 6am and 1pm.

San José (Auto-Transportes Tilarán) ₡3650; four hours; depart 5am, 7am, 9:30am, 2pm and 5pm.

MONTEVERDE & SANTA ELENA

Snug in the misty greenbelt of two cloud-forest reserves, this slim corridor of human habitation consists of the Tico village of Santa Elena and the Quaker settlement of Monteverde. The area, first settled by loggers and farmers who came in the 1930s, later became populated by North American Quakers (a pacifist religious group also known as the 'Friends').

Initially, four Quakers were jailed in Alabama in 1949 for their refusal to be drafted into the Korean War. The incident ignited an exodus and in 1951 members of the group came to set up dairy farms in these greener pastures. In order to protect the vital watershed, the Quaker community established the private reserve that is now Reserva Biológica Bosque Nuboso Monteverde (p569). Tourism grabbed hold when a 1983 *National Geographic* feature described this unique landscape, and subsequently billed the area as *the* place to view one of Central America's most famous birds – the resplendent quetzal. Tourism here hasn't waned since.

Infrastructure is wobbly in these places – the electricity, water and phones blink off when you most need them. Blaming or moaning won't fix it any faster. Instead, kick back for a candlelit dinner. It's part of the rustic charm – you'll see.

Orientation

In the cloud forest at 1200m to 1600m, the community of Monteverde is scattered along the road that leads to the reserve. Most budget hotels and restaurants are in the village of Santa Elena, while the more expensive lodges are found along the road. The Monteverde reserve is 6km southeast of Santa Elena, and the Santa Elena reserve is 5km north and east.

Information

Librería Churches (☎ 2645-5147) has travel and natural history books, US newspapers, laundry service and snacks. Events are posted on the door. The Banco Nacional has an ATM and provides advances on Visa cards.

The town's official website is www.monte verdeforever.com.

Sights

Donning rubbery rain gear and mud boots (for rent at park offices) is a rite of passage for those visiting in search of resplendent quetzals, hummingbirds, howler monkeys, sloths, snakes and more. Just remember that wildlife absconds in the mist, so hold back wild expectations. Hiring a guide is often worth the expense.

BOSQUE ETERNO DE LOS NIÑOS

Founded by school children fed up with the childish squandering of our natural resources, **Bosque Eterno de los Niños** (Children's Eternal Forest; ☎ 2645-5003; www.acmcr.org; adult/student day use US$8/5, guided night hike US$15/10; ☎ 7:30am-5:30pm) is an enormous 220-sq-km reserve providing a home for local wildlife among the primary and secondary forest (and to allow former agricultural land to be slowly reclaimed by the jungle). The night tours here are highly recommended.

RESERVA BIOLÓGICA BOSQUE NUBOSO MONTEVERDE

When Quaker settlers first arrived, they agreed to preserve about a third of their property in order to protect the watershed above Monteverde. Fighting off squatters with the help of the Nature Conservancy and the World Wildlife Fund, they began what is now known as one of the country's most eminent reserves.

Trails in the reserve are clearly marked. The **Sendero Bosque Nuboso** is a pretty 2km (one-way) walk through the cloud forest to the continental divide. From there you can return via the wide **Sendero El Camino**, which branches off to a 25m-high suspension bridge. The circuit takes two

COSTA RICA

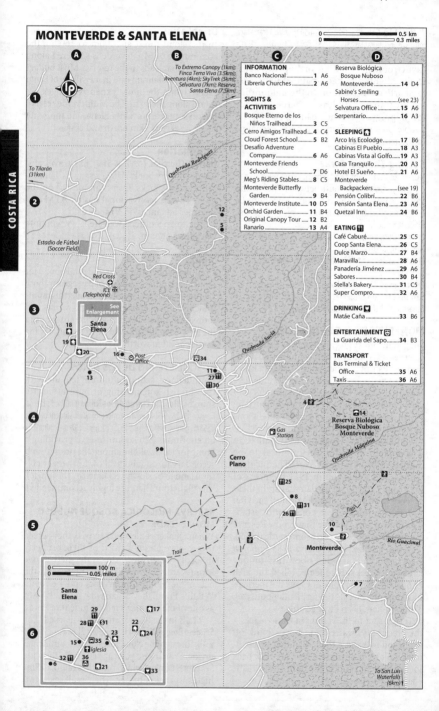

MONTEVERDE & SANTA ELENA

0 _____ 0.5 km
0 _____ 0.3 miles

INFORMATION
Banco Nacional **1** A6
Librería Churches **2** A6

SIGHTS & ACTIVITIES
Bosque Eterno de los
  Niños Trailhead **3** C5
Cerro Amigos Trailhead **4** C4
Cloud Forest School **5** B2
Desafío Adventure
  Company **6** A6
Monteverde Friends
  School **7** D6
Meg's Riding Stables **8** C5
Monteverde Butterfly
  Garden **9** B4
Monteverde Institute **10** D5
Orchid Garden **11** B4
Original Canopy Tour **12** B2
Ranario **13** A4

Reserva Biológica
  Bosque Nuboso
  Monteverde **14** D4
Sabine's Smiling
  Horses .... (see 23)
Selvatura Office **15** A6
Serpentario **16** A3

SLEEPING
Arco Iris Ecolodge **17** B6
Cabinas El Pueblo **18** A3
Cabinas Vista al Golfo **19** A3
Casa Tranquilo **20** A3
Hotel El Sueño **21** A6
Monteverde
  Backpackers .... (see 19)
Pensión Colibrí **22** B6
Pensión Santa Elena **23** A6
Quetzal Inn **24** B6

EATING
Café Caburé **25** C5
Coop Santa Elena **26** C5
Dulce Marzo **27** B4
Maravilla **28** A6
Panadería Jiménez **29** A6
Sabores **30** B4
Stella's Bakery **31** C5
Super Compro **32** A6

DRINKING
Matáe Caña **33** B6

ENTERTAINMENT
La Guarida del Sapo **34** B3

TRANSPORT
Bus Terminal & Ticket
  Office **35** A6
Taxis **36** A6

to three hours. Half-day **tours** (US$15) in English leave at 7:30am; call ahead to reserve a space or to arrange a night walk or bird-watching tour.

You can't camp but three basic **shelters** (dm US$5) provide drinking water, showers, propane stoves and cooking utensils. Hikers need to carry a sleeping bag, candles, food and other necessities (such as toilet paper). Make reservations at least one week in advance for the **dorms** (adult/student US$37/33) near the park entrance. The **visitors center** (☎ 2645-5122; www.cct.or.cr; park entry adult/student & child/child under 6 US$17/9/free; ☽ 7am-4pm) has free trail maps, a snack bar and a restaurant.

RESERVA SANTA ELENA
When Monteverde gets crowded, this park provides a great alternative. An exquisitely misty reserve with 12km of trails, Santa Elena is slightly higher in elevation than Monteverde, with some secondary-growth forest. Open spots help for spotting birds and other animals. Monkeys and sloths may even be seen on the road in. Go on your own or book a **guided tour** (US$15 plus entry fee), leaving from the **information center** (☎ 2645-5390/7107; www.reservasantaelena.org; entry to the reserve adult/student US$14/7; ☽ 7am-4pm) at 7:30am and 11:30am. Call to reserve.

OTHER ATTRACTIONS
The **Monteverde Butterfly Garden** (☎ 2645-5512; www.monteverdebutterflygarden.com; adult/student US$10/8; ☽ 9:30am-4pm) offers fantastic naturalist-led tours (in Spanish, English or German) that include a fascinating walk through live insect exhibits (leave the flyswatter at home). See the greenhouses where butterflies are raised and screened gardens where hundreds flutter about. Mornings are the best time to visit. Visitors can also explore on their own.

Hopping at night, the **Ranario** (☎ 2645-6320; www.ranario.com; adult/student or child US$10/8; ☽ 9am-8:30pm) exhibits over 30 species of frogs, toads and salamanders. For more cold-blooded marvels, the **serpentario** (serpentarium; ☎ 2645-6002; adult/student/child US$8/6/5; ☽ 9am-8pm) has 40 species of snakes.

The roadside **orchid garden** (☎ 2645-5308; www.monteverdeorchidgarden.com; adult/child under 12 US$10/free; ☽ 8am-5pm) has shady trails winding past more than 400 types of orchids organized into taxonomic groups. Peak blooming period is November to February.

Casem (Cooperativa de Artesanía Santa Elena Monteverde; ☎ 2645-5190; www.casemcoop.org; ☽ 8am-5pm Mon-Sat, 10am-4pm Sun high season), a women's arts and crafts cooperative, sells crafts and souvenirs with profits benefiting the community.

A number of art galleries around town are also worth exploring.

Activities

CANOPY TOURS
Aventura (☎ 2645-6388; www.monteverdeadventure.com; adult/student US$40/30; ☽ 7am-4pm) Aventura has 16 platforms that are spiced up with a Tarzan swing and a 15m rappel. It's about 3km north of Santa Elena on the road to the reserve, and transportation from your hotel is included in the price.

Extremo Canopy (☎ 2645-6058; www.monteverdeextremo.com; adult/child US$40/30; ☽ 8am-4pm) The newest player on the Monteverde canopy scene, this outfit runs small groups and doesn't bother with extraneous attractions if all you really want to do is fly down the zip lines. There's also a new Superman canopy ride (US$5 extra), allowing you to fly Superman-style through the air.

Original Canopy Tour (☎ 2645-6950; www.canopytour.com; adult/student/child US$45/35/25; ☽ 7:30am-4pm) On the grounds of Cloud Forest Lodge, this has the fabled zip lines that started the adventure tourism. These lines aren't as elaborate as the others, but with 14 platforms, a rappel through the center of an old fig tree and 5km of private trails worth a wander afterward, you can enjoy a piece of history that's far more entertaining than most museums.

Selvatura (☎ 2645-5929; www.selvatura.com; adult/child US$45/30; ☽ 7:30am-4pm) One of the bigger games in town, Selvatura has 3km of cables, 18 platforms and one Tarzan swing through primary forest. The office is across the street from the church in Santa Elena.

SkyTrek (☎ 2645-5238; www.skywalk.co.cr; adult/student/child US$75/60/48; ☽ 7:30am-5pm) If you're not buying the whole 'eco' element of canopy tours, then this is definitely for you. This seriously fast canopy tour consists of 11 platforms attached to steel towers that are spread out along a road. We're talking serious speeds of up to 40 miles per hour (64km/h), which is probably why SkyTrek is the only canopy tour that has a real brake system.

HIKING
Take a free hike up 1842m **Cerro Amigos** on a clear day for great views of Volcán Arenal, 20km away to the northeast. Near the top of the mountain, you'll pass by the TV towers for channels 7 and 13. The trail leaves Monteverde from behind Hotel Belmar (the road behind the gas station), ascending roughly 300m in 3km. From the hotel, take the dirt road going downhill, then the next left.

The strenuous hike to the **San Luis Waterfall** rewards you with views of a gorgeous stream cascading from the cloud forests into a series of swimming holes just begging for a picnic. It's only a few kilometers, but it's steep and the rocky, mud-filled terrain can get very slick. A taxi from town costs about U$12.

HORSEBACK RIDING

A number of trails and scenic panoramas make the area ideal for horseback riding. Inquire at Pensión Santa Elena for reader-recommended **Sabine's Smiling Horses** (☎ 2645-6894, 8385-2424; www.horseback-riding-tour.com), offering multiday trips and even a five-hour full-moon ride. Also popular is **Meg's Riding Stables** (☎ 2645-5560/052).

Riding from Monteverde and La Fortuna is offered by most outfitters. Overworked horses made the route controversial in the past, but client pressure has really upped local standards. Of the two routes, the Mirador Trail is steep and unmanageably muddy in rainy season while the Lake Trail is flatter and easier. **Desafío Adventure Company** (☎ 2645-5874; www.monteverdetours.com) takes the Lake Trail to La Fortuna (US$85).

VOLUNTEERING

The nonprofit **Monteverde Institute** (☎ 2645-5053; www.mvinstitute.org) offers internships and places student volunteers.

The **Bosque Eterno de los Niños** (Children's Eternal Forest; see p569) is always looking for help. For information visit the website.

To volunteer in the schools, check out opportunities online for the English-language **Monteverde Friends School** (www.mfschool.org) or the **Cloud Forest School** (www.cloudforestschool.org).

Courses

Centro Panamericano de Idiomas (CPI; ☎ 2265-6306; www.cpi-edu.com; classes with/without homestay US$480/330; ⏰ 8am-5pm) Specializes in Spanish-language education, with some courses geared to teens, medical professionals or social workers.

Monteverde Institute (☎ 2645-5053; www.mvinstitute. org) A nonprofit educational institute, founded in 1986, that offers interdisciplinary courses in tropical biology, conservation, sustainable development, women's studies and Spanish, among other topics. Courses are occasionally open to the public – check the website. Internships and volunteer opportunities in education and reforestation are also available.

Monteverde Studios of the Arts (☎ 2645-5053; www.mvinstitute.org) Administered by Monteverde Institute, this offers a variety of classes and workshops, sometimes open to visitors, covering everything from woodworking to papermaking, with a special emphasis on pottery.

Sleeping

An overflow of hotels means you can find many options in addition to those following if need be. These offer hot showers, unless otherwise noted, though air-conditioning is not needed at such great heights.

our pick Pensión Santa Elena (☎ 2645-5051/6240; www.pensionsantaelena.com; campsites per person US$4, dm US$7, d with bathroom US$25-30, d without bathroom US$16-20, cabinas US$35-50; 💻 🛜) This full-service hostel is a perennial favorite, right in central Santa Elena. Ran and Shannon, a brother-sister duo from Austin, Texas, offer budget travellers top-notch, four-star service and *pura vida* hospitality. They're also environmentalists at heart, and work with the local community on projects such as the reduction of gray water by installing a water treatment plant. Each room is different, with something to suit every budget and group.

Monteverde Backpackers (☎ 2645-5844; www.monteverdebackpackers.com/home.html; dm US$10, s/d/tr/q US$20/30/39/44, all incl breakfast; 💻 🛜) Part of the Costa Rica Hostel Network, Monteverde Backpackers is smaller and more basic than some of the other cheapies in town. But it's clean and friendly, with wood-paneled rooms, comfy beds and some of the hottest, most powerful showers we've ever felt.

Cabinas El Pueblo (☎ 2645-6192; www.cabinaselpueblo.com; s with/without bathroom US$20/15, d US$30/20, all incl breakfast; 💻 🛜) This pleasant hostel run by an attentive Tico couple is one of the best value deals in town. The price includes internet and free coffee or tea all day. The well-furnished rooms are big and comfy, with firm mattresses and private hot-water showers. Some rooms also have TV and fridge.

Hotel El Sueño (☎ 2645-5021; www.hotelelsuenocr.com; s/d standard US$20/30, with balcony US$25/35) This hotel has huge wooden rooms with private hot showers. The pricier, upstairs rooms are airier, though the best ones are toward the back. There's a great balcony with sweeping views of the area.

Cabinas Vista al Golfo (☎ 2645-6321; www.cabinasvistaalgolfo.com; s with/without bathroom US$20/15, d US$25/20; 💻 🛜) This is a very comfortable locale run by a congenial Costa Rican family. Rooms are well kept, the showers are hot and the owners will make you feel right at home. The upstairs balcony rooms (US$5 extra) have great views of the rainforest and, on a clear day, the Golfo de Nicoya.

Casa Tranquilo (☎ 2645-6782; www.casatranquilo hostel.com; r per person with/without bathroom incl breakfast US$25/20; 🖳) This wonderful little hotel is owned and managed by a delightful Tico couple, David and Elena (and their little one, Josue). Some of the wood-paneled rooms have skylights and views of the gulf. Check out the great upstairs terrace, perfect for a few late-night ballads on the guitar.

Pensión Colibrí (☎ 2645-5682; r US$20-30) Another popular budget option, this small, family-run *pensión* is on a quiet lane and feels like it's perched among the trees. The larger rooms are worth the money as they have a fridge and balconies overlooking the woods.

Quetzal Inn (☎ 2645-6076; www.quetzalinn.com; s/d without balcony US$30/40, with balcony US$35/45, all incl breakfast; 🖳) Up the same quiet alley as Pensión Colibrí is this lovely little lodge. With wood-plank walls, high-sloped ceilings and green surroundings, this family-run inn embodies the perfect combination of central location, thoughtfully designed accommodations and a personable, hospitable ambience.

Arco Iris Ecolodge (☎ 2645-5067; www.arcoirislodge. com; s US$30-64, d US$40-128, honeymoon ste US$193; 🖳) This clutch of pretty cabins is on a little hill overlooking Santa Elena and the surrounding forests, and has the privacy and intimacy of a mountain retreat. The lodge features a system of private trails that wind throughout the property, including one that leads to a lookout point where you can see the Pacific on a clear day. There are a variety of different room sizes and styles to choose from, so you can either go rustic or live it up.

Finca Terra Viva (☎ 2645-5454; www.terravivacr.com; d US$40, casita US$60, extra person US$5, incl 3 meals US$14; 🖳) This 135-hectare *finca*, 3.5km or so out on the road toward Reserva Santa Elena, is being gradually returned to the forest; about 60% is already there. In the meantime, cattle, pigs, goats, horses and chickens offer guests a typically Costa Rican rural experience. Each of the six rustic, wooden rooms sleeps up to four and has a private hot shower. A few free-standing *casitas* (huts), each sleeping four, and fitted with kitchenette, are available for those desiring more privacy.

Eating

Sabores (☎ 2645-6174; cones ₡560-1700; 🕙 11am-8pm Wed-Mon) Sabores serves Monteverde's own brand of ice cream, plus coffee and a variety of homemade desserts.

Panadería Jiménez (☎ 2645-5035; items ₡560-3000; 🕙 5am-6:30pm Mon-Sat, 5-10am Sun) This bakery has the best goods in town, like whole-wheat breads, pastries and coffee for folks booked on the early bus.

Dulce Marzo (☎ 2645-6568; items ₡650-4500; 🕙 11am-7pm) Yummy home-baked sweets, wraps, sandwiches, good espresso drinks and a favorite-cafe feel make this one of those places to linger over a late-morning coffee as you skim the paper or your guidebook.

Stella's Bakery (☎ 2645-5560; mains ₡800-3200; 🕙 6am-10pm; 🅅) Order your choice of sandwich on delicious homemade breads with a convenient order form (one side is in English), and don't skimp on the veggies, many of which are locally grown (and organic).

Maravilla (☎ 2645-6623; mains ₡1500-3500; 🕙 6am-9pm) Just about the cheapest and most authentic restaurant in Santa Elena, this charming *soda* serves typical Costa Rican specialties, including excellent *casados*.

Café Caburé (☎ 2645-5020; mains ₡2300-5000; 🕙 8am-8pm Mon-Sat; 🛜) Looking for something different? Argentinean owner Susana Salas has created one of the most eclectic menus around, including Mexican chicken *mole* (spicy savoury sauce), chipotle-rubbed steak, sweet-and-sour chicken wraps, curries and mouth-watering, homemade chocolates and other desserts.

The giant **SuperCompro** (☎ 2758-7351; 🕙 7am-9pm) grocery store in Santa Elena has everything you could possibly need, including organic produce. **Coop Santa Elena** (🕙 7:30am-6pm), in Cerro Plano, has a smaller selection, and profits are reinvested in the community.

Drinking & Entertainment

La Guarida del Sapo (☎ 2645-7010; 🕙 6pm-midnight Mon-Thu, until 2am Fri & Sat) This cathedral of music built by the Hotel El Sapo Dorado resembles an old church, right down to the stained-glass windows with Costa Rican nature scenes. Fridays are the most lively nights when the place is transformed into a discotheque. There's live music on most Mondays and Saturdays.

Matáe Caña (☎ 2645-4883; 🕙 noon-late Tue-Sun) Housed in Santa Elana's original tavern, this chic new lounge fills a void that has long been missing in Monteverde. Opened in late 2009 by the folks behind Pensión Santa Elena, Matáe Caña features the same passion and attention to detail. There are numerous padded nooks and crannies where you can sip a drink with your date.

Getting There & Away

All intercity buses stop at the **bus terminal** (☎ 2645-5159; 🕒 5:45-11am & 1:30-5pm Mon-Fri, closes 3pm Sat & Sun) in downtown Santa Elena. Purchase tickets to the Monteverde and Santa Elena reserves at the **Hotel & Info Center Camino Verde** (☎ 2645-6304; www.exploringmonteverde.com/hotel-camino-verde; 🕒 6:30am-10pm) across from the bus terminal.

Destination details are as follows:

Puntarenas ₡1235; three hours; depart from the front of Banco Nacional at 6am.

Reserva Biológica Bosque Nuboso Monteverde ₡600; 30 minutes; depart from front of Banco Nacional at 6:15am, 7:20am, 1:20pm and 3pm, return at 6:45am, 11:30am, 2pm and 4pm.

Reserva Santa Elena ₡1200; 30 minutes; depart from front of Banco Nacional at 6:30am, 8:30am, 10:30am, 12:30pm, 1pm and 3pm, return 11am, 1pm and 4pm.

San José (TransMonteverde) ₡2500; 4½ hours; depart the Santa Elena bus station at 6:30am and 2:30pm.

Tilarán, with connection to La Fortuna ₡1800; seven hours; depart from the bus station at 6am. This is a long ride and you will need to hang around for two hours in Tilarán. If you have a few extra dollars, it's recommended that you take the jeep-boat-jeep option to La Fortuna.

JEEP-BOAT-JEEP

The fastest route between Monteverde–Santa Elena and La Fortuna is a jeep-boat-jeep combo (around US$25 to US$30, three hours), which can be arranged through almost any hotel or tour operator in either town. A 4WD jeep taxi (really a minivan) takes you to Río Chiquito, meeting a boat that crosses Laguna de Arenal, where a taxi on the other side continues to La Fortuna. This is increasingly becoming the primary transportation between La Fortuna and Monteverde as it's incredibly scenic, reasonably priced and saves half a day of rough travel.

LA FORTUNA & VOLCÁN ARENAL
pop 8000

Even without an active volcano popping fireworks overhead, the former farming town of La Fortuna would be a relaxing place to kick back for a few days. The flat grid town is near a playground of cascading waterfalls, steep trails and luxurious hot springs. As rapid development takes its toll, you might find yourself batting off tour-hawkers the minute you step off the bus. Relax, once you get settled in,

these hawkers disperse and you can enjoy nature's many distractions – probably a good thing since it takes time for Volcán Arenal to peek out from the cloud cover.

Orientation & Information

La Fortuna offers few street signs, and most locals give directions using landmarks. The town is centered on a small park adjacent to the taxi stand. The clinic, police station and post office are all within two blocks of the plaza.

Quick internet access is available at **Expediciones** (☎ 2479-9101; per hr ₡450; 🕒 7am-10pm Mon-Sat), across from the parque central. The banks in town all change US dollars and Banco de Costa Rica has a Visa Plus ATM. Pay phones are on the main street and in the parque central.

There is no government-run tourist information center or official tourist information booth in La Fortuna. However, we highly recommend Diego and the staff at Arenal Backpackers Resort and Pete of Gringo Pete's for honest, candid information on local sights and attractions. They also offer some of the best rates for area activities and attractions. If you find cheaper prices, it's probably too good to be true.

Sights & Activities
VOLCÁN ARENAL

Just 15km west of Fortuna, **Parque Nacional Volcán Arenal** (☎ 2461-8499; admission US$10; 🕒 8am-4pm) is home to Arenal – Costa Rica's most active volcano, producing ash columns, explosions and red streamers of molten rock almost daily since 1968. Climbing it is not allowed – hikers have been killed by explosions. Independent travelers can take an 8am bus toward Tilarán (ask to get off at the park) and catch the 2pm bus back to La Fortuna. From the 'Parque Nacional' sign off the main road, a 2km dirt road leads to the park. From the ranger station grab a trail map to choose from trails through old lava flows, tropical rainforest or to the lake.

HOT SPRINGS

What's the consolation prize if you can't actually see the volcano? Why, hot springs, of course, and La Fortuna has some doozies.

Tabacón Hot Springs (☎ 2519-1900; www.tabacon.com; adult day pass incl lunch or dinner US$85, evening pass incl dinner US$70; 🕒 10am-10pm) Enter through a curtain of florid tropical blooms to reveal a 40°C (104°F) waterfall pouring over a cliff, concealing naturalish-looking caves complete with camouflaged cup holders. And lounged across each well-placed stone, in various stages of sweat-induced exhaustion, relax reddening tourists all enjoying what could be called a hot date.

Baldi Hot Springs (☎ 2479-9651; www.baldihot springs.cr; admission with/without buffet US$34/25; ☒ 10am-10pm) A decidedly more budget-friendly option, Baldi sports concrete Roman pillars and a Maya pyramid sprouting waterslides. At night it turns into a veritable club on water, with three swim-up bars, blaring music and a decent buffet to help soak up the booze.

Eco-Termales (☎ 2479-8484; adult/child US$30/20, with dinner US$55/45; ☒ 10am-9pm) The theme here is minimalist elegance, and everything from the natural circulation systems in the pools to the soft, mushroom lighting is understated yet luxurious. Just 100 visitors per slot are welcomed at 10am, 1pm and 5pm, and you must either phone ahead or book online at www.anywherecostarica.com.

We're certainly not going to let out the secret, but there are several free **hot springs** in the area that any local can take you to.

LA CATARATA DE FORTUNA
A ribbon of cold, clear water called **La Catarata de la Fortuna** (admission US$10; ☒ 8am-5pm) pours through a sheer canyon thick with bromeliads and ferns. Though it's dangerous to dive beneath the thundering 70m falls, you can take a dip in its perfect swimming holes (though keep an eye on your backpack). Rent a bike or walk. It's 7km from La Fortuna – all uphill – through pastureland and papaya trees.

Tours
The tour operators listed here are a few of the more established agencies, but this list is by no means exhaustive.

Aventuras Arenal (☎ 2479-9133; www.arenaladven tures.com; ☒ 7am-8pm) Has been around for over 15 years, organizing a variety of local day tours via bike, boat and horseback.

Desafío Adventure Company (☎ 2479-9464; www. desafiocostarica.com; ☒ 6:30am-9pm) This highly recommended company offers a variety of tours including rafting, lava-viewing hikes, horseback riding, mountain biking, spelunking and more. Look for the castle-like building.

Eagle Tours (☎ 2479-9091; www.eagletours.net; ☒ 6:30am-9pm) Budget travelers rave about this professionally run tour agency, with an office about 150m west of the church.

Jacamar Tours (☎ 2479-9767; www.arenaltours.com; ☒ 7am-9pm) Recommended for its incredible variety of naturalist hikes.

Pura Vida Tours (☎ 2479-9045; www.puravidatrips. com; ☒ 7am-10pm)

Sunset Tours (☎ 2479-9800; www.sunsettourcr.com; ☒ 6:30am-9pm) This is La Fortuna's most established tour company, recommended for high-quality tours with bilingual guides.

Sleeping
There's no shortage of sleeping options in La Fortuna.

Gringo Pete's (☎ 2479-8521; gringopetes2003@yahoo. com; campsites per person US$2, dm US$3, r per person with/without bathroom US$5/4; ℗) With a clean and cozy vibe, it's hard to believe that this purple hostel, 100m south of the school, is so cheap! Whether you're in the comfy dorms sleeping four or your own private room with sink and shower, you'll flock to the breezy, covered common areas, which are great spots to chat with other backpackers. Pete can point you toward cut-rate tours and store your bags for you while you're on the tour.

Sleep Inn Guesthouse (☎ 8394-7033; misterlavalava@ hotmail.com; Av Arenal; r with/without bathroom per person US$7/5) If you're looking for a welcoming Tico family to stay with, you've found them. It's owned by Carlos and Cándida. Carlos, whose nickname is Mr Lava-Lava Man, guarantees you'll see lava (or you get to go again for free), and his tours (US$16) are the cheapest in town.

La Choza Inn (☎ 2479-9361; www.lachozainnhostel. com; Av Fort btwn Calles 2 & 4; dm US$7, s/d without bathroom US$13/17, standard s/d US$34/51, deluxe s/d US$51/68, all incl breakfast; ☒ ☒ ☒) This popular budget inn 100m west of the parque central has a great variety of rooms, a well-stocked communal kitchen, an extremely personable staff and is consistently packed with discriminating travelers.

our pick Arenal Backpackers Resort (☎ 2479-7000; http://arenalbackpackersresort.com; Av Central; dm US$14, campsites s/d US$14/20, d/tr/q US$45/75/84; ☒ ☒ ☒ ☒) This self-proclaimed 'five-star hostel' with volcano views is among the cushier hostels in Costa Rica. Dorm rooms have private hot-water bathrooms, and you'll sleep easy on the thick, orthopedic mattresses. Private rooms definitely cater to midrange travelers, though with cable TV, two superior double beds and tiled bathrooms, they're worth the splurge. The newest budget accommodation option is the covered tent city; each raised tent contains a double air mattress, sheets, pillows and electricity. But the real draw is the landscaped pool with swim-up bar, where backpackers spend lazy days lounging with a cold beer.

Hotel Las Colinas (☎ 2479-9305; www.lascolinas arenal.com; Calle 1 btwn Avs Central & Arenal; s/d/tr/q incl breakfast from US$45/60/84/88; ❄ ▯) The superfriendly owners of Las Colinas have completely remodeled this hotel, creating modern, airy rooms and a 2nd-story terrace with great views of the volcano.

Eating

Rainforest Café (☎ 2479-7239; Calle 1 btwn Avs Central & Arenal; pastries ₡750-2750; ❄ 7am-8:30pm; ☎) Superb coffee and espresso is served in what feels like an industrial tent, all glass walls and aluminum bathroom door.

Restaurante El Jardín (☎ 2479-9360; cnr Av Central & Calle 3; mains ₡1400-8000; ❄ 5am-1pm) You can either relax over a shrimp pizza in this bustling eatery 100m east of the parque central, or grab a chair beneath the Pollo Pito Pito sign and snack on a few pieces of greasy (but delicious) fried chicken.

Soda Viquez (☎ 2479-7132; mains ₡1500-4000; ❄ 7am-10pm) Locals swear this is the best *soda* in town, and we won't dispute their opinion. Located just left of the Rainforest Café, this cute, open-air *soda* serves great Tico favorites, including awesome *casados* (₡2700).

Lava Lounge (☎ 2479-7365; Av Central btwn Calles 2 & 4; mains ₡2500-6000; ❄ 11am-10:30pm) This hip, open-air restaurant is a breath of fresh air when you just can't abide another *casado*. There's pasta, fish, burgers, wraps and a fair selection of other such well-executed international standbys, brought to you by friendly staff.

For groceries, stop by the well-stocked **Super Cristian 2** (cnr Av Central & Calle 1; ❄ 7am-9pm) on the southeast corner of the parque central; there's another **branch** (cnr Av Arenal & Calle 2; ❄ 7am-9pm) down by the river. The new **Mega Super** (Ave Arenal; ❄ 7am-9pm Mon-Sat, until 8pm Sun), at the bus terminal, is a good place to visit before boarding a long bus ride.

Getting There & Away

BUS

All domestic buses stop at the **Centro Comercial Adifort bus terminal** (Ave Arenal). The Tica Bus to Nicaragua (₡12,000) passes by El Tanque between 6:30am and 7am daily; to catch the bus you'll have to take an early taxi to El Tanque (15 minutes, ₡4500).

Ciudad Quesada (Auto-Transportes San José-San Carlos) ₡650; one hour; 15 departures per day from 5am to 7pm.

Monteverde ₡1400; six to eight hours; depart 8am (change at Tilarán at 12:30pm for Monteverde).

San José (Auto-Transportes San José-San Carlos) ₡1955; 4½ hours; depart 12:45pm and 2:45pm. Alternatively, take a bus to Ciudad Quesada and change to frequent buses to the capital.

Tilarán (Auto-Transportes Tilarán) ₡1100; 3½ hours; depart 8am and 5:30pm.

JEEP-BOAT-JEEP

The fastest route between La Fortuna and Monteverde–Santa Elena is a jeep-boat-jeep combo (around US$25 to US$30, three hours). For more information, see p574.

LOS CHILES

pop 7000

Sweltering and sleepy, Los Chiles sits three rutted kilometers south of Nicaragua. Originally settled by merchants and fishermen, it recently served as an important supply route for Nicaraguan Contras, with a strong US military presence throughout the 1980s. Today gringo-traffic refers to travelers exploring the scenic water route to Caño Negro or the river route to Nicaragua, a one- to two-hour boat ride. Travelers crossing here must stop in Los Chiles for the necessary paperwork (see boxed text, opposite).

The Banco Nacional changes cash. **Viajes y Excursiones Cabo Rey** (☎ 2471-1251, 8839-7458) provides a boat service to the Caño Negro refuge (from ₡26,009) as well as to El Castillo and the Solentiname Islands in Nicaragua. Cabo himself can usually be found by the dock.

Sleeping & Eating

No Frills Hotel, Bar & Restaurant (☎ 2471-1200/1410; r US$20; ❄) This hotel, about 1km south of Los Chiles just past the gas station, is not, in fact, completely frill-free. Though basic, rooms here are clean and quiet (except for the honking of resident geese) with air-con and TV; some even have a full-sized fridge.

Hotel Tulipán (☎ 2471-1414; www.ranchotulipan.com; s/d/tr US$20/25/35; ❄ ❄ ▯ ☎) Remodeled in 2009, Hotel Tulipán is the most respectable accommodations in town, though it's also home to a very popular (translation: noisy!) bar that becomes a disco on Wednesdays and Fridays. All the rooms have air-con, private hot-water bathrooms and cable TV, and it's conveniently located right across from immigration.

There's the local branch of food outlet Almacén de Los Chiles on the west side of the soccer field to meet all of your grocery needs.

Getting There & Away

Regular boat transportation is limited to quick shuttles across the Nicaraguan border (see boxed text, below) and various day trips throughout the region.

All buses arrive and leave from the terminal behind Soda Pamela, near the intersection of Hwy 35. Timetables are flexible, so play it safe and inquire locally.

San José ₡3000; five hours; depart 5am and 3pm.
Upala via Caño Negro ₡1400; 2½ hours; depart 5am and 4pm.

LA VIRGEN

Steeped in the tangled shores of the wild and scenic Río Sarapiquí, La Virgen prospered in the heyday of the banana trade (no double entendres here). Today it's a little-known destination for world-class kayaking and rafting.

The area has numerous budget options. Our pick of the litter is **Rancho Leona** (☎ 2761-1019; www.rancholeona.com), a shady, riverside spot where you can swap tales of gnarly rapids, detox in the Native American–style sweat lodge and enjoy family-style dinners. Rooms (some private) share hot-water showers and a communal kitchen. **Kayaking trips** (trips from US$75) and guided hikes are arranged on an ad hoc basis.

Down the road is the friendly **Sarapiquí Outdoor Center** (☎ 2761-1123; www.costaricaraft.com; campsites/r US$5/25), where impeccable campsites overlook the river, with access to showers and bathrooms. The simple rooms are a bit overpriced. In addition to rafting and kayaking trips, the owners also arrange horseback rides and guided hikes to a nearby waterfall.

All the buses between San José and Puerto Viejo de Sarapiquí make stops in La Virgen.

PUERTO VIEJO DE SARAPIQUÍ
pop 6500

Banana and coffee booms once made Puerto Viejo the country's most important port. Largely reclaimed by the jungle, today it is redefined as a slightly seedy border town. It isn't to be confused with touristy Puerto Viejo de Talamanca on the Caribbean coast. There are, however, great opportunities here for bird-watching, rafting, boating and jungle exploration.

Sights & Activities
ESTACIÓN BIOLÓGICA LA SELVA

The Organization of Tropical Studies (OTS) runs a **biological research station** (☎ 2524-0697, 2766-6565; www.ots.ac.cr; s/d US$88/166), 5km southeast of Puerto Viejo. On any given day, the station teems with scientists and students researching in the nearby private reserve. La Selva welcomes drop-ins, though it's best to phone ahead and reserve. Rooms here are basic, with fan and bunk beds (a few have doubles), but rates include all meals and activities. Reservations are required for guided hikes (₡22,040/17,400 for a full-/half-day hike; 8am and 1:30pm daily) with a bilingual naturalist guide.

Sleeping & Eating

Trinidad Lodge (☎ 2213-0661, 8381-0621; r per person US$10) Situated on the Río San Juan in the community of Trinidad, this budget lodge is right across from the Nicaragua border crossing and is pretty much the only gig in

---

GETTING TO SAN CARLOS, NICARAGUA

Although there's a 14km-long dirt road between Los Chiles and San Carlos, Nicaragua, using this crossing requires special permission generally reserved for federal employees. Most regular folk go across by boat on the Río Frío, which is easily arranged in Los Chiles. You must first get an exit stamp in your passport at **immigration** (migración; ☎ 2471-1223; ☷ 8am-noon & 1:30-4pm), about 100m east of the dock and directly across the street from Hotel Tulipán. If you are coming from Nicaragua, you must make immigration your first stop.

Regular boats (₡5800, 1½ hours) leave Los Chiles at 12:30pm and 3:30pm daily, with extra boats at 11am and 2:30pm if demand is high. Boats leave San Carlos for Los Chiles at 10:30am and 4pm, with extra boats scheduled as needed. Of course, the Nicaragua–Costa Rica border is not known for its reliability, so confirm these times before setting out. Nicaragua charges a ₡4000 (about US$7.50) entry fee and ₡1150 (US$2) exit fee, which can be paid in US dollars, colones or Nicaraguan córdobas. Los Chiles municipality charges a ₡580 exit and entry fee; after getting your passport stamped at immigration, walk down to the docks and pay the exit fee at the yellow Recaudador Municipal office. Reverse this procedure if you are arriving here from Nicaragua (see p506).

town. Although they're on the rustic side, the bamboo-walled bungalows are charming and very clean, with private cold-water bathrooms. Candle power provides light when the generator shuts off at the end of the night, and meals are available (₡2300 to ₡4600) at the *rancho* (small house or houselike building), with a pool table besides. The lodge is accessible only by boat (₡5800), which departs once daily at 2pm from the main dock of Puerto Viejo de Sarapiquí (35km away).

ourpick **Posada Andrea Cristina B&B** (☎ 2766-6265; www.andreacristina.com; s/d incl breakfast US$28/48, tree house d US$55, extra person US$15) About 1km west of the center, this recommended B&B has eight quiet, immaculate cabins in its garden, each with fan, private hot-water bathroom, hammock and outdoor table and chairs. It's also situated on the edge of the rainforest, so there are plenty of opportunities for birdwatching while you sit outside and eat breakfast. The newest accommodation option is a funky living treehouse with private bathroom and canopy-level balcony from which you can spy on the sloth family living in the nearby trees. The owner, Alex Martínez, is an excellent, amiable guide as well as a passionate frontline conservationist.

There are several *sodas* in Puerto Viejo de Sarapiquí, including the excellent **Soda Judith** (mains ₡1160-2320; ☽ 6am-7pm), one block off the main road, where early risers grab brewed coffee and big breakfasts or an *empanada* (turnover stuffed with meat or cheese) to start their day.

Getting There & Away
BOAT
The small port has a regular service to the Trinidad Lodge in Trinidad, and you are able to arrange transportation anywhere along the river (seasonal conditions permitting) through independent boat captains. Short trips cost about ₡5800 per hour per person for a group of four, or ₡11,600 per hour for a single person. Serious voyages to Tortuguero (p555) and back cost about ₡203,000 for a boat holding five.

BUS
Right across from the park, the **bus terminal** (☎ 2233-4242; ☽ 5am-7pm) sells tickets and stores backpacks (₡870 per day).

Guápiles (Empresarios Guapileños) ₡780; one hour; depart 5:30am, 6:45am, 7:10am, 9:40am, 10:30am, 12:10pm, 2:30pm, 3:45pm, 4:45pm and 7pm.

Puerto Viejo de Sarapiquí ₡350; 30 minutes; frequent local buses.
San José (Autotransportes Sarapiquí) ₡1650; two hours; depart 6:30am, 7:30am, 10am, 11:30am, 1:30pm, 2:30pm, 3:30pm, 4:30pm and 6pm.

GUANACASTE

Like the prized, gnarled shade tree the region is named after, there is something singular and stubborn about Guanacaste. It could be the cowboy culture, which consumes cattle fairs and saddle soap like the rest of the country craves shopping centers. Call it the backwater blessing – a slow, colonial pace means that locals are laid-back and cordial, and roads still lead to nowhere. Of course, this is all poised to change.

With Liberia's expanding international airport, the city is fast in line to being crowned Costa Rica's second city, a status backed up by its easy accessibility to the Interamericana. And although Guanacaste's cities are seemingly at a standstill, Mother Nature looms large in the background. Volcanoes, hot springs and horse packing trips take travelers high above the cowboy plains. Rare, dry tropical forests lead into remote Pacific beaches, turtle havens with riotously sweet surf breaks. In the name of adventure, Guanacaste seems on the verge of being tamed.

CAÑAS
pop 25,000
Hot, dusty streets, custom pickups and machete-wielding cowboys mean you've made it to Cañas. It's typically rural Latin America, where the gait is slow and businesses lock up for lunch. At the crossroads of the Interamericana and the eastern road to Monteverde, Cañas provides visitors with a base for organizing rafting trips on the nearby Río Corobicí or for exploring Parque Nacional Palo Verde.

Wildlife tours take gentle float trips down the Río Corobicí. Book with **Safaris Corobicí** (☎ 2669-6191; www.safaricorobici.com; Interamericana Km 193; ☽ departures 7am-3pm), whose office is on the Interamericana, 4.5km north of Cañas.

At the southeastern end of town, **Cabinas Corobicí** (☎ 2669-0241; cnr Av 2 & Calle 5; r per person US$10) is a good budget option as the friendly management maintains comfortable, good-sized rooms with warmish private showers. And the area is fairly quiet at night.

The newest and most upscale hotel in town, **Caña Brava Inn** (☎ 2669-1294; recepcion canabravainn@hotmail.com; s US$35-57, d US$71-113; ❌ ☎ ☎) has all the modern amenities, including well-insulated rooms with flat-screen TV, wi-fi, huge comfy bedding and contemporary decor.

Rincón Corobicí (☎ 2669-1234; mains ₡1700-6000; ❂ 8am-6pm) is an attractive restaurant 4km north of Cañas on the banks of the Río Corobicí – after lunch, you can take a cool dip.

Getting There & Away

Terminal Cañas sits at the north end of town.
Liberia ₡1050; 1½ hours; depart 4:30am, 5:35am, 6:10am, 6:40am, 7:15am, 7:45am, noon, 1:30pm, 4:30pm and 5:30pm.
Puntarenas ₡1400; two hours; depart 6am, 9:20am, 10:30am, 11:30am, 12:30pm, 3:30pm and 4:30pm.
San José ₡2280; 3½ hours; depart 4am, 4:50am, 5:40am, 6:30am, 8:30am, 11:20am, 1:30pm, 2:30pm and 5:30pm.
Tilarán ₡450; 45 minutes; depart 6am, 8am, 9am, 10:30am, noon, 1:45pm, 3:30pm and 5:45pm.

PARQUE NACIONAL PALO VERDE

Palo Verde has the greatest concentrations of waterfowl and shorebirds in Central America, with over 300 recorded bird species. Visitors can spot large flocks of herons (including rare black-crowned night herons), storks, spoon-bills and scarlet macaws. When the dry season begins in December, birds congregate in lakes and marshes, trees lose their leaves and the flocks become easier to see.

Visitors can **camp** (US$4) near the Palo Verde ranger station, where there are toilets and hot-water showers. Additional dorms at the **ranger station** (☎ 2200-0125; park admission US$10; ❂ 8am-4pm) have mosquito nets and cold showers. Find good accommodations and information at the **Hacienda Palo Verde Research Station** (☎ 2524-0607; www.ots.ac.cr; r per person incl meals adult/child US$65/34), run by the Organization of Tropical Studies (OTS). It also guides recommended **hiking tours** (half-day per 2/3/4 people US$35/60/75) and **bird-watching tours** (half-/full-day per person US$30/38) excursions.

Palo Verde is 30km west of Cañas. Buses connecting Cañas and Liberia (see p581) can drop you at the ACT office on the Interamericana, opposite the turnoff to the park. If you call the office in advance, rangers may be able to drive you on the gravel road from here into the park.

RESERVA BIOLÓGICA LOMAS DE BARBUDAL

The 26-sq-km Lomas de Barbudal reserve forms a cohesive unit with Palo Verde, and protects several species of endangered trees, such as mahogany and rosewood, as well as the common and quite spectacular *corteza amarilla*. In March all the yellow *cortezes* in the forest burst into bloom on the same day, creating a four-day profusion of color. Endangered birds spotted here include king vultures and scarlet macaws.

The **information center** (park admission US$10; ❂ 7am-4pm) offers maps, though you have to wade across the Río Cabuyo to access the actual reserve and a small network of hiking trails. There is no camping or public transportation. Buses can leave you at the turnoff to Lomas de Barbudal at Pijije (on the Interamericana, 2km northwest of Bagaces). Walk or hitch for the remaining 7km.

LIBERIA

pop 50,000

Well, the secret's out. Before the boom in Costa Rican tourism, deciphering the bus timetables and fighting your way through the crowds at the Coca-Cola terminal in San José was a rite of passage for the uninitiated traveler. Even just a few years ago, getting to the beaches on the Península de Nicoya took determination, patience and – depending on the state of Costa Rica's dreadful roads – a little luck. These days, though, travelers are getting their first glimpse of *pura vida* Costa Rica at Liberia's own Aeropuerto Internacional Daniel Oduber Quirós, which is roughly the size of a Wal-Mart parking lot, but more of a breeze to exit.

As an alternative to San José, this airport gives you quick and convenient access to destinations on the Península de Nicoya. Liberia is also a much more user-friendly destination that San José.

Information

Most hotels will accept US dollars, and may be able to change small amounts. If not, Liberia probably has more banks per square meter than any other town in Costa Rica.
BAC San José (☎ 2666-2020; Centro Comercial Santa Rosa; ❂ 9am-6pm Mon-Fri, 9am-1pm Sat) Changes traveler's checks; try this 24-hour ATM if others won't accept your card.
Banco de Costa Rica (☎ 2666-2582; cnr Calle Central & Av 1) Has a 24-hour ATM.

COSTA RICA

COSTA RICA

Cyberm@nia (☎ 2666-7240; Av 1 btwn Calles 2 & Central; per hr ₡600; ⏰ 8am-10pm) With the friendliest staff ever, this spot is also good for cheap long-distance calls, charging ₡150 a minute to most parts of the world.

Hospital Dr Enrique Baltodano Briceño (☎ 2666-0011, emergencies 2666-0318) The hospital is behind the stadium, on the northeastern outskirts of town.

Sleeping

La Posada del Tope (☎ 2666-3876; hotelposadadeltope@ gmail.com; Calle Central btwn Avs Central & 2; r per person US$9-18; ✗ 🖥 📶) This budget hotel is housed in an attractive mid-19th-century house that's decorated with old photos, antiques and mosquito nets, and has a bit of an old-plantation feel to it. Rooms have shared bathrooms and are fairly basic. However, the hotel is recom-

mended; the bilingual Tico owner, Denís, is a wealth of information and can help book tours and transportation.

Hotel Liberia (☎ 2666-0161; www.hotelliberia.com; Calle Central btwn Avs Central & 2; dm US$10, r with/without bathroom US$15/13) Rooms in this rambling, century-old building surround an outdoor lounge complete with TV, hammocks, and jet-lagged backpackers chatting about their past and present travel plans. The hotel is recommended for its vibrant atmosphere that's in part created by the Peruvian manager Beto, whose salty language would make a sailor blush.

Hotel La Casona (☎ 2666-2971; casona@racsa.co.cr; cnr Calle Central & Av 6; s/d with fan US$16/24, with air-con US$20/30; ❄) This pink, wooden house has simple rooms with private bathrooms and cable TV. There's

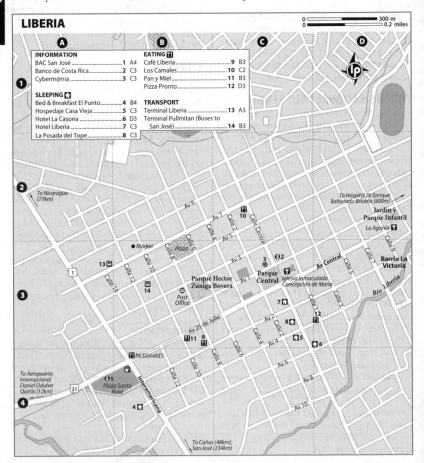

LIBERIA

INFORMATION	
BAC San José	1 A4
Banco de Costa Rica	2 C3
Cyberm@nia	3 C3

SLEEPING 🛏	
Bed & Breakfast El Punto	4 B4
Hospedaje Casa Vieja	5 C3
Hotel La Casona	6 D3
Hotel Liberia	7 C3
La Posada del Tope	8 C3

EATING 🍴	
Café Liberia	9 B3
Los Camales	10 C2
Pan y Miel	11 B3
Pizza Pronto	12 D3

TRANSPORT	
Terminal Liberia	13 A3
Terminal Pullmitan (Buses to San José)	14 B3

To Nicaragua (77km)

To Hospital Dr Enrique Baltodano Briceño (600m)

Jardín y Parque Infantil
La Agonía 🕌

Av 9

Av 7

Av 5

Market
Plaza

Av 3

Barrio La Victoria

Parqué Hector Zuniga Bovera

Parque Central

Iglesia Inmaculada Concepción de María

Río Liberia

Post Office

Av 2

Av 25 de Julio

McDonald's

To Aeropuerto Internacional Daniel Oduber Quirós (12km)

21

Plaza Santa Rosa

Interamericana

Av 6

Av 8

Av 10

To Cañas (48km); San José (234km)

0 .... 300 m
0 .... 0.2 miles

no hot water, and there is also an apartment at the same rates per person as the rooms.

Hospedaje Casa Vieja (☎ 2665-5826; Av 4 btwn Calles Central & 2; s/d with fan US$18/22, with air-con US$36/44; ❆) Just a couple of blocks from Parque Central, this quiet, home-style place has 10 comfortable rooms with private bathroom and TV. Rates do not include breakfast, but there's a small yard out back with a shaded raised patio where you can enjoy the granola that you bring yourself.

Bed & Breakfast El Punto (☎ 2665-2986; www.elpunto hotel.com; Interamericana btwn Avs 25 de Julio & 4; s/d US$60/97; ❆ ▱ ☜) This converted elementary school is now a chic hotel, and would definitely feel more at home in trendy Miami than in humble Guanacaste. The saturated tropical colors of the loft apartments manage also to be understated and minimalist. All rooms have beautifully tiled bathrooms, kitchenettes, hammocks, free wi-fi and colorful modern art.

Eating

Café Liberia (☎ 2665-1660; www.cafeliberia.com; Calle 8 btwn Avs 25 de Julio & 2; items ₡600-3500; ❍ 8:30am-6pm Mon-Fri, 10am-6pm Sat; ❆ ▱ ☜ Ⓥ) Run by a sweet Tica named Radha, this hip spot is a dream, serving organic juices, Costa Rican coffee, fresh sandwiches, salads and crepes, pastries, wines and lots of vegetarian items.

Los Comales (☎ 2666-0105; Calle Central btwn Avs 7 & 5; plates ₡1000-3000; ❍ 6:30-9pm) This convivial, popular local spot is run by a women's collective, and serves native Guanacaste dishes as well as typical cuisine. The specialty is chicken and salsa, but the *casados* are just as tasty.

Pan y Miel (☎ 2666-0718; Av 25 de Julio btwn Calles 10 & 8; mains ₡1100-2800; ❍ 6am-6pm) The best breakfast in town can be had at this branch of the local bakery, which serves its excellent bread as sandwiches and French toast, as well as offering a buffet line with *casado* fixings, pastries and fresh fruit.

Pizza Pronto (☎ 2666-2098; cnr Av 4 & Calle 1; mains ₡2800-5000; ❍ lunch & dinner) Situated in a handsome 19th-century house, this romantic pizzeria is in a class of its own. You can choose from a long list of toppings for your wood-fired pizza, including fresh, local seafood or pineapple; the pastas are just as tasty.

Getting There & Away

AIR

Since 1993, Aeropuerto Internacional Daniel Oduber Quirós (LIR), 12km west of Liberia, has served as the country's second interna-

tional airport, providing easy access to all those beautiful beaches without the hassle of dealing with the lines and bustle of San José. It's a tiny airport, jam-packed with increasing traffic. A new US$35 million airport terminal is currently under construction.

The majority of international flights arrive through the USA; some airlines that fly directly between Liberia and the US include American Airlines, Continental, Delta, United and US Airways. Charter airlines now fly seasonally from Canada, Belgium and the UK.

Domestic airline destinations include the following:

NatureAir (☎ 2220-3054; www.natureair.com) To/from San José, Quepos, Fortuna, Tambor and Tamarindo.

Sansa (☎ 2668-1047; www.flysansa.com) To/from San José and Tamarindo.

BUS

Buses arrive and depart from **Terminal Liberia** (Av 7 btwn Calles 12 & 14) and **Terminal Pulmitan** (Av 5 btwn Calles 10 & 12).

Destination details:

Cañas ₡800; 1½ hours; depart Terminal Liberia 5:30am, 6:30am, 7:30am, noon, 1:30pm, 4:30pm, 5:30pm, 6:45pm and 7:45pm. It's quicker to jump off the San José–bound bus in Cañas.

La Cruz/Peñas Blancas ₡750; 1½/two hours; depart Terminal Pulmitan every hour from 5am to 6pm.

Managua, Nicaragua ₡6000; five hours; depart Terminal Pulmitan 7am, 8am and noon (buy tickets one day in advance). You can also flag down Nicaragua-bound buses on the Interamericana at McDonald's.

Playa del Coco ₡580; one hour; depart Terminal Pulmitan every hour from 5am to 11am, then 12:30pm, 2:30pm and 6:30pm.

Playa Tamarindo ₡1180; 1½ to two hours; depart Terminal Liberia hourly between 3:50am and 6pm. Some buses take a longer route via Playa Flamingo.

Puntarenas ₡1400; three hours; eight buses from 5am to 3:30pm. It's quicker to jump off the San José–bound bus in Puntarenas.

San José ₡2700; four hours; 11 departures from Terminal Pulmitan from 4am to 8pm.

PARQUE NACIONAL RINCÓN DE LA VIEJA

Active Volcán Rincón de la Vieja (1895m) is the steamy main attraction, but the region bubbles with fumaroles, tepid springs, and steaming, flatulent mud pits. (If this doesn't sound like fun, you never read Dr Seuss). All these can be visited on well-maintained but sometimes steep trails, and if you've never visited Yellowstone National Park, this is a good substitute.

The park is home to 300 bird species as well as morpho butterflies, tapirs, monkeys and pumas. Watch out for ticks, especially in grassy areas – wear closed shoes and trousers. About 700m west of Las Pailas ranger station, the Sendero Cangreja leads 5km to **Catarata La Cangreja**, a waterfall plunging from a high cliff into a blue lagoon ideal for swimming. Hiking the volcano **Rincón de la Vieja** is an adventurous 16km round trip. Take a guide or be extra careful to avoid stumbling into geysers (it's happened).

The park is 25km northeast of Liberia, reached by a poor road. There are two entrances with a park ranger station, each with camping areas. Most visitors enter through the **Las Pailas sector** (☎ 2661-8139; www.acguanacaste.ac.cr; admission US$10; ☺ 7am-5pm, no entry after 3pm, closed Mon) on its western flank. (A private road is needed to reach the park and entry to the road costs ₡700 per person.) Going east from the ranger station, a circular trail (about 8km) takes you past boiling mud pools (Las Pailas), sulfurous fumaroles and a miniature volcano. Heading north, trails lead 8km one way to the summit area. There are two waterfalls to the west of the ranger station, the largest dropping from a cliff into a lagoon where you can swim.

The **Santa María ranger station** to the east is the closest to the sulfurous hot springs and also has an observation tower and a nearby waterfall.

Sleeping

Both ranger stations have **campsites** (US$2) with water, pit toilets, showers, tables and grills. No fuel is available, so bring wood, charcoal or a camping stove. Mosquito nets or insect repellent are needed in the wet season.

Just 3km from the park's Santa María sector, **Rinconcito Lodge** (☎ 2200-0074; www.rinconcito lodge.com; campsites per person US$3, standard s/d US$23/35, superior d/tr/q incl breakfast US$55/70/80) is a recommended budget option. Cabins are attractive and rustic and the scenery whispers pastoral and lovely. The lodge is the best place around for inexpensive package deals. Regular shuttles provide transportation to and from Liberia.

Getting There & Away

The Las Pailas sector is accessible via a 20km gravel road beginning at a signed turnoff from the Interamericana 5km north of Liberia. To reach the park you must use a private road

(₡700 per person). Drivers must have 4WD in the rainy season. There's no public transportation, but hotels in Liberia can arrange transportation from Liberia for around US$15 per person each way. Alternately, you can hire a 4WD taxi for about US$25 each way.

The Santa María ranger station is accessible via a rougher road beginning at Barrio La Victoria in Liberia. There is no public bus service. Taxis cost around US$45 each way.

PARQUE NACIONAL SANTA ROSA

The park is a wild space of pristine beaches, tropical dry forests and savannahs of thorn trees and swaying *jaragua* grass. For visitors it's sensory delight. The wildlife on Península Santa Elena is both varied and prolific, especially during the dry season. The rainy months of September and October are best for turtle-watching. Here you'll find *arribadas* (mass-nesting) of up to 8000 olive ridley sea turtles.

The surfing at Playa Naranjo is world renowned, especially near Witch's Rock and Ollie's Point.

Information

The **park entrance** (admission US$10; ☺ 8am-4pm) is on the west side of the Interamericana, 35km north of Liberia. From there, it is another 7km walk to the **Murciélago ranger station** (☎ 2666-5051), where you'll find an information center, campground, museum, research station and nature trail. This is also the administrative center for the Area de Conservación Guanacaste (ACG) and has information about Parque Nacional Rincón de la Vieja and Parque Nacional Guanacaste. A 12km trail leads down to the coast to Playa Naranjo. To drive you need a high-clearance 4WD vehicle for river crossings; inquire with rangers for road conditions.

Sights & Activities

Playa Naranjo, a spectacular beach to the south, has good surfing and is close to the **Witch's Rock** break, famous for its 3m curls (not recommended for beginners). There's a campground with pit toilets, but no potable water. Call ahead regarding road conditions. Although this is a beach break, there are rocks near the river mouth, and be especially careful near the estuary as it's a rich feeding ground for crocodiles during the tide changes. The surfing is equally legendary off Playa Portero Grande at **Ollie's Point**, which boasts the best right-hander in Costa Rica.

The historic Santa Rosa Hacienda unfortunately burnt down in 2001, but has now been completely rebuilt. A small **museum** inside describes the 1856 battle fought here and has displays on Costa Rican life in the 19th century. A few antique artifacts that survived the fire are on display. Another exhibit deals with the ecological significance and wildlife of the park.

Near the museum is a 1km **nature trail**, with signs explaining the varied plant and animal life of Santa Rosa. You will see a fine selection of the park's 240 species of trees and shrubs, and 253 species of bird. Monkeys, snakes, iguanas and other animals are also seen regularly, with bats being the most common: 50 or 60 species have been identified here.

The best turtle beach is **Playa Nancite** in the south, and during September and October you may see as many as 8000 olive ridley turtles on the beach at once. Nancite is a restricted area, but permission can be obtained from the park service to see this spectacle. Flashlights and flash photography are prohibited, as is fishing and hunting.

Sleeping & Eating

Reserve ahead to stay at the **research station** (☎ 2666-5051; dm US$15), with bunk rooms, cold showers and electricity; meals here cost ₡1700 to ₡4000. There is also a shady developed **campground** (per person US$2) close to the park headquarters, along with a picnic area. The campsites have pit toilets and cold-water showers, but no potable water – bring your own.

Getting There & Away

The well-signed main park entrance can be reached by public transportation: take any bus between Liberia and the Nicaragua border of Peñas Blancas and ask the driver to let you off at the park entrance; rangers can help you catch a return bus. You can also arrange private transportation from the hotels in Liberia for about US$20 per person round trip.

To get to the northern Sector Murciélago, go 10km further north along the Interamericana, then turn left to the village of Cuajiniquíl, with a couple of *sodas* and a *pulpería*, 8km away by paved road. Keep your passport handy, as there may be checkpoints. The paved road continues beyond Cuajiniquíl and dead ends at a marine port, 4km away – this isn't the way to Sector Murciélago but goes toward Refugio Nacional de Vida Silvestre Bahía Junquillal. It's about 8km beyond Cuajiniquíl to the Murciélago ranger station by a poor road – 4WD is advised, though the road may be impassable in the wet season. You can camp at the Murciélago ranger station, or continue 10km to 12km on a dirt road beyond the ranger station to the remote bays and beaches of Bahía Santa Elena and Bahía Playa Blanca.

PEÑAS BLANCAS & LA CRUZ

Peñas Blancas is a busy border herding traffic through to Rivas, Nicaragua. As there is no lodging here, spend the night and change money in the hill town of **La Cruz**, 20km south.

Budget travellers and migrant workers grab their Zs at **Cabinas Santa Rita** (☎ 2679-9062; La Cruz; s/d with bathroom US$9/13, with air-con US$15/23; ❄), in dark, clean doubles. Overlooking Bahía Salinas, **Hotel Bella Vista** (☎ 2679-8060; La Cruz; r per person with fan/air-con US$7/10; ❄ ☒) offers well-furnished rooms with hot water, cable TV and terraces. Guests can relax at the pool or enjoy *casados* and beer at the attached restaurant.

Getting There & Away

In La Cruz, a **Transportes Deldú counter** (☒ 7am-12:30pm & 1:30-5pm) sells tickets and stores bags.

GETTING TO RIVAS, NICARAGUA

Peñas Blancas–Rivas is a busy border crossing so get there early. The entry fee into Nicaragua is US$7. There is no charge to enter Costa Rica, but leaving Nicaragua costs US$2, payable in US dollars only (banks on either side will change local colones and córdobas for dollars).

The border posts, generally open 6am to 8pm daily, are 1km apart; you can hire a golf cart (US$2) to make the run. Hordes of totally useless touts will offer to 'guide' you through the simple crossing. If you let them carry your luggage, they will charge you whatever they want. From the border, buses to Rivas (US$1, 45 minutes) depart every 30 minutes.

Alternatively, taxis on the Nicaraguan side of the border can whisk you to Rivas (US$15) or further for a negotiable price.

See p495 for information on crossing the border from Nicaragua.

To catch a TransNica bus to Peñas Blancas, you'll need to flag a bus down on the Interamericana. Buses to the beaches depart from the bus terminal just up the hill from Hotel Bella Vista; a taxi to the beach costs about ₡7000.

Liberia (Transportes Deldú) ₡1000; 1½ hours; eight buses per day from 5:30am to 6:30pm. Alternatively, catch any San José–bound bus.

Peñas Blancas ₡580; 45 minutes; 10 buses per day from 5am to 6:30pm.

San José via Liberia (Transportes Deldú) ₡3400; five hours; depart 4am, 5:45am, 8am, 10am, 11am, 12:30pm, 2pm, 4pm and 6pm.

PENÍNSULA DE NICOYA

The allure of the Península de Nicoya needs no explanation. Archetypal tropical beaches edge this jungle-trimmed rich coast, whose shores have been imprinted on the memories of the millions of marine turtles who return to their birthplaces to nest. So, too, do travelers descend on these beaches, seeking to witness such magical patterns of nature for themselves. Humans, however, make more of an environmental impact than the leatherbacks do.

Development is the name of the game at the moment, and Nicoya is the high-stakes playing field. Easy accessibility to all this beauty may be to blame for its exploitation, but who can be blamed for wanting to play, beckoned by waves that never seem to close out, tropical forests teeming with wild things, the slow, sane pace of *la vida costarricense* and what lies beyond that next turn down a potholed dirt road?

PLAYA DEL COCO

Thirty-seven kilometers west of Liberia and connected by good roads to San José, Playa del Coco is the most easily accessible of the peninsula's beaches. Its name is derived from the cocoa-colored sand that lies between its two rocky headlands, though it can appear, well, dirty. While nearby Tamarindo has become the enclave of moneyed foreigners, Playa del Coco is more the party destination for young Ticos on weekends, and the playground of divers during the week.

Information

The police station and a small post office branch are on the southeast side of the plaza by the beach. Banco Nacional, south of the center on the main road into town, exchanges US dollars and traveler's checks.

Sights & Activities

A prime site to dive or snorkel, El Coco's diverse marine life includes stingrays, turtles, dolphins and whales. Recommended outfitters include **Rich Coast Diving** (☎ 2670-0176, in the USA & Canada 800-434 8464; www.richcoastdiving.com) and Swiss-owned **Summer Salt** (☎ 2670-0308; www.summer-salt.com). The preferred beach for snorkeling and swimming is **Playa Ocotal**, 4km south.

Sleeping

The following lodgings have cold-water showers and fans unless otherwise noted, and primarily cater to Tico weekenders. It's popular for Ticos to camp near the beach, though you need to be careful as things can get dodgy when the clubs let out.

Cabinas Don Carlos (☎ 8887-3192; r per person with/without bathroom US$15/10) The cheapest place in town has simple, clean and tiny rooms, most with shared bathrooms. Pricier rooms have private bathroom, TV and kitchenette. Look for the sign that says 'Rooms for Rent: Backpackers US$8,' advertising the low-season rate.

El Oasis Backpackers Hostel (☎ 2670-0511; dm US$15; ▓ ▣) Playa del Coco's first true hostel is a friendly lodge with segregated men's and women's dorms, communal kitchen and lounge area with TV, DVD, laundry service, bike rentals and a lovely garden with hammocks. It's located behind Papagayo Steak House.

Cabinas Coco Azul (☎ 2670-0431, 8879-3832; cabinas cocoazul_cr@yahoo.com; s/d US$15/20) This two-story, white brick building is the best of several budget *cabinas* located in a gated complex behind the church. Rooms are sparkling clean and comfy.

Pato Loco Inn (☎ 2670-0145; www.costa-rica-beach -hotel-patoloco.com; d US$40-60; ▓ ▣ ▒ ▒) This small inn is one of Coco's most pleasant places to stay, if you don't mind forgetting you're in Costa Rica. It's run by an American whose daughter, Mary, has covered the walls with colorful murals. Each room has a design motif and range of amenities (including hot water) depending on your budget, and the bar in front is a welcoming spot to hang with a beer and shoot the breeze with the other (most likely American) guests.

Eating

El Chinamo Caribeño (mains ₡1000-3500; 7:30am-10pm) East-coast Costa Rican cuisine comes to the Coco at this Caribbean-owned and -operated *soda*, featuring super cheap and tasty Caribbean-style fish, chicken and rice dishes.

La Vida Loca (2670-0181; mains ₡1200-4000; 11am-2am) Opened in 1999 by Oregonian 'Jimbo' Jensen, the beachfront bar specializes in American comfort food, such as burgers, nachos, meat loaf, chili dogs and more.

Suely's Restaurant (2670-1696; sti-costarica@hotmail.com; mains ₡4000-8000; 6pm-10:30pm Mon-Sat) A much-welcomed gourmet addition to Coco's dining scene, the passionate daily changing menu focuses on fresh fish and seafood, like the divine tempura jumbo shrimp in Thai sauce.

For groceries, stock up at **Coco Palms Supermercado** (2670-0367; 24hr), or the massive **Auto Mercado** (2670-2232; 8am-8pm, until 9pm Fri & Sat) at the new Pacifico Plaza shopping center near the entrance of town.

Drinking & Entertainment

The **Lizard Lounge** (3pm-2am) attracts a livelier crowd of dancers. It's a nice place to start out the evening with a game of pool, a cocktail and *bocas* (the Costa Rican equivalent of tapas) on the streetside terrace. **Restaurante CocoMar** (10am-10pm) is a good place for a sunset drink on the beach. Keep the party moving at **La Vida Loca** (2670-0181; 11am-2am), with live music on weekends.

Getting There & Away

All buses arrive at and depart from the main stop on the plaza, across from the police station.

Liberia ₡700; one hour; depart eight times daily from 5:30am to 6pm.

San José (Pulmitan) ₡3200; five hours; depart 4am, 8am and 2pm.

PLAYA TAMARINDO

A little more than 30 years ago Tamarindo was home to around two-dozen Tico families. Then the classic surf film *Endless Summer II* put the town on the map, and it quickly burgeoned into a veritable southern California, sans adequate plumbing and roads to support it. These days, however, the expats who first came to take refuge in a *pura vida* lifestyle now look at their Frankenstein a bit bewildered. The issue? Sustainability. Alas, the sea turtles are long gone, and in their place are high-rise condos, boutique eateries and whole slew of environmental problems.

To be fair, the pace of development is finally slowing down (partly because of the Great Recession), and plenty of people do enjoy themselves in 'Tamagringo.' Call it what you will, this is one place that absolutely caters to tourists' every hedonistic whim, especially if you're looking to party all night long, hook up with strangers and surf some great waves. It may be far from perfect, but with a little airbrushing and creative touch-up, it's close enough to paradise for some.

Tamarindo is also a short distance from Playa Grande, an important nesting site for the *baula* (leatherback turtle) in the Parque Nacional Marino Las Baulas de Guanacaste; see p590.

Information

Tourist information is available from any of the tour operators in town, or your hotel. Keep up on the local happenings by picking up a copy of the *Tamarindo News*, available all over town or online at www.tamarindonews.com.

BAC San José (2653-1617; Plaza Conchal; 8:30am-3:30pm) Has an ATM, and exchanges US dollars and traveler's checks.

Backwash Laundry (8am-8pm Mon-Sat) Get your filthy unmentionables washed, dried and folded for ₡1000 per kilo. Most hotels also offer a laundry service.

Banco de Costa Rica (Plaza Conchal) 24hr ATM

Coastal Emergency Medical Service (2653-0611/1974; 24hr) It does house calls! Can you say that about your hometown doc?

Cyber Bakanos (9am-10pm) On the 2nd floor above a pizza shop, offers high-speed internet connections and international phone calls.

Internet Café del Mar (2653-1740; www.cafedelmarinternet.com; Plaza Conchal; per hr ₡800; 8:30am-9pm)

Jaime Peligro (8820-9004; 9am-6pm Mon-Sat, 10am-3pm Sun) A local spot for new and used foreign-language books and some of the best Central American CDs and DVDs.

Dangers & Annoyances

Tourism has helped spawn a growing drug and prostitution problem. Vendors openly ply their wares (and women) on the main road by the rotunda, and some bars can get rough at closing time. Theft is a problem. Leave your hotel room locked, use room safes and don't leave valuables on the beach. If you're driving, never leave anything in your car.

PENÍNSULA DE NICOYA

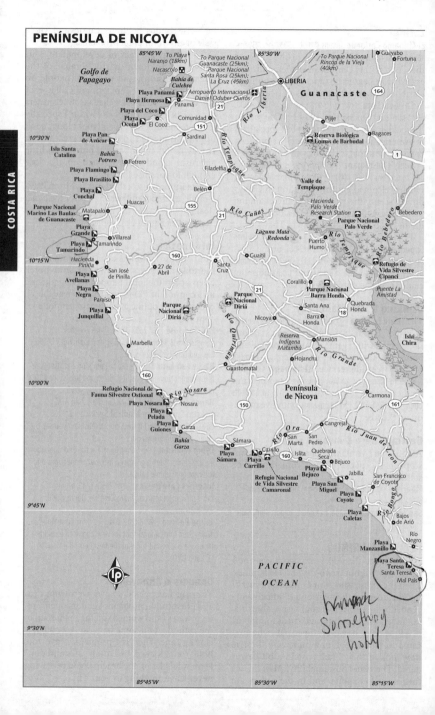

COSTA RICA

Golfo de Papagayo

85°45'W   85°30'W

To Playa Naranjo (18km);
Nacascolo

To Parque Nacional
Guanacaste (25km);
Parque Nacional
Santa Rosa (25km);
La Cruz (45km)

To Parque Nacional
Rincón de la Vieja
(40km)

Guayabo
Fortuna

Bahía de
Culebra

LIBERIA

Guanacaste

164

Playa Panamá
Playa Hermosa
Playa del Coco
Playa Ocotal
El Coco
Playa Pan de Azúcar

Panamá

Aeropuerto Internacional
Daniel Oduber Quirós

21

Comunidad

151

Sardinal

Pijije

Río Liberia

Reserva Biológica
Lomas de Barbudal

Bagaces

1

10°30'N

Isla Santa
Catalina

Bahía
Potrero

Potrero

Playa Flamingo
Playa Brasilito
Playa Conchal

Filadelfia

Río Tempisque

Valle de
Tempisque

Huacas

Belén

155

Río Cañas

Hacienda
Palo Verde
Research Station

Bebedero

Parque Nacional
Marino Las Baulas
de Guanacaste

Matapalo

21

Parque Nacional
Palo Verde

Río Bebedero

Playa
Grande
Playa
Tamarindo

Villareal
Tamarindo

San José
de Pinilla

Laguna Mata
Redonda

Puerto
Humo

Refugio de
Vida Silvestre
Cipancí

10°15'N

Hacienda
Pinilla

27 de
Abril

Santa
Cruz

Guaitil

Coralillo

Río Tempisque

Playa
Avellanas
Playa
Negra

160

Parque
Nacional
Diriá

21

Parque Nacional
Barra Honda

Puente La
Amistad

Playa
Junquillal

Paraíso

Parque
Nacional
Diriá

Nicoya

Santa Ana

Barra
Honda

Quebrada
Honda

18

Isla
Chira

Marbella

Río Quirimán

Guastomatal

Reserva
Indígena
Matambú

Mansión

Hojancha

Río Grande

10°00'N

160

Refugio Nacional de
Fauna Silvestre Ostional

Río Nosara

Nosara

150

Península
de Nicoya

Carmona

161

Playa Nosara
Playa
Pelada
Playa
Guiones

Gatza

Bahía
Garza

Sámara

Playa
Sámara

Playa
Carrillo

Carrillo

Islita

Río Ora

San
Marta

Cangrejal

San
Pedro

Quebrada
Seca

Río Juan de León

Bejuco

Jabilla

San Francisco
de Coyote

Refugio Nacional
de Vida Silvestre
Camaronal

Playa
Bejuco

Playa San
Miguel

Playa
Coyote

Río Bongo

9°45'N

Playa
Caletas

Bajos
de Arío

Río
Negro

Playa
Manzanillo

Playa Santa
Teresa
Santa Teresa
Mal País

PACIFIC

OCEAN

9°30'N

85°45'W   85°30'W   85°15'W

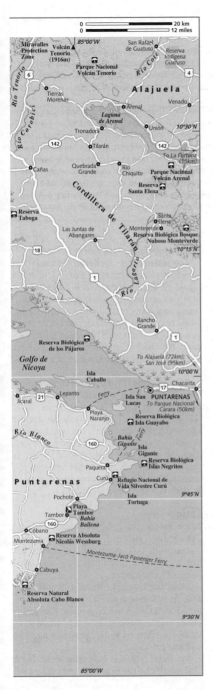

Activities

SURFING

The most popular wave around Tamarindo is a medium-sized right-hander that breaks directly in front of the Diriá Hotel. The waters here are full of beginner surfers learning the ropes. There is also a good left that's fed by the river mouth, a spot also popular with crocodiles during the rising tide (coincidently the best time to surf). Locals know a few other spots in the area, but we're certainly not going to ruin their fun – ask around.

A number of surf schools and surf tour operators line the main stretch of road in Tamarindo. Surf lessons hover at around US$40 for 1½ to two hours and most operators will let you keep the board for a few hours beyond that to practice. All outfits can organize daylong and multiday excursions to popular breaks, rent equipment and give surf lessons.

Banana Surf Club (☎ 2653-0130/2463; www.banana surfclub.com; ⏰ 8am-6pm) This outfit has fair prices on new and used boards.

Blue Trailz (☎ 2653-0114; rasurfshop@yahoo.com; ⏰ 7am-7pm) One of the largest and best shops in town, offers lessons, trips and rents surfboards, body boards and skim boards.

Costa Rica Surf Club (☎ 2653-1270; www.costarica surfclub.com; ⏰ 8am-8pm Mon-Sat, 9am-7pm Sun) Two locations in town offering rentals, lessons, repairs and sales. The main location near the Banana Surf Club even has a falafel stand.

Witch's Rock Surf Camp (☎ 2653-0239; www. witchsrocksurfcamp.com; ⏰ 8am-8pm) Board rentals, surf camps, lessons and regular excursions to Witch's Rock and Ollie's Point are available, though they're pricey. There are beachside accommodations for surfers who sign up for multiday packages.

Tours

Boat tours, snorkeling trips and scooter rentals can be arranged through the various tour agencies in town. Many also rent equipment.

A couple of the most reputable ones:

Hightide Aventuras (☎ 2653-0108; www.tamarindo aventuras.com; scooters per 4hr US$25, dirt bikes per 4hr US$34) Also rents water-sports equipment, including kayaks, snorkeling gear and surfboards.

Papagayo Excursions (☎ 2653-0254; www.papagayo excursions.com) The longest-running outfitter in town organizes a variety of tours, including visits to turtle-nesting sites.

Sleeping

Rates given are for high season but low-season prices are 25% cheaper.

SAVING TAMARINDO

The price of blithely disregarding the pressure on Tamarindo's environment is coming due. At the end of 2007, Playa Tamarindo lost its Bandera Azul Ecológica (Ecological Blue Flag) designation, which marked it as a community with high water quality, safety and environmental responsibility. Frankly, it was about time the flag got pulled, as it was an open secret that the water quality had been deteriorating.

Tamarindo was teetering on the brink of unsustainability. The levels of fecal contamination were so high that visitors were warned against swimming or surfing. Losing the Bandera Azul, and watching the alarming spate of high-density construction rising in the middle of tiny Tamarindo sparked concerned residents and businesses into action. The Asociación Pro Mejoras de Playa Tamarindo and the Save Tamarindo campaign appealed for an urban development plan to curb high-density development and require stricter government regulation. The government's National Water Laboratory, Water Supply and Sewerage (AyA) cited more than 80 businesses and forced them to clean up their act.

So far, their efforts seem to be working. In December 2009, AyA gave Tamarindo's beaches a clean bill of health. At press time, Tamarindo was still awaiting the return of its Bandera Azul.

Coral Reef Hostel (☎ 2653-0291; dm US$6, r per person US$10; 🖳 🛜) The 10 rooms here are clean and fairly basic, without bathrooms. Though it's on a noisy section of the road, the guys running the place are friendly and offer a variety of services, like surfboard rental, internet access and a BBQ area.

La Botella de Leche (☎ 2653-0189; labottelladelcche@racsa.co.cr; dm/s/d US$12/26/36; 🍴 🖳 🛜) With a relaxed vibe and over-the-top cow theme, this spot is highly recommended for its warm and attentive management, fully air-conditioned rooms and dormitories with private bathrooms, and quiet location at the eastern edge of town. Facilities include a shared kitchen, surfboard racks, hammocks and TV lounge.

Beach House Tamarindo (☎ 2653-2848; www.beachhousetamarindo.com; dm incl breakfast US$13; 🖳 🛜) The only hostel located directly on the beach, this funky new resort, opened in late 2009, shows a lot of potential. The small rooms are simple but clean, all with lockers and fans. There's a big communal kitchen, living room, patio, balcony and private beach access.

ourpick **Tamarindo Backpackers** (☎ 2653-4545; www.tamarindobackpackers.com; dm US$15, r per person US$20; 🍴 🖳 🛜 🏊) This intimate, all-star backpacker spot in a gorgeous yellow hacienda is big enough so you'll make new friends, but small enough that it feels more like a home. The common area has a large fully stocked communal kitchen, TV, computers and free coffee all day. Dorm and private rooms are clean and comfy with plenty of storage space (the private room upstairs is the nicest for couples). Outside you'll find lovely tropical gardens, a small pool and hammocks,

all surrounded by woods where you'll hear howler monkeys every morning.

Chocolate Hotel & Hostel (☎ 2653-1311; www.thechocolatehotel.com; dm US$15, s/d US$60/75; 🍴 🖳 🛜 🏊) This sweet little hotel has several well-appointed rooms done up in dark wood and terracotta tile floors, with orthopedic mattresses, fully equipped kitchens and private bathrooms with hot water. Rooms upstairs have higher ceilings and get more light, but all rooms are elegant and comfortable and surround the garden-fringed pool.

Villas Macondo (☎ 2653-0812; www.villasmacondo.com; s/d/tr US$35/40/50, s/d/tr with air-con US$60/65/75, 2-/4-person apt US$105/145, extra person US$10; 🍴 🖳 🛜 🏊) Although it's only 200m from the beach, this establishment is an oasis of serenity in an otherwise frenzied town – it's also one of the best deals around. Beautiful modern villas with private hot showers and hammock-strung patios surround a solar-heated pool and tropical gardens.

Eating

Beach Burger (☎ 2653-2574; burger.beach@gmail.com; ⏰ 24hr) The only 24-hour eatery in Tamarindo, this shack has burgers, subs, hot dogs, *arepas* (corn pancakes) and other hangover-curing treats.

Smilin' Dog Taco Stop (☎ 2653-1370; mains ₡1500-3900; ⏰ 11:30am-10pm Mon-Sat) Those hankering for Mexican grub will appreciate the quality of offerings at this popular eatery, while shoestringers will revel in the generous portions and low prices.

Bar Nogui (☎ 2653-0029; mains ₡1580-14,000; ⏰ 11am-11pm) This beachside restaurant offers upscale *casados* with grilled fish, mixed meats and unbelievable shrimp and lobster.

Eat@Joe's (☎ 2653-1262; mains ₡2200-5000; ☺ 7am-late; 🛜) The best snack in town is at this American-run surf camp, where you can order the famous 'nachos as big as your ass' (or sushi rolls) while sucking down cold ones on the outdoor deck until 2am.

If you're self-catering, the **Super 2001** (☺ 7am-9:30pm Mon-Sat, 8am-8:30pm Sun) and **Super Compro** (☺ 8am-9pm) are well stocked with international groceries.

Drinking & Nightlife

In Tamarindo, all you really have to do is follow the scene wherever it happens to be on that night. On weekends especially, cruising the main drag has the festive feel of a mini Mardi Gras or spring break. And nearly every bar hosts a ladies' night, when women drink free for two hours. With that said, bars and clubs in this town come and go as often as the waves.

Getting There & Away

Buses from San José depart from the Empresas Alfaro office, behind Babylon bar. Other buses depart across the street from Zullymar Hostel. It's possible to get to Montezuma or Mal País/Santa Teresa by bus for about US$10 total, but it will take all day and multiple changes: take the 5:45am bus to Liberia, bus to Puntarenas, ferry to Playa Naranjo, bus to Cobano and bus to Montezuma or Mal Pais.

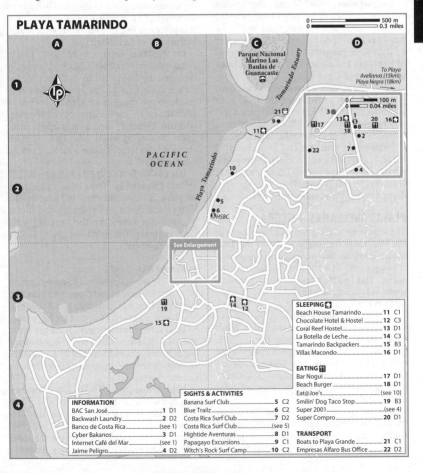

PLAYA TAMARINDO

To Playa Avellanas (15km); Playa Negra (18km)

SLEEPING
Beach House Tamarindo	**11** C1
Chocolate Hotel & Hostel	**12** C3
Coral Reef Hostel	**13** D1
La Botella de Leche	**14** C3
Tamarindo Backpackers	**15** B3
Villas Macondo	**16** D1

EATING
Bar Nogui	**17** D1
Beach Burger	**18** D1
Eat@Joe's	(see 10)
Smilin' Dog Taco Stop	**19** B3
Super 2001	(see 4)
Super Compro	**20** D1

TRANSPORT
Boats to Playa Grande	**21** C1
Empresas Alfaro Bus Office	**22** D2

SIGHTS & ACTIVITIES
Banana Surf Club	**5** C2
Blue Trailz	**6** C2
Costa Rica Surf Club	**7** D2
Costa Rica Surf Club	(see 5)
Hightide Aventuras	**8** D1
Papagayo Excursions	**9** C1
Witch's Rock Surf Camp	**10** C2

INFORMATION
BAC San José	**1** D1
Backwash Laundry	**2** D2
Banco de Costa Rica	(see 1)
Cyber Bakanos	**3** D1
Internet Café del Mar	(see 1)
Jaime Peligro	**4** D2

See Enlargement

COSTA RICA

Liberia ₡1200; 2½ hours; depart 13 times daily from 4:30am to 6:30pm.
San José ₡4860; six hours; depart 3:30am and 5:30am. Alternatively, take a bus to Liberia and change for frequent buses to the capital.

PARQUE NACIONAL MARINO LAS BAULAS DE GUANACASTE

This seaside reserve just north of Tamarindo village includes Playa Grande, which is a major surf destination and one of the most important nesting sites for the *baula* (leatherback turtle). The world's largest turtle, leatherbacks can top 300kg. Nesting season is October to March, when more than 100 turtles can be seen laying their eggs during the course of a night.

The **park office** (☎ 2653-0470; park admission US$10, with guided tour US$25; ☽ 8am-noon & 1-5pm) is by the northern entrance. Visitors must watch the activities from specified areas, accompanied by a guide or ranger, and flash photography or lights are not allowed, as they disturb the laying process.

Be sure to reserve a turtle tour (and transportation) well in advance through your accommodations. If you're looking for a volunteer project, the park office usually accepts volunteers to help monitor nesting.

Boats on the northern end of the beach at Playa Tamarindo can be hired to cross the estuary for daytime visits to the beach at Playa Grande. The ride is roughly ₡690 per person, depending on the number of people.

PLAYAS AVELLANAS & NEGRA

These popular surfing beaches have some of the best, most consistent waves in the area, made famous in *Endless Summer II*. Avellanas is a long stretch of white sand backed by mangroves, and Negra, a few kilometers further south, is a darker, caramel-color beach broken up by rocky outcrops.

At Avellanas, **Little Hawaii** is a powerful and open-faced right at medium tide, while **Beach Break** barrels at low tide (though the surfing is good any time of day). Negra has a world-class right that barrels, especially with a moderate offshore wind. In between is the community of **Playa Lagartillo**, with a few *cabinas* and *sodas* scattered along the road.

The recommended **Avellanas Surf School** (☎ 2652-9042; www.avellanassurfschool.com), near the southern entrance of the beach, has surfboard lessons (US$35) and board rentals (US$15

per day). **Café Playa Negra** (☎ 2652-9351; www.playa negracafe.com; ☽ 7am-9pm) has a laundry service (₡3500 per load) and internet access (₡1000 per hour).

Sleeping & Eating
PLAYA AVELLANAS

Rancho Iguana Verde (☎ 2652-9045; r per person US$5) About 50m from the beach on the road toward Playa Negra, these six *cabinas* are a bit dark but reasonably clean, and share cold-water showers. The owner Josué also runs a great *soda* here, serving up excellent, inexpensive *casados*.

Casa Surf (☎ 2652-9075; www.casa-surf.com; r per person US$12) Look for the 'Casa Surf' across from Cabinas Las Olas, and pull over – if not for espresso and yummy banana bread, then for a clean, quiet place to stay. Run lovingly by Giovanni and Eve, a Tico-Swiss surfer couple, this place has five simple rooms with shared bathrooms and a full kitchen.

Las Avellanas Villas (☎ 2652-9212; www.las avellanasvillas.com; d/tr/q US$65/75/85; ☎) Stunningly designed by Costa Rican architect Victor Cañas, these four *casitas* (cottages) are covetable as permanent residences. With an aesthetic balancing the interior environment with the exterior, they have sunken stone floors crossed by wooden bridges, open-air showers, and large windows looking out on front and back terraces.

Lola's on the Beach (☎ 2652-9097; meals US$5-10; ☽ lunch & dinner Tue-Sun) If the water is looking a bit glassy, Lola's is the place to hang, in low-slung plank chairs on a palm-fringed stretch of Avellanas sand. Try the amazing *poke* (Hawaiian raw-fish salad) or green papaya salad with a beer.

PLAYA NEGRA

Kontiki (☎ 2652-9117; www.kontikiplayanegra.com; dm US$10; ☎) Along the road from Avellanas, this low-key place has a rambling collection of tree-house dorms on stilts that are frequented by both surfers and howlers. In the middle of it all is a rickety pavilion where guests hang out in hammocks and benches. There's a small restaurant serving up traditional Peruvian dishes.

Aloha Amigos (☎ 2652-9023; r with/without bathroom from US$25/15) Friendly, self-described 'haole from Hawaii' Jerry and his son Joey keep basic, screened *cabinas* with shared cold-water bathrooms and more expensive doubles with private hot-water bathrooms. There's a spacious shared kitchen in the center of the grassy grounds, and the atmosphere is about as chilled as it gets.

Café Playa Negra (☎ 2652-9351; www.playanegracafe. com; s/d/tr/q US$25/40/55/70, with air-con US$37/52/67/82, all incl breakfast; 🛏 💻 📶 🍽) This small hotel has a handful of sparkling-clean rooms upstairs from the cafe at street level. Ranging in size to accommodate pairs or small groups, these stylish, minimalist digs have cool, polished concrete floors, elevated beds neatly covered with colorful bedspreads and open-door bathrooms.

Pablo Picasso (☎ 2652-9158; mains ₡1250-4000; 🕑 6am-9pm; 📶) 'Burgers as big as your head' is the house specialty at this American-owned restaurant. Other Yank comfort items include whale-sized fish tacos and Philly cheese steak subs.

Getting There & Away
There is no public transportation here to/from Playa Tamarindo, though accommodations and surf camps can organize trips.

PLAYA SÁMARA
The crescent-shaped strip of pale-gray sand at Sámara is one of the most beloved beaches in Costa Rica – it's safe, tranquil, reasonably developed and easily accessible by public transportation. Not surprisingly, it's popular with vacationing Tico families, backpackers, wealthy tourists, snorkelers and surfers alike (even former President Oscar Arias has a vacation house near here).

Information
Go to www.samarabeach.com to get the skinny on Sámara.

Sámara Beach Travel Center (☎ 2656-0922; www. samara-tours.com; 🕑 9am-9pm) On the main road, this place has an internet cafe (₡1000 per hour), and can book flights and Interbus tickets and arrange tours. Also rents bicycles (US$10 per day), scooters (US$25 per day) and kayaks (US$20).

Activities
SNORKELING & DIVING
The highly recommended **Pura Vida Dive Center** (☎ 2656-0643, 8313-3518; www.puravidadive. com; 2-tank dive incl equipment US$95) arranges diving, snorkeling, fishing and dolphin- and whale-watching tours. Or get your PADI open-water certification (US$400) in three or four days.

SURFING
Experienced surfers will probably be bored with Sámara's inconsistent waves, though beginners can have a blast here.

The experienced and personable Jesse at **Jesse's Sámara Surf School** (☎ 2656-0055; www. samarasurfschool.com) has been teaching wannabe surfers for years, as does his daughter Sunrise. Their friendly, expert instruction (private one-hour lesson US$40) is highly recommended by readers. Jesse also arranges custom surfing safaris to secret spots all over the coast and offers yoga and pilates classes.

Courses
Centro de Idiomas Intercultura (☎ 2656-0127, 2260-8480; www.samaralanguageschool.com) has a campus right on the beach. Language courses begin at US$285 per week, or US$425 with homestay accommodations.

Sleeping
Showers are all cold unless otherwise noted.

Camping Los Coco (☎ 2656-0496; campsites per person US$5) On the eastern edge of the beach, this attractive site has well-maintained facilities but can sometimes be absolutely packed. There are several other campsites along this road if Los Coco has no space.

our pick Hostel Casa Brian (☎ 2656-0315; casabrian@ hotmail.com; dm US$16, s/d US$30/40) The only hostel in town, these spartan but comfy and clean rooms are owned by Brian, a super-friendly Canadian and former commercial fisherman. Amenities include a shared kitchen, all-you-can-eat breakfast (Sunday is banana pancake day) and free use of bikes, snorkeling gear, toys, coolers and more. It's only 60m from the beach, about 300m east of the main road.

Cabinas Kunterbunt (☎ 2656-0235; www.cabinas-villa -kunterbunt.com; s/d/tr with bathroom US$30/40/50, s/d without bathroom US$20/25; 🛏 🍽) Tommy and Antje, the German owners, have built a beachfront house and 'multicolored' (in case you were wondering what Kunterbunt meant) *cabinas* right beside a peaceful section of beach. From the communal outdoor kitchen to the lawn area leading on to the beach, the place has a bare-bones, marooned-on-a-desert-island feel.

Entre Dos Aguas B&B (☎ 2656-0998; www.hoteldos aguas.com; s/d/tr/q incl breakfast US$47/52/60/70; 💻 🍽) This fantastic little inn, on the way into town, is what one reader accurately describes as 'Mercedes Benz accommodations on a Toyota budget.' Seven brightly colored rooms have private stone showers with hot water, vibrant woven linens and homey little touches like incense and candles in every room.

Eating & Drinking

Soda Sheriff Rustic (mains ₡1500-2800; breakfast, lunch & dinner) One of a few classic *sodas* in town, the beachside location sells itself, though the filling breakfasts, killer *casados* and low, low prices aren't too bad either.

Shake Joe's (2656-0252; mains ₡2800-8500; 11am-late) This hip beachside spot is awash with chilled-out electronica and cool, calm travelers lounging on the huge wooden outdoor couches. You can grab a burger here after your surf session, but the ambience is tops when the sun goes down and the drinks start to flow.

Al Manglar (2656-0096; mains ₡3000-5000; 5-10pm) Consistently the best restaurant in town, this thatch-roofed, open-air restaurant serves some of the best Italian food in town at reasonable prices. The pasta dishes, like gnocchi and ravioli, are real winners, and pizza lovers shouldn't miss the Manglar special with ham, bacon, onions, tomatoes and mushrooms, cooked to perfection.

The coolest nightspot in town is the separated beachfront bar at Tabanuco, with a big tiled dance floor and surf videos; Friday is reggae night. La Vela Latina, on the beach, serves sophisticated *bocas* and perfectly blended cocktails and sangria to guests sitting on wooden seats or rocking in comfy leather chairs. To settle in for the evening with some *bocas* and beers with the locals, check out Pablito's Bar way on the west side of town.

Getting There & Away

Nicoya (Traroc) ₡900; two hours; depart 11 times daily from the *pulpería* by the soccer field; there's a more limited schedule on Sundays. From Nicoya, there are frequent buses to Liberia (₡1000, 2½ hours).

San José (Empresas Alfaro) ₡3600; five hours; depart at 4:30am, 8:30am and 1pm Monday to Saturday. On Sundays there is only one bus at 9am. All buses depart from the main intersection just south of Entre Dos Aquas B&B.

PLAYA NARANJO

This small port on the eastern side of the peninsula (not to be confused with the peninsula's west-coast beach of the same name) has neither a beach nor oranges. It serves only as the terminal for the Puntarenas car ferry. There isn't any reason to hang around, and

you probably won't have to as the ferries tend to run reasonably on time.

All transportation is geared to the arrival and departure of the Puntarenas ferry. The **Coonatramar ferry** (2661-1069; www.coonatramar. com; adult/child/car ₡860/515/1850) to Puntarenas departs daily at 8am, 12:30pm, 5:30pm and 9pm and takes 1½ hours. You must have your ticket before boarding.

The right side of the boat has views of Isla San Lucas, the former site of one of Latin America's most notorious prisons. A famous fictionalized memoir, *La Isla de los Hombres Solos* (available in English as *God was Looking the Other Way*) by José León Sánchez tells a gripping tale of life on the inside.

PAQUERA

The tiny village of Paquera is about 25km by road from Playa Naranjo and 4km from the ferry terminal. Paquera is more of a population center than Playa Naranjo, though there's little reason to stay here longer than you have to.

All transportation is geared to the arrival and departure of the Puntarenas ferry. If either is running late, the other will wait. **Ferry Naviera Tambor** (2641-2084; www.navieratambor. com; adult/child/car ₡810/485/1900) departs daily (one hour) at 6am, 9am, 11am, 1pm, 3pm, 5pm, 7pm and 9pm (the last ferry doesn't run in low season). Buses meet passengers at the ferry terminal and take them to Montezuma (₡1400, two hours). The bus can be crowded, so get off the ferry quickly to get a seat.

Many taxi drivers will tell you the bus won't come, but this isn't true. With that said, getting several travelers together to share a taxi is a good option since the ride will take half as long as the bus. The ride to Montezuma is about ₡5000 per person – to Mal País it's about ₡7000.

MONTEZUMA

Up until the late 1990s, a traffic jam in Montezuma was getting off your bike to shoo some cows off the road, a tourist was someone who left after only a month, a night out was rolling a spliff on the beach instead of in your hammock, a good time was… – OK, you get the idea. Montezuma was one of the original 'destinations' in Costa Rica, and its remote location and proximity to Costa Rica's first nature reserve, Cabo Blanco, attracted hippies, artists and dreamers alike. You had to work to get here, and no one had plans to leave quickly.

Montezuma is still a charming village, and foreign travelers continue to be drawn here by the laid-back atmosphere, cheap hotels and sprawling beaches. And while nothing ever stays the same, Montezuma has managed to hang on to its tranquil appeal. Typical touristy offerings, like canopy tours, do a brisk trade here, but you'll see – in the yoga classes, the volunteer opportunities, the arts festivals, the vegan food and the neo-Rastafarians hawking ganja – that the town stays well in touch with its hippie roots. It's no surprise that locals lovingly call this town, 'Montefuma' – *fumar* is the verb 'to smoke' in Spanish.

Information

The only ATM in town is located across from Chico's Bar, and it's regularly empty of cash on busy weekends. Plan ahead.

El Parque (laundry per kilo ₡900; 7am-8pm) The best place in town to get your laundry done. It also rents bikes (US$10 per day) and scooters (US$35 per day).

Librería Topsy (2642-0576; 8am-1pm & 3-5pm Mon-Fri, 8am-noon Sat) Has American newspapers and magazines, and a large lending library with books in several languages. It also serves as the unofficial post service.

Sun Trails (2642-0808; per hr ₡1000; 9am-9pm) Internet access.

Sights & Activities

BEACHES

Picture-perfect white-sand beaches are strung out along the coast, separated by small rocky headlands and offering great beachcombing and tide-pool studying.

The beaches in front of the town are nice enough, but the further northeast you walk, the more isolated and pristine they become. During low tide, the best **snorkeling** is in the tide pools, and at Playa Las Manchas, 1km west of downtown. There's great **surf** if you're willing to walk the 7km up the coastline to Playa Grande, or if you head south about 3km to Playa Cedros.

WATERFALL

A 40-minute river hike leads to a waterfall with a delicious swimming hole. As you head south past Restaurante LaCascada, take the trail to the right just after the bridge. It starts left of the river, crosses and continues on the right. Do not jump the falls – it's the fast-track to a Darwin award. A smaller set of falls is further upriver.

Tours

Tour operators rent everything from snorkeling gear and body boards to bikes. Recommended tour operators:

Cocozuma Traveller (2642-0911; www.cocozumacr. com; 24hr)

Montezuma EcoTours (2642-0467; 8am-9pm)

Zuma Tours (2642-0024; www.zumatours.net; 24hr)

Sleeping

Camping is illegal on the beaches. Also, be careful with your stuff – travelers frequently complain of thefts from hotel rooms in Montezuma.

Campground (campsites per person US$3) There's a small, shaded campground with bathrooms and cold showers a 10-minute walk north of town.

Hotel Lys (2642-1404; www.hotellysmontezuma. net; campsites US$6, r per person US$16) This beachside budget hotel with a laid-back vibe is run by a group of funky Italians who are bursting with creativity. The owners have also launched a project known as Libre Universidad de Montezuma. This evolving concept is based on communication through artistic expression. Unfortunately, maintenance is slipping and the tiny rooms could use a spring cleaning.

Hotel Lucy (2642-0273; dm US$10, s/d US$13/26) This beachside *pensión* was the first budget place to open up in town and is popular with budget travelers. It's an excellent deal in this price range, with hammocks, tables and chairs on the shared terraces. There's free coffee and fruit in the mornings and a communal fridge and a new communal kitchen.

Mochila Inn (2642-0030; d US$19, d/tr cabins from US$25/30) On a quiet hillside north of town, this secluded inn is brimming with wildlife and is silent (except for the sounds of the rainforest) at night. There are a variety of rooms available that cater to different budgets, though everyone can use the outdoor toilets, which offer only a thin curtain between you and nature.

our pick El Pargo Feliz (2642-0065; d US$25-35;) The best budget deal in town, you can't beat the location of these beachfront *cabinas* in the heart of Montezuma. Simple but clean rooms have fans, private bathrooms and free wi-fi. The communal balcony and garden terrace have relaxing hammocks with sea views, and at night the surf will lull you to sleep.

Hotel La Aurora (2642-0051; www.playamontezuma. net/aurora.htm; s US$25-45, d US$30-50, extra person US$5;) Reader-recommended Hotel La Aurora

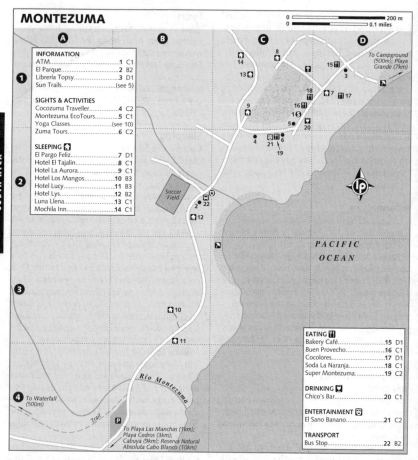

MONTEZUMA

INFORMATION	
ATM..............................1	C1
El Parque.......................2	B2
Librería Topsy................3	D1
Sun Trails....................(see 5)	

SIGHTS & ACTIVITIES	
Cocozuma Traveller...........4	C2
Montezuma EcoTours..........5	C1
Yoga Classes.................(see 10)	
Zuma Tours....................6	C2

SLEEPING	
El Pargo Feliz................7	D1
Hotel El Tajalin.............8	C1
Hotel La Aurora..............9	C1
Hotel Los Mangos............10	B3
Hotel Lucy...................11	B3
Hotel Lys....................12	B2
Luna Llena...................13	C1
Mochila Inn..................14	C1

EATING	
Bakery Café..................15	D1
Buen Provecho................16	C1
Cocolores....................17	D1
Soda La Naranja..............18	C1
Super Montezuma.............19	C2

DRINKING	
Chico's Bar..................20	C1

ENTERTAINMENT	
El Sano Banano..............21	C2

TRANSPORT	
Bus Stop.....................22	B2

Soccer Field

PACIFIC OCEAN

Río Montezuma

To Campground (500m); Playa Grande (7km)

To Waterfall (500m)

Trail

To Playa Las Manchas (1km); Playa Cedros (3km); Cabuya (9km); Reserva Natural Absoluta Cabo Blanco (10km)

has a pretty, vine-covered yellow building with an assortment of 15 comfortable rooms with fan, orthopedic bed and mosquito net; others have varying degrees of cold or hot water and air-con facilities. There's a communal kitchen and plenty of hammocks for chilling out.

Luna Llena (☎ 2642-0390; www.lunallenahotel.com; s US$25, d US$35-50) On the northern edge of town on a hilltop overlooking the bay is this delightful budget option that's terrific value. There are 12 total rooms in a variety of sizes and prices, all with mosquito nettings, fans and safes that are large enough to fit a laptop. All rooms have shared bathrooms except the villa with private bathroom and covered patio.

Hotel El Tajalin (☎ 2642-0061; www.tajalin.com; standard d US$50, superior d US$60-70; ✴ ☎) This delight-

fully quiet hotel is located on a dead-end road behind the church, but still stumbling distance from the beach and bars. The 14 clean and spacious rooms are nothing fancy, but they all have comfy beds, rich wood floors, air-con, wi-fi and private bathrooms. The larger superior rooms also have safe and fridge. Upstairs you'll find hammocks and a communal lounge with satellite TV, comfy couches and free coffee all day.

Hotel Los Mangos (☎ 2642-0076; www.hotellos mangos.com; d with/without bathroom US$75/35, tr bungalows US$95; ☎) This is a charming hotel offering bright, clean orange-and-blue doubles with shared bathroom with hot water in the main building and bungalows with private bathrooms scattered around the mango-dotted gardens.

Eating

Self-caterers should head to the Super Montezuma for fresh food.

Buen Provecho (☎ 2642-0717; mains ₡1500-3500; 6am-1pm & 5-10pm Mon-Sat) By day, it's a quaint cafe with homemade bagels, bread and breakfast sandwiches. At night, it becomes a popular hookah bar with tasty tapas.

Bakery Café (☎ 2642-0458; sanforest@hotmail.com; mains ₡2500-5200; 6am-10pm;) Grab a chair on the outdoor patio of this homey bakery, with an international menu featuring everything from Indian and Thai to Mexican and Italian.

Soda La Naranja (☎ 2642-1001; mains ₡2800-5000; 7:30am-10pm Mon-Sat) Typical food on the main strip, this *soda* has a nice shaded patio and reasonably priced dishes.

Cocolores (☎ 2642-0348; mains ₡4000-11,000; 5-10pm Tue-Sun) One of the best restaurants in Montezuma, beachside Cocolores has a pleasant, thatched-roof patio for candlelit dinners. The menu focuses on French-influenced cuisine, as well as some Tico-fusion standards.

Drinking & Entertainment

There are a few bars in town, including Chico's Bar, which is a sprawling complex of bars, tables, beach chairs and dance space with the music turned up loud – making it party central most nights, especially reggae night Thursdays. You can stop by El Sano Banano to check out which movie it's screening that night.

Getting There & Away

BOAT

A fast passenger ferry connects Montezuma to Jacó in only one hour. At US$37 or so, it's not cheap, but it'll save you a day's worth of travel. Boats depart 9:30am daily and the price includes van transfer from the beach to Jacó bus terminal. Book in advance from any tour operator. Dress appropriately; you will get wet.

BUS

Buses depart Montezuma from a sandy lot on the beach, across from the soccer field. Buy tickets directly from the bus driver. To get to Mal País and Santa Teresa, go to Cobano and change buses.

Cabo Blanco via Cabuya ₡600; 45 minutes; depart 8:15am, 10:15am, 2:15pm and 6:15pm.

Cobano ₡400; 30 minutes; depart every two hours from 8am to 8pm.

Paquera ₡1300; 1½ hours; depart 5:30am, 8am, 10am, noon, 2:15pm and 4pm.

San José ₡5800; six hours; depart 6:15am and 2:30pm.

TAXI

Montezuma Expeditions (www.montezumaexpeditions. com) runs private shuttles to San José (US$40), La Fortuna (US$45), Playa Tamarindo (US$40) and Sámara (US$40).

MAL PAÍS & SANTA TERESA

Situated on little more than a dirt road, these villages are sudden boomtowns for tourists hunting the next great destination. Make no mistake. Unlike most other 'surf towns,' these are all about surfing. While a funky crop of establishments makes staying here more palatable, there is little more to do here than ride the wild rollers. Nightlife means board-waxing, beer in hand. But if it's your scene, you will adore it. A useful website is www.malpais.net.

Five-hundred meters south of Mal País, **Malpaís Surf Camp & Resort** (☎ 2640-0061; www. malpaissurfcamp.com; campsites per person US$13, cabinas US$40, villas US$107, casas US$130;) has dorm beds in an open-air *rancho*.

Heading into Santa Teresa, **Cuesta Arriba** (☎ 2640-0607; www.santateresahostels.com; dm US$13, d US$35, all incl breakfast;) is a gem – each bright, colorful room sleeps six and has a private bathroom with hot water. There are hammocks in the garden, lots of places to lounge, and the scene is happy and relaxed.

Also in town is Asian-inspired guesthouse **Casa Zen** (☎ 2640-0523; www.zencostarica.com; dm US$12, d without bathroom US$24-45, apt from US$55). Emanating plenty of good vibes, there are Buddha statues everywhere that invite a quick belly-rub. Rooms are smart and spare and the shared bathrooms are kept squeaky clean.

Hidden in a jungly garden on the south end of Mal País, **Mary's Restaurant** (☎ 2640-0153; mains ₡3000-7000; 5:30-10pm Thu-Tue) is locally known for the scrumptious wood-fired pizzas, plus fish tacos, burritos, quesadillas and other yummies.

All buses begin and end at Ginger Café, 100m south of Cuesta Arriba; you can flag the bus down anywhere along the road up to Frank's Place, at which point buses turn left and head inland.

A new direct bus from Mal País to San José via the Paquera ferry departs at 6am and 2pm (₡6800, six hours). Local buses to Cobano depart 7am, 11:30am, 2pm and 6:30pm (₡800, 45 minutes).

COSTA RICA

A taxi to/from Cobano costs about ₡12,000. **Montezuma Expeditions** (☎ 2642-0919; www.montezumaexpeditions.com; Centro Comercial Playa El Carmen) offers shuttle van transfers to San José, Tamarindo and Sámara (U$40), plus La Fortuna and Monteverde (US$45).

RESERVA NATURAL ABSOLUTA CABO BLANCO

On the southwestern tip of Península de Nicoya, this is Costa Rica's oldest protected wilderness area, established by pioneering conservationists. Encompassing evergreen forests, pristine white-sand beaches and off-shore islands, the reserve is 11km south of Montezuma by dirt road.

The park was originally established by a Danish-Swedish couple – the late Karen Morgenson and Olof Wessberg – who settled in Montezuma in the 1950s, and were among the first conservationists in Costa Rica. In 1960 the couple was distraught when they discovered that sections of Cabo Blanco had been clear-cut. At the time, the Costa Rican government was primarily focused on the agricultural development of the country, and not on conservation. However, Karen and Olof were instrumental in convincing the government to establish a national-park system, which eventually led to the creation of the Cabo Blanco reserve in 1963. Although the couple continued to fight for increased conservation of ecologically rich areas, Olof was tragically murdered in 1975 during a campaign in the Península de Osa. Karen continued the cause until her death in 1994.

Cabo Blanco is called an 'absolute' nature reserve because prior to the late 1980s, visitors were not permitted. Even though the name has remained, a limited number of trails have been opened to visitors, though the reserve remains closed on Monday and Tuesday to minimize environmental impact.

A **ranger station** (☎ 2642-0093; admission US$10; ☺ 8am-4pm Wed-Sun) offers trail maps. Camping is not permitted. From the ranger station, the **Swedish Trail** and the **Danish Trail** lead 4.5km down to a wilderness beach at the tip of the peninsula. Note that both trails intersect at various points, and it's possible to follow one down and return on the other. Be advised that the trail can get very muddy (especially in the rainy season), and fairly steep in certain parts – plan for about two hours in each direction. From the beach at the end of the trails, it's possible to follow another trail to a second beach, though you should first check with park rangers as this trail is impassable at high tide.

Buses (₡600, 45 minutes) depart from the park entrance for Montezuma at 7am, 9am, 1pm and 4pm. A taxi from Montezuma to the park costs about ₡7000.

CENTRAL PACIFIC COAST

Centered on the boomtown of Jacó, urbanization is primed to transform the coastline. Foreign investment and ex-patriots alike have flooded in, catapulting the central Pacific coast into the ranks of Costa Rica's wealthiest and most cosmopolitan regions. This socioeconomic shift has resulted in drastically improved infrastructure and job creation, though vocal critics in the local media are concerned about future sustainability. While threats of unregulated growth and environmental damage are very real, it's important to see the bigger picture, namely the stunning nature that first put the central Pacific coast on the map.

The central Pacific coast has marked seasons for dry (December to April) and wet (May to November). The dry (high) season rates are given throughout.

PUNTARENAS
pop 150,000

The 'Pearl of the Pacific' is a battered port city at the tip of a sandy peninsula (8km long but only 100m to 600m wide). Lively and hot, the provincial capital served as a major coffee port during the 19th century. During the dry season, Tico vacationers pack the beaches. Otherwise, it's the home of rowdy dockworkers and sailors alongside elderly ladies who scrub their sidewalks and keep the bougainvilleas blooming. Most travelers come here just to catch the ferry to the Nicoya peninsula.

The **Banco de San José** (cnr Av 3 & Calle 3) is connected to the Cirrus network. You can check your email at **Coonatramar** (☎ 2661-9011, 2661-1069; cnr Calle 31 & Av 3; per hr ₡550; ☺ 8am-5pm).

Sleeping & Eating
Hotel Cabezas (☎ 2661-1045; Av 1 btwn Calles 2 & 4; s/d from US$20/25) This no-nonsense budget option is an excellent choice. Pastel-painted rooms have functional overhead fans and screened windows, which means that you'll sleep deeply without needing air-con.

Gran Hotel Imperial (☎ 2661-0579; Paseo de los Turistas btwn Calles Central & 2; s/d from US$25/40) Well situated near the bus stations, this dilapidated and rickety wooden structure still manages to retain a little old-world charm. Cavernous rooms (some with spacious balconies) are cool and clean, and have subtle colonial flourishes, such as wooden furniture and dated paintings to help set the atmosphere.

Self-caterers can head to the **Pali supermarket** (Calle 1 btwn Av 1 & 3) to stock up on just about anything. There's a row of fairly cheap **sodas** (btwn Calles Central & 3) on the beach by the Paseo de los Turistas.

Getting There & Away

BOAT

Car and passenger ferries bound for Paquera and Playa Naranjo depart from the **northwestern dock** (Av 3 btwn Calles 31 & 33). Purchase tickets before boarding.

To Playa Naranjo (for transfer to Nicoya and points west) **Coonatramar** (☎ 2661-1069; adult/car ₡860/1850) ferries depart at 6am, 10am, 2:20pm and 7pm for the two-hour trip.

To Paquera (for transfer to Montezuma and Mal País) **Ferry Peninsular** (☎ 2641-0118; adult/car ₡810/1900) departs at 4:30am, 6:30am, 8:30am, 10:30am, 12:30pm, 2:30pm, 4:30pm, 6:30pm and 8:30pm for the 1½-hour trip.

BUS

Buses for San José depart from the large navy-blue building on the north corner of Calle 2 and Paseo de los Turistas. Book your ticket ahead of time on holidays and weekends.

Buses for other destinations leave from across the street, on the beach side of Paseo de los Turistas.

Jacó ₡800; 1½ hours; depart 5am, 11am, 2:30pm and 4:30pm.

Monteverde/Santa Elena ₡1500; 2½ hours; depart 1:15pm and 2:15pm.

Quepos ₡2100; 3½ hours; depart 5am, 11am, 2:30pm and 4:30pm.

San José ₡1500; 2½ hours; depart every hour from 4am to 9pm.

PARQUE NACIONAL CARARA

Situated at the mouth of the Río Tárcoles, this 52-sq-km park is a green haven during the dry season and an important oasis for wildlife. As the northernmost tropical wet forest on the Pacific coast, its diverse wildlife includes the increasingly rare scarlet macaw, sloths, squirrels and crocodiles. The dry season (December to April) is the best time to go. Visitors can walk the **Sendero Laguna Meándrica**, which penetrates deep into the reserve. From the Río Tárcoles bridge, it is 3km south to the **Carara ranger station** (park admission US$10; ☼ 7am-4pm) where you can get information. Don't travel alone or carry valuables as occasional muggings are reported.

Parque Nacional Carara is 50km southeast of Puntarenas. You can get off at Carara from any bus bound for Jacó or Quepos, though avoid weekends when buses are jam-packed.

JACÓ

Few places in Costa Rica generate as broad a range of opinions and emotions as the beach town of Jacó. In one camp, you have the loyal surfing contingent, resident North American expats and international developers who bill Jacó as the ultimate central Pacific destination, and one of the country's most rapidly developing cities. However, there's another camp of dissatisfied tourists, concerned environmentalists and marginalized Ticos who would urge you to steer clear of Jacó. Like all cases concerning the delicate balance between conservation and development, Jacó is steeped in its fair share of controversy. But it's probably best to ignore the hype and the stereotypes, and make your own decisions about the place. Although the American-style cityscape of shopping malls and gated communities may be off-putting to some, it's impossible to deny the beauty of the beach and the surrounding hillsides, and the consistent surf that first put the beach on the map is still as good as it ever was.

Information

There's no unbiased tourist information office, though several tour offices will give information. Look for the free monthly *Jaco's Guide*, which includes tide charts and up-to-date maps, or go to www.jacoguide.com.

Banco de San José (Av Pastor Díaz, north of Calle Cocal; ☼ 8am-5pm Mon-Fri, 8am-noon Sat) Has a Cirrus ATM open during bank hours on the 2nd floor of the Il Galeone shopping center.

Books & Stuff (Av Pastor Díaz btwn Calles Las Olas & Bohío) Has books in several languages as well as US newspapers.

Mexican Joe's (Av Pastor Díaz btwn Calles Las Olas & Bohío; per hr ₡500; ☼ 9am-9pm Mon-Sat, 10am-8pm Sun) The best place to check email; has multiple computers with high-speed connections and air-con.

Dangers & Annoyances

Drug dealers have set up their candy shop in the street and it's not unusual to be offered a little of this or that before you've hit your hotel. Be aware that Costa Rica is tough on drugs.

Prostitution is also a lucrative business, marketed heavily in bars and dance clubs. If you're suddenly the hottest guy in the room, you might guess why. In addition, some of these girls are definitely not 18.

Partiers should never walk home at night – grab a taxi. Lone walkers have been robbed, particularly on the bridges marking the outskirts of town.

Activities

Jacó is generally safe for swimming, though you should avoid the areas near the estuaries, which are polluted. Although the rainy season is considered best for Pacific coast surfing, Jacó is blessed with consistent year-round breaks. Be advised that the waves can get crowded with beginner surfers who don't always know how to control their boards, so be smart and stay out of their way.

A popular local pastime is following the trail up Mt Miros, which winds through primary and secondary rainforest, and offers spectacular views of Jacó and Playa Hermosa. The trail actually leads as far as the Central Valley, though you only need to hike for a few kilometers to reach the viewpoint. Note that the trailhead is located near the entrance to the canopy tour though it's unmarked, so it's a good idea to ask a local to point it out to you.

Any number of places along the main street rent boards, bikes and mopeds. Virtually every shop, hotel and restaurant in town books tours, as Jacó operates on a lucrative commission-based system.

Sleeping

Camping El Hicaco (☎ 2643-3004; Calle Hicaco; campsites per person US$3) The only proper campground in town: there are picnic tables, bathrooms and a lockup for gear, though its proximity to the bars and clubs means you might not get much shut-eye. Don't leave valuables in your tent as theft is a big problem here.

Las Camas Hostel (☎ no phone; Av Pastor Díaz; dm/d US$14/30; 🖳 🖳) With little more than the word

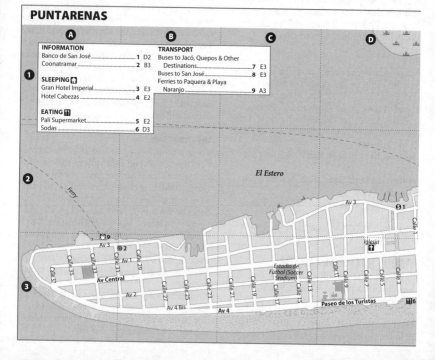

'Hostel' scribbled onto a whitewashed exterior wall, this young backpacker start-up is an understated but highly personable offering. Centrally located next to the KFC, Las Camas puts you steps away from the beach and the nightlife, yet guests seem content spending more of their time on the expansive rooftop deck. Rooms are a bit rough around the edges, but shabbiness is easy to forgive at this price range.

Cabinas Antonio (☎ 2643-3043; cnr Av Pastor Díaz & Blvd; r per person from US$15; ☑) Something of an institution among shoestringers and local Tico families, this clutch of cabins at the northern end of Jacó is one of the best deals in town. Basic rooms are uninteresting at best, but they are clean and cozy, and come with private cold showers and cable TV. And of course, when you're just steps from the surf, it's hard to be too fussy about your surroundings.

Hotel de Haan (☎ 2643-1795; www.hoteldehaan.com; Calle Bohío; dm/r per person from US$19; ☑ ☑) This outpost is one of the top budget bets in town, and is perennially popular with backpackers from around the world. Freshly tiled rooms with steamy hot-water showers are clean and secure, and there's a shared kitchen with fridge, a pool and free internet around the clock. The highlight of the property, however, is the upstairs balcony where you can congregate with fellow backpackers, and swap travel stories over a few cans of Imperial until the wee hours of the morning.

Eating
Soda Flor (Av Pastor Díaz, north of Calle La Central; casados ₡2000-3000) This Jacó institution is a perennial favorite of locals and budget travelers alike. Remarkably, the menu hasn't changed in years despite the fact that nearly every other place in town is now offering everything from sushi to sirloin.

Taco Bar (mains ₡3000-6000) A one-stop shop for Mexican, seafood, salads and smoothies.

Tsunami Sushi (Av Pastor Díaz, north of Calle Cocal; sushi ₡3500-6500) If you've got a hankering for raw fish, don't miss Tsunami, a modern and lively restaurant that serves up an exquisite assortment of sushi, sashimi and Californian-style rolls.

If you're counting your colones, head to **Más X Menos** (Av Pastor Díaz), a Western-style supermarket.

Drinking & Entertainment
There are numerous raging bars and dance clubs that cater to good-times-seeking expats and travelers, but be advised that a good portion of the nightlife in Jacó revolves around prostitution (see Dangers & Annoyances, opposite page).

Le Loft (Av Pastor Díaz) Live DJs spin essential mixes while glam-aspiring customers do their best to look beautiful and act fabulous.

Tabacon (Av Pastor Díaz) Definitely one of the more modest nightspots in town, Tabecon is a casually elegant lounge that occasionally hosts live music.

Jungle (Av Pastor Díaz) The 2nd-story terrace gives you a good vantage point for sizing up your prey, which is a good thing as this place can turn into an unabashed meat market.

Getting There & Away
BOAT
Travelers are increasingly taking advantage of the jet-boat transfer service that connects Jacó to Montezuma. Several boats per day cross the Golfo de Nicoya, and the journey only takes about an hour. At US$37 it's not cheap, but it'll save you about a day's worth of travel. Reservations can be made at most

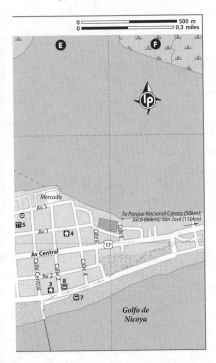

tour operators in town. It's a beach landing, so wear the right shoes.

BUS

Buses for San José stop at the Plaza Jacó mall, north of the center. The bus stop for other destinations is opposite the Más X Menos supermarket. (Stand in front of the supermarket if you're headed north; stand across the street if you're headed south.)

The following are approximate departure times since buses originate in Puntarenas or Quepos – get to the stop early.

Puntarenas ₡800; 1½ hours; depart 6am, 9am, noon and 4:30pm.

Quepos ₡800; 1½ hours; depart 6am, noon, 4:30pm and 6pm.

San José ₡2000; three hours; depart 5am, 7:30am, 11am, 3pm and 5pm.

QUEPOS

pop 12,000

Located just 7km from the entrance to Manuel Antonio, the tiny town of Quepos serves as the gateway to the national park, as well as a convenient port of call for travelers in need of goods and services. Although the Manuel Antonio area was rapidly and irreversibly transformed following the ecotourism boom, Quepos has largely remained an authentic Tico town. Exuding a traditional Latin American charm that is absent from so much of the central Pacific coast, Quepos is a low-key alternative to the tourist-packed trail not far beyond.

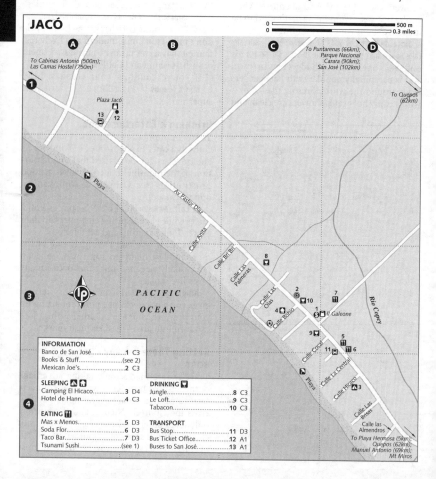

JACÓ

0 — 500 m
0 — 0.3 miles

To Cabinas Antonio (500m);
Las Camas Hostel (750m)

To Puntarenas (66km);
Parque Nacional
Carara (90km);
San José (102km)

To Quepos (62km)

Plaza Jacó

Playa

Av Pastor Díaz

Calle Anita

Calle Bri Bri

Calle Las Palmeras

Calle Las Olas

Calle Bohío

PACIFIC OCEAN

Il Galeone

Río Copey

Calle Cocal

Playa

Calle La Central

Calle Hicaco

Calle Las Brisas

Calle Las Almendros

To Playa Hermosa (5km);
Quepos (62km);
Manuel Antonio (69km);
Mt Miros

INFORMATION	
Banco de San José	**1** C3
Books & Stuff	(see 2)
Mexican Joe's	**2** C3

SLEEPING	
Camping El Hicaco	**3** D4
Hotel de Hann	**4** D3

EATING	
Mas x Menos	**5** D3
Soda Flor	**6** D3
Taco Bar	**7** D3
Tsunami Sushi	(see 1)

DRINKING	
Jungle	**8** C3
Le Loft	**9** C3
Tabacon	**10** C3

TRANSPORT	
Bus Stop	**11** D3
Bus Ticket Office	**12** A1
Buses to San José	**13** A1

Banco de San José and Coopealianza both have 24-hour ATMs on the Cirrus and Plus systems. Check email at **Internet Quepos.com** (per hr ₡750; 8am-8pm Mon-Sat).

Readers recommend **Manuel Antonio Divers** (2777-3483; www.manuelantoniodivers.com) for diving. Adventure outfitter **Iguana Tours** (2777-1262; www.iguanatours.com) offers rafting, sea kayaking, horseback rides, mangrove tours and dolphin-watching excursions.

The beaches are polluted and are not recommended for swimming.

Sleeping

OURPICK Wide-Mouth Frog Backpackers (2777-2798; www.widemouthfrog.org; dm US$11, r with/without bathroom US$40/30;) This backpacker outpost is run by a welcoming couple who are determined to make their little spot one of the best accommodations options in Costa Rica – and so far, they've done everything right. Brightly tiled rooms are centered around an inviting pool with plenty of lounge chairs where backpackers can congregate and swap stories. But what makes this place so memorable is the generally good vibes that radiate throughout the premises, especially in the evenings when everyone unwinds and lets loose over a few drinks.

Hotel Ceciliano (2777-0192; r from US$20) There is no shortage of budget hotels in Quepos catering primarily to Tico travelers, though this family-friendly spot gets good marks for its comfortable rooms and welcoming owners. Although the Ceciliano isn't the newest hotel on the block, everything here is kept spic and span, and the welcoming staff ensures that Costa Rican hospitality reigns true during the entirety of your stay.

Hotel Sirena (2777-0572; www.lasirenahotel.com; s/d/tr US$60/75/85;) An unexpectedly Zen-inducing hotel, the Sirena has whitewashed walls with soft pastel trims that are subtly lit by blue Tiffany lamps. The Mediterranean ambience is soothing, and a world away from the rough-and-ready Quepos street scene. The hotel is also perfectly accented with potted plants and original artwork, and is highlighted by a quaint tiki bar overlooking a tranquil swimming pool.

Eating & Drinking

Escalofrío (gelato ₡1000; Tue-Sun) Here you'll find more than 20 different flavors of gelato, which may just be the perfect way to beat the tropical heat.

Café Milagro (dishes ₡1000-3000; 6am-10pm Mon-Fri) Serving some of the country's best cappuccino and espresso, this is a great place to perk up in the morning – try the *perezoso* (lazy or a sloth), which is a double espresso poured into a large cup of drip-filter coffee, while you indulge in a baked good or a freshly made deli sandwich.

Monchados (dishes ₡4000-7500; 5pm-midnight) Something of a Quepos institution, this long-standing Mex-Carib spot is always bustling with dinner-goers who line up to try traditional Limónese dishes and Mexican standards.

Dos Locos (2777-1526; 7am-11pm Mon-Sat, 11am-10pm Sun) This popular Mexican restaurant also serves as a regular drinking spot for the local expat community, and as a venue for the occasional live band.

Discoteca Arco Iris (10pm-late) This industrial-sized discotheque just north of town brings out the locals with thumping dance beats.

If you want to go local, you can't go wrong with the **mercado central** (central market; hr vary), a vast complex in the center of town that hosts plenty of budget-friendly *sodas* and cafes in addition to fruit-and-vegetable vendors.

Getting There & Away

All buses arrive and depart from the main terminal in the center of town. Buy tickets for San José well in advance at the **Transportes Morales ticket office** (2777-0263; 7-11am & 1-5pm Mon-Sat, 7am-1pm Sun) at the bus terminal. Buses from Quepos depart for the following destinations:

Jacó ₡800; 1½ hours; departs 4:30am, 7:30am, 10:30am and 3pm.

Puntarenas ₡2100; 3½ hours; departs 8am, 10:30am and 3:30pm.

San Isidro de El General, via Dominical ₡2000; three hours; departs 5am and 1:30pm.

San José (Transportes Morales) ₡3500 to ₡3700; four hours; departs 5am, 8am, 10am, noon, 2pm, 4pm and 7:30pm.

Uvita, via Dominical ₡4000; 4½ hours; departs 10am and 7pm.

Getting Around

Buses between Quepos and Manuel Antonio (₡200) depart roughly every 30 minutes from the main terminal between 6am and 7:30pm, and less frequently after 7:30pm. The last bus departs Manuel Antonio at 10:25pm. There are more frequent buses in the dry season.

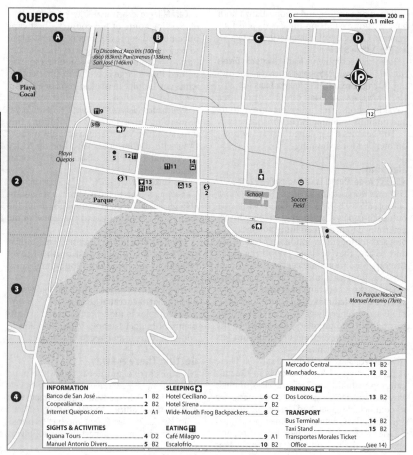

QUEPOS

To Discoteca Arco Iris (100m);
Jacó (63km); Puntarenas (138km);
San José (146km)

Playa Cocal

Playa Quepos

Parque

School

Soccer Field

To Parque Nacional
Manuel Antonio (7km)

INFORMATION			SLEEPING			DRINKING		
Banco de San José	1	B2	Hotel Ceciliano	6	C2	Dos Locos	13	B2
Coopealianza	2	B2	Hotel Sirena	7	B2			
Internet Quepos.com	3	A1	Wide-Mouth Frog Backpackers	8	C2	TRANSPORT		
						Bus Terminal	14	B2
SIGHTS & ACTIVITIES			EATING			Taxi Stand	15	B2
Iguana Tours	4	D2	Café Milagro	9	A1	Transportes Morales Ticket		
Manuel Antonio Divers	5	B2	Escalofrío	10	B2	Office	(see 14)	

Mercado Central	11	B2
Monchados	12	B2

Colectivo taxis between Quepos and Manuel Antonio will usually pick up extra passengers for a few hundred colones; private taxis may cost up to ₡3000 – call **Quepos Taxi** (☎ 2777-0425/734).

MANUEL ANTONIO

From the port of Quepos, the road swings inland for 7km before reaching the beaches of Manuel Antonio Village and the entrance to the national park (see right). This serpentine route passes over a number of hills awash with picturesque views of forested slopes leading down to the palm-fringed coastline. Note that this stretch is hopelessly expensive, though there are fortunately a handful of hostels and eateries where you can get good value for your buck.

Information

La Buena Nota (☎ 2777-1002), at the northern end of Manuel Antonio Village, serves as an informal information center. It sells maps, guidebooks, books in various languages, English-language newspapers, beach supplies and souvenirs.

Sights & Activities

There's a good beach near the entrance to the park, namely **Playa Espadilla**, though you need to be wary of rip currents. There are however some lifeguards working at this beach, though not at the others in the area.

At the far western end of Playa Espadilla, beyond a rocky headland (wear sandals), is **La Playita**, a gay beach frequented primarily by young men and where nude sunbathing is common (use lashings of sunscreen).

Sleeping & Eating

ourpick **Vista Serena Hostel** (☎ 2777-5162; www.vistaserena.com; 13-bed/4-bed dm US$10/15, bungalow without bathroom US$50; 🖳) Catering to the needs of the backpacker, Vista Serena offers spic-and-span white-tiled dorms with shared bathroom, a communal kitchen and a TV lounge, as well as affordable private bungalows for couples that want a bit more privacy. Sonia and her son Conrad, the super-helpful Tico owners, speak fluent English, and are commendable for their efforts in assisting countless travelers. Unsurprisingly, most travelers find themselves getting stuck here for longer than they planned, especially when you can spend your days hiking down from the hostel through a farm to a remote wilderness beach.

Backpackers Paradise Costa Linda (☎ 2777-0304; www.costalinda-backpackers.com; dm or r without bathroom per person from US$10; 🍴 🖳) While it's most definitely not in the same class as competing hostels, this shoestringers' crash pad is decent enough for a night or two, especially considering the rock-bottom price tag and close proximity to the beach. Meals cost between ₡2500 and ₡4500.

El Avión (☎ 2777-3378; dishes ₡3000-6500) This unforgettable airplane bar-restaurant was constructed from the body of a 1954 Fairchild C-123. It was originally purchased by the US government in the '80s for the Nicaraguan Contras, but it never made it out of its hangar in San José because of the ensuing Iran-Contra scandal that embroiled Oliver North and his cohorts in the US government. It's a great spot for a beer, guacamole and a Pacific sunset, and on evenings in the dry season there are regular live-music performances.

Ronny's Place (☎ 2777-5120; mains ₡3000-6500; ⏰ 7:30am-10pm) Head 800m west from the main drag, on the good, well-signed dirt road – it's worth the trip as the view here won't disappoint. Ronny, the bilingual Tico owner, has worked hard to make his rest stop a favorite of locals and travelers alike. Feast on a big burger or some fresh seafood, and then wash down your meal with some of the best sangria in the country, while enjoying views of two pristine bays and 360-degree views of primitive jungle.

Getting There & Away

Buses between Manuel Antonio and Quepos (₡200) operate up and down the main road

and run every 30 minutes between 6am and 7:30pm, and less frequently after 7:30pm. The last bus departs Manuel Antonio at 10:25pm.

Colectivo taxis between Quepos and Manuel Antonio will usually pick up extra passengers for less than ₡500; a private taxi will cost up to ₡3000 – call **Quepos Taxi** (☎ 2777-0425/734).

PARQUE NACIONAL MANUEL ANTONIO

Declared a national park in 1972, Manuel Antonio was spared from being razed and turned into an all-inclusive resort and beachside condos. At 16.25 sq km, it is the country's second-smallest national park. Unfortunately, the volume of visitors that descend on Manuel Antonio can sometimes make it feel like an amusement park. Yet it is absolutely stunning and teeming with wildlife – a coconut-filled paradise.

To avoid the crowds, go early in the morning, midweek or in the rainy season. Taking along snorkeling gear is not a bad idea.

A narrow estuary separates the park entrance from the village. You can wade through it or ferry across for about ₡550. The entrepreneurial ferrymen will tell you it's full of crocs. Look for yourself, the water is clear. The **park entrance** (admission US$10; ⏰ 7am-4pm Tue-Sun) is near the rotunda. Here you can hire naturalist guides (US$20 per person) with telescoping binoculars.

Clearly marked trails wind through rainforest-backed tropical beaches and rocky headlands. With an early start you can see all the sights in a day. Most visitors who spend the day hiking will see monkeys and sometimes sloths, agoutis, armadillos, coatis and lizards. From the park entrance, it's a 30-minute walk to **Playa Espadilla Sur** where there are mangroves and the isthmus widens into a rocky, forested peninsula. A trail leads around the peninsula to **Punta Catedral**, with great views of the Pacific and rocky islets inhabited by brown boobies and pelicans.

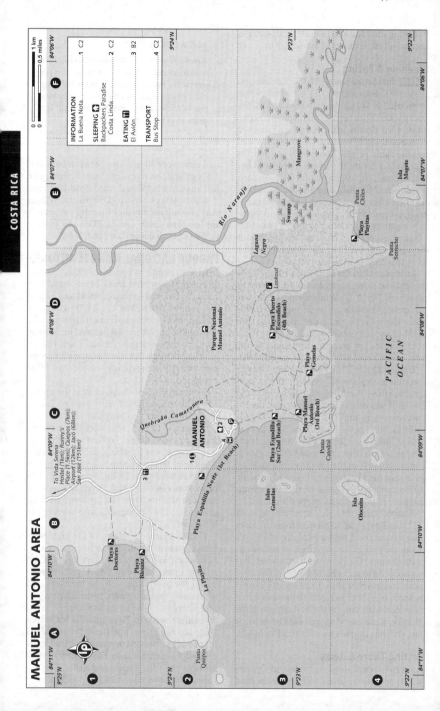

MANUEL ANTONIO AREA

INFORMATION	
La Buena Nota......................1 C2	
SLEEPING 🏠	
Backpackers Paradise	
Costa Linda.......................2 C2	
EATING 🍴	
El Avión...........................3 B2	
TRANSPORT	
Bus Stop..........................4 C2	

0 ___ 1 km
0 ___ 0.5 miles

PACIFIC OCEAN

Río Naranjo

Mangrove

Swamp

Isla Mogote

Punta Chiles

Playa Playitas

Punta Serrucho

Laguna Negra

Lookout

Parque Nacional Manuel Antonio

Playa Puerto Escondido (4th Beach)

Playa Gemelas

Playa Manuel Antonio (3rd Beach)

Punta Catedral

Isla Olocuita

Islas Gemelas

Playa Espadilla Sur (2nd Beach)

Quebrada Camaronera

MANUEL ANTONIO

Playa Espadilla Norte (1st Beach)

La Pistola

Playa Biesainz

Playa Doctores

Punta Quepos

To Vida Serena Hotel (1km); Jenny's Place (1.5km); Quepos (7km); Airport (12km); Jacó (68km); San José (151km)

COSTA RICA

You can continue around the peninsula to **Playa Manuel Antonio**, or you can cut across the isthmus on a direct trail to this beach. A nearby **visitors center** has drinking water, toilets and beach showers. Beyond Playa Manuel Antonio, the trail divides. The steep lower trail descends to the quiet Playa Puerto Escondido. The upper trail climbs to a stunning **lookout** on a bluff. Rangers limit the number of hikers on this trail. Camping is not allowed.

Buses leave from near the national park entrance and will stop along the road to Quepos if you flag them down.

DOMINICAL

With monster waves, mellow vibes and a freewheelin' reputation for reefer madness, Dominical inhales surfers, backpackers and do-nothings. There's little to it, but that's the charm. The village roads are dusty and pot-holed. Its complicated access has spared it the hyper-development fate of other Pacific coast beaches.

Information

There are no banking facilities, but San Clemente Bar & Grill will exchange traveler's checks. It also has a postal service upstairs.
Dominical Internet (per hr ₡1000; 9:30am-7pm Mon-Sat) Check email here, above the San Clemente Bar & Grill.

Dangers & Annoyances

Waves, currents and riptides in Dominical are very strong, and there have been drownings in the past. Watch for red flags (which mark riptides), follow the instructions of posted signs and swim at beaches that are patrolled by lifeguards.

Sights & Activities

Dominical owes its fame to its seriously sick point and beach breaks, though surf conditions here are variable. In general, however, it pays to have a bit of board experience, as you can really get trashed out here if you don't know what you're doing. If you're just getting started, the nearby beach of Dominicalito is tamer.

Of course, one great way to get a bit more experience under your belt is by heading to the reader-recommended **Green Iguana Surf Camp** (8815-3733; www.greeniguanasurfcamp.com). Located on a side road leading to the beach, this camp is run by experienced surfers Jason and Karla Butler, and offers a variety of surf lessons and tours as well as seven- to 10-day surfing camps.

Sleeping

Antorchas Camping (2787-0307; campsites per person US$5, dm US$10) Just a few meters from the beach, this campground is one of the most secure in town, though you should still be extremely diligent about locking up your valuables in the provided lockers. Campers can take advantage of basic amenities, including cold showers and a share kitchen, while more finicky shoe-stringers can bed down in spartan dorms for a few extra dollars a night.

Cabinas San Clemente (2787-0158; r per person US$10-40;) Backpackers gravitate to this classic Dominical spot, which is actually comprised of a variety of different accommodations options. The highlights of the property are the private beach houses that are just steps from the surf, though more budget-conscious travelers can choose from either shiny wooden *cabinas* or simple dorm rooms at the adjacent Dominical Backpackers Hostel.

Tortilla Flats (2787-0033; r US$25-40;) Another popular option, this budget hotel contains 20-odd rooms of varying shapes and sizes, though all feature hot-water showers as well as hammock-strung patios and terraces – a nice option considering the cheap price tag. The downstairs restaurant can get a bit noisy at night, but on the other hand it serves up one of the town's best breakfasts.

Domilocos (787 0244; www.domilocos.net; r US$50;) This Italian-owned property is a solid midrange option, with Mediterranean-inspired grounds and an attractive swimming pool lined with potted plants. Fairly ordinary rooms with solid beds and bamboo-furniture are nothing to write home about, but they're definitely a step up in comfort from the budget hotels.

Eating & Drinking

Complejo Arena y Sol (dishes ₡1500-4500) A local eatery that serves up a hearty *gallo pinto* breakfast spread, this is where you can carbo-load before a serious surf session.

San Clemente Bar & Grill (dishes ₡2000-4500, drinks ₡500-1500) This classic Dominical watering hole complete with broken surfboards on the walls serves up big breakfasts and Tex-Mex dishes.

Maracutú (dishes ₡3000-5500, drinks ₡1000-2000;) The self-proclaimed 'world-music beach bar and Italian kitchen' serves up an eclectic

COSTA RICA

culinary offering that is highlighted by some delicious vegetarian and vegan fare.

Thrusters Bar (sushi ₡4500-8000, drinks ₡500-1500) The local party people congregate here for good times around the pool tables. Next door is a small sushi bar that's definitely worth checking out, as raw fish and tap beer are a blissful combination.

Getting There & Away
BUS
Buses pick-up and drop-off along the main road in Dominical.
Quepos ₡3200; three hours; depart 7:30am, 8am, 10:30am, 1:45pm, 4pm and 5pm.
Uvita ₡800; one hour; depart 4:30am, 10:30am, noon and 6:15pm.

TAXI
Taxis to Uvita cost ₡7500 to ₡10,000, while the ride to San Isidro de El General costs ₡12,500 to ₡15,000, and ₡27,500 to ₡30,000 for Quepos. Cars accommodate up to five people, and can be hailed easily in town from the main road.

UVITA
A loose straggle of farms with back roads swallowed in tall grass, this hamlet 17km south of Dominical shows what coastal Costa Rica was like before the tourist boom. While nightlife may be limited to stargazing, Uvita boasts fantastic stretches of flat sand that comprise Parque Nacional Marino Ballena.

Located 100m inland of the main highway, **Toucan Hotel** (☎ 2743-8140; www.tucanhotel.com; permanent tents US$5, hammocks US$6, dm US$10, tree houses US$12, d US$25-30; ✕ ▣) is the most popular accommodations in Uvita. Run by a delightful family that has made some major changes here in the last few years, the Toucan is home to a variety of options to suit all budgets, from simple tents and hammocks to dormitories, private rooms and the lofty treehouse.

About 2km inland and uphill from Uvita, **Cascada Verde** (☎ 2743-8191; www.cascadaverde.org; dm US$12, shared lofts per person US$12, s/d from US$16/25; Ⓥ) is an organic permaculture farm and holistic retreat that attracts legions of dedicated alternative lifestylers, who typically spend weeks here searching for peace of mind and sound body. Accommodations are extremely basic and somewhat exposed to the elements, though there is ample outdoor communal space for yoga and quiet meditation.

Getting There & Away
Most buses depart from the two sheltered bus stops on the Costanera in the main village.
San Isidro de El General ₡800; 1½ hours; depart 6am and 2pm.
San José, via Dominical ₡2500; seven hours; depart 5am, 6am and 2pm.

Parque Nacional Marino Ballena is accessed from Uvita either by private vehicle or a quick taxi ride – inquire at your accommodations for the latter.

PARQUE NACIONAL MARINO BALLENA
This pristine marine park protects coral and rock reefs in more than 53 sq km of ocean and 110 hectares of land around Isla Ballena, south of Uvita. Although the park gets few human visitors, nesting seabirds, bottle-nosed dolphins and a variety of lizards frequents these beautiful beaches. From May to November (peaking in September and October) both olive ridley and hawksbill turtles bury their eggs in the sand nightly. The star attractions are the pods of humpback whales that pass through from August to October and December to April. The **ranger station** (☎ 2743-8236; admission US$6; ◷ dawn to dusk) is in Playa Bahía, the seaside extension of Uvita.

SOUTHERN COSTA RICA & PENÍNSULA DE OSA

Few used to bother with this other, less convenient Costa Rica, but those who stumbled off the beaten path uncovered isolated charm and a muddy land of contrasts. The mist-shrouded Cordillera de Talamanca is marked with clear, turbulent rivers plunging to the lowlands. Pristine beaches are lapped by rainforest. *National Geographic* penned the Osa peninsula 'the most biologically intense place on earth.' It is certainly one of the few where nature takes *its* course and not ours.

Heading south from San José, the Interamericana reaches its 3491m high point at the Cerro de la Muerte, the so-called mountain of death, fitted with spine-tingling turns (though it was called this before the road was built). San Isidro de El General is the gateway to Parque Nacional Chirripó, with the country's highest peaks. Southeast of San Isidro, farm towns and banana and palm-oil plantations fill the landscape. Most visitors blast through on their way to the magnificent wilderness of Parque Nacional Corcovado.

SAN ISIDRO DE EL GENERAL
pop 45,000

Considering that most settlements in the southern zone are mere mountain villages, it doesn't take much in these parts to be called a 'big city.' Truth be told, San Isidro de El General is little more than a large sprawling town, but since it serves as the region's major transportation hub, you'll likely pass through here at some point in your travels.

Information

Banco Coopealianza Hotel Chirripó (Av 2 btwn Calles Central & 1); Av 4 (Av 4 btwn Calles 2 & 4) Has 24-hour ATMs on the Cirrus network.

BTC Internet (Av 2 btwn Calles Central & 1; per hr ₡500; ☑ 8:30am-8pm Mon-Sat, 10am-4pm Sun) Has speedy connections.

Minae park service office (☎ 2771-3155; aclap@ sinac.go.cr; Calle 2 btwn Avs 2 & 4; ☑ 8am-noon & 1-4pm Mon-Fri) If you're hiking Chirripó (p609), make reservations for the mountaintop hostel here.

Sleeping & Eating

Hotel Chirripó (☎ 2771-0529; Av 2 btwn Calles Central & 1; s/d from US$17/22) Popular with discerning budget travelers, here you'll find bare, whitewashed rooms that are utterly barren but surprisingly dirt- and grime-free. A few flowering plants and a festive mural in the lobby brighten otherwise stark surroundings.

Hotel y Restaurante San Isidro (☎ 770-3444; Interamericana; s/d from US$24/34; ☒ ☐ ☒) This roadside motel does not have much character, but it is clean, comfortable and convenient for those travelers who have no business in San Isidro. Everything you need – from bank to internet to pizza place – is right here in this complex, 2km south of the center.

Hotel Los Crestones (☎ 2770-1200/1500; www.hotel loscrestones.com/es/index.php; Calle Central at Av 14; s/d from US$36/48; ☒) This sharp motor court is decked with blooming flowerboxes and climbing vines outside, which is indeed a welcome sight to the road-weary traveler. Inside, functional rooms feature modern furnishings and fixtures, which are made all the better by the attentive staff that keep this place running efficiently.

Kafe de la Casa (Av 3 btwn Calles 2 & 4; meals ₡3000-6500; ☑ 7am-8pm) Set in an old Tico house, this bohemian cafe features brightly painted

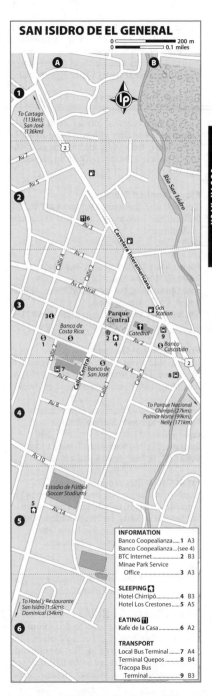

SAN ISIDRO DE EL GENERAL

0 ——————— 200 m
0 ——————— 0.1 miles

To Cartago (113km); San José (136km)

Río San Isidro

Carretera Interamericana

Gas Station

Parque Central

Banco de Costa Rica

Catedral

Banco Cuscatán

Banco de San José

To Parque Nacional Chirripó (27km); Palmar Norte (99km); Neily (171km)

Estadio de Fútbol (Soccer Stadium)

To Hotel y Restaurante San Isidro (1.5km); Dominical (34km)

COSTA RICA

rooms decorated with eclectic artwork, an open kitchen and shady garden seating. With a menu featuring excellent breakfasts, light lunches, gourmet dinners and plenty of coffee drinks, this funky place receives a stream of regulars.

Getting There & Away
BUS
In San Isidro the local bus terminal is on Av 6 and serves nearby villages. Long-distance buses leave from various points near the Interamericana and are frequently packed, so buy tickets early.

From Terminal Tracopa
You will find the **Tracopa bus terminal** (☎ 2771-0468) on the Interamericana, just southwest of Av Central.
Neily ₡3500; six hours; depart 4:45am, 7:30am, 12:30pm and 3pm.
Palmar Norte ₡2000; three hours; depart 4:45am, 7:30am, 12:30pm and 3pm.
Paso Canoas ₡3000; five hours; depart 8:30am, 10:30am, 2:30pm, 4pm, 7:30pm and 9pm.
San José ₡2100; three hours; depart 7:30am, 8am, 9:30am, 10:30am, 11am, 1:30pm, 4pm, 5:45pm and 7:30pm.

From Terminal Quepos
On the side street south of the Tracopa terminal you'll find **Terminal Quepos** (☎ 2771-2550).
Dominical ₡1800; 2½ hours; depart 7am, 8am, 1:30pm and 4pm.
Palmar Norte ₡2000; three hours; depart 6:30am and 3pm.
Palmar Norte/Puerto Jiménez ₡3000; five hours; depart 6:30am and 3pm.
Quepos ₡2000; three hours; depart 7am and 1:30pm.
Uvita ₡800; 1½ hours; depart 8:30am and 4pm.

From Other Bus Stops
The bus for Parque Nacional Chirripó, via San Gerardo de Rivas, originates in San Isidro.
San Gerardo de Rivas, for Parque Nacional Chirripó ₡1800; 2½ hours; departs from Parque Central at 5am and from the local terminal on Av 6 at 2pm.

TAXI
A 4WD taxi to San Gerardo de Rivas will cost between ₡10,000 and ₡16,000.

SAN GERARDO DE RIVAS
If you have plans to climb to the summit of Chirripó, then you're in the right place – the tiny but tranquil town of San Gerardo de Rivas marks the entrance to the national park (see opposite). Here, you can make reserva-tions for accommodations options within the park, pick up a few last-minute supplies and – perhaps most important of all – get a good night's rest, a decent meal and a hot shower before embarking on the trek.

The road to San Gerardo de Rivas winds its way 22km up the valley of the Río Chirripó. The **Chirripó ranger station** (Sinac; ☎ 2200-5348; ⏰ 6:30am-noon & 1-4:30pm) is located about 1km below the soccer field on the road from San Isidro de El General. Stop by here (the earlier the better) to check for space and availability at the mountaintop hostel, and to pay your fees (see opposite) before setting out.

Sleeping & Eating
Cabinas y Restaurante El Descanso (☎ 2742-5061; campsites per person US$5, s/d US$10/30) This quaint and quiet homestead, run by the ever-accommodating Elizondo family, is an excel-lent budget option. Skip the cheaper, cell-like single rooms and spring for a brighter, more spacious unit on the 2nd floor, with private bathroom and balcony.

Cabinas Roca Dura (☎ 2262-7218; campsites per person US$5, r from US$15-35) Conveniently lo-cated in the center of town just opposite the soccer field, this hip hostelry is built right into the side of a giant boulder, lending a *Flintstones* ambience to the quarters. Wall murals brighten the smallest stone rooms, while pricier rooms have tree-trunk furniture and fixtures and views of forested hillsides.

El Urán Hotel y Restaurante (☎ 2742-5003; www.hoteluran.com; dm US$10, s/d US$25/35) Just 50m below the trailhead, this no-nonsense youth hotel is something of an institution for hikers head-ing to/from Chirripó. Budget-friendly rooms of varying shapes and sizes are perfect for a restful snooze, while the onsite restaurant, grocery store and laundry facilities all cater to the shoestring set.

Cabinas y Restaurante El Bosque (☎ 2742-5021; r per person US$10-15) Set in the midst of over-flowing gardens, this family affair offers de-cent rooms with shared bathrooms, as well as newer, more spacious units with private facilities. Some kitsch art by a local painter adorns the restaurant-bar, where you can enjoy fantastic views of the forest and river from the outdoor deck.

Casa Mariposa (☎ 2742-5037; www.hotelcasamariposa.net; dm US$13, s/d US$17/30; 🖳) This warm and welcoming backpacker hostel offers an excellent communal atmosphere that is conducive to picking up a few travel companions for the Chirripó trek. Carved out the side of the mountain, the close but cozy quarters have stone walls and are playfully adorned with colorful tapestries.

Albergue de Montaña El Pelicano (☎ 8382-3000; r/cabins from US$20/40; ⓧ) About 300m below the ranger station, this simple but functional budget lodge has a collection of spartan but spotless rooms that overlook the river valley. The highlight of the property is the gallery of the owner, a late-blooming artist who sculpts whimsical wood pieces.

Getting There & Away

Buses to San Isidro de El General depart from the soccer field at 7am and 4pm (₡1800, 2½ hours). Any of the hotels can call a taxi for you.

PARQUE NACIONAL CHIRRIPÓ

At 3820m Cerro Chirripó is Costa Rica's highest peak and the centerpiece of a gorgeous national park set in the rugged Cordillera de Talamanca. Lush cloud forest, high alpine lakes and bare *paramó* (a highland shrub and tussock grass habitat typical of the southern zone) define the landscape. A well-marked hiking trail leads to the top where trekkers can sleep over in a mountain hostel. It's a two-day climb.

Get ready for mud. The steep 16km ascent goes through constantly changing scenery with abundant vegetation. Wildlife includes the harpy eagle and resplendent quetzal (visible March to May). Start early and allow six to eight hours to reach the hostel. Take plenty of water and all provisions. The grind to the hostel is the hardest part. From there, the terrain flattens and it's a two-hour hike to the summit.

Crestones Base Lodge (Centro Ambientalista El Paramó; dm US$10) houses up to 60 people in dorm-style bunks. A solar panel provides light from 6pm to 8pm and sporadic heat for showers. The lodge rents sleeping bags (US$1.60), blankets (US$0.80), cooking equipment and gas. Spaces fill up quickly, so reserve in advance. All hikers must register at the ranger station in San Gerardo de Rivas (see left) and pay the park entry fee (US$15 for two days, plus US$10 for each additional day). Decent trail maps are for sale. You can also make arrangements here to hire a porter (about US$30 to US$50 for up to15kg) or to store your luggage while you hike.

From San Gerardo de Rivas there is free transportation to the trailhead at 5am from opposite the ranger station, in front of Cabinas El Bosque. Also, several hotels offer early-morning trailhead transportation for their guests.

PALMAR NORTE & PALMAR SUR
pop 6100

This hot and dusty banana-belt town is split into two by the Río Grande de Térraba. For travelers it is the northern gateway to Parque Nacional Corcovado. Facilities such as banks, buses and hotels center in Palmar Norte, while Palmar Sur has a local airstrip.

Lack of allure aside, Palmar is the place to admire **granite spheres** left by pre-Columbian cultures. Some exceed 2m in diameter. They are scattered all over town, including at the airstrip; the most impressive sit in front of the peach-colored school (el colegio) on the Interamericana.

Sleeping & Eating

Hotel Vista al Cerro (☎ 2786-6663; www.vistaalcerro.com; s/d from US$30/35, apt negotiable; ⓧ ⌨ 🛜) On the western edge of town, the Vista al Cerro is a modest family-run hotel with all the required amenities and a decent restaurant to boot. Long-term apartment rentals are available if you find yourself needing a cheap base in the region.

Brunka Lodge (☎ 2786-7489; www.brunkalodge.com; s/f from US$35/45; ⓧ ⌨ 🛜 🅿) The Brunka Lodge is undoubtedly the most inviting option in Palmar Norte. Sun-filled, clean-swept bungalows are clustered around a swimming pool and a popular, pleasant open-air restaurant, and all rooms have hot-water bathrooms, cable TV and high-speed internet connections.

Self-caterers will want to visit **Supermercado Térraba** (Transportes Térraba bus stop) before heading to the Osa, as shopping opportunities are limited in Bahía Drake. The **Panadería Palenquito** (Tracopa bus stop) is a useful breakfast spot if you are catching an early-morning bus.

Getting There & Away

Buses to San José and San Isidro de El General stop on the east side of the Interamericana. Other buses leave from in front of Panadería Palenquito or Supermercado Térraba, a block apart on the town's main street. The bus ticket office is inside the Palenquito.

Neily (Transportes Térraba) ₡800; 1½ hours; depart 5am, 6am, 7am, 9:30am, noon, 1pm, 2:20pm and 4:50pm.

San Isidro de El General (Tracopa) ₡2000; three hours; depart 8:30am, 11:30am, 2:30pm and 4:30pm.

San José (Tracopa) ₡2800; five hours; depart 5:25am, 6:15am, 7:45am, 10am, 1pm, 3pm and 4:45pm.

COSTA RICA

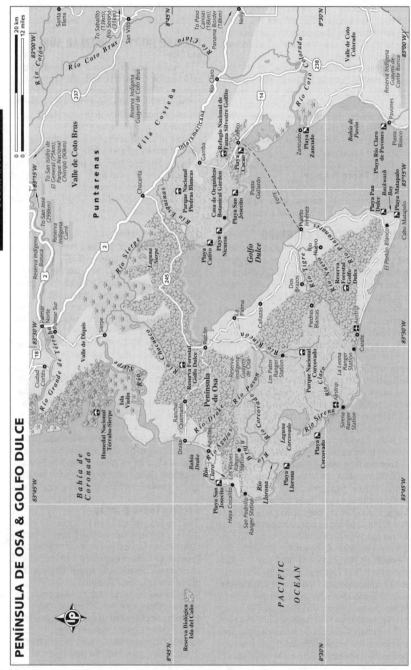

PENÍNSULA DE OSA & GOLFO DULCE

Sierpe (¢650; one hour; depart 4:30am, 7am, 9:30am, 11:30am, 2:30pm and 5:30pm.

SIERPE

This sleepy village on the Río Sierpe is the gateway to Bahía Drake, and if you've made a reservation with any of the jungle lodges further down the coast, you will be picked up here by boat. Beyond its function as a transit point, there is little reason to spend any more time here than it takes for your captain to arrive.

The **Centro Turístico Las Vegas** (☉ 6am-10pm), next to the boat dock, is a catch-all place for tourist information, distributing a wide selection of maps and brochures. It also offers internet access and serves a broad range of food to waiting passengers.

Your lodge will make arrangements for the boat transfer. If for some reason things go awry, there is no shortage of water taxis milling about, though you will have to negotiate to get a fair price.

Buses to Palmar Norte (¢300, 30 minutes) depart from in front of the Pulpería Fenix at 5:30am, 8:30am, 10:30am, 12:30pm, 3:30pm and 6pm. A taxi to Palmar Norte costs about ¢10,000.

BAHÍA DRAKE

This scenic village sits between the great green tangle of Parque Nacional Corcovado and the shimmering bay. It is not only next to Corcovado, but feels like the park's extra appendage, as sightings of macaws, monkeys and other wildlife form part of everyday routine. Traditionally this has been a remote and expensive destination but with the improvement of transportation and hotels, shoestringers can definitely still enjoy it.

Activities

HIKING

All of the lodges offer tours to Parque Nacional Corcovado, usually a full-day trip to San Pedrillo ranger station (from US$75 to US$150 per person), including boat transportation, lunch and guided hikes. Some travelers however come away from these tours disappointed. The trails around San Pedrillo station attract many groups of people, which inhibit animal sightings. Furthermore, most tours arrive at the park well after sunrise, when activity in the rainforest has already quieted down.

SWIMMING & SNORKELING

There are other opportunities for snorkeling on the coast between Agujitas and Corcovado. **Playa San Josecito** attracts scores of colorful species, which hide out among the coral reef and rocks. Another recommended spot is **Playa Cocalito**, a small, pretty beach that is near Agujitas and is pleasant for swimming and sunbathing.

KAYAKING & CANOEING

A fantastic way to explore the region's biodiversity is to paddle through it. The idyllic **Río Agujitas** attracts a huge variety of birdlife and lots of scaly reptiles. The river conveniently empties out into the bay, which is surrounded by hidden coves and sandy beaches ideal for exploring in a sea kayak. Paddling at high tide is recommended because it allows you to explore more territory. Most accommodations options in the area have kayaks and canoes for rent for a small fee.

Tours

Tracie the 'Bug Lady' has created quite a name for herself with a fascinating **nighttime walking tour** (☎ 8382-1619; www.thenighttour.com; admission US$35; ☉ 7:45-10pm) in the jungle. Tracie is a walking encyclopedia on bug facts, and not just the boring scientific detail – one of her fields of research is the military use of insects!

Sleeping & Eating

our pick **Finca Maresia** (☎ 8832-6730; www.fincamaresia.com; dm US$18, s/d US$25/36, standard/superior bungalows US$55/75) After traveling the world for more than 20 years, the owners of this absolute gem of a hotel decided to settle down in their own veritable slice of paradise. Here amid a large *finca* that stretches across a series of hills, Finca Maresia beckons travelers by offering a combination of low prices, high value and good design sense. All seven rooms overlook lush environs, and play a near-continuous audio track of jungle sounds. Beyond the show-stopping natural setting, the decor has been inspired by the owners' extensive travels, evident as you walk from room to room and view the transition from modernist glass walls to Japanese-style sliding rice-paper doors.

Cabinas El Mirador Lodge (☎ 8836-9415; www.miradordrakebay.com; r US$45) High on a hill at the northern end of Agujitas, El Mirador (Lookout Point) lives up to its name, offering spectacular views of the bay from its eight cozy cabins – catch the sunset from the balcony, or climb to the lookout that perches above. The hospitable Vargas family ensures all guests receive a warm welcome, as well as three square meals a day of hearty, home-cooked Costa Rican fare.

Getting There & Away

All of the hotels offer boat transfers between Sierpe and Bahía Drake with prior arrangements. If you have not made advanced arrangements with your lodge for a pick-up, you can always grab a private water taxi in Sierpe for a negotiable price.

From Bahía Drake, it's a four- to six-hour hike along the beachside trail to San Pedrillo ranger station at the north end of Corcovado. If you are heading into the park, make sure you have reservations to camp at the ranger stations – for more information, see opposite page.

PUERTO JIMÉNEZ
pop 8000

Once a gold-mining center, Port Jim (as the gringos call it) retains the air of a flat-out frontier post. While walking through the dusty streets, it's not unusual to spot scarlet macaws roosting on the soccer field, or white-faced capuchins swinging in the treetops adjacent to the main street. Then again, it's not too hard to understand why Puerto Jiménez is brimming with wildlife, given that the town lies on the edge of Parque Nacional Corcovado. As the preferred jumping-off point for travelers heading to the Sirena ranger station (famed for wildlife-watching opportunities), the town is a great place to organize an expedition, stock up on supplies, eat a hot meal and get a good night's rest before hitting the trails.

Information

Check your email at **Cafenet El Sol** (☎ 2735-5719; per hr ₡1000; ☉ 7am-10pm), with wi-fi access. Banco Nacional de Costa Rica has a Plus-system ATM. **Oficina de Área de Conservación Osa** (Osa Conservation Area Headquarters; ☎ 2735-5580; ☉ 8am-noon & 1-4pm Mon-Fri) provides information about Parque Nacional Corcovado and takes camping reservations.

Tours

While independent excursions into Corcovado are possible, the following operators are recommended if you'd like to employ the services of a local guide:

Aventuras Tropicales (☎ 2735-5195; www.aventuras tropicales.com) An operation that offers all sorts of tropical adventures.

Cacique Tours (☎ 8815-8919; www.lasosas.com/index _tours.htm) The affable Oscar Cortés offers a variety of wildlife tours, his specialty being an early-morning bird walk.

Escondido Trex (☎ 2735-5210; www.escondidotrex. com) Specializes in kayak tours, including mangrove paddles, night paddles, sunset tours and kayak-snorkel combos.

Sleeping

Cabinas the Corner (☎ 2735-5328; www.jimenezhotels. com/cabinasthecorner; dm US$5, d US$12) While this ultrabudget crash pad provides little more than a bed in a fan-cooled room for the night, the Corner is kept admirably clean and secure, and resultantly has a growing legion of devoted fans. This is as good a place as any to link up with other potential trekkers, form an expedition party and stock up on invaluable local advice.

Cabinas Oro Verde (☎ 2735-5241; r per person US$15) Simple and central: this is what you are looking for in a budget hotel. Rooms are clean, if a little musty, and the bars on the windows are not pretty, but at least you know the place is safe.

Cabinas Iguana Iguana (☎ 2735-5158; r per person US$20; ☎ ☎) Wood cabins are set on quiet and shady grounds here on the northern edge of town. The onsite bar is among the town's hottest spots on weekend nights so light sleepers should probably stay elsewhere.

Cabinas Carolina (☎ 2735-5696; d with/without air-con US$40/35; ☎) The lack of windows makes this low-priced stalwart feel something like a concrete prison, but at least it's got air-con and a central location. The attached *soda*, Restaurant Carolina, is a Jiménez institution.

Cabinas Bosque Mar (☎ 2735-5681; d with/without air-con US$40/35; ☎ ☎) This hot-pink motel-style building is one of the best bargains in Jiménez, especially considering that all the rooms are large and airy.

Cabinas Eilyn (☎ 2735-5465; d with/without air-con US$40/35; ☎) Hospitality is a family affair at these quiet quarters on the edge of town. High ceilings, tile floors and a comfy porch enhance the decor of the four cozy *cabinas* that are attached to the Tico owners' home.

Eating & Drinking

Café La Onda (light meals ₡1000-3500) A funky and eclectic travelers' cafe that's equally suited for chilling out or chatting up, La Onda sets the stage with homemade pastries accompanied by excellent coffees and fruit smoothies.

Restaurant Carolina (dishes ₡1500-4000) This is *the* hub in Puerto Jiménez. Expats, nature guides, tourists and locals all gather here for food, drinks and plenty of carousing.

Iguana Iguana (🕒 4pm-midnight) At the cabins of the same name, this is a popular watering hole, especially on weekends when the locals join in the action.

Getting There & Away

BOAT

Two passenger ferries travel to Golfito (₡3000, 1½ hours), departing at 6am and 10am daily. Note that these times are subject to change; in this part of the country, schedules often fall prey to the whims of the captain.

A better option than chugging away on the ferries is to hire a private water taxi to shuttle you across the bay. You will have to negotiate, but prices are generally reasonable, especially considering that you'll be free of having to rely on the ferry.

BUS

Most buses arrive at the peach-color terminal on the west side of town. All of these pass La Palma (23km away) for the eastern entry into Corcovado. Buy tickets to San José in advance.

Neily ₡2000; three hours; depart 5:30am and 2pm.

San Isidro de El General ₡3000; five hours; depart 1pm.

San José (Autotransportes Blanco Lobo) ₡5900; eight hours; depart 5am and 11am.

TAXI

Colectivo Transportation (☎ 8837-3120, 8832-8680; Soda Deya) runs a jeep-taxi service to Carate (₡3500) on the southern tip of the national park. Departures are from the Soda Deya at 6am and 1:30pm, returning at 8:30am and 4pm.

Otherwise, you can call and hire a 4WD taxi from **Taxi 348** (☎ 8849-5228; taxicorcovado@racsa. co.cr) or from the **Central Taxi Center** (☎ 2735-5481). Taxis usually charge up to ₡39,500 for the ride to Carate and more than ₡50,000 for the overland trek to Drake.

PARQUE NACIONAL CORCOVADO

The bastion of biological diversity is home to Costa Rica's largest population of scarlet macaws, as well as countless other endangered species, including Baird's tapir, the giant ant-eater and the world's largest bird of prey, the harpy eagle. Corcovado's amazing biodiver-sity has long attracted a devoted stream of visitors who descend from Bahía Drake and Puerto Jiménez to explore the remote location and spy on a wide array of wildlife.

ASK A LOCAL

I always enjoy my time at Restaurant Carolina (see opposite). The food is fresh and the drinks are cold. There is a good mix of people there, so it's energetic and lively. I work in tourism, so I am always happy to see visitors enjoying themselves in Port Jim.

Alejandro, Port Jim

Information

Information and maps are available at the **Oficina de Área de Conservación Osa** (Osa Conservation Area Headquarters; ☎ 2735-5580; park admission US$10; 🕒 8am-4pm) in Puerto Jiménez.

Park headquarters are at **Sirena ranger station** on the coast in the middle of the park. Other ranger stations are located on the park bounda-ries: **San Pedrillo ranger station** in the northwest corner on the coast; the new **Los Planes ranger sta-tion** on the northern boundary (near the village of the same name); **La Leona ranger station** in the southeast corner on the coast (near the village of Carate); and **Los Patos ranger station** in the northeast corner (near the village of La Palma).

Hiking

Paths are primitive and the hiking is hot, humid and insect-ridden, but the challenge of the trek and the interaction with wildlife at Corcovado are thrilling. The main routes across Parque Nacional Corcovado are well marked, making this journey easy enough to complete independently, although guides will provide a much more thorough understanding of the environment. Dry season (December to April) is the best for hiking. Trails lead to all five ranger stations – three border the park boundaries, and Sirena station, the headquar-ters, is in the middle of the park.

The most popular route traverses the park from Los Patos to Sirena, then exits the park at La Leona (or vice versa). This allows hikers to begin and end their journey in or near Puerto Jiménez, which offers easy access to both La Leona and Los Patos. From Carate, it's a 90-minute walk to La Leona ranger station. From there it's a seven-hour hike to Sirena on a coastal trail. From Sirena, hike inland for six hours to Los Patos ranger station and another four hours to La Palma. From there buses travel to Puerto Jiménez.

During the dry season, you can continue along the coast from Sirena to the ranger station at San Pedrillo (eight to 10 hours), then hike out to Drake (five to seven hours). The beach trail between Sirena and San Pedrillo is closed from April to November when the estuaries flood. The coastal trails often involve wading and may have loose sand and no shade – be prepared. Ask the helpful rangers about tide tables and don't get cut off.

Camping (sites per person US$4) is only permitted in stations. Facilities include potable water and latrines. **Dorms** (US$12) and meals are only available at Sirena. Campers must bring all of their own food and pack out their trash.

Reserve 15 to 30 days in advance through the **Oficina de Area de Conservación Osa** (Osa Conservation Area Headquarters; ☎ 2735-5580; 8am-noon & 1-4pm Mon-Fri) in Puerto Jiménez. Don't travel without a compass, flashlight, camping equipment and insect repellent.

Getting There & Away
FROM BAHÍA DRAKE
From Bahía Drake, you can walk the coastal trail that leads to San Pedrillo station (about four hours from Agujitas), or any lodge can drop you here as a part of its regular tours to Corcovado. Alternatively, you can consider heading inland to the Los Planes station, though this is a longer, more heavily forested route.

You can also charter a boat to San Pedrillo (US$80 to US$125) or Sirena (US$125 to US$165). If you have a car, most hotels and lodges along Bahía Drake can watch over it for you for a few dollars a day.

FROM LA PALMA
From the north, the closest point of access is the town of La Palma, from where you can catch a bus or taxi south to Puerto Jiménez or north to San José.

Heading to Los Patos, you might be able to find a taxi to take you partway; however, the road is only passable to 4WD vehicles (and not always), so be prepared to hike the 14km to the ranger station. The road crosses the river about 20 times in the last 6km. It's easy to miss the right turn shortly before the ranger station, so keep your eyes peeled.

FROM CARATE
In the southeast, the closest point of access is Carate, from where La Leona station is a one-hour, 3.5km hike west along the beach.

Carate is accessible from Puerto Jiménez via a poorly maintained, 45km-long dirt road.

This journey is an adventure in itself, and often allows for some good wildlife-spotting along the way. A 4WD jeep taxi travels this route twice daily; prices depend on the size of your party, the season (prices increase in the rainy months) and your bargaining skills.

GOLFITO
pop 16,000

Formerly a bustling banana port, Golfito is now being slowly reclaimed by the jungle behind it. Ticos enthusiastically duty-free shop here but for backpackers it's a mere springboard to either Port Jim or Pavones. If you miss your bus connection, **Cabinas El Tucán** (☎ 2775-0553; r per person with/without air-con US$15/10;) in the town center is welcoming place to stay. Clean spacious rooms of varying sizes and shapes are clustered around the shady, tiled courtyard.

Two passenger ferries (₡3000, 1½ hours) travel to Puerto Jiménez from the Muellecito (Small Dock), departing at 6am and 10am daily. Note that these times are subject to change; schedules often fall prey to the whims of the captain.

Most buses stop at the depot in front of the Muellecito.

Neily ₡800; 1½ hours; depart hourly from 6am to 7pm.
Pavones ₡2500; three hours; depart 10am and 3pm. This service may be affected by road and weather conditions, especially in the rainy season.
San José, via San Isidro de El General (Tracopa) ₡4700; seven hours; depart from the terminal near Muelle Bananero at 5am and 1:30pm.

PAVONES
Narrow gravel lanes and breezy palm-frocked beaches welcome you to Pavones, an end-of-the-road destination a skip away from Panama. The world-class surf, bands of scarlet macaws, and rogue children on evening bike patrol make it feel something like paradise. In light of a budding expat community, the word is out.

Pavones is legendary among surfers for its wicked long left-hander, lasting up to three minutes. When big, the wave schools surfers on the sharp rocks at the end of the bay. The surf can also flatten out for weeks at a time – contact a local business before going for the latest conditions. Conditions are best with a southern swell, usually between April and October.

The town has two areas. Buses arrive first at Pavones, then head further south to Punta Banco where the road ends and jungle stretches to Panama. Transportation between the two areas is scant, but it is a pleasant long walk. Pavones has no bank or gas station, so make sure you have plenty of money and gas prior to arrival.

Sleeping & Eating

Rancho Burica (www.ranchoburica.com; r per person US$8-22) Backpackers can't stop raving about this friendly and youthful outpost, which is literally the end of the road in Punta Banco. All rooms have bathrooms and fans, while the pricier ones have mosquito-netted beds and attractive wood furniture. Hammocks interspersed around the property offer ample opportunity for chilling out. Reservations are not accepted.

    Cabinas Casa Olas (☎ 8826-3693; r per person from US$15; ⓧ) About 100m east of the soccer field, five cabins of varying sizes have wide-plank wood floors, brightly painted walls and an attractive unfinished feel that is appealing if you're one of the laid-back surfer set. All the rooms share access to outdoor kitchen facilities and a covered hammock lounge.

    Cabinas Mira Olas (☎ 8393-7742; www.miraolas.com; r US$30-45) This 4.5-hectare farm is full of wildlife and fruit trees and cabins to suit all tastes. The 'rustic' cabin, incidentally, boasted the first flush toilet in Pavones, though it's quite different from the 'jungle deluxe,' a beautiful, open-air lodging with a huge balcony and elegant cathedral ceiling. To find Mira Olas, turn off at the fishing boats and follow the signs up the steep hill: it's worth the climb!

    Esquina del Mar Cantina (dishes ₡1500-2500) A Pavones institution that has great views of the left break; this is where you should grab a drink after your last ride.

Getting There & Away

Two daily buses go to Golfito (₡2500, three hours): the first leaves at 5:30am and departs from the end of the road at Rancho Burica (but you can pick it up at the bus stop opposite the Riviera); the second leaves at 12:30pm from the Esquina del Mar Cantina. Buses from Golfito depart 10am (to Pavones) and 3pm (to Punta Banco via Pavones) from the stop at the Muellecito.

NEILY

Although it is southern Costa Rica's second-largest 'city,' Neily has retained the friendly atmosphere of a rural town, much like

neighboring Palmar. At just 50m above sea level, steamy Neily also serves as a regional transportation hub and agricultural center, though it is decidedly lacking in tourist appeal. A **Banco Coopealianza** (⏱ 8am-3pm Mon-Fri), just southwest of the *mercado* (market), has a 24-hour ATM on the Cirrus network.

    Few people have reason to stick around town, though you can always grab a clean room and a hot meal at **Centro Turístico Neily** (☎ 2783-3031; r from US$30; ⓧ ⓡ), a low-key resort in a quiet residential part of town. The faux-colonial decorations create a relaxed ambience, as does the tranquil open-air restaurant overlooking the grounds.

    Buses leave from the main terminal on the east side of town.

Golfito ₡800; 1½ hours; depart hourly from 6am to 7:30pm.

Palmar ₡800; 1½ hours; depart 4:45am, 9:15am, noon, 12:30pm, 2:30pm, 4:30pm and 5:45pm.

Paso Canoas ₡250; 30 minutes; depart every half hour from 6am to 6pm.

Puerto Jiménez ₡2000; three hours; depart 7am and 2pm.

San Isidro de El General (Tracopa) ₡3500; six hours; depart 7am, 10am, 1pm and 3pm.

San José (Tracopa) ₡5000; eight hours; depart 4:30am, 5am, 8:30am, 11:30am and 3:30pm.

PASO CANOAS

The main port of entry between Costa Rica and Panama is like most border outposts the world over – hectic, slightly seedy and completely devoid of charm. As you might imagine, most travelers check in and check out of Paso Canoas with little more than a passing glance at their passport stamp.

    Báncredito (⏱ 8am-4:30pm), near the **Costa Rican Migración & Customs** (⏱ 6am-11pm), changes traveler's checks and there is an ATM on the Visa Plus system near the border. Rates for converting excess colones into dollars are not good, but they will do in a pinch. Colones are accepted at the border, but are difficult to get rid of further into Panama.

    Tracopa buses leave for San José (₡5000, six hours) at 4am, 7:30am, 9am and 3pm. The **Tracopa bus terminal** (☎ 2732-2201), or window really, is north of the border post, on the east side of the main road. Sunday-afternoon buses are full of weekend shoppers, so buy tickets as early as possible. Buses for Neily (₡800, 30 minutes) leave from in front of the post office at least once an hour from 6am to 6pm.

GETTING TO DAVID, PANAMA

On the Carretera Interamericana, the **Paso Canoas–David** (☎ 24hr) border crossing is crowded and confusing, especially during vacation periods when shoppers pass through.

Costa Rican immigration is on the eastern side of the highway, north of the Tracopa bus terminal. After securing an exit visa, walk 400m east to the Panamanian immigration post, in a yellow building, to purchase a tourist card (US$5 for US citizens) to enter Panama. You might be asked for an onward ticket and evidence of financial solvency (present a credit card). From here dozens of minivans go to David (US$2, 1½ hours).

See p662 for information on crossing the border from Panama.

COSTA RICA DIRECTORY

ACCOMMODATIONS

The hotel situation in Costa Rica ranges from luxurious and sparkling all-inclusive resorts to dingy, overpriced quarters. The sheer number of hotels means that it's rare to arrive in a town and find nowhere to sleep.

For the most part, this guide's budget category covers lodging in which a typical double costs up to US$40. Cheaper places generally have shared bathrooms, but it's still possible to get a double with a private bathroom for US$25 in some towns off the tourist trail.

In tourist towns, you'll find plenty of *cabinas,* a loose term for cheap to midrange lodging. High-season (December to April) prices are provided throughout this book, though many lodges lower their prices during the low season (May to November). Some beach towns will also charge high-season prices in June and July, when travelers from the northern hemisphere arrive in droves. During Semana Santa (Easter Week) and the week between Christmas and New Year, hotels raise their rates beyond what's listed in this book. During this time, advance reservations are necessary. During school-vacation weekends in January and February it's also advisable to book in advance.

There are numerous independently run hotels around the country, which are considerably cheaper than the Hostelling International (HI) ones. San José has several places, as does Manuel Antonio, Puerto Viejo de Talamanca,

Monteverde and Tamarindo. The least expensive private rooms in budget hotels are often as cheap as hostels.

Most destinations have at least one campground, which usually includes toilets and cold showers, and are crowded, noisy affairs. Campsites are available at many national parks as well; take insect repellent, food and supplies. Camping prices in this book are listed per person, per night.

If you're traveling in from another part of Central America, note that prices in Costa Rica are much higher than in the rest of the region. Sleeping options are listed in order of budget, unless otherwise specified.

ACTIVITIES
Canopy Tours

There's nothing quite like sailing through the rainforest at high speeds in Tarzan-fashion. Operators sell it as a great way to see nature, though all you see are blurry broccoli-sized trees as you whiz by at full throttle. This is a damn-fine adrenaline rush and it seems that the tours are very prolific in tourist towns, though most purists head to Monteverde and Santa Elena (p569), the site of the original zip lines that kicked off the whole craze.

Diving & Snorkeling

Costa Rica's water is body temperature and packed with marine life. As a general rule, water visibility is not good during the rainy months, when rivers swell and their outflow clouds the ocean. At this time, boats to locations offshore offer better viewing opportunities. The country's two top spots are Puerto Viejo de Talamanca (p564) and Playa del Coco (p584).

Hiking

For long-distance hiking and trekking, it's best to travel in the dry season. The best trips include the multiday hike across Parque Nacional Corcovado (p613) and mountain trekking on Chirripó (p609). Assaults and robberies have been reported in some national parks, namely Carara, Braulio Carrillo, Gandoca-Manzanillo and on the road between La Palma and Los Patos near Corcovado. For maximum safety, go in a group or with a guide.

Horseback Riding

Wherever you go in Costa Rica, you will inevitably find someone giving horseback-riding trips. Rates vary from US$25 for an hour or two to over US$100 for a full day. Overnight trips with packhorses can also be arranged, and are a popular way of accessing remote destinations in the national parks. Travelers should continue to recommend good outfitters (and give the heads up on bad ones) by writing to Lonely Planet. Monteverde and Santa Elena (p569) offer a diverse assortment of wilderness trails.

Surfing

Most international airlines accept surfboards (properly packed in a padded board bag) as checked luggage. Domestic airlines accept surfboards (for an extra charge), but the board must be under 2.1m (6.9ft) in length. If the plane is full, there's a chance your board won't make it on because of weight restrictions. It's also possible to buy a board (new or used) in Costa Rica, and then sell it before you leave. Outfitters in many of the popular surf towns – Playa Tamarindo (p585), Jacó (p597), Dominical (p605) and Puerto Viejo de Talamanca (p564) – rent short and long boards, fix dings, give classes and organize excursions.

White-Water Rafting & Kayaking

The months between June and October are considered the wildest months for rafting, but some rivers offer good runs all year. Bring sunblock, a spare change of clothes, a waterproof bag for your camera and river sandals. The epicenter of rafting in Costa Rica is the town of Turrialba (p552).

River kayaking can be organized in conjunction with rafting trips if you are experienced; seasoned kayakers congregate in the town of Puerto Viejo de Sarapiquí (p577) in north central Costa Rica.

Wildlife-Watching

Costa Rica is the easiest country in Central America to spot wildlife; it will often find you. Bird-watching is world-class and most visitors regularly see monkeys, sloths, leaf-cutter ants, morpho butterflies, poison arrow frogs, turtles, crocodiles and iguanas, to name but a few. The national parks are good places for observation, as are the many private reserves. Early morning and late afternoon are the best times to watch for wildlife, and a pair of binoculars will improve your observations tremendously.

Have realistic expectations, as this isn't a zoo; thick rainforest vegetation can make it hard to see wildlife. Walk slowly and quietly, listen as well as look. Hiring a guide vastly improves your chances.

BOOKS

English-language guidebooks can be found in San José bookstores (p535) and in tourist centers. To try out the local lingo pick up Lonely Planet's *Costa Rica Spanish* phrasebook.

For a broad and well-written review of Costa Rican history, culture and economy, read *The Ticos: Culture and Social Change in Costa Rica* by Mavis, Richard and Karen Biesanz.

Costa Rica: A Traveler's Literary Companion, edited by Barbara Ras, compiles 26 short stories by modern Costa Rican writers. Wildlife enthusiasts check out the following guides:

A Guide to the Birds of Costa Rica (F Gary Stiles & Alexander F Skutch) The source for everything avian.

Butterflies of Costa Rica and Their Natural History (Philip J DeVries) Everything you ever wanted to know about butterflies.

Costa Rica: The Ecotravelers' Wildlife Guide (Les Beletsky) A thorough introduction to Central American wildlife that is never boring.

Neotropical Rainforest Mammals: A Field Guide (Louise H Emmons) A color-illustrated field guide to the more than 200 mammal species.

Tropical Nature (Adrian Forsyth) A well-written introduction to the rainforest that will undoubtedly get you excited about your journey.

BUSINESS HOURS

Government offices open 8am to 4pm Monday to Friday, closing between 11:30am and 1pm for lunch. Stores operate from 8am to 7pm Monday to Saturday, with two-hour lunch breaks common in small towns. Banks open Monday through Friday from 8am to 4pm, and some have Saturday hours. Restaurants are usually open from 7am and serve dinner until 9pm, though upscale places may open only for dinner.

CLIMATE

For a small country, Costa Rica's got an awful lot of weather going on. The highlands are cold, the cloud forest is misty and cool, San José and the Central Valley get an 'eternal spring' and both the Pacific and Caribbean coasts are pretty much sweltering year-round. (Get ready for some bad-hair days when you're here.)

For climate charts, see p714.

CUSTOMS

All travelers over the age of 18 are allowed to enter the country with 5L of wine or spirits and 500g of processed tobacco (400 cigarettes or 50 cigars). Camera gear and binoculars, and camping, snorkeling and other sporting equipment, are readily allowed into the country.

DANGERS & ANNOYANCES

The biggest danger that most travelers face is theft, primarily from pickpockets who ply their trade at bus stations, on buses and in crowded areas. Theft is ridiculously commonplace. Don't wear nice jewelry or hang your camera around your neck. Keep your passport and money in the hotel safe and carry a photocopy. Never leave belongings in the overhead compartment on a bus or unattended on a beach.

Of greater concern is the growing rate of armed robberies in San José as well as tourist-heavy areas. In downtown San José, avoid walking around at night – take taxis instead. In the countryside, don't walk around isolated areas at night by yourself. It is always safest to travel in groups. If you are robbed, police reports (for insurance claims) should be filed with the **Organismo de Investigación Judicial** (OIJ; Map p536; ☎ 2222-1365; Av 6 btwn Calles 17 & 19, San José) in the Corte Suprema de Justicia (Supreme Court).

Both coasts have dangerous riptides – strong currents that pull the swimmer out to sea. Additionally, few beaches have lifeguards but some areas flag swimming areas (green) or danger spots (red). River-rafting expeditions may be risky during periods of heavy rain when flash floods can capsize rafts. Use reputable tour operators.

If you are caught in an earthquake, the best shelter in a building is in a doorframe or under a sturdy table. In the open, don't stand near anything that could collapse on you.

The general **emergency number** (☎ 911) is available in the central provinces and is expanding coverage. The **police** (☎ 117) and **fire brigade** (☎ 118) are reachable throughout the country. The main tourist office in San José (p538) publishes a helpful brochure with an up-to-date list of emergency numbers around the country.

EMBASSIES & CONSULATES

Mornings are the best time to go to embassies and consulates, as they are at their quietest. Australia and New Zealand do not have consular representation in Costa Rica; the closest embassies are in Mexico City. For visa information see p622. All of the following are located in San José.

Canada (☎ 2242-4400; Oficentro Ejecutivo La Sabana, Edificio 3, 3rd fl, Sabana Sur) Behind La Contraloría.

El Salvador (☎ 2257-7855) Head 500m north and 25m west of the Toyota dealership on Paseo Colón.

France (☎ 2234-4167) On the road to Curridabat, 200m south and 50m west of the Indoor Club.

Germany (☎ 2232-5533) On the 8th floor of Torre La Sabana, on Sabana Norte, 300m west of the ICE building.

Guatemala (☎ 2283-2555; Curridabat) Casa Izquierda, 500m south and 30m west of Pops.

Honduras (☎ 2291-5147; Urbanización Trejos Montealegre) About 100m west of Banca Promérica, Escazú.

Israel (☎ 2221-6444; Edificio Centro Colón, 11th fl, Paseo Colón)

Italy (☎ 2234-2326; Av Central & Calle 41, Los Yoses)

Mexico (☎ 2257-0633) About 250m south of the Subaru dealership, Los Yoses.

Netherlands (☎ 2296-1490; Oficentro Ejecutivo La Sabana, Edificio 3, 3rd fl, Sabana Sur) Behind La Contraloría.

Nicaragua (☎ 2283-8222; Av Central 2540 btwn Calles 25 & 27, Barrio La California)

Panama (☎ 2281-2442) Head 200m south and 25m east from the *antiguo higuerón* (old fig tree), San Pedro.

Spain (☎ 2222-1933; Calle 32 btwn Paseo Colón & Av 2)

WHAT'S THAT ADDRESS?

Though some larger cities have streets that have been dutifully named, signage is rare and finding a Tico who knows what street they are standing on is even rarer. Everybody uses landmarks when providing directions; an address may be given as 200m south and 150m east of a church. (A city block is *cien metros* – literally 100m – so '250 *metros al sur*' means 2½ blocks south, regardless of the distance.) Churches, parks, office buildings, fast-food joints and car dealerships are the most common landmarks used – but these are often meaningless to the foreign traveler who will have no idea where the Subaru dealership is to begin with. Better yet, Ticos frequently refer to landmarks that no longer exist. In San Pedro, outside of San José, locals still use the sight of an old fig tree *(el antiguo higuerón)* to provide directions.

Confused? Get used to it...

Switzerland (☎ 2221-3229; Edificio Centro Colón, 10th fl, Paseo Colón btwn Calles 38 & 40)

UK (☎ 2258-2025; Edificio Centro Colón, 11th fl, Paseo Colón btwn Calles 38 & 40)

USA (☎ 2220-3939; Carretera a Pavas) Opposite Centro Commercial del Oeste.

FESTIVALS & EVENTS

The following events are listed from January to December:

Las Fiestas de Palmares (mid-January) Ten days of beer drinking, horse shows and other carnival events in the tiny town of Palmares.

Fiesta de los Diablitos (December 31 to January 2 in Reserva Indígena Boruca; February 5-8 in Curré) During the fiesta men wear carved wooden devil masks and burlap masks to re-enact the fight between the *indígenas* and the Spanish. In this version, the Spanish lose.

Día de San José (St Joseph's Day; March 19) Honors the capital's patron saint.

Semana Santa (Holy Week; March or April) The Thursday and Friday before Easter Sunday is the official holiday, though most businesses shut down for the whole week. From Thursday to Sunday bars are closed and alcohol sales are prohibited; on Thursday and Friday buses stop running.

Fiesta de La Virgen del Mar (Festival of the Virgin of the Sea; mid-July) Held in Puntarenas and Playa del Coco, it involves colorful regattas and boat parades.

Día de Guanacaste (July 25) Celebrates the annexation of Guanacaste from Nicaragua.

Virgen de los Ángeles (August 2) The patron saint is celebrated with a particularly important religious procession from San José to Cartago.

El Día de la Raza (Columbus Day; October 12) Puerto Limón celebrates with gusto the explorer's landing at nearby Isla Uvita. The four-day carnival is full of colorful street parades and dancing, music, singing, drinking.

Día de los Muertos (All Souls' Day; November 2) Families visit graveyards and have religious parades in honor of the deceased.

Las Fiestas de Zapote (December 25 to January 1) A weeklong celebration of all things Costa Rican (namely rodeos, cowboys, carnival rides, fried food and a whole lot of drinking) in Zapote, southeast of San José.

FOOD & DRINK

Costa Rican food, for the most part, is basic and fairly bland. The best food is on the Caribbean coast where coconut and chili peppers spice stews. Rice and beans (or beans and rice) are gussied up with *curtido*, pickled hot peppers and vegetables; Tabasco sauce; and *salsa lizano*, the Tico version of Worcestershire sauce.

Breakfast largely consists of *gallo pinto*, a stir-fry of rice and beans, served with eggs,

cheese or *natilla* (sour cream). These are generally cheap (US$2) and filling. Restaurants offer a set meal at lunch and dinner called a *casado*. It usually includes meat, beans, rice and cabbage salad. Veggie *casados* (cheap set meals) can be made on request.

Sodas are cheap lunch counters serving *casados* as well as sandwiches or burgers. Other cheapies include the countless fried and rotisserie chicken stands. (Ticos *love* fried chicken.) Reasonably priced Chinese restaurants and pizza parlors are found in most towns. Better restaurants add a 13% tax plus 10% service to the bill.

Throughout this chapter, eating listings are given in order of budget according to the average price of a meal. The budget category covers meals costing up to ₡5000 while midrange is between ₡5000 and ₡12,500.

GAY & LESBIAN TRAVELERS

The situation facing gay and lesbian travelers is better than in most Central American countries. Homosexual acts between two consenting adults (aged 18 and over) are legal, but most Costa Ricans are tolerant only at a 'don't ask, don't tell' level. Outside of gay spots, public displays of affection are not recommended.

San José offers a good selection of nightclubs ranging from cruising joints to pounding dance clubs to more intimate places (see boxed text, p543). The Pacific resort town of Manuel Antonio (p602) is a popular gay vacation center.

The monthly newspaper *Gayness* and the magazine *Gente 10* (in Spanish) are both available at gay bars in San José. Other resources:

Cipac (☎ 2280-7821; www.cipacdh.org) The leading gay activist organization in Costa Rica.

International Gay & Lesbian Travel Association (IGLTA; ☎ in the USA 800-448-8550, 954-776-2626; www.iglta.org) Maintains a list of hundreds of travel agents and tour operators all over the world.

Tiquicia Travel (☎ 2256-9682; www.tiquiciatravel. com) Makes arrangements at gay-friendly hotels.

Toto Tours (☎ in the USA 800-565-1241, 773-274-8686; www.tototours.com) Gay travel specialists who organize regular trips to Costa Rica, among other destinations.

INTERNET ACCESS

Internet cafes abound in Costa Rica, and you don't have to look very far to find cheap and

COSTA RICA

speedy internet access. Wi-fi access is also on the rise in Costa Rica, and a good number of backpacker hostels offer secure wireless networks to their customers.

INTERNET RESOURCES

Many websites in this chapter may be in Spanish, but we've included them for those that can read the language. Some general resources:

Costa Rica Guide (www.costa-rica-guide.com) Nicely organized website with detailed maps and regional travel information.

Costa Rica Link (www.1costaricalink.com) Provides a great deal of information on transportation, hotels, activities and more.

Guías Costa Rica (www.guiascostarica.com) Has informative links.

Lanic (http://lanic.utexas.edu/la/ca/cr) An exceptional collection of links to sites of many Costa Rican organizations (mostly in Spanish).

Tico Times (www.ticotimes.net) The online edition of Costa Rica's English-language weekly.

LANGUAGE

Spanish is the official language but English is widely understood and spoken exclusively along much of the Caribbean coast. Some Costa Rican slang:

¡adiós! – hello; used as a salutation in remote rural areas; also means 'farewell'

buena nota – OK, excellent; literally 'good grade'

chunche – thing; can refer to almost anything

cien metros – one city block; literally 100m

listo pa' la foto – drunk; literally 'ready for the picture'

maje – dude or buddy

pulpería – corner grocery store

pura vida – super, right on; literally 'pure life,' an expression of approval or greeting

sabanero – Costa Rican cowboy from the province of Guanacaste

salado – too bad, tough luck

Tico – Costa Rican

tuanis – cool

una roja – a red one, literally a 1000-colón note; *'Me costó dos rojas'* means 'It cost me two red ones.'

¿upe? – anybody home? pronounced oo-pay; used in the countryside at people's homes instead of knocking

LEGAL MATTERS

If you get into legal trouble and are jailed, your embassy can offer only limited assistance. Embassy officials will not bail you out and you are subject to Costa Rican laws, not those of your own country.

In many beach towns, police tend to turn a blind eye on marijuana use. However, penalties in Costa Rica for possession of even small amounts of illegal drugs are much stricter than in the USA or Europe. Defendants often spend many months in jail before they are brought to trial and, if convicted, can expect sentences of several years in jail.

Drivers should carry their passport and a valid driver's license. In the event of an accident, leave the vehicles in place until the police arrive and make a report. This is essential for all insurance claims. If the accident results in injury or death, you may be prevented from leaving the country until all legalities are handled.

Prostitution is legal for women over 18. Prostitutes carry cards showing how recently they have had a medical check-up, though these are quite unreliable. Sex with a minor under the age of 18 is illegal in Costa Rica and penalties are severe. Keep in mind that travelers may be subject to the laws of their own country with regard to sexual relations.

MAPS

Detailed maps are hard to come by. An excellent option is the waterproof 1:330,000 *Costa Rica* sheet produced by **International Travel Map** (ITMB; www.itmb.com; 530 W Broadway, Vancouver, BC, V5Z 1E, Canada) with a San José inset.

Available in San José bookstores, **Fundación Neotropica** (www.neotropica.org) has published a 1:500,000 map showing national parks and other protected areas.

The Instituto Costarricense de Turismo (ICT, Costa Rica Tourism Board; see p538) publishes a free 1:700,000 Costa Rica map with a 1:12,500 Central San José map on the reverse.

Online, **Maptak** (www.maptak.com) has maps of Costa Rica's seven provinces and their capitals.

MEDIA

The **Tico Times** (www.ticotimes.net) is the weekly English-language newspaper and hits the streets every Friday. The most widely distributed paper is **La Nación** (www.nacion.co.cr), which has conservative coverage of national and international news. For a liberal perspective, pick up **La Prensa Libre** (www.prensalibre.co.cr), the afternoon daily.

Cable and satellite TV are widely available. There are more than 100 local radio stations.

Radio 107.5 FM is a popular English-language station, playing current hits and providing a regular BBC news feed.

MONEY

The Costa Rican currency is the colón (plural colones), normally written as ₡. Bills come in 500, 1000, 5000, 10,000, 20,000 and 50,000 colones; coins come in denominations of 5, 10, 20, 25, 50 and 100 colones. In 2010, Costa Rica rolled out new banknotes, and old banknotes were subsequently collected, destroyed and no longer deemed legal tender. US dollars are increasingly common, and you can use them to pay for sights and activities, tours, accommodations, and transportation such as international buses and shuttle buses, car rental and flights. Meals, local and intercity bus fares, taxis and small-ticket purchase items should all be paid for in colones.

ATMs

It's increasingly easy to find ATMs (*cajeros automáticos* in Spanish). The Visa Plus network is the standard, but machines on the Cirrus network, which accept most foreign ATM cards, can be found in San José and in larger towns. Some ATM machines will dispense US dollars. Note some machines (eg at Banco Nacional) only accept cards from their own customers. The airport has two ATM machines to get dollars or colones as soon as you arrive.

Bargaining

A high standard of living along with a steady stream of international tourist traffic means that haggling is fast dying out here. Beach communities, especially, have fixed prices on hotels that cannot be negotiated. (Expect some business owners to be offended if you try.) Some smaller hotels in the interior still accept the practice.

Negotiating prices at outdoor markets is acceptable and some bargaining is accepted when hiring long-distance taxis.

Credit Cards

Holders of credit and debit cards can buy colones and sometimes US dollars in some banks. Better hotels and restaurants, car-rental agencies and some travel agencies take plastic. Visa is the most widely accepted, MasterCard less so and American Express (Amex) rarely. Some hotels might charge a 7% fee, in addition to government and service taxes.

Exchange Rates

The table shows currency exchange rates at the time this book went to press.

Country	Unit	₡
Australia	A$1	449
Canada	C$1	496
Euro zone	€1	637
Japan	¥100	577
New Zealand	NZ$1	365
UK	UK£1	772
USA	US$1	517

Exchanging Money

All banks will exchange US dollars, and some will exchange euros; other currencies are more difficult. State-run institutions (Banco Nacional, Banco de Costa Rica and Banco Popular) may have long lines but they don't charge commissions on cash exchanges. Make sure your dollar bills are in good condition or they may be refused.

Hotels and travel agencies are willing to change money for travelers but be aware that many charge hefty commissions. Changing money on the streets is not recommended, except possibly at land borders. Street moneychangers don't give better rates, and scammers abound.

Carry your passport when exchanging currency.

Traveler's Checks

Most banks and exchange houses will cash traveler's checks at a commission of between 1% and 3%.

POST

Airmail letters cost about ₡175 for the first 20g. Parcels can be shipped at the rate of ₡3500 per kilogram. You can receive mail at the main post office of major towns.

RESPONSIBLE TRAVEL

The ubiquitous buzzword 'ecotourism' boils down to marketing claims that are almost never substantiated. Real responsible travel depends on the behavior of your service provider as well as your own. Ecotourism providers accredited by outside institutions can be found at the **ICT sustainable tourism accreditation service** (www.turismo-sostenible.co.cr/en) as well as www.planeta.com. Otherwise, businesses may be evaluated in terms of disposal of wastewater, recycling, energy efficiency, contributions to the local community and living wages for employees.

Visitors should follow the cardinal rules of never littering, never feeding the wildlife, staying on marked trails and not buying endangered products (turtle shell, feathers, skins, coral, shells and exotic hardwoods). An active approach means using mass transportation instead of driving or taking a taxi (if alone), volunteering (see opposite), informing yourself on the local issues and promoting goodwill by respecting local cultures and engaging with locals. For more information, see p529.

SHOPPING

Coffee is the most popular souvenir, and deservedly so. Boozers can fill up on Ron Centenario, the coffee liqueur Café Rica and also *guaro*, the local firewater.

Ceramics and tropical hardwood items are popular. Check to see if wood products are made of endangered hardwoods. Avoid purchasing animal products, including turtle shell, animal skulls and anything made with feathers, coral and shells. See also Responsible Travel (p621).

STUDYING

There is no shortage of language academies ready and willing to teach you Spanish around Costa Rica. Many operate in San José, the Central Valley as well as popular beach towns such as Jacó, Playa Tamarindo and Puerto Viejo de Talamanca.

TELEPHONE

Public phones are found all over Costa Rica and Chip or Colibrí phone cards are available in 1000, 2000 and 3000 colón denominations. Chip cards are inserted into the phone and scanned. Colibrí cards (the most common) require dialing a toll-free number (☎ 199) and entering an access code. Dial '00' followed by the country code and number for international calls. Instructions are provided in English or Spanish. These are the preferred card of travelers since they can be used from any phone. Purchase cards in supermarkets, pharmacies and *pulperías*.

To call Costa Rica from abroad, use the international code (☎ 506) before the eight-digit number (there are no area codes in Costa Rica).

TOILETS

Public restrooms are rare. Restaurants and cafes usually loan their facilities at a small charge – usually a few hundred colones. Bus terminals and other major public buildings have lavatories, also at a charge.

If you're particularly fond of using toilet paper, carry it with you at all times as it is not always available. Just don't flush it down! Costa Rican plumbing is poor and has very low pressure with few exceptions. Dispose of toilet paper in the rubbish bin inside every bathroom.

TOURIST INFORMATION

The government-run tourism board, the Instituto Costarricense de Turismo (ICT), has two offices in the capital (see p538). However, don't expect to be wowed with any particularly insightful travel advice as it's the staff's job to tell you that it's all good in Costa Rica. That said, the ICT can provide you with free maps, a master bus schedule and information on road conditions in the hinterlands. English is spoken.

Consult the ICT's flashy English-language website (www.visitcostarica.com) for information, or in the USA call the ICT's toll-free number (☎ 800-343-6332) for brochures and information.

TOURS

Some well-established companies:

Ecole Travel (☎ 2223-2240; www.ecoletravel.com) Offers a variety of tours.

Euphoria Expeditions (☎ 2849-1271; www.euforia expeditions.com) Specializes in cultural travel and expedition-style adventure trips.

Swiss Travel Service (☎ 2282-4898; www. swisstravelcr.com) Tour agency.

TRAVELERS WITH DISABILITIES

Although Costa Rica has laws on equal opportunity and access for people with disabilities, the law applies only to new or newly remodeled businesses and is loosely enforced. Buses don't have provisions for wheelchairs and few hotels, restaurants or parks have features specifically suited to wheelchair use. One exception is Parque Nacional Volcán Poás (p547).

Outfitter **Vaya con Silla de Ruedas** (☎ 2454-2810; www.gowithwheelchairs.com) offers specialty trips for travelers with wheelchairs.

VISAS

Passport-carrying nationals of the following countries are allowed 90 days' stay with no visa: Argentina, Canada, Israel, Japan, Panama, the USA, and most western European countries.

Citizens of Australia, Iceland, Ireland, Mexico, New Zealand, Russia, South Africa and Venezuela are allowed to stay for 30 days with no visa. Others require a visa from a Costa Rican embassy or consulate. Note that visas cannot be obtained at the border. For the latest info on visas, check out lonelyplanet.com.

Extensions

Extending your stay beyond the authorized 30 or 90 days is a time-consuming hassle. It is far easier to leave the country for 72 hours and then re-enter. Otherwise, go to the **immigration office** (migración; Map p536; ☎ 2220-0355; ⏱ 8am-4pm) in San José, opposite Channel 6, about 4km north of Parque La Sabana. Requirements for extensions change, so allow several working days.

Onward Tickets

Travelers officially need onward tickets before they are allowed to enter Costa Rica. This requirement is not often checked at the airport, but travelers arriving by land should anticipate a need to show an onward ticket.

If you're heading to Panama, Nicaragua or another Central or South American country from Costa Rica, you may need an onward or round-trip ticket before you will be allowed entry into that country or even allowed to board the plane if you're flying. A quick check with the appropriate embassy – easy to do via the internet – will tell you whether the country that you're heading to has an onward-ticket requirement.

VOLUNTEERING

The sheer number of volunteer opportunities in Costa Rica is mind-blowing. 'Voluntourism' is a great way to travel sustainably and make a positive contribution to the local community. Volunteer work is also an amazing forum for self-exploration, especially if you touch a few lives and meet a few new friends along the way. Generally speaking, you will get as much out of volunteering as you put in and the majority of volunteers in Costa Rica walk away from their experiences content.

The following volunteer opportunities provide a general overview of what is currently available in Costa Rica.

English Teaching

Amerispan Unlimited (www.amerispan.com) Offers a variety of educational travel programs in specialized areas.

Cloud Forest School (www.cloudforestschool.org) A bilingual school (kindergarten to 11th grade) in Monteverde offering creative and experiential education.

Sustainable Horizon (www.sustainablehorizon.com) Arranges volunteering trips such as guest teaching spots and orphanage placements.

Forestry Management

Bosque Eterno de los Niños (Children's Eternal Forest; www.acmcr.org) Volunteers are needed to help manage the remarkable achievement – a rainforest purchased by children who raised money to buy and protect it.

Cloudbridge Nature Preserve (www.cloudbridge.org) A private reserve where an ongoing reforestation project is being spearheaded by two New Yorkers.

Fundación Corcovado (www.corcovadofoundation.org) An impressive network of people and organizations committed to preserving Parque Nacional Corcovado.

Monteverde Institute (www.mvinstitute.org) A nonprofit educational institute offering training in tropical biology, conservation and sustainable development.

Organic Farming

Finca La Flor de Paraíso (www.la-flor.org) Offers programs in a variety of disciplines from animal husbandry to medicinal-herb cultivation.

Punta Mona (www.puntamona.org) An organic farm and retreat center that is based on organic permaculture and sustainable living.

Reserva Biológica Dúrika (www.durika.org) A sustainable community that is centered upon a 75-sq-km biological reserve.

Wildlife Conservation

CCC (www.cccturtle.org) Assist scientists with turtle tagging and research on green and leatherback turtles.

Profelis (www.grafischer.com/profelis) A feline conservation program that takes care of confiscated wild cats, both big and small.

WOMEN TRAVELERS

Most female travelers experience little more than a whispered *'mi amor'* (my love) or an appreciative hiss from the local men in Costa Rica. Overall, men are usually gentlemen. But Costa Rican men do consider foreign women to have looser morals than Ticas and some may try to prove that theory. The best way to deal with this is obtaining a black belt in karate. Alternatively, try what Ticas do – ignore it. Women who firmly resist unwanted verbal advances from men are normally treated with respect.

In small highland towns, dress is usually conservative and women rarely wear shorts. On the beach, skimpy bathing suits are OK, but topless and nude bathing are not.

Use normal caution: avoid walking alone in isolated places or through city streets late at night and skip the hitchhiking. Do not take unlicensed 'pirate' cabs (licensed cabs are red and have medallions) as reports of assaults by unlicensed drivers against women have been reported.

Most pharmacies sell birth-control pills without prescription. Tampons are scarce outside of major cities.

WORKING

It's difficult for foreigners to find work in Costa Rica. The government doesn't like anyone taking jobs away from Costa Ricans and the labor laws reflect this sentiment. Basically, the only foreigners legally employed in Costa Rica work for their own businesses, possess skills not found in the country, or work for companies that have special agreements with the government.

Getting a bona fide job necessitates obtaining a work permit – a time-consuming and difficult process. The most likely source of paid employment is as an English teacher at one of the language institutes, or working in the hospitality industry in a hotel or resort. Naturalists or river guides may be able to find work with private lodges or adventure-travel operators, though you shouldn't expect to make more than survival wages from these jobs.

Panama

Blue-green seas, foggy highlands and snaking rivers that fringe a great tropical wilderness. This is Panama as the explorers found it, and as much of it remains today. Many outsiders assume that Panama is all about its capital and commerce. But while the country is racing toward rapid-fire development, the resources Panama has always had and oft neglected have started to attract attention. A third of the country is set aside as protected areas and national parks, and indigenous groups have survived with their cultures largely intact.

Although the canal has defined Panama for the last century, it's what lies just beyond this engineering marvel that could define the next hundred years. Pristine beaches, lush rainforest and big-city nightlife give a taste of the country's outstanding assets. Always a creature of potential, Panama lives with a sharp contrast between its urban and rural counterparts. Panama City is all sparkling skyscrapers, cement mixers and scaffolds, yet an hour outside the capital, indigenous Emberá paddle dugout canoes. Ironically, many residents welcomed the 2009 world economic crisis in relief, and that megadevelopments and real-estate speculation would slow down for a pace as a consequence. For Panama, it's time to get back to natural assets.

PANAMA

FAST FACTS

- **Area** 78,200 sq km (slightly smaller than South Carolina)
- **Budget** US$30 per day
- **Capital** Panama City
- **Costs** Hostel in Bocas US$7, bottle of beer US$1, three-hour bus ride US$6, set lunch US$3.50
- **Country Code** ☎ 507
- **Languages** Spanish, Kuna plus 14 others
- **Money** The balboa – aka the US dollar
- **Population** 3.4 million
- **Seasons** High season runs mid-December to mid-April
- **Time** GMT minus five hours

TRAVEL HINTS

Take a light sweater and a poncho if you plan to hike and camp in the Chiriquí highlands. Get malaria tablets (anything but chloroquine) if you're heading to the Darién.

OVERLAND ROUTES

The principal Costa Rican crossing is on the Interamericana at Paso Canoas. Guabito on the Caribbean side and Río Sereno in the highlands are less chaotic border posts.

HIGHLIGHTS

■ **Bocas del Toro** (p670) Soak up the Caribbean charm of laid-back Isla Colón before exploring the wild beaches and forests of the surrounding islands.

■ **Boquete** (p663) Fire up with mountain-grown coffee before hiking through the cloud forests in search of the elusive quetzal.

■ **Panama City** (p638) Spend the day admiring the faded glory of the old city, then party till sunrise on Calle Uruguay.

■ **Panama Canal** (p653) Marvel at hulking freighter ships raised and lowered through sets of enormous locks.

■ **Comarca de Kuna Yala** (p690) Explore the tiny palm-covered islands of the Archipiélago de San Blás, home to one of Central America's most independent groups, the Kuna.

■ **Off the beaten track** (p694) Head to the virgin jungles and isolated rivers of the Western hemisphere's wildest frontier at Darién Province.

CURRENT AFFAIRS

The lifeline of Panama's economy, the Panama Canal is the world's biggest engineering project and it just got bigger. In 2006, Panamanian voters overwhelmingly endorsed an ambitious US$5 billion project to expand the canal. The sandbox is already being dug up – machinery is widening and deepening existing navigation channels, and creating a third set of locks. This massive makeover – slated for construction in 2014 – should bring on more canal traffic and allow larger vessels for a much needed boost to the economy.

On May 3, 2009, Panama bucked the Latin American leftist trend by electing conservative supermarket magnate Ricardo Martinelli president. Part of the conservative Democratic Change (CD) party, Martinelli was expected to boost big business, but he surprised critics by attacking businesses that evaded taxes and infringed on public lands.

The world economic crisis has left Panama with high inflation. Foreign investors just aren't approaching business opportunities with the same gold-rush aplomb that characterized the first decade of the second millennium. What is certain is that Panama is attracting more and more buzz for its pristine beaches, incredible wildlife and rainforests. While Canadian and US retirees were the first to join the bandwagon, more and more world travelers are following suit.

HISTORY
Lost Panama

The coastlines and rainforests of Panama have been inhabited by humans for at least 11,000 years. Indigenous groups including the Kuna, the Ngöbe-Buglé, the Emberá, the Wounaan, the Bribrí and the Naso were living on the isthmus prior to the Spanish arrival. However, the historical tragedy of Panama is that despite its rich cultural history, there are virtually no physical remains of these great civilizations.

Unlike the massive pyramid complexes found throughout Latin America, the ancient towns and cities of Panama have vanished into the jungles. Tales of lost cities survive in the oral histories of Panama's indigenous communities, and Panamanian archaeologists hope that a great discovery lies ahead.

What is known about pre-Columbian Panama is that early inhabitants were part of an extensive trading zone that extended as far south as Peru and as far north as Mexico. Archaeologists have uncovered exquisite gold ornaments and unusual life-size stone statues of human figures as well as distinctive types of pottery and *metates* (stone platforms that were used for grinding corn). Panama's first peoples also lived beside both oceans, and fished in mangrove swamps, estuaries and coral reefs. Given the tremendous impact that fishing has had on the lives of Isthmians, it seems only fitting that the country's name is derived from an indigenous word meaning 'abundance of fish.'

New World Order

In 1501 the discovery of Panama by Spanish explorer Rodrigo de Bastidas marked the beginning of the age of conquest and colonization in the isthmus. However, it was his first mate Vasco Núñez de Balboa who was to be immortalized in the history books following his discovery of the Pacific Ocean 12 years later.

On his fourth and final voyage to the New World in 1502, Christopher Columbus went ashore in present-day Costa Rica, where he testified to having seen 'more gold in two days than in four years in Spain.' Although fierce local resistance thwarted his attempts to establish a colony at the mouth of the Río Belén in 1503, Columbus petitioned the Spanish Crown to be appointed governor of Veraguas, the stretch of shoreline from Honduras to Panama. With Queen Isabella, his primary benefactor, on her deathbed, the prize went instead to Columbus' rival.

In 1510, Diego de Nicuesa tried to establish a Spanish colony at Río Belén. Local resistance once again beat back the Spanish. Nicuesa fled with a small fleet with 280 starving men aboard. Seeing a protected bay 23km east of what is now Portobelo, he exclaimed: *¡Paremos aqui, en nombre de Dios!* ('Let us stop here, in the name of God!'). Thus was named the town of Nombre de Dios, one of the first Spanish settlements in the New World.

Much to the disappointment of conquistadors, Panama was not rich in gold. Add tropical diseases, inhospitable terrain and less than welcoming natives, and it's easy to see why Nombre de Dios failed several times as an early Spanish colony. Later in 1513, Balboa heard rumors about a large sea and a wealthy, gold-producing civilization across the mountains – likely the Inca Empire of Peru. Driven by ambition and greed, Balboa scaled the continental divide and on September 26, 1513, became the first European to set eyes on the Pacific Ocean. He claimed the ocean and all the lands it touched for the king of Spain.

The Empire Expands

In 1519 a cruel and very vindictive Spaniard named Pedro Arias de Ávila (called Pedrarias by contemporaries) founded the city of Panamá on the Pacific side, near where Panama City stands today. The governor ordered the beheading of Balboa in 1517 on a trumped-up charge of treason. He is also remembered for murderous attacks against the indigenous population, whom he roasted alive or fed to dogs.

Despite a ghastly record, Pedrarias established Panamá as an important Spanish settlement, a commercial center and a base for further explorations, including the conquest of Peru. From Panamá, vast riches of Peruvian gold and Oriental spices were transported across the isthmus by foot. Vestiges of this famous trade route, known as the Sendero Las Cruces (Las Cruces Trail), can still be found throughout Panama.

As the Spaniards grew fat and soft on the wealth of plundered civilizations, the world began to notice the prospering colony, especially the English privateers lurking in coastal waters. In 1573 Sir Francis Drake destroyed Nombre de Dios, and set sail for England with a galleon laden with Spanish gold.

Hoping to stave off further ransacking and pillaging, the Spanish built large stone fortresses at San Lorenzo and Portobelo. However, these fortifications didn't stop Welsh buccaneer Sir Henry Morgan from overpowering Fuerte San Lorenzo and sailing up the Río Chagres in 1671. After crossing the length of the isthmus, Morgan destroyed the city of Panamá, burning it to the ground to return to the Caribbean coast with 200 mules loaded with Spanish loot.

The Spanish rebuilt the city of Panamá a few years later on a cape several kilometers west of its original site. The ruins of the old settlement, now known as Panamá Viejo, and the colonial city of Casco Viejo are located within the city limits of the present-day metropolis.

British privateering didn't cease with the destruction of Panamá. The final nail in the coffin was hammered in when Admiral Edward Vernon destroyed the fortress of Portobelo in 1739. Humiliated by their defeat, the Spanish abandoned the Panamanian crossing in favor of sailing the long way around Cape Horn to the west coast of South America.

The Empire Ends

On October 27, 1807, the Treaty of Fontainebleau, which defined the occupation of Portugal, was signed between Spain and France. Under the guise of reinforcing the Franco-Spanish army occupying Portugal, Napoleon moved tens of thousands of troops into Spain. In an act of treachery and military genius, Napoleon then ordered his troops to seize key Spanish fortifications.

The resulting Peninsular War crippled both countries. As a result of the conflict, as well as the subsequent power vacuum and decades of internal turmoil, Spain lost nearly all of its colonial possessions in the first third of the century.

PANAMA

Panama gained independence from Spanish rule in 1821 and immediately joined Gran Colombia, a confederation of current-day Colombia, Bolivia, Ecuador, Peru and Venezuela, a united Latin American nation that had long been the dream of Simón Bolívar. However, internal disputes lead to the abolishment of Gran Colombia in 1831, though fledgling Panama remained a province of Colombia.

Birth of a Nation

Panama's future forever changed when world powers caught on that the isthmus was the narrowest point between the Atlantic and Pacific Oceans. In 1846 Colombia signed a treaty permitting the USA to construct a railway across the isthmus, though it also granted it free transit and the right to protect the railway with military force. At the height of the California gold rush in 1849, tens of thousands traveled from the east coast of the USA to the west coast via Panama in order to avoid hostile Native Americans living in the central states. Colombia and Panama grew wealthy from the railway, and the first talks of a canal across Central America began to surface.

The idea of a canal across the isthmus was first raised in 1524 when King Charles V of Spain ordered a survey to determine the feasibility of a waterway. Later, Emperor Napoleon III of France also considered the idea. Finally, in 1878, French builder Ferdinand de Lesseps, basking in the glory of the recently constructed Suez canal, was

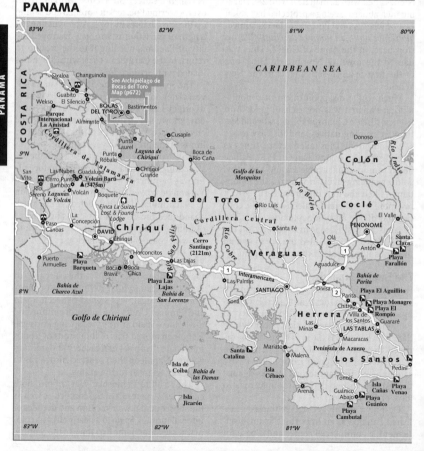

PANAMA

contracted by Colombia to build the canal, bringing his crew to Panama in 1881. Much like Napoleon, Lesseps severely underestimated the task, and over 22,000 workers died from yellow fever and malaria in less than a decade. In 1889 insurmountable construction problems and financial mismanagement drove the company bankrupt.

The USA saw the French failure as a business opportunity. In 1903 Philippe Bunau-Varilla, one of Lesseps' chief engineers, agreed to sell concessions to the USA, though the Colombian government refused. Bunau-Varilla approached the US government to back Panama if it declared independence from Colombia.

On November 3, 1903, a revolutionary junta declared Panama independent, and the US government immediately recognized its sovereignty – the first of a series of American interventions in Panama. Although Colombia sent troops by sea to try to regain control, US battleships prevented them from reaching land. In fact, Colombia did not recognize Panama as a legitimately separate nation until 1921, when the USA paid Colombia US$25 million in 'compensation.'

Growing Pains

Following independence, Bunau-Varilla was appointed Panamanian ambassador to the USA, with his first act of office paving the way for future American interventions. Hoping to profit from the sale of canal concessions to the USA, Bunau-Varilla arrived in Washington,

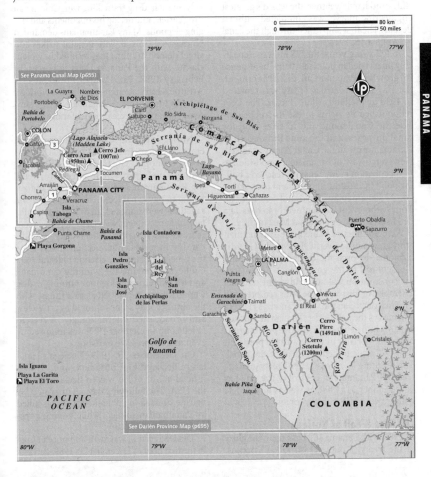

PANAMA

DC before Panama could assemble a delegation. On November 18, 1903, Bunau-Varilla and US Secretary of State John Hay signed the Hay-Bunau-Varilla Treaty, which gave the USA far more than had been offered in the original treaty. In addition to owning concessions to the canal, the USA was also granted 'sovereign rights in perpetuity over the Canal Zone,' an area extending 8km on either side of the canal, and a broad right of intervention in Panamanian affairs.

Despite opposition from the tardy Panamanian delegation as well as lingering questions about its legality, the treaty was ratified, ushering in an era of friction between the USA and Panama. Construction began again on the canal in 1904 and despite disease, landslides and harsh weather, the world's greatest engineering marvel was completed within a decade. The first ship sailed through the canal on August 15, 1914.

In following years, the US military repeatedly intervened in political affairs. In response to growing Panamanian disenchantment, the Hay-Bunau-Varilla Treaty was replaced in 1936 by the Hull-Alfaro Treaty. The USA relinquished its rights to use its troops outside the Canal Zone and to seize land for canal purposes, and the annual sum paid to Panama for use of the Canal Zone was raised. However, a wave of Panamanian opposition to US occupation grew. Tensions reached a boiling point in 1964 during a student protest that left 27 Panamanians dead and 500 injured. Today, the event is commemorated as Día de Los Mártires, or National Martyrs Day.

As US influence waned, the Panamanian army grew more powerful. In 1968 the Guardia Nacional deposed the elected president and took control of the government. Soon after, the constitution was suspended, the national assembly was dissolved, the press censored and the Guardia's General Omar Torrijos Herrera emerged as the new leader. Though he plunged Panama into debt with a massive public works program, Torrijos did convince US president Jimmy Carter to cede control of the canal. The resulting Torrijos-Carter Treaty guaranteed full Panamanian control of the canal as of December 31, 1999, as well as a complete withdrawal of US military forces.

The Rise & Fall of Noriega

In 1981, with Panama still basking in the glory of the treaty, a plane crash killed Torrijos.

Rumors of foul play swept the country. In 1983 Colonel Manuel Antonio Noriega seized the Guardia Nacional, promoted himself to general and made himself the de facto ruler of Panama. Noriega, a former head of Panama's secret police, a former CIA operative and a graduate of the School of the Americas, quickly began to consolidate his power. He enlarged the Guardia Nacional, significantly expanded its authority and renamed it the Panama Defense Forces. He also created a paramilitary 'Dignity Battalion' in every city, town and village, its members armed and ready to inform on any of their neighbors showing less than complete loyalty to the Noriega regime.

Things went from bad to worse in early 1987 when Noriega was publicly accused of involvement in drug trafficking with Colombian drug cartels, murdering his opponents and rigging elections. Many Panamanians demanded Noriega's dismissal, with general strikes and street demonstrations that resulted in violent clashes with the Panama Defense Forces. In February 1988, Panamanian President Eric Arturo Delvalle attempted to dismiss Noriega, but was forced to flee Panama. Noriega subsequently appointed a president more sympathetic to his cause.

Noriega's regime became an international embarrassment. In March 1988, the USA imposed economic sanctions against Panama, ending a preferential trade agreement, freezing Panamanian assets in US banks and refusing to pay canal fees. A few days after the sanctions were imposed, an unsuccessful military coup prompted Noriega to step up violent repression of his critics. After Noriega's candidate lost the presidential election in May 1989, the general declared the election null and void. Guillermo Endara, the winning candidate, and his two vice-presidential running mates, were badly beaten by Noriega's thugs, with the entire bloody scene captured by a TV crew and broadcasted internationally. A second failed coup in October 1989 was followed by even more repressive measures.

On December 15, 1989, Noriega's legislature declared him president, and his first official act of office was to declare war on the USA. The following day, an unarmed US marine dressed in civilian clothes was killed by Panamanian soldiers while leaving a restaurant in Panama City.

The US reaction was swift and unrelenting. In the first hour of December 20, 1989, Panama

City was attacked by aircraft, tanks and 26,000 US troops. The invasion, intended to bring Noriega to justice and create a democracy better suited to US interests, left more than 2000 civilians dead, tens of thousands homeless and destroyed entire tracts of Panama City.

On Christmas Day, Noriega claimed asylum in the Vatican embassy. US forces surrounded the embassy and pressured the Vatican to release him. They bombarded the embassy with blaring rock music. Mobs of angry Panamanians surrounded the embassy, calling for Noriega to be ousted.

After 10 days of psychological warfare, the Vatican embassy persuaded Noriega to give himself up by threatening to cancel his asylum. Noriega surrendered to US forces on January 3, and was flown to Miami where he was convicted of conspiracy to manufacture and distribute cocaine. Although his US prison sentence ended in 2007, as of 2010 he remained captive pending extradition requests from Panama and France. In July 2010 a French court sentenced Noriega to seven years in jail for laundering drug money.

Modern Struggles

After Noriega's forced removal, Guillermo Endara, the legitimate winner of the 1989 election, was sworn in as president, and Panama attempted to put itself back together. The country's image and economy were in shambles, and its capital had suffered damage from both the invasion and the widespread looting that followed. Unfortunately, Endara proved to be an ineffective leader whose policies cut jobs and cost his administration its early popularity. He was voted out of office in 1994 with single-digit approval ratings.

Ernesto Pérez Balladares took office next. Under his direction, the Panamanian government implemented a program of privatization that focused on infrastructure improvements, health care and education. Although Pérez Balladares allocated unprecedented levels of funding for Panama's development, he would later be investigated for corruption in 2010.

In 1999 Mireya Moscoso, the widow of popular former president Arnulfo Arias, and Panama's first female leader and head of the conservative Arnulfista Party (PA), took office. Moscoso's ambitious plans never materialized. As Panama celebrated its centenary in 2003, unemployment hit 18% and parts of the country were without food – yet Moscoso

paid US$10 million to bring the Miss Universe pageant to Panama. She was also accused of looking the other way during Colombian military incursions into the Darién.

Martín Torrijos, a member of the Revolutionary Democratic Party (PRD) and the son of former leader Omar Torrijos, took over in 2004. Although there is still debate regarding the success of his administration, he did implement much-needed fiscal reforms, including an overhaul of the nation's social security system. Furthermore, his proposal to expand the Panama Canal was overwhelmingly approved by national referendum.

On May 3, 2009, Panama became part of the backlash against the Latin American leftist trend by electing conservative supermarket magnate Ricardo Martinelli president. Still in its honeymoon stage, it is early to say where the conservative administration of Martinelli will lead the nation at the crux of Latin American currents.

THE CULTURE
The National Psyche

At the crossroads of the Americas, the narrow isthmus of Panama bridges not only two continents but two vastly different paradigms of Panamanian culture and society. While one sphere of Panama clings to the traditions of the past, the other looks to the modernizing influences of a growing economy.

In some ways, these opposing forces are only natural given the many years that Panama has been the object of another country's meddling. From the US-backed independence of 1903 to the strong-armed removal of Noriega in 1989, with half-a-dozen other interventions in between, the USA left a strong legacy in the country. Nearly every Panamanian has a relative or acquaintance living in the USA. Parts of the country seem swept up in mall-fervor, with consumer inspiration straight out of North America.

Others, however, are not so ready to embrace gringo culture. Indigenous groups such as the Emberá and Kuna are struggling to keep their traditions alive, as more and more of their youth are lured into the Westernized lifestyle of the city.

Given the clash between old and new, it's surprising the country isn't suffering from a serious case of cognitive dissonance. Somehow, the exceptionally tolerant Panamanian character weathers many contradictions – the old and the new, the grave disparity between rich and poor, and the gorgeous natural environment and its rapid destruction.

Lifestyle

In spite of the skyscrapers and gleaming restaurants lining the wealthier districts of Panama City, nearly a third of the country's population lives in poverty. Furthermore, almost a quarter of a million Panamanians struggle just to satisfy their basic dietary needs. The poorest tend to live in the least populated provinces: Darién, Bocas del Toro, Veraguas, Los Santos and Colón. There is also substantial poverty in the slums of Panama City, where an estimated 20% of the urban population lives. Countrywide, 9% of the population lives in *barriados* (squatter) settlements.

For *campesinos* (farmers), life is hard. A subsistence farmer in the interior might earn as little as US$8 per day, far below the national average of US$5510 per capita. In the Emberá villages of the Darién, traditional life continues as it has for hundreds of years. The majority of these people lack clean water and basic sanitation.

The middle and upper class largely reside in and around Panama City with a level of comfort similar to their counterparts in Europe and the USA. They live in large homes or apartments, have a maid, a car or two, and for the lucky few a second home on the beach or in the mountains. Cell phones are de rigueur. Vacations are often enjoyed in Europe or the USA. Most middle-class adults can speak some English and their children usually attend English-speaking schools.

People

The majority of Panamanians (70%) are *mestizo*, which is generally a mix of indigenous and Spanish descent. In truth, many non-black immigrants are also thrown into this category, including a sizable Chinese population – some people estimate that as much as 10% of the population is of Chinese ancestry. There are also a number of other sizable groups: about 14% of Panamanians are of African descent, 10% of Spanish descent, 5% of mixed African and Spanish descent, and 6% are indigenous. Generally, black Panamanians are mostly descendants of English-speaking West Indians, such as Jamaicans and Trinidadians, who were originally brought to Panama as laborers.

Of the several dozen native tribes that inhabited Panama when the Spanish arrived, few remain. The Kuna live on islands along the Caribbean coast in the autonomous region of the Comarca de Kuna Yala. Considered the most politically organized, they regularly send representatives to the national legislature. The Emberá and Wounaan inhabit the eastern Panamá province and the Darién; Panama's largest tribe, the Ngöbe-Buglé live in Chiriquí, Veraguas and Bocas del Toro. The Teribe inhabit Bocas del Toro Province, while the Bribrí are found along the Talamanca Reserve. Despite modernizing influences, each of Panama's indigenous groups maintains its own language and culture.

RELIGION

Panama City is home to scores of Catholic churches, Anglican churches filled with West Indians, synagogues, mosques, a shiny Greek Orthodox church, an impressive Hindu temple and a surreal Baha'i house of worship (the headquarters for Latin America).

Freedom of religion is constitutionally guaranteed in Panama, although the preeminence of Roman Catholicism is also officially recognized, with 85% of the country filling its ranks. In fact, children in school have the option to study theology, though it is not compulsory. Protestant denominations account for 12%, Muslims 4.4% and Baha'i 1.2%. Additionally, the country has approximately 3000 Jews (many of them recent immigrants from Israel), 24,000 Buddhists and 9000 Hindus.

In addition to the mainstream world religions, the various indigenous tribes of Panama have their own belief systems, although these are fading quickly due to the influence of Christian missionaries. As in other parts of Latin America, the evangelical movement is spreading like wildfire.

Although Catholics are the majority, only about 20% of them attend church regularly. The religious orders aren't particularly strong in Panama either – only about 25% of Catholic clergy are Panamanian while the rest are foreign missionaries.

ARTS

Panama's all-embracing music scene includes salsa, Latin and American jazz, traditional music from the central provinces, reggae, reggaetón and Latin, British and American rock 'n' roll. Their biggest export is world-renowned salsa singer Rubén Blades, who even ran for president in 1994, finishing third. The jazz composer and pianist Danilo Pérez is widely acclaimed by critics, while Los Rabanes produces classic Panamanian rock. Heavy on the accordion, Panamanian folk music (called *típico*), is well represented by Victorio Vergara and Samy and Sandra Sandoval. These days reggaetón (also known as *punta*) permeates all social levels in Panama, and its stars include Flex and the now-deceased Danger Man.

Several of Panama's best novels were written mid-20th century. *El ahogado* (The Drowned Man), a 1937 novel by Tristán Solarte, blends elements of the detective, gothic and psychological genres with a famous local myth. *El desván* (In the Garret), a 1954 novel by Ramón H Jurado, explores the emotional limits of the human condition. *Gamboa Road Gang,* by Joaquín Beleño, is about the political and social events surrounding the Panama Canal. Today's notable authors include poet and novelist Giovanna Benedetti, historical novelist Gloria Guardia and folk novelist Rosa María Britton.

The first prominent figure on Panama's art scene, French-trained Roberto Lewis (1874–1949) painted allegorical images in public buildings; look for those in the Palacio de las Garzas in Panama City. In 1913 Lewis became the director of Panama's first art academy, where he and his successor, Humberto Ivaldi (1909–47), educated a generation of artists. Among the school's students were Juan Manuel Cedeño and Isaac Benítez, and mid-20th-century painters Alfredo Sinclair, Guillermo Trujillo and Eudoro Silvera. Newer artists include Olga Sinclair and Brooke Alfaro.

SPORTS

Owing to a strong US legacy, baseball is the national pastime. Although Panama has no professional teams, amateur leagues play in stadiums throughout the country. In the US major leagues, Mariano Rivera, the record-setting Panamanian pitcher for the New York Yankees, is a national hero. The batting champ Rod Carew, another Panamanian star, was inducted into the Hall of Fame in 1991. Former NY Yankee Roberto Kelly is also fondly remembered.

Boxing is another popular spectator sport, and a source of local pride since Panama City native Roberto Durán won the world championship lightweight title in 1972. A legend, he went on to become the world champion in each of the welterweight (1980), light middleweight (1983) and super middleweight (1989) categories.

Panama's first Olympic gold came in 2008 when Irving Saladino won the long jump in Beijing.

ENVIRONMENT
The Land

Panama is both the narrowest and the southernmost country in Central America. The long S-shaped isthmus borders Costa Rica in the west and Colombia in the east. Its northern Caribbean coastline measures 1160km, compared to a 1690km Pacific coastline in the south, and its total land area is 78,056km. By comparison, Panama is slightly bigger than Ireland or Austria.

The Panama Canal effectively divides the country into eastern and western regions. Two mountain ranges run along Panama's spine in both the east and the west. The highest point in the country, Chiriquí's Volcán Barú, is also the country's only volcano.

Like all Central American countries, Panama has large, flat coastal lowlands, with huge banana plantations. There are about 480 rivers in Panama and 1518 islands near its shores. The two main island groups are the San Blás and Bocas del Toro Archipelagos on the Caribbean side, but most of the islands are on the Pacific side.

Wildlife

Panama's position as a narrow land bridge between two huge continents has given it a remarkable variety of plant and animal life. Species migrating between the continents have gathered in Panama, which means that it's possible to see South American armadillos, anteaters and sloths alongside North American tapirs, jaguars and deer. With its wide variety of native and migratory species, Panama is one of the world's best places for bird-watchers.

Panama has more than 940 recorded bird species and more than 10,000 plant species, in addition to 125 animal species found only here. The country's 105 rare and endangered species include scarlet macaws, harpy eagles (the national bird of Panama), golden frogs, jaguars and various species of sea turtle. Panama is one of the best places to see a quetzal. Five species of sea turtle can be seen here, while among the primates are capuchins, tamarins and squirrel, spider and howler monkeys.

Tropical rainforest is the dominant vegetation in the canal area, along the Caribbean coast and in most of the eastern half of the country. The Parque Nacional Darién protects much of Panama's largest tropical rainforest region. Other vegetation zones include Pacific coast grasslands, highland mountain forest, cloud forest on the highest peaks and mangrove forest on both coasts.

National Parks & Reserves

Panama has 12 national parks and more than two dozen officially protected areas. About one-quarter of Panama is set aside for conservation, while about 40% of land remains covered by forest. Panama also has more land set aside for habitat protection than any other Central American country, and it's forests contain the greatest number of species of all New World countries north of Colombia. Yet all of these statistics do not account for the fact that protected lands are often poorly protected.

In many of the national parks and protected areas, *mestizo* and indigenous villages are scattered about. In some scenarios, these communities help protect and maintain parks and wildlife. National environmental authority **ANAM** (Autoridad Nacional del Ambiente; Map p644; ☎ 315-0855; Panama City; ☉ 8am-4pm) manages the national-park system. The admission fee of US$5 (US$20 for marine parks) is paid at

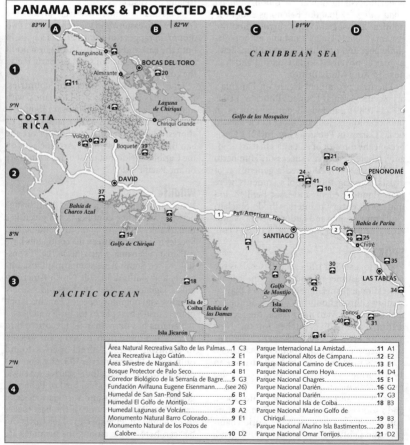

PANAMA PARKS & PROTECTED AREAS

Área Natural Recreativa Salto de las Palmas.......1 C3	Parque Internacional La Amistad................11 A1	
Área Recreativa Lago Gatún.........................2 E1	Parque Nacional Altos de Campana............12 E2	
Área Silvestre de Narganá.........................3 F1	Parque Nacional Camino de Cruces............13 E1	
Bosque Protector de Palo Seco.....................4 B1	Parque Nacional Cerro Hoya.....................14 D4	
Corredor Biológico de la Serranía de Bagre.....5 G3	Parque Nacional Chagres.........................15 E1	
Fundación Avifauna Eugene Eisenmann......(see 26)	Parque Nacional Darién...........................16 G2	
Humedal de San San-Pond Sak....................6 B1	Parque Nacional Darién...........................17 G3	
Humedal El Golfo de Montijo......................7 C3	Parque Nacional Isla de Coiba...................18 B3	
Humedal Lagunas de Volcán.......................8 A2	Parque Nacional Marino Golfo de	
Monumento Natural Barro Colorado..............9 E1	Chiriquí..19 B3	
Monumento Natural de los Pozos de	Parque Nacional Marino Isla Bastimentos.....20 B1	
Calobre...10 D2	Parque Nacional Omar Torrijos...................21 D2	

either the ANAM headquarters in Panama City, a regional ANAM office or at a park ranger station. Permits to camp or stay at an ANAM ranger station (US$5 to US$10) are obtained at the same places.

A few highlights include the following:

Parque Internacional La Amistad Home to several indigenous groups, pristine rainforest and abundant wildlife (p668).

Parque Nacional Darién Unesco World Heritage Site with 576,000 hectares of world-class wildlife-rich rainforest (p699).

Parque Nacional Isla de Coiba Includes the 493-sq-km Isla de Coiba, regarded by scientists as a biodiversity hot spot (p682).

Parque Nacional Marino Golfo de Chriquí Protects 25 islands and numerous coral reefs (p661).

Parque Nacional Marino Isla Bastimentos An important nature reserve for many species of Caribbean wildlife, including sea turtles (p679).

Parque Nacional Soberanía A bird-watcher's paradise in lush rainforest (p654).

Parque Nacional Volcán Barú Surrounds Panama's only volcano and highest peak, 3475m Volcán Barú (p667).

Parque Natural Metropolitano Tropical semideciduous forest within the city limits (p643).

Environmental Issues

Water pollution is a growing issue and most evident around Panama City and Colón, where 90% of Panamanians live. Untreated city sewage is discharged directly into coastal waters and canals. Mangroves, important for maintaining the balance of delicate marine

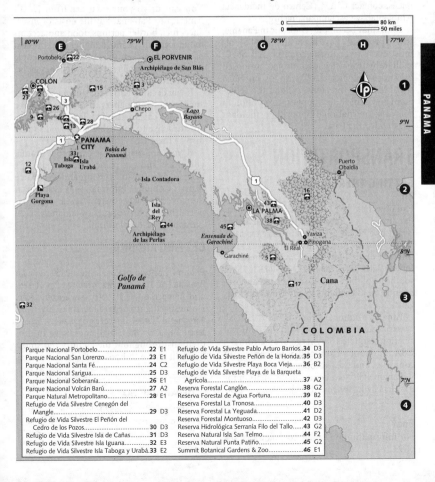

PANAMA

ecosystems, are being destroyed at an unsustainable pace. Coral reefs throughout the Caribbean are also endangered. Deforestation is also devastating, with 800 sq km of Darién rainforest felled in only a decade.

Gold mining is a hot issue in Panama. In 2009, the government approved a proposal by Petaquilla Gold to extract, refine and export gold in the province of Colón. Along with other environmental groups, the **Asociación Nacional para la Conservación de la Naturaleza** (National Association for the Conservation of Nature; Ancon; Map p640; ☎ 314-0060; www.ancon.org, in Spanish) sustains that the income promised the Panamanian state is little compensation compared to the environmental and socioeconomic damage the mine will cause. For more information on mining issues, contact CIAM (Centro de Incidencia Ambiental; www.ciampanama.org).

Dams may become an epidemic in Panama, where proposals have been submitted for almost every river in the country. A US$50-million hydroelectric dam project proposed by Hidroecologica del Teribe SA on Naso tribal territory threatens to flood the settlement and ruin water supplies. In addition to drawing international opposition, the dam has divided the tribe.

TRANSPORTATION

GETTING THERE & AWAY
Air
Panama has two international airports. Panama City's **Tocumen International Airport** (airport code PTY; ☎ 238-4322; www.tocumenpanama.aero), 35km from downtown, receives most international flights. In David, **Aeropuerto Enrique Malek** (airport code DAV; ☎ 721-1072) is 75km southeast of the Costa Rican border, and frequently handles flights to and from San José, Costa Rica.

Panama's national airline, **COPA** (☎ 238-1363; www.copaair.com) is compliant with international aviation standards. Flights go to and from the USA, numerous Latin and South American countries, and the Caribbean.

Panama City is a common destination for travelers flying to/from the region on an open-jaw ticket.

Boat
For information on sailing to Colombia, see p693.

Bus
At all three border crossings with Costa Rica (see p662) you can approach the border via local buses on either side, cross over, board another local bus and continue on your way. Be aware that the last buses leave the border crossings at Guabito and Río Sereno at 7pm; the last bus leaves Paso Canoas for Panama City at 9:30pm.

Panaline (☎ 227-8648; www.viajeros.com/panaline) and **Tica Bus** (☎ 262-2084; www.ticabus.com) have daily direct departures between San José in Costa Rica, and Panama City, departing from the Albrook bus terminal (Map p644). Reserve a few days in advance.

Car & Motorcycle
You can drive your own car from North America to Panama, but the costs of insurance, fuel, border permits, food and accommodations will be much higher than the cost of an airline ticket. As a result, most people opt to fly down and rent cars when they arrive in Panama City.

If you decide to drive to Panama, get insurance, have your papers in order and never leave your car unattended. US license plates are attractive to some thieves, so you should display these from inside the car.

If you are bringing a car into Panama, you must show a passport, valid driver's license, proof of ownership and insurance papers. Complete information is available at the government website: www.ana.gob.pa/portal/index.php/regimenes-aduaneros/120-vehiculos-de-turistas.html.

GETTING AROUND
Air
Panama has two major domestic carriers: **Air Panama** (☎ 316-9000; www.flyairpanama.com/tickets) and **Aeroperlas** (☎ 315-7500; www.aeroperlas.com). Domestic flights depart Panama City from **Aeropuerto Albrook** (Albrook airport, Marcos A Gelabert airport; Map p640; ☎ 315-0403) and arrive in destinations throughout the country. For most flights it's wise to book as far in advance as

---

DEPARTURE TAX

Panama levies a US$20 departure tax for outbound passengers on international flights but it is usually included in the price of your ticket.

possible – this is particularly true of flights to Comarca de Kuna Yala.

Even if you're on a tight budget, one-way domestic flights are never more than US$80, and you can sometimes turn a one- or two-day bus/boat journey into a 45-minute flight.

Bicycle

You can cycle through Panama easily enough, but cycling within larger Panamanian cities – particularly Panama City – is not wise. Roads are narrow, there are no bike lanes, motorists drive aggressively and frequent rains reduce motorists' visibility.

Outside the cities, roads tend to be in fine shape, although parts of the Interamericana are narrow, leaving little room to move aside should a car pass by. Lodging is rarely more than a day's bike ride away.

Boat

Boats are the chief means of transportation in several areas of Panama, particularly in Darién Province, the Archipiélago de Las Perlas, and the San Blás and Bocas del Toro island chains. While at least one eccentric soul has swum the entire length of the Panama Canal, a boat simplifies the transit enormously.

The backpacker mecca of Bocas del Toro on Isla Colón is accessible from Almirante by speedy and inexpensive water taxis – see p677 for details.

Colombian and Kuna merchant boats carry cargo and passengers along the San Blás coast between Colón and Puerto Obaldía, stopping at up to 48 islands to load and unload passengers and cargo. However, these boats are occasionally used to traffic narcotics, and they're often dangerously overloaded. Hiring a local boatman is a wiser option and usually included in lodging – see p691 for more details.

Since there aren't many roads in eastern Darién Province, boat travel is often the most feasible way to get from one town to another, especially during the rainy season. The boat of choice here is a *piragua* (long canoe), carved from the trunk of a giant ceiba tree. Their shallow hulls allow them to ride the many rivers of eastern Panama. Many such boats are motorized. See p698 for more details.

Bus

You can take a bus to just about any community in Panama that is reachable by road. Some are huge, new Mercedes Benzes equipped with air-con, movie screens and reclining seats. These top-of-the-line buses generally cruise long stretches of highway.

The more frequently used Toyota Coaster buses seat 28 people. Affectionately called *chivas*, these provide inexpensive transit to the interior and along the Interamericana.

Urban areas use old American school buses colorfully painted and nicknamed *diablos rojos* (red devils). They're a slow but cheap (US$0.25) way to get around Panama City.

Car & Motorcycle

Due to the low cost and ready availability of buses and taxis, it isn't necessary to rent a vehicle in Panama unless you intend to go to places far off the beaten track. Should you choose to rent, you'll find car-rental agencies in Panama City, David and Chitré. Several agencies also have offices at Tocumen International Airport in the capital. To rent a vehicle in Panama, you must be 25 years of age or older and present a passport and driver's license, though some places will rent vehicles to 21-year-olds if you ask politely, pay higher insurance costs, and supply them with a major credit card.

Prices for rentals in Panama run from US$35 per day for economy models to US$115 per day for a 4WD vehicle (*cuatro por cuatro*). When you rent, carefully inspect the car for minor dents and scratches, missing radio antennae, hubcaps and the spare tire. These damages *must* be noted on your rental agreement; otherwise you may be charged for them when you return the car.

There have been many reports of theft from rental cars, so don't leave valuables or luggage unattended. Many hotels provide parking areas for cars.

Hitchhiking

Hitchhiking is not as widespread in Panama as elsewhere in Central America. Most Panamanians travel by bus and travelers would do best to follow suit. The exception is holiday weekends, when buses are overflowing and hitchhiking may be the only way out of a place. If you get a ride, offer payment upon arrival – '*¿Cuánto le debo?*' ('How much do I owe you?') is the standard courtesy.

Hitchhiking is never entirely safe in any country, but it's not uncommon in rural areas of Panama.

Taxi

Panamanian taxis don't have meters, but there are some set fares. Taxis are cheap, and most of the time plentiful. However, they can be difficult to hail late at night and just before and during holidays. During these times, it's best to call for a radio taxi. Listings for reliable radio taxis can be found in the Yellow Pages of phone directories throughout Panama, under the heading Taxis.

More expensive 'sedan' taxis operate from upscale hotels and malls. These drivers charge at least twice what you'd pay a hailed cab.

Train

For details on the scenic train trip between Panama City and Colón, see p652.

PANAMA CITY

pop 446,000

Undoubtedly the most cosmopolitan capital in Central America, Panama City is both a gateway to the country's natural riches and a vibrant destination in its own right. As a thriving center for international banking and trade, Panama City sports a skyline of shimmering glass-and-steel towers. Residents often joke that Panama City is the 'Miami of the South,' except that more English is spoken.

Although there's no shortage of sophisticated dining and chic dance clubs, visitors to Panama City usually cozy up to the colonial district of Casco Viejo, a dilapidated neighborhood with cobblestones, old churches and scenic plazas reminiscent of old Havana. Casco Viejo lay crumbling on the edge of the sea for decades but has undergone extensive renovation in recent years.

Panama City is at times polluted and chaotic but it is dynamic too. Whether you measure the pulse of the city by the beat of the salsa clubs along Calle Uruguay, or by the staccato voices of street vendors, chances are you'll slip into the rhythm of this Latin playground.

HISTORY

Panama City was founded in 1519 by the Spanish governor Pedro Arias de Ávila (Pedrarias) not long after Balboa first saw the Pacific. The Spanish settlement quickly became an important center of government and church authorities. In 1671 the city was ransacked and destroyed by the Welsh pirate Sir Henry Morgan, leaving only the stone ruins of Panamá Viejo.

Three years later, the city was re-established in the peninsular area of Casco Viejo. Yet after the destruction of the Caribbean port at Portobelo in 1746, the Spanish overland trade route declined. Panama City subsequently faded in importance, though it returned to prominence in the 1850s when gold seekers on the way to California flooded across the isthmus by the Panama Railroad.

After Panama declared its independence from Colombia on November 3, 1903, Panama City was firmly established as the capital. Completed in 1914, the Panama Canal spurred the city to become a hub of international business and trade.

Today, Panama City is by far the wealthiest city in Central America, owed in large part to the Panama Canal. While foreign investment has waned with the 2009 world economic crisis, the pending expansion of the Panama Canal signals a possible future prosperity.

ORIENTATION

Panama City stretches about 20km along the Pacific coast, from the Panama Canal at its western end to the ruins of Panamá Viejo to the east.

Near the canal are Albrook airport, the Fort Amador Causeway and the wealthy Balboa and Ancón suburbs first built for the US canal and military workers. The Puente de las Américas (Bridge of the Americas) arches gracefully over the canal.

The colonial part of the city, Casco Viejo (also called San Felipe and Casco Antiguo), juts into the sea on the southwestern side of town. From here, two major roads head east through the city.

The main drag is Av Central, which runs past the cathedral in Casco Viejo to Parque Santa Ana and Plaza Cinco de Mayo; between these two plazas, the avenue is a pedestrian-only shopping street. At a fork further east, the avenue becomes Av Central España; the section that traverses the El Cangrejo business and financial district is called Vía España. The other part of the fork becomes Av 1 Norte (José D Espinar), Av Simón Bolívar and finally Vía Transístmica as it heads out of town and across the isthmus toward Colón.

Av 6 Sur branches off Av Central not far out of Casco Viejo and undergoes several name changes. It is called Av Balboa as it curves around the edge of the bay to Punta Paitilla, on the bay's eastern point; it then continues under various names past the Centro Atlapa to the ruins of Panamá Viejo. The 2009 expansion of Av Balboa created Cinta Costera, a waterfront green space with walking and biking paths that extends from El Cangrejo to Casco Viejo.

Generally, avenidas (avenues) run east–west, while calles (streets) run north–south. Av Central and Vía España form the boundary – avenidas south of Vía España are labeled *sur* (south) while calles east of Vía España are labeled *este*.

Maps
Just off Av Simón Bolívar opposite the Universidad de Panamá, the **Instituto Geográfico Nacional** (Tommy Guardia; Map p644; ☎ 236-2444; ☽ 8am-4pm Mon-Fri) has an excellent map collection for sale.

INFORMATION
Bookstores
Earl S Tupper Tropical Sciences Library/Smithsonian Tropical Research Institute (STRI; Map p644; ☎ 212-8000; ☽ 10am-4:30pm Mon-Fri) Stocks books on wildlife and the environment, also a library.
Exedra Books (Map p644; ☎ 264-4252; cnr Vías España & Brasil; ☽ 9:30am-9:30pm Mon-Sat, 11am-8:30pm Sun) Among Central America's best bookstores.

Emergency
Ambulance (☎ 228-2187, 229-1133)
Fire (☎ 103)
Police (☎ 104)

Internet Access
Most lodgings have wi-fi, and internet cafes are plentiful in Panama City, especially in the El Cangrejo banking district.
Business Center (Map p644; Calle 49A Oeste; per hr US$0.75; ☽ 24hr) Air-conditioned, fast internet.

Medical Services
Medicine in Panama, especially in Panama City, is of a high standard.
Centro Medico Paitilla (Map p644; ☎ 265-8800, 265-8883; Calle 53 Este & Av Balboa) Has well-trained physicians who speak both Spanish and English.

Money
There are plenty of 24-hour ATMs throughout the city.

HSBC (Map p644; Vía España) Changes Amex traveler's checks with no fee; US$5 transaction for other types.
Panacambios (Map p644; ☎ 223-1800; ground fl, Plaza Regency Bldg, Vía España; ☽ 8am-5pm Mon-Fri) Buys and sells international currencies.

Post
Many hotels sell stamps and some will mail guests' letters.
Main post office (Map p644; Av Balboa btwn Calles 30 & 31; ☽ 7am-5:45pm Mon-Fri, 7am-4:45pm Sat) Holds poste-restante items for 30 days.
Post office (Map p644; Plaza las Americas; ☽ 7am-5:45pm Mon-Fri, 7am-4:45pm Sat) Only post office for mailing packages.

Telephone
Tarjetas (phone cards) in denominations of US$3, US$5 and US$10 can be purchased at pharmacies for local and regional calls, which can be made from any card phone.

Tourist Information
ATP offices give out free maps but few ATP employees speak English.
ATP (Map p640; ☎ 226-7000; www.atp.gob.pa; Vía Israel, San Francisco; ☽ 8:30am-4:30pm Mon-Fri) Panama's tourism bureau is headquartered at the Centro Atlapa in the San Francisco neighborhood. Enter at the rear of the large building.
Autoridad Nacional del Ambiente (ANAM; Map p644; ☎ 315-0855; ☽ 8am-4pm) ANAM can occasionally provide maps and information on national parks. However, they are not organized to provide much assistance to tourists. Located inside Building 804 of the Albrook district.

DANGERS & ANNOYANCES
Casco Viejo is the focus of an ambitious urban renewal program, though it's still a work in progress. Generally speaking, the tip of the peninsula southeast of the Iglesia de la Merced is safe for tourists, especially since the area is heavily patrolled by police officers. But stay where it's well lit and around people. Take taxis at night.

Moving to the base of the peninsula, there are high-density slums where many tourists have been the target of criminals. Other high-crime areas include Curundú, El Chorrillo, Santa Ana, San Miguelito and Río Abajo.

Calle Uruguay, the clubbing hub of the city, also attracts opportunists. Don't take your full wallet out at night. We have heard reports of women going up to male travelers to hug them and taking their wallets.

When walking the city streets, be aware that drivers do not yield to pedestrians. Also, be on the lookout for missing storm and sewer covers, downed wires and high curbs.

SIGHTS
Casco Viejo

Following the destruction of the old city by Henry Morgan in 1671, the Spanish moved their city 8km southwest to a rocky peninsula on the foot of Cerro Ancón. The new location was easier to defend as the reefs prevented ships from approaching the city except at high tide. The new city was also easy to defend as it was surrounded by a massive wall, which is how Casco Viejo (Old Compound; Map p649) got its name.

In 1904, at the time construction began on the Panama Canal, all of Panama City existed where Casco Viejo stands today. As population growth and urban expansion pushed the urban boundaries further east, the city's elite left and the neighborhood rapidly deteriorated into an urban slum.

Today, the Unesco World Heritage Site of Casco Viejo is half-crumbling, half-high-end, with renovations giving a sense of how magnificent the area must have looked in past years. Part of the allure of strolling along Casco Viejo's cobbled streets is the dilapidated charm of the crumbling buildings, modest homes and ruins.

Restoration is still happening, so please be aware of your surroundings, and exercise caution (see p639).

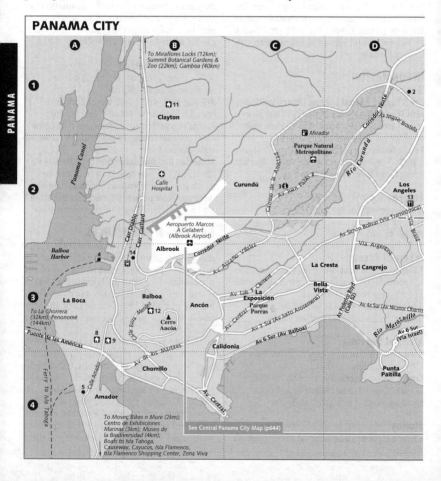

PANAMA CITY

PLAZA DE LA INDEPENDENCIA

This **plaza** (Map p649) is the heart of Casco Antiguo, and was the site where Panama declared its independence from Colombia on November 3, 1903.

IGLESIA DE SAN JOSÉ

This **church** (Map p649; Av A) protects the famous Altar de Oro (Golden Altar), salvaged after Henry Morgan sacked Panamá Viejo. According to local legend, when word came of the pirate's impending attack, a priest painted the altar black to disguise it. The priest told Morgan that the famous altar had been stolen by another pirate, and convinced Morgan to donate handsomely for its replacement. Morgan is said to have told the priest, 'I don't know why,

but I think you are more of a pirate than I am.' Whatever the truth, the baroque altar was later moved from the old city to the present site.

TEATRO NACIONAL

Built in 1907, the interior of this ornate **theater** (Map p649; ☎ 262-3525; Av B) has been completely restored, and boasts red and gold decorations, a once-magnificent ceiling mural by Roberto Lewis and an impressive crystal chandelier. Performances are still held here; for information or a look around, visit the office at the side of the building.

PLAZA DE FRANCIA

At the tip of the point, this **plaza** (Map p649) displays large stone tablets and statues dictating

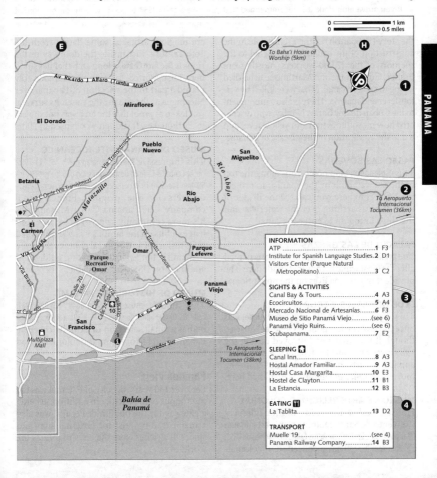

INFORMATION
ATP 1 F3
Institute for Spanish Language Studies. 2 D1
Visitors Center (Parque Natural
   Metropolitano) 3 C2

SIGHTS & ACTIVITIES
Canal Bay & Tours....................... 4 A3
Ecocircuitos.............................. 5 A4
Mercado Nacional de Artesanías........ 6 F3
Museo de Sitio Panamá Viejo.......... (see 6)
Panamá Viejo Ruins...................... (see 6)
Scubapanama.............................. 7 E2

SLEEPING
Canal Inn.................................. 8 A3
Hostal Amador Familiar................. 9 A3
Hostal Casa Margarita.................. 10 E3
Hostel de Clayton....................... 11 B1
La Estancia................................ 12 B3

EATING
La Tablita.................................. 13 D2

TRANSPORT
Muelle 19.................................. (see 4)
Panama Railway Company.............. 14 B3

PANAMA

GETTING INTO TOWN

From the Airports

Tocumen International Airport is 35km northeast of the city center. The cheapest way to get into the city is to exit the terminal, cross the street (to the bus shelter) and catch a city-bound bus. Much faster and costlier, taxis can be hired at the Transportes Turísticos desk at the airport exit, next to posted prices. Or take a *colectivo* (shared taxi) for US$11 per person (for three or more passengers).

Buses to Tocumen depart every 15 minutes from the Albrook Terminal. If you take the Cinta Costera route bus (US$1, one hour), it's twice as fast as the others and air-conditioned. A taxi from downtown to the airport should cost no more than US$20, leaving the airport they tend to charge more (US$25 to US$30).

The Albrook airport north of Cerro Ancón handles domestic flights. The easiest way to get to/from the airport is by taxi, and the ride should be between US$3 and US$5.

From the Bus Terminal

All long-distance buses arrive at the Albrook bus terminal; from here there are connections throughout the city. Routes (such as Vía España, Panamá Viejo) are displayed in the front window and cost US$0.25. If you arrive after dark, it is recommended that you take a taxi (US$3 to US$5) to your destination.

---

the story (in Spanish) of the French role in the construction of the canal. It's dedicated to the memory of the 22,000 workers, mostly from France, Guadeloupe and Martinique, who died trying to create a canal. Most were killed by yellow fever and malaria. There is also a monument to the Cuban doctor Carlos J Finlay, who discovered how mosquitoes transmit yellow fever and led to the eradication of the disease in Panama.

PASEO LAS BÓVEDAS

This **esplanade** (Map p649) runs along the top of the sea wall built by the Spanish to protect the city. From here, you can see the Bridge of the Americas arching over the waterway and the ships lining up to enter the canal.

PALACIO DE LAS GARZAS

The **presidential palace** (Map p649; Av Alfaro) is named after the great white herons that reside here. The president of Panama lives on the upper floor.

CLUB DE CLASES Y TROPAS

This abandoned **ruin** (Map p649; Calle 1a Oeste) was once the favorite hangout of General Noriega, though it was virtually destroyed during the 1989 invasion. Some fresh paint was selectively applied in early 2000, when scenes from the movie *The Tailor of Panama* were filmed here.

MUSEO DE ARTE RELIGIOSO COLONIAL

Housed beside the ruins of the Iglesia y Convento de Santo Domingo, this **art museum** (Map p649; ☎ 228-2897; cnr Av A & Calle 3 Este; admission US$1; ☼ 8am-4pm Tue-Sat) has a collection of colonial-

era religious artifacts, some dating from the 16th century. Just inside the doorway of the ruins is the **Arco Chato**, a long arch that has stood here, unsupported, for centuries. It reportedly played a part in the selection of Panama over Nicaragua as the site for the canal: its survival was taken as proof that the area was not subject to earthquakes. It suddenly collapsed in 2003.

MUSEO DEL CANAL INTEROCEÁNICO

This impressive **museum** (Map p649; ☎ 211-1995; cnr Av Central & Calle 6a Oeste; admission US$2; ☼ 9:30am-5:30pm Tue-Sun) is housed in the former headquarters for the original French canal company. The Panama Canal Museum (as it's more commonly known) presents excellent exhibits on the famous waterway, framed in its historical and political context. Signs are in Spanish, but English-speaking guides and audio tours (US$5) are available.

MUSEO DE HISTORIA DE PANAMÁ

This modest **museum** (Map p649; ☎ 228-6231; Calle 6a Oeste; admission free; ☼ 8:30am-3:30pm Mon-Fri) has a small selection of exhibits covering Panamanian history from the colonial period to the modern era.

Panamá Viejo

For over 150 years, the city of Panamá was the metropolis of the Pacific. In addition to being a gateway for the bullion of Peru, it was also a major trading post for Oriental silks and spices. It's riches were the envy of pirates the world over.

When Panamá fell to Henry Morgan in 1671, the city contained a magnificent cathedral, several beautiful churches, thousands of colonial homes and hundreds of warehouses stocked with foreign goods. Plundering reduced Panamá Viejo to mere beams and stone blocks.

Although the ruins were left intact as recently as 1950, the expansion of the capital resulted in the transformation of Panamá into a squatter camp. Although the government declared the ruins a protected site in 1976 (Unesco followed suit in 1997), most of the old city had already been dismantled and overrun.

Today much of Panamá Viejo lies buried under a poor residential neighborhood, though the ruins are definitely worth visiting, even if only to stand on the hallowed grounds of one of North America's important colonial cities.

PANAMÁ VIEJO RUINS

The **ruins** (Map p640) of Panamá Viejo, founded in 1519, are not fenced in, so you can visit them anytime, though it's probably best to explore the area during the daylight hours. The ruins cover a large area, and you can still see the cathedral with its stone tower, the plaza beside it, the convent of Santo Domingo, the Iglesia de San José, the hospital of San Juan de Dios and the city hall.

MERCADO NACIONAL DE ARTESANÍAS

Panamá Viejo buses (US$0.25) coming from Av Balboa will drop you off at this **artisans market** (National Artisans Market; Map p640; 9am-6pm) behind the first remnant of ruins as you approach from Panama City.

MUSEO DE SITIO PANAMÁ VIEJO

This **museum** (Map p640; admission US$3; 9am-5pm) contains a rather impressive scale model of Panamá Viejo prior to 1671, as well as a few surviving colonial artifacts. All signs are in Spanish, though a brochure and tape recording recount the site's history in English.

Causeway

At the Pacific entrance to the Panama Canal, a 2km palm-tree-lined *calzada* (causeway) connects the four small islands of Naos, Culebra, Perico and Flamenco to the mainland. The Causeway is the popular place to be in the early morning and late afternoon, when residents walk, jog, skate, cycle or simply escape the noise and pollution of the city. The Causeway also offers sweeping views of the skyline and the old city, with flocks of brown pelicans diving into the sea.

On the Causeway, **Bikes n More** (314-0103; 8am-6pm Sat & Sun) operates a booth where you can rent a bicycle.

The interesting **Centro de Exhibiciones Marines** (212-8000 ext 2366; admission US$1; 1-5pm Tue-Fri, 10am-5pm Sat & Sun), operated by the Smithsonian Tropical Research Institute (STRI), includes an informative marine museum with signs in English and Spanish, two small aquariums and a nature trail through a patch of dry forest containing sloths and iguanas.

At the time of publication, construction was well underway on the **Museo de la Biodiversidad** (Museum of Biodiversity; www.biomuseo panama.org; Causeway), Panama's new landmark museum with extensive botanical gardens. World-renowned architect Frank Gehry penned this controversial design of crumpled multicolor forms. Located near the tip of the Causeway, it is slated to open in 2011.

Isla Flamenco is home to an enormous shopping center with open-air restaurants, upscale bars and clubs.

The easiest way to reach the Causeway is by taxi (US$4 to US$6).

Parque Natural Metropolitano

Up on a hill, north of downtown, this 265-hectare national park (Map p640) protects a wild area of tropical forest within the city limits. It has two main walking trails, the **Nature Trail** and the **Tití Monkey Trail**, which join to form one long loop. The 150m-high **mirador** (lookout) offers views of Panama City, the bay and the canal all the way to the Miraflores Locks.

Mammals in the park include *tití* monkeys, anteaters, sloths and white-tailed deer; reptiles include iguanas, turtles and tortoises. More than 250 bird species have been spotted here.

The park was the site of an important battle during the US invasion to oust Noriega. The concrete structures just past the park entrance were used during WWII as a testing and assembly plant for aircraft engines.

The park is bordered on the west and north by Camino de la Amistad; Av Juan Pablo II runs right through the park. For a self-guided tour, get a pamphlet in Spanish and English at the **visitors center** (Map p640; 232-5516; admission

PANAMA

CENTRAL PANAMA CITY

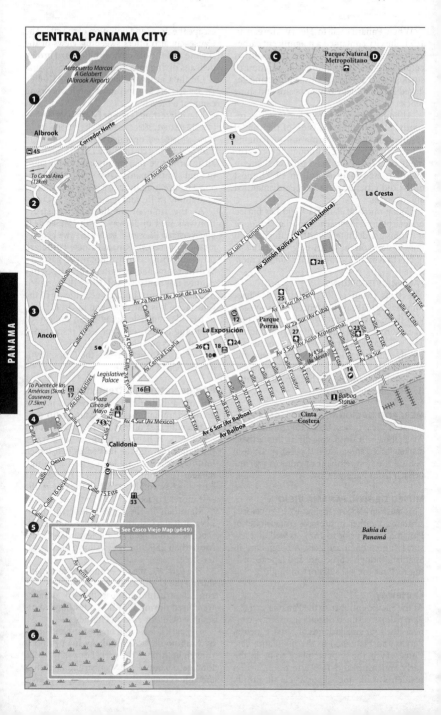

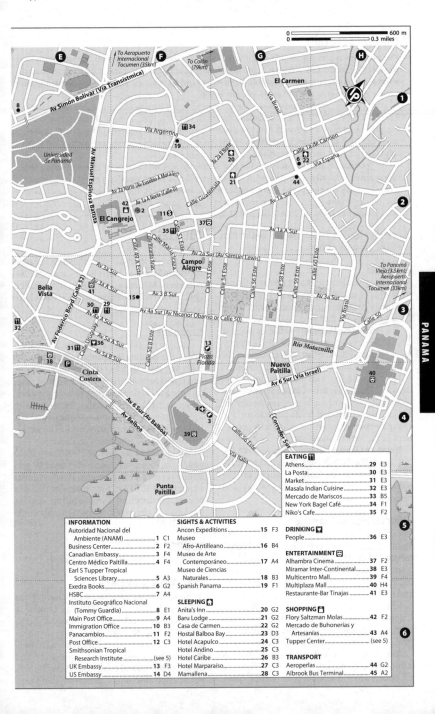

PANAMA

THE JAZZ SOLUTION

This once down-and-out section of the city is writing a new chapter. Making a strong push towards revitalization, Casco Viejo is home to dozens of new restaurants, cafes, shops and renovated historic buildings. In the midst of this architectural revival, another, less tangible one struggles to take place: that of the Panamanian community.

Jazz great and native Panamanian Danilo Perez returned here to establish **Fundación Danilo Perez** (Map p649; ☎ 211-0272; www.fundaciondaniloperez.com; Av A 1069), a musical foundation which has generated over a million dollars in scholarships, many to underprivileged youth. According to Perez, 'Through the discipline of music we can create relevant leaders and good citizens. We can solve many of society's problems.'

The foundation also sponsors the Panama Jazz Festival, a wildly popular city-wide event featuring artists from all over the world. It is held every January. The weeklong event culminates in a free Saturday concert in the Casco's Plaza de la Independencia. The foundation in Casco Viejo also houses a library and musical museum and is open to the public.

US$1; 8am-5pm Mon-Fri, 8am-1pm Sat), about 40m north of the park entrance.

Museums
Sadly, the establishment and preservation of museums is not a governmental priority in Panama City and many collections have not been properly maintained.

The fascinating **Museo Afro-Antillano** (Map p644; ☎ 262-5348; cnr Av Justo Arosemena & Calle 24 Este; admission US$1; 8:30am-3:30pm Tue-Sat) has exhibits on the history of Panama's West Indian community.

Near Av de los Mártires in the Ancón district, **Museo de Arte Contemporáneo** (Map p644; ☎ 262-8012; admission free; 9am-4pm Mon-Fri, 9am-noon Sat, 9am-3pm Sun) hosts permanent and changing contemporary art exhibits by prominent Latin American artists.

Museo de Ciencias Naturales (Map p644; ☎ 225-0645; Av Cuba btwn Calles 29 Este & 30 Este; admission US$1; 9am-3:45pm Tue-Sat) features works on the natural sciences, flora, fauna, geology and paleontology of Panama.

Baha'i House of Worship
Located 11km from downtown on the Transisthmian Hwy, the white-domed **Baha'i temple** (☎ 231-1137; 10am-6pm) looms like a giant egg atop the crest of a hill. It serves all of Latin America and is surprisingly beautiful and breezy.

Information about the faith is available in English and Spanish; readings from the Baha'i writings (also in English and Spanish) are held Sunday mornings at 10am. Any bus to Colón can let you off on the highway, but it's a long walk up the hill. A taxi from Panama City costs around US$20, plus waiting time.

COURSES
Dance
You can try open-air salsa dancing at **Parque Recreativo Omar** (see Map p640). Classes (US$1) run every Saturday at 8:30am. To practice, check out Havana Panamá (p651) in Casco Viejo.

Language
Located in the suburban El Dorado neighborhood, the **Institute for Spanish Language Studies** (ILERI; Map p640; ☎ 260-4424; http://isls.com/panama; Camino de la Amistad) offers four hours of one-on-one instruction per day, five days a week. Costs start at US$395 for the first week (with lodging, meals, trips and activities), and decrease with each subsequent week. The weekly rate without lodging starts at US$265.

Spanish Panama (Map p644; ☎ 213-3121; www.spanish panama.com; Via Argentina, Edificio Americana No 1A) gets strong reviews from travelers. It has a similar structure to ILERI's: four hours of one-on-one classes daily and dorm accommodations for US$375 per week (long-term discounts are available).

TOURS
For listings, please see the Directory, p707.

FESTIVALS & EVENTS
Although not as famous as the celebrations in Rio de Janeiro or New Orleans, **Carnaval** in Panama City is celebrated with equal merriment and wild abandon during the days preceding Ash Wednesday. From Saturday until the following Tuesday, work is put away, and masks, costumes and confetti are brought forth. For a period of 96 hours, almost anything goes.

PANAMA

The **Panama Jazz Festival** (www.panamajazzfestival .com) draws hundreds of thousands of spectators for a weeklong festival in mid-January. For more information, see opposite.

For a list of events, check out the arts section in the Sunday edition of *La Prensa* as well as the back pages of the *Panama News*.

SLEEPING
Casco Viejo

As Casco Viejo (Map p649) sees extensive renovation, this old-world charmer is becoming an excellent option for lodging. Advantages include the great number of restaurants and cafes and its walkability.

Hospedaje Casco Viejo (☎ 211-2027; www.hospedaje cascoviejo.com; Calle 8a Oeste; dm US$9, d with/without bathroom US$18/16; P ☐) Every inch of this old hostel has seen heavy use, from the worn tile bathrooms to bowing beds, but it's hard to get picky at these prices. The best room is the dormitory, with well-spaced single beds. While service is laissez-faire, perks include a communal kitchen, wi-fi and an open-air courtyard. It's on a quiet side street next to the Iglesia de San José.

Luna's Castle (☎ 262-1540; www.lunascastlehostel .com; Calle 9a Este; dm/d/tr incl breakfast US$12/28/36; ☐ ☎) Housed in a creaky, colonial mansion, Luna's Castle blends historic Spanish colonial architecture with funky, laid-back backpacker vibes. Ample dorms are stacked with bunks and the shared bathrooms get a frequent scrub. Perks include internet, laundry service and a basement movie house showing your favorite flicks. A bit loony and very friendly, this is the kind of hostel people keep talking about long after their trip ends.

La Exposición & Bella Vista

The neighborhoods of La Exposición and Bella Vista (Map p644) are home to a number of fairly standard budget and midrange hotels.

Mamallena (☎ 6538-9745; www.mamallena.com; Calle Maria Icaza; dm/d incl breakfast US$11/28; ☐ ☒) For a small, intimate hostel, Mamallena is a top pick. Run by Stuart, an over-working, overplaying Aussie, this place nails the mark on

---

SPEAK PANAMEÑO

You can express your appreciation with *chévere* (cool); *buena leche* is good luck; *un pinta* means a beer while *vaina* just means thing.

---

service. Desk service is 24 hours and guests get free wireless and computer use, pancake breakfasts and access to a DVD library. High-ceiling dorms have air-con at night and the cute motel-style doubles offer considerable privacy. The house itself is homey and cool, on a residential street that's somehow survived the wrecking ball.

Hostal Balboa Bay (☎ 227-6182; Calle 39 No 21; dm incl breakfast US$13, s/d with air-con US$30/40; ☒ ☐) Though quiet and clean, this central hostel gets less traffic than the competition. Service isn't a strong suit, but doubles are ample and airy. The dorm has single beds lined up in a tight row. There's a small kitchen facility and wi-fi costs $5 extra.

Hotel Acapulco (☎ 225-3832; Calle 30 Este; s/d US$39/42; P ☒) A discernible step up from the standard hotel fare that runs chock-a-block in this part of town, the Acapulco offers a certain no-nonsense style. Spotless rooms offer air-con, hot-water showers and balconies off the French doors (make sure yours locks).

Hotel Andino (☎ 225-1162; Calle 35; s/d US$39/50; P ☒) Rooms at the Andino come up short on charm, but they're big, clean and equipped like a start-up apartment. Request a king-size and you can also get a two-burner stove for some self-catering adventures. If you don't feel like leaving the hotel, there's a bar and restaurant, making it a convenient choice to crash overnight between bus departures.

Hotel Marparaíso (☎ 227-6767; Calle 34 Este; s/d incl breakfast US$40/50; P ☒ ☐) If counting pennies, consider that your stay here includes a free airport pickup, satellite TV, wi-fi and continental breakfast. Rooms have bright tropical bedspreads and smell a bit too much of deodorizer. Try for one on the 4th floor or higher. A chill bar and restaurant is a good place to chat up other travelers.

Hotel Caribe (☎ 225-0404; www.caribehotel.net; cnr Calle 28 Este & Av Perú; d/tr incl breakfast US$52/75; P ☒ ☒) Psychedelic and slightly retro – by default rather than design – this large casino-hotel is good on price but short on atmosphere. Its best feature is a rooftop pool overlooking the city. While central, the neighborhood tends to be a little rough.

El Cangrejo & San Francisco

The modern banking district of El Cangrejo is central but also one of the noisier spots in town.

Anita's Inn (Map p644; ☎ 213-3121; www.hostelspanama .com; Av 2a B Norte; dm US$10, dm/s/d without bathroom

US$13/33/39; ⊠ 🖵) Affiliated with Spanish Panama (p646), this student guesthouse occupies a plain peach-colored building. While the location is good, the rooms could use some love and personal presence.

Casa de Carmen (Map p644; ☎ 263-4366; www.lacasa decarmen.com; Calle 1a de Carmen 32, El Carmen; dm/s/d without bathroom US$12/30/35, d US$55; 🅿 ⊠ 🖵) In a cozy colonial near Vía Brasil, this congenial home sports fresh rooms with high ceilings. Guests of all ages congregate in the communal kitchen, lounge area or on the lush hammock patio. The owners offer a wealth of knowledge of the city and countryside. Be sure to book ahead.

Baru Lodge (Map p644; ☎ 393-2340; www.barulodge .com; Calle 2nda Norte H-7, El Carmen; s/d incl breakfast US$55/88; ⊠ 🖵) Tasteful and cordial, this subdued inn sits on a residential street central to the action. Rooms are sleek and modern, with subdued colors and soft lighting. Cable TV, wi-fi, air-con and air purifiers are among the perks. The garden patio has wicker seating where continental breakfasts are served and soon will have a pool.

ourpick Hostal Casa Margarita (Map p640; ☎ 394-5557; www.hostalcasamargarita.com; Calle Los Claveles, casa 97, San Francisco; s/d/tr/q incl breakfast US$66/77/110/132; 🅿 ⊠ 🖵) Irresistibly cozy and chic, this is a great addition to the Panama City B&B scene. Rooms in this stucco house are smart and simple, with colorful touches, flat-screen TVs and minifridges. A huge garden and breakfast patio offers ample space to lounge or dally over a complete breakfast with fresh fruit. Guests also get kitchen use and wi-fi, but the real treasure here is the warm Venezuelan family.

Canal Zone

For quieter digs, this is your best bet. The neighborhood of Balboa sits right before the Causeway, while Clayton is further out, adjacent to Miraflores Locks. You're a taxi ride away from downtown, but staying out here is a welcome respite from the noise and congestion of Panama City.

Hostel de Clayton (☎ 317-1634; www.hosteldeclayton .com; Calle Guanabana, Edificio 605B, Clayton; dm US$14, d with/without bathroom US$40/35; 🅿 ⊠ 🖵) Reminiscent of an army barracks, this friendly hostel is located on the site of the former US army base of Clayton, a well-heeled residential area. The rooms and amenities are perfectly suited to the budget traveler, but for those without a rental car or the budget for taxis, the location leaves you adrift in suburbia.

Hostal Amador Familiar (☎ 314-1251; www .hostalamadorfamiliar.com; Calle Akee, casa 1519, Balboa; dm incl breakfast US$15; d with fan/air-con US$30/35 🅿 ⊠ 🖵 🛜) A big yellow canal house with airy, high-ceiling bedrooms and a private garden with open-air kitchen. Breakfast comes with cereal or eggs, toast and coffee. Tiled rooms with rod iron beds and sashed windows sport the quirks and creaks of old buildings. The location is just off the Causeway, US$3 to downtown by taxi.

Canal Inn (☎ 314-0112; www.canal-inn.com; Calle Ernesto J Castillero, Casa 7, Balboa; s/d incl breakfast US$77/88; 🅿 ⊠ 🖵 🛜 🏊) Catering mostly to couples and older independent travelers, this personable inn offers excellent service and a selection of snug, bright rooms. Some mattresses are worthier than others. The best room is No 17, sporting its own balcony. While the ethnic decor gets a little overly enthusiastic, it's still a sweet and relaxing spot. The quiet neighborhood is ideal for jogging or strolling out to the Causeway.

La Estancia (☎ 314-1417; www.bedandbreakfast panama.com; Casa 35, Quarry Heights, Ancón; d incl breakfast US$83; 🅿 ⊠ 🖵 🛜) Perched atop Cerro Ancón and surrounded by tropical flora and fauna, La Estancia is a small cement apartment building converted into a tranquil B&B. Rooms are clean and uncluttered but slim on personality. Breakfasts are excellent, best enjoyed on the patio while gazing upon the Puente de las Américas. It's a US$5 to downtown by taxi.

EATING

Panama City is a paradise for those who love to dine out. There are literally hundreds of places to eat, from holes in the wall to garden bistros.

Casco Viejo

Casco Viejo hosts a unique mix of upscale eateries, and the city's cheapest dives.

Café Coca Cola (Map p649; Av Central; plates US$1-3; ⏱ 7:30am-11pm) A neighborhood institution, this old-school diner serves hearty platefuls of rice, beans and the featured meat of the day, all with air-conditioning.

Granclement (Map p649; Av Central; gelato US$2.50-3.50; ⏱ noon-8pm) Pure pleasure defines these intense tropical fruit gelatos and intense, creamy flavors like basil, orange-chocolate and ginger. A few scoops of these fussy French creations sweeten any stroll through the Casco.

ourpick Mercado de Mariscos (Map p644; Av Balboa; mains US$2.50-8; ⏱ lunch Mon-Sat) Above a bristling fish market in a new building donated by Japan, this unassuming restaurant is *the* place to get your seafood fix. *Ceviche* starts at US$2.50 and you can also get a whole fried fish with salad (US$5). A cavernous bowl of 'Get Up Lazarus' soup supposedly cures hangovers.

Super Gourmet (Map p649; Av A; sandwiches US$3.50-9; 7am-7pm Mon-Sat, 10am-3pm Sun;) Stocking gourmet goods that range from wine to wasabi peas, this is the perfect pre-picnic stop. You can also grab soup or a baguette deli sandwich with roasted chicken and peppers, pastrami or three cheeses; the half-portion is probably enough.

Diablo Rosso (Map p649; Av A; lunch US$3.50-6; 9am-7pm Mon-Sat) This art cafe with biting social commentary and quirky folk art would be perfectly at home in Buenos Aires' Palermo.

You can also enjoy a frothy cup of cappuccino, cheesy *arepas* (corn cakes) piled high with eggs, hearty vegetarian soup or spinach quesadillas. Check for art openings or Tuesday night dinner-and-a-movie.

Frit Arte (Map p649; Av Central; set menu US$3.80; 8am-4pm Mon-Sat) A fine lunchtime fix with a cheap rotating menu with home-cooked dishes. You can also get breakfast, a variety of vegetarian dishes and *fritura* (fried food) such as gourmet *carimañolas* (deep-fried rolls with meat and yucca) stuffed with gouda, or grilled *arepas*. Service is superfriendly and the walls are lined with kooky crafts and art for sale.

Café Per Due (Map p649; Av A; pizza US$5-8; 9am-10pm Tue-Sun) Our pick for a quick bite, this casual Italian-run eatery serves scrumptious

CASCO VIEJO

0 ——— 200 m
0 ——— 0.1 miles

PANAMA

INFORMATION
French Embassy	**1** B4
Fundación Danilo Perez	**2** A2
Tourist Police	**3** C3

SIGHTS & ACTIVITIES
Club de Clases y Tropas	**4** C3
Iglesia de San José	**5** A2
Museo de Arte Religioso Colonial	**6** B3
Museo de Historia de Panamá	**7** B3
Museo del Canal Interoceánico	**8** B3
Palacio de las Garzas	**9** C2
Plaza de Francia	**10** B4
Plaza de la Independencia	**11** B2
Teatro Nacional	**12** C3

SLEEPING
Hospedaje Casco Viejo	**13** A3
Luna's Castle	**14** B1

EATING
Café Coca Cola	**15** A1
Café Per Due	**16** B3
Diablo Rosso	**17** B3
Frit Arte	**18** B3
Granclement	**19** B3
Manolo Caracol	**20** C3
Super Gourmet	**21** B3

DRINKING
Bar Relic	**22** B1
Havana Panamá	**23** B1

thin-crust pizzas. Check out the bacon and blue cheese or the fresh tomato, basil and garlic. Mozzarella is not skimped on. For privacy, try the tiny brick courtyard with a couple of tables.

Manolo Caracol (Map p649; ☎ 228-4640; Av Central; 5-course lunch US$25; ◷ noon-3pm & 7-10:30pm Mon-Fri, 7-11pm Sat) Manolo's immerses you in tropical tastes. Tiny courses pair opposite flavors and textures, such as beef tongue sprinkled in sea salt, fire-roasted lobster drizzled in olive oil, and tart mango salad with crunchy greens. Not every dish sings, but the fun is adventuring through them in a lovely colonial atmosphere. Drinks are extra.

El Cangrejo & Bella Vista

La Tablita (Map p640; Transistmica; mains US$2-8) Classic in the beat-up, rundown sense of the word, La Tablita is a smoking open-air grill with worn checkered tiles, surly wait service and delicious charred meat.

Niko's Cafe (Map p644; Calle 51 Este near Vía España; mains US$3-8; ◷ 24hr) Spawned from a Greek immigrant who once sold food from a cart, Niko's has become one of Panama City's most successful chains, with locations throughout the city. These sprawling 24-hour cafeterias serve hearty portions of inexpensive food ranging from made-to-order breakfasts, Panamanian dishes and desserts.

New York Bagel Café (Map p644; Plaza Cabeza de Einstein, near Vía Argentina; mains US$3-8; ◷ 7am-8pm Mon-Fri, 8am-8pm Sat, 8am-3pm Sun; ☞) More San Francisco than Brooklyn, this fully American creation nonetheless packs in expats with fresh baked bagels, lox and oversized breakfasts. The setting offers jazz, soft sofas and an assortment of laptop geeks.

Athens (Map p644; Calle 50, Bella Vista; mains US$5; ◷ 11am-11:30pm) Fresh, delicious and casual, this Greek eatery serves warm pitas with hummus, satisfying Greek salads, gyros and pizzas. It's ideal for families and large groups, with extensive opening hours and plenty of indoor and outdoor seating.

Masala Indian Cuisine (Map p644; ☎ 225-0105; Calle 42 Este, Bella Vista; mains US$8; ◷ noon-11pm) A fiery plate of Indian curry and an ice-cold Kingfisher lager are a perfect match for the tropical climate. Cozied up with floor pillows and colorful textiles, Masala offers a full complement of traditional dishes ranging from tikka masala to lamb vindaloo, with a good selection for vegetarians.

Market (Map p644; Calle Uruguay & Calle 47, Bella Vista; mains US$9-28) With blackboard specials, brick and bustle, this bistro is more Manhattan than Calle Uruguay, but here it is. The emphasis is on style and quality. Salads come in oversized bowls and you can top off your order of Angus beef with interesting sides such as creamed spinach or green beans with bacon. It is wildly popular for weekend brunch.

La Posta (Map p644; ☎ 269-1076; www.lapostapanama .com; Calle Uruguay, Bella Vista; mains US$11-24; ◷ noon-2:30pm & 7-10:30pm Mon-Sat) For contemporary Panamanian cuisine, this is the place. The tropical setting says hacienda and a seasonal menu features local meats and produce. Start with sashimi-style fish with seared herb crust and choose from flavorful mains such as seafood risotto or wood-fire roasted pork chops. Mangrove wood supplies a sweet smoky flavor to dishes; the restaurant also supports its reforestation. The warm chocolate cake made with organic Bocas chocolate oozes with goodness.

DRINKING

Bars and clubs open and close with alarming frequency in Panama City, where the nightlife is stylish, sophisticated and fairly pricey. The well-to-do denizens love a good scene, so it's worth scrubbing up, donning nice threads and parting with a bit dough. You might regret blowing your budget in the morning, but that's the price you pay to party with the beautiful people.

Big areas for nightlife include Casco Viejo, Bella Vista and the Causeway. Vía Argentina is an up-and-coming spot – look for new bars and clubs on this fashionable avenue. The district of Bella Vista is home to Calle Uruguay, a strip of trendy bars and clubs reminiscent of Miami's South Beach. The scene is young and you can expect to pay to play here. Moreover, clubs change hands quickly in this neighborhood, so it's best to ask locals about the latest and greatest additions.

For the latest on what's happening in the city, be sure to pick up a copy of *La Prensa* (www.prensa.com, in Spanish). Weekend listings are available in the Thursday and Friday editions or on its website; look for the 'De Noche' section.

Generally, the best gay scene in Panama City is actually found at the city's hippest bars and clubs, not in gay-specific establishments. Website www.farraurbana.com (in Spanish) lists new gay clubs as well as upcoming parties.

Although half the fun of partying it up in Panama City is finding a hidden gem, here's a few of our favorite spots to get you started.

Bar Relic (Map p649; Calle 9a Este; 8:30pm-late Tue-Sat) Wildly popular with travelers and hip young Panamanians, this cavernous hostel bar knows the right thing at the right time. Service is friendly and patrons easily mingle in the ample courtyard with shared picnic tables. Not only are you outside (a rarity in Panama City bars) but you're partying next to the historic wall of the city.

Cayucos (Map p640; Causeway) Located on the Causeway, this open-air resto-bar sits on the water with excellent views of the city. While more a restaurant than bar, it's perfect for the first cold beer of the evening.

Havana Panamá (Map p649; Av Alfaro; cover US$10; Thu-Sat) Old school rules this vintage salsa bar replete with bandstand and leather booths. You'll have to don your finest threads (there's a dress code) and enter behind a swooshy velvet curtain. A salsa band rocks the house.

People (Map p644; Calle Uruguay) A favored spot for the beautiful people and their hangers-on, this polished club attracts a babyfaced crowd to dance to pop hits.

Zona Viva (Map p640; Isla Flamenco, Amador) On the Causeway, Zona Viva is a closed compound hosting a number of nightlife spots, ranging from packed dance clubs to more low-key watering holes. Shop around and pick the theme that you like, be it a pirate bar or an Egyptian club. For some it's *pura racataca* (without class), for others it's a fishbowl of fun. Identification is checked at the gate to the complex, so the area is considered more secure than most.

ENTERTAINMENT

If you're not looking to get blotto, there are numerous ways to spend a moonlit (or rainy) evening in the city. A good place to start is the arts section in the Sunday edition of *La Prensa*, or the back pages of the *Panama News*.

Panamanians have a love affair with Hollywood, and there is no shortage of air-conditioned cinemas in and around the city. For a little escapism, **MultiCentro** (Map p644; Av Balboa) and **Multiplaza Mall** (Map p644; Vía Israel & Vía Brasil; 10am-9pm) show the latest Hollywood releases in English, with Spanish subtitles. If you're more independently minded, the **Alhambra Cinema** (Map p644; Vía España) screens art-house films.

Panamanians love to gamble, and there are flashy casinos scattered around the city. Even if you're not a big card-player, it's hard to pass up US$5 blackjack, especially when the drinks are free – a good spot is the **Miramar Inter-Continental** (Map p644; Av Balboa).

A good place to see some traditional Panamanian folk dancing is the **Restaurante-Bar Tinajas** (Map p644; 263-7890; Av 3a A Sur near Calle 52; Mon-Sat). Sure, it's touristy, but nicely done just the same. Shows are staged here on Tuesday, Thursday, and Friday and Saturday nights at 9pm; there's a US$5 entertainment fee, as well as a US$5.50 minimum per person for drinks and food. Make a reservation before dining.

For a little culture, the **Teatro Nacional** (Map p649; 262-3525; Av B) offers dance, music and live performances, though just sitting in this historic theater is enjoyable enough.

SHOPPING

Merchandise from around the world is sold very cheaply in Panama. Clothes, radios, shoes and textiles (including fabrics the Kuna purchase to make clothes) spill onto the pedestrian walkway along Av Central.

Authentic handicrafts can be found at the following places:

Flory Saltzman Molas (Map p644; Calle 49 B Oeste near Vía España) Has the best selection of authentic *molas* (colorful hand-stitched textiles made by the Kuna) outside the islands.

Mercado de Buhonerías y Artesanías (Map p644) A bustling outdoor market.

Mercado Nacional de Artesanías (Map p640) Crafts market recently moved to the first ruins approaching Panamá Viejo.

Tupper Center of the Smithsonian Tropical Research Institute (STRI; Map p644) At STRI's bookstore, opposite the Legislative Palace in the Ancón district, you'll find a nice selection of *tagua* nut carvings (from the egg-sized *tagua* nut).

GETTING THERE & AWAY
Air

International flights arrive at **Tocumen International Airport** (238-4160), 35km northeast of the city center.

Panama's airlines are **Air Panama** (316-9000; www.flyairpanama.com/tickets) and **Aeroperlas** (Map p644; 315-7500; www.aeroperlas.com).

Domestic flights depart from **Albrook airport** (315-0403), aka Aeropuerto Marcos A Gelabert, in the former Albrook Air Force Station near the canal.

PANAMA

For information on getting to town from the airports see boxed text, p642.

All flights within Panama last under one hour and prices vary according to season and availability. Both Aeroperlas and Air Panama fly to the following destinations: Bocas del Toro and David (one way US$80), El Porvenir and Playón Chico for San Blás (US$40), Isla Contadora (US$35), La Palma and Sambú for Darién (US$48).

Boat

For Isla Taboga, **Barcos Calypso** (☎ 314-1730; round trip US$11) has regular departures from the Causeway, see p658.

Bus

The Albrook bus terminal (p644), near Albrook airport, is a convenient one-stop location for most buses leaving Panama City. The terminal includes a food court, banks, shops, a sports bar, storage room, bathrooms and showers. The mall next door has a supermarket and cinema. Before you board your bus you must pass through a turnstile and pay US$0.10 tax to the terminal.

Local buses from the city's major routes stop at the terminal, and behind the station there are direct buses to and from Tocumen International Airport. To get to the station from the city, take any of the frequent buses that pass in front of the Legislative Palace or along Vía España (look for the 'via Albrook' sign in the front window).

Inside, **Información** (☎ 303-3040; 24hr) offers assistance.

Both **Panaline** (www.viajeros.com/panaline) and **Tica Bus** (www.ticabus.com) serve San José, Costa Rica; see their websites for hours.

Canal Zone buses with Cooperativa SACA depart from the Albrook bus terminal to Balboa and Clayton (both US$.025), Miraflores Locks (US$0.35), and Gamboa (US$0.65), leaving every 45 minutes.

Car

Many car rental agencies lie clustered around Calle 49 B Oeste in El Cangrejo. Daily rates start from US$35 per day for the most economical cars, including insurance and unlimited kilometers.

Rental-car companies in Panama City include the following:

Avis Albrook airport (☎ 264-0722, 315-0434); Tocumen airport (☎ 238-4056)

Barriga (☎ 269-0221, 238-4495; Tocumen airport)

Budget Albrook airport (☎ 263-8777, 315-0201); Tocumen airport (☎ 238-4069)

Hertz Albrook airport (☎ 264-1111, 315-0418); Tocumen airport (☎ 238-4081)

Train

The **Panama Railway Company** (☎ 317-6070; www.panarail.com; Carretera Gaillard) operates a glass-domed luxury passenger train from Panama City to Colón (one-way/round-trip US$22/38), leaving at 7:15am and returning at 5:15pm daily. It's a lovely ride that follows the canal, and at times the train is surrounded by nothing but thick vine-strewn jungle. If you want to relive the heyday of luxury train travel for an hour or two, this is definitely the way to do it.

BUSES FROM PANAMA CITY

Destination	Cost (US$)	Duration (hr)	Frequency
Changuinola	24	10	8pm daily
Chitré	7.50	4	hourly
Colón	2.50	2	every 20min
David	12.50-15	7-8	15 daily
El Valle	3.50	2½	hourly
Las Tablas	8	4½	hourly
Penonomé	4.35	2½	48 daily
Pesé	8	4½	6 daily
San José, Costa Rica	25-35	16	2 daily
Santiago	7.50	4	20 daily
Soná	8	6	6 daily
Villa de Los Santos	8	4	18 daily
Yaviza	14	6-8	8 daily

A taxi to the station, located in the town of Corazal, from Panama City centre costs about US$3.

GETTING AROUND
Bicycle
The only spot to rent bicycles in Panama City is at the start of the Causeway. Both **Moses** (☎ 221-3671; ⌚ 9am-7pm Sat & Sun) and **Bikes N More** (☎ 314-0103; ⌚ 8am-6pm Sat & Sun) operate booths with rentals starting at US$3.50 per hour for mountain bikes. You can also rent tandems and rickshaw bikes.

Bus
Panama City has a good network of local buses (nicknamed *diablos rojos* or 'red devils'), which run every day from around 5am to 11pm. A ride costs US$0.25, and we promise you've never seen anything quite like these tricked-out street rockets.

Buses run along the three major west–east routes: Av Central–Vía España, Av Balboa–Vía Israel, and Av Simón Bolívar–Vía Transístmica. The Av Central–Vía España streets are one-way going west for much of the route; eastbound buses use Av Perú and Av 4 Sur; these buses will take you into the banking district of El Cangrejo. Buses also run along Av Ricardo J Alfaro (known as Tumba Muerto).

There are plenty of bus stops along the street, but you can usually hail one from anywhere. Many of these buses stop at the Albrook bus terminal.

Taxi
Taxis are plentiful but some do not travel (or even know) the whole city, so don't be surprised if they leave you standing on the sidewalk upon hearing your destination.

Taxis are not metered, but there is a list of standard fares by zone. One zone runs a minimum of US$2; Canal Zone destinations run up to US$6. An average ride, crossing a couple of zones, would cost US$3 to US$4, more for additional passengers or if it's late. Always agree on a fare before you get into the taxi, or ask your hotel to estimate the fare to your destination so you can hand the driver the correct change upon arriving. Taxis can also be rented by the hour.

You can phone for a taxi:
America (☎ 223-7694)
America Libre (☎ 223-7342)
Latino (☎ 224-0677)
Metro (☎ 264-6788)
Taxi Unico Cooperativa (☎ 221-3191)

AROUND PANAMA CITY

No visit to Panama City would be complete without taking a day trip to its famous waterway – just remember that the Canal Zone is much, much more than just the canal. The rainforest surrounding the canal is easily accessed and one of the best places to view a variety of Central American wildlife.

PANAMA CANAL
The canal is truly one of the world's greatest engineering marvels. Stretching for 80km from Panama City on the Pacific side to Colón on the Atlantic side, the canal cuts right through the Continental Divide. Nearly 14,000 vessels pass through the canal each year, and ships worldwide are built with the dimensions of the Panama Canal's locks in mind: 305m long and 33.5m wide.

Ships pay according to their weight, with the average fee around US$30,000. The highest amount, around US$200,000, was paid in 2001 by the 90,000-ton French cruise ship *Infinity*; the lowest amount was US$0.36, paid in 1928 by Richard Halliburton, who swam through.

The canal has three sets of double locks: Miraflores and Pedro Miguel Locks on the Pacific side and Gatún Locks on the Atlantic side. Between the locks, ships pass through a huge artificial lake, Lago Gatún, created by the Gatún Dam across the Río Chagres (when created they were the largest dam and largest artificial lake on Earth), and the Gaillard Cut, a 14km cut through the rock and shale of the isthmian mountains. With the passage of each ship, a staggering 52 million gallons of fresh water is released into the ocean.

In 2006, Panamanian voters overwhelmingly endorsed an ambitious project to expand the Panama Canal. One of the biggest transportation projects in the world, this US$5.25 billion mega-project will stretch over seven years and finish in conjunction with the canal's centennial in 2014. New locks will be 60% wider and 40% longer, and container traffic is expected to triple.

For more information on the history of the canal, see p629.

Sights

MIRAFLORES LOCKS

The easiest and best way to visit the canal is to go to the **Miraflores Visitors' Center** (☎ 276-8325; www.pancanal.com; viewing deck/full access US$5/8; ☯ 9am-5pm), located just outside Panama City. The recently inaugurated visitors' center features a large, four-floor museum, several viewing platforms and an excellent restaurant that overlooks the locks. A tip: the best time to view big liners passing through is from 9am to 11am and from 3pm to 5pm.

To get there, take any Paraíso or Gamboa bus from the bus stop on Av Roosevelt across from the Legislative Palace in Panama City. These buses, passing along the canal-side highway to Gamboa, will let you off at the 'Miraflores Locks' sign on the highway, 12km from downtown. It's about a 15-minute walk to the locks from the sign. A taxi should cost less than US$15 for the round trip – agree on the price beforehand.

OTHER LOCKS

Further north, beyond the Miraflores Locks, are the **Pedro Miguel Locks**. You will pass them if you're taking the highway to Gamboa. The only facilities here are a parking lot, from where you can see the locks.

On the Atlantic side, the **Gatún Locks** have a viewing stand for visitors. You can also drive across the locks themselves; you will pass over them if you cross the canal to visit Fuerte San Lorenzo. For more details on these locks, see p687.

Activities

CANAL TRANSITS

Reader-recommended **Canal Bay & Tours** (☎ 314-1339; www.canalandbaytours.com) offers partial canal transits every Saturday morning. Boats depart from Muelle (Pier) 19 (Map p640) in Balboa, a western suburb of Panama City, travel through the Miraflores Locks to Lago Miraflores and back, and then cruise out into the bay for scenic views of the city. These tours last 4½ hours and cost US$115 per person – it's a good idea to make reservations in advance.

One Saturday every month, the company also offers full transits from Balboa to Cristóbal on the Caribbean coast, passing all three sets of locks. The transit takes all day, from 7:30am to 5:30pm, and costs US$165. Check the company's website for dates of upcoming transits.

A one-way taxi fare to Muelle (Pier) 19 should cost around US$6.

FISHING

If you're looking to reel in the big one, get in touch with **Panama Canal Fishing** (☎ 6699-0507; www.panamacanalfishing.com). Its signature tour is fishing for peacock bass in Lago Gatún and the Río Chagres. Introduced by an American looking to boost his pastime, peacock bass are now considered a plague and fishing them does a great favor to the lake.

AROUND THE CANAL

Although no visit to Panama would be complete without visiting the world-famous canal, the surrounding area is home to impressive attractions, especially wildlife-watching and bird-watching. On a day trip from Panama City, you could first visit the Miraflores Locks, then the Summit Botanical Gardens & Zoo, and finish at the Parque Nacional Soberanía and the Panamá Rainforest Discovery Center. The last two stops are only 25km from the center of Panama City, but they seem like a different world.

These attractions are located along the highway that runs from Panama City to Gamboa, the small town where the Río Chagres enters Lago Gatún. They can be reached by taking the Gamboa bus from Albrook terminal.

Summit Botanical Gardens & Zoo

Ten kilometers past the Miraflores Locks is the **Summit Botanical Gardens & Zoo** (☎ 232-4854; admission US$1; ☯ 8am-4pm), which was established in 1923 to introduce, propagate and disseminate tropical plants from around the world into Panama. Later, a small zoo was added to help American soldiers identify tropical animals while they were out in the field. Many of the plant species are marked along a trail.

Under the jurisdiction of the Panama City municipality, Summit depends on city funding and organization, thus improvements are often slow to implement. The star attractions at the zoo include an enormous harpy-eagle compound, a tapir area and a rapidly expanding jaguar enclosure. Since the aim of the park is to promote environmental education, natural enclosures mimic rainforest habitats highlighting the native flora and fauna of Panama.

Parque Nacional Soberanía

A few kilometers past Summit, across the border into Colón Province, the 221-sq-km

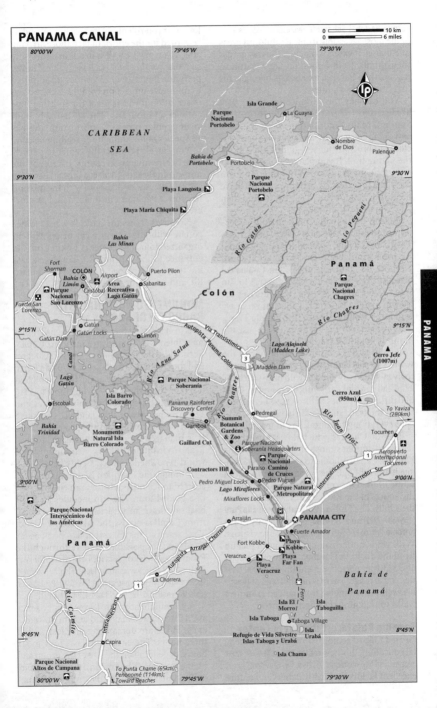

PANAMA CANAL

0 — 10 km
0 — 6 miles

80°00'W   79°45'W   79°30'W

CARIBBEAN SEA

Isla Grande

La Guayra

Parque Nacional Portobelo

Nombre de Dios

Palenque

Bahía de Portobelo

Portobelo

9°30'N   9°30'N

Playa Langosta

Parque Nacional Portobelo

Playa María Chiquita

Panamá

Bahía Las Minas

Río Gatún

Río pequeni

Fort Sherman

COLÓN

Bahía Limón

Airport

Puerto Pilon

Sabanitas

Parque Nacional Chagres

Parque Nacional San Lorenzo

Cristobal

Área Recreativa Lago Gatún

Colón

Río Chagres

Fuerte San Lorenzo

Gatún

Gatún Locks

Limón

Vía Transístmica

9°15'N   9°15'N

Gatún Dam

Autopista Panamá-Colón

Río Agua Salud

Lago Alajuela (Madden Lake)

Cerro Jefe (1007m)

Canal

3

Madden Dam

Lago Gatún

Isla Barro Colorado

Parque Nacional Soberanía

Río Chagres

Cerro Azul (950m)

To Yaviza (280km)

Escobal

Panama Rainforest Discovery Center

Pedregal

Río Juan Díaz

Tocumen

Bahía Trinidad

Monumento Natural Isla Barro Colorado

Gamboa

Summit Botanical Gardens & Zoo

Gaillard Cut

Parque Nacional Soberanía Headquarters

Aeropuerto Internacional Tocumen

Contractors Hill

Paraiso

Parque Nacional Camino de Cruces

1

Pedro Miguel Locks

Pedro Miguel

Lago Miraflores

Parque Natural Metropolitano

Corredor Sur

9°00'N   9°00'N

Miraflores Locks

Parque Nacional Interoceánico de las Américas

Arraiján

Balboa

PANAMA CITY

Fuerte Amador

Autopista Arraiján-Chorrera

Fort Kobbe

Playa Kobbe

Panamá

Veracruz

Playa Far Fan

Playa Veracruz

Bahía de Panamá

Interamericana

1

La Chorrera

Ferry

Isla El Morro

Isla Tabogilla

8°45'N   8°45'N

Río Caimito

Isla Taboga

Taboga Village

Isla Urabá

Capira

Refugio de Vida Silvestre Islas Taboga y Urabá

Isla Chama

Parque Nacional Altos de Campana

To Punta Chame (65km); Penonomé (114km); Toward Beaches

80°00'W   79°45'W   79°30'W

PANAMA

Parque Nacional Soberanía (admission US$5) is one of the most accessible tropical rainforest areas in Panama. It extends much of the way across the isthmus, from Limón on Lago Gatún to just north of Paraíso, and boasts hiking trails that brim with wildlife.

You can pay the entrance fee at the **park headquarters** (☎ 276-6370) at the turnoff to Summit. Maps, information about the park and camping permits are available here, including a brochure for self-guided walks along the nature trail. If you plan on hiking, please note that the trailheads are quite far from park headquarters. If arriving by taxi, have the driver wait for you to pay the fee and then take you to the trailhead.

Hiking trails in the park include a section of the old **Sendero Las Cruces** (Las Cruces Trail), used by the Spanish to transport gold by mule train between Panama City and Nombre de Dios, and the 17km **Camino del Oleoducto (Pipeline Rd)**, providing access to Río Agua Salud, where you can walk upriver for a swim under a waterfall. A shorter, very easy trail is the **Sendero El Charco** (the Puddle Trail), signposted from the highway, 3km past the Summit Botanical Gardens & Zoo.

Pipeline Rd is considered to be one of the world's **premier bird-watching sites** – not surprisingly, it's intensely popular with bird-watchers, especially in the early morning hours. Over 500 different species of birds have been spotted on the trail, and it's fairly likely you will spot everything from toucans to trogons.

The Río Chagres, which flows through the park and supplies most of the water for the Panama Canal, is home to several **Emberá communities**. Although the Darién is the ancestral home of the Emberá, a wave of migration to the shores of the Río Chagres commenced in the 1950s. The Emberá community of **Ella Puru** (☎ 6537-7223) and Wounaan community of **San Antonio** (☎ 6637-9503) regularly receive visitors. With prior notice you can arrange a pickup from the docks in Gamboa. Tour prices start at US$30 per person, depending on the activities you arrange. There is no shortage of possible excursions, ranging from guided rainforest walks to watching traditional dances.

Panama Rainforest Discovery Center

Geared toward ecotourism and environmental education, this new **center** (☎ 6588-0697; www .pipelineroad.org; adult/child US$20/4; ◷ 6am-4pm) is an excellent facility for bird-watchers and nature lovers. If you roll out of bed early, you will be rewarded for the effort. In fact, those arriving after 10am pay US$5 less in admission, a sure sign that coming later is a lesser value. During premium hours, only 25 visitors are admitted to minimize impact on wildlife. A 32m-high observation tower is great for spotting blue cotinga and toucans. The sustainably built visitor center provides information and has 13 species of hummingbirds feeding nearby.

You can also contact the center to participate in bird migration counts. It's run by the non-profit **Fundación Avifauna Eugene Eisenmann** (☎ 264-6266; www.avifauna.org.pa) with the mission to protect Panama's bird fauna and rainforest habitat.

No buses access the park. It is best to negotiate with a taxi, rent a car or go with an organized tour. The center is 1.6km from the entrance to the Pipeline Rd. You must pass the town of Gamboa, at the end of Gaillard Rd, and follow the signs.

MONUMENTO NACIONAL ISLA BARRO COLORADO

This lush island in the middle of Lago Gatún is most intensively studied area in the neotropics. Formed by the damming of the Río Chagres and the creation of the lake, in 1923 Isla Barro Colorado (BCI) became one of the first biological reserves in the New World. Home to 1316 recorded plant species, 381 bird species and 120 mammal species, the island also contains a 59km network of marked and protected trails. It is managed by the Smithsonian Tropical Research Institute (STRI), which administers a world-renowned research facility here.

Although the 15-sq-km island was once restricted to scientists, visitors can enter as part of a guided tour. The trip includes an STRI boat ride down an attractive part of the canal, from Gamboa across the lake to the island. Tour reservations are essential – book as far in advance as possible. Reserve through the Panama City visitor services office of **STRI** (Map p644; ☎ 212-8026; www.stri.org; Tupper Bldg, Av Roosevelt, Ancón district; foreign adult/student US$70/40, Panamanian adult/student US$25/12; ◷ 8:30am-4:30pm Mon-Fri).

A 45-minute boat ride leaves Gamboa pier at 7:15am on weekdays and at 8am on weekends. Hikes are demanding and last two to three hours. The entire trip lasts four to six hours, depending on the size of the group and on the weather. A buffet lunch (with vegetarian options) is included. For more information, you can download the free pdf on the STRI website.

ISLA TABOGA

A tropical island with only one road and no traffic, Isla Taboga is a pleasant place to escape the hustle and bustle of Panama City, just 20km offshore. First settled by the Spanish in 1515, quaint Taboga is also home to the second-oldest church in the Western hemisphere. However, the main appeal is sandy beaches lapped by warm waters, which can rejuvenate even the most hardened urbanite.

Rumors abound that the now-defunct Hotel Taboga will be knocked down to make way for a upmarket resort. In the meantime, Taboga is still a laid-back day trip from Panama City, for a little fun in the sun.

History

Taboga is part of a chain of islands once inhabited by indigenous peoples who resided in thatch huts and lived off the bounty of the sea. In 1515, Spanish soldiers announced their arrival on Taboga by killing or enslaving the islanders and establishing a small colony. However, peace did not reign, especially since a number of pirates, including Henry Morgan and Francis Drake, frequented the island, and used it as a base from which to attack Spanish ships and towns. Aside from a few live rounds fired by the US Navy during a WWII session of target practice, recent years have been peaceful.

Orientation & Information

Ferries from Panama City tie up at a pier near the north end of the island. As you exit the pier, you'll see the entrance to the abandoned Hotel Taboga to your right. To your left, you'll see a narrow street that is the island's main road. From this point, the street meanders for 5.2km before ending at the old US military installation atop the island's highest hill, Cerro El Vigia.

For more information on the island, check the excellent English-language site, www.taboga.panamanow.com.

Sights & Activities

There are fine **beaches** in Taboga, all free, in either direction from the ferry dock. Many visitors head straight for the Hotel Taboga, to the right as you walk off the ferry dock; the hotel faces onto the island's most popular beach, arcing between Taboga and tiny Isla El Morro.

On weekends, when most visitors arrive, fishermen at the pier take passengers around the island, showing it from all sides and stopping at some good **snorkeling** spots. The caves on the island's western side are rumored to hold golden treasure left there by pirates. During the week you can still snorkel around Isla El Morro, which doesn't have coral but attracts some large fish.

Walk left from the pier along the island's only road for about 75m until you reach the fork. The high road leads to a modest **church**, in front of which is a simple square. Founded in 1550, it is the second-oldest church in the western hemisphere; inside is a handsome altar and lovely artwork. Further down the road is a beautiful public garden, which bears the statue of the island's patroness, **Nuestra Señora del Carmen**.

For a fine view, you can walk up the hill on the east side of the island, **Cerro de la Cruz**, to the cross on the top. Another trail leads to a viewpoint atop **Cerro El Vigia**, on the western side of the island.

A wildlife refuge, the **Refugio de Vida Silvestre Isla Taboga y Urabá**, covers about a third of the island, as well as the island of Urabá just off Taboga's southeastern coast. This refuge is home to one of the largest breeding colonies of brown pelicans in the world. May is the height of nesting season, but pelicans can be seen from January to June.

On your way to and from the island, keep an eye on the ocean. On rare occasions during August, September and October, migrating humpback and sei whales can be seen in spectacular displays.

Festivals & Events

Taboga's **annual festival** takes place on July 16, the day of its patron saint, Nuestra Señora del Carmen. The statue of the saint is carried upon the shoulders of followers to the shore, placed on a boat and ferried around the island. Upon her return, she is carried around the island while crowds follow.

Sleeping & Eating

Most people choose to visit Isla Taboga as a day trip from Panama City, though there are a few affordable places to stay.

Zoraida's Cool (☎ 6471-1123, 6566-9250; d/tr US$30/35) Overlooking the bay, this family lodging is lovingly run by Zoraida. Rooms are small and mattresses plastic-wrapped, but this is the best bargain on the island. The best feature is a hammock deck ideal for a snooze with Pacific views. Turn left as you exit the dock and walk for a few minutes until you see a sign leading you up the hill.

Vereda Tropical Hotel (☎ 250-2154; http://veredatropicalhotel.com; d from US$71; ❄ ▣) Atop a hill with commanding views (it's about 100m up a winding path), this boutique hotel charms with tropical tones, mosaic tiles and rod-iron railings. The dining patio has gaping views and Julio Iglesias serenading from the speakers. Unfortunately, service is slack.

Cerrito Tropical (☎ 390-8999; www.cerritotropicalpanama.com; d incl breakfast US$75, 2-person apt US$100-170; ❄ 🛜) This smart Canadian-owned B&B occupies a quiet nook at the end of a steep road. Rooms are stylish but small, and have access to a large shady deck. Extras range from Spanish lessons to barbecues and picnic lunches. To arrive, go right uphill at the end of Calle Francisco Pizarro.

Donde Pope Si Hay (mains US$4-7; ☺ 8am-8pm) A simple cement eatery serving fresh fish, green coconut water and *patacones* (fried plantains).

Getting There & Away

The scenic boat trip out to Isla Taboga is part of the island's attraction. **Barcos Calypso** (☎ 314-1730; round trip US$11) has departures from Panama City at 8:30am and 3:00pm Monday and Friday, 8:30am on Tuesday and Thursday, and 8:30am, 10:30am and 4:00pm on weekends. Ferries depart Isla Taboga at 9:30am and 4:00pm Monday and Friday, 4:30pm on Tuesday and Thursday, and 9:00am, 3:00pm and 5:00pm on Saturday and Sunday.

Ferries depart from La Playita de Amador, which is located behind the Centro de Exhibiciones Marinas on the Causeway. The easiest way to reach the dock is by taxi (US$4 to US$6).

CHIRIQUÍ PROVINCE

Chiricanos claim to have it all, and there's an element of truth in what they say: Panama's tallest mountains, longest rivers and most fertile valleys are in Chiriquí. The province is also home to spectacular highland rainforests as well as the country's most productive agricultural and cattle-ranching regions. Not surprisingly, many *chiricanos* often dream about creating an independent República de Chiriquí.

Bordering Costa Rica to the west, Chiriquí is often the first province in Panama encountered by overland travelers. It also serves as a suitable introduction to the not-so-subtle beauty Panama has to offer. Although the mist-covered mountains near Boquete are slowly being colonized by waves of North American and European retirees, the town serves as a good base for exploring the flanks of towering Volcán Barú, Panama's only volcano and its highest point (3475m). The region is also home to the Parque Internacional La Amistad, a bi-national park shared by Costa Rica and Panama. The park offers excellent hiking through lush rainforests, largely unfettered by tourist crowds.

DAVID

pop 124,000

Panama's second-largest city is the capital of Chiriquí Province and a major agricultural center. Though David has a large town feel, it's rapidly growing in terms of wealth and importance as foreign capital arrives via North American and European retirees moving in. But the trend has somewhat stabilized.

For most travelers, David serves as an important transportation hub for anyone heading to/from Costa Rica, the Chiriquí highlands, Golfo de Chiriquí, Panama City and Bocas del Toro. Although the city has few attractions in its own right, David is a pleasant enough place to stay, and there's no shortage of interesting things to see and do in the surrounding area.

Orientation

David is halfway between San José in Costa Rica and Panama City – about seven hours by road from either place. The Interamericana does not enter the town, but skirts around its northern and western sides. The city's heart is its fine central plaza, the Parque de Cervantes, about 1.5km southwest of the highway.

Information

BOOKSTORES

Livraría Regional (Av Bolívar) Modest bookstore with a handful of titles in English including coffee-table books on Panama.

INTERNET ACCESS

Internet Fast Track (Av 2 Este; per hr US$0.75; 24hr)

Planet Internet (Calle Central; per hr US$0.75; 9am-midnight)

MEDICAL SERVICES

Chiriquí Hospital (777-8814; cnr Calle Central & Av 3 Oeste) One of the best hospitals in the country.

MONEY

HSBC (Av Central) With branches on Calle C Norte near the park and on Av Obaldía north of the bus station.

POST

Post office (Calle C Norte; 7am-6pm Mon-Fri, 7am-4:30pm Sat)

TOURIST INFORMATION

ATP (775-2839; Av Central; 8:30am-4:30pm Mon-Fri) Provides information on Chiriquí Province.

Autoridad Nacional de Ambiente (ANAM; 775-7840; fax 774-6671; 8am-4pm Mon-Fri) Provides tourist information and gives permits to camp in the national parks. It's near the airport.

Sights & Activities

David serves as a base for exploring the Chiriquí lowlands. For tips on attractions see boxed text, right.

The modest **Museo de Historia y de Arte José de Obaldía** (Av 8 Este btwn Calles Central & A Norte; admission US$1; 8:30am-noon & 12:45-4:30pm Mon-Sat) is a two-story colonial home constructed in 1880, still furnished with its original art and decor. Named after the founder of Chiriquí Province, the museum also houses local archaeological artifacts and old photos of the canal constructions.

If you're looking to get your adrenaline fix, consider spending the day **white-water rafting**

EXPLORE MORE AROUND DAVID

Spice things up with these Lonely Planet author-tested excursions:

- **Rest those bones in hot springs** Take a bus to the town of Caldera, and hike the dirt road for 45 minutes to Los Pozos de Caldera.

- **Develop your rum palate** Go on a private tour of the Carta Vieja Rum Factory on the outskirts of town.

- **Swim with *chiricanos* at Balneario Majagua or Balneario La Nueva Barranca** Hop on a Boquete- or Concepción-bound bus and jump off at either of these popular local swimming spots.

- **Beat the heat at nearby Playa Barqueta** Grab some friends and take a taxi from David to the lovely dark-sand beach of Playa Barqueta for a day of fun in the sun.

on the Río Chiriquí or the Río Chiriquí Viejo. Tour operators in Boquete pass by David on their way to the launch point and with advanced notice, they'll be happy to pick you up at your accommodations. For more information, see p665.

Festivals & Events

The **Feria de San José de David**, held for 10 days each March, is a big international fair. La Concepción, half an hour west of David, celebrates it's **saint's day** on February 2.

Sleeping

Purple House (774-4059; www.purplehousehostel.com; cnr Calle C Sur & Av 6 Oeste; dm/d US$8/20;) The first hostel in David continues as a welcoming good deal. Tile bunk rooms are clean and tidy, and the doubles come with á la carte options of hot water (US$2), air-con (US$5) and cable TV (US$2). Andrea proves to be an incredible resource, and can direct guests to binders of information or suggest economical transport to the coast or elsewhere. The house also recycles and has a community partnership selling Ngöbe-Buglé crafts without commission.

Bambu (730-2961; www.bambuhostel.com; Calle de la Virgencita, San Mateo Abajo; dm US$8, d with/without bathroom US$30/25;) This is an ideal crash pad for backpackers wanting a little rock 'n' roll. Run by a NYC musician, it features two dorms

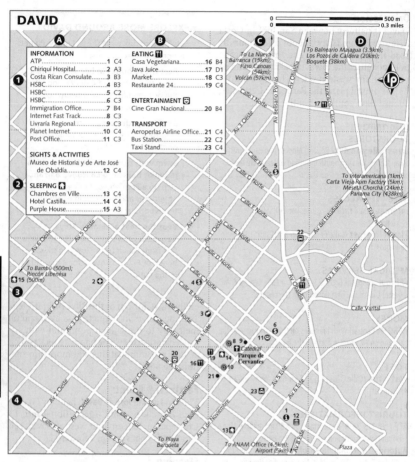

DAVID

0   500 m
0   0.3 miles

INFORMATION
ATP.............................1 C4
Chiriquí Hospital................2 A3
Costa Rican Consulate........3 B3
HSBC.............................4 B3
HSBC.............................5 C2
HSBC.............................6 C3
Immigration Office............7 B4
Internet Fast Track...........8 C3
Livraría Regional..............9 C3
Planet Internet................10 C4
Post Office.....................11 C3

SIGHTS & ACTIVITIES
Museo de Historia y de Arte José
de Obaldía.....................12 C4

SLEEPING
Chambres en Ville............13 C4
Hotel Castilla..................14 C4
Purple House..................15 A3

EATING
Casa Vegetariana.............16 B4
Java Juice......................17 D1
Market..........................18 C3
Restaurante 24................19 C4

ENTERTAINMENT
Cine Gran Nacional..........20 B4

TRANSPORT
Aeroperlas Airline Office...21 C4
Bus Station....................22 C2
Taxi Stand.....................23 C4

To La Nueva
Barranca (15km);
Paso Canoas
(54km);
Volcán (57km)

To Balneario Majagua (3.9km);
Los Pozos de Caldera (20km);
Boquete (38km)

To Interamericana (1km);
Carta Vieja Rum Factory (5km);
Meseta Chorcha (24km);
Panama City (438km)

To Bambú (500m);
Rincón Libereña
(500m)

Calle Varital

Parque de
Cervantes

Catedral

Plaza

To Playa
Barqueta

To ANAM Office (4.5km);
Airport (5km)

---

and doubles with low-slung beds, cable TV and air-con. The best feature is the swimming pool with requisite hammocks.

Chambres en Ville (☎ 775-7428; www.chambresen ville.info; Av 5ta Este; r with/without air-con US$30/20; 🖳 🔊) This cute house opens to a big interior courtyard with access to smart, small rooms. Rooms are clean and the ample swimming pool proves a nice added bonus. Morning coffee is included and you can get extra services such as transfers and tours.

Hotel Castilla (☎ 774-5260; Calle A Norte; r from US$40; 🅿 🔀 🖳) Professional and super clean, this hotel offers cheerful rooms with matching beds and desk sets in deco style. Each is equipped with air-con, a hot-water shower, phone and cable TV.

Eating & Drinking

If you're looking for cheap produce, don't miss the bustling **market** (cnr Avs Bolívar & Obaldía).

Casa Vegetariana (Av 2 Este; meal US$2; 🕙 7am-4pm) This cheerful Chinese-style mini-cafeteria packs in the crowds for inexpensive plates of sautéed greens, eggplant, fried rice and beans served on no-nonsense metal plates.

Restaurant 24 (Av 2 Este; mains US$2-3; 🕙 till late) Popular with locals for its grilled meats and inexpensive lunch specials – this is the perfect spot to get your fill without breaking the budget.

Java Juice (Av Francisco Clark; mains US$2.50-4; 🕙 11am-11pm Mon-Sat, 4-10pm Sun) Iced coffee, fresh-fruit smoothies, healthy salads and grilled burgers are the fare at this charming outdoor cafe northeast of the bus terminal.

Rincón Libenésa (Interamericana; mains US$4-7) The homemade hummus, tabouleh and *baba ghanooj* at this authentic Lebanese restaurant provide welcome relief from a steady diet of rice and beans. It's located three blocks past the McDonald's off the Interamericana.

Entertainment

Cine Gran Nacional (Av 1 Este btwn Calles Central & A Sur) David's small cinema screens mostly American new releases.

Getting There & Away

AIR

David's airport, the Aeropuerto Enrique Malek, is about 5km from town. There are no buses to the airport; take a taxi (US$5).

Air Panama (☎ 721-0841; www.flyairpanama.com/tickets) and **Aeroperlas** (☎ 721-1195; www.aeroperlas.com) fly direct from Panama City to David (US$80, 45 minutes), both with multiple flights daily. Aeroperlas also flies at 10am on Monday, Wednesday and Friday to Bocas del Toro (US$36, 40 minutes).

BUS

The David **bus station** (Av del Estudiante) is about 600m northeast of the central plaza. Most buses begin service by 7am.

For Guadalupe, passengers can get on a Cerro Punta bus, which continues on; passengers for Volcán also take the Cerro Punta bus, but get off earlier. For Las Lajas, visitors will have to continue to the beach via taxi (US$5).

Tracopa (☎ 775-8853) operates direct buses between David and San José, Costa Rica (US$14, eight hours). Buses depart from the bus station every day at 8:30am from the David bus station. From San José, buses depart for the return trip to David at 7:30am. Tickets can be purchased up to two days in advance.

GOLFO DE CHIRIQUÍ

The undisputed gem of the Chiriquí lowlands is **Parque Nacional Marino Golfo de Chiriquí**, a national marine park with an area of 147 sq km protecting 25 islands, 19 coral reefs and abundant wildlife. The marine park also protects the 30-sq-km **Isla Boca Brava** (accessed via mainland Boca Chica), a lovely little island crisscrossed by hiking trails and home to monkeys, nesting sea turtles and 280 recorded bird species. Whether you want to lie on the beach, snorkel clear waters or go wildlife-watching underneath the rainforest canopy, there's something for everyone in this off-the-beaten-path destination.

our pick **Hotel Boca Brava** (☎ 851-0017; www.hotelbocabrava.com; Isla Boca Brava; hammocks/dm US$7/10, d without bathroom US$25, standard/deluxe r US$35/50) has been renovated and revamped under the enthusiastic new management of a young couple. Offering a wide selection, from the ultrabudget to air-con comfort, this is a great getaway spot to mingle with other travelers. The hotel can arrange any number of excursions around the islands, involving snorkeling, whale-watching or just lounging on a gorgeous island (prices range from US$12 to US$70 depending on the tour and the number of participants). The breezy restaurant-bar (meals US$4 to US$8) cooks up fresh fish and burgers.

PANAMA

BUSES FROM DAVID

Destination	Cost (US$)	Duration	Frequency
Boquete	1.50	1hr	every 20min until 9:30pm
Caldera	2	45min	hourly until 7:30pm
Cerro Punta	3	2¼hr	every 20min until 8pm
Changuinola	8	4½hr	hourly until 6:30pm
Guadalupe	3.50	2½hr	every 20min until 8pm
Horconcitos	1.50	45min	11am & 5pm
Las Lajas	2.25	1½hr	four daily
Panama City	13-15	6-8hr	every 45min, 6:45am-8pm
Paso Canoas	1.75	1½hr	every 10min until 9:30pm
Puerto Armuelles	3	2½hr	every 15min until 9pm
Río Sereno	4	2½hr	every 30min until 5pm
Santiago	7.25	3hr	hourly until 9pm
Volcán	2.50	1¾hr	every 20min until 8pm

GETTING TO COSTA RICA

The most heavily trafficked Panama–Costa Rica border crossing is at **Paso Canoas** (⊗ 24hr), 53km west of David on the Interamericana. Allow at least one to two hours to get through the formalities on both sides. Buses from David depart frequently for the border (US$1.50, 1½ hours, every half hour) from 4:30am to 9:30pm. On the Costa Rican side of the border, you can catch regular buses to San José or other parts of the country.

The less traveled border post at **Guabito–Sixaola** (⊗ 8am-6pm), just north of Changuinola, is more straightforward. Buses from Changuinola (US$1.80, 30 minutes, every half hour) depart from 6am to 7pm. The Costa Rican side has regular buses on to Puerto Limón and San José, as well as regional destinations.

The least trafficked crossing is **Río Sereno** (⊗ 9am-5pm Mon-Sat, 9am-3pm Sun), located 47km west of Volcán. Buses to the border depart from David and travel via La Concepción, Volcán and Santa Clara (US$4, three hours, every 30 minutes). On the Costa Rican side, take a 15-minute bus or taxi to San Vito, where buses leave for regional destinations.

Travelers may be asked for an onward ticket if entering Costa Rica. If you do not possess one, it is acceptable to buy a return bus ticket back to Panama. Note that Costa Rica is one hour behind Panama – opening and closing times are given here in Panama time.

For crossing in the opposite direction, see p616 and p567.

To reach Boca Chica, first take a David bus (US$1.50) to the Horconcitos turnoff, located 39km east. You can also take any passing bus (those heading from David to Panama City), as long as you ask the driver to drop you at the Horconcitos turnoff.

From the turnoff, a bus (US$3, 50 minutes) leaves four times daily for Boca Chica, or you can take a taxi (US$20). For transportation hours, call **Jimi** (☎ 6857-2094). At the Boca Chica dock, hire a water taxi (per person US$2) to take you 200m to the Boca Brava island dock at Restaurante Boca Brava.

PUNTA BURICA

This lush peninsula jutting into the Pacific is a lovely spot for absorbing the beauty of both the rainforest and the coastline. **Mono Feliz** (☎ 6595-0388; monofeliz@gmail.com; cabin per person US$22, campsite per person US$10; ℗ ☺) offers visitors a chance to enjoy this untouched natural beauty. Wildlife is a key feature here, and the Mono Feliz (happy monkey) certainly has its share of its namesake.

Facilities include three stand-alone cabins – two in the garden and one on the beach. There is also a large pool (fed by cool spring water, and you may be surrounded by monkeys at times), freshwater showers and an outdoor kitchen for guest use. Those who'd rather not cook can pay US$30 per day extra for three home-cooked meals, ranging from fresh seasonal fish to conch or lobster when available (individual meals available for US$8 to

US$12). Beds have mosquito nets. Camping on the beach is also available (bring your own gear), and you have access to pool and bathrooms.

The friendly American owner Juancho offers a range of activities including nature walks (an excursion to **Isla Burica** at low tide is a highlight), fishing, bird-watching, surfing (several boards available) and horseback riding. Remedial massage and yoga is available for guests in need of deeper relaxation. All activities except horseback riding (US$10 plus guide fee) are free. The owner speaks English, French and Spanish.

Owing to its isolation, reaching Mono Feliz requires a bit of work. You'll first need to go to the small coastal town of Puerto Armuelles. Departures from David to Puerto Armuelles leave every 15 minutes (US$3, 2½ hours). Be sure to arrive in Puerto Armuelles no later than noon.

The bus drops you off in the *mercado municipal*, and from there take a truck to Bella Vista. It's approximately a one-hour walk down the hill from here to Mono Feliz. You can also exit at El Medio, the last stop before the trucks go inland to Bella Vista. From El Medio it's an hour's walk along the beach. Mono Feliz is directly in front of Isla Burica.

For private transportation from Puerto Armuelles, contact Spanish-speaking **Tonio** (☎ 6662-9533, 6584-8456; per person one-way US$10) or **Otto** (☎ 6595-0388); weather permitting, either can take you directly to Mono Feliz.

PLAYA LAS LAJAS

Playa Las Lajas, 51km east of David and 26km south of the Interamericana, is one of several long, palm-lined beaches along this stretch of the Pacific coast. Playa Las Lajas gathers crowds on the weekends, but often lies empty during the week, when you can have serious stretches of sand all to yourself.

Saturated with beachgoers on the weekend, **Las Lajas Beach Cabins** (☎ 720-2430, 618-7723; 3-person campsites US$10, 2-/3-person r or cabins US$20/30) has nine rustic *cabañas* right on the beach, a clam's toss from the surf. Bathrooms are communal in a nearby concrete structure. An additional concrete structure offers six private rooms. None of them have fans and all could use a good sweep.

Comfortable and stylish **Las Lajas Beach Resort** (☎ 832-5463; www.laslajasbeachresort.com; d/ste US$99/150; ☽ closed Oct; ☒) is a sweet splurge. Rooms are impeccable, with beds decked in embroidered *molas* and amenities include an infinity pool. Even nonguests might pop in for American-style breakfasts or big cheeseburgers.

Back where the road dead-ends at the beach sits **La Estrella del Pacifico** (mains US$4), serving simple fish dishes with great ocean views.

To reach Las Lajas, take any bus from David (US$2.25, 90 minutes) that travels by the Las Lajas turnoff on the Interamericana. At the turnoff, take a taxi (US$5) to where the road reaches the sea. Turn right and proceed 1.5km until you arrive at the cabins.

BOQUETE

pop 5000

The mountain town of Boquete, the Napa Valley of coffee, is known throughout Panama for its cool, fresh climate and pristine natural setting. Flowers, coffee, vegetables and citrus fruits flourish in Boquete's rich soil, and the friendliness of the locals seems to rub off on everyone who passes through.

Boquete was very much intent on remaining a small town, but was faced with changes beyond anyone's control – baby boomers started getting old. One decade ago, *Modern Maturity* magazine of the American Association for Retired Persons chose Boquete as one of the four top places in the world to retire, and a flock of foreign retirees started snatching up mountain plots. Today, gated communities dot the hillsides and the face of Boquete is slowly being transformed.

For travelers, Boquete is one of the country's top destinations for outdoor lovers. From here you can hike, climb, raft, visit coffee farms, soak in hot springs, study Spanish or go on a canopy tour. And of course there's nothing quite like starting your day with a glass of freshly squeezed OJ, or perking up with a cup of locally grown coffee.

Orientation & Information

Boquete's central area is only a few square blocks. The main road, Av Central, comes north from David, passes along the western side of the plaza and continues up the hill past the church.

ATP (☽ 8am-5:30pm) About 1.5km south of Boquete, this office sits atop a bluff overlooking town. Here you can grab a Kotowa coffee, pick up maps and obtain information on area attractions. A 2nd-floor exhibit details the history of the region (Spanish only).
Banco Nacional de Panama (Av Central) A 24hr ATM.
Centro Medico San Juan Bautista (☎ 720-1881)
Global Bank (Av Central)
Internet Kelnix (Av Central; per hr US$0.75; ☽ 8am-11pm Mon-Sat, 10am-11pm Sun)
Post office (☽ 7am-6pm Mon-Fri, 7am-5pm Sat)

Sights

COFFEE PLANTATIONS

No trip to Boquete is complete without learning the secrets of a perfectly blended cup of joe.

Located on the main road about 600m north of the town center, **Café Ruíz** (☎ 720-1392; www.cafe ruiz.com; 3hr tour US$30) is Panama's most famous coffee-grower and makes the award-winning Gesha coffee. The tour includes transportation to a nearby coffee farm, a presentation on the history of coffee in Boquete, a visit to the roasting facility and a tasting session. Tours start at 9am daily except Sundays and holidays; advance reservations are required.

Kotowa Coffee Estate (☎ 720-1430; 2½hr tour US$28) is a gourmet grower offering the most comprehensive coffee-estate tour in the area. It features a description of the estate's history, a full tour of the production facilities and processing mill, and again, the obligatory tasting session. The estate requests 24 hours' notice prior to your visit. You can also have a cup at an outlet in the ATP information center.

GARDENS & ZOOS

Mi Jardín es Su Jardín (admission free; ☽ dawn-dusk), just uphill from Café Ruíz, is a magnificent garden surrounding a luxurious private estate. The residence is off-limits to the public, but you are free to stroll about the garden.

PANAMA

El Explorador (☎ 775-2643; Calle Jarmillo Alto; admission US$3; ☺ 10am-6pm daily mid-Dec–mid-Apr, Sat & Sun only mid-Apr–mid-Dec) is a private garden in a hilly area 45 minutes' walk from the town center. It's like something out of *Alice in Wonderland,* with no shortage of quirky eye-catching displays.

Working in conjunction with ANAM, the family-run **Paradise Gardens** (☎ 6615-6618; www .paradisegardenspanama.com; Calle Volcancito Principal; suggested donation US$5; ☺ 10am-4pm Thu-Tue) has taken in confiscated, orphaned and abandoned birds, sloths, monkeys, anteaters and the occasional feline. Animals have large enclosures and are very well taken care of. The landscaped grounds are a delight to roam too. Educational material is in English and

Spanish. It's several kilometers before Boquete on the road to Volcancito.

HOT SPRINGS

Boquete is a good base for exploring the **Los Pozos de Caldera** (admission US$2; ☺ dawn-dusk), an undeveloped hot spring rumored to have health-giving properties. A round-trip taxicab from Boquete to the hot springs should cost about US$30. A bus from the center runs to Caldera (US$1.45) every two hours; from here there's a walk (inquire at your hotel).

Activities
HIKING

With its breathtaking vistas of mist-covered hills and nearby forests, Boquete is one of the

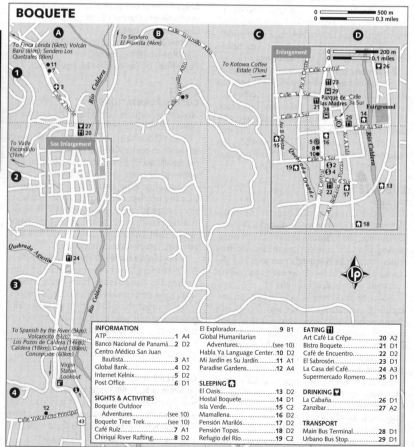

BOQUETE

0 _____ 500 m
0 _____ 0.3 miles

INFORMATION
ATP...1 A4
Banco Nacional de Panamá....2 D2
Centro Médico San Juan
 Bautista.......................................3 A1
Global Bank.................................4 D2
Internet Kelnix............................5 D2
Post Office....................................6 D1

SIGHTS & ACTIVITIES
Boquete Outdoor
 Adventures...........................(see 10)
Boquete Tree Trek...............(see 10)
Café Ruíz.......................................7 A1
Chiriquí River Rafting.............8 D2

El Explorador..............................9 B1
Global Humanitarian
 Adventures........................(see 10)
Habla Ya Language Center...10 D2
Mi Jardín es Su Jardín..........11 A1
Paradise Gardens...................12 A4

SLEEPING
El Oasis.......................................13 D2
Hostal Boquete........................14 D1
Isla Verde...................................15 C2
Mamallena.................................16 D2
Pensión Marilós........................17 D2
Pensión Topas...........................18 D2
Refugio del Río........................19 C2

EATING
Art Café La Crêpe....................20 A2
Bistro Boquete..........................21 D1
Café de Encuentro...................22 D2
El Sabrosón................................23 D1
La Casa del Café......................24 A3
Supermercado Romero..........25 D1

DRINKING
La Cabaña..................................26 D1
Zanzibar.....................................27 A2

TRANSPORT
Main Bus Terminal..................28 D1
Urbano Bus Stop......................29 D1

most idyllic regions for hiking and walking. Several good paved roads lead out of town into the surrounding hills, passing coffee plantations, fields and farms, gardens and virgin forest.

Although saunterers will be content with picturesque strolls along the river, the more ambitious can climb **Volcán Barú** (3475m), Panama's highest point and only volcano. There are several entrances to the park, but the trail with easiest access to the summit starts near Boquete. For more information, see p667.

You can also access the **Sendero Los Quetzales** (Quetzals Trail; see p667) from Boquete; the trail is uphill from here though – you'll have an easier time if you start hiking from Cerro Punta (see p668).

A pleasant day hike is along the **Sendero El Pianista** (Pianist Trail), which winds through dairy land and into humid cloud forest. To access the trail head, take the first right fork out of Boquete (heading north) and cross over two bridges. Immediately before the 3rd bridge, about 4km out of town, a track leads off to the left between a couple of buildings. You need to wade across a small river after 200m, but then it's a steady, leisurely incline for 2km before you start to climb a steeper, narrow path. The path winds deep into the forest, though you can turn back at any time.

WHITE-WATER RAFTING

Those who seek a bit of adventure shouldn't miss the excellent white-water rafting within a two-hour drive of Boquete. The Río Chiriquí and the Río Chiriquí Viejo both flow from the fertile hills of Volcán Barú, and are flanked by forest for much of their lengths. At some places, waterfalls can be seen at the edges of the rivers, and both pass through narrow canyons with awesome, sheer rock walls.

The Río Chiriquí is most often run from May to December, while the Chiriquí Viejo is run the rest of the year; the rides tend to last four and five hours, respectively. Depending on the skill level of your party, you can tackle thrilling Class III and Class IV rapids or some seriously scary Class V rapids.

For quality white-water trips, **Boquete Outdoor Adventures** (☎ 720-2284; www.boqueteout dooradventures.com; Av Central, Plaza Los Establos) is a reputable outfitter, also offering kayak and sportfishing on the Chiriquí coast. Another good option is **Chiriquí River Rafting** (☎ 720-1505; www.panama-rafting.com; Av Central). Both staff

bilingual employees. All-day rafting trips are offered for around US$90, depending on the run and the size of the party.

CANOPY TOURS

Although canopy tours are about as prevalent as rice and beans in Costa Rica, they're still quite new to the Panama tourist scene. For the uninitiated, a canopy tour consists of a series of platforms anchored into the forest canopy and connected by zip lines. Although they were originally used by biologists to study the rainforest canopy, today they function primarily as a way for gringos to get their ecokicks.

If you're game, **Boquete Tree Trek** (☎ 720-1635, 6450-2599; www.aventurist.com; Av Central, Plaza Los Establos; ⏰ 7:30am-12:15pm & 1:15-4:30pm) offers a three-hour tour (US$70) with 12 zip lines, a rappel and a Tarzan-swing in secondary forest. These lines pick up some serious speed, so you might want to consider going a little heavy on the hand-brake.

VOLUNTEERING

Does your experience of Central America include challenging local kids to soccer or reading one a story in your brand new Spanish? **Global Humanitarian Adventures** (GHA; ☎ in USA 1-877-442-4255, in Boquete 6907-0781; www.gogha.org; Av Central, Plaza Los Establos; ⏰ 8am-4pm Mon-Fri, 8am-noon Sat) is a Red Cross–affiliated project that matches travelers with a range of fantastic volunteer opportunities.

Volunteers are needed in a range of areas from the environment to education. GHA matches your skills and interest to the job. Placement is free, no Spanish is required and there's no minimum stay. The office is shared with Boquete Outdoor Adventures.

Courses

Spanish by the River (☎ /fax 720-3456; www.spanishat locations.com) is the sister school to the popular Spanish school in Bocas del Toro. Rates for group/private lessons are US$150/290 for 20 hours, a one-week course. Cheaper rates are available for more comprehensive packages and longer stays. Students can choose homestays (US$15 per night with breakfast), simple dorms (US$10 per night) or private rooms (US$15 per night). Spanish by the River is located 5km south of Boquete near the turnoff to Palmira.

The reader-recommended **Habla Ya Language Center** (☎ 720-1294; www.hablayapanama.com; Central Av,

Plaza Los Establos; 8am-6pm Mon-Fri, 9am-noon Sat) offers both group and private lessons. A week (20 hours) of group/private lessons is US$225/295.

Both Spanish schools can arrange tours and hook up travelers with volunteer opportunities.

Festivals & Events

The town's annual festival is the **Feria de las Flores y del Café** (Flower and Coffee Fair), held for 10 days each January. Another popular event is the **Feria de Las Orquídeas** (Orchid Fair), held every April.

Sleeping

Because of the cool climate, all the places to stay in Boquete have hot showers.

Pensión Marilós (☎ 720-1380; marilos66@hotmail .com; cnr Av A Este & Calle 6 Sur; s/d without bathroom US$7/10, d US$16; P) With the feel of a well-worn family home, Marilós offers a bit of peace and quiet at bargain rates. Rooms are warmly decorated with assorted knick-knacks and doo-dads reminiscent of the guest bedroom at grandma's house. Wi-fi is in the works.

Pensión Topas (☎ 720-1005; www.pension-topas .com; Av Belisario Porras; s/d without bathroom US$10/12, s/d/ tr US$22/32/36; P 🖥 🛜 🏊) Built around a small organic garden and pool, this agreeable German-run lodging features Tintin murals and tidy rooms. A shady outdoor patio provides ample shared space and perks include an outdoor solar-heated shower, foosball and volleyball.

Refugio del Río (☎ 720-2088; www.refugiodelrio.com; dm/d/tr US$10/25/35; P) With the comfy feel of a large, well-kept home, this budget stop rises above mere hostel living. Featuring high ceilings and fine hardwood details, the sprawling rooms are pleasant and well furnished. A refreshing escape from bunk-bed living, the dormitory features a row of single beds with snug covers. The tidy lawn borders a babbling river, a background sound sure to give sweet dreams.

Mamallena (☎ 730-8342; www.mamallenaboquete.com; Av Central; dm incl breakfast US$11, d with/without bathroom US$33/28; P 🛜) On the central plaza, this creaky boardinghouse has been converted into a backpacker hub, complete with fresh paint, complimentary bicycles and free pancake breakfasts. Dorms are on the small side and private rooms are in the process of being upgraded – don't expect anything fancy. Service-oriented, it's a good place to get local information.

Hostal Boquete (☎ 720-2573; Calle 4a Sur; dm US$12, d/tr US$33/43, d/tr with view US$38/48; P 🖥 🛜) Overlooking the Río Caldera, Hostal Boquete is both attentive and attractive. It's a worthy deal for budget travelers, especially considering the attentive service given by its American owner David. While rooms are basic and functional, the best features are the riverfront terraces. There is also a decent onsite restaurant and scooter rentals.

El Oasis (☎ 720-1586; www.oasisboquete.com; Calle de la Feria; d with/without view US$55/50, ste US$75-120; P 🖥 🛜) Fresh and modern, this good-value inn sits across the river from Boquete proper, ideal for couples or groups of friends. The garden-side restaurant serves satisfying and reasonably priced meals (US$6 to US$12), which range from smoked trout with roquefort to rosemary lamb or pastas. Breakfast is included in the prices above.

Isla Verde (☎ 720-2533; islaverde@cwpanama.net; Av B Oeste; d/ste US$80/100, cabin from US$100; P 🖥 🛜) Set riverside in a beautiful, lush garden, these delicious two-story Alpine cabins feature luxuriant mattresses, vaulted ceilings, complete kitchens and roomy bathrooms. It's probably the best in-town retreat, with prompt and professional service and even professional massages available. Cabins cost US$20 extra for each additional person (US$10 for kids).

Eating & Drinking

Supermercado Romero (Av A Este; 24hr) One block east of the plaza, this has the best selection of groceries.

La Casa del Café (Av Central; coffee US$1.50; 8am-8pm) Just before the Texaco gas station, this tiny shop is the only spot in town to sample a wide variety of brands and brews, with 20 to 40 varieties, plus sandwiches and frappes.

El Sabrosón (Av Central; mains US$2-3) This much-loved local institution cooks up cheap and filling Panamanian cuisine served cafeteria style.

our pick Café de Encuentro (Calle 6 Sur; breakfast US$6; 7am-midnight) In a converted carport and garden, this family-run eatery is a true find. Eggs in warm *ranchera* sauce are a favorite, and the menu ranges from Panamanian fare to pancakes and bacon. Expect a line out the door.

Art Café La Crêpe (Av Central; mains US$6-13; 11am-9pm Tue-Sun) Fresh and festive, this cafe serves delicious incarnations of its namesake. There is a daily lunch special (US$12) with dessert and appetizer. There's also brunch on weekends.

Boquete Bistro (Av Central; mains US$10-12; 11am-10pm) Decent fare for fussy travelers, but service is slow. The steak fajitas appetizer and garden salads satisfy lesser appetites for fewer dollars. By strange election, all burgers are served on English muffins.

Zanzibar (Av Central) A low-key jazz bar with the cure for what ails ya, Zanzibar is the place to mingle with travelers and locals. Your best chance of hearing live music is on weekends, though most nights of the week you'll find a friendly face sitting at the bar. Happy hour runs from 5pm to 7pm.

La Cabaña (Calle de la Feria; cover US$2; ⏱ 7pm-2am Fri & Sat) Boquete's only disco is riverside, with DJs, reggaetón, a young crowd and a steady current of rum and Cokes to keep it flowing.

Getting There & Around

Buses to Boquete depart David's main bus terminal regularly (US$1.50, one hour, every 30 minutes from 6am to 9:30pm). Buses to David depart from the northern side of Boquete's plaza (every 30 minutes from 5am to 6:30pm). A taxi between David and Boquete costs around US$18.

Boquete's small size lends itself to easy exploration, and walking is a great way to see the area. The local *(urbano)* buses winding through the hills cost US$0.50. They depart from the main road one block north of the plaza. Taxis charge US$1 to US$2 to get to most places around town.

For scooter or bike rentals (about US$3 per hour), check out Mamallena (left) or Boquete Tree Trek (p665).

PARQUE NACIONAL VOLCÁN BARÚ

This 143-sq-km national park is home to Volcán Barú, which is Panama's only volcano as well as the dominant geographical feature of Chiriquí. Volcán Barú is no longer active (there is in fact no record of its most recent eruption), and it has not one but seven craters. Its summit, which tops out at 3475m, is the highest point in Panama; on a clear day it affords views of both the Pacific and Caribbean coasts.

The national park is also home to the Sendero Los Quetzales, one of the most scenic treks in the entire country. It is home to its namesake bird, plus over 250 bird species as well as pumas, tapirs and the *conejo pintado* (a spotted raccoon-like animal).

Unfortunately, landslides in 2009 severely damaged the trail. Until it is repaired, hikers may have to hire a guide to navigate the tricky terrain. Inquire with rangers before setting out.

Information

Admission to the park (US$5) is paid at either of the trailheads leading to the summit or at the ranger station on the Cerro Punto side of the Sendero Los Quetzales.

The best time to visit is during the dry season, especially early in the morning when wildlife is most active.

Overnight temperatures can drop below freezing, and it may be windy and cold during the day, particularly in the morning – dress accordingly.

Sights & Activities
VOLCÁN BARÚ

There are entrances to the park, with summit access, on the eastern and western sides of the volcano. The eastern access to the summit, from Boquete, is the easiest, but it involves a strenuous uphill hike along a 14km dirt/mud road that goes from the park entrance – about 8km northwest of the center of Boquete – to the summit. If you drive or take a taxi as far up as you can and then walk the rest of the way, it takes about five or six hours to reach the summit from the park gate; walking from town would take another two or three hours each way. It's best to camp on the mountain for at least one night, but be prepared for the cold. Camping will also allow you to be at the top during the morning, when the views are best.

The other park entrance is just outside the town of Volcán, on the road to Cerro Punta. The rugged 4WD-only road into the park goes only a short way off the main road to the foot of the volcano. The view of the summit and nearby peaks from this entrance is impressive, and a lovely loop trail winds through secondary and virgin forest. The climb from this side is steep and technical.

Sendero Los Quetzales

The park's most accessible trail is the scenic Sendero Los Quetzales (Quetzal Trail) near Cerro Punta. One of the most beautiful in Panama, this trail runs for 8km between Cerro Punta and Boquete, crossing back and forth over the Río Caldera. The trail can be done in either direction, but is easiest from west to east: the town of Cerro Punta is almost 1000m higher than Boquete, so hiking east is more downhill.

Please note that a recent landslide has made sections of this trail very difficult to follow. It is under repair, but progress will surely be slow. Always check on the state of the trail

PANAMA

before starting your hike, and whether a guide may be required.

In good conditions, the trail itself takes about four to five hours walking west to east, though getting to and from the trailhead will take another couple of hours of walking on either side. A 4WD taxi can take you to the start of the trail on the Cerro Punta side for about US$12; taxi drivers know the area as Respingo. The trail is 5km uphill from the main road and 2km from the last paved road. When you exit the trail, it's another 8km along the road to Boquete, though you may be able to catch a taxi along the road.

In total, the hike is about 23km, so plan accordingly if you intend to walk the length of the trail.

After arriving in Boquete, you can stay overnight or take a bus to David and then Cerro Punta; note that the last Cerro Punta bus leaves David at 6pm. You can also leave your luggage at one of the hotels in David and save yourself the hassle of backtracking. Take only the bare essentials with you on the walk (and a little cash for a good meal and/or lodging in Boquete).

Sleeping
Camping (US$5) is available in the park and on the trail to the summit from the Boquete side, along the Sendero Los Quetzales or at the ranger station at the entrance to the Sendero Los Quetzales on the Cerro Punta side.

Getting There & Away
See Volcán Barú (p667) and Sendero Los Quetzales (p667) for information.

CERRO PUNTA
At an altitude of 1800m, this small town is surrounded by beautiful, rich agricultural lands, and offers spectacular views across a fertile valley to the peaks of Parque Internacional La Amistad. Although the scenery is inspiring enough, the main reason travelers pass through here is to access the Sendero Los Quetzales or the Parque Internacional La Amistad.

The modest **Hotel Cerro Punta** (☎ 771-2020; hotelcer@hotmail.com; s/d US$25/31; P) offers a row of mint-green concrete rooms that are a bit tired and beat up. If you're on your way to either national park, enjoy the private hot-water bathroom – it's the last one you'll see for awhile.

Buses run from David to Cerro Punta (US$3, 2¼ hours, every 20 minutes from 5:30am to 8pm). If you're coming from Costa Rica, you can catch this bus at the turnoff from the Interamericana at Concepción.

PARQUE INTERNACIONAL LA AMISTAD
This 4070-sq-km national park was established jointly by Panama and Costa Rica – hence its name, La Amistad (Friendship). In Panama, the park covers portions of Chiriquí and Bocas del Toro Provinces, and is home to members of three indigenous groups: the Teribe, the Bribrí and the Ngöbe-Buglé.

The bi-national park also contains large swaths of virgin rainforest that remain home to a recorded 90 mammal species (including jaguars and pumas) and more than 300 bird species (including resplendent quetzals and harpy eagles). Although most of the park's area is high up in the Talamanca Mountains and remains inaccessible, there is no shortage of hiking and camping opportunities available for intrepid travelers.

Information
Admission to the **park** (admission US$5, campsite US$5; ◷ 8am-4pm) is paid at either of the two Panamanian entrances: one at Las Nubes, near Cerro Punta on the Chiriquí side and one at Wekso, near Changuinola on the Bocas del Toro side. Permits to camp in the park are available at the ranger station.

If you plan to spend much time at Las Nubes, be sure to bring a jacket. This side of the park, at 2280m above sea level, has a cool climate. Temperatures are usually around 24°C (75°F) in the daytime and drop to about 3°C (38°F) at night.

Sights & Activities
LAS NUBES
Three main trails originate at Las Nubes ranger station. The **Sendero La Cascada** (Waterfall Trail) is a 3.4km round-trip hike that takes in three *miradors* (lookout points) as well as a 45m-high waterfall with a lovely bathing pool. The **Sendero El Retoño** (Rebirth Trail) loops 2.1km through secondary forest, crosses a number of rustic bridges and winds through bamboo groves. The **Vereda La Montaña** (Mountain Lane) is a more strenuous 8km round-trip hike that ascends Cerro Picacho.

The Las Nubes entrance is about 7km from Cerro Punta; a sign on the main road in Cerro Punta marks the turnoff. The road starts out paved, but by the time you reach the park, it's a rutted track suitable only for 4WD vehicles. A taxi will bring you from Cerro Punta for US$4 for up to two people, then US$2 per extra person.

WEKSO

To reach Wekso, you first have to catch a bus from Changuinola to the hamlet of El Silencio (US$0.75, 40 minutes, every 20 minutes), and then take a 45-minute boat ride up the Río Teribe. In El Silencio, you can hire a five-person boat for around US$60 to US$75. If you contact the **ANAM office** (☎ 758-8967) in Changuinola about visiting Wekso, they can radio ahead and make sure there is someone at the river's edge.

Once on the river, you'll pass hills blanketed with rainforest and intermittent waterfalls; the backdrop is always the glorious Talamanca range. After about 45 minutes on the river, you'll see a sign on the right bank that announces your arrival at Wekso, which is actually a protected area but still some way from the park. There's a 3.5km loop trail at Wekso that cuts through secondary and virgin rainforest, with excellent bird-watching. You can also take a dip in the river (the water is too swift for crocodiles), but be careful not to wade out very far or the current will carry you downstream.

Sleeping

The ranger station at Las Nubes has a **dorm** (dm US$12) with bunk beds. Due to their popularity, guests need to reserve ahead via ANAM in David (p659). Guests have kitchen access; stock up on provisions in Cerro Punta. You'll also need to bring your own bedding.

Wekso has a Naso-run **guest lodge** (lodging per person US$15, 3 meals US$13) which benefits the tribe, staffed by members of the local community. Rooms are basic but there is a secure water supply, flush toilets and an outdoor shower. Workers can also prepare meals for you, lead you on guided tours through the jungle and answer all your questions about Naso culture and history. It's a five-hour hike from Wekso to the Parque Internacional La Amistad.

Wekso is administered by **ODESEN** (Organization for the Sustainable Development of Naso Ecotourism; eco turismo_naso@yahoo.es; ☎ 6569-3869), a community-based development organization that promotes ecotourism in the park as well as the cultural preservation of the Naso. Their direct contact is Raul Quintero.

Getting There & Away

See Las Nubes (opposite page) and Wekso (left) for transportation information.

THE ROAD TO BOCAS PROVINCE

If you travel along the paved road that crosses the Cordillera Central from the Interamericana to Chiriquí Grande, providing access to Bocas del Toro, you will pass a few wonderful accommodations that boast relaxation and incredible hiking opportunities. Both are located high in the Talamanca range about 41km from the Interamericana.

Sleeping & Eating

our pick **Lost & Found Lodge** (☎ 6432-8182; www .lostandfoundlodge.com; dm/d without bathroom US$12/30) A backpacker community in the cloud forest, this original lodge offers a utopian take on jungle living. The trail-accessed lodge sits perched on a steep hill facing a gaping mountain panorama. Bunks are stacked high, though you can also choose a private room that's basic but clean. Shared bathrooms are stall-style and well maintained. The young Canadian owners have plotted out every detail, from foosball tournaments to a tricked-out treasure hunt that takes visitors mucking through rivers and labyrinths, competing for a coveted bottle of cheap wine.

You don't need to lug food up here – the shelves of the open-air kitchen are stocked with the basics (pasta, eggs, sauces and vegetables) to cook, though you can also order meals if you prefer. Activities are plentiful and well-priced. Guests can visit a local coffee producer who produces organic farming or peruse the trails (those of Finca La Suiza are accessible for a fee). Lost & Found supports the local community by using community-organized tours and local guides and offering volunteer liaisons to work in farming, English teaching or outreach. If you have some extra time on your hands, ask about volunteer opportunities.

While Rocky the resident kinkajou is here because he cannot be released into the wild, other animals come for the buffet of bananas left out for them – not the best wildlife practice, but one you might see throughout the country and should discourage.

Given the isolation, it's necessary to call or email your reservation 24 hours in advance.

Finca La Suiza (☎ 6615-3774, in David 774-4030; afinis@chiriqui.com; s/d US$55/66; ⦿ closed mid-Sep–mid-Nov) Featuring 200 hectares of cloud forest and some of the best views in Panama, this is a recommended mountain retreat. The low-key lodge has three clean, comfortable rooms with private hot-water bathrooms and large picture windows. On a clear day, you can see the bright blue expanse of the Golfo de Chiriquí. The enthusiastic and warm German owners will also provide a home-cooked breakfast for about US$4 to US$7 and dinner for US$8 to US$16.

Several kilometers of well-marked hiking trails pass through primary forest. The scenery features towering trees, hundreds of bird species and views of the Reserva Forestal Fortuna, the Chiriquí mountains and the Pacific islands. Highlights include waterfalls, dipping ponds and superb vantage points across the forest canopy. Be advised that the owners keep dogs that roam freely at night, and for morning bird-watching you'll need to ask for them to be tied up. Entrance to the trails costs guests US$8 for the duration of their stay; nonguests pay US$8 per day.

English, Spanish and German are spoken. Since it's isolated, it is best to make reservations in advance. The best time to call is between 7pm and 9pm.

Getting There & Away

Lost & Found Lodge provides shuttle transportation from David (US$30), or you can take the bus (US$3 from David). After one hour, the bus reaches a yellow tollbooth followed by a sign near Km 42 that says 'You have found the lost paradise.' From here, hike up a path for 15 minutes, following the signs. You can also take a bus from the Bocas side, starting in Changuinola or Almirante (around US$8).

To get to Finca La Suiza, take any Changuinola-bound bus from David (hourly starting at 5am) and ask the driver to drop you off. Coming from the Interamericana, the lodge is to the right just after the only gas station on the road. Coming from the north, the lodge is on the left 1.3km after a toll plaza for trucks. You can leave luggage with the caretaker near the entrance gate while hiking.

BOCAS DEL TORO

Where primary rainforest meets banana plantation and Caribbean islands dot a shock of blue waters, Bocas del Toro Province promises all that is tropical. Located 32km from the Costa Rican border, the Archipiélago de

Bocas del Toro consists of six densely forested islands, scores of uninhabited islets and Panama's oldest marine park, Parque Nacional Marino Isla Bastimentos. Naturally beautiful and half-tame, Bocas is Panama's principal tourist draw, the place for a hefty dose of sun and surf.

In addition to being the longtime roost of Chiquita Banana, the mainland is home to the Panamanian half of the binational Parque Internacional La Amistad, home of megafauna such as the elusive jaguar, as well as Ngöbe-Buglé settlements. Deep in the forest live the last remaining Naso, one of the only tribes in the Americas to retain their traditional monarchy.

Few visitors are disappointed with the perfect Bocas cocktail of water fun and thatched luxury. Unfortunately, the secret has leaked, and there's no sign that development will slow down. The real-estate boom has brought bulldozers and bullying interests, making locals debate the merits of increased tourism when there may not be the infrastructure to support it.

ISLA COLÓN

Relaxed as it is, Isla Colón has ridden a major development boom. Since the mid-1990s, foreign investors have been buying up land like crazy, with new hotels, restaurants and condos constantly springing up. Fortunately, there's still a heavy dose of local flavor, and the lack of beachside Pizza Huts is testament to the fact that development is still years behind similar destinations in nearby Costa Rica.

ACTIVITIES
Diving & Snorkeling

With nearly 40 rivers unloading silt into the seas around Bocas del Toro, the archipelago's waters are notorious for poor visibility. For example, if it has rained a lot in recent days, visibility may be limited to only 3m; at best visibility is about 15m. Although experienced divers accustomed to crystal-clear Caribbean diving may be disappointed with Bocas, the islands still have much to offer.

The emerald green waters of the archipelago are home to barracuda, stingrays, dolphins and nurse sharks. Better sites nearby include **Dark Wood Reef**, northwest of Bastimentos; **Hospital Point**, a 50ft wall off Cayo Nancy; and the base of the **Punta Juan buoy** north of Isla Cristóbal.

PADI-certified **Starfleet Eco Adventures** (Map p674; ☎ 757-9630; www.starfleetscuba.com; Calle 1A) and

Bocas Water Sports (Map p674; ☎/fax 757-9541; www .bocaswatersports.com; Calle 3) offer diving trips. They cost around US$60 for a two-tank dive and US70 for a full-day tour. PADI open-water and advanced-diver courses are available. Both dive shops also offer snorkeling on their boat tours.

Boat Tours

The most popular tours in the area are all-day snorkeling trips, which are perfect for nondivers who want a taste of the area's rich marine life. A typical tour costs US$20 per person, and goes to Dolphin Bay, Cayo Crawl, Red Frog Beach and Hospital Point. A trip to the distant Cayos Zapatillas costs US$25 (plus an additional US$10 for admission to the marine park), and includes lunch, a laze on the beach and a jungle walkabout on Cayo Zapatilla Sur.

In addition to the dive operators listed earlier, a recommended tour operator is **J&J Tours** (Map p674; ☎ 757-9915; transparentetour@hotmail .com; Calle 3).

Many 'tours' are really little more than boat transportation to a pretty spot. If you have your own snorkel gear (or if you rent it), you can also get the local boatmen to take you around the area in their small, motorized canoes. Agree on a price before you go.

Surfing

Although everyone (and their grandmother) seems to have picked up surfing in nearby Puerto Viejo, Bocas del Toro is still emerging as an international surf destination. It offers an excellent mix of beginner beach breaks, ripping reefs breaks and some seriously suicidal breaks.

For surfing information on nearby Isla Bastimentos and Isla Carenero, see p679 and p677 respectively.

Beginner surfers looking for a bit of reef experience should check out **Playa Punch**, which offers a good mix of lefts and rights. Although it can get heavy when big, Punch generally offers some of the kindest waves around.

Just past Punch on route to Playa Bluff is a popular reef break known as **Dumps**. This left break can get up to 3m, and should only be ridden by experienced surfers as wiping out on the reef here is a dangerous affair. There is also an inner break known as **Inner Dumps**, which also breaks left, but is more forgiving than its outer brother.

Be careful walking out on the reefs as they are sharp and full of urchins – wear booties. If you wipe out and get cut up, be sure to properly disinfect your wounds. Although salt water heals, sea water doesn't, especially in the Caribbean where the water temperature means that the ocean is full of live bacteria.

The island's most notorious surf spot is **Playa Bluff**, which throws out powerful barreling waves that break in shallow water along the beach, and have a reputation for snapping boards (and occasionally bones). Though waves close quickly, the tubes here are truly awesome, especially when the swells are strong.

You can rent surfboards from **Tropix Surf** (Map p674; ☎ 757-9727; Calle 3; ☼ 9am-7pm) or Mondo Taitú (see p675). If heading out to Isla Bastimentos or Isla Carenero, arrange your board in advance as there are no surf shops on either island.

Kayaking

Although you will need to be wary of boat traffic and the occasional swell, a great way to travel between islands is by sea kayak. Bocas Water Sports rents kayaks for US$3 per hour.

Cycling

Whether you're heading to Boca del Drago on the paved road or taking the dirt path to Playa Bluff, a bike can seriously increase your mobility. Note that the bike ride to Boca del Drago is taxing, especially when the sun is beaming. If you're unsure of your fitness level, it's advised that you head to Punta Bluff instead, even though the road can flood after heavy rains.

Hiking

If you're looking to get well off the beaten path, there is a network of undeveloped hiking trails that fan out across the island. One of the more popular hikes starts at the end of the coastal road in Mimbi Timbi and carries on along the coast to Boca del Drago. You will need about six hours of daylight to complete the hike and you must carry in all your fresh water. The trail winds past caves, caverns and plenty of vine-entangled jungle. A bike will help speed things up a bit, though you will be carrying it part of the way, especially if it's been raining recently.

Sailing

With affordable overnight adventures and options for snorkeling, fishing and dolphin-watching, **Catamaran Sailing Adventures** (Map p674; ☎ 757-9710; www.bocassailing.com; Av Sur; snorkel tour US$40) has popular tours on a 42-foot catamaran that are kid-friendly too.

PANAMA

PANAMA

ARCHIPIÉLAGO DE BOCAS DEL TORO

0   5 km
0   3 miles

SIGHTS & ACTIVITIES
Bocas Butterfly Farm....................1 C3
Dark Wood Reef............................2 D3
La Gruta (Communidad Bahia
    Honda)..3 B2
Nivida Cave...................................4 E4
Punta Juan Buoy..........................5 B4

SLEEPING 🛏
Aqua Lounge...............................6 C3
Cabañas Estefany.......................7 A1
Casa Acuario..............................8 C3
La Coralina.................................9 C2

EATING 🍴
Bibi's...10 C3
Island Time Thai.........................11 D3
Up in the Hill..............................12 D3

82°15'W

CARIBBEAN SEA

Punta
Cauto

*Boca
del
Drago*

Punta
Norte

Isla Colón

Punta
Ricosa

Playa
Bluff

Punta
Bluff

Playa
Puuch

Bahía
Pass Head

Big
Creek

Playa
El Istmito

BOCAS DEL
TORO

Isla
Carenero

Hospital
Point

Old
Bank

Wizard
Beach

Playa
Segunda

Red Frog
Beach

Playa
Larga

Parque Nacional
Marino Isla
Bastimentos

Isla
Bastimentos

Quebrada Sal

Isla
Solarte

Cayo
Nancy

Conch Point

Punta
Runcho

*Bahía de
Almirante*

Isla
Cristóbal

82°15'W

Fishing
The best budget option for aspiring anglers is to go surf casting with the local water-taxi drivers. The hand lines are a bit tricky at first, though you'll get the hang of it. It's best to go early in the morning when the fish are biting; prices are negotiable.

Bocas del Toro
The archipelago's largest and most developed island is home to the provincial capital, Bocas del Toro, a colorful town of wooden houses built by the United Fruit Company in the early 20th century. Today, Bocas is a slow-paced community of West Indians, Latinos and resident gringos. It serves as a convenient base for exploring the marine national park, as *taxis marinos* (water taxis) can whisk you away to remote beaches and snorkeling sites.

ORIENTATION
Bocas town is laid out in a grid pattern with most of the hotels and restaurants on Calle 3. The airport is on Av E, four blocks from Calle 3.

Note that the town, the archipelago and the province all share the name Bocas del Toro. Isla Colón and Bocas del Toro town are also referred to as Bocas Isla. It rains a lot in Bocas – even in the dry season, there can be long periods of constant showers.

INFORMATION
For more information on the islands, see the useful English website www.bocas.com or check out the island's monthly bilingual publication, *The Bocas Breeze* (www.thebocas breeze.com).

ANAM (Map p674; ☎ 757-9442; Calle 1) Not really set up as a tourist information office, though they can answer questions about the national park or other protected areas. If you want to camp out in any of the protected areas, you must first get a permit from an ANAM office.

ATP tourist office (Map p674; ☎ 757-9642; ☽ 8:30am-3:30pm Mon-Fri) In Centro de Facilidades Turísticas e Interpretación (Cefati) on the eastern waterfront. A color map in English and Spanish is available.

Banco Nacional de Panamá (Map p674; cnr Calle 4 & Av E; ☽ 8am-2pm Mon-Fri, 8am-noon Sat) Exchanges traveler's checks and has a 24-hour ATM.

Bocas Internet Café (Map p674; Calle 3; per hr US$1.50; ☽ 8am-10pm)

Bocas Sustainable Tourism Alliance (Map p674; ☎ 6086-2331; www.discoverbocasdeltoro.com; Calle 3) English-speaking with good reference information for travelers. Arranges tours and visits to a Ngöbe crafts workshop on Isla San Cristobal. You can recycle plastic bags here (they get made into very cool purses by local women) and get water refills to avoid buying more plastic.

Cable & Wireless (Map p674; Calle 1) International calls can be made here.

Hospital (Map p674; ☎ 757-9201; Av G; ☽ 24hr) The island's only hospital has a 24-hour emergency room.

Post office (Map p674; Governmental Bldg, Calle 3)

DANGERS & ANNOYANCES
The surf can be quite dangerous on some beaches, with frequently strong riptides – use caution when going out into the waves. If you get caught in a rip, swim parallel to the shore and don't panic.

Tap water is not safe to drink in Bocas del Toro. Bocas Sustainable Tourism Alliance refills water bottles.

Bocas del Toro is a conservative place, and local law prevents both men and women from walking down the streets topless. Even if you are on your way to the beach, wear a shirt or you will be sent back to your hotel if spotted by the police.

SIGHTS
Boca del Drago
Located on the western side of Isla Colón, this sleepy beach (Map p672) is famed for its huge numbers of starfish. The calm and relaxed vibe at Boca del Drago is perfect for beach bums. The swimming and snorkeling here is good, especially when the sea is calm and the water is clear. Although it's not as stunning as the wilderness beaches on Isla Bastimentos, the lack of surge here means that this is the safest spot in the archipelago for nonsurfers.

Cabañas Estefany (p675) is the one place to stay here. To get here from Bocas, take a

---

ASK A LOCAL

Mass tourism has been hard on Bocas, so when you go, think sustainable. Avoid using small plastic water bottles; support sustainable tourism with a visit to the Ngöbe-run restaurant in Communidad Bahía Honda (p675); make sure your boat in Dolphin Bay keeps a respectable distance from the dolphins, and use the co-op of local boaters (p687) who show more consciousness in their boating practices.

Daniel, Bocas del Toro

local bus, water taxi (US$15 to US$20 round-trip) or taxi (US$15 one way). The bus leaves from Bocas plaza (US$0.70, one hour) at 7am, 10am, noon, 3pm and 5pm. Return trips go at 8am, 11am, 1pm, 4pm and 6pm, though afternoon trips tend to experience delays.

Other Beaches

A string of beaches on the eastern side of Isla Colón can be reached by a road that skirts up the coast from town. There's no public transportation to the beaches, but a 4WD taxi will take you to any of them and pick you up at an appointed time for a negotiable price – expect to pay US$40 for a round-trip taxi to Playa Bluff, since road conditions may be poor.

The closest beach to town, **Playa El Istmito** (Map p674), is plagued by *chitras* (sand flies). Since it's not the most attractive beach, it's worth heading further north.

Further up the coast is **Playa Punch** (Map p672), which is dangerous for swimming but good for surfing.

After you round Punta Bluff, the road takes you along **Playa Bluff** (Map p672), a secluded wilderness beach that is pounded by intense waves. Although you wouldn't want to get into the water here without a board, the soft, yellow sand and palm-fringed shores are pristine and well worth the trip. Playa Bluff stretches for 5km all the way to Punta Rocosa, and serves as a nesting area for sea turtles from May to September.

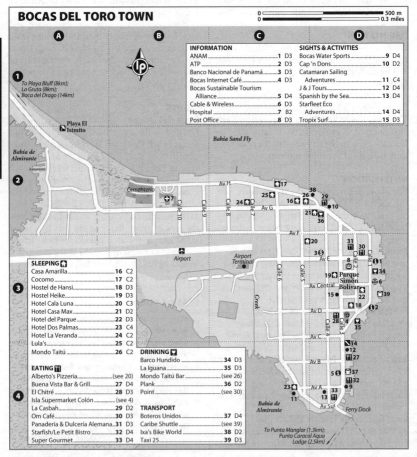

BOCAS DEL TORO TOWN

0 — 500 m
0 — 0.3 miles

INFORMATION	
ANAM	1 D3
ATP	2 D3
Banco Nacional de Panamá	3 D3
Bocas Internet Café	4 D3
Bocas Sustainable Tourism Alliance	5 D4
Cable & Wireless	6 D3
Hospital	7 B2
Post Office	8 D3

SIGHTS & ACTIVITIES	
Bocas Water Sports	9 D4
Cap 'n Dons	10 D2
Catamaran Sailing Adventures	11 C4
J & J Tours	12 D4
Spanish by the Sea	13 D4
Starfleet Eco Adventures	14 D4
Tropix Surf	15 D3

SLEEPING	
Casa Amarilla	16 C2
Cocomo	17 C2
Hostel de Hansi	18 D3
Hostel Heike	19 D3
Hotel Cala Luna	20 C3
Hotel Casa Max	21 D2
Hotel del Parque	22 D3
Hotel Dos Palmas	23 C4
Hotel La Veranda	24 C2
Lula's	25 C2
Mondo Taitú	26 C2

EATING	
Alberto's Pizzeria	(see 20)
Buena Vista Bar & Grill	27 D4
El Chitré	28 D3
Isla Supermarket Colón	(see 4)
La Casbah	29 D2
Om Café	30 D3
Panadería & Dulcería Alemana	31 D3
Starfish/Le Petit Bistro	32 D3
Super Gourmet	33 D4

DRINKING	
Barco Hundido	34 D3
La Iguana	35 D3
Mondo Taitú Bar	(see 26)
Plank	36 D2
Point	(see 30)

TRANSPORT	
Boteros Unidos	37 D4
Caribe Shuttle	(see 39)
Ixa's Bike World	38 D2
Taxi 25	39 D3

To Playa Bluff (8km);
La Gruta (8km);
Boca del Drago (14km)

Playa El Istmito

Bahía de Almirante

Bahía Sand Fly

Cementerio

Av H
Av G
Av F
Av E
Av Central
Av D
Av C
Av B
Av A
Av Sur

Calle 10
Calle 9
Calle 8
Calle 7
Calle 6
Calle 5
Calle 4
Calle 3
Calle 2
Calle 1

Airport
Airport Terminal

Creek

Parque Simón Bolívar

Bahía de Almirante

Ferry Dock

To Punta Manglar (1.3km);
Punta Caracol Aqua
Lodge (2.5km)

PANAMA

La Gruta

If sun, sand and surf aren't your persuasion, then consider taking a trip to the indigenous **Communidad Bahía Honda**. Here you'll find **La Gruta** (The Cavern; Map p672), a cave where you can wade through waist-high water while trying not to disturb the thousands of sleeping bats overhead. The entrance to the cave, which is marked by a statue of the Virgin Mary, is located 8km from Bocas town along the road to Boca del Drago. There is also a small community restaurant. A taxi should cost about US$15 round trip or take the bus.

Bocas Butterfly Farm

A great morning trip from Bocas, this adorable **butterfly farm** (Map p672; ☎ 757-9008; www.bocas butterfly.com; adult/child US$5/2; ☖ 9am-3pm Mon-Sat, 9am-noon Sun) houses species from every corner of Panama. There is no road access – hire a water taxi from Bocas town for US$1 one way.

COURSES

A reader-recommended language school, **Spanish by the Sea** (Map p674; ☎ /fax 757-9518; www .spanishbythesea.com; Calle 4) offers affordable Spanish classes in a relaxed setting. Group lessons are US$150 per week for 20 hours. The school also offers a popular survival Spanish course to jump-start your travels.

Homestays can be arranged (US$15 per night with breakfast), or you can bunk down in clean and comfy dorms (US$10) or private rooms (US$15). Spanish by the Sea also organizes parties, dance classes and open lectures. English, Spanish, French, German and Dutch are spoken.

FESTIVALS & EVENTS

Bocas celebrates all of Panama's holidays, with a few enjoyable local ones besides. Annual events celebrated on Bocas and Bastimentos include the following:

May Day (May 1) A Maypole dance performed by local girls.

Día de la Virgen del Carmen (third Sunday in July) Pilgrimage to La Gruta caves for a mass in honor of the Virgen del Carmen.

Feria del Mar (September 28 to October 2) Held on Playa El Istmito, a few kilometers north of Bocas.

Fundación de la Provincia de Bocas del Toro (November 16) A big affair celebrating the foundation of the province in 1904 with parades and other events.

Día de Bastimentos (November 23) Bastimentos Day is celebrated with a huge parade and drumming exhibitions.

SLEEPING

Reservations are a good idea between December and April and during national holidays and local festivals.

Cabañas Estefany (Map p672; ☎ 6624-9246; campsite per person US$5, kitchen use US$5, d US$35, 5-/7-person cabin US$20/65) Located at Boca del Drago, this is one of the few beach lodgings on Isla Colón. Its wooden *cabañas* are bare bones, some without fans and all with cold showers. Secure a room with a fan as it can get quite buggy. Cabins are often booked with scientific researchers, so it's recommended that you call ahead.

Mondo Taitú (Map p674; ☎ /fax 757-9425; www.mondo taitu.com; Av H; dm/d US$10/22, dm with air-con US$12; ✂ 🖥) Though it looks like a strong wind could collapse it, this is Bocas' backpacker hub. Built on good vibes, this hostel makes good with a chill social atmosphere, freebies and nightlife. There's a communal kitchen, lounge area, laundry facilities, free bikes and surfboards.

our pick **Hostel Heike** (Map p674; ☎ 757-9708; www .hostelheike.com; Calle 3; dm with/without air-con US$17/10; ✂ 🖥) Awash with colorful murals and natural woods, Heike is the perfect spot for chilling Caribbean-style. Expertly managed by a friendly Panamanian, it gets rave reviews from travelers. The sprawling roof deck with fans and hammocks is the perfect spot to indulge in a cold beer and a good book.

Hostel de Hansi (Map p674; ☎ 757-9085; Calle 3; s without bathroom US$11, d US$25) This cheery German-run lodging recently underwent major renovations. It prides itself on a quiet, family-friendly setting. Spotless rooms have fans; doubles sport their own balcony and guests have use of an ample kitchen.

Hotel La Veranda (Map p674; ☎ 757-9211; www .explorepanama.com/veranda.htm; Av G; d without bathroom US$29, d/tr US$56/66) This lovely residence-turned-inn was built in 1910 and has been maintained down to its gleaming hardwood floors. The six unique guest rooms have early-20th-century antique furnishings. The veranda is perfect for an afternoon sundowner.

Hotel Casa Max (Map p674; ☎ 757-9120; casa1max @hotmail.com; Av G; d US$35) This Dutch-owned spot offers brightly painted wooden rooms with firm beds and high ceilings. Guests get hot-water showers, though some bathrooms are dated and worn. Dreamy balconies overlook the town and the ocean, and a breakfast of fresh fruits and strong coffee sweetens the deal.

Hotel Dos Palmas (Map p674; ☎ 757-9906; Av Sur; d US$35) Proudly '100% Bocatoreño,' Dos Palmas offers basic wooden rooms with old-fashioned furnishings. Run by a friendly matriarch, it's not some cookie-cutter lodging, though some might find it a little musty. It sits above the water and boasts exceptional views of the bay.

Hotel del Parque (Map p674; ☎ 757-9008; Calle 2; s/d/tr US$37/45/50; 🅿 🛜) A classic Caribbean house fronting the plaza, this tranquil place has B&B style within budget reach. Ample rooms have big windows, cool cement floors and firm beds in crisp linens. The terraces provide views of the action on the plaza and hammocks for cat naps.

Hotel Cala Luna (Map p674; ☎ 757-9066; www.calaluna bocas.com; Calle 5; s/d/tr US$45/55/65; 🅿 🖳) Built atop legendary Alberto's Pizza, the Italian-owned Cala Luna features cathedral windows, tasteful wood details and crisp, functional rooms. As an added bonus, guests can watch planes coming in for a landing 30m above their heads from a pair of lookouts on the roof.

Casa Amarilla (Map p674; ☎ 757-9938; Calle 5; d US$50; 🅿 🖳) In a cute yellow house, these four motel-style rooms come decked out with amenities. Each has a laptop with internet connections, flat-screen TV and hot water. The American owners are usually around to help or to share a morning cup of coffee with you.

Lula's (Map p674; ☎ 757-9057; www.lulabb.com; Av Norte; d/tr/q incl breakfast US$55/66/77; 🅿 🖳) A place of rockers and porches, this lovely B&B is a welcome addition to the Bocas scene. Rooms are immaculate, with hot-water showers and a snug design. The American hosts give first-rate service, in addition to big southern breakfasts.

La Coralina (Map p672; ☎ 6788-8992; www.lacoralina .com; Punta Bluff; d with/without bathroom US$100/60, ste US$120; 🅿 🛜) On the way to Punta Bluff, this attentive resort in a cool colonial offers airy rooms, sprawling decks and sea views. The location – facing two world-class surf breaks, stuns those with tubes on the brain. Active travelers can take advantage of the private nature trails and horseback riding on offer.

Cocomo (Map p674; ☎ 757-9259; www.cocomoonthe sea.com; cnr Av Norte & Calle 6A; s/d/tr incl breakfast US$66/83/94; 🅿 🖳) A sweet clapboard house with a tropical garden and hammock deck on the sea, Cocomo wants for nothing. A local pioneer, this American-run bed and breakfast knows service. Rooms have hot water, and breakfast includes fresh pastries, fruit, yogurt and omelets. Kayaks are complimentary.

EATING

Bocas town has some of the best dining options in Panama. All are on Map p674. On Saturdays, a farmers market operates in Parque Simon Bolívar. Food carts sell roast chicken and juices, but ask for bottled water in your *batido*.

Isla Supermarket Colón (Calle 3) The largest supermarket on the island.

Super Gourmet (Calle 3) Stocks specialty items such as rotisserie chicken, Mexican food, wine and frozen bagels.

Panadería & Dulcería Alemana (Calle 2; pastries US$1-3; 🕑 7am-8pm Mon-Sat, 8am-4pm Sun) Frothy cappuccinos, whole-grain bread and moist slabs of carrot cake are the order of the day at this German bakery.

El Chitré (Calle 3; plates US$2-3) Patronized by locals and travelers alike, this no-frills cafeteria is the best spot in town for cheap but tasty grub.

Buena Vista Bar & Grill (Calle 1; mains US$5-12) This waterfront restaurant serves nachos, bacon cheeseburgers and brownie sundaes to hungry expats. Dinner ups the ante with seafood and fish dishes.

Starfish/Le Petit Bistro (Calle 1; tapas US$4-6; 🕑 8am-noon & 6-10pm Mon-Sat, 9am-2pm Sun) With homespun charm, Starfish is a coffee and smoothie bar by day, with stacks of fashion mags and comfy chairs. By night it's candlelit and serves good French cuisine, tapas and sashimi. Foreign-run and friendly, it's worth a try.

Alberto's Pizzeria (Calle 5; pizzas US$9; 🕑 noon-10pm Mon-Sat) Sardinian-run Alberto's is a favorite local haunt where you can even play ping-pong while anticipating your dinner. Fresh pizzas with toppings such as artichokes, kalamata olives and gorgonzola satisfy big appetites.

Om Café (Av H; mains US$6.50-15; 🕑 8am-noon & 6-10pm Fri-Tue) Guaranteed to make your brow sweat, this welcoming Indian cafe cooks up classic curries and vindaloo with crisp hot naan. Service may be slow, so order up a cocktail to keep you company (try the Tipsy Turban – a dizzy mix of passion fruit, rum and sugar).

La Casbah (☎ 6477-4227; Av H; mains US$8-15; 🕑 6-10pm Tue-Sat) Popular with locals and travelers alike, this Mediterranean restaurant serves up gazpacho, goat's cheese salad and well-prepared meats and seafood. The fish of the day comes in cucumber and coconut sauce and there's a nice baked veggie plate for non-meat-eaters. Reserve ahead.

DRINKING

Kick off your crazy Bocas night at **La Iguana** (Calle 1), a popular surfer/skate bar that will start you off with a US$1.50 beer-tequila combo. You probably won't be in the mood for the dancing pole yet, though.

Next, head to backpacker central, namely the **Mondo Taitú Bar** (Av I), which always guarantees a good time. On Tuesdays and Fridays, the party-loving owners entertain their guests with a variety of themed events, though the creative cocktail list and hookahs (US$5) make Mondo a good choice any night. If you're feeling brave (and cheap), order a tequila suicide – a snort of salt, a squeeze of lime in the eye and a shot of the worst tequila they can find (at least it's free!).

Caribbean pub and bar **Plank** (Av 1; 5-11pm) has bar seating on faded decks to live music that spans from reggae to disco. Happy hour is daily from 7pm to 9pm and women get free drinks on Tuesdays and Fridays. Another spot is **Point** (Av H), a chill hangout located below Om, with pool tables and US$1 shots.

Most nights in Bocas end at the **Barco Hundido** (Calle 1), an open-air bar that's affectionately known as the 'Wreck Deck' – the name comes from the sunken banana boat that rests in the clear Caribbean waters in the front. A short boardwalk extends from the bar to an island seating area perfect for stargazing.

All of these places are on Map p674.

GETTING THERE & AWAY

Air

Both **Aeroperlas** (757-9341) and **Air Panama** (757-9841) offer daily flights connecting Bocas with Panama City (US$100, one hour, one to two daily). Aeroperlas also has flights from David to Bocas (US$55, 50 minutes, daily from Monday to Friday). **Nature Air** (in USA 800-235-9272; www.natureair.com) has flights from San José, Costa Rica to Bocas (US$160, 1½ hours, 7am on Sunday, Wednesday and Friday).

Boat

If you don't fly into Bocas you'll have to take a water taxi (US$4) from Almirante on the mainland (for more information, see p680). On the waterfront, Taxi 25 makes the half-hour trip every half hour from 6am to 6:30pm. To reach Puerto Viejo, Costa Rica, **Caribe Shuttle** (757-7048; www.caribeshuttle.com) offers a combination boat-bus trip (US$28) daily at 9am, arriving in Puerto Viejo at 11:30am

(Costa Rica time). They provide a hotel pickup but you must reserve one day in advance.

GETTING AROUND

To reach nearby islands, you can hire boaters operating motorized boats and canoes along the waterfront. As a general rule, you should always sort out the rate beforehand, and clarify if it is for one way or round trip. Rates vary but you will get a better deal if you speak Spanish, are with a group and arrange for a pickup.

Locals claim **Boteros Unidos** (Calle 3) consistently offer fair prices; the staff is also trained in safe boating and sustainable tourism practices. Round-trip rates are generally US$8 to the near side of Isla Bastimentos and US$2 to Isla Carenero. Although you should always pay on the return leg – this guarantees a pickup – most boaters will want some money upfront so that they can buy petrol.

You can rent a wide selection of bicycles from **Ixa's Bike World** (Av H; 8am-6pm) for US$10 per day.

ISLA CARENERO

A few hundred meters from Isla Colón, the oft-forgotten island of Isla Carenero takes its name from 'careening,' nautical talk for leaning a ship on one side for maintenance. In October, 1502 Columbus docked his fleet here for careening while he recovered from a bellyache.

Today, the wave of development that transformed Isla Colón is also making headway on Isla Carenero. Staying on the island is a quiet alternative to Isla Colón.

Orientation

Water taxis dock at the small marina on the tip of the island. From here, a path that leads to the island's fledgling town, and continues across the island.

Activities

Those serious about **surfing** can tackle Silverbacks, an enormous barreling right that breaks over a reef, with heights of over 5m. On a good day Silverbacks is a world-class break that wouldn't look out of place on Hawaii's North Shore. Since it breaks off the coast, a water taxi is required to reach it.

For surf classes (three hours US$45) or kayak rentals (half-day US$10), check out Bibi's (see p678), where Argentine surf instructor **Luis** (www.escueladelmarsurf@gmail.com) offers tailored trips.

PANAMA

PANAMA

EXPLORE MORE OF BOCAS DEL TORO

Skip the crowds by hiring a boat and checking out:

- **Cayo Crawl** Get lost in these mangrove-dotted channels near Isla Bastimentos.

- **Cayos Zapatillas** Set out for these pristine white-sand beaches and virgin forests.

- **Dolphin Bay** Spot dolphins frolicking at this densely populated breeding ground.

- **Swan Cay** Spot red-billed tropic birds and white-crowned pigeons in this cay near Isla de Los Pájaros.

Sleeping & Eating

Although not as popular as Isla Colón or Isla Bastimentos, Isla Carenero is a good option for travelers who want a different view of the islands.

Aqua Lounge (Map p672; ☎ 757-9042; www.bocas aqualounge.com; dm US$10) This backpacker palace is a rustic matchstick construction on the dock facing Bocas. Guests love it or leave it, but it says Spring Break in so many ways. The onsite bar is hugely popular, then there's the aquatic trampoline…

Casa Acuario (Map p672; ☎ 757-9565; d US$85-94;) Visually dreamy, this tropical inn sits above crystal-blue waters teeming with tropical fish. Rooms are impeccably outfitted with smart fixtures and rustic, crafty touches. The big draw is the private decks and open-air dining.

Bibi's (Map p672; mains US$5-10; Wed-Mon) This thatched, over-the-water restaurant and surf outfitter makes fresh salads, tasty soups and lightly fried fish. The service couldn't be friendlier and the sea views will keep you lingering.

Getting There & Away

Isla Carenero is a quick and easy US$1 boat ride from Bocas town.

ISLA BASTIMENTOS

Although it's a mere 10-minute boat ride from the town of Bocas del Toro, Isla Bastimentos is a different world. The northern coast of the island is home to palm-fringed wilderness beaches that serve as nesting grounds for sea turtles, while most of the southern coast consists of mangrove islands and coral reefs within the boundaries of the Parque Nacional

Marino Isla Bastimentos. The main settlement is the historic West Indian town of Old Bank, which has its origins in the banana industry. The island is also home to the Ngöbe-Buglé village of Quebrada Sal, separated from Old Bank by a huge swath of jungle.

Long the stronghold of Afro-Caribbean culture in Bocas, Bastimentos is changing in nature, not in small part to Red Frog Beach Rainforest Resort & Marina, a luxury development project that puts destination real estate front and center.

Orientation

The small village of Old Bank has no roads, just a wide, concrete footpath lined on both sides with colorfully painted wooden houses. From the town, there is a path leading across the island to Wizard Beach and Red Frog Beach, though the route can turn into a virtual swamp following the rains.

On the southeastern side of the island is the remote Ngöbe-Buglé village of Quebrada Sal. Tropical forest covers the interior of the island; you can explore it, but go only with a guide, as it's very easy to get lost.

Dangers & Annoyances

Readers have reported muggings on the trail to Wizard Beach. Never go on any trail after dark and always travel with a friend. The alternate trail (follow the signs from town to Island Time Thai and beyond) is slightly longer but more secure.

Sights

OLD BANK

Although very poor and somewhat depressed, Old Bank has a much more pronounced Caribbean vibe than Bocas town, and it's a relaxing place to stroll around and soak up the atmosphere. You may hear Guari-Guari, the Spanish-English Creole language.

BEACHES

Bastimentos has some amazing beaches, though be careful swimming as the surf can really pick up on the north coast of the island.

The most beautiful beach on the island is **Wizard Beach** (also known as Playa Primera), which is awash in powder-yellow sand and backed by thick vine-strewn jungle. Although Wizard Beach is connected to Old Bank via a wilderness path, the mere 30-minute walk can turn into an all-day trek through the muck if it's been raining heavily.

Assuming the weather is cooperating, you can continue walking along the coast to **Playa Segunda** (Second Beach) and **Red Frog Beach**. Like Wizard, both beaches are stunning and virtually abandoned, though it's likely that this will change as development on the island continues. If the weather isn't cooperating, you can access Red Frog Beach by water taxi via a small marina on the south side of the island; entrance to the beach is US$2. While you are on Red Frog beach, keep an eye out for the *rana rojo* (strawberry poison-dart frog) as they might not be on the island for too much longer.

The path continues past Red Frog Beach to **Playa Larga** (Long Beach), where sea turtles nest from April to August. Playa Larga and much of the eastern side of the island fall under the protection of Parque Nacional Marino Isla Bastimentos.

PARQUE NACIONAL MARINO ISLA BASTIMENTOS

Established in 1988, this was Panama's first **marine park** (admission US$10). Protecting various areas of the Bocas del Toro Archipelago including parts of Isla Bastimentos and the Cayos Zapatillas, the marine park is an important nature reserve for countless species of Caribbean wildlife.

You can get current park information from the ATP or ANAM offices in Bocas del Toro (p673). The dive operators and boatmen in Bocas are also good sources of information about the park and its attractions. If you want to camp out anywhere in the park, you are required to first obtain a permit from ANAM.

QUEBRADA SAL

On the southeastern edge of Bastimentos at the end of a long canal cut through the mangrove forest is the Ngöbe-Buglé village of Quebrada Sal (Salt Creek). The community consists of 60-odd thatch and bamboo houses, an elementary school, a handicrafts store, a general store and a soccer field. Water taxis can drop you off at the entrance to pay the US$1 entry fee and sign the visitors' log.

The Quebrada Sal is slowly modernizing along with the rest of the archipelago. The villagers are friendly and open to visitors, especially if you can speak Spanish. If you have the time, it's worth hiring a local guide to walk with you along the cross-island trail that leads to Playa Larga (about one hour each way).

Activities
DIVING & SNORKELING
Diving trips are offered by **Dutch Pirate** (☎ 6567-1812; www.thedutchpirate.com), with an office in Old Bank, though it's best to phone ahead to make a reservation. For more information on diving and snorkeling, see p670.

SURFING
If you're looking for a solid beach break, both Wizard Beach and Red Frog Beach offer fairly constant sets of lefts and rights that are perfect for beginner and intermediate surfers. When the swells are in, Wizard occasionally throws out some huge barrels, though they tend to close up pretty quickly.

SPELUNKING & HIKING
The fascinating **Nivida cave** is one of the island's natural wonders, and half the fun is getting there. At Roots (see p680) you can arrange a trip with Oscar (prices negotiable), a reliable local guide. You'll then travel by small motorboat up a channel through lush vegetation full of wildlife. A short walk through the jungle leads to a massive cavern complete with swarms of nectar bats and a swimmable subterranean lake.

Oscar can also arrange a challenging cross-island hike to **Laguna de Bastimentos**, a jungle lake completely surrounded by dense vegetation. This swath of rainforest is the terra firma section of the Parque Nacional Marino Isla Bastimentos.

Sleeping
Hostel Bastimentos (☎ 757-9053; Old Bank; dm US$6, d US$12-20, d with air-con US$40; ✗) On a hill off the main path, this sprawling yellow clapboard has a bright selection of 28 rooms and hammock decks. Spaces are creaky but serviceable and the host, Dixon, couldn't be nicer. Backpacker-ready, it has two kitchens and a common room with a bar, TV and dartboard.

Beverly's Hill (☎ 757-9923; www.beverlyshill.blogspot .com; Old Bank; d US$40-50, s/d without bathroom US$14/20) Run by Simon from Brighton, these jungle cabins occupy a lush green garden replete with red frogs. Immaculate thatched rooms feature fans and firm mattresses. Hammocks abound and some rooms offer hot-water showers. The onsite composting and water filtration system makes this one of the most environmentally friendly hotels on the island.

El Jaguar (Old Bank; d/tr US$20/24) This simple boarding house is distinguished by the irrepressible personality of its owner – El Jaguar. A local schoolteacher, he is also known to serenade guests with impromptu ditties on the guitar. There is an outdoor kitchen and some rooms have bathrooms.

Pension Tío Tom (☎ /fax 757-9831; tiotomscabin@gmail.com; Old Bank; d US$20-25, 2-person bungalow US$30) This plank-and-thatch building has been offering cheap, clean and unfussy rooms for years. All rooms now come with private baths and a waterfront deck is strewn with hammocks. German-run, they can also provide hearty meals (dinner US$6), organize tours and rent kayaks.

Point (☎ 757-9704; Old Bank; d US$30) At the northern tip of Bastimentos, these standard rooms boast excellent views of the point break (bring your own board). Service may be indifferent, but there are creature comforts like hot-water showers, and a fridge and coffee maker.

Eating & Drinking

Although you're just a short boat ride away from Isla Colón, there are a handful of interesting spots on the island that are worth checking out.

Rooster (Old Bank; mains US$2-4) Welcome to Panama's only fry-free zone. Using the region's fresh fruits and vegetables, chef Pete makes everything from banana waffles to lobster tails taste fresh and healthy. Its new location occupies the deck of a colorful house.

Roots (Old Bank; mains US$3-10) This Bocas institution is famous for its masterfully prepared local meats and seafood, perfectly accented with fresh coconut milk. Co-owner Oscar Powell has also done much for the community of Isla Bastimentos and he's a personable fellow with a sharp sense of humor.

ourpick Island Time Thai (☎ 6844-7704; dishes US$6; 12:30-8pm) Well worth the muddy 20-minute jungle trek and a one-hour wait, this is real and red-hot, made by Nui, a loveable Thai transplant. Red curry and cold Balboas are enjoyed on a forested deck in view of resident sloths. To get here, follow the signs uphill from the cement plaza in Old Bank and leave your shoes at the door.

Up in the Hill (www.upinthehill.com; chocolate from US$2) Organic chocolate and gourmet coffee are reason enough to hike to this charming

outpost on Bastimentos. To get there, head right from the docks onto the main road and follow the signs (it is past Island Time Thai).

Getting There & Away

To get to Isla Bastimentos from Bocas del Toro, just walk down to the waterfront and ask a boatman to take you over. The ride will cost about US$2 to get to the near side of the island or US$4 to the far side.

ALMIRANTE

On the mainland, this sad, garbage-strewn village is the point of entry for Bocas del Toro. Water taxis depart here. Seeing disoriented travelers arrive, local taxis will try to charge US$5 for the trip between the bus station and the dock, but the walk only takes five minutes. Taxi 25 has a water shuttle to Bocas del Toro (US$4, 30 minutes). An air-conditioned bus to Changuinola (US$1) leaves every 15 minutes between 6am and 8pm. Taxis to Changuinola (US$5 to US$15) can be bargained, particularly if you start your walk from the dock to the bus station.

CHANGUINOLA

pop 50,000

Headquarters of the Chiriquí Land Company, the very same people that bring you Chiquita bananas, Changuinola is a hot and rather dusty town surrounded by a sea of banana plantations. Although there is little reason to linger here, overland travelers en route from Costa Rica to Isla Colón stop here.

Changuinola also serves as the access point for the Wekso entrance to the Parque Internacional La Amistad. The **ANAM** (☎ 758-6603, 767-9485; 8am-4pm Mon-Fri) office near the center of town has information on the park.

Sleeping & Eating

Hotel Hawaii (☎ 758-6025; Av 17 de Abril; s/d US$20/24;) These ample plain rooms have clean bathrooms with spigot showers and beds clad in white sheets. There's an internet cafe in the lobby.

Resto Cotty's (Av 17 de Abril; meals US$2.50; 24hr) On the main road, this clean cafeteria-style restaurant prepares Panamanian fare. A plate of curried chicken and rice is gratifying and quick.

Getting There & Away

Buses for Costa Rica depart next to the gas station. Other buses depart from **Terminal**

Urrica (☎ 758-8115) with departures between 6am and 7pm.

Almirante (with boat connections to Isla Colón; US$4; 45min) Every half hour.

David (US$8; 4½hr) Every half hour.

El Silencio (Parque Internacional Amistad; US$0.65; 30min) Every 20 minutes.

Guabito-Sixaola (US$1.80; 30min) Every half hour.

Panama City (US$25; 10hr) Daily at 7am.

San José (Costa Rica; US$12; 6hr) Daily at 10am.

You can take a taxi from Changuinola to the Costa Rican border at Guabito (US$2.50 per person, 15 minutes).

THE INTERIOR

Between Chiriquí and Panama City, the regions of Veraguas, Península de Azuero and Coclé – all part of the interior – have long been overshadowed by the flash of the capital, the coolness of the highlands and the lure of the Caribbean. For Panama's heart and soul, this may be the best place to look. Here, some of the friendliest Panamanians reside in laid-back colonial towns and hillside villages. Founded by the Spanish four centuries ago, many settlements retain original, well-preserved colonial churches and colonial character.

Some of Panama's oldest traditions live on here, with old-world festivals held throughout the year. The region's economy is primarily based on agriculture, though the interior also produces exquisite handicrafts. The region is also home to Santa Catalina, one of the best surf destinations in Central America, as well as the scenic mountain towns of Santa Fé and El Valle. The Pedasí coast is an up-and-coming destination for off-track beaches and surf.

SANTA FÉ

This tiny mountain is a perfect destination for independent-minded hikers and birdwatchers looking to escape the crowds.

Lovely mountain streams abound. There's a lovely swimming hole at **Río Bulava**, a 20-minute walk. Head along the right branch of the fork at the southern edge of town, take the second right, and you'll soon reach several spots that make for a nice dip. The refreshing **Cascada de Bermejo** is an excellent half-day hike – you can get directions at the hostel.

To see an organic family farm up close, visit with **Chong & María** (☎ 6525-4832; per person half-

day US$5, lunch US$2), hospitable *campesino* hosts happy to show you around their very small-scale operation. Make sure you book ahead.

If you are interested in visiting a Ngöbe-Buglé community, **Inocencio & Pedra Virola** (☎ 6738-9906; per person US$30) offer tours of Río Piedra.

The perfect base camp for area adventures, **Hostal La Qhia** (☎ 954-0903, 6592-5589; www.panamamountainhouse.com; dm US$11, d & tr with/without bathroom US$33/28; P) is a an oasis of lovely gardens and comfortable beds. It's also an excellent source of information, offering maps and detailed instructions for area hikes and river trips.

Frequent buses travel from Santiago to Santa Fé (US$2.40, 1½ hours, every 30 minutes), from 5am to 6pm. From Santiago you can catch frequent buses to David (US$7, three hours) and Panama City (US$7.50, four hours).

SANTA CATALINA

Santa Catalina is home to several hundred people who lead simple lives as fishers. The town has a laid-back feel to it, with one good outdoor pizzeria that forms the nexus of the dining and nightlife scene. However, the real-estate signs are starting to go up, and rumors run the gamut from constructing a mega-resort and airstrip to establishing a protected area and a marine park. It's hard to know what the future of Santa Catalina holds, but in the meantime, enjoy it while it's still remote, undeveloped and home to some seriously wicked surf.

Sleeping & Eating

If you want to be on the beach, follow the road out of town – a number of signed turnoffs advertise accommodations. Most are a 1km walk to the center on mostly flat but unshaded terrain.

Surfer's Paradise (camping per person US$5, d/tr/q US$33/36/44, deluxe q US$100; P) You could watch the tubes roll in all day at this hilltop camp with a box seat to the waves. Guests can take surf classes (2½ hours, US$40) and rent boards (US$15 to US$20). To arrive, take the turnoff on the left after arriving in town and follow the signs.

Cabañas Rolo (☎ 6598-9926; dm $10, d/tr with bathroom US$55/65, without bathroom US$40/50; P) These rustic cabins are a favorite of baby-faced surfers from around the world. Each has one to three good beds, a fan, and a shared cold-water bathroom that sees much traffic. Truckstop-quality coffee is free in the morning and guests get use of an open-air kitchen.

PANAMA

SPLURGE: ISLA DE COIBA

With the exception of Galápagos and Isla de Coco, few Latin destinations are as exotic (and difficult to access) as this national park just 20km offshore from the Golfo de Chiriquí. Coiba is a veritable lost world of pristine ecosystems and unique fauna. Left alone for the past century while it hosted a notorious penal colony on its shores, Coiba offers intrepid travelers the chance to paddle the Pacific, hike through primary rainforest, snorkel and dive in a marine park and come face to face with increasingly rare wildlife. However, with virtually no tourist infrastructure in place, a tour is key.

For a multiday ocean-kayak trip (starting at around US$400 for three days and two nights), contact Boquete Outdoor Adventures or Fluid Adventures; see p702.

The owner, Rolo Ortega, speaks Spanish and English, rents surfboards (US$10 to $US15 per day), and can arrange surf trips to Isla Cébaco (per group US$200).

our pick **Hibiscus Garden** (☎ 6615-6097; www.hibiscus garden.com; s/d US$23/39, without bathroom US$15/25; P ✖ ☐) On Playa La Gartero (10km before Santa Catalina), these mellow German-run lodgings fuse modern with rustic, with stylish installations and minimal fuss. Rooms have recycled driftwood beds and private hammock terraces. The gulf beach is calm, secluded and very swimmable. For some, the distance will be a drawback, though you can ride the horse-carriage shuttle into town for only US$1, or the faster Flying Sausage for US$5. You won't get bored here; horseback riding (three hours US$15), surf lessons and fishing trips are offered. The restaurant serves salads and sandwiches, as well as a daily special.

Oasis Surf Camp (☎ 6588-7077; surfoasis@hotmail .com; d with fan/air-con US$35; ☿ closed Oct; P ☎) This Italian-run surf camp has long been a staple of Santa Catalina and its beachfront setting is one of the best. Cabins overlooking the black-sand beach have simple but adequate facilities including cold-water showers and ample hammocks. Breakfast (US$3) and authentic Italian meals (around US$7) are served at the open-air restaurant. They also rent a variety of surf boards (US$10 to US$15). It's 2km from Santa Catalina's main road, on Playa Estero near the mouth of the river.

La Buena Vida (☎ 6572-0664; www.labuenavida .biz; cabins US$55-100; P ✖) Three bright cabins feature sea-themed mosaics and colorful tiles, original designs crafted by the American couple that has welded, tiled and painted the place into eclectic perfection. The owners have ironed out every little detail here, from local tips and recommendations to quality lunchboxes for tours. La Buena Vida composts and recycles, and runs a community art workshop, with local artisans' work sold onsite. It is located on the main street in Santa Catalina.

Pizzeria Jamming (pizza US$5-8; ☿ 6:30-11pm Tue-Sun) A much-loved local institution on the road to the beach-facing hotels. Delicious thin-crust pizzas are made from fresh ingredients, and the open-air *rancho* is Santa Catalina's liveliest gathering spot.

Getting There & Away

To reach Santa Catalina from Panama City, first take a bus to Soná where you can take one of the three daily buses to Santa Catalina, leaving at 7am, noon and 4pm (US$3.80, 1½ hours). Unless the driver is pushed for time, he may be able to take you to any one of the hotels listed for an additional fee. If you miss the bus, you can hire a taxi from Soná to Santa Catalina for around US$30.

From Santa Catalina, daily buses to Soná leave at 7am, 8am and 2pm. In Santa Catalina, the bus stops at the intersection to the beach road. Note that there are never taxis in town, unless of course someone is arriving from Soná.

CHITRÉ
pop 40,000

The mellow, cowboy-esque capital of Herrera Province links visitors to the lovely Península de Azuero.

Sights & Activities

Chitré is centered on its understated **cathedral**, which is striking for its elegant simplicity and fine balance of gold and wood. The town is also home to the modest **Museo de Herrera** (☎ 996-0077; cnr Paseo Enrique Geenzier & Av Julio Arjona; admission US$1; ☿ 8am-noon & 1-4pm Tue-Sat, 8-11am Sun), a small anthropology and natural history museum.

Bird-watchers can explore **Playa El Agallito**, 7km from Chitré, a mudflat hosting thousands of migratory birds. The **Humboldt Ecological Station** studies them; you're welcome to stop by and visit the displays. A bus leaves the Chitré station for the beach every 20 minutes or so during

DETOUR: REMOTE AZUERO

Most visitors access the Azuero via Chitre, but a few hours south of Santiago, the west coast of the peninsula is an amazing off-the-beaten-path attraction. Between December and February, three species of turtles hatch on the beaches of Malena. To join community volunteers working toward their preservation, contact **Malena Beach Conservation Association** (Asociación Conservacionista de Playa Malena; www.playamalena.org; per week incl meals & lodging US$150). Basic Spanish is necessary. The organization also offers horseback riding (US$10 per hour), boat tours and nature walks.

Providing luxury camping and rooms, **Tanager Tourism Ranchos** (☎ 6866-9652, 6667-6447; www .tanagertourism.com; luxury campsite s/d incl breakfast US$25/20, s/d incl breakfast US$40/55) are thoughtfully crafted by a Dutch couple who offer area tours and promote sustainable local tourism. From Santiago, coaster buses leave hourly to Mariato, which will pass Palmilla (1½ hours, US$3). Get off at Tanager Tourism (known as Casa de los Holandeses).

daylight hours. The one-way fare is US$0.50. A taxi ride from town costs US$3 one way.

Sleeping & Eating

There's no shortage of cheap hotels in town.

Hotel Santa Rita (☎ 996-4610; cnr Calle Manuel Maria Correa & Av Herrera; d with/without air-con US$22/18; P ⊠) One of the city's first hotels, Santa Rita has slid in status to simply economical. High-ceiling rooms feel musty around the edges and bathrooms smell scoured with bleach. Perks include some private balconies and there's wi-fi and cable TV.

Hotel Rex (☎ 996-4310; Calle Melitón Martín s/n; s/d US$36/49; P ⊠ ☎) With a prime location on Parque Union and good dining downstairs, Rex is a solid midrange choice. Clean tiled rooms have brick walls, fresh towels and water thermoses. There's TV in the rooms, two terminals with internet and wi-fi available throughout.

Restaurante El Meson (Calle Melitón Martín s/n; mains US$4-12; ☺ 7:15am-10pm; ☎) Has a long list of offerings, from sandwiches to steak and seafood. The chicken tacos will fully satisfy small appetites. Full breakfasts include fried yucca or *tortillas de maiz* with eggs and coffee. The ambience is glass tables and tall wooden chairs.

Getting There & Away

Chitré is a regional bus transportation center. Buses arrive and depart from the **Terminal de Transportes de Herrera** (☎ 996-6426), 1km south of downtown. Buses go to Las Tablas (US$1.25, 40minutes, every 20 minutes) and on to Pedasí (US$3.25, one hour, hourly) and other places on the peninsula. To get there, **Radio Taxi** (☎ 996-4442) charges US$1 to US$2. The 'Terminal' bus (US$0.25) leaves from the intersection of Calle Aminta Burgos de Amado and Av Herrera.

To get to David or Panama City from Chitré, take a bus to Divisa and then catch a *directo* (direct bus) to either city (US$7 or US$8, six hours). Buses leave every half hour from the Delta station at the intersection of the Interamericana and the Carretera Nacional.

PEDASÍ
pop 2400

For years, this sleepy retreat bloomed only at festival times. But outsiders are discovering the big appeal of small-town life and wilderness beaches. Almost without warning, Pedasí has become the focus of an intensive push to develop the southwestern coastline, with lofty comparisons to Tuscany and California.

Helpful but slow, the **ATP office** (☎ 995-2339; ☺ 9:30am-5:30pm) lies one block past the main road in the north of town. The **ANAM** (☺ 8am-4pm, Mon-Fri) office in the south of town has extremely poor service, but in theory provides information about Isla Iguana and Isla de Cañas.

Pedasí serves as the gateway to the Azuero coastline; the closest beaches are **Playa El Toro** and **La Garita**, both reached by a 2km road (walk or take a taxi, US$6 to US$8). It's also a convenient base for exploring the **Refugio de Vida Silvestre Isla Iguana** a 55-hectare island wildlife refuge. Though ravaged by El Niño, the surviving coral is pretty spectacular and the water is shallow enough to be snorkeled.

Snorkeling and diving around the nearby islands surrounded by large coral reefs are a major attraction. The PADI-certified **Pedasí Sports Club** (Buzos de Azuero; ☎ 995-2894; www .pedasisportsclub; Calle Central s/n) offers two-tank dives (US$85 and up) to Isla Frailes and Isla Iguana. Snorkelers (US$35) can join dive trips to Iguana. They also offer a river kayak

PANAMA

LOS FIESTAS DE AZUERO

Famous throughout Panama, the traditional festivals in Azuero were created by Spanish settlers. Few foreigners see this wild side of Panama. While you may sacrifice a day or two to a thumping head, these are parties you'll never forget. Some of the best:

- **Carnaval** – the four days before Ash Wednesday (February/March) in Chitré, Parita, Las Tablas and Villa de Los Santos.

- **Semana Santa** – March/April in Pesé and Villa de Los Santos.

- **Feria de Azuero** – late April/early May in Villa de los Santos.

- **Fiesta de Corpus Christi** – 40 days after Easter in Villa de Los Santos.

- **Patronales de San Pablo & San Pedro** – June 29 in Pedasí and La Arena.

- **Feria de la Mejorana, Festival de la Virgen de las Mercedes** – September 23 to 27 in Guararé.

For more information, see the various town and city listings in this chapter and Panama City bus schedules (p652).

---

tour or kayak rentals (US$40), sportfishing, turtle-watching (US$65) and horseback riding (US$45 to US$65). Staff speak English, Turkish and Spanish.

Every year, thousands of olive ridley sea turtles nest at **Isla de Cañas** (admission US$10). There is no public transportation to the island but trips can be arranged through the ATP office.

The bare-bones **Residencial Moscoso** (☎ 995-2203; Av Central s/n; s/d US$20/25; P ✗ ▣) offers clean but worn dark-tile rooms. The friendly **Dim's Hostal** (☎ 995-2303; Av Central s/n; s/d incl breakfast US$33/49; P ✗ ▣) has a coveted backyard patio with hammocks and a mango tree; the breakfasts are made to order.

Ask around for local restaurant recommendations. The amiable **Restaurante Angela** (Av Central s/n; mains US$2.50; ⏰ 7am-8:30pm) is a good spot to grab a quick lunch of *típico*, grilled fish or chicken or shrimp in garlic herb sauce.

Buses from Las Tablas leave every 45 minutes between 6am and 4pm (US$2, one hour) from in front of Restaurante Angela. Buses to Playa Venado (US$2) leave at 7am, 10am and noon.

Playa Venao

Past Pedasí, the long, protected beach of Playa Venao is transforming from a wild beach to an outright destination. Surfers lay the first claim to its waters – waves are consistent and break in both directions.

On the jungle side of the main access road, **Eco Venao** (☎ 832-0530; www.venao.com; campsite per person US$5.50, dm US$11, d without bathroom US$28, 2-person cabin US$44; P ▣) offers a cool mountain ambience and kind prices. The eight-person dorm is rustic but comfy, with mosquito nets, kitchen and shady porch ringed with hammocks. The colonial-style guesthouse is simply lovely. You can also rent horses (US$10), surfboards (US$20 per day), kayaks (US$25 per day) and do beachfront yoga. Internet (US$4) may be dear, but consider your location. 'Eco' means that trash separation and recycling are practiced, and instead of building big infrastructure the property was left mostly intact, with small footpaths that lead to the beach. The property has a 15-minute waterfall hike.

The Playa Venao turnoff is 33km by road southwest of Pedasí. The Cañas–Las Tablas bus (US$2) passes between 8am and 9am and makes the return journey in the evening. Confirm exact times with your hotel. You can also take a taxi from Pedasí (US$30).

EL VALLE
pop 6000

Picturesque El Valle de Antón is nestled in the crater of a giant extinct volcano that blew its top three million years ago. El Valle is a popular weekend getaway for urbanites in need of a little fresh air and scenery. It's a superb place for walking, hiking or horseback riding.

Sights & Activities

In addition to outdoor pursuits, El Valle's main attraction is its Sunday **handicrafts market** (mercado; ⏰ 8am-2pm) where Ngöbe-Buglé, Kuna, Emberá and Wounaan sell quality baskets, woodwork, ceramics, soapstone carvings, flowers and plants (including orchids) as well as a variety of fresh produce.

The excellent **El Valle Amphibian Conservation Center** (Evacc; ☎ 6676-8094; www.houstonzoo.org/amphibians) works to save amphibians from the deadly kitrid virus threatening amphibians around the world. You can see native Panamanian species including the golden frog. It's on the grounds of El Níspero zoo, 1km north of Av Central.

El Valle's famous *arboles cuadrados* or **square trees**, an unusual native species, are located in a thicket along a hiking trail behind the Hotel Campestre, east and north of the town center.

On the west side of town (follow the signs), **Pozos Termales** (Thermal Baths; Calle los Pozos; admission US$1; 8am-5pm) is the perfect place to soak the afternoon away. In a remote, forested area, the recently renovated complex features a series of pools with varying temperatures and supposed curative properties.

The hills around El Valle are excellent for walking and horseback riding; Residencial El Valle (below) hires out both bikes and horses. The trails are well-defined since they're frequently used by locals. **Piedra El Sapo** (Toad Stone), west of town near **La India Dormida** (a mountain ridge that resembles a sleeping Indian girl), is said to have some of the most beautiful trails. Nearby, in the neighborhood of La Pintada, are some unusual ancient **petroglyphs** depicting humans, animals and other shapes.

The most famous waterfall in the El Valle area is the 85m-high **Chorro El Macho** (admission US$3.50; 8am-4pm), accessed via a short hike. The waterfall is 2km northwest of town, reachable by the bus to La Mesa (US$0.35). A lovely rainforest swimming hole just below the falls – bring your swimsuit.

Sleeping & Eating

La Casa de Juan (6453-9775; www.lacasadejuan panama.blogspot.com; Calle Cocorron No 4; dm/d US$10/20) This bare-bones Sanford and Son setup brims with the clutter of ATV vehicles, outdoor weight-lifting equipment and wagon wheels. Though decrepit, the house is clean and Señor Juan is a social host also offering guided walks.

Santa Librada (6591-9135; Av Central; d US$15) Behind the popular restaurant, a passageway leads to three basic but clean doubles, adding another much-needed value option ideal for couples.

Residencial El Valle (983-6536; residencialelvalle@ hotmail.com; Av Central; d/tr/q US$44/55/66; P) Visitors become loyalists, given the high level of service offered at this motel-style lodging. This long-standing hotel offers clean no-fuss rooms and like the nearly identical Don Pepe next door, it has a nice roof deck and bike rentals. Attached is a popular restaurant.

Restaurante Santa Librada (Av Central; mains US$2-4.50) Cheap and cheerful, the Santa serves hearty portions of Panamanian staples such as *bistec picado* (spicy shredded beef), as well as sandwiches and breakfast.

El Valle Gourmet & Coffee Shop (Av Central; sandwiches US$5; 9am-6pm Thu-Sun) With gourmet sandwiches and smoothies, this is also a good stop to stock up on picnic items before heading for the trails. You can find goat cheese, cured meats and olives here.

Getting There & Away

Buses leave Panama City for El Valle (US$3.50, 2½ hours, hourly from 7am to 7pm).

The center of town is small, but many of El Valle's attractions are a distance from there. Taxis within town cost no more than US$2. Buses to La Mesa (US$0.35) pass by Chorro El Macho, and run along El Valle's main street.

COLÓN PROVINCE

With an edgy reputation more true crime than travel, Colón rarely makes travel wish lists. But there is more to this Caribbean province than its notorious capital. Extending for over 200km along the Caribbean coast from Veraguas Province in the west to the Comarca de Kuna Yala in the east, Colón Province is mostly undeveloped and virtually inaccessible. However, the province is also home to the Spanish colonial city of Portobelo, which at one time was the most prominent port on the Caribbean, as well as the famed tropical getaway of Isla Grande.

Although the city of Colón can be dangerous, the surrounding area features everything from pristine beaches and lowland rainforests to colonial splendors and modern engineering marvels. Portobelo, with its growing music and art scene, shows the best of vibrant Congo culture. And of course, it's worth mentioning that the luxury train connecting Panama City to Colón is one of the greatest rail journeys in the Americas.

COLÓN
pop 45,000

With its colonial grandeur crumbling and its neighborhoods marginalized, historical Colón is sadly the city that Panama forgot, in spite of vigorous renovations underway in isolated sectors to court Caribbean cruise ships. Prior to 1869, the railroad connecting Panama City and Colón was the only rapid transit across the continental western hemisphere. However, the establishment of the US

PANAMA

transcontinental railroad put Colón out of business almost overnight. The last whiff of prosperity was seen during the construction of the Panama Canal.

In an attempt to revive the city, the Zona Libre (Free Zone) was created on the edge of Colón in 1948. Today, it's the largest free-trade zone in the Americas. Unfortunately, none of the US$10 billion in annual commercial turnover seems to get beyond the compound's walls and the Zona Libre exists as an island of materialism floating in a sea of unemployment, poverty and crime.

The improved Ruta 3 between Panama City and Colón is now a four-lane highway, resulting in much quicker travel times.

History
Colón was founded in 1850 as the Caribbean terminus of the Panama Railroad, though it faded into obscurity less than 20 years later. At the peak of its economic depression in 1881, the French arrived in Colón to start construction of an interoceanic canal, though the city was burnt to the ground four years later by a Colombian hoping to spark a revolution. In the years to follow, Colón entered a second golden age as the city was entirely rebuilt in French Colonial architectural style. Rivaling Panama City in beauty and wealth, life in the top of the Canal Zone was pleasurable and highly profitable.

Following its economic ruin in 1914, the city spiraled into the depths of depravity. Today, most of the colonial city is still intact, though the buildings are on the verge of collapse.

Orientation & Information
The city is reached via two major roads on the southern side of town. The roads become Av Amador Guerrero and Av Bolivar at the entrance to the town, and run straight up the grid-patterned city, ending near Colon's northern waterfront.

Perpendicular to these avenues are numbered streets. Calle 16 is the first of these you'll cross as you enter the town while Calle 1 is at the northern end of town. The Zone Libre occupies the southeastern corner of the city while the city's cruise-ship port, Colón 2000, is located just north of the Free Zone.

Given Colón's high rate of crime, the safest place to withdraw money is the BNP ATM in the Colón 2000 cruise port.

Dangers & Annoyances
Despite Colón's new cruise port on the eastern side of the city, Colón is still a dangerous slum. Crime is a serious problem, and you need to exercise caution when walking around. Paseo de Washington, the renovated waterfront area, and Av Bolívar are safe to peruse by day. The train and bus stations are under 300m away and walkable during daylight hours. Always travel by taxi at night.

Sights
For some great sights just outside of Colón, see opposite.

ZONA LIBRE
The Free Zone is a huge fortresslike area of giant international stores selling items duty free. It's the world's second-largest duty-free port after Hong Kong. However, most of these stores only deal in bulk merchandise; they aren't set up to sell to individual tourists, and simple window-shopping is not very interesting. Many travelers leave disappointed. If you do buy something, the store usually sends it to the Tocumen International Airport in Panama City, where you can retrieve your purchase before departing the country. You can enter the Zona Libre by presenting your passport at the security office.

COLÓN 2000
Only a decade old, this sterile shopping and entertainment sector geared toward cruise-ship travelers sits on the east side of Colón. Though lacking in any Panamanian flavor, it is safe to peruse and features a good selection of restaurants and souvenir shops as well as a casino.

Sleeping & Eating
There's no shortage of hotels in Colón, though most are in seedy areas and have serious security issues. The following options have 24-hour security guards.

Meryland Hotel (☎ 441-7055; cnr Calle 7 & Av Santa Isabel; s/d US$50/60; P ✗ ☐ ☎) A massive stone building, this business hotel fronts an attractive city park. Small tile rooms with gold tones and rod-iron furniture have air-con, cable TV and hot-water bathrooms, though you're paying for security, not luxury. The restaurant saves you the trouble of having to leave the hotel at night.

Radisson (☎ 446-2000; www.radisson.com; Colón 2000; s/d US$119/220; P ✗ ☐ ☎) Really you could be anywhere, but this luxury chain hotel has the friendliest staff and the best digs in Colón.

Rooms are comfortable and sufficiently stylish, with minibar and flat-screen TVs, and you can always let off steam with some laps in the pool. Get in on big off-season discounts by looking for specials on the web.

Getting There & Away
BUS
From Panama City, a regular bus service to Colón (US$2.50, one hour, every 30 minutes) departs from the Albrook Bus Terminal.

Colón's Terminal de Buses is at the intersection of Calle Terminal and Av Bolívar. It serves towns throughout Colón Province, including the following:

La Guayra (US$2.85; 2hr; hourly) In La Guayra, you can catch the boat to Isla Grande.

Nombre de Dios (US$3.75; 2½hr; hourly)

Portobelo (US$1.30; 1½hr; hourly)

TRAIN
The **Panama Railway Company** (☎ 317-6070; www
.panarail.com; Carretera Gaillard) operates a glass-domed luxury passenger train along the canal and through jungle to/from Panama City (US$22/38 one-way/round-trip, one hour), leaving Colón at 5:15pm daily. The Colón train station is in the city but is best accessed by taxi. If you are arriving via train, the bus terminal is close by and shouldn't be a problem to walk to.

Getting Around
While in Colón, it's a good idea to not wander around on foot. Fortunately, taxis congregate at the bus station, train station and the Zone Libre, and fares across the city are usually around US$1.

AROUND COLÓN
Gatún Locks
The **Gatún Locks** (admission free; ⏰ 8am-4pm), just 10km south of Colón, raise southbound ships 29.5m from Caribbean waters to the level of Lago Gatún. From there, ships travel 37km to the Pedro Miguel Locks, which lower southbound ships 9.3m to Lago Miraflores, a small body of water that separates the two sets of Pacific locks. The ships are lowered to sea level at the Miraflores Locks.

The Gatún Locks are the largest of the three sets, and their size is truly mind-boggling. In his superlative book *The Path Between the Seas*, David McCullough notes that if stood on its end, a single lock would have been the tallest structure on Earth at the time it was built, taller by several meters than even the Eiffel Tower.

From a well-placed viewing stand opposite the control tower, you can watch the locks in action. The whole process takes about two hours; it's probably the most interesting stage of the Canal transit, and the English brochure does a good job of describing what you're watching.

Buses to the Gatún Locks leave the Colón bus terminal hourly (US$1.25, 20 minutes). If you arrive by taxi you can stop here before heading on to Gatún Dam – another 2km away. A taxi ride from Colón to the locks and dam and back should cost US$60 per party but agree on a price before leaving.

Parque Nacional San Lorenzo
Centered on the ruins of the crumbling Spanish colonial fortress of Fuerte San Lorenzo, the 97-sq-km **park** (www.sanlorenzo.org
.pa) is perched at the mouth of the Río Chagres. This river floated Welsh pirate Henry Morgan to the interior in 1671, enabling him to sack the original Panama City.

This Spanish fortress is built of blocks of cut coral with rows of old cannons jutting out. Among the many Spanish cannons, you might spot a British one – evidence of the time when British pirates overcame the fort. Much of the fort is well preserved, including the moat, the cannons and the arched rooms.

There is unfortunately no public transportation to Fuerte San Lorenzo from Colón. However, a round-trip taxi ride from Colón should cost around US$40.

PORTOBELO
pop 4100
This Caribbean fishing village is so laid-back and languorous, it's incredible to ponder that it was once the greatest Spanish port in Central America. Mules once carried Peruvian gold and Oriental treasures to Panama City via the fortresses at Portobelo. Though English privateers destroyed them several times throughout their history, many of these atmospheric colonial fortresses still stand. Throughout the village, homes are situated among these atmospheric ruins.

Portobelo is experiencing something of a cultural rival, with recent interest surging in Congo art and dancing. Visitors can explore the extensive ruins, boat to remote beaches and dive at interesting underwater attractions.

PANAMA

History

Portobelo, the 'beautiful port,' was named by Columbus in 1502, when he stopped here on his fourth New World voyage. For the next 200 years, Portobelo served as the principal Spanish Caribbean port in Central America.

Aiming to disrupt the Spanish treasure route, British admiral Edward Vernon destroyed Portobelo in 1739. Discouraged, the Spanish abandoned the overland Panama route, and instead started sailing the long way around Cape Horn to and from the western coast of South America.

Though rebuilt in 1751, Portobelo never attained its former prominence, and in time became a virtual ruin. The outermost fortress was dismantled to build the Panama Canal, with larger stones used in the construction of the Gatún Locks. Yet there are still considerable parts of the town intact, protected as a national park and historic site.

Orientation & Information

Located 43km from Colón, Portobelo consists of about 15 blocks of homes and businesses that line a paved, two-lane road. This road intersects with the Panama City–Colón road at the town of Sabanitas, 33km to the west.

East of Portobelo, the road forks after 9km. The left branch extends 11km to the village of La Guayra, where you can hire boats to Isla Grande.

Just off the main road, **ATP** (☎ 448-2200, 6485-7028; ⏱ 9:30am-5:30pm Tue-Fri & Sun) has good information. Ask Mireya Jimenez for information about congo dance workshops or volunteering with the school; Spanish-only spoken. Across the street from the tourist office, an **internet cafe** (per hr US$1.50; ⏱ 8:30am-4pm Mon-Fri) also serves as a small library.

Sights

The remnants of **Fuerte San Jerónimo** and **Fuerte Santiago** can still be seen near town, and the ruins of **Fuerte San Fernando** occupy a grassy flat across the bay. The ruins of Santiago, 500m west of Portobelo's center, include officers' quarters, an artillery shed, a sentry box, a barracks and batteries. You can climb up a hill behind the fort for a fine view overlooking the ruins and bay. At the center of Portobelo, Fuerte San Jerónimo is a more complete fort than Santiago.

The restored **Real Aduana de Portobelo** (Customs House; admission US$1), also known as the *contaduría* (counting house), has interesting exhibits of Portobelo's history as well as a three-dimensional model of the area.

The large **colonial church**, built in 1776, contains a life-size statue of the Black Christ, which is believed to have miraculous powers.

On the way to Portobelo, the black-sand **Playa María Chiquita** and the white-sand **Playa Langosta** are two attractive beaches.

Activities

Although the clarity of the water here is not spectacular, Portobelo enjoys a good diving reputation due to two unique sites off the coast, namely a 33m (110ft) cargo ship and a C-45 twin-engine plane.

An open-water course costs US$275; a discovery dive for first-timers runs US$110. If you're planning to dive, it's best to phone ahead or make a reservation via the internet. Outfitter **Scubaportobelo** (☎ 261-3841; www.scubapanama.com) offers all-inclusive scuba packages.

Festivals & Events

On October 21 each year, the **Festival of the Black Christ** attracts hundreds of pilgrims, many dressed in the same royal purple color as the statue's clothes. The statue is paraded through the streets starting at 6pm, and street festivities follow. **Holy Week** is also an interesting time to be here.

The most intriguing local tradition is **Festival de Diablos y Congos** (www.diablosycongos .org), a festival of rebellion and ridicule that mocks the colonial Spaniards. During the festivity, blacks assume the role of escaped slaves and take 'captives.' It is held two weeks after Carnaval, sometimes coinciding with March 20, Portobelo's patron saint day.

In addition, on the last Sunday of each month there is an **Afro Mass** with a town fair displaying local food and traditional crafts.

ASK A LOCAL

'To see authentic Portobelo, see the **Festival de Diablos y Congos** where we celebrate our *cimarrón* (ex-slave) ancestors, slaves who survived by rebellion. We dance, and instead of wearing our Sunday best, we wear clashing rags. We speak in reverse, as *cimarrones* did, to keep the Spaniards guessing. Survival is all about liberty, it's a beautiful thing to see.'

Aristela Blandon, Portobelo

Sleeping & Eating

Local families may rent out spare rooms for around US$15, particularly during festivals – ask at ATP (opposite).

Coco Plum Eco Lodge (☎ 448-2102; www.coco plumpanama.com; s/d/tr US$45/55/65; P ⚡) An attractive, motel-style lodging, the friendly Coco Plum has been around for years. At the time of writing, the scuba shop was undergoing transition to new management. On the waterfront, the feel of the place is ocean kitsch, replete with nets, shells and pastels, but the effect is cozy. A salon has games and TV. The attached bar-restaurant (mains US$7.50 to US$15) is popular with travelers – check out the octopus in coconut milk or the seafood stew.

Scubaportobelo (☎ 448-2147; www.scubapanama .com; d US$50, d/q cabins US$61/72; P ⚡) Nondivers are welcome at this comfortable seafront lodging. A new structure has motel-style doubles with balconies, electric showers and air-con. The cute cabins are charming but pocket-sized – best for a couple or a family with small children.

our pick **Casa de la Bruja** (☎ 226-2035; sandraeleta@ gmail.com; d US$50, 4-person loft US$75, 2-bedroom house US$150; P ⚡) Quite out of the ordinary, this chill photographer's home is adapted for guests. Side by side there are two ample houses; just lovely, with a grassy seafront perfect for lounging. The bright, open interiors showcase photography and local Congo art. It is fine to cook here or you can pay extra for prepared meals. Guests can organize onsite excursions to snorkel and sightsee or take a Caribbean cooking workshop (US$15 per person) from Doña Cecelia.

Getting There & Away

Buses to Portobelo (US$1.30, 1½ hours, every 30 minutes) depart from Colón's Terminal de Buses from 6:30am to 6pm.

From Panama City you can avoid passing through Colón. Take the Colón bus and get off at El Rey supermarket in Sabanitas, 10km before Colón. Next, catch the bus coming from Colón to Portobelo when it passes through Sabanitas (US$1, 1¼ hours). It's often full, so try to take as little luggage as possible.

ISLA GRANDE

Palm trees and white-sand beaches form the backdrop to this lovely island 15km northeast of Portobelo. A popular getaway for Panama City folk, Isla Grande is an ideal setting for

---

PORTOBELO'S TOP FIVE ESCAPES

▥ Take a water taxi to Puerto Francés for private swims and jungle hikes.

▥ Snorkel around Spanish cannons encrusted in the coral landscape.

▥ Kayak up the tranquil Río Claro.

▥ See a sunset from El Fuerte de San Fernando.

▥ Join a Congo dance workshop and sweat to cool African rhythms.

---

snorkeling, scuba diving or simply soaking up the island's relaxed vibe. About 300 people of African descent live on the island, most of whom eke out a living from fishing and coconuts – you'll get a taste of both when you sample the fine island cuisine.

Activities

Some lovely **beaches** on the northern side of the island can be reached by boat (hire a water taxi at the dock in front of Cabañas Super Jackson) or on foot (there's a water's-edge trail that loops around the 5km long, 1.5km wide island, as well a slippery cross-island trail).

If you're looking for a good **surf** break, take a water taxi out to La Guayra where you can find a good reef break that peaks right and left.

The trail across the island leads to **Bananas Village Resort** (☎ 263-9766; www.bananasresort.com), where US$35 will get you use of the facilities, a welcome cocktail and lunch. Some fine snorkeling and dive sites are within a 10-minute boat ride of the island. **Isla Grande Dive Center** (☎ 223-5943), located 50m west of Cabañas Super Jackson, offers a variety of dives around the island and in the San Blás archipelago.

For US$30, one of the boatmen in front of Cabañas Super Jackson will take you on a half-day adventure – the possibilities are quite appealing. The mangroves east of Isla Grande are fun to explore, or you could go snorkeling off the coast of the nearby islets.

Festivals & Events

The **Festival of San Juan Bautista** is celebrated on June 24, with swimming and canoe races. The **Virgen del Carmen** is honored on July 16, with a land and sea procession, baptisms and masses.

Carnaval is also celebrated here in rare form. Along with the dancing, there are also satirical songs about current events and a lot of joking in the Caribbean calypso tradition.

Sleeping & Eating

Cabañas Super Jackson (☎ 448-2311; d with fan/air-con US$20/35; ⊠) Closest to the main pier, this Isla Grande landmark offers a handful of cheap and cheerful rooms with private bathrooms. There are definitely more comfortable spots on the island, but it's hard to beat the price, the convenience factor and the humorous name.

Hotel Sister Moon (☎ 236-8489; www.hotelsister moon.com; s/d incl breakfast US$49/98; ⊠ ⓡ) A 10-minute walk east of the Super Jackson takes you to these cabins on a hillside at the end of the island. Surrounded by swaying palms and crashing waves, each boasts fabulous views from a front-porch hammock. The hotel bar-restaurant is built right over the water and features the island's famous coconut-infused seafood.

Getting There & Away

Buses from Colón go to La Guayra (US$2.50, 1½ hours, hourly). A 10-minute boat ride from there to Isla Grande costs US$3 to US$5. Parking costs US$2.50 per day.

COMARCA DE KUNA YALA

Imagine a turquoise archipelago with one island for every day of the year. With white sand and waving palms, these Caribbean islands cheat no one's version of paradise. The Comarca de Kuna Yala is home to the Kuna, an autonomous indigenous group who run San Blás with minimal interference from the national government. The Kuna was the first indigenous group in Latin America to gain such independence and today are a unique example of successful indigenous autonomy.

The Comarca is a narrow, 226km-long strip on the Caribbean coast that includes the Archipiélago de San Blás, which stretches from the Golfo de San Blás to the edge of the Colombian border. While the majority of the islands are postcard perfect, only community islands are inhabited. These acre-sized cays packed with bamboo huts, livestock and people are integral to the strong Kuna sense of community. In tourism, the Kuna is protectionist: no foreigner may run a business here (even Panamanian) and visitors are often charged a fee to land.

San Blás is no longer the off-the-beaten-path tourist destination it once was. In 2009, the road to Cartí was completed, making the region more accessible. However, visitors still have a choice between vibrant community life and complete and total isolation.

HISTORY

The Kuna have lived in Eastern Panama for at least two centuries, though scholars fiercely debate their origins. Language similarities with people who once lived several hundred kilometers to the west would indicate that the Kuna migrated eastward. However, oral tradition has it that the Kuna migrated to San Blás from Colombia after the 16th century, following a series of devastating encounters with other tribes armed with poison-dart blowguns.

Scholars agree that life on the islands is relatively new for the Kuna. Historians at the end of the 18th century wrote that the only people who used the San Blás islands at the time were pirates, Spaniards and the odd explorer.

Today, there are an estimated 70,000 Kuna; 32,000 live on the district's islands, 8000 live on tribal land along the coast and 30,000 live outside the district. So communal are the island Kuna that they inhabit only 40 of the 400 cays – the rest are coconut farms with sea turtles and iguanas. The inhabited islands are packed with traditional bamboo-sided, thatched-roof houses in sometimes unsanitary conditions.

Historically, the Kuna subsisted on freshly caught seafood including fish, lobster, shrimp, Caribbean king crab and octopus. This was accompanied by food crops, including rice, yams, yucca, bananas and pineapples grown on the nearby mainland. Today, this traditional diet is supplemented by food products obtained by bartering coconuts with passing Colombian ships.

ORIENTATION

Up until recently, the only practical way to visit the Comarca region was to fly and inaccessibility helped preserve traditional Kuna culture. Recently, road access via Cartí was added – now visitors can take a 4WD taxi to the edge of the mainland and boat to the islands. At the northwest end of the province, airport-equipped El Porvenir is the traditional gateway to the San Blás islands. From here, boat transportation can be arranged to islands with basic hotels. If you're planning on staying at any of the far-flung islands, you can also fly into Río Sidra or Playón Chico.

INFORMATION

Although a trip to the Archipiélago de San Blás may not fit in the budget, these culturally rich Caribbean islands are a good place for a splurge if you can swing it. Prices vary, but if you stick to the cheaper hotels, you can survive on about US$45 per day; this includes meals, lodging and daily boating excursions.

Owing to the limited number of flights to the area, you should book as far in advance as possible. It's also recommended that you reserve your hotels in advance, especially since package deals are pretty much the norm in the Comarca. You're also going to want to hit an ATM before you touch down on the islands.

The Kuna are very particular about what foreigners do on their islands (see p692). As a result, they require that tourists register and pay a visitation fee (between US$3 and US$12) on the main islands. On smaller, privately owned islands, visitors must seek out the owner, receive permission and pay a fee (around US$2).

Visitors must also pay for any photo they take of the Kuna. If you want to take someone's photo, ask their permission first and be prepared to pay US$1 per subject (some Kuna expect to be paid US$1 per photo). You may not be expected to pay for a photo taken of an artisan from whom you buy crafts from, but it depends on the subject. Some islands may charge you US$50 just for possessing a video camera.

ACTIVITIES

Most hotels are complete packages, where a fixed price gets you a room, three meals a day and boat rides to neighboring islands for swimming, snorkeling and lounging on the beach. If you seek community life, you can also arrange visits to more populated islands. Before swimming off the shores of a heavily populated island, however, take a look at the number of outhouses built over the ocean – they may change your mind.

Snorkeling is good in places, but many of the coral reefs in the region are badly damaged. You can often rent snorkeling equipment from your hotel, but serious snorkelers should bring their own gear. Hikers can also arrange jaunts to the mainland jungles, but these trips should not be attempted without

PANAMA

KUNA LIVING 101

Lodging considerations in the Comarca are vastly different from those on the mainland. Here, a spot in a thatched hut with sand floor can cost anywhere between US$30 and US$130 per night. What's the difference?

Often it has more to do with access, ambience and organization than anything. Densely populated community islands are more likely to have budget options, but they will not live up to your image of a remote tropical paradise. Resort islands generally have a higher price tag, but may not offer many opportunities to interact with locals. When planning, consider why you're going and the following:

- **Space** Does the island have shade? Privacy? Are there pleasant areas to swim or do you have to boat to swim and snorkel sites?
- **Access** Is the island too remote, requiring expensive transfers to do anything?
- **Hospitality** Ask other travelers about their experience.
- **Water** Is it potable? Consider bringing a filter.
- **Bathrooms** Are there modern installations or does the toilet sit at the end of a dock?
- **Safety** Do excursion boats have life vests and good motors?

Lodgings generally include three meals (but not drinks), one outing per day (eg snorkeling, a community visit) and transportation to or from the airport or Cartí, but do confirm ahead. Fees to visit Kuna islands and drinking water may be separate. It is always wise to bring snacks, insect repellent, a first-aid kit and a flashlight. Rates are generally lower from April to November.

When booking, remember that internet is not prevalent and any mobile phone number is only good until that phone accidentally falls into the ocean. But approach your hosts with good humor and patience and they will probably reciprocate in spades.

RESPONSIBLE TRAVEL IN KUNA YALA

When visiting the Comarca de Kuna Yala, please consider how your visit may affect the community. Tourism revenue can play a vital role in the development of the region, particularly if you are buying locally produced crafts or contracting the services of a Kuna guide. However, indigenous tourism can be an exploitative force. Western interests have already caused an irreversible amount of damage to the region. Be aware of your surroundings and be sensitive to your impact.

One look at the paradisiacal setting, the rainbow flag and the distinctive Kuna dress and you might feel transported into the pages of *National Geographic*. Don't snap that shutter just yet. If the Kuna appear unfriendly, consider their predicament. When cruise ships visit, the number of people on an already congested island can triple. Nonetheless, nearly two-thirds of the populace (the tourists) turns paparazzi on the other third (the Kuna). It's an unsavory scene that is repeated again and again.

Trash is a problem on the islands, and there is no effective plan for its removal. You may see litter and burning piles of plastics. For the Kunas, the cost of removal to the mainland is too costly, there is no designated site or 'culture' of waste management, since all refuse was relatively innocuous until outside influence prevailed. With no current solution to the issue, do what you can to pack out your own garbage and try to consume fresh products with minimal packaging, eg choose coconut water over Coca Cola.

The way you dress (or fail to) is another issue. Kuna men never go shirtless and Kuna women dress conservatively, with their cleavage, bellies and most of their legs covered. Arriving in Kuna villages in bikinis or shirtless is nearly always interpreted as a sign of disrespect. In general, it is not worth the risk of offending local sensibilities.

To rein in the situation, the Kuna charge fees for photographs taken of them as well as visitation fees for each island. Forget the way things work back home. Remember this is their territory and their rules apply. If you can't afford the photo fee, just tuck away your camera and strike up a conversation instead.

---

a guide. Activities aside, most travelers to Kuna Yala are content with simply soaking up the Caribbean sun and perfecting their hammock-swaying.

SLEEPING & EATING

In a protectionist move to preserve local culture, the Kuna Congress passed a law several years ago that prohibits outsiders from owning property in the Comarca. Hotels in the Comarca are 100% owned by local families.

For tips on lodging, see p691. Since there are no restaurants, each hotel provides meals for guests. Seafood features widely. Quality varies, as stocks have been depleted through overfishing; there is always a healthy stock of fresh coconuts on hand. It's a good idea to bring packaged snacks with you.

The following hotels are listed by location (west to east) instead of by price.

Hotel Corbiski (☎ 6708-5254; www.corbiski.com; r per person incl 3 meals & tour US$45) A new bamboo-walled lodging with laminated floors and neat and spacious rooms on a busy community island. Clean shared bathrooms occupy cement stalls. Lodgings include purified water and transportation to and from Cartí or Porvenir.

The owner, Elias Pérez, is the school principal, speaks English and can arrange local excursions or facilitate volunteering at the school.

Cartí Homestay (☎ 6734-3454, 6517-9850; www.carti homestay.blogspot.com; r per person incl 3 meals & tour US$30) Catering to backpackers, this popular hostel on a crowded community island is friendly and cozy. Certainly it is the best place to meet young Kunas and strike up a conversation, though the inflatable Jägermeister bottle in the corner is a good indicator of the kind of cultural interactions you might expect. The hosts can also coordinate sailing trips to Colombia.

Robinson's Cabins (☎ 6721-9885; r per person incl 3 meals & tour US$30) Occupies one side of Naranjo Chico. There is little to do here, but dining outdoors around the picnic table provides the perfect opportunity to mix with fellow travelers. At the time of writing, bathrooms with plumbing were in the process of installation. In low season, rates are discounted but transfers to Cartí (US$15) are charged separately. If Robinson is full, his cousin Ina's place next door offers identical rates and lodgings. Defected from a previous location known as Robinson's Island, the location can be confusing for boat drivers. Access via Cartí, El Porvenir or Río Sidra.

our pick **Cabañas Kuanidup** (☎ 6635-6737, 6742-7656; r per person incl 3 meals & tour US$75) A clutch of solar-powered bamboo-and-thatch cabins with sandy floors and private bathrooms. They are extremely professional, with secure boats, and purified drinking water included. Interesting outings include night diving, a waterfall hike, and a visit to the prized Cayos Holandeses or to the nudist island next door. The island fronts a lovely beach and there's volleyball, but most pass the time swinging in the hammocks. Regional transportation is included. Access via Cartí, El Porvenir or Río Sidra.

Cabañas Tigre (☎ 333-2006; r per person US$10, child US$5) On a quiet tip of a lovely community island, these bamboo-and-thatch *cabañas* have cement floors and shared facilities. Meals are extra (US$4 to US$7). The grounds are strung up with colorful hammocks and the ocean here is clear and placid, perfect for kayaking or snorkeling (US$1). Local guide Leonard Serrano can guide kayaking trips, hiking (US$15 for two) or snorkeling (US$20 to US$26 for two, depending on location). Fly into Corazón de Jesus.

Yandup Lodge (☎ 261-7229; www.yandupisland.com; cabins per person incl 3 meals & tour US$125) Just five minutes by boat from Playón Chico, tiny islet

Yandup is run by an attentive Spaniard-Kuna family. The octagonal thatched-roof cabins have private bathrooms, solar-generated light and clean water. Guests can request vegetarian meals and get tailored excursions, which include cultural visits as well as the usual snorkeling and hiking. The island's grassy grounds and powder-fine beach might be reason enough to just stay put.

SHOPPING

Molas are the most famous of Panamanian traditional handicrafts. Made of brightly colored squares of cotton fabric sewn together, the finished product reveals landscape scenes, birds, sea turtles or fish – often surrounded by a mazelike pattern. Craftsmanship varies considerably between *molas*, and prices only start at US$10, going into the hundreds. You can find *molas* on the islands (or rather, the *mola*-sellers will find you).

GETTING THERE & AWAY
Air

Both **Air Panama** (☎ 316-9000; www.flyairpanama.com) and **Aeroperlas** (☎ 315-7500; www.aeroperlas.com) fly to the Archipiélago de San Blás. Air Panama has one flight per day to Achutupu, Cartí, Corazón

SAILING THE KUNA YALA TO COLOMBIA

Don't mind roughing it? Here's an adventure. Small sailboats can take passengers to Colombia via Archipiélago de San Blás for the price of a flight. However, these boats are not official charters. Passengers help out in exchange for cheap passage, a few days of sun and sand in the San Blás, and a snorkeling trip or two. Half the trip is the open-sea passage to Cartagena, which can be quite rough. Before you book, find out:

- Do you get a cabin or floor space?
- What's the size of boat and the number of passengers?
- Are there adequate life boats and life vests for all passengers?
- Is there adequate safety equipment and a functioning radio?
- Does the captain have a charter license?
- What are the meals like? (some boats serve beans and rice three times a day)

Reports are mostly good, but travelers have complained about boats skimping on meals, overcrowding or traveling despite bad weather. Bring snacks and ask ahead if the boat needs fresh groceries (since boats spend extended periods at sea). During trade-wind season (December to April) you should bring motion-sickness medication. Don't skimp on research – check a boat or captain's existing references with hostels and other travelers before committing. If you are only traveling for the novelty of sailing, consider a trip that sticks to the Kuna Yala.

The best place to inquire about scheduled departures is at any of the youth hostels in Panama City (p647). A typical five-day sailing trip including food, and activities (but not island fees) costs around US$385.

de Jesús, El Porvenir, Playón Chico and Río Sidra. Aeroperlas has three flights per day to all of these destinations, except Achutupu.

Book as far in advance as possible as demand far exceeds supply. Note that planes may stop at other islands in the archipelago, loading and unloading passengers or cargo before continuing on.

Flights depart from Albrook Airport in Panama City and arrive at their destinations in about 30 minutes to an hour. A one-way flight ticket to each destination is around US$60; prices vary according to season and availability.

Car

Recently completed, the only road that leads into the district connects the town of El Llano, on the Carretera Interamericana 70km east of Panama City, to the San Blás coastal hamlet of Cartí. The road begins near El Llano at the turnoff for Nusagandi, and has one river crossing that sometimes may be impassable. It's best to take a shared 4WD with a powerful engine, a winch and good tires. Ask your Panama City hostel to arrange transportation or call driver **Germain Perez** (☎ 6734-3454; www .cartihomestaykunayala.blogspot.com; per person US$25).

You can also get around the islands by boat (see boxed text, p693).

DARIÉN PROVINCE

The Darién has a rogue reputation fed by its reputation as the playground of Colombian guerrillas and narcotraffickers. While the dangers of the province shouldn't be underestimated, they should at least be contextualized. The issues surrounding the Darién are complex and require careful consideration. With the right planning, the Darién can show prudent travelers something truly wild.

In a stroke of irony, the lower Darién has remained so pristine because of its volatile reputation. Parque Nacional Darién is a 5760-sq-km national park where the primeval meets the present, its landscape virtually unchanged in a million years. Emberá and Wounaan people maintain many of their traditional practices and retain generations-old knowledge of the rainforest. Parque Nacional Darién is also one of world's richest biomes and home to the legendary bird-watching destination of Cana.

But while the southern Darién features Panama's most spectacular rainforests, the north faces the worst scenes of habitat destruction. Most news items focus on Colombian conflicts spilling over into Panama's borders, but the real battle lines surround the province's rapidly disappearing forests.

History

Indigenous groups living within the boundaries of the Darién emigrated from the Chocó region of Colombia thousands of years ago. Anthropologists place the Chocóes in two linguistic groups – the Emberá and the Wounaan. With the exception of language, their cultural features are virtually identical but they prefer to be distinguished as two separate peoples.

Before the introduction of the gun, the Emberá and Wounaan were expert users of the *boroquera* (blowgun) and they envenomed their darts with lethal toxins from poisonous frogs and bullet ants. Many scholars believe that they forced the Kuna out of the Darién and into the Caribbean coastal area.

During occupation, the US Air Force turned to the Emberá and Wounaan for jungle survival. Since both groups thrive in the tropical wilderness, many were added to the corps of instructors that trained US astronauts and air force pilots at Fort Sherman, near Colón.

Today, the majority of the 8000 Emberá and Wounaan in Panama live deep in the rainforests of the Darién, particularly along the Sambú, Jaqué, Chico, Tuquesa, Membrillo, Tuira, Yape and Tucutí rivers. Along with subsistence agriculture, hunting, fishing and poultry raising, they also work on nearby commercial rice and maize plantations.

Orientation & Information

The Interamericana terminates in the frontier town of Yaviza, beyond which lies the vast wilderness region of the Darién. The highway starts again 150km further on in Colombia. This break between Central and South America is known as the Darién Gap – literally the end of the road.

International authorities eager to improve transportation and trade between the continents are lobbying to push the Interamericana through the Darién Gap now that Colombia has become more stable. However, proponents must deal with Panamanian fears that it is not stable enough. In addition, a road could also

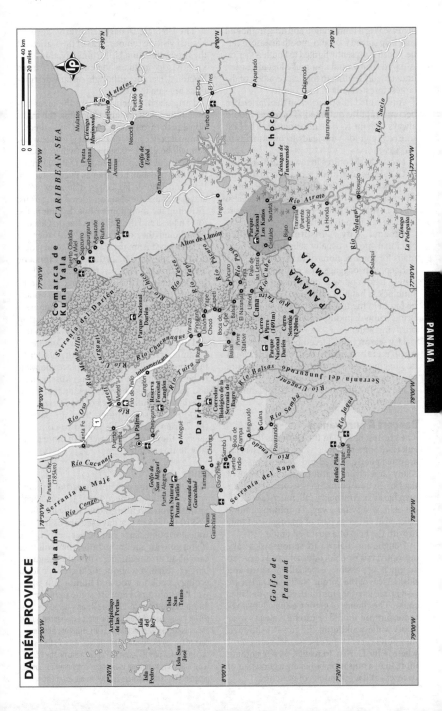

DARIÉN PROVINCE

PANAMA

increase illegal immigration and drug traffic and may help spread foot-and-mouth disease in cattle, which is presently limited to South America. A paved road would also make logging easier, undoubtedly leading to the deforestation of the largest forested area in the country.

Any printed information on the Darién can become rapidly outdated. Travelers should always seek up-to-date information. The best source is a guide who leads frequent trips to the area.

Local ANAM offices in towns such as Yaviza or La Palma can provide some information on the park and potentially help find guides (usually rangers with days off). Travelers must also check in with the police in these towns before heading out into the jungle.

Panama City's Instituto Geográfico Nacional (p639) usually sells topographical maps for some regions of the Darién.

Keep your baggage to a minimum on any jungle trek. You will need insect repellent, sunblock, a hat and rain gear. Food can only be found in the towns, not at ranger stations. Bring some drinking water and a means of purifying water.

Dry season (mid-December through mid-April) is the best time to visit; otherwise, you'll be slogging your way through thick mud and swatting at moth-size mosquitoes.

For more information on trip planning, see opposite.

Dangers & Annoyances

The greatest hazard in the Darién is the difficult environment. Trails, when they exist at all, are often poorly defined and are never marked. Many large rivers that form the backbone of the Darién transportation network create their own hazards. Any help at all, much less medical help, is very far away. To minimize these risks, visit either as part of an organized tour or with the help of a qualified guide.

Dengue and malaria are serious risks. Take a prophylaxis or chloroquine – and cover up as much as possible, especially at dawn and dusk. Areas of the Parque Nacional Darién are also prime territory for the deadly fer-de-lance snake. The chance of getting a snakebite is remote, but you should be careful – always wear boots while walking in the forest. Although they don't carry Lyme disease, ticks are everywhere in the Darién. In reality, they're nothing more than a nuisance, but bring a good pair of tweezers and a few books of matches.

The US State Department warns travelers against visiting remote areas of the Darién off the Interamericana.Unfortunately, this blanket advisory includes the entirety of Parque Nacional Darién, although certain destinations are safe to visit.

Particularly treacherous are the areas between Boca de Cupe and Colombia, the traditional path through the Darién Gap – there is minimal police presence, and it is unlikely that you will be given assistance if (when) trouble arises. It's also recommended that you avoid the towns of Balsal, El Naranjal, Púcuro, Limón, Paya and Palo de las Letras. The areas north and east of this are also considered dangerous, including the mountains Altos de Limón, the Río Tuquesa and the trail from Puerto Obaldía.

Although the no-go zones in the Darién are well removed from the traditional tourist destinations, the dangers in these spots cannot be underestimated. Narcotraffickers utilize these jungle routes and they don't appreciate bumping into travelers trekking through the woods. Parts of the Darién Gap have also become areas of activity for guerrillas from neighboring Colombia, although they usually come to rest and hide, not to attack. However, Colombian paramilitary forces often cross the border to hunt the guerrillas and the last place you want to be is caught in the crossfire. Missionaries and travelers alike have been kidnapped and killed in the southern area of the Darién.

Despite these warnings, there are parts of the Darién that can be visited in complete safety – these areas are covered in more detail later in this chapter.

Tours

The Darién is the only major part of Panama where a guide is necessary. If you speak Spanish, you can hire guides locally for about US$10 to US$20 per day (see opposite). But transportation costs can be very expensive. If you go with a tour operator, they will take care of all arrangements without a language barrier, teach you about the incredible local ecology, cook for you and humor you when you blisters. Here are some options:

Ancon Expeditions (p707) The sole operator in the Darién for many years, Ancon has the most experienced guides and operate highly professional tours. Trips run from four days to two weeks. Destinations include Ancon's field station in Cana, a private lodge in Punta Patiño on the Pacific coast and visits to remote indigenous communities. Special programs for bird-watchers and hikers are excellent.

SURVIVING THE DARIÉN

Parque Nacional Darién is the most ecologically diverse land-based national park in all Central America yet it is one of the least-visited parks too. Chalk it up to reputation – with its high stakes and poisonous snakes, the Darién isn't for everyone. Yet as a destination it is fascinating and fulfilling – provided you take the necessary precautions and go prepared.

Security

When planning your trip, first consider your destination. Established routes are recommended both for your safety and for legal reasons. The police have been known to detain those on unauthorized routes and suspect their activity – even if they are with a guide.

Safety

Even if you have crossed Central America by bus alone, solo travel here is not recommended. First off, trails are unmarked and it is terribly easy to get lost. Second, no one is likely to come to your aid. Third, poisonous snakes and scorpions could end your trip (or your life) unexpectedly.

Preparations

Though remote, the Darién is not cheap. Travelers should make a careful trip budget. Most people loathe to take tours do so here. Decide whether going with an independent guide and paying all the fuel and food costs separately will really work out to your advantage – fuel can be astronomical. Those who contract a local guide should speak Spanish themselves, so solutions can be discussed when problems arise.

Engines break, flights are delayed...in short, travel delays are about as common as raindrops in the Darien. Go with extra food and cash, a flashlight, matches, good personal equipment and flexibility in your schedule.

Guides

Paying more usually means getting more. A naturalist guide will have a different skill set than a *guía local* (local guide). Consider your needs and criteria when making a selection. The following are essential:

- Experience in the area
- Extensive local contacts and problem-solving skills
- A planned itinerary with realistic travel times and contracted transportation
- Good equipment (tents, etc) if you do not have your own
- Any necessary permits

The following are desired:

- Skill at spotting animals
- Knowledge of local history, animals and plants
- Knowledge of English (or another language)
- First-aid kit and skills
- Handheld radio and/or cell phone for areas with coverage

Fellow travelers can be excellent guide references but it is important to meet your guide – particularly if you will be traveling solo. If contracting your guide in the Darien, converse with locals, find someone you trust and ask them for references.

Find out ahead of time if gas, transportation, food and fees are included. Perhaps the most important factor for a local guide is that they have extensive contacts in the region who can help arrange logistics, and know the actual terrain. Don't assume that a local guide is experienced – some have never before set foot in the national park. ANAM is a good point of reference.

PANAMA

Ecocircuitos (p707) With a focus on sustainable tourism, Ecocircuitos offers volunteer vacations in a rural community of the Darién. Projects include working on an organic farm, assisting a nonprofit crafts cooperative or improving community infrastructure.

Panama Exotic Adventures (☎ 314-3013; www .panamaexoticadventures.com) With an ecolodge in Metetí (right), this French-run outfit offers three- to eight-day trips with hands-on visits to indigenous communities, kayaking and outings.

Volunteering

An excellent organization that sometimes takes volunteers is the **Fundación Pro-Niños de Darién** (☎ in Panama City 264-4333, in Metetí 299-6825; www.darién.org.pa). The nonprofit foundation aims to improve the lives of children through educational and nutritional programs. 'Godparents' can sponsor a child for US$20 per month. They also help residents develop sustainable agriculture.

Also see the listing for Ecocircuitos (p707).

Getting There & Away

The Interamericana journeys 266km from Panama City to Yaviza, passing through Chepo, El Llano, Ipetí, Tortí, Higueronal and smaller, unmapped communities in Panamá Province before crossing into the Darién. Serving these towns, there are eight buses daily from Panama City to Yaviza between 3:30am and 7am (US$14, six to eight hours). Be sure to tell the bus driver your destination.

With varying frequency, **Air Panama** (☎ 316-9000; www.flyairpanama.com/tickets) has flights to La Palma (US$40, one hour) and El Real Sambú (US$35, 15 minutes) up to several times per week.

Getting Around

In the vast jungles of the Darién Province, rivers are often the only means of getting from one point to another, with *piraguas* providing the transport. In La Palma you can hire a motorized boat for US$175 to US$200 per day, which can take you to the Río Mogué or the Río Sambú. From either of these rivers you'll have to negotiate with indigenous villagers (in Mogué or La Chunga) to take you further upriver in *piraguas*. Hiring boats in Río Jaqué is possible but strongly ill-advised owing to the dangers of guerrilla activity. A shorter (and cheaper) boat trip goes from Puerto Quimba to La Palma.

METETÍ

On the road to Yaviza, Metetí buzzes with passing traffic. It's also a key stepping stone to La Palma via a scenic boat ride. Lodging options here are preferable to those in Yaviza. New additions include an ecolodge and an airstrip in the works. For last-minute purchases there is a good-sized grocery store.

The bleach-scented **Hotel Felicidad** (☎ 299-6544; d with fan/air-con US$10/15) is one of the decent hotels, with clean cement rooms. The nearby **Restaurante Johana** (mains US$2.50) serves meat dishes with rice and plantain, and fresh juice (but no beer).

Run by Panama Exotic Adventures, ecolodge **Filo de Tallo** (☎ 6780-2945, 6673-5381; www .panamadarien.com; 4-day package per person US$600) is an elegant take on jungle living, with three well-spaced thatched huts containing beds draped with mosquito netting and attached bathrooms set with pastel river stones. Activities include crabbing in the mangroves, kayaking and visiting a Wounaan village. Although it's on a deforested sector just entering the Darién, it's one of the best lodgings in the region. It is also certified as carbon-neutral by Forest Finance. Packages include all meals and activities and transportation to/from Panama City.

For the boat to La Palma, take the turnoff for Puerto Quimba, a port on the Río Iglesias. The paved road between Metetí and Puerto Quimba is about 20km long. A passenger pickup shuttles between Metetí and Puerto Quimba every 30 minutes from 6am until 9pm (US$1.50), or take a taxi (US$10). From Puerto Quimba, unscheduled boats to La Palma leave several times a day between 7:30am and 6:30pm (US$3); they depart from La Palma roughly between 5:30am and 5pm. A one-way charter (US$30) may also be an option.

Traveling to La Palma by boat from Puerto Quimba is an excellent alternative to flying straight in from Panama City. The scenery along this 30-minute river trip is virgin jungle and dense mangrove forests – and you're bound to meet interesting characters onboard.

YAVIZA
pop 3300

Part bazaar and part bizarre, this concrete village is the end of the road. Here the Interamericana grinds to a halt and beyond lies the famous Darién Gap. Rough-edged and misshapen, it's hardly a holiday destination unless you had cockfighting in mind. For travelers, it is an essential stop to check in for entry to Parque Nacional Darién.

Recently relocated from El Real, the **ANAM** (☎ 299-4495) office of Parque Nacional Darién (right) can offer updated information on trails and safety; register here and pay your park fee (foreigners US$10). The office also can suggest local guides (US$10 to US$20 per day). If you do not need a local guide, your best bet is to register with ANAM in Panama City and take the boat to La Palma from Puerto Quimba.

The best sleeping option is **Ya Darien** (☎ 294-4334; d with fan/air-con US$15/20), where tidy rooms have cold-water showers and the help is slow as molasses. If you have a pressing need to spend the night in Yaviza, the **Hotel 3Americas** (☎ 299-4439; r from US$20) has worn, plain rooms and the distraction of a cockfighting pit.

There are eight buses daily between Panama City and Yaviza (US$14, six to eight hours). To arrange a private boat to El Real (US$60 to US$80 for three passengers), contact **Chicho Bristan** (☎ 299-6566, 6539-2007) of El Real to pick you up in Yaviza.

EL REAL
pop 1300
El Real dates from the days of the early conquistadors, when they constructed a fort beside the Río Tuira to prevent pirates from sailing upriver and attacking Santa María. Gold from mines in the valley of Cana, to the south, was brought to Santa María, and stored until there was a quantity sufficient to warrant assembling an armada and moving the bullion to Panama City. Today, El Real is one of the largest towns in the Darién, though it's still very much a backwater settlement.

El Real is the last sizable settlement before the national park. Those heading up to Rancho Frío must either hire a local guide or be part of a tour – ANAM will not let you proceed unescorted. Before your arrival, you must register at ANAM in Yaviza or Panama City, where you can pay the entry fee (foreigners US$10).

Options are slim here and it is really best to make food purchases prior for the hike. If you arrive in town too late to start the trek to Rancho Frío, you can spend the night at **Macho de Monte** (☎ 299-6566, 6539-2007; r per person US$10), a rustic *pensión*. At **Fonda Doña Lola** (meals US$3) you can have a heaping plate of rice and chicken.

Currently, El Real is only accessed by boat or air charter. Veteran boatman **Chicho Bristan** (☎ 299-6566, 6539-2007) offers charter boat trips between Yaviza and El Real (US$60 to US$80 for three passengers). Though the park cannot be accessed by vehicle, Chicho can arrange a 4WD vehicle (US$25) to take you partway, leaving you in Pirre 1, a 1½-hour hike to Rancho Frío.

PARQUE NACIONAL DARIÉN
Rancho Frío (Pirre Station)
Thirteen kilometers south of El Real, as the lemon-spectacled tanager flies, is the Rancho Frío sector of Parque Nacional Darién. It's home to **Pirre Station**, the most accessible section of the national park, with two good hiking trails. A two-day hike to Mount Pirre ridge requires a tent and complete self-sufficiency. A second trail winds through jungle to a series of cascades about an hour's hike away. Neither should be attempted without a ranger or local guide as they are not well marked and if you get lost out here, you're finished.

Pirre Station has **barracks** (cots per person US$10) with fold-out cots, a rustic dining area and kitchen, cold stall showers and an outhouse. There is also a shady **campsite** (per person US$5) where you can either pitch a tent or string up a hammock. Electricity is run off batteries and use must be kept minimal.

Visitors must bring their own food and purified water. Cooking fuel is scare, so let the rangers do the cooking (US$10 a day is most appreciated).

Beware: most of Parque Nacional Darién is prime fer-de-lance territory, and these very deadly snakes have been found near the station. Always wear boots and long trousers when you're walking in camp at night or entering the forest at any time.

Pirre Station can only be reached by hiking or by a combination of hiking and boating or 4WD transportation (see El Real, left). The four-hour hiking route takes the 'road' connecting El Real and Rancho Frío, yet this barely discernible path is pretty much impossible without a guide (though you can contract one in Pirre 1 for US$10).

Only 15km separate Pirre Station and Cana, yet between the two there's nothing but virgin rainforest.

LA PALMA
pop 4200
The provincial capital of Darién Province, La Palma is a one-street town located where the wide Río Tuira meets the Golfo de San Miguel. Pastel stilt houses lord over the

---

GETTING TO COLOMBIA

The Interamericana stops at the town of Yaviza and reappears 150km further on, far beyond the Colombian border. Although a trickle of travelers have walked through the infamous Darién Gap, the presence of Colombian guerrillas, paramilitaries, smugglers and bandits make this a potentially suicidal trip.

The Caribbean crossing between Puerto Obaldía, Panama and Capurganá, Colombia is not recommended. From Puerto Obaldía, a traveler must either walk or boat to the Colombian village of Sapzurro. On foot, this takes about 2½ hours, but the track is indistinct in places, and the presence of rogue factors in the area makes boating the better option. From Sapzurro it's a two-hour walk further to Capurganá. There is a fair amount of risk crossing here and anyone attempting it should get solid information about the security situation beforehand. Tourists have made it safely to Colombia along this route, though the point worth emphasizing is that not everyone has made it.

For information on sailing to Colombia, which is by far the safest option after flying, see boxed text, p693.

---

muddy waterfront, a scene abuzz with commerce, bars and evangelist messages.

Most travelers pass through La Palma to take transport to somewhere else. The two most popular boating destinations are Reserva Natural Punta Patiño and the Emberá villages that line the banks of the Río Sambú.

Every facility of possible interest to the traveler is located on the main street, which is within 300m of the airstrip. La Palma is home to the only bank in the Darién Province, the Banco Nacional de Panamá. There are also a hospital, a port and a police station (if you intend to go anywhere near the Colombian border and you speak Spanish, you should talk to the police here first), as well as hotels, bars and several food stands.

The waterfront **Hospedaje Pablo & Benita** (☎ 299-6490; Calle Central Abajo; s/d/tr US$10/15/20) has thin walls and mattresses but good sea views. The friendly owners can help arrange visits to the Emberá community of Mogue. The comparatively upscale **Hotel Biaquira Bagara** (☎ /fax 299-6224; d with/without bathroom US$20/15, d with air-con US$25; ⊠) is simple and sweet, with hardwood decks, wicker furniture and firm beds. Below there is a basic market: if you're boating upriver, stock up on groceries here.

There's no shortage of cheap and somewhat cheerful eateries in town. **La Unción** (☎ 299-6372; mains US$2-4) offers decent *comida criollo* (typical food) served along with fiery sermons on the satellite TV.

For flights, **Air Panama** (☎ 316-9000; www .flyairpanama.com/tickets) flies twice weekly from Panama City to La Palma (US$46, one hour).

To hire a boat and a guide, look in the vicinity of the dock for a responsible cap-

tain with a seaworthy motorboat (US$120 to US$200 per day, gas included).

Reserva Natural Punta Patiño

Twenty-five kilometers south of La Palma, Punta Patiño is a private **wildlife reserve** owned by the government conservation group Ancon. The 263-sq-km preserve contains species-rich primary and secondary forest, and is one of the best places in Panama to spot harpy eagles. It is also a great place to rack up the bird count, and there's a good chance of seeing everything from three-toed sloths and howler monkeys to crocodiles. The only way to reach the preserve is by boat or plane.

Ancon Expeditions (p707) offers a package tour that includes the round-trip airfare between Panama City and Punta Patiño, lodging, food and activities. You can book lodgings at the reserve without a guided tour, but you must notify it in advance of your arrival.

SAMBÚ

Riverside Sambú is an interesting stop, populated by Emberá people and *cimarrones* (whose ancestors escaped the slave trade by living in the jungle). Urban by Darién standards, it has an airstrip, hospital and pay phone. Given the ease of flying in here, it makes a good launch point to visit riverside Emberá and Wounaan communities and absorb the slow jungle pace.

From Sambú, visitors can plan trips to **Puerto Indio** (with permission from the Emberá and Wounaan) and visit petroglyphs or mangrove forests. **Bocaca Verano** is a lagoon with crocodiles and prolific birdlife. Local guide Lupicinio, found in front of Sambú house, guides hiking excursions ($15 per person) to see harpy eagles and tours to Bocaca Verano in dry season. For boat tours, Juan Murillo takes visitors **fishing** (4 passengers US$120) in the Golfo de San Miguel in his 75-horsepower boat. Since there are no phones, ask around for either guide.

Facing the airstrip, **Hotel Fiesta** (☎ public phone 333-2512; r with air-con US$25) is Sambú-deluxe, boasting the village's only air-conditioned lodgings. It's above a store also run by the friendly Telma and Ricardo. Next door, **Mi Lindo Sueño** (☎ public phone 333-2512; r without bathroom US$10) has plain concrete rooms.

ourpick Sambu Hause (☎ 6687-4177; http://sambu hausedarienpanama.com; r per person incl breakfast US$25) is the only jungle B&B around. It's an attractive yellow clapboard run by friendly Mabel. Cozy but simple, this might be the only place to get pancake breakfasts in the Darién. You can also arrange cultural tours here.

The Emberá community runs Werara Puru, a *choza* (hut) built to lodge tourists, located a 10-minute walk from town. When we visited the space was under renovation.

You can get cheap and tasty meals at **Comidas Benedicta** (meals US$2.50), where Anthony Bourdain dined when in Sambú. If it's a party you want, check out **Mis Cabañas del Nuevo Milenio** (☽ Sat & Sun), a woodsy juke-joint with music blasting half the village away. You can get a beer here, though it may not be cold.

Air Panama (☎ 316-9000; www.flyairpanama.com/tickets) flies twice weekly from Panama City (US$46, one hour). Always confirm your return ticket in advance.

Boat **Barco Buen Pastor** (☎ 6772-2435) travels between Panama City and Sambú (12 hours, US$15) weekly; contact Señora María Teresa on the phone number above for details.

The *panga* boat to Puerto Quimba (US$20) goes three times a week, with one stop in La Palma. Trips are not scheduled far in advance, ask around and try to confirm a date for a return trip.

CANA

Nestled in foothills on the eastern slope of Pirre Ridge, the Cana valley is the most isolated place in Panama. It's also the heart of the Parque Nacional Darién, and is regarded as one of the finest bird-watching spots in the world. In addition to four species of macaw, Cana is known for its harpy eagles, black-tipped cotingas, dusky-backed jacamars, rufous-cheeked hummingbirds and golden-headed quetzals.

Ancon Expeditions is the exclusive operator here. Their base is the ANAM/Ancon field station, a wooden structure built by gold workers during the 1970s, and enlarged in mid-1998. The building has rustic dorms, shared bathrooms and candlelit evenings. Ancon Expeditions (see p707) offers an excellent five-day, four-night package that includes private charter flights between Panama City and Cana, an English-speaking guide, all meals and accommodations (including tent camping along the Pirre Mountain Trail, with all provisions carried by porters).

PANAMA DIRECTORY

ACCOMMODATIONS

Prices cited are high-season rates including Panama's 10% tax on hotel rooms. High season is from mid-December to mid-April. Rates may spike up to 50% higher for Easter week and between Christmas and New Year's. Low-season rates are generally about 15% lower.

There is usually no shortage of places to stay in Panama, except during holidays or special events outside Panama City, when advance reservations may be necessary.

Budget lodgings typically range from US$7 per person and up to US$35 for a double room. Hotels in the midrange category usually charge about US$36 to US$90 for a double room.

ACTIVITIES
Bird-Watching

With more than 900 species of birds in Panama, all you need to do to spot feathered friends is to get a good pair of binoculars and hit the trails. Two popular spots include **Camino del Oleoducto** (Pipeline Rd; p656) in Parque Nacional Soberanía and **Parque Nacional Volcán Barú** (p667), home of the resplendent quetzal, the Maya bird of paradise.

Panama's avian species are at their best in the legendary Cana Valley, which is regarded as one of the top bird-watching destinations in the world. This phenomenal wildlife preserve can only be accessed via organized tour with Ancon Expeditions (p707).

The **Panama Audubon Society** (☎ 224-9371; www.panamaaudubon.org), located in Panama City, organizes the annual Christmas bird count on Pipeline Rd, and runs bird-watching expeditions throughout the country.

PANAMA

PANAMA

Diving & Snorkeling

Panama has numerous islands with good snorkeling and diving sights. On the Caribbean coast, **Bocas del Toro** (p679) and the **San Blás Archipelago** (p691) are prime spots. Dive shops on Bocas del Toro rent snorkeling and diving gear, and offer PADI-certified classes, while snorkeling in San Blás is more of the do-it-yourself variety. There is also good diving and snorkeling around **Portobelo** (p688) as well as a couple of reputable dive shops in town.

On the Pacific coast, there is good snorkeling in the **Golfo de Chiriquí** (p661) and in the **Archipiélago de las Perlas** (p658). Although coral reefs in the Pacific are not as vibrant as their Caribbean counterparts, you're bound to see some big fish here as well as the occasional pelagic creature.

You can rent equipment at the destinations listed above, but avid snorkelers should bring their own. **Scubapanama** (Map p640; ☎ 261-3841; www.scubapanama.com), based in Panama City, offers diving trips throughout the country.

Fishing

With 1518 islands, 2988km of coast and 480 rivers, there's no problem finding a fishing spot in Panama. Possibilities include deep-sea fishing, fishing for bass in **Lago Gatún** on the Panama Canal, trout fishing in the rivers running down **Volcán Barú** and surf casting on any of Panama's Pacific and Caribbean beaches.

Hiking

Hiking opportunities abound in Panama. In the Chiriquí highlands, the **Sendero Los Quetzales** (p667) winds through Parque Nacional Volcán Barú, and is regarded as the country's top hike – check conditions before going. **Parque Internacional La Amistad** also has some fine, short trails, starting near its Cerro Punta (p668) entrance.

From Boquete, you can summit **Volcán Barú** (p664), Panama's highest point and only volcano. **El Valle** (p684), nestled in a picturesque valley, is a fine place for casual walkers.

Near Panama City on the shores of the canal, **Parque Nacional Soberanía** (p654) contains a section of the old Sendero Las Cruces used by the Spanish to cross between the coasts. **Parque Natural Metropolitano** (p643), on the outskirts of Panama City, also has some good walks leading to a panorama of the city.

You can also trek through lush rainforests in the **Parque Nacional Darién** (p699), though this is

---

THE TRANSPANAMA TRAIL

Linking all of Panama by trail, this **cross-country circuit** (www.transpanama.org) has spectacular landscapes spanning from coastline to rainforest and mountains. The trail is a work in progress and is currently 60% finished, running from the border of Costa Rica toward Panama City. The Camino Real – the historic land crossing made redundant by the Panama Canal – is part of it.

The trail can be done in short three- to four-day segments, accessed by public transportation. Highlights include the segments between Boquete and Costa Rica, Parque Nacional Campana and El Valle (three to four days), and the Coclé–Veraguas crossing from Huacas el Quise to Laguna de La Yeguada. More information is available on the website, where you can also download GPS tracks for free.

---

best arranged through a reputable guide owing to the guerrilla activity in the region.

See p704 for advice on hiking.

Surfing

The country's top surfing destination is the Caribbean archipelago of **Bocas del Toro** (p679), which attracts strong winter swells and surfers from around the world. Although it remains an off-the-beaten-path destination, **Santa Catalina** (p681) on the Pacific coast has some of the most challenging breaks in Central America. There is also uncrowded surfing on the laid-back Caribbean island of **Isla Grande** (p689) and at **Playa Venao** (p684) on the Península de Azuero.

White-Water Rafting & Kayaking

Whether you take to the water by raft or kayak, Panama boasts some excellent opportunities for river running. The country's most famous white-water runs are the Ríos Chiriquí and Chiriquí Viejo, though there are also opportunities for sea kayaking in both Bocas del Toro and Chiriquí Provinces.

The unofficial river-running capital of Panama is the highland town of Boquete (p665). Located near the Ríos Chiriquí and Chiriquí Viejo, Boquete is home to the country's top rafting outfits, namely **Boquete Outdoor Adventures** (☎ 720-2284; www.boqueteoutdoor adventures.com) and **Chiriquí River Rafting** (☎ 720-1505; www.panama-rafting.com).

Boquete Outdoor Adventures run river kayak trips during the rainy season (April to November). They also run sea kayak trips in the Golfo de Chiriquí, as do **Fluid Adventures** (☎ 6560-6558; www.fluidadventurespanama.com). The only adventure tour operator to offer kayaking in San Blás is **Ecocircuitos** (☎ 314-0068; www .ecocircuitos.com). Also on the Caribbean coast, independently minded travelers can rent kayaks at **Cap 'n Dons** (Map p674; ☎ 757-9248) on Isla Colón.

BOOKS
Excellent books dealing with facets of Panamanian history include the following:

The Sack of Panamá: Sir Henry Morgan's Adventures on the Spanish Main, by Peter Earle, is a vivid account of the Welsh pirate's looting and destruction of Panama City in 1671.

The Path Between the Seas: The Creation of the Panama Canal, by David McCullough, is a readable and exciting account of the building of the Panama Canal. It's 700 pages long and reads like a suspense novel.

How Wall Street Created a Nation: J.P. Morgan, Teddy Roosevelt and the Panama Canal, by Ovidio Diaz Espino, probes deeply into the dark alliances and backroom deals that culminated in the Canal's construction.

Inside Panama, by Tom Barry and John Lindsay-Poland, is a look at the political, economic and human-rights scenes in Panama, with special emphasis on Panamanian society since the 1960s and on US–Panama relations from that time through to the mid-1990s.

BUSINESS HOURS
Opening hours for travel agents, tour operators and other businesses are normally 8am to noon and 1:30pm to 5pm weekdays, and 8am to noon on Saturdays. Government offices, including post offices, are open 8am to 4pm on weekdays and don't close for lunch. Most banks are open 8:30am to 1pm or 3pm on weekdays; some have Saturday hours as well. Shops and pharmacies are generally open from around 9am or 10am until 6pm or 7pm Monday to Saturday.

Grocery stores are generally open from 8am to 9pm, though some stay open 24 hours.

Restaurants usually open for lunch from noon to 3pm and dinner from 6pm to 10pm. Those that offer breakfast open from 7am to 10am. On Sundays, many restaurants are closed. In Panama City and David, restaurants open later on Fridays and Saturdays, until about 11pm or midnight. Most bars are open from around noon to 10pm, later on Friday and Saturday nights (typically 2am). Nightclubs in Panama City open around 10pm or 11pm and close at 3am or 4am.

CLIMATE
Panama's tourist season is the dry season (from mid-December to mid-April). This is true for the Pacific slope, but the Caribbean side can get rain throughout the year. The weather can be hot and steamy in the lowlands during the rainy season, when the humidity makes the heat oppressive. But it won't rain nonstop; rain in Panama, as elsewhere in the tropics, tends to come in sudden short downpours that freshen the air, and is followed by sunshine. It's more comfortable to do long, strenuous hiking in the dry season.

COURSES
Panama is home to several Spanish-language schools, which are located in Panama City (p646), Boquete (p665) and Bocas del Toro (p675).

DANGERS & ANNOYANCES
Crime is a problem in certain parts of Panama City. The city's better districts, however, are safer than in many other capitals: witness the all-night restaurants and activity on the streets at night. On the other hand, it is not safe to walk around at night on the outskirts of Casco Viejo – be careful in the side streets of this district, even in the daytime. In general, stay where it's well lit and there are plenty of people around.

Colón has some upscale residential areas, but the city is widely known for street crime. Consult your hotel on areas to avoid.

Certain areas in the Darién Province bordering Colombia are extremely dangerous. Few travelers have reason to be in these areas. In the past, it has been used as a staging ground by criminals, human traffickers, the Colombian paramilitary and guerrillas. The area that is particularly treacherous goes beyond Boca de Cupe to Colombia, the traditional path through the Darién Gap.

Numerous Colombian boats travel the Caribbean through the Archipiélago de San Blás between the Zona Libre in Colón and Cartagena, Colombia. There have been cases of boats trafficking drugs on northbound voyages. Take this possibility into account if you plan on taking one of these slow cargo boats. On the Pacific there have been incidences as well.

PANAMA

Hiking Safety

Though tropical, Panama runs the gamut from hot to cold and hiking is not easy here. You should go adequately prepared. Always ask about the conditions of the trail before heading out – either with local outfitters or rangers. Carry plenty of water, even on short journeys, and always bring food, matches and adequate clothing – jungles get quite a bit colder at night, particularly at higher elevations.

Hikers have been known to get lost in rainforests, even seemingly user-friendly ones such as Parque Nacional Volcán Barú and the Sendero Los Quetzales. Landslides, storms and vegetation growth can make trails difficult to follow. In some cases, even access roads can deteriorate enough for transport to leave you a few miles before your intended drop-off point. This is just the reality of the jungle. Many hikers have gotten lost and there is no official rescue organization to help. If you are heading out without a guide, let your plans be known at your hotel and tell them the number of days you will be gone.

Never walk in unmarked rainforest; if there's no trail going in, you can assume that there won't be one when you decide to turn around and come back out. Always plan your transportation in advance – know where and when the last bus will pass your terminus, or arrange for a taxi pickup with a responsible, recommended transporter.

EMBASSIES & CONSULATES

More than 50 countries have embassies or consulates in Panama City. For contact details see the Panama White Pages, listed under 'Embajada de [country]' or 'Consulados.' With the exception of the USA and France, you'll find most embassies in the Marbella district of Panama City.

Ireland, Australia and New Zealand have no representation in Panama.

Canada (☎ 294-2500; www.canadainternational.gc.ca/panama; Torre de las Americas, Tower A, Piso 11, Punta Pacifica)

Colombia (☎ 264-9266; World Trade Center, Calle 53 Este, Marbella)

Costa Rica David (Map p660; ☎ /fax 774-1923; Calle C Sur btwn Avs 1 & 2 Este); Panama City (☎ 264-2980; fax 264-4057; Av Samuel Lewis)

France (Map p649; ☎ 228-7824; Plaza de Francia, Paseo las Bóvedas, Casco Viejo)

Germany (☎ 263-7733; www.panama.diplo.de; World Trade Center, Calle 53 Este, Marbella)

Netherlands (☎ 264-7257; Calle 50, Marbella)

UK (Map p644; ☎ 269-0866; www.ukinpanama.fco.gov.uk/en; Swiss Tower Calle 53 Este, Marbella)

USA (Map p644; ☎ 207-7000; www.panama.usembassy.gov; cnr Av Balboa & Calle 37 Este, La Exposición)

FESTIVALS & EVENTS

Panama has a range of colorful festivals that encompass everything from traditional folkloric fests to indigenous celebrations. For the lion's share of the country's revelry, head to the interior, where some of Panama's most famous events take place. For more details see p684.

The following events are the country's better known celebrations:

Carnaval (February/March) On the four days preceding Ash Wednesday, costumes, music, dancing and general merriment prevail in Panama City and in the Península de Azuero towns of Las Tablas, Chitré, Villa de Los Santos and Parita.

Semana Santa (March/April) On Holy Week (the week before Easter), the country hosts many special events, including the re-enactment of the crucifixion and resurrection of Christ; on Good Friday, religious processions are held across the country.

Corpus Christi (May/June) Held 40 days after Easter, this religious holiday features colorful celebrations in Villa de Los Santos. Masked and costumed dancers representing angels, devils, imps and other mythological figures enact dances, acrobatics and dramas.

Festival of the Black Christ On October 21, thousands of visitors come to honor the black Christ in Portobelo.

FOOD & DRINK
Food

Panama's national dish is *sancocho* (chicken and vegetable stew). *Ropa vieja* (literally 'old clothes'), a spicy shredded beef combination served over rice, is another common and tasty dish. Rice is the staple of Panama.

Breakfast staples and snacks are *tortillas de maíz* (thick, deep-fried cornmeal cakes) and *hojaldras* (deep-fried mass of dough served hot and covered with sugar). For lunch, simple *comida corriente* is an inexpensive set meal of beef, chicken or fish served with rice, black beans, fried plantain, chopped cabbage and maybe an egg or an avocado.

Meat figures prominently in the Panamanian diet. You'll find specialties such as *carimañola*, a yucca roll filled with chopped meat then deep-fried. The most common snack is the *empanada* (turnover filled with ground meat and fried), and tamales (cornmeal with a few spices and chicken or pork, all wrapped in banana leaves and boiled) are another favorite. Seafood is abundant and includes shrimp, Caribbean king crab, octopus, lobster and *corvina* (sea bass). Along the Caribbean coast you'll also find a West Indian influence to the dishes, such as coconut rice and coconut bread, or seafood mixed with coconut milk.

In Panama City you'll often see men pushing carts and selling *raspados,* cones filled with shaved ice topped with fruit syrup and sweetened condensed milk.

Drinks

Fresh fruit drinks, sweetened with sugar and mixed with water or milk, are called *chichas,* and are extremely popular. *Chicheme* is a concoction of milk, sweet corn, cinnamon and vanilla. Coffee is traditionally served very strong and offered with cream or condensed milk. Milk is pasteurized and safe to drink.

The national alcoholic drink is made of *seco,* milk and ice. *Seco,* like rum, is distilled from sugarcane, but it doesn't taste anything like the rum you know. This is the drink of *campesinos* (farmers). Popular in the central provinces, *vino de palma* is fermented sap extracted from the trunk of a palm tree called *palma de corozo.* By far the most popular alcoholic beverage in Panama is *cerveza* (beer). A large Atlas at a typical *cantina* can cost as little as US$1; the same beer can cost you US$3 at a decent restaurant.

GAY & LESBIAN TRAVELERS

Panamanians are more out than in recent years, though the trend is much more prevalent in the capital than anywhere else. More than in other parts of Central America, you will probably meet openly gay locals, though the culture generally follows an unspoken 'don't ask, don't tell' policy.

The **New Men and Women Association of Panama** (Asociación de Hombres y Mujeres Nuevos de Panamá; www .ahmnpanama.org) has information on national issues and events.

Panama City has a few gay and lesbian clubs (not openly advertised). Outside the capital, gay bars are hard to come by and discrimination is more prevalent. In most instances, gays and lesbians just blend in with the straight crowd at the hipper places and avoid cantinas and other conventional lairs of homophobia. Panamanian website www.farraurbana.com lists upcoming gay and lesbian events and

parties, new club openings and political issues in Panama City. You'll need at least a little Spanish to maneuver through the site.

HOLIDAYS

New Year's Day January 1
Martyrs' Day January 9
Carnaval February to March
Semana Santa (Holy Week) March to April
Labor Day May 1
Founding of Old Panama August 15
All Souls' Day November 2
Independence from Colombia November 3
First Call for Independence November 10
Independence from Spain November 28
Mothers' Day December 8
Christmas Day December 25

INTERNET ACCESS

With the exception of the Kuna Yala and Darién regions, internet cafes and wi-fi are widely available throughout the country. Most cafes charge US$1 per hour.

INTERNET RESOURCES

ATP (Autoridad de Turismo Panamá; www.atp.gob.pa) Panama's tourist website in Spanish. Also has a sister site in English, www.visitpanama.com.
Lanic (http://lanic.utexas.edu/la/ca/panama) Has an outstanding collection of links from the University of Texas Latin American Information Center.
Panama info (www.panamainfo.com) Also in English.

MAPS

The **Instituto Geográfico Nacional** (Tommy Guardia; Map p644; ☎ 236-2444; ☉ 8am-4pm Mon-Fri), in Panama City, sells topographical maps of selected cities and regions. Various free tourist publications distributed in Panama also have maps.

MEDIA
Newspapers & Magazines

La Prensa (www.prensa.com, in Spanish) is the most widely circulated daily newspaper in Panama. Other major Spanish-language dailies include *La Estrella de Panamá, El Panamá América, El Universal* and *Crítica.*

The **Panama News** (www.thepanamanews.com) is published in English every two weeks. It is distributed free in Panama City. *The Visitor,* written in English and Spanish and targeted towards tourists, is another free publication. The *Miami Herald International Edition* is available in some upscale hotels.

Radio & TV

There are three commercial TV stations in Panama (channels two, four and 13) and two devoted to public broadcasting (five and 11). Many hotels have cable TV with Spanish and English channels.

Panama has over 90, mostly commercial, radio stations. Popular radio stations include 97.1 and 102.1 (salsa), 88.9 (Latin jazz), 88.1 (reggae), 94.5 (traditional Panamanian), 106.7 (Latin rock) and 98.9 (US rock).

MONEY

Panama uses the US dollar as its currency. The official name for it here is the balboa, but it's exactly the same bill, and in practice people use the terms 'dólar' and 'balboa' interchangeably. Panamanian coins are of the same value, size and metal as US coins; both are used. Coins include one, five, 10, 25 and 50 *centavos* (or *centésimos*); 100 *centavos* equal one balboa. Be aware that most businesses won't break US$50 and US$100 bills and those that do may require you to present your passport. For exchange rates at the time of research, see below.

ATMs

Throughout Panama, ATMs are readily available except in the most isolated places. Look for the red *'sistema clave'* signs to find an ATM. They accept cards on most networks (Plus, Cirrus, MasterCard, Visa and Amex).

These places have no banks, and it's a long way to the nearest ATM: Santa Catalina, Santa Fé, Boca Brava, Isla Contadora, Isla Grande, Portobelo, Isla de Coiba and the Darién.

Credit Cards

Although accepted at travel agencies, upscale hotels and many restaurants, credit cards can be problematic almost everywhere else. In short, carry enough cash to get you to the next bank or ATM.

Exchange Rates

The table shows currency exchange rates at the time this book went to press.

Country	Unit	US$
Australia	A$1	0.81
Canada	C$1	0.93
Euro zone	€1	1.19
Japan	¥100	1.09
New Zealand	NZ$1	0.66
UK	UK£1	1.44

Taxes

A tax of 10% is added to the price of hotel rooms – always ask whether the quoted price includes the tax. Hotel prices given in this book include the tax. A 5% sales tax is levied on nonfood products.

Tipping

The standard tipping rate in Panama is around 10% of the bill; in small cafes and more casual places, tipping is not necessary. Taxi drivers do not expect tips.

Traveler's Checks

Although they can be cashed at a few banks, traveler's checks are rarely accepted by businesses, and traveler's checks in currencies other than US dollars are not accepted anywhere in Panama. Some banks will only accept American Express traveler's checks. The banks that do accept traveler's checks typically charge an exchange fee equal to 1% of the amount of the check.

POST

Panama's mail is handled by **Correos de Panama** (www.correos.gob.pa). Airmail to the USA takes five to 10 days; to Europe and Australia it takes 10 days. Panama has neither vending machines for stamps nor drop-off boxes for mail. Upscale hotels may send post.

In Panama City, packages can only be mailed from the Plaza de las Americas Post Office. Bring all packing materials yourself.

Most post offices are open from 7am to 6pm weekdays and from 7am to 4:30pm Saturday. General delivery mail can be addressed to '(name), Entrega General, (town and province), República de Panamá.' Be sure the sender calls the country 'República de Panamá' rather than simply 'Panamá,' or the mail may be sent back.

RESPONSIBLE TRAVEL

Traveling sensitively in Panama means being mindful of the environment around you. Try to patronize local businesses and industries, and spend your money where it will go directly to the people working for it.

Don't support businesses that keep caged animals around. It's an offense to keep a parrot, toucan or macaw in a cage. In some restaurants you may see endangered species on the menu; avoid *tortuga* (sea turtle), *huevos de tortuga* (turtle eggs), *cazón* (shark), *conejo pintado* (paca), *ñeque* (agouti) and *enado* (deer).

For information on responsible tourism in the Comarca de Kuna Yala, see the boxed text (p692).

For information on responsible tourism in Bocas del Toro, see boxed text, p673.

SHOPPING

A remarkable variety of imported goods, including cameras, electronic equipment and clothing, is sold in Panama, both in Colón's tax-free Zona Libre (p686) and in Panama City (p651).

The favorite handicraft souvenir from Panama is the *mola*, a colorful, intricate, multilayered appliqué textile sewn by Kuna women of the Archipiélago de San Blás. Small, simple souvenir *molas* can be bought for as little as US$10, but the best fetch several hundred dollars.

It's possible to purchase high-quality replicas of *huacas* – golden objects made on the isthmus centuries before the Spanish conquest and placed with Indians at the time of burial. These range in price from US$15 to more than US$1000.

Other handicrafts that can be purchased include wood carvings (from the *cocobolo* tree), *tagua* carvings (from the egg-sized *tagua* nut) and baskets – all made by the Wounaan and Emberá tribes.

TELEPHONE

Panama's country code is ☎507. To call Panama from abroad, use the country code before the seven-digit Panamanian telephone number. There are no local area codes in Panama.

Telephone calls to anywhere within Panama can be made from pay phones. Local calls cost US$0.10 for the first three minutes, then US$0.05 per minute. You can buy Telechip phonecards at pharmacies, corner shops and Cable & Wireless offices (the national phone company) in denominations of US$3, US$5, US$10 and US$20. You then plug this into the phone and dial the local number. Some public phones accept both cards and coins, but many accept only cards. Note that calling cell phones (which typically begin with a '6') is much pricier (US$0.25 per minute).

TOURIST INFORMATION

The **Autoridad de Turismo Panamá** (ATP, Panama Tourism Authority; Map p640; ☎226-7000; www.atp .gob.pa; Atlapa Convention Center, Vía Israel, San Francisco,

Panama City), formerly known as IPAT, is the national tourism agency. In addition to this head office, ATP runs offices in Bocas del Toro, Boquete, Colón, David, Paso Canoas, Penonomé, Portobelo, Santiago, Villa de Los Santos, Las Tablas, El Valle and Pedasí. There are smaller information counters at the ruins of Panamá Viejo, in Casco Viejo, and in both the Tocumen International Airport and the Albrook domestic airport.

ATP has a few useful maps and brochures, but often has a problem keeping enough in stock for distribution to tourists. Most offices are staffed with people who speak only Spanish, and the helpfulness of any particular office depends on the person at the counter. Some employees really try to help, but others are just passing the time. As a general rule, you will get more useful information if you have specific questions.

TOURS

Though increasingly navigable for the independent traveler, Panama does have special conditions (complex logistics, limited public access and big wilderness) which make contracting a tour operator a good option. The Darién is relatively inaccessible without a guide. Some recommended operators:

Ancon Expeditions (Map p644; ☎269-9415; www .anconexpeditions.com; El Dorado Bldg, Calle Elvira Mendez) Operating all over Panama, Ancon employs the country's best nature guides. The company is also the exclusive operator for the world-famous Cana field station popular with bird-watchers, and the Punta Patiño lodge, both in the Darién.

Ecocircuitos (Map p640; ☎314-0068; www.ecocircuitos .com) With a focus on sustainable tourism, Ecocircuitos offers a range of tours throughout the country, including wildlife-watching, kayaking in the Comarca Kuna Yala and volunteer vacations in the Darién.

Scubapanama (Map p640; ☎261-3841; www.scuba panama.com) Located in the El Carmen area of Panama City, Scubapanama is the country's oldest and most respected dive operator, and offers a variety of dive trips throughout Panama.

TRAVELERS WITH DISABILITIES

The government-created **Instituto Panameño de Habilitación Especial** (IPHE, Panamanian Institute for Special Rehabilitation; ☎261-0500; Camino Real, Betania, Panama City; ☉7am-4pm) assists all disabled people in Panama, including foreign tourists. However, the law does not require – and Panamanian businesses do not provide – discounts for foreign tourists with disabilities.

Panama is not wheelchair-friendly; with the exception of wheelchair ramps outside a few upscale hotels, parking spaces for the disabled and perhaps a few dozen oversized bathroom stalls, accommodation for people with physical disabilities rarely exists in Panama, even at top hotels. The international **Travelin' Talk Network** (TTN; ☎ in USA 303-232-2979; www.travelintalk .net; membership per year US$20) is a member-based organization offering those with various disabilities a network about travel.

VISAS

Every visitor needs a valid passport and an onward ticket to enter Panama, but further requirements vary by nationality and change occasionally. Anyone planning a trip to Panama would be advised to check the government website (www.migracion.gob.pa) for the latest information on entry requirements. Ticketing agents of airlines that fly to Panama and tour operators that send groups there often can provide this information.

Citizens of the UK, Germany, the Netherlands, Switzerland, Austria, Spain, Finland, as well as a few South and Central American countries, need only a passport. Most other nationals, including US, Canadian, Australian and New Zealand citizens, may enter with a US$5 tourist card filled out at the airport or some border posts upon entry.

Nationals of countries not listed above should obtain a visa prior to travel at Panamanian embassies and consulates abroad. The cost is around US$20, depending on the country.

If you are heading to Colombia, Venezuela or some other South American country, you may need an onward ticket before you'll be allowed entry, or even allowed to board the plane out.

A quick check with the appropriate embassy – easy to do by telephone in Panama City – will tell you whether the country you're heading to has a requirement to have an onward ticket.

You are required by law to carry either your passport or a copy with you at all times, and police officers reserve the right to see your identification at any time.

Visas and tourist cards are both good for 90 days. To extend your stay, contact the **Immigration office** (Migración y Naturalización; Map p644; ☎ 225-1373; cnr Av Cuba & Calle 29 Este; ◷ 8am-3pm Mon-Fri) in La Exposición. They also have offices in David and Chitré. You must bring your pass-

port and photocopies of the page with your personal information and of the stamp of your most recent entry to Panama. You must also bring two passport-size photos, an onward air or bus ticket and a letter to the director stating your reasons for wishing to extend your visit. You must have proof of funds (US$500) for the remainder of your stay. You will have to fill out a *prórroga de turista* (tourist extension) and pay US$250. You will then be issued a plastic photo ID card. Go early in the day as the whole process takes about two hours.

If you have extended your time, you will also need to obtain a *permiso de salida* (permit) to leave the country. For this, bring your passport and a *paz y salvo* (a certificate stating you don't owe any back taxes) to the immigration office. *Paz y salvos* are issued at Ministerios de Economia y Finanzas, found in towns with immigration offices, which simply require that you bring in your passport, fill out a form and pay US$1.

VOLUNTEERING

Volunteer opportunities are on the rise in Panama and there are excellent causes to donate your time to. Nonprofit **Fundación Pro-Niños de Darién** (☎ 254-4333; www.darien.org.pa) is targeted at the improvement of the lives of children throughout the Darién through education, health and nutrition programs. The organization also works to help residents develop sustainable agriculture. You can also take part in volunteer vacations in the Darién (p707).

With a base in Boquete, **Global Humanitarian Adventures** (GHA; ☎ in USA 1-877-442-4255, in Boquete 6907-0781; www.gogha.org) is a Red Cross–affiliated project involved in literacy programs, health projects, orphanages, community outreach and more. Opportunities can be tailored to match volunteer skills and there is no minimum time or language requirement for participation. This expanding program has offshoots throughout the country, though most volunteers start at the main office. For further information, see p665.

WOMEN TRAVELERS

While there is no doubt Panama is a Latin culture, female travelers usually find it safe. A minority of Panamanian men may make flirtatious comments, hiss, honk their horn or stare, even if you're accompanied. Don't take it as a challenge. A kind of hormonal babble, this behavior is as much about male bonding as the female passerby. The best response is to follow the lead of Panamanian women: give these men a broad berth, ignore their comments and look away.

While locals might get away with skimpy, stretchy clothing, travelers will naturally attract less attention with a more conservative approach. Wearing shorts outside of a beach setting marks you as a tourist. In the interior, dress is more formal, with skirts and nice sandals the norm. Even in beach towns, women should save their bathing suit for the beach.

Women traveling solo will get more attention than those traveling in pairs or groups. Although assault and rape of foreign travelers is rare, avoid placing yourself in risky scenarios. In general, don't walk alone in isolated places, don't hitchhike and always pay particular attention to your surroundings.

If you are taking a long-distance bus, sit down next to a woman or a family if you are nervous about come-ons. Be picky about your taxis: though shared taxis may be the norm (between unknown parties), avoid those with more than one man in them. If the driver tries to pick up another fare, you can offer to pay more to travel alone.

WORK

It's difficult for foreigners to find work in Panama. The government doesn't like anyone taking jobs away from Panamanians, and the labor laws reflect this sentiment. Basically, the only foreigners legally employed in Panama work for their own businesses, possess skills not found in Panama or work for companies that have special agreements with the Panamanian government.

Central America Directory

CONTENTS

This chapter provides general information on Central America. Country-specific details are included in the Directory at the back of each country chapter. Also, each country title page displays 'key facts' information, such as travel tips and popular border crossings.

ACCOMMODATIONS

Central America's sleeping options range from thin-wall sand-floor shacks to luxury beach resorts. This book focuses on budget accommodations such as hostels, *casas de huéspedes* (guesthouses) with fan-cooled rooms and shared bathrooms, lean-to *cabañas* (bungalows) on a beach, or simply trees to hang a hammock from. Some midrange choices and worthy splurges are also included.

BOOK YOUR STAY ONLINE

For more accommodations reviews and recommendations by Lonely Planet authors, check out the online booking service at www.lonelyplanet.com/hotels. You'll find the true, insider low-down on the best places to stay. Reviews are thorough and independent. Best of all, you can book online.

Unless otherwise noted, prices listed in the book reflect high-season rates (roughly July and August, Christmas to Easter) and include applicable national taxes. Prices do change; use the prices in this book as a gauge, not law. Showing the price listed in the book is a far less successful tactic to getting a lower rate than simply asking for a discount. When business is slow or over a several-night stay, it's often possible to get a cheaper rate. Be prepared to take 'no' for an answer.

Generally Nicaragua, Honduras and Guatemala are the cheapest countries, Mexico and Belize (and many beach destinations), the most expensive. Features like a private bathroom, hot water and air-con jack up prices. Generally, hostels are around US$7 to US$15 per person, and OK hotels (with shared bathroom and fan) are about US$20 to US$40 per double in the bulk of Central America.

Reservations are not possible at many places, much less needed. Key exceptions are tourist areas during peak season, particularly during Semana Santa (Easter Week) and the week between Christmas and New Year's, when locals are traveling around the region too.

Camping

Organized campgrounds aren't commonly found in the region. If you plan on camping, bring your own gear – and bug repellent. Facilities at campgrounds can vary: some have fire pits, latrines and water. Others have *nada*. Nothing.

Some hostels set aside areas for campers. Some national parks and reserves (particularly in Costa Rica) have basic facilities, but they can be hit-and-miss – sometimes packed and noisy. Prices range from US$5 to US$10 per person. In some places it's feasible to ask to camp on private land.

Guesthouses & Hotels
The most popular places to stay are the cheap guesthouses and hotels. Many are small (10 or so rooms) and family-run, and (depending on the family) can be fun, attractive and offer cheap deals that practically plead for another night. That said, you can also expect a night or two on a dumpy bed with smeared mosquito remains on the walls and a smelly leaky-faucet shower (thankfully) down the hall.

Most rooms have a fan and shared bathroom. Many do not provide a towel or soap. Rooms with air-con and TV (generally US$20 and up) start at double the price of a room with fan. Generally breakfast is not included in the overnight rate.

'Hot water' can be lukewarm and working only at certain hours of the day. Beware of the electric shower: a cold-water showerhead juiced by an electric heating element. Don't touch it, or anything metal, while in the shower or you may get a shock.

Used toilet paper should be placed in the receptacle provided.

We've done our best to avoid including places used by the 'hourly' crowd or prostitutes. If you stumble on some we've included, please let us know.

Hammocks & Bungalows
Sleeping in a hammock can make for a breezier night than sleeping in a stuffy room. Many beach towns have hammock rooms or areas for the same price as a dorm. Beach *cabañas* (or *cabinas*) provide memorable stays on the beach or in the jungle. Many of these are simple thatched-roof huts with a dirt or sand floor; others are electrified deals, with fans and fine decor.

Homestays
Nothing offers more insight into local culture than staying with a local family. In towns with Spanish-language school scenes, such as Antigua or Quetzaltenango in Guatemala, or Granada in Nicaragua, schools can arrange homestays for their students. Many can even arrange for you to stay with a family for a week or longer, even if you're not studying. Homestays can be arranged in many other towns as well. A week's stay ranges from US$70 to US$150 per person, including most

meals. See Courses in individual towns or in the country Directory for more information.

Hostels
Hostels are found throughout Central America, and generally charge around US$7 to US$15 for a bunk, though your Hostelling International (HI) membership isn't particularly useful here, as many hostels are independently run. Mexico and Costa Rica are exceptions, with many HI-affiliated hostels.

ACTIVITIES
Coastal fun is Central America's most popular draw for tourists: the Pacific is booming on surfers' itineraries, while the Caribbean has the best diving and most of the white-sand beaches. Mountains and volcanoes run through most of the region, offering many compelling (and often tough) hiking and cycling options.

See also p17 for an activity-based itinerary.

Canopy Tours
These zip-line trips sliding over jungle and mountains may not be the most natural of Central American activities, but you can at least tickle your inner Tarzan. Costs average US$45. You'll find opportunities all over Costa Rica, including in Monteverde (p571). In Honduras the options are at La Ceiba (p397) or the Garífuna villages nearby (p402). You can also zip down Volcán Mombacho outside Granada, Nicaragua (p490).

Cycling
Many shops rent bicycles for local exploring. Some offer guided cycling trips – such as to Maya villages from San Cristóbal de Las Casas, Mexico (p43), and coffee plantations or ridge rides from Antigua, Guatemala (p109). Cycling is also a fine way to explore local villages in other countries, though it is best to bring your own bike for these trips (along with proof that you own the bike).

See p731 for a quick rundown on the joys and pitfalls of cycling your way around the region.

Diving & Snorkeling
Some of Latin America's (and the world's) finest diving and snorkeling spots are found along the barrier reefs off Central America's Caribbean shores. Sites up and down the coast – from Mexico to Panama – offer rich marine life, sunken ships and deep holes. Some of the

---

SAFETY GUIDELINES FOR DIVING

Before embarking on a scuba-diving, skin-diving or snorkeling trip, carefully consider the following points to ensure a safe and enjoyable experience.

- Possess a current diving certification card from a recognized scuba-diving instructional agency (if scuba diving).

- Be sure you are healthy and feel comfortable diving.

- Obtain reliable information about physical and environmental conditions at the dive site (eg from a reputable local dive operator).

- Be aware of local laws, regulations and etiquette relating to marine life and the environment.

- Dive only at sites within your realm of experience; if available, engage the services of a competent, professionally trained dive instructor or dive master.

- Be aware that underwater conditions vary significantly from one region, or even site, to another. Seasonal changes can significantly alter any site and dive conditions. These differences influence the way divers dress for a dive and what diving techniques they use.

---

most famous dive spots can be found at Bay Islands, Honduras (p410); Cozumel, Mexico (p69); the reefs off Belize's northern cays (p231); and the more low-key Corn Islands, Nicaragua (p513).

Honduras' Bay Islands are famous for good-value dives and scuba courses; taking the four-day Professional Association of Diving Instructors (PADI) open-water diving certification course here costs about US$315.

Region-wide, snorkeling day trips out to a couple of reef spots can be taken for US$15 to US$45 or so, and dives start at around US$36 in Honduras or US$56 in Mexico. Most dive shops will rent diving equipment – always check it carefully before going under. Be sure to bring evidence of your certification if you plan to dive.

It's possible to dive in the Pacific too, though conditions are generally murkier. Panama has great dive sites in the Pacific and Caribbean (p702). The best time for diving in the Pacific is October to February. San Juan del Sur (p497) in Nicaragua also has a dive shop. The crater lakes in Laguna de Apoyo, Nicaragua (see p490), are another good option.

Mexico offers otherworldly dives in cenotes (limestone sinkholes filled with rain water). Check out some options reachable from Tulum (p69).

For safety considerations see boxed text, above.

Also check out Lonely Planet's *Diving & Snorkeling Cozumel* and *Diving & Snorkeling Belize* guides.

Hiking

Central America's stunning natural environment, volcanoes and abundant wildlife make for great hiking. The terrain ranges from cloud forests and rainforests to lowland jungles, river trails and palm-lined beaches.

Jungle trekking can be strenuous, and hikers should be prepared. If you want to camp, bring your own gear as its availability is limited here.

Popular hikes in the region range from volcanoes around Antigua in Guatemala (p108) or El Imposible in El Salvador (p306), to prehistoric rock carvings on Nicaragua's Isla de Ometepe (p500), a wilderness beach at Costa Rica's Península de Nicoya (p596) or coffee-scented hills around Panama's only volcano, Volcán Barú, in the Chiriquí highlands (p667).

The ultimate would be the 60km hike to Guatemala's El Mirador (p207), a sprawling, largely unexcavated Maya city reached by an intense hike into the El Petén jungle, a couple of days each way. Less demanding, but no shorter, is the hike through modern Maya villages from Nebaj (p136) to Todos Santos Cuchumatán, also in Guatemala.

Surfing

Surfing's popularity is on the rise in Central America, with many places renting boards to tackle 'perfect' breaks. Costa Rica has the most developed scene, but low-key spots in El Salvador and Nicaragua are, to some, the best places. If you've never surfed, you can find surf lessons for cheap, and board rentals starting at US$10. Hot spots include El Salvador's Balsam Coast (p293), San Juan del

Sur in Nicaragua (p497), and Costa Rica's increasingly popular Mal País (p595) on the Península de Nicoya.

White-Water Rafting

Some of the best white-water rafting in the tropics can be found in Central America, and rafting is fast becoming popular all over Latin America. Guatemala, Honduras and Panama are developing a rafting industry, and have a number of rivers there offer anything from frothing Class IV white water to easy Class II floats. Costa Rica leads the pack in river adventure sports, with many tour operators to choose from. See the countries' Directory sections for more details on rafting opportunities.

Wildlife-Watching

The unexpected appearance of a toucan, howler monkey, sloth, crocodile, iguana, dolphin or puma makes for the greatest rush on your trip, and the wildlife-viewing and bird-watching opportunities in every part of Central America are world-class. A system of national parks, wildlife refuges, biosphere reserves and other protected areas throughout the region facilitates independent bird- and wildlife-viewing. Even private areas such as gardens around hotels in the countryside can yield a sample of birds, insects, reptiles and even monkeys.

Early morning and late afternoon are the best times to watch for wildlife activity anywhere.

Leading the rest in terms of wildlife density is Costa Rica, with remarkable places such as the pristine Parque Nacional Corcovado (p613) and many others.

The elusive quetzal – and hordes of other implausibly colorful birds – can be seen at many places; a couple of spots include Honduras' Lago de Yojoa (p360) and Panama's Volcán Barú in the Chiriquí highlands (p667). Belize's Crooked Tree Wildlife Sanctuary (see boxed text, p239) is another hot spot for bird-watchers. Morning bird-watching tours at Tikal, Guatemala (p204) add to the experience of seeing the ruins.

Howler monkeys (named for their frightening tiger-like roar) can be seen in treetops around the region, such as on an unforgettable walk through the Yaxchilán Maya ruins (p48), throughout Panama and on the Mexico–Guatemala border. The black howler monkey lives only in Belize, and can be seen at the Bermudian Landing Community Baboon Sanctuary (p237).

The best places to see sea turtles are Parque Nacional Tortuguero (p555) in Costa Rica, Isla de Cañas (p684) in Panama and Refugio de Vida Silvestre La Flor (p499) in Nicaragua. Coral reefs are an excellent place to see sea turtles, stingrays, sharks and tons of smaller, more colorful creatures. See p711 for some of Central America's top dive sites.

Also see *Where to Watch Birds in Central America, Mexico & the Caribbean*, by Nigel Wheatley.

BOOKS

The following books will help with pretrip preparation (and dreaming). See also boxed text, p22.

Lonely Planet

Along with country-specific guidebooks to the region, Lonely Planet publishes an in-depth guide to Caribbean Mexico: *Cancún, Cozumel & the Yucatán*. If you're heading south from Central America, pick up a copy of *South America on a Shoestring*.

Other useful titles from Lonely Planet include *Healthy Travel Central & South America*, a guide to minimizing common health risks on the road; *Lonely Planet's Guide to Travel Photography*, which provides some excellent advice on getting the most out of your travel photos; and *Travel With Children*.

Also consider getting a copy of Lonely Planet's *Latin American Spanish* phrasebook.

Travel Literature

The number of books on Central America (travelogues and political essays) swelled during the turbulent '80s and into the early '90s,

---

TOP SURFING SPOTS

Here's our pick of the best on offer.

Costa Rica Experts-only Salsa Brava, at Puerto Viejo de Talamanca (see boxed text, p566) or Pavones' three-minute left (p614)

El Salvador Punta Roca, at La Libertad (p291)

Guatemala Sipacate (p161)

Nicaragua Las Salinas (west of Rivas; p500)

Panama Waves at Santa Catalina (p681) and Bocas del Toro's (p679)

For more top surfing spots, see boxed texts, p293 (El Salvador), and p500 (Nicaragua).

but have waned in the years since. Many good ones are unfortunately no longer in stock.

Travelers' Tales Central America: True Stories, edited by Larry Habegger, is a collection of glories and failures of trips in the region. John L Stephens' widely available classic *Incidents of Travel in Central America, Chiapas and Yucatan,* in two volumes, dates from the 1840s. These volumes provided the world with the first glimpses of the Maya cities and are still regarded as a good, popular overview.

Guatemala: Eternal Spring – Eternal Tyranny by Jean-Marie Simon uses first-hand accounts and more than 130 photographs in a moving, harrowing documentation of human-rights abuses during the civil war. Other interesting portraits include *Salvador* by Joan Didion, a moving account of the early days of El Salvador's civil war. Gioconda Belli's *The Country Under My Skin: A Memoir of Love and War* profiles Nicaragua. *The Darkest Jungle* by Todd Balf chronicles the US Army's disastrous 1854 Darién expedition in Panama.

Costa Rica: A Traveler's Literary Companion (edited by Barbara Ras) is a compilation of short stories by modern Costa Rican writers. Bruce Barcott's *The Last Flight of the Scarlet Macaw* is an account of one activist making a difference in Belize. *The Soccer War* by Ryszard Kapuscinski is an entertaining and harsh account of the 100-hour war between Honduras and El Salvador.

BUSINESS HOURS

Much of Central America takes lunch off: that includes some tourist offices, banks and even a restaurant or two. Though opening hours can vary region-wide (see country Directories for details), generally banks don't break for siesta; some are open on Saturday mornings as well. Sunday is a real shut-down day in much of the region.

Government offices tend to work shorter hours (8am to 4pm or 5pm) weekdays only, with a couple of hours off at midday. Other businesses are open similar hours (closed for siesta from 12:30pm to 2pm or so), but often have Saturday hours too. Restaurants are expected to be open roughly from 8am to midnight, bars from 8am to 2am or so, shops from 10am to 8pm, and tourist information offices from 8am to 5pm Monday to Friday or Saturday.

In this guidebook only variations on standard business hours are included in reviews; otherwise standard hours are assumed.

CLIMATE

Central America is within the tropics, but there's a lot of variation in climate within this small region. The land rises from sea level to over 4000m, dividing the region into three primary temperature zones according to altitude, but there is little variation in temperature throughout the year.

In the lowlands (sea level to about 1000m) daytime temperatures range from 29°C to

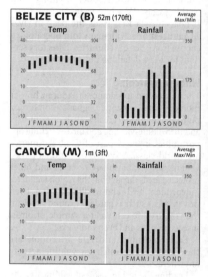

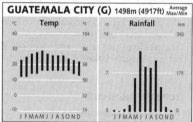

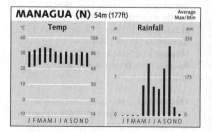

32°C (84°F to 90°F), and nighttime temperatures from 21°C to 23°C (70°F to 74°F).

The temperate zone (from around 1000m to 2000m) has a pleasant climate, with daytime temperatures ranging from 23°C to 26°C (74°F to 79°F) and nighttime temperatures from about 15°C to 21°C (59°F to 70°F).

The cold zone (above 2000m) has similar daytime temperatures to the temperate zone but is colder at night, around 10°C to 12°C (50°F to 54°F). The very few areas over 4000m are characterized by an alpine climate.

The rainy season, which runs from May to November or early December in most of Central America, is called *invierno* (winter). The rest of the year constitutes the dry season and is called *verano* (summer). This book's country Directories explain regional variations. The Caribbean side of Central America gets much more rainfall than the Pacific side – often more than twice as much. Hurricane season fluctuates, but it can be as long as June to November. Panama is one country not affected by hurricanes.

CUSTOMS REGULATIONS

All visitors leaving and entering a Central American country go through customs. Be prepared for quick bag checks at airports and land borders too. Most are just a quick gaze-and-poke, more of a formality than a search – but not always. Do not have any illegal drugs (or drug paraphernalia) on you. And it's wise to always be polite with officials and dress conservatively.

DANGERS & ANNOYANCES

Travel in Central America poses a number of potential dangers that require caution, but don't be put off. Most areas are quite safe, and with sensible precautions you are unlikely to have any problems. For most travelers, the worst thing to happen is paying a few dollars more than expected to a cab driver, a few (dozen) mosquito or sand-fly bites, and the inevitable bout or two of diarrhea. Specific warnings are listed in country Directories and for applicable cities or towns throughout this guide.

The protracted civil wars in El Salvador, Nicaragua and Guatemala are over, but these dangers have been replaced by an alarming rise in the general crime rate and gang activity. Much of it doesn't involve foreign visitors, but there have been occasions of grab-and-run theft, assault, rape, carjacking and the occasional murder. Capital cities tend to have the highest rates of crime. Many sexual assaults occur on isolated beaches.

Parts of Nicaragua's sparse north still have uncovered land mines from the 1980s conflict. Areas in Panama's Darién Province, which borders Colombia, may be extremely dangerous because of guerrilla activity.

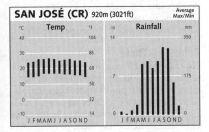

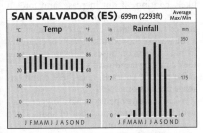

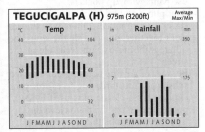

Avoid night buses (with the possible exception of Mexico and Panama), as highway robberies often happen at night.

The **UK Foreign & Commonwealth Office** (FCO; www.fco.gov.uk/travel) lists excellent overviews on all countries on their website. Up-to-date 'travel warnings' are available from the **US Department of State** (www.travel.state.gov).

Will you run into trouble? No one can say. Tens of thousands of foreign visitors enjoy the incomparable beauties of the region and the friendliness of its people every year, the huge majority without untoward incidents of any kind. But then there are the unlucky few or those who don't take precautions.

Ask, ask, ask for updates – from other travelers, tourist offices, police, guesthouse owners and Lonely Planet's **Thorn Tree** (http://thorntree.lonelyplanet.com).

Discrimination

In many Latin American countries, the lighter one's skin tone, the higher their social status is perceived to be. In areas not inhabited by Afro-Caribbean cultures (which include the Garífuna villages in Belize, Honduras' Bay Islands and Panama's Archipiélago de Bocas del Toro), travelers of African descent may encounter some discrimination (eg being refused entry into a nightclub, a stare, a flip remark).

It's sad to say it, but it can help to let locals know you're a foreign tourist (either by speaking English or saying so), thus presumably wealthy.

Asian travelers are less likely to face discrimination in Central America.

Drugs

Marijuana and cocaine are available in many places but are illegal everywhere in the region, and penalties are severe. Avoid any conversation with someone who offers you drugs. If you are in an area where drug trafficking is prevalent, ignore it and do not show any interest whatsoever, since drugs are sometimes used to set up travelers for blackmail and bribery.

Roll-your-own cigarettes or cigarette papers may arouse suspicion.

Natural Hazards

Central America is prone to a wide variety of natural disasters, including earthquakes, hurricanes, floods and volcanic eruptions. General information about natural-disaster preparedness is available from the **US Federal Emergency Management Agency** (FEMA; www.fema.gov).

Police & Military

Corruption is a very serious problem among Latin American police, who are generally poorly paid and poorly supervised. In many countries, they are not reluctant to plant drugs on unsuspecting travelers or enforce minor regulations to the letter in the hope of extracting *coimas* (bribes).

If you are stopped by 'plainclothes policemen,' never get into a vehicle with them. Don't give them any documents or show them any money, and don't take them to your hotel. If the police appear to be the real thing, insist on going to a bona fide police station on foot.

The military often has considerable influence, even under civilian governments. Don't approach military installations, which may display warnings translated as 'No stopping or photographs – the sentry will shoot.' Military checkpoints are frequent in places such as Chiapas, Panama's Darién Province and El Salvador. Most involve routine passport checks.

Robbery & Theft

No matter where you are, getting your gear stolen is a possibility, particularly in larger cities and transit points such as bus stations. Most theft is of the pickpocket or grab-and-run variety. As economic woes build up in Central America, these types of crimes will likely continue if not increase, and foreign tourists are often singled out as they are presumed to be 'wealthy' and carrying valuables.

Be wary of food, drinks, sweets or cigarettes from strangers on buses, trains or in bars, as they could be laced with sedatives.

To protect yourself, take these common-sense precautions:

- Wear a money belt to keep a bigger stash of money or passport out of sight. Have small amounts of cash in your pockets; use pants with zip pockets.
- Any purse or bag in plain sight can be slashed or grabbed. Often two thieves work together, one cutting the strap, the other grabbing as you walk along the street.
- Be wary of anyone pointing out a spilled substance (mustard, dog feces) on your clothes. It's a classic ploy used by pickpocket teams: one helps to clean the victim, the other robs them.

- Avoid taking night buses.
- Take taxis after dark, particularly in big cities. Don't wander alone down empty city streets or in isolated areas.
- When possible, keep most of your cash, traveler's checks and valuables (such as airline tickets or jewelry) sealed in a signed envelope in a hotel safe.
- Make sure your room lock works. And consider locking your (locked) backpack to something immovable in your room, such as bathroom pipes.
- Lock your room every time you leave it – even just for a quick bathroom visit down the hall.
- If you're staying in a room that has a dodgy lock (or none), such as a beach *cabaña,* try to keep your valuables in left luggage.
- Don't camp overnight on beaches or in the countryside unless you can be sure it's safe.
- Ask around for advice – guesthouse owners, tourist offices, other travelers.
- If you're being robbed, fork over whatever they want. Many thieves are armed; it's not worth resisting.

Go to the police after a robbery if you'll need a police statement to present to your insurance company. Otherwise, there's little point. In Spanish-speaking areas, say *'Quiero poner una acta de un robo'* (I want to report a robbery). You may have to write up the report yourself, then present it for an official stamp and signature.

Swimming Safety

Hundreds of people drown each year at Central America's beaches, with about 150 to 200 drownings recorded annually at Costa Rican beaches alone. Of these, 80% are caused by riptides – strong currents that pull the swimmer out to sea. They can occur even in waist-deep water. The best advice of all: ask about conditions before entering the water. If it's dangerous, don't tempt the ocean.

DISCOUNT CARDS

A Hostelling International (HI) membership card isn't terribly useful in Central America, except in Mexico and Costa Rica, where some hostels offer minimal discounts to cardholders. Those going on to South America, however, may want to invest in the membership as the card is more commonly accepted there (see www.iyhf.org for information).

Carriers of the International Student Identity Card (ISIC) can get very good discounts on travel insurance, as well as discounted air tickets. Check www.isic.org for details.

EMBASSIES & CONSULATES

For embassy and consulate addresses and phone numbers, see individual country Directories. General embassy information can be found at www.embassyworld.com.

As a visitor in a Central American country, it's important to realize what your own country's embassy can and can't do. Generally speaking, it won't be much help in emergencies when you're even remotely at fault. Remember that you are bound by the laws of the country you are in. Your embassy will not be sympathetic if you end up in jail after committing a crime locally, even if such actions are legal in your own country.

In genuine emergencies you may get some assistance, but only if other channels have been exhausted. For example, if you have all your money and documents stolen, the embassy might assist in getting a new passport, but a loan for onward travel is out of the question.

FESTIVALS & EVENTS

National holidays *(días feriados)* are taken seriously in Central America, and banks, public offices and many stores close. The big national holidays are dictated by the Roman Catholic Church calendar. Christmas and Semana Santa (Holy Week), the week leading up to Easter, are the most important. Panama hosts some of the most famous Carnaval celebrations (February), and Mexico's Día de los Muertos (Day of the Dead), on November 2, is another huge celebration.

During events such as these, hotels are usually booked well in advance, especially in beach areas and in towns that have particularly elaborate celebrations, such as Antigua, Guatemala. Bus services may be limited or nonexistent on the Thursday afternoon and Friday leading into Easter, and many businesses are closed for the entire week preceding the holiday. In general, public transportation tends to be tight on all holidays and the days immediately preceding or following them, so book tickets in advance.

GAY & LESBIAN TRAVELERS

On the whole, Central America is a pitifully unwelcoming place for gay men, and although lesbians have it a bit better, homosexuality is generally shunned in much of the region. The silver lining is in Mexico, where same-sex marriage was made legal in 2009. Advocacy groups in other Central American countries are eager to follow suit.

In Nicaragua there is a statute criminalizing homosexual behavior, and although enforcement is inconsistent, harassment of gays does occur. The absence of such laws elsewhere does not prevent official harassment. Misinformation about homosexuality in general, and AIDS in particular, has made Latin America that much more inhospitable for gay people.

In general, public displays of affection will not be tolerated, and gay men (and possibly women) could find themselves the target of verbal or physical abuse. Discretion is definitely the rule, especially in the countryside of Central America. Lesbians are generally less maligned than gay men, and women traveling together should encounter few, if any, problems.

Venues

There is usually at least one gay bar in big cities, which makes meeting people easier. Here's a rundown of some of the more in-the-open gay and lesbian scenes in Central America:

Costa Rica San José's thriving scene; beach hangout at Manuel Antonio.

El Salvador Gay scene around San Salvador's Blvd de los Héroes; mountain town San Vicente is gay-friendly.

Guatemala Drag shows in Quetzaltenango; bars in Guatemala City.

Mexico Cancún's bars and May festival; Playa del Carmen's clubs.

Panama Gay float at Carnaval parade in Panama City.

Internet Resources

As well as websites listed in the country Directories, good gay/lesbian websites include:

www.advocate.com Features international news and a travel section.

www.damron.com Publishes annual gay/lesbian guides, plus has a database of gay sites.

www.gay.com Travel page with info on Mexico, Guatemala, Panama and Costa Rica.

www.iglhrc.org Site for International Gay & Lesbian Human Rights Commission.

Additional information on gay and lesbian travel in Latin America can be found through the **International Gay & Lesbian Travel Association** (Iglta; www.iglta.com), whose website has information on group tours, and links to gay- and lesbian-friendly hotels.

INSURANCE

A travel insurance policy covering theft, loss, accidents and illness is highly recommended. Some policies compensate travelers for misrouted or lost luggage. Also check that the coverage includes worst-case scenarios: ambulances, evacuations or an emergency flight home. Some policies specifically exclude 'dangerous activities,' which can include scuba diving, motorcycling or even trekking. Read the small print.

There is a wide variety of policies available; rates start at around US$100 for the first month. **World Nomads** (www.worldnomads.com) has good-deal policies, and those handled by STA Travel and other student-travel organizations usually offer good value too. If a policy offers lower and higher medical-expense options, the low-expenses policy should be OK for Central America – medical costs are not nearly as high here as elsewhere.

If you have baggage insurance and need to make a claim, the insurance company may demand a receipt as proof that you bought the stuff in the first place. You must usually inform the insurance company by airmail and report the loss or theft to local police within 24 hours. Make a list of stolen items and their value. At the police station, you need to complete a *denuncia* (statement), a copy of which is given to you for your claim. The *denuncia* usually has to be made on *papel sellado* (stamped paper); it's cheap and available at stationery stores.

For information on vehicle insurance, see p729, and for health insurance, go to p734.

INTERNET ACCESS

Internet cafes are available nearly everywhere except in the smallest towns. Rates are often under US$1 per hour, rising to US$8 per hour on touristy islands. A wi-fi boom is being felt in bigger cities – some have free wi-fi in cafes and restaurants. See city and town Information sections in this book for access points.

INTERNET RESOURCES

Lonely Planet's discussion board **Thorn Tree** (http://thorntree.lonelyplanet.com) is the best way to get and share tips with fellow travelers before, during and after a trip. Check the Central

---

WHERE IT'S @

The cute little *arroba* (@) can be vexing to find on Latin American keyboards. Either cut and paste it from another email address or hold down the 'Alt' key and hit '6' key, then '4' key on the number pad (*not* at the top of the keyboard, and be sure 'Num Lock' is on). Or try 'Alt-Gr' (to the right of the space bar), then '2.' If that doesn't work, ask someone '¿Cómo se hace arroba?' (How do you type '@'?).

America or Mexico pages. See also www.lonely planet.com for country summaries.

Suggested websites appear in relevant sections throughout the book; see boxed text, p22, for pretrip inspiration, and p4 for responsible-travel websites. Some general websites with information on Central America include the following:

CIA World Fact Book (www.odci.gov/cia/publications/factbook) Frequently updated background info on every country.

Latin American Network Information Center (http://lanic.utexas.edu/subject/countries.html) University of Texas site with oodles of Latin American links.

Latin World (www.latinworld.com) Loads of links, by country.

Revue (www.revuemag.com) Free online English-language Guatemala mag with excellent Central America coverage.

South American Explorers (www.saexplorers.org) Handy if you're heading on to South America.

UK Foreign & Commonwealth Office (FCO; www.fco.gov.uk/travel) British government site with travel advisories etc.

US Department of State (www.travel.state.gov) Rather alarmist travel advisories and tips.

LEGAL MATTERS

Police officers in Central American countries are sometimes (if not often) part of the problem rather than the solution. The less you have to do with the law, the better. See p716 for more information.

Whatever you do, don't get involved in any way with illegal drugs: don't buy, sell, use or carry them, or associate with people who do – even if the locals seem to do so freely. As a foreigner, you are at a disadvantage, and may be set up by others for bribes or arrest. Drug laws in all of these countries are strict, and though enforcement may be uneven, penalties are severe. See also p716.

MAPS

The best map of the region is the fold-up color 1:1,100,000 *Traveller's Reference Map of Central America* (US$13), produced by **International Travel Maps & Books** (ITMB; www.itmb.com) in Canada. ITMB also publishes separate maps covering each of the Central American countries and various regions of Mexico, as well as several maps of South America.

Other websites that deal with map sales include **Maplink** (www.maplink.com) and London-based **Stanfords** (www.stanfords.co.uk).

MONEY

Generally travelers go with a combination of cash and credit/bank cards, and possibly some traveler's checks, though they can be more hassle than convenience these days. By far the most accepted currency is the US dollar: two countries (El Salvador and Panama) use it as their own, and Costa Rica and Nicaragua widely accept it. Use up the local currency during your stay, as it is often not accepted outside the region – or even outside the country!

The guide lists prices for Mexico, Guatemala, Honduras and Belize in local currency. El Salvador and Panama, which officially use the US dollar, have costs listed in dollars. For Costa Rica and Nicaragua, our use of either US dollars or local currency in this book reflects the preferred currency for a given type of service; see these two chapters' Directories for details.

For sample costs and average daily budgets, see Fast Facts on the title page of each country chapter. For general tips on saving money, see boxed text, p20.

ATMs

Bring an ATM (or debit) card. ATMs are available in most cities and large towns, and are almost always the most convenient, reliable, secure and economical way of getting cash.

The exchange rate from ATMs is usually as good as (if not better than) at any bank or legal money changer. Many ATMs are connected to the MasterCard/Cirrus or Visa/Plus networks. Bring two cards in case one is lost or stolen, and keep an emergency phone number for your bank in a separate place. Some banks that issue ATM cards charge a fee for international transactions; check the policy before leaving home and notify your bank of your travel plans so foreign-made transactions are not barred.

Bargaining

The art of bargaining can be acquired through practice, and you'll get some in Central America's markets, particularly for souvenirs and craft goods. Most accommodations prices are fixed, but for long-term stays (or during low season) it's worth asking for a discount. Indoor shops (such as groceries) generally have fixed prices. You may need to negotiate a price with a taxi driver, but fares for buses are standardized. Always approach bargaining with patience and humor, and you'll often end up with a price agreeable to both you and the seller.

Black Market

The black market (mercado negro) – also known as mercado paralelo (parallel market) – is generally limited to money changers at borders, who may or may not be legal. They are known to slip in torn bills or shortchange on occasion, though they accept local currencies that banks elsewhere sometimes don't take. Such unofficial exchange rates for the US dollar can be lower than official bank rates, which may be artificially high for political reasons.

Cash

It's a good idea to always have a small amount of US dollars handy – enough to get a room, a meal and a taxi, at least – because they can be exchanged practically anywhere. It's particularly useful when crossing the border or when an ATM or exchange service for traveler's checks isn't available. Central American currencies don't always fly in the next country and it can be hard finding anyone willing to change leftover quetzals, for example – but generally it's possible to use US dollars. Plan ahead before you head to remote areas; take more than enough cash.

Getting change for bigger notes in local currency is a daily concern. Notes worth even US$20 can sometimes be difficult to change.

Credit Cards

A credit card can be handy in emergencies and it enables you to obtain cash or enjoy an unexpected luxury somewhere along the way. It can also be useful if you're asked to demonstrate 'sufficient funds' when entering a country.

American Express, Visa and MasterCard are the most widely accepted credit cards in Central America. Depending on the country, credit cards can often be used to withdraw cash at ATMs. Some credit-card websites have ATM locators that show which towns have this service.

Some travelers rely on cash advances to reduce the need for traveler's checks, but this isn't always possible (particularly in smaller towns). Always inquire about transaction charges for cash advances; in some countries you may be charged a fee in addition to that charged by the card company back home. Some card companies also charge a fee (usually around 2%) for international transactions.

The amount you actually pay your credit-card company will depend on the exchange rate. Consider prearranging monthly payments to your account if you're planning to be on the road for some time.

Keep your cards separate from your cash as well as emergency phone numbers for the companies. Hold onto your receipts so you can later double-check payments.

Exchanging Money

Change traveler's checks or foreign cash at a bank or a casa de cambio (currency exchange office). Rates are usually similar, but in general casas de cambio are quicker, less bureaucratic and open longer or on weekends. Street money changers, who may or may not be legal, will only handle cash. Sometimes you can also change money unofficially at hotels or in shops that sell imported goods (electronics dealers are an obvious choice). Big cities tend to offer better exchange rates. Some money-changing services are listed in town Information sections in this guide. Compare exchange rates and commission fees before you commit.

Don't accept torn notes, as most locals won't when you try to use them.

International Transfers

If you're in a pinch, **Western Union** (www.western union.com) has offices in all Central American countries, and can arrange transfers. Generally it's cheapest to arrange this through an agent, but you can also send money by phone or internet. Charges vary from a set fee starting at US$10 to 8% of the balance.

Bank money transfers are possible, but they take longer and can run into complications. Ask for a cable transfer (not a mail draft); you'll need to provide a local bank's branch information.

Tipping

Diners are generally expected to tip about 10% at restaurants. Some restaurants add a service charge of 10% to 20% to the bill; to be sure, ask ¿La cuenta incluye el servicio? (Does the bill include service charge?).

A small tip for taxi drivers or for the cleaning staff at your hotel is not necessary, but is appreciated.

Traveler's Checks

Fewer people are carrying them, but traveler's checks from companies such as American Express, Visa, Thomas Cook and Citibank, which offer replacement in case of loss or theft, remain the safest way to carry money. Don't use those issued by smaller banks. To facilitate replacement in case of theft, keep a record of check numbers and the original bill of sale in a safe place.

In some countries traveler's checks are more difficult to cash, however, and banks and casas de cambio charge high commissions. Check if there's a fixed transaction fee (regardless of the value of the checks) or a percentage fee (usually 1% to 3%); if the fee is fixed, consider cashing larger amounts.

PHOTOGRAPHY & VIDEO

Consumer electronics are readily available in cities though costs may be higher than in your home country.

Digital cameras make photography easy for travelers. Consider bringing a memory stick or external hard drive to store photos and back up using online storage. It is also possible to burn photos to a CD in most cyber cafes.

If you're still in the 35mm world, film is widely available throughout the region. For slide or black-and-white film, bring your own. Developing the film is relatively expensive, and sometimes not great quality. Avoid mailing unprocessed film back, as that goes through more powerful X-rays than those in airports.

Always ask before photographing individuals, particularly indigenous people. In some places, like the Comarca de Kuna Yala in Panama, indigenous people may take offence at being photographed; elsewhere they may ask for a small payment. People may also take offence if you photograph images in their local church. Some areas will charge extra for bringing cameras or video cameras.

Taking photographs of military installations or security-sensitive places, such as military checkpoints in Chiapas and El Salvador, is very unwise (and probably illegal).

Note that some tourist sites charge an additional fee for tourists with cameras; others charge fees only for use of video cameras.

POST

The quality of the postal service in the region varies and can be a very uncertain business. Letters airmailed to Europe and North America typically take 14 days to arrive, sometimes longer. Generally, important mail and parcels should be sent by registered or certified service, and if you want something to arrive within a reasonable amount of time, be sure to specify airmail (correo aéreo or por avión). Sending parcels can be awkward, as often a customs officer must inspect the contents before a postal clerk can accept them. Note that the place for posting overseas parcels is sometimes different from the main post office. UPS, FedEx, DHL and other shipping and private courier services are available in some countries, providing an efficient but expensive alternative.

The simplest way of receiving mail is to have letters sent to you poste restante (general delivery; known in Latin America as lista de correos) to all of Central America except Guatemala. A post-office box is known as apartado (abbreviated to 'Ap' or 'Apto') or casilla de correos ('Casilla' or 'CC').

Note that mail theft can happen. This is primarily a problem with mail sent from the USA to points in Central America, presumably because many Central Americans live and work in the USA and send money home to their families. Postcards make it through more easily.

STUDYING

One of Central America's greatest attractions is the language schools. As part of a trip to Central America, studying Spanish (or an indigenous language such as Quiché) is a terrific way to absorb local culture, have a sense of purpose in a secondary town most travelers blaze through, and actually learn something. Schools often work to help the disadvantaged in their communities. Many schools are excellent, and prices throughout the region are cheaper than in Mexico. Outside Mexico it's generally possible to study for four hours a day with a private experienced teacher and stay and eat with a local family for around US$220 per week.

Antigua, Guatemala (p109), is by far the most celebrated language-school haven, with several dozen schools catering to the buzzing traveler scene.

Quetzaltenango, Guatemala (p143) – big enough to maintain interest for weeks, but far from the main travel circuit – and Estelí, Nicaragua (p471), are a couple of Central America's best places to get serious. It's certainly feasible to study-hop your way around the region – if you don't know Spanish yet, you will before you get to Panama!

It may be possible to show up at a school on Monday morning to start that week. It's preferable, though, to plan ahead and arrange it by phone or email. Many schools require some sort of one-time registration fee; ask if they'll waive it – often they will. Levels of teaching experience (and engagement) vary wildly. If you're not happy, say so. Most schools are accommodating and will switch teachers.

You can also book courses in the region with an outside organization such as **AmeriSpan** (www.amerispan.com). These courses are generally excellent but cost about twice the price as one booked locally. **ICAD** (www.icadscr.com) combines responsible travel with its year-long immersion courses in Costa Rica. It's about US$1700 per year, plus US$400 to US$600 monthly expenses.

Do try to stay with a family – it can offer a fascinating glimpse into local life not seen from the hostel. You'll witness such phenomena as the 'Latin bed' (the whole family sleeping in one room – don't worry, you'll get a private room) and the fluid family count, as new cousins suddenly pop up for a few days, then leave just as unexpectedly.

TELEPHONE

Prepaid phone cards, available for national telecommunications systems in each country, allow local and long-distance (and international in some countries, such as Costa Rica and Mexico) calls, with 'units' of time displayed on public pay phones. These are bought from newsstands and shops in set denominations.

Local, long-distance and international phone and fax services are available at centralized telephone offices in every city and town. Avoid credit-card phones in Mexico, and the black 'press button' phones in Guatemala, which charge extortionate rates.

Often a far cheaper alternative is using online phone services from internet cafes, where international rates start at US$0.04 per minute to the USA, US$0.25 to Europe.

Note that it is not possible to make collect (reverse-charge) calls to a number of countries from Central America – collect calls will only be accepted in countries having reciprocal agreements with the country from which you are calling; check with the telephone office. You can usually place them to the USA. It is sometimes cheaper to make a collect or credit-card call to Europe or North America than to pay for the call where you are. Often the best way is to make a quick international call and have the other party call you back (some telephone offices allow this).

Direct lines abroad, accessed via special numbers and billed to an account at home, have made international calls much simpler. There are different access numbers for each telephone company in each country – get a list from your phone company before you leave home.

Cell (mobile) phones are in wide use around Central America's bigger towns and cities, but using one can be quite expensive. Prepaid SIM cards are available. Central America doesn't subscribe to a consistent system. El Salvador, Guatemala and Honduras use the GSM 1900/850 (like the USA); Belize, Mexico and Nicaragua GSM 1900; Costa Rica GSM 1800 and Panama GSM 850 (like the UK's GSM 1800/850 system). It's sometimes possible to rent cell phones; cheapies cost about US$25.

TOILETS

The toilets of Central America are fine, it's just the plumbing that has issues. Nowhere in the region should you deposit toilet paper or anything else in the toilet unless a sign specifies that it's OK to do so. Wastebaskets are generally provided for that purpose.

Some public toilets have attendants who charge a small fee (US$0.10 or so) and provide paper. It's a good idea to keep a spare roll of toilet paper handy.

TOURIST INFORMATION

Travelers will find a tourist office in the capital city of each country; some countries have them in outlying towns as well. If you're a student, look for student travel agencies in the capital cities of Costa Rica and Panama, and in Cancún, Mexico.

Check www.visitcentroamerica.com (in Spanish only), which has standard tourist-board coverage of all countries.

South American Explorers (www.saexplorers.org) is a helpful membership-based organization with information for travel in Latin America, particularly South America. It has traveler clubhouses in Lima, Cuzco, Quito and Buenos

Aires; its **US office** (☎ 607-277-0488; 126 Indian Creek Rd, Ithaca, NY 14850) publishes the quarterly magazine, *South American Explorer*.

TRAVELERS WITH DISABILITIES

Latin America generally isn't well equipped for disabled travelers, and services (such as phones, toilets, or anything in Braille) are rare to the point of nonexistence. Expensive international hotels are more likely to cater to guests with disabilities than cheap hotels; air travel or prearranged transportation will be more feasible than most local buses; off-the-beaten-track destinations will be less accessible than well-developed ones. Careful planning and communication is a must, though information isn't always easy to come by.

If you have a disability and want to communicate with a person with disabilities who might have been to Central America recently, consider becoming a member of **Travelin' Talk Network** (TTN; ☎ in USA 303-232-2979; www.travelintalk. net; membership US$20). This organization offers a worldwide directory of members with various disabilities who communicate among themselves about travel.

Other organizations:

Access-Able Travel Source (☎ in USA 303-232-2979; www.access-able.com; PO Box 1796, Wheat Ridge, CO 80034) An excellent website with many links.

Mobility International USA (☎ in USA 541-343-1284; www.miusa.org; 132 E Broadway, Ste 343, Eugene, OR 97440) Advises disabled travelers on mobility issues and runs an educational exchange program.

Society for Accessible Travel & Hospitality (SATH; ☎ in USA 212-447-7284; www.sath.org; 347 Fifth Ave, Ste 610, New York, NY 10016) Lobbies for better facilities and publishes *Open World* magazine.

VISAS & DOCUMENTS
Visas

Presently citizens of the USA, EU, Canada, Australia, New Zealand and many other nations can arrive in all Central American countries (including Mexico) without arranging a visa beforehand. Check ahead from your country before planning your trip, as this may change.

Many countries charge an entry or tourist fee upon arrival – from US$5 to US$20. Check country Directory sections for country-specific visa information, as well as the Transportation sections in country chapters for departure-tax fees.

Note that if you need a visa for a certain country and arrive at a land border without one, you will probably have to return to the nearest town that has a consulate and obtain a visa. Airlines will not normally let you board a plane to a country for which you don't have the necessary visa. Also, a visa in itself may not guarantee entry: in rare cases, you may still be turned back at the border if you don't have 'sufficient funds' or an onward or return ticket.

Sufficient Funds & Onward Tickets

Checking passports is a routine procedure upon arriving in a country, but some officials may ask about your financial resources either verbally or on the application form. If you lack 'sufficient funds' for your proposed visit, officials may limit the length of your stay. (US$500 per month of your planned stay is generally considered sufficient; traveler's checks, and sometimes a credit card, should qualify toward the total amount.)

Several Central American countries require you to have a ticket out of the country (see boxed text, p727).

Visa Extensions

Once you are inside a country, you can always apply for an extension at the country's immigration office *(migración)*. Usually there is a limit to how many extensions you can receive; if you leave the country and re-enter, your time starts over again. See individual country's Directory sections for more on this.

VOLUNTEERING

Considering that well over half the population of countries such as Nicaragua and Guatemala live in poverty, volunteering can both make a trip more meaningful and help out the region

---

¡VIVA EL CA-4!

Guatemala, Honduras, El Salvador and Nicaragua's 'CA-4 Border Control' agreement allows free travel for up to 90 days within this subregion for citizens of the four countries and many foreign nationals (including residents of the USA, Canada, the UK and Australia). On paper, at least, you should only have to pay a tourist fee once to enter these four countries. The catch is that many border patrols try to sneak in a few dollars (for 'paperwork') when you're crossing borders. This is not true – if they ask, politely remind them of the 'CA-4.'

you visit. On offer are programs to teach those who can't afford classes, help build homes, work to preserve the environment, or help out at hill-town medical clinics. Many who volunteer end up staying longer than expected and find it to be the best part of a bigger trip. Volunteers – sometimes working alone, seven days a week – usually work hard. Note that studying Spanish at schools that pool profits to help communities is another way of contributing (see p721).

You can find volunteering organizations once in Central America (which is cheaper), or arrange programs with international organizations before your trip. Be aware that some volunteering organizations seek a minimum-period commitment, and may prefer that you organize your visit before turning up at the doorstep.

For more information on volunteering, get a copy of Lonely Planet's *Volunteer: A Traveller's Guide to Making a Difference Around the World.*

International Organizations

Many international organizations will help you peg a program to match job/school requirements, and get college credit for it. Nearly all programs cost money – usually a bit more than you'd pay on a trip. Some volunteers find sponsors – at school or privately – to fund a program. Spanish is not mandatory for all. Often programs begin with a few weeks of Spanish classes, as part of the on-location transition. A sample three-month program in Guatemala, for example, including four weeks of Spanish study, runs at about US$2500 (not including the airfare). Costa Rica has the most opportunities (such as in Monteverde), and Guatemala and Mexico have many too.

Travel agencies such as **STA Travel** (www.statravel.com) can arrange volunteering projects. A few other organizations that offer a variety of programs for Latin America include the following. (Prices don't include transportation to the region unless otherwise noted.)

AmeriSpan (☎ in USA 800-879-6640, 215-751-1100, ☎ in UK 020-8123 6086; www.amerispan.com) Sends volunteers to Costa Rica, Guatemala and the Yucatán on varied programs – building homes, teaching children, working with animals. Programs in Guatemala run from US$790 for four weeks (including homestay).

Amigos de las Américas (www.amigoslink.org) Youth-oriented summer programs – costing about US$4600 (including flight to/from USA) – ranging from national-park work to community development in Honduras, Costa Rica and Mexico.

Habitat for Humanity (www.habitat.org) Generally is more about funding than on-field programs, though it listed several options in Costa Rica at research time.

i-to-i (www.i-to-i.com) Has UK, US and Ireland offices; four- to 24-week volunteer and study programs in Guatemala, Honduras, Costa Rica and Mexico, with no language requirement. Prices range from US$1000 to US$3000, including a homestay and most meals.

Idealist.org (www.idealist.org) Hundreds of links for volunteering opportunities around the world.

International Volunteer Programs Association (www.volunteerinternational.org) Lists many programs in Latin America, most from US$900 for a couple of weeks.

ResponsibleTravel (www.responsibletravel.com) UK-based ecofriendly tour operator with many volunteer trips.

Transitions Abroad (www.transitionsabroad.com) Heaps of volunteer links; look under Central America.

Organizations in Central America

There are many smaller, privately run volunteer organizations in Central America, and it's not difficult to find short-term (one or two weeks) or longer programs once you're on the road. This will save you the higher costs of pre-arranging a program, but opportunities aren't always easy to find. We have listed volunteer programs by town and in individual country Directories.

Here are some options that can be arranged by local organizations, often during your trip:

■ Teaching English to Maya children outside Quetzaltenango, Guatemala (p144)

■ Helping monitor sea-turtle nests in Costa Rica (p556)

■ Learning organic farming at a sustainable agriculture ranch in Costa Rica (see boxed text, p553)

■ Providing English courses in San Salvador (p329)

■ Playing with children in an orphanage in Boquete, Panama (p665)

WOMEN TRAVELERS

Women traveling solo through Central America typically find that popular perceptions overestimate the dangers faced. Take all the normal precautions you would elsewhere in new territory or big cities. The biggest adjustment is getting used to a very vocal male population who hoot, hiss and whistle. Ignore this behavior and most of the time you will be simply left alone. Certain bars and soccer games tend to be testosterone territory and your incursion will invite attention.

Dress according to local norms to avoid unwanted attention (often this means wearing longer skirts or pants instead of shorts). Match locals' formality in dress as disheveled clothing can be a sign of disrespect. Being gracious and behaving somewhat formally will win you allies. Talk to locals to find out which areas to avoid.

Locals, particularly families, will often go out of their way to help a single female traveler. Keep in mind, though, that it's more typical for Latin American women to socialize with other women. Women in Central America's more conservative societies rarely have male friends. Befriending someone's husband can attract resentment and befriending guys in general is a little unusual – it's probable that they will think you want more than their friendship.

Though there's no need to be paranoid, women travelers should be aware that sexual assault, rape and mugging incidents do occur. The greatest risk is in remote or dark areas, on lone stretches of beach, or sometimes when trekking. Always keep enough money for a taxi ride to your accommodations – it's not wise to be walking after dark.

In general, Central American police are not likely to be very helpful in rape cases. The tourist police may be more sympathetic, but it's possibly better to contact your embassy and see a doctor.

JourneyWoman (www.journeywoman.com) is a useful online resource for female travelers, with lots of tips and advice.

WORK

According to law you must have a permit to work in any of the countries covered in this guide. In practice people may get paid under the table or through some bureaucratic loophole, if they can find suitable work. Many travelers work short-term jobs – through the aforementioned loophole – in restaurants, hostels or bars geared to international travelers, for survival wages. Before taking such a job, consider volunteering instead (see p723), as many of these jobs could just as well be performed by locals.

Teaching English is another option. Consult the classified advertisements in local newspapers (both English- and Spanish-language papers), browse the bulletin boards in spots where foreigners gather and ask around. Big cities offer the best possibilities for schools or private tutoring. Generally this doesn't involve big money, but often you could trade classes for room and board. If you do teach, teach well. Even small fees can be big sacrifices for locals trying to learn a language to better their chances in school or at work. It's not as easy as it looks. Many schools will require Teaching English as a Foreign Language (TEFL) teaching certificates.

Some international organizations help place individuals in various work jobs; see opposite page.

Transitions Abroad (www.transitionsabroad.com) is an excellent web magazine and internet resource center with work- and study-abroad options. The website has many useful links.

Transportation

CONTENTS

GETTING THERE & AWAY

Most visitors reach Central America by air or overland from Mexico. Flights, tours and rail tickets can be booked online at www.lonely planet.com/travel_services.

AIR

All Central American countries have international airports. The major ones are Cancún, Mexico (airport code CUN); Guatemala City, Guatemala (GUA); Belize City, Belize (BZE); San Salvador, El Salvador (SAL); San Pedro Sula (SAP) and Tegucigalpa (TGU), Honduras; Managua, Nicaragua (MGA); San José, Costa Rica (SJO); and Panama City, Panama (PAC). A limited number of international flights also reach Flores, Guatemala (FRS); Roatán, Honduras (RTB); and David, Panama (DAV).

THINGS CHANGE...

The information in this chapter is particularly vulnerable to change. Check directly with the airline or a travel agent to make sure you understand how a fare (and ticket you may buy) works and be aware of the security requirements for international travel. Shop carefully. The details given in this chapter should be regarded as pointers and are not a substitute for your own careful, up-to-date research.

Other than South American flights, nearly all go via US gateways (particularly Houston, Miami or New York's JFK) or Mexico City.

Airlines

The following offer frequent service to Central America:

Aeroméxico (airline code AM; www.aeromexico.com) To San José, San Pedro Sula and Cancún from many US cities and Madrid.

American Airlines (airline code AA; www.americanair lines.com) All of Central America from Dallas and Miami.

British Airways (airline code BA; www.britishairways. com) Flights to Belize City, Guatemala City, San José and Panama City via Miami.

Continental Airlines (airline code CO; www.continental. com) All of Central America from Newark and Houston.

COPA (airline code CPA; www.copaair.com) Hub in Panama City with flights to New York, Washington DC, Miami and Los Angeles, as well as Central and South American cities.

Delta Airlines (airline code DL; www.delta.com) Flights to Central America from Atlanta and Los Angeles.

Jet Blue (airline code B6; www.jetblue.com) Connects Boston and New York with Cancún.

Mexicana (airline code MX; www.mexicana.com) To Cancún, Guatemala City, San Salvador, San José, Panama City and Tuxtla Gutierrez, Mexico, via Mexico City.

TACA (airline code TA; www.taca.com) Hub in San Salvador with flights within Central America and to North and South America.

United Airlines (airline code UA; www.united.com) Reaches several Central American cities.

US Airways (airline code US; www.usairways.com) Goes to Guatemala City, San José and Cancún from Charlotte, Las Vegas, Phoenix and Philadelphia.

Tickets

Central America's slender isthmus shape makes 'open jaw' tickets – flying into one place (say Cancún or Guatemala City) and out from another (eg Panama City) – an attractive option, and the good news is that it's often not much more expensive than a round-trip ticket. If you're flexible on where you start and end, shop around – discount fares come and go.

You might think going to a hub city – such as San Salvador on TACA – would save money, but sometimes it's *more* expensive; we found some tickets through San Salvador to Belize City from Los Angeles, for exam-

---

ONWARD-TICKET REQUIREMENTS

If you're planning on flying into one country and back from another, note that increasingly immigration officials require travelers show proof of onward or continuing travel. The restriction is there mainly to ensure nonresidents don't stay long-term in the country without permission.

Showing 'continuing travel' from another country (say a flight home) and explaining how you'll get there is almost always enough. Most travelers are never asked; as one travel agent summed up, 'It's rarely a problem, but it's up to the mood of the person checking your passport and whether their supervisor is watching or not.'

It's a good idea to ask the airlines, as they can be fined for bringing in a passenger without proper documentation. Also, it may be worth showing a print-out of a 'bus reservation' out of the country, emailed from a local travel agency.

This requirement also pops up at land borders on occasion. Crossing into Costa Rica, for instance, it's sometimes necessary to purchase a bus ticket at the border leaving Costa Rica – even if you don't plan to use it. If you enter by private car, no onward ticket is required, obviously, but proper documentation for the car is needed.

If you're continuing on to South America, check beforehand for similar restrictions in those countries.

---

ple, to be cheaper than return tickets to San Salvador. The reason – in the confusing world of airline ticket pricing – is airlines trying to compete with more direct options. Again, shop around.

Typically, Panama City is more expensive to reach from the US gateways than Guatemala City, but otherwise no Central American city is consistently cheaper than another.

High-season rates (generally July and August, Christmas to New Year, and around Semana Santa) can be US$100 to US$250 more expensive.

Student travel agencies such as **STA Travel** (www.statravel.com) offer student discounts for those under 26.

If you're flying from Europe or Australia, chances are you can get a free stopover in a US gateway city such as Los Angeles or Miami.

See individual country Transportation sections for information on the departure taxes collected when leaving from Central American airports.

RTW TICKETS

Round-the-world (RTW) tickets are an option if coming from the USA or Europe, but lack of flight connections between Australasia and Central America have all but put Latin America off RTW ticket options from that part of the world.

From Australia & New Zealand

No direct flights to Central America from Australia or New Zealand exist. (Sydney and Auckland do have services via Argentina and Chile.) The cheapest option to Central America is through the USA, usually Los Angeles or Miami. It is often considerably cheaper to get two individual tickets – one to the USA, another to Central America.

Two of the best travel agents specializing in cheap airfares are **STA Travel** (☎ 1300 733-035, 03-9207-5900; www.statravel.com.au) and **Flight Centre** (☎ 133 133; www.flightcentre.com.au). Both have many offices nationwide.

For discount tickets in New Zealand, also try **STA Travel** (☎ 0800 474 400; www.statravel.co.nz) or **Flight Centre** (☎ 0800 243 544; www.flightcentre.co.nz). Both have offices in Auckland and other cities.

For online fares try www.travel.com.au or www.zuji.com from Australia, and www.goholidays.co.nz or www.zuji.co.nz from New Zealand.

From Continental Europe

The best deals are often found at 'student' travel agencies (nonstudents are welcome too) in Amsterdam, Brussels, Paris, Berlin and Frankfurt, and sometimes Athens. Alternatively, you can try booking via a London agent.

In Paris, student or discount travel agencies include **Nouvelles Frontières** (☎ 08 25 00 07 47; www.nouvelles-frontieres.fr), with nationwide offices, including services in Belgium. Another is **Havas Voyages** (☎ 01 48 51 86 19; www.havasvoyages.fr).

In the Netherlands, the official student agency **NBBS Reizen** (☎ 010-2891 891; www.nbbs.nl) is good.

STA Travel (www.statravel.com) has offices throughout Germany and in Austria, Denmark, Finland, Sweden and Switzerland.

From South America

TACA and COPA airlines connect Central American cities to and from Venezuela, Colombia, Ecuador, Peru, Chile and Argentina. Some US airlines, such as American Airlines, have a few connections too.

If you're planning to visit both Central America and South America on a trip, note that TACA (and other airlines) often allows a free stopover (in San José for TACA), meaning you can visit Central America for no extra charge. Panama City is generally the cheapest link to and from South America, with Colombia, Ecuador and Venezuela, unsurprisingly, offering the least expensive deals.

Note that many South American countries require onward air tickets upon arrival (see boxed text, p727).

Helpful travel agencies and services in South America include the following:

South American Explorers (www.saexplorers.org) Buenos Aires (☎ 011-5275-0137; Apt A, 7th fl, Roque Saenz Peña 1142); Lima (☎ 01-445-3306; Calle Piura 135, Miraflores); Quito (☎ 02-222-5228; Apt 17-21-431, Eloy Alfaro)

Trotamundos (☎ 1-288-2399; www.trotamundos.com.co; Diagonal 35 No 5-73; Bogotá, Colombia)

From the UK

No flights link the UK directly with Central America. British Airways has weekly flights direct to Mexico City, which run at about £150 to £180 less than Central American fares. Otherwise it's possible to reach any Central American country in a day via the USA (where it's necessary to clear customs, even if you're only making a connection). It's possible to get free stopovers in US cities such as Houston or New York on Continental Airlines, or Atlanta, Cincinnati, Los Angeles or San Francisco on Delta Airlines. British Airways and Iberia often go via Miami.

Book way ahead if you're planning to go from mid-December through January, or from July through mid-September.

If planning on globe-trotting, ask about discounted one-way tickets through Central and South America. Check the weekend editions of national newspapers for airfare listings.

DEPARTURE TAXES

Air taxes in Central American countries vary. Costa Rica and Panama have the smallest taxes (5%), while Guatemala and El Salvador have a 20% tax jacking up airfares. These taxes are generally included in fares quoted by travel agents (but not when booking online), both abroad and in Central America. Departure taxes are covered in the Transportation sections of individual country chapters.

For student discounts, **STA Travel** (☎ 0871-230 0040; www.statravel.co.uk) has offices throughout the UK. An excellent travel agency geared toward trips in the region is **Journey Latin America** (☎ 020-874 7108; www.journeylatinamerica.co.uk), with offices in London and Manchester.

Bucket shops selling discounted fares abound in London and in the UK. Check for travel agents that are bonded by organizations (such as ATOL, ABTA or AITO) which give some protection to ticket buyers if the company goes broke.

From the USA & Canada

Most flights from the USA and Canada go through Dallas/Fort Worth, Houston, Los Angeles or Miami. Other major gateways are Atlanta, Chicago, Newark, New York, San Francisco, Charlotte, Toronto and Washington, DC.

Tickets bought here usually have restrictions, including a two-week advance-purchase requirement. Often prices rise if you stay over three or four months.

Travel agencies known as 'consolidators' have some of the best deals; they buy tickets in bulk, then sell at discounts.

A couple of excellent Latin American–focused agencies are worth contacting, even if you're not in their immediate area: the Colorado-based **Exito Travel** (☎ 800-655-4053, 925-952-9322; www.exitotravel.com) and San Francisco–based **Americas Travel** (☎ 888-703-9955, 415-703-9955; www.americastravel.net).

The USA's largest student travel agency is **STA Travel** (☎ 800-781-4040; www.statravel.com), with nationwide offices and cheaper prices for students. Booking tours and tickets, the **Adventure Travel Company** (☎ in USA or Canada 888-238-2887; www.atcadventure.com) has offices in the USA and Canada.

A few online ticket services include www. cheaptickets.com, www.expedia.com and www.travelocity.com. You can try bidding for a cheaper one at www.priceline.com or www.skyauction.com.

LAND

For details on border crossings between Central American nations and also country-specific requirements, see Transportation sections and the border-crossing boxed texts in each country chapter. For general advice on crossing borders, see boxed text, p730.

From Mexico

BUS & BOAT

It's possible to bus from the USA or Canada into Mexico and directly into Central America. The three most convenient land borders between Mexico and Central America are at the Chetumal–Corozal (Belize) border in Quintana Roo (Yucatán Peninsula; see p71); as well as Ciudad Cuauhtémoc–La Mesilla (Guatemala; see p154) and Ciudad Hidalgo–Ciudad Tecún Umán (Guatemala; see p155) in Chiapas state (about 38km to the south of Tapachula).

Another popular border crossing is by boat across the Río Usumacinta at the Frontera Corozal–Bethel (Guatemala) border, south of Palenque (see p47).

CAR & MOTORCYCLE

Most people driving to Central America do so from the USA (or Canada). Buying a car in the region (including Mexico) is very complicated. If you drive, you will *not* save money, but it can make for a great trip. But there are a lot of fees, paperwork, red tape, tolls and parking worries involved. You'll need to be prepared to stop for passport checks at military checkpoints. Also, highway robberies aren't unknown. Avoid driving at night.

Note that you'll need liability insurance that covers Mexico and Central America – your policy back home isn't recognized here. It's available at many border towns. Texas-based **Sanborn's Insurance** (☎ 800-222-0158; www.sanbornsinsurance.com) sells separate coverage (only) for Mexico and Central America. A two-week liability/full-coverage policy in Mexico is US$126/183; in Central America, sadly, coverage doesn't include Belize or Nicaragua. Monthly rates for liability/full coverage are US$186/386. It's possible to get a policy by phone or online – so you can get Mexico coverage on the road in Central America for your return through Mexico.

A few other pretrip considerations:
- You need a valid driver's license from your home country (see p732).
- Unleaded gas/petrol is now available throughout Central America.

CLIMATE CHANGE & TRAVEL

Climate change is a serious threat to the ecosystems that humans rely upon, and air travel is the fastest-growing contributor to the problem. Lonely Planet regards travel, overall, as a global benefit, but believes we all have a responsibility to limit our personal impact on global warming.

Flying & Climate Change

Pretty much every form of motor travel generates CO_2 (the main cause of human-induced climate change) but planes are far and away the worst offenders, not just because of the sheer distances they allow us to travel, but because they release greenhouse gases high into the atmosphere. The statistics are frightening: two people taking a return flight between Europe and the US will contribute as much to climate change as an average household's gas and electricity consumption over a whole year.

Carbon Offset Schemes

Climatecare.org and other websites use 'carbon calculators' that allow jetsetters to offset the greenhouse gases they are responsible for with contributions to energy-saving projects and other climate-friendly initiatives in the developing world – including projects in India, Honduras, Kazakhstan and Uganda.

Lonely Planet, together with Rough Guides and other concerned partners in the travel industry, supports the carbon offset scheme run by climatecare.org. Lonely Planet offsets all of its staff and author travel.

For more information check out our website: lonelyplanet.com.

TRANSPORTATION

TRANSPORTATION

- Make sure that the shock absorbers and suspension are in good shape for the bumpy roads.
- A spare fuel filter, and other spare parts, could be invaluable.
- Check with a national tourist board or consulate for any changes of bringing a car into Mexico, or Central America, before showing up in your vehicle.

From South America

There are no road connections between South America and Central America (via Panama), and instability in the border region with Colombia (plus the difficulty of travel) have essentially made the trip over the Darién Gap on foot an impossibility. Visitors to the Darién must register with the police, who currently do not permit crossing on foot.

SEA

Unless you're a filthy-rich yachtie or on a cruise ship, options for boat travel heading to/from the region are very limited and very expensive. The most plausible way is going on a chartered sailboat from the Archipiélago de San Blas, Panama, to Cartagena, Colombia (per person US$385). The five-day trip usually includes a few days on the islands and two days' transit to/from Colombia. See boxed text, p693, for more information.

In Cartagena, check with the hostel **Casa Viena** (☎ 05-664-6242; www.casaviena.com; Calle San Andrés 30-53, Getsemaní) for schedule info. Note that cargo boats are a risky business; smuggling is common on the Colón–Cartagena cargo route.

GETTING AROUND

Like buses? They are the cheapest and most accessible way to get around Central America, particularly along the Pan-American Hwy (also called the Pan-Americana or Interamericana – we've alternated usage based on local parlance), which runs through all of the countries except Belize.

Because of the region's skinny stature, a flight can save several hours of backtracking. Islands and some borders are served by various types of boat. See p15 for suggested itineraries.

AIR

Many flights connect the region by some international carriers as well as the national airlines; see p726 for listings. Some smaller

---

HINTS FOR BORDER CROSSINGS

Going from one of Central America's seven countries (or Mexico) into another can be a frenetic, confusing, even scam-ridden experience. But with a little planning it's usually a breeze (make that a *slo-o-ow* breeze). Some considerations:

- Before you leave one country for another, read that country's entry requirements in the Visas section of the Directory at the back of the chapter.
- Don't leave a country without getting your passport stamped at that country's immigration office. Occasionally, no one will flag you down to do this; be on the lookout for it.
- Often you'll be changing buses at the border, perhaps walking a few hundred meters across, or catching a *colectivo* (shared taxi or minibus taxi) to the nearest bus station. Not all of the borders are open 24 hours, but bus schedules tend to match opening hours.
- Many travel agents offer organized trips across the border; many travelers prefer the ease of having someone there (a driver, for example) to help if things get sticky.
- Money changers linger around nearly all borders; rates can be fair but some changers do try to shortchange; count carefully. If you're carrying only local currency, try to change at least some before moving on, as it's possible no one will accept it once you're across the border.
- Note that, technically, there's a border agreement between Guatemala, Honduras, El Salvador and Nicaragua, allowing travel up to 90 days in the four-country region – and you shouldn't have to pay to cross into another country; see boxed text, p723

See also Overland Routes boxed texts at the beginning of each country chapter for border information. Border-crossing details appear in boxed texts in relevant sections throughout the book.

SAMPLE AIRFARES

Origin	Destination	One-way (US$)	Round-trip (US$)
Cancún	Guatemala City	351	447
Guatemala City	Panama City	295	383
Guatemala City	San José	295	289
Managua	Guatemala City	306	410
Managua	Panama City	US$335	400

domestic airlines provide service too; see the Transportation sections of country chapters for more information. Occasionally it will be necessary to change planes in the carrier's hub city (eg a Managua–Panama City flight may change planes up north in San Salvador).

Prices are an obstacle. Despite relatively short distances, individual one-way and round-trip tickets within Central America (either bought abroad or in the region) can be very expensive. Note that if you fly to Central America on TACA, they sometimes sell regional flights – generally to or from San José – at a discount. Not infrequently, one-way tickets run just a few dollars less than a round-trip ticket.

Flights can sometimes be overbooked; reconfirm yours before arriving at the airport. See boxed text, p727, for potential problems with entering one country and flying out of another.

Sample Airfares

What you're about to see borders on sacrilege. Airfares can vary wildly – depending on the length of stay, time of year and special promotions – so treat the high-season fares listed in the table above as a rough gauge only in identifying potential routes.

Note that San Salvador and San José are the most popular hubs – promotional flights between them are sometimes as low as US$139 return. Occasionally a promotional return flight may be even cheaper than a one-way fare.

Worthwhile domestic flights include Managua to Corn Islands (about US$164 return), which saves a two-day bus/boat trip each way (about US$50 return). Flights to Panama's Comarca de Kuna Yala and Darién Province are similarly cheap.

BICYCLE

Long-distance cycling in the region can be dangerous, as few drivers are accustomed to sharing narrow streets in cities or (often) shoulderless two-lane highways with bicycles. That said, cycling is on an upswing – with mountain rides and coffee-plantation tours (including guide and bike) available all over Central America.

You can rent bicycles in several cities and traveler hangouts, such as San Cristóbal de Las Casas (Mexico), Flores (Guatemala), Granada (Nicaragua) and Panama City. There are many mountain-bike tours available (notably in cooler locales such as Guatemala's highlands and San Cristóbal de Las Casas). Consider the seasons if you're planning to cycle a lot. The dry season (roughly December to April) should spare you from soakings.

If you're planning to bike across borders, keep a document of your ownership handy for immigration officials.

Check out www.downtheroad.org which documents the ongoing worldwide cycling odyssey of Tim and Cyndie Travis; entries are detailed and include Central America. Though dated, the staple guide to cycling the region is *Latin America by Bike: A Complete Touring Guide* (1993), by Walter Sienko. Richard Ballantine's *Richard's New Bicycle Book* helps understand the parts. Ian Benford and Peter Hodkinson's *Cycle Central America* covers southern Mexico, Belize, Guatemala and Honduras.

BOAT

Aside from domestic water-related activities (such as white-water rafting or boating to volcanic islands), a few water journeys connect Central American countries. Travelers between Palenque, Mexico, and Flores, Guatemala, cross the Río Usumacinta near Frontera Corozal, Mexico, and Bethel, Guatemala (see boxed text, p47). Another interesting crossing is between Punta Gorda, Belize, and Puerto Barrios (and sometimes Lívingston), Guatemala (see p183). There's a rather off-track river border crossing between San Carlos, Nicaragua, and Los Chiles, Costa Rica (see boxed text, p506).

Key domestic water journeys include the ride down the Río Escondidas to Bluefields, Nicaragua, and then out to the Corn Islands in the Caribbean (see boxed text, p508, and p511). Guatemala's Río Dulce (see p177) is another famous ride. Other Caribbean islands that are reached by boat include Honduras' Bay Islands, Belize's Caye Caulker and Mexico's Cozumel and Isla Mujeres.

The Panama Canal is one of the world's most important waterways, connecting the Caribbean and the Pacific.

BUS

Many about your trip will be of how you got around by bus. Bus service is well developed throughout the region, though not always comfortable. While some buses are air-conditioned with reservable reclining seats, you're sure to bounce a time or 20 in one of the famed 'chicken buses.' These are often colorfully repainted former US school buses with a liberal 'bring on what you want' policy (ie chickens).

Avoid night buses throughout the region (with the possible exception of Mexico), as these have been popular targets for highway robbers.

First-class and some 2nd-class buses depart on scheduled times from a *terminal de autobuses* (long-distance bus station); others leave from parking-lot bus terminals once they are full (these stop to collect more passengers all along the way – thus, you're likely to get a lift from the highway if need be). Be aware that many cities have more than one bus station. Bus companies can have their own terminals as well.

Bus frequency can vary. In bigger cities and on more popular routes, smoke-spewing giants troll the streets every few minutes, while in remote places, if you oversleep you'll be staying another night.

Luggage may be stored in a lower compartment or piled on the roof of the bus. Keep an eye on your luggage on bus trips if you can, particularly on the easily accessible racks in a packed bus. Always keep your valuables tucked away on your person. Watch out for pickpockets on crowded buses and in bus stations.

In some places, travel agents run shuttle services (mostly vans with air-con) to popular destinations. They're more comfortable and more expensive (and carry a lot less street cred). An example: Antigua to Guatemala City is about US$10 by shuttle; or you can take three chicken buses and do the route for about US$0.50.

Getting There & Away sections following towns and cities throughout this book list most bus routes and fares; see also the Transportation sections in individual country chapters.

Colectivos & Minibuses

Around Central America, and usually connecting hub towns with smaller ones on short-haul trips, are an array of minibuses of various conditions and nomenclature (called *rapidito* in Honduras, *chiva* in Panama, and *colectivo* in Costa Rica and Mexico). These are cheaper transportation options than 1st-class buses, when available, and they go frequently – the catch is that they make frequent stops and that the driver knows no word for 'full.'

Sample Bus Durations

Seeing most of Central America by bus is not difficult, but you'll need time. Here are the durations of some sample bus journeys. Remember that bus connections and border-crossing formalities can add extra time to the trip.

Origin	Destination	Duration (hr)
Cancún (M)	Belize City (B)	9-10
Flores (G)	Guatemala City (G)	8-10
Guatemala City (G)	Copán Ruinas (H)	5
Managua (N)	San José (CR)	9
San Cristóbal de Las Casas (M)	Antigua (G)	11
San José (CR)	Panama City (P)	15
San Salvador (ES)	Tegucigalpa (H)	8
Tegucigalpa (H)	Managua (N)	8

CAR & MOTORCYCLE
Driver's License

If you're planning to drive anywhere, check before you leave to see if your country's driver's license is honored in all the countries you plan to hit the road in. It's possible you may need an International Driving Permit (IDP), which is issued by automobile associations worldwide.

Be prepared for police checkpoints – always stop and have your papers handy.

Hire & Insurance

Central America is relatively easy to explore by private vehicle, and would be more popular if it weren't for the cost (rental and gas) and hassle. Rentals range from about US$15 per day in Nicaragua to US$80 per day in Belize.

However, rentals are usually not allowed to leave the country – though Budget, for example, allows it if you rent from Nicaragua or Guatemala only. But renting can make for a memorable splurge day or two, and get you into areas you might otherwise miss (such as isolated beaches south of Tulum in Mexico and around Costa Rica's Península de Nicoya).

In many cases it's cheaper to arrange (even same-day) rentals with major car-rental agencies on their websites; during research in Tulum we saved 50% on the quoted local fare by going to an internet cafe next door and booking a car online!

4WD vehicles are more expensive (generally US$80 to US$100 per week), and gas is about US$1.25 to US$2.50 per liter.

Insurance is required – and your coverage back home isn't recognized here. Make sure you have at least collision damage insurance coverage.

To rent a car, you'll need a passport and a driver's license. Some agencies rent to those 21 and over, while others to only those 25

and over. All of Central America drives on the right-hand side of the road.

Scooters and bigger motorcycles are available in some places, the latter usually costing about the same price as a compact car.

For more information and general advice on driving in Central America, including liability insurance, see p729.

HITCHHIKING

Hitchhiking (*tomando un jalón* – literally 'taking a hitch') is never entirely safe in any country in the world, and Lonely Planet does not recommend it. However, it is common in parts of Central America. Side roads – or wherever the last bus just went by – may tempt you to try. If you do, try to be in groups. Solo women should never hitchhike. If you get a ride, offer to pay gas money, even if the driver may turn it down.

TRAIN

The only train trip in the region is a very scenic, glass-domed luxury ride from Panama City to Colón, Panama, along the Panama Canal (see p687).

TRANSPORTATION

Health Dr David Goldberg

Travelers to Central America need to be concerned about food-borne as well as mosquito-borne infections. Most of these illnesses are not life-threatening, but they can certainly ruin your trip. Besides getting the proper vaccinations, it's important that you bring along a good insect repellent and exercise great care in what you eat and drink.

BEFORE YOU GO

Bring medications in their original containers, clearly labeled. A signed, dated letter from your doctor describing medical conditions and medications (including generic names) is a good idea. If carrying syringes, take a physician's letter documenting their medical necessity.

INSURANCE

If your health insurance does not cover you for medical expenses abroad, consider supplemental insurance. Check www.lonelyplanet.com for more information. US travelers can find a list of recommended doctors abroad and emergency evacuation details on the website of the **US State Department** (www.travel.state.gov). Find out in advance if your insurance plan will make payments directly to providers or reimburse you later for overseas health expenditures. If the latter, be sure to collect receipts.

RECOMMENDED VACCINATIONS

Since most vaccines don't produce immunity until at least two weeks after they're given, visit a physician four to eight weeks before departure. Ask your doctor to provide you with an international certificate of vaccination (the yellow booklet), which will list all the vaccinations you've received. This is mandatory for countries that require proof of yellow-fever vaccination upon entry, but it's a good idea to carry it wherever you travel.

The only required vaccine is yellow fever, and that's only if you are arriving from a yellow fever–infected country in Africa or South America. However, there are a number of vaccines that are recommended. Note that some of these are not approved for use by children and pregnant women – check with your physician.

MEDICAL CHECKLIST

- acetaminophen/paracetamol (Tylenol) or aspirin
- adhesive or paper tape
- antibacterial ointment (eg Bactroban) for cuts and abrasions
- antibiotics
- antidiarrheal drugs (eg loperamide)
- antihistamines (for hay fever and allergic reactions)
- anti-inflammatory drugs (eg ibuprofen)
- bandages, gauze and gauze rolls
- DEET-containing insect repellent for the skin
- iodine tablets (for water purification)
- oral rehydration salts
- permethrin-containing insect spray for clothing, tents and bed nets
- pocketknife
- scissors, safety pins and tweezers
- steroid cream or cortisone (for poison ivy and other allergic rashes)
- sunblock
- syringes and sterile needles
- thermometer

INTERNET RESOURCES

The **World Health Organization** (www.who.int/ith/) publishes a superb book called *International Travel and Health,* which is revised annually and is available on its website at no cost. Its website lists updated risks and worldwide vaccination certificate requirements. Another website of general interest is **MD Travel Health** (www.mdtravelhealth.com), which provides complete travel health recommendations for every country, updated daily, also at no cost.

It's usually a good idea to consult your government's travel health website before departure, if one is available.

Australia (www.smarttraveller.gov.au)
Canada (www.hc-sc.gc.ca/index_e.html)
UK (www.doh.gov.uk)
USA (www.cdc.gov/travel)

Up for an appetite killer? Browse through the US Food and Drug Administration's *Bad Bug Book.* You can also download it free at www.cfsan.fda.gov/~mow/intro.html.

FURTHER READING

For further information, see *Healthy Travel Central & South America* from Lonely Planet. If you're traveling with children, Lonely Planet's *Travel with Children* will be useful. The *ABC of Healthy Travel,* by E Walker et al, and *Medicine for the Outdoors,* by Paul S Auerbach, are other valuable travel health resources.

IN TRANSIT

DEEP VEIN THROMBOSIS (DVT)

Blood clots may form in the legs during plane flights, chiefly because of prolonged immobility. The longer the flight, the greater the risk. Though most blood clots are reabsorbed uneventfully, some may break off and travel through the blood vessels to the lungs, where they could cause life-threatening complications.

The chief symptom of deep vein thrombosis is swelling or pain in the foot, ankle or calf, usually but not always on just one side. When a blood clot travels to the lungs, it may cause chest pain and difficulty in breathing. Travelers with any of these symptoms should immediately seek medical attention.

To prevent the development of deep vein thrombosis on long flights, you should walk about the cabin, perform isometric compressions of the leg muscles (ie contract the leg muscles while sitting), drink plenty of fluids and avoid alcohol and tobacco.

JET LAG & MOTION SICKNESS

Jet lag is common when crossing more than five time zones, and is characterized by insomnia, fatigue, malaise or nausea. To avoid jet lag, try drinking plenty of fluids (nonalcoholic) and

HEALTH

RECOMMENDED VACCINATIONS

Vaccine	Recommended for	Dosage	Side effects
chickenpox	travelers who've never had chickenpox	2 doses 1 month apart	fever, mild case of chickenpox
hepatitis A	all travelers	1 dose before trip; booster 6-12 months later	soreness at injection site, headaches, body aches
hepatitis B	long-term travelers in close contact with the local population	3 doses over 6-month period	soreness at injection site, low-grade fever
measles	travelers born after 1956 who've had only 1 measles vaccination	1 dose	fever, rash, joint pains, allergic reactions
rabies	travelers who may have contact with animals and may not have access to medical care	3 doses over 3- to 4-week period	soreness at injection site, headaches, body aches
tetanus-diphtheria	all travelers who haven't had a booster within 10 years	1 dose lasts 10 years	soreness at injection site
typhoid fever	all travelers	4 capsules by mouth; 1 taken every other day	abdominal pain, nausea, rash
yellow fever	required for travelers arriving from a yellow fever–infected area in Africa or South America	1 dose lasts 10 years	headaches, body aches; severe reactions are rare

eating light meals. Upon arrival, get exposure to natural sunlight and readjust your schedule (for meals, sleep etc) as soon as possible.

Antihistamines such as dimenhydrinate (Dramamine) and meclizine (Antivert, Bonine) are usually the first choice for treating motion sickness. Their main side effect is drowsiness. A herbal alternative is ginger, which works like a charm for some people.

IN CENTRAL AMERICA

AVAILABILITY & COST OF HEALTH CARE

Good medical care is available in most of the region's capital cities, but options are limited elsewhere. In general, private hospitals are more reliable than public facilities, which may experience significant shortages of equipment and supplies.

Many doctors and hospitals expect payment in cash, regardless of whether you have travel health insurance. If you develop a life-threatening medical problem, you'll probably want to be evacuated to a country with state-of-the-art medical care. Since this may cost tens of thousands of dollars, contract insurance before the trip.

Many pharmacies are well supplied, but important medications may not be consistently available. Be sure to bring along adequate supplies of all prescription drugs.

INFECTIOUS DISEASES
Cholera

Cholera is an intestinal infection acquired through ingestion of contaminated food or water. The main symptom is profuse, watery diarrhea, which may be so severe that it causes life-threatening dehydration. The key treatment is drinking an oral rehydration solution. Antibiotics are also given, usually tetracycline or doxycycline, though quinolone antibiotics such as ciprofloxacin and levofloxacin are also effective.

Cholera outbreaks occur periodically in parts of Central America, but the disease is rare among travelers. A cholera vaccine is no longer required, and is in fact no longer available in some countries, including the US, because the old vaccine was relatively ineffective and caused side effects. There are new vaccines that are safer and more effective, but they're not available in many countries and are only recommended for those at particularly high risk.

Dengue Fever

Dengue fever is a viral infection found throughout Central America. Dengue is transmitted by aedes mosquitoes, which bite predominantly during the daytime and are usually found close to human habitations, often indoors. They breed primarily in artificial water containers, such as jars, barrels, cans, cisterns, metal drums, plastic containers and discarded tires. As a result, dengue is especially common in densely populated, urban environments.

Dengue usually causes flu-like symptoms, including fever, muscle aches, joint pains, headaches, nausea and vomiting, often followed by a rash. The body aches may be quite uncomfortable, but most cases resolve themselves uneventfully in a few days. Severe cases usually occur in children under the age of 15 who are experiencing their second dengue infection.

There is no treatment for dengue except to take analgesics such as acetaminophen/paracetamol (Tylenol) and to drink plenty of fluids. Severe cases may require hospitalization for intravenous fluids and supportive care. There is no vaccine. See also Mosquito Bites, p739.

Hemorrhagic Conjunctivitis

Outbreaks of hemorrhagic conjunctivitis (pink-eye) have recently been reported in several Central American countries, including El Salvador, Guatemala and Nicaragua. The chief symptoms are redness, discomfort, and swelling around the eyes, usually associated with a discharge. Hemorrhagic conjunctivitis may be spread by the hands (after an infected person has rubbed their eyes) or by inanimate objects, such as towels. It doesn't usually cause any long-term eye problems, but it's highly contagious and extremely uncomfortable. You can reduce your risk by washing your hands frequently and having good personal hygiene.

Hepatitis A

Hepatitis A occurs throughout Central America. It's a viral infection of the liver that is usually acquired by ingestion of contaminated water, food or ice, though it may also be acquired by direct contact with infected persons. The illness occurs all over the world, but the incidence is higher in developing nations. Symptoms may include fever, malaise, jaundice, nausea, vomiting and abdominal pain. Most cases resolve themselves uneventfully, though hepatitis A occasionally causes severe liver damage. There is no treatment.

The vaccine for hepatitis A is extremely safe and highly effective. If you get a booster six to 12 months later, it lasts for at least 10 years. You really should get it before you go to Central America or any other developing region. Because the safety of the hepatitis A vaccine has not been established for pregnant women or children under the age of two, they should instead be given a gamma-globulin injection.

Hepatitis B

Like hepatitis A, hepatitis B is a liver infection that occurs worldwide but is more common in developing nations. Unlike hepatitis A, the disease is usually acquired by sexual contact or by exposure to infected blood, generally through blood transfusions or contaminated needles. The vaccine is recommended only for long-term travelers (on the road more than six months) who expect to live in rural areas or have close physical contact with the local population. Additionally, the vaccine is recommended for anyone who anticipates sexual contact with the local inhabitants or a possible need for medical, dental or other treatments while abroad, especially if a need for transfusions or injections is expected.

Hepatitis B vaccine is safe and highly effective. However, a total of three injections are necessary to establish full immunity. Several countries added hepatitis B vaccine to the list of routine childhood immunizations in the 1980s, so many young adults are already protected.

Malaria

Malaria occurs in every country in Central America. It's transmitted by mosquito bites, usually between dusk and dawn. The main symptom is high spiking fevers, which may be accompanied by chills, sweats, headache, body aches, weakness, vomiting or diarrhea. Severe cases may involve the central nervous system and lead to seizures, confusion, coma and death.

Taking malaria pills is recommended for rural areas in certain parts of Central America; to find out which areas, go to the website of the **Centers for Disease Control and Prevention** (www.cdc. gov/travel/regionalmalaria/camerica.htm). Transmission is greatest during the rainy season (June through November). Except in Panama, the first-choice malaria pill is chloroquine, taken once weekly in a dosage of 500mg, starting one to two weeks before arriving in Central America and continuing through the trip and for four weeks after departure. Chloroquine is safe, inexpensive and highly effective. Side effects are typically mild and may include nausea, abdominal discomfort, headache, dizziness, blurred vision or itching. Severe reactions are uncommon. In Panama, either mefloquine (Lariam), atovaquone/proguanil (Malarone) or doxycycline should be taken.

See also Mosquito Bites, p739.

If you may not have access to medical care while traveling, you should bring along additional pills for emergency self-treatment, which you should undergo if you can't reach a doctor and you develop symptoms that suggest malaria, such as high spiking fevers. One option is to take four tablets of Malarone once daily for three days. If you self-treat for malaria, it may also be appropriate to start a broad-spectrum antibiotic to cover typhoid fever and other bacterial infections. The drug of choice is usually a quinolone antibiotic such as ciprofloxacin (Cipro) or levofloxacin (Levaquin). If you start self-medication, try to see a doctor at the earliest possible opportunity.

If you develop a fever after returning home, see a physician, as malaria symptoms may not occur for months.

Rabies

Rabies is a viral infection of the brain and spinal cord that is almost always fatal. The rabies virus is carried in the saliva of infected animals and is typically transmitted through an animal bite, though contamination of any break in the skin with infected saliva may result in rabies. Rabies occurs in all Central American countries. Most cases are related to bites from dogs or bats.

The rabies vaccine is safe but a full series requires three injections and is quite expensive. Those at high risk for rabies, such as animal handlers and spelunkers (cave explorers), should certainly get the vaccine. In addition, those at lower risk for animal bites should consider asking for the vaccine if they might be traveling to remote areas and might not have access to appropriate medical care if needed. The treatment for a possibly rabid bite consists of the rabies vaccine with rabies immune globulin. It's effective but must be given promptly. Most travelers don't need rabies vaccine.

See also Animal Bites, p739.

Typhoid Fever

Typhoid fever is common throughout Central America. The infection is acquired by ingestion of food or water contaminated by a species of salmonella known as salmonella typhi. Fever occurs in virtually all cases. Other symptoms may include headache, malaise, muscle aches, dizziness, loss of appetite, nausea and abdominal pain. Either diarrhea or constipation may occur. Possible complications include intestinal perforation, intestinal bleeding, confusion, delirium and (rarely) coma.

Unless you expect to take all your meals in major hotels and restaurants, a typhoid vaccine is a good idea. It's usually given orally, but is also available as an injection. Neither vaccine is approved for use in children under the age of two.

The drug of choice for typhoid fever is usually a quinolone antibiotic such as ciprofloxacin (Cipro) or levofloxacin (Levaquin), which many travelers carry for treatment of traveler's diarrhea. However, if you self-treat for typhoid fever, you may also need to self-treat for malaria, since the symptoms of the two diseases may be indistinguishable.

Yellow Fever

Yellow fever no longer occurs in Central America, but many Central American countries, including Belize, El Salvador, Guatemala, Honduras and Nicaragua, require you to have a yellow-fever vaccine before entry if you're arriving from a country in Africa or South America, where yellow fever is known to occur. If you're not arriving from a country with yellow fever, the vaccine is neither required nor recommended. The vaccine is given only in approved yellow-fever vaccination centers, which provide validated international certificates of vaccination ('yellow booklets'). The vaccine should be given at least 10 days before departure and remains effective for approximately 10 years. It is not recommended for pregnant women or children less than nine months old. Reactions to the vaccine are generally mild and may include headaches, muscle aches, low-grade fevers, or discomfort at the injection site. Severe, life-threatening reactions have been described but are extremely rare.

Other Infections

BRUCELLOSIS

Brucellosis is an infection of domestic and wild animals that may be transmitted to humans by direct animal contact or by consumption of unpasteurized dairy products from infected animals. Brucellosis occurs in the northern part of Central America. Symptoms may include fever, malaise, depression, loss of appetite, headache, muscle aches and back pain, and may linger for months if not treated. Complications may include arthritis, hepatitis, meningitis and endocarditis (heart valve infection).

CHAGAS' DISEASE

Chagas' disease is a parasitic infection that is transmitted by triatomine insects (reduviid bugs), which inhabit crevices in the walls and roofs of substandard housing in South and Central America. The triatomine insect lays its feces on human skin as it bites, usually at night. A person becomes infected when they unknowingly rub the feces into the bite wound or any other open sore. Chagas' disease is extremely rare in travelers. However, if you sleep in a poorly constructed house, especially one made of mud, adobe or thatch, be sure to protect yourself with a bed net and a good insecticide.

HISTOPLASMOSIS

Histoplasmosis is caused by a soil-based fungus that is acquired by inhalation, often when the soil has been disrupted. Initial symptoms may include fever, chills, dry cough, chest pain and headache, sometimes leading to pneumonia.

HIV/AIDS

HIV/AIDS has been reported in all Central American countries. Be sure to use condoms for all sexual encounters. Avoid needles, including those used for tattoos and body-piercing.

LEISHMANIASIS

Leishmaniasis occurs in the mountains and jungles of all Central American countries. The infection is transmitted by sand flies, which are about one-third the size of mosquitoes. Leishmaniasis may be limited to the skin, causing slowly growing ulcers over exposed parts of the body, or (less commonly) disseminate to the bone marrow, liver and spleen. The disease may be particularly severe in those with HIV. There is no vaccine for leishmaniasis. To protect yourself from sand flies, follow the same precautions as for mosquitoes (see opposite), except that netting must be made of a finer mesh (at least 18 holes to the linear inch).

LEPTOSPIROSIS

Leptospirosis is acquired by exposure to water contaminated by the urine of infected animals. Outbreaks often occur at times of flooding, when sewage overflow may contaminate water sources. The initial symptoms, which resemble a mild flu, usually subside uneventfully in a few days, with or without treatment, but a minority of cases are complicated by jaundice or meningitis. There is no vaccine. You can minimize your risk by staying out of bodies of fresh water that may be contaminated by animal urine. If you're visiting an area where an outbreak is in progress, you can take 200mg of doxycycline once weekly as a preventative measure. If you actually develop leptospirosis, the treatment is 100mg of doxycycline twice daily.

TRAVELER'S DIARRHEA

To prevent diarrhea, avoid tap water unless it has been boiled, filtered or chemically disinfected (with iodine tablets); only eat fresh fruits or vegetables if cooked or peeled; be wary of dairy products that might contain unpasteurized milk; and be highly selective when eating food from street vendors.

If you develop diarrhea, be sure to drink plenty of fluids, preferably an oral rehydration solution containing lots of salt and sugar. A few loose stools don't require treatment, but if you start having more than four or five stools a day, you should start taking an antibiotic (usually a quinolone drug) and an antidiarrheal agent (such as loperamide). If diarrhea is bloody or persists for more than 72 hours or is accompanied by fever, shaking chills or severe abdominal pain, you should seek medical attention.

ENVIRONMENTAL HAZARDS
Animal Bites

Do not attempt to pet, handle or feed any animal, with the exception of domestic animals known to be free of any infectious disease. Most animal injuries are directly related to a person's attempt to touch or feed the animal.

Any bite or scratch by a mammal, including bats, should be promptly and thoroughly cleansed with large amounts of soap and water, followed by application of an antiseptic such as iodine or alcohol. The local health authorities should be contacted immediately for possible postexposure rabies treatment, whether or not you've been immunized against rabies. It may also be advisable to start an antibiotic, since wounds caused by animal bites and scratches frequently become infected.

One of the newer quinolones, such as levo-floxacin (Levaquin), which many travelers carry in case of diarrhea, would be an appropriate choice.

Mosquito Bites

The best solution is prevention. To prevent mosquito bites, wear long sleeves, long pants, hats and shoes (rather than sandals). Bring along a good insect repellent, preferably one containing DEET, which should be applied to exposed skin and clothing but not to eyes, mouth, cuts, wounds or irritated skin. Products containing lower concentrations of DEET are as effective, but for shorter periods of time. In general, adults and children over 12 years of age should use preparations containing 25% to 35% DEET, which usually lasts about six hours. Children between two and 12 years of age should use preparations containing no more than 10% DEET, applied sparingly, which will usually last about three hours. Neurological toxicity has been reported from DEET, especially in children, but appears to be extremely uncommon and generally related to overuse. DEET-containing compounds should not be used on children under the age of two.

Insect repellents containing certain botanical products, including oil of eucalyptus and soybean oil, are effective but last only 1½ to two hours. DEET-containing repellents are preferable for areas where there is a high risk of malaria or yellow fever. Products based on citronella are not effective.

For additional protection, you can apply permethrin to clothing, shoes, tents and bed nets. Permethrin treatments are safe and remain effective for at least two weeks, even when items are laundered. Permethrin should not be applied directly to skin.

Don't sleep in buildings with the window open unless there is a screen. If sleeping outdoors or in accommodations that allow entry of mosquitoes, use a bed net, preferably treated with the permethrin, with edges tucked in under the mattress.

The mesh size should be less than 1.5mm. If the sleeping area is not otherwise protected, use a mosquito coil, which will fill the room with insecticide through the night. Repellent-impregnated wristbands are not effective.

Snake Bites

Snakes are a hazard in some areas of Central America. The chief concern is the fer-de-lance, a heavy-bodied snake up to 2m in length. In the event of a venomous snake bite, place the

HEALTH

victim at rest, keep the bitten area immobilized and move the victim immediately to the nearest medical facility. Avoid tourniquets, which are no longer recommended.

Scorpion Bites
Scorpions are a problem in some regions. If stúng, you should immediately apply ice or cold packs, immobilize the affected body part and go to the nearest emergency room. To prevent scorpion stings, be sure to inspect and shake out clothing, shoes and sleeping bags before use, and wear gloves and protective clothing when working around piles of wood or leaves.

Sun
To protect yourself from excessive sun exposure, you should stay out of the midday sun, wear sunglasses and a wide-brimmed sun hat, and apply sunscreen with SPF 15 or higher, with both UVA and UVB protection. Sunscreen should be generously applied to all exposed parts of the body approximately 30 minutes before sun exposure and should be reapplied after swimming or vigorous activity. Travelers should also drink plenty of fluids and avoid strenuous exercise when the temperature is high.

Water
Tap water in Central America is generally not safe to drink. Vigorous boiling for one minute is the most effective means of water purification. At altitudes greater than 2000m (6500 feet), boil for three minutes.

Another option is to disinfect water with iodine pills. Instructions are usually enclosed and should be carefully followed. Or you can add 2% tincture of iodine to one quart or liter of water (five drops to clear water, 10 drops to cloudy water) and let it stand for 30 minutes. If the water is cold, longer times may be required. The taste of iodinated water may be improved by adding vitamin C (ascorbic acid). Iodinated water should not be consumed for more than a few weeks. Pregnant women, those with a history of thyroid disease and those allergic to iodine should not drink iodinated water.

A number of water filters are on the market. Those with smaller pores (reverse osmosis filters) provide the broadest protection, but they are relatively large and are readily plugged by debris. Those that have somewhat larger pores (microstrainer filters) are ineffective against viruses, although they do remove other organisms. Manufacturers' instructions must be carefully followed.

TRAVELING WITH CHILDREN
In general, it's safe for children and pregnant women to go to Central America. However, because some of the vaccines listed on p734 are not approved for use in children and pregnant women, these travelers should be particularly careful not to drink tap water or consume any questionable food or beverage. Also, when traveling with children, make sure they're up to date on all routine immunizations. It's sometimes appropriate to give children some of their vaccines a little early before visiting a developing nation. You should discuss this with your pediatrician. Lastly, if pregnant, bear in mind that should a complication such as premature labor develop while abroad, the quality of medical care may not be comparable to that in your home country.

Since the yellow-fever vaccine is not recommended for pregnant women or children less than nine months old, these travelers, if arriving from a country with yellow fever, should obtain a waiver letter, preferably written on letterhead stationary and bearing the stamp used by official immunization centers to validate the international certificate of vaccination.

Language

CONTENTS

Spanish is the most commonly spoken language in Central America. While English is the official language of Belize, both Spanish and a local Creole are also widely spoken there. British and US influences have left other English-speaking pockets in the region, most notably among the descendants of West Indian settlers on the Caribbean coast, but also in Panama, particularly in the Canal Zone. Maya languages are the most common of a number of indigenous languages and dialects spoken throughout the region.

Every visitor to Central America will benefit from learning some Spanish, and it's easy to pick up the basics. Don't hesitate to practice your new skills – Latin Americans generally meet attempts to communicate in their language with enthusiasm and appreciation.

CENTRAL AMERICAN SPANISH

The Spanish of the Americas comes in many varieties. Depending on the areas in which you travel, consonants may be glossed over, vowels squashed into each other, and syllables dropped entirely. Slang and regional vocabulary, much of it derived from indigenous languages, can further add to the mix. For example, in Guatemala and Honduras a soft drink is called a *refresco*, a *gaseosa* in El Salvador and Nicaragua, and a *soda* in Panama. Frequent travel among the small Central American republics is common, however, so people are generally familiar with these variations; you should have few problems being understood.

Throughout Latin America, the Spanish language is referred to as *castellano* more often than *español*. Unlike in Spain, the letters **c** and **z** are never pronounced as lisped in Latin America.

Another notable difference between Latin American Spanish and the variety spoken in Spain is that the plural of the informal *tú* (you) is *ustedes* rather than *vosotros*; the latter term will sound quaint in the Americas. In many parts of El Salvador, Honduras and Costa Rica, the term *vos* is used instead of *tú*, and as a result some verb endings can vary slightly. To avoid complication, we haven't used the *vos* form in this chapter. It's a variant that only affects informal speech, so no offence will be taken when you use *tú* and you'll still be understood everywhere without problem.

For a more in-depth guide to the Spanish of Central America, get a copy of Lonely Planet's *Latin American Spanish* phrasebook. Lonely Planet also offers the *Costa Rican Spanish* and *Mexican Spanish* phrasebooks for those interested in the language varieties of these destinations. Another useful resource is the compact *University of Chicago Spanish–English, English–Spanish Dictionary*.

PRONUNCIATION

Spanish spelling is phonetically consistent, meaning that there's a clear and consistent relationship between what you see in writing and how it's pronounced. Also, most Spanish sounds have English equivalents, so English speakers shouldn't have trouble being understood. The phrases in this language guide are all accompanied by guides to pronunciation, so the task of getting your message across is made even simpler.

LANGUAGE

Vowels

a	as the 'a' in 'father'
ai	as in 'aisle'
ay	as in 'say'
e	as the 'e' in 'met'
ee	as the 'ee' in 'meet'
o	as the 'o' in 'more' (without the 'r')
oo	as the 'oo' in 'zoo'
ow	as in 'how'
oy	as in 'boy'

Consonants

Pronunciation of Spanish consonants is similar to their English counterparts. The exceptions are given in the following list.

kh	as the throaty 'ch' in the Scottish *loch*
ny	as the 'ny' in 'canyon'
r	as in 'run' but stronger and rolled, especially at the beginning of a word and in all words with *rr*
s	not lisped

The letter 'h' is invariably silent (ie never pronounced) in Spanish.

Note also that the Spanish **b** and **v** sounds are very similar – they are both pronounced as a very soft 'v' in English (somewhere between 'b' and 'v').

There are some variations in spoken Spanish as part of the regional accents across Latin America in general. The most notable of these variations is the pronunciation of the letter *ll*. In some parts of Latin America it's pronounced as the 'll' in 'million,' however throughout Central America it's pronounced as 'y' (eg as in 'yes'), and this is how it's represented in our pronunciation guides.

Word Stress

In general, words ending in vowels or the letters **n** or **s** have stress on the second-last syllable, while those with other endings have stress on the last syllable. Thus *vaca* (cow) and *caballos* (horses) both carry stress on the second-last syllable, while *ciudad* (city) and *infeliz* (unhappy) are both stressed on the last syllable.

Written accents will almost always appear in words that don't follow the rules above, eg *sótano* (basement), *América* and *porción* (portion). When a word with a written ac-

cent appears in capital letters, the accent is often not written, but is still pronounced.

GENDER & PLURALS

Spanish nouns are either masculine or feminine, and there are rules to help determine gender (with the obligatory exceptions). Feminine nouns generally end with -**a** or with the groups -**ción**, -**sión** or -**dad**. Other endings typically signify a masculine noun. Endings for adjectives change to agree with the gender of the noun they modify (masculine/feminine -**o**/-**a**). Where both masculine and feminine forms are included in this chapter, they are separated by a slash, with the masculine form given first, eg *perdido/a*.

If a noun or adjective ends in a vowel, the plural is formed by adding -**s** to the end. If it ends in a consonant, the plural is formed by adding -**es** to the end.

ACCOMMODATIONS

I'm looking for a ...	*Estoy buscando ...*	e·*stoy* boos·*kan*·do ...
Where's a ...?	*¿Dónde hay ...?*	*don*·de ai ...
cabin	*una cabaña*	*oo*·na ka·*ba*·nya
camping ground	*un terreno de camping*	oon te·*re*·no de *kam*·peen
guesthouse	*una pensión/ una casa de huéspedes*	*oo*·na pen·*syon*/ *oo*·na *ka*·sa de *we*·spe·des
hotel	*un hotel*	oon o·*tel*
youth hostel	*un albergue juvenil*	oon al·*ber*·ge khoo·ve·*neel*
I'd like a room.	*Quisiera una habitación ...*	kee·*sye*·ra *oo*·na a·bee·ta·*syon* ...
double	*doble*	*do*·ble
single	*individual*	een·dee·vee·*dwal*
twin	*con dos camas*	kon dos *ka*·mas
How much is it per ...?	*¿Cuánto cuesta por ...?*	*kwan*·to *kwes*·ta por ...
night	*noche*	*no*·che
person	*persona*	per·*so*·na
week	*semana*	se·*ma*·na

Does it include breakfast?
¿Incluye el desayuno?   een·*kloo*·ye el de·sa·*yoo*·no
Can I see the room?
¿Puedo ver la habitación?   *pwe*·do ver la a·bee·ta·*syon*
I don't like it.
No me gusta.   no me *goos*·ta

MAKING A RESERVATION

(for phone or written requests)

From ...	De ...
To ...	A ...
Date	Fecha
I'd like to book ...	Quisiera reservar ...
in the name of ...	en nombre de ...
for the nights of ...	para las noches del ...
credit card	tarjeta de crédito
expiry date	fecha de vencimiento
number	número
Please confirm ...	¿Puede confirmar ...?
availability	la disponibilidad
price	el precio

It's fine, I'll take it.
  OK, la alquilo.   o·kay la al·kee·lo

From (July 2) to (July 6).
  Desde (el dos de julio)   des·de (el dos de khoo·lyo)
  hasta (el seis de julio).   as·ta (el says de khoo·lyo)

For (three) nights/weeks.
  Para (tres) noches/semanas.   pa·ra (tres) no·ches/se·ma·nas

Please wake me at (seven).
  Por favor, despiérteme a   por fa·vor des·pyer·te·me a
  (las siete).   (las sye·te)

I'm leaving now.
  Me voy ahora.   me voy a·o·ra

cheaper	más económico	mas e·ko·no·mee·ko
discount	descuento	des·kwen·to
private/shared	baño privado/	ba·nyo pree·va·do/
bathroom	compartido	kom·par·tee·do
too expensive	demasiado caro	de·ma·sya·do ka·ro

CONVERSATION & ESSENTIALS

In their public behavior, Latin Americans are very conscious of civilities. When approaching a stranger, always extend a greeting, such as *buenos días* or *buenas tardes*, and use only the polite form of address, especially with the police and public officials.

Central America is generally more formal than many of the South American countries. The polite form *usted* (you) is used in all cases in this chapter; where options are given, the form is indicated by the abbreviations 'pol' and 'inf.'

The three most common greetings are often abbreviated to simply *buenos* (for *buenos días*) and *buenas* (for *buenas tardes* and *buenas noches*).

Hello.	Hola.	o·la
Good morning.	Buenos días.	bwe·nos dee·as
Good afternoon.	Buenas tardes.	bwe·nas tar·des
Good evening/	Buenas noches.	bwe·nas no·ches
night.		
Goodbye.	Adiós.	a·dyos
See you later.	Hasta luego.	as·ta lwe·go
Yes./No.	Sí./No.	see/no
Please.	Por favor.	por fa·vor
Thank you.	Gracias.	gra·syas
Many thanks.	Muchas gracias.	moo·chas gra·syas
You're welcome.	Con mucho gusto.	kon moo·cho goos·to
Pardon.	Perdón.	per·don
Excuse me.	Con permiso.	kon per·mee·so
(to ask permission)		
Sorry.	Disculpe.	dees·kool·pe
(when apologizing)		

How are you?
  ¿Cómo está/estás?   ko·mo es·ta/es·tas (pol/inf)

Fine, thanks. And you?
  Bien, gracias.   byen gra·syas
  ¿Y usted/tú?   ee oos·te/too (pol/inf)

What's your name?
  ¿Cómo se llama?   ko·mo se ya·ma (pol)
  ¿Cómo te llamas?   ko·mo te ya·mas (inf)

My name is ...
  Me llamo ...   me ya·mo ...

It's a pleasure to meet you.
  Mucho gusto.   moo·cho goos·to

Where are you from?
  ¿De dónde es/eres?   de don·de es/e·res (pol/inf)

I'm from ...
  Soy de ...   soy de ...

Can I take a photo?
  ¿Puedo sacar una foto?   pwe·do sa·kar oo·na fo·to

DIRECTIONS

How do I get to ...?
  ¿Cómo puedo llegar a ...? ko·mo pwe·do ye·gar a ...

What's the address?
  ¿Cuál es la dirección?   kwal es la dee·rek·syon

Can you show me (on the map)?
  ¿Me lo podría indicar   me lo po·dree·a een·dee·kar
  (en el mapa)?   (en el ma·pa)

Is it far?
  ¿Está lejos?   es·ta le·khos

here	aquí	a·kee
left	a la izquierda	a la ees·kyer·da
on the corner	en la esquina	en la es·kee·na
right	a la derecha	a la de·re·cha
straight ahead	todo derecho	to·do de·re·cho
there	allí	a·yee

EMERGENCIES

Help!	¡Socorro!	so·ko·ro
Stop!	¡Pare!	pa·re
Fire!	¡Fuego!	fwe·go
Go away!	¡Váyase!	va·ya·se
Watch out!	¡Cuidado!	kwee·da·do
I was robbed.	Me robaron.	me ro·ba·ron

Call ...!	¡Llame a ...!	ya·me a ...
an ambulance	una	oo·na
	ambulancia	am·boo·lan·sya
a doctor	un médico	oon me·dee·ko
the police	la policía	la po·lee·see·a

It's an emergency.
Es una emergencia.   es oo·na e·mer·khen·sya
Can you help me, please?
¿Me puede ayudar,   me pwe·de a·yoo·dar
por favor?   por fa·vor
I'm lost.
Estoy perdido/a.   es·toy per·dee·do/a
Where are the toilets?
¿Dónde están los baños? don·de es·tan los ba·nyos

north	norte	nor·te
south	sur	soor
east	este	es·te
west	oeste	o·es·te

avenue	avenida	a·ve·nee·da
block	cuadra	kwa·dra
highway	carretera	ka·re·te·ra
street	calle	ka·ye

EATING OUT

Can you recommend a bar/restaurant?
¿Puede recomendar un   pwe·de re·ko·men·dar oon
bar/restaurante?   bar/res·tow·ran·te
Do you have an English menu?
¿Hay un menú en inglés? ai oon me·noo en een·gles
What would you recommend?
¿Qué me recomienda?   ke me re·ko·myen·da
What's the local specialty?
¿Cuál es la especialidad kwal es la es·pe·sya·lee·dad
local?   lo·kal
I'll have (that).
Yo quiero (eso).   yo kye·ro (e·so)
I'd like it with/without ...
Lo quisiera con/sin ...   lo kee·sye·ra kon/seen ...
I'm a vegetarian.
Soy vegetariano/a.   soy ve·khe·ta·rya·no/a
That was delicious.
Estaba buenísimo.   es·ta·ba bwe·nee·see·mo

I'll buy you a drink.
Te invito a una copa.   te een·vee·to a oo·na ko·pa
Please bring the drink list.
Por favor nos trae la   por fa·vor nos tra·e la
lista de bebidas.   lees·ta de be·bee·das
Cheers!
¡Salud!   sa·lood
The bill, please.
La cuenta, por favor.   la kwen·ta por fa·vor

HEALTH

I'm sick.
Estoy enfermo/a.   es·toy en·fer·mo/a
I need a doctor.
Necesito un médico.   ne·se·see·to oon me·dee·ko
Where's the hospital?
¿Dónde está el hospital? don·de es·ta el os·pee·tal
I'm pregnant.
Estoy embarazada.   es·toy em·ba·ra·sa·da
I've been vaccinated.
Estoy vacunado/a.   es·toy va·koo·na·do/a

I'm allergic to ...	Soy alérgico/a ...	soy a·ler·khee·ko/a ...
antibiotics	a los antibióticos	a los an·tee·byo·tee·kos
nuts	a las nueces	a las nwe·ses
penicillin	a la penicilina	a la pe·nee·see·lee·na

I'm ...	Soy ...	soy ...
asthmatic	asmático/a	as·ma·tee·ko/a
diabetic	diabético/a	dya·be·tee·ko/a
epileptic	epiléptico/a	e·pee·lep·tee·ko/a

I have (a) ...	Tengo ...	ten·go ...
diarrhea	diarrea	dya·re·a
headache	dolor de cabeza	do·lor de ka·be·sa
nausea	náuseas	now·se·as
sore throat	dolor de garganta	do·lor de gar·gan·ta

LANGUAGE DIFFICULTIES

Do you speak English?
¿Habla/Hablas inglés?   a·bla/a·blas een·gles (pol/inf)
Does anyone here speak English?
¿Hay alguien que   ai al·gyen ke
hable inglés?   a·ble een·gles
I (don't) understand.
Yo (no) entiendo.   yo (no) en·tyen·do
How do you say ...?
¿Cómo se dice ...?   ko·mo se dee·se ...
What does ... mean?
¿Qué significa ...?   ke seeg·nee·fee·ka ...

SIGNS

Abierto	Open
Cerrado	Closed
Comisaría de Policía	Police Station
Entrada	Entrance
Información	Information
Prohibido	Prohibited
Salida	Exit
Servicios/Baños	Toilets
Hombres/Varones	Men
Mujeres/Damas	Women

Could you	*¿Puede ...,*	*pwe·*de ...
please ...?	*por favor?*	por fa·*vor*
repeat that	*repetirlo*	re·pe·*teer·*lo
speak more	*hablar más*	a·*blar* mas
slowly	*despacio*	des·*pa·*syo
write it down	*escribirlo*	es·kree·*beer·*lo

NUMBERS

0	*cero*	*se·*ro
1	*uno*	*oo·*no
2	*dos*	dos
3	*tres*	tres
4	*cuatro*	*kwa·*tro
5	*cinco*	*seen·*ko
6	*seis*	says
7	*siete*	*sye·*te
8	*ocho*	*o·*cho
9	*nueve*	*nwe·*ve
10	*diez*	dyes
11	*once*	*on·*se
12	*doce*	*do·*se
13	*trece*	*tre·*se
14	*catorce*	ka·*tor·*se
15	*quince*	*keen·*se
16	*dieciséis*	dye·see·*says*
17	*diecisiete*	dye·see·*sye·*te
18	*dieciocho*	dye·see·*o·*cho
19	*diecinueve*	dye·see·*nwe·*ve
20	*veinte*	*vayn·*te
21	*veintiuno*	vayn·tee·*oo·*no
30	*treinta*	*trayn·*ta
31	*treinta y uno*	*trayn·*ta ee *oo·*no
40	*cuarenta*	kwa·*ren·*ta
50	*cincuenta*	seen·*kwen·*ta
60	*sesenta*	se·*sen·*ta
70	*setenta*	se·*ten·*ta
80	*ochenta*	o·*chen·*ta
90	*noventa*	no·*ven·*ta
100	*cien*	syen
101	*ciento uno*	*syen·*to *oo·*no
200	*doscientos*	do·*syen·*tos
1000	*mil*	meel
10,000	*diez mil*	dyes meel
100,000	*cien mil*	syen meel
1,000,000	*un millón*	oon mee·*yon*

SHOPPING & SERVICES

I'd like to buy ...
Quisiera comprar ...   kee·*sye·*ra kom·*prar* ...

I'm just looking.
Sólo estoy mirando.   *so·*lo es·*toy* mee·*ran·*do

May I look at it?
¿Puedo verlo?   *pwe·*do *ver·*lo

How much is it?
¿Cuánto cuesta?   *kwan·*to *kwes·*ta

That's too expensive.
Es demasiado caro.   es de·ma·*sya·*do *ka·*ro

Could you lower the price?
¿Podría bajar un poco   po·*dree·*a ba·*khar* oon *po·*ko
el precio?   el *pre·*syo

I don't like it.
No me gusta.   no me *goos·*ta

I'll take it.
Lo llevo.   lo *ye·*vo

Do you	*¿Aceptan ...?*	a·*sep·*tan ...
accept ...?		
American	*dólares*	*do·*la·res
dollars	*americanos*	a·me·ree·*ka·*nos
credit cards	*tarjetas de*	tar·*khe·*tas de
	crédito	*kre·*dee·to
traveler's	*cheques de*	*che·*kes de
checks	*viajero*	vya·*khe·*ro
more	*más*	mas
less	*menos*	*me·*nos
large	*grande*	*gran·*de
small	*pequeño*	pe·*ke·*nyo
Where's the ...?	*¿Dónde está ...?*	*don·*de es·*ta* ...
ATM	*el cajero*	el ka·*khe·*ro
	automático	ow·to·*ma·*tee·ko
bank	*el banco*	el *ban·*ko
bookstore	*la librería*	la lee·bre·*ree·*a
chemist	*la farmacia*	la far·*ma·*sya
embassy	*la embajada*	la em·ba·*kha·*da
exchange	*la oficina de*	la o·fee·*see·*na de
office	*cambio*	*kam·*byo
general store	*la tienda*	la *tyen·*da
laundry	*la lavandería*	la la·van·de·*ree·*a
post office	*los correos*	los ko·*re·*os
(super)market	*el (super-)*	el (*soo·*per·)
	mercado	mer·*ka·*do
tourist office	*la oficina de*	la o·fee·*see·*na de
	turismo	too·*rees·*mo

PAPERWORK

birth certificate	certificado de nacimiento
car registration	registro del carro
car-owner's title	título de propiedad
customs	aduana
departure tax	impuesto de salida
driver's license	licencia de conductor
identification	identificación
immigration	inmigración
insurance	seguro
passport	pasaporte
tourist card	tarjeta de turista
visa	visado

What time does it open/close?
  ¿A qué hora abre/cierra? a ke o·ra a·bre/sye·ra
I want to change some money/traveler's checks.
  Quiero cambiar dinero/ kye·ro kam·byar dee·ne·ro/
  cheques de viajero. che·kes de vya·khe·ro
What is the exchange rate?
  ¿A cómo está el tipo a ko·mo es·ta el tee·po
  de cambio? de kam·byo
I want to call ...
  Quiero llamar a ... kye·ro ya·mar a ...

airmail	correo aéreo	ko·re·o a·e·re·o
black market	mercado negro	mer·ka·do ne·gro
cell phone	teléfono celular	te·le·fo·no se·lu·lar
letter	carta	kar·ta
registered	certificado	ser·tee·fee·ka·do
stamps	estampillas	es·tam·pee·yas

TIME & DATES

What time is it?	¿Qué hora es?	ke o·ra es
It's one o'clock.	Es la una.	es la oo·na
It's (10) o'clock.	Son las (diez).	son las (dyes)
Quarter past (two).	Las (dos) y cuarto.	las (dos) ee kwar·to
Half past (two).	Las (dos) y media.	las (dos) ee me·dya
Quarter to (two).	Las (dos) menos cuarto.	las (dos) me·nos kwar·to

in the morning	de la mañana	de la ma·nya·na
noon	mediodía	me·dyo·dee·a
in the afternoon	de la tarde	de la tar·de
at night	por la noche	por la no·che
midnight	medianoche	me·dya·no·che

yesterday	ayer	a·yer
today	hoy	oy
now	ahora	a·o·ra
tonight	esta noche	es·ta no·che
tomorrow	mañana	ma·nya·na

Monday	lunes	loo·nes
Tuesday	martes	mar·tes
Wednesday	miércoles	myer·ko·les
Thursday	jueves	khwe·ves
Friday	viernes	vyer·nes
Saturday	sábado	sa·ba·do
Sunday	domingo	do·meen·go

January	enero	e·ne·ro
February	febrero	fe·bre·ro
March	marzo	mar·so
April	abril	a·breel
May	mayo	ma·yo
June	junio	khoo·nyo
July	julio	khoo·lyo
August	agosto	a·gos·to
September	septiembre	sep·tyem·bre
October	octubre	ok·too·bre
November	noviembre	no·vyem·bre
December	diciembre	dee·syem·bre

TRANSPORTATION
Public Transportation

At what time does the ... leave/arrive?	¿A qué hora sale/llega el ...?	a ke o·ra sa·le/ye·ga el ...
bus	autobús	ow·to·boos
plane	avión	a·vyon
ship	barco	bar·ko
train	tren	tren

airport	aeropuerto	a·e·ro·pwer·to
bus station	estación de autobuses	es·ta·syon de ow·to·boo·ses
bus stop	parada de autobuses	pa·ra·da de ow·to·boo·ses
left-luggage office	consigna para equipaje	kon·seeg·na pa·ra e·kee·pa·khe
ticket office	boletería	bo·le·te·ree·a
timetable	horario	o·ra·ryo
train station	estación de tren	es·ta·syon de tren

I'd like a ticket to ...
  Quisiera un boleto a ... kee·sye·ra oon bo·le·to a ...
What's the fare to ...?
  ¿Cuánto cuesta a ...? kwan·to kwes·ta a ...

1st class	primera clase	pree·me·ra kla·se
2nd class	segunda clase	se·goon·da kla·se
child's	infantil	een·fan·teel
one-way	de ida	de ee·da
round-trip	de ida y vuelta	de ee·da ee vwel·ta
student's	de estudiante	de es·too·dyan·te
taxi	taxi	tak·see

ROAD SIGNS

Acceso	Entrance
Aparcamiento	Parking
Ceda el Paso	Give Way
Despacio	Slow
Dirección Única	One Way
Mantenga Su Derecha	Keep to the Right
No Adelantar	No Passing
No Estacionar	No Parking
No Rebase	No Passing
Pare	Stop
Peaje	Toll
Peligro	Danger
Prohibido Aparcar	No Parking
Prohibido el Paso	No Entry
Salida de Autopista	Freeway Exit

Private Transportation

I'd like to	Quisiera	kee·sye·ra
hire a ...	alquilar ...	al·kee·lar ...
4WD	un todo terreno	oon to·do te·re·no
bicycle	una bicicleta	oo·na bee·see·kle·ta
car	un carro	oon ka·ro
motorbike	una moto	oo·na mo·to
hitchhike	hacer dedo	a·ser de·do
truck	camión	ka·myon

Is this the road to ...?
¿Se va a ... por esta carretera? — se va a ... por es·ta ka·re·te·ra

Where's a gas station?
¿Dónde hay una gasolinera? — don·de ai oo·na ga·so·lee·ne·ra

Please fill it up.
Lleno, por favor. — ye·no por fa·vor

I'd like (20) liters.
Quiero (veinte) litros. — kye·ro (vayn·te) lee·tros

diesel	diesel	dee·sel
gas	gasolina	ga·so·lee·na
leaded (regular)	gasolina con plomo	ga·so·lee·na kon plo·mo
unleaded	gasolina sin plomo	ga·so·lee·na seen plo·mo

(How long) Can I park here?
¿(Por cuánto tiempo) Puedo aparcar aquí? — (por kwan·to tyem·po) pwe·do a·par·kar a·kee

Where do I pay?
¿Dónde se paga? — don·de se pa·ga

I need a mechanic.
Necesito un mecánico. — ne·se·see·to oon me·ka·nee·ko

The car has broken down (in ...).
El carro se ha averiado (en ...). — el ka·ro se a a·ve·rya·do (en ...)

The motorbike won't start.
No arranca la moto. — no a·ran·ka la mo·to

The battery is flat.
La batería está descargada. — la ba·te·ree·a es·ta des·kar·ga·da

I have a flat tire.
Tengo un pinchazo. — ten·go oon peen·cha·so

I've run out of gas.
Me quedé sin gasolina. — me ke·de seen ga·so·lee·na

I've had an accident.
Tuve un accidente. — too·ve oon ak·see·den·te

TRAVEL WITH CHILDREN

Do you mind if I breast-feed here?
¿Le molesta que dé de pecho aquí? — le mo·les·ta ke de de pe·cho a·kee

Are children allowed?
¿Se admiten niños? — se ad·mee·ten nee·nyos

I need (a) ...	Necesito ...	ne·se·see·to ...
baby seat	un asiento para bebé	oon a·syen·to pa·ra be·be
babysitter (who speaks English)	una niñera (de habla inglesa)	oo·na nee·nye·ra (de a·bla een·gle·sa)
child-minding service	un servicio de cuidado de niños	oon ser·vee·syo de kwee·da·do de nee·nyos
children's menu	un menú infantil	oon me·noo een·fan·teel
(disposable) diapers/ nappies	pañales (de usar y tirar)	pa·nya·les (de oo·sar ee tee·rar)
milk formula	leche en polvo	le·che en pol·vo
potty	una bacinica	oo·na ba·see·nee·ka
stroller	un cochecito	oon ko·che·see·to

Latin American **Spanish**

with 3500-word two-way dictionary

Also available from
Lonely Planet:
Latin American Spanish
phrasebook

Glossary

See the Language chapter, p741, for other useful words and phrases.

aguardiente – clear, potent liquor made from sugar-cane; also referred to as *caña*

aguas de frutas – fruit-flavored water drink

alcaldía – mayor's office

almuerzo – lunch; sometimes used to mean an inexpensive set lunch

apartado – post-office box

artesanía – handicraft

Av – abbreviation for avenida (avenue)

ayuntamiento – municipal government

bahía – bay

bajareque – traditional wall construction, where a core of stones is held in place by poles of bamboo or other wood then covered with stucco or mud

balboa – national currency of Panama

balneario – public beach or swimming area

barrio – district; neighborhood

bistec – grilled or fried beef steak

Black Caribs – see *Garífuna*

bocas – appetizers, often served with drinks in a bar

caballeros – literally 'horsemen,' but corresponds to the English 'gentlemen'; look for the term on bathroom doors

cabaña – cabin or bungalow

cabina – see *cabaña;* also a loose term for cheap lodging in Costa Rica (in some cases it refers to cabins or bungalows, in others it refers merely to an economical hotel room)

cafetería – literally 'coffee shop'; any informal restaurant with waiter service (not a self-service establishment as implied by the English 'cafeteria')

cafetín – small *cafetería*

cajero automático – automated teller machine (ATM)

calle – street

callejón – alley; small, narrow or very short street

calzada – causeway

camión – truck; bus

camioneta – pickup truck

campesino – farmer

caña – see *aguardiente*

Carretera Interamericana – Interamerican Hwy, or Interamericana (also referred to as the Pan-American Hwy, or Panamericana); the nearly continuous highway running from Alaska to Chile (it breaks at the Darién Gap in Panama)

casa de cambio – currency exchange office

casa de huéspedes – guesthouse

casado – cheap set meal, usually served at lunchtime

cascada – waterfall

caseta telefónica – telephone call station

catedral – cathedral

cay – small island of sand or coral fragments

caye – see *cay*

cayo – see *cay*

cayuco – dugout canoe

cenote – large, natural limestone cave used for water storage or ceremonial purposes

cerro – hill

cerveza – beer

ceviche – seafood marinated in lemon or lime juice, garlic and seasonings

Chac – Maya rain god; his likeness appears on many ruins

chacmool – Maya sacrificial stone sculpture

chamarra – thick, heavy woolen blanket (Guatemala)

chapín – citizen of Guatemala; Guatemalan

chicha – fruit juice mixed with sugar and water (Panama)

chicken bus – former US school bus used for public transportation

cine – movie theater

ciudad – city

cocina – literally 'kitchen'; small, basic restaurant, or cookshop, usually found in or near municipal markets

cofradía – religious brotherhood, particularly in highland Guatemala

colectivo – shared taxi or minibus that picks up and drops off passengers along its route

colón – national currency of Costa Rica

comedor – basic and cheap eatery, usually with a limited menu

comida a la vista – meal served buffet- or cafeteria-style

comida corrida – meal of the day; set meal of several courses, usually offered at lunchtime

comida corriente – mixed plate of different foods typical of the local region

comida típica – typical local-style meal or food

conquistador – any of the Spanish explorer-conquerors of Latin America

Contras – counterrevolutionary military groups fighting against the Sandinista government in Nicaragua throughout the 1980s

cordillera – mountain range

córdoba – national currency of Nicaragua

correo aéreo – airmail

corte – piece of material 7m to 10m long that is used as a wraparound skirt

costa – coast

criollo – Creole; born in Latin America of Spanish parentage; on the Caribbean coast it refers to someone of mixed African and European descent; see also *mestizo* and *ladino*
cuadra – city block
cueva – cave

damas – ladies; the usual sign on bathroom doors

edificio – building
empanada – Chilean-style turnover stuffed with meat or cheese and raisins
entrada – entrance
expreso – express bus

faja – waist sash that binds garments and holds what would otherwise be put in pockets
finca – farm; plantation; ranch
fritanga – sidewalk barbecue, widely seen in Nicaragua
fuerte – fort

gallo pinto – common meal of blended rice and beans
Garífuna – descendants of West African slaves and Carib Indians, brought to the Caribbean coast of Central America in the late 18th century from the island of St Vincent; also referred to as *Black Caribs*
Garinagu – see *Garífuna*
gaseosa – soft drink
gibnut – small, brown-spotted rodent similar to a guinea pig; also called *paca*
golfo – gulf
gringo/a – mildly pejorative term used in Latin America to describe male/female foreigners, particularly those from North America; often applied to any visitor of European heritage
gruta – cave
guacamole – a salad of mashed or chopped avocados, onions and tomatoes
guaro – local firewater made with sugarcane (Costa Rica)

hacienda – agricultural estate or plantation; treasury, as in Departamento de Hacienda (Treasury Department)
hospedaje – guesthouse
huipil – long, woven, white sleeveless tunic with intricate, colorful embroidery (Maya regions)

iglesia – church
indígena – indigenous
Interamericana – see *Carretera Interamericana*
internacionalistas – volunteers from all over the world who contributed to rebuilding Nicaragua when the Sandinistas assumed power
invierno – winter; Central America's wet season, which extends roughly from April through mid-December
isla – island
IVA – *impuesto al valor agregado*; value-added tax

junco – type of basket weaving

ladino – person of mixed indigenous and European parentage, often used to describe a *mestizo* who speaks Spanish; see also *mestizo* and *criollo*
lago – lake
laguna – lagoon; lake
lancha – small motorboat
lempira – national currency of Honduras
leng – colloquial Maya term for coins (Guatemalan highlands)
licuado – fresh fruit drink, blended with milk or water
lista de correos – poste restante (general delivery) mail

malecón – waterfront promenade
mar – sea
marimba – xylophone-like instrument
menú del día – fixed-price meal of several courses
mercado – market
Mesoamerica – a geographical region extending from central Mexico to northwestern Costa Rica
mestizo – person of mixed ancestry, usually Spanish and indigenous; see also *criollo* and *ladino*
metate – flat stone on which corn is ground
migración – immigration; immigration office
milpa – cornfield
mirador – lookout
mola – colorful hand-stitched appliqué textile made by Kuna women
muelle – pier
municipalidad – town hall
museo – museum

Navidad – Christmas

oficina de correos – post office
ordinario – slow bus

paca – see *gibnut*
PADI – Professional Association of Diving Instructors
palacio de gobierno – building housing the executive offices of a state or regional government
palacio municipal – city hall; seat of the corporation or municipal government
palapa – thatched, palm-leaf-roofed shelter with open sides
pan de coco – coconut bread
panadería – bakery
Panamericana – see *Carretera Interamericana*
panga – small motorboat
parada – bus stop
parque – park; sometimes also used to describe a plaza
parque nacional – national park
peña – folkloric club; evening of music, song and dance
pensión – guesthouse
petén – island
plato del día – plate (or meal) of the day

plato típico – mixed plate of various foods typical or characteristic of a place or region
playa – beach
pollera – Spanish-influenced 'national dress' of Panamanian women, worn for festive occasions
pozo – spring
propina – tip; gratuity
pueblo – small town or village
puente – bridge
puerta – gate; door
puerto – port; harbor
pulpería – corner store; minimart
punta – point; traditional Garífuna dance involving much hip movement
pupusa – cornmeal mass stuffed with cheese or refried beans, or a mixture of both (El Salvador)

quebrada – ravine; brook
quetzal – national currency of Guatemala, named for the tropical bird

rancho – thatched-roof restaurant
refresco – soda, or soft drink; drink made with local fruits (Costa Rica)
río – river
ropa vieja – literally 'old clothes'; spicy shredded beef and rice dish (Panama)
rotisería – restaurant selling roast meats
Ruta Maya – Maya Route, describing travels to the Maya sites of Mexico, Guatemala and Belize (chiefly), but also El Salvador and Honduras

sacbé – ceremonial limestone avenue or path between Maya cities
salida – exit
sancocho – spicy meat-and-vegetable stew, the 'national dish' of Panama
santo – saint

Semana Santa – Holy Week, the week preceding Easter
sendero – path or trail
sierra – mountain range; saw
soda – place that serves a counter lunch; soda or soft drink (Panama)
sorbetería – ice-cream parlor
stela, stelae – standing stone monument of the ancient Maya, usually carved
supermercado – supermarket, from a corner store to a large, Western-style supermarket

taller – shop; workshop
tamale – boiled or steamed cornmeal filled with chicken or pork, usually wrapped in a banana leaf
tapado – rich Garífuna stew made from fish, shrimp, shellfish, coconut milk and plantain, spiced with coriander
templo – temple; church
terminal de autobus – bus terminal
Tico/a – male/female inhabitant of Costa Rica
tienda – small shop
típica – see *típico*
típico – typical or characteristic of a region, particularly used to describe food; also a form of Panamanian folkloric music
traje – traditional handmade clothing
turicentro – literally 'tourist center'; outdoor recreation center with swimming facilities, restaurants and camping (El Salvador)

vegetariano/a – male/female vegetarian
venado – deer; venison
verano – summer; Central America's dry season, roughly from mid-December to April
viajero/a – male/female traveler
volcán – volcano

Zapatistas – members of the left-wing group Ejército Zapatista de Liberación Nacional (EZLN), fighting for indigenous rights in Chiapas, Mexico

Behind the Scenes

THIS BOOK

The 7th edition of *Central America on a Shoestring* was coordinated by Carolyn McCarthy, who also wrote the Panama chapter and the front and back sections of this book. The authors of the other destination chapters were Greg Benchwick (Mexico's Yucatán & Chiapas), Lucas Vidgen (Guatemala), Joshua Samuel Brown (Belize), Tom Spurling (El Salvador), Kevin Raub (Honduras), Alex Egerton (Nicaragua) and Matthew D Firestone (Costa Rica). Dr Allan Maca contributed to the Copán Archaeological Site text in the Honduras chapter. Dr David Goldberg wrote the Health chapter. Daniel Schechter's work on the 4th edition of *Guatemala* contributed to this book's Guatemala chapter, and the work of Carolina A Miranda and César G Soriano on the 9th edition of *Costa Rica* contributed to the Costa Rica chapter. The previous edition of this book was coordinated by Robert Reid, who wrote the text along with Jolyon Attwooll, Matthew D Firestone, Carolyn McCarthy, Andy Symington and Lucas Vidgen. This guidebook was commissioned in Lonely Planet's Oakland office, and produced by the following:

Commissioning Editor Catherine Craddock
Coordinating Editors Martine Power, Branislava Vladisavljevic
Coordinating Cartographers Mark Griffiths, Valentina Kremenchutskaya
Coordinating Layout Designer Jacqui Saunders
Managing Editor Annelies Mertens
Managing Cartographers Alison Lyall, Herman So
Managing Layout Designers Indra Kilfoyle, Celia Wood
Assisting Editors Andrew Bain, Chris Girdler, Trent Holden, Helen Koehne, Alison Ridgway, Gina Tsarouhas
Assisting Cartographers Andras Bogdanovits, Valeska Cañas, Brendan Streager
Cover Designer James Hardy, lonelyplanetimages.com
Internal Image Research Sabrina Dalbesio, lonely planetimages.com
Project Manager Rachel Imeson

Thanks to Lucy Birchley, Helen Christinis, Daniel Corbett, Melanie Dankel, Bruce Evans, Craig Kilburn, Lisa Knights, Katie Lynch, Averil Robertson, John Taufa, Juan Winata

THANKS
CAROLYN MCCARTHY
Sincere thanks go out to all the Panamanians, travelers and expats whose experiences and sto-

ries enriched these pages. Many individuals generously offered their time and expertise to improve this edition. You guys rock. Fellow authors Lucas, Greg, Matt, Tom, Kevin, Joshua and Alex, I thank you for tireless work in the face of thin mattresses, dodgy bus rides and one coup. Matt, good luck in greener pastures. I am also indebted to commissioning editor Cat Craddock for her cool counsel and the excellent team of cartographers and editors at Lonely Planet.

GREG BENCHWICK
The biggest and bravest of thanks goes to my darling bride Alejandra. *Te quiero verde y para siempre*, baby! I'd also like to thank my father for taking me to Akumal and Cozumel when I was just a boy. And to the great travel companions I met along the way, especially Sandra Blum, Balint Vekerdy, Peter Blake, Christel Van Dyk, Richard from Sweden, Terri and Rick from Florida, Don Kevin, and Marcia from Utah. And *muchísimas gracias* to the book's coordinating author Carolyn McCarthy. And last but not least, a huge amount of love and gratitude goes out to my dear mother.

JOSHUA SAMUEL BROWN
Joshua would like to thank everyone in Belize who made exploring, researching and blogging all the more worthwhile this time around. Special thanks to Vitalano in Corozal, Christopher and the Nesbitt family at MMRF, and Dave in Dangriga. Special thanks to Jen and the kids in California for keeping me anchored.

ALEX EGERTON
Big thanks to all the folk in Nicaragua, whose passion for the country made this job so much easier, and all the travelers who were so willing to share their experiences. Specific big ups go out to Franjaz and Hakeem; Nicholas Kazu for traveling so far to visit us; Ras Ariel, Edwin and Zander; Juanita Boyd; Oliver and Debo in Managua; Kurt van Blum and Juan Lasso. And of course, thanks to Cat Craddock for sending me out there and to Carolyn for not blocking me from her Gmail chat.

MATTHEW D FIRESTONE
My family has gotten bigger since the publication of this book, so first off, I'd like to extend a

warm welcome to my wonderful wife, Aki. We've traveled the world from east to west, but there is still so much more for us to discover together. And of course, I can't overlook the overwhelming support that my parents and sister have shown me over the years, which has guided me over more hurdles and around more obstacles than I care to mention. And finally, a tip of the hat to my Lonely Planet coworkers, namely commissioning editor extraordinaire Catherine Craddock, and coordinating author and all-around-star Carolyn McCarthy.

KEVIN RAUB

Special thanks to my wife, Adriana Schmidt, who I left for another two-month stint. At Lonely Planet, Catherine Craddock, Carolyn McCarthy and Greg Benchwick. On the road in Honduras: my in-country angel, Karla Calidonio, who made the unmakeable happen in a country in turmoil; Jorge Salverri, Nicole Marder, Efrain Bueso, Sandra Bastidas, Kevin Braun, Captain Vern, Pamy Marinakys, Lu Seapy, Dale Brandenburger, Sonia Regalado-Baumgartner, Dr Allan Maca, Dr Chris Begley, Howard Rosenzweig and Marco Cáceres.

TOM SPURLING

Massive high fives to Lawler for officially smashing El Salvador. Big love to my wife Lucy and son Oliver for letting Deadbeat Dad run away for a bit. Thanks to Rene at Suchitoto Outfitters and Chalchuapa's bad boys, Luis and George! Thanks to Manolo in Tacuba! *Feliz Navidad* to Guillermo Perdomo and Ana Lynn at Pinacoteca. Cheers to Trenta for injecting the freshness! Thanks to Richard in Tunco and Tom at La Tortuga Verde in El Cuco – two fine ambassadors for the good life. Thanks also to Letty in San Salvador, Cesar in Juayua, Alex in El Zonte, Lidby and Robert in Suchitoto. *Guanaco* for life!

LUCAS VIDGEN

Firstly, I'd really like to thank all the Guatemalans for making such a great country to live, travel and work in. Sure, we've got our problems, but we're getting there, *poco a poco*. Out on the road, Virgilio Molina, Encarnación Morán, Daniel Vásquez and Daantje for standing still long enough to let me quote them. To the guy who ran into my car in Esquipulas and drove off without leaving a note: thanks very much. To Geert in Copán, Glenn in Guatemala City and Dennis in Mariscos: awesome work, guys – see you next time. My coauthor on the Guatemala country guide, Danny Schechter, whose work on the Highlands, El Petén and Antigua I adapted for this book. And the home-fire crew: James and Alma for taking care

of business and of course to Sofía and América – the best traveling companions a guy could ask for.

OUR READERS

Many thanks to the travelers who used the previous edition and wrote to us with helpful hints, useful advice and interesting anecdotes:

A Cristian Abud, Allie Ackland-Prpic, Jill Amery, Tim Anderson, Lorenz Artaker **B** Catherine Bach, Laurel Baker, Ryan Bates, Allen Beach, Stephen Benjamin, Dewi Blom, Takeyu Boström, Peter Brugger, Michael Burr **C** Connie Colten, Heather Crickere, Laura Cullen, Jim Curtis **D** Jessica Daley, Hans Danelius, Charles-Etienne Daoust, Henry De Marigny, Sharon Dequine, Genevieve Dionne, Peter Divine, Paul Drabsch **E** Jenny Ellinghaus, Mike Evans **F** Amanda Fernandez, Ralph Ferrusi, Lilia Fick, Melissa Fishburne **G** Chris Gleed-Owen, Eliane Godement, Emily Golan, Joseph Goldman, Suzanne Grasso, Michelle Griffin **H** Tamara Hajsky, George Michael Hakim, Scott Harrington, Lars Havig Berge, Mark Heptinstall, Kevin Hill, Jade Horan, Phil Hornsby, Scott Housman, Kenneth Hoyt, Jadrino Huot **J** Morten Jacobsen, Elissa James, Mollie Jameson, Britta Jensen, Andreas Johnsen **K** Barry Kaiser, Anne Karbe, Marlise Kast, Jemi Katko, Gillian Kirkwood, Dar Kleinbach, Sabine Klotz, Yaniv Kriger, Kevin Krol **L** Cathy Larson, Oliver Lawn, Jerome Luepkes, Rene Daniel Luisman **M** Leigh Malcolmson, Christian Martin, Marcel Matte, Johanna Mau, Andrew Miller, Jonathan Mischke, Dennis Mogerman, Anthony Moore, Anne Mulcair **N** Paige Newman, Lisa Nolan, Kim Nørgaard,

Guilherme Nunes **O** Terry O'Brien, Emma Ogunbiyi, Sally O'Sullivan **P** Eric Paine, Bob Penner, Matt Pepe, Edo Plantinga, Thomas Preinl **R** Isolde Raftery, Linda Reynolds, Sharon Rosenfeld, Mary & Mike Rossignoli **S** Frank Schoen, Tal Sela, Ana Slevec, Yvonne Smiertka, Diego Sogorb, Kelly Spencer **T** Stephen Tapply, Amanda Thompson, Connie Tobolsky, Monica Toth, Kariina Tshursin, Tristan Tuftnell **V** Hank Van Den Bosch, Cathelijne Van Weelden, Peter Vang Jensen, Timothy Veldhuizen, Greta Von Bernuth **W** Dustin Weaver, Martin Weinhold, Evian White, Bronwynn Whiteley, Teresa Widmer, Cindy Williams, Kenneth Wood, Lexie Woodward, Natasha Woollcombe, Julia Wüst **Y** Dan Yack, Shiri Yaniv **Z** Mike Zipf, Rodolfo Zosel

ACKNOWLEDGMENTS

Many thanks to the following for the use of their content:

Globe on title page ©Mountain High Maps 1993 Digital Wisdom, Inc.

Index

INDEX

INDEX

GreenDex

GOING GREEN

The following listings have been selected for their demonstrated commitment to sustainability. Eating listings may offer organic food, maintain traditional cooking techniques or support local producers. Accommodations may be considered environmentally friendly because of responsible water use, a commitment to recycling or energy conservation. Attractions listed are involved in conservation or environmental education. GreenDex national parks listings indicate unique habitats that present exceptional biodiversity in a pristine state. We also include local, grass-roots organizations and community services worth supporting.

For a small region, Central America boasts excellent cultural and biological diversity. Country chapters include information about responsible travel in culturally or ecologically sensitive areas. For more tips, turn to p4.

If you think we've omitted a listing, or if you disagree with our choices, email us at talk2us@lonelyplanet.com.au and set us straight for next time. For more information about sustainable tourism and Lonely Planet, see www.lonelyplanet.com/responsibletravel.

THE LONELY PLANET STORY

Fresh from an epic journey across Europe, Asia and Australia in 1972, Tony and Maureen Wheeler sat at their kitchen table stapling together notes. The first Lonely Planet guidebook, *Across Asia on the Cheap*, was born.

Travelers snapped up the guides. Inspired by their success, the Wheelers began publishing books to Southeast Asia, India and beyond. Demand was prodigious, and the Wheelers expanded the business rapidly to keep up. Over the years, Lonely Planet extended its coverage to every country and into the virtual world via lonelyplanet.com and the Thorn Tree message board.

As Lonely Planet became a globally loved brand, Tony and Maureen received several offers for the company. But it wasn't until 2007 that they found a partner whom they trusted to remain true to the company's principles of traveling widely, treading lightly and giving sustainably. In October of that year, BBC Worldwide acquired a 75% share in the company, pledging to uphold Lonely Planet's commitment to independent travel, trustworthy advice and editorial independence.

Today, Lonely Planet has offices in Melbourne, London and Oakland, with over 500 staff members and 300 authors. Tony and Maureen are still actively involved with Lonely Planet. They're traveling more often than ever, and they're devoting their spare time to charitable projects. And the company is still driven by the philosophy of *Across Asia on the Cheap*: 'All you've got to do is decide to go and the hardest part is over. So go!'

Published by Lonely Planet Publications Pty Ltd
ABN 36 005 607 983

© Lonely Planet Publications Pty Ltd 2010

© photographers as indicated 2010

Cover montage by James Hardy. Photographs by Lonely Planet Images: Bill Bachmann, Tom Boyden, Paul Kennedy, Alfredo Maiquez, Chris Mellor, Damian Turski, Eric Wheater.

Many of the images in this guide are available for licensing from Lonely Planet Images: www.lonelyplanetimages.com.

Printed by Toppan Security Printing Pte. Ltd.
Printed in Singapore

Lonely Planet and the Lonely Planet logo are trademarks of Lonely Planet and are registered in the US Patent and Trademark Office and in other countries.

Lonely Planet does not allow its name or logo to be appropriated by commercial establishments, such as retailers, restaurants or hotels. Please let us know of any misuses: www.lonelyplanet.com/ip.

LONELY PLANET OFFICES

Australia
Head Office
Locked Bag 1, Footscray, Victoria 3011
☎ 03 8379 8000, fax 03 8379 8111
talk2us@lonelyplanet.com.au

USA
150 Linden St, Oakland, CA 94607
☎ 510 250 6400, toll free 800 275 8555
fax 510 893 8572
info@lonelyplanet.com

UK
2nd fl, 186 City Rd,
London EC1V 2NT
☎ 020 7106 2100, fax 020 7106 2101
go@lonelyplanet.co.uk

Mixed Sources
Product group from well-managed forests and other controlled sources
www.fsc.org Cert no. SGS-COC-005002
© 1996 Forest Stewardship Council